THE ENCYCLOPEDIA OF THE
MEXICAN-AMERICAN WAR

THE ENCYCLOPEDIA OF THE
MEXICAN-AMERICAN WAR

A Political, Social, and Military History

VOLUME I: A–L

Dr. Spencer C. Tucker
Editor

James Arnold and Roberta Wiener
Editors, Documents Volume

Dr. Paul G. Pierpaoli Jr.
Associate Editor

Dr. Thomas W. Cutrer
Dr. Pedro Santoni
Assistant Editors

 ABC-CLIO

Santa Barbara, California   Denver, Colorado   Oxford, England

Library of Congress Cataloging-in-Publication Data

The encyclopedia of the Mexican-American War : a political, social, and military history / Spencer C. Tucker, editor ; James Arnold and Roberta Wiener, editors, documents volume ; Paul G. Pierpaoli Jr., associate editor ; Thomas W. Cutrer and Pedro Santoni, assistant editors.
     v. cm.
  Includes bibliographical references and index.
  Contents: volume I. A-L — volume II. M-Z — volume III. Documents.
  ISBN 978-1-85109-853-8 (hardcover : acid-free paper) — ISBN 978-1-85109-854-5 (ebook)
  1. Mexican War, 1846–1848—Encyclopedias. 2. Mexican War, 1846–1848—Sources. I. Tucker, Spencer, 1937– II. Arnold, James R., 1952– III. Wiener, Roberta, 1952– IV. Pierpaoli, Paul G., 1962– V. Cutrer, Thomas W. VI. Santoni, Pedro.
  E404.E62   2013
  973.6'2—dc23

                                      2012032450

ISBN: 978-1-85109-853-8
EISBN: 978-1-85109-854-5

16 15 14 13 12   1 2 3 4 5

This book is also available on the World Wide Web as an eBook.
Visit www.abc-clio.com for details.

ABC-CLIO, LLC
130 Cremona Drive, P.O. Box 1911
Santa Barbara, California 93116-1911

This book is printed on acid-free paper ∞
Manufactured in the United States of America

For my friend Mike Hubbard

About the Editors

Spencer C. Tucker, PhD, held the John Biggs Chair of Military History at his alma mater, the Virginia Military Institute in Lexington, for 6 years until his retirement from teaching in 2003. Before that, he was professor of history for 30 years at Texas Christian University, Fort Worth. He has also been a Fulbright Scholar and, as a U.S. Army captain, an intelligence analyst in the Pentagon. Currently the senior fellow of military history at ABC-CLIO, he has written or edited 42 books and encyclopedias, including the award-winning *Encyclopedia of the Arab-Israeli Conflict*, the comprehensive *A Global Chronology of Conflict*, and the *Encyclopedia of the Middle East Wars*, all published by ABC-CLIO.

James R. Arnold is the author of more than 20 military history books and has contributed to numerous others. His published works include *Jeff Davis's Own: Cavalry, Comanches, and the Battle for the Texas Frontier* and *Napoleon Conquers Austria: The 1809 Campaign for Vienna*, which won the International Napoleonic Society's Literary Award in 1995. His two newest titles are *The Moro War: How America Battled a Muslim Insurgency in the Philippine Jungle, 1902–1903*, and *Napoleon's Triumph: The Friedland Campaign, 1807*.

Roberta Wiener is managing editor for the the *Journal of Military History*. She has written *The American West: Living the Frontier Dream* and coauthored numerous history books for the school library market, including ten volumes on *The Revolutionary War* (2002) and the thirteen-volume set *13 Colonies* (2005).

Contents

List of Entries

List of Maps

List of Tables

Foreword

In March 1847, a small United States army landed at Veracruz on Mexico's east coast. In the six months that followed, it marched over 250 miles, won six major battles, captured the Mexican capital of Mexico City, and pacified much of the countryside in the process. It was one of the most brilliant military operations in American history, conducted by one of the greatest generals the country has ever produced. As the culminating campaign of a two-year war, it helped pave the way for a treaty that transferred over half a million square miles from Mexico to the United States, including all or part of Arizona, California, Colorado, Nevada, New Mexico, Utah, and Wyoming.

Despite the significance of these events, most Americans know little about the Mexico City Campaign, Winfield Scott, or the Treaty of Guadalupe Hidalgo. That is because most Americans know so little about the Mexican-American War which was fought from 1846 to 1848.

The conflict played an important formative role in nineteenth-century American history, completing the nation's westward push to the Pacific Ocean. It was the country's first major foreign war and it served as a proving ground for several hundred Civil War generals. War costs exceeded $100 million and 13,000 lives, which made it, as a percentage of those who served, second only to the Civil War as the bloodiest conflict in American history. The war also produced two presidents in the years immediately following.

In 1848 soldiers returned home as conquering heroes. They believed that they had participated in the great epic event of the century, one that would be remembered forever. Indeed, towns across the country, especially in the South, were named for Mexican War battles and leaders; among the most common are Buena Vista, Cerro Gordo, Quitman, Ringgold, and Saltillo. The state of Iowa has no fewer than seven counties with names associated with

the war. Veterans, however, were wrong about their deeds being remembered. Ask the average American today about the Mexican-American War, and one is likely to receive a blank stare or, at best, a vague comment about the Alamo, the sinking of the battleship *Maine*, or Pancho Villa.

There are several reasons for this historical amnesia, but three are especially prominent. First, just over a decade after the Treaty of Guadalupe Hidalgo, a much bigger and far bloodier conflict gripped the nation, obscuring the war with Mexico in its long shadow. The great national struggle between North and South gave rise to new heroes, larger battles, and much more bloodshed, all of which continued to dominate the country's attention for generations to come. The second reason has to do with the nature of the war and was best expressed by Ulysses S. Grant, who served as a lieutenant in Mexico. In his memoirs forty years later, he characterized the war as "one of the most unjust ever waged by a stronger against a weaker nation." Because it was regarded then and is still regarded today by many people as a dishonorable land grab, it is difficult to view the war with patriotism and pride and rather more convenient to forget that chapter of American history. As a result, historians have given comparatively little attention to the Mexican War in the 16 decades since it ended, and that fact constitutes the third reason for the conflict's relative anonymity.

The timely publication of this new *Encyclopedia of the Mexican-American War* reflects a trend of growing interest in the conflict, which has fostered a still thin but growing list of works that will hopefully help pull the war out of the shadow that has hidden its significance for more than a century and a half. Current economic issues and demographic changes along with an ongoing immigration controversy make a greater knowledge and a deeper understanding of our relationship with our southern neighbor imperative. For, while Americans have generally forgotten the war and its antecedents, Mexicans have not.

A variety of societal forces converged in the early decades of the nineteenth century to set the stage for the war with Mexico. Attitudes of nationalism, especially in the years following the War of 1812, had engendered an aggressive foreign policy. Also, Americans possessed a pride in the liberty that they enjoyed which convinced them of the importance of spreading the benefits of freedom across the continent. To some people, that even meant exporting republican forms of government to other countries. Additionally, the religious revivalism called the Second Great Awakening created a sense of missionary zeal and spiritual fervor that demanded the spread of Christianity to neighboring regions. These factors came together in a way that complemented and reinforced each other in the 1840s, and as a result many Americans came to the conclusion that expansion was their national mission.

John L. O'Sullivan, creator and editor of *The United States Magazine and Democratic Review*, called this missionary expansionism "Manifest Destiny." Writing in 1845 in support of the annexation of Texas, he asserted that the acquisition of western land would be "the fulfillment of our manifest destiny to overspread the continent allotted by Providence for the free development of our yearly multiplying millions." In other words, O'Sullivan and others believed that American expansion, even as far as the Pacific Ocean, was part of God's design. The American mission was to spread its superior institutions across the continent and their accompanying liberty, market economy, and religious freedom. In an earlier essay entitled "The Great Nation of Futurity," O'Sullivan had written that American exceptionalism had set the United States apart from other nations of the world, and its forward march would write a new chapter of progress in the history of human experience. These were the ideas that drove American settlers into northern Mexico and all the way to the Pacific Ocean. So steady was American migration into Texas in the 1820s and 1830s that on the eve of the Texas Revolution in 1835, transplanted Americans outnumbered native Mexicans by ten to one. Indeed, Mexico had an immigration problem.

Conditions in Mexico seemed in American minds to justify the ideas associated with Manifest Destiny. Catholicism was the state religion, which made the country incompatible with American ideals of religious freedom and its dominant Protestantism. By the time the war started in 1846, the Mexican government had had 35 heads of state in its 25 years of existence, which lends credence to one historian's recent description of the government as being more like a prize to be commandeered than a means of governing the country. It was that very political instability, coupled with suspicions (unfounded it now seems) of British designs on portions of Mexico, that fueled Americans' desire to spread their influence across the continent. To many Americans, the fact that Spain had lost its 300-year-old grip on that portion of its colonial empire meant that the southwestern quadrant of the continent was up for grabs. The strongest nation and the most enlightened institutions, they thought, would end up in control.

President James K. Polk was the principal agent of manifest destiny. While American settlers were already pushing to the west coast, Polk saw to it that the nation's borders followed them. He ran on an expansionist platform in 1844, and when elected left no doubt about his intentions to acquire western lands. He was, as a recent biographer put it, "the man who transformed the presidency and America." But historians disagree on whether Polk's actions in this drama are laudable or culpable. His questionable policy toward Mexico caused a border dispute along the Rio Grande, which in turn precipitated a border clash and declaration of war in May 1846. The end result two years later was the transfer of Mexico's northern territories to the United States. Polk defenders have pointed to the fact that his diplomatic overtures were ignored by the Mexican government and that the bloodshed that started the war was the result of a Mexican attack. The president's critics, however, charge that his bold actions amounted to nothing short of naked aggression, and that his provocative actions instigated the opening clash of the conflict.

Polk's role leading up to the outbreak of war is not the only controversy associated with its origins. While the annexation of Texas and the subsequent border dispute attracted headlines, events in California took on an air of intrigue when Brevet Captain of Engineers John C. Frémont arrived in spring 1846 at the head of a column of armed "explorers." Mexican officials were already suspicious of U.S. intentions because of an 1842 incident in which the commander of the U.S. Pacific Squadron, Commodore Thomas ap Catesby Jones, believing that a state of war existed between the United States and Mexico, had seized the town of Monterey, California. Mexican Comandante General José María Castro confronted Frémont and ordered him to leave California. Frémont then took his men north into the Oregon Country. But after receiving a mysterious dispatch of unknown origin, Frémont and his men returned in time to assist in the Bear Flag Revolt whereby rebels (mostly American immigrants) declared their independence from Mexico and later cooperated with U.S. naval vessels that arrived off California's coast. These colorful events remain largely unknown to the general public today.

The war itself afforded fame to a host of individuals, but the two principal generals captured most of the attention and emerged as national heroes. One was a new hero, the other an old one. After the initial clashes at Palo Alto and Resaca de la Palma, Brigadier General Zachary Taylor and his army crossed the Rio Grande and took possession of several towns in northern Mexico. By fall 1846, Taylor had captured the city of Monterrey after a hard-fought battle, and back in the states where he was already the object of hero worship, his name was being mentioned as a possible presidential candidate in 1848. The following year, at about the time Taylor's army was fighting its last battle at Buena Vista, Winfield Scott, who first became famous in the War of 1812, invaded central Mexico and began his skillful march to Mexico City. On September 14, 1847, a triumphant Scott rode into the captured capital after victories at Veracruz, Cerro Gordo, Contreras, Churubusco, El Molino del Rey, and Chapultepec. Scott's sophisticated pacification plan made his campaign one that was ahead of its time. The Whig general might have realized his lifelong dream of becoming president had it not been for his feuding with fellow officers and his embarrassment at the hands of Democratic President Polk.

There are several noteworthy points regarding the conduct of the war. American forces typically fought offensively (the only significant battle in which they fought on the defensive was Buena Vista), and an unbroken string of victories apparently taught young officers to seize the initiative by being aggressive on the battlefield. Moreover, the tactics were Napoleonic in nature with turning movements and flank attacks. The conduct of numerous Civil War battles was reminiscent of Mexican War battles, where scores of Civil War generals learned their first lessons of war. Also, the war in Mexico was the first in which West Point graduates made their mark. Staff officers such as P. G. T. Beauregard, Robert E. Lee, George B. McClellan, Gustavus W. Smith, Isaac I. Stevens and numerous others gained valuable experience in reconnaissance, logistics, and map making. So valuable was their service that after the fall of Mexico City Scott toasted West Point at a dinner gathering, stating that without the academy his army would never have reached Mexico City. Truly, if one did a roll call of lieutenants and captains in the Mexico-American War, it would quickly become obvious that it was in many respects a Civil War training ground.

Connections between Mexican War experience and the way the Civil War was conducted is one theme in current historiography. It seems like an obvious relationship and a topic rich with research possibilities, but until recent years the only effort to make such a case was Alfred Hoyt Bill's *Rehearsal for Conflict*, which is over sixty years old. More work is needed on this topic. Other historiographical trends have emphasized the social history of the U.S. Army as well as the political instability and class factions within Mexico that help to account for its relatively weak attempt to turn back the North American invaders. The cruelty of some U.S. soldiers as they marched through Mexico is well documented, but recent studies have balanced that version by suggesting that there were significant efforts, at least within Scott's army, to pacify the countryside by purchasing food and supplies while respecting private property and religious structures. Contributors to this encyclopedia have produced some of the best scholarship on the war to appear in years. Despite a bibliography that has slowly grown in the past twenty years, there are areas of research that remain unexplored.

Perhaps the most significant reason why the Mexican-American War deserves greater notice is its role in deepening sectional conflict and hastening the Civil War. The great land expansion that resulted from the Treaty of Guadalupe Hidalgo brought to the forefront the dilemma of slavery expansion. In the pre–Civil War period, anytime slavery and expansion collided, political turmoil was the natural byproduct. The Compromise of 1850 proved to be only a temporary band-aid that was unable to stop what one historian called "the impending crisis." Indeed, the celebrations over the victory in Mexico had hardly subsided when one of the most turbulent decades in American history began. Thanks to this encyclopedia, the general public now has at its fingertips the people, events, causes, and consequences of this little known chapter of American history.

Thanks to ABC-CLIO and to editor Spencer Tucker, Associate Editor Paul Pierpaoli, and Assistant Editors Thomas W. Cutrer and Pedro Santoni, information about the Mexican-American War will now be more accessible to the general public. This three-volume work is impressive in its size, scope, and quality. Its 800 entries and 146 important primary documents related to the war will be useful to the general reader and essential to historians working the field, or anyone for that matter who is interested in the kind of research that brings deeper understanding to simple chronological facts. The encyclopedia is one of the best research tools available.

TIMOTHY D. JOHNSON
LIPSCOMB UNIVERSITY

Preface

The war between the United States and Mexico during 1846–1848 was a pivotal event in U.S. history. It came at a time when many Americans believed that it was the destiny of the United States to control the North American continent from the Atlantic to the Pacific. "Manifest Destiny" and American nationalism were the key factors behind the war. Nationalism also played a role on the Mexican side. When the Mexican government refused to entertain President James K. Polk's offer to purchase California (the chief prize in the war), in a splendid example of *Realpolitik* Polk goaded Mexico into war over the Texas boundary.

Many European observers thought that Mexico might win the war. After all, Mexico had a far larger professional army than did the United States. But Mexican political instability served to undermine the courage and dedication of many of its soldiers in the field, who paid a heavy price for generally inept senior military leadership.

The well-served American artillery proved decisive in many encounters, most notably the Battle of Buena Vista, while Major General Winfield Scott's Mexico City Campaign was one of the most brilliant in U.S. military history. The U.S. Navy also quickly neutralized the small Mexican Navy, assisted in the occupation of California, and isolated Mexico from overseas arms shipments. The war amply demonstrated the importance of steamers in providing logistical support.

The war added significantly to U.S. territory, with Mexico ceding to the United States all of Texas to the Rio Grande boundary, New Mexico (including the future states of New Mexico, Arizona, Colorado, Utah, and Nevada), and upper California (including San Diego). The war also hastened such military technologies as the percussion rifled musket, the telegraph, railroads, and steam warships. The young West Point-trained officers gave good account of themselves, and then war proved to be a valuable training ground for many young officers who would later fight in the Civil War.

This is the most comprehensive encyclopedia of the Mexican-American War to appear to date. The two volumes of entries contain 800 entries totaling some 570,000 words. Subjects covered include key individuals in the military and political realms, battles, political developments, diplomacy, economics, social movements, literature, and the arts. We also have what I believe to be the most detailed chronology of the war itself, an extensive bibliography of works on the war, a glossary of military terms, and information on military awards and decorations and ranks. The documents volume, ably edited by Jim Arnold and Roberta Weiner, who have also provided introductions for the documents, provides much useful background material.

As always I am grateful to my splendid associate editor, Dr. Paul G. Pierpaoli, Jr. for his invaluable assistance in helping to plan the encyclopedia, securing contributors and their work, then recording the entries, as well as writing a great many entries himself and helping me edit the entire encyclopedia. We are fortunate in having two highly respected specialists on the war, Dr. Thomas W. Cutrer of the Department of History and American Studies, Arizona State University, and Dr. Pedro Santoni of the Department of History, California State University San Bernardino. Both are well published scholars on the war. I am also grateful to Dr. Timothy Johnson of Lipscomb University, another well-known specialist on the war, who wrote the fine introduction.

SPENCER C. TUCKER

General Maps

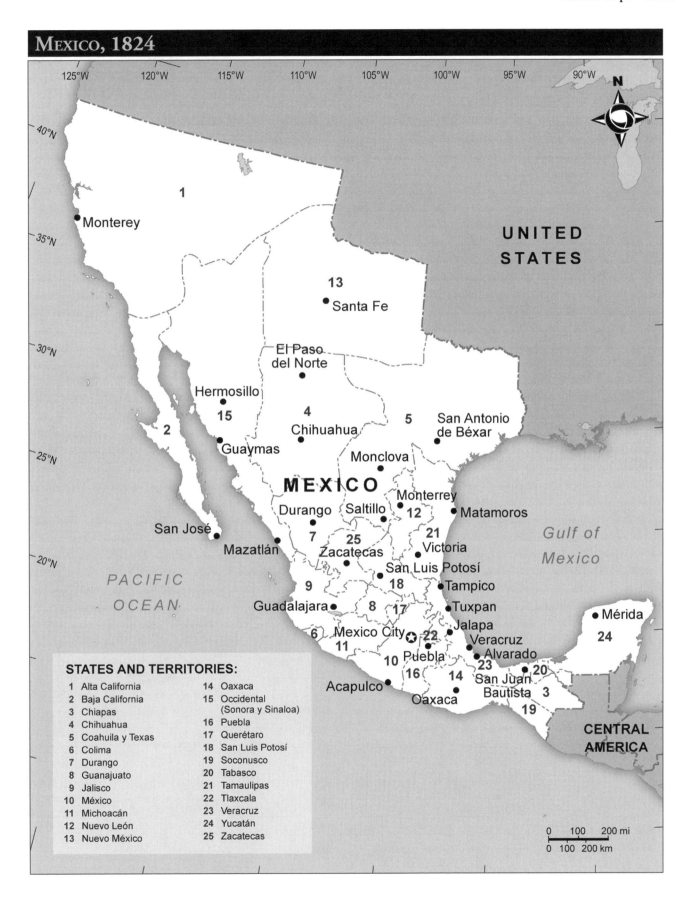

MEXICO, 1824

UNITED STATES

1

Monterey

13

Santa Fe

El Paso
del Norte

Hermosillo

15

4

Chihuahua

5

San Antonio
de Béxar

2

Guaymas

Monclova

MEXICO

Monterrey

San José

Durango   Saltillo   12   Matamoros

Gulf of
Mexico

7   25   21

Mazatlán   Zacatecas   Victoria

PACIFIC   9   San Luis Potosí

OCEAN   18   Tampico

Guadalajara   8   17   Tuxpan

6   Mexico City   Jalapa   Mérida

11   22   Veracruz   24

10   Puebla   Alvarado

16   23

Acapulco   14   San Juan
Bautista   20

Oaxaca   3

19

CENTRAL
AMERICA

STATES AND TERRITORIES:

1	Alta California	14	Oaxaca
2	Baja California	15	Occidental (Sonora y Sinaloa)
3	Chiapas	16	Puebla
4	Chihuahua	17	Querétaro
5	Coahuila y Texas	18	San Luis Potosí
6	Colima	19	Soconusco
7	Durango	20	Tabasco
8	Guanajuato	21	Tamaulipas
9	Jalisco	22	Tlaxcala
10	México	23	Veracruz
11	Michoacán	24	Yucatán
12	Nuevo León	25	Zacatecas
13	Nuevo México		

0   100   200 mi
0   100   200 km

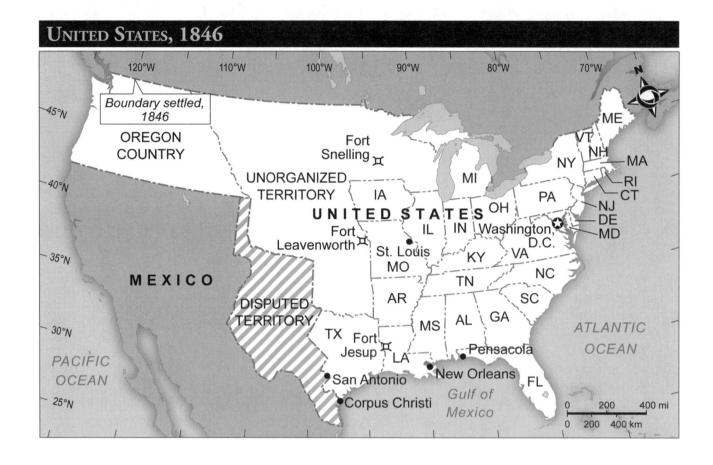

UNITED STATES, 1846

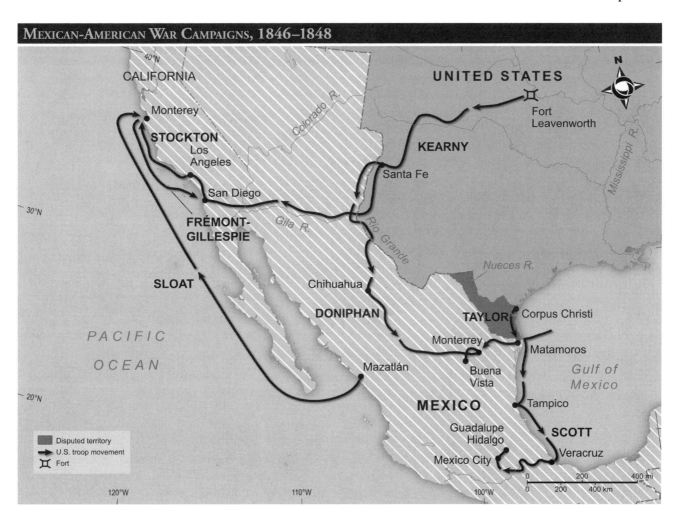

NORTH AMERICA AND THE EXPANSION OF THE UNITED STATES, 1824–1854

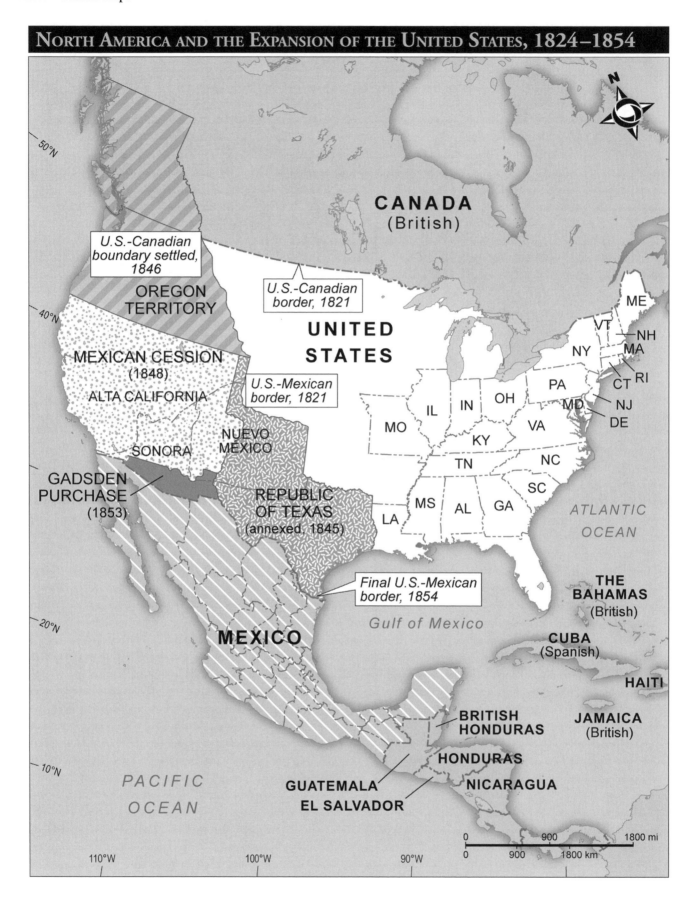

Overview

In 1820, Connecticut-born entrepreneur Moses Austin traveled to San Antonio de Béxar to present to Spanish authorities his plan to bring North American colonists into Spanish-held Texas. Austin pledged to Antonio Mario Martínez, the governor of Coahuila y Texas, that Texan colonists would learn the Spanish language, convert to Catholicism, serve as a buffer between Mexico and raiding Comanches and, after ten years, sever all economic ties with the United States and trade exclusively within the Spanish empire. Although he had misgivings, Martínez accepted Austin's offer. Moses Austin then returned to Missouri to recruit the 300 families stipulated in the treaty with Spain, but he died soon thereafter. His son, Steven Fuller Austin, now took up his father's agenda and assumed his father's role as *empresario*.

Austin chose as the site for the settlement the rich bottom lands of the Colorado and Brazos Rivers, east of San Antonio. There he and his colonists planned to expand the slave-based plantation economy of the lower South. Although Austin had no trouble finding recruits for his colony, the plan was dealt a near fatal blow when, on September 27, 1821, Spanish royalist Colonel Agustín de Iturbide marched into Mexico City at the head of a rebellious army, overthrew the Spanish viceroy, and established Mexican independence. Undeterred, however, Austin made contact with the new government in Mexico City, which duly ratified his father's contract.

By the end of 1824, 300 families had settled the Austin colony, content under the federal Mexican Constitution of 1824, which bore much resemblance to that of the United States. By the end of 1835, 41 *empresarios* had received land grants from the Mexican government that permitted 13,500 families to settle in Texas, bringing the Anglo-American population of the Mexican province to a total of approximately 30,000, in addition to their 5,000 African-American slaves. At the same time, an estimated 3,470 Hispanics lived north of the Rio Grande River.

Two circumstances doomed the harmonious relationship between the Republic of Mexico and its colonists in Texas. First, a steady stream of North Americans entered Texas illegally, exacerbating Mexican fears of American expansionism. For this reason, the central government passed a series of measures that imposed more rigorous tax collection, blocked the further importation of slaves, occupied Texas with military garrisons, and culminated with the Decree of April 6, 1830, which prohibited any further immigration of North Americans into Texas. Second, the government of the Republic of Mexico was highly unstable, and consequently it could not devote its full attention to affairs in Texas. On January 3, 1833, General Antonio López de Santa Anna led an army into Mexico City, and three months later he was elected president of the Republic. His administration was forced to confront the growing tensions in Texas.

Indeed, the laws designed to assert Mexican control over Texas had led to armed resistance in 1832, with skirmishes at Anahuac. Then, the Turtle Bayou Resolutions of June 13, 1832 clearly expressed the colonists' resentment of the Mexican government's policies and seeming abandonment of the principles set forth in the 1824 constitution. In April 1833, a convention of Anglo-American colonists drafted a petition calling for the recognition of Texas as a separate state within the Mexican federation rather than as a province of Coahuila, as it was then configured. Against his better judgment, Austin delivered this petition to authorities in Mexico City where, after experiencing a series of disappointments, he drafted a letter encouraging the colonists to establish a separate state government, with or without the approval of the Mexican government. This letter was intercepted and Austin was placed under arrest; he spent the next year in prison. Not only did this experience compel the moderate Austin into a less conciliatory stance regarding the Mexican central government, but it stirred up a great deal of the anti-Mexican sentiment among Anglo colonies.

By 1835, moreover, a minority of Mexican legislators, capitalizing on fears that federalism had only promoted social chaos, had begun to restructure the Mexican government, vesting all power in a central authority and largely stripping the states of their powers. Several of Mexico's states were quick to respond to this abrogation of the Constitution of 1824 with military resistance. Resistance to the new centralist government was especially strong in Zacatecas, Tamaulipas, and Yucatán. To stamp out the flames of rebellion, in May 1835 Santa Anna led his army into Zacatecas, routed the state's militia, and sacked the state capital.

Then, following the clash at Anahuac in July 1835 between Mexican soldiers and Texan militiaman, Santa Anna ordered the garrisons in Texas to be reinforced. The Anglo-Texan community responded with a call to arms. On October 2, 1835, a column of Mexican lancers sent by General of Brigade Martín Perfecto Cos to take possession of a small cannon at the village of Gonzalez clashed with a group of Texan militiaman fighting under a banner inscribed with the words "Come and Take It." Although the skirmish itself was nearly bloodless, the action may be viewed as the beginning of the Texas Revolution.

From the nucleus of the Gonzalez militia grew the Army of the People, as settlers from all of Texan colonies rushed to join in what they viewed as a fight against Mexican tyranny. Under the command of Stephen F. Austin this "army"—in fact, little more than a rabble in arms—set out for San Antonio and a battle with Mexican forces there under the command of General Cos. Austin's small force arrived at San Antonio on October 9 to begin a lengthy and ill-coordinated siege. Despite several minor tactical victories, including a fight at Mission Concepción on October 20 in which volunteers under James Bowie and James Walker Fannin drove back a strong Mexican sortie, and the so called "Grass Fight," which interdicted the forage supply of the Mexican cavalry, as autumn phased into winter, the Army of the People began to grow demoralized.

On the verge of collapse from lack of leadership—Austin was in Washington heading a delegation seeking assistance from the United States—as well as internal disputes, the army rallied for an assault on the Mexican garrison on the morning of December 5, 1835. After five days of hand-to-hand combat in the streets of the villa in which the insurrectionists were greatly assisted by the arrival of two companies of volunteers from Louisiana, the New Orleans Greys, the Mexican troops withdrew into the walls of the former Franciscan mission known as the Alamo. There, on December 9, General Cos surrendered with the understanding that he would withdraw his troops beyond the Rio Grande and that they would make no further resistance to the reestablishment of the Federal Constitution of 1824.

While the siege of Béxar was under way, delegates from the Anglo colonies met at San Felipe de Austin to create a government.

This convention authorized the creation of a regular army under the command of Sam Houston, issued a Declaration of Causes stating that the rebellion in Texas had been precipitated by the abrogation of the Constitution of 1824, and sent a commission, headed by Steven F. Austin, to Washington to seek support for the Texan cause. The delegates further appointed Henry Smith of Brazoria as governor and constituted themselves a legislative body known as the General Counsel.

Following their success at San Antonio, the loosely organized Texas government planned an expedition against Matamoros. Outside of San Antonio, the largest contingent of Texan volunteers was located at Goliad on the San Antonio River about 100 miles downstream. From there Frank W. Johnson and Dr. James Grant launched an expedition toward the Rio Grande, only to be intercepted and routed by a Mexican counteroffensive under General of Brigade José Urrea. Urrea's strike force was one of two columns that Santa Anna had sent into Texas in reaction to Cos' surrender of San Antonio. The other, under Santa Anna's personal command, crossed the Rio Grande late in January 1836, marching for San Antonio. Santa Anna's army reached Béxar on February 23 and began its siege of the Alamo. The garrison, initially a mere 150 men, was divided between Texas regulars under Lieutenant Colonel William Barrett Travis and volunteers under James Bowie. Travis' call for reinforcements was heeded by only 18 volunteers who fought their way into the fortress from Gonzales. After a 13-day siege, Santa Anna's 3,000-man army stormed the Alamo at dawn on March 6, 1836, overwhelming the garrison and leaving no male survivors.

At the same time Urrea's column, having crushed the Texans at San Patricio on February 26 and at Agua Dulce Creek on March 2, marched toward the mission La Bahía at Goliad, which the rebel garrison under James Walker Fannin had renamed Fort Defiance. Fannin, realizing himself to be outnumbered, vacillated, determining first to hold the fort and then to fall back, first on Travis's position at the Alamo and then on Sam Houston's nucleus of an army at Victoria. He delayed doing either for too long, however, and was pinned down by Mexican cavalry near Coleto Creek. Urrea's infantry and artillery arrived, and Fannin was forced to surrender. His 300 troops were marched back to Goliad where on March 27, 1836, they were shot to death under Santa Anna's orders.

By then, a second congress, known as the Convention of 1836, had met at Washington-on-the-Brazos. There, on March 2, while the Alamo was under siege and on the very day that Fannin surrendered to Urrea, the delegates signed a declaration of independence from Mexico. Ironically, the defenders of the Alamo died fighting under the Mexican flag, never knowing that Texas was then an independent republic.

With the destruction of Travis's command at the Alamo and Fannin's at Goliad, the republic showed no sign of being able to outlive its birth. Only Sam Houston and a handful of men at Gonzalez remained in arms against Santa Anna's army, and, on learning of the fall of the Alamo, Houston began a rapid retreat across east Texas toward Louisiana. In a mass evacuation known as the

Runaway Scrape, almost all of the Anglo-Texan colonists fled their homes for the safety of the United States.

Confident that Texas resistance had collapsed, Santa Anna, with a 1,000-man vanguard, moved rapidly in pursuit of Houston's fleeing force, sure of destroying it. But as Houston approached the Sabine River, he was steadily reinforced by a stream of volunteers from the United States, and on April 21, 1836, with an army of some 900 men, he surprised and overran Santa Anna's camp on the San Jacinto River. Shouting the battle cries "Remember the Alamo!" and "Remember Goliad!" the Texan army killed more than 630 Mexican soldiers and captured 730 others in a bloody eighteen-minute battle. Houston's casualties were only nine killed and thirty wounded.

Santa Anna, captured by the victorious Texan forces, was offered the option of signing the Treaty of Velasco, which would give Texas its independence and national territory extending all the way to the Rio Grande, or face immediate execution by hanging. Santa Anna chose the former. He sent orders to his subordinate commanders to immediately evacuate Texas, while he himself was put aboard ship and sent to Washington, D.C., where he met with President Andrew Jackson.

Not surprisingly, the Mexican Congress failed to ratify the Treaty of Velasco and continued to regard Texas as part of the Mexican national territory. Thus, for a 10-year period, the Republic of Mexico and the breakaway Republic of Texas carried on a desultory border war of raid and counter raid, with neither side able to win a decisive victory over the other.

Hoping to make good its claim to all territory on the left bank of the Rio Grande, the 321-man Santa Fe Expedition, led by Colonel Hugh McCloud, marched out of Austin in June, 1841 and ventured as far west as modern-day Tucumcari, New Mexico, only to be surrounded by Mexican forces and captured on September 17, 1841. The brutal treatment of the Santa Fe prisoners gave Anglo Texans further reason to seek vengeance against their Mexican neighbors.

Hoping to at least remind its breakaway province that Mexico still claimed sovereignty over Texas, 400 Mexican soldiers under Colonel Rafael Vásquez crossed the Rio Grande and marched into San Antonio on March 5, 1842. After occupying the town for only three days, however, the column returned to Mexico before Texas authorities could gather a force to resist it. Later that same year, on September 10, a second Mexican incursion of 1,082 troops, led by General Adrian Woll, again briefly retook San Antonio. A hastily-organized Texan counteroffensive clashed with Woll's column at Salado Creek, just outside of San Antonio, on September 18. Both sides claimed victory, but Woll withdrew his force below the Rio Grande.

Seeking to secure its territory from further Mexican incursions and to regain lost national honor, the Republic of Texas prepared a counterstrike. The Houston administration authorized Alexander Somervell to organize a 700-man force to be known as the Southwestern Army of Operations with the objective of invading northern Mexico. Somervell's command departed San Antonio late in November 1842, and on December 8 captured Laredo. Demoralization and insubordination, however, caused the army to stall at that point, whereupon Somervell ordered the men to demobilize and return to their homes. Some 300 of them, however, refused to give up the campaign and, selecting William S. Fisher as their commander, crossed the Rio Grande on December 23 and occupied Mier. There, on Christmas Day, they were surrounded by Mexican regulars under General Pedro de Ampudia, and after a 24-hour siege, Fisher surrendered his command. The prisoners were marched to Salado where, at the command of acting president Nicolás Bravo, every tenth man—those who drew black beans rather than white ones from an earthen jar—was executed by firing squad. Those who survived the decimation were marched to the state of Veracruz, where they experienced confinement at the notorious Perote Prison.

In addition to its ongoing war with Mexico, Texas was increasingly beset by Comanche war parties raiding its western frontier. Beginning with the attack on Parker's Fort on May 19, 1836 and culminating with the Council House Fight on March 19, 1840 and the Great Comanche Raid and the decisive Battle of Plum Creek on August 12, 1840, Indian warfare absorbed much of Texas's resources and slowed the republic's westward expansion.

Perhaps the sole positive aspect of Texas's war with Mexico occurred at sea. The Navy of the Republic of Texas dominated the Gulf of Mexico for ten years and gave considerable assistance to the rebels in Yucatán. In the naval battle of Campeche off the coast of Yucatán, April 30, 1843, Commodore Edwin Ward Moore, commanding the Texan sloop-of-war *Austin* and brig *Wharton* defeated two of the most advanced warships of the time, the Mexican steamship-of-war *Guadalupe* and the equally formidable *Moctezuma*. The Texas Navy died an ignominious death, however, when President Sam Houston ordered its ships sold at auction because the Republic could not afford their upkeep.

With finances of their nation in a perilous state and the constant threat of re-annexation by Mexico, the prospect of becoming a state in the American union was entirely pleasing to a majority of Texans. Sam Houston, as the first president of the Republic of Texas, sought annexation, but, because Texas would have entered the Union as a slave state, its entry was for ten years blocked by abolitionist elements in the United States Congress. And not all Texans wanted to become part of the United States. Maribeau B. Lamar, for example, the Republic's second president, fought to maintain Texas sovereignty.

After a decade of diplomatic proposals from Texas and rebuffs by the American congress, at last, President John Tyler, a Tennessee planter and slave-owner, finessed an agreement that admitted Texas to the Union. The United States Senate signed the annexation agreement on February 27, 1845 and the House of Representatives followed suit on the day following. The state's admission was formalized in Austin, Texas on February 19, 1846.

Not surprisingly, Mexico viewed this acquisition by the United States of what it still considered to be its own territory as a blatant land grab. Mindful that war with Mexico might be the result of Texas annexation, in mid-1845 President Polk ordered Brigadier General Zachary Taylor to Fort Jesup, Louisiana, to take command there of the regiments of the regular United States Army to be known as the Army of Observation. As the possibility of war with Mexico increased, on July 25, 1845, Polk ordered Taylor's 3,400-man force to Corpus Christi, Texas, on the Nueces River, provocatively close to the disputed zone between the Nueces and the Rio Grande.

An attempt at finding a diplomatic solution to the U.S.-Mexico border dispute failed when, in December 1845, Mexican authorities refused to treat with Polk's emissary, John Slidell. Exerting further pressure on the Mexican government to recognize Texas's annexation, on January 13, 1846, Polk ordered Taylor's command (renamed the Army of Occupation when it entered Texas) to the Rio Grande. The army arrived at the site of the present-day city of Brownsville, Texas, on March 28 and began construction of fortification that it called Fort Texas (later Fort Brown).

Mexican authorities, viewing this U.S. movement into an area that it still believed to be part of the state of Coahuila, responded by sending General of Division (Major General) Pedro de Ampudia at the head of the Army of the North to Matamoros, opposite Fort Texas. Ampudia was shortly thereafter replaced by General Mariano Arista. A period of uneasy watchfulness was shattered on April 25 when a sizable Mexican force under Colonel Anastasio Torrejón overwhelmed a squadron of U.S. dragoons commanded by Captain Seth Thornton north of the Rio Grande. This incident proved to be the immediate catalyst for the U.S. war declaration the following month.

Taylor's primary problem was one of logistics, and on May 1, 1846 he marched the largest part of his command out of Fort Texas to establish a line of communication and supply with Point Isabel at the mouth of the Rio Grande. Seeking to take advantage of Taylor's exposed position, Arista's army crossed the Rio Grande and, on May 8, 1846, attacked the American army—then marching back to Fort Texas—at Palo Alto. There the Mexican army, although greater in numbers, was defeated, largely by superior American artillery. The following day, May 9, the opposing forces clashed again, this time with Arista's army fighting a defensive battle. The result was another U.S. victory. At this point, the demoralized Army of the North withdrew to Matamoros where Arista was relieved of command by General Ampudia, and Taylor's men continued their march to the relief of Fort Texas, which had been under siege since May 1.

Although Washington had not yet received word of the fighting at Palo Alto and Resaca de la Palma, on May 11, 1846 President Polk called a joint session of Congress and, based on the attack on Thornton's dragoons, called for a declaration of war against Mexico, claiming that "American blood has been shed on American soil." Although Congressman Abraham Lincoln of Illinois and a few other Whigs raised their voices in protest, war was declared on May 13 and remained generally popular in the south and west where the belief in America's Manifest Destiny was es-

pecially strong and where the desire for new farmlands, especially land where slavery could be practiced, made northern Mexico a tempting target for takeover. Southern hopes of a southwestern empire for slavery were somewhat diminished by the introduction of the Wilmot Proviso, a rider to the house appropriations bill that funded the war, which stipulated that no territory taken from Mexico would ever be a home to slavery. The proviso easily passed in the House of Representatives, and although it failed to gain a majority in the Senate, it served as a dire warning to the South that its labor system and, indeed, its whole way of life were in peril.

Following the twin Mexican defeats at Palo Alto and Resaca de la Palma, Ampudia shifted the conduct of the war from an offensive strategy to one of defense, deep in his home territory, behind the forbidding deserts of northern Mexico that he hoped would exhaust any U.S. column that sought to pursue his army. The Army of the North, therefore, abandoned Matamoros and fell back 175 miles to the fortress city of Monterrey. Taylor's army followed, occupying Matamoros on May 17–18. Then, led by patrols of Texas Rangers that scouted out water sources and forage for the army's draft animals, the Americans marched out of Matamoros in September and began their trek toward Monterrey.

With the war now well underway, the Polk administration was faced with two major tasks. The first of these was raising an army. The regular United States army, in 1846, numbered only 7,500 officers and men. The soldiers were, by and large, well-disciplined and ably led, largely by a cadre of fine junior officers recently graduated from the United States Military Academy at West Point. Their numbers, however, were obviously much too small to win a war with Mexico. To augment his force of regulars, Polk called upon the states to raise regiments of volunteers to be mustered into United States service. Support for the war in the South and West made recruitment there an easy job, but in the Northeast, particularly in New England, where the war was much less popular, volunteers were scarce.

While generally enthusiastic and eager for adventure, volunteers proved to be highly resistant to military discipline and liable to committing atrocities against Mexican civilians. Their officers, elected by the men or appointed by state governors, were of uneven quality, varying from very good—John A. Quitman and Alexander Doniphan—to abominable, such as Gideon J. Pillow, the President's former law partner commissioned a major general solely on his loyalty to the Democratic Party. In all, the administration raised 73,532 volunteers for the war.

Polk's second task lay in devising a strategy for the war. When his initial hope that Mexico would give up the fight and cede not only Texas but California and what is now the American Southwest to the United States after the North Americans won a battle or two on the Rio Grande proved illusory, the president realized that a longer, more complex war was at hand. With the help of Secretary of War Randolph B. Marcy and Major General Winfield Scott, the Polk administration initially devised a two-part strategy, first sending Taylor into Mexico to occupy the republic's northern provinces as bargaining chips at the negotiating table. Concurrently, Polk authorized the formation of a second, smaller army—the Army of the West—to march down the Santa Fe Trail, capture the important trading center of Santa Fe, and then to march overland to California to assist in the conquest of that greatly desired province. The United States Navy, operating in the Pacific, would aid in this mission by capturing such Alta California ports as San Diego, Los Angeles, and Monterey.

Taylor, having arrived at Walnut Springs, three miles north of Monterrey on September 19, planned to use three of his four divisions, those of Brigadier General John A. Quitman, Brigadier General David Emanuel Twiggs, and Major General William Butler, to smash the city's defenses from the north and east. At the same time, he would send his fourth division, that of Brigadier General William Jennings Worth, on a sweeping flanking maneuver around to the west of city to interdict the highway to Mexico City and to serve as the anvil against which he planned to hammer the Mexican army. On September 20, Taylor threw the three divisions against Arista's forces, but was able to make no headway against the heavily fortified city. On its eastern outskirts, Mexican engineers had made a formidable fortress of buildings; all of Taylor's attempts to breach this line were costly failures.

Worth, however, had better luck. Arriving at the rear of the city, he stormed and captured two major fortresses: the Bishop's Palace atop Independence Hill and *El Soldado* on Federation Hill, and then entered Monterrey, clearing the western half of the city in hand-to-hand fighting. Taylor, however, unaware of his subordinate's success and mindful of his own heavy losses, requested a truce. Arista, realizing, as Taylor did not, that he was surrounded and in danger of annihilation, was happy to negotiate an armistice under the terms of which he evacuated the city on September 24, but moved out with his entire army with all of its arms, baggage, and equipment. The terms of the capitulation also stipulated that the two armies would observe a two-month truce.

Taylor was pleased with the terms of this agreement, but the Polk administration immediately abrogated the truce, reminding Taylor in a scathing letter that his job was not to make treaties but to "kill the enemy." The president was genuinely anxious to carry the war through to a successful conclusion because the American people were beginning to lose their enthusiasm for the conflict. He was also concerned about Taylor's rising political star. "Old Rough and Ready," as Taylor had come to be known by his adoring public, was the hero of Palo Alto, Resaca de la Palma, and now Monterrey, *and* he was a Whig. Polk was hooked on the horns of a political dilemma. He could scarcely fire his most successful and popular general, but to give him the opportunity to achieve further military glory was certain to sweep Taylor into the White House in the election of 1848. The president, therefore, attempted a difficult middle course by ordering Taylor to discontinue his invasion of Mexico and stand on the defensive at Monterrey. While this order made some strategic sense—the hundreds of miles of barren, desert terrain between Monterrey and Mexico City would have been almost impossible for a horse- and mule-drawn army to

traverse—it infuriated the sensitive Taylor who, although largely apolitical to that point, was beginning to harbor strong presidential ambitions. Taylor, therefore, in defiance of the war department's instructions, moved south out of Monterrey and, on November 16, 1846, occupied Saltillo.

While Taylor was waging his campaign in northern Mexico, the second front was opening in California and the Southwest. Even before the war had begun, the Polk administration had sent brevet Captain John C. Frémont to California with a group of soldiers in civilian clothing on an ostensible scientific expedition. Politely, but firmly, California authorities expelled Frémont, who then drifted north toward the Oregon Territory to await developments. On May 9, 1846, the same day that Taylor was fighting Arista at Resaca de la Palma, Frémont returned to California, intent upon fomenting rebellion among the American settlers in the Mexican state.

On July 4, 1846, Frémont declared California independent from Mexico and helped instigate the so-called Bear Flag Republic. In support of this insurrection, Commodore John Drake Sloat, in command of the Pacific Squadron, seized Monterey, California, July 7, and on August 12 his replacement, Commodore Robert Field Stockton, occupied Los Angeles.

To further the administration's ambition to annex the Mexican state of Alta California, on June 5, 1846 Colonel Stephen Watts Kearny marched out of Fort Leavenworth, Kansas, at the head of the Army of the West. This patchwork army of 1,700 men was to seize Santa Fe and then assist in the conquest of the Pacific coast. Manuel Armijo, the governor of New Mexico, attempted to rally the citizens of his province to the defense of its capital, but his numbers were insufficient and ill-trained, and dispersed as Kearny approached. The Army of the West, therefore, bloodlessly occupied Santa Fe on August 18, 1846. When a second regiment of Missouri mounted volunteers arrived at Santa Fe some weeks afterward, commanded by Colonel Sterling Price, Kearny, with his dragoons, departed the city on September 25, 1846, undertaking a grueling march of 850 miles across the Sonoran Desert for San Diego. En route, he encountered veteran scout Christopher "Kit" Carson, eastbound as a courier bearing dispatches to the effect that Frémont and the navy had already pacified California. Assuming, therefore, that his men would not be needed, he turned back all but 121 of his 300 dragoons.

Unbeknownst to Kearny, however, the *Californios* had revolted against American rule at Los Angeles on September 22-23, 1846 and had regained control of much of the region for Mexico. The situation in California was, then, much different than Kearny expected when, on December 6, 1846, his exhausted dragoons encountered a force of Ranchero cavalry at San Pasqual, a few miles north of San Diego. Although his forces were near the point of starvation after the desert crossing and his ammunition was wet from a recent rainfall, on Carson's advice Kearny determined to disburse the enemy horsemen. Although Kearny's men were initially successful, the Mexicans, under command of Don Andrés Pico, turned and counterattacked when they saw that American horses were failing, and the Mexican lancers were able to ride down the American horsemen whose guns would not fire. Kearny himself was severely wounded, and his 60 surviving dragoons were forced to take a defensive position on Mule Hill, holding out until Carson and Edward Fitzgerald "Ned" Beale were able to reach San Diego and return with a relief column from Stockton's flotilla. The battle of San Pasqual is considered the only significant engagement of the Mexican War that the United States lost.

Kearny, who arrived at San Diego on December 12, took command of all U.S. forces on the West Coast and, on January 8, 1847, defeated the Mexican insurgents at the Battle of San Gabriel. On January 10, 1846, Commodore Stockton reoccupied Los Angeles, effectively bringing to an end resistance to the American occupation of California.

Kearny had left the 1st Missouri Mounted Volunteers, under Colonel Alexander Doniphan, at Santa Fe to suppress Indian raids and to keep in check any New Mexican unrest resulting from the American occupation. With the arrival of Price's regiment and the appearance that the province was thoroughly pacified, Doniphan's regiment rode out of Val Verde on December 12, 1846, heading south down the Rio Grande to invade Chihuahua.

Before departing for California, Kearney appointed Charles Bent as territorial governor of New Mexico. Although the situation there appeared calm, many New Mexicans and Native Americans, in fact, resented the U.S. takeover of their territory and feared that Mexican land titles would not be recognized by the new government. On the morning of January 19, 1847, insurrectionists, led by Pablo Montoya and Tomás Romero, revolted in Taos. A group under Romero broke into the home of Governor Bent, and wounded and scalped him in the presence of his family. When the assailants left, Bent sought assistance but was discovered and murdered. Also killed and scalped that day were three other local officials. On the following day, a force of some 500 Mexicans and Indians killed from six to eight men at Arroyo Hondo and seven American traders at Mora.

Price moved swiftly against the rebels. During February 3-5, his men surrounded some 1,500 Mexicans and Indians in Taos and, after breaching the adobe walls with cannon fire, stormed the pueblo, killing an estimated 150 rebels and capturing 400 others. A second column of U.S. troops defeated and dispersed the rebel force at Mora. Ultimately, 15 men were found guilty of murder and treason and sentenced to death; six of them were hanged in Taos Plaza on April 9. On April 25 another five were executed. Altogether, some 28 people were executed for having taken part in the revolt. Tomás Romero was murdered in his cell before trial, while Montoya was among those tried, sentenced to death, and hanged. Some sporadic fighting continued in the ensuing months, but the rebellion was crushed.

By the time of the Taos revolt, Doniphan's regiment was in Mexico. On Christmas Day the Missourians defeated Colonel Antonio Ponce's 2,000-man force at the battle of El Brazito, and two days later occupied El Paso. After a month of rest and refitting

there, Doniphan again moved south, defeating General of Brigade José A. Heredia's force of nearly 4,000 regulars and militiamen, supported by 16 guns at the Battle of Río Sacramento on February 28, 1847, and occupying Chihuahua on March 1. From there, "Doniphan's Thousand," as they came to be known, moved east across northern Mexico, absolutely unopposed. On May 22 they connected with Taylor's army at Saltillo and from there moved on to the port of Brazos Santiago, where they were taken aboard transports and sailed to New Orleans. From there they steamed up the Mississippi River to Saint Louis and ultimately to Saint Joseph, the point of their departure. The men of the First Missouri Mounted Rifles had traveled 3,600 miles overland and 2,000 by water and fought two significant battles, but otherwise had faced little serious resistance. Doniphan's March was of little strategic significance, but it did capture the imagination of the American people and demonstrated that if American raiders were unable to hold the territory they traversed, neither did they incite local people to attempt to expel them.

Yet another large-scale incursion into northern Mexico was led by Brigadier General John E. Wool, who led 900 American soldiers out of San Antonio on September 25, 1846, the same day that Kearny departed New Mexico for California, bound for Chihuahua. Wool occupied Monclova without opposition on October 29, 1846 and, on December 5, the city of Parras, and from there joined Taylor's army at Saltillo. Like Doniphan's March, Wool's was of little strategic value, but gave further evidence of the fact that the common Mexican people had little interest in the war.

General Santa Anna, who had been exiled to Cuba in 1845 in the wake of his failed fifth presidential administration, was eager to return to power in Mexico. He thus concluded a deal with the Polk administration in which he promised to end the war and deliver a favorable boundary resolution to the United States in return for passage to Veracruz and a payment of $30 million. Santa Anna returned to Mexico on August 16, 1846. He then reneged on his agreement to befriend the Polk administration, and vowed to drive the Yankee invaders from his country. President Polk, saddled with an increasingly unpopular war, had discovered that the occupation of Mexican territory was not driving the enemy to the negotiating table and, perhaps worse, his most successful general was of the wrong political party. He therefore engineered a change in strategy, determining to strike at the enemy's capital and thus force Mexico to terms. Bypassing Taylor, Polk appointed Major General Winfield Scott to command the new expedition. Scott had been denied a field command at the beginning of the war because he, like Taylor, was a Whig, a potential presidential candidate, and a bitter political foe of the commander in chief. Nevertheless, most likely realizing that of all his generals only Scott had the necessary military skills to successfully carry out such an operation, on November 18, 1846 the president appointed Scott to command of a new American army. Its task was to undertake an amphibious landing on Mexico's Gulf coast, capture the vital port city of Veracruz, and then march inland to Mexico City.

Scott had been given an army without troops, and so was forced, on January 3, 1846, to remove from Taylor's command almost all of the regular regiments of the United States army. This stripping of his army of its best units stirred Taylor to great resentment of the president and of his fellow general, a resentment that would have lasting repercussions when Taylor became president in 1848.

Stung by the evisceration of his army and the lack of respect, on February 5, 1847, Taylor, in defiance of Polk's orders to remain at Monterrey, moved his diminished army to an advanced position at Agua Nueva. Santa Anna, aware that Scott's invasion was imminent, rightly perceived that he and the Mexican army were about to be caught between two American forces. Faced with the choice of meeting Scott's landing force on the beaches below Veracruz or attacking Taylor in his advanced position at Agua Nueva, the Mexican general chose the latter, hoping to destroy Taylor's weakened army and then march north into Texas.

Santa Anna put this bold and daring plan into action, raising a new army and marching north, catching Taylor virtually by surprise. Only astute reconnaissance by a company of Texas Rangers warned him of the enemy's presence in time to fall back to a strong defensive position at Buena Vista on February 21. The two-day Battle of Buena Vista (February 22–23, 1847) was closely contested and came near to being a decisive Mexican victory. Superior American artillery and the stand of the First Mississippi Rifles under Colonel Jefferson Davis broke the spirited Mexican attacks, however, and, with both armies largely shattered, Santa Anna withdrew to Mexico City. There he declared a victory and recruited a new army with which to face Scott.

Santa Anna, however, did not have time to fully raise, equip, and organize an army before Scott arrived. He was certain, nevertheless, that the walls of Veracruz and the seemingly impregnable fortress of San Juan de Ulúa, with their combined garrison of 4,390 men, could hold the American army on the beach long enough for him to march to the rescue or that the dreaded yellow fever ("vómito negro"), so prevalent in the Mexican low country, would destroy the United States army without a fight. Thus, on March 9, 1847, Scott's armies splashed ashore just below Veracruz unopposed. With remarkable speed, Scott's West Point-trained engineers erected heavy batteries around Veracruz and began a systematic siege and bombardment. Within three days the walls were breached, and on March 29, 1847, the Mexicans surrendered the city.

With equal rapidity, Scott prepared his army to move to the Mexican interior, out of reach of the yellow fever mosquitoes. On April 8, he began to move inland using the port of Veracruz as his base. Ever hopeful that each American success would bring peace, on April 15 Polk appointed Nicholas Trist of the State Department as commissioner plenipotentiary and sent him to negotiate a peace with Santa Anna. The Mexican general, however, was not prepared to discuss peace, instead moving his new army into a superb defensive position at Cerro Gordo, the only route that Scott could take into the highlands and on to the Mexican capital. Santa Anna's position appeared impregnable, but engineer Captain Robert E. Lee,

in a daring reconnaissance, discovered a path around his flank and Scott was able to move his regulars into position on the enemy left and rear. Utterly surprised by an attack from that quarter, the Mexican army scattered, and its general barely escaped from the field, leaving behind his personal carriage, the army's payroll, and one of his several wooden legs.

Scott moved quickly inland and, on April 22, his vanguard, led by Brigadier General William J. Worth, occupied Perote, and on May 15, Puebla, the second largest city in Mexico. There, however, the invasion ground to a halt when 4,000 of Scott's volunteers, their enlistment periods up, insisted upon being allowed to return home. The army, therefore, remained halted at Puebla until August, waiting for replacement troops to arrive from the United States. The energetic Santa Anna took full advantage of this delay and raised yet another army for the defense of his capital.

At last, with his army reinforced by new recruits, Scott again began his advance. Santa Anna had used time wisely, surrounding Mexico City with a chain of powerful fortifications, but once again Scott's remarkable young engineers performed heroic reconnaissance missions to locate a soft spot in the enemy line. On August 20, having found a trail across an apparently impassable lava bed called El Pedregal, Scott engaged the Northern Division under the command of General of Division Gabriel Valencia at the Battle of Contreras, and the Army of the Center, led by General of Division Manuel Rincón, at Churubusco. Both of these actions were decisive U.S. victories, breaching Santa Anna's defenses and leaving open the way to Mexico City, then only five miles distant.

The Americans, however, hoped for a negotiated settlement rather than a continuation of the bloody and increasingly unpopular war; Scott also feared that Mexican congressmen would scatter if Mexico City were captured, making the negotiation and ratification of a treaty almost impossible. Therefore, on August 24 he and Santa Anna agreed upon an armistice, ostensibly to provide an opportunity for Trist and the Mexican commissioners to meet and discuss a conclusion to the war. Neither side was to reinforce its army or to construct defensive works while the armistice was in effect. Almost immediately, however, Santa Anna broke the terms of the agreement, repulsing American supply trains and strengthening the capital's defenses. Therefore, on September 6, Scott terminated the Tacubaya Armistice and prepared again for offensive operations.

Acting on a flawed piece of intelligence that had located a cannon foundry at El Molino del Rey, Scott determined to make his next strike there. He left tactical control of the battle, however, to William J. Worth, who failed to carry out proper reconnaissance before launching his troops in a frontal assault on the breast-high walls of the mill. Although the American army carried the position with the bayonet, routing its defenders, Molino Del Rey, fought on September 8, 1847, was the single most costly battle of the war for the United States.

At however high a cost, control of Molino del Rey brought Scott's army one step closer to the final assault on Mexico City. Only the key fortress of Chapultepec Castle remained between them and the gates of the city. Formerly the home of the Spanish viceroy, this castle was now the Mexican national military academy, and alongside the regular Mexican soldiers, the cadets, ever after known as "*Los Niños Héroes*," defended their school. After an intense artillery bombardment, Scott's infantry surged forward on September 13, 1847, scaled the walls, and overran the citadel. With no further organized resistance outside its walls, U.S. soldiers quickly secured the capital's gates and began a street-by-street, house-by-house battle for control of the city. Scott entered the capital early in the morning of September 14, and his troops assumed full control of Mexico City following a two-day riot led by members of Mexico City's underclass. That same day, September 16, Santa Anna, who had fled with the remains of his army in the early morning hours of September 14, relinquished the presidency but continued a brief and sporadic campaign against Scott's attenuated supply line.

Meanwhile, Trist's apparent lack of progress toward a peace settlement angered the president, and on October 8 Polk ordered his recall. Not until November 16, however, did Trist receive word of his dismissal, and, in view of the fact that the capital had fallen since Polk had issued his recall and negotiations with Mexican officials were well underway, he determined to defy the president's order and remain in Mexico. After months of negotiations, on February 2, 1848 Trist and the Mexican commissioners signed the Treaty of Guadalupe Hidalgo. It stipulated, in brief, that the present-day states of California, Utah, New Mexico, Nevada, most of Arizona, and parts of Colorado and Wyoming—a total of 525,000 square miles—would be ceded to the United States. In return Mexico would receive $15 million in restitution, and all debts owed to American citizens by the Republic of Mexico—some $3.25 million—would be paid by the United States Treasury. On March 10, 1848 the treaty was ratified by the United States Senate; on March 25 the Mexicans ratified it. On June 12, Americans troops evacuated Mexico City.

While the American conquest of California and the Southwest represented a huge and potentially highly valuable land acquisition, this growth did not come without tremendous cost. Gold discovered at Sutter's Mill, California, in 1848—ironically, almost simultaneously with the signing of the Treaty of Guadalupe Hidalgo—brought to the United States fabulous wealth. It also brought to the political forefront the question of whether or not slavery should be allowed in the newly acquired territories. Gold fever drew tens of thousands of settlers to California, and they, of course, soon demanded statehood. The question of whether the state, as well as the other territories taken from Mexico, would enter the Union as slave or free became the most burning issue of the next decade of American political debate.

The Compromise of 1850, which brought California into the Union as a free state but left the remaining territories free to choose their status under the concept of "popular sovereignty," settled this vexing question, but only temporarily. The rancor and animosity engendered between the two sides of this debate were instrumental in driving a sharp wedge between the North and the South, leading inevitably to Southern secession and civil war by 1861. As the American philosopher Ralph Waldo Emerson had rightly predicted, "Mexico will poison us."

THOMAS W. CUTRER

References

Clary, David A. *Eagles and Empire: The United States, Mexico, and the Struggle for a Continent.* New York: Bantam, 2009.

Hardin, Stephen L. *Texian Iliad: A Military History of the Texas Revolution.* Austin: University of Texas Press, 1994.

Lack, Paul D. *The Texas Revolutionary Experience: A Political and Social History, 1835-1836.* College Station: Texas A&M University Press, 1992.

Johannsen, Robert W. *To the Halls of the Montezumas: The Mexican War in the American Imagination.* New York: Oxford University Press, 1985.

McCaffrey, James M. *Army of Manifest Destiny: The American Soldier in the Mexican War, 1846-1848.* New York: New York University Press, 1992.

Winders, Richard Bruce. *Polk's Army: The American Military Experience in the Mexican War.* College Station: Texas A & M University Press, 1997.

A

Abolitionism

A relatively broad-based social reform movement in the United States that advocated the abolition of the institution of slavery. Although abolitionism had existed in North America since colonial times, it gained considerable momentum beginning in the 1830s. Abolitionists were divided over the means by which slavery should be eradicated in the United States. Some abolitionists were pacifists and were opposed to armed conflict in general, while others perceived the Civil War of 1861–1865 as an opportunity to finally destroy the institution, pressing President Abraham Lincoln to make the conflict an antislavery crusade.

Abolitionists opposed slavery for a variety of reasons. A number were opposed to it on religious and moral grounds. Some ultimately saw it as an institution that would eventually destroy the United States. Still others opposed slavery because they believed it stood as an impediment to economic growth and maturation.

Opposition to slavery during colonial times was manifested by religious groups such as the Society of Friends, or Quakers. Antislavery sentiments were also apparent in the natural rights ideology of the American Revolution, and slavery was abolished by most northern states following independence in 1776. Slavery, however, grew in the South, especially after Eli Whitney's invention of the cotton gin in 1793 and the expansion of cotton production into the western territories. Concerned with the spread of slavery and also concerned that racial prejudice would prevent freed slaves from participating in American life, some antislavery advocates formed the American Colonization Society in 1817. This organization advocated transporting freed slaves back to Africa. Between 1817 and 1867, approximately 15,000 blacks were sent to the Republic of Liberia, in West Africa, but the colonization approach foundered because of high costs and the fact that many slaves were already generations removed from Africa.

The growing abolitionist movement was fueled in the 1830s by the religious ferment of the Second Great Awakening and evangelists such as Theodore Weld, who preached that slavery was a sin. Weld's antislavery endeavors were supported by wealthy New York merchants Arthur and Lewis Tappan, who paid the young abolitionist's way to Lane Theological Seminary in Cincinnati, Ohio. While attending the seminary, Weld led an 18-day debate on slavery, which led to his expulsion. Weld and his Lane followers then moved throughout the Midwest spreading the gospel of abolition. In 1839, Weld published *Slavery as It Is,* one of the most influential tracts describing the brutality of the slave system.

With the impetus of the British abolition of slavery in the West Indies in 1833 and the Second Great Awakening, the American Anti-Slavery Society was founded in 1833. Under the leadership of William Lloyd Garrison, editor of the antislavery newspaper the *Liberator,* abolitionists pushed for the immediate emancipation of slaves as opposed to the gradualist approach of the American Colonization Society. Among Garrison's most important early supporters was the eloquent Boston patrician Wendell Phillips, who refused to eat cane sugar or wear cotton shirts, as these items were produced by slave labor. Abandoning the idea of reform within the churches, Garrisonians also advocated other more universal reforms such as temperance, women's rights, improved working conditions, and nonviolence.

Women such as Angelina Grimké, Elizabeth Cady Stanton, Lydia Maria Child, Lucy Stone, and Abby Kelley played leading roles in the movement, but the inclusion of women was considered controversial by some abolitionists. They maintained that linking women's rights with antislavery would divide the movement and postpone the end of slavery. Garrison's argument that the U.S. Constitution was proslavery caused considerable controversy, and in 1844 the American Anti-Slavery Society passed a resolution calling for the dissolution of the Union, believing that without northern financial support the southern economy and slavery system would collapse.

The highly diverse abolitionist movement also included former slaves fighting for the liberation of their brethren. Sojourner Truth, with her proclamation "Ain't I a Woman Too?" was a forceful advocate for both women's rights and antislavery. Harriet Tubman escaped from slavery in 1849 but risked her freedom by working with the Underground Railroad, returning to the South more than a dozen times and aiding approximately 300 slaves in their flight to freedom.

Perhaps the best-known black abolitionist was Frederick Douglass, who escaped bondage in 1838. The highly articulate Douglass soon became a prominent speaker at abolitionist rallies and began publishing the antislavery newspaper the *North Star.* He increasingly believed that abolitionists would need to become more involved with politics to eradicate slavery.

In 1840 the Liberty Party was formed, calling for no further expansions of slavery as the first step to abolishing the institution. In 1844, the party's presidential candidate, James J. Birney, received only 2 percent of the nation's popular vote. Many in the North actually feared that abolitionist agitation might provoke a war and disrupt trade, thus threatening jobs and white social mobility. Mob violence, such as the 1837 murder of Elijah Lovejoy in Alton, Illinois, became a threat to northern abolitionists during the 1830s and 1840s.

Perceptions of abolitionism in the North began to change, however, following the vast territorial expansion brought about by the 1846–1848 Mexican-American War and the passage of the Fugitive Slave Law as part of the Compromise of 1850. Indeed, after 1848, slavery became a highly incendiary political and social issue, which threatened to tear the nation apart. Sectional tensions were further exacerbated with the publication of Harriet Beecher Stowe's novel *Uncle Tom's Cabin* (1852), passage of the 1854 Kansas-Nebraska Act, and the violence in what came to be known as Bleeding Kansas. Fearing southern domination of Kansas, abolitionists supported the efforts of the New England Emigrant Aid Company, which dispatched about 2,000 antislavery settlers to the South. Prominent New York minister and abolitionist Lyman Beecher helped to raise funds to arm the abolitionist forces under attack by proslavery forces from Missouri. The violence of Bleeding Kansas became personified in the actions of abolitionist John Brown and his sons, who killed five slave owners at Pottawatomie Creek in May 1856. Brown fled prosecution in Kansas and was welcomed to Massachusetts by the writer and protester Henry David Thoreau.

Supported by wealthy abolitionists such as Samuel Gridley Howe, Theodore Parker, and Thomas Wentworth Higgenson, Brown next planned a raid on the federal armory at Harpers Ferry to arm slaves in Virginia. The October 16, 1859, raid on Harpers Ferry proved unsuccessful, and abolitionists were divided in their response. Douglass, whose son had participated in the action, proclaimed Brown a martyr, while Garrison described the raid as "well intended but sadly misguided."

The election of Abraham Lincoln in 1860 followed by southern succession and the firing on Fort Sumter in April 1861 led to war, and many abolitionists were forced to confront their conflicting views on war and antislavery. The Quaker Lucretia Mott continued to insist that slavery could be toppled without resorting to violence. Gerrit Smith, president of the American Peace Society, attempted to qualify his support for the war by insisting that the conflict was simply a rebellion that the federal government had the right to suppress. Other abolitionist pacifists, such as Adin Ballou and Josiah Warren, continued to oppose the war, insisting that slavery could be ended without resorting to violence and enhancing the power of the state.

In contrast, abolitionists such as Phillips and Garrison reluctantly embraced the conflict as an opportunity to eradicate slavery. Pro-war abolitionists pressured Lincoln to expand the aims of the war beyond preserving the Union to include the destruction of slavery. Abolitionists in Congress were angered by Lincoln's November 1861 rescinding of Major General John C. Frémont's proclamation confiscating secessionist property and emancipating the slaves in Missouri. Congressional Republicans passed legislation freeing the slaves in the nation's capital on April 16, 1862, while slavery in the territories was abolished on June 19, 1862. Abolitionists rallied in Chicago on September 7, 1862, calling for immediate emancipation. Lincoln agreed to meet with a delegation headed by William W. Patton and began discussing with his cabinet the option of employing emancipation as a war aim.

Following the Union victory at Antietam on September 17, 1862, Lincoln believed that the time had come to expand the war's purpose. Moving against slavery would also gain support from the British government and public, which were opposed to the institution. On September 22, 1862, the president issued the Preliminary Emancipation Proclamation, declaring forever free on January 1, 1863, the slaves in Southern states remaining in rebellion. While the directive did not apply to the slave-owning border states, the proclamation clearly foreshadowed the end of slavery. The Emancipation Proclamation also satisfied the demand of many abolitionists, including Douglass, by allowing the enrollment of free blacks in the military. During the war, approximately 180,000 African Americans served in the Union military, providing an important source of manpower.

Slavery was formally ended with approval of the Thirteenth Amendment to the U.S. Constitution on December 18, 1865, but as Douglass noted, abolition would not be complete until freedmen were allowed to vote and had secured their full rights as citizens. The Civil War ended slavery, but the status of the former slaves remained tenuous. Indeed, it would take another century before African Americans received full citizenship and voting rights and enjoyed access to institutions theretofore closed to them.

RON BRILEY

See also
Garrison, William Lloyd; Liberty Party; Mexican Cession; Second Great Awakening; Slavery; Thoreau, Henry David.

References
Azevedo, Celia M. *Abolitionism in the United States and Brazil: A Comparative Perspective.* New York: Garland, 1995.

Davis, David Brion. *The Problem of Slavery in the Age of Revolution, 1770–1823.* Ithaca, NY: Cornell University Press, 1975.

Lowance, Mason, ed. *Against Slavery: An Abolitionist Reader.* New York: Penguin Books, 2000.

McKivigan, John R., ed. *History of the American Abolitionist Movement.* New York: Routledge, 1999.

Stewart, James Brewer. *Holy Warriors: Abolitionists and American Slavery.* New York: Hill & Wang, 1976.

Adams, John Quincy
Birth Date: July 11, 1767
Death Date: February 23, 1848

Diplomat, congressman, senator, secretary of state (1817–1825), president of the United States (1825–1829), vociferous opponent of the Mexican-American War. Few Americans have ever compiled a record of public service as extensive and distinguished as that of John Quincy Adams. Born in Braintree (Quincy), Massachusetts, on July 11, 1767, Adams spent many of his early years traveling abroad with his famous father, John Adams, the second president of the United States.

With a penchant for languages, at age 14 young Adams was employed as an assistant to the foreign secretary to Russia. He graduated from Harvard College in 1788. During the 1790s, he served successive stints as the American foreign minister to Holland, Portugal, and Prussia. Returning to the United States in 1802, Adams was elected to the U.S. Senate as a Federalist that same year, where he remained until 1808. Resigning in 1808, he left the Federalist Party and became a Democratic-Republican. He soon was appointed minister to Russia, a post he held until 1814.

At Saint Petersburg, Adams first prepared negotiations for a conclusion to the War of 1812. Previous efforts at an armistice between the United States and Britain having failed, in March 1813 Russia offered to help mediate a peace. President James Madison was pleased by the idea and dispatched three commissioners to join Adams in Saint Petersburg. There they waited for six months. The British rejected Russian mediation and instead requested direct negotiations with the United States early in 1814. Madison obliged and selected five Americans for the forthcoming conference. John Quincy Adams chaired the president's peace delegation, and the Americans agreed that Ghent, Belgium, would afford a neutral and accessible site for peace talks.

Negotiations convened on August 8, 1814. The recent defeat of Napoleon, which freed up British military strength, did not bode well for the American cause. Buoyant over the victory, the British government could now focus the brunt of its forces against America

if it so decided. The British delegation quickly went on the offensive, demanding significant territorial and military concessions. Adams and his fellow commissioners were greatly displeased and rejected the demands, despairing of any real prospect for peace. The British delegation, however, began to retreat that October as news of British military failures at Baltimore and Plattsburg reached England, British debts and tax protests threatened to grow, and the court of European public opinion decidedly shifted in favor of the Americans. By December the British had relinquished their territorial demands, insistence on a Native American reserve in the Northwest Territory had been dropped, and American fishing rights were reestablished in Canadian waters. The Treaty of Ghent was finalized on Christmas Eve, 1814. Pleased by his performance in Ghent, Madison next assigned Adams to serve as minister to Great Britain, the most important U.S. diplomatic assignment of the 19th century. In 1817 President Monroe selected Adams as secretary of state, a post in which he contributed his most important career legacies. These included design of the 1819 Adams-Onís Treaty and the 1823 Monroe Doctrine, which Adams himself authored.

Adams was elected president in 1824 by the House of Representatives after none of the five candidates won the necessary number of electoral votes in the November elections. As president,

Former president of the United States John Quincy Adams (1825–1829) was one of the strongest opponents of the Mexican-American War, chastizing the conflict as both "unrighteous" and unconstitutional. (Library of Congress)

he promoted an ambitious agenda for the development of various national infrastructure projects and institutions. But the Democratic-Republicans, many of whom had backed Andrew Jackson in 1824, blocked him at nearly every opportunity. The bitter Jackson soundly defeated Adams in the election of 1828.

Not satisfied by retirement, in 1831 the former president won election to the U.S. House of Representatives, an office he held for 17 years until his death. A leading antislavery voice in Congress, Adams battled the "gag rule" for nine years and uncompromisingly fought to prevent any expansion of the "peculiar institution." Indeed, he submitted numerous proposals and petitions calling for the ending of slavery and the slave trade in Washington, D.C., and other areas. Admirers called him "the conscience of New England" and "Old Man Eloquent"; adversaries considered the sobriquet "Madman of Massachusetts" more appropriate.

In his final days of public service, Adams was among the Mexican-American War's most outspoken critics, viewing the conflict as "unrighteous" as well as unconstitutional. Adams strongly opposed the "robbery" of Texas from Mexico, which is what he termed the December 1845 annexation of that state, lamenting the event as "a signal triumph of the slave representation." Indeed, he predicted in late 1845 that Texan annexation would be tantamount to "the blast of the trumpet for a foreign, civil, servile, and Indian war." Sure enough, war with Mexico soon followed. In 1846 Adams openly accused President James K. Polk of having fraudulently engineered the conflict, and he led a small group of congressmen who tried in vain to prevent war. As an ultra Whig, Adams subsequently rejected measures to honor the war's participants. Praising the 1846 Wilmot Proviso, he demanded that troops be withdrawn immediately from Mexico with peace provided on generous terms. Adams died in Washington, D.C., on February 23, 1848, just prior to the conclusion of the war.

JEFFREY W. DENNIS

See also

Democratic Party; Polk, James Knox; Slavery; Texas; Whigs; Wilmot Proviso.

References

Falkner, Leonard. *The President Who Wouldn't Retire: John Quincy Adams, Congressman from Massachusetts.* New York: Coward McCann, 1967.

Hickey, Donald R. *The War of 1812: A Forgotten Conflict.* Urbana: University of Illinois Press, 1989.

Richards, Leonard L. *The Life and Times of Congressman John Quincy Adams.* New York: Oxford University Press, 1986.

Adams-Onís Treaty
Event Date: February 22, 1819

Formal treaty negotiated and signed in Washington, D.C., by U.S. secretary of state John Quincy Adams and Spanish minister to the United States Luis de Onís on February 22, 1819. The treaty

The Adams-Onís Treaty was in response to Andrew Jackson's Florida incursion in 1818. Signed on February 22, 1819, and ratified in 1821, the treaty granted the United States all Spanish lands east of the Mississippi River, including Florida. (Library of Congress)

entered into force exactly two years later. Formally known as the Treaty of Amity, Settlement, and Limits between the United States of America and His Catholic Majesty and also known as the Florida Treaty, the document settled a number of outstanding issues between the United States and Spain in North America. The most significant impact of the agreement was that it established the borders between Spanish North America and the United States, but it also dealt with a number of other issues.

Major General Andrew Jackson's spring 1818 military incursion into Florida during the First Seminole War (1817–1818) prompted the American-Spanish negotiations of 1819. In pursuit of the Seminoles, Jackson also seized Spanish-held posts at Pensacola and Saint Marks, which caused a minor crisis in U.S.-Spanish relations. Jackson's moves were tied directly to Adams's ability to negotiate a highly favorable treaty with Onís. After the post seizures, Adams approached Onís, arguing that the United States had legitimate concerns about its borders with Spanish Florida. By the summer of 1818, Spain was already willing to turn over all of Florida to the United States, although it would be another six months before the remaining details could be worked out.

The Adams-Onís Treaty opened with a promise of friendship between the two powers but quickly moved to the resolution of outstanding territorial issues. It is perhaps best known for transferring all Spanish lands east of the Mississippi River to the United States, an area that included both West and East Florida. West Florida (the Alabama and Mississippi Gulf Coast and the so-called Florida parishes of Louisiana—that is, those east of the Mississippi River) was already under de facto U.S. control but had been an area of contention between the two countries since the 1803 Louisiana Purchase. East Florida encompassed all of the Florida peninsula as well as the Florida panhandle. The treaty also settled the eastern and northern boundaries of Spanish possessions in North America, thus resolving the question of the western border of the Louisiana Purchase. In addition, the Spanish gave up their claims to modern-day Oregon, Washington, and British Columbia, while the United States gave up any claims to Texas and settled on the Sabine River as the Spanish-U.S. border.

The agreement covered a number of other issues important to both sides at the time. It promised that newly acquired Florida would be integrated into the United States as soon as practical and that the citizens of newly acquired areas would have the freedom to continue practicing their chosen religion. The United States and Spain also both renounced many of their claims dating back to the Napoleonic Wars. In addition, the Americans agreed to cover future claims against Spain up to $5 million. Both sides agreed to the return of deserters from vessels in their ports and that the Spanish would not pay higher duties than American vessels in either Pensacola or Saint Augustine, Florida, for 12 years after the agreement.

DONALD E. HEIDENREICH JR.

See also
Adams, John Quincy; Jackson, Andrew; Louisiana Purchase; Onís y González-Vara, Luis de; Sabine River; Spain; Texas.

References
Adams, John Q. *The Diary of John Quincy Adams, 1794–1845.* Edited by Allan Nevins. New York: Longmans, Green, 1928.
Adams, John Q. *John Quincy Adams and American Continental Empire: Letters and Speeches.* Edited by Walter LaFeber. Chicago: Quadrangle Paperback, 1965.
Brooks, Philip Coolidge. *Diplomacy and the Borderlands: The Adams-Onis Treaty of 1819.* Berkeley: University of California Press, 1939.
Lewis, James E., Jr. *John Quincy Adams: Policymaker for the Union.* Wilmington, DE: SR Books, 2001.

African Americans

African Americans played an important role in the U.S. victory in the Mexican-American War. Although the conflict saw the least amount of direct participation by African Americans of any declared war in U.S. history, they nevertheless furnished important support to the troops in the field. In 1846, slightly more than 3 million African Americans lived in the United States, of whom some 400,000 were free; the remainder were enslaved or indentured. The South claimed 55 percent of the African American population, while 45 percent resided in the North.

Despite the large number of African Americans, states undertook to prevent them from participating in the conflict. On February 18, 1820, the U.S. Army issued a general order, followed by general regulations in 1821, that excluded all African Americans from military duty. State militias also refused to accept African Americans. Delaware's Volunteer Militia Act, passed on the eve of the Mexican-American War, restricted all military units—artillery, infantry, cavalry, dragoons, riflemen, and grenadiers—to "free white male citizens." Despite efforts to exclude African Americans from the military, however, some managed to participate as soldiers, although they were not officially recognized as such. At least one mulatto slave defied army regulations and enlisted by using the government's call for volunteers as a disguise to escape to freedom in Mexico. Another African American civilian, a free mulatto barber from Galveston, is identified as having voluntarily followed the army. Many African Americans in the army worked as personal servants and assumed camp duties or other noncombatant assignments.

Commanders from the northern states used large numbers of black servants. Pay vouchers for officers of the New York Volunteers indicate that 7 of 15 servants were African American, and not all of them came from the free black community. Some officers took slaves with them across the Rio Grande into Mexico. Major Generals Winfield Scott and William O. Butler each had 4 black servants. The officers received compensation for securing slave servants, and they established quotas thanks to the national government's emphasis on utilizing slave servants.

African Americans represented as many as two-thirds of all military servants in the Mexican-American War. A slave named Samuel served at the Battle of Buena Vista (February 23, 1847) with the 2nd Illinois Volunteer Regiment. African American males comprised a majority of the servants, but a few African American women also served in that capacity. An African American female servant named Blanche worked for the 2nd Indiana Volunteers and faced danger in her duties, similar to other servants in the war camps. African American servants often had to defend themselves in the line of duty, and they failed to receive recognition for their valor.

Numerous African American servants risked their lives to prove their loyalty or to protect their masters. During various battles, African Americans fulfilled important combat duties by providing necessary services under deplorable conditions. Their service consisted of cooking, laundering, and general labor in the war camps. During the battles and marches, they also often cared for the horses and other animals and nursed the sick and wounded.

In 1847, Lieutenant Colonel John C. Frémont took Jacob Dodson, a free African American servant, on an 840-mile mission to California, because Dodson had essential expertise in training

The African American Population in the United States, 1820–1860

Census Year	Number of African Americans	% of Total U.S. Population	Slaves	% Slaves	% Non-Slaves
1820	1,771,656	18%	1,538,022	86.8%	13.2%
1830	2,328,642	18%	2,009,043	86.3%	13.7%
1840	2,873,648	17%	2,487,355	86.6%	13.4%
1850	3,638,808	16%	3,204,313	88.1%	11.9%
1860	4,441,830	14%	3,953,760	89.2%	10.8%

horses. George B. McClellan secured the services of a free black man named Songo from the plantation of his brother-in-law in Alabama and wrote often of his servant's character and deeds in his Mexican War journal and in his letters to his family. In July 1845, Lieutenant Ulysses S. Grant had an African American servant with him while stationed at New Orleans. Another free black man, Lewis Addams of Copiah County, Mississippi, served in Mexico as the servant of a volunteer captain.

African Americans also served in the navy, as crew members on navy vessels stationed off the Mexican coast and in California. Some slaves served in the navy as personal servants of officers, while others worked as carpenters, cooks, coopers, and dock hands.

The war also enabled African American slaves to take advantage of opportunities and escape from slavery by fleeing to Mexico. Many slaves sought refuge in Mexico because slavery already had been abolished in that country. Captains William S. Henry and Philip N. Barbour documented numerous cases of slaves running away. Many slaves chose to remain with their masters, however, perhaps because of the language barrier or fear that conditions in Mexico might not be any better.

Compared to white Americans, African Americans died at a much higher rate, mainly because of exposure to communicable diseases and unsanitary conditions. As was the case with Anglo-American soldiers, far more African Americans died from diseases than from hostile action. Poor personal hygiene, minimum medical training, and shortages of medicines and medical supplies all contributed to the high death rate. The status of African Americans divided the nation during the war, and this division became far more intense at war's end. By the early 1850s, the abolitionist movement gained significant momentum, and the divisions between North and South came to a head in the secession crisis of 1860–1861, which in turn precipitated the Civil War.

LaVonne Jackson Leslie

See also

Abolitionism; Army Life, Mexican and U.S.; Barbour, Philip Norbourne; Buena Vista, Battle of; Butler, William Orlando; Frémont, John Charles; Grant, Ulysses Simpson (Hiram Ulysses Grant); Scott, Winfield; Slavery; United States Army; United States Navy.

References

Astor, Gerald. *The Right to Fight: A History of African Americans in the Military.* New York: Ballantine Books, 1998.

Donaldson, Gary. *The History of African Americans in the Military: Double V.* Melbourne, FL: Krieger, 1991.

Foos, Paul. *A Short, Offhand, Killing Affair: Soldiers and Social Conflict during the Mexican-American War.* Chapel Hill: University of North Carolina Press, 2002.

Langley, Harold D. "The Negro in the Navy and Merchant Service, 1789–1860." *Journal of Negro History* 52 (1967): 279–280.

May, Robert E. "Invisible Men: Blacks in the United States Army during the Mexican War." *Historian* 49 (August 1987): 463–477.

Agriculture, United States and Mexico

During the 1840s the agricultural systems of the United States and Mexico were both in a period of transition. In the case of the United States, agriculture was moving steadily away from subsistence farming in the direction of a more commercial, market-oriented endeavor. Large tracts of fertile land had been opened to the plow in the years prior to the Mexican-American War, particularly in the Midwest and Great Plains. Indeed, American desire to secure Mexican-owned farm land in California and other places in the Southwest had helped precipitate the conflict between the two nations. Mexican agriculture, however, was moving in the opposite direction, reverting from a market orientation toward a more subsistence type of agriculture as a result of a number of social disruptions in the years leading up to the Mexican War, a circumstance frequently and disparagingly remarked on by U.S. soldiers—most of whom were farmers in civilian life—in their letters home and in their journals.

With the assistance of new technologies such as the steel plow, the seed drill, various cultivating and swathing devices, and the mechanical reaper, American farmers had opened up the vast prairies of Indiana, Illinois, Iowa, Wisconsin, and the Oregon Territory to agriculture in the 1840s. Federal land policy in the United States increasingly favored yeoman farmers by reducing the cost of land while making tracts available in smaller, more affordable plots. This was opposed to previous land policies that had favored speculators who bought large plots and then sold them in parcels to smaller farmers.

American farmers were also helped by an activist federal government that, beginning in the 1840s, offered material and scientific help to agrarians by searching the planet for new crop types, compiling statistics, and offering advice on improving stock through modern breeding principles. By the time of the Mexican-American War, numerous agricultural societies had also promoted new types of fertilizers and other farm improvements.

By 1862 the federal government had created the U.S. Department of Agriculture, a cabinet-level agency, to further help farmers become more productive and market-responsive. Even with this increased market orientation, many farmers continued to produce a variety of goods, such as butter, cheese, and cloth, both for subsistence needs and for occasional bartering for supplies that could not be produced on the farm. American farmers were also aided by major government investments in transportation infrastructure, including improved roads, canal projects, rail lines, and eventually the subsidization of the railroad industry.

In the American South, raw cotton had already emerged as the nation's top agricultural export by the time of the Mexican War. Fueled by technological and scientific innovations, as well as the expansion of slave labor, the desire to spread the cotton economy into new territories was another leading factor that propelled the United States into war with Mexico in 1846. By 1850 cotton was by far the chief export of the United States, helping fuel a worldwide revolution in the textile and clothing industry. Farmers in the northern reaches of the South, where cotton did not grow well, grew hemp to provide rope for the U.S. Navy, as well as packing material for the cotton trade. Rice and sugarcane were other major agricultural products, while farmers in Kentucky and Missouri also raised mules for export to the cotton economy in the Deep South. Tobacco, once the major export of southern farms, continued to be an important export crop, although there were far fewer farmers growing tobacco than in previous decades. Vagaries in the agricultural process caused by overproduction or bad weather and economic recessions hurt all farmers in the United States, and these economic challenges were particularly hard on the southern economy, which, unlike the North, was predominantly driven by agriculture.

Even though most southerners did not own slaves, the institution of slavery was usually very profitable for slave owners. Southern agriculture tended to be somewhat traditional in that land was seen as a commodity to be used up, rather than nurtured for long-term production. With little knowledge of crop rotation and new fertilizers, vast tracts of southern lands were "farmed out" by abusive practices, thereby creating an incessant need to develop new areas for cultivation. Eventually, farmers planted "green manure" crops, such as clover, to help restore fertility; they also added manufactured nutrients to denuded farm land.

In the years leading up to and during the Mexican-American War, agriculture in Mexico was less commercially developed than in the United States. In many areas of Mexico large haciendas and ranchos with substantial numbers of peasant laborers raised cattle and sheep, as well as pigs for the production of lard. Crops of wheat, often grown by smaller-scale farmers of American Indian or mestizo descent, were often complemented by small vegetable gardens, although in some areas Mexican farmers grew irrigated crops of wheat, beans, peas, barley, and corn. Often, these subsistence crops were augmented by vineyards and orchards.

Several factors, however, hampered Mexican agriculture in the 1840s. Much of the country is arid, and only a small fraction of Mexican agriculture was regularly irrigated in the 1840s. In addition to the lack of rain, two-thirds of Mexico is mountainous, where agricultural pursuits are difficult, if not impossible. Ongoing political unrest and periodic civil insurrections following the end of the wars of independence from Spain in 1821 led to frequent changes in governments and a diminution of the tax base, as well as the death of numerous farmers and the demise of many haciendas in the agriculturally rich areas of central Mexico. Peasant revolts against large landowners also periodically plagued the Mexican countryside.

Agriculture in many areas regressed from export-driven farms to smaller, less productive farms oriented to subsistence or self-sufficiency. Also, cheap imports of foreign textiles, especially from the United States, hurt the indigenous cotton and wool growers. Silver mining, which provided both capital and markets for Mexican agriculture, declined precipitously in the first half of the 19th century. Miners required a great amount of calories to sustain their hard work, and mining concerns provided a strong market for mules. When silver mining declined, the need for agricultural goods declined as well. Eventually, Mexican agriculture began to introduce modern farming and marketing techniques, but it would take decades to recover from the disruptions in the years surrounding the Mexican-American War. It was not until the 1880s that Mexico's agricultural system began to recover from the tumult that wracked the nation from the 1820s to the 1860s.

RANDAL BEEMAN

See also
Mexico; United States, 1821–1854; Slavery.

References
Bogue, Alan G. *From Prairie to Corn Belt: Farming on the Illinois and Iowa Prairies in the Nineteenth Century.* Ames: Iowa State University Press, 1994.
Coatsworth, John. "Obstacles to Economic Growth in Nineteenth-Century Mexico." *American Historical Review* 83, no. 1 (1978): 82–84.
Fehrenach, T. R. *Fire and Blood: A History of Mexico.* New York: Macmillan, 1973.
Hurt, R. Douglas. *American Agriculture: A Brief History.* Ames: Iowa State University Press, 1993.
Weber, David J. *The Mexican Frontier: The American Southwest under Mexico.* Albuquerque: University of New Mexico Press, 1982.

Agua Fria, Skirmish at
Event Date: November 2, 1847

One of numerous clashes involving Mexican guerrillas and U.S. Army troops during the American occupation of Mexico. The skirmish at Agua Fria occurred on November 2, 1847, near Marín in the northeastern state of Nuevo León. As it became clear to the Mexicans that they were losing the conventional war, they initiated guerrilla operations. At first they attacked American garrisons, but they soon learned that such assaults were fruitless and costly and so turned to ambushing American detachments patrolling the countryside. Although such attacks were rare in northern Mexico in 1847, one occurred on the morning of November 2 at Agua Fria, near Marín, on the Camargo-Monterrey road.

That day, Lieutenant Reuben C. Campbell of the 2nd Dragoons was leading a body of 25 dragoons and Texas Rangers, part of U.S. forces under Major General John E. Wool, in an attempt to secure this route against guerrilla threat, when he was attacked by between 124 and 150 Mexican guerrillas. The Mexicans were led by Marco Martinez, nicknamed *El Mucho* or *La Mancho*. Campbell's position seemed dire. Not only was he greatly outnumbered, but he also faced the man whom Major General Zachary Taylor had declared to be the most active guerrilla leader in northern Mexico.

Undaunted, the Americans took cover behind dead horses, cacti, and brush and used discarded Mexican lances as protection against enemy horsemen. They loaded their musketoons with double shot or six .31 caliber buckshot and, while suffering from intense heat and thirst, lay down a formidable fire against their attackers for more than an hour. Martinez, rashly exposing himself to enemy fire, was shot out of his saddle and fell mortally wounded. Campbell's men also killed five others of the attackers and wounded many more. The Americans then fought their way through the weakened guerrilla force and made their escape. They suffered three killed, nine wounded, and several horses killed or wounded. Five days later, U.S. forces defeated another guerrilla band near Ramos, and U.S. military officials declared the Camargo-Monterrey road to be free of threat.

PAUL DAVID NELSON

See also

Guerrilla Warfare; Northern Mexico Theater of War, Overview; Ramos; Taylor, Zachary; Wool, John Ellis.

References

Bauer, K. Jack. *The Mexican War, 1846–1848*. New York: Macmillan, 1974.
Foos, Paul. *A Short, Offhand, Killing Affair: Soldiers and Social Conflict during the Mexican-American War*. Chapel Hill: University of North Carolina Press, 2002.
Levinson, Irving W. *Wars within War: Mexican Guerrillas, Domestic Elites, and the United States of America, 1846–1848*. Fort Worth: Texas Christian University Press, 2005.
Winders, Richard Bruce. *Mr. Polk's Army: The American Military Experience in the Mexican War*. College Station: Texas A&M University Press, 1997.

Agua Nueva

Small village in the Mexican state of Coahuila, about 17 miles south of Saltillo, which served as a staging area for U.S. and Mexican armies in northern Mexico. Agua Nueva was also occupied by both sides during the 1847 Buena Vista Campaign. On September 24, 1846, Major General Zachary Taylor captured Monterrey and on November 16 marched into Saltillo.

Brigadier General John E. Wool's men occupied Agua Nueva on December 21. To Wool's disgust, some soldiers raped several women and perpetrated other offenses against the citizenry there. On February 14, 1847, Taylor's army of 4,650 men encamped at Agua Nueva. The soldiers' repose was frequently disturbed by the ill will between them and the citizens. Taylor, deploring his soldiers' depredations against the townspeople, finally dismissed two companies of Arkansas volunteers from the army for their offenses.

In late February 1847, General Antonio López de Santa Anna marched against Taylor, who fell back to La Angostura. His men burned supplies and buildings in Agua Nueva as they departed. Santa Anna followed, engaged, and was defeated by the Americans in the Battle of Buena Vista on February 23, 1847. He then retreated to Agua Nueva but abandoned the town on February 26. Taylor occupied Agua Nueva from February 27 to March 9 and then returned to Monterrey. For the remainder of the war, American forces in northern Mexico were on the defensive while holding captured territory.

PAUL DAVID NELSON

See also

Buena Vista, Battle of; Saltillo; Santa Anna, Antonio López de; Taylor, Zachary; Wool, John Ellis.

References

Bauer, K. Jack. *The Mexican War, 1846–1848*. New York: Macmillan, 1974.
Clary, David A. *Eagles and Empire: The United States, Mexico, and the Struggle for a Continent*. New York: Bantam Books, 2009.
Eisenhower, John S. D. *So Far from God: The U.S. War with Mexico, 1846–1848*. Norman: University of Oklahoma Press, 1989.
Singletary, Otis A. *The Mexican War*. Chicago: University of Chicago Press, 1960.

Aguascalientes, Plan of
Event Date: 1848

Abortive plan of government for Mexico proposed by General Mariano Paredes y Arrillaga in June 1848. As a result of the Treaty of Guadalupe Hidalgo, which was signed on February 2, 1848, and the policies of *moderado* President Jose Joaquín de Herrera, whose government had been installed on June 3, 1848, General Paredes y Arrillaga, along with Manuel Doblado and Celestino Dómeco de Jarauta, launched a rebellion to oust the Mexican government. Paredes y Arrillaga had dislodged Herrera from office once before, in December 1845, and had installed himself as president on January 1, 1846; his government lasted for barely seven months before he too was unseated.

Paredes y Arrillaga bitterly denounced the *moderados'* war policies and their seeming willingness to accommodate the North Americans. Further, he decried the Treaty of Guadalupe Hidalgo, terming it a cowardly sellout to U.S. interests. In the spring of 1848, he began mobilizing troops at Aguascalientes and, working together with guerrilla leader Jarauta, attempted to foment a rebellion, oust Herrera from power, and continue the war with the United States. He also drafted a plan for a new government that he himself planned to head, which would temporarily grant individual Mexican states virtual autonomy until a better central government could be established.

Early on, Paredes y Arrillaga managed to capture Lagos de Moreno and Guanajuato, but in fewer than two months the rebellion was crushed, forcing the upstart general into hiding. The vast majority of the Mexican population, exhausted from war and the deprivations that it had engendered, refused to embrace Paredes y Arrillaga's cause. Although the insurrection failed, it nevertheless showcased the continuing fragility of the Mexican government and the instability that suffused Mexican politics in the middle third of the 19th century.

PAUL G. PIERPAOLI JR.

See also
Guadalupe Hidalgo, Treaty of; Herrera, José Joaquín de; Jarauta, Celestino Dómeco de; Moderados; Paredes y Arrillaga, Mariano; Politics, Mexican.

References
DePaolo, William A. *The Mexican National Army, 1822–1852.* Albuquerque: University of New Mexico Press, 1997.
Robertson, F. D. "The Military and Political Career of Mariano Paredes y Arrillaga, 1797–1849." PhD diss., University of Texas, 1949.

Alamán y Escalada, Lucas Ignacio
Birth Date: October 18, 1792
Death Date: June 2, 1853

Conservative Mexican politician and historian who served as minister of interior and foreign relations on three occasions during the early decades of Mexican independence. Born on October 18, 1792, in Guanajuato, Mexico, into a prominent family, Lucas Ignacio Alamán y Escalada was one of the best-educated men in Mexico during the first half of the 19th century. Having witnessed the violence unleashed by a potential class war by Father Miguel Hidalgo in 1810, Alamán was a lifelong supporter of conservative political values and lauded the virtues of Spanish colonial rule.

Following the overthrow of Emperor Agustín, Alamán served as the minister of interior and exterior relations from 1823 to 1825. He subsequently served in the same capacity from 1830 to 1832. Alamán fully supported the Law of April 6, 1830, which prohibited any further immigration of Americans into Texas. In 1831, he signed a treaty with the United States that ratified the borders established between the United States and Mexico in the Transcontinental (Adams-Onís) Treaty of 1819. In 1840, Alamán prophetically suggested that recognition of Texan independence would eliminate the potential of future conflict with the United States, and he accurately predicted the negative impact on Mexico

of war with the United States. In 1849, he founded the Mexican Conservative Party. Between 1849 and 1852, he published a five-volume history of Mexico. His third term as minister of interior and exterior relations lasted from 1851 until his death in Mexico City on June 2, 1853.

MICHAEL R. HALL

See also
Adams-Onís Treaty; Mexico.

References
González Navarro, Moises. *El pensamiento político de Lucas Alamán.* Mexico City: El Colegio de Mexico, 1952.
Hamnett, Brian R. *A Concise History of Mexico.* New York: Cambridge University Press, 2006.

Alamo, Battle of the
Event Date: March 6, 1836

Military engagement between Texas revolutionaries and the Mexican army at an 18th-century Spanish colonial mission known as the Alamo, located in San Antonio, Texas. The Battle of the Alamo was the culmination of a 13-day siege of the outpost. Although Mexican general Antonio López de Santa Anna's forces eventually crushed the defenders at the Alamo, the siege and storming of the Alamo quickly became enshrined in the U.S. public mind as one of the most heroic moments in American history. The cry "Remember the Alamo!" became a potent slogan for the Texas Revolution.

In the early days of the Texas Revolution, a provisional government was established to organize resistance against the Mexicans, and Sam Houston was named the commander of the Texan army. Believing San Antonio to be too isolated to defend successfully, Houston sent Jim Bowie to withdraw the garrison stationed there. Bowie, however, became enamored of an abandoned mission, San Antonio de Valero, better known as the Alamo, which for several decades had served as a barracks for Mexican troops. With some captured Mexican artillery and hard work, the garrison had already begun shoring up the crumbling mission. Bowie sent word to Houston that he would stay and defend the Alamo. Almost immediately, he argued with Colonel William B. Travis, the garrison's permanent commander, but the two decided to share command and make a stand at the Alamo. Only 150 men, including legendary frontiersman Davy Crockett, were in the Alamo when Santa Anna's force, numbering about 1,500 troops, arrived there on February 23, 1836.

Santa Anna quickly ordered his force, which was reinforced to 3,000–4,000 men on March 2, to surround the Alamo. He then commenced an around-the-clock bombardment to which the defenders were barely able to respond. They had cannon, but gunpowder was in painfully short supply. The encirclement was not secure, and Travis (who assumed command when Bowie became ill) sent three riders out to summon aid. In answer to his appeals, 32 men rode in from Gonzales and forced their way at night through the

Fall of the Alamo---Death of Crockett.

Depiction by an unknown artist of the death of frontiersman Davy Crockett at the Battle of the Alamo on March 6, 1836. Crockett achieved mythical status after his death. (Library of Congress)

incomplete Mexican investment. Thus the final defense numbered about 187 men, although the exact count remains in dispute. In any case, it was an impossibly small force to defend a perimeter encompassing the church and two sets of barracks around a very large open courtyard. The adobe walls were originally built to keep out the Comanches, but they were not sufficiently stout to withstand prolonged artillery fire.

On the night of March 5, the bombardment ceased. In the darkness, the Mexican troops quietly positioned themselves for a dawn attack. Only an overly eager soldier's cry alerted the garrison to the imminent danger before the attackers were upon them. The morning darkness, coupled with the inexperience of many of the Mexican troops, made the opening assault unsuccessful, but the Mexicans re-formed, and on their second attempt breached the walls. Once inside, they had such an overwhelming numerical advantage that the Texans had little chance of survival. Travis reportedly died early in the battle and Bowie, according at least to legend, fought from his sickbed for a short time. The men inside the church building held out the longest but did not have the firepower to survive for very long. Mexican sources state that many of the defenders, possibly as many as half, fled the makeshift fortress to the southeast but were ridden down by Mexican cavalry anticipating just such a move.

By 8:00 a.m. the battle was over. All 187 Texan defenders, including Bowie and Crockett, were killed. The victorious Mexicans spared some 20 women, children, and African American slaves who had taken refuge in the Alamo. Mexican army casualties have been estimated at anywhere from 400 to 1,600.

In the 1970s, a diary allegedly kept by José Enrique de la Peña, one of Santa Anna's staff officers, came to light. Although its veracity has been challenged, the journal describes the final moments of the battle in a way that brought the traditional accounts into question. Since 1836, the generally accepted view was that all the defenders died in battle, but de la Peña's diary states that a handful, including Crockett, were taken prisoner. Although most of the officers recommended mercy, Santa Anna's reputation for ruthless suppression of rebellion showed itself again when he ordered the prisoners executed as traitors.

Although the siege at the Alamo slowed the Mexican campaign in Texas only by some two weeks, it provided the spark that motivated many to join General Sam Houston's motley force. At the Battle of San Jacinto on April 21, 1836, Houston's forces destroyed the vanguard of the Mexican army and captured Santa Anna, who was forced to accept Texan independence.

TIM WATTS

See also

Bowie, James; Houston, Samuel; San Antonio; San Jacinto, Battle of; Santa Anna, Antonio López de; Texas Revolution; Travis, William Barret.

References

Casteñeda, Carlos E., ed. *The Mexican Side of the Texas Revolution.* Dallas, TX: P. L. Turner, 1956.

de la Peña, José Enrique. *With Santa Anna in Texas: A Personal Narrative of the Revolution.* Edited by James E. Crisp. College Station: Texas A&M University Press, 1997.

Dimmick, Gregg. *Sea of Mud: The Retreat of the Mexican Army after San Jacinto, an Archeological Investigation.* Austin: Texas State Historical Association, 2006.

Hansen, Todd, ed. *The Alamo Reader: A Study in History.* Mechanicsburg, PA: Stackpole Books, 2003.

Hardin, Stephen L. *Texian Iliad: A Military History of the Texas Revolution.* Austin: University of Texas Press, 1994.

Matovina, Timothy M. *The Alamo Remembered: Tejano Accounts and Perspectives.* Austin: University of Texas Press, 1995.

Moore, Stephen L. *Eighteen Minutes: The Battle of San Jacinto and the Texas Independence Campaign.* Plano: Republic of Texas Press, 2004.

Newell, Chester. *History of the Revolution in Texas; Particularly of the War of 1835 & '36.* New York: Wiley and Putnam, 1838.

Winders, Richard Bruce. *Sacrificed at the Alamo: Tragedy and Triumph in the Texas Revolution.* Abilene, TX: State House Press, 2003.

Alcorta, Lino José

Birth Date: 1794
Death Date: 1854

Mexican brigadier general during the Mexican-American War. Lino José Alcorta was born in Veracruz, Mexico, in 1794. In July 1813 he entered military service as a cadet in the Cazadores de América Regiment. As a royalist during the Mexican wars for independence he participated in numerous clashes with independence forces, earning the reputation as an intrepid soldier. In 1821, however, Alcorta subscribed to the Plan of Iguala and swore his loyalty to Agustín de Iturbide. He rose steadily through the ranks and distinguished himself during the 1829 Spanish invasion of Tampico, during which he helped repel Spanish forces and ended Spain's attempt to retake its former colony. Thereafter Alcorta held a series of increasingly important military posts.

By 1840, Alcorta had been promoted to brigadier general. That same year, he was instrumental in quashing a rebellion in Mexico City against President Anastasio Bustamante's centralist government fomented by Brigadier General José Urrea. During the 12-day struggle, Alcorta sustained a serious head wound, but he refused to relinquish his command. In 1844, he became military commander at San Luis Potosí, and when the Mexican-American War began two years later Alcorta was chief of the general staff. He oversaw the early struggles against Major General Zachary Taylor's forces in northern Mexico and quickly became one of General Antonio López de Santa Anna's most trusted subordinates and confidantes. After the April 17–18, 1847, Battle of Cerro Gordo, Alcorta began serving as minister of war and marine, a post he held for the remainder of the conflict.

Realizing that Mexican forces could not overcome the Americans' far superior firepower and discipline, Alcorta came to favor multiple, simultaneous hit-and-run attacks against U.S. forces by Mexican contingents of no more than 2,000 men each. After the raids Mexican forces could quickly disappear into the countryside to avoid capture and detection. He strongly believed that large, pitched battles should be avoided. It was the Americans, however, and not the Mexicans, who largely determined the size and pacing of set-piece engagements. After the Battle of Chapultepec on September 13, 1847, and as U.S. troops were breaching the gates of Mexico City, Alcorta was among three of Santa Anna's senior commanders who recommended a quick capitulation of the capital city to avoid unnecessary civilian casualties.

After the end of the war, Alcorta remained in the army for a time but in 1851 became vice president of the Mexican Society of Geography and Statistics. He held that position until becoming minister of war—again—in Santa Anna's last government. Alcorta died in office in Mexico City in 1854.

PAUL G. PIERPAOLI JR.

See also

Bustamante y Oseguera, Anastasio; Cerro Gordo, Battle of; Chapultepec, Battle of; Mexico City, Battle for; Santa Anna, Antonio López de; Taylor, Zachary; Urrea y Elías Gonzales, José de.

References

Clary, David A. *Eagles and Empire: The United States, Mexico, and the Struggle for a Continent.* New York: Bantam Books, 2009.

Clendenen, Clarence C. *Blood on the Border: The United States Army and the Mexican Irregulars.* New York: Macmillan, 1969.

DePalo, William A., Jr. *The Mexican National Army, 1822–1852.* College Station: Texas A & M University Press, 1997.

Alexander, Edmund Brooke

Birth Date: October 6, 1802
Death Date: January 3, 1888

U.S. Army officer. Edmund Brooke Alexander was born at Hay Market, Prince William County, Virginia, on October 6, 1802. He attended the U.S. Military Academy, West Point, graduating in the class of 1823 with future U.S. Army generals George S. Greene and Lorenzo Thomas. After graduation, Alexander was commissioned a second lieutenant of infantry and served in a string of frontier assignments until the Mexican-American War began in 1846.

At the beginning of the war, Alexander was a captain in the 3rd Infantry Regiment. He saw considerable action during Major General Winfield Scott's Mexico City Campaign, including the Battles of Cerro Gordo (April 17–18, 1847) and Contreras (August 20, 1847). At the August 20, 1847, Battle of Churubusco, Alexander led an assault against a well-fortified former convent, where vicious hand-to-hand combat ensued. Alexander received two brevet promotions for his service during the war—one to major and another to lieutenant colonel.

In 1851 Alexander was promoted to major. In 1855, he was promoted to colonel and assigned to command of the 10th Infantry when that newly authorized regiment was formed that same year. During 1857–1858, he participated in the Utah Expedition. When the Civil War began in 1861, Alexander was serving as acting assistant provost marshal general for the city of Saint Louis, Missouri, which was strongly divided between pro-Southern and pro-Union sentiments. He also subsequently served as chief recruiting and disbursing officer for the state of Missouri. Although he did not hold a field command during the Civil War, his diplomacy was credited with keeping that state in the Union and preventing large outbreaks of partisan fighting there.

In March 1865, Alexander was brevetted brigadier general and given command of Fort Snelling (Minnesota), which post he held until his retirement in February 1869. Alexander died in Washington, D.C., on January 3, 1888. He is buried in Saint Paul, Minnesota, where he had settled after his retirement from the army.

PAUL G. PIERPAOLI JR.

See also

Cerro Gordo, Battle of; Churubusco, Battle of; Contreras, Battle of; Mexico City Campaign; Scott, Winfield.

References

Eisenhower, John S. D. *So Far from God: The U.S. War with Mexico, 1846–1848.* Norman: University of Oklahoma Press, 2000.

Heitman, Francis Bernard. *Historical Register and Dictionary of the United States Army, from Its Organization, September 29, 1789, to March 2, 1903.* Washington, DC: Government Printing Office, 1903.

Johnson, Timothy D. *Winfield Scott: The Quest for Military Glory.* Lawrence: University of Kansas Press, 1998.

Alleye (de Billon) de Cyprey, Isidore Elisabeth Jean Baptiste, Baron

Birth Date: 1784
Death Date: Unknown

French diplomat who precipitated a major incident with the Mexican government in 1845. Isidore Elisabeth Jean Baptiste Alleye (de Billon) de Cyprey was born in 1784 in Basse-Terre, Guadeloupe, part of the French West Indies. Known for his choleric temper and tactless ways, he entered diplomatic service as a young man and held a series of increasingly important diplomatic postings, mostly in Europe. In 1830 he was ennobled and took the surname Alleye de Cyprey, and by the end of the decade he was chargé d'affaires at the French legation in Frankfurt. There he ran afoul of François Guizot, who became France's foreign minister under King Louis Philippe in 1840.

Anxious to place the boorish Alleye de Cyprey in a less delicate position, in January 1840 Guizot reassigned him to the French legation in Mexico City. Although Alleye de Cyprey would be the senior French diplomat in Mexico, the move was considered to be a significant step down on the career ladder. He arrived in Mexico City in February 1840, largely uninformed regarding Mexican culture and politics. Almost immediately he began to lobby for the establishment of a Bourbon monarchy in Mexico, to be underwritten by France, arguing that the Mexicans were ill-suited for a republican style of government. Guizot, who was trying to act as an honest broker in the steadily worsening relationship between the

United States and Mexico, ignored Alleye de Cyprey's dispatches and instructed him to remain neutral. Nevertheless, the diplomat continued to press the issue, instigating a series of confrontations involving diplomatic protocol, hoping that one of them might invite a French military response.

On May 25, 1845, Alleye de Cyprey and his staff precipitated a major rift between the French legation and the Mexican government in the so-called Baño de las Delicias Affair. The Baño de las Delicias was a livery stable used by the diplomat and his staff. When the baron's grooms berated a group of Mexican stable boys for their alleged mistreatment of a horse, a fight ensued. Alleye de Cyprey soon arrived on the scene, where an angry mob of Mexicans had gathered. The baron became involved in the skirmish and exchanged gunfire with several members of the crowd.

When the melee was over, Alleye de Cyprey angrily demanded a formal apology from the Mexican government and reparations for "damages" incurred to his horses and livery staff. The Mexican government refused to comply, and Alleye de Cyprey, without authorization from Paris, severed diplomatic ties between France and Mexico. He also publicly called for French military intervention in Mexico. A few months later Alleye de Cyprey, still in Mexico City, reportedly spit in the face of a Mexican journalist who he claimed had tarnished his reputation. In October, just as Guizot was preparing to recall his rogue diplomat, the Mexican government asked Alleye de Cyprey to leave the country "for his own safety."

Coming as it did on the eve of the Mexican-American War, Alleye de Cyprey's undignified and hasty departure left France with no representation in Mexico at a critical diplomatic juncture. Thus, whatever diplomatic pressure that Guizot might have exerted on Washington and Mexico City to avert war was largely lost. The fact that Alleye de Cyprey stayed in his post for nearly five years, however, seemed to amply demonstrate the low regard of the French government for Mexico.

PAUL G. PIERPAOLI JR.

See also

Diplomacy, Mexican; Diplomacy, U.S.; Europe and the Mexican-American War; France; Mexico.

References

Barker, Nancy Nichols. *The French Experience in Mexico, 1821–1861: A History of Constant Misunderstanding.* Chapel Hill: University of North Carolina Press, 1979.

Pletcher, David M. *The Diplomacy of Annexation: Texas, Oregon, and the Mexican War.* Columbia: University of Missouri Press, 1979.

All of Mexico Movement

Campaign spearheaded by expansionist-minded U.S. politicians, southern slave owners, and radical members of the press to annex all of Mexico rather than just the northern part that was eventually ceded to the United States in 1848. The "All of Mexico" movement was closely linked to the concept of Manifest Destiny and in fact had gained traction beginning in the mid-1830s during the Texas Revolution, well before the Mexican-American War began in 1846. Some expansionists envisioned the United States possessing the entirety of Mexico for political and ideological reasons, namely that the United States would gain important economic and strategic advantages and that the country was morally preordained to spread its system of governance over all of North America. Slave owners, meanwhile, coveted the fertile lands in central Mexico, where they hoped to establish plantations powered by slave labor.

The movement reached its apex of popularity in the fall of 1847, when a good number of Americans, weary of the war and its growing cost in blood and money, believed that Mexico might capitulate more quickly if complete annexation were sought. Not surprisingly, many other Americans decried the campaign's goals, believing that they were being pursued solely for the personal gain of a relative few.

Not surprisingly, ideas of race and racism informed both those who sought complete annexation and those who rejected it. And the concept of Manifest Destiny was employed by both sides. Some advocates of Manifest Destiny, including John O'Sullivan, who coined the term, believed that it should not be applied to people against their will, making the All of Mexico movement a violation of that tenet. Democratic U.S. senator John C. Calhoun (South Carolina) rejected the movement because it would mean extending U.S. citizenship to millions of Mexicans. Speaking for many who opposed complete annexation, Calhoun essentially argued that the incorporation of nonwhite Mexicans into the United States would be a grave mistake that would threaten the supremacy of America's white population. On the other hand, those who championed the movement and who embraced the "mission" aspect of Manifest Destiny, which held that the United States had a morally bound duty to lift up "inferior" peoples and introduce them to democracy, believed that annexing all of Mexico would fulfill this purpose. Thus, racism fueled both sides of the debate.

The movement found some of its most ardent adherents among expansionist-minded Democrats in Congress. They included Sen. Ambrose H. Sevier of Arkansas and Congressmen Robert Dale Owens (Indiana), John W. Tibbatts (Kentucky), and Alexander D. Sims (South Carolina). They were supported by a vocal minority in the national press, including the influential journalist Jane (McManus Storms) Cazneau. Most Whigs, including a young congressman from Illinois by the name of Abraham Lincoln, decried the All of Mexico movement; some in fact believed it a mistake to extract from Mexico any territory at all upon the conclusion of the war. Many journalists also opposed the movement, including poet/journalist Walt Whitman, who expressed in the *Brooklyn Daily* in July 1846 his adamant opposition to the All of Mexico campaign.

As U.S. forces made steady headway in the war in 1846 and 1847, and as California fell practically undefended, the movement gained momentum, reaching its zenith when Winfield Scott's army took Mexico City on September 14, 1847. At that point, President James K. Polk discussed the idea of annexing all of Mexico

with his cabinet. The idea attracted some supporters, but not enough to form a mandate. In the military, Brigadier General John A. Quitman was the most vocal proponent of full annexation. By mid-autumn of 1847, when it became clear that the Mexican government would not discuss a peace that was acceptable to the Polk administration, and as the fighting wore on with the attendant costs rising, the All of Mexico campaign began to lose ground. Many Americans wanted the war to end and longed for the return of American troops from Mexico.

At the same time, a number of Americans began to examine the potential pitfalls of complete annexation and came to the conclusion that such a course was simply too risky. First, the annexation of Mexico would likely require voting rights for Mexicans and representation in Congress, which would badly skew political power in the United States because the central Mexican states were heavily populated. Second, much of central Mexico's most fertile lands were already privately owned, so some U.S. slave owners realized that building large plantations there would be exceedingly difficult. Third, the racial complexities of absorbing millions of nonwhite people and eventually making them citizens unnerved most Americans. Fourth, complete annexation would likely involve an expansion of slavery and upset the fragile balance between free and slave states. Finally, many Americans came to realize that bringing peace and stability to Mexico would be a very costly proposition in terms of money and lives. Indeed, parts of the country were already involved in a virtual civil war with the central government; pacifying these areas would require large U.S. troop deployments potentially lasting for years.

As peace talks dragged on with no foreseeable end in sight, the All of Mexico movement deflated in the winter of 1847–1848. The American public heartily embraced the announcement that U.S. envoy Nicholas Trist had concluded the Treaty of Guadalupe Hidalgo in February 1848, although Trist had concluded the agreement without Polk's full knowledge or support. Indeed, Polk was still holding out for the annexation of Baja California (in addition to Alta California and the vast Nuevo Mexico region), but he was hardly in a position to reject the treaty agreement. In the end, the Mexican cession only included California and lands north of the Rio Grande for an indemnity to the Mexican government of $15 million. Mexican sovereignty over most of its territory remained intact.

PAUL G. PIERPAOLI JR.

See also

Cazneau, Jane McManus Storms; Democratic Party; Expansionism and Imperialism; Guadalupe Hidalgo, Treaty of; Lincoln, Abraham; Manifest Destiny; Mexican Cession; Mexico City, Battle for; Opposition to the Mexican-American War, U.S.; Quitman, John Anthony; Sevier, Ambrose Hundley; Slavery; Trist, Nicholas Philip; Whigs; Whitman, Walter (Walt).

References

Fuller, John Douglas Pitts. *The Movement for the Acquisition of All of Mexico, 1846–1848.* Baltimore, MD: Johns Hopkins University Press, 1936.

Pletcher, David L. *The Diplomacy of Annexation*. Columbia: University of Missouri Press, 1973.

Stacy, Lee. *Mexico and the United States*. Tarrytown, NY: Marshall Cavendish, 2002.

Almonte, Juan Nepomuceno
Birth Date: May 15, 1803
Death Date: March 21, 1869

Key political, military, and diplomatic official in Mexico from the 1820s to the 1860s. The illegitimate son of the famous independence leader José María Morelos, Juan Almonte was born in Necupétaro, Michoacán, on May 15, 1803. Almonte accompanied his father on various military campaigns and was wounded in the arm in one attack. On August 9, 1814, at age 11, his father made him a brigadier general, an appointment confirmed by the revolutionary congress.

The next year Almonte formed part of a delegation sent by his father to the United States to seek recognition and military

Mexican general and politician Juan Nepomuceno Almonte served as ambassador to the United States in the years just before the Mexican-American War and was later minister of war. (Library of Congress)

supplies for the independence movement. He arrived at New Orleans on November 1, 1815. That same month, Spanish forces captured his father, who was then executed on December 22, 1815. Almonte spent the period from 1815 to 1821 in New Orleans. Following the triumph of the Mexican independence movement in 1821, he served as a colonel in Texas in 1822 and as a diplomat in London in 1824, Paris in 1826, and South America in 1831.

In 1834, once again as a colonel, Almonte was assigned to Texas to determine the boundary between Mexico and the United States. Almonte later filed a "secret report" evaluating the grievances of the Anglo settlers and the strength of the independence party in Texas. After the outbreak of revolution in Texas in late 1835, he joined the forces led by General Antonio López de Santa Anna. Almonte participated in the Battles of the Alamo (February 23–March 6, 1836) and San Jacinto (April 21, 1836), where he was taken prisoner by the victorious Texan forces.

In the rapidly changing world of Mexican politics, Almonte's involvement in the loss of Texas did little harm to his political and military careers. In 1839 he became a brigadier general, and he served as minister of war between 1839 and 1841. In 1842 he became Mexican ambassador to the United States. Almonte was serving in that position in March 1845 when the U.S. Congress passed the resolution providing for the annexation of Texas. Almonte responded to this action by breaking relations and returning to Mexico.

The process of annexing Texas was coming to a conclusion in December 1845 when Almonte joined with other Mexican generals to overthrow President José Joaquín de Herrera, whose search for a peaceful settlement with the United States had cost him domestic political support. The coup led to Almonte's appointment as minister of war in January 1846, a position he held only until February 21. He took up the same post again that August and served until his resignation in December. Amid political instability and military setbacks, Almonte tried to organize the nation's defenses. Almonte held no national leadership positions during the remainder of the war, but he did run unsuccessfully for the presidency in Mexico's first postwar election in May 1848.

Almonte continued to play an important role in Mexican history after the war with the United States. He served the liberal government as ambassador to England and France in 1856 but sided with the losing conservatives in the civil war from 1858 to 1860. As an exile in Europe, Almonte played an important role in bringing about the French intervention in 1862 and the establishment of Maximilian's puppet empire in Mexico in 1864. He was in France on a diplomatic mission for Maximilian when the empire collapsed in 1867. Almonte remained in Paris until his death there on March 21, 1869.

Don M. Coerver

See also

Alamo, Battle of the; Herrera, José Joaquín de; Mexico; San Jacinto, Battle of; Santa Anna, Antonio López de; Texas; Texas Declaration of Independence; Texas Revolution.

References
Cotner, Thomas Ewing. *The Military and Political Career of José Joaquín de Herrera, 1792–1854.* Austin: University of Texas Press, 1949.
Jackson, Jack, ed. *Almonte's Texas: Juan N. Almonte's 1834 Inspection, Secret Report and Role in the 1836 Campaign.* Austin: Texas State Historical Association, 2003.

Alvarado Expeditions
Event Dates: October 15, 1846–April 1, 1847

The first U.S. operation against the Mexican port city of Alvarado, located three miles upriver from the Gulf of Mexico astride the Rio Papaloapán, occurred on October 15, 1846. That spring several Mexican gunboats had sought refuge at Alvarado, and in the summer Commodore David Conner decided to seize the port. He ordered a naval assault on the city on August 7, which failed because river currents were too fast and the drafts on the U.S. warships too deep.

Determined to attempt another expedition against Alvarado in the early fall, Conner requisitioned two shallow draft revenue cutters. In the meantime, Mexican forces, having anticipated another U.S. assault, strengthened the fortifications and enlarged the garrison in and around the port.

Conner launched the second expedition against Alvarado from Antón Lizardo. The Americans arrived near the mouth of the Papaloapán on October 15, 1846. Early in the day, the steamer *Mississippi* fired on the outer forts of the city as other warships attempted to cross the sandbar in the river. The *Mississippi*'s guns proved nearly useless, however, because the ship's deep draft would not allow it to approach within effective range. Rough surf further complicated the mission.

In the afternoon, with the surf having subsided, Conner ordered a second advance up the river. He was commanding in the *Vixen,* with two schooner-gunboats in tow. The *McLane,* a revenue cutter, was towing three additional schooner-gunboats, while the *Mississippi* remained behind to provide gunfire support. Although the column safely passed over the bar, the *McLane* ran aground before the U.S. warships could reach the main port. Although the captain of the *McLane* managed to refloat his vessel, Conner called off the expedition. The Americans sailed back into the Gulf and returned to Antón Lizardo. Conner reported no casualties except for a few men slightly wounded. The Mexicans apparently suffered no losses. The Mexicans were temporarily buoyed by the Americans' failure to take Alvarado, but the repulse may have given them the faulty notion that they could successfully defend other ports along the coast. Alvarado remained in Mexican hands until the spring of 1847. On March 9, 1847, the campaign to take Mexico City had begun with Major General Winfield Scott's landing on the beaches south of Veracruz. Over the period of several weeks, Scott's troops laid siege to the city, and on March 29, Veracruz capitulated, opening the gateway to Mexico City.

Scott planned to march inland as quickly as possible in order to escape the low-lying coastal region before the coming of the yellow fever season that summer. Because most of his men would join the march, he needed horses and mules to help transport the tons of supplies that would be required to sustain his army in the field. Even if sufficient livestock could have been brought from the United States, the voyage often left animals unfit for service in Mexico. The solution was to purchase or seize as many horses and mules as could be obtained locally.

Requiring large numbers of draft animals for his Mexico City Campaign, Winfield Scott assigned the task of requisitioning livestock to Major General John A. Quitman and his brigade containing the Georgia, Alabama, and South Carolina volunteer regiments supported by two companies of U.S. dragoons, and one section of U.S. artillery. Their arrival at Alvarado would coincide with a landing by U.S. sailors under Commodore Matthew C. Perry.

The combined American force reached Alvarado on April 1, 1847. According to American accounts, after the initial panic caused by the appearance of the soldiers and sailors subsided, the residents were both friendly and eager to sell livestock to them. In addition to some 500 horses, the Americans secured more than 20 pieces of artillery and a quantity of small arms from Alvarado and its environs. Quitman's brigade was back in Veracruz by April 6.

Although the mission was accomplished without a battle, the expedition produced hard feelings among the troops that took part in it. The march had been hard and the volunteers believed that they had been assigned to carry out a task that was beneath their dignity.

There was dissension among the naval ranks as well. Navy lieutenant Charles G. Hunter, commander of the screw steamer *Scourge* (three guns), had disobeyed Perry's orders and moved against Alvarado prematurely, upsetting the timing of the operation. Through the evening of March 30 and the following morning the *Scourge*'s 32-pounder long gun shelled into submission the La Vigía Battery that guarded the mouth of the river. The Mexican captain of the port then put out in a boat and informed Hunter that the inhabitants had evacuated the town during the night, that all naval vessels had been burned, and that the Americans were free to enter. Hunter then landed a small party to take possession of Alvarado.

Learning that Mexican vessels laden with munitions had withdrawn upriver, Hunter proceeded there in the *Scourge,* capturing the *Relamago* and three other Mexican schooners, one of which had grounded and had to be burned. Hunter next took the surrender of the village of Tlacotalpán.

Hunter had no authority for these actions, and in fact his actions had caused the Mexicans to drive off horses the expedition was designed to secure. Hunter was later found guilty of insubordination and disobeying orders of a superior officer and was sentenced to a reprimand and immediate dismissal from the squadron but not from the navy.

BRUCE WINDERS, SPENCER C. TUCKER, AND PAUL G. PIERPAOLI JR.

See also

Antón Lizardo; Conner, David; Hunter, Charles G.; Mexico City Campaign; Perry, Matthew Calbraith; Quitman, John Anthony; Scott, Winfield; United States Navy; Veracruz.

References

Bauer, K. Jack. *Surfboats and Horse Marines: U.S. Naval Operations in the Mexican War, 1846–1848.* Annapolis: U.S. Nanal Institute, 1969.

May, Robert E. J*ohn A. Quitman: Old South Crusader.* Baton Rouge: Louisiana State University Press, 1995.

Morison, Samuel Eliot. *"Old Bruin": Commodore Matthew Calbraith Perry.* New York: Little, Brown, 1967.

Smith, Justin. *The War with Mexico.* 2 vols. 1919. Reprint, Gloucester, MA: Peter Smith, 1963.

Álvarez, Juan

Birth Date: January 27, 1790
Death Date: August 21, 1867

Mexican army officer and politician who commanded the Mexican Army's Division of the South during the Mexican-American War. To a greater extent than any other Mexican leader of the period, Álvarez personified the political and ethnic tensions that weakened Mexico before and after the conflict. Born on January 27, 1790, at Santa Maria de la Concepcíon Atoyac in the present-day Mexican state of Guerrero, Juan Álvarez fought against the Spanish during Mexico's War of Independence (1810–1821), joining the army of José María Morelos y Pavón as a private in 1810 and rising to take Acapulco from royalist forces and become the commander there in 1821.

After Mexico secured its independence, Álvarez became a prominent member of the Liberal Party, repeatedly leading armed revolts against Conservative governments that sought to strengthen the authority of the national government in Mexico City. His main bases of political support as well as his land holdings were in the present-day Mexican states of Guerrero and Oaxaca. By 1830, Álvarez was a brigadier general, and in 1841 he was promoted to general of division.

Four years before the start of the war with the United States, Álvarez rose in armed revolt against the Mexican government's effort to carve a new administrative jurisdiction out of territory in which he was the political master. Although the men of primarily mixed ancestry (mestizos) and American Indians whom he roused to revolt initially fought the central government, they soon turned against estate owners. Faced with an uncontrollable situation that ultimately resulted in widespread devastation over an area of some 60,000 square miles, Álvarez was forced to make an alliance with the national government that he detested in order to restore order.

During the Mexican-American War, many Mexicans in impoverished rural communities took advantage of the weakened state of the Mexican army to rebel. Álvarez sought to restore order in some areas, but he enjoyed only limited success. Appointed by General Antonio López de Santa Anna to command the Mexican cavalry and operate against U.S. major general Winfield Scott's supply lines stretching from Veracruz toward Mexico City, his performance was at best ineffectual.

Ordered by Santa Anna to assist in the defense of the Mexican capital, Álvarez took part in the Battle of El Molino del Rey on September 8, 1847. Santa Anna ordered Álvarez to launch his force in a flank attack against Scott's army, but Álvarez refused, later arguing that a Mexican infantry battalion had stood in the path of his men and that consequently a charge could not have been made. However, Mexicans of that era and many historians believed that Álvarez sought to conserve his forces for a civil war that he correctly believed would be fought between Mexicans once the Americans had departed. It has also been suggested that Álvarez feared U.S. artillery and that he was inexperienced in fighting pitched battles.

From 1850 to 1853 Álvarez served first as interim governor and then governor of the state of Guerrero. In 1854, he launched the Ayutla Revolution, an armed revolt against Santa Anna in the name of the Liberal Party. Two years later, his victorious forces entered Mexico City and sent Santa Anna into exile. Álvarez became interim president of the republic on October 5, 1855, but remained in the post for only 74 days. Frustrated by the constant bickering within liberal ranks, he resigned on December 12 to return to his beloved Acapulco. He died on August 21, 1867, at his hacienda in La Providencia, Guerrero. On December 25, 1922, the Mexican government moved his remains to the Rotunda of Illustrious Men in Mexico City, a site reserved for the most honored of Mexican citizens.

IRVING W. LEVINSON

See also

Chapultepec, Battle of; Mexico; Mexico City, Battle for; Mexico City Campaign; Santa Anna, Antonio López de, Scott, Winfield.

References

Díaz Díaz, Fernando. *Caudillos y caciques.* Mexico City: El Collegio de México, 1972.

Guardino, Peter F. *Peasants, Politics, and the Formation of Mexico's National State: Guerrero, 1800–1857.* Stanford, CA: Stanford University Press, 2002.

Meyer, Michael C., and William H. Beezley, eds. *The Oxford History of Mexico.* New York: Oxford University Press, 2000.

Raat, W. Dirk. *Mexico: From Independence to Revolution, 1810–1910.* Lincoln: University of Nebraska Press, 1982.

Alvarez, Manuel

Birth Date: 1794
Death Date: 1856

Prosperous trader, trapper, and U.S. consul in Santa Fe, New Mexico, during the Mexican-American War. Born in 1794 in northern Spain and educated in France and Spain, Manuel Alvarez traveled to Mexico and Cuba in the early 1820s and then spent time in New York City before deciding to seek his fortunes in Saint Louis in 1824. Later that same year, he settled in Santa Fe, New Mexico, where he became a successful trader and trapper, benefitting from the robust trade between Saint Louis and Santa Fe and between Santa Fe and Chihuahua. Around 1833 he began to operate a lucrative general store that catered to traders and travelers along the Santa Fe–Chihuahua Trail. In the process, he became quite wealthy and a highly regarded local figure.

Alvarez, ever the shrewd and perceptive businessman, eventually came to believe that New Mexico would likely prosper under American control, so he publically championed U.S. policies toward Texas and New Mexico, particularly in the aftermath of the 1835–1836 Texas Revolution. In 1843 the U.S. government took the highly unusual step of appointing Alvarez as U.S. consul in Santa Fe despite the fact that he was not an American citizen.

Late in the summer of 1846, after the Mexican-American War had begun, Alvarez provided considerable assistance to U.S. occupation forces under Brigadier General Stephen W. Kearny as the Americans consolidated their hold on Santa Fe. Indeed, he had attempted to convince New Mexico governor Manuel Armijo that capitulation to U.S. occupation forces would benefit New Mexico in both the short and long term.

After the war, Alvarez continued to be a central political figure in New Mexico and championed its statehood as early as 1850. He died in Santa Fe in 1856.

PAUL G. PIERPAOLI JR.

See also
Armijo, Manuel; Kearny, Stephen Watts; New Mexico; Santa Fe–Chihuahua Trail; Texas Revolution.

References
Chávez, Thomas E., ed. *Conflict and Acculturation: Manuel Alvarez's 1842 Memorial.* Santa Fe: Museum of New Mexico Press, 1988.
Chávez, Thomas E. *Manuel Alvarez, 1794–1856: A Southwestern Biography.* Boulder: University Press of Colorado, 1990.
Weber, David J. *The Taos Trappers.* Norman: University of Oklahoma Press, 1971.

American Peace Society

Significant pacifist organization founded in the United States in 1828. The American Peace Society (APS) was formed in early 1828 by Congregationalist minister and head of the Massachusetts Peace Society Noah Worcester and New York City merchant and leader of the New York Peace Society David Low Dodge. Worcester wrote the organization's constitution, while the society's leadership fell to Harvard College graduate and New England sea captain William Ladd. As early as May 1828, the APS began publishing its own journal, *Harbinger of Peace.* Located initially in New York City, the society moved to Hartford, Connecticut, in 1835 and to Boston in 1837.

Those attracted to the APS's cause were primarily upper- to middle-class Americans whose professions ranged from preaching, to law, to commerce, to public service. In the pre–Civil War years the society focused its efforts on addressing wars of aggression. Questions of basic philosophy relating to peace, however, led to a serious split within the organization. Only 10 years after its founding, William Lloyd Garrison broke away to form his own peace group, the New England Non-Resistance Society, and in 1846, Elihu Burritt established the League of Universal Brotherhood.

Despite contentious debates over the issues of "defensive war" and "respectability," the society received a boost when one of its executive committee members, Boston lawyer Charles Sumner, made an impassioned speech during the city's Fourth of July celebration in 1845. Wary of the expansionist policies of Democratic president James K. Polk and how they might further promote the spirit of Manifest Destiny while engaging the United States in a war with Mexico, Sumner's talk, titled "True Grandeur of Nations," condemned war and the "heathen patriotism" that propelled it. The rousing speech called for disarmament, the abolition of war, and the establishment of a permanent peace based on Christian and humanitarian principles.

Antiwar sentiment and the society's activities only increased with the Mexican-American War (1846–1848). The society's protests were strongest in New England, taking direct aim at federal enlistments. Leading New England intellectuals such as Ralph Waldo Emerson and Henry David Thoreau aided the society's efforts by criticizing the illiberal warmongering tendencies of the U.S. government. The APS issued pamphlets and arranged for speeches criticizing the greed and ambitions of the Polk administration. Its journal, by that time called the *Advocate of Peace* and edited by George C. Beckwith, published numerous articles critical of the Mexican-American War.

Operating out of society headquarters in Boston, members of the APS continued to garner support for a peace settlement with Mexico. Unitarian minister Theodore Parker opposed the war on political grounds and called upon all supporters of peace to support the march of progress "by anything rather than bullets." Although the war once again divided the society on the issue of its basic philosophy toward peace, as witnessed by the growing tolerance for violence to end slavery on the part of the Garrisonian abolitionists, its antiwar criticisms did help force Polk to agree to a more limited acquisition of land in the Southwest. That came with a price, however. A serious upheaval at the leadership level led to a withdrawal of the society's pacifist element while forcing a reorientation of its basic policies in a more conservative direction.

When the Mexican-American War ended early in 1848, the organization continued moving in a more "respectable" direction. Unlike Burritt's efforts to reach out to the working masses with a more radical pacifist critique of war, the society began adopting proposals fostering international arbitration and the idea of a congress of nations. Fearful of offending public opinion and being labeled "ultraists," the APS embarked on a more cautious approach to world peace in the later antebellum years. During the Civil War (1861–1865), many society members left in support of the Union cause and abolitionism. The society issued a declaration stating that the conflict was an internal police action and not within its field of jurisdiction.

After the Civil War, the society continued its efforts to attract people of wealth on behalf of international arbitration and the establishment of a permanent court of international justice. Following World War I (1914–1918), and in spite of the efforts of its most influential leader, Benjamin Franklin Trueblood, the society's importance waned as more nonviolent, direct action groups such as the Fellowship of Reconciliation, War Resister's League, and the Women's International League for Peace and Freedom took center stage in the 20th-century organized movement against war.

Since 1911, the society has been headquartered in Washington, D.C. From 1932, its efforts have been directed mainly at publishing a quarterly journal, *World Affairs* (its present name), on international relations. Throughout its history, the APS represented the more conservative, respectable wing of the organized peace movement.

CHARLES F. HOWLETT

See also

Abolitionism; Emerson, Ralph Waldo; Expansionism and Imperialism; Garrison, William Lloyd; Public Opinion and the War, U.S.; Thoreau, Henry David.

References

Brock, Peter. *Pacifism in the United States: From the Colonial Era to the First World War.* Princeton, NJ: Princeton University Press, 1968.

Chatfield, Charles, with Robert Kleidman. *The American Peace Movement: Ideals and Activism.* New York: Twayne, 1992.

Davis, Harold E. "One Hundred and Fifty Years of the American Peace Society." *World Affairs* 141 (Fall 1981): 92–103.

DeBenedetti, Charles. *The Peace Reform in American History.* Bloomington: Indiana University Press, 1980.

Howlett, Charles F. *The American Peace Movement: References and Resources.* Boston: G. K. Hall, 1991.

Whitney, Edson L. *The American Peace Society: A Centennial History.* Washington, DC: American Peace Society, 1928.

Ampudia, Pedro de

Birth Date: 1803
Death Date: August 7, 1868

Mexican military officer. Pedro de Ampudia was born in Cuba in 1803. He began his military career in the Spanish army but migrated to Mexico after that country's independence in 1821. Ampudia served with the Mexican army against forces of the Republic of Texas in the siege of the Alamo (February 23–March 6, 1836) and at the Battle of San Jacinto (April 21, 1836).

During the period of Texan independence (1836–1845), Ampudia led Mexican troops in frequent border skirmishes against Texan forces. In December 1842 Ampudia, who was commander of the Mexican forces at Matamoros, defeated a Texan invasion force, known as the Mier Expedition, and marched his prisoners to Matamoros. Mexican president Antonio López de Santa Anna, not wishing to execute all the prisoners, allowed them to draw black beans (death) and white beans (freedom) to determine their fate. Each 10th man was executed.

In 1846, at the beginning of the Mexican-American War, Santa Anna placed Ampudia in charge of the Mexican Army of the North. Because of political infighting, however, Santa Anna replaced Ampudia as general in chief with Mariano Arista in mid-April. After Arista's defeat at the Battles of Palo Alto and Resaca de la Palma on May 8 and 9, 1846, Ampudia sharply criticized Arista's military strategy. During the Mexican Army of the North's retreat, Santa Anna once again gave Ampudia command of the Mexican Army of the North.

As general in chief of the Mexican Army of the North, Pedro de Ampudia led 7,300 Mexican troops at the Battle of Monterrey (September 21–23, 1846). Despite orders from Santa Anna to retreat farther south to the city of Saltillo, Ampudia chose to hold his position at Monterrey. After three days of fighting and with U.S. forces led by Major General Zachary Taylor having penetrated the city in vicious house-to-house combat and his lines of communication with Mexico City having been cut, Ampudia negotiated a truce with Taylor and surrendered the city under terms that allowed the Mexican forces to withdraw with full military honors and with their weapons.

Mexican general Pedro de Ampudia commanded the Army of the North at the beginning of the Mexican-American War and again during the Battle of Monterrey (September 21–23, 1846). (Library of Congress)

After the battle, both Ampudia and Taylor were harshly criticized by their respective political leaders for agreeing to the truce. Ampudia believed that his troops, frustrated by constant retreats from battle, were on the point of rebelling against his command, and this had led him to make a stand at Monterrey. His decision to surrender the city nonetheless enraged Santa Anna. President James K. Polk was equally furious with Taylor for the truce, which allowed the entire Mexican Army of the North to escape.

Following the battle, Ampudia retreated to Saltillo but was unable to defend the city, and Santa Anna removed him from his command. Following the Mexican-American War, in 1854 Ampudia was appointed general in chief and governor of Nuevo Laredo. In the War of the Reform (1858–1860), Ampudia sided with the liberals, and he also supported that cause and its leader, Benito Juárez, during the reign of Maximilian von Habsburg (1864–1867) as he led Juárez's Army of the East. Ampudia died on August 7, 1868, in Mexico City.

MICHAEL R. HALL

See also

Alamo, Battle of the; Arista, Mariano; Juárez, Benito; Matamoros; Mier Expedition; Monterrey, Armistice of; Monterrey, Battle of; Palo Alto, Battle of; Resaca de la Palma, Battle of; Saltillo; San Jacinto, Battle of; Santa Anna, Antonio López de; Taylor, Zachary; Texas; Texas Revolution.

References

Bauer, K. Jack. *Zachary Taylor: Soldier, Planter, Statesman of the Old Southwest.* Baton Rouge: Louisiana State University Press, 1993.

Dana, Napoleon J. *Monterrey Is Ours! The Mexican War Letters of Lieutenant Dana, 1845–1847.* Lexington: University Press of Kentucky, 1990.

DePalo, William A., Jr. *The Mexican National Army, 1822–1852.* College Station: Texas A&M University Press, 1997.

Anáhuac Disturbances

See Texas Revolt

Anaya, Pedro María de

Birth Date: May 20, 1795
Death Date: March 21, 1854

Twice president of Mexico (1847–1848) and a general who fought under General Antonio López de Santa Anna in the battles for the Valley of Mexico during the Mexican-American War. Born on May 20, 1795, in Huichipán, Hidalgo, Mexico, Pedro María de Anaya decided on a military career as a youth and fought with pro-independence forces during Mexico's War of Independence (1810–1821). He earned numerous promotions, achieving the rank of brigadier general in 1833. Like many prominent Mexicans of that era, he repeatedly crossed the line separating the armed forces from the civil government. As a *moderado* liberal, Anaya decried

Vice President Valentín Gómez Farías's attempt to confiscate Catholic Church assets to prosecute the war in early 1847 and so supported the resulting Polkos Revolt, which began in February.

On April 2, 1847, after Gómez Farías had been removed from office, Anaya was appointed interim president by General Santa Anna. At the time, Santa Anna was fighting Major General Winfield Scott's army in eastern Mexico. Following Santa Anna's defeat on April 17–18, 1847, at Cerro Gordo, Anaya acted promptly to stiffen Mexico City's defenses in anticipation of a U.S. assault and declared the capital city in a state of siege. He also ordered the formation of a mounted partisan force, known as the *Cuerpo Ligero* (Light Corps), to attack American supply lines. It was hoped that these units would pose formidable opposition to U.S. Army convoys until the end of the conflict.

Anaya's term as president ad interim ended when Santa Anna again assumed the presidency on May 20, 1847. Anaya then returned to duty with the army and was given responsibility for the perimeter defenses of Mexico City. On August 20, 1847, he commanded the 1,600-man force that stoutly defended the Convent of San Mateo during the Battle of Churubusco. The discipline of the Mexican defenders there enabled them to inflict heavy casualties on the U.S. attackers. However, American artillery fire and flanking maneuvers, as well as an ammunition shortage, led to a Mexican surrender. When the commander of the attacking forces, Brigadier General David Twiggs, entered the convent, he asked Anaya where the Mexicans kept their ammunition. In a famous reply, the Mexican informed his foe that if he had any remaining ammunition, Twiggs would not have been standing where he was.

Although the Americans briefly held him as a prisoner of war, Anaya obtained release and proceeded to Querétaro, the temporary seat of the Mexican government following the fall of the capital. There legislators chose him as president on November 14, 1847. He remained in that post until January 8, 1848. During this brief period, Anaya appointed a peace commission to begin negotiations that culminated in the Treaty of Guadalupe Hidalgo. In Querétaro, Anaya continued to support the *moderados,* a faction of the Liberal Party that occupied the middle ground between the anticlerical and antimilitary *puro* liberals and the conservatives, who looked backed fondly to the social order of the colonial era.

Anaya's decision to fight to the last bullet at Churubusco and his reply to Twiggs made him a hero to Mexicans. After his second tenure as president, he went on to serve as postmaster general and minister of war. After his death on March 21, 1854, a bronze statue of him in uniform was placed atop a 23-foot-high pedestal in Mexico City. The statue was later moved to the grounds of the San Mateo convent, the scene of his heroic stand at Churubusco.

IRVING W. LEVINSON

See also

Cerro Gordo, Battle of; Gómez Farías, Valentín; Guadalupe Hidalgo, Treaty of; Mexico City Campaign; *Moderados*; Polkos Revolt; *Puros*; Santa Anna, Antonio López de; Twiggs, David Emanuel.

References

Eisenhower, John S. D. *Agent of Destiny: The Life and Times of General Winfield Scott.* New York: Free Press, 1997.

Galeana, Patricia, ed. *En defensa de la patria, 1847–1997.* Mexico, DF: Archivo General de la Nación, 1997.

Leon-Portilla, Miguel, ed. *Diccionario porrua de historia, biografia, y geografia de México.* México, DF: Editorial Porrua, 1997.

Anderson, Robert

Birth Date: June 14, 1805
Death Date: October 26, 1871

U.S. Army officer, artillery specialist, and commander of Fort Sumter, South Carolina, at the start of the Civil War. Robert Anderson was born near Louisville, Kentucky, on June 14, 1805. He graduated from the U.S. Military Academy at West Point in 1825 and was posted to the 3rd Artillery Regiment. He saw action during the 1832 Black Hawk War and the Second Seminole War (1835–1842) in Florida, where he was brevetted for gallantry. His keen interest in artillery tactics helped secure him a teaching appointment at West Point, where he further refined his ideas on artillery deployment. Fluent in French, Anderson also translated papers on French artillery tactics, which in turn were used by Major Samuel Ringgold to develop the so-called

An engraving of U.S. Army major Robert Anderson (1805–1871), circa 1848. Anderson's letters to his wife are a primary source for the Mexico City Campaign during the Mexican-American War. (Getty Images)

flying artillery that would be employed with much success during the war with Mexico.

Anderson served with distinction in the Mexican-American War, and he heartily supported the American war effort and its aims. "Poor deluded nation," he wrote of Mexico in 1847, "the people are not fit for self government, and we are, perhaps, instruments intended to open this country to the world and finally establish enlightened and free government in it." That March he oversaw the placement and operation of the siege mortars employed during the siege of Veracruz. He saw action in several subsequent battles, including El Molino del Rey (September 8, 1847), where he was wounded in the arm. He was subsequently brevetted major. His collected letters to his wife, published in 1911 as *An Artillery Officer in the Mexican War, 1847–1848: Letters of Robert Anderson,* have become one of the standard primary source documents concerning Scott's Mexico City Campaign.

Anderson remained in the army after the war and served in a variety of assignments. In November 1860, Secretary of War John B. Floyd ordered him to take command of the garrison at Fort Sumter in Charleston harbor, South Carolina. This was in anticipation of potential conflict with the southern states. In early April 1861, the Confederates demanded the surrender of Fort Sumter; Anderson, although a Kentuckian and a member of a slave-owning family, refused. On April 12, Confederate brigadier general Pierre G. T. Beauregard ordered the fort shelled. After almost 34 hours of continual bombardment Anderson capitulated, but only after the walls of the fort had been breached, the main entrance ruined, and the powder magazine surrounded by fire. Anderson left the post on April 14 in orderly fashion, colors flying. His brave stand made him an instant war hero in the North.

On May 15, 1861, to honor his bravery, President Abraham Lincoln secured Anderson's promotion to brigadier general and assigned him to the command of the Department of Kentucky and, later, the Department of the Cumberland. By 1863, Anderson's health was precarious, however, and he was compelled to resign his commission and retire from military service. Nevertheless, on April 14, 1865, with the temporary brevet rank of major general, Anderson returned to Fort Sumter on the fourth anniversary of its surrender and raised the U.S. flag over the post. Anderson died in Charleston, South Carolina, on October 26, 1871.

PAUL G. PIERPAOLI JR.

See also

Artillery; Flying Artillery; El Molino del Rey, Battle of; Ringgold, Samuel; Veracruz, Landing at and Siege of.

References

Anderson, Robert. *An Artillery Officer in the Mexican War, 1847–1848: Letters of Robert Anderson.* Edited by E. A. Lawton. New York: G. P. Putnam's Sons, 1911.

Dillon, Lester R., Jr. *American Artillery in the Mexican War, 1846–1847.* Austin, TX: Presidial Press, 1975.

Warner, Ezra J. *Generals in Blue: Lives of the Union Commanders.* Baton Rouge: Louisiana State University Press, 2006.

Andrade, Juan José
Birth Date: 1796
Death Date: 1844

Mexican army officer and politician. Born in Mexico City in 1796, Juan José Andrade entered military service with the Spanish army in 1809, enlisting as a cadet in the Regiment Provincial Durango and seeing action in 27 skirmishes and 4 major battles against insurrectionists during the Mexican War of Independence. In 1821 Andrade supported the cause of independence when he endorsed the Plan de Iguala, turning against the Spanish cause and joining Colonel Agustín de Iturbide's Army of the Three Guarantees. Fighting in 3 more battles and 7 skirmishes against his former comrades, he was rewarded after the conflict with the rank of major general of cavalry.

Serving in both the military and political spheres, Andrade was the governor of Puebla in the 1820s before accepting the post of commandant general of San Luis Potosí. During the suppression of the Zacatecan rebellion in May 1835, Andrade's cavalry played an important role in the Battles of Guadalupe and Zacatecas, duping the Zacatecan cavalry through a feint and attacking the rear of the Zacatecan formation. In 1836, Andrade commanded a brigade of cavalry in the invasion of Texas led by General Antonio López de Santa Anna.

After the fall of the Alamo on March 6, 1836, Andrade remained in San Antonio in command of the captured post. Although ordered to return to San Luis Potosí by Santa Anna on April 1 in anticipation of a Texan rout, his troops still occupied the Alamo on April 24. On that day, following Santa Anna's defeat at San Jacinto, he received orders from Major General Vicente Filisola, second in command of Mexican forces in Texas, to destroy those fortifications and march to Goliad. His troops pulled down walls and set fires, spiked any cannon that could not be moved with their forces, and joined Filisola at Goliad. The combined Mexican force then continued the retreat toward Matamoros.

On June 12, Filisola received notification that Major General José Urrea had replaced him as commander of Mexican forces in Texas. Because Urrea was not with Filisola's troops, Filisola turned command over to Andrade. Despite orders from Urrea to the contrary, Andrade and Filisola followed the orders received from a captured Santa Anna and continued the evacuation of Goliad. Despite again receiving orders on June 12 from Urrea to return to Goliad, Andrade continued his movement toward Matamoros. He arrived in that city on June 18, thus ending the Texas Campaign.

Following the campaign in Texas, Andrade became commandant general of Mexico. In late 1843 he began his last assignment as governor of the Department of Sinaloa. He died in Mazatlán in early 1844.

JEFFREY D. PEPPERS

See also
Alamo, Battle of the; Filisola, Vicente; San Jacinto, Battle of; Matamoros; Mazatlán; Puebla; San Luis Patosí; Santa Anna, Antonio López de; Texas Revolution; Urrea y Elías Gonzales, José de; Zacatecas.

References
Bancroft, Hubert Howe. *History of the North Mexican States and Texas.* San Francisco: History Company, 1886.
The Handbook of Texas. Austin: Texas State Historical Association, 1986.
Harden, Stephen. *Texian Iliad: A Military History of the Texas Revolution, 1835–36.* Austin: University of Texas Press, 1994.
Roberts, Randy, and James S. Olson. *A Line in the Sand.* New York: Free Press, 2001.

Andrade, Manuel
Birth Date: 1800
Death Date: Unknown

Mexican army general. Born in Puebla in 1800, Manuel Andrade entered military service as a cadet in Spain's Escuadrón de Tulancingo in 1814 and became a cavalry officer. In 1823 he supported Antonio López de Santa Anna and rose steadily through the ranks. By the eve of the Mexican-American War, he was a general of division and had command of a cavalry division under General Juan Álavarez.

Andrade took part in numerous engagements during the war against the United States, including the Battle of Buena Vista on February 22–23, 1847, and the Battle of El Molino del Rey on September 8, 1847. Andrade's performance at the latter engagement remains controversial. When U.S. infantry began to charge the stone fortifications at El Molino del Rey, Andrade was ordered to confront the American attack and scatter the infantry. After much hesitation, Andrade's force moved forward but then collapsed completely in a chaotic retreat. This compelled other Mexican cavalry units to follow suit, and the battle was eventually lost. General Álvarez later blamed the loss on Andrade's timidity.

Andrade continued his association with the military following the Mexican-American War. Secretary of War Mariano Arista, himself the veteran of many battles with Texas and the United States, selected Andrade to head a commission to recommend reforms to improve the army's performance. The commission revived many older recommendations made by General Pedro García Conde, who had been tasked with the same assignment after the disastrous Texas Campaign of 1836. A few of Conde's ideas had been implemented prior to the Mexican-American War, but the war with the United States put others on hold. In April 1849, Andrade's commission endorsed the previous plan almost without change.

Thereafter Andrade continued his service in the Mexican army. A liberal, he took part in the fight against the French and their Austrian allies in the 1860s. In September 1865, troops commanded by Andrade engaged a larger Austrian column around the town of Tlapacoyan in the state of Veracruz. Even though he was outnumbered, Andrade reported that he was able to force the enemy to withdraw from the area.

The date and manner of Andrade's death are unknown.

BRUCE WINDERS

See also

Álvarez, Juan; Arista, Mariano; Buena Vista, Battle of; El Molino del Rey, Battle of; García Conde, Pedro.

References

DePalo, William P. *The Mexican National Army, 1822–1852*. College Station: Texas A&M University Press, 1997.

Ramsey, Albert C., ed. *The Other Side: Notes for the History between Mexico and the United States.* New York: John Wiley, 1850.

Anglo-American Press in Mexico

From the start of the Mexican-American War, the publication of English-language American newspapers was common in the cities occupied by U.S. forces. Numerous American printers and editors served in the volunteer regiments and, in addition to sending war reports to home papers they represented, they also established their own newspapers in several Mexican cities. After the defeat of the Mexican army in the fall of 1847, the American press in Mexico worked as an important political and diplomatic tool for U.S. occupation officials and the U.S. government.

In February 1847 Jason R. Barnard founded the *Sentinel* in Tampico, and in Veracruz, together with John H. Peoples and William Jewell, in April 1847, less than a month after U.S. forces occupied the port city, they began to publish the *Vera Cruz Eagle*. Peoples, for his part, had also begun to publish the *American Star* in Jalapa, Veracruz, a paper that later would move to the city of Puebla and finally to Mexico City. The *American Star* began by circulating every other day, but in less than one month it had begun to sell daily, which was proof of its enormous demand. It provided news regarding the war, the occupation of the city, and the official dispositions of occupation forces. The daily also published opinion pieces by the military commanders.

Many of the Anglo newspapers catered to a dual audience: English-speaking and Spanish-speaking individuals. The *American Star,* for example, was divided into two parts. The first was published in English and included a section with dispatches and reports for the occupation army. The second, and shorter part of the paper, published in Spanish, provided national news and information about entertainment in the capital.

Occupation newspapers also served as a mouthpiece for members of the U.S. Army in which they expressed their complaints and claims regarding robberies, deaths, and threats incurred by U.S. military personnel. Warnings about dangerous places to avoid, likely attack strategies practiced by the locals, and ways to protect oneself in Mexico City were frequent topics. The American

press in Mexico City also published accounts detailing the corporal punishment of Mexicans who had refused to conform to the rules of occupation officials. Newspapers also printed stories about more uplifting subjects, including suggestions on where to enjoy good food and where to attend shows and dances.

One of the most interesting aspects of the U.S. press during the occupation was that newspapers also trumpeted the alleged benefits of Manifest Destiny and the glories of war and conquest. Papers were full of anecdotes about soldiers' bravery on the battlefield, which, swathed in the romanticism of the time, created popular heroes in the public imagination. Upon returning to the United States, these men were treated as conquerors. Also, the coverage of American military victories seemed to confirm the idea that Americans had been given the unique mission of expanding democratic, republican values into other parts of the world.

Not surprisingly, publishing a newspaper in a foreign country presented challenges. Obtaining paper often proved difficult. Printing was mostly done on Mexican printing presses, the designs of which publishers were not familiar with, and training personnel who would be responsible for the publication could be troublesome.

In general, the U.S. press in Mexico responded well to the needs of troops on the front lines and readers at home, as there was a constant demand for news at the end of a battle. Further, the occupation press allowed members of the army to maintain ties with their families and friends and, above all, to endure the daily monotony of life in a military camp. On the other hand, the Anglo press also reported the dispositions issued by U.S. Army personnel in an effort to control the Mexican population and keep peace and order in occupied cities.

FABIOLA GARCÍA RUBIO

See also

Associated Press; Jalapa; Kendall, George Wilkins; Manifest Destiny; Mexico, Occupation of; Mexico City; Public Opinion and the War, Mexican; Public Opinion and the War, U.S.; Puebla; Tampico and Victoria, Occupation of; Taylor, Zachary; Veracruz.

References

García Rubio, Fabiola. *La entrada de las tropas estadunidenses a la ciudad de México: La mirada de Carl Nebel.* México, DF: Instituto de Investigaciones Dr. José María Luis Mora, 2002.

Johannsen, Robert W. *To the Halls of the Montezumas: The Mexican War in the American Imagination.* New York: Oxford University Press, 1985.

Reilly, Thomas William. "American Reporters and the Mexican War, 1846–1848." Unpublished PhD diss., University of Minnesota, 1975.

Roth, Michael. "Journalism and the U.S.-Mexican War." In *Dueling Eagles: Reinterpreting the U.S.-Mexican War, 1846–1848,* edited by Douglas W. Richmond and Richard Francaviglia, 103–126. Fort Worth: Texas Christian University Press, 2000.

Angostura, Battle of

See Buena Vista, Battle of

Antiwar Sentiment

Although the Mexican-American War was generally quite popular in the United States from its beginning, the conflict nonetheless produced staunch opposition from a small but resolute collection of protestors throughout its duration. This antiwar sentiment was driven primarily by politicians from the Whig Party, including such noted statesmen as John Quincy Adams and Abraham Lincoln, who articulated skepticism over the conflict with Mexico even before the first shots were fired. These dissenters recognized how warmongering by many U.S. citizens caused them to overlook the suspect causes allegedly justifying a U.S. invasion of Mexico. Indeed, they attempted to draw attention away from the prospects of military glory and heroics to the discrepancies in the Democrats' hawkish rhetoric.

Arguably the loudest protests against the war came from northern abolitionists, both within and outside of the Whig Party. They identified the conflict as a scheme hatched by southern politicians to expand the institution of slavery and bolster the powerbase of proslavery elements in the national government and society. In the most publicized support of this conviction, in the summer of 1846 renowned New England author Henry David Thoreau spent a night in jail for refusing to pay poll tax as a public demonstration of his objection to the war. The American Peace Society, whose membership included a rather eclectic array of individuals including clergymen, abolitionists, academics, lawyers, merchants, and general peace proponents, was especially active during the two-year-long war.

Once the war began in earnest, many Whig supporters abandoned their oppositional stance in order to gain political advantage, particularly opportunistic Whig army officers such as Zachary Taylor and Winfield Scott, who saw the war as an opportunity for a possible future bid for the White House. This two-faced approach to the war caused dissension and confusion among Whigs in Congress, and they leveled as much criticism at their own party as they did at the James K. Polk administration.

Opposition leaders also shifted the focus of their arguments from the causes of the war to its consequences. As before the war, President Polk was placed at the center of antiwar criticism as the cause of all of its difficulties. Skeptics dubbed the conflict "Mr. Polk's War" and lambasted his management of the war, from charges that he was frivolously adding to the national debt to his hypocrisy in attempting to spread republican institutions in Mexico through the use of force.

Opposition to the war occurred within the U.S. Army itself when more than 200 immigrant Catholic soldiers deserted to the Mexican army, finding they had more ideologically in common with their enemy. Mexican general Antonio López de Santa Anna formed them into a unit known as the San Patricio Battalion (Batallon de San Patricio), named after the Catholic patron saint of Ireland, Saint Patrick. These deserters fought bravely with

A cartoon making fun of the Democrats' position on the annexation of Texas. The artist presents Texas as the ugly hag War or Chaos, embodying the threat of war with Mexico, feared by American opponents of annexation. (Library of Congress)

Mexican forces in several key engagements, including the August 20, 1948, Battle of Churubusco on the outskirts of Mexico City. Their capture by their former comrades caused international controversy when American authorities executed many of them.

When the war ended in 1848, its critics continued to demonize Polk for his diplomatic failures in the delay in securing peace with the defeated Mexican government. Several Whigs blamed Polk's overt territorial ambitions as the cause of the Mexicans' reluctance to appear at the negotiating table.

BRADFORD WINEMAN

See also

Abolitionism; Adams, John Quincy; American Peace Society; Emerson, Ralph Waldo; Lincoln, Abraham; Polk, James Knox; San Patricio Battalion; Santa Anna, Antonio López de; Scott, Winfield; Slavery; Taylor, Zachary; Thoreau, Henry David; Whigs.

References

Chatfield, Charles, with Robert Kleidman. *The American Peace Movement: Ideals and Activism.* New York: Twayne, 1992.

Holt, Michael. *The Rise and Fall of the American Whig Party: Jacksonian Politics and the Onset of the Civil War.* New York: Oxford University Press, 1999.

Miller, Robert Ryal. *Shamrock and Sword: The Saint Patrick's Battalion in the U.S.-Mexican War.* Norman: University of Oklahoma Press, 1989.

Schroeder, John H. *Mr. Polk's War: American Opposition and Dissent, 1846–1848.* Madison: University of Wisconsin Press, 1973.

Antón Lizardo

Small fishing village located some 12 miles south of Veracruz, Mexico. The village's population at the time of the Mexican-American War was probably fewer than 1,000 people. In February 1847, U.S. Navy commodore David E. Conner selected Antón Lizardo for his base of operations, to be used during the impending U.S. amphibious landing that would precede the assault on Veracruz. Conner favored the spot because it was close to the actual landing area at Collado Beach, located approximately 2.5 miles south of the city of Veracruz.

Army transport ships first transported soldiers and material to Lobos, an island near Tampico. From there, the men and supplies were sent on by ship to Antón Lizardo, which they reached on March 4. The upcoming landing would be the largest one to date in U.S. military history, involving 30 ships in all and some 12,000 troops. It was a Herculean task, but Conner and Major General Winfield Scott worked well together. U.S. Navy captain French Forrest had charge of the embarkation of troops preparing to leave Antón Lizardo. He also had initial charge of the landing operation at Collado Beach. After waiting out inclement weather, the landing proceeded on March 9, 1847, with troops going ashore at Collado Beach. There were few hitches and virtually no enemy resistance. By March 27, Veracruz had fallen. In 1952, Antón Lizardo, with a population of about 4,500 people, became home to Mexico's naval academy.

PAUL G. PIERPAOLI JR.

See also

Collado Beach; Conner, David; Forrest, French; Scott, Winfield; Veracruz, Landing at and Siege of.

References

Bauer, K. Jack. *Surfboats and Horse Marines: U.S. Naval Operations in the Mexican War.* Annapolis, MD: U.S. Naval Institute, 1969.

Clary, David A. *Eagles and Empire: The United States, Mexico, and the Struggle for a Continent.* New York: Bantam Books, 2009.

Apache Canyon

Defensible position on Brigadier General Stephen W. Kearny's line of advance against Santa Fe, New Mexico, during early to mid-August 1846. Apache Canyon is a narrow pass that cuts through rugged hills about 12 miles southeast of Santa Fe and was the site of the village of Cañoncito.

As Kearny's Army of the West, numbering 1,458 men, approached the canyon, Manuel Armijo, governor of New Mexico, appealed to the citizens on August 8 to gather under the command of Colonel Manuel Pino to repel the Americans. A day later, some 3,000 Mexicans, including soldiers, militiamen, and guerrillas, along with a number of Native Americans armed with a variety of weapons including bows and arrows, met the call. They gathered at Cañoncito, where the canyon walls were only 40 feet apart. Although not a cohesive unit, they constructed an abatis and emplaced eight cannon to command the approaches.

When Kearny learned of the Mexicans' defensive preparations, he considered bypassing them. However, on August 17 he decided to assault Pino's numerically superior army, even though it might prove costly. As he advanced, an *alcalde* (a municipal magistrate) rode up to Kearny on a mule and informed him that the defenders had decamped. Armijo and Pino had wanted to fight, but a junta that included Diego Archuleta had voted on August 17 to retreat. Thus, the American forces on August 18 passed unmolested through Apache Canyon and went on to occupy Santa Fe.

PAUL DAVID NELSON

See also

Archuleta, Diego; Armijo, Manuel; Cañoncito, Battle of; Kearny, Stephen Watts; New Mexico; Santa Fe.

References

Bauer, K. Jack. *The Mexican War, 1846–1848.* New York: Macmillan, 1974.

Clary, David A. *Eagles and Empire: The United States, Mexico, and the Struggle for a Continent.* New York: Bantam Books, 2009.

Connor, Seymour V., and Odie B. Faulk. *North America Divided: The Mexican War, 1846–1848.* New York: Oxford University Press, 1971.

Reséndez, Andrés. *Changing Identities at the Frontier: Texas and New Mexico, 1800–1850.* Cambridge, UK: Cambridge University Press, 2004.

Apaches

Generic term used to describe numerous separate Native American groups who traditionally habituated the American Southwest (Arizona, Texas, and New Mexico principally). The name *Apache* was bestowed on them by the Zuni tribe of New Mexico in whose language the word means "enemy." The Apaches referred to themselves as "the people."

The activities of four bands of Apaches were especially noteworthy during the 1830s and 1840s: the Lipans, Mescaleros, Gila and Mimbres, and the Chiricahuas. The Lipan Apaches were the easternmost band and ranged in what is now west Texas from the Edwards Plateau to the Rio Grande. The Mescaleros ranged in the Sierra Blanca and Sacramento Mountains of south central New Mexico. The Gila Apaches, which included the Mimbres, ranged in the upper regions of the Gila River along the New Mexico–Arizona border from the Datil Mountains south to the state of Chihuahua. The Chiracahuas ranged from the Dragoon Mountains of southern Arizona into northern Mexico.

The Lipans, ironically, were among the first to suffer the consequences of American expansion. After all, they had befriended the first Anglo-American settlers who had been invited to settle in Texas after Mexico achieved its independence and had supported them during the Texas Revolution of 1835–1836. Subsequently, after Texas won independence in 1836, the Lipans were among the first allies of the new Republic of Texas, even joining in military actions against the Comanches. The Lipans also supported Texas when Mexico's Army of the North briefly reoccupied San Antonio and several nearby towns in 1842. While the Texans were raising a militia force to oppose this raid, Lipan warriors defended Austin, Houston, and other Texas cities from surprise attack by Mexican forces. And that November, when Alexander Somervell led a daring punitive expedition into Mexico, Lipan warriors rode alongside him, prompting Texas president Sam Houston to promise that Texas would always be "kind" to the Lipans.

Nevertheless, an incident in which a young Lipan chief, Flacco the Younger, was killed began to sour Lipan-Texas relations. Unfortunately for the Lipans, the United States subjected the state's Native Americans to its national policies of Indian removal after it annexed Texas in 1845. In response, the Lipans regularly raided both U.S. and Mexican settlements through the 1850s before being brutally subdued by U.S. forces two decades later.

Farther east, the Mescaleros, from the Spanish "mescal makers," had traditionally warred with the Comanches and routinely raided the Pueblos as well as both Anglo and Mexican settlements and ranches. After Texas's independence in 1836, Texas Rangers attempted, quite ineffectually, to stop such activity. During the Mexican-American War, the Mescaleros, always intrepid warriors, conducted raids against U.S. supply trains in both New Mexico and Chihuahua; they also occasionally ambushed small American and Mexican detachments.

The Mescaleros had a visceral hatred of the Mexicans, and so when Brigadier General Stephen W. Kearny arrived in New Mexico in 1846, the Mescaleros sought a treaty of alliance with the United States. American officials, including Kearny, rebuffed their overtures, however, and warned the tribe that they would be punished militarily if raids continued. The Mescaleros paid little heed to U.S. threats and continued terrorizing settlers and overland trade routes until they were finally subdued in the 1860s.

The Gila/Mimbre Apaches waged grueling guerrilla-style warfare against Mexico beginning in 1830. They finally sued for peace in August 1832, but amity remained elusive, and within a few months the Gilas had resumed their raids against Mexican settlements. When the Americans arrived in Apacheria at the beginning of the Mexican-American War, the Gilas initially greeted them cordially and offered to fight alongside them in order to defeat their common enemy. The Americans demurred, but throughout the conflict the Gilas launched repeated raids into Mexico. Even after the conflict ended they continued this low-level warfare aimed at both Mexicans and Americans, and the United States seemed ill equipped to stop it. Not until 1863, when Gila leader Mangas Coloradas was killed by U.S. troops, did their attacks subside.

The Chiricahua Apaches, who proved the most difficult to subdue, warred against the Mexicans from about 1831 until 1836, by which time they had signed peace agreements with the Mexican government. By 1840, however, the truce had been broken and the Chiricahuas renewed their offensive. After the Chiricahuas went to war against the state of Sonora in 1844, they suffered a severe setback when Mexican forces killed 100 Chiricahuas in August 1844. In July 1847, a Mexican mercenary was responsible for the murder and mutilation of 148 peaceful Chiricahuas.

The Chiricahuas greeted the Americans warmly at the beginning of the Mexican-American War, but relations between the two eventually deteriorated. During that conflict, the Chiricahuas waged war against the Mexicans throughout Sonora. Through the 1850s the Chiricahuas remained at peace with the United States, but relations had plummeted by the early 1860s and the U.S. Army launched offensives against them. The Apaches, however, turned out to be one of the most difficult adversaries that the United States would face during the Indian Wars of the 19th century.

Justin D. Murphy, Patrick R. Ryan, and Paul G. Pierpaoli Jr.

See also
Arizona; Comanches; Kearny, Stephen Watts; Native Americans; Navajos; New Mexico; Pueblos; Texas; Texas Revolution.

References
Aleshire, Peter. *Reaping the Whirlwind: The Apache Wars.* New York: Facts on File, 1998.
DeLay, Brian. *War of a Thousand Deserts: Indian Raids and the U.S.-Mexican War.* New Haven, CT: Yale University Press, 2008.
Schilz, Thomas F. *Lipan Apaches in Texas.* El Paso: Texas Western Press, 1987.
Sturtevant, William C., ed. *Handbook of North American Indians.* Vol. 10, *Southwest.* Washington, DC: Smithsonian Institution, 1983.

Thrapp, Dan L. *The Conquest of Apacheria*. Norman: University of
    Oklahoma Press, 1967.
Worcester, Donald E. *The Apaches: Eagles of the Southwest*. Norman:
    University of Oklahoma Press, 1979.

Archuleta, Diego
Birth Date: March 27, 1814
Death Date: March 24, 1884

New Mexico politician, soldier, and militia leader who organized
resistance to the U.S. occupation of New Mexico in the fall of
1846. Diego Archuleta was born on March 27, 1814, at Alcade,
New Mexico, and was schooled locally and then came under the
tutelage of Father Antonio José Martinez, a Catholic priest with
whom he would later plot a revolt against the Americans in New
Mexico. Archuleta studied eight years in Durango in preparation
for the priesthood but never took his final vows after deciding that
life as a clergyman did not suit him. In 1840 he settled near Rio
Arriba, New Mexico, and shortly thereafter secured a commission
as a captain in the local militia. During the 1841 Santa Fe Expedition, when a contingent of volunteers marched from Texas to
New Mexico in an attempt to claim the region for the Republic of
Texas, Archuleta helped defeat the incursion and took a number of
Texans prisoner. In 1843 he was elected as a deputy to the national
Mexican Congress, serving until 1845.

When the U.S. invasion of New Mexico began in August 1846,
Archuleta, who then held the rank of colonel and was second in
command of New Mexican forces under Governor General Manuel
Armijo, advocated a rapid and potent counteroffensive. The New
Mexicans had assembled a force of about 3,000 men who were supposed to confront Brigadier General Stephen W. Kearny's force at
Apache Canyon. However, after Armijo called a council of war, the
will to repel the American advance evaporated, and the New Mexican force disbanded. Armijo and many others fled to Chihuahua,
but Archuleta and other hard-liners opted to remain in New Mexico.

Soon thereafter, James Magoffin, an American interpreter and
emissary who had accompanied Kearny's force from Fort Leavenworth to Santa Fe, secretly met with Archuleta. Magoffin hoped
to convince him to abandon his calls for resisting the American
army and apparently informed Archuleta that the Americans were
interested only in taking the disputed east bank of the Rio Grande,
claimed by both the Republic of Mexico and the Republic of Texas
under the controversial Treaty of Velasco. Indeed, Magoffin
offered to make Archuleta the military commander of all of western New Mexico. In return, Archuleta agreed not to take up arms
against Kearny's force.

By early September, however, Archuleta surmised that the
Americans planned to seize all of New Mexico. Incensed by the
seeming American duplicity, he, along with other insurgents who
included Father Martinez, Augustín Duran, and Tomás Ortiz,
began to plot against the occupiers. By late fall they had developed a plan to assassinate acting governor Charles Bent and
Colonel Sterling Price, then commanding U.S. occupation forces.
Price learned of the scheme and ordered Archuleta and the others involved in it arrested. Archuleta and many of his coconspirators fled into northern Mexico, but the scheme to assassinate
Bent went forward in January 1847, resulting in his death and the
beginning of the Taos Revolt, which was quashed after several
weeks of violence. Archuleta remained at large for the remainder
of the Mexican-American War.

In 1848, Archuleta, who remained quite popular among New
Mexicans, was permitted to return to his native New Mexico. He
swore an oath of loyalty to the United States and became involved
in local politics. In 1857, he was named U.S. Indian agent for the
southern Utes and Apaches, a post he held for several years. In
1861, at the outset of the Civil War, he was commissioned a lieutenant colonel of volunteers before being named Indian agent for
the Utes and Apaches. He was also made a brigadier general of the
New Mexican Militia. Archuleta was perhaps the first person of
Hispanic ancestry to hold flag rank in an American military force.
Subsequently, he served multiple terms in the New Mexico territorial legislature and ran unsuccessfully for a seat in the U.S. House
of Representatives. Archuleta died on March 24, 1884, in Santa Fe.

PAUL G. PIERPAOLI JR.

See also

Armijo, Manuel; Bent, Charles; Duran, Augustín; Kearny, Stephen Watts;
    Magoffin, James Wiley; Martinez, Antonio José; New Mexico; Ortiz,
    Tomás; Price, Sterling; Santa Fe; Taos Revolt.

References

Coldsmith, Don. *Trail from Taos*. New York: Bantam Books, 1990.
Crutchfield, James Andrew. *Tragedy at Taos: The Revolt of 1847*. Plano:
    Republic of Texas Press, 1995.
Twitchell, Ralph Emerson. *The History of the Military Occupation of the
    Territory of New Mexico from 1846 to 1851 by the Government of the
    United States*. 1909. Reprint, New York: Arno Press, 1976.

Arista, Mariano
Birth Date: July 26, 1802
Death Date: August 7, 1855

Mexican army officer and president (1851–1853). Born in San
Luis Potosí on July 26, 1802, Mariano Arista initiated his military
career as a cadet in the provincial militia of Puebla, fighting on
the royalist side in Mexico's 1810–1821 independence wars. His
superiors recognized Arista's zeal with a promotion in 1818 to
standard-bearer for the Dragones de México (a militia dragoon
regiment); *alférez* (rank equivalent to second lieutenant) in September 1820; and lieutenant in May 1821.

In June 1821, however, Arista changed his allegiance and
joined the independence movement of Mexican-born Spanish
officer Agustín de Iturbide. Arista fought royalists with the same

Mexican general Mariano Arista commanded the Army of the North against U.S. forces under Brigadier General Zachary Taylor in the battles of Palo Alto and Resaca de la Palma on May 8 and 9, 1846, both of which were Mexican defeats. (Library of Congress)

fervor he once employed against insurgents. In 1824 and again in 1829, after Mexico had achieved independence in 1821, the federal government recognized Arista's contributions by promoting him to captain and lieutenant colonel, respectively.

On December 4, 1829, Vice President Anastasio Bustamante staged a coup against President Vicente Guerrero, claiming it as necessary to impede the radical and dictatorial actions by the president. Arista backed the revolt and secured the presidency for Bustamante, which endured from 1830 to 1832. For his services to the new administration, President Bustamante promoted Arista to colonel on February 12, 1831, and to brigadier general that August.

On November 27, 1838, a French fleet arrived to force the Mexican government to pay 600,000 pesos to France, as compensation for damages inflicted on French-owned shops in Mexico City during the 1828 Parián riot. The riot had occurred because Guerrero's supporters had refused to accept his loss in the 1828 presidential election to Manuel Gómez Pedraza and had sacked the Parián Market in protest. Because the Mexican government would not meet France's demands, the French took over the San Juan de Ulúa fortress off Veracruz. To repel the invasion, which came to be known as the Pastry War, Bustamante summoned Brigadier General Arista to aid General Antonio López de Santa Anna in leading the Mexican defenses. A detachment of French troops who entered Veracruz on the morning of December 5 captured and imprisoned Arista, but the French freed him after hostilities concluded in late January 1839.

Later that year President Bustamante, concluding his second term in office (1837–1839), promoted Arista to commanding general of the Army of the North, with responsibility for protecting Coahuila, Texas, Nuevo León, and Tamaulipas. The promotion was for his role in defeating a rebellion against Bustamante in mid-1839.

With the rupture in diplomatic relations between Mexico and the United States in 1845 after the U.S. annexation of Texas, both countries cautiously prepared for what seemed an inevitable war. During this time, Arista constantly kept the government informed of the need for additional arms, equipment, and supplies. On May 8, 1846, General Zachary Taylor's Army of Occupation and Arista's Army of the North engaged in what became the first major battle of the U.S.-Mexican War, the Battle of Palo Alto. On the morning of May 9, due to the high number of Mexican casualties, Arista ordered his army to withdraw southward. By that afternoon, the armies met again and fought the second key encounter in the war, the Battle of Resaca de la Palma. Taylor emerged with a definitive victory over Arista's army, which led to his removal as commander of the Army of the North by then-president Mariano Paredes y Arrillaga.

In June 1848 then-president José Joaquín de Herrera cleared Arista of any wrongdoing at Palo Alto and Resaca de la Palma, naming him minister of war. In 1851 Artista was elected president, in the first such election since the early 1820s. Nevertheless, Arista's presidency was short-lived. On July 26, 1852, supporters of Antonio López de Santa Anna initiated a rebellion to overthrow and replace him with Santa Anna. Witnessing the increasing popularity of the rebellion, Arista resigned the presidency on January 6, 1853. He died on August 7, 1855, while exiled in Portugal.

RICARDO A. CATÓN

See also

Bustamante y Oseguera, Anastasio; Guerrero, Vicente; Herrera, José Joaquín de; Palo Alto, Battle of; Paredes y Arrillaga, Mariano; Pastry War; Resaca de la Palma, Battle of; Santa Anna, Antonio López de; Taylor, Zachary.

References

DePalo, William A. *The Mexican National Army, 1822–1852.* College Station: Texas A&M University Press, 1997.

Fowler, Will. *Santa Anna of Mexico.* Lincoln: University of Nebraska Press, 2007.

Rivera Cambas, Manuel. *Los gobernantes de México: Mariano Arista.* [Mexico]: Colección Suma Veracruzana, 1972.

Sanchez, Joseph P. "General Mariano Arista at the Battle of Palo Alto." *Journal of the West* 24 (April 1985): 8–21.

Arizona

State located in the southwestern region of the United States. Bordered by Mexico to the south and by California and Nevada to the west, Utah to the north, and New Mexico to the east, Arizona's extreme northeastern border also touches the tip of Colorado's southwestern border. The southern portion of the present state of

Arizona was part of New Spain's Pimería Alta region during the era of Spanish control, which lasted until 1821. Northern Arizona, under both Spanish and Mexican rule, was divided between the territories of Alta California and Nuevo Mexico. Tucson, founded in 1775, and Phoenix are the two largest cities in Arizona. Arizona covers 113,988 square miles.

Arizona's diverse geography and climate are mostly due to differences in altitude. The state is traversed by many mountain ranges, low and high plateaus, and both high and low deserts. The San Francisco Peaks' Humphreys Peak, at 12,633 feet, is the state's highest point. The Grand Canyon is the best-known geological feature, and the Colorado River that runs through the canyon is the lowest point in Arizona at 70 feet above sea level. Other notable rivers include the Verde, Salt, Santa Cruz, and San Pedro. In the north, where elevations are high, winter snow is frequent and deep. In the south, with the exception of mountainous regions, snow is infrequent and rare. Much of the south is desert, ranging from the low deserts of the western regions, which average fewer than 6 inches of precipitation per year, to the higher deserts (including the Sonora Desert), which can receive up to 12 inches per year. The Sonora Desert, which extends well into Mexico, is one of the greenest deserts in the world and is the only place where the giant saguaro cactus grows.

Amerindians were the earliest inhabitants of Arizona, and they overwhelmingly outnumbered the non-Amerindian population throughout the Spanish, Mexican, and early U.S. eras. The non-Amerindian population was quite small, often numbering in the hundreds to the low thousands. A number of different Native American groups lived in Arizona, including the Pimas, Yumas, Navajos, and Apaches. Arizona's current population is approximately 6.5 million people, with about 60 percent white, 29 percent Hispanic, 6 percent Amerindian, and 3 percent other.

Early Spanish settlements in Arizona primarily consisted of Catholic missions, and neither Spain nor Mexico established large settlements in Arizona. Generally, the territory was divided into large sections and given to various Mexican individuals or families willing to settle in the region. Most took up farming and ranching.

During the Mexican-American War, no major combat operations occurred in Arizona, although Brigadier General Stephen Watts Kearny, commander of the U.S. Army of the West, led his troops through southern Arizona on his way to conduct military operations against Mexican forces in California.

The 1848 Treaty of Guadalupe Hidalgo, which ended the war, resulted in the United States acquiring control over most of modern-day Arizona. The southern tier of the state, known as the Gadsden Purchase, was purchased from Mexico in 1853 during President General Antonio López de Santa Anna's term in office; the purchase was ratified by the U.S. Congress in 1854. The land was purchased ostensibly to build a transcontinental railroad linking the Deep South with Southern California.

Initially, most of Arizona was part of the New Mexico Territory. However, during the Civil War (1861–1865), both the Confederate

States of America and the United States created their own Arizona Territories, in 1861 and 1863, respectively. In the post–Civil War era, Arizona remained a territory until it was granted statehood on February 14, 1912.

WYNDHAM E. WHYNOT

See also

Apaches; Army of the West, United States; Gadsden Purchase; Guadalupe Hidalgo, Treaty of; Kearny, Stephen Watts; Navajos; New Mexico; Santa Anna, Antonio López de.

References

Sheridan, Thomas E. *Arizona: A History*. Tucson: University of Arizona Press, 1995.

Walker, Henry Pickering, and Don Bufkin. *Historical Atlas of Arizona*. 2nd ed. Norman: University of Oklahoma Press, 1986.

Armijo, Manuel
Birth Date: 1790
Death Date: December 9, 1853

Mexican politician who served as governor of New Mexico at the outbreak of the Mexican-American War. Born in 1790 in Belen (near Albuquerque, New Mexico) into a large landowning family, Manuel Armijo and his brothers became prominent fixtures in the public life of Albuquerque. Throughout his political career, Armijo was engaged in power struggles with the political elite of Santa Fe, New Mexico. He served as *alcalde* (mayor) of Albuquerque in 1822, 1824, 1825, and 1830. His brothers served as *alcalde* in 1820, 1823, 1827, 1828, 1831, and 1834.

The first of Armijo's three terms as governor of New Mexico lasted from May 1827 to March 1829, when he resigned. Armijo was especially concerned about the smuggling of goods into New Mexico and the illegal trapping of beaver by Americans. He then returned to Albuquerque, where he became *alcalde* and amassed considerable wealth as an entrepreneur. In August 1837 a group of angry residents in Santa Fe murdered the governor and launched the Rebellion of 1837. Armijo then led a contingent of Mexican troops to Santa Fe, crushed the rebellion, and declared himself governor.

In 1841 Armijo orchestrated the capture of the members of the Texas–Santa Fe Expedition and sent them to be incarcerated in Perote Castle, Veracruz. He resigned his position as governor in 1844. Armijo was not well liked by many of those he governed, largely because of the spoils system he created that favored his friends and political allies.

In 1845 Armijo was appointed governor of New Mexico for the third time. Following the outbreak of the Mexican-American War in 1846, he attempted to organize the defense of New Mexico. With the assistance of Diego Archuleta, a young Mexican army officer, Armijo assembled a poorly trained and poorly equipped force of about 3,000 men. The plan was to stop an American force, moving in from the north, at Apache Canyon. By August 1846, realizing the weakness of his forces and the threat posed to the inhabitants of Santa Fe, Armijo fled to Chihuahua, Mexico, thus allowing Brigadier General Stephen Watts Kearny's army to capture Santa Fe on August 16 without a fight. What remained of Armijo's defense force scattered into the nearby hills.

Armijo was charged with treason and cowardice but was acquitted in a Mexican court. Charges that Armijo had accepted a bribe from American merchants in New Mexico to withdraw from the scene without resistance are unsubstantiated. After the Mexican-American War, Armijo returned to New Mexico, settling on a ranch near Socorro. He died at his home in Lemitar, New Mexico, on December 9, 1853. His will specified that $1,000 be set aside to establish a public secondary school in New Mexico.

MICHAEL R. HALL

See also

Archuleta, Diego; Kearny, Stephen Watts; New Mexico; Perote Castle; Santa Fe.

References

Keleher, William Aloysius. *Turmoil in New Mexico.* Santa Fe, NM: Rydal Press, 1951.

Reséndez, Andrés. *Changing Identities at the Frontier: Texas and New Mexico, 1800–1850.* Cambridge, UK: Cambridge University Press, 2004.

Tyler, Daniel. "Governor Armijo's Moment of Truth." *Journal of the West* 11 (April 1972): 307–316.

Armistead, Lewis Addison

Birth Date: February 18, 1817
Death Date: July 5, 1863

U.S. Army officer. Lewis Addison Armistead was born on February 18, 1817, in New Berne, North Carolina. He came from a prominent family; his father was a high-ranking U.S. Army officer, and his grandfather was a U.S. congressman. Armistead enrolled at the U.S. Military Academy, West Point, in 1834, but he experienced academic problems, especially in French. Armistead also smashed a mess hall plate over the head of fellow cadet Jubal A. Early, who would go on to become a celebrated Confederate general. The event brought about Armistead's expulsion. Thanks to his father's intervention, however, Armistead received a commission as a second lieutenant in the 6th U.S. Infantry in 1839.

Armistead saw action in Florida during the Second Seminole War (1835–1842), where he earned a reputation for bravery and the respect of his men. During the Mexican-American War, he fought in Major General Winfield Scott's army during its advance from Veracruz to Mexico City. Armistead distinguished himself at the Battles of Contreras and Churubusco, earning a brevet promotion to captain in 1847. During the Battle of Chapultepec (September 13, 1847), Armistead was one of the first to leap into the deep trench surrounding Chapultepec Castle, which guarded access to

Lieutenant Lewis A. Armistead of the 6th Infantry Regiment received brevets to captain and major for his role in the American victories in the battles of Contreras, Churubusco, and El Molino del Rey. (North Wind Picture Archives)

Mexico City from the west. He immediately began scaling the fortress's high walls, exhorting others to follow him. Not long after he began his ascent, he was felled by a musket ball and seriously wounded. For his bravery at Chapultepec and the earlier Battle of El Molino del Rey, he was brevetted major.

After the war, Armistead served mainly in the American West. He was promoted to the permanent rank of captain in 1855. When the Civil War began, Armistead cast his lot with the Confederacy, resigning his U.S. Army commission in May 1861. He then became colonel of the 57th Virginia Infantry, a post he held until April 1, 1862, when he became a brigadier general. Armistead performed well at the May 31–June 1, 1862 Battle of Seven Pines and during the Seven Days' Battles (June 25–July 1, 1862) under General Robert E. Lee. He also took part in the Second Battle of Bull Run (August 29–30, 1862). During the September 3–17 Antietam Campaign Armistead served as Lee's provost marshal, a demanding post because of the high number of desertions occurring that month. At the Battle of Fredericksburg (December 13, 1862), he served in Major General George Pickett's division.

On July 2, 1863, Armistead and his brigade arrived at Gettysburg. The next day, they took part in Pickett's ill-fated charge against the center of the Union line. Armistead reached a stone fence on Cemetery Ridge with approximately 100 other Confederates. Determined to take a Union artillery battery, he fell to the ground badly wounded by three bullets. Transported to a nearby Union field hospital, he died there on July 5. Of six Confederate generals who died at Gettysburg, Armistead is thought to have been the one most suited to higher command.

PAUL G. PIERPAOLI JR.

See also

Chapultepec, Battle of; Churubusco, Battle of; Contreras, Battle of; Mexico City Campaign; El Molino del Rey, Battle of; Scott, Winfield.

References

Eicher, John H., and David J. Eischer. *Civil War High Commands.* Stanford, CA: Stanford University Press, 2001.
Hess, Earl J. *Pickett's Charge—the Last Attack at Gettysburg.* Chapel Hill: University of North Carolina Press, 2001.
Singletary, Otis A. *The Mexican War.* Chicago: University of Chicago Press, 1968.

Army Life, Mexican and U.S.

During the Mexican-American War army life was uniformly unpleasant for the enlisted soldier of both sides. Both armies contended with the problems of campaigning in the heat of northern and central Mexico while wearing wool uniforms. Each faced the onset of the yellow fever season, particularly when campaigning in the coastal regions near Veracruz. The armies also had great difficulty maintaining adequate supplies because of long supply routes, the slow speed of horse-drawn wagons, and the constant threat of interdiction by the enemy. Most troops were additionally burdened by slow-firing, short-ranged, smoothbore muskets, characterized by an ignition system that failed to fire 15 percent of the time, even under optimal conditions. Morale was negatively affected by the poor rewards each nation offered for service in the military, and neither army could fall back on extensive training or professional leadership to improve the lives of the men. In short, army service during the war was often a miserable experience, especially for enlisted personnel.

Soldiers in the Mexican army could look to General Antonio López de Santa Anna as an effective tactician, but it was evident that he did not care deeply about the conditions for his troops. Santa Anna faced invasions on two fronts, but his efforts to personally manage resistance to each incursion largely eluded him. Mexican troops fought in a defensive capacity, and this motivated many in the defense of their homes. Nevertheless, most of the Mexican army was conscripted, poorly trained, poorly equipped, poorly fed, and the soldiers resented the harsh discipline meted out by Santa Anna and his officers.

Although the Mexican army had the numerical advantage in every major battle of the war, it was hindered by a lack of proper logistical support. Ammunition and gunpowder were constantly in short supply, and the army did not possess a substantial amount of artillery. The lack of artillery meant that the Mexican soldiers were often subjected to fire from American field pieces without the capacity to return fire. The weapons possessed by the Mexican army tended to be obsolete models, long abandoned by the armies of Europe. Some Mexican units were not issued firearms at all because of a general shortage and instead were issued other weapons such as lances.

Mexican troops were kept in the ranks largely by rule of force. Punishments for disciplinary infractions were harsh, arbitrary, and unevenly applied. Desertion rates were high, as soldiers abandoned distant postings in order to return to their homes. This problem became magnified in the wake of major American victories that humiliated the proud troops and threatened the most populous regions of the country, as during the Mexico City Campaign. Often the troops felt abandoned by their officers, many of whom escaped losing battles on horseback, leaving the enlisted personnel to be captured.

Corruption permeated the leadership of the Mexican army, too. Membership in the officer corps, largely restricted to the landed elite, offered the promise of fame, glory, and a potential source of income. Officers appeared to care little for their men or the effectiveness of their fighting units. They often collected pay for men who had died or deserted, and government rations "disappeared," sold by officers to enrich themselves at the expense of their troops.

When American captors offered to parole the Mexican prisoners of war, many of the released prisoners deserted the Mexican army and went home, only to be impressed into the military once more. American generals reported that Mexican troops repeatedly violated their parolee oaths but did not mention why the oath breaking occurred. Modern historians have argued that this probably occurred from simple ignorance or under threats by the Mexican government.

On campaign, Mexican troops rarely received sufficient food to meet their daily needs. Their health was further endangered by the almost total lack of medicine and the scant attention paid to sanitation among the enlisted personnel. The poor supply system greatly hindered the effectiveness of Mexican troops in the field. Not only was ammunition in limited quantity, but the quality of the munitions available to Mexican troops was extremely poor.

Entertainment revolved around music, whether played by a band or sung. Mexican units were accompanied by a large number of noncombatants, which further strained the supply system of the army but improved the morale of the troops. Catholic priests accompanied every regiment and served in much more than a symbolic fashion. In addition to the traditional chaplain's duties of receiving confession, delivering blessings, offering absolution, and performing last rites, Catholic priests also served as a check on the behavior of the units they accompanied.

In spite of the best efforts of the clergy, however, gambling and drunkenness permeated the Mexican army. Mexican soldiers were also accompanied by *soldaderas,* women occupying the traditional roles of camp followers. Some followed husbands along a campaign, others pursued financial gain by offering services such as laundering and cooking, and some worked as prostitutes, following their customers across the Mexican countryside.

American army units fared little better on the battlefields of Mexico. The American peacetime army had numbered fewer than 9,000 troops and required rapid augmentation to fight against Mexico. Congress authorized President James K. Polk to call for 50,000 volunteers, who were often integrated into existing units. As such, each unit was a motley assortment of career regulars and wartime volunteers. Veterans of battles larger than a border skirmish with Native American warriors were almost nonexistent. They were augmented by Texas Rangers, who tended to be undisciplined, brutal men motivated by conquest of territory bordering their home state.

There was insufficient time for more than rudimentary training in the basics of army life. Many of the enlistees were illiterate, and virtually none had more than an elementary education. Fully 40 percent of the volunteers were recent immigrants to the United States.

As a largely volunteer army, discipline was relatively poor; American soldiers were accused of theft, rape, and murder wherever the invading forces traveled in Mexico. Many soldiers, upon experiencing the harsh campaign conditions, reconsidered their decision to don a uniform and deserted their units. During the Mexican-American War, U.S. forces had the highest desertion rate of any war in American history. Enough deserters left the American service and shifted allegiances that the Mexican army was able to field two battalions of foreigners (namely the San Patricio Battalion), almost all of them American deserters. Recent immigrants to the United States proved particularly susceptible to Mexican offers of free land in exchange for service.

American leadership varied greatly by regiment. Many future general officers of the American Civil War saw their first wartime service in Mexico. Junior officers, mostly trained at the U.S. Military Academy, proved capable and effective in the field. The senior leadership, however, contained a substantial number of political appointees who were included to ensure regional support for the war. Some proved to be excellent tacticians, while others were unmitigated disasters.

American units in Mexico faced tremendous logistical problems. They often could not secure their supply lines from the depredations of partisans in the countryside. Both Major General Zachary Taylor, commanding U.S. forces in northern Mexico, and Major General Winfield Scott, commanding the force sent to capture Mexico City, were forced to leave troops in garrisons along the route of march to ensure a secure supply route. Nonetheless, American troops often had to purchase food from the local populace or to forage and confiscate food. The latter approach had the predictable effect of creating more partisans among the enemy civilian population, and Scott at least worked hard to prevent it.

Soldiers had to endure long marches through a hot, dry climate while carrying 30 or 40 pounds of gear. Upon reaching a bivouac site, American soldiers erected canvas tents that offered little protection from the weather. Six men filled each tent to bursting, sleeping in uncomfortable bedrolls. The U.S. soldier's rations included preserved meat, hard bread, and poor-quality vegetables. Coffee, sugar, and salt were all in chronically short supply, and the small amounts available were typically monopolized by officers. Soldiers cooked their own meals by squads; camp kitchens did not exist on the campaigns into Mexico.

The medical corps of the U.S. Army was considerably better supplied and trained than its Mexican counterpart. Nevertheless, many more American soldiers died of disease than on the battlefield. Soldiers were subjected to dysentery, malaria, measles, smallpox, and yellow fever, and doctors did not understand the causes of any of these diseases. Treatments often caused more harm than good. The medical situation was exacerbated by poor hygiene and sanitation. Often, treated wounds became infected, resulting in amputations or death.

American troops, like their Mexican counterparts, pursued numerous entertainments. Some relied on the local civilian population for music and dancing, while others turned to alcohol or gambling as forms of escape. Both of these vices were against regulations, yet most enlisted personnel engaged in one or both on a regular basis. Most found army life to be harsh, inglorious, and boring. Few who did not volunteer for the duration of the war would reenlist. Among the duration volunteers, desertion was the highest as a percentage of the enlisted population. A sizable number of African Americans accompanied U.S. troops into battle, but all except a small few acted in ancillary, noncombat roles, such as personal assistants and servants to officers, cooks, launderers, and nurses. Their contributions, while significant, failed to elicit much recognition at the time.

Overall, American forces received more training and better supplies than their opponents, which offset the difference in the size of the armies. Well-drilled soldiers proved more effective on the battlefield than the massive numbers of raw conscripts fielded by Santa Anna. Success on the battlefield created higher morale among American units, but the improved morale was often offset by the slow pace of the campaigns in Mexico and the harsh climatic conditions. Despite facing one another on battlefields throughout Mexico, the lives of enlisted personnel on each side of the line greatly resembled one another, a series of shared miseries not usually experienced by the leadership of the armies.

PAUL J. SPRINGER

See also

African Americans; Atrocities; California Theater of War, Overview; Desertion; Logistics, Mexican; Logistics, U.S.; Military Medicine; Northern Mexico Theater of War, Overview; San Patricio Battalion; Weapons, Mexican; Weapons, U.S.

References

Bauer, K. Jack. *The Mexican War*. New York: Macmillan, 1974.

Clary, David A. *Eagles and Empire: The United States, Mexico, and the Struggle for a Continent*. New York: Bantam Books, 2009.

DePalo, William A. *The Mexican National Army*. College Station: Texas A&M University Press, 1997.

Fowler, Will. *Military Political Identity and Reformism in Independent Mexico: An Analysis of the* Memorias de Guerra *(1821–1855)*. London: ILAS, 1996.

Mahin, Dean B. *Olive Branch and Sword: The United States and Mexico, 1845–1848*. Jefferson, NC: McFarland, 1997.

McCaffrey, James M. *Army of Manifest Destiny: The American Soldier in the Mexican War, 1846–1848*. New York: New York University Press, 1992.

Olivera, Ruth R., and Liliane Crete. *Life in Mexico under Santa Anna, 1822–1855*. Norman: University of Oklahoma Press, 1991.

Weems, John Edward. *To Conquer a Peace*. College Station: Texas A&M University Press, 1988.

Winders, Richard Bruce. *Mr. Polk's Army: The American Military Experience in the Mexican War*. College Station: Texas A&M University Press, 1997.

Army of the West, United States

In May 1846, President James K. Polk ordered Stephen Watts Kearny, colonel of dragoons at Fort Leavenworth, Kansas, to put together a force and, with it, to conquer New Mexico and California. Kearny was a career officer with more than 30 years of frontier experience. Dragoons used horses to get to their destination but then dismounted to fight as infantry equipped with carbines, heavy pistols, and sabers. Kearny's resulting Army of the West's professional units were his 1st Dragoons (six companies) and the Topographical Engineers under Lieutenant William H. Emory. Its volunteer units consisted of Colonel Alexander W. Doniphan's 1st Missouri Mounted Volunteers (eight companies); a Missouri infantry battalion of two companies; two Missouri light artillery companies; the Laclede Rangers, a Missouri cavalry troop; and the Mormon Battalion. Altogether, Kearny's force numbered more than 1,600 men. Once in California, Kearny was to assume command of all U.S. land forces there, including Captain John C. Frémont's topographers and the California Volunteers.

Departing Fort Leavenworth in June 1846, Kearny's force headed along the Santa Fe Trail. Advanced to brigadier general en route, Kearny took the city of Santa Fe, New Mexico, without bloodshed on August 18, 1846. On September 25, he departed for California with five dragoon companies, leaving Charles Bent in charge as military governor of New Mexico. Kearny left Lieutenant Colonel Philip St. George Cooke behind to command the Mormon Battalion once it arrived. Doniphan was to lead the 1st Missouri down the Rio Grande and into Chihuahua.

Brigadier General Sterling Price's 2nd Missouri Mounted Volunteers arrived in Santa Fe three days later, and Price then assumed command of troops in New Mexico. Near Socorro, New Mexico, Kearny met eastward-bound Lieutenant Christopher "Kit" Carson

carrying dispatches about a peaceful California. Hearing the news, Kearny reduced his command to two companies. Unbeknownst to them, however, the Californios revolted two days later.

Arriving in California, Kearny fought the Battle of San Pascual against General Andrés Pico during December 6–11, 1846. Commodore Robert F. Stockton and a wounded Kearny then won two fights with Pico outside Los Angeles on January 8 and 9, 1847, retaking that place two days later. The retreating Californios surrendered to Frémont, who later refused to obey Kearny's orders and relinquish command of California to him. Frémont accompanied Kearny east in June 1847 and was then arrested for mutiny. His court-martial became a national event.

The Mormon Battalion mobilized on August 1, 1846, and arrived in Santa Fe during October 9–12. It left with Cooke on October 19, with orders to find a wagon road to California. Marching through northern Mexico (Chihuahua and Sonora), it arrived in San Diego on January 30, 1847. The battalion mustered out in July 1847 without seeing any action.

Doniphan's orders were to support Brigadier General John Ellis Wool's conquest of Chihuahua after pacifying the Native Americans. After signing treaties with all tribes in New Mexico, he marched south on December 12, 1846. On Christmas Day, the American forces repulsed a Mexican attack at El Brazito, 30 miles north of El Paso. On February 28, 1847, Doniphan defeated Mexican forces under General Pedro García Conde at Sacramento Creek, taking Chihuahua the next day. Marching east in late April, Doniphan's regiment reached the Gulf Coast of Mexico, from which it was transported to New Orleans and was mustered out in June 1847.

RICHARD GRISET

See also

Brazito, Battle of; California; California Theater of War, Overview; Californios; Carson, Christopher Houston "Kit"; Cooke, Philip St. George; Doniphan, Alexander William; Emory, William Hemsley; Frémont, John Charles; García Conde, Pedro; Kearny, Stephen Watts; Mormon Battalion; New Mexico; Pico, Andrés; Price, Sterling; Sacramento; San Pascual, Battle of; Santa Fe; Santa Fe–Chihuahua Trail; Stockton, Robert Field; Topographical Engineers; Wool, John Ellis.

References

Clarke, Dwight Lancelot. *Stephen Watts Kearny, Soldier of the West*. Norman: University of Oklahoma Press, 1961.

De Voto, Bernard. *The Year of Decision: 1846*. Boston, MA: Little, Brown, 1943.

Martinez, Orlando. *The Great Land Grab: The Mexican-American War*. London: Quartet Books, 1975.

Nardo, Don. *The Mexican-American War*. San Diego: Lucent Books, 1991.

Arroyo Colorado

Distributary channel of the Rio Grande that winds for 90 miles across the plains north of the river, emptying into the Laguna Madre about 30 miles from the river's mouth. Not much more than a stream of brackish water, the Arroyo Colorado was the site of the first contact between Mexican and U.S. forces in March 1846.

On March 8, 1846, as Brigadier General Zachary Taylor marched his 3,600-man Army of Occupation southward from Corpus Christi toward the Rio Grande, the Arroyo Colorado loomed as a likely point for an attack on his advancing column. There the army would be vulnerable as it descended the steep, brush-covered banks and forded its chest-deep waters. In anticipation of an attack, Taylor drew his separate brigades together and prepared to force his way across on March 20. The day before, he had sent a squadron of the 2nd Dragoons forward toward the Arroyo Colorado; they met immediate resistance from elements of the Mexican cavalry, but no shots were fired.

War now seemed imminent. As Taylor positioned artillery to cover his advance, several Mexican soldiers approached under a flag of truce and warned that any American crossing would be sharply contested. Sounds and movement across the river suggested that a large Mexican force waited in the brush. A resolute Taylor dismissed these threats and ordered his men down the bank and into the water on March 20. After a few tense moments, the first companies reached the far shore without incident. The Mexicans had abandoned their position and were withdrawing to Matamoros.

Taylor's men ridiculed their foes for fleeing, but the Mexicans had little choice given that General Francisco Mejía could muster only about 200 militia troops to fortify the arroyo. His plea for reinforcements had been met with a command to avoid confrontation and focus on defending the city of Matamoros. The Mexican troops at the Arroyo Colorado reluctantly accepted these orders, and Taylor's army was allowed to march onward to the Rio Grande.

DOUGLAS MURPHY

See also

Corpus Christi; Matamoros; Mejía, Francisco; Rio Grande; Taylor, Zachary; United States Army of Observation.

References

Alcaraz, Rámon, Alejo Barreiro, José María Castillo, Félix María Escalante, José María Iglesias, Manuel Muñoz, Ramón Ortiz, et al. *Apuntes para la historia de la guerra entre México y los Estados Unidos*. Mexico City: Tipografia de Manuel Payno, 1848.

Bauer, K. Jack. *The Mexican War, 1846–1848*. New York: Macmillan, 1974.

Clary, David A. *Eagles and Empire: The United States, Mexico, and the Struggle for a Continent*. New York: Bantam Books, 2009.

Henry, William Seaton. *Campaign Sketches of the War with Mexico*. New York: Harper and Brothers, 1847.

Arroyo Hondo, Skirmish at
Event Dates: January 19–20, 1847

Outbreak of violence involving an American mill owner and liquor distiller whose property was assaulted and besieged on January 19–20, 1847, at Arroyo Hondo, located several miles outside Taos, New Mexico. The Arroyo Hondo incident was part of the larger Taos Revolt (January 19–February 9, 1847), which involved an insurrection by Mexican nationals and allied Pueblo Indians against the U.S. occupation government in New Mexico.

U.S. Army forces under Colonel Stephen Watts Kearny had easily captured Santa Fe, New Mexico, in August 1846. The Mexican governor, Manuel Armijo, evacuated the city without offering any resistance. Kearny then moved on to California and placed Colonel Sterling Price in charge of securing New Mexico; he also named Charles Bent as territorial governor. Almost immediately after Kearny's departure, however, numerous Mexican nationals began plotting to overthrow the U.S.-installed regime. The conspirators planned to stage a rebellion around Christmas 1846 but were forced to postpone their action when American officials learned of the scheme. Meanwhile, rough behavior and drunkenness on the part of soldiers of Price's 2nd Missouri Mounted Rifles had led to increased tensions between the American government and New Mexican natives.

The insurrectionists made their move on the morning of January 19, 1847, when they launched a series of attacks in Taos. A band of Native Americans attacked Bent's official residence, killing and then scalping him. Three other American officials were also killed. That afternoon, a group of as many as 500 Mexicans and allied Pueblos assaulted the mill and distillery owned by Simon Turley, located at Arroyo Hondo. Turley, who had lived in the area since 1830, was married to a Mexican woman and had employed local New Mexicans as well as Native Americans to help him produce his corn-based liquor, known affectionately as "Taos Lightning." Turley himself was forced to defend against the large, angry, and well-armed force with only eight other men. Having received advance warning that the mob was approaching, Turley locked the gates to his complex and waited.

During the course of the next two days, the rebel force laid siege to Turley's mill, killing most of his livestock and horses. Several of his outbuildings were set ablaze, destroying them in short order. Turley and his men put up a brave fight, but they were no match for the vastly superior force. Several of Turley's men were killed by arrows or gunfire. Turley himself attempted to escape with three other men, but they were tracked down and killed. It is believed that only two men survived the siege and the assault that followed.

In the meantime, other attacks were occurring in New Mexico in an effort to drive the American occupation forces out of the region. Price hit back hard and instituted martial law. The insurrection was subdued by February 9. Price then created an ad hoc tribunal, which began systematically trying captured rebels. In all, 28 insurrectionists were hanged, many of them in the Taos town square. The Taos Revolt marked the last significant opposition to U.S. rule in New Mexico.

PAUL G. PIERPAOLI JR.

See also

Bent, Charles; Kearny, Stephen Watts; New Mexico; Price, Sterling; Pueblos.

References

Coldsmith, Don. *Trail from Taos*. New York: Bantam Books, 1990.

Crutchfield, James Andrew. *Tragedy at Taos: The Revolt of 1847*. Plano: Republic of Texas Press, 1995.

McNierney, Michael. *Taos 1847: The Revolt in Contemporary Accounts*. Boulder, CO: Johnson Publications, 1980.

Sando, Joe. *The Pueblo Indians*. San Francisco: Indian Historian Press, 1976.

Art

The Mexican-American War of 1846–1848 may be considered America's first media war. It was covered by the press with correspondents in the field, it was depicted in popular lithographic prints as well as in fine art, and it saw the first use of the camera in a war zone involving U.S. troops—albeit on a very limited scale. Prior to the Civil War, the Mexican campaign was the most extensively recorded event in American history.

Several artists accompanied U.S. forces into Mexico, and their names have survived through the prints that were published based on their paintings. These were the German-born Carl Nebel (1808–1855), the British-born James Walker (1818–1889), U.S. Navy lieutenant Henry Walke (1808–1896), and the soldier-artist Captain Daniel Powers Whiting (1808–1892). Other soldiers such as Ange (Angelo) Paldi, Major Joseph Horace Eaton (1815–1896),

and Samuel E. Chamberlain (1829–1908) recorded their experiences in sketches and watercolors.

Back in the United States, lithographic publishers were eager to produce prints of the war and portraits of the leading commanders, which would find a ready market among the art-buying public, and the companies of Nathaniel Currier, Napoleon Sarony, Henry B. Major, James S. Baillie, and David W. Kellogg emerged as leading purveyors of lithographic prints during this period. While the majority of these popular prints were inaccurate, they were often based on newspaper accounts and tried to present a realistic impression of the events as they transpired. During the war and in the years immediately following, the public could purchase popular illustrated histories of the war, and some of the artists represented in these works included Felix O. C. Darley (1821–1888) and Alonzo Chappel (1828–1887). Their pictures, however, were similarly highly inaccurate.

In contrast to these imaginary pictures of the war is the series of large lithographic plates published in portfolio form by George Wilkins Kendall after paintings by Carl Nebel. Both had been in Mexico prior to the fighting, and once the war began Kendall sent back accounts of the fighting that were published in various newspapers. Nebel had visited Mexico City earlier but was in Europe during the campaign and only returned to the country once the fighting had ceased. Nevertheless, his on-the-spot sketches of the various battlefields were generally accurate in terms of the

Painting by Carl Nebel depicting American forces storming Chapultepec Castle on September 13, 1847. Mexico City surrendered the next day. (Library of Congress)

topography. The finished lithographs were accompanied by a text written by Kendall. They portrayed the war's major battles including Monterrey, Buena Vista, Cerro Gordo, Chapultepec, and Palo Alto.

James Walker, who served as an interpreter on Brigadier General William Worth's staff, had lived and worked in Mexico prior to the war. He witnessed the actions at Contreras, Churubusco, and Chapultepec and was with the army when it occupied Mexico City. Throughout the campaign he made abundant sketches of the various scenes and may also have used a camera. At the end of the war he returned to New York, where he completed several small paintings of the various battles in addition to two large murals depicting the fighting at Chapultepec that hang in the Capitol in Washington, D.C. In a similar way, he later produced a number of important paintings of Civil War battles. His pictures can be considered combat art and are highly representational, although his style of depicting soldiers in some of the paintings perhaps lacks life and movement.

Lieutenant Henry Walke covered naval aspects of the war in watercolors and drawings made from his ship, the bomb brig *Versuvius*, during operations off Veracruz and in the riverine expeditions up the Tuxpan and Tabasco Rivers. Some of his pictures were reproduced as lithographs and published by Nathaniel Currier as the *Naval Portfolio* in 1848. Corresponding to this was the *Army Portfolio*, published in the same year by G. & W. Endicott, containing five lithographs after Captain Daniel Powers Whiting of the land campaign.

Graphic representation of the Mexican War ranged from the accurate to the inaccurate, depending on whether the artists observed the action or not. Nonetheless, the war witnessed some of the emerging new developments in visual communication, especially lithography and photography. While many of the popular lithographs are inaccurate, they provide a glimpse into contemporary attitudes toward war and soldiering of mid-19th-century America—ideas of gallantry, glory, heroes, leadership, and the representations of death and the enemy.

PETER HARRINGTON

See also
Currier, Nathaniel; Lithographs; Photography; War Correspondents; Worth, William Jenkins.

References
Goetzmann, William H. *Sam Chamberlain's Mexican War: The San Jacinto Museum of History Paintings.* Austin: Published for the San Jacinto Museum of History by the Texas State Historical Association, 1993.
McNaughten, Marian R. "James Walker—Combat Artist of Two American Wars." *Military Collector & Historian* 9 (Summer 1957): 31–35.
Sandweiss, Martha A., Rick Stewart, and Ben W. Huseman. *Eyewitness to War: Prints and Daguerreotypes of the Mexican War, 1846–1848.* Fort Worth, TX: Amon Carter Museum, 1989.
Tyler, Ronnie C. *The Mexican War: A Lithographic Record.* Austin: Texas State Historical Association, 1973.

Artillery

Artillery refers to heavy ordnance, such as cannon, capable of firing large projectiles in combat, rather than small arms such as pistols and muskets. Artillery was widely used during the Mexican-American War, although both the United States and Mexico entered the war in 1846 with artillery systems little changed from those in use a century earlier. Artillery pieces were thus smoothbore, muzzle-loaded weapons of various calibers and cast of either iron or bronze. For the most part, however, American artillery was superior to that of Mexico thanks in large part to recent reforms and innovations in equipment manufacturing and procurement procedures, and in the training of gun crews.

Artillery was classified according to its use and other factors. Field artillery was the lightest, most mobile of the categories. Its guns generally fired 6- or 12-pound projectiles. Siege and coastal artillery guns were heavier and designed for use in fixed positions, firing projectiles weighing 18 pounds and heavier. With mobility not a factor as with field artillery, naval artillery tended to fire heavier rounds than field guns.

Field artillery fell into three basic types. The gun was the most widely used field piece and fired a projectile at high velocity and long range in a relatively flat trajectory. Owing to the primitive sights available, gunners relied on direct fire—firing at a target within view—rather than indirect fire, or firing at a target out of the crews' line of sight. Mortars were short-barreled weapons that fired explosive projectiles at high trajectories (usually fixed, with range determined by the size of the powder charge). Although relatively short-ranged, mortars were especially useful in firing over barriers. Shorter than the gun yet longer than the mortar, the howitzer was the third basic type of field artillery. It was a hybrid weapon and proved very versatile in the field. It lacked the range of the gun yet chambered the full array of ammunition. Its higher trajectory made it particularly effective at firing explosive rounds timed to detonate over enemy troops.

Ammunition chests, or caissons, contained a variety of projectiles designed for specific situations. Solid shot, a simple cast iron ball, was the most commonly used type of projectile and was effective at long range against dense enemy formations. The common shell was a hollow sphere fitted with a simple time fuse designed to detonate a bursting charge and shatter into deadly fragments. Developed in England by Lieutenant Henry Shrapnel, spherical case shot also had a bursting charge and was also filled with musket balls to add to its destructive capabilities. At close ranges, grapeshot and canister were the most lethal antipersonnel loadings, as they effectively turned the gun into a giant shotgun. Grapeshot consisted of a dowel attached to a wood base plate with a number of iron balls around it within a cloth bag secured by twine. The whole looked very much like a bunch of grapes. It would break apart on firing. Grapeshot was employed against troops, wagons, or boats. Canister was a tinned can filled with iron or lead balls and used at short range against troops.

In 1846 the Mexican army mustered three brigades of artillery armed with Spanish field pieces as well as British-made garrison guns. Although Mexican gun crews were usually well trained, their powder was often defective and their heavy iron artillery pieces were mounted on less maneuverable carriages than those of the United States.

In both equipment and tactics, U.S. artillerymen held a distinct advantage over their Mexican counterparts. In September 1838, U.S. secretary of war Joel R. Poinsett had called for the refitting and training of one company of each regiment as horse-drawn light field artillery, and in 1841 the United States began eliminating iron field pieces in favor of lighter and more dependable bronze weapons.

Commanded by Captain Samuel Ringgold, the first U.S. horse artillery unit, Company C, 3rd Artillery, fought in Mexico with the latest Model 1841 bronze 6-pounder guns. In contrast to the other four mounted artillery companies, whose crews usually walked beside their guns, every man in Company C was mounted. Capable of moving quickly and decisively in tactical situations, Company C earned the designation "flying artillery," whereas the other companies were known as "mounted artillery." Although Ringgold received a mortal wound at the Battle of Palo Alto (May 8, 1846), the new American field artillery consistently outperformed its Mexican counterparts, firing eight times to the Mexicans' one, an achievement maintained in later actions, most notably at the Battle of Buena Vista on February 22–23, 1847.

JEFF KINARD

See also
Anderson, Robert; Buena Vista, Battle of; Flying Artillery; Mexico, Army; Palo Alto, Battle of; Poinsett, Joel Roberts; Ringgold, Samuel.

References
Dillon, Lester R., Jr. *American Artillery in the Mexican War, 1846–1847*. Austin, TX: Presidial Press, 1975.
Eisenhower, John S. D. *So Far from God: The U.S. War with Mexico, 1846–1848*. New York: Random House, 1989.
Kinard, Jeff S. *Artillery: An Illustrated History of Its Impact*. Santa Barbara, CA: ABC-CLIO, 2007.
Manucy, Albert. *Artillery through the Ages: A Short History of Cannon, Emphasizing Types Used in America*. Washington, DC: Government Printing Office, 1949.

Ashmun Amendment

Amendment introduced in the U.S. House of Representatives on January 3, 1848, by Massachusetts Whig politician George Ashmun, which condemned the Mexican-American War as "unnecessary and unconstitutional." George Ashmun, born in Blandford, Massachusetts, in 1804, was elected as a Whig to the U.S. Congress House of Representatives from the Sixth District of Massachusetts in March 1845. He held that office until March 3, 1851. While in the U.S. Congress, Ashmun served as a member of the committees on the judiciary, Indian affairs, and rules.

A staunch critic of slavery, Ashmun sharply condemned the James K. Polk administration's expansionist policies, which he believed would result in more slaveholding territory in the United States. He first offered a House resolution on February 3, 1846, calling upon Polk to provide justification for moving U.S. forces toward Mexico prior to the outbreak of actual hostilities. On May 13, 1846, after fighting had commenced in late April, he was one of only 14 members of Congress who voted against military appropriations for the war.

During Polk's third annual message to Congress on December 7, 1847, the president referred to the military conflict with Mexico as "a just war." Two weeks later, on December 22, 1847, a freshman member of the House from Illinois, Abraham Lincoln, introduced what became known as the "Spot Resolutions," challenging Polk's assertion that American blood had been spilled on U.S. soil by Mexican forces before war had been declared. Ashmun applauded Lincoln for his stand. Although the House did not act on Lincoln's Spot Resolutions, a new measure was immediately introduced at the start of the new term aimed at censuring Polk for starting the Mexican War. The original intent of this measure—the army supply bill—was to bring a quick resolution to the war given its growing unpopularity and increasing financial burden.

On January 3, 1848, with the Whigs now in control of the House, Ashmun offered to amend the supply bill by adding the words, "in a war unnecessarily and unconstitutionally begun by the President of the United States." It passed by a vote of 85–81. Ashmun's amendment censuring Polk for "unnecessarily and unconstitutionally" provoking the war with Mexico became the focal point for continued spirited debates in both houses of Congress in efforts to force the president to end all military action.

Ashmun did not seek reelection to the U.S. Congress when his term expired in 1850. Instead, he returned to Springfield, Massachusetts, and resumed his law practice. In later years, he served as chairman of the Republican National Convention at Chicago in 1860, which nominated Lincoln for president, and he was director of the Union Pacific Railroad Company. He was also a delegate to the Union National Convention in Philadelphia in 1866. Ashmun died in Springfield, Massachusetts, on July 16, 1870.

CHARLES F. HOWLETT

See also
Congress, U.S.; Democratic Party; Lincoln, Abraham; Opposition to the Mexican-American War, U.S.; Politics, U.S.; Polk, James Knox; Whigs.

References
Bullard, F. Lauriston. "Abraham Lincoln and George Ashmun." *New England Quarterly* 19, no. 2 (June 1946): 184–211.
Katcher, Phillip R. *The Mexican American War, 1846–1848*. New York: Random House, 1989.
Schroeder, John H. *Mr. Polk's War: American Opposition and Dissent, 1846–1848*. Madison: University of Wisconsin Press, 1973.

Associated Press

Group of loosely associated U.S. newspapers formed in New York City in 1846 to pool resources in order to facilitate the collection and dissemination of news. The Associated Press (AP) soon expanded to become the single largest news source covering both domestic and international events in the nation. The AP originated with Moses Yale Beach and allowed news events to be quickly transferred for rapid publication, beating the competition to the stories.

Beach, the publisher of the *New York Sun,* first hired Pony Express riders to bring breaking news from the front lines during the Mexican-American War. Dispatches were then sent via Great Southern Mail from Mobile to Montgomery, Alabama, then transferred again to a telegraph station in Richmond, Virginia. This process was both time-consuming and expensive, however.

In 1846 Beach offered to sell the reports to all of New York's newspapers, with the papers equally sharing the news stories and the costs. Although at first only four took Beach up on his offer, the AP was nevertheless born. The first official dispatches were printed in the *Sun* on May 29, 1846. Services expanded rapidly, with regular reports first sent from New York and Washington on June 5, 1846, and later from New York to Boston on June 27, 1846. The New York to Albany and Buffalo branch and services from Philadelphia to Harrisburg, Pennsylvania, completed the regional network by the end of 1847.

In 1848 the Harbor News Association was created to share reports transmitted from a news vessel stationed in New York harbor. The national election of 1848 was a historic first, with newspaper reports tallying same-day returns. A second Harbor News Association was established in 1849, with the addition of the *New York Tribune* and European reports emanating from Halifax, Nova Scotia, carried by steamer to the Boston telegraph station, where they were disseminated to telegraph operators throughout the country and sold to independent newspapers.

A formal charter for the General News Association of the City of New York was established in 1856. Each newspaper would receive a general summary of the national news as part of the service. The Associated Press continued to expand its coverage and played an important role reporting news during the Civil War, including the accurate text of President Abraham Lincoln's Gettysburg Address and a description of Confederate general Robert E. Lee's surrender at Appomattox, Virginia. The Associated Press continues operation to the present day and is one of the country's most important print news services.

PAMELA LEE GRAY

See also
Penny Press; War Correspondents.

References
Associated Press. *Breaking News: How the Associated Press Has Covered War, Peace and Everything Else.* New York: Princeton Architectural Press, 2007.

Americans on a hotel porch react to news of the Mexican-American War. Even before the beginning of hostilities in April 1846, correspondents were reporting on U.S. military activities in Texas. (Library of Congress)

Moreno, Luis Gerardo Morales, Jesus Velasco Marques, and Krystyna Libura, eds. *Echoes of the Mexican-American War.* Toronto, ON: Groundwood Books, 2004.

Atlixco, Skirmish at
Event Date: October 19, 1847

A small military engagement between U.S. troops and Mexican guerrillas, one of the last noteworthy actions of the Mexican-American War, occurred at Atlixco on October 19, 1847. Atlixco is a town in the southwestern part of the state of Puebla, about 15 miles from the city of Puebla. Located in a fertile and well-watered valley on the slopes of Mount Popocatepetl, the area proved an ideal base of support for one of the many irregular partisan groups that struck at Major General Winfield Scott's supply lines during and after the American advance from Veracruz to Mexico City (March 7, 1847, to September 13, 1847).

These groups, collectively known as the Cuerpo Ligera (Light Corps), struck with such effectiveness that U.S. Army convoys proceeding along the route routinely required escorts of at least 1,500 men. Following his capture of Mexico City in September 1847, Scott launched a two-pronged effort to eliminate Mexican partisans. The first consisted of posting semipermanent garrisons of 500 to 1,000 men along his supply route. The second involved the formation of a mounted pursuit force led by Brigadier

Skirmish at Atlixco, October 19, 1847

	United States	Mexico
Killed	1	219
Wounded	3	319

General Joseph Lane, and charged with the duty of tracking and destroying partisan formations. One of Lane's targets was the Pueblan guerrilla group led by Brigadier General Joaquín Rea. Lane's force included an artillery section and a contingent of Texas Rangers as well as regular army troops, numbering some 1,500 men.

During the evening of October 19, 1847, this American force came under fire from Rea's forces in Atlixco. Lane responded by posting his artillery on a hill overlooking the community and ordering a rapid and intense bombardment of the town center. Following a 45-minute shelling, he sent an advance force into Atlixco and later moved his entire force into the town. Lane considered his action a success for several reasons. He had silenced the hostile fire, seized Atlixco, and inflicted hundreds of casualties on the Mexicans. Lane reported only two U.S. casualties. As a result of the "terror" (his term) of his attack, Lane reported, the town would cause him no difficulty in the future.

Although Atlixco well may have been terrorized by casualties that the Mexicans set at 219 killed and 319 wounded, the bombardment failed to completely destroy Rea's unit. He and an undetermined number of his men escaped with their artillery in tow. During the following months, Rea continued to attack U.S. convoys, and his group remained active until the end of the war.

By the standards of the 19th century, Lane's conduct at Atlixco was justified. The community was serving as a base for hostile forces and therefore could be attacked. By modern standards, however, the American attack violated several principles of anti-insurgent warfare. In demolishing much of the town, Lane alienated the civilian population, which ideally he should have befriended. Moreover, his decision to begin his attack with an artillery bombardment rather than with encirclement or an immediate attack allowed the guerrillas who were his primary target to escape and regroup.

IRVING W. LEVINSON

See also

Guerrilla Warfare; Lane, Joseph; Mexico City Campaign; Puebla; Rea, Joaquín; Scott, Winfield.

References

Lane, Joseph. *Report of 22 October 1847, Executive Document Number 1, Report of the Secretary of War to the Thirtieth Congress.* Washington, DC: Wendell and Van Benthuysen, 1847.

León-Portilla, Miguel, ed. *Diccionario porrúa de historia, biografía, y geografía de México.* México, DF: Editorial Porrúa, 1997.

Levinson, Irving. *Wars within War: Mexican Guerrillas, Domestic Elites, and the United States of America.* Fort Worth: Texas Christian University Press, 2005.

Atocha, Alexander José

Birth Date: Unknown
Death Date: Unknown

Mexican secret agent. Alexander José Atocha's Mexican-American War antecedents are obscure, and there is virtually no information on the circumstances of his birth, early years, or death. He claimed to be Spanish-born but apparently became a naturalized American citizen. Prior to the diplomatic mission for which he is remembered, Atocha was a speculator in Mexican government contracts and sporadically lived in New Orleans.

In mid-February 1846, in the midst of the crisis precipitated by the U.S. annexation of Texas in late 1845, Atocha met with President James K. Polk. He claimed to carry a secret letter from former Mexican president Antonio López de Santa Anna, who was in exile in Havana, Cuba, at the time. In that letter Santa Anna offered—in exchange for $30 million and U.S. help in returning to power in Mexico—to recognize the Rio Grande as the southern boundary of Texas and to extend the Mexican-American boundary line to San Francisco, California. The offer was attractive because the Mexican government had long insisted that the Nueces River was the Texas boundary, and it had showed no inclination to negotiate the sale of other territories.

U.S. emissary to Mexico John Slidell had been trying since December 1845 to persuade the Mexicans to part with Texas, New Mexico, and California in exchange for $30 million and the liquidation of all claims by U.S. citizens against Mexico, but he had received a hostile reception in Mexico. Santa Anna's note to Polk recognized that his offer would be politically unpalatable in Mexico, so it suggested a staged drama for public consumption: Slidell would leave Mexico for a U.S. warship, where he would demand immediate payment of all debts owed by Mexico to U.S. citizens. Polk would send additional warships to Veracruz and U.S. troops into the disputed territory between the Rio Grande and Nueces River. The popular outcry from these developments would give Santa Anna the pretext he needed to gain support for an overthrow of the government of Mariano Paredes y Arrillaga.

The elaborate ruse was vintage Santa Anna, but Polk was suspicious of Atocha from the very beginning. He brought up the scheme before his cabinet, where it encountered strong opposition from Secretary of State James Buchanan and was never acted on.

Atocha appeared in Washington again in January 1847, after hostilities had begun, claiming once more to represent Santa Anna as an emissary of peace. He proposed a settlement similar to the earlier proposal, agreeing to go to Mexico City in an unofficial capacity with a sealed message from U.S. leaders announcing U.S. willingness to send peace commissioners to Mexico. For its part, Mexico would have to agree to accept them and to suspend hostilities as soon as the first meeting took place.

Unfortunately for Atocha, by the time he arrived in Mexico City the political situation had changed. Power was in the hands of acting chief executive Valentín Gómez Farías, who had no wish to come to terms with the United States. Gómez Farías concocted a falsified version of the terms the United States had proposed in the note Atocha carried and sent this version to Congress and the press in order to further inflame public opinion. He also ordered Atocha confined for a time outside Mexico City.

Atocha subsequently spent many years pressing claims in U.S. courts against the Mexican government for financial damages he claimed to have suffered upon being expelled from that country.

TIMOTHY J. HENDERSON

See also

Buchanan, James; Causes of the War; Diplomacy, U.S.; Gómez Farías, Valentín; Nueces River; Paredes y Arrillaga, Mariano; Politics, Mexican; Polk, James Knox; Rio Grande; Santa Anna, Antonio López de; Slidell, John; Trans-Nueces.

References

Pletcher, David M. *The Diplomacy of Annexation: Texas, Oregon, and the Mexican War.* Columbia: University of Missouri Press, 1973.
Seigenthaler, Arthur Meier. *James K. Polk.* New York: Henry Holt, 2004.
Soto, Miguel. *La conspiración monárquica en México, 1845–1846.* Mexico City: EOSA, 1988.

Atrocities

The passions aroused by the Mexican-American War, not to mention the usual fog that surrounds combat and warfare, led to violent acts that exceeded the normally accepted boundaries of combat. A number of these atrocities involved members of American volunteer units, particularly mounted regiments from Texas and Arkansas. Colonel John (Jack) C. Hays's regiment, the 1st Texas Mounted Rifles (unofficially known as the Texas Rangers), included men who had been engaged in the 1835–1836 Texas Revolution. While they were excellent partisan warriors, many of these Texans harbored long-standing animosity against Mexicans, which occasionally manifested itself as wanton and gratuitous violence.

After the September 1846 Battle of Monterrey, Major General Zachary Taylor reported trouble with volunteer units in the occupation of that city. Indeed, members of American volunteer units reportedly robbed, raped, and murdered Mexicans. Often atrocities occurred after resentment between American soldiers and local citizens festered into a series of attacks and retaliations. For instance, a group of Mexican rancheros ambushed and mutilated a number of Texas Rangers after the Rangers had burned three or four of their ranches, which had been done in retaliation for the earlier murder of another member of the Rangers.

One of the bloodiest incidents occurred in early February 1847 near Agua Nueva, Coahuila, a small town 17 miles south of Saltillo, after some local residents roped and dragged a member of an Arkansas volunteer regiment to death in retaliation for the molestation of local women by the victim's Arkansas volunteer unit. To avenge their comrade's murder, the Arkansas unit tracked down whom it believed to be the murderers in a cave near Cataña and shot and scalped nearly two dozen Mexican civilians. This atrocity

shocked and outraged General Taylor, who dismissed the soldiers involved and sent them back to the Rio Grande. In a similar incident in October 1847, more than 200 drunken American soldiers, many of them volunteers, pillaged the Mexican town of Huamantla after a resident of the town shot and killed a Texas Ranger captain, Samuel H. Walker, from a window. In an act of crazed revenge, the Americans raped and murdered numerous Mexican civilians and destroyed a number of homes, businesses, and churches.

During the American occupation of Mexico City, beginning in September 1847, some Mexicans claimed that Texas Rangers assaulted men without cause and groped local women indecently. As an act of defiance, a group of Mexican robbers slashed one Ranger so severely with their knives that the victim's heart could reportedly be seen through his ribs. By noon the following day, the Rangers had retaliated by shooting 80 Mexican men and leaving their corpses lying in the streets.

Occasionally, atrocities were simply isolated incidents. After the September 8, 1847, Battle of El Molino del Rey, American officers reported seeing Mexican gun emplacements firing on American medics in their clearly marked ambulances as they searched for wounded soldiers on the battlefield. Typically, however, Mexican-American War atrocities seem to have been fueled by the existing animosities between Mexicans and Americans and by a lack of discipline among American volunteer units. Atrocities were committed by both sides, but the worst and largest incidents appear to have been perpetrated by U.S. soldiers.

DEREK R. MALLETT

See also

Agua Nueva; El Molino del Rey, Battle of; Hays, John Coffee; Huamantla, Battle of; Mexico City, Occupation of; Texas Rangers; Taylor, Zachary; Volunteers, U.S.; Walker, Samuel Hamilton.

References

Bauer, Karl Jack. *The Mexican War, 1846–1848.* New York: Macmillan, 1974.
Collins, Michael L. *Texas Devils: Rangers and Regulars on the Lower Rio Grande, 1846–1861.* Norman: University of Oklahoma Press, 2008.
Eisenhower, John S. D. *So Far from God: The U.S. War with Mexico, 1846–1848.* New York: Random House, 1989.
Foos, Paul. *"A Short, Offhand, Killing Affair": Soldiers and Social Conflict during the Mexican-American War.* Chapel Hill: University of North Carolina Press, 2002.
Wheelan, Joseph. *Invading Mexico: America's Continental Dream and the Mexican War, 1846–1848.* New York: Carroll and Graf, 2007.

Austin, Stephen Fuller
Birth Date: November 3, 1793
Death Date: December 27, 1836

Businessman, politician, and Texas *empresario* who helped settle Mexico's northern Texas frontier with U.S. settlers. Austin is considered the father of Anglo-American Texas. Stephen Fuller Austin was born on November 3, 1793, in Wythe County on the

STEPHEN F. AUSTIN.

Stephen F. Austin, having secured land grants from the Mexican government, led hundreds of American settlers into Texas to help colonize the Mexican frontier. Austin is considered the founder of Anglo-American Texas. (Getty Images)

southwestern frontier of Virginia. His parents, Moses and Maria Brown Austin, moved to Missouri in 1798. His father founded the town of Potosi (present-day Washington County, Missouri) and sent his son to school in Colchester, Connecticut. Austin entered Transylvania University in Lexington, Kentucky, graduating in 1810. That April he returned to Missouri and found employment in his father's general store, ultimately taking over his father's lucrative lead business, which included mining, smelting, and manufacturing operations.

At Potosi, Austin served as an adjutant of a militia battalion and from 1814 to 1820 served in the Missouri territorial legislature. In 1816 he helped obtain a charter for the Bank of Saint Louis, but the bank and the Austin family businesses failed after the Panic of 1819, and Austin moved to the Arkansas Territory. In 1820, at the age of 27, he was appointed a territorial circuit judge of the First Judicial District of Arkansas. Shortly thereafter he left Arkansas and sought his fortune in Natchitoches, Louisiana, but within a matter of months after his move there he moved to New Orleans to study law.

Meanwhile, the elder Austin had traveled to San Antonio, Texas (Coahuila y Texas), where in January 1821 he obtained a land grant from the Mexican government to oversee the settlement of 300 American families in Texas. In exchange for helping

Spain colonize its northern frontier in Mexico as an *empresario,* the elder Austin would also receive a generous personal land grant in Texas. The senior Austin died later in 1821 while Mexico fought its war for independence with Spain, but his son was granted permission to assume his father's contract. In January 1822, Austin established the first legal settlement of Anglo-Americans in Texas.

Three years later, in 1825, Austin completed the terms of his contract, and the Mexican government granted him another *empresario* contract that allowed him to settle an additional 500 families. Austin received three additional contracts between 1827 and 1831 and eventually settled more than 1,000 families in Texas. As a whole, 41 *empresarios* received contracts that permitted 13,500 families to settle in Texas between 1821 and 1835, but Austin was the most successful by far in fulfilling his obligations to the Mexican government.

As an *empresario* Austin did more than settle colonists. He acted on behalf of the state government of Coahuila y Texas by overseeing the enforcement of laws in the colony. He also mapped and charted the region's bays and rivers, promoted commerce with the United States, and encouraged the growth of commercial enterprises and the establishment of schools. While Austin's attitude toward slavery was inconsistent, after 1833 he fully supported the institution of slavery in Coahuila y Texas, where free labor was difficult to obtain.

Austin had pledged his allegiance to Mexico by becoming a Mexican citizen, but by 1830 friction had begun to develop between Anglo-American settlers in Texas and the Mexican government. While Austin favored settling disputes peaceably, in 1833 he met with a group of Texans interested in petitioning Mexico to divide the single state of Coahuila y Texas into two separate states. Coahuila had nine times the population of Texas, and separating the two regions would allow Texas greater political autonomy.

Austin then traveled to Mexico City to request that Texas be made a separate Mexican state. His request was denied, and in 1834 Mexican officials imprisoned him under false pretenses. Austin was released from custody the following year, and shortly after his return to Texas the fight for Texas independence began. At the end of October 1835, Austin was called to command a volunteer army of Texans, but after the Texans organized a provisional government Austin participated in a diplomatic mission to the United States. On May 14, 1836, in the Treaty of Velasco, Mexico recognized Texas's independence. Austin returned to Texas in June 1836 and ran for president of the Republic of Texas. He lost to military hero Sam Houston but was appointed secretary of state.

On December 27, 1836, just months after Texas had won its independence, Austin died in Austin, Texas, at the age of 43 after suffering a bout of malaria.

ALICIA RODRIQUEZ

See also

Coahuila y Texas; *Empresarios*; Houston, Samuel; Land Grants; Texas; Texas Revolution; Velasco, Treaties of.

References

Cantrell, Gregg. *Stephen F. Austin: Empresario of Texas.* New Haven, CT: Yale University Press, 1999.

Fehrenbach, T. R. *Lone Star: A History of Texas and the Texans.* New York: Macmillan, 1968.

Reichstein, Andreas V. *Rise of the Lone Star: The Making of Texas.* College Station: Texas A&M University Press, 1989.

Ayutla Revolution
Event Date: 1854

Military uprising that began on March 1, 1854, and sought to overthrow the dictatorship of Antonio López de Santa Anna. By that time Santa Anna's regime had earned the enmity of many liberal politicians, as well as of peasants and local elites in the state of Guerrero.

The Ayutla uprising, which began in the town of the same name located in the state of Guerrero (southwest of Mexico City), was led by Florencio Villarreal, Juan N. Álvarez, and Ignacio Comonfort. Others who soon joined the revolt included liberal politicians Benito Juárez and Melchor Ocampo, whom Santa Anna had exiled and who were living in New Orleans. The insurrectionists rejected the presidency of Santa Anna and called for a special congress to draft a new constitution.

All the southern towns subscribed to the revolution, despite Santa Anna's threats to put to death anyone possessing a copy of the revolution's manifesto. Santa Anna, with some 5,000 men at his command, personally led the campaign against the uprising, but Comonfort's forces repulsed him at Acapulco. Santa Anna, who assumed that Juan Álvarez's troops were superior in numbers to his own force, decided to retreat to Mexico City. As he returned to the capital, however, Santa Anna destroyed ranches and haciendas, actions that further fueled animosity toward him.

As the revolution grew in size and intensity (by mid-1854 the states of Tamaulipas, Guanajuato, San Luis Potosí, and Mexico, as well as various guerrilla forces, had all joined the rebellion), the government resorted to terror in an attempt to quash it. On August 9 Santa Anna departed Mexico City for Veracruz, and by mid-month he had boarded the steamboat *Iturbide,* which took him to exile in Colombia.

Álvarez assumed the role of president within weeks of Santa Anna's departure. He filled his cabinet with a new generation of liberals who would set the agenda for Mexican politics for the next two and a half decades. These men included Ocampo as minister of foreign affairs, Juárez as minister of justice, Guillermo Prieto as minister of treasury, and Comonfort as minister of war. Their leadership ushered in a new era—commonly known as *La Reforma*—that sought to diminish the power of the Catholic Church, foster the creation of a secular state, and encourage the growth of private investment. Many of these changes were enshrined in a new charter, the Constitution of 1857, which for the next 60 years stood as a symbol of that era.

Fabiola García Rubio

See also

Álvarez, Juan; Catholic Church, Mexico; Constitutions, Mexican; Juárez, Benito; Mexico; Mexico, 1821–1854; *Moderados*; Ocampo, Melchor; Politics, Mexican; Puros; Salas, José Mariano; Santa Anna, Antonio López de.

References

Guardino, Peter F. *Peasants, Politics, and the Formation of Mexico's National State: Guerrero, 1800–1857.* Stanford, CA: Stanford University Press, 1996.

Johnson, Richard A. *The Mexican Revolution of Ayutla, 1854–1855.* Rock Island, IL: Augustana College Library, 1939.

McGowan, Gerald L. *Prensa y poder: La revolución de Ayutla; El Congreso Constituyente.* Mexico City: El Colegio de México, 1978.

Vázquez Mantecón, Carmen. *Santa Anna y la encrucijada del Estado: La dictadura (1853–1855).* Mexico City: Fondo de Cultura Econoómica, 1986.

Aztec Club

Fraternal, hereditary organization founded in Mexico City in September 1847 by U.S. Army officers then serving in the Mexican-American War. The Aztec Club's formal name is the Military Society of the Mexican War, although it is more popularly known by the former.

By September 1847, Major General Winfield Scott's army had entered Mexico City to bring the conflict to a close, at least militarily. As American forces began their occupation of the Mexican capital, a number of U.S. officers decided to form an association to commemorate their service during the war. The Aztec Club held its first formal meeting in Mexico City on October 13, 1847, and initial membership numbered some 160 officers. In the words of Brevet First Lieutenant DeLancey Floyd-Jones of the 4th Infantry Regiment, "The Club was organized for the purpose of forming a resort for officers, as a promoter of good fellowship, and of furnishing a home where they could pass their leisure hours in social intercourse, and where more palatable and healthful viands could be procured at a reduced price than at the best Fondas of the city."

The founders of the Aztec Club sought to emulate the Society of the Cincinnati, which had been established in 1783 by officers who had served in the Revolutionary War. Like that society, the Aztec Club's membership would be hereditary and would be passed on to direct male descendants or the closest male blood relative. The first meeting was convened at the residence of Mexico's former minister to the United States, José María Bocanegra, on the Plaza de la Constitución. "We have a magnificent club house, and it is a source of great pleasure and comfort to us," wrote George B. McClellan. "We go there and are sure that we will meet none but gentlemen."

John A. Quitman was the organization's founding president, and the charter founders included Franklin Pierce, future president of the United States. Among the original members were such luminaries as Winfield Scott, Zachary Taylor, and Ulysses S. Grant; the latter two also became president of the United States.

On January 13, 1848, the club adopted a constitution and levied a membership fee of $20 per year. In addition to army officers, navy and marine officers were also invited to join.

Membership in the club remained relatively constant throughout the 19th century. In 1892 the Aztec Club's constitution was altered, and the purpose of the club was more explicitly defined. The aim was stated as "cherishing the memories and keeping alive the traditions that cluster about the names of those officers who took part in the Mexican War . . . and also aiding other patriotic societies in efforts to inculcate and stimulate patriotism."

Reunions and meetings have been held annually since 1867. With a current membership of about 425, the Aztec Club's chief goal today is to preserve and disseminate the history of the Mexican-American War. The Aztec Club was a predecessor to such military organizations as the Grand Army of the Republic and the Military Order of the Loyal Legion of the United States, both of which were formed by Civil War veterans.

PAUL G. PIERPAOLI JR.

See also

Grant, Ulysses Simpson (Hiram Ulysses Grant); McClellan, George Brinton; Mexico, Occupation of; Pierce, Franklin; Scott, Winfield; Taylor, Zachary.

References

Breithaupt, Richard. *The Aztec Club of 1847: The Military Society of the Mexican War.* Van Nuys, CA: Walika, 1998.

B

Backus, Electus, Jr.
Birth Date: February 17, 1804
Death Date: June 7, 1862

U.S. Army officer who commanded the captured Mexican fort at San Juan de Ulúa in Veracruz, Mexico, from April 4, 1847, to January 1, 1848, during the Mexican-American War. Born on February 17, 1804, in Rensselaerville, New York, Electus Backus Jr. was the son of Lieutenant Colonel Electus Backus Sr., who was killed at Sackets Harbor, New York, during the War of 1812. Backus graduated from the U.S. Military Academy at West Point in 1824 and was commissioned a second lieutenant. He served as an aide to Brigadier General Hugh Bradley from 1827 to 1837. His first wife, Sarah, and second wife, Mary, were both daughters of Bradley. Backus was promoted to first lieutenant in 1831 and to captain in 1837. He fought in the Second Seminole War (1835–1842) from 1837 to 1840.

During the Mexican-American War, Backus saw combat at the Battle of Monterrey (September 21–23, 1846). For his effective service there, Backus was brevetted major on September 23, 1846. He also participated in the 20-day siege of Veracruz, Mexico's principal seaport, during March 9–29, 1847, which ended with the city's occupation. Backus then commanded the fortress of San Juan de Ulúa, which controlled the harbor of Veracruz, while Major General Winfield Scott marched the majority of his forces to Mexico City.

After the Mexican-American War, Backus recruited for the army in Buffalo, New York, until 1850 when he was promoted to the permanent rank of major. In 1851, the army sent him to the Arizona Territory to oversee construction of Fort Defiance to establish a military presence in Navaho territory. Between 1855 and 1856, Backus was the superintendent of the general recruiting service for the U.S. Army. He returned to Fort Defiance in 1858 and served in the October–November 1858 campaign against the Navaho. The troops under his command did not sustain any casualties. Backus was promoted to lieutenant colonel in 1859. At the outset of the Civil War, Backus was in command of Fort Ringgold, Texas. In 1861, after Texas seceded from the Union, Backus successfully relocated his troops to Fort Jefferson, Missouri. He was reassigned to Detroit, Michigan, and served as a mustering and disbursing officer. Although his rapidly declining health prohibited him from engaging in active combat, Backus was promoted to colonel in 1862. He died on June 7, 1862, in Detroit.

MICHAEL R. HALL

See also
Mexico City Campaign; Monterrey, Battle of; San Juan de Ulúa; Scott, Winfield; Veracruz; Veracruz, Landing at and Siege of.

References
Ferrell, Robert H., ed. *Monterrey Is Ours! The Mexican War Letters of Lieutenant Dana, 1845–1847.* Lexington: University Press of Kentucky, 1990.

Wheelan, Joseph. *Invading Mexico: America's Continental Dream and the Mexican War, 1846–1848.* New York: Carroll and Graf, 2007.

Baja California

Baja California, which means "Lower California" in Spanish, is a 1,250-mile-long peninsula extending from Tijuana in the north to Cabo San Lucas in the south. It is also one of the states of Mexico. Baja California separates the Gulf of California (or Sea of Cortez) from the Pacific Ocean. In 1539 the Spanish began exploration of the peninsula, and during the 18th century they established settlements along its coast. On May 19, 1773, Roman Catholic officials divided California into Alta California, or "Upper California," and Baja California. This occurred at the line separating Franciscan missions in the north from Dominican missions in the south. Spanish authorities formally acknowledged the division in 1804.

During the Mexican-American War, the U.S. government was primarily concerned with acquiring Alta California. Nevertheless, a series of naval operations attempted to secure Baja California for the United States. Throughout, the U.S. naval campaigns on Mexico's Pacific coast were consistently overextended for the assets available. Although U.S. naval forces had virtually secured the coast of Alta California by August 1846, attempts at securing the coast of Baja California and Mexico proved sporadic and largely ineffectual. That same month two U.S. ships were sent to blockade the coast of Baja California and Mexico, and in September U.S. Navy commander Samuel F. Du Pont obtained a promise of neutrality from Francisco Palacios Miranda, the governor of Baja California.

On April 14, 1847, U.S. forces led by Commander John B. Montgomery occupied La Paz, on the southeast corner of Baja California. Miranda readily agreed to Montgomery's terms of surrender, which included full rights of United States citizens and U.S. protection for the Mexican inhabitants acknowledging American control of the region. In essence, Montgomery promised Mexicans in the Baja full rights as U.S. citizens in return for their loyalty. Many residents, however, considered Miranda a traitor and remained loyal to Mexico. Du Pont now sailed the sloop of war *Cyane* along the coast of Baja California to provide the pro-American Mexicans with a semblance of protection. Regardless, without sufficient ships and support, the U.S. Navy could not protect friendly Mexicans or suppress unfriendly ones.

On November 19, 1847, Mexican captain Manuel Piñeda attacked La Paz. Lacking support from the local population because of his harsh recruitment practices and plundering of private supplies, Piñeda's attack failed. On December 7, 1847, President James K. Polk announced that Baja California was under American control and would never be surrendered to Mexico. Nevertheless, the February 1848 Treaty of Guadalupe Hidalgo left Mexico in possession of Baja California. Indeed, Secretary of State James Buchanan had instructed treaty negotiator Nicholas P. Trist that the acquisition of Baja California was not a priority and should not inhibit treaty negotiations.

After the conclusion of peace, when American forces withdrew from Baja California, they took with them to the United States hundreds of disappointed and disillusioned Mexican collaborators, including Palacios Miranda. In 1853, American filibuster William Walker briefly occupied La Paz and declared himself president of the Republic of Lower California. His self-declared presidency did not last long, however.

In 1930, the Mexican government divided Baja California into northern and southern territories. Northern Baja California became Mexico's 29th state in 1952, and Southern Baja California became Mexico's 31st state in 1974.

MICHAEL R. HALL

See also

Buchanan, James; California; Du Pont, Samuel Francis; Guadalupe Hidalgo, Treaty of; Gulf of California (Mar de Cortés); La Paz; Montgomery, John Berrien; Polk, James Knox.

References

Barrett, Ellen. *Baja California, 1535–1956*. New Castle, DE: Oak Knoll Press, 1999.

Halleck, Henry W. *Mexican War in Baja California*. Los Angeles: Dawson's Books, 1977.

Harlow, Neal. *California Conquered: The Annexation of a Mexican Province, 1846–1850*. Berkeley: University of California Press, 1989.

Meadows, Don. *The American Occupation of La Paz*. Los Angeles: Glen Dawson, 1955.

Moyano Pahissa, Angela. *La resistencia de las Californias a la invasión norteamericana (1846–1848)*. Mexico City: Consejo Nacional para la Cultura y las Artes, 1992.

Richmond, Douglas W. "A View of the Periphery: Regional Factors and Collaboration during the U.S.-Mexico Conflict, 1845–1848." In *Dueling Eagles Reinterpreting the U.S.-Mexican War, 1846–1848*, edited by Richard Francaviglia and Douglas W. Richmond, 127–154. Fort Worth: Texas Christian University Press, 2000.

Baker, Edward Dickinson
Birth Date: February 24, 1811
Death Date: October 21, 1861

Whig (later Republican) politician and lawyer who served as a U.S. Army officer during the Mexican-American War and the U.S. Civil War. Born on February 24, 1811, in London, England, Edward Dickinson Baker immigrated with his family to Philadelphia, Pennsylvania, in 1816. The family joined Robert Owen's ill-fated utopian community in New Harmony, Indiana, in 1825. Baker subsequently moved to Carrollton, Illinois, and was admitted to the bar in 1830. He was elected to the Illinois House of Representatives in 1837 and the Illinois Senate in 1840. Baker won a seat in the U.S. House of Representatives in 1844, defeating his close friend Abraham Lincoln.

On July 4, 1846, during the Mexican-American War, Baker was commissioned a colonel of the 4th Regiment of the Illinois Volunteer Infantry, resigning his seat in the U.S. House on December 24, 1846. On April 18, 1847, Baker participated in the Battle of Cerro Gordo, and his troops took control of the strategic road to Jalapa. After his commanding officer, Brigadier General James Shields, was severely wounded during the battle, Baker took command and led the brigade in a charge that overwhelmed the Mexican rear. He led the brigade, still at the rank of colonel, for the remainder of

Edward D. Baker of Illinois resigned from Congress to serve as a colonel in the U.S. Army during the Mexican-American War. Distinguishing himself in the fighting, he won reelection to Congress after the war. (Library of Congress)

the war, seeing action in almost all of the major battles during the Mexico City Campaign.

Returning to Illinois, he was reelected to the U.S. House of Representatives, serving from 1849 to 1851. Baker moved to San Francisco, California, in 1851. He moved to Oregon in 1860 and was elected as a Republican to the U.S. Senate. By that time he had earned a reputation as a gifted orator, giving soaring and patriotic speeches on the floor of the Senate.

Upon the outbreak of the Civil War, Baker was offered a commission as brigadier general, which would have compelled him to resign his Senate seat. He turned down the commission but recruited, organized, and was elected colonel of a regiment of Pennsylvania volunteer infantry. Enthusiastic but largely unschooled in tactics or strategy, Baker hoped for a quick and colorful victory, which would bolster his political career. On October 21, 1861, while leading the 71st Pennsylvania Infantry, Baker was killed at the Battle of Ball's Bluff in Virginia. He was the only sitting senator killed in battle during the Civil War. Baker's death and the Union's poor showing at Ball's Bluff were largely his own making. However, after the Committee on the Conduct of the War investigated the actions of October 21, it wrongfully concluded that Brigadier General Charles P. Stone bore the blame for reversal at Ball's Bluff. This all but ruined Stone's career as a professional soldier but saved the image of a martyred senator

who was well liked and admired. Many have since asserted that Baker acted recklessly in advancing his own career rather than contributing to a well-reasoned military engagement for the Union.

MICHAEL R. HALL

See also
Cerro Gordo, Battle of; Lincoln, Abraham; Mexico City Campaign; Shields, James.

References
Bauer, K. Jack. *The Mexican War, 1846–1848.* New York: Macmillan, 1974.
Matheny, James H. "A Modern Knight Errant: Edward Dickinson Baker." *Journal of the Illinois State Historical Society* 9, no. 1 (April 1916): 23–42.

Balbontín, Manuel
Birth Date: August 30, 1824
Death Date: December 17, 1894

Mexican army officer and historian. Manuel Balbontín was born in Mexico City on August 30, 1824. He began his military career on March 26, 1845, as a cadet in Mexico City's Military College. That July the college promoted Balbontín to corporal, and he rose to sublieutenant of the college's 1st Artillery Brigade in November. After the break in diplomatic relations between Mexico and the United States in early 1846 caused by the U.S. annexation of Texas, the Mexican government ordered the enlistment of all Military College officers into the army's infantry and artillery regiments in Mexico City. Balbontín entered the 1st Artillery Battalion as a sublieutenant.

On September 21, 1846, during the first day of the Battle of Monterrey (September 21–23, 1846), Major General Zachary Taylor's forces captured Balbontín, but he was exchanged on September 24, and he was with his command at the Battle of Buena Vista (February 22–23, 1847). On August 21, 1847, Balbontín was promoted to lieutenant.

After the conclusion of the U.S.-Mexican War in 1848, Balbontín took part in the Mexican civil war known as the War of the Reform (1858–1861); the French Intervention (1862–1863), when French troops attempted to conquer Mexico; and during the monarchical rule of Maximilian von Habsburg (1864–1867), when he fought against the monarch's forces. He also served as military commander at Tampico during 1861–1862.

Manuel Balbontín retired from the army as a colonel in March 1876. Along with an active military career, Balbontín chronicled the history of the Mexican army, particularly its actions during the Mexican-American War in a work titled *La invasión americana, 1846 a 1848: Apuntes del subteniente de artillería Manuel Balbontín* (1888). Balbontín died in Mexico City on December 17, 1894.

RICARDO A. CATÓN

See also

Ampudia, Pedro de; Buena Vista, Battle of; Monterrey, Battle of; Taylor, Zachary.

References

Balbontín, Manuel. *La invasión americana, 1846 a 1848: Apuntes del subteniente de artillería Manuel Balbontín.* San Luís Potosí, México: Tip. de G. A. Esteva, 1888.

Balbontín, Manuel. *Memorias del Coronel Manuel Balbontín.* San Luís Potosí, México: Tip. de la Escuela I. Militar, dirigida por Aurelio B. Cortés, 1896.

DePalo, William A. *The Mexican National Army, 1822–1852.* College Station: Texas A&M University Press, 1997.

Balderas, Lucas

Birth Date: October 18, 1797
Death Date: September 8, 1847

Mexican politician and patriot. Lucas Balderas was born in humble circumstances on October 18, 1797, in San Miguel de Allende, Guanajuato, Mexico. His family was unable to provide him with a formal education, and as a boy he was apprenticed to a tailor. In 1813 his family moved to Mexico City where Balderas was employed by a Spanish tailor, Manuel Alcalde. Two years later Balderas joined the Fieles de Fernando VII, a loyalist militia unit organized by the Spanish viceroy in 1810. He served with that unit until it was disbanded in 1820.

Mexican Army officer and war hero Lucas Balderas capably led the national guard Mina Battalion during the Mexican-American War but was killed in the Battle of El Molino del Rey on September 8, 1847. (Library of Congress)

Following Mexico's declaration of independence in 1821, Balderas supported the creation of a federal republic. In 1825 he joined the radical York Rite Masons, which opposed the elitist Scottish Rite Masons. The York Rite Masons, who mobilized the support of Mexico City's urban masses, favored the expulsion of the Spaniards from Mexico.

In 1826, Balderas was elected to Mexico City's town council. To limit the power of the national army and elitist interests, the Yorkist-dominated government authorized the creation of a civic militia (also known as the National Guard) in 1827, and Balderas served as the inspector general of this force in Mexico City from 1833 to 1834. In 1835, after pro-centralist legislators took control of the Mexican government, Balderas began to conspire against it. He was jailed because of his participation in the unsuccessful July 1840 attempt to overthrow President Anastasio Bustamante, and on December 6, 1844, Balderas participated in the popular revolt that overthrew then president Antonio López de Santa Anna. In late December 1845, however, elitist elements in Mexico City, fearful of the growing power of the masses, orchestrated a military coup that toppled the government that had succeeded Santa Anna's and disbanded the civic militia.

In August 1846, during the Mexican-American War, the federal government issued a decree that reestablished the National Guard. Conservative elements in Mexico City, however, fearful of increasing the power of the lower classes, organized their own militias and excluded participation by the urban poor. Because most guardsmen in these units belonged to the propertied classes, they became known as the Polkos, a reference to the polka dance that was popular with the elites. One of these units, the Mina Battalion, was made up almost entirely of artisans and led by Balderas, who by now had abandoned his radical rhetoric and adopted the outlook of the middle class.

The Mina Battalion engaged U.S. forces on September 8, 1847, in the Battle of El Molino del Rey in which Balderas suffered fatal wounds and died in the arms of his son. On September 8, 1856, his remains were transferred to and interred in a monument built by the Mexican government at Molino del Rey to honor the role of the National Guard in the defense of Mexico.

MICHAEL R. HALL

See also

Bustamante y Oseguera, Anastasio; Chapultepec, Battle of; El Molino del Rey, Battle of; Freemasonry; Mexico City; Mexico City, Battle for; Mexico City Campaign; Polkos Revolt; Santa Anna, Antonio López de.

References

Santoni, Pedro. "Lucas Balderas: Popular Leader and Patriot." In *The Human Tradition in Mexico,* edited by Jeffrey M. Pilcher, 41–56. Wilmington, DE: Scholarly Resources, 2003.

Santoni, Pedro. "Where Did the Other Heroes Go? Exalting the *Polko* National Guard Battalions in Nineteenth-Century Mexico." *Journal of Latin American Studies* 34, no. 4 (November 2002): 807–844.

Warren, Richard A. *Vagrants and Citizens: Politics and the Masses in Mexico City from Colony to Republic.* Wilmington, DE: Scholarly Resources, 2001.

Bancroft, George
Birth Date: October 3, 1800
Death Date: January 17, 1891

Prominent U.S. historian, author, educator, secretary of the navy (1845–1846), and ambassador to Great Britain (1846–1849) and Prussia and the German Empire (1867–1874). Born in Worcester, Massachusetts, on October 3, 1800, George Bancroft graduated from Phillips Exeter Academy, Harvard College (BA, 1817), and the University of Göttingen in Prussia (PhD, 1820). He established himself as America's preeminent historian during the 19th century with his comprehensive, best-selling *History of the United States* (10 volumes, 1834–1874). Early on, Bancroft earned the reputation as an extraordinary writer and essayist, and cofounded the Round Hill School in Northampton, Massachusetts, in 1823. He also became an avid adherent of rigorous secondary education. In 1837 President Martin Van Buren appointed Bancroft collector of customs for the port of Boston, a post he held until 1844; that same year, he ran unsuccessfully as the Democratic candidate for the governorship of Massachusetts.

President James K. Polk appointed Bancroft secretary of the navy in March 1845, a political reward for Bancroft's significant role in securing the 1844 Democratic Party presidential nomination for Polk. As secretary, Bancroft pursued an agenda of modernization and economy, advocating such reforms as merit promotion, the establishment of a retired list for the U.S. Navy, the abolition of arbitrary and illegal forms of flogging as punishment for enlisted sailors, the elimination of wasteful expenditures and unnecessary officer positions, the introduction of professional competency examinations for naval personnel, and the creation of an improved system of naval officer education.

Bancroft's greatest success and legacy as navy secretary was his founding of the U.S. Naval Academy at Annapolis, Maryland, on October 10, 1845. Congress had opposed the establishment of a naval academy for decades, citing the high financial cost, the alleged superiority of the U.S. Navy's traditional method of educating midshipmen on board ships at sea, and the desire to avoid the perceived elitism of the U.S. Military Academy at West Point. Bancroft overcame congressional opposition by using only the authority of the executive branch to create a working naval academy at Fort Severn, a former U.S. Army post in Annapolis, Maryland, without consulting or securing financial support from Congress until after the school had been in operation for almost two months.

Bancroft served as secretary of the navy during the first five months of the Mexican-American War. Although he was the only member of Polk's cabinet to oppose war with Mexico initially, he supported a declaration of war after learning of the Mexican attack on Brigadier General Zachary Taylor's army in Texas, which had occurred on April 25, 1846. Anticipating hostilities with Mexico, Bancroft issued orders to Commodore John D. Sloat, commander of the Pacific Squadron, to capture San Francisco, California, and to blockade or occupy Mexico's other Pacific coast ports. He also ordered Commodore David Conner's Home Squadron to blockade Mexican ports in the Gulf of Mexico. Acting on orders from Bancroft, Commodore Robert F. Stockton established the authority of the United States in California by creating a civil administration there. Although a routine part of Bancroft's job as secretary, his orders helped to secure the acquisition of California by the United States.

Bancroft resigned as secretary of the navy in September 1846 to become the U.S. minister to Great Britain, serving until 1849. There he became a close friend and confidant of the acclaimed British historians Thomas Babington Macaulay and Henry Hallam. Bancroft later served as minister to Prussia from 1867 to 1871 and minister to the German Empire from 1871 to 1874. In 1866, the U.S. Congress awarded Bancroft the singular honor of delivering a formal eulogy for President Abraham Lincoln, who had been assassinated in April 1865. George Bancroft died in Washington, D.C., on January 17, 1891.

WILLIAM P. LEEMAN

See also
Conner, David; Polk, James Knox; Sloat, John Drake; Stockton, Robert Field; United States Navy.

References
Bauer, K. Jack. "George Bancroft." In *American Secretaries of the Navy*, edited by Paolo E. Coletta, 1:217–229. Annapolis, MD: Naval Institute Press, 1980.
Bauer, K. Jack. *Surfboats and Horse Marines: U.S. Naval Operations in the Mexican War, 1846–48*. Annapolis, MD: Naval Institute Press, 1969.
Handlin, Lilian. *George Bancroft: The Intellectual as Democrat*. New York: Harper & Row, 1984.
Nye, Russel B. *George Bancroft: Brahmin Rebel*. New York: Knopf, 1944.

Bandini, Juan
Birth Date: October 4, 1800
Death Date: November 4, 1859

California ranchero and political leader. Born on October 4, 1800, in San Marcos de Arica, Peru, Juan Bandini was the son of Spanish sea captain José Bandini. His family descent may be traced to Italy and shares lineage with Bernardo Bandini, the assassin of Lorenzo de' Medici's brother Guilliano.

José Bandini arrived in Alta California in 1818, transporting Spanish troops to defend the capital at Monterey. Having settled in Southern California (near San Diego) on the promise of a land grant from the Mexican government, Bandini became active in the political and military affairs of Alta California. He also came to own considerable tracts of land.

At the time, California, which was far removed from the capital of Mexico City, often fell into de facto dictatorship under the constitutionally appointed governor. With little division of power, Mexican governors in California tightly controlled politics, the military, and the judiciary. Sectionalism became rampant in Mexican California, with northern (*norteño*) politicians located near Monterey, opposing southerners (*sureños*). One of the most contentious issues was the secularization of Spanish missions. Bandini, a proponent of secularization, led a revolt in the early 1830s that resulted in the resignation of Governor Manuel Victoria, who had not supported secularization. Bandini then lobbied the next governor, José Figueroa, for such a measure. On August 9, 1834, under pressure from Bandini and other *sureños,* Figueroa capitulated, secularizing California's missions, an action that earned Bandini the title "Destroyer of the California Missions."

Two years later, in 1836, Bandini supported newly appointed governor Carlos Carillo in another power struggle. Carillo, younger brother to José Antonio Carillo, was refused the governorship by the incumbent, Juan Bautista Alvarado. Bandini, along with Pío de Jesús Pico, led a revolt against Alvarado's forces near the new capital at Los Angeles. Pro-Alvarado forces repulsed the attack, and Bandini and Pico fled to San Diego to evade arrest. For the next decade Bandini managed his enormous tracts of land, which stretched from Tijuana to the San Bernardino Mountains. He also remained influential in California politics.

When the United States declared war on Mexico in 1846 American troops under the leadership of Captain John C. Frémont entered Northern California. He then moved into Southern California and entered San Diego on July 29, 1846, where he was welcomed by the American flag hung by the family of Juan Bandini. Bandini's support of the American occupation was no small event. He aided the American troops by providing food and shelter and also allowed them free movement through his ranches. More than anything else an opportunist, and gambling on an American victory, Bandini sought to protect his land from seizure. California was weakly defended by the Mexican government, so the prospect of losses during an American invasion overwhelmed any Mexican patriotism Bandini may have felt.

After the war, Bandini, having successfully protected his property, was heralded as a supporter of both California and the United States. He remained an important force in California politics, even serving briefly on a legislative council for the American governor, Robert F. Stockton. Until his death on November 4, 1859, near San Diego, Bandini was a true California socialite, well respected both for his wealth and his cordiality. Poor financial decisions later in life resulted in his losing a good amount of his fortune, but Bandini's contributions to the American war effort in California unquestionably helped to transform the region from a distant Mexican territory to American statehood.

Jim Piecuch and Jason Lutz

See also

California; California Theater of War, Overview; Frémont, John Charles; Missions; Pico, Pío de Jesús; Rancheros; Stockton, Robert Field

References

Baker, Patricia. "The Bandini Family." *The Journal of San Diego History* 15, 1 (Winter 1969): 33–54.

Beattie, George William. "San Bernardino Valley Before the Americans Came." *California Historical Society Quarterly* 12, 2 (June 1933): 111–124.

Harlow, Neal. *California Conquered: War and Peace on the Pacific, 1846–1850.* Berkeley: University of California Press, 1982.

Banditry

A culture of banditry developed in Mexico at the time of its independence movement from 1810 to 1821. The conflict between royalists and rebels left a power vacuum in some regions into which local strongmen moved. Many of these strongmen hired their own mercenaries to ensure control over their territory. Most historians have labeled these men and their followers as bandits or brigands. Travelers passing through the bandit-controlled territories frequently faced robbery and murder unless they were accompanied by a strong, well-armed escort.

Bandit activity continued after independence, becoming a way of life for some Mexicans, particularly in the northern border areas. Bandits often figured into Mexican politics because they sold their services to the highest bidder and frequently switched allegiances based on how much they were being paid.

During the Mexican-American War, bandits plagued American forces throughout Mexico. Stragglers and small military detachments frequently faced capture and death at the hands of bandits. American commanders relied on mounted units, especially those whose members had once been Texas Rangers, to combat the menace. The roads linking Camargo to Saltillo and Veracruz to Mexico City, where banditry was rife, were particularly dangerous routes.

Banditry in Mexico has made it difficult for historians to gauge the actual level of guerilla activity that developed in opposition to the U.S. invasion. The Mexican government issued orders for guerrillas to operate against the Americans; however, guerrillas and bandits operated in much the same way, making it hard to distinguish between the two. Moreover, many known guerrillas were former bandits, a fact that further confuses the issue.

In central Mexico, Lieutenant Colonel Ethan Allen Hitchcock, Major General Scott's inspector general, resorted to hiring Mexican bandits to help the Americans control the route to Mexico City. Hitchcock convinced Manuel Domínguez, a local bandit leader, to recruit two scouting companies from among his accomplices to work for Scott. They were designated Mexican spy companies, and their task was to gather intelligence and keep the roads safe. At the end of the war, Domínguez and his followers left Mexico to escape retribution for their service to the U.S. Army.

After the war ended in 1848, the newly drawn border between the United States and Mexico gave new life to Mexican banditry. In the Lower Rio Grande Valley, where banditry had been historically endemic, bandits used the new border to their advantage, launching raids in one country and then fleeing into the other. It took nearly another half century before the governments of Mexico and the United States permitted their police forces to pursue bandits over the border onto the other's soil. The tightly centralized Mexican governments that had come to power in the last half of the 19th century also helped curb banditry, but their efforts to entirely extinguish it proved unsuccessful.

BRUCE WINDERS

See also

Guerrilla Warfare; Hitchcock, Ethan Allen; Mexican Spy Company; Mexico; Mexico, 1821–1854; Texas Rangers.

References

Clendenen, Clarence C. *Blood on the Border: The United States Army and the Mexican Irregulars.* New York: Macmillan, 1969.

Croffut, W. A., ed. *Fifty Years in Camp and Field: Diary of Major General Ethan Allen Hitchcock.* New York: Putnam and Sons, 1909.

Frazer, Chris. *Bandit Nation: A History of Outlaws and Cultural Struggle in Mexico, 1810–1920.* Lincoln: University of Nebraska Press, 2006.

Levinson, Irving W. *Wars within War: Mexican Guerrillas, Domestic Elites, and the United States of America, 1846–1848.* Fort Worth: Texas Christian University Press, 2005.

Vanderwood, Paul J. *Disorder and Progress: Bandits, Police, and Mexican Development.* Wilmington, DE: Scholarly Resources, 1992.

Bankhead, Charles

Birth Date: 1797
Death Date: November 3, 1859

British diplomat and minister plenipotentiary to Mexico (1843–1847). Charles Bankhead was born in England in 1797; little else is known about his early life. As a young adult, he served as an apprentice to various British foreign ministers, and by 1824 he was a foreign office attaché in Frankfurt, where he met his future wife, Maria Horatia Paul. The Paul family, long-standing British aristocrats, did not think Bankhead a suitable match for their daughter but relented after recognizing Bankhead's potential in the foreign service. The two married in 1826.

Bankhead's marriage clearly provided increased career opportunities, and in 1826 he was appointed secretary of the British legation to the United States and served twice as interim chargé d'affaires (1831–1833 and 1835–1836). In 1836, Bankhead, under instructions from the British government, acted as a mediator between the United States and France when the French government refused to pay an outstanding debt. Bankhead assured President Andrew Jackson that Great Britain would mediate the affair in hopes of avoiding war between the two nations. Eventually, France reversed its decision and paid the debt. In 1841, Bankhead was promoted to secretary of the British embassy in the Ottoman Empire at Constantinople.

With almost two decades of experience in diplomatic affairs, Bankhead was sent to Mexico City in 1843 as Britain's top diplomat. His arrival coincided with a period of turmoil in both U.S.-Mexican relations and Anglo-American relations, which had been badly strained over the ongoing Oregon boundary dispute. Bankhead's main goals in Mexico were to protect British-Mexican trade and prevent a full-scale war between Mexico and the United States. Following Mexico's independence from Spain in 1821, any foreign presence in Mexico, particularly European, proved highly contentious among many Mexican officials, who tended to view outsiders as profiteers and exploiters. Many Mexicans believed that the British were trying to assert control over Alta California, and perhaps the Yucatan as well.

Bankhead sought to maintain peace between Mexico and the United States, although his motives were not solely humanitarian. When Texas declared its independence from Mexico in 1836, Bankhead, who was then chargé d'affaires in Washington, repeatedly appealed to Mexican officials to recognize Texas as an independent nation and negotiate a permanent boundary treaty and assurances of security with U.S. officials. Bankhead believed that by continuing its warlike posturing toward Texas, Mexico would compel the newly independent nation to seek protection from the United States, including possible annexation. Furthermore, the British wanted to restrict further American expansion into the Southwest and develop their own lucrative trade with the burgeoning cotton plantations in Texas.

Bankhead had also warned, presciently, that U.S. annexation of Texas would likely lead to U.S. conquest of Mexico. In February 1844, Bankhead became the first person in Mexico to learn that the United States had informally proposed annexation to the Texas government. Mexicans were outraged by the news. Bankhead, along with Charles Elliot, British chargé d'affaires in Texas, brokered a tentative agreement between Mexico and Texas known as the Smith-Cuevas Treaty. The agreement, needing only ratification by the Mexican Congress, acknowledged the independence of Texas. However, anti-British sentiment torpedoed the deal and helped drive Mexicans like Antonio López de Santa Anna and others to openly discuss the retaking of Texas. Despite Bankhead's efforts, Texas was formally annexed by the United States in February 1845. Bankhead later tried to convince Mexican foreign minister Manuel de la Peña y Peña to again enter into discussions with the Texans and Americans to avert war, but his pleadings went unheeded. War between Mexico and the United States began in the late spring of 1846.

Once the war began, Bankhead continued to advise Mexican officials. In August 1846 the Mexican government debated issuing letters of marque to disrupt trade in American ports like New Orleans. Bankhead, with France and Spain in agreement, strongly advised against this measure, because Mexican privateers might disrupt American cotton exports to Europe. Nearly one year later, in June 1847, Bankhead began to work as an intermediary for peace. Holding the confidence of both sides, particularly Santa Anna and the American negotiator, Nicholas P. Trist, Bankhead routinely delivered communications between the warring nations. Bankhead's efforts came to fruition on February 2, 1848, with the signing of the Treaty of Guadalupe Hidalgo. By the time the treaty was signed, however, Bankhead had been replaced by Percy

William Doyle (in October 1848). He returned to Mexico in 1850 as chargé d'affaires and remained there until 1859. Bankhead then came back to Britain that year, where he died on November 3.

JIM PIECUCH AND JASON LUTZ

See also

Boundary Disputes, U.S. and Mexican; Diplomacy, Mexican; Great Britain; Guadalupe Hidalgo, Treaty of; Oregon Boundary Dispute; Peña y Peña, Manuel de la; Santa Anna, Antonio López de; Texas; Texas Revolution; Trist, Nicholas Philip.

References

Pletcher, David M. *The Diplomacy of Annexation: Texas, Oregon, and the Mexican War.* Columbia: University of Missouri Press, 1973.

Smith, Justin H. "The Mexican Recognition of Texas." *American Historical Review* 16, no. 1 (October 1910): 36–55.

Smith, Justin H. *The War with Mexico.* 2 vols. Boston: Peter Smith, 1963.

Barbour, Philip Norbourne
Birth Date: April 14, 1813
Death Date: September 21, 1846

U.S. infantry officer. Born in Henderson, Kentucky, on April 14, 1813, Philip Norbourne Barbour studied in Kentucky until 1828, when he went to Washington, D.C. There he secured an appointment to the U.S. Military Academy, West Point, from which he graduated in 1834 and was commissioned as a second lieutenant in the 3rd Infantry Regiment. After service at several posts in the West, he saw his first combat action in 1842 in Florida during the Second Seminole War, where he was brevetted captain.

In 1845 Barbour's regiment was deployed to Texas and assigned to Brigadier General Zachary Taylor's Army of Occupation at Corpus Christi to defend the newly annexed state of Texas from a potential Mexican invasion. After Taylor's army had marched to the Rio Grande in early 1846, Barbour's regiment participated in the Battle of Palo Alto on May 8, 1846. It also played a decisive role at the Battle of Resaca de la Palma on May 9, 1846, repulsing a unit of Mexican lancers. Barbour's leadership in the battle earned him another brevet to major.

Later that year, Barbour's regiment participated in the Battle of Monterrey (September 21–23, 1846), where General Taylor attacked Major General Pedro de Ampudia's Mexican Army of the North. Barbour died during the battle (on September 21) while leading his regiment across a heavily defended canal on the outskirts of the city.

CHRIS DISHMAN

See also

Ampudia, Pedro de; Monterrey, Battle of; Northern Mexico Theater of War, Overview; Palo Alto, Battle of; Resaca de la Palma, Battle of; Taylor, Zachary.

References

Barbour, Philip and Martha. *The Journals of Major Philip Norbourne Barbour.* Edited by Rhoda Van Bibber Tanner Doubleday. New York: G.P. Putnam's Sons, 1901.

Bauer, K. Jack. *The Mexican-American War, 1846–1848.* New York: Macmillan, 1974.

Cullum, George W. *Register of the Officers and Graduates of the U.S. Military Academy.* Vol. 1. New York: J. F. Trow, 1850.

Dishman, Christopher. *The Perfect Gibraltar: The Battle for Monterrey, Mexico.* Norman: University of Oklahoma Press, 2010.

Bartlett, John Russell
Birth Date: October 23, 1805
Death Date: May 28, 1886

Noted ethnologist, author, and boundary commissioner who supervised the American component of the binational American-Mexican team of surveyors charged with implementing the boundary provisions of the Treaty of Guadalupe Hidalgo from 1850 to 1853. Born on October 23, 1805, in Providence, Rhode Island, John Russell Bartlett's family moved to Kingston, Ontario, in 1806. While the family lived in Canada, Bartlett attended boarding school at the Lowville Academy, a private school established in 1808 in upstate New York.

In 1824 Bartlett returned to Providence and entered the banking profession four years later. Bartlett moved to New York City in 1836 and opened a bookshop that sold literary and scientific publications with his friend Charles Welford. In 1842 Bartlett and Albert Gallatin founded the American Ethnological Society, the first professional anthropological organization in the United States, to encourage research in the emerging field of ethnology. Bartlett published *The Progress of Ethnology* in 1847 and the *Dictionary of Americanisms* the following year.

Despite Bartlett's unfamiliarity with the American Southwest, on June 15, 1850, Whig president Zachary Taylor chose him to lead the team of American surveyors assigned to chart the new boundary between the United States and Mexico as a result of the 1848 Treaty of Guadalupe Hidalgo. The decision to appoint Bartlett to head the boundary commission was primarily based on Bartlett's membership in the Whig Party and the friendships that he had formed with influential Whigs. Bartlett, who had long desired to visit the Southwest and study the local Native Americans, eagerly accepted the appointment.

Bartlett's team of surveyors departed New York City on August 3, 1850, and arrived in Indianola, Texas, 27 days later. As leader of the American team, Bartlett was charged with coordinating his efforts with Pedro García Conde, the director of the Mexican team of surveyors. After meeting with García Conde in December, Bartlett agreed to make the southern boundary of New Mexico and Arizona 42 miles north of El Paso, giving to the Mexicans some 6,000 square miles of territory that many Americans deemed essential for the construction of a southern continental rail line. The U.S. Congress rejected the line proposed by the Bartlett-Conde Agreement, however, and refused to continue funding the survey. The controversy surrounding the southern boundary of New

John Russell Bartlett had charge of the Americans in the binational surveying team that, during 1850–1853, set the boundary between Mexico and the United States in accordance with the 1848 Treaty of Guadalupe-Hidalgo. (Dictionary of American Portraits)

Mexico was eliminated in 1853 when the United States and Mexico concluded the Gadsden Purchase.

In 1853, after the Whigs lost control of the White House, Bartlett was removed as commissioner of the American team. By then his tenure had become increasingly controversial. Allegations surfaced that he had misappropriated public funds and transportation, and that he had been generally negligent in his duty to provide for the safety and welfare of those under his charge.

Bartlett returned to Providence in 1853 and one year later published the *Personal Narrative of Explorations and Incidents in Texas, New Mexico, California, Sonora, and Chihuahua, Connected with the United States and Mexican Boundary Commission, during the Years 1850, '51, '52, and '53.* Bartlett served as Rhode Island's secretary of state from 1855 to 1872 and subsequently published numerous other works. He died on May 28, 1886, in Providence.

MICHAEL R. HALL

See also

Bartlett-Conde Agreement; Gadsden Purchase; García Conde, Pedro; Guadalupe Hidalgo, Treaty of; Taylor, Zachary.

References

Bartlett, John Russell. *Personal Narrative of Explorations and Incidents in Texas, New Mexico, California, Sonora, and Chihuahua, Connected with the United States and Mexican Boundary Commission, during the Years 1850, '51, '52, and '53.* New York: D. Appleton, 1854.
Hine, Robert V. *Bartlett's West: Drawing the Mexican Boundary.* New Haven, CT: Yale University Press, 1968.

Bartlett-Conde Agreement
Event Date: December 25, 1850

Statement of agreement signed on December 25, 1850, that set the beginning point for the official survey of the new border between the United States and Mexico. The agreement was named for U.S. boundary commissioner John Russell Bartlett and General Pedro García Conde, who represented the Mexican government. The framework for the talks that led to the agreement had been established in Article V of the 1848 Treaty of Guadalupe Hidalgo. That clause stipulated that the U.S.-Mexico border was to follow the Rio Grande to New Mexico's southwestern border, then align with the Gila and Colorado Rivers, and finally move west in a straight line to the Pacific, just south of San Diego, California. Article V also stipulated that a boundary commissioner from each nation would oversee the survey. In November 1850 President Zachary Taylor appointed Bartlett as the American commissioner and, on December 3, Bartlett and Conde met for the first time in El Paso, Texas.

The boundary survey faced immediate problems. First, the maps used for the Guadalupe Hidalgo negotiations in 1848 had been inaccurate. Second, during the ratification process, the Americans had used one version of a map delineating the New Mexico border, while the Mexicans had employed another. Neither was accurate, and they also differed rather substantially. Preliminary surveys showed that the location of the Rio Grande was off by two degrees, or about 138 miles (one degree in latitude is equal to approximately 69 miles). Also, these initial surveys found that El Paso had been located too far to the north on both maps used in the ratification process. To make matters even more confusing, other parts of the treaty instructions were contradictory, and there was no agreement on the key starting points for the survey. Both sides thus had much to gain or lose as the survey got under way.

Conde and Bartlett agreed to a number of concessions and decided to locate the initial point on the Rio Grande at the latitude indicated on the maps, with no reference to the location of El Paso. The boundary line was then extended to the west by three degrees. Once the two men had agreed on these arrangements, the formal agreement was signed on Christmas Day 1850.

After Bartlett left El Paso, the treaty was presented to the U.S. Senate's Committee on Foreign Relations for discussion and approval before being submitted to Congress as a whole. A number of Americans were critical of Bartlett's concessions, arguing that they had given up potentially valuable territory to the Mexicans, including the productive Mesilla Valley in southern New Mexico. Nicholas Trist, however, who had been the chief negotiator of the Treaty of Guadalupe Hidalgo, approved of Bartlett's work.

Not surprisingly, when the Bartlett-Conde Agreement was debated on the floor of the Senate, heated and exhaustive arguments ensued. In the end, the pact was approved, but many continued to believe that Bartlett had conceded far too much to the Mexican government. The survey went forward, and the official boundaries were codified by both the United States and Mexico.

Had Bartlett agreed to the original boundary intent, the United States would have come into possession of southern New Mexico's Mesilla Valley. That area was eventually purchased from Mexico in the 1853 Gadsden Purchase, which saw the United States take possession of almost 30,000 square miles of land that now composes the southern tier of New Mexico and Arizona. The purchase was ostensibly designed to facilitate the construction of a southern transcontinental railway line, but it was also designed to lessen tensions between Mexico and the United States over security in the region.

PAUL G. PIERPAOLI JR.

See also

Bartlett, John Russell; Gadsden Purchase; García Conde, Pedro; Guadalupe Hidalgo, Treaty of; New Mexico; Rio Grande; Trist, Nicholas Philip.

References

Bauer, K. Jack. *The Mexican War, 1846–1848.* New York: Macmillan, 1974.

Griswold del Castillo, Richard. *The Treaty of Guadalupe Hidalgo: A Legacy of Conflict.* Norman: University of Oklahoma Press, 1990.

Weems, John Edward. *To Conquer a Peace: The War between the United States and Mexico.* College Station: Texas A&M University Press, 1974.

Bartolo Ford, Battle of

See San Gabriel River, Battle of

Battalon de San Patricio

See San Patricio Battalion

Baz y Palafox, Juan José

Birth Date: 1820
Death Date: October 1887

Mexican *puro* politician. Juan José Baz y Palafox was born in Guadalajara, Jalisco, in 1820. He studied at that city's Lancasterian School and then law in Mexico City. By the time of his graduation in 1841 Baz had become involved in the nation's political and military affairs. In 1838 he took part in the defense of San Juan de Ulúa Port during the Pastry War with France, and three years later, in 1841, he supported the rebellion that toppled President Anastasio Bustamante. Baz also tried his hand at journalism.

During 1842 and 1843, he served as the editor of the *Diario del gobierno,* and he was the cofounder of another journal, *El ateneo Mexicano.*

Within a few months of the outbreak of hostilities with the United States and on the heels of the *puros* taking control of the government following the August 4, 1846, *pronunciamiento* of the Ciudadela, Baz was elected to the Mexico City *ayuntamiento.* He quickly made a name for himself at a September 8 public meeting, thanks to several impassioned remarks that threatened the Catholic Church's privileged position. The following January, during the Mexican-American War, acting president Valentín Gómez Farías named Baz governor of the Federal District, and he was tasked with enforcing the controversial January 11 decree that authorized the government to raise 15 million pesos through the seizure or mortgaging or selling of church property (up to 20 million pesos) in order to raise monies to fight the invading U.S. armies.

By the late summer of 1847 Baz served as head of the National Guard of the Federal District and in that capacity took part in the defense of Mexico City. On August 20, together with other prominent citizens who accompanied General Antonio López de Santa Anna throughout the encounters fought in and around the capital, Baz helped deliver ammunition and orders to the defenders of the convent at Churubusco. Little is known, however, about Baz's actions in the other clashes with U.S. troops.

After the war, Baz was a deputy for the state of Veracruz, and in 1851 President Mariano Arista named him alderman of the Mexico City Municipal Council. Two years later, he was exiled by President Antonio López de Santa Anna and went to Europe. He returned to Mexico in 1856 following the successful Ayutla Revolution and Santa Anna's final ouster from power. Baz once more became governor of the Federal District and also served as counsel to the state of Colima and as a constituent deputy from 1856 to 1857 during the drafting of the 1857 Constitution.

Baz then took part in the Reform War to combat the conservatives. He was defeated at the Battle of Salamanca in March 1858 and was soon thereafter imprisoned by conservative president Felix María Zuloaga. Baz managed to escape from prison and, in the city of Morelia in the state of Michoacán, founded *La bandera roja* newspaper.

Beginning in June 1863, a short time before the French occupation began, Baz again held the office of governor of the Federal District. With the establishment of Emperor Maximilian's regime, he went into self-imposed exile in New York City, where he joined the Aid Junta against the French intervention. After the fall of Maximilian's government in 1867, he once again served as governor of the Federal District, where he ordered the creation of Independencia and Cinco de Mayo Streets and founded the Tecpan de Santiago Asylum and the Industrial School for Orphans.

During August–November 1876, Baz was minister of the interior under the Sebastián Lerdo de Tejada government and returned to Congress as a federal deputy for the state of Hidalgo in

1884 and 1887. Baz died in Mexico City in October 1887, three days after resigning from his post.

FABIOLA GARCÍA RUBIO AND PEDRO SANTONI

See also

Arista, Mariano; Ayutla Revolution; Chapultepec, Battle of; Churubusco, Battle of; El Molino del Rey, Battle of; Gómez Farías, Valentín; Mexico City; Politics, Mexican; Pastry War; *Puros*; San Juan de Ulúa; Santa Anna, Antonio López de.

References

Alcaraz, Ramón. *Apuntes para la historia de la guerra entre México y los Estados Unidos.* Mexico City: Consejo Nacional para la Cultura y las Artes, 1991.

Carreño, Alberto María. *Jefes del ejército mexicano en 1847: Biografías de generales de división y de brigada y de coroneles del ejército mexicano por fines del año de 1847; Manuscrito anónimo, adicionado en gran parte y precedido de un estudio acerca de la participación del ejército en la vida política de México durante la primera mitad de siglo XIX con numerosos documentos inéditos por Alberto M. Carreño.* Mexico City: Imprenta y Fototipia de la Secretaría de Fomento, 1914.

Santoni, Pedro. *Mexicans at Arms:* Puro *Federalists and the Politics of War, 1845–1848.* Fort Worth: Texas Christian University Press, 1996.

Beach, Moses Yale

Birth Date: January 7, 1800
Death Date: July 19, 1868

Inventor, journalist, and publisher who served as a secret agent of the U.S. government during the Mexican-American War. Moses Yale Beach was born in Wallingford, Connecticut, on January 7, 1800. His mother was a descendant of Connecticut scion Elihu Yale, a major benefactor of Yale University, which bears his name. After apprenticing to a cabinetmaker as a teenager, Beach purchased his release and went into business for himself in Northampton, Massachusetts. Around 1820, he married Nancy Day.

An avid inventor, Beach developed a popular rag-cutting machine for use in paper mills. In 1829 Beach moved with his family to Saugerties, New York, where he engaged in the paper milling business. Four years later, Beach's brother-in-law, Benjamin H. Day, founded the *New York Sun,* the first successful penny daily newspaper in the United States. It quickly attained the largest circulation in New York City. Beach was taken in as a partner in 1835 after briefly serving as a reporter. Three years later, Day sold his share of the *Sun* to Beach, who eventually became the sole proprietor of the newspaper. The paper would become a major mouthpiece for the Democratic Party. During the Mexican-American War, Beach had helped found the New York Associated Press, a cooperative of some leading U.S. newspapers.

Beach was an ardent expansionist who championed the U.S. annexation of Texas in 1845. He editorialized in favor of the Manifest Destiny of the United States to spread across the North American continent. Strongly favoring the United States'

declaration of war against Mexico in May 1846, Beach pursued investment opportunities in the banking and transportation sectors of the Mexican economy. He also offered to help the U.S. government broker a peace with Mexico in hopes of someday gaining the transit rights across Mexico's isthmus of Tehuantepec. After meeting with U.S. president James K. Polk and U.S. secretary of state James Buchanan in Washington, D.C., Beach was commissioned as a confidential executive agent of the State Department in November 1846.

Beach sailed from New York to Cuba to Mexico accompanied by his wife and Jane McManus Storms Cazneau, a journalist and expansionist advocate who regularly contributed to the *Sun.* The three traveled incognito using false British passports, but their mission soon became known to Mexican President Antonio López de Santa Anna through his loyal contacts in Cuba. Entering Veracruz in January 1847, Beach traveled to Mexico City and began cooperating with U.S. consul John Black and other U.S. agents. Beach and Cazneau attempted to persuade disgruntled influential Mexican businessmen, politicians, and Roman Catholic clergy to capitulate to the United States. Beach tried to convince businessmen and government officials, including Mexican vice president Valentín Gómez Farías, that the United States would help industrialize Mexico following its surrender.

With Santa Anna off fighting Major General Zachary Taylor's forces in northern Mexico, the anticlerical Gómez Farías decreed on January 11, 1847, that Roman Catholic Church property would be confiscated and sold at auction to raise money for Mexico's war effort. Thus, several Roman Catholic bishops came to believe that Mexico's war effort endangered the church. Convinced that powerful clergy could influence the Mexican government to end the war on favorable terms for the United States, Beach asserted that the U.S. government would protect church assets in Mexico.

On February 27, 1847, Mexicans angered at Gómez Farías's decree initiated the Polkos Revolt, which created civil unrest in Mexico City for nearly a month. Exhausted by two days of fighting at the Battle of Buena Vista (February 22–23), Santa Anna returned to Mexico City, removed Gómez Farías from office, and rescinded the controversial decree. Believing that Beach had played a part in instigating the Polkos Revolt, Santa Anna posted a reward for Beach and declared that anyone found with a copy of the *New York Sun* would be punished as a traitor.

His mission a failure, Beach escaped Mexico and met with President Polk in Washington, D.C., in May 1847. Using his newspaper to stress the potential importance of the right of way across the isthmus of Tehuantepec for U.S. commerce, Beach unsuccessfully advocated for the U.S. annexation of all Mexico. In the editorial pages of the *Sun,* Beach lamented that the Treaty of Guadalupe Hidalgo had ended the Mexican-American War in February 1848 without mention of Tehuantepec transit rights.

That December Beach turned the *New York Sun* over to two of his sons; the newspaper remained family-controlled for 20 more years. With a considerable fortune, Beach retired and engaged in local philanthropy in Wallingford, Connecticut, where he died on July 19, 1868.

DAVID M. CARLETTA

See also

All of Mexico Movement; Black, John; Buchanan, James; Buena Vista, Battle of; Catholic Church, Mexico; Cazneau, Jane McManus Storms; Gómez Farías, Valentín; Manifest Destiny; Polk, James Knox; Polkos Revolt; Santa Anna, Antonio López de; Taylor, Zachary.

References

Eisenhower. John S. D. *So Far from God: The U.S. War with Mexico, 1846–1848.* New York: Random House, 1989.

Farnham, Thomas J. "Moses Y. Beach, Confidential Agent." *New-England Galaxy* 12, no. 2 (1970): 25–32.

Hudson, Linda S. *Mistress of Manifest Destiny: A Biography of Jane McManus Storms Cazneau, 1807–1878.* Austin: Texas State Historical Association, 2001.

Nelson, Anna K. "Mission to Mexico—Moses Y. Beach, Secret Agent." *New-York Historical Society Quarterly* 59, no. 3 (July 1975): 227–245.

Beale, Edward Fitzgerald
Birth Date: February 4, 1822
Death Date: April 22, 1893

U.S. Navy officer, California militia brigadier general, diplomat, frontiersman, surveyor, and hero of the December 6, 1846, Battle of San Pascual. Edward Fitzgerald Beale, more commonly known as Ned, was born in Washington, D.C., on February 4, 1822. His father, George, was a paymaster in the U.S. Navy and had earned a congressional commendation for valor during the War of 1812. His grandfather had been a commodore in the U.S. Navy.

While Edward Beale was studying at Georgetown College, his mother appealed to President Andrew Jackson for her son's appointment as a midshipman. Beale received a warrant on December 14, 1836. He was promoted to passed midshipman on July 1, 1842. Beale then spent two years on cruises in the Mediterranean and off South America. In 1845, he was assigned to Captain Robert F. Stockton's Pacific Squadron.

After his promotion to acting sailing master and private secretary to Stockton, Beale sailed for California and Oregon in October 1845 in the frigate *Congress*. While on the high seas, Stockton ordered Beale to board a Danish ship and sail to England incognito to ascertain information about British feelings toward the Oregon boundary dispute. In March 1846, Beale reported to President James K. Polk that Great Britain seemed to be making preparations for war. Beale then sailed for Panama, and he rejoined Stockton and the *Congress* in Peru in May 1846. When the *Congress* finally reached Monterey, California, on July 20, 1846, war between the United States and Mexico had begun.

Stockton immediately sailed to San Diego, where he assigned Beale to serve with U.S. land forces. Along with a small force under the command of Captain Archibald Gillespie, Beale joined Brigadier General Stephen Kearny's column just prior to the Battle of San Pascual on December 6, 1846. On that day, Californios surrounded Kearny's forces and began inflicting heavy casualties. Beale, along with legendary frontiersman Christopher "Kit" Carson, stole away through enemy lines and journeyed 28 miles to San Diego to bring reinforcements. Stockton immediately dispatched 200 sailors and marines who then dispersed the Californios and escorted Kearny's battered troops back to San Diego.

The following two years witnessed Beale undertaking six cross-country journeys delivering dispatches to and from American military forces and the federal government in Washington, D.C. Advanced to master on August 1, 1849, Beale achieved the rank of lieutenant on February 28, 1850. He resigned his commission on March 5, 1852, and returned to California.

During his remaining years, Beale was active in a number of areas. On March 3, 1853, President Millard Fillmore appointed him superintendent of Indian affairs for California and Nevada. In 1857, California governor John Bigler commissioned him with the rank of brigadier general in the California militia to facilitate peace treaties with Native Americans in the state. That same year, President James Buchanan selected Beale to survey a wagon road from Fort Defiance, New Mexico, to the Colorado River. During this expedition, he used camels imported from Tunis as pack animals to test their endurance in rugged terrain. In 1861, shortly after the outbreak of the Civil War, President Abraham Lincoln convinced

U.S. Navy officer Edward F. Beale and frontiersman Christopher ("Kit") Carson made their way through Mexican lines and walked 28 miles to San Diego to bring up reinforcements for the Americans besieged by Californian rebels following the Battle of San Pascual, December 6, 1846. (Library of Congress)

Beale to forego a Union Army command in favor of becoming surveyor general of California and Nevada.

At the conclusion of the Civil War in 1865, Beale retired to Rancho Tejon, a 270,000-acre estate he purchased in 1866, near present-day Bakersfield, California. In 1871, Beale purchased the house built by War of 1812 naval hero Stephen Decatur opposite the White House in Washington, D.C. In 1876, President Ulysses S. Grant appointed Beale as minister to Austria-Hungary, a post he held for one year. Beale died at Decatur House on April 22, 1893, and was buried in Chester, Pennsylvania. Beale Air Force Base in California is named in his honor.

CHARLES F. HOWLETT

See also

Californios; Carson, Christopher Houston "Kit"; Gillespie, Archibald H.; Kearny, Stephen Watts; San Pascual, Battle of; Stockton, Robert Field.

References

Bonsal, Stephen. *Edward Fitzgerald Beale, a Pioneer in the Path of Empire.* New York: G. P. Putnam's Sons, 1912.

Coy, Owen C. *The Battle of San Pasqual.* Sacramento: California State Printing Office, 1921.

Lesley, Lewis B. *Uncle Sam's Camels: The Journal of May Humphreys Stacy Supplemented by the Report of Edward Fitzgerald Beale (1857–1858).* Cambridge, MA: Harvard University Press, 1929.

Thompson, Gerald. *Edward F. Beale and the American West.* Albuquerque: University of New Mexico Press, 1983.

Bear Flag Revolt
Event Dates: June 14–July 9, 1846

Rebellion on June 14, 1846, among Americans living in Mexican-controlled Sonoma, California, that resulted in the short-lived Bear Flag Republic. From the time of Mexican independence in 1821, government officials in Mexico City never exerted much authority over Alta California, as California was then known. By 1845 California had a population of some 7,000 Californios, or people born in California of Hispanic ancestry. Most Californios considered themselves distinct, if not better, than other Mexicans. At the same time, a group of wealthy local families who owned vast tracts of land dominated the political economy in California. By the early 1840s, Mexican control of California was becoming weaker.

The 1844 election of James K. Polk to the American presidency convinced most Californio elites that their power would be jeopardized if their allegiance remained with the Mexican government. Polk's support of Manifest Destiny, in addition to British, French, and Russian territorial aspirations in the Pacific region, essentially forced the Californios to reconsider their political loyalties. Alta California's governor, Pío de Jesús Pico, favored the British, but the Mexican military commander there, Mariano Guadalupe Vallejo, favored the United States, as did a number of his supporters. Nevertheless, Vallejo was concerned by the presence of about 800 American settlers in California. These settlers, some of whom favored an independent California—a concept that Vallejo viewed as a threat to the established social order—became more agitated when rumors began to circulate in the fall of 1845 that the Mexican government was planning to expel all settlers who were not Mexican citizens.

Settlers in the Grigsby-Ide party were especially upset by these rumors. The group, led by trail boss John Grigsby and William B. Ide, initially planned to settle in Oregon. However, they were lured to the Sacramento Valley by an agent of John Sutter, who owned almost 50,000 acres in the region. Sutter, who envisioned building an agricultural utopian community, initially supported the French annexation of California but later sided with the settlers who favored independence.

The Grigsby-Ide party arrived at Sutter's Fort on October 25, 1845. While at Sutter's Fort, members of the Grigsby-Ide party, who were unable to purchase land in California because of a new Mexican law, met with U.S. Army captain John C. Frémont. Frémont had been exploring and mapping the region. Although documentation is lacking, it is probable that Frémont spread rumors of the Mexican plan to expel American settlers and encouraged the members of the Grigsby-Ide party to forcibly acquire land that the Mexican government would not sell to them.

At dawn on June 14, 1846, a group of about 30 disgruntled settlers, explorers, and trappers, initially led by fur trapper Ezekiel Merritt, arrived at Vallejo's fortified home in Sonoma. Rumors that Vallejo was planning to supply the Mexican governor with 300 horses convinced the settlers to attack. Clearly outnumbered, the pragmatic Vallejo quickly surrendered his residence. As the terms of capitulation were being agreed on, Vallejo offered the negotiating party large quantities of brandy. By the end of the day, the rebellious settlers who had remained outside the home had become disillusioned with the now inebriated Merritt and chose Ide as their leader. The rebels then escorted Vallejo and three other men in his home to Sutter's Fort, where Vallejo contracted malaria. After promising to remain neutral in the Mexican-American War, Vallejo and his friends were eventually released on August 1, 1846, and allowed to return to Vallejo's estate in Sonoma.

At dusk on June 14, the victorious settlers, unaware of the U.S. declaration of war on Mexico of May 13, 1846, proclaimed California independent of Mexico. To announce the new California Republic, commonly known as the Bear Flag Republic, the Bear Flaggers, as they became known, hoisted a flag made by Abraham Lincoln's nephew, William L. Todd. Todd had painted the flag on brown cloth. It had a lone red star, supposedly representing Texas, a red stripe, a poorly drawn grizzly bear, and the words "California Republic." Ironically, the bear was so crudely constructed that many who saw the flag thought that the bear was a pig. Although this flag was destroyed in the 1906 San Francisco earthquake, it served as the basis of California's current state flag.

The Bear Flaggers immediately proclaimed Ide their first president. Ide issued a proclamation, based on the U.S. Constitution and Declaration of Independence, which guaranteed liberty and freedom for everyone in California.

On July 7, 1846, Commodore John Sloat captured the port of Monterey, California, from the Mexicans. Sloat, who claimed California for the United States, informed Frémont that a state of war existed between Mexico and the United States. Two days later, on July 9, U.S. Navy lieutenant Joseph Warren Revere (Paul Revere's grandson) rode to Sonoma and informed the Bear Flaggers that the Mexican-American War had begun. Notwithstanding claims to all of California, rebel control had never extended beyond the immediate region of Sonoma. The Bear Flaggers now joined the American war effort, took down the Bear flag, and hoisted the American flag. Although the Bear Flag Republic lasted for only 25 days, it facilitated the U.S. occupation of California during the Mexican-American War.

MICHAEL R. HALL

See also

California; Frémont, John Charles; Ide, William Brown; Manifest Destiny; Pico, Pío de Jesús; Polk, James Knox; Sloat, John Drake; Sutter, John Augustus; Sutter's Fort; Vallejo, Mariano Guadalupe.

References

Jackson, Donald. *Expeditions of John Charles Frémont: The Bear Flag Revolt and the Court-Martial.* Urbana: University of Illinois Press, 1973.

Papp, Richard Paul. *Bear Flag Country: Legacy of the Revolt.* Santa Rosa, CA: Analecta, 1996.

Walker, Dale L. *Bear Flag Rising: The Conquest of California, 1846.* New York: Forge, 1999.

Warner, Barbara. *The Men of the California Bear Flag Revolt and Their Heritage.* Spokane, WA: Arthur H. Clark, 1996.

Beaubien, Carlos (Charles)
Birth Date: October 1800
Death Date: 1864

French Canadian trapper and trader who became a major landholder in New Mexico and Colorado. Born Alexis Beaubien in Saint-Jean-Baptiste de Nicolet, Quebec, in October 1800, Beaubien studied for the priesthood until the age of 20, at which time he changed his first name to Charles and moved to the vicinity of Saint Louis, Missouri, where he entered the trading business around 1823.

By the mid-1820s Beaubien had joined other traders, some of whom were fellow French Canadians, in Mexican-held New Mexico. He eventually settled in the area around Taos, became a prosperous fur trader, and learned Spanish. During this time, he again changed his first name, to Carlos—the Spanish equivalent of Charles. He then married a Mexican woman and became a vital part of New Mexico's economic and social fabric. Hoping to expand his business holdings, in 1840 he applied for a massive 1.7-million-acre land grant from the Mexican government, which New Mexican

governor Manuel Armijo approved in early 1841. The land grant was located on the eastern side of the Sangre de Cristo Mountains.

Several years later, Beaubien sold off part of his grant to Charles Bent in exchange for Bent's help in establishing ranches in other parts of New Mexico. In 1844 he received another land grant, this time in southern Colorado, which encompassed nearly 1 million acres. That grant was placed in his son's name because he had already received a land grant from the Mexican government.

In August 1846, when Brigadier General Stephen W. Kearny's army occupied New Mexico, Beaubien applauded the U.S. presence and vowed to cooperate with the occupation force. Recognizing the benefit in allying with Beaubien, General Kearny appointed him a judge in Charles Bent's U.S.-sponsored government. In January 1847, when the Taos Revolt broke out, which resulted in the murder of Governor Bent, Beaubien's son Narciso was among others killed in the initial wave of violence. After the insurrection was quelled several weeks later, Beaubien presided over the proceedings that sought to convict the insurrectionists, including those who had killed his son. Most were found guilty and hanged.

After the Mexican-American War ended in 1848, Beaubien remained an influential and well-connected New Mexican citizen. He largely retired from public life in 1851 but remained tied to his vast land holdings and other enterprises until his death in New Mexico in 1864.

PAUL G. PIERPAOLI JR.

See also

Bent, Charles; Kearny, Stephen Watts; New Mexico; Taos Revolt.

References

Twitchell, Ralph Emerson. *The History of the Military Occupation of the Territory of New Mexico.* New York: Arno Press, 1976.

Weber, David J. *The Taos Trappers.* Norman: University of Oklahoma Press, 1971.

Beauregard, Pierre Gustave Toutant
Birth Date: May 28, 1818
Death Date: February 20, 1893

U.S. and Confederate Army officer. Born into an important Louisiana family of Creole background in Saint Bernard Parish on May 28, 1818, Pierre Gustave Toutant Beauregard graduated second in his class from the U.S. Military Academy, West Point, in 1838. Commissioned a second lieutenant of engineers, his first assignment was to Fort Adams near Newport, Rhode Island, after which he made first lieutenant in June 1839. Helping to supervise the construction of coastal defenses, he was then stationed at Pensacola, Florida, and in Louisiana.

During the Mexican-American War, Beauregard served on the staff of Major General Winfield Scott and took part in his Mexico City Campaign, chiefly as a scout and engineer. Prior to the U.S. landing at Veracruz in March 1847, Beauregard and Captain Robert

E. Lee conducted reconnaissance to ascertain that city's defenses. That same month, Beauregard fell ill and was largely bedridden until early April. At the Battle of Cerro Gordo, he helped scout a route that allowed U.S. forces to outflank the Mexican army. Prior to the Battle of Contreras in August 1847, Beauregard and Lee opened a pathway though the *pedregal,* a massive lava field that protected the approaches to Mexico City. With the help of some 500 men, Lee and Beauregard cleared a pathway large enough to accommodate wagons and artillery. The Mexicans had believed the *pedregal* impassable and so did not expect the U.S. Army to take this route.

As American forces neared Mexico City, Beauregard was among the junior officers who helped convince General Scott that the capital city should be attacked via Chapultepec Castle. Beauregard was wounded twice during the Mexican-American War and was rewarded with a brevet to captain for his role in the Battles of Contreras and Churubusco and to major for the Battle of Chapultepec.

Following the war, Beauregard returned to New Orleans as a chief engineer. He also dabbled in Democratic politics. Beauregard became superintendent of West Point in January 1861. Only five days after assuming the position, however, Beauregard resigned when Louisiana seceded from the Union. He subsequently resigned his army commission, and, on March 1, 1861, he secured a commission as brigadier general in the Confederate Army. Assigned to Charleston, South Carolina, he commanded its defenses, confronting the Union enclave at Fort Sumter, where the first shots of the Civil War were fired.

During the First Battle of Bull Run, Beauregard commanded the Confederate Army of the Potomac and was advanced to full general on August 31, 1861. He then commanded the Potomac District of the Department of Northern Virginia (October 1861–January 1862). Continually disagreeing with Confederate president Jefferson Davis over military strategy, Beauregard was exiled to the Western Theater, where he served under Confederate commander General Albert S. Johnston. During the first day of the Battle of Shiloh (April 6–7, 1862), when Johnston was killed, Beauregard assumed command of attacking Confederate forces, but, in a controversial decision, he called off the attack, and Davis blamed him for the ensuing Confederate retreat.

When Beauregard became ill in June 1862, he relinquished command to General Braxton Bragg. Beauregard was subsequently relegated to command of the Department of South Carolina, Georgia, and Florida, with his headquarters at Charleston, which he ably defended against Union sea and land attacks. In April 1864, Beauregard was assigned command of the Department of North Carolina and Southern Virginia. In this position, he assisted General Robert E. Lee in the defense of Richmond. Beauregard continued to serve under Lee in an awkward command relationship until September, when Davis ordered Beauregard to command the Military Division of the West.

The last months of the war found Beauregard in a series of unredeemable situations as his subordinate General John Bell Hood carried out his disastrous campaign into Tennessee in late 1864. The end of the war found him second in command to General Joseph E. Johnson. He left the army in April 1865 and returned to New Orleans.

In the postwar years, Beauregard declined offers to command the armies of Romania and Egypt. He prospered in a variety of business ventures, including a railroad presidency, wrote his memoirs, and served in several public offices before his death in New Orleans on February 20, 1893.

STEVEN RAMOLD AND SPENCER C. TUCKER

See also

Chapultepec, Battle of; Churubusco, Battle of; Contreras, Battle of; Lee, Robert Edward; Mexico City Campaign; *Pedregal*; Scott, Winfield; Veracruz, Landing at and Siege of.

References

Basso, Hamilton. *Beauregard: The Great Creole.* New York: Scribner's, 1933.

Roman, Alfred. *The Military Operations of General Beauregard in the War between the States.* 2 vols. New York: Harper and Brothers, 1884.

Williams, T. Harry. *P. G. T. Beauregard: Napoleon in Gray.* Baton Rouge: Louisiana State University Press, 1954.

Williams, T. Harry, ed. *With Beauregard in Mexico: The Mexican War Reminiscences of P. G. T. Beauregard.* Baton Rouge: Louisiana State University Press, 1956.

Bee, Barnard Elliot
Birth Date: 1787
Death Date: April 9, 1853

Early Texas settler, politician, and diplomat for the Republic of Texas. Barnard Elliot Bee was born into a prominent family in Charleston, South Carolina, sometime in 1787. His father, Thomas Bee, was a delegate to the Continental Congress. Bee studied law in Charleston and served as an aide to South Carolina governor James Hamilton, his brother-in-law, from 1830 to 1832. During the Nullification Crisis of 1832, when South Carolina declared the Tariffs of 1828 and 1832 void in that state, Bee supported states' rights Democrats such as Vice President John C. Calhoun and James Hamilton. The Nullification Crisis, which epitomized the growing schism between North and South, convinced Bee that slavery, in order to survive, needed to expand. Therefore, during the early 1830s, for both economic and political reasons, Bee became interested in settling Texas. Shortly after the Battle of San Jacinto (April 21, 1836), the decisive clash in the Texas revolt against Mexico, Bee relocated to Texas and settled near the present city of Houston.

Bee joined the army of the Republic of Texas that same year but resigned within a few weeks to serve as secretary of the treasury in David Burnet's interim government. During Sam Houston's first term as president of Texas, from October 22, 1836, to December 10, 1838, Bee served as secretary of war. In 1837, Bee accompanied Mexican president Antonio López de Santa Anna, who had been taken prisoner after San Jacinto, to Washington, D.C. In 1838, after Sam Houston's political enemy Mirabeau B. Lamar became the president of Texas, Bee was appointed secretary of state. Early the next year, however, Bee resigned this position to enter the diplomatic service. That February Lamar sent Bee to Mexico to seek Mexican recognition of Texan independence. Bee was authorized to offer the Mexican government $5 million in return for official diplomatic recognition. Three months later, Mexican authorities, imbued with a reinvigorated sense of national pride following the conclusion of the so-called Pastry War, refused Bee's offer.

On April 20, 1840, Lamar appointed Bee as Texan minister plenipotentiary to the United States. Ill health, however, kept him away from Washington, D.C., for the rest of the year. Bee spent most of the time convalescing with his family in South Carolina. In 1841, Bee attempted to negotiate a treaty between Texas and Spain. He pointed out that an alliance between Spain and Texas was natural because both Spanish Cuba and Texas supported slavery. Although the Spanish government refused to enter into any such treaty, it did grant the Republic of Texas free trade with Cuba.

During the summer of 1841, Bee was able to negotiate a treaty of commerce and extradition with the United States, which was ratified on January 16, 1843. Houston, who favored annexation to the United States, was reelected president in 1841. Citing Bee's ill health, Houston removed Bee, who was against annexation, from his diplomatic position. Following the annexation of Texas to the United States in 1845, Bee returned to South Carolina, where he died near Charleston on April 9, 1853. He is buried in Saint Paul's Episcopal Churchyard in Pendleton, South Carolina.

MICHAEL R. HALL

See also

Houston, Samuel; Lamar, Mirabeau Buonaparte; Pastry War; Santa Anna, Antonio López de; Slavery; Texas; Texas Revolution.

References

Davis, William C. *Lone Star Rising: The Revolutionary Birth of the Republic of Texas.* New York: Free Press, 2004.

Lack, Paul D. *The Texas Revolutionary Experience: A Political and Social History, 1835–1836.* College Station: Texas A&M University Press, 1992.

Weems, John Edward. *Dream of Empire: A History of the Republic of Texas, 1836–1846.* New York: Barnes & Noble Books, 1995.

Wooten, Dudley Goodall, ed. *A Comprehensive History of Texas.* Austin: Texas State Historical Association, 1987.

Belknap, William Goldsmith

Birth Date: September 7, 1794
Death Date: November 10, 1851

U.S. Army general who served in the War of 1812, the Second Seminole War (1835–1842), and achieved distinction during the Mexican-American War. A career soldier, William Goldsmith Belknap was born in Newburgh, New York, on September 7, 1794. At age 19, during the War of 1812, he was commissioned a second lieutenant in the 23rd Infantry on April 5, 1813. Nine years later he was promoted to the rank of captain and served with the 3rd Infantry Regiment. Belknap was promoted to major in 1842, and his actions in the Second Seminole War led to him being brevetted lieutenant colonel that March.

Following the U.S. annexation of Texas, Belknap was assigned to Brigadier General Zachary Taylor's Army of Occupation at Corpus Christi. On May 1, 1846, Taylor gave him temporary command of a brigade. At the May 9, 1846, Battle of Resaca de la Palma fought against General Mariano Arista's Army of the North, Belknap led his brigade from the front and seized a Mexican battle flag. His leadership earned Belknap a brevet promotion to colonel that same day.

Belknap also played an important role in the Battle of Buena Vista on February 23, 1847, when his men were instrumental in repulsing assaults by Mexican troops led by General Antonio López de Santa Anna. The day after the battle, Belknap was brevetted brigadier general. Subsequently, he was appointed inspector general on Major General Taylor's staff for the duration of the war.

After the conclusion of the Mexican-American War in 1848, Belknap reverted to his original rank of lieutenant colonel and was placed in command of the 5th Infantry Regiment. He then had charge of Fort Gibson in Indian Territory (Oklahoma) as commander of Military District Number Seven, north of Texas and Louisiana, from December 1848 through May 1851. He died

Lieutenant Colonel William Belknap, a career army officer who had fought in the War of 1812 and the Second Seminole War, played a key role in the U.S. victories of Resaca de la Palma and Buena Vista. (Library of Congress)

while commanding a post in Young County, Texas, on November 10, 1851. The post was renamed Fort Belknap in his honor. His son, William Worth Belknap, later became secretary of war in the Ulysses S. Grant administration.

CHARLES F. HOWLETT

See also
Arista, Mariano; Buena Vista, Battle of; Palo Alto, Battle of; Resaca de la Palma, Battle of; Santa Anna, Antonio López de; Taylor, Zachary.

References
Heitman, Francis B. *Historical Register and Dictionary of the United States Army: From Its Organization, September 29, 1789, to March 2, 1903.* Washington, DC: Government Printing Office, 1903.
Ledbetter, Barbara A. *General William Goldsmith Belknap (1794–1851), Fort Belknap, Young County, Texas.* Archer City, TX: McCrain, 1975.
Smith, George Winston, and Charles Judah, eds. *Chronicles of the Gringos: The U.S. Army in the Mexican War, 1846–1848.* Albuquerque: University of New Mexico Press, 1966.
Smith, Justin. *The War with Mexico.* 2 vols. New York: Macmillan, 1919.

Bell, Peter Hansbrough
Birth Date: May 12, 1812
Death Date: March 8, 1898

American politician who served as the third governor of Texas from 1849 to 1853. Born on May 12, 1812, at Culpeper in Spotsylvania County, Virginia, Peter Hansbrough Bell attended public schools in Virginia before moving to Texas in 1836 to fight in the Texas Revolution against Mexico (1835–1836). During that brief conflict, he served as a private in a cavalry company and saw action at the Battle of San Jacinto on April 26, 1836. After the proclamation of Texas independence later that year, Bell served as adjutant general and inspector general of Texan forces (in 1837 and 1839, respectively).

Bell joined the Texas Rangers in 1840 and two years later served in the Somervell Expedition, a punitive raid against Mexico in retaliation for three predatory expeditions made by Mexican military forces against Texas. At the outset of the Mexican-American War in 1846, Bell was commander of the Corpus Christi District. He subsequently served as a lieutenant colonel in the 2nd Texas Mount Rifles, a regiment led by Colonel George T. Wood, and fought at the Battle of Buena Vista on February 22–23, 1847. By the end of the war, Bell had rejoined the Texas Rangers to protect the Rio Grande frontier.

In the 1849 gubernatorial election Bell defeated fellow Democrat George T. Wood, who had been elected Texas governor in 1847. Wood's defeat was due in large part to his failure to resolve the boundary dispute with the New Mexico Territory. The major event during Bell's four-year tenure as governor was the resolution of this dispute, which occurred in 1850.

The controversy had begun with the Boundary Act of 1836, a Texas law that had proclaimed the entire length of the Rio Grande as the southern and western boundary of the newly created Republic of Texas. The 1848 Treaty of Guadalupe Hidalgo had confirmed the Rio Grande as the southern boundary of Texas, but by 1850 the people of the New Mexico Territory had ratified a proposed constitution that defined the boundaries of the territory to include lands claimed by Texas.

Bell now convened a special session of the Texas legislature to enforce the state's claims. Meanwhile, he had requested troops to occupy Santa Fe, and the governor of Mississippi promised help if the federal government sent troops to intervene. President Millard Fillmore warned Bell that any attempt to impose Texan control by force over the disputed region would be met with intervention by the U.S. Army. A series of bills were then presented in the U.S. Congress in an attempt to diffuse the volatile situation. One measure proposed by Maryland senator James A. Pearce, a Whig, offered Texas $10 million in exchange for ceding 67 million acres of disputed territory. The compromise was acceptable to the federal government and the Texan legislature. Half the payment was designated to pay the outstanding foreign debt accrued by the Republic of Texas. Texan voters accepted the compromise by a 3–1 majority, and Bell signed the act on November 25, 1850.

A few months before the end of his second gubernatorial term, Bell resigned to take a vacant seat in the U.S. House of Representatives. After serving two terms, Bell declined to run for a third in 1856 and returned to Texas. In March 1857 Bell married Ella Reeves Eaton Dickens and moved to Warrenton, North Carolina, to manage her father's estate. During the Civil War Bell served as a colonel in the Confederate Army. In 1890 the Bells sold their property in Warrenton and moved to Littleton, North Carolina, where Bell died on March 8, 1898.

MICHAEL R. HALL

See also
Buena Vista, Battle of; Fillmore, Millard; Guadalupe Hidalgo, Treaty of; New Mexico; San Jacinto, Battle of; Texas; Texas Rangers; Texas Revolution.

References
Cutrer, Thomas W., ed. "'A Lion in Her Path': Texas, New Mexico, and the United States Army, 1850." *Military History of the West*, no. 34 (2005): 75–80.
Keleher, William A. *Turmoil in New Mexico, 1846–1868.* Santa Fe, NM: Sunstone Press, 2007.
Stegmaier, Mark J. *Texas, New Mexico, and the Compromise of 1850: Boundary Dispute and Sectional Crisis.* Kent, OH: Kent State University Press, 1996.

Bent, Charles
Birth Date: November 11, 1799
Death Date: January 17, 1847

American pioneer and merchant who in 1846 served as the first civilian governor under American rule of the New Mexico Territory. Born on November 11, 1799, in Charleston, West Virginia, Charles Bent moved to Saint Louis, Missouri, with his family in

One of the most prominent citizens and businessmen in New Mexico at the beginning of the Mexican-American War, Charles Bent became the first civilian governor of that territory when it passed under American control. (Mercaldo Archives)

1806. Bent joined the Missouri Fur Company in 1822, becoming a partner three years later. Finding too much competition in the Missouri fur trade, Bent and his brother William led a trading expedition down the Santa Fe Trail in 1828.

Discovering trade in Mexican-controlled New Mexico to be profitable, the Bent brothers formed the Bent and St. Vrain Company with local fur trader Ceran St. Vrain in 1832. The company subsequently built a series of fortified trading posts along the Santa Fe Trail, the most important of which was a massive adobe brick structure at La Junta, Colorado, called Bent's Fort (or Bent's Old Fort), constructed between 1833 and 1834. Located just across the Arkansas River on the boundary between Mexico and the United States, Bent's Old Fort would be an important staging ground for military expeditions into New Mexico during the Mexican-American War.

In 1835, Bent, who had a very low opinion of local Latinos, built his home in Taos, New Mexico. In August 1846 Brigadier General Stephen Watts Kearny's force of 1,700 American troops captured Santa Fe without encountering any resistance. On September 22 of that year, Kearny, before departing for California, appointed Bent as territorial governor of the New Mexico Territory. Bent was determined to efficiently govern the territory and immediately

requested money from Washington, D.C., to create schools, a mail system, and other essential services. Ignoring warnings from locals in Santa Fe that he should remain there, Bent returned to his home in Taos in early January 1847. Unbeknownst to Bent, a group of disaffected Mexicans was plotting to overthrow the American regime and kill him.

On January 17, a group of *nuevo mexicanos* and Native American insurrectionists murdered Bent and several of his friends at his home, thus igniting the Taos Revolt, a local insurrection against American rule. Before it could be quashed, the revolt saw the death of 17 other Anglo-Americans. Sixteen of the leaders of the Taos Revolt were eventually captured, tried, convicted, and hanged in a square in Taos.

MICHAEL R. HALL

See also

Bent, William; Bent's Old Fort; Kearny, Stephen Watts; New Mexico; Santa Fe; Taos Revolt.

References

Crutchfield, James A. *Tragedy at Taos: The Revolt of 1847*. San Antonio: Republic of Texas Press, 1995.

McNierny, Michael, ed. *Taos 1847: The Revolt in Contemporary Accounts*. Boulder, CO: Johnson, 1980.

Bent, William

Birth Date: May 23, 1809
Death Date: May 19, 1869

American fur trapper and merchant who managed Old Bent's Fort, a privately owned fortified trading post of the Bent and St. Vrain Company, located on the border between the United States and Mexico along the Arkansas River (modern-day southeastern Colorado). Born on May 23, 1809, in Saint Louis, Missouri, William Bent was the younger brother of Charles Bent (who briefly served as governor of the New Mexico Territory until he was murdered at the start of the Taos Revolt in 1847). In 1832, the Bent brothers formed the Bent and St. Vrain Company with Ceran St. Vrain and built a series of fortified trading posts along the Santa Fe Trail, the most important being a massive adobe brick structure at La Junta, Colorado, called Bent's Old Fort (or Bent's Fort). Located just across the Arkansas River on the boundary between Mexico and the United States, Bent's Fort, constructed in 1833, facilitated trade with New Mexico as well as with local Native Americans. In 1835, William Bent married a Cheyenne woman and established friendly relations with Cheyenne chief Black Kettle, which further increased trade with the local Native American population.

During the Mexican-American War, Bent's Fort served as an important staging area for military expeditions into New Mexico. Bent, however, became annoyed by the outbreak of disease caused by the presence of so many American troops at the fort. After the war, Bent offered to sell the fort to the United States, but the War

Department refused the offer because the fort's strategic value had greatly diminished once the U.S.-Mexico boundary had been moved much farther south as a result of the Treaty of Guadalupe Hidalgo. On August 21, 1849, a disgruntled Bent burned Fort Bent and terminated his business relationship with St. Vrain. Bent died on May 19, 1869, in Westport, Kansas.

MICHAEL R. HALL

See also

Bent, Charles; Guadalupe Hidalgo, Treaty of; Santa Fe–Chihuahua Trail; Taos Revolt.

References

Crutchfield, James A. *Tragedy at Taos: The Revolt of 1847.* San Antonio: Republic of Texas Press, 1995.

Lavender, David. *Bent's Fort.* Lincoln: University of Nebraska Press, 1972.

Benton, Thomas Hart
Birth Date: March 14, 1782
Death Date: April 10, 1858

Attorney, Democratic Party politician, and one of the chief U.S. proponents of Manifest Destiny. Thomas Hart Benton was born on March 14, 1782, in Hillsboro, North Carolina, the oldest of seven children. His father died when Benton was eight years old, leaving the boy as the oldest male of the family. Benton attended the University of North Carolina and the College of William and Mary.

In 1801 Benton moved to Tennessee to tend to a family estate, known as Widow Benton's Settlement, near Nashville. He was admitted to the state bar four years later and commenced a legal practice in 1805. He was elected to the Tennessee Senate in 1809, where he became involved in land ownership issues and the rights of slaves in capital trials, and served until 1811.

After serving as a colonel in the War of 1812, Benton moved to Saint Louis, Missouri, where he practiced law and became editor of the *St. Louis Enquirer.* In 1820 he was elected to the U.S. Senate from Missouri, a seat he would hold for 30 years. Benton stood against restricting slavery in that state, but by 1828 he had come to favor the gradual abolition of slavery. As a firm advocate of acquiring new territory and nationally improving road and river communications, Benton was beginning to view slavery as an impediment to the development of the West, an issue that quickly attained prominence in his political agenda. Benton tirelessly promoted the career of his controversial son-in-law, John C. Frémont, a western explorer who had married his daughter Jessie in October 1841. Although initially opposed to the union, Benton avidly followed Frémont's exploits and shared his son-in-law's interest in the development of the West.

An advocate of Andrew Jackson's Democratic Party, Benton supported Jackson's position on the Tariff of 1828 and his decision to compel South Carolina to accept the tariff. Always the moderate, Benton believed in the rights of states, but not in nullification.

Thomas Hart Benton served as a U.S. senator from Missouri for 30 years. One of the most prominent statesmen of the antebellum period, he was a staunch advocate of Manifest Destiny. (Library of Congress)

Once again following Jackson's lead, Benton was the Senate floor leader during Jackson's war on the national bank, an institution Benton thought bred inequalities. Nicknamed "Old Bullion," Benton avidly backed gold coinage and paying for public lands in hard currency and thus opposed the national bank's power to issue notes. In 1831 he introduced a resolution opposing the scheduled rechartering of the national bank and endorsed removal of government deposits prior to the expiration of the charter. His support undermined congressional efforts to override Jackson's veto of the bank charter.

During the mid-1830s, Benton was initially opposed to the annexation of Texas because it was tied to the expansion of slavery, but he later—and reluctantly—accepted Texas statehood as part of a larger design for Manifest Destiny. In 1845 Benton had urged the formation of a presidential commission tasked with negotiating a peaceful annexation of Texas with the Mexican government. When that failed, Benton, a doggedly loyal Democrat and confidant of President James K. Polk, cast a reluctant vote for war with Mexico in May 1846. Indeed, he believed that the potential annexation of California and New Mexico far outweighed the drawbacks of U.S. expansion into the Southwest. During the war, Benton met often with Polk, advising him on matters involving the military as well as politics. As the war progressed, however, and Major General Zachary Taylor's triumphs in northern Mexico did not result in a Mexican capitulation, he grew exasperated with the conflict and pushed Polk into authorizing the Mexico City Campaign in early 1847. Polk offered Benton a commission as major general in 1847, but Benton refused because he would not have overall command of U.S. troops in Mexico.

By early 1848, Benton and Polk had had a falling out over the court-martial of Benton's son-in-law, John Frémont, who had been brought up on charges of insubordination in a feud with Brigadier General Stephen W. Kearny. Benton was furious that Polk had approved of the tribunal, even though the president later pardoned Frémont, who had been found guilty. Largely out of spite, Benton refused to vote for the 1848 Treaty of Guadalupe Hidalgo during the ratification process.

While opposed to outright abolition, Benton endorsed the right of Congress to legislate on slavery in the territories. Eventually, he began to see the intransigent defense of slavery by Southern leadership as a grave threat to peace and the preservation of the Union. Benton's opposition to southern demands during the debate on the Compromise of 1850 cost him his support in Missouri, and he lost the Senate seat he had held for 30 years. Though he had championed such essential western interests as the Pony Express, the telegraph, and the building of a transcontinental railroad, his constituents could not tolerate what they saw as his antislavery views.

Undeterred, Benton won a seat in the House of Representatives in 1852, and there he fought against the repeal of the Missouri Compromise (necessary for the passage of the Compromise of 1850), only to lose his seat there as well in 1854. He was defeated in a run for the Missouri governorship in 1856 and retired from political life to write several books. Benton died on April 10, 1858, in Washington, D.C.

STEVEN G. O'BRIEN AND PAUL G. PIERPAOLI JR.

See also

Benton-Brown Compromise; Congress, U.S.; Democratic Party; Frémont, John Charles; Guadalupe Hidalgo, Treaty of; Manifest Destiny; Politics, U.S.; Polk, James Knox; Slavery.

References

Benton, Thomas H. *Thirty Years View, or, A History of the American Government for Thirty Years from 1820–1850*. 2 vols. 1854, 1856. Reprint, New York: Greenwood Press, 1968.

Clary, David A. *Eagles and Empire: The United States, Mexico, and the Struggle for a Continent*. New York: Bantam Books, 2009.

Smith, Elbert B. *Magnificent Missourian: Thomas Hart Benton*. Philadelphia: Lippincott, 1957.

Benton-Brown Compromise
Event Date: 1845

Congressional measure that reconciled a measure advocated by Whig representative Milton Brown of Tennessee and another advocated by Democratic senator Thomas Hart Benton of Missouri to bring about the U.S. annexation of Texas. Brown's resolution passed the House of Representatives on January 25, 1845, by a vote of 128–98; Benton's resolution passed the Senate on February 27, 1848, by a narrow two-vote margin (27–25).

Buoyed by the recent victory of the pro-expansion Democrats in the November 1844 election, expansionist-minded congressmen rushed to bring about the annexation of Texas during the new legislative session that began in January 1845. Brown, an expansionist Whig, presented his resolution in mid-January. It called for the immediate annexation of Texas but was silent on several controversial issues, including the boundary dispute with Mexico, the absorption of the Republic of Texas's debts, and the disposition of public lands.

Meanwhile, the annexation issue faced a more difficult test in the Senate because that body was controlled by Whigs, many of whom were against expansion and annexation. Although Senator Benton had previously pushed for the annexation of Texas, he had tempered that position by insisting that such a move be undertaken only with Mexican advice and consent. Benton then came under great pressure to push for annexation without such a stipulation. Thus, he offered a resolution that would create a presidential commission of five individuals who would help secure Texas annexation. This proposal did not, however, advocate immediate annexation.

In an effort to avoid a deadlock between the House and Senate, several senators, including Robert J. Walker (Democrat, Mississippi) and William Allen (Democrat, Ohio), heavily lobbied their colleagues to pass an annexation measure that would employ Benton's proposal as a way to reconcile the House and Senate annexation efforts. The resulting bill would empower the president to either grant immediate annexation or choose to pursue further negotiations using a presidential commission. On February 27, the Senate narrowly endorsed the Benton-Brown Compromise, with the House concurring the following day. On March 1, 1845, President John Tyler signed the legislation into law; he chose to seek immediate annexation of Texas without further negotiations. On July 4, the Texas Convention endorsed the proposal, and by year's end Texas was admitted to the Union.

PAUL G. PIERAPAOLI JR.

See also

Benton, Thomas Hart; Congress, U.S.; Democratic Party; Expansionism and Imperialism; Texas; Whigs.

References

Clary, David A. *Eagles and Empire: The United States, Mexico, and the Struggle for a Continent*. New York: Bantam Books, 2009.

Eisenhower, John S. D. *So Far from God: The U.S. War with Mexico, 1846–1848*. New York: Free Press, 1997.

Merk, Frederick. *Slavery and the Annexation of Texas*. New York: Alfred A. Knopf, 1972.

Bent's Old Fort

Major staging area for U.S. military operations against Mexico during the Mexican-American War. In 1833, William Bent, Charles Bent, and Ceran St. Vrain constructed Bent's Old Fort in modern-day southeastern Colorado, on the north bank of the upper Arkansas River, as a convenient base for their burgeoning trade with Native Americans. The fort became a frequent stopping place for

Illustration of Bent's Old Fort on the Santa Fe Trail, ca. 1845. (Library of Congress)

travelers on the Santa Fe Trail and was in fact the only such haven between Independence, Missouri, and Santa Fe, New Mexico.

In early 1846 relations between the United States and Mexico grew tense over disputed territory in West Texas and along the Rio Grande. Mexico's refusal to sell California also increased tensions. To demonstrate American readiness for war, President James K. Polk sent a number of military expeditions into the disputed territory. Colonel Stephen Watts Kearny led 250 dragoons westward along the Oregon Trail, then southward to Bent's Old Fort, where he replenished supplies before returning eastward. Shortly after Kearny's departure, two survey parties passed through Bent's Old Fort, one led by Lieutenant Colonel John C. Frémont on the way to California, the other by Lieutenant J. W. Albert, bound southward toward the Washita and Canadian Rivers. All these activities, while lucrative for the owners of Bent's Old Fort, nevertheless disrupted local trade and Native American life.

On May 13, 1846, the United States declared war on Mexico. Kearny, with his Army of the West at Fort Leavenworth, was ordered to march west to conquer New Mexico, Arizona, and California. To the chagrin of the Bent brothers and St. Vrain, Kearny appropriated Bent's Old Fort as a rendezvous point for his supply columns and troops. The partners were powerless to stop him.

By late July 1846 Kearny's forces had converged on the fort and had to be accommodated, even though the facility was not stocked to serve such large numbers. Army officers vied for space to camp and graze their horses, and quartermasters demanded storage and repair facilities. Traders traveling with the army worried about their markets. Soon the company's business was ruined, its storerooms stripped, and its repair shops gutted.

Kearny marched south toward Santa Fe on August 2 and captured that city 16 days later. He then named Charles Bent governor of the territory and marched on to California. Bent was assassinated on January 19, 1847, during the Taos Revolt. Two years later, William Bent and St. Vrain abandoned Bent's Old Fort because disease and the removal of many of the local Native American tribes had destroyed their business. Six years later, Bent constructed Bent's New Fort at Big Timber, 40 miles down the Arkansas River.

PAUL DAVID NELSON

See also

Colorado; Frémont, John Charles; Kearny, Stephen Watts; Polk, James Knox; Santa Fe; Santa Fe–Chihuahua Trail; Taos Revolt; Trade.

References

Comer, Douglas C. *Ritual Ground: Bent's Old Fort, World Formation, and the Annexation of the Southwest.* Berkeley: University of California Press, 1996.

Garst, Shannon. *William Bent and His Adobe Empire.* New York: Messner, 1957.

Lavender, David. *Bent's Fort.* Garden City, NY: Doubleday, 1954.

Bermúdez de Castro, Salvador
Birth Date: August 6, 1817
Death Date: March 23, 1883

Spanish poet, historian, diplomat, and minister to Mexico, 1844–1847. Born at Jerez de la Frontera, Cádiz, Spain, on August 6, 1817, into an aristocratic family, Salvador Bermúdez de Castro dabbled in writing history and poetry, publishing *Ensayos poéticos* in 1840. He assumed his duties as Spanish minister to Mexico in 1844, bearing oral instructions from Spanish first minister Ramón María Narváez to restore a monarchy in that country. Spanish and Mexican conservatives clung to the notion that Mexico's only hope for political stability lay in the crowning of a European prince—preferably a Spanish Bourbon—as its king, although Spain's own recent political history hardly proved that monarchy was necessarily conducive to stability.

Bermúdez de Castro found an enthusiastic coconspirator in Lucas Alamán y Escalada, Mexico's most eminent conservative intellectual and statesman. Bermúdez de Castro and Alamán persuaded General Mariano Paredes y Arrillaga to seize power and convene a promonarchist congress, which then would invite Spain to send a prince to Mexico. In support of the plot, Spain sent warships to Havana and placed funds in the Cuban treasury to cover expenses. Bermúdez assured his home government that the scheme would gain resounding support from Mexican conservatives, the Catholic Church, and wealthy Mexican property owners. The Spanish government, for its part, believed that a Spanish prince on the Mexican throne would help obstruct U.S. expansionism and aid Spanish commercial interests in Mexico.

The rebellion began on December 14, 1845, and General Paredes assumed leadership of the movement the following day. The rebels charged that the government of José Joaquín Herrera was planning to receive American envoy John Slidell, with whom it intended to negotiate the cession of Texas and thus avoid what Paredes called "a glorious and necessary war." Their proclamations did not mention monarchism but called instead for the new Congress to adopt a constitution that best suited the nation. Paredes and the rebels then marched toward Mexico City, and on December 30 Herrera resigned.

Nearly one month later, on January 24, 1846, Bermúdez de Castro and Alamán founded *El tiempo* to publicize their views. They sought support from the Britith minister, Charles Bankhead, but were rebuffed. Bermúdez de Castro also urged his home government to broach the topic of a Mexican monarchy with England and France, both of which declared they would welcome such a regime should the Mexican people freely choose that option. Unfortunately for Bermúdez de Castro and his fellow conspirators, the success of the plan depended on Paredes, who had become interim president in early January, remaining in office, which, in turn, hinged on Mexico's successful prosecution of the war with the United States. After news arrived in the capital of Mexico's defeat in the first battles of the war in mid-May, Paredes jettisoned the idea of transforming Mexico into a monarchy and instead sought to remain in office by portraying himself as a staunch defender of republicanism. *El tiempo* ceased publication, and the monarchist conspiracy was abandoned.

The failed monarchist plot in Mexico accomplished little beyond providing a particularly compelling demonstration of the dysfunction of Mexico's political system as it embarked on war with the United States. It also demonstrated that there was little popular support in Mexico for the idea of importing a Spanish prince.

Bermúdez de Castro went on to serve as Spain's ambassador to the Court of Naples (Two Sicilies) (1853–1864) and Paris (1865–1866). He died in Rome on March 23, 1883.

TIMOTHY J. HENDERSON

See also

Alamán y Escalada, Lucas; Diplomacy, Mexican; Diplomacy, U.S.; Herrera, José Joaquín de; Mexico; Paredes y Arrillaga, Mariano; Politics, Mexican; Slidell, John; Spain.

References

Delgado, Jaime. *La monarquía en México (1845–1847)*. Mexico City: Editorial Porrúa, 1990.

Pletcher, David M. *The Diplomacy of Annexation: Texas, Oregon, and the Mexican War*. Columbia: University of Missouri Press, 1973.

Santoni, Pedro. *Mexicans at Arms: Puro Federalists and the Politics of War, 1845–1848*. Fort Worth: Texas Christian University Press, 1996.

Soto, Miguel. *La conspiración monárquica en México, 1845–1846*. México: EOSA, 1988.

Béxar, Siege of
Event Date: December 1835

Early engagement of the Texas Revolution that secured the town of San Antonio de Béxar (or Béjar) (now San Antonio) and the Alamo. The Siege of Béxar was undertaken by a volunteer Texan army during December 5–9, 1835. By 1835 the Americans living in the Mexican province of Texas (Coahuila y Texas) had become increasingly disillusioned with the central government in Mexico, particularly given its decision to set up a centralist republic. In early October American settlers gathered in Gonzales to stop Mexican troops from seizing a small cannon. The resulting clash (known as the Battle of Gonzales) launched the Texas Revolution. American volunteers continued to assemble in Gonzales and soon established the Texan army. They elected well-respected local leader Stephen F. Austin as their commander with the rank of colonel, despite his overall lack of military experience.

Since 1803 the Mexican army had maintained a garrison at the Alamo, a former Roman Catholic monastery built in 1724 just outside the village of San Antonio de Béxar. In mid-October 1835 an informal army of some 400 Texas volunteers encamped near the town, resulting in a virtual standoff with the Mexican garrison of about 750 soldiers, commanded by Mexican general Martín Perfecto de Cos, who was also Santa Anna's brother-in-law. By mid-November the Texan army was running short of supplies, and Austin, along with two other commissioners, left the camp bound for the United States in hope of obtaining both support and recognition.

By then the various commanders at Béxar were divided in their desire to take the village. Lieutenant Colonel Edward Burleson, the overall commander, proposed that the Texans withdraw to Goliad for the winter. However, Colonels Benjamin R. Milam and Francis

W. Johnson, with some 300 volunteers of their own, arrived at Béxar before dawn on December 5 and strongly opposed a retreat. Milam asked for volunteers to assault the now fortified village, and some 300 responded. Burleson led another 400 men to protect the Texans' supply line, forcing Cos to divide his forces between the town and the Alamo.

Early on December 5, the Texans, led by Milam and Johnson, began their attack. They skirmished with the Mexican soldiers for two days against heavy odds, as they were outnumbered in both numbers of men and artillery. On December 7 Milam died after being shot by a sniper. His death seemed to inspire the Texans, however, as they engaged in house-to-house combat in the town for the next two days. As a result, on December 9 Cos asked for surrender terms. The Texans lost only 4 men killed, including Milam, and 15 wounded during the siege. Mexican losses are not known.

According to the terms of the capitulation signed on December 11, 1835, Cos agreed not to engage Texan forces in the future and to withdraw beyond the Rio Grande with his men. Their departure effectively removed the last Mexican soldiers from Texas. The Texans secured all of the public property, including guns and ammunition, in San Antonio, and they now controlled one of the most important strongholds in Texas. Convinced that the war was over, most members of the Texan army returned to their homes. Within a few months, however, a much larger Mexican army, personally led by General Antonio López de Santa Anna, returned to Texas to retake the town during the bloody siege and Battle of the Alamo (February 23–March 6, 1836). The Texan army later reversed this by capturing both Santa Anna and General Cos in the Battle of San Jacinto.

ROBERT B. KANE

See also

Alamo, Battle of the; Austin, Stephen Fuller; Burleson, Edward; Cos, Martín Perfecto de; Gonzales, Battle of; San Jacinto, Battle of; Santa Anna, Antonio López de; Texas Revolution.

References

Barr, Alwyn. *Texans in Revolt: The Battle for San Antonio, 1835.* Austin: University of Texas Press, 1990.

Davis, William C. *Three Roads to the Alamo.* New York: Harper Collins, 1998.

Hardin, Stephen L. *Texian Iliad: A Military History of the Texas Revolution.* Austin: University of Texas Press, 1994.

Biddle, James
Birth Date: February 18, 1783
Death Date: October 1, 1848

U.S. Navy captain. James Biddle was born into a prominent Philadelphia family on February 18, 1783. Between 1798 and 1800 he attended the University of Pennsylvania but did not earn a degree. Biddle received a warrant as a midshipman in the navy on February 14, 1800. During the Quasi-War with France (1798–1800) he served under Captain Thomas Truxtun.

Although President Thomas Jefferson reduced the size of the navy in 1801, Biddle was one of 150 midshipmen selected to remain in the service. Assigned to the frigate *Philadelphia,* he served in the Mediterranean in the war against Tripoli under Captain William Bainbridge. On October 31, 1803, while in pursuit of a Tripolitan vessel off Tripoli, the *Philadelphia* ran aground on Kaliusa Reef, an uncharted sandbar. Bainbridge was subsequently forced to surrender his ship, and Biddle was held captive at Tripoli with the rest of the ship's crew until June 1805. Promoted to lieutenant on February 11, 1807, he served on gunboat duty until he was assigned as first lieutenant to Commander Jacob Jones in the sloop of war *Wasp.*

During the War of 1812, off the Virginia coast, the *Wasp* defeated and captured the British sloop *Frolic* on October 18, 1812. Biddle had charge of the boarding party and personally took down the British flag. Both ships were severely damaged in the engagement and shortly thereafter were recaptured by the British ship of the line *Poictiers.* Biddle was then held prisoner with Jones and the remainder of the crew in Bermuda for two weeks until a prisoner exchange could be arranged.

Promoted to commander on March 6, 1813, following his release, Biddle received command of the sloop *Hornet,* but because of the British blockade, he was not able to get his ship to sea until November 1814. On March 23, 1815, the *Hornet* defeated the slightly larger *Penguin* off the coast of Tristan da Cunha in the south Atlantic. During the encounter, Biddle was severely wounded. Later the British ship of the line *Cornwallis* chased the *Wasp* for several hours, and the American ship was able to escape only because Biddle ordered its cannon thrown overboard. Biddle returned his ship to New York City to receive a gold medal and promotion to captain on February 28, 1815.

In August 1818, the Navy Department sent Biddle to the Columbia River to lay formal claim to the Oregon Territory for the United States. In 1830, Biddle participated in negotiating the first commercial treaty between the United States and the Ottoman Empire.

In March 1845, Secretary of the Navy George Bancroft gave Biddle command of the East India Squadron. On December 25, 1845, Biddle's flagship, the ship of the line *Columbus,* arrived off the coast of Canton, China. On December 31, Biddle helped formalize the Treaty of Wangxia (1844), the first written diplomatic agreement between China and the United States. In July 1846, he sailed into the mouth of Tokyo Bay in an attempt to open Japan to American trade, but the Japanese rebuffed his efforts.

In September 1846, the navy recalled the *Columbus* to the United States for the war with Mexico. A northern Whig, Biddle personally opposed the war, which he viewed as a southern plot initiated by President James K. Polk to expand slavery. On March 3, 1847, Commodore Biddle arrived in Monterey, California, in the *Columbus* and encountered rivalry among the U.S. military leaders. As senior U.S. military officer in California until July 25, 1847,

Biddle selected Captain William Shubrick over Captain Robert Stockton to command U.S. naval operations along the California coast. Biddle canceled Stockton's ineffectual paper blockade of the entire Mexican Pacific coast and ordered an effective blockade of Mazatlán and Guaymas. He also ordered Shubrick to capture towns in Baja California and to treat the Mexicans with respect.

Biddle sailed for Hampton Roads, Virginia, on July 25, 1847. He died of unknown causes at his brother's estate of Andalusia just north of Philadelphia on October 1, 1848.

MICHAEL R. HALL AND SPENCER C. TUCKER

See also

Baja California; Bancroft, George; Blockade, Naval; California; California Theater of War, Overview; Monterey, California; Shubrick, William Branford; Stockton, Robert Field.

References

Harlow, Neal. *California Conquered: The Annexation of a Mexican Province, 1846–1850.* Berkeley: University of California Press, 1989.

Henson, Curtis T. *Commissioners and Commodores: The East India Squadron and American Diplomacy in China.* Tuscaloosa: University of Alabama Press, 1982.

Long, David F. *Sailor-Diplomat: A Biography of Commodore James Biddle, 1783–1848.* Boston: Northeastern University Press, 1983.

Billings, Eliza Allen
Birth Date: January 27, 1826
Death Date: Unknown

American author who published a memoir titled *The Female Volunteer, or, The Life, Wonderful Adventures and Miraculous Escapes of Miss Eliza Allen, a Young Lady of Eastport, Maine* (1851). The book describes the purported experiences of a young woman fighting with the U.S. Army during the Mexican-American War. Born on January 27, 1826, into an elite family in Eastport, Maine, Eliza Allen fell in love with William Billings, a common laborer and Canadian immigrant who worked for Allen's father. The Allen family, horrified at their daughter's infatuation with Billings, was pleased that the young man enlisted in the U.S. Army at the outbreak of the Mexican-American War in 1846.

Allen supposedly disguised herself as a man and enlisted in the U.S. Army. Most women who attempted this venture, however, were promptly discovered and sent home. Allen's entertaining memoir, however, claims that the young woman served in combat and was wounded in battle at Cerro Gordo. Although possible, but not very probable, the memoir is a dramatic tale that culminates with Allen's marriage to Billings after the war.

Like many fictional representations of female warriors masquerading as male soldiers in 19th-century literature, the book was written to entertain audiences and teach moral lessons. Billings disappeared from the historical record after publishing her book. Scholars continue to cast doubts on the validity of Billings's book.

MICHAEL R. HALL

See also

Cerro Gordo, Battle of; Literature.

References

Johannsen, Robert W. *To the Halls of the Montezumas: The Mexican War in the American Imagination.* New York: Oxford University Press, 1985.

Bishop's Palace, Monterrey, Action at
Event Date: September 19–25, 1846

Imposing stone edifice located on a high hill (Independencia) guarding the western approach to the Mexican city of Monterrey. Bishop's Palace (Palacio del Obispo, or the Obispado), built in 1789, had been the official residence of the regional Catholic bishop. After independence from Spain in 1821 the Mexican government fortified both the palace and surrounding area to provide a high, forward defensive position for Monterrey, which lay in the valley below. At the time of the Mexican-American War Lieutenant Colonel Francisco Berra commanded the post, which had a garrison of about 200 men and also mounted an artillery battery.

On September 19, 1846, a 6,600-man U.S. army under the command of Major General Zachary Taylor reached the outskirts of Monterrey. Taylor knew that the city itself was well defended by a Mexican force under Major General Pedro de Ampudia. Guarding the western approaches to Monterrey were two steep hills, Independencia and Federación.

Brigadier William J. Worth's division stormed and seized Federación Hill with surprisingly light resistance on September 21. The assault on Bishop's Palace was scheduled for the following day. In the predawn hours of September 22, amid a heavy downpour, an advance U.S. force led by Lieutenant Colonel Thomas Childs and Colonel John Coffee Hays slowly made its way up the steep western edge of Independencia Hill. Taking a small Mexican redoubt located near the apex of the hill by surprise, the Americans then mounted a howitzer—which they had dragged up the hill—and opened fire on the Bishop's Palace. Simultaneously, an artillery battery captured by U.S. forces on Federación Hill the day before also opened fire on the palace.

The shelling demolished the gates of the palace, allowing the advancing U.S. troops to storm the structure. A brief fight ensued, much of it hand-to-hand, before the Mexicans withdrew, fled down the hill, and took refuge in Monterrey itself. The taking of Bishop's Palace was the turning point in the battle. It gave American forces unfettered access to Monterrey from the west. Although Taylor and the three U.S. divisions attempting to break into the city from the east were checked by Mexican defenses, Worth's men penetrated the heart of Monterrey, and after two additional days of street fighting, the Mexicans surrendered on September 25, 1846.

The number of fatalities during the storming of the Obispado is unknown. Later in the 19th century, Bishop's Palace served as a

The storming of the Bishop's Palace in Monterrey by U.S. troops on September 22, 1846. Lithograph published by Currier & Ives, 1847. (Library of Congress)

hospital; in 1913 the Mexican bandit and revolutionary Francisco "Pancho" Villa sought refuge within the palace walls. Today, the restored building serves as a regional museum.

PAUL G. PIERPAOLI JR.

See also

Ampudia, Pedro de; Hays, John Coffee; Monterrey, Battle of; Taylor, Zachary; Worth, William Jenkins.

References

Bauer, K. Jack. *The Mexican War, 1846–1848*. Lincoln: University of Nebraska Press, 1974.

Dishman, Chris D. *A Perfect Gibraltar: The Battle for Monterrey, Mexico, 1846*. Norman: University of Oklahoma Press, 2010.

Eisenhower, John S. D. *So Far from God: The U.S. War with Mexico, 1846–1848*. New York: Random House, 1989.

Bissell, William Henry
Birth Date: April 25, 1811
Death Date: March 18, 1860

U.S. politician and volunteer army officer. Born in Hartwick, Otsego County, New York, on April 25, 1811, William Henry Bissell graduated from the Philadelphia Medical College in 1835. After practicing medicine in New York for two years, he moved to Monroe County, Illinois, to practice medicine there.

By 1840 Bissell had decided that he would rather pursue a career in law and politics than continue to practice medicine. Running as a Democrat, he was elected to the Illinois House of Representatives that year and served until 1842. Two years later Bissell earned a law degree from Transylvania College in Lexington, Kentucky, and was admitted to the bar in Belleville, Saint Claire County, Illinois. He then served as a prosecuting attorney in the Second Illinois Judicial District from 1844 to 1846.

During the Mexican-American War, Bissell was elected as captain of Company G, 2nd Illinois Volunteer Infantry and rose to be its colonel and commanding officer. He saw service during the war under Brigadier General John E. Wool in the expedition to Chihuahua before being ordered to Saltillo to join forces under Major General Zachary Taylor. Bissell's regiment fought with distinction in the Battle of Buena Vista on February 22–23, 1847, helping to secure a U.S. victory. Positioned on the left flank and outnumbered by Mexican forces, the 22nd Illinois executed a slow fighting withdrawal that ultimately checked an advance by Mexican general Manuel Lombardini's division. The 22nd Illinois then helped Colonel Jefferson Davis's Mississippi Rifles fight off a Mexican cavalry flanking attack.

Following the Mexican-American War, Bissell served in the U.S. House of Representatives from 1849 to 1855. Disillusioned with the Democratic Party, he ran as an Independent for his third term. Reportedly, while in Washington Bissell and Davis had several heated arguments over which regiment had won the Battle of Buena Vista.

During 1851–1855, Bissell chaired the Committee on Military Affairs. He suffered a stroke in 1852 that left his legs paralyzed and forced him to walk with crutches for the remainder of his life. Because of his health and political disillusionment, Bissell did not run for Congress again in 1854 but returned to Illinois.

Bissell became close friends with Abraham Lincoln and was, with him, one of the founding members of the Illinois Republican Party in February 1856. Running as a Republican, Bissell won election as governor of Illinois in November 1856 and took office in January 1857. Bissell signed a bill creating the Illinois State Normal University (now Illinois State University, the state's oldest public university) and he encouraged railroad construction in Illinois. Bissell was an adamant supporter of the colonization in Africa of freed black slaves as a way to alleviate the potential social problems of emancipation on American society. Bissell also actively encouraged Lincoln to run for the presidency. In early 1860, Bissell contracted pneumonia and died in Springfield, Illinois, on March 18, 1860.

Michael R. Hall

See also
Buena Vista, Battle of; Davis, Jefferson Finis; Lincoln, Abraham; Lombardini, Manuel María; Republican Party; Saltillo; Taylor, Zachary; Wool, John Ellis.

References
Church, Charles A. *History of the Republican Party in Illinois, 1854–1912.* Rockford, IL: Press of Wilson Brothers, 1912.

Jensen, Richard J. *Illinois: A History.* Urbana: University of Illinois Press, 2001.

Black, John
Birth Date: Unknown
Death Date: Unknown

U.S. diplomat and consul to Mexico (1843–1861). Virtually nothing is known about John Black, including the circumstances of his birth or early years. It seems likely that he entered foreign service in the 1830s and was named U.S. consul to Mexico in 1843, which made him the highest-ranking permanent American official in Mexico during the Mexican-American War. During the early months of 1845, as tensions between the United States and Mexico mounted, Black corresponded numerous times with journalist Moses Y. Beach, who also often acted as an informal secret agent for President James K. Polk. Beach, an ardent expansionist, had tried to convince Black to engage in discussions with key Mexican leaders, including those of the Catholic Church, to effect the sale of California and New Mexico to the United States.

In September 1845 Secretary of State James Buchanan instructed Black, via letter, to sound out the Mexican government to see if it would receive an American emissary with full powers to negotiate "all the questions in dispute between the two governments." By then the Mexicans had broken off official diplomatic relations as a result of the pending U.S. annexation of Texas. On October 11, Mexico's minister of foreign affairs, Manuel de la Peña y Peña, met with Black, and the two men engaged in a long discussion. Four days later, the Mexican foreign minister sent a letter to Black in which he agreed to discussions with an American emissary to be appointed by President James K. Polk to settle "the present dispute." Black duly informed Buchanan of his success, but he apparently did not inform him that the Mexican government had agreed to discuss only "the present dispute" (namely, the annexation of Texas), and not the other issues that the Americans hoped to settle, including the sale/cession of Mexican territory and the Texas border dispute.

Black's omission likely arose from misunderstanding and carelessness rather than a conscious attempt to sabotage the upcoming talks, although it should be noted that Black was the type of civil servant who told his superiors what he believed they wanted to hear. Indeed, he had repeatedly sent overly optimistic reports to Washington in the months leading up to the war that seemed to suggest that the Mexican government was more malleable than it actually was.

Polk promptly appointed John Slidell as U.S. minister to Mexico with full powers to negotiate all outstanding issues between the United States and Mexico. He arrived in Mexico City on December 6, 1845, and only then did the magnitude of Black's omission become fully known. Indeed, Peña y Peña now indicated that his government was willing to discuss *only* the issue of Texas. The Mexicans refused to meet with Slidell, who remained in Mexico City until May 1846, by which time tensions between the United States and Mexico had boiled over into war.

The best assumption about the diplomatic impasse is that Black and Peña y Peña probably never discussed exactly what the "questions in dispute" actually were, which was certainly a shortcoming on Black's part. In March 1847, when Veracruz fell to U.S. forces under Major General Winfield Scott, the Mexican government expelled Black, who returned to Mexico City at the war's end and continued as consul to Mexico until 1861. Black then again fell out of the historical record, and nothing is known of his later years and death.

Paul G. Pierpaoli Jr.

See also
Beach, Moses Yale; Buchanan, James; Causes of the War; Peña y Peña, Manuel de la; Polk, James Knox; Slidell, John; Texas.

References
Clary, David A. *Eagles and Empire: The United States, Mexico, and the Struggle for a Continent.* New York: Bantam Books, 2009.

McAfee, Ward M. "A Reconsideration of the Origins of the Mexican-American War." *Southern California Quarterly* 62 (1980): 49–65.

Black Bean Episode
Event Date: March 25, 1843

Dramatic execution of Texans by Mexicans on March 25, 1843, in the aftermath of a Texan border raid against Ciudad Mier, Mexico, on December 23, 1842. The Mier Expedition, as it came to be known, was the last of a number of raids by Texans against Mexico during the years of the Republic of Texas (1836–1845). It grew out of an expedition of 700 Texans, led by Alexander Somervell, who marched against the Mexican town of Guerrero on November 25, 1842. Somervell seized the town but found himself overextended, so he ordered his men to disband on December 19. A group of 308 refused to heed this command, however, and elected William S. Fisher as their leader. The next day they moved along the northern bank of the Rio Grande toward the Mexican town of Ciudad Mier. Crossing the river, they captured that town on December 23 but withdrew into Texas when the *alcalde* (municipal magistrate) promised to deliver supplies to them. The arrival of Major General Pedro de Ampudia and Brigadier General Antonio Canales Rosillo with an army of 3,000 men thwarted the delivery, however.

On December 25, Fisher and 261 of his men recrossed the Rio Grande and attacked the Mexicans, killing 600 and wounding 200 others, while suffering 31 casualties. They surrendered on December 26, with the understanding from Ampudia that they would be treated with consideration. Ampudia nevertheless sentenced them to death, although he reversed his decree on December 27.

The prisoners were marched to Matamoros, en route to Mexico City, all the while planning their escape. At Salado, on February 11, 1843, they made a break for the Rio Grande. Becoming separated and lost, they were captured singly and in small groups. Within seven days, 176 of them were returned to Salado; only 3 managed to escape to Texas.

General Antonio López de Santa Anna, then president of Mexico, ordered all the prisoners executed, but Governor Francisco Mejía, who had charge of them, refused to comply. Meanwhile, foreign diplomats in Mexico City intervened in the case, and Santa Anna agreed to modify his decree. He now ordered every 10th man to be executed. To determine who would die, Colonel Domingo Huerta, who had superseded Francisco Mejía at Salado, had 159 white beans and 17 black beans placed in an earthen pot. He had the Texans blindfolded, and in alphabetical order they drew the beans.

The unlucky men who drew the black beans were allowed to write letters home. Then, on the evening of March 25, 1843, they were executed by firing squad. The survivors were marched to

Captured Texans shown drawing beans from a jar at Salado on March 25, 1843. The 159 who drew white beans were spared, while the 17 drawing black beans were allowed to write a letter home and were then executed by firing squad. The illustration is from the *Journal of the Texian Expedition against Mier,* 1845. (Library of Congress)

Mexico City. Not surprisingly, the episode stirred up much anti-Mexican sentiment in the United States.

After repairing roads during the summer of 1843, the remaining prisoners were transferred to a prison in Perote Castle. There some died, a few escaped, and a few others were released because foreigners intervened on their behalf. The majority remained captive until Santa Anna ordered them released on September 16, 1844. The black bean incident is the subject of a famous painting by Frederick Remington.

PAUL DAVID NELSON

See also
Ampudia, Pedro de; Canales Rosillo, Antonio; Fisher, William S.; Mejía, Francisco; Mier Expedition; Perote Castle; Santa Anna, Antonio López de.

References
Eisenhower, John S. D. *So Far from God: The U.S. War with Mexico, 1846–1848.* Norman: University of Oklahoma Press, 1989.
Green, Thomas Jefferson. *Journal of the Texan Expedition against Mier.* New York: Harper and Brothers, 1845.
Haynes, Sam M. *Soldiers of Misfortune: The Somervell and Mier Expeditions.* Austin: University of Texas Press, 1990.
Nance, Joseph Milton. *Attack and Counterattack: The Texas-Mexican Frontier, 1842.* Austin: University of Texas Press, 1964.
Nance, Joseph Milton. *Mier Expedition Diary.* Edited by Joseph D. McCutchan. Austin: University of Texas Press, 1978.
Stapp, William Preston. *The Prisoners of Perote.* Austin: University of Texas Press, 1977.
Walker, Samuel H. *Samuel H. Walker's Account of the Mier Expedition.* Edited by Marilyn McAdams Sibley. Austin: Texas State Historical Association, 1978.

Blake, Jacob Edmund
Birth Date: January 1812
Death Date: May 9, 1846

U.S. Army officer and topographical engineer. Jacob Edmund Blake was born in January 1812 in Philadelphia, Pennsylvania. He matriculated at the U.S. Military Academy, West Point, in July 1829 and graduated with the class of 1833, along with the grandson of diplomat and politician Rufus King and future brevet Major General George W. Cullum, Blake's later biographer. Blake was commissioned a second lieutenant on July 1, 1833, in Colonel Henry Atkinson's 6th U.S. Infantry Regiment. That unit would be commanded by Colonel Zachary Taylor from 1843 to 1846. Blake served as the Military Academy quartermaster from May 25, 1835, to July 29, 1836. He was posted to Washington, D.C., two days later, and on September 6 was promoted to first lieutenant in the adjutant general's office, a post he held from November 1837 to July 7, 1838.

On July 5, 1838, Colonel J. J. Albert's new corps of topographical engineers was created, and Blake immediately joined it. He served in Florida during the Second Seminole War from 1838 to 1839, helped construct harbors at Lake Erie (1839–1841), and surveyed along the U.S.-Texas boundary (1841–1842); he also briefly worked on the defenses at New Orleans. From 1842 to 1845, Blake was back in Florida working with brevet Brigadier General William J. Worth's surveying staff.

In the late winter of 1845, Blake was posted to Brigadier General Zachary Taylor's Army of Occupation in Texas. Just prior to the Battle of Palo Alto on May 8, 1846, Taylor dispatched two engineers—Blake and Lloyd Tilghman—on a reconnaissance mission to gauge Mexican troop strength and armaments. Blake and Tilghman reached within 100 yards of the Mexican Army of the North, commanded by General Mariano Arista. Using field glasses, the two engineers were able to provide a rough estimate of the size of the Mexican force and also reported numerous artillery pieces hidden amid tall grass. Arista was aware of the two Americans' presence but instructed his men to hold their fire according to the rules of engagement. It is not known what role, if any, Blake played in the ensuing battle, which ended in a U.S. victory. The day after Palo Alto, on May 9, Blake accidentally shot himself with his own pistol as he stopped for water. He died that same day.

VANCE E. BURKE

See also
Arista, Mariano; Palo Alto, Battle of; Taylor, Zachary; Worth, William Jenkins.

References
Cullum, George W., ed. *Biographical Register of the Officers and Graduates of the United States Military Academy from 1802 to 1867.* New York: Miller and Company, 1879.
Frost, John. *The Mexican War and Its Warriors, Comprising a Complete History of All Operations of the American Armies in Mexico: With Biographical Sketches and Anecdotes of the Most Distinguished Officers in the Regular Army and Volunteer Force.* New Haven, CT: Mansfield, 1848.
Traas, Adrian George. *From the Golden Gate to Mexico City: The U.S. Army Topographical Engineers in the Mexican War, 1846–1848.* Washington, DC: Office of History, Corps of Engineers, and Center of Military History, United States Army, 1993.
Winders, Richard Bruce. *Mr. Polk's Army: The American Military Experience in the Mexican War.* College Station: Texas A&M University Press, 2001.

Blanco, Santiago
Birth Date: 1815
Death Date: 1883

Mexican army officer. Santiago Blanco was born in Campeche in 1815. Entering the Colegio Militar (Mexican Military Academy) at Chapultepec, he was among the first generation of graduates in 1827. He was commissioned as a lieutenant and taught mathematics at the college until 1832. Well versed in engineering as well as artillery tactics, Blanco subsequently saw action repressing rebellions as an artillery officer. He also erected fortifications and led surveying parties as an engineering officer. In the early 1840s Blanco traveled to the United States to examine that country's early railroad infrastructure, and by 1843 he had attained the rank of colonel.

At the start of the Mexican-American War in 1846 Colonel Blanco had earned the reputation of an efficient, hardworking officer who, unlike many of his contemporaries, was able to work seamlessly with both his superiors and subordinates. Blanco distinguished himself just prior to and during the Battle of Buena Vista. On February 22, the day before the main battle commenced, he led troops in several minor engagements with American forces in the hills surrounding Hacienda Buena Vista. On the day of the battle (February 23), Blanco, operating under the command of General Ignacio Mora y Villamil, bolstered General Antonio López de Santa Anna's left flank along the road near La Angostura. As he tried to push forward toward the American position, however, his men suffered high casualties from U.S. artillery fire. Nevertheless, Blanco's decisive and intrepid leadership earned him promotion to the rank of general, in command of the Battalion of Army Engineers.

Blanco also played a key role at the Battle of Contreras on August 20, 1847, as American troops moved ever-closer to the Mexican capital. As U.S. soldiers made their way through the perilous *pedregal* (lava fields) that surrounded Churubusco and partially obstructed the approaches to Mexico City, Blanco personally directed the Mexican artillery batteries that helped slow the Americans' advance. Blanco's deadly fire prevented General Gabriel Valencia's Army of the North, then in a poorly chosen defensive position, from being overrun by U.S. forces. Blanco, who was completely exposed as he directed the Mexican artillery fire, was severely wounded in the battle.

After the war, Blanco, an inveterate conservative, remained in the army, mostly as commander of the Battalion of Army Engineers. In 1853 he served as minister of war under President Santa Anna and became the commandant of the Colegio Militar the following year. He also served as a deputy for Campeche (1853–1855). Blanco remained a staunch opponent of liberals and liberal policies. He supported the French intervention in the early 1860s, and after the end of that struggle in 1867 he was imprisoned for two years at Tacubaya. Thereafter, Blanco remained largely out of the public spotlight. He died in Mexico City in 1883.

PAUL G. PIERPAOLI JR.

See also

Buena Vista, Battle of; Chapultepec, Battle of; Contreras, Battle of; Mexican Military Academy (Colegio Militar); Mora y Villamil, Ignacio; *Pedregal*; Santa Anna, Antonio López de; Tacubaya; Valencia, Gabriel.

References

Carreño, Alberto María. *Jefes del ejército mexicano en 1847: Biografías de generales de division y de la brigade y de coronels del ejército mexicano por fines del año de 1847*. Mexico City: Secretaría de Fomento, 1914.
Johnson, Timothy D. *A Gallant Little Army: The Mexico City Campaign*. Lawrence: University Press of Kansas, 2007.
Lavender, David. *Climax at Buena Vista: The American Campaigns in Northeastern Mexico, 1846–47*. Philadelphia, PA: Lippincott, 1966.

Bliss, William Wallace Smith
Birth Date: August 17, 1815
Death Date: August 5, 1853

U.S. Army officer, aide to and later son-in-law of Major General Zachary Taylor. William Wallace Smith Bliss was born in Whitehall, New York, on August 17, 1815. A highly intelligent man and extraordinary student, he graduated from the U.S. Military Academy at West Point in 1833, after beginning his studies there at age 14. He was commissioned a second lieutenant in the 4th Infantry Regiment in 1833 and served at Fort Mitchell, Alabama, before returning to West Point in 1834 as a mathematics instructor, a post he held until 1837. In 1840–1841 he served in the Second Seminole War (1835–1842). Known for his fastidiousness and slavish attention to detail, Bliss soon earned the nickname "Perfect."

Bliss served in several posts thereafter before being attached to then brigadier general Zachary Taylor's force in southern Texas in 1845. He was at the time a captain. General in Chief Winfield Scott, mindful of Bliss's skills as an administrator, personally assigned Bliss to Taylor's staff as adjutant when the Mexican-American War commenced in 1846. Taylor took an immediate liking to Bliss, marveling at his diplomatic and military skills, not to mention his proclivity for writing simple, cogent, and elegant reports and letters. Rare was the time that Bliss was not by Taylor's side. In May 1846, immediately after the Battle of Palo Alto, during which Bliss performed admirably, he was promoted to major. For his gallant and meritorious service during the February 1847 Battle of Buena Vista, Bliss was again brevetted—to lieutenant colonel. In the immediate aftermath of that engagement, Taylor dispatched Bliss to Agua Nueva to discuss prisoner exchanges and care of wounded and sick soldiers with the Mexican high command.

Bliss remained doggedly loyal to Taylor even after the war ended, serving as his personal secretary during 1849–1850, in the early days of the Taylor presidency. He also earned the equivalent of a master's degree from Dartmouth College in 1848 and married Taylor's youngest daughter, Mary Elizabeth, that same year. From 1850 to 1853 he served as adjutant general of the army's Western Division. On a trip to New Orleans in the summer of 1853, Bliss contracted yellow fever and soon died at Pascagoula, Mississippi, that August 5; he was only 37 years old. Fort Bliss, Texas, was named in his honor in 1854.

PAUL G. PIERPAOLI JR.

See also

Buena Vista, Battle of; Palo Alto, Battle of; Taylor, Zachary.

References

Bauer, K. Jack. *Zachary Taylor: Soldier, Planter, Statesman of the Old Southwest*. Baton Rouge: Louisiana State University Press, 1985.

Dyer, Brainerd. *Zachary Taylor.* New York: Barnes and Noble, 1967.

Singletary, Otis A. *The Mexican War.* Chicago: University of Chicago Press, 1960.

Blockade, Naval

A blockade is a naval operation that seeks to prevent ships from entering or leaving an enemy's ports. Blockades are of two types. A military blockade seeks to contain or deny free passage by an enemy's warships. A commercial blockade denies the use of the sea to an enemy's merchant marine. These types of blockades may be used individually or in combination depending on strategic objectives. Blockades may also be "close," whereby the blockading warships operate as closely as possible to an enemy coastline, and "distant," in which warships operate at a distance from the enemy's coastline.

At the time of the Mexican-American War, for a blockade to be legal under international law, blockading ships had to be present in the ports that were being subjected to the declared blockade. The United States blockaded most Mexican ports during the conflict, especially those on the Gulf Coast. Simply declaring a blockade with no means of enforcement, often known as a "paper blockade," had no international legal standing. During 1846–1848, the U.S. Navy stopped and seized only those ships displaying the Mexican flag, which was in accordance with the long-standing American position vis à vis neutral shipping rights. Non-Mexican vessels were permitted to pass through the blockade without harassment. During the conflict, the Mexican Navy, which possessed only two warships of any import—the steamers *Guadalupe* and *Moctezuma*—posed no viable threat to U.S. shipping or the U.S. Navy. The British repossessed the two ships, however, when the war began.

Besides supplying ground troops and staging the amphibious landing at Veracruz in March 1847, blockade duties were the U.S. Navy's principal activity during the Mexican-American War. The American naval strategy in the event of war with Mexico envisioned a combination of blockade, bombardment where feasible, and amphibious operations. The blockade of Mexican ports was implemented by the U.S. Home Squadron in the Gulf of Mexico and the Pacific Squadron on the coast of Alta California. The Home Squadron, commanded by Commodore David Conner since December 30, 1843, consisted of the steamer *Mississippi,* two frigates, three sloops, and three brigs. Conner requested shallow-draft vessels that could operate close to shore and in rivers, but the request was denied, largely for monetary reasons.

In August 1845, Secretary of the Navy George Bancroft issued preparatory orders to Conner to blockade Mexico's ports if one of two actions on the part of Mexico took place. These were either Mexican troops crossing the Rio Grande River into the disputed trans-Nueces region, or an American ship coming under attack by Mexican forces.

Depiction of the capture of Yerba Buena by American forces under Commodore John Sloat on July 7, 1846. The coastal port was named San Francisco the next year. (Naval Historical Center)

When the war began Conner positioned his flagship *Mississippi* off Veracruz and issued detailed instructions to his captains regarding blockade operations. Neutral rights were to be observed at all times and the blockade was limited to ports where American warships were stationed. Ships displaying the Mexican flag were subject to capture. The Home Squadron carried out Conner's orders precisely, as evidenced by the fact that all captures were later sustained by admiralty courts. On March 21, 1847, Commodore Conner was relieved by Commodore Matthew C. Perry.

The U.S. naval blockade proved highly successful. Only one Mexican privateer managed to capture a U.S.-flagged ship during the entirety of the conflict. U.S. ships closed off the principal ports at Veracruz and Tampico and other smaller ports, and few ships made it through the blockade. Such success was all the more impressive given the complexity of the operation and the distances involved. The closest U.S. naval base was at Pensacola, Florida, some 900 miles from Veracruz. Disease and poor weather often hampered naval operations, as did the paucity of natural harbors in Mexico and the lack of reliable coastal charts. Conner eventually expanded his fleet to include five fast schooners captained by senior lieutenants; other ships were also added.

The blockade of the Pacific coast by the Pacific Squadron, under the initial command of Commodore John D. Sloat, was complicated by politics, poor communications, and frequent changes of command. On May 24, 1845, anticipating war with Mexico, Secretary of the Navy George Bancroft ordered Sloat to occupy San Francisco and blockade or occupy other Mexican ports as permitted by existing American naval forces.

With no direct telegraph communications with the West, Sloat received very little information about events farther east. On July 15, 1846, the U.S. frigate *Congress* arrived off Northern California under the command of Commodore Robert F. Stockton. He assumed command of the Pacific Squadron later that month, with orders to hold San Francisco and Monterey and occupy San Diego and Los Angeles. He was also to blockade as many remaining Mexican ports as his forces would permit.

In January 1847, John Y. Mason succeeded Bancroft as secretary of the navy while Commodore James Biddle assumed command of the Pacific Squadron under the same orders for blockade as Stockton.

Blockade duty was arduous and possessed of a tedium that tried the patience of sailors and officers alike. Yet in view of the almost complete lack of Mexican ships to challenge the U.S. Navy, the blockade became the navy's major contribution to the Mexican-American War. No significant amount of war matériel made its way into Mexican ports during 1846–1848.

HAROLD N. BOYER SR.

See also

Bancroft, George; Biddle, James; Conner, David; Mexico, Navy; Perry, Matthew Calbraith; Semmes, Raphael; Sloat, John Drake; Stockton, Robert Field; United States Navy; Veracruz, Landing at and Siege of; Warships.

References

Bauer, K. Jack. *Surfboats and Horse Marines: U.S. Naval Operations in the Mexican War, 1846–1848.* Annapolis, MD: U.S. Naval Institute, 1969.

Hagan, Kenneth J. *This People's Navy: The Making of American Sea Power.* New York: Free Press, 1991.

Love, Robert W., Jr. *History of the U.S. Navy.* Vol. 1, *1775–1941.* Harrisburg, PA: Stackpole Books, 1992.

Bocachicacampo, Skirmish at
Event Date: February 13, 1848

A minor military engagement that was part of the general fighting around the port of Guaymas on the Gulf of California (state of Sonora y Sinaloa), after Guaymas had been captured by U.S. naval forces commanded by Captain Elie A. F. Lavallette in the frigate *Congress* on October 19–20, 1847. When the port fell, its Mexican commander, Colonel Antonio Campuzano, withdrew his garrison of 400 men to Bocachicacampo, a rocky peninsula four miles up the coast. His camp, which included barracks and storage facilities, stood on a stony outcrop.

The rugged terrain provided very little cover for an attacking force. Hence, the Americans in Guaymas were hesitant to assault Campuzano's position even though he continued to harass them from there. On November 17 Campuzano led 350 men back into Guaymas, which Captain Lavallette had left ungarrisoned due to manpower shortages. These Mexicans had to be expelled by an American landing party of 65 sailors and marines led by Commander Thomas A. Selfridge, captain of the sloop *Dale.*

Finally, in early 1848, Lieutenant Edward M. Yard, who had replaced the wounded Selfridge as captain of the *Dale,* decided to eliminate Campuzano's camp at Bocachicacampo, regardless of the danger. On February 12 he ordered Lieutenant Fabius Stanly of the sloop *Libertad* to lead a party of about 60 seamen and marines in a surprise frontal assault against Campuzano's unsuspecting men before they could offer any resistance. Shortly after midnight the next day, Stanly's party went ashore near Guaymas. The Americans separated into three groups and silently converged on the sleeping Mexican camp from the west, southwest, and northwest. Achieving complete surprise, they charged from the three directions when the first Mexican shot was fired. The Mexicans fled, abandoning most of their arms, ammunition, artillery, and equipment, and the Americans returned to Guaymas.

Mexican casualties in the brief skirmish are unknown; the Americans suffered no losses. A week later, Lieutenant Stanly returned with 19 men to the still-empty camp and burned all the barracks and storage sheds.

PAUL DAVID NELSON

See also

Baja California; Campuzano, Antonio; Guaymas, Battle of; Gulf of California (Mar de Cortés); Lavallette, Elie Augustus Frederick; United States Navy.

References

Bauer, K. Jack. *The Mexican War, 1846–1848*. New York: Macmillan, 1974.

Bauer, K. Jack. *Surfboats and Horse Marines: U.S. Naval Operations in the Mexican War, 1846–1848*. Annapolis, MD: U.S. Naval Institute, 1969.

Kemble, John Haskell, ed. "Amphibious Operations in the Gulf of California, 1847–1848." *American Neptune* 5 (1945): 121–136.

Bocanegra, José María de
Birth Date: June 25, 1787
Death Date: July 23, 1862

Mexican lawyer and politician who twice served as minister of foreign relations (1837, 1841–1844). José María de Bocanegra was born on June 25, 1787, at the hacienda Ciénega de Mata in Aguascalientes, located in the province of Zacatecas. He studied grammar and rhetoric at the seminary of Guadalajara from which he graduated in 1802. Bocanegra went on to study philosophy at the University of Guadalajara and obtained his degree in 1804. He then took up the study of law at the Antiguo Colegio de San Ildefonso in Mexico City, graduating in 1807 and obtaining his lawyer's certification in 1813.

Bocanegra represented Zacatecas in the first Mexican Constituent Congress and the Junta Nacional Instituyente in 1822, but at the beginning of 1823 the Casa Mata rebellion invalidated the legitimacy of both bodies. He remained on the political sidelines for some years thereafter because he had supported the empire of Agustín de Iturbide. Bocanegra then entered the Chamber of Deputies in 1827 and was reelected in 1829, 1844, and 1848. He was also elected as a senator in 1834. He worked in different consultative bodies, such as the Supremo Poder Conservador (Supreme Conservative Power) during 1837–1841 and the Consejo de Estado (Council of State) in 1844 and 1853.

Bocanegra collaborated with the York-Rite Masons (*Yorquinos*) and established close relationships with several of its most notable members; the most noteworthy were two high-profile generals, Vicente Guerrero and José María Tornel y Mendivil. The bonds he maintained with this Masonic society helped him attain two cabinet positions—minister of internal and external affairs and minister of economic affairs in 1829—and interim president on December 18, 1829. Bocanegra again served as minister of economic affairs in 1835, as well as a judge on the Mexican Supreme Court (1835–1841).

Bocanegra returned to national politics in late 1837. He briefly served as minister of foreign affairs under Anastasio Bustamante (October 27–November 6, 1837) and again during the presidency of Antonio López de Santa Anna (1841–1844). From this post he vigorously opposed the so-called Catesby Affair, in which U.S. commodore Thomas ap Catesby Jones temporarily occupied Monterey (Alta California) in 1842 under the mistaken assumption that the United States and Mexico had gone to war. He also objected to the 1842 Mier Expedition, an attempt of Texas filibusters to invade northern Mexico. Bocanegra also made clear his adamant opposition to the potential U.S. annexation of Texas and objected to the way Texans behaved toward Mexico.

After leaving office in 1844 Bocanegra largely retired from national politics. He subsequently worked as a lawyer and collected documents from his public life in order to write his memoirs. Although he spent nearly 20 years writing, he never completed this work (it was published posthumously). Bocanegra died after a prolonged illness on July 23, 1862, in the village San Ángel on the outskirts of Mexico City.

ANA ROMERO-VALDERRAMA

See also

Bustamante y Oseguera, Anastasio; Freemasonry; Guerrero, Vicente; Jones, Thomas ap Catesby; Mier Expedition; Monterey, California; Santa Anna, Antonio López de; Texas; Tornel y Mendivil, José María de; Webster, Daniel.

References

Bocanegra, José María de. *Memorias para la historia de México independiente, 1822–1836*. 3 vols. Mexico City: INEHRM/FCE, 1987.

Bocanegra, José María de. *Memorias del secretario de Estado y del despacho de Relaciones Exteriores y Gobernación de la República Mexicana correspondiente a la Administración provisional en los años 1841, 42 y 43*. Mexico City: Vicente G. Torres, 1844.

Romero-Valderrama, Ana. "Soberanía y federación: Vida política; José María de Bocanegra (1822–1844)." Unpublished diss., Universidad Autónoma del Estado de Morelos, 2005.

Bomb Brig

A two-masted, shallow-draft sailing vessel, traditionally mounting either large mortars or heavy cannon employed in shore bombardment. The U.S. Navy employed four bomb brigs during the Mexican-American War, all of which had been former coastal freighters purchased in 1846 and converted for naval use. The ships were the *Etna* (the third U.S. Navy ship of that name, ex-*Walcott,* purchased at Boston for $17,000), *Stromboli* (ex-*Howard,* Boston, $17,000), *Vesuvius* (the second navy ship of that name, ex–*St. Marys,* New York, $12,500), and the *Hecla* (ex–*I. L. Richardson,* New York, $34,478). These vessels were 182–239 feet in length and of 182–239 tons burden. The first two ships were converted at Boston and the last two at New York. A drawing in the National Archives (Record Group 19, #107–15–4A) shows the internal arrangements of the *Etna* fitted at the Boston Navy Yard in February 1847 with one 10-inch columbiad gun on a pivot mount amidships.

Columbiads were large guns specifically designed to fire shell in flat trajectory. Although tests were conducted with the largest 12-inch columbiad, which fired a 172-pound shell, at some 25,000 pounds it was found too heavy for sea service. The 10-inch columbiad weighed 15,400 pounds and fired a 128-pound projectile up to 4,800 yards.

The bomb brigs were intended to assist in the attack on the San Juan de Ulúa fortress at Veracruz. None reached there in time, however, because of bad weather and other causes. The *Hecla* arrived on March 29, 1847, only to see Veracruz surrender. Commodore Matthew C. Perry subsequently took advantage of the bomb brigs' shallow draft to employ them in operations against coastal towns and in blockade duty. They took part in the April 1847 capture of Tuxpan and in operations against Tabasco on the Tabasco (today Grijalva) River in mid-June 1847. All four of the Mexican War bomb vessels were sold out of the navy after the war, in 1848.

JEFFERY SEYMOUR AND SPENCER C. TUCKER

See also

Blockade, Naval; Perry, Matthew Calbraith; San Juan de Ulúa; Tabasco River Expeditions; Tuxpan; Tuxpan, Battle of; United States Navy; Veracruz; Veracruz, Landing at and Siege of.

References

Bauer, K. Jack. *The Mexican War, 1846–1848.* Lincoln: University of Nebraska Press, 1992.

Bauer, K. Jack. *Surfboats and Horse Marines: U.S. Naval Operations in the Mexican War, 1846–48.* Annapolis, MD: United States Naval Institute, 1969.

Emmons, George F. *The Navy of the United States: From the Commencement, 1775 to 1853; with a Brief History of Each Vessel's Service and Fate as Appears upon Record.* Washington: Gideon and Co., 1853.

Jeffers, William N. *A Concise Treatise on the Theory and Practice of Naval Gunnery.* New York: D. Appleton and Co., 1850.

Tucker, Spencer C. *Arming the Fleet: U.S. Navy Ordnance in the Muzzle-Loading Era.* Annapolis, MD: Naval Institute Press, 1989.

Bonham, Milledge Luke

Birth Date: December 25, 1813
Death Date: August 27, 1890

U.S. Army officer and subsequently U.S. congressman (1857–1860), Confederate Army officer and congressman (1862–1863), and governor of South Carolina (1863–1864). Born in Edgefield District, South Carolina, on December 25, 1813, Milledge Luke Bonham began his formal education at local academies before entering South Carolina College at Columbia. In 1834 he graduated second in his class and then took up the study of law. After the Second Seminole War began, Bonham received a captain's commission in his state's volunteer militia on April 9, 1836. He then went to Florida to pursue warriors led by Osceola, but by July he had returned home to resume the study of law. He was admitted to the Edgefield bar in 1837 and began a successful law practice. A leader in his community, Bonham began a four-year term as his district's state representative in 1840.

The commencement of hostilities with Mexico prompted Bonham to reenter the military, and on March 3, 1847, he was commissioned a lieutenant colonel in the 12th U.S. Infantry Regiment. The next month his regiment was deployed to Mexico under Major General Winfield Scott. On August 19, 1847, seven days after he

was promoted to full colonel, Bonham accidentally shot himself in the hand at Contreras, one day before the Battle of Churubusco. Bonham and his regiment followed General Scott until Mexico City fell on September 15, 1847. After the war officially ended on February 2, 1848, he remained in Mexico as an occupational military governor before returning to his home state in July 1848.

On March 4, 1857, Bonham filled a seat in the U.S. House of Representatives that was formerly held by his cousin, Preston Brooks, who had died earlier in the year. One day after South Carolina seceded from the Union on December 21, 1860, Bonham resigned his seat to support his home state during the Civil War. On February 10, 1861, he became major general and commander in chief of South Carolina's state militia. He spent the next two months defending the coast under the overall command of Brigadier General P. G. T. Beauregard during the Fort Sumter crisis. On April 23, 1861, he was promoted to brigadier general in the Confederate Army. At the First Battle of Bull Run on July 21, 1861, Bonham distinguished himself by holding his brigade together under heavy pressure. Despite this, Confederate president Jefferson Davis passed him over for promotion. Bonham resigned from the Confederate Army on January 29, 1862.

On February 18, Bonham began serving as a representative in the First Confederate Congress, but in January 1863 he resigned his seat to serve as governor of South Carolina, an office he held until December 18, 1864. As both a Confederate congressman

Milledge L. Bonham served as a colonel in the U.S. Army during the Mexican-American War. Later, he was a member of Congress, then governor of South Carolina during the Civil War. (Library of Congress)

and governor, Bonham sought to empower the states with more authority over military affairs, especially conscription. He bickered constantly with the Jefferson Davis administration, which he distrusted enormously. He vigorously contested Davis's orders to requisition state supplies for use by the army.

On February 9, 1865, Bonham reentered the Confederate Army as a brigadier general, organizing and commanding a cavalry brigade for several weeks before the war ended in April. From October 1865 until December 1866, Bonham again served as a state representative. He was appointed as South Carolina's first railroad commissioner in 1878 by Governor Wade Hampton, a fellow Confederate Army officer whose campaign Bonham had supported. He retained this position until his death at Sulfur Springs, North Carolina, on August 27, 1890.

ANGELA D. TOOLEY AND JIM PIECUCH

See also

Churubusco, Battle of; Mexico, Occupation of; Mexico City Campaign; Scott, Winfield.

References

Freeman, Douglas Southall. *Lee's Lieutenants: A Study in Command.* Vol. 1. New York: Charles Scribner and Sons, 1943.

Borden, Gail, Jr.
Birth Date: November 9, 1801
Death Date: 1874

Publisher, surveyor, and inventor who plotted the towns of Houston and Galveston, Texas. He also drew that state's first topographical map and established its first permanent newspaper. He is credited with inventing condensed milk. Born on November 9, 1801, in Norwich, New York, Gail Borden Jr. and his family moved to New London, Indiana, in 1816. With fewer than two years of formal public schooling, Borden relocated to Mississippi to find a milder climate to improve his fragile health.

First apprenticed to a surveyor, Borden became the official county surveyor in Amite County, Mississippi, in 1826. In December 1829 Borden moved to Galveston Island, Texas, and by February 1830 he had been appointed the official surveyor of Stephen Austin's colony in east Texas. In October 1835 Borden, his brother Thomas, and Joseph Baker established the *Telegraph and Texas Register* in San Felipe, the first permanent newspaper in Texas. That same year Borden published the first topographical map of Texas. Borden was appointed customs and tax collector for the Brazos Department in 1835 and held that position until 1837. He also surveyed and plotted Houston in late 1836.

In 1837 Borden sold his interests in the *Telegraph and Texas Register* and was appointed customs and tax collector in Galveston, the most important port of the newly established Republic of Texas. His first term as collector ended in late 1838, but Borden was reinstated in his position in 1841. He remained collector until he resigned in 1843 after a dispute with Republic of Texas president Sam Houston. From 1839 until 1851, Borden was an agent for the Galveston City Company, which owned most of Galveston Island. Borden surveyed and plotted Galveston and helped to sell hundreds of plots of land in the town. He was also instrumental in developing insular defenses in Galveston against the ever-present threat of a Mexican invasion.

MICHAEL R. HALL

See also

Austin, Stephen Fuller; Houston, Samuel; Texas.

References

Frantz, Joe B. *Gail Borden: Dairyman to a Nation.* Norman: University of Oklahoma Press, 1951.
Kienzle, George J. *The Story of Gail Borden: The Birth of an Industry.* Whitefish, MT: Kessinger, 2007.
Wharton, Clarence R. *Gail Borden, Pioneer.* San Antonio, TX: Naylor, 1941.

Border Culture

The area on both sides of the Rio Grande, which came to serve as the border between the United States and Mexico, produced its own distinct culture. The three groups who contributed most to this border culture were the indigenous American Indians, the Spanish and their Mexican descendants, and Anglo-Americans from the United States.

When they conquered Mesoamerica, the Spanish did not move into an unpopulated area of the continent. Indigenous peoples had lived in Mexico and the American Southwest for thousands of years, and their civilization was based largely on nature and natural phenomena. Climate and physical terrain shaped life in very distinct ways. The Indians living along what would become the border between Mexico and the United States were predominantly hunter-gatherers who depended on small game and seasonal fruits, nuts, and berries for food. Some basic agriculture existed, but only in areas with enough rainfall to produce a crop. In general, much of the region was arid or semi-arid, so water tended to be scarce. Although life may have appeared simple, these were complex societies that developed relationships with other people, nature, and their gods.

The arrival of the Spanish dramatically changed the life of these indigenous people. The Spanish introduced two major technological innovations: horses and firearms. Initially, only people willing to become allies with the Spanish were given access to these powerful resources. Eventually, however, through trading, raiding, and natural loss, enemies of the Spanish and their Indian allies obtained these valuable commodities.

More than any other item introduced by the Spanish, livestock revolutionized life in this traditionally dry region. The horse dramatically increased the distance one could travel and how much an individual could carry. Cattle brought to the New World by the

Spanish helped form the foundation of a future way of life based on ranching.

The Spanish wanted to do more than simply occupy the land, however. Their goal was to transform indigenous people into Spanish subjects and convert them to Christianity. This was accomplished principally through the mission system that was most prevalent in Mexico's frontier regions, ranging from Texas to Alta California to northern Mexico; much of this land later became the border region. Indians introduced to a mission were taught certain skills (weaving, ranching, and stone work, for example) to make them self-sufficient and contributing members of the larger community. They were taught the Spanish language and converted to Catholicism, Spain's official religion. They were also educated in the Spanish system of government and trained to become local leaders. The mission system was largely successful in transplanting Spanish culture to the border region. In reality, however, the cultures at play—Spanish and indigenous—augmented each other, creating a new way of life in the region that reflected both. This helped give birth to the unique border culture.

By 1800 a third group of people had begun to make inroads into the border region. Americans, chiefly Anglos from the recently established United States, were drawn south and west to the mysteries and economic opportunities that the Spanish territories seemed to hold. At first these individuals numbered only a few explorers, trappers, and traders. By 1822, however, Missouri merchants were organizing annual trade expeditions along the Santa Fe Trail to Santa Fe, New Mexico. American ships routinely stopped at Southern California ports to pick up hides and tallow, and colonists from the United States began to flood into Texas, enticed there by the newly independent Mexican Republic's generous land policies.

Americans hoped that Mexico's break with Spain in 1821 would usher in more opportunities to settle in and profit from the Spanish borderlands (now Mexican borderlands). The Spanish had feared that the United States wanted to seize this territory for its own, so they had tried to keep Americans out. Mexico believed that it could control foreign access to Texas through laws limiting immigration, such as the Decree of 1830, which forbade further Anglo settlement in Texas, but the government quickly realized that the Americans' demand for Texas land outmatched its ability to control its border with the United States. When connected to political events in Mexico, the situation in Texas led to the Texas Revolution and the establishment of the independent Republic of Texas in 1836.

During the era of the Republic of Texas (1836–1845) life in the borderlands continued to change. Americans kept making inroads into south Texas, New Mexico, and California, and the presence of competing peoples (Americans, Mexicans, Tejanos, and still-independent Indians) meant that conflict became a part of everyday life in the region. Raids by one party on another frequently occurred.

Following the 1846–1848 Mexican-American War, the border region fell under the control of the United States as a result of the Treaty of Guadalupe Hidalgo. Border culture thereafter was reflected in many different ways, and it continued to thrive. Many of the region's residents continued to speak Spanish or became bilingual. The area's food, music, religion, art, and architecture retained a decidedly Mexican flair. Tex-Mex cuisine is a fine example of border culture, combining Mexican food and products with Anglo culinary influences. The cowboy heritage, which continues to exist, is a quintessential by-product of border culture, and western ranches still exhibit the vaquero influence. Western states' adherence to common law and water rights based on Spanish law and custom are also products of border culture, which inherited it from the Spanish legal system before 1821. Today, especially in areas like southern Texas, New Mexico, Arizona, and Southern California, many inhabitants are bilingual and bicultural. They move between the Mexican and Anglo cultures fluidly and often engage in cross-border business pursuits. They also frequently celebrate both U.S. and Mexican traditions and adhere to the Catholic faith. The downside to this border culture is that it makes American citizens of Mexican or American Indian extraction more susceptible to discrimination and violence.

BRUCE WINDERS

See also

Arizona; Borderlands; California; Cattle; Cattle Hide Industry; Decree of 1830; Missions; Native Americans; New Mexico; Rio Grande; Santa Fe–Chihuahua Trail; Tejanos; Texas; Texas Revolution.

References

Hall, Dawn, ed. *Drawing the Borderline: Artist-Explorers of the U.S.-Mexico Boundary Survey*. Albuquerque, NM: Albuquerque Museum, 1996.

Paredes, Américo. *Folklore and Culture on the Texas-Mexican Border*. Austin: CMAS Books, Center for Mexican American Studies, University of Texas at Austin, 1993.

Stoddard, Ellwyn R., Richard L. Nostrand, and Jonathan P. West, eds. *Borderlands Sourcebook: A Guide to the Literature on Northern Mexico and the American Southwest*. Norman: University of Oklahoma Press, 1983.

Thompson, Jerry D. *A Wild and Vivid Land: An Illustrated History of the South Texas Border*. Austin: Texas State Historical Association, 1997.

Tijerina, Andrés. *Tejano Empire: Life on the South Texas Ranchos*. College Station: Texas A&M University Press, 1998.

Borderlands

The term "borderlands" in this context generally refers to the region on both sides of the border between the United States and Mexico, including the present-day states of Texas, New Mexico, Arizona, Nevada, Utah, Colorado, and California and the Mexican states of Baja California Norte, Sonora, Chihuahua, Coahuila, Nuevo León, and Tamaulipas In the borderlands, Mexican, Native American, and Anglo-American cultures have clashed and blended since their initial encounters with one another. Because of weak and unstable governments and ongoing fiscal woes, Mexico had a difficult time governing its northern borderlands, which were often located a thousand miles or more from the capital of Mexico City.

Mexico inherited the region from Spain after it gained independence in 1821, and Mexican leaders accurately foresaw that the country would have to defend the borderlands from an expansionist-minded United States. Many in the United States contended that Texas had been part of the Louisiana Purchase and wanted the area for its agricultural potential. Expansionists in the United States also desired California because of its excellent Pacific harbors for trade with South and East Asia.

In the early 1800s, in addition to sending Lewis and Clark to the Pacific Northwest, President Thomas Jefferson dispatched Zebulon Pike to explore Colorado and New Mexico while they were still in Spanish hands. Many American merchants saw the potential in trade between Chihuahua and Santa Fe. After several false starts, merchants regularly traveled from Missouri to New Mexico along the Santa Fe Trail, exchanging American manufactured goods for Mexican silver.

One of Mexico's first acts after independence was to assure that Texas would have a loyal and prosperous population that would form a buffer between the country's heartland and the threats it faced: Americans seeking land and Comanches looking for plunder. The policy had the support of many Texans, who realized that Mexico City had neither the resources nor the inclination to provide for their defense. Their chances of attracting immigrants from Mexico were slight, however, because few Mexicans wished to live on the wild frontier, subject to Native American depredations. As a solution, the Mexican government began recruiting colonists from the United States and Europe through a system of government-appointed land agents known as *empresarios.* As American settlers arrived, especially in Texas and New Mexico, Mexican frontiersmen welcomed them as allies against the Native Americans and as agents of economic progress.

Progress came at a price, however. The trickle of Anglo settlers and traders quickly became a flood, and the Mexican government could not control the border areas. By the late 1820s, nearly 30,000 Americans had flooded into Texas, where they became the majority population.

The United States had offered on several occasions to buy Texas, but the Mexican government refused to sell any territory. For their part, many Texans and Tejanos were becoming increasingly disillusioned with the distant Mexican government and wanted Texas to be a separate state with its own capital. Some Texans owned slaves, which caused more friction between Texans and Mexico City. The inhabitants of Texas were further alienated in 1834 when President Antonio López de Santa Anna abolished the Constitution of 1824 and replaced the federal system that shared power with the states with one that concentrated control in Mexico City.

Texas broke into open revolt in late 1835. Rebel forces captured several key points, including San Antonio and Goliad, and drove all forces loyal to Santa Anna from Texas. In response, Santa Anna personally led an army back into Texas, brutally crushing the rebels at the Alamo (San Antonio) and Coleto Creek (Goliad). On April 21, 1836, however, Texas forces surprised and decisively defeated Santa Anna in the Battle of San Jacinto. Santa Anna, who was captured by the Texans the following day, subsequently signed the Treaties of Velasco that recognized the sovereignty of the Republic of Texas and established the Rio Grande as the boundary between it and Mexico. The Mexican legislature refused to ratify the Treaties of Velasco. The new government of Texas, however, continued to claim the Rio Grande, with its headwaters in Colorado, as its southern and western boundary.

After 1836 and independence, Texas established formal diplomatic ties with Britain, France, and the United States. Most Texans favored annexation by the United States. After much wrangling, Texans finally received what they had sought for more than a decade. Texas was admitted to the Union on December 29, 1845, still claiming the Rio Grande as its southern and western border. The disputes between the United States and Mexico were a major cause of the Mexican-American War (1846–1848), which quickly followed on the heels of Texas's annexation.

In the summer of 1846, Brigadier General Stephen W. Kearny led a column designated the Army of the West from eastern Kansas to New Mexico. On August 18, the general entered and occupied Santa Fe without a fight, announcing to the town's inhabitants that the region was now a part of the United States. He appointed officers from the regiment of Missourians who had accompanied him to establish a territorial government for New Mexico.

News that war had broken out did not reach California until mid-July. Meanwhile, U.S. consul Thomas O. Larkin tried unsuccessfully to keep peace between the United States and the small Mexican military garrison. U.S. Army captain John C. Frémont and about 60 armed men had entered California in December 1845 and were making their way slowly north to Oregon when they heard that war between the United States and Mexico was imminent. On June 15, 1846, some 30 settlers, most of whom were U.S. citizens, staged a revolt, later called the Bear Flag Revolt, and seized the small Mexican garrison at Sonoma. The revolt lasted one week until Frémont and the U.S. Army took control on June 23, 1846.

Commodore John Drake Sloat and his naval and marine forces then occupied San Francisco until he was replaced by Commodore Robert Stockton. On July 18, Frémont and his men entered Monterey in a joint operation with some of Stockton's sailors and marines. The U.S. forces easily captured San Francisco, Sonoma, and Sutter's Fort near modern-day Sacramento. An additional detachment of U.S. dragoons under Kearny arrived overland from New Mexico to reinforce Stockton. Their combined forces marched north from San Diego, entering the

Los Angeles area on January 8, 1847, linking up with Frémont's men. The U.S. forces, totaling 660 soldiers and marines, fought and defeated an equal-sized Californio force in the Battle of Rio San Gabriel. On January 12, 1847, the last significant contingent of Californios surrendered to U.S. forces, marking the end of the war in California.

On January 28, 1847, U.S. Army lieutenant William T. Sherman and other army forces arrived in Monterey, California, and the next day Lieutenant Colonel Philip St. George Cooke and his Mormon Battalion arrived at San Diego after a march from Council Bluffs, Iowa. More U.S. forces arrived, including Colonel Jonathan D. Stevenson's 7th Regiment of New York Volunteers on March 15, 1847. In February 1848, the United States and Mexico signed the Treaty of Guadalupe Hidalgo, ending the war. The United States now controlled almost all of Mexico's northern borderlands. Mexico lost more than 500,000 square miles of territory. The U.S. acquisition of California was made even more important with the news that gold had been discovered at Sutter's Fort (Mill).

The unprecedented rush of people to California at the start of the Gold Rush allowed territorial officials to ask for statehood in an amazingly short period of time. The Compromise of 1850 granted California the statehood it sought. The problem the nation now faced was how to connect this far western state with the east.

The solution was to build a railroad that would stretch across the continent. Southerners, who wanted the route laid across the South, pointed out that high mountain ranges would have to be conquered if a northern route was selected. In order to ensure the flattest roadbed possible, the United States pressed Santa Anna, again the president of Mexico, to sell the Mesilla River Valley. Called the Gadsden Purchase, the 1853 acquisition of the valley formed the southern boundaries of the modern states of New Mexico and Arizona.

KATHLEEN WARNES AND BRUCE WINDERS

See also

Arizona; Bear Flag Revolt; California; California Theater of War, Overview; Californios; Colorado; *Empresarios*; Gadsden Purchase; Gold Rush, California; Land Grants; Mexican Cession; Mormon Battalion; Nevada; New Mexico; Santa Fe–Chihuahua Trail; Sutter's Fort; Tejanos; Texas; Texas Revolution; Utah.

References

Bannon, John Francis. *The Spanish Borderlands Frontier, 1513–1821*. Santa Fe: University of New Mexico Press, 1974.

Reséndez, Andrés. *Changing National Identities at the Frontier: Texas and New Mexico, 1800-1850*. Cambridge, UK: Cambridge University Press, 2005.

Weber, David J. *The Mexican Frontier, 1821–1846: The American Southwest under Mexico*. Albuquerque: University of New Mexico Press, 1981.

Weber, David J., ed. *New Spain's Far Northern Frontier: Essays on Spain in the American West, 1540–1821*. Albuquerque: University of New Mexico Press, 1982.

Weber, David J. *The Spanish Frontier in North America*. New Haven, CT: Yale University Press, 1992.

Borginnis, Sarah
Birth Date: June 5, 1813[?]
Death Date: December 23, 1866

Heroine during the siege of Fort Texas (renamed Fort Brown) in May 1846. Sarah Knight was reportedly born in Clay County, Missouri, on June 5, 1812, yet she appears in the 1850 New Mexico census as Sarah Bourgette, b. 1817, Tennessee; and the 1860 U.S. census in Arizona County of New Mexico Territory lists her as Sarah Bowman, b. 1813, with the place of birth as Tennessee. She told the census taker in 1860 that she was 47. Married to a U.S. soldier named John Langwell by 1840, she served the U.S. Army as a laundress. Her duties included washing clothes and cooking for officers, as well as caring for the sick and wounded.

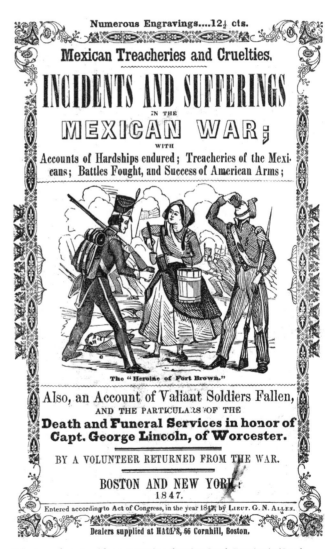

Dime novel cover with an engraving showing Sarah Borginnis (Sarah Bowman) serving coffee to soldiers during the Siege of Fort Texas (later named Fort Brown) in May 1846. Borginnis was remembered by the U.S. soldiers as a heroine who served meals, dressed wounds, and loaded weapons for them during the Mexican attack. (Library of Congress)

Reportedly strong yet graceful, Langwell stood over 6 feet tall and reportedly had an hourglass figure. Her attractive appearance brought her much attention. Langwell's nickname, "The Great Western," was inspired by the name of the largest steamer of the day.

Anticipating trouble in 1845 over the U.S. annexation of Texas, U.S. President James K. Polk authorized Brigadier General Zachary Taylor to assemble the largest number of U.S. military troops since the American Revolutionary War. Langwell and her husband joined Taylor's forces in Corpus Christi, Texas. She reportedly idolized Taylor and was outspokenly confident in his leadership skills. By May 1846, Langwell was apparently married to her second husband, a soldier named Borginnis (spellings vary).

When orders came from Washington, D.C., for Taylor's forces to move toward Mexico, Borginnis drove south in her donkey cart full of supplies. On the Rio Grande opposite Matamoros, Mexico, Taylor hurriedly constructed Fort Texas. After the war officially began, Taylor maneuvered to protect his supply base, leaving Major Jacob Brown in charge of the fort and its 500 inhabitants. When the Mexicans laid siege to Fort Texas for seven days in May 1846, Borginnis repeatedly exposed herself to danger while serving meals, dressing wounds, and loading muskets.

Borginnis achieved national attention when news of her courage and composure under attack appeared in the U.S. press. "The Great Western" thus entered Western lore as the heroine of Fort Brown. Accompanying Taylor's forces in several battles, especially the defense of the American baggage train at Buena Vista, she maintained her reputation for courage under fire. After her second husband was killed in combat later in 1846, she took several other male companions and spouses. A woman of great business acumen despite being unable to either read or write, Borginnis was reportedly fluent in Spanish and subsequently managed two hotels, both called the American House, in the Mexican cities of Saltillo and Monterrey. The hotels provided soldiers with entertainment, food, liquor, lodging, and women. One of Samuel Chamberlain's Mexican War paintings is of Borginnis tending her bar.

The war's end in early 1848 coincided with the discovery of gold in California. Borginnis, now having married her fourth husband, Albert J. Bowman, a Mexican-American War veteran, moved with him to what became El Paso, Texas, where federal troops were stationed to protect westward-migrating Americans. Borginnis is remembered as El Paso's first Anglo female resident, as well as its first madam. A few years later, Borginnis moved west with a new man and the couple settled at Fort Yuma, Arizona, where Borginnis, Yuma's first Anglo female resident, created a business cooking and cleaning for officers while Bowman pursued mining interests. Soon, Borginnis was running a restaurant, bar, boarding house, and brothel across from the fort.

Borginnis's final years were spent managing her various businesses in Arizona, most of them in Yuma. The only woman laid to rest in Fort Yuma's cemetery, Borginnis died on December 23, 1866, supposedly from a spider bite, and was buried with full military honors. Her body was later reinterred at San Francisco National Cemetery, where her gravestone is marked "Sarah A. Bowman."

DAVID M. CARLETTA

See also
Brown, Jacob; Fort Texas (Fort Brown); Saltillo; Taylor, Zachary.

References
Eisenhower, John S. D. *So Far from God: The U.S. War with Mexico, 1846–1848.* New York: Random House, 1989.
Elliott, James F. "The Great Western: Sarah Bowman, Mother and Mistress to the U.S. Army." *Journal of Arizona History* 30, no. 1 (Spring 1989): 1–26.
Johannsen, Robert W. *To the Halls of the Montezumas: The Mexican War in the American Imagination.* New York: Oxford University Press, 1985.
Sandwich, Brian. *The Great Western: Legendary Lady of the Southwest.* El Paso: Texas Western Press, 1991.

Borland, Solon
Birth Date: September 21, 1808
Death Date: January 1, 1864

Physician, journalist, U.S. soldier, U.S. senator, and diplomat. Solon Borland was born in Suffolk, Virginia, on September 21, 1808, and moved with his family to North Carolina as a youth. After attending local preparatory schools, he studied medicine and opened a medical practice. In 1843, after the death of his second wife, he moved to Little Rock, Arkansas, where he founded the pro–Democratic Party newspaper *Arkansas Banner*. When the Mexican-American War began in 1846, he volunteered for service in the 1st Arkansas Volunteer Cavalry, commanded by Colonel Archibald Yell, with the rank of major. Mirroring its commanding officer and many of its men, the Arkansas Cavalry was notoriously undisciplined and prone to tactical errors. Indeed, the outfit became known for the atrocities it perpetrated, earning the sobriquet "Arkansas Ransackers." Borland, who had previously challenged a rival newspaperman to a duel in Little Rock, had a short temper and so fit in well with the rest of his unit.

On January 18, 1847, Majors Borland and John P. Gaines, with a detachment of 90 men, were sent on a scouting mission to determine the position of General Antonio López de Santa Anna's army, just south of Saltillo, Coahuila. On the evening of January 22, the detachment bivouacked for the night in an abandoned ranch building. Foolishly, neither Borland nor Gaines posted sentries. The next morning, when the detachment awoke, it was surrounded by some 3,000 Mexican cavalrymen under the command of General José Vicente Miñón. The general allegedly quipped to Borland that he hoped his men had not awakened the Americans too early. The Americans, including Borland, were taken prisoner.

Borland managed to escape some days later, making it back to his unit, but only after Yell had been killed at the Battle of Buena

Vista. The Arkansas Cavalry mustered out in June 1847, but Borland remained in Mexico, serving as Brigadier General William Worth's aide-de-camp. Despite the embarrassment of his capture, Borland's reputation was not tarnished, and he stayed with Worth for the remainder of the war.

In 1848 Borland was elected to the U.S. Senate representing Arkansas, taking the seat vacated by Ambrose Sevier, who had recently died. Borland's Senate tenure was not without controversy; his advocacy of states' rights angered many of his colleagues, and his sometimes boorish behavior shocked his contemporaries. During a debate on states' rights in 1850, he physically assaulted Mississippi senator Henry Foote. Realizing that he had alienated many of his constituents, Borland resigned his Senate seat in 1853, becoming minister to Nicaragua, a post he held until April 1854. He committed a major faux pas there when he called for the United States to annex Nicaragua, which earned him an official rebuke by the secretary of state. He then served as minister to Costa Rica, Honduras, and Guatemala, respectively, between April and December 1854.

Returning to Arkansas in late 1854, Borland opened a medical practice in Little Rock; he declined a presidential appointment to become governor of the New Mexico Territory. At the start of the Civil War, he became commander of the state militia. He was soon replaced but remained active in the militia, helping recruit troops and requisition supplies for the Confederate cause. Borland later became colonel of the 3rd Arkansas Cavalry. In poor health, he resigned his commission in June 1862. Borland died on January 1, 1864, outside Houston, Texas.

PAUL G. PIERPAOLI JR.

See also

Miñón, José Vicente; Sevier, Ambrose Hundley; Worth, William Jenkins; Yell, Archibald.

References

Caruso, A. Brooke. *The Mexican Spy Company: United States Covert Operations in Mexico, 1845–1848*. Jefferson, NC: McFarland, 1991.

Hughes, William. *Archibald Yell: An American Hero*. Fayetteville: University of Arkansas Press, 1988.

Boundary Commissions

As a result of the 1848 Treaty of Guadalupe Hidalgo, which formally ended the Mexican-American War and codified the Mexican land cession to the United States, several boundary commissions were established between 1849 and 1855. These agencies were frequently fraught with political impediments, both in the United States and Mexico, and they also triggered frayed relations between Mexico City and Washington.

Compounding the difficulties faced by the commissions was the vague language contained in the 1848 treaty regarding the postwar U.S.-Mexican border. The principal responsibility of the boundary commissions was to establish scientific inquiries and information to inform surveying parties working from the Rio Grande Valley west to the Pacific coast in Southern California. In the process, much other scientific information was gathered as well, to include astronomical, geologic, hydrologic, zoological, and botanical identification and sample collecting.

The work of the joint commission proceeded in five stages, beginning in 1849 at San Diego and ending in 1855 at Nogales, Arizona, with the surveying work resulting from the 1853 Gadsden Purchase. From 1849 to 1851, work took place in California; in 1851, the commission established the Bartlett–García Conde Compromise Line; later that year the Gila River was surveyed; from 1851 to 1853 the Rio Grande was surveyed; and finally, in 1855, the confines of the Gadsden Purchase were finalized by surveying parties.

The joint commission included six commissioners—four Americans and two Mexicans. The Americans were John B. Weller, John Russell Bartlett, Robert Blair Campbell, and William H. Emory. The two Mexican commissioners were Pedro García Conde and José Salazar Ilarregui. In addition, there were two U.S. surveyors and one Mexican surveyor, two of whom also served as commissioners (Emory and Salazar), and six secretaries—four American and two Mexican.

The work in California ground to a halt in March 1850 because of an earlier mapping error and disputes over the boundary headed east from the Pacific Ocean. That December, the commissions reconvened at El Paso, Texas. Bartlett finally agreed to recognize the Mexican boundary claim along the 32-degree, 22-minute latitude, but only if the Mexicans would abandon their claim to a longitude approximately one degree west of the Rio Grande for a line three degrees west of the Rio Grande. The resulting Bartlett–García Conde Agreement prompted bitter recriminations on both sides, however, and it was never completed. Indeed, the U.S. Congress suspended work on it in December 1852, pending agreement on the New Mexico dispute.

Next, the commission moved to the Gila River's intersection with the western border of New Mexico and to its intersection with the Rio Grande at 32 degrees, 22 minutes. This stage proved arduous, as surveying teams battled a drought and harsh elements for months. Making matters worse, García Conde died before the section was completed in 1852.

In 1851 another surveying team began the difficult task of sorting out the Rio Grande boundary, which endured until 1853. That November commissioners agreed to divide the work on the long river into six segments. Both the Mexicans and Americans would survey the first and sixth segments; Americans would survey the second and fourth, while the Mexicans would survey the third and fifth. The work along the Rio Grande proved the most difficult due to financial, logistical, and climatic difficulties and sporadic Native American raids. In November 1853, U.S. and Mexican officials convened to set the final portion of the Rio Grande boundary.

The commissions' final work revolved around the 1853 Gadsden Purchase, which included parts of southern Arizona and New

Mexico. Scientific work got under way at El Paso in January 1855 and worked west to Nogales, Arizona. This phase was concluded that November. The work of the commissions and their teams of surveyors and scientists was impressive, especially given the daunting political, financial, and environmental challenges they faced.

PAUL G. PIERPAOLI JR.

See also

Bartlett, John Russell; Bartlett-Conde Agreement; Boundary Disputes, U.S. and Mexican; Emory, William Hemsley; Gadsden Purchase; García Conde, Pedro; Guadalupe Hidalgo, Treaty of; Rio Grande.

References

Clary, David A. *Eagles and Empire: The United States, Mexico, and the Struggle for a Continent.* New York: Bantam Books, 2009.

Griswold del Castillo, Richard. *The Treaty of Guadalupe Hidalgo: A Legacy of Conflict.* Norman: University of Oklahoma Press, 1990.

Hietala, Thomas R. *Manifest Design: Anxious Aggrandizement in Late Jacksonian America.* Ithaca: Cornell University Press, 1990.

Werne, Joseph Richard. *The Imaginary Line: A History of the United States and Mexican Boundary Survey, 1848–1857.* Fort Worth: Texas Christian University Press, 2007.

Boundary Disputes, U.S. and Mexican

Under the heady influence of expansionism and Manifest Destiny, the United States had various boundary disputes with Great Britain, Spain, and Mexico during the 19th century. It also acquired vast new territories from Mexico as a result of the Mexican-American War. As the United States rapidly expanded in both population and settlements, it began to clash with its neighbors over its western and southern boundaries. After the end of the Revolutionary War in 1783, the American western boundary ran roughly along the Mississippi River and stood unchallenged for 20 years.

In 1803, however, the Louisiana Purchase erased the original western boundary, doubling the size of the country while using ambiguous language to describe its limits. President Thomas Jefferson unsuccessfully attempted to claim parts of Spanish-held Texas based on original French claims. Finally, the United States compromised with Spanish officials and created a neutral zone between the conflicting claims. Americans violated the agreement, however, beginning with the 1803–1806 Lewis and Clark Expedition to the Pacific. Despite a previous Spanish claim to the area, the United States jointly claimed occupancy of the Columbia River region with Great Britain. In 1810 the United States annexed Spanish West Florida, and after Mexico declared its independence from Spain in 1821 it inherited a legacy of boundary disputes with the Americans.

In the 1820s American immigrants began to settle in Texas, encouraged by the Mexican government. Eventually the Anglo population began to overwhelm the Mexican population in Texas, and the Mexicans recognized the threat that these new citizens might pose to Texas sovereignty. President Andrew Jackson, an ardent expansionist, offered to buy Texas from Mexico on more than one occasion but was rebuffed. Indeed, some people suspected Jackson of sending agents, including his friend Sam Houston, into the area to agitate for Texas independence.

In 1836 the reality of Texan independence, a result of the 1835–1836 Texas Revolution, once again changed the U.S.-Mexican boundary. Immediately, however, a controversy arose over the Texas-Mexico boundary. Texas claimed the Rio Grande as the boundary, while the Mexicans claimed the Nueces River.

Texans seeking independence from Mexico had also to consider the boundaries of the Cherokees and other east Texas bands of Native Americans. If the Native Americans sided with the Mexicans, the Texan revolt could have ended disastrously. Hoping to ensure the tribes' neutrality, the provisional government of Texas promised to respect the land rights of the Native Americans of east Texas and establish clear boundaries with the various tribes. The Texas government appointed three commissioners to deal with the problem, including Sam Houston, whom the Cherokees had adopted as a member of their nation. In February 1836 Houston negotiated a treaty with the Cherokees and east Texas tribes that set aside the land between the Angelina, Neches, and Sabine Rivers and the Old San Antonio Road for the Native Americans. After the Texas Convention of 1836 refused to ratify the treaty, however, the tribes felt betrayed, and the threat of a boundary war between Native Americans and Texans hovered over the republic for most of the year.

The decade in which Texas was a sovereign nation (1836–1846) only further complicated the boundary disputes between the United States and Mexico. Although Mexican president Antonio López de Santa Anna signed the Treaties of Velasco, giving Texas sovereignty over the left bank of the Rio Grande from its headwaters in the present state of Colorado to its mouth on the Gulf of Mexico, the Mexican Congress refused to ratify them, and a state of war continued between the Republic of Texas and Mexico. Mexico never did recognize Texan independence, but the United States, Great Britain, and France did, even though the western and southern borders of Texas remained in question. In 1836 Texas pressed a claim south to the Rio Grande and west to its source, throwing the trans-Nueces region as well as most of Nuevo Mexico (New Mexico) into dispute. In subsequent years, successive Texas legislatures claimed even more Mexican territory, eventually laying claim to Upper and Lower California as well. Beginning in 1841 Texas also unsuccessfully tried to occupy eastern New Mexico, an attempt culminating in the disastrous Santa Fe Expedition.

Texas diplomats worked to have their republic annexed by the United States, and most citizens of that republic supported their efforts. The uncertainty over Texas borders, however, made annexation difficult because abolitionists feared that Texans would help extend slavery across the continent. On July 4, 1845, the United States annexed Texas by a joint resolution of Congress and subsequently settled its dispute with Great Britain over the Oregon Territory.

In 1844, Texas and Mexico reached an agreement that recognized Texas independence, but the Mexican government still disputed the Texan boundaries. The United States accepted the Texas claim of the Rio Grande border, while Mexico claimed territory as far north as the Nueces River, about 150 miles north of the Rio Grande. After the U.S. Congress voted to annex Texas in February 1845, both sides began making war preparations.

President James K. Polk sent troops to occupy Texas to protect that state but then ordered them into the disputed territory south of the Nueces River—the so-called Nueces Strip—under the claim that this land was part of the Louisiana Purchase and that it rightly belonged to the United States. By October 1845, as many as 4,000 U.S. troops were positioned on the northern bank of the Rio Grande. Mexico scoffed at such an idea, and sent an army to Matamoros to challenge the so-called Army of Occupation. The two forces clashed the following spring, sparking the war that Polk had sought.

As he worked for war between the United States and Mexico, Polk also tried to purchase Mexican territory. In the fall of 1845 he dispatched John Slidell, a Louisiana lawyer, to Mexico City. His assignment was to secure Mexican recognition of the Rio Grande as the border between Texas and the United States, negotiate the purchase of the New Mexico area for $5 million, and purchase California for as much as $30 million, offering in return American forgiveness of the claims of U.S. citizens against the Mexican government. Slidell's mission failed, and the border dispute between the United States and Mexico erupted into war on April 24, 1846. On that day, in what came to be known as the Thornton Affair, a Mexican cavalry unit ambushed an American army unit in disputed territory. After two years of often bitter and bloody fighting, the United States prevailed, resulting in the American conquest of more than half of Mexico's national territory.

Boundary adjustments led to further conflict even after the United States and Mexico signed the Treaty of Guadalupe Hidalgo in 1848. The boundary commissioners of the two nations could not agree where to begin their surveys, but eventually diplomats from both countries resolved the issue through negotiation and compromise. In 1853 the Gadsden Purchase, which saw the United States purchase the southern parts of Arizona and New Mexico (29,670 square miles) from Mexico for $10 million, settled most of the remaining issues regarding the disputed border between the United States and Mexico.

KATHLEEN WARNES

See also

Boundary Commissions; Cherokees; Conventions of 1832 and 1833; Gadsden Purchase; Guadalupe Hidalgo, Treaty of; Houston, Samuel; Louisiana Purchase; Nueces River; Oregon Boundary Dispute; Polk, James Knox; Rio Grande; Slidell, John; Texas; Texas Revolution; Thornton Affair; Trans-Nueces.

References

Clary, David A. *Eagles and Empire: The United States, Mexico, and the Struggle for a Continent.* New York: Bantam Books, 2009.

Francaviglia, Richard V., and Douglas Richmond, eds. *Dueling Eagles: Reinterpreting the U.S.-Mexican War, 1846–1848.* Fort Worth: Texas Christian University Press, 2000.

Fuller, Douglas Pitts. *The Movement for the Acquisition of All Mexico, 1846–1848.* Baltimore, MD: Johns Hopkins University Press, 1936.

Bowie, James
Birth Date: April 10, 1796
Death Date: March 6, 1836

Slave trader, land speculator, adventurer, soldier, and advocate of Texan independence. James Bowie was born in Logan County, Kentucky, on April 10, 1796. By 1802 his family had moved to Louisiana where Bowie lived until moving to San Antonio, Texas, in 1830. Between 1812 and 1814 or so, Bowie and his brother Rezin made a small fortune in the illegal slave trade, allegedly teaming up with the French pirate Jean Lafitte. After that venture, Bowie engaged for a time in land speculation in southern Louisiana. In 1827 Bowie was involved in an infamous melee in Natchez, Mississippi, known as the Sandbar Fight, in which several men were killed or wounded, among them Bowie himself. During the brawl Bowie made a name for himself with his extraordinary knife-fighting abilities. Furthermore, it is said that as a result of having been injured in the Sand Bar Fight Bowie created the knife that bears his name, a multipurpose implement with a large single blade and unique shape.

Bowie arrived in Texas about 1830, and his natural charm and fluency in the Spanish language made him seem like a solid citizen to Mexican authorities. Bowie's public image helped him marry, on April 25, 1831, Ursula de Veramendi, the daughter of the vice governor of Coahuila y Tejas (Texas) and goddaughter of Mexican president and general Antonio López de Santa Anna. These connections, along with Bowie's natural affability toward those he

Slave trader, land speculator, and Indian fighter James Bowie was a larger-than-life, legendary figure even in his own time. His death as a defender of the Alamo cemented his reputation as a martyr for Texan independence. (Texas State Library)

liked, led many Mexicans in and around San Antonio to befriend him and predisposed them as well to be sympathetic toward the American-led Texas rebellion. When Bowie settled in Texas for good, he took an oath of allegiance to the government of Mexico and soon thereafter became a Mexican citizen.

Before long, the restless Bowie was again involved in land speculation. His aggressive tactics in this regard came to anger Stephen Austin, the Texas *empresario* and soon-to-be leader of the Texas independence movement. Between 1831 and 1833, Bowie embarked on a number of exploration trips to far western Texas.

Bowie actively fought against Mexican officials' attempts to disarm Anglo settlers in Texas. In 1833 he had served as a delegate to the Colonial Convention, which requested independent statehood for Texas from Mexico, and two years later, in preparation for a possible war against Mexico, Bowie visited the Shawnee and Cherokee tribes in the region to determine the extent of their loyalty to Mexico.

Bowie played a key role in the Texans' victory at the October 18, 1835, Battle of Concepción, and when he heard that Mexican forces had crossed the Rio Grande to attack San Antonio, Bowie and 30 volunteers went there to help defend the Alamo in February and March 1836.

Once Bowie arrived at the Alamo conflict broke out almost immediately between the commissioned officer in charge there, Lieutenant Colonel William B. Travis, and the popular but not commissioned Bowie. Eventually the two men worked out an agreement of joint command, but the arrangement ended when Bowie accidentally fell from a scaffold. That accident, combined with a mysterious ailment thought now to be tuberculosis or pneumonia, restricted Bowie to his cot. Mexican soldiers killed him when they overran the Alamo on March 6, 1836. The death of Bowie has been glorified in half a dozen Alamo movies, from D. W. Griffith's 1915 *Martyrs of the Alamo* to John Lee Hancock's 2004 *The Alamo* and including Walt Disney's 1955 *Davy Crockett: King of the Wild Frontier* and John Wayne's 1960 *The Alamo,* and is very much a part of the Bowie mystique. Two other popular films, *Iron Mistress* (1952), staring Alan Ladd and Virginia Mayo and based on a novel by Paul I. Wellman, and *Last Command* (1955), staring Sterling Hayden, are specifically about Bowie and his "martyrdom." Bowie remains a legendary hero in Texas.

PAUL G. PIERPAOLI JR. AND DAVID SLOAN

See also
Austin, Stephen Fuller; Alamo, Battle of the; Concepción, Battle of; Texas; Texas Revolution; Travis, William Barret.

References
Chariton, Wallace O. *Exploring the Alamo Legends.* Plano: Republic of Texas Press, 1992.
Davis, William C. *Three Roads to the Alamo: The Lives and Fortunes of David Crockett, James Bowie, and William Barret Travis.* New York: Harper Collins, 1998.
Hopewell, Clifford. *James Bowie, Texas Fighting Man: A Biography.* Austin, TX: Eakin Press, 1994.

Bowles, William Augustus
Birth Date: 1799
Death Date: March 28, 1873

American physician and businessman who served as colonel of the 2nd Indiana Volunteer Infantry Regiment during the Mexican-American War. Born in 1799 in Maryland, William Augustus Bowles was the son of Thomas C. Bowles, a druggist. Bowles moved to Paoli, Indiana, in 1828 and began to practice medicine. In 1833, with the financial assistance of his father, Bowles purchased 15,000 acres of land in nearby French Lick, one of the many salt licks in southern Indiana. In 1840 he began to sell Pluto's Water, a popular laxative, and opened the first French Lick Springs Hotel in 1845.

At the onset of the Mexican-American War, Bowles, a Democrat who supported American expansion and slavery, assumed command of the 2nd Indiana Volunteer Infantry Regiment with the rank of colonel. He had no prior military experience. On February 22, 1847, at the Battle of Buena Vista, Bowles's troops performed poorly, and he issued a hasty call for retreat. His premature withdrawal precipitated the collapse of the U.S. left flank.

Although subsequently cleared of wrongdoing in court-martial proceedings, the tribunal determined that Bowles lacked judgment as a commander. Future Confederate president Jefferson Davis, a friend of Bowles, came to his defense at the proceedings. Bowles did not help his case, however, when he suggested that his men had acted in cowardly fashion.

Much more skilled in medicine, Bowles returned to Paoli after the war to continue his practice, eventually being joined by his brother Lewis. During the 1850s, Bowles joined the Knights of the Golden Circle, a secret society to protect and promote slavery, and illegally imported slaves into Indiana. In 1864 a military court convicted Bowles of treason for his attempt to sabotage Union-owned property, but he was released in 1866 when the U.S. Supreme Court declared that he should have been tried in a civil court. Bowles returned to manage his hotel at French Lick, where he died on March 28, 1873.

MICHAEL R. HALL

See also
Buena Vista, Battle of; Davis, Jefferson Finis; Slavery.

References
Perry, Oran. *Indiana in the Mexican War.* Indianapolis, IN: Burford, 1908.
Smith, John Martin. *French Lick and West Baden Springs.* Dover, NH: Arcadia, 2007.

Boyd, Linn
Birth Date: November 22, 1800
Death Date: December 17, 1859

Democratic politician and outspoken proponent of U.S. expansionism. Linn Boyd was born in modest circumstances in

Nashville, Tennessee, on November 22, 1800. He moved to Kentucky with his family as a young boy but received little education as a youth. Boyd worked as a farmhand, yet he later read for the law and gained admittance to the Kentucky bar.

In 1827, Boyd began his political career when he ran successfully for a seat in the Kentucky House of Representatives. In 1832, he ran unsuccessfully for the U.S. House of Representatives as a Democrat, but two years later he won election and took his seat in the U.S. House in 1835. His initial tenure was short, however, as he lost a reelection bid to his Whig opponent in 1836. Undeterred, Boyd again ran for a House seat in 1838 and won; he retained his seat until 1855.

Boyd became an extremely deft legislator and forged a close relationship with President Andrew Jackson. He clung closely to the Democratic Party platform and was an ardent supporter of American expansionism. In 1845, he was influential in shepherding the annexation of Texas through Congress. Not surprisingly, Boyd supported President James K. Polk's policies that culminated in the Mexican-American War. Indeed, as chairman of the House Committee on Military Affairs, he engaged in recurring discussions with Polk and his war cabinet on matters pertaining to the conflict. When Polk submitted an appropriations bill to Congress to pay for the war in 1846, Boyd appended an amendment that called for 50,000 more troops and a $10 million appropriation to bring the war to a quick conclusion. The amendment was not approved, but it clearly showed the deep level of support Boyd was willing to give to the Polk administration.

After the Mexican-American War ended in 1848, Boyd became chairman of an ad hoc committee that was charged with organizing the territory gained by the Mexican land cession. In 1850, he was instrumental in getting the important Compromise of 1850 through Congress. That compromise helped defuse rising sectional tensions over the disposition of slavery in newly acquired U.S. territories.

Largely because of his efforts in 1850, Boyd was elected speaker of the House in 1851, which post he held until he left Congress in 1855. He returned to Kentucky to practice law and once again became involved in state politics. He was elected lieutenant governor of the state in 1859 but died shortly after taking office on December 17, 1859, in Paducah.

PAUL G. PIERPAOLI JR.

See also
Congress, U.S.; Democratic Party; Expansionism and Imperialism; Polk, James Knox; Slavery.

References
Francaviglia, Richard V., and Douglas Richmond, eds. *Dueling Eagles: Reinterpreting the Mexican-American War, 1846–1848.* Fort Worth: Texas Christian University Press, 2000.
Nevin, David. *The Mexican War.* Alexandria, VA: Time-Life Books, 1978.

Bradburn, Juan Davis
Birth Date: 1787
Death Date: April 20, 1842

U.S.-born filibusterer and Mexican army officer. Juan Davis Bradburn, also known as John Davis Bradburn, was born in Virginia, possibly near Richmond, in 1787. His family settled in Kentucky, most probably in the 1790s. Bradburn became a merchant in Springfield, Tennessee, and eventually made his way to Louisiana. While there, it is possible he joined the Gutiérrez-Magee filibustering expedition into Spanish Texas in 1812–1813; however, no firm evidence supports this claim.

In December 1814, Bradburn enrolled in the Louisiana militia, which had been called up in the event of a British attack during the War of 1812. He served as a lieutenant in the militia and was sent with his regiment to New Orleans on January 8, 1815. He arrived on January 24, too late to take part in Andrew Jackson's victory at the Battle of New Orleans. Bradburn therefore saw no combat and was released from duty in March 1815.

Following his release, Bradburn joined another filibustering campaign into the Spanish-held province of Texas led by the Mexican insurgent Juan Pablo Anaya and an American by the name of Henry Perry. Bradburn served in the expedition as a sergeant major. The effort floundered on the Texas Gulf Coast in 1816; however, members of the expedition, including Bradburn and Perry, joined another excursion led by the insurgent Francisco Xavier Mina that same year to capture the Mexican port of Tampico, departing in April 1817. Bradburn rose to second in command of the American volunteers under Mina's cohort, Colonel Guilford D. Young.

Although initially successful, the rebels eventually found themselves besieged inland. Colonel Young's death in battle left Bradburn in command of the Americans. Unable to negotiate acceptable terms with the Spanish forces, Bradburn led a breakout of the American volunteers.

Bradburn continued his activities in Mexico's struggle for independence against Spain. By 1818, he found his way into Vicente Guerrero's revolutionary army. In December 1820, however, he switched sides and joined Agustín de Iturbide's Spanish forces as a colonel, a rank he would hold for the remainder of his military career. In 1821 Mexico declared its independence from Spain and Iturbide became emperor of Mexico in 1822.

Iturbide sent Bradburn as envoy to the United States, and Bradburn returned with news that the United States was preparing to recognize Mexican independence. Bradburn continued his career in the Mexican army and cultivated relationships with prominent conservatives, including General Manuel Mier y Terán, who in 1830 appointed Bradburn commander of a post on Galveston Bay in Texas. In that capacity Bradburn was charged with enforcing the provisions of the Decree of April 6, 1830, that imposed restrictions on American colonization of Texas and new tariffs. While serving at Galveston Bay, Bradburn founded the town of Anahuac.

Bradburn faced the challenges of maintaining the distant post, as well as enforcing restrictions on land ownership, commerce, and shipping in the face of rising Anglo-American protest. Matters came to a head in 1832, when he ordered the arrest on a charge of sedition of colonists William Barrett Travis and Patrick Jack, along with several others. A number of colonists revolted, capturing a detachment of Bradburn's cavalry. Bradburn eventually acquiesced to the colonists' demands, releasing the prisoners and resigning his post. He left Galveston Bay for Matamoros, Mexico, where he died on April 20, 1842.

DAVID K. SMITH

See also

Decree of 1830; Guerrero, Vicente; Mier y Terán, José Manuel Rafael Simeón de; Texas.

References

Davis, William C. *Three Roads to the Alamo: The Lives and Fortunes of David Crockett, James Bowie, and William Barrett Travis.* New York: Harper Perennial, 1999.

Henson, Margaret Swett. *Juan Davis Bradburn: A Reappraisal of the Mexican Commander at Anahuac.* College Station: Texas A&M Press, 1982.

Bragg, Braxton
Birth Date: March 22, 1817
Death Date: September 27, 1876

U.S. and Confederate Army officer. Braxton Bragg was born on March 22, 1817, in Warrenton, North Carolina, and graduated from the U.S. Military Academy, West Point, in 1837. He was commissioned a second lieutenant in the 3rd Artillery Regiment and sent to Florida to participate in the removal of the Seminoles. Bragg's health failed as a result of the poor living conditions and stress, and he spent most of 1838 recovering. Bragg also gained a reputation as a rigid commander who was quarrelsome, tactless, and critical of faults of superiors and subordinates alike.

In 1845, Bragg was assigned to the Army of Occupation under Major General Zachary Taylor in Texas. During the 1846–1848 Mexican-American War, Bragg distinguished himself by his ability to mold raw recruits into disciplined fighting men as well as for his administrative skills. He was also hated by his men, some of whom reportedly tried to kill him—once in August 1847 and again that October. Bragg especially distinguished himself as an artillery battery commander in the February 23, 1847, Battle of Buena Vista, where his highly mobile and accurate guns repulsed numerous Mexican infantry charges. Zachary Taylor's command, "A little more grape, Captain Bragg," became a catch phrase that helped propel "Old Fuss and Feathers" into the White House in 1848. For his actions in the battle, Bragg was brevetted lieutenant colonel.

Following the war, Bragg became dissatisfied with the lack of progress in his military career and resigned his commission as a lieutenant colonel in 1855 and purchased a sugar plantation in Louisiana. When Louisiana seceded from the Union in 1861, Bragg became head of its army. He was appointed a brigadier general in the Confederate Army in March 1861 and sent to confront Fort Pickens. Following the fall of Forts Donelson and Henry in Tennessee in February 1862, Bragg led his men from Florida to join General Albert Sidney Johnston's Army of Mississippi at Corinth, Mississippi.

As a major general, Bragg distinguished himself in the Battle of Shiloh on April 6–7, 1862, where he commanded a corps. He continued in corps command during the Battle of Corinth (October 3–4). In June 1862, Bragg's friend President Jefferson Davis appointed him a full general and named him to command the Army of Mississippi, which was renamed the Army of Tennessee on November 20, 1862.

Bragg performed well in Tennessee in the late summer of 1862 and he mounted an invasion of Kentucky, but he was forced to withdraw following the Battle of Perryville (October 8). On December 31, 1862, and January 2, 1863, Bragg attacked Union major general William S. Rosecrans's Army of the Cumberland in the Battle of Stones River and was defeated. Rosecrans then maneuvered Bragg out of Chattanooga, but Bragg counterattacked and caught Rosecrans off guard and defeated him in the Battle of Chickamauga (September 19–20). Bragg, however, failed to follow up the victory, and when he alienated his men through his harsh discipline and his chief subordinates through his incessant criticism and refusal to accept responsibility for mistakes, his generals urged President Davis to relieve him, without success. Davis even traveled to Chattanooga to assess the situation in person but determined that the complaints were the work of malcontents.

Bragg then suffered a major defeat in the Battle of Chattanooga (November 25, 1862), largely as a consequence of poor placement of artillery, and he resigned his command under pressure on November 29. Unable to part with his friend, Davis brought Bragg to Richmond as his military adviser. In this position, Bragg improved conscription and the supply system and reduced corruption. Sent to Fort Fisher near Wilmington, North Carolina, in October 1864 to defend the Confederacy's last Atlantic seaport, Bragg bungled the defense and Fort Fisher fell in January 1865. Bragg ended his military career as a subordinate to General Joseph E. Johnston in the Army of Tennessee. Bragg's last action was the Battle of Bentonville (March 19–21, 1865).

Following the war, Bragg, having lost his plantation, worked as superintendent of the water works in New Orleans, then later in an insurance firm. In 1874 he accepted a position as the chief engineer for the Gulf, Colorado, and Santa Fe Railroad. Bragg died in Galveston, Texas, on September 27, 1876.

TIM WATTS AND SPENCER C. TUCKER

See also

Artillery; Buena Vista, Battle of; Davis, Jefferson Finis; Taylor, Zachary.

References

Hallock, Judith Lee. *Braxton Bragg and Confederate Defeat.* Vol. 2. Tuscaloosa: University of Alabama Press, 1991.

Lavender, David. *Climax at Buena Vista: The American Campaigns in Northeastern Mexico, 1846–47.* Philadelphia, PA: Lippincott, 1966.

McWhiney, Grady. *Braxton Bragg and Confederate Defeat.* Vol. 1, *Field Command.* New York: Columbia University Press, 1969.

Winders, Richard Bruce. *Mr. Polk's Army: The American Military Experience in the Mexican War.* College Station: Texas A&M University Press, 1997.

Bravo Rueda, Nicolás
Birth Date: September 10, 1787
Death Date: April 22, 1854

Mexican army officer and politician who twice served as vice president of Mexico (1824–1828, 1846) and as interim president three times (1839, 1842–1843, 1846). Nicolás Bravo Rueda was born on September 10, 1787, in Chilpancingo (in the modern-day state of Guerrero) and joined the independence forces to effect the overthrow of Spanish rule. In 1822, a year after Mexico won its independence, Bravo was given the official honorific of "national hero."

Bravo opposed the rule of Emperor Agustín Iturbide and raised troops to help oust him in 1823. Bravo then became a member of a triumvirate that held executive authority and subsequently served as vice president of Mexico under President Guadalupe Victoria from 1824 to 1828. Returning to his military duties, he

Nicolás Bravo Rueda was one of the most influential military and political figures in Mexico from 1821 through the Mexican-American War. Three times interim president, he also commanded the Army of the East that resisted the advance of Major General Winfield Scott toward Mexico City in 1847. (Library of Congress)

accompanied General Antonio López de Santa Anna's failed expedition in 1836 to retake Texas during the Texas Revolution.

In 1843, President Pedro María Anaya gave Bravo command of all troops in the Federal District. In early 1846, Bravo again served as vice president under Mariano Paredes y Arrillaga, and in late July, when Paredes vacated the presidency to take command of Mexico's armies, Bravo briefly assumed the office. The following year, Santa Anna named Bravo commander of the Army of the East and charged him with repulsing the U.S. advance under Major General Winfield Scott from Veracruz to Mexico City. Bravo was hamstrung, however, by acute supply and arms shortages, ill-trained and ill-disciplined soldiers, and the lack of an overall strategic plan from Mexico City. Establishing his headquarters at Puebla, Bravo attempted to form a credible guerrilla force to harass the American line of communication, but this effort disintegrated because the guerrillas seemed more interested in robbing Mexicans than harassing Americans.

By August 1847, as U.S. troops approached the capital city, Bravo had formed a loose defensive line running from Mexicalzingo to Churubusco to San Antonio but was unable to much slow the American advance. In September, Bravo was given command of Chapultepec Castle on the outskirts of Mexico City. He had at his disposal a ragtag garrison of fewer than 1,000 men, including the young cadets of the Colegio Militar. The castle's fortifications were incomplete, and he could not expect reinforcement. In other words, he stood little chance against the numerically superior Americans, who boasted vastly superior arms and well-seasoned soldiers. Despite their best efforts, Bravo's men were unable to hold Chapultepec, and he was forced to surrender on September 13, 1847. He reportedly offered his gem-studded sword to the U.S. victors, who refused to accept it. Many Americans were apparently impressed by Bravo's cool courage under fire.

General Santa Anna, however, who had a love-hate relationship with Bravo and eyed him as a political rival, was not as impressed with Bravo's stand at Chapultepec. The general promptly ordered his arrest and demanded that he be tried for surrendering prematurely and abandoning his post. The charges were scurrilous, and few Mexicans would have seen fit to convict Bravo, who was eventually cleared of all charges.

In 1848, Bravo served as governor of Puebla, and two years later he served in the National Assembly representing the newly formed state of Guerrero. On April 22, 1854, Bravo died under somewhat mysterious circumstances at his home in Chilpancingo. His death came just one day after Santa Anna had visited the city, and many concluded that the general played some role in Bravo's demise.

Paul G. Pierpaoli Jr.

See also
Anaya, Pedro María de; Chapultepec, Battle of; Guerrilla Warfare; Los Niños Héroes; Mexican Military Academy (Colegio Militar); Mexico City Campaign; Paredes y Arrillaga, Mariano; Santa Anna, Antonio López de; Texas Revolution; Victoria, Guadalupe.

References

DePalo, William A., Jr. *The Mexican National Army, 1822–1852.* College Station: Texas A&M University Press, 1997.

Johnson, Timothy D. *A Gallant Little Army: The Mexico City Campaign.* Lawrence: University Press of Kansas, 2007.

Parrish, Leonard. "The Life of Nicolás Bravo." Unpublished PhD diss., University of Texas at Austin, 1951.

Brazito, Battle of
Event Date: December 25, 1846

Engagement, also known as the Battle of Temascalitos, between U.S. forces and elements of the Mexican army on December 25, 1846, at Brazito (Texas). Brazito, meaning "little arm," was a nondescript locale on the Rio Grande's left bank about 25 miles north of El Paso. The Army of the West, commanded by Colonel Stephen Watts Kearny, was one of three columns ordered to seize northern Mexico. Kearney captured New Mexico by taking Santa Fe on August 18, 1846. After Kearny departed for California with elements of the 1st Dragoons, Colonel Alexander Doniphan marched south on December 14, 1846, with the mission of meeting Brigadier General John E. Wool's force in Chihuahua, Mexico. Doniphan, a volunteer officer, commanded the 900 mounted riflemen of his own 1st Missouri Volunteer Regiment and 100 more from the 2nd Missouri Volunteers, plus three regular army advisers.

After a grueling 90-mile march through barren and forbidding country, Doniphan camped at Brazito on the afternoon of December 25 with about half his force and no artillery; the remainder of his troops were some miles behind. An advancing 1,000-man force of Mexican cavalry, infantry, and artillery appeared. Fortunately, its commander, Mexican brevet lieutenant colonel Antonio Ponce de León, deployed his force about a half mile away, giving Doniphan time to prepare for his first battle. Doniphan arranged his troops in line and dismounted, placing a small mounted element behind his line as a reserve and gathering his supply wagons at his left rear.

The Mexicans approached with cavalry on the flanks and infantry, supported by a single artillery piece in the center. The action began with a volley from the Mexican infantry from about 400 yards. Because the Mexicans were armed with old, smoothbore muskets that had an effective range of only about 100 yards, this accomplished little. In an attempt to deceive the Mexicans, however, Doniphan directed some of his soldiers to lie down. After another ineffective volley from 300 yards, more Americans appeared to go down. Doniphan had ordered his troops to hold their fire until the Mexicans were 100 yards distant. At that range, American rifle fire was deadly.

When it appeared that the Mexicans might envelop his left, Doniphan moved some of his men to that flank. The Mexicans thought he was retreating and charged. At that point, Doniphan shouted for his men to stand and fire, which caused the Mexican infantry to falter.

León's lancers then charged the American left flank while his infantry tested the American right. American fire, however, stopped both. León was wounded and a bugle call was misinterpreted by many of his soldiers as a call to withdraw. The Mexican attack fell apart. Captain John Reid then led his mounted reserve in a charge against the Mexican artillery piece, driving its crew away. The Mexicans were now in complete retreat. The engagement had lasted less than an hour, and the way to El Paso was open. The Americans had sustained 7 men wounded; the Mexicans lost more than 40 killed and many more wounded.

Philip L. Bolté

See also

Doniphan, Alexander William; Doniphan's March; Kearny, Stephen Watts; Wool, John Ellis.

References

Dawson, Joseph G. *Doniphan's Epic March: The 1st Missouri Volunteers in the Mexican War.* Lawrence: University Press of Kansas, 1999.

Francaviglia, Richard V., and Douglas W. Richmond, eds. *Dueling Eagles: Reinterpreting the Mexican-American War.* Fort Worth: Texas Christian University Press, 2000.

Breese, Samuel Livingston
Birth Date: October 6, 1794
Death Date: December 17, 1870

U.S. Navy officer. Born in Whitestown, New York, on October 6, 1794, Samuel Livingston Breese was the brother of Sidney Breese, future senator from Illinois. Breese received a midshipman's warrant on December 17, 1810. During the War of 1812, he participated in the Battle of Lake Champlain on September 11, 1814, for which he was awarded a sword and voted the Thanks of Congress.

Breese was promoted to lieutenant on April 17, 1816, and served in the Mediterranean in 1826–1827. He was promoted to master commandant on December 22, 1835, and was assigned to the Philadelphia Navy Yard in 1836. Promoted to captain on September 8, 1841, he commanded the frigate *Cumberland* in the Mediterranean Squadron in 1845.

During the Mexican-American War, Breese served as captain of the sloop *Albany* of 22 guns. He took part in the landing at Veracruz on March 9, 1847, the siege of the city, and the capture of Tuxpan, of which he briefly served as military governor.

From 1853 to 1855, Breese commanded the Norfolk (Gosport) Navy Yard. Breese commanded the U.S. Mediterranean Squadron from 1855 until 1858, and in 1858 he assumed command of the Brooklyn (New York) Navy Yard. Breese was promoted to commodore on the retired list effective July 16, 1862, and effective September 3, 1862, he was advanced to rear admiral on the retired list. He was appointed lighthouse inspector on his retirement and also served on the court-martial board during the Civil War. Breese died in Mount Airy, Pennsylvania, on December 17, 1870.

SPENCER C. TUCKER

See also

Tuxpan; Tuxpan, Battle of; United States Navy; Veracruz, Landing at and Siege of.

References

Bauer, K. Jack. *Surfboats and Horse Marines: U.S. Naval Operations in the Mexican War, 1846–48.* Annapolis, MD: United States Naval Institute, 1969.

Callahan, Edward W., ed. *List of Officers of the Navy of the United States and of the Marine Corps from 1775 to 1900.* New York: L. R. Hamersley Co., 1901.

Thompson, Kenneth E. *Civil War Commodores and Admirals: A Biographical Directory of All Eighty-Eight Union and Confederate Navy Officers Who Attained Commissioned Flag Rank during the War.* Portland, ME: Thompson Group, 2001.

Brevet Rank

A temporary rank bestowed on a military officer. The term "brevet" originated in France and came to mean a commission. The English adopted the term in the mid-1600s, also as a means of special patronage and promotion. Brevet ranks were bestowed for extraordinary service or heroism in battle. Usually an officer with a brevet rank was permitted to hold that title and to wear the insignia of the brevet rank but did not receive the higher pay. The exception to this was when a higher ranking officer was not present and the brevet officer was fulfilling his duties. Brevet ranks generally terminated with the end of a war, when the officer reverted to his permanent rank.

Both the British Army and the Continental Army employed brevet ranks during the American War for Independence. Brevet rank was first authorized for the U.S. Army in the Articles of War of 1806. It was employed during the War of 1812 and continued during the Mexican-American War, when it caused sufficient unrest among the officers in the army that President James K. Polk was forced to issue a declaration to the effect that brevet rank was inferior to actual rank. When he learned that Colonel David E. Twiggs outranked him, Brevet Brigadier General William J. Worth left the army just before the beginning of the war. He later returned, allegedly vowing to earn either a grave or a grade. During the Mexican War, Second Lieutenant Ulysses S. Grant received two brevet promotions, advancing him to brevet captain, and Robert E. Lee won brevets from captain through colonel.

The Civil War witnessed an enormous number of awarded brevets, with some 4,000 given to more than 2,000 Union officers. A number of brevets were also awarded to officers in volunteer units and militias. Throughout the first half of the 19th century, a number of recent graduates from the U.S. Military Academy at West Point were named brevet second lieutenants because there were not a sufficient number of billets for regular second lieutenants in the army.

One estimate holds that some 1,700 Union officers held the brevet ranks of brigadier general and major general. The possibility existed of an individual holding four separate ranks: actual volunteer rank, brevet volunteer rank, actual regular rank, and brevet regular army rank. Thus, George Armstrong Custer was a major general of volunteers at the end of the Civil War but reverted to the rank of lieutenant colonel in the regular army thereafter and was still serving in that rank when he was killed in the Battle of the Little Big Horn in 1876.

The U.S. Marine Corps also made use of brevet ranks during the Civil War and thereafter until World War I. The Marine Corps actually submitted brevet promotions to Congress for confirmation. In the 1920s, the Marine Corps created the now-obsolete Brevet Medal to recognize those officers who were awarded brevet commissions subsequently confirmed by Congress. The medal ranked directly below the Medal of Honor and ahead of the Navy Cross. Only several dozen were awarded.

The Confederate Army did not employ brevet ranks during the Civil War. The practice of brevet ranks was largely discontinued after the Civil War, although a few were awarded during the Indian Wars, the Spanish-American War, and World War I. Temporary and permanent ranks were applied during World War II.

DAVID SLOAN, SPENCER C. TUCKER, AND DAVID T. ZABECKI

See also

Mexico, Army; United States Army.

References

Neave-Hill, W. B. R. "Lieutenant-Colonel Brevet Rank." *Journal of the Society for Army Historical Research* 48, no. 194 (1970): 85–104.

Winders, Richard Bruce. *Mr. Polk's Army: The American Military Experience in the Mexican War.* College Station: Texas A&M University Press, 1997.

Brooke, George Mercer
Birth Date: October 16, 1785
Death Date: March 9, 1851

U.S. Army officer. George Mercer Brooke was born on his family's plantation, Mantapike, in King William County, Virginia, on October 16, 1785. Brooke entered the army in 1808 as a lieutenant in the U.S. 5th Infantry Regiment. Promoted to captain on May 1, 1810, Brooke served with that unit until May 1, 1814, when he was transferred to the 23rd Infantry Regiment as a major.

Brooke jointly commanded a battalion during the 1814 Niagara Campaign with Major Daniel McFarland and succeeded him when the latter fell in the Battle of Lundy's Lane on July 25, 1814. Brooke particularly distinguished himself throughout the ensuing siege of Fort Erie, being brevetted lieutenant colonel for actions during the nighttime British attack on August 15 and colonel for distinguished leadership during the sortie of September 17.

Brooke was retained in the peacetime establishment after the war, serving with the new 4th Infantry Regiment. During the course of the next four decades, he had a varied and far-ranging career. Brooke took part in Major General Andrew Jackson's Florida Campaign in 1817–1818. In 1824 he supervised the construction of Fort Brooke at the site of present-day Tampa, Florida. He was brevetted brigadier general on September 17, 1824, and promoted to full colonel commanding the 5th Infantry Regiment as of July 15, 1831.

Brooke next took charge of Military Department Number Four (Ohio, Indiana, Michigan, Wisconsin, Illinois, Iowa, and Missouri), and on June 10, 1846 he became commander of the Western Division—comprising U.S. territory west of the Mississippi River and headquartered at New Orleans, Louisiana. Brooke replaced Brigadier General Edmund P. Gaines, who had been removed for exceeding his authority in raising thousands of militiamen for the war that the government could not use. As commander of the Western Division, Brooke garnered great praise for efficiently forwarding supplies to the armies of Major Generals Zachary Taylor and Winfield Scott in Mexico. He subsequently presided over the court-martial of Lieutenant Colonel John C. Frémont.

Brooke rose to major general on May 30, 1848. On July 1, he was superseded by General Taylor and thereafter commanded Military Department Number One (Alabama, Mississippi, Louisiana, Tennessee, Kentucky, and Florida) and the following year took command of Department Number Eight in eastern Texas. Brooke died in San Antonio, Texas, on March 9, 1851. His son, John Mercer Brooke, was a U.S. Navy and later Confederate Navy officer who helped design the ironclad CSS *Virginia* as well as heavy naval guns for the Confederacy.

JOHN C. FREDRIKSEN

See also

Frémont, John Charles; Gaines, Edmund Pendleton; Scott, Winfield; Taylor, Zachary.

References

Bauer, K. Jack. *The Mexican War, 1846–1848.* New York: Macmillan, 1974.

Brooke, George M., Jr. *John M. Brooke: Naval Scientist and Educator.* Charlottesville: University Press of Virginia, 1980.

Brooke, St. George Tucker. "The Brooke Family of Virginia." *Virginia Magazine of History and Biography* 11 (1903): 444–446.

Brooks, William Thomas Harbaugh

Birth Date: January 28, 1821
Death Date: July 19, 1870

U.S. Army officer. William Thomas Harbaugh Brooks was born on January 28, 1821, in New Lisbon, Ohio. He graduated from the U.S. Military Academy, West Point, at the bottom of his class in 1841 and was assigned to the 3rd Infantry. He was stationed on the western frontier and subsequently saw combat toward the end of the Second Seminole War (1835–1842), remaining in Florida until 1843.

Brooks again served on the frontier until his regiment was ordered to Mexico to serve under Brigadier General Zachary Taylor. He participated in the opening battles of the Mexican-American War at Palo Alto (May 8, 1846) and Resaca de la Palma (May 9, 1846). Promoted to first lieutenant in September 1846, Brooks also served at the Battle of Monterrey on September 21–23, 1846, for which he was brevetted to captain for his meritorious service. Reassigned to Major General Winfield Scott's army in early 1847, Brooks participated in the siege of Veracruz (March 9–29, 1847) and at the Battle of Cerro Gordo (April 17–18, 1847). Before the latter engagement, he was credited with locating a mule path that helped the Americans turn the Mexicans' left flank. On the day prior to the Battle of Contreras (August 20, 1847), Brooks was dispatched on a nighttime scouting mission, along with Captain Robert E. Lee; the path they reconnoitered was used by Scott's attacking troops the next day. The Battle of Contreras ended in an American victory, and Brooks was promoted to major for his important reconnaissance efforts.

Brooks went on to fight at the Battle of Churubusco (August 20, 1847) and the Battles for Mexico City (September 8–15, 1847). He was appointed as adjutant on Brigadier General David Twiggs's staff, retaining the position until 1851, during which time he was promoted to the substantive grade of captain.

The postwar years found Brooks serving on the western frontier in the territories newly acquired from Mexico, mainly Texas and New Mexico. He participated in several campaigns against Native Americans that ultimately took a toll on his health.

Shortly after the outbreak of the Civil War, on September 28, 1861, Brooks was promoted to brigadier general of volunteers, serving with the Army of the Potomac during the Peninsular Campaign (March–August 1862) and the Battle of Antietam (September 17, 1862). He led a division at the Battles of Fredericksburg (December 13, 1862) and Chancellorsville (May 1–4, 1863) but ran afoul of Major General Ambrose Burnside, who held him partly culpable for the loss at Fredericksburg. Promoted to major general of volunteers on June 10, 1863, Brooks commanded the Department of the Monongahela until April 1864. From April to July 1864, he commanded a division at the Battle of Cold Harbor (June 1–3, 1864) and in the opening part of the Petersburg Campaign (June 15, 1864–April 3, 1865).

Years on the frontier and successive Civil War commands had taken their toll on Brooks's health, and he was forced to retire on July 14, 1864. He bought a farm in Huntsville, Alabama, and lived there until his death on July 19, 1870.

WILLIAM E. WHYTE

See also

Cerro Gordo, Battle of; Churubusco, Battle of; Contreras, Battle of; Lee, Robert Edward; Mexico City Campaign; Mexico City, Battle for; Monterrey, Battle of; Palo Alto, Battle of; Resaca de la Palma, Battle of; Scott, Winfield; Taylor, Zachary; Twiggs, David Emanuel; Veracruz, Landing at and Siege of.

References

Heitman, Francis B. *Historical Register and Dictionary of the United States Army: From Its Organization, September 29, 1789, to March 2, 1903.* Washington, DC: Government Printing Office, 1903.

Smith, Justin H. *The War with Mexico.* 2 vols. New York: Macmillan, 1919.

Stevens, George T. *Three Years in the Sixth Corps.* Charleston, SC: BiblioLife, 2009.

Brown, Jacob
Birth Date: July 19, 1789
Death Date: May 9, 1846

U.S. Army officer. Jacob Brown was born in Charlton, Massachusetts, on July 19, 1789. On August 3, 1812, he enlisted as a private in the 11th Infantry. Rising to the rank of sergeant, on April 15, 1814, he was commissioned as an ensign for his role in the Battle of Crysler's Farm. Brown gained promotion to third lieutenant on May 1, 1814, and to second lieutenant on September 1, 1814, for his role in the Battles of Chippewa and Lundy's Lane.

On May 17, 1815, Brown was transferred to the 6th Infantry. From 1818 through 1825, he was stationed at Council Bluffs on the Missouri River as quartermaster and commissary of subsistence. He took part in the Yellowstone Expedition of 1819. Brown was promoted to first lieutenant on August 18, 1819, and to captain on April 7, 1825.

From 1831 until 1840, Brown was on detached service in Little Rock, where he speculated in commercial and agricultural property in eastern Arkansas. There, too, while still on active duty, he was elected president of the Bank of Arkansas, serving a controversial one-year term during the Panic of 1837.

Brown rejoined the 6th Infantry in 1840 and on February 27, 1843, was promoted to major. In August 1845 he was assigned as acting commander of the 7th Infantry. With the beginning of the Mexican-American War, Brown and his regiment were assigned to Brigadier General Zachary Taylor's Army of Occupation at Corpus Christi, Texas. When the army advanced to the Rio Grande, opposite Matamoros, Taylor ordered the construction there of Fort Texas.

Fort Texas was not yet complete when, on May 1, Taylor marched with his army to Point Isabel to secure his line of communication and supply, leaving Brown in command there. On May 3, Mexican forces at Matamoros began a siege of Fort Texas with a heavy bombardment. On the afternoon of May 6, while walking the rounds of the post with his adjutant, Brown stopped to give instructions to a group of soldiers. At that moment, a Mexican shell struck the parapet, burying itself in the sand but failing initially to explode. When it did go off, it took off one of Brown's legs. His mangled limb was then amputated above the knee. The wound became infected, however, and Brown died on May 9, 1846.

When Taylor returned and heard the news of Brown's death, he renamed the post Fort Brown. Brownsville, Texas, established in 1846 at the same location, is named in his honor.

THOMAS W. CUTRER

See also

Fort Texas (Fort Brown); Point Isabel; Taylor, Zachary.

References

Doubleday, Rhoda Van Bibber Tanner Barbour, ed. *The Journals of Major Philip Norbourne Barbour.* New York: G. P. Putnam's Sons, 1901.

Ferrell, Robert H., ed. *Monterrey Is Ours! The Mexican War Letters of Lieutenant Dana, 1845–1847.* Lexington: University of Kentucky Press, 1990.

Heitman, Francis B. *Historical Register and Dictionary of the United States Army: From Its Organization, September 29, 1789, to March 2, 1903.* Washington, DC: Government Printing Office, 1903.

Buchanan, James
Birth Date: April 23, 1791
Death Date: June 1, 1868

Democratic Party politician, diplomat, secretary of state during the administration of James K. Polk (1845–1849), and 15th president of the United States (1857–1861). Buchanan was the last president to be born in the 18th century, the last secretary of state to become president, and the only bachelor president. James Buchanan was born on April 23, 1791, in Cove Gap, near Harrisburg, Pennsylvania. At age 16, he entered Dickinson College in Carlisle, graduating with honors in 1809. In 1813, he began practicing law in Lancaster, Pennsylvania, and served for a short period of time in a volunteer light dragoon unit during the War of 1812. After the war, he returned to his law practice in Lancaster where he made a substantial fortune.

At age 23, Buchanan was elected to the Pennsylvania House of Representatives as a Federalist, where he served from 1814 until 1819. That year he fell in love with Ann Coleman, but her family opposed her marriage to Buchanan. A few days after calling off the engagement, Coleman died, and Buchanan never again became seriously involved with another woman. During his tenure as president, Harriet Lane, an orphaned niece whom he had adopted, served as his First Lady.

Buchanan won election to the U.S. House of Representatives in 1820, serving in Congress from 1821 until 1831. There he became noted as a constitutional lawyer and served on the House Judiciary Committee. With the Federalist Party in decline, he supported the fledgling movement that would become the modern Democratic Party. In 1828, Buchanan led the Democratic presidential campaign in Pennsylvania and helped Andrew Jackson win that year's presidential election.

Shortly after Jackson's reelection in 1832, the president appointed Buchanan minister to Russia. After negotiating a trade treaty with

James Buchanan was U.S. secretary of state during the Mexican-American War. Initially counseling President James K. Polk to eschew territorial claims against Mexico, he subsequently supported the annexationist Treaty of Guadalupe Hidalgo. Buchanan was president of the United States during 1857–1861. (Library of Congress)

Russia, Buchanan returned to the United States the following year. He then won election to the U.S. Senate, where he chaired the important Senate Foreign Relations Committee. Buchanan served in the Senate from December 1834 until March 1845.

In 1844, Buchanan fervently hoped to receive the Democratic nomination for president, but that went to James K. Polk instead. Polk went on to win the election and appointed Buchanan as his secretary of state; he took office on March 10, 1845. Both Polk and Buchanan believed in Manifest Destiny and were strong proponents of U.S. westward expansion. In 1846, Buchanan negotiated the Oregon Treaty with the British minister to Washington, Richard Pakenham, which ended conflicting British and American claims on the Oregon Territory. The pact extended the current border between the United States and British Canada along the 49th parallel of latitude to Vancouver Sound and gave all of Vancouver Island to British Canada. The U.S. Senate ratified the treaty on June 18, 1846.

Buchanan also supported the efforts of outgoing president John Tyler to annex Texas by a joint resolution of Congress, a resolution that eventually helped spark the Mexican-American War in 1846. During that war, Buchanan shifted his view as to how much Mexican territory the United States should annex according with military fortunes. Initially, he counseled Polk to refrain from demanding territorial claims, but in the end he supported the 1848 Treaty of Guadalupe Hidalgo, directly negotiated by Nicholas Trist, chief clerk of the State Department. The treaty established the Rio Grande as the border between Mexico and Texas and ceded most of northern Mexico (the American Southwest), 55 percent of Mexico's pre-war territory, to the United States for $15 million. Buchanan, however, believed that the treaty should have included Baja California and the northern provinces of Mexico.

Buchanan's tenure in office was not an entirely happy one. He did not like the pressures of the office and the ambivalent relationship with Polk, who frequently questioned his motives and who suspected him of harboring presidential aspirations. He left his position as secretary of state in March 1849 and then attempted to gain the Democratic presidential nomination in 1852. Buchanan sparred with Stephen A. Douglas, U.S. senator from Illinois, over the nomination, but after 24 ballots failed to produce a majority for either candidate the Democrats turned to a little-known New Englander, Franklin Pierce, as a compromise candidate. Pierce went on to win the presidency.

The newly elected President Pierce then named Buchanan as minister to Britain. The posting to London kept Buchanan in politics while it also distanced him from the trouble of the disastrous Kansas-Nebraska Act of 1854. As minister, Buchanan helped draft the Ostend Manifesto, which proposed that the United States obtain Cuba as a place suitable for plantation agriculture using slaves. The manifesto angered antislavery forces and failed to achieve its goal, but Buchanan gained the favor of proslavery southerners.

In 1856, Buchanan again sought the presidency and this time was elected. He served from March 1857 to March 1861. Buchanan supported the U.S. Supreme Court's *Dred Scott* decision, which declared slaves to be property anywhere in the United States, and the Lecompton Constitution, which would have allowed Kansas to enter the Union as a slave state. In a December 3, 1860, message to Congress, he stated that while the states could not legally secede from the Union, the U.S. government could not legally prevent them from doing so. He watched silently as South Carolina and six other cotton states seceded in late December 1860 to form the Confederate States of America, leaving it to his successor, Abraham Lincoln, to take action.

In 1866, Buchanan published *Mr. Buchanan's Administration on the Eve of the Rebellion,* the first published presidential memoir. In it he defended his actions as president. Buchanan died on June 1, 1868, at his home at Wheatland, Pennsylvania.

ROBERT B. KANE

See also

Democratic Party; Douglas, Stephen Arnold; Guadalupe Hidalgo, Treaty of; Oregon, Treaty of; Oregon Boundary Dispute; Manifest Destiny; Mexican Cession; Ostend Manifesto; Pakenham, Richard; Polk, James Knox; Slavery; Texas; Trist, Nicholas Philip.

References

Bergeron, Paul H. *The Presidency of James K. Polk.* Lawrence: University of Kansas, 1987.

Binder, Frederick Moore. *James Buchanan and the American Empire.* Cranbury, NJ: Associated University Press, 1994.

Borneman, Walter R. *Polk: The Man Who Transformed the Presidency and America.* New York: Random House, 2008.

Clary, David A. *Eagles and Empire: The United States, Mexico, and the Struggle for a Continent.* New York: Bantam Books, 2009.

Buchanan, Robert Christie

Birth Date: March 11, 1811
Death Date: November 29, 1878

U.S. Army officer. Born on March 11, 1811, in Baltimore, Maryland, Buchanan, a nephew of President John Quincy Adams by marriage, graduated from the U.S. Military Academy at West Point in 1830. Commissioned as a second lieutenant in the 4th Infantry Regiment, he was then posted to the U.S. Army Baton Rouge Arsenal and Ordnance Depot in Louisiana. In 1832 he was assigned to Fort Crawford, Wisconsin, where he served in the Black Hawk War, commanding gunboats on the Wisconsin River. During 1836–1838, Buchanan was with the 4th Infantry in Florida, fighting in the Second Seminole War (1835–1842). Promoted to first lieutenant (March 1836), in 1838 Buchanan participated in the transfer of Cherokees from Georgia to Oklahoma, along the so-called Trail of Tears. Promoted to captain that November, he returned to Florida three years later to fight the Seminoles again.

Still a captain with the 4th Infantry in 1845, Buchanan accompanied Brigadier General Zachary Taylor's force when it was dispatched to Corpus Christi. After seeing action at the Battle of Palo Alto on May 8, 1846, Buchanan was instrumental in outflanking the Mexicans at Resaca de la Palma the following day. After locating a path through the chaparral, Buchanan led his company directly toward the Mexican left flank, taking it by surprise. After vicious hand-to-hand combat, his men seized a Mexican artillery battery. The Mexican defenders quickly panicked, and by day's end the Americans had scored another victory. Buchanan was brevetted to lieutenant colonel for his bravery. He also fought at the Battles of Monterrey, Churubusco, and Chapultepec. Advanced to the permanent rank of major in the 4th Infantry (February 1855), Buchanan served as superintendent of the Western Recruiting Service in Newport, Kentucky, during 1857–1859.

At the beginning of the Civil War, Buchanan was on frontier duty in Oregon and California. Promoted to lieutenant colonel in the 4th Infantry in September 1861, he served in the defense of Washington, D.C., from November 1861 to March 1862. Buchanan commanded the 4th Infantry in the Virginia Peninsula Campaign (March to July 1862). He subsequently fought in the Second Manassas (Bull Run) Campaign (August to September 1862), the Maryland Campaign (September to November 1862), and the Rappahannock Campaign (from December 1862 to January 1863). During March and April 1863, Buchanan was the commander of Fort Delaware, which housed political prisoners as well as captured Confederate officers and soldiers. From April 1863 to November 1864, he was superintendent of Volunteer Recruiting Services in New Jersey. Promoted to colonel of the 1st Infantry (February 1864), he commanded it in Louisiana from December 1864 to August 1865. He was brevetted major general in March 1865.

From January 1868 to March 1869, Buchanan commanded the District of Louisiana. During his administration of the state, Louisiana was readmitted to the Union. Buchanan oversaw the imposition of an African American governor and a Republican legislature. He retired from the U.S. Army in December 1870 and died in Washington, D.C., on November 29, 1878.

MICHAEL R. HALL

See also

Chapultepec, Battle of; Churubusco, Battle of; Monterrey, Battle of; Palo Alto, Battle of; Resaca de la Palma, Battle of; Taylor, Zachary.

References

Dawson, Joseph G. *Army Generals and Reconstruction: Louisiana, 1862–1877.* Baton Rouge: Louisiana State University Press, 1994.

Winters, John D. *The Civil War in Louisiana.* Baton Rouge: Louisiana State University Press, 1991.

Buckner, Simon Bolivar

Birth Date: April 1, 1823
Death Date: January 8, 1914

U.S. and Confederate Army officer. Simon Bolivar Buckner was born on April 1, 1823, at the family plantation of Glen Lily in Hart County, Kentucky. He graduated from the U.S. Military Academy, West Point, in 1840 and was commissioned a second lieutenant. He then served in a number of assignments, including teaching at West Point.

In the spring of 1846 Buckner was assigned to the 6th U.S. Infantry Regiment, which eventually joined Brigadier General John Wool's army at Saltillo, Mexico. In March 1847, he took part in the siege of Veracruz, and that August he became quartermaster for the 6th Infantry. He also saw action at the Battles of Churubusco, Contreras, and El Molino del Rey. For his performance in the latter engagement, he was brevetted to captain. Buckner also took part in the Battle of Mexico City and then was assigned to occupation duty there, where he joined the Aztec Club with other U.S. officers.

After the war, Buckner remained in the army. He resigned his commission in 1855, however, to manage the family business in Chicago, but his continuing interest in military affairs led to his appointment as adjutant general of the Illinois militia.

Buckner returned to Kentucky in 1858, where he commanded the elite Citizen Guard of Louisville before Governor Beriah Magoffin appointed him in March 1860 to command Kentucky's state guard. Under Buckner, the 5,000-man state guard gained a reputation as the best-drilled and best-officered military unit outside of the U.S. Army. When the pro-Union Kentucky legislature ordered the state guard to turn in its weapons in July 1861, Buckner resigned in protest. He had already turned down offers of a general's commission in the Union Army.

Confederate troops occupied Kentucky in September 1861, and Buckner accepted a brigadier general's commission in the Confederate Army that same month. He led a force that briefly occupied Bowling Green, then withdrew to Fort Donelson on the Cumberland River in Tennessee and was its third ranking officer in February 1862 when it came under attack by Union forces. While his two superiors, Brigadier Generals Gideon J. Pillow and John B. Floyd, chose to escape, Buckner opted to remain with his men, and he surrendered the fort to federal troops under Brigadier General Ulysses S. Grant on February 16.

Buckner was a prisoner of war until August 1862. During his confinement, he was promoted to major general. On his release he commanded a division in the Army of Tennessee.

After a brief period in command of the District of the Gulf, Buckner assumed control of the Department of East Tennessee in May 1863. In August, he participated in the Chickamauga Campaign, and his men played a key role in breaking the Union line at the Battle of Chickamauga on September 20, 1863. Buckner then returned to eastern Tennessee.

On April 28, 1864, Buckner was transferred to the Trans-Mississippi Department and he assumed command of west Louisiana, where he built up Confederate forces to defend against a federal invasion. On May 26, 1865, Buckner surrendered the Trans-Mississippi Department, the last Confederate commander to do so.

After the war, Buckner was not permitted to leave Louisiana until 1868. He found employment as a newspaper writer, commission merchant, and president of an insurance company. When he returned to Kentucky, Buckner brought suit to recover his and his wife's confiscated property. He was successful in both instances, and by 1871, Buckner's personal fortune was estimated at more than $1 million.

Buckner was elected governor of Kentucky in 1887 and headed a reform-minded administration. Many of his programs, such as education and prison reforms and trust and railroad regulation, were blocked by special interests. He left office in 1892. In 1896, Buckner ran for vice president on the so-called Gold Democrats' ticket, helping to ensure that the populist William Jennings Bryan lost the election. Buckner died at his home in Glen Lily on January 8, 1914.

TIM WATTS

See also

Aztec Club; Churubusco, Battle of; Contreras, Battle of; El Molino del Rey, Battle of; Mexico City, Battle for; Veracruz, Landing at and Siege of; Wool, John Ellis.

References

Powell, Robert A. *Kentucky Governors.* Danville, KY: Bluegrass Printing Company, 1976.

Stickles, Arndt Mathis. *Simon Bolivar Buckner: Borderland Knight.* Chapel Hill: University of North Carolina Press, 1940.

Buena Vista, Battle of
Event Dates: February 22–23, 1847

Battle that pitted some 4,700 U.S. troops commanded by Major General Zachary Taylor against a Mexican army of 15,000 commanded by Mexican general Antonio López de Santa Anna on February 22–23, 1847. In the preceding months, Taylor had crossed the Rio Grande into Mexico and had besieged the city of Monterrey. Following its capture on September 23, 1846, President James K. Polk approved shifting most of Taylor's forces to Major General Winfield Scott for an advance on Mexico City from Veracruz. Much to Taylor's displeasure, these forces were gradually siphoned off beginning in January 1847. Taylor then decided to concentrate what was left of his army around the city of Saltillo. When a U.S. courier was killed and his dispatches taken, Santa Anna, located at San Luis Potosí, some 250 miles to the south, learned of the approximate size of Taylor's force and Scott's intention to attack the Mexican capital. Santa Anna quickly gathered an army to march north in hopes of pushing Taylor's reduced army out of Mexico, then returning south to meet Scott.

Santa Anna set out with some 20,000 men, but only about 15,000 were able to make the difficult march north. At first unwilling to believe that Santa Anna was moving against him, Taylor learned for certain on February 21, 1847, that the Mexican army was nearby. Taylor then decided to leave Saltillo as Santa Anna's army approached. The Americans first advanced seven miles to Agua Nueva but then backtracked to the more easily defended Angostura Mountain pass, situated halfway between Agua Nueva and Saltillo. The Americans named the resulting battle for the nearby Hacienda Buena Vista, while the Mexicans remember it by the name of the pass.

Taylor ordered his second in command, Brigadier General John Wool, to set up a defensive position. The Americans chose the difficult high ground in large part to offset the Mexican advantage in cavalry. As the Americans prepared to meet the Mexican attack, Santa Anna arrived at Agua Nueva with his exhausted troops. Taylor

Battle of Buena Vista, February 22–23, 1847

	United States	Mexico
Total Mobilized	4,800	16,000
Casualties		
Killed	267	500
Wounded	456	1,000
Captured	0	300*
Missing	23	Unknown

* Includes some wounded

BATTLE OF BUENA VISTA, FEBRUARY 22–23, 1847

N

Hacienda Buena Vista

MEXICO

Angostura R.

3. *U.S. forces successfully defend Hacienda Buena Vista from Mexican cavalry*

U.S. camps

25°N

TAYLOR

Bragg 1st MS

3rd IN

3rd IN

Washington

1st IL

4. *Mexican column repulsed by realigned U.S. forces*

1. *Initial Mexican advance repulsed by U.S. artillery*

2. *Main Mexican attack turns U.S. left flank*

2nd KY

2nd IL

Blanco

Sherman

Bragg

2nd IN

1st KY 1st AR

O'Brien

Ortega

Pacheco

Lombardini

Juvera

Torrejón

SANTA ANNA

Ampudia

■ U.S. troops
□ Mexican troops
→ U.S. troop movement
→ Mexican troop movement
✺ Major battle
∥ Artillery battery
⌂ U.S. headquarters
⌂ Mexican headquarters

0   1/8   1/4 mi
0   1/8   1/4 km

101°W

Lithograph depicting the Battle of Buena Vista during February 22–23, 1847, between a Mexican army commanded by General Antonio López de Santa Anna and U.S. major general Zachary Taylor's Army of Occupation. This final battle in northern Mexico was a significant turning point in the Mexican-American War. (Library of Congress)

returned from Saltillo on the morning of February 22 to see the Mexicans deploying. Perceiving Taylor's withdrawal as weakness, Santa Anna demanded that the Americans surrender, which Taylor promptly rejected. The battle opened that afternoon when Mexican light infantry under General Pedro de Ampudia, who had previously faced Taylor while in command of Mexican forces at Monterrey, tried to scale the mountain on the American left but was rebuffed. By evening, skirmishing between the two sides had ceased.

A light rain fell that night as both sides repositioned their forces for the main battle expected the next day. Early on February 23, Santa Anna ordered the main assault. Advancing up the Saltillo Road, the Mexicans were halted by fire from an American artillery battery in the pass commanded by Captain John M. Washington. Meanwhile, the Mexicans were having success on the American left. There two Mexican divisions drove back the vastly outnumbered American 2nd Indiana Regiment and three artillery pieces. American reinforcements were rushed forward to slow the Mexican advance, while Wool, who exercised tactical control of the battle, ordered the center slowly to retire, supported as it did so by artillery fire. Taylor arrived to help rally the men.

Meanwhile, Mexican cavalry moved around the American left to attack Hacienda Buena Vista in the American rear. There the cavalry was met, and repulsed, by wagon train guards and some of the troops who had retreated earlier. Wool was able to form a

new battle line and halt the Mexican breakthrough. A U.S. counterattack that afternoon was repulsed by the Mexicans, who then launched their own attack in turn and took two American artillery pieces. American artillery, which played perhaps the key role in the battle, halted any further Mexican advance.

That afternoon, Santa Anna withdrew and the battle was over. During the night the Mexicans began retracing their steps south so that Santa Anna might defend against Scott's invasion force. The badly outnumbered Taylor expected a renewal of the Mexican attack the next day and was surprised to learn of the Mexican departure. He did not pursue.

The Battle of Buena Vista claimed U.S. casualties of 267 dead, 456 wounded, and 23 missing. Mexican losses were far higher: 600 killed, 1,000 wounded, and 1,800 missing. The battle brought Taylor additional laurels and assisted him in his successful bid for the presidency in 1848. Although Santa Anna had suffered significant losses at Buena Vista, he was nonetheless able to reconstitute his forces to face Scott.

PAUL J. SPRINGER AND SPENCER C. TUCKER

See also

Agua Nueva; Ampudia, Pedro de; Artillery; Bragg, Braxton; Mexico City Campaign; Monterrey, Battle of; Polk, James Knox; Saltillo; San Luis Potosí; Santa Anna, Antonio López de; Taylor, Zachary; Washington, John Macrae; Wool, John Ellis.

References

Lavender, David. *Climax at Buena Vista: The American Campaigns in Northeastern Mexico, 1846–47*. Philadelphia, PA: Lippincott, 1966.

Nichols, Edward J. *Zach Taylor's Little Army*. Garden City, NY: Doubleday, 1963.

Winders, Richard Bruce. *Mr. Polk's Army: The American Military Experience in the Mexican War*. College Station: Texas A&M University Press, 1997.

Burleson, Edward
Birth Date: December 15, 1798
Death Date: December 26, 1851

Soldier and statesman of the Texas Revolution and Texas Republic. Born on December 15, 1798, in Buncombe County, North Carolina, Edward Burleson served in the War of 1812 as a private in the Alabama militia. Moving to Missouri following the war, he was elected captain of local militia in 1817, later rising to colonel, and served as colonel in the Tennessee militia from 1823 to 1830. Burleson moved to Texas—then still a province of Mexico—in May 1830 where he earned a reputation as a frontier soldier, Indian fighter, and military leader.

Applying for and receiving a league of land from Texan *empresario* Stephen F. Austin in 1831, Burleson went back to Tennessee briefly before returning to Texas with his family later that year to settle his land. Located on the outer reaches of the Austin land grant, the Burleson league required its owner to engage in frequent altercations with hostile Native Americans. Proving himself adept and fierce as an Indian fighter, Burleson soon became a local military leader and an individual other colonists looked to for political leadership. He became a member of the governing *ayuntamiento* for several Texan counties in 1832 and was later elected lieutenant colonel of the Austin area militia. Following the Battle of Gonzales in early October 1835 at the start of the Texas Revolution, Burleson was elected lieutenant colonel in Stephen F. Austin's army, serving in the infantry.

During the siege of San Antonio de Béxar (November–December 1835), Burleson was elected to replace Austin—who had resigned his position to head a delegation to Washington, D.C.—as commanding officer of the Texan volunteers who began a partial siege of the city. Finding it difficult to get the militia to attack Béxar, Burleson ordered a retreat from the city, only to be contradicted by one of his subordinates, Ben Milam, who rallied most of the volunteers. Fearing that he would lose control of his forces, Burleson supported Milam's attack on Béxar on December 5 and captured the city four days later. The volunteer army disbanded shortly thereafter, and Burleson later became commanding officer of the 1st Regiment, commanding it at the Battle of San Jacinto, on April 21, 1836, when he accepted the surrender of Mexican forces.

Burleson continued his participation in Texan political and military matters during the era of the Texas Republic (1836–1845). He led frontier militia forces on numerous occasions, engaging hostile Native American tribes and defending against occasional Mexican incursions into Texas. Burleson served in the Texan senate on two occasions and was elected as vice president of Texas in 1841.

Then, during the Mexican-American War, Burleson was a senior aide-de-camp with the rank of major and served as a spy at Monterrey and Buena Vista. Burleson particularly distinguished himself during the Battle of Monterrey. Unwilling to simply stand by as a staff officer, he organized some 20 Texas volunteers to conduct a reconnaissance. Successfully completing his mission, he made his report to Brigadier General William Worth, who was struggling to take Independence Hill. Worth then ordered Burleson to charge a stout force of Mexican cavalry and artillery near the base of the hill. After several hours of heated combat, Burleson's impromptu force played a leading role in the Americans gaining control of the hill. The capture of Independence Hill marked an important event that resulted ultimately in an American victory. Burleson was later cited for his extraordinary bravery.

Burleson again served in the Texas Senate following the war until his death from pneumonia on December 26, 1851, in Austin, Texas.

KELLY E. CRAGER

See also

Almonte, Juan Nepomuceno; Austin, Stephen Fuller; Béxar, Siege of; Buena Vista, Battle of; Monterrey, Battle of; San Jacinto, Battle of; Texas; Texas Revolution; Worth, William Jenkins.

References

Brands, H. W. *Lone Star Nation*. New York: Doubleday, 2004.

Campbell, Randolph B. *Gone to Texas: A History of the Lone Star State*. New York: Oxford University Press, 2003.

Dishman, Christopher. *The Perfect Gibraltar: The Battle for Monterrey, Mexico*. Norman: University of Oklahoma Press, 2010.

Jenkins, John H., and Kenneth Kesselus. *Edward Burleson: Texas Frontier Leader*. Austin, TX: Jenkins, 1990.

Burnett, Ward B.
Birth Date: 1810
Death Date: June 24, 1884

U.S. engineer and army officer who was severely wounded during the September 1847 Battle of Chapultepec. Ward B. Burnett was born in 1810 in New York and attended the U.S. Military Academy at West Point, graduating in 1832. Commissioned a second lieutenant in the 2nd U.S. Artillery Regiment shortly thereafter, he saw service during the 1832 Black Hawk War in Illinois and modern-day Wisconsin. He subsequently taught infantry tactics at West Point and was reassigned to the Corps of Engineers, a posting that was more suited to his proclivities. In 1836, Burnett resigned his commission and pursued a career in civil engineering.

When the Mexican-American War began in 1846, Burnett volunteered for service, becoming colonel of the 2nd New York

Volunteer Infantry Regiment. Dispatched to Mexico sometime thereafter, he led his unit admirably during the Siege of Veracruz and the Battles of Cerro Gordo, Contreras, and Churubusco. On September 13, 1847, as U.S. troops moved toward Mexico City during the Battle of Chapultepec, Burnett's New York Volunteers were among the first units set to storm the castle of Chapultepec. Burnett, leading his men during the initial storming of the Mexican defenses, crossed a minefield under heavy small-arms fire. As his unit advanced toward the high walls of the castle, he was struck by a musket ball and seriously wounded. Lieutenant Colonel Charles Baxter took command as Burnett was carried to a field hospital at Hacienda Misoac.

After he was sufficiently recovered, Burnett left the war front for home. Brevetted brigadier general for his service in Mexico, he mustered out in 1848 and held a series of important engineering jobs, including superintendent of the navy dry docks at the Philadelphia Navy Yard and the Brooklyn Navy Yard. Burnett also served as chief engineer for the Brooklyn Water Works. Subsequently, he served as U.S. surveyor general in the Kansas and Nebraska Territory before retiring to the Washington, D.C., area. Burnett died in Washington, D.C., on June 24, 1884.

PAUL G. PIERPAOLI JR.

See also
Cerro Gordo, Battle of; Chapultepec, Battle of; Churubusco, Battle of; Contreras, Battle of; Veracruz, Landing at and Siege of.

References
Bauer, K. Jack. *The Mexican-American War, 1846–1848.* New York: Macmillan, 1974.
Dupuy, R. Ernest. *Men of West Point: The First 150 Years of the United States Military Academy.* New York: W. Sloane, 1951.

Bustamante, Carlos María de
Birth Date: November 4, 1774
Death Date: September 29, 1848

Mexican statesman, historian, and prolific author who used the accomplishments of Mexico's extensive and well-developed ancient civilizations to help cultivate a sense of Mexican nationalism after independence in 1821. Carlos María de Bustamante was born in Antequera de Oaxaca, Mexico, on November 4, 1774. He began studying law in 1794 in Mexico City, returned to Oaxaca in 1800 after receiving his bachelor's degree, and became a lawyer in Guadalajara in 1801. In 1805, he became the editor of the *Diario de Mexico.*

After 1810, Bustamante participated in the nascent Mexican independence movement and published pro-independence articles in a variety of periodicals. Because of his pro-independence stance, he was imprisoned several times by the royalist government. In 1820 Bustamante joined forces with Antonio López de Santa Anna and became his secretary, and the next year he supported the efforts of a creole officer in the Spanish army, Colonel Agustín de Iturbide, to grant Mexico its independence.

After independence, however, Bustamante opposed Iturbide's successful effort to turn Mexico into a hereditary monarchy. Consequently, Bustamante was again imprisoned, and at least once the government confiscated his possessions, including his manuscripts, and later sold them at public auction. Despite these setbacks, Bustamante received appointments to several important government positions. He served, off and on, as the representative from Oaxaca to the Mexican legislature from 1824 until his death in 1848, and as one of five members of the supreme executive power, a fourth branch of government under the 1835 centralist constitution, from 1837 to 1841.

In addition to his government service, Bustamante established himself as a prominent historian and writer. He believed that the accomplishments of Mexico's ancient civilizations were on the same level as those of Europe. He selected exemplary accounts of past Mexican civilizations, many of which had existed only as partly forgotten manuscripts, to make them better known to the Mexican people. Bustamante particularly used the extraordinary nature of Mexico's native heritage to further ideas of Mexican nationalism among his fellow intellectuals. Around 1830 Bustamante published a contemporary version of the *Historia general de las cosas de Nueva España* (*General History of the Things of New Spain*), also known as the *Florentine Codex,* originally written by Fray Bernardino de Sahagún (1499–1590). He also published the chronicle of Francisco López de Gómara (1511?–1566?), a Spanish historian from Seville, particularly noted for his works on the early-16th-century expedition by Hernán Cortés that conquered the Aztec Empire in Mexico. In all he authored 117 works that total 19,142 pages.

Bustamante was also an astute observer of public life in early republican Mexico, and his articles, in which he voiced his opinions with regard to the frequent political upheavals that shook the nation from 1821 to 1848, appeared almost daily in the country's vibrant press. As recent research shows, in addition to his commitment to Mexico's indigenous cultures, Bustamante's political ideology proved highly distinctive. Although he preferred centralism, he did not turn away from his commitment to constitutionalism and republicanism.

Bustamante was particularly chagrined by the Mexican-American War of 1846–1848. His history of that war, *El Nuevo Bernal Díaz Del Castillo, o sea, historia dela invasión de los Anglo-Americanos en México,* published in 1847, provided a sad record of the decay and disintegration that afflicted Mexico at the time. He wrote frankly and unsparingly about the conduct of the war on the Mexican side, and directed his frustration at one man—General Antonio López de Santa Anna—whom he accused of handing over Mexico to the United States. Adversely affected by the war and the death of his wife in August 1846, Bustamante died in Mexico City on September 29, 1848.

ROBERT B. KANE AND PEDRO SANTONI

See also
Mexico; Public Opinion and the War, Mexican; Santa Anna, Antonio López de.

References
Castelán Rueda, Roberto. *La fuerza de la palabra impresa: Carlos María de Bustamante y el discurso de la modernidad.* Mexico City: Fondo de Cultura Económica, 1997.

Fowler, Will. *Mexico in the Age of Proposals, 1821–1853*. Westport, CT: Greenwood Press, 1998.

Fowler, Will. *Santa Anna of Mexico*. Lincoln: University of Nebraska, 2007.

Santoni, Pedro. "The View from the Other Side: Mexican Historiographical Perspectives on the 1846–1848 War with the United States." In *Ready, Booted, and Spurred: Arkansas in the U.S.-Mexican War*, edited by William A. Frazier and Mark K. Christ, 74–101. Little Rock: Butler Center for Arkansas Studies, 2009, 74–101.

Bustamante y Oseguera, Anastasio
Birth Date: July 27, 1780
Death Date: February 8, 1853

Conservative Mexican politician and president of Mexico (1830–1832, 1837–1841). Anastasio Bustamante was born on July 27, 1780, in Jiquilpan, Michoacán. His parents, who were *peninsulares* (Spaniards born on the Iberian Peninsula), sent him to study religion at the seminary in Guadalajara and then medicine in Mexico City. After completing his studies, he became the family physician to Félix María Calleja, the military commander of San Luis Potosí. Bustamante fought with Calleja's forces against the anti-Spanish rebellion instigated by Father Miguel Hidalgo y Costilla. He distinguished himself in the encounter that put an end to Hidalgo's movement, the January 17, 1811, Battle of Calderón Bridge.

In 1821 Bustamante abandoned the royalist cause and joined Agustín Iturbide, who conspired to separate Mexico from Spain and authored the Plan de Iguala (February 24, 1821). The proposal declared Mexico's independence and established a constitutional monarchy. Iturbide then appointed Bustamante commander of the Mexican cavalry.

Following the achievement of independence that September, Bustamante became a member of the Provisional Junta of Government, which ruled until Iturbide was crowned emperor of Mexico on July 21, 1822, and he continued to support Iturbide even after his abdication in March 1823. Bustamante remained in the military for the next few years, and in 1828 he won the vice presidency. Then, in late 1829, Bustamante led a successful coup against then president Vicente Guerrero. Bustamante assumed the presidency early the next January, the first of his two terms in that office (1830–1832). Ousted by liberal forces, Bustamante then went into the first of his two European exiles. He returned to Mexico in time to fight in the Texas revolt and became president again in 1837. Bustamante's second presidential term ended when he was deposed in 1841, after which he again sailed for Europe to begin three years of exile.

Bustamante returned to Mexico in mid-June 1845, and although he did not engage in combat with U.S. forces during the Mexican War he nonetheless played a significant role in Mexican domestic affairs during the conflict. By year's end Bustamante, a staunch supporter of then president General José Joaquín Herrera,

served as commander of the Mexico City garrison. As such he was preparing the city's defenses to resist the pro-monarchist rebellion led by General Mariano Paredes y Arrillaga. On December 30, however, he resigned his position when the troops under his command joined Paredes's revolt. Then, late in 1846, he served as the commander in chief of Mexico's Army of the West, and twice in 1848 Bustamante helped the *moderado*-led government remain in power. That January he refused to support a revolt in San Luis Potosí, the leaders of which sought to continue hostilities against the U.S. Army, and in June he subdued another rebellion led by General Paredes.

Bustamante remained in the army and continued to be active in national politics in the years that followed the war. He commanded the forces that crushed the peasant uprising known as the Sierra Gorda Rebellion in 1848–1849, as well as another antigovernment revolt in Guanajuato early in 1851. He died in San Miguel de Allende, Guanajuato, on February 8, 1853.

MICHAEL R. HALL AND PEDRO SANTONI

See also
Decree of 1830; Mexico; Pastry War; Santa Anna, Antonio López de; Texas; Texas Revolution.

References
Andrews, Catherine. *Entre la espada y la constitución: El General Anastasio Bustamante, 1780–1853*. Tamaulipas: Universidad Autónoma de Tamaulipas, 2008.

Costeloe, Michael P. *The Central Republic in Mexico, 1836–1846: Hombres de Bien in the Age of Santa Anna*. New York: Cambridge University Press, 2002.

DePalo, William A., Jr. *The Mexican National Army, 1822–1852*. College Station: Texas A&M University Press, 1997.

DiTella, Torcuato S. *National Politics in Early Independent Mexico, 1820–1847*. Albuquerque: University of New Mexico Press, 1996.

Fowler, Will. *Mexico in the Age of Proposals, 1821–1853*. Westport, CT: Greenwood Press, 1998.

Santoni, Pedro. *Mexicans at Arms: Puro Federalists and the Politics of War, 1845–1848*. Fort Worth: Texas Christian University Press, 1996.

Butler, Anthony Wayne
Birth Date: 1787
Death Date: 1849

U.S. lawyer, soldier, politician, and diplomat. Born sometime in 1787 in Clarendon County, South Carolina, Anthony Wayne Butler was commissioned a lieutenant colonel in the U.S. Army at the outbreak of the War of 1812 and was later promoted to colonel and commanded the 2nd Rifle Regiment, serving under Major General Andrew Jackson. After the war, he settled in Kentucky and built a large plantation near Russellville.

Butler went on to serve two terms in the Kentucky legislature before running unsuccessfully for the state governorship in 1820. He moved to Mississippi in 1829, and later to Coahuila y Texas, where he engaged in land speculation. Believing himself to be an expert on

Mexico, Butler contacted his old friend Jackson, now president of the United States, and lobbied him to appoint him U.S. minister to Mexico. Jackson chose Butler to serve as chargé d'affaires to Mexico in 1829, succeeding the botanist and statesman Joel R. Poinsett.

Butler, like Jackson, was a strong proponent of the U.S. acquisition of the Mexican province of Texas. Indeed, this may have been the sole reason he was appointed to the post. Butler spoke no Spanish, was thoroughly ignorant of diplomatic protocol, and had the reputation of being a swashbuckling, ethically challenged bully, traits hardly useful for a diplomat.

Jackson asked Butler to present a proposal for the American acquisition of Texas and Northern California, which never materialized. His tenure in Mexico was forgettable, and he only antagonized Mexican officials with his unscrupulous and undiplomatic behavior. Butler even tried to offer a bribe of $5 million to the Mexican government to cede to the United States the desired territory, but he was turned down. Texan Sam Houston had little use for his undiplomatic ways and underhanded tactics, and even Jackson concluded that his friend was a scoundrel. Nevertheless, Butler retained his post for nearly six years. He was recalled from Mexico in 1835 but remained in the country of his own accord and continued to make periodic reports to Jackson on the state of Texas affairs in Mexico. Finally, an outraged Mexican government demanded that Butler be recalled and leave Mexico immediately.

Butler subsequently took up residence in Texas and was elected to the territorial legislature in 1838. Upon the outbreak of the Mexican-American War in 1846, Butler offered his services to Major General Zachary Taylor but ended up moving north in 1847. He died on the Mississippi River in 1849 in the act of saving fellow passengers from a burning steamboat.

RUSSELL D. JAMES

See also
Coahuila y Texas; Houston, Samuel; Jackson, Andrew; Mexico; Texas.

References
Lamar, Curt. "A Diplomatic Disaster: The Mexican Mission of Anthony Butler." *The Americas* 45 (1988): 1–17.
Smith, Justin H. *The War with Mexico*. 2 vols. New York: Macmillan, 1919.
Williams, Amelia W., and Eugene C. Barker, eds. *The Writings of Sam Houston, 1813–1863.* 8 vols. Austin: University of Texas Press, 1938–1943.

Butler, Pierce Mason
Birth Date: April 11, 1798
Death Date: 1847

U.S. Army officer and politician. Pierce Mason Butler was born in Edgefield District (later county), South Carolina, on April 11, 1798, and was the brother of two other well-known South Carolinians—Andrew Pickens Butler and William Butler Jr. He was educated at the Willington Academy in Willington, South Carolina, and in 1818 was appointed a second lieutenant in the

U.S. Army. Through distinguished service, he rose to the rank of captain but resigned his commission in 1829 to become active in South Carolina politics and to begin a career as a banker. Butler eventually became the president of the State Bank of South Carolina. He subsequently served in the South Carolina militia, rising to the rank of lieutenant colonel and distinguishing himself during the early years of the Second Seminole War of 1835–1842.

Largely because of the popularity he had gained as a soldier serving his state, Butler was elected governor of South Carolina in 1836. He served a two-year term and chose not to run for reelection. While governor, Butler sought to heal the wounds brought about by the 1832 Nullification Crisis, a movement that he had endorsed at the time. He was also one of the first governors in the United States to support a public, state-supported education system. In 1841, at the end of his second term as governor, Butler secured a presidential appointment as U.S. agent to the Cherokee Nation at Fort Gibson (present-day Muskogee, Oklahoma), a post he held until 1846, when he resigned because of ill health.

In December 1846, after the beginning of war with Mexico, Butler secured appointment as colonel of the Palmetto Regiment of South Carolina Volunteers, encompassing 10 companies of former professional soldiers and volunteers. The Palmetto Regiment was assigned to the brigade commanded by Brigadier General John A. Quitman, and when Quitman was promoted to major general and assigned to the command of a division, his old brigade was given to Brigadier General James Shields. Butler's regiment performed well during the Mexico City Campaign, fighting in the siege of Veracruz and the Battles of Contreras (August 19, 1847), Churubusco (August 20, 1847), and Chapultepec (September 12–13, 1847).

Butler was often sick during the march from Veracruz to Mexico City and had to be carried on a litter at the head of his regiment when he was unable to ride horseback or walk. While still suffering the effects of his illness, he led his regiment in its midnight march to fight in the Battle of Churubusco. Butler was wounded in the leg by an errant musket ball during the opening hours of the battle and was heard to yell, "The South Carolinians will follow you to death!" a battle cry that caused a cheer from his men and a charge into the heat of battle. Butler died that same day from a second musket ball to his head, as his men swept forward and helped win the battle for the United States. His body was shipped back to South Carolina for burial in Edgefield, where he was given a full military funeral. Butler's regiment went on to be among the vanguard during the final push into Mexico City in September 1847 and claimed to be the first U.S. unit to raise its flag on the walls surrounding the city.

RUSSELL D. JAMES

See also
Chapultepec, Battle of; Churubusco, Battle of; Contreras, Battle of; Mexico City Campaign; Quitman, John Anthony; Shields, James; Veracruz, Landing at and Siege of.

References

Claiborne, J. F. H. *Life and Correspondence of John A. Quitman.* Vol. 2. New York: Harper and Brothers, 1860.

Meyer, Jack A. *South Carolina in the Mexican War: A History of the Palmetto Regiment, 1846–1847.* Columbia: South Carolina Department of Archives and History, 1996.

Butler, William Orlando

Birth Date: April 19, 1791
Death Date: August 6, 1880

U.S. attorney, Democratic Party politician, and army officer. William Orlando Butler was born on April 19, 1791, in Jessamine County, Kentucky, and graduated from Transylvania University in 1812. After briefly studying law in Lexington, he enlisted as a volunteer private in September 1812, operating with Kentucky forces. That same month, he was dispatched to Fort Wayne to serve under Brigadier General James Winchester. On January 13, 1813, Butler was wounded and taken prisoner during action at the river Raisin. After being incarcerated for a time at Fort Niagara, Butler was exchanged and commissioned a captain of volunteers. In 1814, he saw action in Alabama and New Orleans under Major General Andrew Jackson. He was brevetted major for his performance in the Battle of New Orleans (January 8, 1815). During 1816–1817, he served on Jackson's staff.

In 1817, Butler resigned his commission, returned to his legal studies, was admitted to the bar, and commenced a law practice in Carrollton, Kentucky. From 1817 to 1818, he served in the Kentucky House of Representatives. From 1839 to 1843, Butler, a Democrat, served in the U.S. House of Representatives, and in 1844 he ran unsuccessfully for the governorship of Kentucky.

On June 29, 1846, at the outset of the Mexican-American War, Butler obtained a commission as a major general of volunteers from President James K. Polk. He received command of the 3rd Division, composed of volunteers from Ohio, Tennessee, Kentucky, Mississippi, and Texas, in Major General Zachary Taylor's army. On September 21, 1846, during the Battle of Monterrey, Butler was severely wounded in the leg while personally leading an assault against a Mexican position. He next commanded the U.S. garrisons at Monterrey and Saltillo but was sent home in early 1847 because his wound had not properly healed. In March, Congress passed a resolution honoring Butler's action at Monterrey and awarded him with a ceremonial sword.

Butler did not return to Mexico until the end of 1847, after the major battles had ended and Mexico City was occupied. In January 1848 President Polk chose to replace Major General Winfield Scott with Butler, who assumed overall command of U.S. forces in Mexico on April 22. As such, he supervised the evacuation of American troops from Mexico City and left for home in June 1848.

William O. Butler, who fought in the War of 1812, secured a major generalcy of volunteers during the Mexican-American War. While in command of the 3rd Division, he was severely wounded on September 21, 1846, during the Battle of Monterrey. (Library of Congress)

That same year, Butler ran unsuccessfully on the Democratic ticket as the vice-presidential nominee with presidential nominee Lewis Cass. Cass and Butler lost the election to Whigs Zachary Taylor and Millard Fillmore. Butler thereafter practiced law and remained active in Democratic politics. In 1855, President Franklin Pierce offered Butler the governorship of the Nebraska Territory, but he turned it down. During the Civil War, Butler remained loyal to the Union, and in February 1861 he served as a delegate to the abortive peace convention held in Washington, D.C., designed to avert the conflict. Although he himself was a slaveholder, Butler denounced attempts to expand slavery beyond its current confines and advocated gradual emancipation. He died in Carrollton, Kentucky, on August 6, 1880.

PAUL G. PIERPAOLI, JR.

See also

Democratic Party; Fillmore, Millard; Mexico City; Monterrey, Battle of; Polk, James Knox; Scott, Winfield; Taylor, Zachary.

References

Clary, David A. *Eagles and Empire: The United States, Mexico, and the Struggle for a Continent.* New York: Bantam Books, 2009.

Eisenhower, John S. D. *So Far from God: The U.S. War with Mexico, 1846–1848.* New York: Random House, 1989.

Roberts, Gerald F. "William O. Butler: Kentucky Cavalier." Master's thesis, University of Kentucky, 1962.

C

Cabinet, U.S.

The cabinet is an advisory board to the president of the United States composed of the heads of the major departments of the executive branch, which in 1844 were state, navy, war, treasury, justice, and the post office. After his election in November 1844, James K. Polk attempted to form a cabinet that would fairly represent the country's geographical sections while conciliating all the major factions of the Democratic Party. Intending to serve only a single four-year presidential term, he sought to stabilize the cabinet by demanding that appointees not seek the Democratic nomination for president in 1848.

Polk failed his purpose in choosing as secretary of state James Buchanan of Pennsylvania, a Polk supporter in a state cool toward Polk's plans for tariff reduction. Not only did Buchanan's appointment annoy Vice President George M. Dallas, a rival of Buchanan's for control of the Pennsylvania Democratic Party, but Buchanan was determined to position himself as Polk's successor and would promise to resign from the cabinet only should he become a strong candidate for the nomination.

Polk failed also in his choice of William Marcy of New York as secretary of war. This appointment infuriated supporters of former president Martin Van Buren, who thought Marcy was instrumental in making Polk the party nominee in 1844 rather than his fellow New Yorker, Van Buren. Less controversial was Polk's naming of the third northerner, George Bancroft of Massachusetts, a perceptive and forthright historian, as secretary of the navy.

The other cabinet secretaries were southerners. Mississippi's Senator Robert J. Walker was made secretary of the treasury for his support of Polk's candidacy for the presidential nomination despite warnings from former president Andrew Jackson that Walker might involve the treasury in helping to rescue land speculators from their bad investments. John Y. Mason of North Carolina, a college classmate of Polk's with cabinet experience in President John Tyler's administration, became attorney general as head of the Justice Department. For postmaster general, the official traditionally in charge of distributing jobs and other political patronage, Polk chose his best friend, Tennessee congressman Cave Johnson.

In 1846 Bancroft left the cabinet to become minister to Great Britain, and John Mason took over the Navy Department. Mason was succeeded as attorney general by Nathan Clifford of Maine, who himself left the cabinet in 1848 to negotiate the peace treaty with Mexico. Isaac Toucey of Connecticut was Polk's last attorney general. Thus, five of the six original appointees served for Polk's entire term, making it an extremely stable cabinet.

Polk planned for the cabinet to meet twice weekly, on Tuesdays and Saturdays at noon, with emergency meetings as necessary. He was determined to achieve four goals: settling the Texas and Oregon questions, acquiring California, reducing the tariff, and establishing a truly independent treasury. He expected his cabinet to support these aims, to avail him of their knowledge and wisdom, and to seek honest consensus on the issues and problems facing the government. As a former Speaker of the U.S. House of Representatives, Polk was well versed in negotiating toward a workable consensus with others but found Buchanan a source of constant frustration. Barely six months into the administration, in a meeting on August 26, 1845, Buchanan obstinately opposed Polk over negotiating with Britain about Oregon. The rest of the cabinet was dismayed at Buchanan's attitude, and Polk went home that night to write his version of the quarrel, which became a daily habit resulting in an invaluable diary of the politics of his administration. As events proceeded, Buchanan's presidential ambitions led him to swing as the political winds shifted. Having demanded at the beginning of the war with Mexico that Polk repudiate any claims on Mexican territory, Buchanan became a champion of territorial acquisition as the war went on and he gauged the public mood.

Although Polk lost a certain amount of credibility among people astonished by his tolerance of Buchanan's sudden changes of direction and his duplicity, he kept Buchanan to the end. Overall, however, the cabinet supported Polk's goals, helped develop policies and strategies, and drafted letters and other documents for the president's use.

JOSEPH M. MCCARTHY

See also

Bancroft, George; Buchanan, James; Clifford, Nathan; Dallas, George Mifflin; Democratic Party; Marcy, William Learned; Mason, John Young; Politics, U.S.; Polk, James Knox; Van Buren, Martin; Walker, Robert John.

References

Borneman, Walter R. *Polk: The Man Who Transformed the Presidency and America.* New York: Random House, 2008.
Merry, Robert W. *A Country of Vast Designs: James K. Polk, the Mexican War and the Conquest of the American Continent.* New York: Simon and Schuster, 2009.
Seigenthaler, John. *James K. Polk.* New York: Times Books, 2004.

Caddos

A Native American nation of scattered autonomous villages and complexes. The Caddo people resided throughout the lower Red River area, which comprises much of present-day Oklahoma, Texas, Louisiana, and Arkansas. The word "Caddo" is a French abbreviation of *Kadohadacho,* derived from the term *kaadi,* meaning "chief." The term identifies both the nation and the language spoken by the Wichitas, Kichais, Pawnees, and Arikaras. Spanish references to the Caddos such as *Tejas* or *Teches,* meaning "friend," eventually became the name of the state of Texas.

The Caddos were composed of several dozen loosely organized tribes and confederacies, the most important of which were the Hasinais, Natchitoches, Caddos proper (Kadohadachos or Cadodachos), Adais, Eyishes, and Tulas. In 17th-century records, the Caddos were recognized as having controlled their lands prior to the Spanish exploring expedition as far west as present-day eastern Oklahoma under Hernando de Soto during 1539–1543. By 1686 the Caddos had allied with their old rivals, the Wichitas, and were in conflict with the Choctaws, Chickasaws, Osages, and Tonkawas.

The French established early in their colonizing efforts their control over all the Caddo tribes, excepting the Adais, where the Spanish had located. In 1714 the French founded a trading post at present-day Natchitoches, Louisiana, and by 1730 there were several hundred dwellings near the post. The Caddos hoped to remain neutral, trading with both colonial powers, but this proved impossible. In fighting between France and Spain, the Adais particularly suffered, their villages being divided between the two colonial powers.

In the 1762 Treaty of Fontainebleau, France compensated Spain for losses incurred while fighting on the French side in the Seven Years' War (1756–1763) by giving it the Louisiana Territory. The transaction was not completed until 1769, but it angered the Caddos, who believed the French did not have the right to cede their land. The Spanish succeeded in winning Caddo loyalty, however, through the fur trade and presents. Caddo chief Tinihiouien, meanwhile, negotiated several treaties ceding land to the Spanish.

When the United States took control of the Louisiana Territory in 1803, a number of Caddos were compelled to move west into Spanish-controlled Texas. After the successful Texas Revolution of 1836, the government of the Republic of Texas did not adequately protect the tribe from white aggression, and so by the early 1840s they had relocated again to the Brazos River Valley. Eventually, the Caddos settled in Indian Territory (modern-day Oklahoma) on a reserve along the Washita River.

RAESCHELLE POTTER-DEIMEL AND SPENCER C. TUCKER

See also

Native Americans; Texas; Texas Revolution.

References

Hudson, Charles. *Knights of Spain, Warriors of the Sun.* Athens: University of Georgia Press, 1997.
John, Elizabeth A. H. *Storms Brewed in Other Men's Worlds: The Confrontation of Indians, Spanish, and French in the Southwest, 1540–1795.* College Station: Texas A&M University Press, 1975.
Smith, F. Todd. *The Caddo Indians: Tribes at the Convergence of Empires, 1542–1854.* College Station: Texas A&M University Press, 1995.
Swanton, John Reed. *The Indians of the Southeastern United States.* Washington, DC: Smithsonian Institution Press, 1979.

Cadwalader, George
Birth Date: May 16, 1806
Death Date: February 3, 1879

U.S. Army general during both the Mexican-American War and the Civil War. George Cadwalader was born in Philadelphia on May 16, 1806. His grandfather was a Revolutionary War militia general. Cadwalader studied law at the University of Pennsylvania and was later admitted to the Pennsylvania bar. In 1830 he married Fanny Butler Mease, granddaughter of Pierce Butler, a U.S. senator from South Carolina. He went on to enjoy success in business with Philadelphia's Mutual Assurance, or Green Tree Company, one of the earliest insurance underwriters of policies designed to protect domestic property against fire.

In 1826 Cadwalader became a member of the popular 1st City Troop of the Philadelphia Cavalry and six years later was promoted to captain. In 1844, now a brigadier general of the 1st Brigade, 1st Division of the Pennsylvania militia, Cadwalader commanded

George Cadwalader received a commision from the James K. Polk administration as a brigadier general of volunteers and commanded a brigade during the 1847 campaign from Veracruz to Mexico City. (Library of Congress)

troops in Philadelphia during the anti-Catholic riots there inspired by the Know-Nothing Party.

Cadwalader received a commission from the James K. Polk administration in March 1847 as a brigadier general of volunteers. Arriving at Veracruz in June, he marched his brigade to the interior, joining Major General Winfield Scott at Puebla in June. His brigade was designated the 2nd Brigade and served in Major General Gideon Pillow's 3rd Division. Cadwalader fought in the Battles of Churubusco (August 20, 1847), El Molino del Rey (September 8, 1847), and Chapultepec (September 12, 1847), as well as in the final assault on Mexico City.

While Cadwalader did not particularly distinguish himself in field command, he also did not make any major blunders and was rewarded for his part in the taking of Chapultepec Castle by being brevetted major general. Following the cessation of hostilities, he served for a short time as governor of the Mexican state of Toluca. Following the war, Cadwalader returned to his law practice and business interests.

At the beginning of the Civil War in 1861, Cadwalader, now age 55, was appointed a major general of volunteers and given command of the 1st Division of the Pennsylvania troops. In this capacity, he served in garrison commands and as an adviser to President Abraham Lincoln and Secretary of War William Stanton, as well as on numerous military commissions and boards of inquiry.

Cadwalader's Civil War notoriety came not on the battlefield but in matters of constitutional law, when, having charge of Fortress Monroe and in deference to President Abraham Lincoln's proclamation suspending the writ of habeus corpus, he rejected Chief Justice of the Supreme Court Roger B. Taney's ruling that the suspension of the writ in regard to Maryland secessionist John Merryman was unconstitutional. Taney cited Cadwalader for contempt of court and rebuked the general in his written opinion in *Ex parte Merryman.* Lincoln, however, supported Cadwalader, who remained in federal service until after the end of the war.

Cadwalader devoted the remainder of his life to estate law and became chairman of the board of Mutual Assurance. Cadwalader died at his Philadelphia home on February 3, 1879.

CHARLES F. HOWLETT

See also
Chapultepec, Battle of; Churubusco, Battle of; El Molino del Rey, Battle of; Mexico City, Battle for; Mexico City Campaign; Pillow, Gideon Johnson; Puebla; Scott, Winfield; Veracruz.

References
Baltzell, E. Digby. *Philadelphia Gentlemen.* Philadelphia: University of Pennsylvania Press, 1979.
Burt, Nathaniel. *The Perennial Philadelphians.* New York: Arno Press, 1975.

Cahuenga, Treaty of
Event Date: January 13, 1847

Treaty signed on January 13, 1847, at Campo de Cahuenga, located in modern-day North Hollywood, California, which ended hostilities between Mexican and U.S. forces in Alta California. The Treaty of Cahuenga, sometimes referred to as the Capitulation of Cahuenga, was initiated by Mexican captain (and governor of Alta California) Andrés Pico. Pico was the de facto governor and military commander of the Californios, or Mexicans living in Alta California. After several skirmishes between U.S. forces and Mexican Californio irregulars in modern-day Southern California, an American military-naval force under Commodore Robert F. Stockton and Brigadier General Stephen Watts Kearny occupied Los Angeles on January 10, 1847. Meanwhile, the impetuous Lieutenant Colonel John C. Frémont, commanding the California Battalion, was advancing steadily toward Los Angeles. On January 11, his force clashed with a small Californio contingent at Rancho Los Verdugos. When Pico received word of Frémont's advance, he dispatched several officers to meet with the Americans and negotiate a cease-fire.

On January 12, Francisco de la Guerra, Francisco Rico, and Augustín Olvera—representing the Californios—entered into talks with Frémont, Majors P. B. Reading and William H. Russell, and Captain Louis McLane. Frémont agreed to the negotiations without official authorization and without notifying his superior officer, General Kearny. Frémont's insubordinate actions, coupled with his open clash with Kearny over who should be military governor of California, eventually led to his court-martial and resignation from the army.

The terms of the Cahuenga treaty were generous. They allowed all Californios to return to their homes on parole or leave California at the conclusion of the war. Californios who agreed to surrender were offered protection by U.S. occupation forces. They were not required to swear an oath of loyalty to the United States and would receive the same rights as Americans living in California. The Treaty of Cahuenga essentially ended hostilities in California and set the stage for a relatively peaceful U.S. occupation. On January 14, Frémont's battalion of 400 men arrived in Los Angeles to a hero's welcome, much to the chagrin and annoyance of Kearny. They were feted by Los Angelinos, honored by an impromptu parade, and congratulated by an evening ball.

PAUL G. PIERPAOLI JR.

See also

California; California Battalion; California Theater of War, Overview; Californios; Frémont, John Charles; Kearny, Stephen Watts; Pico, Andrés; Stockton, Robert Field.

References

Chaffin, Tom. *Pathfinder: John Charles Frémont and the Course of American Empire.* New York: Hill and Wang, 2002.

Harlow, Neal. *California Conquered: War and Peace on the Pacific, 1846–1850.* Berkeley: University of California Press, 1982.

Roberts, David. *A Newer World: Kit Carson, John C. Frémont, and the Claiming of the American West.* New York: Touchstone, 2001.

Calhoun, John Caldwell
Birth Date: March 18, 1782
Death Date: March 31, 1850

U.S. lawyer, Democratic Party politician, U.S. congressman (1811–1817), secretary of war (1817–1825), vice president (1825–1832), U.S. senator (1832–1843, 1845–1850), and secretary of state (1844–1845). John Caldwell Calhoun, one of the most dominant political figures in the United States during the first half of the 19th century, was born on March 18, 1782, in what became Abbeville, South Carolina. He graduated from Yale College in 1804 and studied law with the noted Tapping Reeve in Litchfield, Connecticut. He returned to South Carolina in 1807 and was admitted to the bar. Although a gifted lawyer, he disliked the profession and decided he could best serve his state and country as a planter and in public service.

Calhoun was elected to the South Carolina legislature in 1808 as a Democratic-Republican. In 1810 he was elected to the U.S. House of Representatives for the first of three terms, serving until November 1817. Calhoun quickly established himself as one of the war hawks, calling for an aggressive stance toward Great Britain during the Napoleonic Wars. During the War of 1812 he did his

best to raise funds to prosecute the war, to weed out unfit officers and cabinet members, and to strengthen the unity of the nation. Following the war, Calhoun became known as a nationalist. He called for federal support of internal improvements such as canals and roads. He drafted a bill to create the Second Bank of the United States, and he supported a protective tariff.

From 1817 to 1825 Calhoun served as secretary of war in President James Monroe's cabinet and turned out to be one of the most effective such functionaries in the nation's history. He established military posts in the West, created the first general staff, and established the position of commanding general of the army. He also developed the "expansible army" concept, or what would be known as skeletonizing today. It called for an officer-heavy force that could be rapidly expanded by volunteers in time of war. Congress rejected the plan because of its expense, however. Calhoun also wanted to court-martial Major General Andrew Jackson for his unauthorized invasion of Spanish Florida, but the president countermanded him.

In 1824 Calhoun was the presidential candidate selected by the Democratic-Republican congressional caucus. In the past,

South Carolinian John C. Calhoun was one of the most prominent political figures in the United States in the first half of the 19th century. As secretary of state during 1844–1845, he strongly supported the annexation of Texas, but Calhoun also opposed war with Mexico in 1846. (Library of Congress)

this choice was the party's certain nominee. By 1824, however, local party organizations were exerting their power, and Calhoun could not overcome Jackson, Henry Clay, and John Quincy Adams. Calhoun was nominated for vice president and was inaugurated in 1825 with President-Elect John Quincy Adams. Calhoun joined a pro-Jackson faction and worked for Jackson's election in 1828. He was again elected vice president. Calhoun soon became alienated from the president, however, and his earlier attempt to censure Jackson over Florida remained a sensitive issue.

In 1832 Calhoun resigned the office of vice president and was elected senator from South Carolina. He held the office for practically the rest of his life, serving as secretary of state for a short interval under John Tyler. As senator, Calhoun helped negotiate the Compromise Tariff of 1833 that ended the Nullification Crisis. He became best known as a champion of slavery and states' rights. While serving as secretary of state (1844–1845), Calhoun argued forcefully for the annexation of Texas, seeing Texas as additional slave territory and believing that it could be a buffer between the United States and British interests in Mexico. Conversely, Calhoun opposed the Mexican-American War in 1846. He feared that the United States would add vast new territories from Mexico that would bring the question of slavery's spread to the fore and expand the scope and powers of the federal government. Calhoun also thought that Mexicans, whom he deemed inferior to Americans, would make poor U.S. citizens. Calhoun also opposed the admission of Oregon and California as free states in 1848 and 1849 because that move would upset the regional balance in the Senate. Not surprisingly, Calhoun was a vociferous opponent of the Wilmot Proviso, which would have forbidden the extension of slavery into new U.S. territories.

Toward the end of his life, Calhoun warned that the dissolution of the Union was likely if the federal government did not protect slavery. On March 4, 1850, at a meeting of representatives of the slave states in Nashville, Tennessee, Calhoun gave a fiery speech against any compromise. He died that March 31 in Washington, D.C., before the Compromise of 1850 was reached. He had warned darkly—and presciently—that the Union would be dissolved within 12 years if slavery were not guaranteed.

Tim Watts

See also

Congress, U.S.; Expansionism and Imperialism; Opposition to the Mexican-American War, U.S.; Politics, U.S.; Slavery; Texas; Wilmot Proviso.

References

Bartlett, I. H. *John C. Calhoun: A Biography*. New York: W. W. Norton, 1993.

Capers, Gerald M. *John C. Calhoun, Opportunist: A Reappraisal*. Gainesville: University of Florida Press, 1960.

Lander, E. M. *Reluctant Imperialists: Calhoun, the South Carolinians, and the Mexican War*. Baton Rouge: Louisiana State University Press, 1980.

California

California, known as Alta (Upper) California by the Mexicans, was formally acquired by the United States in the Treaty of Guadalupe Hidalgo of 1848, but it was practically brought into the Union by its conquest by the U.S. military in 1846–1847 during the opening months of the Mexican War. California was admitted to the Union as a state on September 9, 1850. Encompassing 158,706 square miles, California is the third-largest state in the United States in land mass, surpassed only by Alaska and Texas. It has a long shoreline along the Pacific Ocean and today borders on Oregon to the north, Nevada and Arizona to the east, and Baja California (Mexico) to the south. It has widely varying climates, which include low desert, high desert, Mediterranean style (close to the coast), and a temperate climate inland and in the north. The state is traversed by numerous small and large mountain ranges. The 1846 population was estimated to be only 75,000–80,000 people—a sparse number for so large an area.

The Spanish had the oldest colonial claim to California and began creating a series of missions in the region in the early 18th century. Significant numbers of settlers did not begin arriving there until the mid-18th century, however. The Spanish claim was accepted by the United States and solidified by the drawing of the boundary between British Columbia and New Spain at the 42nd parallel in the 1819 Adams-Onís Treaty, but the treaty's long-term significance would not apply to Spain. The region became a part of Mexico upon the latter's formal independence from Spain in September 1821.

Americans pushing west moved first into Louisiana, then Texas, and by the mid-1820s had begun moving into California. But the numbers of North Americans migrating to the region had not been great.

There were numerous reasons for American interest in California on the eve of the Mexican-American War. The fine, natural ports that California offered, such as San Francisco Bay and San Diego Bay, were ideally situated for opening the United States to trade with Asia. The state also offered abundant and profitable natural resources, including huge tracts of lumber, various mineral deposits, and millions of acres of land and climate suitable for large-scale agriculture. In addition, the concept of Manifest Destiny asserted that it was the proper, God-given role of the United States to overtake the whole of the North American continent, including California. The idea of adding California to the Union had advocates in high places, including President James K. Polk, who left little doubt among the leaders in Washington about his desire to annex California to the United States. Indeed, securing California from Mexico was Polk's chief aim in his negotiations with Mexico. When his attempts to purchase the territory failed, Polk goaded Mexico into war to secure his aims.

The Mexican-American War in California was short but had two distinct phases: the rebellion and the occupation. In January 1846, Captain John C. Frémont, an army officer and explorer, led a survey mission to Oregon. The group had stopped in California to rest and was to play a significant role in what would be called the Bear Flag Revolt. His command of 60 men, small by most standards, was large for California for the day.

The rebellion fomented by Americans against the Mexican government in California broke out on June 14, 1846, with the arrest in Sonoma of General Mariano Guadalupe Vallejo and the creation of the Bear Flag Republic. Frémont and his party now moved to Sonoma. He encouraged the rebellion, which at first was focused in the north, and saw American forces take control of Sutter's Fort, a key point for control of the northern half of California's Central Valley. John Sutter, a Swiss German immigrant to California, had established the fort near the confluence of what are now known as the Sacramento and American Rivers. In one of the ironies of the war, Sutter lost control of his fort to Frémont, and in August 1846 was made a lieutenant in the U.S. Army and second in command in his own fort.

The California (Bear Flag) Republic only lasted a few weeks until the arrival of the U.S. Navy's Pacific Squadron under the command of Commodore John Drake Sloat. On July 7, 1846, Sloat sent a shore party to claim possession of Monterey, California's territorial capital. He then moved to occupy Yerba Buena (modern-day San Francisco). Sloat's time in California was short, however. His replacement, Commodore Robert Stockton, quickly took control of such vital locations along the California coast as Santa Barbara, San Pedro, and Los Angeles. Unlike Sloat, Stockton worked closely with Frémont, whom he promoted to major.

While the north was relatively quiet, Mexican forces did have success in recapturing parts of the south. Brigadier General Stephen Watts Kearny moved a small part of his army from Santa Fe, New Mexico, to California. When he heard that Stockton had secured California, he sent the majority of this force back to Santa Fe, a mistake that would have adverse consequences. In the meantime, a Mexican rebellion had broken out in the south and had succeeded in recapturing parts of the region. When Kearny arrived, therefore, he had to fight his way into Southern California. On December 5, 1846, his forces ran into a force of Mexican irregular cavalry at San Pascual. The battle there was inconclusive, but it forced Kearny to wait for reinforcements, the first of which arrived on December 11 in the form of sailors and marines dispatched by Stockton.

After Stockton and Kearny had joined forces, they advanced against the Mexicans at San Gabriel. The Americans' victories there, on January 8, 1847, and the following day at La Mesa, finally secured California for the United States. On January 10, 1847, U.S. forces moved into Los Angeles, bringing an effective end to military operations in California. On January 13, 1847, Frémont signed the Treaty of Cahuenga, or the capitulation of Cahuenga, formally ending hostilities in California.

More fighting occurred after the surrender of California, but it was largely between the American occupation leaders. Both Stockton and Kearny each saw themselves as having the authority to command U.S. operations in the region. Kearny appears to have paid some deference to Stockton while he was in the region. When Stockton left, he appointed Frémont governor. Kearny, however, saw both his orders from Washington and his status as a superior officer as giving him the authority to take control of the civil government. Frémont refused to obey Kearny's orders based on his appointment by Stockton. Kearny subsequently had Frémont arrested and court-martialed for disobeying orders; he was convicted, but the sentence would be suspended. After the winter of 1847, California's role in the war would be insignificant, as American forces drove on toward Mexico City, well south of California.

DONALD E. HEIDENREICH JR.

See also
Bear Flag Revolt; Cahuenga, Treaty of; California Theater of War, Overview; Frémont, John Charles; Kearny, Stephen Watts; La Mesa, Battle of; Manifest Destiny; Polk, James Knox; San Gabriel River, Battle of; San Pascual, Battle of; Sloat, John Drake; Stockton, Robert Field; Sutter's Fort; Vallejo, Mariano Guadalupe.

References
Bornemann, Walter R. *Polk: The Man Who Transformed the Presidency and America.* New York: Random House, 2008.

Eisenhower, John S. D. *So Far from God: The U.S. War with Mexico, 1846–48.* Norman: University of Oklahoma Press, 1989.

Harlow, Neal. *California Conquered: War and Peace on the Pacific, 1846–1850.* Berkeley: University of California Press, 1982.

California Battalion

Ad hoc military unit formed in California in the early summer of 1846, commanded by Brevet Captain John C. Frémont, to effect the occupation of Alta California and control its valuable Pacific Ocean deepwater harbors at the beginning of the Mexican-American War. The battalion grew out of a U.S. military exploration expedition of the Topographic Engineers sent west under Frémont. Critics of the Mexican-American War claimed that Frémont's men had been pre-positioned near the West Coast in order to seize California on the commencement of hostilities.

The revolt in California began on June 14, 1846, when a group of American residents of Northern California captured Sonoma and General Mariano Guadalupe Vallejo, the Mexican commandant of the region. The rebels proclaimed the formation of a new republic, known as the Bear Flag Republic because the image of a grizzly bear appeared on the flag the volunteers later carried. The republic, however, had a short life, lasting less than a month.

On June 23, 1846, Frémont arrived on the scene with a small detachment that included the official members of his expedition and other volunteers who had joined him. He took possession of California for the United States, even though news that the United States and Mexico were at war would not reach the West Coast until July.

Frémont was not the only senior officer in the region, however. The U.S. Navy had long kept a naval squadron in the Pacific to keep track of events in California. On July 7, 1846, Commodore John D. Sloat, its commander, landed sailors and marines at San Francisco and Monterey. More ports quickly fell to Commodore Robert F. Stockton, who replaced Sloat in late July. Four more cities had fallen to the Americans by month's end: Santa Barbara, San Pedro, San Diego, and Los Angeles. By the end of the summer, it appeared that California was safely in U.S. hands.

Not all Californios were happy to see their land change hands, however. Throughout the summer, Governor Pío de Jesús Pico and General José María Castro marshaled local forces to resist the U.S. occupation, and their actions threatened the stability of the new administration. By the end of the summer, Californio forces were ready to strike back, and on September 29 men under José María Flores recaptured Los Angeles.

To counter this local resistance, Frémont and Stockton formed the California Battalion, which was officially authorized on July 24, 1846, and was formally known as the California Battalion of Mounted Riflemen. The unit was composed of American volunteers who had joined Frémont's expeditionary force and U.S. sailors and marines from Stockton's command. The battalion, with Frémont acting as its commander with the volunteer rank of lieutenant colonel, comprised six companies of mounted riflemen, two companies of artillery, one company of local Californios, one scout company of local Indians, and one company of infantry. These companies were commanded by a mixture of volunteer officers and U.S. naval and marine personnel. The battalion numbered just over 500 men at peak strength.

In December 1846 an additional U.S. commander entered California. Brigadier General Stephen W. Kearny had led an American column to Santa Fe, New Mexico, in the late summer of 1846. Acting on news that California had already been conquered, Kearny left the bulk of his troops behind and marched off to California with only two companies of dragoons, about 60 men in all. Arriving in Southern California in early December with his small column nearly exhausted from the arduous trip, Kearny was surprised to learn that the military action in California was far from over. Indeed, he and his men were nearly defeated by local ranchers on December 6 at the Battle of San Pascual. From his hilltop defense on Mule Hill, Kearny was forced to call on Stockton for rescue.

The Americans regained control of California shortly after the start of the New Year. The California Battalion, now augmented by Kearny's two companies of U.S. Dragoons, launched a punitive campaign against the Californios with the goal of retaking Los Angeles and other strategic points. On January 7, 1847, the two sides clashed on the San Gabriel River, an action that went in favor of the Americans. The following day, the Americans again bested Californio forces, and on January 10 the American flag was again raised over Los Angeles.

With California seemingly safe, the American commanders began to fight each other. On January 12, without consulting Stockton, Frémont signed a peace treaty (Treaty of Cahuenga) with Andrés Pico. Stockton was furious, but he had to recognize its

terms or face continued resistance. The disagreement over command of California developed into a two-way struggle between Stockton and Kearny as each claimed the office of military governor. Stockton, whose time in California was coming to an end, ultimately appointed Frémont governor. Kearny, Frémont's superior officer, fiercely objected and later had Frémont brought before a court-martial for insubordination.

The California Battalion remained in service until April 1847. By then, however, the force had largely disintegrated, with many volunteers and Californios simply disappearing into the rugged countryside. The relatively few remaining soldiers were folded into the regular U.S. Army stationed at Los Angeles.

BRUCE WINDERS

See also

Bear Flag Revolt; Cahuenga, Treaty of; California; California Theater of War, Overview; Californios; Castro, José María; Flores, José María; Frémont, John Charles; Kearny, Stephen Watts; Mule Hill; Pico, Andrés; Pico, Pío de Jesús; San Gabriel River, Battle of; San Pascual, Battle of; Sloat, John Drake; Stockton, Robert Field; Vallejo, Mariano Guadalupe.

References

Cleland, Robert G. *From Wilderness to Empire: A History of California.* New York: Alfred A. Knopf, 1970.

Harlow, Neal. *California Conquered: The Annexation of a Mexican Province, 1846–1850.* Berkeley: University of California Press, 1989.

Jackson, Donald, and Mary Lee Spence. *The Expeditions of John Charles Fremont.* Vol. 2, *The Bear Flag Revolt and the Court-Martial.* Champaign: University of Illinois Press, 1973.

Walker, Dale L. *Bear Flag Rising: The Conquest of California, 1846.* New York: Forge Books, 1999.

Winders, Richard Bruce. "Mr. Polk's Army: Politics, Patronage, and American Military in the Mexican War." Unpublished PhD diss., Texas Christian University, 1994.

California Gold Rush

See Gold Rush, California

California Theater of War, Overview

The California Theater of Operations stretched from San Francisco in central California, south to San Diego, and involved elements of the U.S. Army, Navy, and Marine Corps, as well as settlers, all engaged in fighting Californios or Californianos (Californians of Mexican descent). Battles in California included Los Angeles (August 13, 1846); Dominguez Rancho (October 8, 1846); Natividad (November 11, 1846); San Pascual (December 6, 1846); San Gabriel (January 8, 1847); and La Mesa (January 9, 1847). The January 13, 1847, Treaty of Cahuenga ended combat operations in California.

By 1846 American citizens were deeply interested in Alta (Upper) California. Much of what they knew of this Mexican province came from two books, Richard Henry Dana's *Two Years Before the Mast,* and U.S. Army lieutenant John C. Frémont's account of his expedition there. Both praised California in glowing terms. Its potential was all too apparent, as were the thin bonds that tied it to Mexico. Indeed, barely 6,000 white men lived there. The key prize in President James K. Polk's expansionist agenda was the acquisition of Upper California, which the president was determined to win for the United States. San Francisco and San Diego were splendid harbors and there was concern in Washington that Britain or even Russia might secure California. When Mexico rebuffed Polk's offers to buy the provinces, the president goaded Mexico into a war in which California was to be the chief prize.

Although war was declared on May 13, 1846, the official declaration did not reach California until mid-July. In June 1846, meanwhile, a group of Californios, unhappy with rule by the central government of Mexico, joined a group of U.S. settlers to organize a rebellion to overthrow the Mexican government in Sonoma, California, and proclaim the Republic of California. The settlers feared that a war between the United States and Mexico might cost them their lands, and they were determined to protect them. This Bear Flag Revolt, as it came to be called, received assistance from Lieutenant Colonel John C. Frémont, then in California on yet another exploring expedition. On June 24, Mexican government forces from Monterey under the command of Joaquín de la Torre clashed with Frémont's men from Sonoma in the Battle of Olompali, north of San Rafael. Little more than a skirmish, it saw two Americans and five or six Californios killed. On July 1, Frémont crossed to the presidio with his Republic of California forces and there spiked 10 Spanish cannon. Frémont also gave the name of "Chrysopylae" ("Golden Gate") to the bay's entrance. Returning to Sonoma, on July 5, 1846, Frémont organized the Bear Flaggers into the California Battalion.

Meanwhile, when Commodore John D. Sloat, commanding the Pacific Squadron, received word of the Sonoma rebellion and Frémont's support for it, he offered his own assistance. Sloat had instructions that, should war be declared, he was to blockade all major ports along the California coast. Sloat was loath to act, however, lest he repeat the earlier error of Commodore Thomas ap Catesby Jones in 1842, who, believing war had begun between the United States and Mexico, had seized the port for the United States only to have to return it. But on July 7, 1846, claiming that he feared the British might act, Sloat sent U.S. sailors and marines ashore to occupy both San Francisco and Monterey. U.S. forces later took the ports of Santa Barbara, San Pedro, and San Diego.

Sloat was replaced by Commodore Robert F. Stockton. On August 13, 1846, a force of 50 U.S. marines under the command of Lieutenant Archibald Gillespie entered Los Angeles unopposed. Los Angeles contained a large pro-Mexican government population and, when Gillespie instituted martial law, a group of Californios incited a popular rebellion against the occupation. Faced with an ultimatum to leave and vastly outnumbered, Gillespie chose to withdraw to U.S. ships offshore. On September 29, 1846, Mexican forces led by Commandant General José María Flores retook Los Angeles.

That same month, President Polk ordered Brigadier General Stephen W. Kearny and a force from Santa Fe to augment forces in California. Kearny left the majority of his force behind at Santa Fe, which he had taken on September 25, to pacify New Mexico, and, believing a false report that Frémont had already secured the area, he arrived in California in early December with his Army of the West of only 100 men and two mountain howitzers. Once there, Kearny was met by Gillespie's marines and, with an aggregate force of 136 men, they marched toward San Diego. Near San Diego in the valley of San Pascual, on December 6, 1846, Kearny attempted to surprise a force of some 75 Californios led by Major Andrés Pico.

The Americans mismanaged the Battle of San Pascual from the beginning. Unfamiliar with the terrain, Kearny ordered a charge before his troops were actually close to the Mexican encampment; the men were also exhausted and they became separated from the cavalry. Additionally, American powder failed because of wet conditions, forcing many soldiers to rely on their sabers alone. The Californios, armed with firearms, sabers, long lances, and lariats, won the battle, killing 21 Americans and wounding 17 (including both Kearny and Gillespie). The Californios lost probably 6 dead and 12 wounded. Kearny immediately appealed to Stockton at San Diego for reinforcements. Stockton dispatched more than 200 sailors and marines, whose arrival three days later caused the Californios to disperse and permitted Kearny's battered force to proceed to San Diego.

Other battles of the California Theater of Operations included Dominguez Rancho on October 7, 1846. In this encounter Californios under Captain José Carrillo held off some 300 U.S. marines under the command of U.S. Navy captain William Mervine, who attempted to retake Los Angeles. The Battle of Natividad, fought on November 16, 1846, in the Salinas Valley, was also significant. Although technically a skirmish with 15 Californios attacking 50 Americans, it resulted in 3 Americans killed and 7 wounded and only 5 Californios wounded.

Finally, the Battle of La Mesa on January 9, 1847, near present-day Pasadena, California, saw some 300 Californios fight off some 600 Americans who employed firearms. In the battle one American and one Californio were killed. The Americans had five men wounded, while the Californios suffered an unknown number wounded. The Californios fell back to Pasadena, and on January 10, 1847, Kearny and Stockton retook Los Angeles. Three days later, on January 13, the Capitulation (or Treaty) of Cahuenga, signed by Frémont and Mexican governor general Andrés Pico in what is now North Hollywood, Los Angeles, ended organized resistance to American rule in California.

Kearny and Stockton then clashed over who was the legitimate military governor of California. Stockton, preparing to leave for naval operations against Acapulco, refused to recognize Kearny, and on January 16, 1847, commissioned Frémont as governor.

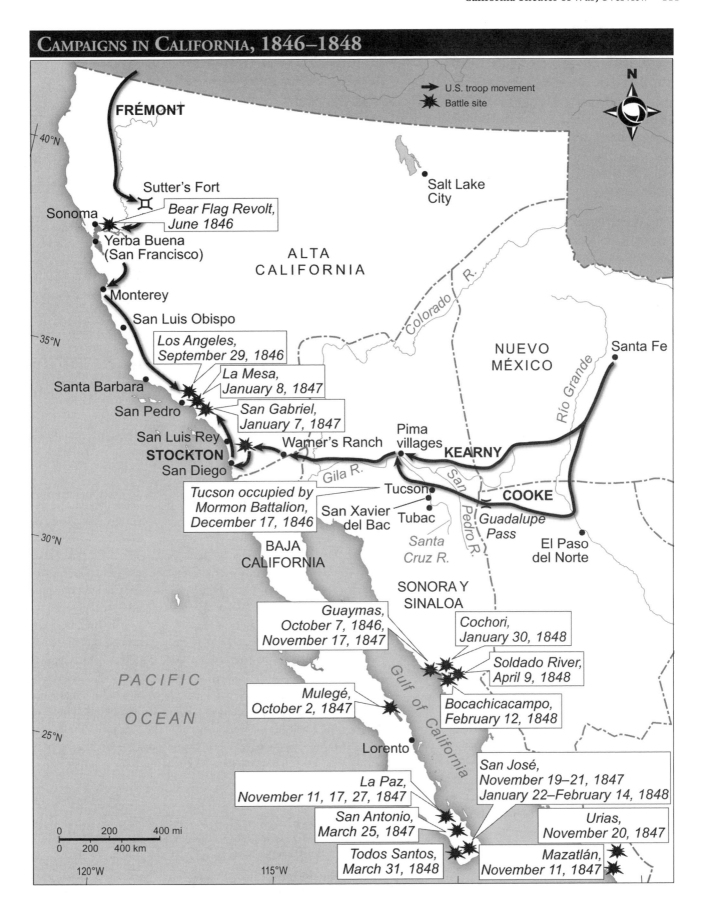

CAMPAIGNS IN CALIFORNIA, 1846–1848

→ U.S. troop movement
✸ Battle site

N

FRÉMONT

40°N

Sutter's Fort

Salt Lake City

Sonoma

Bear Flag Revolt, June 1846

Yerba Buena (San Francisco)

ALTA CALIFORNIA

Monterey

San Luis Obispo

35°N

Los Angeles, September 29, 1846

Santa Barbara

La Mesa, January 8, 1847

San Pedro

San Gabriel, January 7, 1847

NUEVO MÉXICO

Santa Fe

San Luis Rey

STOCKTON

Warner's Ranch

Pima villages

KEARNY

San Diego

Tucson occupied by Mormon Battalion, December 17, 1846

Tucson

COOKE

San Xavier del Bac

Tubac

Guadalupe Pass

El Paso del Norte

30°N

BAJA CALIFORNIA

Santa Cruz R.

SONORA Y SINALOA

Guaymas, October 7, 1846, November 17, 1847

Cochori, January 30, 1848

Soldado River, April 9, 1848

PACIFIC

Mulegé, October 2, 1847

Bocachicacampo, February 12, 1848

OCEAN

25°N

Lorento

San José, November 19–21, 1847 January 22–February 14, 1848

La Paz, November 11, 17, 27, 1847

Urias, November 20, 1847

San Antonio, March 25, 1847

Todos Santos, March 31, 1848

Mazatlán, November 11, 1847

0   200   400 mi
0   200   400 km

120°W

115°W

Colorado R.

Río Grande

Gila R.

San Pedro R.

Gulf of California

Kearny temporarily acquiesced but appealed the decision to the War Department. When Commodore William Branford Shubrick arrived to replace Stockton, he brought orders from Polk investing Kearny with governmental authority until such time as California was completely pacified. Kearny took command of the California Battalion and placed it under normal military regulations, leading many men to depart and in effect disbanding Frémont's base of power. This caused Frémont to leave California in a huff for Washington, D.C., where he faced dismissal from the army for insubordination. Kearny thus received recognition as the conqueror of California as well as being brevetted major general.

The fighting in California led to its acquisition by the United States and its admission as a state in 1850. The territories acquired from the Mexican-American War, including California, however, sharply raised sectional tensions over whether to admit the new territories as free or slave states.

PATRICK M. ALBANO AND SPENCER C. TUCKER

See also

Bear Flag Revolt; Cahuenga, Treaty of; California; California Battalion; Californios; Flores, José María; Frémont, John Charles; Gillespie, Archibald H.; Jones, Thomas ap Catesby; Kearny, Stephen Watts; La Mesa, Battle of; Los Angeles; Manifest Destiny; Mervine, William; Monterey, California; San Gabriel River, Battle of; Pico, Andrés; Polk, James Knox; Rancho Dominguez, Skirmish at; San Pascual, Battle of; Shubrick, William Branford; Sloat, John Drake; Stockton, Robert Field.

References

Bauer, K. Jack. *The Mexican War, 1846–1848*. New York: Macmillan, 1974.

Clary, David A. *Eagles and Empire: The United States, Mexico, and the Struggle for a Continent*. New York: Bantam, 2009.

Eisenhower, John S. D. *So Far from God: The U.S. War with Mexico, 1846–1848*. New York: Random House, 1990.

Harlow, Neal. *California Conquered: War and Peace on the Pacific, 1846–1850*. Berkeley: University of California Press, 1982.

Henry, Robert Selph. *The Story of the Mexican War*. Indianapolis: Bobbs-Merrill, 1950.

Californios

Peoples of European and mixed-race descent in Mexican-held (Alta) California. Californios numbered approximately 7,500 people in 1845 in all of what is currently the state of California. The Californios were ruled by wealthy landowners known as dons, or *gente de razon* (people of reason). Operating large ranchos (ranches) deeded in land grants by both the Spanish and Mexican governments, the leading members of Californio society lived a rich frontier lifestyle based on cattle raising for hides and the tallow trade.

The Californios led an interesting social life dominated by work, religion (Roman Catholicism), and frontier recreation. Although most of the hard work was accomplished by Native Americans existing in a slave-like status on the large ranchos, the Californios and their vaqueros (cowboys) had to oversee rodeos (roundups) of their cattle, drive them to the coast, and oversee the *matanza,* or the process of killing the cattle and dressing the hides, which were then ferried to offshore ship via small boats. At the ranchos, missions, and other holdings Californios also practiced subsistence and small-scale market agriculture, including the cultivation of vegetables, grapes, and other crops. Californio families tended to be large, and they placed much emphasis on celebrating religious holidays and other fiestas. During the Mexican period, there were only a few schools in the region, one printing press, and a limited number of literate citizens.

Governing Mexican-era California was an arduous and a frequently chaotic task. Immense distance separated California from the Mexican government in Mexico City. Mexican government officials offered little financial assistance to the Californios, and soldiers in the province were frequently ill equipped and unpaid. There was also frequent political strife between the mission padres, the military *alcaldes* (regional captains), and the civilian government, leading to periodic revolts and skirmishes. There was also an ongoing debate over whether California should declare independence, as well as struggles between northern and southern factions as to who should assert more control. California was also a dumping ground for Mexican convicts, and the presence of these so-called cholos led to much violence and banditry. Additionally, by inviting non-Mexican settlers into the territory, the Californios were repeating the same mistake that had resulted in the Mexican loss of Texas in 1836.

Promised full U.S. citizenship rights under the 1848 Treaty of Guadalupe Hidalgo, some Californios remained distinguished citizens in the new state, but many others faced discrimination and land usurpation after the Mexican-American War. The Foreign Miners Tax of 1850 was often illegally applied to Spanish speakers, even if they were U.S. citizens. Also, the Land Law of 1851 required the dons to offer proof of their titles. Because record keeping was haphazard in the Mexican period and many of the land claims were ill documented or even fraudulent, a great number of the Californios' ranches were divided and resold to Anglo-American farmers. While some of the leading Californio families, such as the Peraltas in the San Francisco Bay area, held on to their land and power, many of the former dons were reduced to second-class citizen status. Long after the Mexican period ended, Anglo-Californians contributed to the rebuilding of the missions, and Hollywood to this day has continued to romanticize the Mexican period of California and the Californios.

RANDAL BEEMAN

See also

California; Cattle; Cattle Hide Industry; Guadalupe Hidalgo, Treaty of; Land Grants; Mexico.

References

Beebe, Rose Marie, and Robert M. Senkowicz. *Lands of Promise and Despair: Chronicles of Early California, 1535–1846*. Berkeley, CA: Heyday Books, 2001.

Californios were Spanish-speaking residents of Alta California. They numbered some 7,500 people on the eve of the Mexican-American War. (North Wind Picture Archives)

Beebe, Rose Marie, and Robert M. Senkowicz. *Testimonios: Early California through the Eyes of Women.* Berkeley, CA: Heyday Books, 2006.

Pitt, Leonard. *The Decline of the Californios: A Social History of the Spanish Speaking Californians.* Berkeley: University of California, 1966.

Weber, David. *The Mexican Frontier: The American Southwest under Mexico.* Albuquerque: University of New Mexico Press, 1982.

Camargo

Mexican town located in the state of Tamaulipas, utilized by Major General Zachary Taylor as a staging area during the U.S. invasion of northern Mexico in 1846. Camargo is strategically situated on the San Juan River just three miles upriver from the Rio Grande.

After prevailing in the Battles of Palo Alto (May 8, 1846) and Resaca de la Palma (May 9), Taylor readied his Army of Occupation to advance toward Monterrey. Moving almost 12,000 men and their supplies and equipment over such distances in unfamiliar terrain and a hostile climate proved challenging. Having chosen Camargo as a staging area, Taylor ordered his men to set up camp there; most were transported by steamer up the Rio Grande during July and August.

When the American force began converging on Camargo, the town had a population of about 3,000 people. It was thus ill equipped for a sudden influx of people four times its entire population. Located in an arid valley, the town had limited fresh water supplies, and its low-lying areas near the river were breeding grounds for mosquitoes, which were vectors for such communicable diseases as yellow fever. To make matters worse, the weather was torrid, with daytime temperatures easily exceeding 100 degrees and rarely falling below 80 at night. The majority of the U.S. camps were situated along the San Juan River, an area teaming with ants, spiders, tarantulas, scorpions, and snakes. The dust was so thick when the men moved about that the area was frequently shrouded in great dust clouds.

Not surprisingly, Camargo became a hotbed of disease and death. Soldiers had little choice but to drink water from the San Juan River, which was polluted upstream with both human and animal waste, and many fell gravely ill with dysentery and uncontrollable diarrhea. Others who managed to escape this dim fate were struck down by yellow fever. Poor sanitation only compounded the suffering. Hospital tents became quickly filled to capacity while the death rate became so high that bodies had to be removed from the camp twice a day. When the wood supply for coffins had been depleted, men were buried only in blankets in unmarked graves. By late August, nearly one-third of Taylor's entire army was too ill to be moved. Those arriving late were forced to make camp in the poorest low-lying areas, and almost 50 percent of newly arriving volunteer forces fell ill after arrival. The squalid conditions in camp, combined with boredom and U.S. antipathy toward the Mexicans, also produced frequent violence aimed at the townspeople.

In early September Taylor began moving much of his force south toward Monterrey, anxious to abandon the camps at Camargo. By September 6, all but 2,000 men had left the town. The men who remained behind were tasked with caring for the sick, burying the dead, and transporting supplies and dispatches. Taylor's hasty exit, however, meant that his army was now poorly supplied.

Taylor was victorious at the September 21–23, 1846, Battle of Monterrey, but it was a costly triumph. Of the estimated 12,000 men who had camped at Camargo, 1,500 had died of disease and illness. Many of the soldiers remain buried along the banks of the San Juan River.

PAUL G. PIERPAOLI JR.

See also

Monterrey, Battle of; Palo Alto, Battle of; Resaca de la Palma, Battle of; Taylor, Zachary; Yellow Fever.

References

Chamberlain, Samuel E. *My Confession: The Recollections of a Rogue.* New York: Harper & Brothers, 1956.
Ferrell, Robert H., ed. *Monterrey Is Ours! The Mexican Letters of Lt. Dana, 1845–1847.* Lexington: University of Kentucky Press, 1990.

Cameron, Ewen
Birth Date: 1811
Death Date: April 25, 1843

Kentucky volunteer who fought in the Texas Revolution and also participated in the ill-fated Mier Expedition of 1842. Born in Scotland in 1811, Ewen Cameron, a stonemason, migrated to Kentucky in the early 1830s. When the Texas Revolution broke out in 1835, he joined a Kentucky company of volunteer soldiers who were subsequently deployed to Texas. He served two short stints in the Texas army, the second as a private in Captain Clark L. Owen's Company A of the 1st Regiment of Permanent Volunteers. Cameron mustered out in December 1836. For his service to Texas, he received a land grant of 1,920 acres in San Patricio County.

After the Texas Revolution, Cameron became a prominent citizen in southern Texas, earning the reputation as a fearless fighter against both Native Americans and Mexicans. He also engaged in a lucrative cattle-rustling venture in the Trans-Nueces region. In July 1842 he was credited with stoutly defending a Texan position against an assault led by Mexican general Antonio Canales Rosillo.

That fall Cameron was made a captain in the Somervell Expedition. When the venture disintegrated in late November

1842, Cameron chose to press on with a group of others, determined to storm and seize Ciudad Mier in northern Mexico. The Battle for Mier went badly for the Texans, however, and Cameron and numerous others were taken prisoner on December 26 and marched toward Mexico City. On February 11, 1843, Cameron led a daring escape from the Hacienda del Salado, where the prisoners had been encamped for the night. Cameron and his men managed to elude the Mexicans for a time, but several days later a shortage of food and water compelled them to surrender for a second time. They were returned to Salado, and President Antonio López de Santa Anna ordered all 176 Texas to be summarily executed.

After intercession from both U.S. and Mexican officials, in what has come to be called the Black Bean Episode, all but 17 of the men (those who had drawn the black beans) were spared execution. Cameron was among the 159 survivors who were then marched to Mexico City. As the Texas contingent neared Mexico City, Santa Anna learned that Cameron was not among the 17 executed and issued a death warrant for him. In Huehuetoca, outside Mexico City, Cameron was shot to death by a firing squad on April 25, 1843. He was likely executed because he had been the leader of the earlier escape at Salado and because of his cattle rustling and attacks against Mexicans in the Trans-Nueces.

PAUL G. PIERPAOLI JR.

See also

Black Bean Episode; Canales Rosillo, Antonio; Mier Expedition; Santa Anna, Antonio López de; Texas Revolution; Trans-Nueces.

References

Haynes, Sam W. *Soldiers of Misfortune: The Somervell and Mier Expeditions.* Austin: University of Texas Press, 2000.
Jenkins, John Holland. *Recollections of Early Texas.* Austin: University of Texas Press, 1958.
Sibley, Marilyn M., ed. *Samuel H. Walker's Account of the Mier Expedition.* Austin: Texas State Historical Association, 1978.

Campbell, William Bowen
Birth Date: February 1, 1807
Death Date: August 19, 1867

Lawyer, officer during the Mexican-American War, and governor of Tennessee. William Bowen Campbell was born in Sumner County, Tennessee, on February 1, 1807. After studying law with his uncle, Daniel R. Campbell, in Abington, Virginia, he returned to Tennessee in 1829 and opened a law practice at Carthage. In 1831 the legislature selected him as attorney general of the Fifth District of Tennessee, but he resigned before the end of the year. In 1835 he was elected to the state House of Representatives, but he resigned the next year to serve as the captain of a company in the Second Seminole War (1835–1842). Campbell represented Tennessee during three terms in the U.S. House of Representatives, from 1837 to 1843. He then retired to practice law and was made major general of the state militia.

When war with Mexico began Campbell was elected colonel of the 1st Tennessee Volunteer Regiment, known as the "Bloody 1st." Campbell and his unit won distinction in the Battles of Monterrey, Veracruz, and Cerro Gordo. During the Battle of Monterrey he is reported to have yelled "Boys, follow me," as he plunged into battle. At Veracruz he served in Brigadier General Gideon J. Pillow's brigade. Campbell did not think much of Pillow as a general. He was furious at Pillow's performance in the Battle of Cerro Gordo and he tried hard to press the attack.

Elected unanimously as circuit judge on his return from the war, Campbell ran successfully for governor of Tennessee on the Whig ticket in 1851 under the slogan of "Boys, follow me." At the end of his term in 1853 he refused to stand for reelection and moved to Lebanon to become president of the Bank of Middle Tennessee.

In 1861 Campbell strongly opposed secession. On July 23, 1862, he was commissioned a brigadier general in the U.S. Army but resigned after only two months. In 1865 he was elected to Congress but because of Reconstruction could not take his seat until June 1866. Campbell died in Lebanon, Tennessee, on August 19, 1867. Fort Campbell, Kentucky, is named in his honor.

SPENCER C. TUCKER

See also

Cerro Gordo, Battle of; Monterrey, Battle of; Pillow, Gideon Johnson; Veracruz, Landing at and Siege of.

References

Eisenhower, John S. D. *So Far from God: The U.S. War with Mexico, 1846–1848.* Norman: University of Oklahoma Press, 2000.

Johnson, Timothy D. *A Gallant Little Army: The Mexico City Campaign.* Lawrence: University Press of Kansas, 2007.

Camp Followers, Mexican and U.S.

The term "camp follower" commonly has a negative connotation, as it can describe persons such as prostitutes who travel in the wake of an army. However, the term may also refer to a whole host of civilians who are attached either officially or unofficially to an army and who perform many useful tasks for soldiers. The word "army" automatically brings to mind combat soldiers and their officers. Armies, after all, exist to fight battles, yet combat operations made up only a small portion of military life during the Mexican-American War. The rest was taken up with the often dull routine of daily existence, including foraging, cooking, laundering, cleaning, and the like.

Armies, then as now, are intended to be self-sufficient organizations. Departments are dedicated to providing uniforms and equipment, food and fodder, ordnance, and housing, as well as maintaining the mountains of paperwork created to document the army's activities. Although all of a soldier's "official" needs may have been met through official channels, some needs were not addressed. One particularly pressing need was that of married enlisted soldiers to care for their families. Unlike today's military,

no provision was made for feeding and housing the families of soldiers. As a result, wives who followed their husbands from post to post often were forced to live on the outskirts of the military compound, finding whatever work they could to provide for themselves. In the U.S. Army, a few wives (four per company) were employed as laundresses. With the outbreak of the Mexican-American War, however, the U.S. Army ordered wives to stay behind, essentially leaving them to fend for themselves. Not all followed this directive, however.

The same problem existed for soldiers in the Mexican Army. However, Mexican women—wives, mothers, and girlfriends—frequently accompanied the soldiers on active campaigns. With a wholly inefficient supply system, these *soldaderas* fanned out from camp and foraged for food for themselves and their men. *Soldaderas* also cared for those who fell ill on the march or suffered wounds in battle and served as cooks and laundresses. Thus, the Mexican army came to depend on these women for the care of most of its soldiers. Countless *soldaderas* died in the service of their families and country. Some *soldaderas* would take up arms and actually fight in battle. Such heroines during the Mexican-American War included María Josefa Zozaya, who died at the Battle of Monterrey while tending to wounded Mexican and American soldiers.

An entire category of camp followers strived to meet the creature comforts of an army. Numerous vendors trailed armies, hoping to sell soldiers things that the army did not provide, like cakes, pastries, stationery, sewing implements, and liquor. Others enticed soldiers to try their luck at such games of chance as faro, roulette, and twenty-one, which they would set up outside of camp. The gamblers, along with ever-present prostitutes, created the persistent idea that all camp followers were by nature of low moral character.

Once in Mexico, the U.S. Army had to contend with Mexican camp followers who showed up wherever the army went. Mexican farmers brought in produce and meat to sell to U.S. soldiers; others sold Mexican mustangs, often poorly broken to the saddle, to soldiers who were tired of walking. One Mexican merchant was caught selling buzzard eggs as chicken eggs. Few attempts were made by Mexicans to sell American soldiers deliberately tainted or poisoned food or drink, however.

Few records document female camp followers in the U.S. Army, but we know from memoirs, diaries, and contemporary reports that they did indeed exist. Most were wives of enlisted men, many of them foreign-born, coming either from Ireland or Germany. Many provided cooking, laundering, sewing, and nursing services. Reports indicate that there were women—and perhaps even some children—at most of the battles fought in northern Mexico during 1846. And despite official orders that women and camp followers not accompany U.S. forces into Mexico's interior, some certainly did. Perhaps the most noteworthy woman to accompany the army was Sarah Borginnis, who tended to wounded soldiers at Fort Texas (later called Fort Brown), Monterrey, and Buena Vista.

BRUCE WINDERS

See also

Army Life, Mexican and U.S.; Borginnis, Sarah; Buena Vista, Battle of;
Fort Texas (Fort Brown); Mexico, Army; Monterrey, Battle of; United
States Army; Women, Mexican; Women, U.S.; Zozaya, Maria Josefa.

References

Olivera, Ruth R., and Liliane Crété. *Life in Mexico under Santa Anna,
1822–1855.* Norman: University of Oklahoma Press, 1991.

Salas, Elizabeth. *Soldaderas in the Mexican Military: Myth and History.*
Austin: University of Texas Press, 1990.

Vance, Linda. "Women and the Mexican War." *Mexican War Journal* 3,
no. 2 (1994): 5–11.

Winders, Richard Bruce. *Mr. Polk's Army: The American Military
Experience in the Mexican War.* College Station: Texas A&M
University Press, 1997.

Campuzano, Antonio

Birth Date: 1810
Death Date: 1866

Mexican army officer and partisan for General Antonio López de
Santa Anna. Antonio Campuzano was born in 1810 in Mexico City.
He entered military service as a teenager after Mexican independence in 1821 and was posted to Veracruz and Texas before leaving the army in 1839. While on active duty he was befriended by
General Santa Anna, who was impressed with his loyalty and dedication. In 1841 Santa Anna insisted that Campuzano join him as
he prepared to put down a rebellion in Sonora y Sinaloa. Campuzano went on active duty once more with the rank of major, often
serving as one of Santa Anna's staff officers.

By the time the Mexican-American War began in 1846, Campuzano was a colonel. The following year, he was sent to Guaymas, a strategic port city in northwestern Mexico (state of Sonora
y Sinaloa) on the Gulf of California (Sea of Cortez) where he was
ordered to repel a potential U.S. landing. By the autumn of that
year, Campuzano commanded about 400 troops and had at his
disposal some half dozen artillery pieces.

When U.S. Navy commander Samuel F. Du Pont arrived off
Guaymas on October 6, 1847, with the sloop of war *Cyane* (22
guns), he demanded that Campuzano surrender the ships in the
port, but the Mexican officer refused. The next day, Du Pont dispatched a boarding party to seize and burn the Mexican brig *Condor* and two gunboats. Thereafter, the port was blockaded.

On October 17, Captain Elie Lavallette, commanding the frigate
Congress (52 guns), accompanied by Commander John B. Montgomery in the sloop *Portsmouth* (22 guns), arrived off the coast
of Guaymas. On October 19, the Americans again demanded that
Campuzano surrender Guaymas, and he again refused. The next
morning American ships shelled Guaymas for an hour, doing considerable property damage and killing one civilian. Campuzano
then surrendered, and U.S. marines went ashore and occupied
the town. On October 21 they destroyed Mexican fortifications

and collected arms and ammunition from the city's inhabitants.
Lavallette, lacking the men to garrison the town securely, charged
Commander Thomas A. Selfridge, captain of the sloop of war *Dale*
(16 guns), to anchor in the roadstead and maintain order. Campuzano's men harassed the Americans in the next few weeks, and on
November 17, 350 of them moved back into Guaymas.

Determined to repulse the Americans at virtually any cost,
Campuzano carefully rationed food, water, and supplies, as the
port city was virtually blockaded by both land and sea. Campuzano subsequently pinned down a U.S. landing party from the
Dale, until the ship's guns drove the Mexicans from the town.
Between the end of November 1847 and April 1848, numerous
American landing parties wore down Campuzano's force. Meanwhile, as rations, supplies, and ammunition became increasingly
scarce, Campuzano's small army began to dissolve, with many
men simply abandoning their posts. By war's end, virtually every
building in Guaymas had been damaged in the fighting, but Campuzano had steadfastly refused to give up.

Santa Anna and other commanders were impressed with
Campuzano's tenacity in the face of great odds, and he held
a number of significant military posts in the postwar period,
including prefect of Guaymas in 1853. During Santa Anna's last
term in office, from 1853 to 1855, Campuzano served as a military
inspector and then military commander at Guaymas. Thereafer
Campuzano, having lost his major patron, held few positions
of authority, although he remained in the military through the
French intervention that began in late 1861. Campuzano died in
1866 in Mexico City.

PAUL G. PIERPAOLI JR.

See also

Bocachicacampo, Skirmish at; Du Pont, Samuel Francis; Guaymas,
Battle of; Gulf of California (Mar de Cortés); Lavallette, Elie Augustus
Frederick; Montgomery, John Berrien; Santa Anna, Antonio López
de; Sonora y Sinaloa.

References

Bauer, K. Jack. *Surfboats and Horse Marines: U.S. Naval Operations in the
Mexican War.* Annapolis, MD: U.S. Naval Institute, 1969.

Craven, Tunis A. M. *A Naval Campaign in the Californias—1846–1848:
The Journal of Lieutenant Tunis Augustus Macdonough Craven,
U.S.N., United States Sloop of War* Dale. San Francisco: Book Club of
California, 1973.

Canales Rosillo, Antonio

Birth Date: 1802
Death Date: 1869

Mexican lawyer, politician, military officer, and guerrilla leader.
Antonio Canales Rosillo was born in Monterrey, Nuevo León, in
1802 but was reared largely in Camargo in the state of Tamaulipas. He wed Refugio Molano, Juan Nepomuceno Molano's sister,

thereby linking himself closely with a political cabal that dominated the politics of Tamaulipas until the early 1850s. Canales studied law, earning his license in 1829, and also practiced as an official surveyor for the state of Tamaulipas. He also joined the local militia and became one of its leaders, waging frequent raids against the Apaches and Comanches. A state representative beginning in 1838, he opposed General Antonio López de Santa Anna's centralist agenda. That year Canales helped foment a federalist rebellion against Mexico City's centralist regime, going so far as to establish a rump government of Mexico's eastern departments. Learning that some Texans were interested in forming a Republic of the Rio Grande in the Trans-Nueces region, he visited San Antonio in 1839 to raise troops for the upstart republic.

In January 1840 Canales, along with Antonio Zapata and other federalist rebels, convened at Guerrero and officially proclaimed the Republic of the Rio Grande. There they drafted a constitution and chose Laredo as the capital. Canales was appointed secretary of war and commander in chief of the army. As Canales and others had planned it, the new republic would have encompassed the states of Tamaulipas, Coahuila, Nuevo León, and portions of the Trans-Nueces. The republic was short-lived, however. Centralist troops decimated federalist forces, and Zapata was executed in March 1840. Canales soon surrendered, abandoned his Texas allies, embraced the centralist government, and was offered a generalship in Santa Anna's army, serving under General Mariano Arista. Thereafter, he led numerous raids against Anglo-Texans in and about the Trans-Nueces region. In 1842 Canales, along with General Pedro de Ampudia, helped defeat the Mier Expedition, which had been dispatched into northern Mexico by Texas president Sam Houston in retaliation for Mexican forays into southern Texas and New Mexico.

By the early 1840s, Canales had rightly earned the reputation as a brutal and shrewd guerrilla tactician. Until the outbreak of war with the United States in 1846, he continued to do battle with Texas Rangers along the Texas-Mexico border and was widely detested by Texans and Mexicans alike, as he and his men frequently raided and looted Mexican ranches and settlements.

When the Mexican-American War began in May 1846, Canales commanded an auxiliary regiment from Tamaulipas, and he participated in the Battles of Palo Alto and Resaca de la Palma that same month. At Palo Alto, he personally led a 500-man cavalry contingent in an unsuccessful effort to outflank Brigadier General Zachary Taylor's army. The following month he was ordered to wage a guerrilla war against Taylor's army and supply lines with a contingent of some 600 guerrillas and rancheros.

In the fall of 1846, when Taylor moved his army from Monterrey to Saltillo, Canales's guerrillas inflicted considerable havoc on the Americans and their supply lines. Late in 1846, Canales teamed up with General José Urrea, and together they increased the frequency and intensity of Mexican guerrilla raids. In February 1847 Canales unleashed a particularly damaging series of guerrilla assaults before joining Santa Anna at the February 23 Battle of

Buena Vista. In that single month alone, Canales's guerrillas killed more than 150 U.S. soldiers. By the spring, however, Canales's force had been degraded by sickness, desertions, and battle losses. His ability to continue the guerrilla activities was further impeded by the Mexican civilians' reluctance to harbor guerrillas or provide them with supplies.

After the war, between 1848 and 1852, Canales served in the legislature of Tamaulipas, as state surveyor general, senator in the national congress, and as an interim governor in 1851–1852. He also maintained his military connections, leading government forces that suppressed the 1852 Rebelión de la Loba. Canales died at Miquihuana, Mexico, in 1869.

PAUL G. PIERPAOLI JR.

See also

Ampudia, Pedro de; Apaches; Comanches; Guerrilla Warfare; Houston, Samuel; Mier Expedition; Monterrey, Battle of; Northern Mexico Theater of War, Overview; Palo Alto, Battle of; Resaca de la Palma, Battle of; Rio Grande, Republic of the; Saltillo; Tamaulipas; Santa Anna, Antonio López de; Texas; Texas Rangers; Trans-Nueces; Taylor, Zachary; Urrea y Elías Gonzales, José de.

References

Lindheim, Milton. *The Republic of the Rio Grande: Texans in Mexico, 1839–40*. Waco, TX: Morrison, 1964.

Nance, Joseph Milton. *After San Jacinto: The Texas-Mexican Frontier, 1836–1841*. Austin: University of Texas Press, 1963.

Zorilla, Juan F., and Carlos Gonzáles Salas. *Diccionario biográfico de Tamaulipas*. Victoria, Tamaulipas: Universidad Autónoma de Tamaulipas, 1984.

Canalizo, Valentín

Birth Date: January 17, 1794
Death Date: February 20, 1850

Mexican general and president (1843–1844). Born in Monterrey, Nuevo León, on January 14, 1794, Valentín Canalizo joined the royalist army during Mexico's independence wars and then supported Colonel Agustín de Iturbide's bid for independence in 1821. Canalizo was known for his extremely conservative and centralist views and his close friendship with Antonio López de Santa Anna, for whom he often served as proxy. The esteemed 19th-century Mexican writer Guillermo Prieto once disparagingly referred to Canalizo as "Santa Anna's toy soldier." It was Santa Anna who promoted him to the rank of brigadier general in 1841.

Canalizo joined an insurrection in 1841 that installed Santa Anna as chief executive military dictator. Santa Anna disliked the routines of governing, however, and would often retire to his hacienda, leaving presidential responsibilities to subordinates. Thus Canalizo served as interim president from October 4, 1843, until June 4, 1844, and again from September 21, 1844, to December 4, 1844. During this latter period, Santa Anna charged Canalizo with the impossible task of silencing the opposition press and securing funds for the reconquest of Texas, all without raising taxes. As opposition built steadily in congress, Santa Anna ordered Canalizo to disband that body, something that he attempted to do on December 1. The heavy-handed undertaking sparked a rebellion that brought General José Joaquín de Herrera to power and sent both Canalizo and Santa Anna into exile.

Canalizo returned to Mexico in late 1846, by which time both Herrera and his successor, General Mariano Paredes y Arrillaga, had been overthrown in the liberal Revolt of the Ciudadela. Santa Anna was elected to the presidency in December 1846, but by that time he had taken command of the army in northern Mexico, leaving his vice president, Valentín Gómez Farías, in charge in Mexico City. Gómez Farías appointed Canalizo minister of war, although Canalizo served only briefly in this capacity. In February 1847 he resigned to rejoin the army, where he took charge of the defense of the Gulf Coast against the invasion led by U.S. Army major general Winfield Scott. During this time, government efforts to finance the war effort by taxing the church provoked proclerical elements to rise up in the so-called Polkos Rebellion. Canalizo was able to prevent his own men from joining that rebellion and helped negotiate an end to the revolt as well.

Otherwise, Canalizo's activities in the war against the United States were undistinguished. He was relieved of his command of the eastern forces by Santa Anna, who suffered a crucial defeat at the Battle of Cerro Gordo in April 1847. Canalizo subsequently had a falling out with Santa Anna and took no part in the defense of Mexico City later that year. He retired to private life after the war and died in obscurity in Mexico City on February 20, 1850.

TIMOTHY J. HENDERSON

See also

Cerro Gordo, Battle of; Gómez Farías, Valentin; Herrera, José Joaquín de; Paredes y Arrillaga, Mariano; Politics, Mexican; Polkos Revolt; Santa Anna, Antonio López de.

References

Costeloe, Michael. *The Central Republic in Mexico, 1835–1846: Hombres de Bien in the Age of Santa Anna*. Cambridge: Cambridge University Press, 1993.

Prieto, Guillermo. *Memorias de mis tiempos*. Vol. 1, *1828 a 1848*. Paris: Librería de la Vda. de C. Bouret, 1906.

Santoni, Pedro. *Mexicans at Arms: Puro Federalists and the Politics of War, 1845–1848*. Fort Worth: Texas Christian University Press, 1996.

Cañoncito, Battle of
Event Dates: August 17–18, 1846

Confrontation in Apache Canyon, New Mexico, as an invading U.S. Army military force advanced on Santa Fe. On August 2, 1846, Brigadier General Stephen W. Kearny, commanding the Army of the West, marched southward into New Mexico on the Santa Fe Trail. Kearny's force consisted of 1,458 men, including dragoon regulars, Missouri volunteers, and artillerists with 12 6-pounders and 4 12-pounder howitzers. Kearny's army debouched from Raton Pass on August 7 and proceeded southward toward Apache Canyon, a narrow defile about 12 miles southeast of Santa Fe, site of the village of Cañoncito, and the most accessible route into Santa Fe. As the Americans advanced, Kearny heard disquieting reports that Manuel Armijo, governor of New Mexico, was collecting 12,000 troops and building defensive works at Cañoncito to oppose him.

Indeed, Governor Armijo was working assiduously to stop General Kearny's march short of Santa Fe, but he never had a hope of collecting anywhere close to 12,000 defenders. Receiving no support from army commanders at Chihuahua and Durango, Armijo summoned the citizens of New Mexico on August 8 to gather under the command of Colonel Manuel Pino to repel the Americans. A day later, 3,000 men, mostly raw conscripts, untrained militia, old soldiers, and Native Americans, answered the call. In the next few days Pino had them working at Cañoncito, where the canyon walls were as close together as 40 feet, constructing an abatis and placing a battery of eight cannon to command the approaches. He and Armijo knew that the position was far from impregnable, that it was vulnerable to being flanked, and that their men were unreliable. But it was the best they could do.

As Kearny approached Apache Canyon in mid-August, he considered bypassing Pino's numerically superior force and the defenses at Cañoncito, but by August 17 he had decided to advance through Apache Canyon even though it might prove risky. He was relieved when Nicholas Quintaro, secretary of state of New Mexico, rode into his camp with news that Armijo and his troops had "gone to Hell" and that the canyon was clear. Armijo and Pino had wanted to fight, but Armijo's chief military aide, Colonel Diego Archuleta, and a junta had voted on August 17 to disband the militia, spike the cannon, and flee. Armijo so ordered and then retreated with an escort of 90 dragoons toward Chihuahua. He arrived there two weeks later. On August 18, Kearny led the Army of the West through Cañoncito and Apache Canyon without a shot being fired. Just before sunset, his troops marched smartly into Santa Fe, where they were welcomed by Lieutenant Governor Juan Bautista Vigil y Alared.

PAUL DAVID NELSON

See also

Apache Canyon; Armijo, Manuel; Kearny, Stephen Watts; Pino, Manuel.

References

Bauer, K. Jack. *The Mexican War, 1846–1848*. New York: Macmillan, 1974.

Connor, Seymour V., and Odie B. Faulk. *North America Divided: The Mexican War, 1846–1848*. New York: Oxford University Press, 1971.

Keleher, William Aloysius. *Turmoil in New Mexico, 1846–1868*. Santa Fe, NM: Rydal Press, 1952.

Singletary, Otis A. *The Mexican War, 1846–1848*. Chicago: University of Chicago Press, 1960.

Carbajal, Francisco
Birth Date: Unknown
Death Date: Unknown

Mexican writer and politician. Although scholars know little about Francisco Carbajal's early life and postwar activities (including the circumstances of his birth and death), the historical record reveals that in the 1840s he played a prominent role in the complex political struggles that engulfed 19th-century Mexico. A supporter of the pro-war *puro* political bloc and a popular chief who served both as a member of Mexico City's municipal government and a National Guard officer, his activities shed light both on the strategic role of the country's urban masses and the divisions that bedeviled *puro* politicians.

In the spring of 1845, Carbajal wrote for *El estandarte nacional,* a journal that echoed the *puros'* goals of recovering Texas and restoring federalism under the auspices of the 1824 Constitution. Carbajal also served as a *regidor* in the Mexico City *ayuntamiento* and in that capacity vigorously insisted on the need to develop a National Guard to arm the populace and help repel the expected U.S. invasion.

Carbajal reentered the political scene in July 1846 through his election as secretary of Mexico City's Junta Patriótica, an organization established in 1825 to commemorate Independence Day festivities, one of the most important in the country's ritual calendar. The following month, residents of the capital spontaneously took up arms in support of the August 4 *pronunciamiento* of the Ciudadela, and immediately thereafter new demands were made for the prompt reorganization of the National Guard. Carbajal benefitted from the unrest. On August 10, a large crowd met at the Santo Domingo convent and acclaimed him colonel of what eventually became known as the Abasolo National Guard Battalion. Later that month, government officials appointed him to the five-man commission that drew up a September 11, 1846, decree that reestablished the National Guard in Mexico's states, districts, and territories. Then, on September 27, Carbajal was among *puro* supporters (and five National Guard colonels) chosen to serve as Mexico City's primary electors to the upcoming constitutional congress, which opened its sessions that December.

By October 1847, with U.S. forces in control of Mexico City, Carbajal had come to believe that continuing the war was futile. He feared that Mexico would lose its sovereignty if hostilities continued. Carbajal thus broke ranks with *puro* leader Valentín Gómez Farías, whose bellicose disposition remained steadfast. Carbajal then became the editor of *La razón,* a newspaper that clamored for peace and promoted the establishment of a U.S. protectorate. Indeed, Carbajal wanted the U.S. Army to remain in Mexico to ensure basic civil liberties, including trial by jury and freedom of religion, as well as the abolition of internal custom duties and the military and ecclesiastical *fueros* (privileges).

These reforms, Carbajal believed, would rejuvenate Mexico and enhance social progress.

PEDRO SANTONI

See also
Fueros; Gómez Farías, Valentín; Mexico City; *Puros.*

References
Pletcher, David. *The Diplomacy of Annexation: Texas, Oregon, and the Mexican War.* Columbia: University of Missouri Press, 1973.
Santoni, Pedro. *Mexicans at Arms: Puro Federalists and the Politics of War, 1845–1848.* Fort Worth: Texas Christian University Press, 1996.
Zamora, Rubén Amador. "El manejo del fusil y la espada: Los intereses partidistas en la formación de la guardia nacional en la ciudad de México, agosto–octubre 1846." Unpublished BA thesis, Universidad Nacional Autónoma de México, 1997.

Carmen

Port city located in the southwestern Mexican state of Campeche, about halfway between Veracruz to the west and Mérida to the east, on the Yucatán Peninsula. Today known as Ciudad del Carmen, the city is situated on the southwestern side of Carmen Island near the mouth of the Laguna de Términos on the Gulf of Mexico. The city has also been part of the states of Yucatán and Tabasco.

The area was strategically important well prior to European colonization, and it served as an entrepôt between the Mayan and Aztec civilizations. The Spanish later used it as a trade hub between Spain and New Spain, and it also became a focal point for pirates. By the mid-1840s the port at Carmen bustled with activity, mostly commercial and fishing, and had a population of between 10,000 and 12,000 people.

At the start of the Mexican-American War, Carmen served as a strategic center of illicit trade between the Yucatán Peninsula and interior Mexico. The port itself was protected by several small barrier islands near the entrance to Laguna de Términos. Even after the United States had instituted a naval blockade against Mexico, small vessels still made their way into Carmen, allowing the Mexicans to move contraband into the country's interior. Determined to stop such traffic, Commodore David Conner, commander of the Home Squadron, decided to occupy the port city. In early December 1846 Commodore Matthew C. Perry was dispatched to install an occupation force at Carmen. He got under way about two weeks later, taking with him the side-wheeler steam frigate *Mississippi,* the steamer *Vixen,* and sailing schooners *Bonita* and *Petrel.* Perry's orders called for him to seize or destroy all military supplies at Carmen, including vessels used to smuggle contraband.

On December 20, Perry's squadron anchored in Laguna de Términos. Without a shot being fired, the Mexicans surrendered the city and Perry's men seized sizable amounts of gunpowder. They also destroyed munitions and military supplies. Once the military and smuggling threat had been neutralized, Perry placed

Commander Joshua R. Sands in charge as U.S. military governor of Carmen. The American military regime remained in place until the spring of 1847, at which point a pro-American Mexican municipal government was installed. The blockade was loosened considerably after that time, although trade with the interior of Mexico continued to be prohibited.

Carmen remained a sleepy fishing village until the 1970s, when discoveries of large oil reserves in the area brought with them large infusions of money and people. Its current population is about 150,000 people, a good number of whom are foreign workers in the oil industry, including many Texans. The areas around Carmen have also become tourist destinations, and parts of Carmen Island are known for their beautiful beaches.

PAUL G. PIERPAOLI JR.

See also

Blockade, Naval; Conner, David; Perry, Matthew Calbraith; Trade; Yucatán.

References

Bauer, K. Jack. *Surfboats and Horse Marines: U.S. Naval Operations in the Mexican War, 1846–48*. Annapolis, MD: United States Naval Institute, 1969.

Nugent, Daniel, ed. *Rural Revolt in Mexico: U.S. Intervention and the Domain of Subaltern Politics*. Durham, NC: Duke University Press, 1998.

Carricitos Ranch, Skirmish at

See Thornton Affair

Carson, Christopher Houston "Kit"

Birth Date: December 24, 1809
Death Date: May 23, 1868

Fur trapper, guide, soldier, and renowned Indian fighter. Christopher Houston "Kit" Carson was born in Madison County, Kentucky, on December 24, 1809. Before he was two years old his family moved to Missouri, where he spent most of his youth. At age 14 Carson was apprenticed to a saddlemaker, but he later ran away and joined a wagon train headed west to Santa Fe, New Mexico. Carson soon found himself as a fur trapper and mountaineer, and this provided the foundation for almost everything he did for the rest of his life. Carson traveled all over the West as far as California, hunting, trapping, and ranching, and often living with various Native American tribes. In the process he took at least two Native American wives and also learned at least four Native American languages.

In 1846 Carson joined John C. Frémont's California Expedition as a guide and hunter. After the brief Bear Flag Revolt in June of that year, Carson became a citizen-soldier (holding no rank) in Frémont's impromptu brigade. In July, when the California Battalion was organized, Carson was given a commission as a second

lieutenant. Two months later Carson embarked on an official trip to Washington, D.C., where he was to brief officials on the situation in California and carry written orders to U.S. military commanders. He made it only as far as New Mexico, however, where Brigadier General Stephen W. Kearny ordered him to return to California. Carson then joined Kearny's march to California and took part in the unsuccessful Battle of San Pascual in December 1846. After Kearny's force was encircled by Californio forces on Mule Hill, not far from San Pascual, Carson and Edward Beale made their way through the Mexican lines and reached San Diego, where they requested reinforcements. Sailors and marines from the Pacific Squadron were immediately dispatched to relieve Kearny's force.

Carson next saw action at San Gabriel on January 8, 1847, and in the second occupation of Los Angeles on January 10. On February 25 Carson embarked on a second trip to Washington, D.C., arriving in the capital in late May. He met with President James K. Polk on three occasions, and in June Polk appointed Carson a second lieutenant in the Regiment of Mounted Rifles. He left the capital that same month, arriving in California in October. For the next several months, Carson was at Téjon Pass on patrol duty.

Cover of an 1850s dime novel featuring legendary American frontiersman Christopher "Kit" Carson. (Library of Congress)

Carson left on his third and final trip to Washington on May 4, 1848. As he passed through Santa Fe, he was informed that his U.S. Army commission had been rescinded by Congress because of his close ties to Frémont, who had been discredited for his actions in California. He nonetheless pressed on, reaching the capital in August, where he presented dispatches that he had been instructed to deliver.

After the war Carson continued to hunt, trap, scout, and served as an Indian agent for the Utes from 1854 to 1861. With the outbreak of the Civil War in 1861, Carson resigned this post and was commissioned a colonel in the New Mexico volunteers. He saw action in the Southwest and was soon tasked with the removal of Native Americans from their ancestral lands to remote reservations. Carson's campaign against the Navajos would be the most high profile of his actions against Native American tribes.

Beginning in July 1863, Carson led five missions through Navajo country, conducting a campaign of "total war." By the end of January 1864, between 6,000 and 8,000 Navajos (between one-half to two-thirds of the tribe) had come forward to be removed to the Bosque Redondo. The long march to the remote reservation resulted in many more Navajo deaths. Carson conducted other smaller campaigns against Native Americans in the Southwest until the Civil War ended in April 1865. Meanwhile, Carson had been granted a brevet commission as brigadier general in 1865. He then moved to Colorado to command Fort Garland before leaving the post in 1866 because of poor health. Carson died near Fort Lyons, Colorado, on May 23, 1868.

DAVID SLOAN

See also

Bear Flag Revolt; California Battalion; California Theater of War, Overview; Californios; Frémont, John Charles; Kearny, Stephen Watts; Los Angeles; Mule Hill; Polk, James Knox; San Gabriel River, Battle of; San Pascual, Battle of.

References

Carter, Harvey Lewis. *Dear Old Kit: The Historical Christopher Carson.* Norman: University of Oklahoma Press, 1968.
Gordon-McCutchan, R. C., ed. *Kit Carson: Indian Fighter or Indian Killer?* Boulder: University Press of Colorado, 1996.
Roberts, David. *A Newer World: Kit Carson, John C. Fremont, and the Claiming of the American West.* New York: Simon & Schuster, 2000.

Cartography

Cartography refers to the making and studying of maps designed to portray the physical characteristics of a given body of land or water or man-made features built on land, such as a city, town, fort, or defensive works. The Texas Revolution and the Mexican-American War brought about revolutionary changes in cartography, because the vast area in what would become the American Southwest was surveyed and mapped in detail for the first time. In addition, technological innovations during the 1830s and 1840s further transformed modern mapmaking. The history of modern printed maps began shortly after the invention of movable type by German printer Johannes Gutenberg in 1454. Printers quickly discovered that they could print maps by pressing engraved metal plates, which contained a reversed etching of the image, onto paper using the same style press. By the early 19th century, cartography and the sale of maps had become a substantial business in Europe and North America.

In the United States, Philadelphia, New York, and Boston became the center of the printing industry. Most printing (books and maps) was done by family-owned businesses. By the time of the Mexican-American War, however, even small, family-owned businesses began to rely on new steam-powered rotary printing presses. Printing became not only faster but more profitable for sellers and cheaper for the buyer. The use of lithography, still a relatively new technological advance, along with the increasing employment of paper made from wood pulp, also made the printing of maps easier and cheaper by the early 1840s.

Several types of maps dominated the market at the time. Pocket maps were designed to be carried folded by travelers, while larger, home atlases became part of the home library. School atlases were produced to fill the demand created by the emerging public education system in the United States. Mapmakers always claimed that their maps represented the latest discoveries. Major American mapmakers and sellers of the era included Samuel A. Mitchell, Joseph Hutchins Colton, Roswell C. Smith, William C. Woodbridge, Emma Willard, and James H. Young.

The U.S. Topographical Engineers, along with the U.S. Army Corps of Engineers, produced a plethora of maps for the U.S. government's use. These maps often contained information gathered during army expeditions sent to explore unknown regions, a number of which occurred in the West and Southwest. Civilian mapmakers continually updated their own works using these military maps.

Mexico was not an unknown land during the first half of the 19th century. For several hundred years, Mexico had been represented on European maps depicting New Spain, and Alexander von Humboldt's pioneering work on the geography of Mexico became available around 1811. Mexico also had its own mapmakers operating out of Mexico City and other larger cosmopolitan population centers. Although these maps lacked the accuracy of modern maps, they nevertheless provided a rough picture of Mexico and the American Southwest. It should be noted, however, that Mexico's northern border regions—particularly New Mexico and Texas—were the least well mapped of all of Mexico's landmass. During the Mexican-American War, families of soldiers often relied on commercially available maps and atlases to locate specific places mentioned in newspaper reports and letters from soldiers on the front.

The best-known map of the war was captured on the battlefield of Resaca de la Palma in May 1846. The property of Mexican general Mariano Arista, the map was revised and widely reproduced by American mapmaker John Disturnell and sold to the public. The Disturnell map was later selected as the official map used by

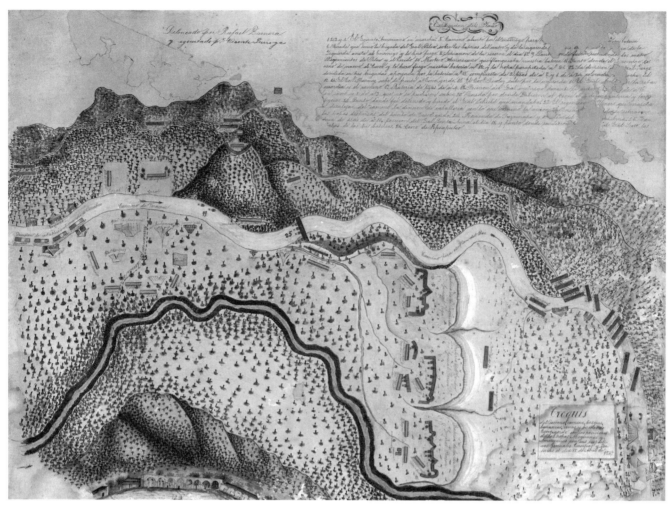

Map of the Battle of Cerro Gordo, April 18, 1847. Illustration by Rafael Zamora. (Getty Images)

U.S. and Mexican negotiators working on the 1848 Treaty of Guadalupe Hidalgo, which would establish the new boundary separating the two countries. Unknown to the negotiators, however, the map contained significant errors that were discovered by surveyors sent to mark out the boundary. El Paso (Texas) was mistakenly placed 30 miles too far north, while the position of the Rio Grande was set two degrees too far to the west.

The error ultimately resulted in the 1853 Gadsden Purchase, by which the United States paid Mexico $15 million for the Mesilla Valley, in what is now southern Arizona and New Mexico. Congress approved the transaction the following year because this region seemed the most likely route for a southern transcontinental railway that would link California to the East Coast. The Mexican-American War and its immediate aftermath not only resulted in the first detailed, relatively accurate mapping of the U.S. Southwest but also fueled the public's interest in maps.

BRUCE WINDERS

See also

Arista, Mariano; Boundary Commissions; Boundary Disputes, U.S. and Mexican; Engineering, Military; Gadsden Purchase; Mexico, Geography, Topography, Hydrology, and Climate; Guadalupe Hidalgo,

Treaty of; Lithographs; Mesilla Valley; Resaca de la Palma, Battle of; Rotary Printing Press; Topographical Engineers.

References

Martin, James. *Maps of Texas and the Southwest, 1513–1900*. Austin: Texas State Historical Association, 1999.

Reinhartz, Dennis, and Charles C. Colley, eds. *The Mapping of the American Southwest*. College Station: Texas A&M University Press, 1987.

Ristow, Walter W. *American Maps and Mapmakers: Commercial Cartography in the Nineteenth Century*. Detroit: Wayne State University Press, 1985.

Werne, Joseph Richard. *The Imaginary Line: A History of the United States and Mexican Boundary Survey, 1848–1857*. Fort Worth: Texas Christian University Press, 2007.

Carvajal, José María de Jesús
Birth Date: ca. 1805
Death Date: 1874

Mexican revolutionary, politician, soldier, and filibusterer. José María de Jesús Carvajal was born circa 1805 at San Fernando de

Béxar (later San Antonio). As a young man he went to Kentucky, where he apprenticed as a tanner and saddlemaker for two years. He then lived for a short while in Virginia, where he renounced his native Catholicism and became a Protestant. Under the tutelage of *empresario* Stephen F. Austin, Carvajal went back to Texas in the late 1820s as a surveyor and helped lay out the town of Victoria. In 1830 he married the daughter of Martín de Léon, a successful Texas *empresario,* thus permanently connecting himself to the political elite in Texas. In the early 1830s he served as the secretary for the municipal council of Béxar, and for a time he also served in the state legislature of Coahuila y Texas.

In 1835, the military commander of Coahuila y Texas exiled Carvajal for his alleged rebellious activities. Carvajal then traveled to New Orleans to help exiled Texans foment a rebellion, which would soon become part of the larger Texas Revolution. He chartered a small ship, the *Hannah Elizabeth,* and departed New Orleans for Texas in the late fall of 1835. The vessel was intercepted by the Mexicans, however, and Carvajal was captured and imprisoned. He managed to escape and returned to Texas, where he became involved in the Goliad Declaration of Independence in December 1835. Carvajal was elected as a delegate to the Texas Convention of 1836, although he did not attend.

In 1839 Carvajal led a contingent of Texas volunteers on an expedition into Mexico and was badly wounded in fighting outside Mier, Mexico. Long a proponent of an independent republic in northern Mexico, he fully supported the creation of the Republic of the Rio Grande, which General Antonio Canales had tried unsuccessfully to establish.

When the Mexican-American War began in the late spring of 1846, Canales commanded a Mexican army volunteer contingent against the U.S. invasion, not wanting to see the country annexed by the Americans. Canales, however, fought largely for the creation of an independent northern Mexico, and not because of any fealty toward the Mexican government.

After the war, Carvajal continued his rebellious ways. He resided along the Texas-Mexico border and between 1850 and 1853 spearheaded a number of cross-border raids and filibustering expeditions, composed chiefly of U.S. merchants and soldiers of fortune. The resulting low-level border warfare soon became known as the Merchants War. American officials twice arrested Carvajal for his illegal activities, but he was quickly released, much to the annoyance of the Mexican government.

In 1861 Carvajal was commander of troops in the state of Tamaulipas and led them in an effort to support the state government of Jesús de la Serva, which was under attack from insurgents. Carvajal, however, was defeated at Matamoros. In 1862, during the early stages of the French intervention, he joined the liberals in their mission to oust the French from Mexico. During the mid-1860s Carvajal served as the governor of the states of Tamaulipas and San Luis Potosí. In 1865 he was sent to Washington, D.C., to arrange a loan from the U.S. government. Carvajal later moved to Texas, and by 1872 he was living in Soto la Marine, Tamaulipas, where he died in 1874.

PAUL G. PIERPAOLI JR.

See also
Austin, Stephen Fuller; Canales, Antonio Rosillo; Coahuila y Texas; Filibusters; Rio Grande, Republic of the; San Antonio; Texas; Texas Revolution.

References
Bancroft, Hubert Howe. *History of Mexico.* 6 vols. San Francisco: A. L. Bancroft and the History Company, 1883–1889.
Chance, Joseph E. *José María de Jesús Carvajal: The Life and Times of a Mexican Revolutionary.* San Antonio, TX: Trinity University Press, 2006.

Casey, Silas
Birth Date: July 12, 1807
Death Date: January 22, 1882

U.S. Army officer. Silas Casey was born on July 12, 1807, in East Greenwich, Rhode Island. He graduated from the U.S. Military Academy at West Point in 1826. Upon graduation and commissioning as a second lieutenant of infantry, Casey served on the frontier and in various posts on the Great Lakes, including Sackets Harbor, New York; Fort Niagara, New York; and Fort Gratiot, Michigan. He was promoted to first lieutenant in 1836 and served in the Second Seminole War, during which he was promoted to captain in 1839. Casey returned to the Great Lakes and was assigned to Buffalo, New York, and Fort Mackinac, Michigan, before serving under Major General Winfield Scott in the Mexican-American War.

Casey served with distinction during the Battles of Contreras (August 20, 1847), Churubusco (August 20, 1847), and El Molino del Rey (September 8, 1847). For his actions at the former two engagements, he was brevetted to major. During the September 13, 1847, Battle of Chapultepec, where he was badly wounded in his leg, Casey led one of two attacking wings of 250 men charged with storming Chapultepec Castle. He was brevetted to lieutenant colonel on September 14, 1847, and received an official thanks from the Rhode Island legislature for his gallant service during the war.

The years between the Mexican War and the Civil War found Casey serving at various posts on the Pacific coast. In 1855 he was selected as a member of a board to revise the army's *Manual of Infantry Tactics.* He then wrote the three-volume *System of Infantry Tactics,* which expanded on William J. Hardee's two-volume manual published in 1855 by applying Hardee's tactics to the brigade and division levels. The War Department adopted the new manual in 1862, and it proved highly useful to the many volunteer officers who filled Union ranks during the Civil War. In 1863, Casey published *Infantryman Tactics for Colored Troops,* which was adopted that same year. Following action against Native Americans in the Pacific Northwest and garrison duty on San Juan

Island, Casey began the Civil War as a lieutenant colonel in the 9th Infantry Brigade. He was soon promoted to brigadier general of volunteers.

As a division commander during the Peninsula Campaign (March–August 1862), Casey's troops were overrun at the Battle of Fair Oaks (Seven Pines) on May 31–June 1, 1862. Casey was promoted to major general of volunteers and brigadier general in the regular army on May 31, 1862. He spent the remainder of the war in Washington, D.C., mostly in administrative assignments.

Casey was promoted to major general in the regular army on March 13, 1865, and retired from active duty on July 8, 1868. He died in Brooklyn, New York, on January 22, 1882.

WILLIAM E. WHYTE

See also
Chapultepec, Battle of; Churubusco, Battle of; Contreras, Battle of; El Molino del Rey, Battle of; Scott, Winfield.

References
Heitman, Francis B. *Historical Register and Dictionary of the United States Army: From Its Organization, September 29, 1789, to March 2, 1903.* Washington, DC: Government Printing Office, 1903.
Rafuse, Ethan S. *McClellan's War: The Failure of Moderation in the Struggle for the Union.* Bloomington: Indiana University Press, 2005.
Smith, Justin H. *The War with Mexico.* 2 vols. New York: Macmillan, 1919.

Castes

Groups into which Mexicans were classified on the basis of ethnic ancestry during the Spanish colonial period and during much of the postcolonial independence era. First introduced by the Spanish, this classification system and its remnants existed well after Mexico became independent.

Castes rested on the belief that Christian Spaniards—with no Islamic or Jewish antecedents—were at the pinnacle of the caste hierarchy and were thus entitled to participate in the governance of their society. In Mexico, the Spanish established many additional distinctions based on ancestry. At the top, of course, they placed themselves. Ranked next, and regarded by Spaniards as inferior, stood the criollos (whites born in Mexico). Next came the mestizos (or people born to a Spanish father and a Native American mother). The fully developed caste system included 24 different gradations, some with dismissive labels such as *lobo* (wolf). Although wealth could mitigate the effect of one's classification, barriers still remained. During four centuries of colonial rule, only one criollo and no Native American or mestizo ever held the highest administrative post in the colony (viceroy).

Although the 1821 victory of the independence forces under Colonel Agustín de Iturbide removed the Spanish governing system from Mexico and promised to secure equality for all Mexicans, the caste system remained largely unchanged. Criollos, who constituted some 10 percent of the population of postindependence Mexico, often proved far more interested in exercising the prerogatives of a dominant caste than in effectively abolishing the system. Castes remained so significant that American ambassador to Mexico Waddy Thompson Jr. (1842–1844) wrote that Mexican distinctions of color were as great as those in the United States. While upward movement between groups proved possible for the exceptionally talented, sharp distinctions remained in a deeply polarized nation in which the preponderance of political and economic power lay in criollo hands.

From 1821 to 1847 sporadic rebellions broke out among the most disadvantaged of Mexicans, most notably the Juan Álvarez Rebellion of 1842. Poor Indians in southwest México used the tumult to embark on a campaign of destruction that spread over 60,000 square miles. Ultimately, only the power of the Mexican army could break the rebels' force.

By mid-1847 the U.S. Army's destruction of Mexican forces had reached the point at which the Mexican government no longer possessed the force necessary to crush internal revolts. Throughout the more heavily Indian southern half of Mexico, and particularly on the Yucatán Peninsula, rebellions grew to the extent that the Mexican government feared the loss of several major cities. In Yucatán, Governor Manuel Barbachano, who found his area of control reduced to just two cities, considered the so-called Caste War an effort by native Maya peoples to exterminate whites.

Consequently, in both the Truce Agreement of March 6, 1848, and in the Treaty of Guadalupe Hidalgo, Mexico's government sought and obtained U.S. assistance to deal with this problem. This included an American commitment to break up any group of armed Mexicans not sanctioned by the Mexican government that U.S. forces might encounter. The United States also agreed to return all captured arms and forts as soon as the treaty was ratified and began selling weapons to the Mexican army well before that ratification occurred. By December 1848, a Mexican army of 21,278 men, which was slightly larger than the force General Antonio López de Santa Anna had used to defend Mexico City against the Americans, was fighting revolts by lower-caste Mexicans. Of these forces, 16,000 fought the Maya in Yucatán, while the remaining 5,278 men combated rebellion in other parts of the nation, particularly the Huasteca, a region in northeastern Mexico that comprises parts of the states of Veracruz, Tamaulipas, San Luis Potosí, and Hidalgo.

IRVING W. LEVINSON

See also
Guadalupe Hidalgo, Treaty of; Mexico; Santa Anna, Antonio López de.

References
Katz, Friedrich, ed. *Riot, Rebellion, and Revolution: Rural Social Conflict in Mexico.* Princeton, NJ: Princeton University Press, 1988.
Katzew, Ilona. *Casta Painting: Images of Race in Eighteenth-Century Mexico.* New Haven, CT: Yale University Press, 2005.
León-Portilla, Miguel, ed. *Diccionario Porrúa de Historia, Biografía, y Geografía de México.* México, DF: Editorial Porrúa, 1997.

Reina, Leticia. *Las rebeliones campesinas en México (1819–1906)*. Mexico City: Siglo Veintiuno, 1980.

Rugeley, Terry. *Yucatán's Maya Peasantry and the Origins of the Caste War*. Austin: University of Texas Press, 1996.

Thompson, Waddy. *Recollections of México*. New York: Wiley and Putnam, 1846.

Castro, José María

Birth Date: ca. 1810
Death Date: 1860

Prominent Californio and military commander of Alta California at the time of the Mexican-American War. José María Castro was born circa 1810, probably in the vicinity of Monterey in (Alta) California. Little is known of his early years or rise to prominence. What is certain is that Castro was fiercely proud of his Californio heritage and believed that Alta California should be an independent republic, free from both Mexican and U.S. control. Castro ultimately became the military commander of Alta California, where he was headquartered at Monterey, along the coast in the northern part of the territory. Despite his suspicion of Americans residing in California, Castro maintained close personal and political ties with John A. Sutter, proprietor of Sutter's Fort.

In December 1845, Captain John C. Frémont arrived at Sutter's Fort with a contingent of some 60 men. Frémont then traveled west to Monterey, where he was to meet with Castro and obtain his permission to scout the region, purportedly to prevent the British from seizing control. Castro was highly suspicious of the American's motives, however, and permitted Frémont to stay temporarily in Alta California but not along the coast. When Frémont violated the arrangement, Castro requested that he leave California. The brash American refused. Castro now began to recruit and mobilize men for a potential showdown with American forces.

Meanwhile, the governor of Alta California, Pío Pico de Jesús, who resided some distance away in Los Angeles, grew suspicious of Castro's activities, fearing that the military commander was attempting to seize power for himself. The two men rarely saw eye to eye, which made governing the vast territory all the more daunting. After the Bear Flag Revolt began on June 14, 1846, Castro's troops fought against the Bear Flaggers at the skirmish at Olompoli Rancho on June 24. The engagement was something of a draw, but Castro realized that he would be unable to resist the upstart independence movement without help. In July, Monterey fell to a U.S. force under Captain William Mervine, and later that month Castro traveled to Los Angeles to meet with Pico. The two men sought to attain British intervention, which was not forthcoming, and then appealed to Commodore Robert Stockton, imploring him to allow California to become an independent republic. That effort also failed.

On August 10, Pico and Castro fled Los Angeles, which Stockton occupied on August 13. During the autumn of 1846 Castro joined forces with Captain José María Flores, and the Californios managed to reoccupy Santa Barbara and San Diego. Meanwhile, on September 25, Los Angeles was captured by Californio forces. Castro appealed directly to the Mexican government for aid and reinforcements, but his pleas were ignored. By January 1847 the Californios were defeated, and Alta California remained in U.S. control for the remainder of the Mexican-American War.

When the war ended in 1848, Castro, who had taken refuge in Sonora, returned to Monterey. In 1853 he resettled in Baja California, where he held several positions in the local government. He died there in 1860.

PAUL G. PIERPAOLI JR.

See also

Baja California; Bear Flag Revolt; California; California Theater of War, Overview; Californios; Flores, José María; Frémont, John Charles; Los Angeles; Mervine, William; Monterey, California; Olompoli Rancho, Skirmish at; Pico, Pío de Jesús; Stockton, Robert Field; Sutter, John Augustus; Sutter's Fort.

References

Harlow, Neal. *California Conquered: War and Peace on the Pacific, 1846–1850*. Berkeley: University of California Press, 1982.

Pitt, Leonard. *The Decline of the Californios: A Social History of the Spanish Speaking Californians, 1846–1890*. Berkeley: University of California Press, 1966.

Stone, Irving. *Men to Match My Mountains: The Opening of the Far West, 1840–1900*. New York: Doubleday, 1956.

Casualties, Mexico

Approximately 82,000 Mexicans served in the Mexican-American War, either as regular army troops or as partisan fighters. There is considerable disagreement over the total number of Mexican casualties, however. Estimates range from a low of 14,700 killed and wounded to as many as 50,000. The actual number is likely toward the lower end of the range, but poor Mexican record keeping makes pinpointing the number nearly impossible. In some cases, the only casualty figures come from U.S. battlefield reports, which are mostly estimates.

As with their American opponents, the high mortality rate among Mexican soldiers can, in part, be accounted for by the ineffectiveness of medical care. Infection made any penetrating wound dangerous. There were few surgical options for open wounds of the head or chest, and wounds that penetrated an abdominal viscus were virtually always fatal. Because of the high incidence of subsequent infection, any open fracture of an extremity was taken as cause for amputation.

As was typical of other 19th-century conflicts, infectious disease accounted for far more deaths than battle trauma. Yellow fever, malaria, dysentery, and epidemic measles, mumps, and even occasional smallpox were problems both on campaign and in camp.

Mexican soldiers suffered greater casualties than did their American enemies in large measure because of their inferior weapons. The Mexican army lacked long-range cannon, while the United States was able to rely on its superior artillery to inflict hundreds of mass casualties from a distance. For Mexican soldiers, this disparity in ordnance made charging the American lines particularly deadly. This discrepancy became evident in the initial fighting along the Rio Grande at the Battles of Palo Alto and Resaca de la Palma. American casualties in these two confrontations amounted to 38 killed and 137 wounded, whereas the Mexicans suffered 256 killed and 334 wounded. Official reports of Mexican casualties may be understated, since Major General Zachary Taylor claimed to have buried at least 200 Mexican soldiers after the battle.

The disproportionately greater Mexican casualties continued throughout the war. The Battle of Cerro Gordo produced almost 4,000 Mexican prisoners of war, as well as large numbers of dead and wounded, at a cost of only 63 Americans killed and 368 wounded. At Churubusco, Mexican casualties totaled 4,297 killed and wounded compared with the loss of 133 Americans killed and 865 wounded. Finally, the battle for Mexico City cost the defending Mexican forces an estimated 2,200 casualties, whereas the attacking Americans suffered only 130 killed and 703 wounded.

Likewise, Mexican general Antonio López de Santa Anna's forced march to confront Taylor's force at Buena Vista in February 1847 resulted in heavy losses. In the course of the 240-mile march north almost 5,000 of his 20,000-man force were unable to fight because of starvation, dehydration, exhaustion, and exposure. The Mexicans then suffered 2,000 casualties in the ensuing battle. Short of food, Santa Anna was forced to withdraw and march the 240 miles back to San Luis Potosí. In roughly a month's time he had lost more than 10,000 men—half of his army. Santa Anna's attempt to counter Major General Winfield Scott's march from Veracruz to Mexico City had similar results.

The number of Mexican civilian casualties is difficult to ascertain. Most scholars place civilian losses at about 1,000 (killed and wounded) for the Battles of Monterrey, Veracruz, Mexico City, and Huamantla alone.

Derek R. Mallett

See also
Atrocities; Casualties, United States; Military Medicine.

References
Bauer, K. Jack. *The Mexican War, 1846–1848.* New York: Macmillan, 1974.
Eisenhower, John S. D. *So Far from God: The U.S. War with Mexico, 1846–1848.* New York: Random House, 1989.
Gillett, Mary. *The Army Medical Department: 1818–1865.* Washington, DC: Center of Military History, United States Army, 1987.
Henderson, Timothy J. *A Glorious Defeat: Mexico and Its War with the United States.* New York: Hill and Wang, 2007.
Johannsen, Robert W. *To the Halls of the Montezumas: The Mexican War in the American Imagination.* New York: Oxford University Press, 1985.
Wheelan, Joseph. *Invading Mexico: America's Continental Dream and the Mexican War, 1846–1848.* New York: Carroll and Graf, 2007.

Casualties, United States

Between the summer of 1845, when troops assembled near Corpus Christi, Texas, and the end of the Mexican-American War on February 2, 1848, a total of 26,922 regular army troops and 73,260 volunteers served on the American side. Of this total of 100,182 men, 3,393 were wounded in action, 1,044 were killed in action, 505 died of wounds, and 10,196 died of disease. The seven to one ratio of death from disease to death from wounds can be compared to the Civil War, where the ratio was approximately two to one. Jefferson Davis's Mississippi Rifles suffered the most combat deaths, 59, of any volunteer regiment in the war, with the Palmetto Regiment from South Carolina second, losing 56 men.

The high mortality of American servicemen can largely be attributed to the poor state of medical care at the time. Any battlefield wound, or noncombat accident for that matter, could become life-threatening, especially those to the head or chest. Abdominal wounds most often proved fatal, and doctors frequently amputated arms or legs that suffered serious damage through the carrying away of sections of bone. Military hospitals lacked appropriate antibiotics and operated in largely unsanitary conditions. The 12 percent death rate in army hospitals was, however, not that different from civilian facilities in the United States and far better than that of military hospitals of the belligerents in the Crimean War nearly a decade later.

Poor food, unsanitary practices, and lack of immunity to certain diseases carried off many men. Infection and disease were the largest killers of American soldiers. The connection between mosquitoes and diseases such as malaria and yellow fever was yet to be discovered. Yellow fever (*vómito*), in particular, frequently made its deadly rounds through American army camps. Furthermore, with American soldiers drinking often-polluted river water and disregarding basic sanitary measures, not to mention the mixing of men from all parts of the country, other diseases took their toll as well. Measles, mumps, and smallpox, along with dysentery ("the bloody flux") and simple diarrhea ("the blues"), brought

Estimated Casualty Statistics of the Mexican-American War

	United States	Mexico
Total Mobilized (Regular and Guerrilla)	104,556	82,000
Killed in Action or Died of Wounds	1,733	5,000
Died of Disease or Other Causes	12,229	Unknown
Wounded	4,152	20,000
Missing	695	10,000

The Night After the Battle. Burying the Dead, a lithograph by Nathaniel Currier, 1846. (Beinecke Rare Book & Manuscript Library)

their own brand of misery and claimed the lives of many American soldiers.

American volunteer units tended to be less disciplined about field sanitation than regular army units. Thus, greater numbers of volunteers died from disease than did regulars. Also not surprisingly, disease epidemics often hit American soldiers from rural areas harder than they did their urban counterparts, likely because the city dwellers had developed proportionately more immunity to these.

The high frequency of epidemics, coupled with the relative scarcity of wood in many areas where the war was fought, meant routine shortages of coffins. The deceased would thus often be given a "soldier's grave," which meant that their bodies would simply be wrapped in a blanket and buried directly in the ground. At the American encampment at Camargo in late summer and early fall of 1846, the death rate was so high that the local mockingbirds were alleged to have begun imitating "The Dead March," the song military bands played for soldiers' funerals.

DEREK R. MALLETT

See also

Atrocities; Camargo; Casualties, Mexico; Davis, Jefferson Finis; Military Medicine.

References

Eisenhower, John S. D. *So Far from God: The U.S. War with Mexico, 1846–1848.* New York: Random House, 1989.

Henderson, Timothy J. *A Glorious Defeat: Mexico and Its War with the United States.* New York: Hill and Wang, 2007.

Wheelan, Joseph. *Invading Mexico: America's Continental Dream and the Mexican War, 1846–1848.* New York: Carroll and Graf, 2007.

Catana, Massacre at
Event Date: February 10, 1847

Massacre of between 20 and 30 Mexican civilians by U.S. volunteer soldiers near the village of Catana, Mexico, on February 10, 1847. Catana was located in north central Mexico (Coahuila), just outside Agua Nueva, which is set some 17 miles south of Saltillo. Following his victory at the Battle of Monterrey on September 21–23, 1846, Major General Zachary Taylor expected Mexican general Antonio López de Santa Anna to move his army northward from San Luis Potosí. He thus chose Agua Nueva as the site for an encampment, from which he would monitor Santa Anna's movements. By early February 1847 some 4,500 U.S. troops, a good number of them ill-trained volunteers, had set up camp around Agua Nueva.

Boredom soon set in among the troops, and some engaged in acts of violence against the local townspeople. Others stole from or looted shops and ranches. Most of the U.S. regulars behaved honorably, but several volunteer units perpetrated many of the depredations.

By the end of December, the situation had become desperate. On Christmas Day, U.S. troops raped several Mexican women. Among the worst offenders was the 1st Arkansas Volunteer Cavalry under the command of Colonel Archibald Yell. By then, that outfit's reputation for poor discipline and use of excess force with civilians had earned it the nickname "Arkansas Ransackers."

The rape of women especially outraged the locals, some of whom retaliated on February 9 by killing a private from Yell's regiment just outside the army camp. Determined to seek retribution, about 100 men from Yell's brigade fanned out into the countryside on the following day. Although details about what took place next remain sketchy, the men apparently cornered 20–30 civilians in a cave outside Catana and systematically began killing them; some were shot and others beaten to death. Receiving word of the massacre in progress, Brigadier General John E. Wool, who had only recently arrived at Agua Nueva, dispatched a contingent of U.S. regulars to investigate.

When the regulars arrived on the scene they immediately stopped the carnage, but by then most of the damage had been done. At least 20 Mexicans lay dead, some of whom had been scalped and mutilated. Several more lay dying of gunshot wounds or crushed skulls from savage beatings. Wool subsequently demanded that Colonel Yell produce those individuals responsible for the massacre, but Yell never complied. Wool then dismissed Companies B and G from Yell's regiment, the men of which were later sent home. No further punishment was meted out. General Taylor, sickened by the reports he received, wrote, "Such deeds . . . cast disgrace upon our arms and reputation of our country." Nevertheless, Taylor did not order any other disciplinary measures against the Catana Massacre perpetrators.

PAUL G. PIERPAOLI JR.

See also
Atrocities; Taylor, Zachary; Wool, John Ellis; Yell, Archibald.

References
Chamberlain, Samuel F. *My Confession: The Recollections of a Rogue.* New York: Harper & Brothers, 1956.

Eisenhower, John S. D. *So Far from God: The U.S. War with Mexico, 1846–1848.* New York: Random House, 1989.

Foos, Paul. *A Short, Offhand, Killing Affair: Soldiers and Social Conflict during the Mexican-American War.* Chapel Hill: University of North Carolina Press, 2003.

Catholic Church, Mexico

The Roman Catholic Church has been one of Mexico's most powerful and enduring institutions. During the colonial era (1519–1821), the Roman Catholic Church functioned as a virtual department of government, was the principal instrument of social control for the crown, and played a leading role in the economy. In this last role, the Catholic Church was Mexico's largest landowner and most important financial institution for a colony with no banking system and limited surplus capital. It was the Catholic Church's economic and financial role that drew increasing criticism in the decades immediately after independence in 1821. While Mexican politics nominally revolved around a conservative-liberal competition for power, a more important struggle developed between a wealthy church and a poor state.

Reformers first moved to curb the powers of the Catholic Church in 1833–1834, but the reforms were largely undone with the return to power in 1834 of Mexico's most famous general and president, Antonio López de Santa Anna. Politicians of all political persuasions looked to the church as a potential source of major government financing, but church officials were reluctant to financially support any Mexican administration, regardless of supposed political philosophy.

During the Mexican-American War, various Mexican regimes sought to tap church wealth to help finance the war effort, and in May 1846 the government of General Mariano Paredes y Arrillaga issued a decree calling on the Catholic Church to lend it 2.4 million pesos. Although most church organizations pledged cooperation, in fact no money changed hands. That November the government, then headed by interim chief executive General José Mariano Salas, tried a new approach; it proposed to sell bills to the general public worth 2 million pesos, with the bills to be secured by church property. In December, however, the government agreed to abandon this approach in return for a promise from the Catholic Church of a loan of 850,000 pesos.

By 1847 the financial situation of the Mexican government was so desperate that it issued a controversial decree on January 11 authorizing the mortgaging or sale of church property up to a maximum of 15 million pesos. On February 4, the Mexican congress authorized the mortgage or sale of an additional 5 million pesos of church property. Domestic opposition to this financial "attack" quickly grew, and on February 27 an uprising, known as the Revolt of the Polkos, broke out in Mexico City.

The rebellion forced Santa Anna to leave the northern front (the Battle of Buena Vista had just concluded) and return to the capital. Santa Anna quickly brought an end to the unrest, agreeing to annul the decree of January 11 in return for a promise by the Catholic Church to guarantee a new sale of bills by the government of up to 1.5 million pesos. Church-state financial negotiations during the war concluded with an agreement in August 1847 in which the Catholic Church guaranteed 144,000 pesos in promissory notes issued by the government. Clearly, the Catholic Church had not proved the ready source of funds hoped for by the Mexican government in its war with the United States.

The Catholic Church also had a significant impact on the war effort through its active involvement in the factional politics that characterized 19th-century Mexico. In fact, church officials helped to plan and finance the Polkos' Revolt in an attempt to end the governmental threat to church property. The political instability in Mexico, to which the church had contributed since the 1820s, made it difficult for Mexico to present a united front against U.S.

This 1846 lithograph, entitled *The Mexican Rulers Migrating from Matamoros with Their Treasures,* illustrates the anti-Catholic view of the Mexican clergy prevalent in the United States during the Mexican-American War. Special privileges enjoyed by the Church led to some corruption. (Library of Congress)

expansionist policies. The conflict between church and state during the Mexican-American War was, however, only a preview of the even more bitter struggle between the two institutions that would lead to civil war in the late 1850s.

DON M. COERVER

See also

Buena Vista, Battle of; Congress, Mexican; Politics, Mexican; Polkos Revolt; Religion; Santa Anna, Antonio López de.

References

Costeloe, Michael P. "Church-State Financial Negotiations in Mexico during the American War, 1846–1847." *Revista de historia de América* 60 (1965): 91–123.

Costeloe, Michael P. "The Mexican Church and the Rebellion of the Polkos." *Hispanic American Historical Review* 46 (1966): 170–78.

Santoni, Pedro. *Mexicans at Arms: Puro Federalists and the Politics of War, 1845–1848.* Fort Worth, TX: Texas Christian University Press, 1996.

Tenenbaum, Barbara A. *The Politics of Penury: Debts and Taxes in Mexico, 1821–1856.* Albuquerque: University of New Mexico Press, 1986.

Cattle

Cattle provided a crucial food source for Americans during the Mexican-American War. Cattle also tended to be at the root of numerous problems between Anglo settlers and Native Americans in Texas, and between Anglos and Mexicans.

The early cattle industry had gradually spread westward from the eastern seaboard to the Midwest and then to the open grasslands of Texas and the Great Plains. In addition to dairy products, first provided by cattle in Upstate New York and, later, in Wisconsin, cattle also provided meat on the hoof, especially after Texas became an independent republic in 1836. By then, vast herds of longhorn cattle capable of living on the sparse and arid grasslands of Texas were available for market. In the 1840s they were being driven northward to Missouri. Prior to refrigeration and refrigerated railcars, which did not appear until the late 1870s, cattle were transported on the hoof (meaning while still alive). In order to maintain a healthy weight, they could be moved only about 15 miles a day, making the process a prolonged and costly affair.

As Anglo ranchers in Texas expanded their cattle herds, inevitable conflicts arose between Texans and Native Americans, particularly the Comanches. White encroachment on Indian lands outraged Texas tribes, leading to raids and the larceny—and sometimes destruction—of significant herds of cattle. Anglo ranchers were also sometimes engaged in a low-level conflict against Mexicans and Mexican bandits, especially near the border, where they engaged in frequent cattle rustling.

During the Mexican-American War, Texas cattle in particular helped feed U.S. Army soldiers. Army quartermasters sometimes contracted with Texas ranchers and ranch hands who delivered cattle—on the hoof—to U.S. Army camps. This did not happen often, however, because the logistical challenges of moving cattle over long distances were daunting. Any cattle requisitioned had to be herded by ranchers and cowboys to their destination. Major General Zachary Taylor's army, operating near the Texas border and in far northern Mexico, occasionally requisitioned cattle for food, but such orders became impossible as the war progressed and American forces moved further away from Texas. Instead, Taylor and Major General Winfield Scott on occasion requisitioned local cattle from Mexican ranchers, but this did not happen with much frequency.

After the U.S. Civil War (1861–1865), cattle ranching on the Great Plains gave birth to the famous cattle drives, boomtowns, and the meat-packing industry in Chicago. Gustavus Swift and Philip Armour, both from Chicago, and the Cudahy Brothers in Omaha became pioneers in the thriving meat-packing industry, especially after the introduction of the insulated refrigeration railcar in 1877. Meanwhile, the extension of railroads westward across Kansas and to the West Coast provided junctions where the cattle drives ended, and processing centers in the Midwest allowed dressed beef to be hauled quickly and cheaply to population centers throughout the East. Eventually, farmers fenced off prairie lands, and other train lines soon connected Texas and other western states with the East Coast so that cattle drives became a thing of the past. Nevertheless, beef remained an important part of military procurement from the 1870s onward.

LARRY SCHWEIKART AND PAUL G. PIERPAOLI JR.

See also

Logistics, U.S.; Quartermaster Services, U.S. and Mexican; Scott, Winfield; Taylor, Zachary; Texas; Texas-Comanche Relations.

References

Birzer, Bradley, and Larry Schweikart. *The American West.* New York: Wiley, 2003.

Dykstra, Robert R. *The Cattle Towns.* New York: Knopf, 1968.

Jordan, Terry G. *Trails to Texas: Southern Roots of Western Cattle Ranching.* Lincoln: University of Nebraska Press, 1981.

Kujovich, Mary Yeager. "The Refrigerator Car and the Growth of the American Dressed Beef Industry." *Business History Review* 44 (1970): 460–482.

Swift, Lewis F., and Arthur Van Vlissington. *The Yankee of the Yards: The Biography of Gustavus Swift.* New York: A. W. Shaw, 1928.

Cattle Hide Industry

The cattle industry was immensely important in the economies of both the United States and Mexico during the first half of the 19th century. Cattle provided the economic foundation of California during this period, with their hides serving as a prominent form of currency called California bank notes. The hides and tallow (rendered beef fat) were more important than the meat, to the extent that carcasses were sometimes left to rot in the sun after the hide and tallow products were harvested. In addition to a form of exchange, hides had myriad uses as beds, blankets, saddles, shoes, furniture, luggage, door and window coverings, fencing, and rope. Eastern industry consumed large numbers of cattle hides. The value of leather tanned in the Mississippi Territory was second only to cotton cloth in the early decades of the century. The tallow was also extremely important and was employed for cooking, candles, and soap. Rendered tallow was usually placed into leather bags and shipped. The cattle hide industry played an important role in the escalating conflict between the United States and Mexico leading to the Mexican-American War of 1846–1848.

In the early decades of the 19th century, the prospect of raising cattle drew American settlers to the northern Mexican province of Texas, which was ideally suited for cattle ranching on a large scale. The Mexican government also actively encouraged American settlement in Texas following independence from Spain in 1821 to develop the region's economy, as well as to provide a buffer between Mexican citizens and bands of raiding Indians in the north. By 1830 Texas had become a cattle powerhouse, reaping huge revenues from its shipments of beef, tallow, and hides.

Nevertheless, the large influx of Americans into Texas led the impoverished Mexican government to issue the Decree of April 6, 1830, a law that included heavy taxation on Texas imports and exports (Texas settlers had heretofore been exempt from such taxes). Mexico then sent customs officials, along with soldiers, to collect the taxes, which resulted in smuggling and armed conflict between the Texans and the Mexican representatives. The April 6 decree also mandated an end to Anglo-American immigration and to slavery in Texas (Mexico had earlier abolished it). Texans' anger over these three points directly contributed to outbreaks of violence between Mexican regulars and Texas militia and to the Texas Revolution, which resulted in Texan independence in 1836.

The Mexican government maintained that Texas was still a Mexican province, however. Conflict continued between the Texans and the Mexican government between 1836 and 1845 and led to increased violence, property seizures, and accusations of unjust imprisonment of Texans and even murder. The annexation of Texas by the United States in 1845 escalated the ongoing violence, which ultimately helped bring war between the United States and Mexico in the spring of 1846.

DEBRA J. SHEFFER

See also

California; Cattle; Decree of 1830; Texas; Texas Revolution.

References

Birzer, Bradley, and Larry Schweikart. *The American West.* New York: Wiley, 2003.

Dana, Richard Henry. *Two Years before the Mast: A Personal Narrative.* New York: Harper and Brothers, 1840.

Guice, John D. W. "Cattle Raisers of the Old Southwest: Reinterpretation." *Western Historical Quarterly* 8 (April 1977): 167–187.

Worcester, Don. *The Texas Longhorn: Relic of the Past, Asset for the Future.* College Station: Texas A&M University Press, 1987.

Causes of the War

The Mexican-American War resulted from the interplay of Manifest Destiny in which Americans claimed not only Texas but California, Arizona, and New Mexico with Mexican honor and nationalism. Meanwhile, European leaders were preoccupied with revolutionary developments in their continent that drew their attention away from the Western Hemisphere. The James K. Polk administration took advantage of these dynamics, which were only enhanced by the 1803 Louisiana Purchase and ascendant American views of superiority and exceptionalism, particularly after the War of 1812. American public opinion had favored expansion since the Revolutionary War, first into Louisiana, and then into Texas, Arizona, and California because of the steady migration of American farmers and ranchers by the 1820s into these areas. And the many Americans who championed or benefited from slavery saw western expansion as a way to spread slavery beyond the general confines of the Southeast.

Economic systems, foreign policy goals, and the governments of Mexico and the United States were also starkly different. Like the United States, Mexico had been a European colony. However, Mexico was a debtor nation, owing sums both to the United States and European powers. The postindependence period (since 1821) was also marked by political unrest with a rapid turnover of governments. Added to that were independence movements in the northern Mexican states.

The U.S. government, on the other hand, was quite stable during the same period. For much of the 19th century the American economy and foreign policy were geared toward the ideal of Manifest Destiny—the belief that it was a divine right or preordination for the United States to occupy the North American continent from the Atlantic to the Pacific. Also inherent in this belief was that no obstacles—be they Native Americans or Mexico—would stand in the way of this goal. Additionally, Manifest Destiny suggested that Anglos were ideologically and racially superior to Mexicans (and Native Americans). Historian Norman A. Graebner suggests that economic considerations in the West also drove Manifest Destiny. Northeastern merchants had long-standing relationships with trading partners in the Pacific. These merchants sought ports on the West Coast for trade with Asia, and therefore they lobbied U.S. presidents from Andrew Jackson to James K. Polk to pursue western expansion. Proslavery forces, of course, hoped to extend slavery into newly won lands in the West.

American goals under this rubric were to keep imperial European powers out of the Americas and to compete economically all around the world. Certainly, the 1823 Monroe Doctrine was a clear enunciation of this thinking. U.S. leaders wanted to emulate the traditional European nation-state. But some Americans were concerned that European powers might invade Mexico or other Latin American nations, thereby threatening American sovereignty in the Western Hemisphere. According to many policy makers of the era, the only logical way to avoid this scenario was to invade Mexico.

Race was also a factor in the differences between Mexicans and Americans. Mexico was a hybrid society that had emerged from the interplay of Spanish and Native American cultures. Conversely, the United States in the early 19th century was an essentially racist society that relegated all but white, Anglo-Saxon Protestants to the sidelines, enslaved African Americans, legally barred miscegenation, and believed fervently in Anglo superiority.

Mexico also held differing racial ideologies and views on slavery. The Mexican government had abolished slavery. It did not want slavery in Texas, something that angered the Anglos of Texas, but it lacked the resources to enforce this policy. Many Mexicans also realized that, if Mexico were to be annexed by the United States, they would most likely be treated in the same manner as African Americans, Native Americans, and other ethnic and religious minorities.

Meanwhile, by the 1830s and 1840s, slavery had become a divisive issue in the United States. Southern slave owners demanded that slavery be allowed into any new territories acquired from Mexico and thus strongly pushed for the annexation of Texas in 1845. In contrast, many Whigs and northern Democrats decried the potential expansion of slavery, but their sentiments were in the minority, at least in Congress. Most of the American Southwest, however, is arid and not well suited for slave-based agriculture. Some scholars thus argue that because of Manifest Destiny many American leaders coveted not only the Southwest, but all of Mexico as a way to dull the growing division surrounding slavery. Such an acquisition would have given proslavery forces all of Mexico below the Compromise of 1821 line and would not have upset the balance between free and slave territories.

Another cause of the war was the tension between the American and Mexican governments over Texas. Mexico had allowed settlement in Texas by American citizens after 1821, provided that they obeyed Mexican laws and respected their culture. However, many white settlers in Texas refused to comply with these policies, producing ideological conflict and causing resentment among Anglos over what they perceived as their harsh treatment at the hands of the Mexican government.

By 1830, however, demographics in Texas had changed, with American settlers now greatly outnumbering Mexican citizens. Mexico now feared it would lose the entire Southwest to American expansion. The May 1836 Treaties of Velasco, negotiated by Texans and Santa Anna, put an end to the Texas Revolution, granted Texans their independence, and established the Rio Grande, near Brownsville, as the southern border of Texas. However, these agreements caused great resentment in Mexico. The Mexican government refused to ratify the treaties or recognize the border at the Rio Grande. Instead, Mexico claimed that the Texas border was the Nueces River, near Corpus Christi.

After Texan independence, raids by bands of Mexican nationals across the border caused nearly $2 million in property damage to Texas residents. The failure of the Mexican government to deal with these raids caused outrage among Texans. The Mexican government actually borrowed money from the United States to pay for the damages but defaulted on these loans because it was nearly bankrupt. In 1845, President James K. Polk now demanded repayment and suggested that Mexico cede California and New Mexico to the United States to cover the cost of the loans. Mexican president José Joaquín Herrera, seeking to avoid a war, actually considered such a move. But in late December of that year he was removed from power in a coup led by General Mariano Paredes y Arrillaga, who seemed to relish a conflict with the United States and flatly refused Polk's demands.

In February 1845 the United States annexed Texas. This did not bring war, however. That came when Polk sought to provoke Mexico by sending U.S. forces south of the Nueces River, the traditional southern boundary for Texas, to the Rio Grande, in support of Texas claims of that stream as its border with Mexico. By mid-August 1845, U.S. brigadier general Zachary Taylor and 3,500 troops had occupied Corpus Christi, Texas. On January 13, 1846, Polk ordered these troops to move south and enforce a naval blockade of the Rio Grande. The Mexican government viewed this as a blatant act of war.

Then, upon reaching Port Isabel on March 8, 1846, Taylor's men discovered that fleeing residents had burned the settlement. These soldiers had captured the mouth of the Rio Grande by the end of the month, and consequently Mexican general Pedro de Ampudia warned Taylor that if he remained in the area armed conflict would result. On April 25, 1846, a Mexican cavalry unit crossed the Rio Grande and skirmished with American troops at Carricitos Ranch, killing several and taking 47 as prisoners, in what came to be known as the Thornton Affair.

Polk had already drafted a declaration of war based on Mexico's failure to repay loans and its refusal to meet with presidential envoy John Slidell. Slidell had been sent to Mexico City late in 1845 to negotiate the boundary dispute and other issues. Upon hearing the news of the April 25 skirmish, a new American declaration was made claiming that the Mexican army had "invaded" the United States and "had shed American blood upon American soil." Congress—almost unanimously—declared war on May 9, 1846.

Under the guise of Manifest Destiny, the United States waged a war of aggression against Mexico. Old feelings of resentment toward their northern neighbor were rekindled and left many Mexicans "yankeephobic," especially after the discovery of gold deposits in California in 1848. Mexico suffered tremendous losses in the war (50,000 casualties) compared to the United States (13,000 casualties). What's more, the war cost Mexico half its land mass and one-third of its population as the 1848 Treaty of Guadalupe Hidalgo ceded the American Southwest to the U.S for $15 million, leaving the United States four times larger than Mexico in land mass.

JEFFERY O. MAHAN

See also

All of Mexico Movement; Ampudia, Pedro de; Congress, U.S.; Democratic Party; Election of 1844, U.S.; Europe and the Mexican-American War; Expansionism and Imperialism; Herrera, José Joaquín de; Louisiana Purchase; Manifest Destiny; Mexican Cession; Mexico; Monroe Doctrine; Nueces River; Paredes y Arrillaga, Mariano; Politics, Mexican; Politics, U.S.; Point Isabel; Polk, James Knox; Racism; Rio Grande; Santa Ana, Antonio Lopéz de; Slavery; Slidell, John; Taylor, Zachary; Texas; Thornton Affair; Trans-Nueces; Velasco, Treaties of; Whigs.

References

Clary, David A. *Eagles and Empire: The United States, Mexico, and the Struggle for a Continent.* New York: Bantam Books, 2009.

Campbell, Randolph B. *An Empire for Slavery: The Peculiar Institution in Texas.* Baton Rouge: Louisiana State University Press, 1989.

DeLeon, Arnoldo. *They Called Them Greasers.* Austin: University of Texas Press, 1980.

Francaviglia, Richard V., and Douglas W. Richmond, eds. *Dueling Eagles: Reinterpreting the U.S.-Mexican War, 1846–1848.* Fort Worth: Texas Christian University Press, 2000.

Fuller, John D. P. *The Movement for the Acquisition of All of Mexico, 1846–1848.* New York: Da Capo Press, 1969.

Graebner, Norman A. *Empire on the Pacific: A Study in American Continental Expansion.* New York: Ronald Press, 1955.

Johannsen, Robert W. *To the Halls of the Montezumas: The Mexican War in the American Imagination.* Oxford, UK: Oxford University Press, 1985.

Price, Glenn W. *Origins of the War with Mexico.* Austin: University of Texas Press, 1967.

Weber, David J. *The Mexican Frontier, 1821–1846: The American Southwest under Mexico.* Albuquerque: University of New Mexico Press, 1982.

Cavalry and Dragoons

Both sides in the Mexican-American War employed significant numbers of mounted units. Generally lumped together under the name "cavalry," these units performed diverse duties that included reconnaissance, screening their own forces from those of the enemy, and participation in battles. The U.S. Army included both regular and volunteer cavalry units, some of which were armed with the latest type of firearms. The Mexican cavalry was composed of nearly all regular units but was armed with weapons unique to its organization.

Following the War of 1812, U.S. regular mounted troops were disbanded. Not until 1832 did Congress authorize the formation of a battalion of Mounted Rangers for the defense of the extended

A dramatic portrayal of dragoons engaging Mexican infantry. Dragoons were mounted infantry that usually fought on foot. Dragoons of the period were armed with sabre, carbine (or musketoon), and pistol. (Library of Congress)

western frontier. A year later, the battalion was expanded to create the 1st Regiment of U.S. Dragoons. Unlike cavalry, the dragoons were intended to fight on foot and use their horses chiefly for transportation. In practice, army officials quickly realized the need for mounted tactics when fighting Native Americans. In 1835, a cavalry school was established at Carlisle Barracks, Pennsylvania. Four years later, a course in horsemanship was introduced at the U.S. Military Academy at West Point to give future cavalry officers a basic knowledge of their mounts. Three young officers, including Philip Kearny, were sent that same year to France, where they studied French cavalry tactics at the Royal School of Cavalry at Samur. When they returned, they put together the first U.S. manual for training mounted troops.

Meanwhile, in 1836, Congress authorized a second regiment of dragoons. Many of the mounted troopers served in the Second Seminole War in Florida, but they usually fought in company units instead of by regiments. When that war ended in 1842, the dragoons were scattered among the various frontier posts.

When the United States annexed Texas in late February 1845, Mexico threatened war. To defend the southern border, President James K. Polk ordered an Army of Observation to be formed under Brigadier General Zachary Taylor at New Orleans. It took up station at Corpus Christi, Texas, in August 1845. After Taylor moved on Polk's orders to the Rio Grande, in territory claimed by Mexico,

in April 1846 a patrol of dragoons was ambushed by a much larger force of Mexican cavalry in the so-called Thornton Affair, an incident that helped spark the Mexican-American War. Congress then approved an expansion of the regular army and allowed the president to call for volunteers. A third dragoon regiment, named the U.S. Regiment of Mounted Rifles, was authorized and quickly filled. Six of the volunteer regiments were also mounted and organized according to a pattern similar to that of the regulars. Most of these regiments served with Taylor's army in the early stages of the war. An exception was some 400 troopers of the 1st U.S. Dragoons, who accompanied Colonel (later brigadier general) Stephen Watts Kearny on his march to Santa Fe and California from Fort Leavenworth.

In 1847 the main focus of the U.S. effort changed from northern Mexico to an invasion via Veracruz on that country's eastern coast. Major General Winfield Scott's army made the first amphibious landing in U.S. history on its way to Mexico City. Scott was accompanied by an ad hoc battalion of companies from both the 1st and 2nd U.S. Dragoons. The U.S. Mounted Rifles also joined the invasion. Most of the latter unit's horses were lost during the sea voyage. The surviving horses were given to the dragoons, so most of the Mounted Rifles spent the remainder of the war on foot. Two regiments of Texas Mounted Rifles were also landed at Veracruz in later September 1847. They spent most of the remainder of the war hunting for Mexican guerrillas along the lines of communication to Mexico City.

The U.S. Dragoons carried weapons suitable to their mounted role. Full-size muskets and rifles were unwieldy, so carbines with shortened barrels were supplied to mounted troops. The basic weapon was the Model 1833 Hall carbine. It used a percussion firing system, instead of the older flintlock method, so it was more reliable. The Hall carbine had some unusual features. One was a spike under the barrel that slid forward to lock in place as a bayonet. The firing mechanism could also be removed from the carbine. Many dragoons removed it while off duty and used it as a single-shot pistol. Some troopers were also armed with a Model 1847 cavalry musketoon, which had a larger caliber. It also had a swivel on the barrel, so it could be hung from a strap around the dragoon's neck. Both the musketoon and the carbine were smoothbore weapons with a limited effective range.

U.S. dragoons were also armed with pistols. Most were single-shot flintlock weapons, but some models were converted to use percussion caps. They were large weapons, carried in holsters on either side of the pommel of the dragoon's saddle. Multishot revolvers also made their appearance during the war. Texas Rangers who had joined Taylor's Army of Observation were armed with Colt revolvers originally ordered for the Texas navy. The six-shooters gave them a tremendous advantage in firepower. During the war, Samuel Colt collaborated with Samuel W. Walker, former ranger and captain in the U.S. Mounted Rifles, to design an improved model. The Walker Colt was the largest revolver ever made, weighing about 4.5 pounds. They were issued in pairs to the Mounted Rifles.

The Mexican army also had a large mounted contingent. During the war it raised 14 regular cavalry and dragoon regiments, and six militia cavalry regiments. The cavalry was the premier arm of the Mexican army. Splendidly uniformed and mounted on small, fast horses, it had been used by different governments to impress and intimidate the Mexican people as required. Some regiments were armed with lances, which were striking and had great shock value. The 8-foot-long lance had four cutting edges on an 8-inch blade, and a pennant was fixed at the end to scare enemy horses. Lancers were regarded as the elite of Mexico's cavalry. In the very short ranges of a mounted melee, however, lances were of limited use. The main firearms used by the Mexican cavalry were older weapons manufactured by the British, such as the Paget flintlock carbine and the *escopeta,* a blunderbuss dating back to the Napoleonic Wars. Mexican cavalry also used sabers and lassos, the latter to snare unwary enemies.

In battle, the Americans found the men in Mexican cavalry units to be brave but limited by their lack of quality weapons. The firepower and discipline of most U.S. mounted units were usually sufficient to overcome their opponents. U.S. observers also commented on the ability of larger U.S. horses to overrun smaller Mexican mounts if they tried to stand their ground.

TIM WATTS

See also

Colt, Samuel; Kearny, Stephen Watts; Lancers; Mexico, Army; Revolvers; Scott, Winfield; Taylor, Zachary; Texas Rangers; Thornton Affair; United States Army; Veracruz, Landing at and Siege of; Weapons, Mexican; Weapons, U.S.

References

Bauer, K. Jack. *The Mexican War, 1846–1848.* New York: Macmillan, 1974.
Collins, Michael L. *Texas Devils: Rangers and Regulars on the Lower Rio Grande, 1846–1861.* Norman: University of Oklahoma Press, 2010.
DePalo, William A. *The Mexican National Army, 1822–1852.* College Station: Texas A&M University Press, 1997.
Merrill, James M. *Spurs to Glory: The Story of the United States Cavalry.* Chicago: Rand McNally, 1966.
Urwin, Gregory J. *The United States Cavalry: An Illustrated History 1776–1944.* Norman: University of Oklahoma Press, 2003.
Winders, R. Bruce. *Mr. Polk's Army: The American Military Experience in the Mexican War.* College Station: Texas A & M Press, 1997.

Cazneau, Jane McManus Storms
Birth Date: April 6, 1807
Death Date: December 10, 1878

Journalist who may have coined the term "Manifest Destiny" and who also argued for the annexation of all Mexican territory in the aftermath of the Mexican-American War. Jane Maria Eliza McManus was born on April 6, 1807, in Troy, New York. Educated at an all-girls academy in Troy, she married Allen Storms in 1825. Facing economic hardship after her divorce from Storms in 1831, Jane McManus Storms investigated land speculation opportunities in Texas. In 1832 she traveled to Texas, then still Mexican territory, with her brother and acquired a land grant in Matagorda.

In 1835 Storms openly supported Texan independence from Mexico and advocated annexation to the United States. She subsequently published numerous articles supporting her position in American newspapers and journals, often using the pseudonym "Cora Montgomery." In the March 1845 issue of *United States Magazine and Democratic Review,* she wrote an article in which she coined the term "Manifest Destiny." Although the term was initially credited to the journal's editor, John L. O'Sullivan, recent historical research suggests that the unsigned article in question may have been written by Storms.

During the Mexican-American War Storms served as the first female war correspondent, providing American readers with coverage of the conflict from behind enemy lines. In November 1846 President James K. Polk authorized *New York Sun* editor Moses Yales Beach to initiate a secret mission to investigate the terms of a possible peace treaty with Mexico. Assisted in his efforts by Storms, Beach returned to the United States in April 1847 as his mission was unsuccessful. Regardless, Storms can be considered the first unofficial female diplomat in U.S. history.

In addition to her earlier journalistic endeavors, Storms, writing as Cora Montgomery, insisted that the United States annex all Mexican territory in the aftermath of the Mexican-American War. As such, she became one of the most vocal champions of the "All of Mexico" movement in the United States. She was especially interested in acquiring the Isthmus of Tehuantepec in Oaxaca as a possible rail and canal route to connect the Gulf of Mexico with the Pacific Ocean. Northern abolitionists who feared the potential expansion of slavery into Mexican lands and others who believed that it would be impossible to incorporate the culturally diverse Mexicans into mainstream American society, however, successfully countermanded Storms's insistence on annexing all of Mexico.

In 1849 Storms married Texan businessman and politician William Cazneau, and the the couple lived at Eagle Pass, Texas, from 1850 to 1852. Jane Cazneau now devoted herself to writing and furthering the cause of U.S. territorial and commercial expansion. Her efforts to reconcile sectional attitudes toward American expansion exemplified the desires of nationalistic Democrats. Motivated by a complex combination of altruistic ideological justifications and self-serving economic imperatives, following the Mexican-American War Cazneau supported the expansion of U.S. political and economic hegemony in Mexico, the Dominican Republic, Cuba, and Nicaragua.

Cazneau died when the steamship *Emily B. Souder* sank in a storm off the coast of North Carolina en route from New York to Santo Domingo, on December 10, 1878.

MICHAEL R. HALL

See also

All of Mexico Movement; Expansionism and Imperialism; Manifest Destiny; War Correspondents; Women, U.S.

References

Cazneau, Jane Maria McManus. *Eagle Pass, or, Life on the Border.* Austin, TX: Pemberton Press, 1966.

Hudson, Linda S. *Mistress of Manifest Destiny: A Biography of Jane McManus Storms Cazneau, 1807–1878.* Austin: Texas State Historical Association, 2001.

Cerralvo

Mexican town located in the state of Nuevo León used as a forward supply base for U.S. troops during the Mexican-American War. Situated in the northeastern region of Nuevo León, about 50 miles southwest of Camargo, Cerralvo was founded in 1579 by José Luis Carvajal de la Cueva; the first settlement in the area appeared three years later, in 1582. Cerralvo served as Nuevo León's first state capital and was the center of very lucrative silver mining activities in the region for many decades. Lead was also mined in large quantities there.

In 1846, Cerralvo had an estimated population of about 1,800 people. As Major General Zachary Taylor's forces moved from Camargo toward Monterrey in the summer of 1846, the Americans occupied Cerralvo and established a forward supply depot there.

Then, in the early winter of 1847, General Antonio López de Santa Anna commenced operations designed to push Taylor's force out of northern Mexico. Santa Anna charged General José Urrea's force with severing Taylor's supply and communication lines between Saltillo, where Taylor had temporarily headquartered his army, and the Rio Grande. Urrea's men took Cerralvo in February 1847, thereby badly disrupting U.S. supply lines just as the Battle of Buena Vista was about to begin. After nearly a month of Mexican occupation, a small U.S. force managed to retake Cerralvo, much to Taylor's relief. Cerralvo remained in U.S. possession thereafter until the end of the war, although its garrison was subjected to numerous attacks by Mexican partisans.

Cerralvo remains a small town, with a current estimated population of about 8,500 people. Mining is no longer central to the local economy, which is now heavily influenced by agriculture.

PAUL G. PIERPAOLI JR.

See also

Buena Vista, Battle of; Camargo; Guerrilla Warfare; Northern Mexico Theater of War, Overview; Saltillo; Taylor, Zachary; Urrea y Elías Gonzales, José de.

References

Clary, David A. *Eagles and Empire: The United States, Mexico, and the Struggle for a Continent.* New York: Bantam Books, 2009.

Lavender, David. *Climax at Buena Vista: The American Campaigns in Northeastern Mexico, 1846–47.* Philadelphia, PA: Lippincott, 1966.

Cerro Gordo, Battle of
Event Dates: April 17–18, 1847

Engagement between Mexican and American forces at Cerro Gordo, Mexico, on April 17–18, 1847, which was part of the American Mexico City Campaign. A large hill, officially named El Telégrafo but known by the local residents as Cerro Gordo, dominated the area and gave the battle its name. Just west of Plan del Río, the National Road entered a defile. There Mexican general Antonio López de Santa Anna established a defensive position, hoping to trap U.S. major general Winfield Scott's forces. Not only did Santa Anna seek a decisive victory on the battlefield, but he also hoped to delay Scott's march from the coast, thereby keeping the American forces in the lowlands for the upcoming yellow fever season. To avoid the onset of disease in his forces, Scott was forced to offer battle in terrain that greatly favored the Mexican defenders.

Learning of Santa Anna's position, Scott sent Brigadier General David Twiggs ahead with some 2,600 men and artillery. Twiggs arrived in Plan del Río on April 11 and sent his engineer, Lieutenant Pierre G. T. Beauregard, out to scout the Mexican positions. Beauregard reported that the Mexicans could be flanked if the Americans secured the hill of La Atalaya, just before El Telégrafo. Twiggs, however, made preparations for a frontal assault on the

Lithograph depicting U.S. Army colonel William S. Harney leading a charge at the Battle of Cerro Gordo (April 17–18, 1847), an impressive U.S. victory during the Mexico City Campaign. (Library of Congress)

Mexican positions and so informed Scott. Twiggs estimated Mexican strength at 4,000 men, whereas Santa Anna in fact had at his disposal some 14,000 men.

Major General Robert Patterson's division of volunteers arrived on April 12. Patterson's brigade commanders, Brigadier Generals Gideon Pillow and James Shields, talked Twiggs out of an assault that day. On April 14, Patterson, previously bedridden with fever, postponed any attack until Scott's arrival. When Scott arrived at Plan del Río, he ordered a thorough reconnaissance of the Mexican positions, refusing to commit his army to a hastily planned assault on unknown forces. Captain Robert E. Lee reported that Santa Anna had sent few men to defend the Mexican left flank, convinced that the rough terrain in that sector would prevent any American attack there. He also noted that the left flank of the Mexican line was indeed passable, and that U.S. forces might thereby bypass Mexican defenses unobserved and envelop the entire Mexican line. In effect, if sufficient troops could move down the path without being detected, they could seize the Jalapa Road behind El Telégrafo at the village of Cerro Gordo. American forces would then be in position to trap Santa Anna's entire force.

Scott ordered the trail Lee had discovered to be widened, with an attack to occur on the morning of April 18. Lee would lead Twiggs's division, supported by Shields's brigade, around the

Mexican line. On April 17, Twiggs and Shields began their flanking maneuver. A brief skirmish with Mexican pickets soon expanded into a full-blown battle, however, alerting Mexican forces on La Atalaya to the American presence. Colonel William S. Harney led an attack on that hill, routing the Mexican defenders and chasing them to Cerro Gordo. Because of Twiggs's attack on La Atalaya, Santa Anna believed that Scott's objective was the capture of El Telégrafo, not the Jalapa Road, despite information provided on Scott's plan by a U.S. deserter that Scott intended to capture the National Road beyond the Mexican positions.

On the morning of April 18, Harney led an assault on El Telégrafo. Despite reinforcements dispatched by Santa Anna, the defenders could not prevent the Americans from taking its summit. At the same time, Shields's brigade, supported by a brigade under Colonel Bennett Riley, moved around the hill, outflanking the Mexican defenders, and struck the Mexican camp at Cerro Gordo. The surprise appearance of American troops in the rear of their positions panicked the now-disorganized Mexican forces, turning a tactical defeat into a rout.

After two days of hard fighting, American casualties totaled 63 killed and 353 wounded. The Mexican army lost approximately 1,000 killed and wounded, with an additional 3,000 captured and paroled under oath not to participate in further fighting. The

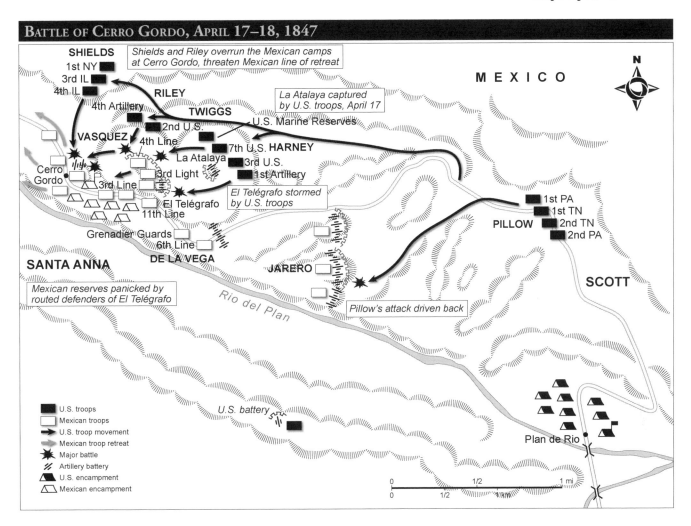

BATTLE OF CERRO GORDO, APRIL 17–18, 1847

Americans also secured 43 guns and virtually the entire Mexican baggage train including personal effects belonging to Santa Anna and his staff. Although the majority of Santa Anna's force managed to escape up the National Road to Jalapa, Scott was able to move his army out of the yellow fever belt and reorganize it for the movement into the Valley of Mexico.

PAUL J. SPRINGER AND SPENCER C. TUCKER

See also

Beauregard, Pierre Gustave Toutant; Harney, William Selby; Lee, Robert Edward; Mexico City Campaign; Patterson, Robert; Pillow, Gideon Johnson; Riley, Bennett; Santa Anna, Antonio López de; Scott, Winfield; Shields, James; Twiggs, David Emanuel.

References

Bauer, K. Jack. *The Mexican War, 1846–1848.* New York: Macmillan, 1974.

Clary, David A. *Eagles and Empire: The United States, Mexico, and the Struggle for a Continent.* New York: Bantam Books, 2009.

Eisenhower, John S. D. *So Far from God: The U.S. War with Mexico, 1846–1848.* New York: Random House, 1989.

Johnson, Timothy D. *A Gallant Little Army: The Mexico City Campaign.* Lawrence: University Press of Kansas, 2007.

Weems, John Edward. *To Conquer a Peace: The War between the United States and Mexico.* College Station: Texas A&M University Press, 1988.

Chapultepec, Battle of
Event Dates: September 12–13, 1847

Significant U.S. victory over the forces of Mexican general Antonio López de Santa Anna at Chapultepec Castle, a defensive position just west of Mexico City, on September 12–13, 1847. By early September 1847, U.S. major general Winfield Scott and some 7,000 of his men were camped just outside Mexico City to the southwest near the castle of Chapultepec; another large contingent was stationed not far away. The castle was perched on a 200-foot-high promontory and was the site of a military college. It also commanded the key causeways into the capital city.

On September 12, despite disagreement from his engineers and some of his senior officers, Scott decided to storm the castle. Part of his plan was to keep Santa Anna and his 15,000 troops uncertain about his primary battle plan. Scott thus ordered part of his force to move south and southeast of Mexico City while his artillery began hammering the castle at dawn and throughout most of the day. Defending Chapultepec were about 1,000 soldiers, including 100 cadets from the military college, under the command of General Nicolás Rueda Bravo. The total Mexican force in the area was almost 5,000 men.

The storming of Chapultepec by U.S. forces on September 13, 1847. Mexico City fell to U.S. forces the next day. (Library of Congress)

The next morning, after halting the artillery barrage, Scott ordered Brigadier General John A. Quitman's division, with a select storming party of handpicked troops from Brigadier General David E. Twigg's division led by Captain Silas Casey, to move against the south and east walls of the castle. Heading Casey's storming party were 40 marines followed by Brigadier General James Shields's brigade of volunteers. At the same time, Brigadier General Gideon J. Pillow's division, led by another select storming party under Captain Samuel Mackenzie and followed by three assault columns from Brigadier General George Cadwalader's brigade, fought its way ahead from the west with assistance from Brigadier General William J. Worth's forces.

Both storming parties met with artillery fire and stiff resistance. A brief lull ensued as the attacking American forces waited for the arrival of scaling ladders. When they reached the western walls and the ladders were hoisted, the attackers began moving up the rocky summit using pickaxes. In desperate hand-to-hand combat, American forces steadily made their way to the top of the hill. After two hours of fighting, the Mexican commander surrendered the castle.

With the castle secured, Scott immediately set out to seize Mexico City and ordered Worth's division to march on La Verónica Causeway for the main attack against the San Cosme

Gate. Meanwhile, Quitman's forces headed east down the Belén Causeway, where they encountered strong resistance and became the center of the attack as they forced the castle's defenders back into the city. His forces finally breached the Belén Gate in the early afternoon. To the north, Brevet Major Robert E. Lee led Worth's attackers as they marched toward the San Cosme Gate. There Worth's forces beat back a Mexican counterattack by 1,500 cavalry; Lieutenant Ulysses S. Grant and his battery mounted a howitzer atop the bell tower of San Cosme Church and began firing into the defenders. At this point, Lieutenant George Terrett led a group of marines behind the Mexican defenders and unleashed a devastating volley of gunfire. By evening, Worth's troops had broken through the gate and were just inside the city. As night fell, fighting ceased. Fortunately for the American forces, Mexican authorities decided against trying to prevent the capture of Mexico City. Santa Anna withdrew his forces under cover of darkness, and the next day Scott triumphantly marched into the city.

The Battle of Chapultepec was a major victory for U.S. forces and led to the immediate capture of Mexico City. The actual attack lasted for about 24 hours, but it was both brutal and costly. Three American generals, Twiggs, Pillow, and Shields, were wounded. Most American casualties occurred during the attack on Belén Gate; for instance, Quitman's entire staff died during fierce fighting

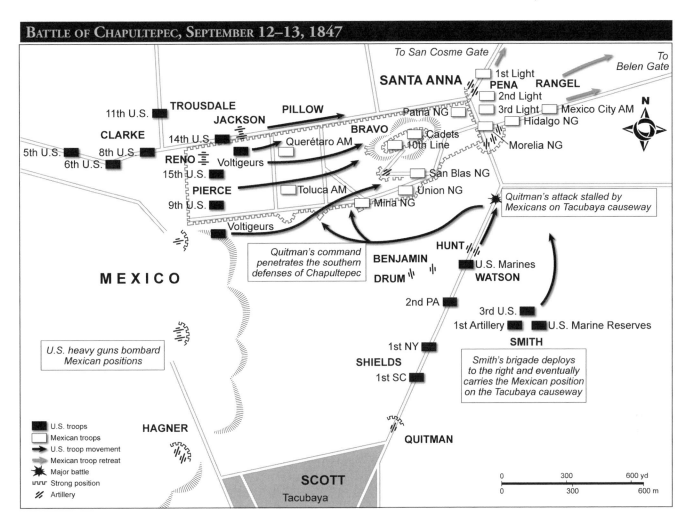

BATTLE OF CHAPULTEPEC, SEPTEMBER 12–13, 1847

To San Cosme Gate
To Belen Gate

SANTA ANNA

1st Light
PENA   RANGEL
2nd Light
3rd Light   Mexico City AM
Hidalgo NG

11th U.S.   TROUSDALE
JACKSON   PILLOW
Patria NG

CLARKE   14th U.S.   BRAVO
Querétaro AM   Cadets
10th Line   Morelia NG

5th U.S.   8th U.S.
6th U.S.   RENO
Voltigeurs
15th U.S.
PIERCE
9th U.S.   Toluca AM   San Blas NG

MEXICO
Union NG
Mina NG

Voltigeurs

Quitman's command penetrates the southern defenses of Chapultepec

Quitman's attack stalled by Mexicans on Tacubaya causeway

HUNT
BENJAMIN   U.S. Marines
DRUM   WATSON

2nd PA

3rd U.S.
1st Artillery   U.S. Marine Reserves
SMITH

1st NY
SHIELDS   Smith's brigade deploys to the right and eventually carries the Mexican position on the Tacubaya causeway
1st SC

U.S. heavy guns bombard Mexican positions

U.S. troops
Mexican troops
U.S. troop movement   HAGNER
Mexican troop retreat
Major battle   QUITMAN
Strong position
Artillery

SCOTT
Tacubaya

0   300   600 yd
0   300   600 m

on the Belén Causeway. American casualties and losses totaled 862, including 130 killed and 703 wounded. As for the Mexicans, five generals, including Bravo, were captured, and one general (Juan N. Pérez) was killed. The total number of Mexican losses was 2,623, including approximately 655 killed and 1,145 wounded. Within a month of the fall of Mexico City, the war had ended.

CHARLES F. HOWLETT

See also

Bravo Rueda, Nicolás; Cadwalader, George; Grant, Ulysses Simpson (Hiram Ulysses Grant); Lee, Robert Edward; Los Niños Héroes; Mexico City; Mexico City, Battle for; Mexico City Campaign; Pillow, Gideon Johnson; Quitman, John Anthony; San Patricio Battalion; Santa Anna, Antonio López de; Scott, Winfield; Shields, James; Twiggs, David Emanuel; Worth, William Jenkins.

References

Bauer, K. Jack. *The Mexican War, 1846–1848.* New York: Macmillan, 1974.

Johnson, Timothy D. *A Gallant Little Army: The Mexico City Campaign.* Lawrence: University Press of Kansas, 2007.

Singletary, Otis. *The Mexican War.* Chicago: University of Chicago Press, 1960.

Smith, Justin. *The War with Mexico.* 2 vols. New York: Macmillan, 1919.

Chase, Anna McClarmonde
Birth Date: 1809
Death Date: 1874

Irish-born wife of Franklin Chase, the U.S. consul to the Mexican port of Tampico. During the Mexican-American War, Anna Chase was an American spy known as "The Heroine of Tampico." Anna (Ann) McClarmonde Chase was born in Northern Ireland and emigrated to the United States with her family in 1818. After a living in New Orleans for a number of years, McClarmonde and her brother moved to Tampico, Mexico, in 1836, where she met and married Franklin Chase. During the Mexican-American War, when Mexico expelled U.S. citizens from its territory, Tampico's military command allowed Anna Chase to remain behind because she was still a British subject. Anna Chase proceeded to spy on Mexican troop movements and spread disinformation among Mexican officials.

In late October 1846, Anna Chase observed how Mexican forces were withdrawing from the city. She then sent word to Commodore David Conner, commander of the U.S. Navy Home Squadron, about these movements, and raised the Stars and Stripes over the consulate. Conner took the city without incident on November 14.

The U.S. troops who landed in the city named their fortifications Fort Ann, in honor of Anna Chase.

Anna Chase's role in the fall of Tampico made her a celebrity. She and her husband remained in Tampico until 1871. Chase died sometime in 1874.

CHRISTOPHER CONWAY

See also

Conner, David; Tampico; Tampico and Victoria, Occupation of.

References

The American Annual Cyclopaedia and Register of Important Events of the Year: 1874. Vol. 14. New York: D. Appleton, 1875.

Slagle, Jay. *Ironclad Captain: Seth Ledyard Phelps and the U.S. Navy, 1841–1864.* Kent, OH: Kent University Press, 1996.

Chaves, Manuel Antonio
Birth Date: October 18, 1818
Death Date: January 1889

Mexican rancher, trader, soldier, and scout for the U.S. Army. Manuel Antonio Chaves was born in Atrisco, outside modern Albuquerque, New Mexico, on October 18, 1818. Chaves became involved in trade along the Santa Fe Trail at a young age and also had experience in cattle ranching.

The cousin of Mexican general Manuel Armijo, Chaves's first taste of combat was likely in the summer 1837 Santa Fe Uprising during which Armijo's force quelled the unrest and instituted a military government there. Two years later, Chaves became a sublieutenant in the rural New Mexico militia. For a time he lived in Saint Louis, but he returned to New Mexico in early 1841, settling in Santa Fe and becoming a prosperous rancher. It is believed that he participated in the negotiations that led to the surrender of the 1841 Texas Santa Fe Expedition, led by military personnel and civilians from Texas.

When the Mexican-American War began in 1846, Chaves offered his service to Armijo, now governor of New Mexico, as a militia officer. Armijo, however, surrendered the territory to the Americans, and Chaves then became involved in several plots to overthrow the U.S. occupiers. In particular, he helped plan what would become the Taos Revolt. U.S. occupation officials had Chaves arrested for possible seditious activity, but he was found innocent of treason in January 1847. He subsequently took an oath of allegiance to the United States and served unofficially in the U.S. Army as a scout, turning down a brevet officer's commission. Chaves served bravely and efficiently during the Taos Revolt, which began on January 19, 1847, and saved his company commander during the siege of Pueblo de Taos on February 5 by clubbing to death a Native American who had dragged the captain off his horse and was preparing to shoot him.

Throughout the remainder of the 1840s and 1850s, Chaves continued his ranching and trade enterprises and earned a reputation as an intrepid Indian fighter. Indeed, he was given the sobriquet *el lioncito* (little lion) for his exploits against hostile Native Americans. Later on, during the U.S. Civil War, Chaves commanded a local New Mexican militia company and worked closely with U.S. forces to fight the Navajos and Apaches. In early 1862, during Confederate Brigadier General Henry H. Sibley's New Mexico Campaign, which sought to capture New Mexico for the Confederate cause, Chaves and his militia fought alongside Union forces. He was present at the Union defeat at the Battle of Valverde and helped disrupt the Confederates' supply lines during the March 1862 Battle of Glorietta Pass, which ultimately forced the Confederates to retreat into Texas.

After the war, Chaves moved to southwestern New Mexico and remained an active trader and rancher and occasionally participated in retaliatory actions against local Native Americans. He died there in January 1889.

PAUL G. PIERPAOLI JR.

See also

Armijo, Manuel; New Mexico; Pueblo de Taos, Skirmish at; Santa Fe; Taos Revolt.

References

Simmons, Marc. *The Little Lion of the Southwest: A Life of Manuel Antonio Chaves.* Chicago: Swallow Press, 1973.

Twitchell, Ralph Emerson. *The History of the Military Occupation of the Territory of New Mexico from 1846 to 1851.* New York: Arno Press, 1976.

Cherokees

One of the so-called Five Civilized Tribes and the largest single Native American group in the Southeast upon first European contact. The word "Cherokee" probably comes from the Creek *tciloki,* "people who speak differently." Their self-designation was *Aniyun-wiya,* "Real People." With the Creeks, Choctaws, Chickasaws, and Seminoles, the Cherokees were one of the so-called Five Civilized Tribes (a European designation) because by the early 19th century these tribes dressed, farmed, and governed themselves nearly like white Americans. Cherokee is an Iroquoian language and had three dialects that were mutually intelligible with difficulty.

Significant Cherokee depopulation resulted from several mid-18th-century epidemics. Some Cherokees who lived near Chattanooga, Tennessee, relocated in 1794 to Arkansas and Texas and in 1831 to Indian Territory (Oklahoma). Between 1819 and 1821, another small band relocated to Spanish-held Texas. These people eventually became known as the western Cherokees.

The discovery of gold in their traditional southeastern territory led in part to the 1830 Indian Removal Act, requiring the Cherokees (among other tribes) to relocate west of the Mississippi River. When a small minority of Cherokees signed the Treaty of New Echota, ceding the tribe's last remaining eastern lands, local nonnatives immediately began appropriating their land and

Estimated Cherokee Population, 1809–1866

Year	Population
1809	13,395
1826	17,713
1835	21,542
1851	15,802
1866	15,566

plundering their homes and possessions. Native Americans were forced into internment camps, where many died, although more than 1,000 escaped to the mountains of North Carolina, where they became the progenitors of what came to be called the eastern band of Cherokees.

The removal, known as the Trail of Tears, began in earnest in 1838. The Cherokees were forced to walk some 1,000 miles through severe weather without adequate food and clothing. About 4,000 Cherokees, almost a quarter of the total, died during the removal, and more died once the people reached the Indian Territory, where they joined—and largely absorbed—the group already there.

The band of Cherokees that went to Texas during 1819–1821 was led by Chief Bowl (Duwali). In 1822, the Mexican government officially recognized the tribe and granted it citizenship. The Mexicans also permitted the Cherokees to settle in east Texas. There they farmed, traded, and lived in relative peace with the Mexicans. The formation of the Republic of Texas in 1836 proved troubling for the Cherokees in Texas, however. Indeed, by 1839, the Texas army displaced most of them from their lands. Some went north to Indian Country (Oklahoma), but some went south, allying with Mexico and setting up camps along the upper Brazos River. Between 1839 and 1842, these Cherokees engaged in several expeditions alongside Mexican troops in a vain attempt to dislodge the Anglo-Texans and retake Texas.

Perhaps realizing that the Cherokees were not likely to give up without further bloodshed, the Texas government signed peace treaties with them and other area tribes—one treaty in September 1843 and another in October 1844. From 1844 to 1848, numerous Cherokees continued to reside in both Mexico and Texas, and there was an uneasy truce between the Native Americans and Texans. However, when the Mexican-American War began in 1846, the Cherokees were threatened repeatedly by U.S. offensives into northern Mexico. There is, however, little evidence that the Cherokees played any significant role in the war or engaged in guerrilla tactics against American forces.

By the early 20th century, many eastern Cherokees were engaged in subsistence farming and in the local timber industry. Having resisted allotment, the tribe took steps to ensure that it would always own its land. The western Cherokees, however, had mostly been assimilated into Mexican culture, or had moved—reluctantly—to Indian Territory after 1848.

BARRY M. PRITZKER

See also

Native Americans; Texas; Texas Revolution.

References

Clarke, Mary Watley. *Chief Bowles and Texas Cherokees.* Norman: University of Oklahoma Press, 2001.

Ehle, John. *Trail of Tears: The Rise and Fall of the Cherokee Nation.* New York: Anchor Books, 1997.

Everett, Dianna. *The Texas Cherokees: A People between Two Fires, 1819–1840.* Norman: University of Oklahoma Press, 1995.

Newcomb, W. W., Jr. *The Indians of Texas.* Austin: University of Texas Press, 1961.

Winfrey, Dorman. *The Indian Papers of Texas and the Southwest, 1825–1916.* Austin: Pemberton Press, 1966. Reprint, Austin: Texas State Historical Association, 1995.

Chihuahua, State of

Located in north central Mexico, directly south of what would be the U.S. Territory of New Mexico, Chihuahua was one of the 19 states that comprised the Mexican Republic in the early 19th century. It is bordered on the south by the states of Durango and Coahuila, Texas to the east, and the Mexican states of Sonora and Sinaloa to the west. Its capital is Chihuahua City. Today, Chihuahua is the largest of Mexico's 31 states and covers 94,571 square miles, making it slightly larger than the United Kingdom.

Chihuahua had long benefitted from its location astride the only overland route between Mexico City and northern Mexico and Santa Fe. This vital trade and transportation route, the Royal Road to the Interior (El Camino Real de Tierra Adentro), ran through Chihuahua City and crossed the Rio Grande at El Paso del Norte (modern-day El Paso, Texas). Chihuahua is the location of the Chihuahuan Desert, which features a harsh, arid climate and rugged geography. But it also includes some rich agricultural lands and the Sierra Madre Occidental mountain range, which runs through the western portions of the state. Chihuahua also has dense forests in higher altitudes. The state's primary natural resources are in mineral deposits, although some agricultural development had been undertaken during Spanish rule.

Trade, always a significant factor in the economy of Chihuahua, increased with the opening of the Santa Fe–Chihuahua Trail in 1821. The Santa Fe Trail connected Missouri with Santa Fe and, by extension, the United States with Mexico. Chihuahua thus quickly benefitted from overland trade with the United States. Because of its broad economic ties with the United States, residents of Chihuahua were less than enthusiastic with the beginning of war between that country and Mexico.

Chihuahua's strategic location and difficult terrain were notable factors during the war. Because of its location bordering American operations both in New Mexico and south of the Rio Grande, Chihuahua assumed strategic importance in both Mexican and American war planning. U.S. president James K. Polk ordered a large force under Brigadier General John E. Wool to march from

San Antonio, Texas, in September 1846 to secure Chihuahua. Travel and supply difficulties impeded Wool's efforts, and he returned east without accomplishing his objective.

The governor of Chihuahua during the war, Ángel Trías Álvarez, proved to be a resourceful leader who successfully mobilized his state for war. Battlefield success eluded him, however. A column of troops dispatched north from Chihuahua was defeated at the Battle of Brazito north of El Paso on December 25, 1846, by American forces led by Colonel Alexander Doniphan. Doniphan's invasion of Chihuahua enjoyed greater success than that of Wool because his force was smaller in number and the men were already hardened marchers.

Governor Trías then assembled 3,000 men under the command of General José Antonio de Heredia to defend Chihuahua City, but Doniphan defeated him in the Battle of Río Sacramento on February 28, 1847, and went on to occupy Chihuahua City from March 2 through April 28, 1847. A number of American traders had accompanied Doniphan on his march south to trade in Chihuahua, and some chose to remain in Chihuahua when he left for Saltillo. Doniphan negotiated with Mexican forces regarding the status of these traders, an example of the continuing tug and pull in Chihuahua between economic self-interest and war fervor.

After Doniphan departed, Governor Trías reoccupied Chihuahua City. However, in February 1848, Brigadier General Sterling Price launched an invasion of Chihuahua with a small force in response to erroneous reports of a Mexican advance. Approaching Chihuahua City and unconvinced by Trías's claims that a peace treaty had been signed, he captured the capital on March 7, 1848, and defeated Trías's forces at the Battle of Santa Cruz de Rosales on March 16, 1848, the last battle of the Mexican-American War.

JOSHUA B. MICHAEL

See also

Brazito, Battle of; Doniphan, Alexander William; Doniphan's March; Heredia, José Antonio de; Price, Sterling; Río Sacramento, Battle of; Santa Cruz de Rosales, Battle of; Santa Fe–Chihuahua Trail; Trías Álvarez, Ángel; Wool, John Ellis.

References

Bauer, K. Jack. *The Mexican War*. New York: Macmillan, 1974.

Dawson, Joseph G., III. *Doniphan's Epic March: The First Missouri Volunteers in the Mexican War*. Topeka: University of Kansas Press, 1999.

Jáuregui, Luis. "Chihuahua en la tormenta, su situacion política durante la Guerra con los Estados Unidos. Septiembre de 1846–julio de 1848." In *México al tiempo de su Guerra con los Estados Unidos (1846–1848)*, coordinated by Josefina Zoraida Vázquez, 134–156. Mexico City: Secretaría de Relaciones Exteriores, El Colegio de México, y Fondo de Cultura Económica, 1997.

Childs, Thomas
Birth Date: March 16, 1796
Death Date: October 8, 1853

U.S. Army officer. Thomas Childs was born on March 16, 1796, in Pittsfield, Massachusetts, the son of a physician and Revolutionary War veteran. Two months after his graduation from the U.S. Military Academy, West Point, on March 11, 1814, Childs was commissioned a third lieutenant of artillery. He fought in the Niagara Campaign in the War of 1812 and distinguished himself in the July 25, 1814, Battle of Lundy's Lane and in defense of Fort Erie in Canada. He was promoted to second lieutenant on May 1, 1814. After the war, Childs remained in the service.

From 1836 to 1842, Childs fought in the Second Seminole War in Florida, and for his service he received a promotion to captain on August 21, 1836, and to major on February 1, 1841. In 1846 Childs was part of Brigadier General Zachary Taylor's Army of Occupation along the Rio Grande in Texas. He was brevetted to lieutenant colonel for his role in the May 8, 1846, Battle of Palo Alto, where he commanded an artillery battalion in the first brigade, and at the Battle of Resaca de la Palma on May 9, 1846. During the September 22, 1846, Battle of Monterrey, Childs led American forces up Independence Hill and captured a Mexican position that General Pedro de Ampudia had believed was unassailable. This move helped the Americans achieve victory at Monterrey.

During Major General Winfield Scott's 1847 Mexico City Campaign, Childs acted as chief of staff to Brevet Major General William J. Worth at Veracruz. From April to June of that year, he was military governor in Jalapa, with instructions to keep open the supply lines for Scott's army. On April 13, 1847, Scott appointed Childs military and civil governor at Puebla, with a force of just 400 men and some 2,000 sick and convalescing soldiers. After Mexico City fell to Scott's forces in September 1847, Childs's garrison at Puebla was surrounded by some 4,000 Mexicans under Brigadier General Joaquín Rea. Childs, however, refused to surrender and managed to fight off repeated attacks until reinforcements arrived on October 1. For his dogged defense of the city during the four-week siege, Childs was brevetted to brigadier general on October 12, 1847.

Childs's 39 years of active service culminated in his last three as commander of Fort McHenry and Baltimore harbor in Maryland and duty in Florida, first at Pensacola and then in charge of military operations in east Florida. On October 8, 1853, after a bout with yellow fever, Childs died in his headquarters at Fort Brooke (Tampa), Florida. Upon hearing of Childs's death, General Scott, then the commanding general of the army, ordered all his officers to wear black crepe for 30 days.

GARY KERLEY

See also

Ampudia, Pedro de; Jalapa; Mexico City Campaign; Monterrey, Battle of; Palo Alto, Battle of; Puebla; Puebla, Siege of; Resaca de la Palma, Battle of; Rea, Joaquín; Santa Anna, Antonio López de; Scott, Winfield; Taylor, Zachary; Worth, William Jenkins.

References

Bauer, K. Jack. *The Mexican War, 1846–1848*. Lincoln: University of Nebraska Press, 1974.

Fredriksen, John C. "Thomas Childs." In *American National Biography*, vol. 4, edited by John A. Garraty and Mark C. Carnes, 815–816. New York: Oxford University Press, 1999.

Smith, Justin H. *The War with Mexico*. Vol. 2. New York: Macmillan, 1919.

Churubusco, Battle of
Event Date: August 20, 1847

Major military engagement fought on August 20, 1847, at Churubusco, some four miles from Mexico City, as part of Major General Winfield Scott's final offensive against the Mexican capital. The battle occurred on the same day as the Battle of Contreras, some seven miles distant.

While Major General Zachary Taylor maintained a holding action on captured ground in northern Mexico, Scott opened a second front with an amphibious landing at Veracruz on March 9, 1847. From there, Scott pushed back Mexican forces under General Antonio López de Santa Anna, driving steadily inland toward the Mexican capital in a brilliant campaign. Nonetheless, by early August Santa Anna had assembled 30,000 defenders in position to block Scott from taking the capital. Meanwhile, Scott had received reinforcements from the United States to bring his strength up to some 11,000 men.

The most direct route to Mexico City was through Ayutla (or Ayotla) on the east, but Scott found that impractical because of stout Mexican fortifications. He planned, therefore, to attack the city from the south, which approach was defended by Mexican forces at Contreras and Churubusco. Thanks to a reconnaissance by Major Robert E. Lee, Scott's forces found a mule path around the enemy and were able to surprise the Mexican defenders under General Gabriel Valencia at Contreras early in the morning on August 20.

After suffering heavy casualties inflicted by the American forces, the remnants of the Mexican army withdrew to Churubusco, with Scott's army in pursuit. During their retreat, the Mexicans lost another 500 men captured by U.S. forces under Brigadier General William J. Worth. That was in addition to the 700 killed and wounded and 813 captured at the Battle of Contreras.

General Santa Anna now concentrated his forces around the monastery at Churubusco and prepared his defense. The terrain offered no real natural defense for the Mexicans with the exception of the small Churubusco River to their front. Meanwhile, Scott's forces advanced from two directions.

In his haste, Scott had not carried out an adequate reconnaissance of Churubusco and failed to realize that the monastery was heavily defended. The Mexican forces there numbered some 1,300 to 1,800 men; they included 680 national guardsmen mustered in the Independencia and Bravos National Guard Battalions and around 200 soldiers from the elite unit known as the San Patricio (Saint Patrick) Battalion composed of Irish American deserters from Scott's army. Seven cannon supported the Mexican defenders.

Scott directed Brigadier Generals William J. Worth and David E. Twiggs to lead the assault, but their effort was repulsed. The heaviest fighting took place at the small bridge that crossed the river. Future U.S. president Franklin Pierce, now a brigadier general of volunteers, led one of the first units across the river, soon followed by other American regiments. Pierce, whose leg had been

The Battle of Churubusco, fought some four miles from Mexico City on August 20, 1847, as part of Major General Winfield Scott's campaign to capture the Mexican capital. A lithograph by Currier & Ives. (Library of Congress)

Battle of Churubusco, August 20, 1847

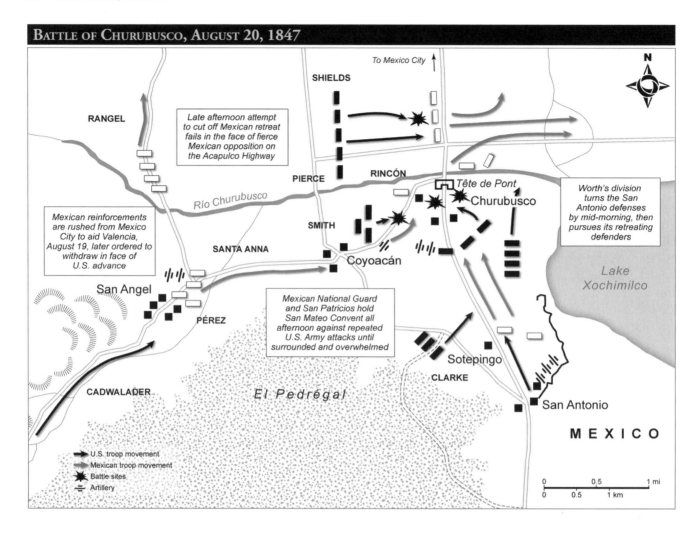

injured the day before when his horse fell on him, refused to quit the fight, but the pain was so great that he passed out during the battle and had to be carried from the field. Ironically, years later his political opponents would use the incident against him, accusing him of deserting his men in the heat of combat.

The fighting at the monastery was fierce, due both to spirited resistance by both the national guardsmen and the San Patricio Battalion. Members of the latter rightly feared serious reprisals by U.S. Army officials if captured. They used the cover of the monastery's stone walls and made the American attackers pay in blood for every inch of ground they took. The U.S. forces prevailed, however, after a second American force led by Brigadier General William J. Worth hit the monastery from the north. A Mexican officer raised a white flag, but the San Patricios tore it down. Eventually, U.S. captain James M. Smith raised another white flag over the monastery to restrain impassioned American soldiers from massacring those San Patricios who had survived. Once the fighting ended, the American officers paid their respects and saluted the Mexican officers. They then demanded the Mexicans surrender their ammunition. The Mexican commander, General Pedro María Anaya, replied matter-of-factly that if they had had any ammunition remaining, the Americans would not be there.

The Battles of Contreras and Churubusco were costly for both sides. Of some 25,000 engaged, the Mexicans lost more than 4,000 killed and wounded and 2,700 captured, including eight generals and 200 other officers. U.S. losses were also heavy—higher than the two previous engagements combined. Casualties for the 8,500 Americans engaged totaled 137 killed and 877 wounded. The Battles of Contreras and Churubusco had a demoralizing effect on the Mexican army and people, especially because they had been defeated by a much smaller force. The battle also set the stage for the final surrender of Mexico City, which followed one month later.

Both Mexican and American historians have criticized Scott for fighting what some have termed an unnecessary battle. They point out that Churubusco was an isolated fortress some four miles from Mexico City and could simply have been bypassed. That would have been unwise, however, for it would have left a large, hostile force to Scott's rear. Others disapprove of Scott's decision for a direct, frontal assault on the monastery. Much of this latter-day analysis benefits from hindsight that Scott did not have at the time of the battle, yet one critique does have merit—that Scott attacked the monastery at Churubusco without making his usual meticulous reconnaissance.

ALAN K. LAMM

See also

Contreras, Battle of; Lee, Robert Edward; Mexico City Campaign; Pierce, Franklin; San Patricio Battalion; Santa Anna, Antonio López de; Taylor, Zachary; Twiggs, David Emanuel; Valencia, Gabriel; Worth, William Jenkins.

References

Bauer, K. Jack. *The Mexican War, 1846–1848*. New York: Macmillan, 1974.

Johnson, Timothy D. *Winfield Scott: The Quest for Military Glory*. Lawrence: University of Kansas Press, 1998.

Eisenhower, John S. D. *So Far from God: The U.S. War with Mexico, 1846–1848*. Norman: University of Oklahoma Press, 2000.

Henderson, Timothy J. *A Glorious Defeat: Mexico and Its War with the United States*. New York: Hill & Wang, 2007.

Citadel, Monterrey

A massive fort occupied by Mexican troops during the Battle of Monterrey, Mexico, on September 21–23, 1846. An old, abandoned cathedral, the Citadel, known to American troops as the Black Fort, occupied a strategic position on the plain north of the city, the most likely approach for an American attack. The church was constructed of 20-foot-high stone walls, held up by 12 massive pillars, and it was enclosed by a quadrangular bastioned earthwork some 12 feet tall. Surrounding that structure was a deep—albeit unfinished—moat. Mexican soldiers covered the walls in tufa, a gray, soft, rocklike material that would help the structure absorb artillery shot. They also constructed artillery platforms on each of the building's four corners. These could hold 8 guns each, for a total of 32, and the entire structure could house up to 400 men.

At the time of the Battle of Monterrey, Mexican major general Pedro de Ampudia had garrisoned the Citadel with about 300 men. When the engagement began, U.S. major general Zachary Taylor approached Monterrey from the north as expected, and the Citadel's gunners fired the first shots of the battle at Taylor's small advance force. Indeed, the gunners here played a key role in the battle by shelling Taylor's men as they marched across the northern plain toward the city, inflicting significant casualties. Some of the Citadel's artillerists were likely San Patricios, former U.S. army soldiers who had deserted to the Mexican side earlier while in Texas. Taylor did not try to take the Citadel, and Ampudia surrendered it in the armistice that ended the fighting.

CHRIS DISHMAN

See also

Ampudia, Pedro de; Monterrey, Battle of; Northern Mexico Theater of War, Overview; Taylor, Zachary.

References

Dishman, Christopher. *The Perfect Gibraltar: The Battle for Monterrey, Mexico*. Norman: University of Oklahoma Press, 2010.

Thorpe, Thomas Bangs. *Our Army in Monterrey*. Philadelphia, PA: Carey and Hart, 1847.

Claims and Damages, U.S. and Mexican

Both Mexico and the United States sought damage claims against the other, some of which originated during the Mexican War of Independence of 1810–1821, at which time Mexico was still under Spanish rule. Other claims reached as far forward as the 1850s and 1860s, during which time various Mexicans pursued damage claims against the U.S. government for filibustering expeditions led by the Republic of Texas during the late 1830s and early 1840s to recompense for Mexican naval ships that had been damaged or captured in Mexican territorial waters by the Texas navy and for Indian raids staged from the United States. Yet the Joint Claims Commission, which sought to settle all outstanding damage claims by both nations, was not established until 1868. By then, the Mexican government and Mexican citizens had pressed 998 claims totaling a staggering $86,661,891. Of that amount, however, only 167 claims were actually processed, totaling just $150,500. Some 336 claims, filed between 1848 and 1853 and totaling $31 million, were dismissed out of hand, with the United States arguing that the 1848 Treaty of Guadalupe Hidalgo had absolved it from liability.

Of the 167 Mexican claims that the Joint Commission deemed legitimate, about 150 involved residents of Piedras Negras, Coahuila, located along the Rio Grande, whose personal property and homes had been destroyed by American troops in 1855. Residents of Sabinas Hidalgo, Coahuila (now Nuevo León), received approximately $24,000 for claims filed as a result of a raid on their village by a band of Texas volunteers after the Treaty of Guadalupe Hidalgo had been signed in 1848.

American damage claims against the Mexican government were far more numerous and complicated and turned into a perennial thorn in the side of Mexican-American relations for decades. Although some claims went back as far as 1812, when Mexico was still under Spanish suzerainty, the U.S. government had begun, as early as 1826, to press claims for bodily injuries, death, and property/financial losses that dated back to the early part of the century. In general, Mexico City accepted responsibility for most of these, but near-constant financial crises and weak and shifting governments did not allow it to settle them.

In 1843 the U.S. government forced the issue by compelling the Mexicans to sign a treaty in which they promised to pay $2.5 billion in damage claims, an amount which an international arbitration board had set in 1839. That figure evolved from a total of $11,850,589 worth of claims that the board had considered. That same treaty left open the door for further negotiations to settle other claims (and subsequent ones) not examined by the 1839 board. In the United States, the issue of long unsettled claims became a rallying cry for pro-war politicians, and in 1845, soon after taking office, President James K. Polk proposed going to war with Mexico to force payment of the outstanding claims.

Late in 1845, Polk dispatched John Slidell to Mexico City to discuss outstanding issues between the two governments and empowered him to offer the Mexicans $5 million and the U.S. assumption of all outstanding damage claims against Mexico in return for Mexico's acceptance of the Rio Grande as the Texas-Mexican border. Slidell was also authorized to purchase Alta California. The Mexican government refused to even see Slidell, handing Polk another reason to wage war against Mexico in 1846. Indeed, during his war message to Congress in May 1846, the president specifically mentioned the unsettled claims against the Mexican government.

American damage claims also played a central role in the negotiation of the 1848 Treaty of Guadalupe Hidalgo. Indeed, the amount the United States was willing to pay for the Mexican land cession, $15 million, was determined in part by the amount of unsettled and unpaid monetary claims against the Mexican government. The United States also agreed to assume $3.25 million in claims made by U.S. citizens against Mexico. Mexico insisted, however, that the United States be held responsible for future Indian raids into Mexico from U.S. territory, which gave the Mexicans some leverage.

After the war, Mexico and the United States finally hammered out an agreement on the payment of outstanding claims against the Mexican government, amounting to about $5 million, but this did not, of course, settle the issue definitively.

PAUL G. PIERPAOLI JR.

See also

Boundary Disputes, U.S. and Mexico; Diplomacy, Mexican; Diplomacy, U.S.; Filibusters; Guadalupe Hidalgo, Treaty of; Mexico; Polk, James Knox; Slidell, John; United States, 1821–1854.

References

Clary, David A. *Eagles and Empire: The United States, Mexico, and the Struggle for a Continent.* New York: Bantam Books, 2009.
Griswold del Castillo, Richard. *The Treaty of Guadalupe Hidalgo: A Legacy of Conflict.* Norman: University of Oklahoma Press, 1992.
Pletcher, David M. *The Diplomacy of Annexation: Texas, Oregon, and the Mexican War.* Columbia: University of Missouri Press, 1973.

Clark, Meriwether Lewis
Birth Date: January 10, 1809
Death Date: October 28, 1881

Architect, engineer, politician, and U.S. and Confederate Army officer. Meriwether Lewis Clark, the son of explorer William Clark of the Lewis and Clark Expedition, was named after the elder Clark's friend and associate, Meriwether Lewis. Clark was born in Saint Louis on January 10, 1809. After graduating from the U.S. Military Academy at West Point in 1830, he was commissioned a second lieutenant in the 6th Infantry Regiment. He saw action during the Second Seminole War but resigned his commission in 1833 to become an architect and civil engineer.

Returning to Saint Louis, Clark designed and built several important buildings there, including St. Vincent de Paul Catholic Church. In 1836, he entered politics and was elected to the

Missouri General Assembly. In 1840, he became the chief engineer for the city of Saint Louis.

When the Mexican-American War began, Clark once again entered military service, this time as a volunteer major in an artillery battalion in Brigadier General Stephen W. Kearny's Army of the West. He marched with Kearny's army from Fort Leavenworth to Santa Fe in the fall of 1846 and then continued on to Chihuahua under Colonel Alexander Doniphan and commanded that unit's artillery at the February 28, 1847, Battle of Río Sacramento. His accurate and intense fire is credited with having forced the Mexican withdrawal there. For the remainder of the war, Clark saw mostly garrison duty in northern Mexico.

After the war, Clark became the federal surveyor general for Illinois and Missouri, a post he held from 1848 to 1853. Thereafter, he worked on a number of private engineering and architectural projects. Clark, who was strongly prosecessionist, became a brigadier general in the Missouri State Guard in 1861. That November, he resigned that commission to accept a commission as a major in the Confederate artillery. Later promoted to colonel, he held several staff positions and was named head of the Confederate Ordnance Department in Richmond, Virginia. He held that post until November 1864, when he joined General Robert E. Lee's army as an infantry brigade commander with the rank of colonel. During the Battle of Sayler's Creek on April 6, 1865, he was captured by Union forces.

After the Civil War, Clark moved to Louisville, Kentucky, and resumed his engineering interests. He designed and supervised the construction of numerous state buildings and also served for a time as commandant of cadets at the Kentucky Military Institute. Clark died in Frankfort, Kentucky, on October 28, 1881. Clark's son, Meriwether Lewis Clark Jr., became a prominent Kentuckian, and was a horse-racing enthusiast who built the famed Churchill Downs in Louisville.

PAUL G. PIERPAOLI JR.

See also

Chihuahua, State of; Doniphan, Alexander William; Doniphan's March; Kearny, Stephen Watts; Río Sacramento, Battle of.

References

Eicher, John H., and David J. Eicher. *Civil War High Commands.* Stanford, CA: Stanford University Press, 2001.
Hughes, John Taylor. *Doniphan's Expedition, Containing an Account of the Conquest of New Mexico.* New York: Arno Press, 1973.

Clay, Cassius Marcellus
Birth Date: October 19, 1810
Death Date: July 22, 1903

Wealthy Kentucky planter, Whig politician, abolitionist, and captain of a Kentucky militia unit during the Mexican-American War. Cassius Marcellus Clay was born in Madison County, Kentucky, on October 19, 1810, the son of Green Clay, one of Kentucky's wealthiest planters and slave owners. Clay's cousin was famed Whig politician Henry Clay; another cousin was Clement Comer Clay, who served as governor of Alabama.

After attending Centre College (Kentucky), Clay graduated from Yale College in 1832, having already earned a reputation as an impetuous hothead. While he was a student at Yale, he heard noted abolitionist William Lloyd Garrison deliver a speech against slavery and was smitten with the growing abolitionist movement, although initially he favored a more gradualist approach over the more radical approach espoused by Garrison. Despite his wealth and ties to slavery, he returned to Kentucky in 1832, believing that slavery should eventually be abolished, a position that did not endear him to his Kentucky contemporaries.

After briefly studying law, Clay opted for a political career, successfully running for the state legislature in 1834 as a Whig. He began serving in 1835 but was defeated in 1841, largely because of his increasingly militant stand against slavery and his frequent outbursts and arguments with political adversaries. In 1844 he campaigned actively for his cousin Henry Clay's unsuccessful presidential campaign against Democrat James K. Polk. The following year, he began publishing an abolitionist newspaper titled *True American,* which brought death threats. Not long after, the newspaper offices were ransacked by an angry mob. Rather than give in to the violence, Clay shifted publication to Cincinnati, Ohio.

Not surprisingly, Clay opposed Texas annexation, fearing that it would lead to the spread of slavery. Nevertheless, he volunteered for service when the Mexican-American War began in 1846, believing that military service would bolster his political aspirations and abolitionist platform. Clay took a commission as captain of a Kentucky volunteer cavalry company. His cousin Henry Clay, meanwhile, had become a vociferous opponent of war with Mexico. During Major General Zachary Taylor's Buena Vista Campaign, Clay was involved in an embarrassing faux pas that resulted in his being taken prisoner by Mexican forces. Clay, who completely lacked military experience, led a scouting patrol in mid-January 1847 to ascertain the position of Mexicans. On January 23, Clay and his entire patrol were surrounded and taken prisoner at La Encarnación because Clay had not posted sentries before he and his men fell asleep. Clay and his men were later exchanged and fought in subsequent engagements.

Clay returned to his home state in 1848 and left the Whig Party two years later to run for the Kentucky governorship on an antislavery platform. He lost the contest but nevertheless received 5,000 votes. He later helped found Berea College and joined the new Republican Party, becoming a close friend of Abraham Lincoln.

In 1860, Clay was one of the top candidates to run as Lincoln's vice president. In 1861, newly elected president Lincoln dispatched Clay to Russia as the U.S. minister. Within a year, he had returned to the United States and was offered a commission as a major general of volunteers in the Union Army. Clay would not accept the commission unless Lincoln issued an emancipation proclamation. Lincoln then sent Clay on a fact-finding mission to gauge public support for the issuance of an emancipation proclamation. When Clay returned to Washington, Lincoln issued the proclamation soon thereafter, but by now Clay was uninterested in becoming a Union general. He nevertheless took partial credit for the Emancipation Proclamation. In 1863, he returned to Russia as minister, remaining there until 1869.

Upon his return, Clay surmised that Republican Reconstruction efforts had gone far astray of Lincoln's vision, and so he left the Republican Party. In 1872, he was among the disaffected Republicans who founded the short-lived Liberal Republican faction that put Horace Greeley on that year's presidential ticket. Greeley was crushed by war hero Ulysses S. Grant. In the 1876 and 1880 presidential elections, Clay actively supported Democratic candidates, but in 1884 he returned to the Republican fold. Clay died at Whitehall, Kentucky, on July 22, 1903.

Paul G. Pierpaoli Jr.

See also
Abolitionism; Clay, Henry; Slavery.

References
McQueen, Kevin. *Cassius M. Clay: Freedom's Champion.* Whitehall, KY: Turner, 2001.
Robinson, H. Edward. *Cassius Marcellus Clay: Firebrand of Freedom.* Lexington: University Press of Kentucky, 1976.

Clay, Henry
Birth Date: April 12, 1777
Death Date: June 29, 1852

Famed orator and U.S. congressman, senator, and secretary of state who was vociferously opposed to the Mexican-American War. Clay began his political career as a Democratic-Republican, then joined ranks with the anti-Jackson National Republican Party, and finally became a member of the Whig Party. Henry Clay was born on April 12, 1777, in Hanover County, Virginia. As a young man he moved to Versailles, Kentucky, where his family ran a tavern.

After his stepfather secured him a position with the Court of Chancery in Virginia, the young Clay demonstrated a keen aptitude for the law. He was soon befriended by the prominent Virginia jurist George Wythe, who hired him as his personal assistant. Wythe later secured Clay a job in the Virginia attorney general's office. He then studied law at the College of William and Mary under Wythe's tutelage and was admitted to the bar in 1797. That same year, Clay relocated to Lexington, Kentucky, where he quickly earned a reputation as a stellar lawyer and orator.

Clay entered politics in 1803, successfully running for a seat in the Kentucky General Assembly, where he became a prominent

MR. CLAY TAKING A NEW VIEW OF THE TEXAS QUESTION.

A political cartoon of February 1847 lampooning Henry Clay's opposition to the Mexican-American War. Clay believed the war would lead to the expansion of slavery and plunge the nation into crisis. Clay's opposition grew with the death of his son in the Battle of Buena Vista (February 22–23, 1847). (Library of Congress)

member. His fine work led to two brief appointments as Kentucky's junior U.S. senator, the first lasting from 1806 to 1807 and the second from 1810 to 1811. In both cases he completed the terms of men who had resigned their seats; notably, he was allowed to be seated in 1806, even though he had not yet reached the mandatory age of 30. In 1811 he was elected to the U.S. House of Representatives, when he became the only freshman congressman in history—before or since—who was immediately elected as Speaker of the House. He served three nonconsecutive terms as House Speaker: 1811–1814, 1815–1820, and 1823–1825. In Congress Clay became known as the "Great Compromiser," renowned for his oratorical skills and ability to seek accommodation from both sides of the aisle. Interestingly, despite his objections to the Mexican-American War, he was among the so-called war hawks who had championed war with Great Britain prior to the War of 1812.

Clay remained in the House of Representatives until 1825, and during this time he and fellow House member John C. Calhoun put in place an economic scheme to aid American industry known as the American System. In 1820, when tensions arose over the extension of slavery into the Missouri Territory, Clay helped broker the Missouri Compromise. Five years later Clay became secretary of

state in the John Quincy Adams administration, a position he held until 1829.

In 1831 Clay ran successfully for the U.S. Senate, quickly becoming one of its most influential members. Almost immediately Clay was thrust into action when he helped arrange a workable compromise that ended the Nullification Crisis and lowered the 1828 protective tariff, which had set off a South Carolina secessionist movement. Clay ran against Andrew Jackson for the presidency the following year but lost by a large margin. Again in 1844 Clay made a run for the presidency on the Whig ticket but lost to Democrat James K. Polk, who ran on an unabashed platform of expansionism, including the immediate annexation of Texas. Clay opposed adding Texas as a state because he believed it would risk war with Mexico, and because it would inflame sectional tensions over the slavery issue.

Although he had left the Senate in 1842, Clay was adamantly opposed to the Mexican-American War and offered repeated public criticisms of it. Having brokered the Missouri Compromise nearly two decades before, Clay knew that the issue of the expansion of slavery into newly won territories would soon plunge the nation into crisis, a prediction that proved quite prescient. His opposition to the war grew stronger after his son Henry Jr. was killed at the Battle of Buena Vista. Clay also abhorred the All of Mexico movement, taking every opportunity to discredit it.

Clay again ran for the U.S. Senate, taking his seat in March 1849. His last great act as a legislator came in the drafting of the Compromise of 1850, which once again temporarily deferred the slavery question and postponed sectional crisis and civil war. Clay died of tuberculosis in Washington, D.C., on June 29, 1852. Clay is considered one of the greatest legislators in American history and was among the "Great Triumvirate" in the Senate during the first decades of the 19th century, which also included John C. Calhoun and Daniel Webster.

Paul G. Pierpaoli Jr.

See also

All of Mexico Movement; Buena Vista, Battle of; Democratic Party; Expansionism and Imperialism; Missouri Compromise; Polk, James Knox; Slavery; Whigs.

References

Baxter, Maurice G. *Henry Clay and the American System.* Lexington: University Press of Kentucky, 1995.

Baxter, Maurice G. *Henry Clay the Lawyer.* Lexington: University Press of Kentucky, 2000.

Remini, Robert V. *Henry Clay: Statesman for the Union.* New York: W. W. Norton, 1991.

Clay, Henry, Jr.
Birth Date: April 10, 1811
Death Date: February 23, 1847

U.S. attorney, politician, and volunteer army officer. Henry Clay Jr. was born on April 10, 1811, on his family's estate of Ashland, near Lexington, Kentucky. His father, Henry Clay, was the famed Whig politician and U.S. senator from Kentucky. The senior Clay, who authored the 1820 Missouri Compromise, ran unsuccessfully for president on the 1844 Whig ticket and was a vociferous opponent of the Mexican-American War.

Henry Clay Jr. attended Transylvania University, where he first met Jefferson Davis, who became a lifelong friend and confidant. After securing his degree from Transylvania in 1828, Clay went on to the U.S. Military Academy, West Point, where he graduated in 1831. Clay did not enter the army, however, and instead returned to Kentucky where he read for the law. He was admitted to the state bar in 1833 and commenced a law practice. Clay also served in the Kentucky House of Representatives from 1835 to 1837.

At the outset of the Mexican-American War in 1846, despite his father's staunch opposition to the conflict, Clay accepted a commission as a lieutenant colonel of the 2nd Kentucky Volunteer Infantry Regiment, for which he helped recruit soldiers. He soon joined Major General Zachary Taylor's force in northern Mexico and saw action in several engagements with Mexican troops. During the first hours of the Battle of Buena Vista on February 23, 1847, he was instrumental in preventing the disintegration of Taylor's left flank, thus greatly contributing to the American victory there. As he led his men, Clay was shot in the thigh and could not walk. Several of his men carried him to the top of a hill and stayed with him. Not wanting to jeopardize their lives, Clay ordered the men to rejoin the main force. Shortly thereafter, Clay was bayoneted and killed there by retreating Mexican forces.

Clay's performance at Buena Vista was lauded by General Taylor, and his friend, Colonel Jefferson Davis, insisted that he personally escort Clay's body back to Kentucky, where he was buried.

PAUL G. PIERPAOLI JR.

See also
Buena Vista, Battle of; Clay, Henry; Davis, Jefferson Finis; Taylor, Zachary.

References
Lavender, David. *Climax at Buena Vista: The American Campaigns in Northeastern Mexico, 1847–48.* New York: J. B. Lippincott, 1966.
Remini, Robert V. *Henry Clay: Statesman for the Union.* New York: W. W. Norton, 1991.

Clayton-Bulwer Treaty
Event Date: April 19, 1850

Agreement between Great Britain and the United States signed on April 19, 1850, that guaranteed mutual cooperation in the construction of an isthmian canal in Central America to link the Pacific and Atlantic Oceans. Ratification of this treaty by the U.S. Senate was the culmination of steady American territorial and commercial expansion during the 1840s, which was best exemplified by the gains made in the Mexican-American War. It was also the result of growing friction between the two nations over Central America and the possible construction of an isthmian canal through Nicaragua. The agreement was a step toward accomplishing a long-held American goal of building a canal across Central America.

Until the mid-1840s the British had dominated affairs in Central America, but several factors—including the acquisition of Oregon, California, Arizona, New Mexico, and Texas, the California Gold Rush, and a growing interest in trade with the Far East—turned American attention toward Central America. Much of this expansionist enthusiasm had been awakened and fostered by the Mexican-American War. Both American and British politicians and businessmen recognized the need to ship goods swiftly from the Atlantic coast to the Pacific coast. American speculators and businessmen soon recognized an opportunity to profit by escorting travelers from the East to the West Coast across the isthmus. The British, however, controlled numerous strategic sites on the Atlantic coast of Central America that might hinder the American development of a possible canal route. Among the areas where British influence was highest were the Mosquito Coast in Nicaragua and Belize on the border of Guatemala. Also of increasing interest to the British was Panama, then a part of the Republic of Great Colombia.

In order to undermine British influence in the region, U.S. diplomatic personnel began to exploit Latin American fears of British imperialism. In 1846, U.S. minister to Colombia Benjamin Bidlack signed a treaty giving the U.S. transit rights across Panama in return for an American guarantee of transit rights for other parties. The Senate delayed ratification of the Bidlack Treaty until 1848, however, recognizing that the agreement was tantamount to an entangling alliance. The treaty did have the advantage of allowing the United States to build the first transcontinental railroad across Panama during the 1850s, and it would provide President Theodore Roosevelt with a pretext for breaking Panama away from Colombia to build the current canal in 1904. Similar treaties were then negotiated with Nicaragua and Honduras, which then aggravated British concerns about American intentions in Central America. Before long, rumors of war between the United State and Britain began to circulate.

Neither country wanted war with the other, and to avoid that possibility British minister to Washington Sir Henry Bulwer-Lytton and U.S. secretary of state John Clayton negotiated an agreement. The two diplomats arranged for a treaty containing the following provisions: first, neither country would build a canal in Central America unless the other power gave its consent or cooperation; second, neither nation would fortify the region or establish new colonies in the area; and third, if a canal were to be built at some future time, both nations would guarantee its neutrality.

Getting the British to agree to the treaty was a significant diplomatic victory for the Zachary Taylor administration. The Clayton-Bulwer Treaty both recognized the United States as an equal in Central America and further strengthened the 1823 Monroe Doctrine's noncolonization principle in the Western Hemisphere.

Members of the Whig Party in the Senate were pleased that canal rights had been preserved while war with the British had been avoided. The Democrats, however, under the leadership of Senator Stephen A. Douglass of Illinois, attacked the administration for compromising with Great Britain. Critics could also point out that any American attempt to build a canal in Central America would require British acquiescence.

Following the American Civil War (1861–1865), U.S. interest in a Central American canal increased. In 1867, Secretary of State William H. Seward unsuccessfully attempted to negotiate a transit agreement with Nicaragua. Two years later, he was able to complete a similar pact with Colombia, but the Colombian senate rejected the treaty. The opening of the Suez Canal in 1869 sparked further interest in an isthmian canal, and the Ulysses S. Grant administration successfully negotiated a treaty giving the United States canal rights in Panama. However, the Colombian senate attached several amendments to the treaty that, in turn, led the U.S. Senate to reject the treaty.

A number of attempts to abrogate the Clayton-Bulwer Treaty occurred after 1850, but the British government refused to surrender its rights under it. Secretary of State James G. Blaine, who took office in 1881, opened talks with Nicaragua about a canal route, ignoring the terms of the Clayton-Bulwer agreement. Blaine's successor, Frederick J. Frelinghuysen, completed the talks in 1884 by arranging a treaty with Nicaragua that gave the United States exclusive rights to build a canal across Panama, guaranteed Nicaragua's territorial integrity, established a permanent alliance, and, in direct violation of the Clayton-Bulwer Treaty, stated the principle of an American-owned and -operated canal. This treaty, however, was never ratified.

Finally, in 1901, the British gave in and agreed to abrogate the Clayton-Bulwer Treaty. The 1901 Hay-Pauncefote Treaty allowed the United States to build, own, and fortify an isthmian canal. This step would allow the Theodore Roosevelt administration to complete the process of securing a canal route across Panama and would lead to the eventual construction of today's Panama Canal, which was completed in 1914. While it took place more than 50 years after the Clayton-Bulwer Treaty, the building of an isthmian canal in Central America was a logical step in the progression of American expansionism, commercialism, and Manifest Destiny that had gained so much credence during and after the Mexican-American War.

GREGORY MOORE

See also

Expansionism and Imperialism; Gold Rush, California; Great Britain; Manifest Destiny; Monroe Doctrine; Taylor, Zachary.

References

Jones, Howard, and Donald A. Rakestraw, eds. *Prologue to Manifest Destiny*. Lanham, MD: Scholarly Resources, 1997.

McCullough, David. *The Path between the Seas: The Creation of the Panama Canal, 1870–1914*. New York: Simon & Schuster, 1978.

Potter, David M. *The Impending Crisis, 1848–1861*. New York: Harper and Row, 1976.

Clifford, Nathan
Birth Date: August 18, 1803
Death Date: July 25, 1881

American politician, diplomat, and jurist who served as President James K. Polk's envoy extraordinary and minister plenipotentiary to Mexico during 1848–1849. Born on August 18, 1803, to a humble farming family in Rumney, New Hampshire, Nathan Clifford attended the Haverhill Academy in Haverhill, New Hampshire, before finishing his studies at the New Hampton Literary Institute in New Hampton, New Hampshire. After reading for the law with Josiah Quincy, he was admitted to the New Hampshire bar in 1827 and moved to Newfields, Maine, to practice.

Clifford joined the Democratic Party and was elected to the Maine House of Representatives, serving there from 1830 to 1834. He spent the next four years serving as Maine's attorney general. When John Fairfield resigned his seat in the U.S. House of Representatives after being elected governor of Maine in 1838, Clifford was elected to his seat, representing Maine's First Congressional District from 1839 to 1843. Clifford chose not to run in the 1842 elections and was replaced by fellow Democrat Joshua Herrick.

On October 17, 1846, Polk appointed Clifford attorney general of the United States to replace John Mason, who returned to his position as secretary of the navy, a post he had previously held during the presidency of John Tyler. Clifford served as attorney general until March 17, 1848. In this post Clifford often served as a facilitator between Polk and Secretary of State James Buchanan, who had sharp differences concerning the war. Clifford was an expansionist and favored taking the state of Tamaulipas in northeastern Mexico, and indeed all Mexico should the Mexican government resist the annexation.

When the Treaty of Guadalupe Hidalgo was amended by the U.S. Senate, Polk appointed Clifford as envoy extraordinary and minister plenipotentiary to Mexico and sent him and Senator Ambrose H. Sevier, chairman of the Foreign Relations Committee, to Mexico City to secure Mexican approval of the changes. Clifford then remained in Mexico City, helping to establish postwar relations between the two countries. On September 6, 1849, Clifford left the diplomatic corps and returned to Maine to resume the practice of law.

In 1858 President James Buchanan appointed Clifford to the U.S. Supreme Court. The only man nominated to that body during Buchanan's presidency, Clifford's confirmation was narrowly approved by the U.S. Senate. Most of the senators who voted against Clifford were concerned about placing another proslavery Democrat on the Supreme Court. Clifford, however, believed in a strict delineation between state and federal powers when interpreting the Constitution. Following the controversial presidential election of 1876, Clifford served as the president of the Electoral Commission established by Congress in 1877 to determine the outcome of the election. The Electoral Commission consisted of 15 members: 5 U.S. representatives, 5 U.S. senators, and 5 Supreme

Nathan Clifford was attorney general of the United States during the Mexican-American War. During 1848–1849 he was envoy extraordinary and minister plenipotentiary to Mexico. (Library of Congress)

Court justices. The 8 Republicans and 7 Democrats voted along party lines, which assured the election of Rutherford B. Hayes. Clifford died following a stroke on July 25, 1881, in Cornish, Maine.

MICHAEL R. HALL

See also

Buchanan, James; Guadalupe Hidalgo, Treaty of; Politics, U.S.; Polk, James Knox; Sevier, Ambrose Hundley; Tamaulipas.

References

Clifford, Philip Greely. *Nathan Clifford: Democrat (1803 to 1881)*. New York: G.P. Putnam's Sons, 1922.

Griswold del Castillo, Richard. *The Treaty of Guadalupe Hidalgo: A Legacy of Conflict*. Norman: University of Oklahoma Press, 1992.

Coahuila y Texas

A state in Mexico between 1824 and 1836, part of which became the Republic of Texas in 1836. Also known as Coahuila y Tejas, Coahuila y Texas encompassed 193,600 square miles bordered by the Red River to the north, the territory of Nuevo Mexico (New Mexico) to the northwest, Chihuahua to the west, Durango to the southwest and south, Zacatecas and San Luis Potosí to the south, Nuevo León to the south and southeast, Tamaulipas and the Gulf of Mexico to the southeast, and the Sabine River and United States to the east. The physical geography was quite diverse, including deserts, mountains, forests, and prairies as well as numerous rivers including the Rio Grande and the Nueces. The state's capital moved at various times between Saltillo and Monclova.

Various Amerindian groups inhabited the region in the pre-Columbian era, but Spanish exploration and conquest of the area resulted in the founding of Saltillo in 1577. Later expeditions by soldiers and Jesuit missionaries established other small settlements throughout Coahuila, centered on presidios and missions. Most residents were engaged in farming or ranching, with some small-scale mining. Located in the northeastern frontier region, the area remained sparsely populated. In 1833, 12 years after Mexico achieved independence, the state had approximately 87,000 inhabitants. In an attempt to settle Texas, the Mexican government authorized land grants to American settlers, including Moses and Stephen F. Austin, the latter of whom brought the first 300 Anglo-American families to the region between 1824 and 1828.

American settlers brought their own ideas and institutions to Coahuila y Texas, including slavery, which became illegal in Mexico after 1829. Increasingly dissatisfied over government policies and the necessity of dealing with an administration in the state capital that was several hundred miles away, the Americans were essentially waiting for a reason to revolt. Mexico's congress provided that reason in 1835, when it revoked the Constitution of 1824 and established a new constitution that greatly restricted state autonomy. The change led to revolts in various states, and Texans, both Tejanos and Americans, followed suit late in 1835. The Texas Revolution (October 2, 1835–April 21, 1836) succeeded, and Coahuila y Texas no longer existed as a unified state, despite the fact that the Mexican government did not officially recognize Texas's independence. Mexico warned the United States that Mexico would oppose any U.S. attempts to annex Texas.

A few years later some Coahuilan citizens joined with others in the neighboring states of Tamaulipas and Nuevo León to rebel against the Mexican government and form the so-called Republic of the Rio Grande. This effort to break away from Mexico failed, however, as the rebels failed to acquire either domestic or international support.

The disputed areas between the Nueces River and the Rio Grande, both of which ran through Coahuila y Texas, served as a basis for events leading to the Mexican-American War. During the war, U.S. forces under Major General Zachary Taylor marched through Coahuila, occupying Saltillo in November 1846. The Battle of Buena Vista (Angostura) was fought in Coahuila on February 22–23, 1847, against General Antonio López de Santa Anna's forces.

The independence of Texas and annexation by the United States was finally accepted by the Mexican government, but Coahuila remains an important part of Mexico. During the Mexican Revolution, from 1910 to 1920, various military operations took place in Coahuila. Since the end of the revolution, the state has been rebuilt and has become an important industrialized state within Mexico.

WYNDHAM E. WHYNOT

See also

Buena Vista, Battle of; Nueces River; Rio Grande; Saltillo; Santa Anna, Antonio López de; Taylor, Zachary; Texas; Texas Revolution.

References

Brands, H. W. *Lone Star Nation: The Epic Story of the Battle for Texas Independence.* New York: Anchor Books, 2005.

Kessell, John L. *Spain in the Southwest: A Narrative History of Colonial New Mexico, Arizona, Texas, and California.* Norman: University of Oklahoma Press, 2003.

Sheridan, Cecilia. "Coahuila y la invasión norteamericana." In *México al tiempo de su Guerra con los Estados Unidos (1846–1848),* coordinated by Josefina Zoraida Vázquez, 157–188. Mexico City: Secretaría de Relaciones Exteriores, El Colegio de México, y Fondo de Cultura Económica, 1997.

Weber, David J. *The Spanish Frontier in North America.* New Haven, CT: Yale University Press, 1994.

Cochori, Skirmish at
Event Date: January 30, 1848

Minor, brief military engagement between a detachment of Mexican irregulars and U.S. forces at Cochori, Mexico, on January 30, 1848. Cochori, a tiny Mexican fishing village, was located about eight miles east of Guaymas, Sonora, along the margin of a small bay known as La Laguna. For much of the Mexican-American War, Cochori served as a supply station for the U.S. Navy operating along the Pacific coast, and local Native Americans sold fish and other locally procured foods to the U.S. ships.

In an attempt to disrupt U.S. supply lines, a detachment of Mexican irregulars, the size of which remains unknown, moved into the village in late January 1848. Before daybreak on January 30, some 100 U.S. sailors and marines under the command of Lieutenant Tunis Augustus McDonough Craven crossed La Laguna in small boats from the sloop *Dale*. At dawn, the U.S. contingent landed about three miles south of Cochori and moved swiftly toward the village. Once the Americans had surrounded Cochori, they launched an assault, taking the Mexicans by surprise.

Outnumbered and outgunned, the Mexican defenses quickly collapsed. By noon, the fighting was over, and the Americans had secured Cochori. The Mexicans suffered 3 killed, 5 wounded, and 15 taken prisoner. There were no U.S. casualties. The skirmish at Cochori effectively eliminated one of the last pockets of Mexican resistance in the Guaymas region.

PAUL G. PIERPAOLI JR.

See also

Guaymas, Battle of; Sonora y Sinaloa; United States Marines; United States Navy.

References

Bauer, K. Jack. *Surfboats and Horse Marines: U.S. Naval Operations in the Mexican War.* Annapolis, MD: U.S. Naval Institute, 1969.

Craven, Tunis A. M. *A Naval Campaign in the Californias—1846–1848: The Journal of Lieutenant Tunis Augustus McDonough Craven, U.S.N. United State Sloop of War* Dale. San Francisco: Book Club of California, 1973.

Coleto Creek, Battle of
Event Dates: March 19–20, 1836

The Battle of Coleto Creek occurred on March 19–20, 1836, and was the culmination of the Goliad Campaign during the Texas Revolution of 1835–1836. It took place near Coleto Creek in Goliad County, southeastern Texas, and was originally known as the Battle of the Prairie and la Batalla del Encinal del Perdido (the Battle of Oak Grove Creek). It pitted Texan forces commanded by James Walker Fannin Jr. against Mexican forces under General José de Urrea y Elías Gonzales and is considered one of the most important battles of the Texas Revolution.

Fannin and some 500 men were stationed at Goliad's Presidio La Bahía, or Fort Defiance as Fannin named it. Fannin had spent considerable time fortifying that post and was reluctant to give it up. His men were also confident and eager to confront the Mexicans. Yet, after the fall of the Alamo on March 6, General Sam Houston ordered Fannin and his men to withdraw from Goliad to Guadalupe Victoria, 28 miles distant, "as soon as practical on receipt of this order." Fannin knew that the port of Copano had already been lost, reducing the significance of his own position, yet he was slow to obey.

Much of the blame for what was to happen to his men indeed rested with Fannin. Beginning on March 10, 1836, he weakened his own force by sending contingents totaling some 150 men, first under Amon B. King and then under William Ward, to Refugio in order to assist in the evacuation of settlers from there to Goliad. Fannin, however, sent with them wagons and teams he would need in any subsequent evacuation. He also delayed because he was hoping to receive oxen and wagons from Guadalupe Victoria. But the main reason Fannin did not implement Houston's order immediately was that he insisted on first hearing from the dispatched contingents before he moved with the main body. Meanwhile, Mexican general Urrea was swiftly advancing on Goliad with some 1,400 men. Having captured Fannin's couriers, he was well aware of his plans, while Fannin was largely unaware of Urrea's strength and location.

On March 17 Fannin learned of the defeat of King and Ward at Refugio, but he still delayed ordering a withdrawal to Guadalupe Victoria until the next day. Yet no movement occurred until early on March 19. Even then progress was slow, for Fannin insisted on taking nine cannon and some 1,000 muskets. This decision allowed Urrea's forces to close. Fannin, however, had taken sufficient food and water for only several meals.

By the time Fannin had departed, however, Urrea's cavalry had already closed on Goliad. Urrea was preparing to lay siege to Presidio La Bahía when he learned from his scouts that Fannin was withdrawing. He immediately detached a force to garrison La Bahía, and set out with an advance formation of some 360 horsemen in pursuit of the Texans, then two hours ahead. Urrea caught up with Fannin at about 1:30 p.m. on March 19 while the Texans were crossing a stretch of some six miles of open prairie. He quickly ordered his cavalry to halt the Texans before they could reach protective timber, about one mile away, or Coleto Creek, some two miles distant. Fannin responded by deploying his force in a moving hollow square, but when the Texans were about a mile from the creek, and in a low area trying to get to higher ground 400–500 yards distant, the ammunition wagon broke down. Fannin then called a council of war to consider taking what ammunition they could carry and try to make the timber, but Urrea attacked with both cavalry and infantry.

Although Urrea's men were unable to penetrate the Texan formation, they had killed 10 Texans and wounded another 60, 40 of these seriously, by the end of the battle after nightfall. Fannin was among the wounded. Fannin's men were also running out of ammunition, and they had no water. Still, their spirits remained high, confident in the expectation that they would receive reinforcements from Guadalupe Victoria.

The battle resumed the next morning, March 20, when Urrea, who had brought up reinforcements during the night and increased his strength to between 700 and 1,000 men, opened fire on the Americans with several artillery pieces from higher ground at close range. Following several Mexican rounds, Fannin became convinced that further resistance was futile and agreed to treat with Urrea. What transpired in their meeting is still debated, but Fannin certainly believed that in surrendering he had received terms for himself and his men. Urrea said that he had made it clear he could accept only unconditional surrender but that he would also seek to intercede on the Americans' behalf. Indeed, the extant capitulation documents show that the Texans surrendered "subject to the disposition of the supreme government."

While Urrea continued on to Victoria with the bulk of his forces, the unwounded Texan prisoners were returned to Goliad. A number of the wounded went unattended and many, including Fannin, were not transported to Goliad for two or three days. There they were joined by other prisoners, bringing the number of men held to more than 350. Although the Texans had assumed they would be treated honorably, General Antonio López de Santa Anna bypassed Urrea and ordered Colonel José Nicolás de la Portilla, the Goliad commander, to implement the congressional decree of December 30, 1835, which called for captured armed rebels to be executed as pirates.

On March 27, 1836, Palm Sunday, Fannin's men and the other prisoners were marched out of Goliad and were summarily executed. More than 20 escaped, however, carrying news of the massacre to Anglo settlements. The wounded Fannin was not marched out with the others. He asked to be shot in the chest and afforded a proper burial. Despite his request, the Mexicans shot him in the head and buried Fannin's body in a mass grave with others.

The Battle of Coleto Creek not only removed a large Texan fighting force but assured the Mexican military control of the port of Copano and the coastal region south of the Brazos River. It also instilled a sense of overconfidence in the Mexicans that would cost them later. The execution of the prisoners from the battle hardened opinion against Mexico in the United States and also gave the Texans another point in their rallying cry, now "Remember the Alamo! Remember Goliad!"

ASHLEY R. ARMES AND SPENCER C. TUCKER

See also

Alamo, Battle of the; Fannin, James Walker; Goliad Massacre; Houston, Samuel; Santa Anna, Antonio López de; Texas; Texas Revolution; Urrea y Elías Gonzales, José de.

References

Hardin, Stephen L. *Texian Iliad: A Military History of the Texas Revolution.* Austin: University of Texas Press, 1994.

Pruett, Jakie L., and Everett B. Cole. *Goliad Massacre: A Tragedy of the Texas Revolution.* Austin, TX: Eakin Press, 1985.

Roell, Craig H. "Coleto, Battle of." In *The New Handbook of Texas,* vol. 2, edited by Ron Tyler, Douglas E. Barnett, and Roy R. Barkley, 205–211. Austin: Texas State Historical Association, 1996.

Collaboration, Mexican

Collaboration between U.S. forces and Mexican citizens greatly assisted the invaders' military operations while hampering those of Mexico during the Mexican-American War. Suffering from an unstable political system, class and racial unrest, and an economic crisis, the Mexican government lacked the ability to sustain public support for the war or conduct effective operations against the American invaders. Little of this collaboration emerged as active military alliances with the Americans, however. Instead, it came in the form of passive political or economic ties through the promise of active American military support to various independence movements. American economic assistance also served to further destabilize the Mexican government.

After gaining its independence in 1821, and three years after a failed experiment in constitutional monarchy, a weak Mexican federalist government ruled a vast territory of varying geography, ethnicities, and languages. Many of Mexico's 19 states regarded themselves as a "small homeland," or *patria chica*, largely autonomous from the central government's authority. The southern states of the Yucatán Peninsula, with a large indigenous population and in rebellion against a renewed plan of Mexican centralism in the mid-1830s, had traditionally maintained their autonomy from Mexico City, and during the late 1830s and early 1840s they agreed to collaborate with the Texans to stave off threats of an invasion by forces from the central government. Yucatán elites greatly valued American trade, and Mayan uprisings allowed the United States to exploit these internal divisions and to seize areas vital to the Veracruz landing in March 1847. Indeed, the Yucatán leaders nearly acceded to a plan to send American troops to assist in the quelling of racial violence between Mexicans and the Mayans.

Residents of the territory on Mexico's northern frontier engaged in more overt collaboration with the Americans in hopes of continued economic relationships and the potential for American annexation. California (Alta California) had never been truly integrated into the Mexican economy, and in consequence foreign commerce dominated Californians' interests. The additional flood of Americans into the region further undermined Mexican authority. When the Americans initiated the short-lived Bear Flag Revolt in the summer of 1846, Mariano Guadalupe Vallejo, a Spanish-born, wealthy landowner and commander of the Mexican garrison at Sonoma, extended to them a generous meal and surrendered the presidio without a single shot being fired. Vallejo continued to collaborate with the Americans and became an influential figure in California politics.

Nuevo Mexicanos (New Mexicans), to the east of California, also enjoyed strong economic ties with the United States and possessed a strong distaste for edicts issued from Mexico City. Furthermore, residents of New Mexico believed that the Americans could deal with hostile Native American tribes better than the Mexican government. American merchants in New Mexico routinely supplied intelligence to the Americans and persuaded the territory's governor to allow U.S. military forces to occupy the region with little resistance. With such high levels of collaboration, U.S. troops were able to enter Santa Fe on the same day Congress declared war, May 13, 1846, and quickly pacify the region.

Just to the south of Alta California and the Rio Grande in Baja California, Americans collaborated with Mexican officials and assisted the upper classes in their civil war with the guerrilla movements involving the lower classes. Several sensational guerrilla attacks on U.S. forces and supply trains resulted in the implementation of collective responsibility on the civilian population to prevent such happenings in the future, but such severe incidents of guerrilla warfare were relatively rare. Indeed, they actually served to strengthen the resolve of many Mexicans to sever the popular support so essential for such guerrilla movements to survive.

American forces permitted many local officials to remain in office after the occupation began and extended citizenship rights to those in Baja California. Although the American naval blockade denied supplies to guerrillas, and the inability of Mexico City to assist the loyalists further eroded morale, the guerrillas enjoyed some success and prevented pro-American elites from achieving their goal of annexation to the United States. After the war, many in Baja California's upper classes emigrated to the United States rather than face the middle- and lower-class guerrilla leaders who subsequently assumed control.

Many inhabitants of the other Mexican states, particularly those in the North, collaborated actively and passively with the Americans, and none of the states outside of central Mexico supplied their manpower quotas when the government instituted conscription to bolster the military defenses. American forces had additional advantages in the significant number of Mexican spies and guides to provide invaluable intelligence, most notably Chapita Sandoval at Matamoros. Then, after he established a base of operations in Puebla in the spring of 1847, Major General Winfield Scott hired local bandits to spy for him and paid other Mexicans to help protect his troops and supply lines as they moved into central Mexico. By the time the Mexico City Campaign had moved into high gear, Scott had formed some 200 Mexican bandits and criminals into five spy companies, enticing them into collaboration with the then lofty salary of $20 per month.

Mexican women in particular performed a number of menial tasks for American troops, including cooking, laundering, and tailoring, and often entered into sexual liaisons with them, some of which resulted in marriage. Other Mexican women attended sick, wounded, and dying American soldiers, while wealthy women provided goods and hospitality to U.S. troops, recognizing the potential for an economic windfall by doing business with them.

The Americans permitted many municipalities, including those in central Mexico and the capital, to keep their local governments, and more than a few flourished under American occupation. Many of these decisions to collaborate with the Americans stemmed from a desire to maintain internal stability. As the Americans began to depart Mexico following the war, many groups within Mexico appealed to the United States for annexation. With some justification, they believed that the absence of American troops would bring renewed social, political, and economic conflicts.

Most American troops in Mexico had strict orders to conduct themselves in a humane and helpful manner vis-à-vis Mexican civilians, which undoubtedly helped in forming collaborative relationships between the occupied and the occupiers. While atrocities did occur involving U.S. soldiers (especially among volunteers in Major General Zachary Taylor's army), such incidents were few and far between in Winfield Scott's army. Scott, in fact, was very mindful of the need to cultivate the good will and support of the local Mexican population and strictly enforced his orders that U.S. troops not engage in untoward behavior. He also insisted that goods and services procured from local populations be paid for in full, often in U.S. currency. During the occupation of Mexico City, Scott even hired a local administrator for three months, who helped the Americans procure and pay for needed supplies and who acted as a liaison between occupation forces and local suppliers. In the final analysis, Mexican collaboration with U.S. forces diluted the Mexican war effort, undermined the central government, weakened resistance toward the occupiers, and helped secure more acquiescence toward U.S. proposals, including the cession of large parts of Mexican territory.

DEREK W. FRISBY

See also

Atrocities; Baja California; Bear Flag Revolt; California; California Theater of War, Overview; Espionage; Guerrilla Warfare; Matamoros; Mexico; Mexico, Army; New Mexico; *Patria Chica*; Public Opinion and the War, Mexican; Scott, Winfield; Taylor, Zachary; Trade; Veracruz, Landing at and Siege of; Vallejo, Mariano Guadalupe; Yucatán.

References

Foos, Paul. *"A Short, Offhand, Killing Affair": Soldiers and Social Conflict during the Mexican-American War.* Chapel Hill: University of North Carolina Press, 2002.

Johnson, Timothy D. *A Gallant Little Army: The Mexico City Campaign.* Lawrence: University Press of Kansas, 2007.

Levinson, Irving W. *Wars within War: Mexican Guerrillas, Domestic Elites, and the United States of America.* Fort Worth: Texas Christian University Press, 2005.

Richmond, Douglas W. "A View from the Periphery: Regional Factors and Collaboration During the U.S.-Mexican Conflict, 1845–1848." In *Dueling Eagles: Reinterpreting the U.S.-Mexican War, 1846–1848,* edited by Richard V. Francaviglia and Douglas W. Richmond, 127–154. Fort Worth: Texas Christian University Press, 2000.

Collado Beach

Landing site for Major General Winfield Scott's army as it began the Mexico City Campaign in March 1847. The landing at Collado Beach also marked the beginning of the siege of Veracruz. After seizing and securing the port city of Veracruz, Scott's army would move west toward Mexico City.

Collado Beach, now part of Veracruz proper, was during the Mexican-American War located approximately 2.5 miles south of the port city. Scott chose it as the site of his amphibious landing because of its gently sloping terrain and light currents. He also picked Collado Beach because it lay just out of range of Mexican artillery situated in Veracruz and was partly blocked by nearby Isla Sacrificios (Sacrificios Island). The placement of the island shielded it from strong winds, and the Mexicans had not built any defensive works near the beach.

In February 1847, in anticipation of an amphibious landing along Mexico's southeastern coast, Scott requested a contingent of 15,000 men and 50 ships, ranging in size from 500 to 750 tons. His request was reduced so that he would have some 12,000 men at his disposal and a somewhat smaller contingent of ships. Scott wanted the landing in early March, but inclement weather, including several "northers," delayed the landing. Finally, on March 9, the weather cleared and the U.S. landing began. It proved to be the first major amphibious landing in American military history, and was the United States' largest amphibious operation until the 1942 North Africa Campaign during World War II.

The largest ships participating in the landing were frigates, including the *Raritan* and *Potomac,* which carried about 2,500 men each. Smaller sloops, which included the *Albany* and *St. Mary's,* carried about 1,000 men each. The men employed specially constructed surfboats and landing barges (about 140), which allowed them to row ashore after leaving the larger ships in deeper water. The landings went off without major problem, and by dusk some 10,000 men had moved ashore. The Americans encountered virtually no defenders save for a few snipers and skirmishers, who were quickly neutralized. Once the beachhead was secured, Scott began the siege of Veracruz, which lasted until Mexican forces there capitulated on March 27, 1847.

PAUL G. PIERPAOLI JR.

See also

Scott, Winfield; Veracruz; Veracruz, Landing at and Siege of.

References

Bauer, K. Jack. *Surfboats and Horse Marines: U.S. Naval Operations in the Mexican War.* Annapolis, MD: U.S. Naval Institute, 1969.

Clary, David A. *Eagles and Empire: The United States, Mexico, and the Struggle for a Continent.* New York: Bantam Books, 2009.

Colorado

Sparsely populated northern extreme of Mexican territory ceded to the United States as a result of the 1848 Treaty of Guadalupe Hidalgo. The area that is now Colorado has been inhabited by humans for at least 13,000 years. Over the centuries, Colorado became home to numerous Native American tribes, including the Pueblos, Apaches, Arapahos, Cheyennes, Comanches, Shoshones, and Utes.

The first Europeans to reconnoiter the region were the Spanish conquistadors in the early to mid-1500s, although it is difficult to say for certain if they traveled as far north as Colorado. In 1787 Juan Bautista de Anza founded the Spanish settlement of San Carlos, near present-day Pueblo, Colorado. That venture quickly failed, however, and the Spanish never again attempted to settle Colorado, although they did engage in trade with cooperative Native American tribes. Colorado's rugged terrain (which includes the Rocky Mountains), severe climate, and hostile Native Americans kept Spaniards from making permanent homes there.

In 1803, the United States staked a claim to eastern Colorado under the Louisiana Purchase. The French had previously claimed the area as part of their territory, but that claim had not been pursued by either side. Three years later, in 1806, Zebulon Pike led an American expedition into the disputed area, but he and his men were captured by Spanish cavalrymen in the San Luis Valley and taken to Chihuahua. After being held and questioned, they were released and warned not to return. In the 1819 Adams-Onís Treaty, Spain ceded Florida to the United States and agreed to establish a firm border between its holdings and those of the United States in the west. This gave the United States sovereignty over the southern and eastern portion of Colorado, with the Arkansas River as the official boundary. When Mexico achieved independence in 1821, the portion of Colorado controlled by Spain was ceded to the Mexicans.

Until the advent of the Mexican-American War in 1846, western and northern Colorado remained largely populated by Native Americans, as few Mexicans ventured into the region. In the east and southeast, however, white settlers, trappers, and traders created numerous towns and trading posts. Included among them was Bent's Old Fort and Fort Pueblo on the Arkansas River, and Fort St. Vrain along the South Platte River. Furs and buffalo hides were the chief trade items. When the Army of the West under the command of Brigadier General Stephen Watts Kearny began its march into New Mexico in 1846, Bent's Old Fort was used as a supply and staging area. The area saw little military activity during the Mexican-American War.

Upon the conclusion of the war, all of Colorado was ceded to the United States. Colorado was then split, becoming part of the New Mexico, Utah, Kansas, and Nebraska Territories. Although most Americans avoided settling or even traversing the Rocky Mountains of Colorado, the first Anglo-American settlement in what would become Colorado took hold in 1851 at San Luis, which was then part of the New Mexico Territory. Gradually, the western territories were reduced and combined so that the Territory of Colorado was established in 1861. Colorado was admitted to the Union in 1876.

PAUL G. PIERPAOLI JR.

See also
Bent's Old Fort; Kearny, Stephen Watts.

References
Abbot, Carl, Stephen J. Leonard, and Thomas J. Noel. *Colorado: A History of the Centennial State.* 4th ed. Boulder: University Press of Colorado, 2005.
Lecompte, Janet. *Pueblo, Hardscrabble, Greenhorn: The Upper Arkansas, 1832–1856.* Norman: University of Oklahoma Press, 1977.

Colt, Samuel
Birth Date: July 19, 1814
Death Date: January 10, 1862

American inventor and industrialist. Samuel Colt was born in Hartford, Connecticut, on July 19, 1814. Indentured to a farm in Glastonbury at age 11, Colt attended school there and became fascinated by the *Compendium of Knowledge,* a scientific encyclopedia. This led to his decision to become an inventor and produce a firearm that could shoot multiple times without reloading.

In 1829 Colt began working in his father's textile mill in Ware, Massachusetts, and thus gained access to tools and skilled workers. He built a galvanic cell (a primitive battery) and used it to explode a charge in Lake Ware. In 1832, Colt's father sent him to

Samuel Colt of Connecticut became famous for perfecting a revolving-barrel firearm in the 1830s. His .36 caliber revolver of 1838 was the first revolving-cylinder pistol in general use. (Hayward Cirker, ed., *Dictionary of American Portraits,* 1967)

sea with the intention that he would become a sailor. On his first voyage, Colt built a model revolver, said to have been inspired by the movement of the ship's wheel and the clutch mechanism that held it.

Returning home that same year, Colt again worked for his father, who financed the manufacture of his first two pistols. Both failed, however, because they had been poorly made of inferior materials. That same year, 1832, Colt applied for a patent on his revolver. Colt then traveled and made a modest living performing nitrous oxide (laughing gas) demonstrations. In 1835 he traveled to Britain and there secured a patent for his revolver. Colt returned to the United States in 1836 and then secured a patent for his "revolving gun."

That same year Colt formed the Patent Army Manufacturing Company in Paterson, New Jersey. Its first product was a small, five-shot .28 caliber revolver, but its most famous early design was the 1838 Colt Holster Model Paterson Revolver No. 5. Better known as the Texas Paterson, it was .36 caliber, had five cylinders, and came in 4- to 12-inch barrel lengths. This was the first revolving cylinder pistol in general use. Each chamber was separately loaded from the muzzle end, and each had its own nipple for the copper percussion caps. The drum chamber moved each time the hammer was cocked. The Mexican-American War brought an order for 1,000 of his revolvers, establishing his business. These were first employed by Texas Rangers against the Comanches in the Battle of Walker Creek on June 8, 1844. The California Gold Rush and western expansion greatly assisted the business, and his patent gave him a virtual monopoly. Colt revolvers were adopted by both the army and navy and saw wide service in the Mexican-American War, the U.S. Civil War, and fighting with Native Americans in the West.

Colt did not claim to have invented the revolver, which is attributed to Elisha Collier of Boston, but he greatly improved and popularized it. His was the first truly practical revolver and repeating firearm. Colt also greatly accelerated the employment of interchangeable parts in manufactured goods. He also experimented with underwater mines, and tensions with Great Britain led Congress to appropriate funds for his project at the end of 1841. The next year, Colt destroyed a small ship with a mine in a demonstration for President John Tyler. He also developed an underwater telegraph cable to capitalize on Samuel Morse's invention of the telegraph. In 1855 he completed construction of a new plant at Hartford, at the time the largest arms manufacturing facility in the world. Colt was apparently a model employer, building factory housing for his workers and mandating a 10-hour work day and a 1-hour lunch break. He also established a club for his employees where they could relax and read newspapers.

On the outbreak of the Civil War, Colt accepted a commission as a colonel from the State of Connecticut in May 1861 in the 1st Regiment Colts Revolving Rifles of Connecticut, armed with his revolving rifle. The unit never was established, however, and Colt was discharged the next month. Colt died in Hartford on January 10, 1862. At the time of his death his estate was estimated at $15 million.

Colt's resolute wife, Elizabeth, carried on the firm after his death. Probably the most famous early revolver in U.S. history was the Colt .45 Peacemaker. Designed for the U.S. Army trials of 1873 and still in production, it was widely used in the American West in fighting against the American Indians. The cavalry version had a 7.5-in barrel and was officially known as the Single Action Army Revolver, Model 1873 Six-Shot Caliber .45 in Colt.

SPENCER C. TUCKER

See also

Morse, Samuel Finley Breese; Revolvers; Tyler, John.

References

Grant, Ellsworth S. *The Colt Legacy.* Providence, RI: Mowbray, 1982.

Hosley, William. *Colt: The Making of an American Legend.* Amherst: University of Massachusetts Press, 1996.

Kelner, William L. "On Samuel Colt and the Patent Arms Manufacturing Company, New Jersey." Unpublished MA thesis, Fairleigh Dickinson University, 1969.

Kinard, Jeff. *Pistols: An Illustrated History of Their Impact.* Santa Barbara, CA: ABC-CLIO, 2003.

Taylorson, A. *The Revolver.* 3 vols. London: Arms and Armour, 1966–1970.

Comanches

A Native American group of the southern Plains. The Comanches were an offshoot of the Shoshones of the upper Platte River area of Wyoming. Between 1650 and 1700 or so, they became an autonomous group, although they were never really a unified tribe. Rather, they were subdivided into as many as 12 independent groups. Their language was of the Uto-Aztekan family, and they were linguistically, and in many ways culturally, identical to the Shoshones, whose wider range had been in the Great Basin and Rocky Mountain area. The first European contact with the Comanches occurred in New Mexico in 1705, when the Spaniards first encountered them.

After the split with the Shoshones, the Comanches migrated east and south for a time, toward eastern Wyoming and Colorado, western Nebraska, and Kansas before settling on the southern Plains. The Comanches had obtained horses early; by the time of their first encounter with the Spanish, they already had substantial herds. Indeed, their culture was dominated by the horse, the bison, and raiding.

From the 1700s on, their principal range became northwestern Texas, western Oklahoma, eastern Colorado, and southern Kansas. The area in time became known as the Comancheria. The area in which they conducted raids, however, was much larger, stretching from eastern Kansas and Nebraska deep into Mexico, and from the Gulf Coast of Texas to Santa Fe, New Mexico. At their peak, it is believed that the Comanches numbered about 20,000 people.

The Comanches were bellicose and aggressive, driving various Apache tribes off the southern Plains and then raiding into both the regions of the Lipan Apaches and the various Apache groups of eastern New Mexico. They warred almost constantly with the Utes and engaged in raids deep into Mexico until their free roaming days drew to a close in the 1870s. In addition, the Comanches warred against tribes to their east in Texas, Oklahoma, and against Prairie tribes such as the Osages and Pawnees. Throughout the early 1800s, the Comanche presence on the southern Plains effectively stopped Mexican expansion from New Mexico and Texas and halted French penetration of the area. Texan and American expansion, while not halted, was slowed as the fortunes of the Comanches and the Americans ebbed and flowed.

The purpose of warfare for the Comanches initially was to maintain their hold on Comancheria, their bison hunting grounds. Additionally, they raided for horses, captives, and material goods. The Comanches raided other tribes, the Mexicans, Texans, American settlers, and even the U.S. Army for horses. The Comanches also angered and frightened settlers with their habit of taking captives, the youngest of whom were routinely adopted into the tribe.

Through the years of Texas colonization, relations between the Comanches and the Anglo-Texan settlers had been friendly, but as the Anglo settlements began to reach onto the plains of central Texas—the Comanches' buffalo-hunting territory—those amicable relations began to sour. In May 1836, only weeks after the Republic of Texas had achieved its independence from Mexico, a party of Comanche and Kiowa warriors overran Parker's Fort, a civilian settlement of some 34 persons in present-day Limestone County, killing several settlers and taking five hostages, among them the nine-year-old Cynthia Ann Parker who was adopted into the tribe and later became the wife of prominent chief Peta Nocona and the mother of the last of the great Comanche chiefs, Quanah Parker. A 26-year search for the captive girl at last resulted in her return to her white family, but by that time so acculturated was she into Comanche life that she was unable to reestablish herself in white society and died soon after her return to "civilization." The classic John Wayne film *The Searchers* is based on this incident.

Comanche raids intensified as white settlements pushed farther west, often resulting in the taking of captives. By the end of the decade, with both sides wishing for a cease-fire along the frontier, the Texans and Comanches sought to make peace. Accordingly, 65 Comanches arrived in San Antonio on March 19, 1840, to begin negotiations. The Texas commissioners demanded the return of all captives, including those who, like Cynthia Ann Parker, had been adopted into the tribe. In what they seem to have intended as a show of good faith, the Indians produced Matilda Lockhart, a 16-year-old white captive who told of repeated physical and sexual abuse at the hands of her captors. Her story was corroborated by severe facial mutilation. The outraged Texans demanded the immediate return of all captives, and when the Comanches informed them that this was not possible, the Texans responded by taking the delegates hostage. When the Indians resisted, 30 warriors, as well as some 5 women and children, were killed in what came to be known as the Council House Fight.

Outraged by what they perceived as Texan perfidy, the Comanches retaliated by launching a spectacular raid that reached all the way to the Gulf Coast port of Linnville, which the Indians overran and sacked on August 8, 1840. The raiding party, numbering as many as 1,000 warriors and camp followers, then turned back toward Comancheria with more than 3,000 horses and a number of captives. On their return, however, they were intercepted in the vicinity of the present town of Lockhart and attacked by a body of militiamen and Texas Rangers under General Felix Huston, Colonel Edward Burleson, and Ben McCulloch. In the ensuing Battle of Plum Creek, on August 11, 1840, the Comanches were decisively defeated, and their military power broken until it enjoyed a temporary resurgence with the absence of United States soldiers and Texas Rangers attendant to the Civil War.

There is little evidence that the Comanches played anything more than a subsidiary role during the Mexican-American War, but Texas officials and the U.S. government were always wary of reports—most of them unsubstantiated—that the Mexicans were instigating the Comanches to take up arms against American forces.

To avoid such a scenario, U.S. government officials signed a peace treaty with the Penateka Commanches in the spring of 1846, and a small delegation of Panatekas subsequently traveled to Washington, D.C., to meet with President James K. Polk. During 1847–1848, raids along the Santa Fe–Chihuahua Trail by an alliance of Comanche, Apache, Pawnee, and Kiowa warriors wrought damage, but the extent of the damage is anecdotal and not easily substantiated. Perhaps as many as 20 whites were killed on the trail, although some accounts claim that close to 50 were killed. Furthermore, it cannot be clearly established that the Comanches were even involved in the attacks.

After the war ended, Anglos and Comanches lived together uneasily, and there continued to be sporadic raids and captive taking on the part of the Comanches. During the American Civil War (1861–1865), the Comanches forcefully drove back the Texas frontier by as much as 100 miles. The reign of the Comanches in the southern Plains came to an end in June 1875, however, when the last of the major Comanche bands under the Comanche leader Quanah Parker surrendered to U.S. officials following devastating defeats at the Battles of Adobe Walls and Palo Duro Canyon on the Texas Panhandle and moved to the reservation at Fort Sill in Oklahoma.

JOHN THOMAS BROOM

See also

Apaches; Native Americans; Santa Fe–Chihuahua Trail; Texas-Comanche Relations.

References

Brice, Donlay E. *The Great Comanche Raid: Boldest Indian Attack of the Republic of Texas*. Austin: Eakin Press. 1987.

Ferhenbach, T. R. *Comanches: The History of a People*. New York: Alfred A. Knopf, 1979.

Wallace, Ernest, and E. Adamson Hoebel. *The Comanches: Lords of the South Plains*. Norman: University of Oklahoma Press, 1952.

Communications

Wartime communications may be divided into two principal applications—tactical and strategic. Tactical communications are largely limited to the passage or exchange of information on the battlefield, or sometimes within a confined geographical area, such as a portion of a theater of operations. Strategic communications refer to the exchange of information over long distances, such as between the battlefield and the capital city of a nation, or the homefront in general. During the Mexican-American War, tactical communications remained little changed from earlier wars. However, taking place as it did on the cusp of the transportation and long-distance communications revolution of the 19th century, the conflict witnessed quite radical changes in the processing of strategic communications.

At the tactical level, military commanders continued to depend on designated couriers to pass information to their subordinates. These couriers operated either on foot or horseback. To aid in the dissemination of information, commanders almost always chose to wage battles at or near central locations that would remain near the front lines. Most also chose to set up headquarters that would not be far removed from the battle lines and supply lines. While fighting was in progress, bugles, drums, and a wide variety of flags helped to pinpoint the location of specific units. Signal lights and signal flags were also sometimes used before and during battle to convey messages to the troops. These tactical modes of communication had remained virtually unchanged for many hundreds of years. And because the Mexicans lacked technology such as railroads and telegraphs, they conducted strategic communications in much the same way—principally by trusted couriers operating on horseback.

During the Mexican-American War, the United States employed three relatively new 19th-century technologies to revolutionize the speed and accuracy of strategic, or long-distance, communications—steam-powered boats and ships, railroads, and the telegraph. Compared to the last major conflict the United States had waged—the War of 1812—long-distance communications had witnessed quantum improvements in speed. Steamboats were in their early infancy during the War of 1812, but by the 1840s they were being used on many U.S. waterways as well as in the Gulf of Mexico and Gulf of California. Much faster and more reliable than sailing vessels or river barges that relied mainly on currents or animal power operating ashore, these steam-powered vessels could carry information over great distances in record time. Because railroads were virtually nonexistent in Mexico and the Southwest, U.S. couriers usually rode to an inland port, seaport, or rail depot, where the information they carried was transmitted by water to New Orleans, which was linked by telegraph to Washington, D.C., and other large cities along the East Coast. Steamboats had been in use since 1808 when Robert Fulton's *North River* (also known as the *Clermont*) made a successful run up the Hudson River from lower Manhattan to Albany. By the early 1830s railroads had begun operating in the East, and within 15 years more than 5,000 miles of rail tracks had been laid in the United States.

Without doubt, the use of the telegraph, which was still in its infancy during the war, helped revolutionize communications for U.S. commanders. Not put into commercial use in the United States until 1844, when inventor Samuel Morse sent the first message ("What hath God wrought!"), telegraphy was highly dependent on railroads because telegraph lines were mainly strung along railroad rights-of-way adjacent to the tracks. Thus, railroad stations and depots soon became telegraphy centers where messages could be received, deciphered, and sent. Although the telegraph did not play a central role during the Mexican War because few lines extended much beyond Virginia, the implications of the technology were amply demonstrated.

In the United States, the changes in strategic communications were impressive. Unlike past American wars (all of which had been fought not far from the population center), most news from the battlefields arrived in a matter of days instead of weeks. This allowed civilian policy makers and military commanders in Washington to react far more quickly to changing strategic circumstances and also helped them mold public opinion in ways that they heretofore could not. However, newspapers received war news far more quickly, which could be both a boon and hindrance

to public opinion, depending on what kinds of news the public received. Finally, the communications revolution in progress during the war helped U.S. logistics and supply enormously, because requisitions and information concerning times and places of delivery could be relayed much quicker. All of these improvements allowed the United States to successfully wage a war several thousand miles away from its main population centers.

PAUL G. PIERPAOLI JR.

See also
Logistics, Mexican; Logistics, U.S.; Morse, Samuel Finley Breese; Railroads; Steamships; Telegraph.

References
Clary, David A. *Eagles and Empire: The United States, Mexico, and the Struggle for a Continent.* New York: Bantam Books, 2009.
Coe, Lewis. *The Telegraph: A History of Morse's Invention and Its Predecessors in the United States.* Jefferson, NC: McFarland, 1993.
Flexner, James Thomas. *Steamboats Come True.* New York: Little, Brown, 1944.
Winders, R. Bruce. *Mr. Polk's Army: The American Military Experience in the Mexican War.* College Station: Texas A&M University Press, 1997.

Compromise of 1850

Congressional legislation passed on September 9, 1850, comprising five bills and authored chiefly by U.S. senator Stephen A. Douglas from Illinois, which sought to bridge sectional divisions related to the expansion of slavery. The Compromise of 1850 was a direct consequence of the Mexican-American War and the Mexican land cession that resulted from it in 1848. Among the issues confronting Congress in 1850 were the admission of California, Deseret (Utah), and New Mexico to the Union, the establishment of firm Texas boundaries and the clearing of Texan debt, fugitive slaves, and the abolition of the slave trade in Washington, D.C. Congress faced these daunting challenges amid a divisive political scene and a nation increasingly polarized by mounting sectional tensions, many of which revolved around the issue of slavery.

On January 29, 1850, Whig senator Henry Clay of Kentucky introduced eight resolutions that attempted to address these contentious issues. Clay's first proposal sought to grant California statehood. Under proposal two, the territories of Deseret (Utah) and New Mexico would gain territorial governments without any restrictions or conditions addressing slavery. Resolutions three and four stated that Texas's boundaries would be reduced and its debt paid at an unspecified amount at a later date. Resolution five held that slavery could continue in Washington, D.C. The last resolution stipulated that Congress could not make any decisions regarding the slave trade in the southern states. Clay argued that the northern states should think about sectional issues from the southern point of view.

After seven months of heated debate, Clay's resolutions failed to win the requisite support in the Senate. Soon thereafter, Senator

Lithograph depicting the confrontation between Senator Henry S. Foote of Mississippi and Senator Thomas Hart Benton of Missouri during a debate on the Compromise of 1850. Foote threatened Benton with a pistol. (Library of Congress)

Stephen A. Douglas proposed five new resolutions that sought to break the deadlock over the extension of slavery into new territories gained from Mexico. The final versions of the resolutions authored by Douglas sought to strike a delicate compromise between the free and slave states.

The first three resolutions addressed statehood and territorial matters. Douglas's first resolution established the northern and western boundaries of Texas and ceded the disputed territory outside of those boundaries to the United States; in return, the federal government assumed the debts incurred by the Republic of Texas from 1836 to 1845. Most of this debt was in the form of government bonds purchased by citizens of slaveholding states that had wished to see Texas gain its independence from Mexico and thus provide room for the South's "peculiar institution" to expand westward. Although Texas would have preferred to have maintained sovereignty over that portion of New Mexico Territory east of the Rio Grande that it had claimed under the 1836 Treaty of Victoria (the state having already defaulted on its bonds), southern bondholders, promised to have their bonds redeemed at par, threw their political weight behind the compromise measure. The same act addressing Texan concerns also established the territorial government for New Mexico (which included modern-day Arizona). The second resolution admitted California to the Union as a free state, and the third one renamed Deseret "Utah" and set its boundaries

and established its territorial government. New Mexico and Utah were to be organized under the concept of popular sovereignty, meaning that the residents in those territories would decide for themselves whether slavery would be permitted.

The two remaining resolutions impacted existing slavery legislation and enacted a new law. First, the compromise allowed the practice of slavery to continue in the District of Columbia but prohibited the sale or transfer of slaves intended for other states in the district beginning on January 1, 1851.

Since the South came out relatively behind in its first four resolutions, a fifth was designed to balance the compromise along regional lines. To please the South, Congress voted to revise and strengthen the Fugitive Slave Act of 1793. This detailed the powers of the commissioners and courts regarding fugitives. Douglas's five compromise resolutions passed both the House of Representatives and the Senate on September 9, 1850. The Zachary Taylor administration had opposed the measures, but the president's sudden and unexpected death in July 1850 paved the way for President Millard Fillmore's support of the compromise. Between September 9 and 20, the president signed all five bills into law.

The Compromise of 1850 briefly mended sectional disputes by granting a stronger fugitive slave act to mollify the South. However, the addition of California upset the balance between free states and the slave states, giving the free states the majority representation in the Senate. The issues addressed by the compromise did not stop or reverse the growing sectionalism in the United States and in fact contributed greatly to the eventual secession of the southern states beginning in 1860, precipitating the Civil War in 1861. Indeed, the Compromise of 1850 lasted only four years at which time the highly controversial Kansas-Nebraska Act essentially nullified both the 1820 Missouri Compromise and the Compromise of 1850.

THERESA STOREY HEFNER-BABB

See also

Abolitionism; California; Clay, Henry; Douglas, Stephen Arnold; Fillmore, Millard; Mexican Cession; Missouri Compromise; New Mexico; Nevada; Politics, U.S.; Popular Sovereignty; Slavery; Taylor, Zachary; Utah.

References

Hamilton, Holman. *Prologue to Conflict: The Crisis and Compromise of 1850.* Louisville: University of Kentucky Press, 1964.
Sewell, Richard. *A House Divided: Sectionalism and Civil War.* Baltimore, MD: Johns Hopkins University Press, 1988.
Waugh, John C. *On the Brink of Civil War: The Compromise of 1850 and How It Changed the Course of American History.* Farmington Hills, MI: Scholarly Resources, 2003.

Concepción, Battle of
Event Date: October 28, 1835

Early battle of the Texas Revolution. Fought on October 28, 1835, near San Antonio, this engagement pitted some 90 members of the Texas army against 275 Mexican army troops. Following the skirmish at Gonzales on October 2, 1835, and other small engagements between Texans and Mexican forces, Stephen F. Austin led 400 men of the Texas army against San Antonio de Béxar, held by Mexican general Martín Perfecto de Cos and some 750 Mexican soldiers.

Arriving at San Francisco de la España Mission near San Antonio on October 27, Austin ordered James Bowie, James W. Fannin Jr., and 90 men to search for a protected position closer to San Antonio. While on their reconnaissance, the Texans briefly engaged some Mexican scouts before reaching Mission Concepción. There Bowie and Fannin decided to make camp for the night in a wooded bend of the San Antonio River, rather than return immediately to the main body as Austin had ordered. The Texans put out pickets to provide warning of any Mexican attack.

Aware of the small size of the Texan force at Concepción, Cos decided to attack it early on October 28. Before dawn he sent Colonel Domingo de Ugartechea and 275 men, most of them cavalry, and two artillery pieces against the Texan rebels. Ugartechea and 200 cavalrymen formed on the west bank of the San Antonio River to cut off any Texan retreat, while Lieutenant Colonel José María Mendoza led the remaining 75 infantry and artillerymen with the two guns in an attack from the east. Texan pickets sounded the alarm, and while the early morning fog gave the attackers an initial

advantage, most of their fire went high. Added to this, the Mexican gunpowder proved defective. That was not the case with the defenders, who repelled three Mexican charges with accurate fire, killing or wounding many of the infantry and artillerymen. After about a half hour, the Texans themselves charged, driving back the Mexican infantry and capturing one of their artillery pieces.

Hearing the sound of distant gunfire, Austin and the remaining Texans rode to the rescue, but they arrived too late to do much more than harry the already rapidly withdrawing Mexicans. In the Battle of Concepción, the first major battle of the Texas Revolution, Mexican losses were 14 killed and 39 wounded, some mortally; the Texans lost only 1 killed, Richard Andrews, and 1 wounded.

Austin favored an immediate assault on San Antonio de Béxar but was dissuaded in this by his subordinates, who believed it too well fortified. The Texans nonetheless held their position and initiated a siege.

SETH A. WEITZ AND SPENCER C. TUCKER

See also

Austin, Stephen Fuller; Bowie, James; Cos, Martín Perfecto de; Fannin, James Walker; Gonzales, Battle of; San Antonio; Texas Revolution; Ugartechea, Domingo de.

References

Barr, Alwyn. *Texans in Revolt: The Battle for San Antonio, 1835.* Austin: University of Texas Press, 1990.
Davis, William C. *Lone Star Rising: The Revolutionary Birth of the Texas Republic.* New York: Free Press, 2004.
Hardin, Stephen L. *Texian Iliad: A Military History of the Texas Revolution.* Austin: University of Texas Press, 1996.
Winders, Richard B. *Sacrificed at the Alamo: Tragedy and Triumph in the Texas Revolution.* Abilene, TX: State House Press, 2004.

Congress, Mexican

Although personalist leadership like that of General Antonio López de Santa Anna played a key role in the public affairs of 19th-century Mexico, institutions such as the national congress also contributed to the nation's historical development. Three different such legislatures convened during the war with the United States, and each influenced, in varying degrees, Mexican domestic and external policies between 1846 and 1848.

Preparations for the first of these congresses began late in January 1846 when the government of General Mariano Paredes y Arrillaga, which had come into power earlier that month following a rebellion that unseated the regime of General José Joaquín Herrera, moved to fulfill one of the main goals of the uprising. It then issued bylaws that called for elections to a new constitutional congress; the regulations ensured that representatives would be prosperous individuals, thereby eliminating every vestige of popular participation from national politics. This legislature was also intended to help pave the way for Paredes and his conservative allies to establish a monarchical regime. By the time Congress convened on June 6, however, two factors—the fury that the aforementioned endeavors had evoked among many politically conscious Mexicans and the defeats suffered by the Mexican army one month earlier at the Battles of Palo Alto and Resaca de la Palma—had sealed both its fate and that of Paredes's administration. Two months later, a coalition headed by erstwhile rivals General Santa Anna and radical (*puro*) federalist leader Valentín Gómez Farías capitalized on these circumstances and staged a revolt that overthrew Paredes's regime.

As with Paredes's rebellion, the uprising that enthroned Santa Anna and Gómez Farías sought to elect a congress that would bestow Mexico with a new constitutional structure, and in May 1847 this legislature approved the Acta de Reformas, a bill that sanctioned some minor modifications to the 1824 federal constitution. Political turmoil, nonetheless, hampered the effectiveness of this congress. Although regulations to elect members of the legislature were to follow those of 1823, which allowed for voting on the basis of universal male suffrage and would thus help advance the *puros'* agenda, when congress assembled on December 6 it was almost evenly divided between *puros* and *moderados* (moderate federalists). Legislators, as a result, failed to construct a united front to confront the U.S. military threat and instead quarreled over key issues. A prime example of this state of affairs was the January 11, 1847, decree that empowered the government to mortgage or sell ecclesiastical property in order to finance the war effort. The law, however, exacerbated existing political tensions and paved the way for the so-called rebellion of the *polkos,* which broke out on February 27 and submerged the capital in a bloody civil war that lasted for nearly one month. The ensuing struggle prevented the government from lending assistance to the eastern port of Veracruz, which was attacked by U.S. expeditionary forces under Major General Winfield Scott and surrendered late in March 1847.

News of the capitulation of Veracruz awakened patriotic feelings among *puro* and *moderado* lawmakers, who immediately proposed a flurry of combative pieces of legislation. Their efforts resulted in the decree of April 9, 1847, which authorized the government to organize the National Guard and to secure arms to defend the country's independence. The Mexican armies, however, failed to halt the U.S. advance into central Mexico, and by the early summer Santa Anna and congress engaged in much gamesmanship as they both tried to avoid the stigma of bearing sole responsibility for entering into peace negotiations with the United States.

The fall of Mexico City to U.S. armies in mid-September 1847 meant that the issue of whether to continue the war could no longer be avoided, and it fell to yet another Mexican national congress, the third that convened during the conflict, to resolve the matter. Members of this legislature convened in the city of Querétaro early in May 1848 to consider whether or not to accept the terms of the Treaty of Guadalupe Hidalgo, signed that February 2. After listening to several speakers who expounded on the merits of both the pro-war and pro-peace positions, the majority of legislators voted

to ratify the accord. In so doing they hoped to end the U.S. military occupation and avoid the ongoing economic crisis and likely loss of additional territory. One additional factor prompted their decision. Most of these congressmen were new actors on the political stage, and their future careers might well have depended on an alliance with the incumbent *moderado* president. A vote against the treaty could jeopardize those aspirations, and thus they cast their ballots to end the war.

Since the advent of independence in 1821, members of the Mexican national legislature steadfastly endeavored to assert their prerogatives against overbearing chief executives. The three Mexican national legislatures that assembled during the conflict with the U.S. acted on weighty matters in a tumultuous time and in so doing demonstrated that congress was indeed an important political actor in early republican Mexico.

PEDRO SANTONI

See also

Guadalupe Hidalgo, Treaty of; Herrera, José Joaquín de; Palo Alto, Battle of; Resaca de la Palma, Battle of; Santa Anna, Antonio López de; Scott, Winfield; Veracruz, Landing at and Siege of.

References

Costeloe, Michael P. *The Central Republic in Mexico, 1835–1846: Hombres de Bien in the Age of Santa Anna.* Cambridge, UK: Cambridge University Press, 1993.

Santoni, Pedro. *Mexicans at Arms: Puro Federalists and the Politics of War, 1845–1848.* Fort Worth: Texas Christian University Press, 1996.

Sordo Cedeño, Reynaldo. "El congreso y la guerra con Estados Unidos de América, 1846–1848." In *México al tiempo de su guerra con Estados Unidos (1846–1848),* coordinated by Josefina Zoraida Vázquez, 47–103. Mexico City: Secretaría de Relaciones Exteriores, El Colegio de México, and Fondo de Cultura Económica, 1997.

Congress, Texan

Legislative body that governed the Republic of Texas from the adoption of its constitution on March 16, 1836 to its annexation by the United States and admittance as a state on December 29, 1845. On March 1, 1836, a convention of 59 American colonists in Texas met at Washington-on-the-Brazos and, on the next day, adopted a Declaration of Independence. The constitutional convention then elected an interim government with David G. Burnet as president and began work on a constitution. As General Antonio López de Santa Anna's army marched toward Washington-on-the-Brazos, the new Texas government completed the constitution, formally adopted it at midnight on March 16, adjourned the next day, and fled to Harrisburg (now within the city limits of Houston) near Galveston Island, 100 miles to the east.

The Constitution of 1836 generally followed the U.S. Constitution but also included portions of Mexican laws. It established a government with a president and a vice president and a bicameral legislature, consisting of a House of Representatives and a Senate, and created 23 counties. The Texas Congress had the same general legislative powers as the U.S. Congress, including the levying of taxes, regulating currency and commerce, establishing a postal system, maintaining an army and a navy, activating the militia, and passing laws needed to govern the republic. It also possessed the power to declare war.

Initially, the House of Representatives would have between 24 and 40 members until the population of the republic exceeded 100,000, at which point the number of representatives would increase to between 40 and 100 members. Each county, created by the constitution, had at least one representative. A representative had to be at least 25 years old, a citizen of the republic, and a resident of his district for six months. House terms lasted only one year. The House chose its Speaker and had the power of impeachment.

The number of senators would be between one-third and one-half of the number of representatives. Each senator represented a district that had approximately the same number of free men as possible, excluding free blacks and Native Americans. Each Senate district had only one senator. A senator had to be at least 30 years old, a citizen of the republic, and a resident of his district for one year. Senators served a three-year term, with one-third of them elected each year. The vice president presided over the Senate but only voted in case of a tie vote for any action before it. The Senate chose its own officers, including the president pro tempore, and had the responsibility to try impeachments.

The first Texas Congress convened at Columbia on October 3, 1836, and had 30 representatives and 14 senators. The interim vice president, Lorenzo de Zavala, served as president of the Senate until October 22, when Mirabeau B. Lamar was inaugurated as vice president and Richard Ellis was elected president pro tempore of the Senate. Ira Ingram was elected as the first Speaker of the House. During the Texas Revolution, the Texas Congress met at Washington-on-the-Brazos, Harrisburg, Galveston, Velasco, and Columbia. In 1837, the new city of Houston became the capital of Texas. In 1839, the capital moved again to a tiny frontier settlement on the Colorado River named Waterloo, which was later renamed Austin. During its history as a republic, Texas had nine congresses.

Because there were no true political parties in the Republic of Texas, the Congress played a somewhat different role in Texas politics, especially as compared to the U.S. Congress. Instead, political factions developed, which were usually tied to a specific leader, like Sam Houston, or which were opposed to a particular leader. This meant that congressmen did not follow regular or prescribed strategies of legislation. Because Texas had low taxes and limited, unstable credit, Congress had a hard time appropriating funds. Voter dissatisfaction thus made the Congress often critical of presidential administrations that could not exercise fiscal constraint, which often made the presidential-congressional relationship an adversarial one. With congressional terms so short, few alliances could form in Congress, and many members ended up obstructing presidential initiatives. In the end, Congress had virtually no

control over spiraling debt and attendant inflation; Texas's debt burden increased from $1.2 million in 1836 to over $12 million by 1845.

With the admittance of Texas to the United State as a state, the Texas Congress transformed itself into the state legislature. In the final analysis, the Congress of Texas functioned about as well as could be expected under the novel circumstances of its history. Furthermore, it did act as a fairly effective counterbalance to presidential prerogatives.

ROBERT B. KANE

See also

Congress, U.S.; Constitution, Texan; Houston, Samuel; Politics, Texan; Texas; Texas Declaration of Independence; Texas Revolution.

References

Campbell, Randolph B. *Gone to Texas: A History of the Lone Star State.* New York: Oxford University Press, 2003.

Ferhenbach, T. R. *Lone Star: A History of Texas and Texans.* New York: Macmillan, 1968.

Lack, Paul D. *The Texas Revolutionary Experience: A Political and Social History, 1835–1836.* College Station: Texas A&M University Press, 1995.

Siegel, Stanley. *A Political History of the Texas Republic, 1836–1845.* Austin: University of Texas Press, 1956.

Congress, U.S.

Established by the U.S. Constitution as the legislative branch of the U.S. government, the U.S. Congress is tasked with the responsibility of writing laws, ratifying treaties, declaring war, and other duties. Congress members also act as representatives for the people of their respective states. Congress is divided into two houses: the U.S. Senate and the U.S. House of Representatives.

The United States had two major political parties during the 1840s—the Democratic Party and the Whig Party. The 1844 elections for the 29th Congress (March 4, 1845–March 3, 1847) resulted in a victory for the Democrats, who controlled both Houses, having 34 senators and 142 representatives compared to the Whigs' 24 senators and 79 representatives. American Party (also known as the Know-Nothing or American Republican Party) candidates won 6 seats, leaving 1 seat vacant. Additionally, two territorial delegates attended House sessions. During the 29th Congress, Democrats selected Indiana's representative John Wesley Davis as Speaker of the House. Willie Person Mangum, a Whig from North Carolina, and Democratic senators Ambrose Hundley Sevier and David Rice Atchison, from Arkansas and Missouri, respectively, all served as president pro tempore during the 29th Congress. In general, the Democrats were expansionist-oriented, while the Whigs tended to be far more cautious about adding new territories to the United States.

The 28th Congress (March 4, 1843–March 3, 1845) had approved a joint resolution on March 1, 1845, authorizing the annexation of Texas. The 29th Congress approved an additional

Political Makeup of the United States Congress during the Mexican-American War

	Democratic Party	Whig Party	Independents and Other Parties	Vacancies
29th Congress (1845–1847)*				
House	137	77	12	2
Senate	31	24	1	2
30th Congress (1847–1849)*				
House	110	115	5	0
Senate	36	23	1	0

* All statistics are as of the end of each congressional session

joint resolution authorizing Texas statehood, which Democratic president James K. Polk signed, admitting Texas to the Union as a state on December 29, 1845. During the 29th Congress, Polk requested that the Democrat-controlled Congress declare war against Mexico in response to alleged Mexican attacks against U.S. troops. On May 13, 1846, the Senate, voting 40–2, and the House, voting 173–14, overwhelmingly decided to declare war against Mexico. Throughout the war, Whig congressmen and some northern Democrats opposed the war and attempted to impose restrictions on the use of any lands acquired from Mexico. One of the biggest concerns among antiwar congressmen was the potential spread of slavery into newly acquired lands in the Southwest.

In an attempt to prevent slavery from spreading to new territories, Pennsylvania's representative David Wilmot (Democrat) submitted the Wilmot Proviso on August 8, 1846, which would have prohibited slavery in any lands acquired from the war; the proviso barely passed in the House but failed in the Senate. Future Democratic and Whig attempts to pass similar legislation followed the same pattern. Other significant legislation of the 29th Congress included the admission of Iowa as a state on December 28, 1846; the Walker Tariff, which lowered tariff rates; the 1847 Passenger Act; and District of Columbia Retrocession, which returned some District of Columbia territory back to Virginia.

The 1846 congressional elections for the 30th U.S. Congress (March 4, 1847–March 3, 1849) resulted in a victory for the Democrats in the Senate and for the Whigs in the House. Democrats won 38 Senate seats compared to 21 for the Whigs and 1 Independent Democrat in the Senate; the Whigs won a narrow victory in the House, with 116 seats to 110 for the Democrats, 1 for the American Party, 2 Independent Democrats, and 1 Independent candidate. Senator Atchison remained president pro tempore, while the Whigs elected Massachusetts representative Robert Charles Winthrop as the Speaker of the House. Notably, Whig candidate Abraham Lincoln was elected to represent Illinois during the 30th Congress, but he accomplished little of note, his antiwar stance notwithstanding. He served only one two-year term.

Members of the 30th Congress continued to deal with the ongoing war with Mexico but were responsible for dealing with other matters as well. The U.S. Senate ratified the Treaty of Guadalupe Hidalgo (38–14) on March 10, 1848. Congress authorized Wisconsin's entry into the Union as a state on May 29, 1848; created two new territories, Oregon and Minnesota, on August 14, 1849, and March 3, 1849, respectively; and passed the 1849 Gold Coinage Act. Congress also passed a bill establishing the Department of the Interior on March 3, 1849. The 30th Congress essentially continued congressional support for the war, albeit in a somewhat more circumspect fashion in the House owing to the Whig's razor-thin majority there. An attempt to add the Wilmot Proviso to the Treaty of Guadalupe-Hidalgo was resoundingly defeated by senators, and thus the divisive slavery issue, which would spark the Civil War, was placed into the hands of future politicians.

WYNDHAM E. WHYNOT

See also

Abolitionism; Antiwar Sentiment; Democratic Party; Free Soil Party; Guadalupe Hidalgo, Treaty of; Lincoln, Abraham; Polk, James Knox; Slavery; Texas; Whigs; Wilmot, David; Wilmot Proviso.

References

Curry, David P. *The Constitution in Congress: Democrats and Whigs, 1829–1861.* Chicago: University of Chicago Press, 2005.

Curry, David P. *The Constitution in Congress: Descent into the Maelstrom, 1829–1861.* Chicago: University of Chicago Press, 2005.

Holt, Michael F. *The Rise and Fall of the American Whig Party: Jacksonian Politics and the Onset of the Civil War.* New York: Oxford University Press, 2003.

Conner, David

Birth Date: 1792
Death Date: March 20, 1856

U.S. naval officer. David Conner was born in Harrisburg, Pennsylvania, in 1792 and entered the navy as a midshipman on January 16, 1809. He was assigned to the frigate *President*. In 1811 Conner transferred to the sloop of war *Hornet* and served in it throughout the War of 1812, save for a brief period early in the war when he was a prisoner of war of the British.

Conner won promotion to lieutenant on July 24, 1813. He participated in the engagement with the British sloop of war *Peacock* on February 24, 1813, in which he was reportedly the last man to leave the sinking British ship, and the capture by the *Hornet* of the British brig sloop *Penguin* on March 23, 1815, an encounter where he suffered a severe hip wound. Congress awarded him a medal for his gallantry.

Thereafter Conner served in the Pacific, ashore at the Philadelphia Navy Yard, and in command of the schooner *Dolphin*. Advanced to commander on March 23, 1825, he commanded in succession the sloops of war *Erie* and *John Adams*. Conner was promoted to captain on March 3, 1835. During 1841–1842 he served on the Board of Navy Commissioners. He was then the first chief of the new Bureau of Construction, Equipment, and Repair.

Late in 1843 Conner assumed command of the Home Squadron, consisting of all U.S. Navy vessels in the Gulf of Mexico and Caribbean. Conner's position was the most important naval command of the war. His ships not only had to maintain the lines of communication and supply to the United States but carry out a blockade of the Mexican coasts. Conner was also expected in the event of hostilities to seize Mexican ships, to secure Mexican ports, and to cooperate with and support U.S. forces ashore. With war with Mexico looming, Conner concentrated his ships off the Mexican port of Veracruz, but he did not believe that Mexico would resort to hostilities.

In 1846 Conner's ships instituted a highly effective blockade of the Mexican Gulf Coast. Despite a shortage of suitable vessels for such operations, Conner attempted an operation up the Alvarado River to seize Mexican ships that had taken refuge at Tlacotalpan. Lacking sufficient shallow-draft vessels, his attempts in July, August, and October were unsuccessful. On November 14, 1846, however, Conner took Tampico with a view to using it for future operations against Mexico City. This operation also provided valuable experience for the subsequent operation against Veracruz. Because of the shallow coastal waters and his lack of small steamers, Conner was cautious in the employment of his larger ships, which was the correct approach but one that nonetheless frustrated President James K. Polk.

Conner's greatest success in the war was the conduct of the U.S. landing at Veracruz, the largest amphibious landing in U.S. history to that point. On March 9, 1847, Conner's ships put ashore in surfboats 10,000 men and supplies of Major General Winfield Scott's invasion force. Thereafter Conner oversaw substantial assistance by his ships and men in the siege operations leading to the capture of Veracruz on March 29.

Conner had been in poor health for some time and had held his command for 15 months beyond a normal tour. Consequently, Secretary of the Navy John Young Mason secured President Polk's permission to relieve him. On March 21 Conner's second in command, Commodore Matthew C. Perry, took charge of the Home Squadron. Although it was done for health reasons, the timing of his relief robbed Conner of much recognition for his Veracruz accomplishment. Eventually recovering his health, Conner assumed command of the Philadelphia Naval Yard. He died in Philadelphia on March 20, 1856.

SPENCER C. TUCKER

See also
Blockade, Naval; Perry, Matthew Calbraith; Polk, James Knox; Tampico; United States Navy; Veracruz; Veracruz, Landing at and Siege of.

References
Bauer, K. Jack. *Surfboats and Horse Marine: U.S. Naval Operations in the Mexican War.* Annapolis, MD: U.S. Naval Institute, 1969.
Conner, Philip Syng Physick. *The Home Squadron under Commodore Conner in the War with Mexico.* N.p.: n.p., 1896.

Constitution, Texan

Document that established the blueprint for the government of Republic of Texas, promulgated on March 17, 1836. The Mexican Constitution of 1824 had established Mexico as a federal republic and combined the regions of Texas and Coahuila into a single state (Coahuila y Texas). It also mandated that each state write its own constitution, which Texas y Coahuila did in 1827. This constitution favored the Spanish-speaking and Catholic inhabitants of Coahuila, however, at the expense of those in Texas. For example, of the 12 delegates in the state legislature, only 2 came from Texas. Catholicism also was proclaimed the official religion of the state.

The 1824 Mexican Constitution also prohibited slavery. The Texans, mostly recently arrived Americans from the southern slaveholding states, were dissatisfied with their union with Coahuila and hoped to maintain the practice of slavery in Texas. As a result, they drafted and proposed a constitution in 1833 that would have made Texas a separate state within the Mexican Republic. The Mexican government, however, rejected this proposal.

Two years later, in 1835, Mexican president Antonio López de Santa Anna suspended the 1824 Constitution and together with his allies in congress placed into effect a new charter that centralized political power. Growing dissatisfaction with the Mexican government led the Americans in Texas to call a convention at Washington-on-the-Brazos in early 1836. As the delegates prepared to convene, Santa Anna led an army into Texas to quash the growing rebellion, the vanguard of which arrived at San Antonio on February 23. On February 1, Texas had elected a convention of 59 colonists. It met for the first time on March 1, and the next day adopted the Texas Declaration of Independence, written primarily by George Childress.

On March 6, Mexican forces under Santa Anna's army captured the Alamo at San Antonio. Sam Houston, one of the delegates and the commander in chief of the army, convinced the deputies to remain and continue their work on establishing a government. The constitutional convention then elected an interim government with David G. Burnet as president and began work drafting a constitution. Under the threat of the Mexican army, the delegates drafted the constitution quickly, incorporating large portions of the constitution of the United States, taking many clauses verbatim from the U.S. Constitution and paraphrasing others, but also including portions of Mexican laws. The Constitution of 1836 governed the Republic of Texas until its admittance into the United States in 1845.

As Santa Anna's army marched toward Washington-on-the-Brazos, the new government completed the constitution, formally adopted it on March 17, and adjourned. The newly elected government then fled to Harrisburg (now within the city limits of Houston) near Galveston Island, 100 miles to the east.

The 1836 Constitution established a government with a president and a vice president and a bicameral legislature, consisting of a House of Representatives and a Senate. The representatives and senators were elected for terms of one and three years, respectively. However, the president, elected by popular vote instead of by an Electoral College as the U.S. president was, served a three-year term and could not run directly for reelection (he could do so indirectly). To reduce religious influences in the government, the constitution prohibited clergy from holding office. The constitution also established a judicial branch, consisting of courts at four levels: justice, county, district, and supreme.

Although the 1836 Texas Constitution had a Bill of Rights, it also reflected the slaveholding status of many of the Americans living in Texas. It legalized slavery and denied citizenship to African Americans and Native Americans. Additionally, the constitution made it illegal for slave owners to free their own slaves without the consent of the Texas Congress. It also provided for adult male suffrage and a sizable grant of land to the head of each household.

In 1845, when Texas joined the United States, a new state constitution superseded the Constitution of the Republic of Texas. In early 1861, the Secession Convention modified the Constitution of 1845 to transfer Texas statehood from the United States of America to the Confederate States of America. After the war, the Constitution of 1866 nullified the Ordinance of Secession, abolished slavery, provided some civil rights for freedmen (but not the right to vote or hold office), and repudiated the Confederate war debt. In 1869, Texas again modified its constitution to include some proposals of the Radical Republicans in the U.S. Congress. Texas adopted its current constitution in 1876, soon after the end of Reconstruction in Texas. With its various amendments, this document has endured since.

ROBERT B. KANE

See also

Alamo, Battle of the; Austin, Stephen Fuller; Catholic Church; Congress, Texas; Houston, Samuel; Santa Anna, Antonio López de; Slavery; Texas; Texas Declaration of Independence; Texas Revolution.

References

Binkley, William C. *The Texas Revolution.* Baton Rouge: Louisiana State University Press, 1952.

Campbell, Randolph B. *Gone to Texas: A History of the Lone Star State.* New York: Oxford University Press, 2003.

Lack, Paul D. *The Texas Revolutionary Experience: A Political and Social History, 1835–1836.* College Station: Texas A&M University Press, 1995.

Richardson, Rupert Norval. *The Lone Star State.* 2nd ed. Englewood Cliffs, NJ: Prentice-Hall, 1958.

Constitutions, Mexico

Between 1824 and 1845 Mexican legislators experimented with several constitutions in an effort to provide the nation with a legal framework that would ensure political stability and economic growth following the achievement of independence from Spain in 1821.

Mexico adopted its first constitution, one largely modeled after Spain's 1812 charter and not that of the United States, in 1824. It preserved certain features reminiscent of the Spanish colonial regime, such as making Catholicism the official religion of the nation and guaranteeing special legal privileges for both the church and the army, as it upheld progressive principles like that of popular sovereignty by granting broad suffrage rights to adult males. The constitution also provided for shared sovereignty between the states and the national government, called for a bicameral legislature, and established an executive branch with a president and vice president elected for four-year terms. Unlike the United States, however, the president and vice president were to be elected by the state congresses, and not by popular vote.

Although the 1824 charter awakened expectations of grandeur, bitter partisan politics were among the factors that prevented such hopes from becoming a reality. In the mid-1820s competing factions, organized around Masonic lodges, tried to gain or preserve political power at the national, state, and local levels. York Rite Masons (who came to be identified as *yorkinos*) began to mobilize the urban masses in pursuit of electoral victory, and these efforts culminated with the Parián Riot of December 1828, during which a crowd of approximately 5,000 pillaged shops and stores in Mexico City's central square.

The chaos unleashed by the riot dampened the democratic idealism of the early republic, and the events of 1833–1834, when then vice president Valentín Gómez Farías, with the help of his allies in congress, attempted to curtail the privileges of the church and the army, further convinced many in the upper echelons of the middle class that only a stronger national government could remove the threat of social chaos, as well as guarantee progress and order. These men preached in newspapers and pamphlets that federalism was not a suitable form of government for a country in its infancy, and late in 1835, following the ouster of Gómez Farías by President General Antonio López de Santa Anna, a minority of legislators dismantled the federal republic.

Mexico then experimented with various forms of centralized rule during the next 11 years. Legislators first ratified the constitution commonly known as the Siete Leyes in December 1836. Hoping to provide stability, the charter stipulated that presidents were to serve for eight years and transformed states into departments that would be ruled by governors appointed by the national government. The Siete Leyes also sought to restrict popular participation in public life to prevent the social and economic upheaval that federalism had seemed to nourish. Full citizenship, which carried with it the right to vote, was restricted to men with a yearly income of at least 100 pesos, while qualifications to serve in public office were more stringent; for instance, election to the Chamber of Deputies required a man to have a minimum income of 1,500 pesos.

But the Siete Leyes alone could not restore economic growth or consolidate a long-lasting, stable government, and in June 1842 a constituent congress met to revise Mexico's political structure. The legislature's proposal for a new, more progressive federalist charter that attacked the church's and military's legal privileges, however, threatened Santa Anna, who had served as provisional president since late 1841. Consequently, in mid-December 1842 he and his allies orchestrated a nationwide cycle of military rebellions. Santa Anna then dissolved the constituent congress and called on an assembly of notables to draft a new charter. The deliberations produced the code commonly known as the Bases Orgánicas of 1843.

The Bases, in accordance with *Santanista* (as followers of Santa Anna were known) ideology, tried to secure the foundations for a centralist republic. Although they sanctioned the usual division of powers, they dropped a feature of the Siete Leyes, the so-called Supreme Conservative Power (Supremo Poder Conservador), a fourth branch of government charged with determining the national will if circumstances demanded it. The Bases also widened the powers of the executive branch, further restricted popular participation, gave the national government almost total control over the departments, and protected the legal privileges of both the army and the church. Pundits thus claimed that the Bases allowed Santa Anna to set up a personalist dictatorship, and consequently many politically conscious Mexicans expected the government of General José Joaquín Herrera, which took power following a December 1844 revolt, to immediately discard the Bases as Mexico's legal charter. Herrera failed to do so, however, and the Bases remained in effect until late December 1845, at which time General Mariano Paredes y Arrillaga, on the heels of a yet another successful rebellion, suspended that charter.

Although members of Mexico's first political elite could not set up a constitution that consolidated a strong and effective government during the early republic, their efforts should not be considered a failure. Rather, one should commend this generation of public-spirited Mexicans for their steadfast endeavors to further refine their ideas in order to set up a legal framework as the basis for a strong, stable nation-state.

SETH A. WEITZ AND PEDRO SANTONI

See also

Catholic Church; Congress, Mexican; Herrera, José Joaquín de; Mexico; Politics, Mexican; Santa Anna, Antonio López de.

References

Costeloe, Michael P. *The Central Republic in Mexico, 1835–1846: Hombres de Bien in the Age of Santa Anna.* Cambridge: Cambridge University Press, 1993.

Fowler, Will. *Mexico in the Age of Proposals, 1821–1853.* Westport, CT: Greenwood Press, 1998.

Fowler, Will. *Santa Anna of Mexico.* Lincoln: University of Nebraska Press, 2007.

Noriega Elío, Cecilia. *El constituyente de 1842.* Mexico City: Universidad Nacional Autónoma de México, 1986.

Rodríguez O., Jaime E. "The Constitution of 1824 and the Formation of the Mexican State." In *The Evolution of the Mexican Political System,* edited by Jaime E. Rodríguez O., 71–90. Wilmington, DE: Scholarly Resources, 1993.

Contreras, Battle of
Event Dates: August 19–20, 1847

Battle fought about 15 miles south of Mexico City during Major General Winfield Scott's advance toward that city. The Mexican forces in Padierna, mistakenly identified by the Americans as Contreras, were defeated on August 20, 1847, and the misnaming of the battle has endured. Total U.S. forces in the area were estimated at 8,500 men. The Mexicans fielded about 5,000 men.

General Scott had already decided to advance to Mexico City from the south instead of the more direct approach from the east, which would have required reducing the strong Mexican position at El Peñon. On August 15, he ordered his army to march to San Agustin via the Chalco route, thus bypassing Mexican positions at El Peñon and Nexicalzingo. While he considered whether to advance directly toward Churubusco or bypass the strong position at San Antonio, he sent a reconnaissance westward to determine the practicality of an alternate route. An assault on San Antonio would have produced excessive casualties, as it was protected by a lake on the east and on the west by a lava bed known as the *pedregal*, a mass of black, jagged rocks and crevices about three miles across. Reconnaissance conducted by Robert E. Lee showed that an old mule path that skirted the south side of the *pedregal* could be improved to pass infantry and artillery. This route would join a good road leading north along the west side of the *pedregal*.

Before making a final decision, Scott ordered a 500-man contingent of Brigadier General Gideon J. Pillow's division to improve the road. They were to be protected by Brigadier General David Emanuel Twiggs's division and the remainder of Pillow's division. Initially, the work went well.

Although General Antonio López de Santa Anna had ordered General Gabriel Valencia and some 5,000 men of the Army of the North to prevent any American advance from San Agustín, and the latter had taken a position in San Ángel to block the aforementioned western road, he had unwisely moved troops forward to an isolated position in Padierna. When the American force progressed about a mile, they encountered Mexican resistance. General Scott, who could see the Mexican forces from his headquarters at San Agustín, told Pillow that the Mexicans appeared to be in strength and ordered Pillow not to bring on a general engagement for which he was not ready.

When Pillow reached a hill called Zacetepec, he could see beyond the *pedregal*. To his front lay about 600 yards of ground, broken by jagged rocks, crevices, and defiles that sloped gradually down to a

Illustration depicting the Battle of Contreras (August 19–20, 1847) during the American advance on Mexico City. (N. C. Brooks, *A Complete History of the Mexican War*, 1849)

ravine through which a stream passed, running roughly parallel to the San Ángel Road. Pillow could see the enemy position in Padierna and the heavily fortified high ground beyond it. His immediate concern was Mexican skirmishers scattered in the rocks. To protect his working party, he decided to push the enemy back. His initial effort was countered when Valencia added artillery support to his skirmishers.

Ignoring Scott's order, Pillow added artillery and infantry in an unsuccessful attempt to drive the Mexicans from their positions. Valencia, soon believing that he had achieved a great victory, thought he could easily defeat the Americans and refused an order from Santa Anna to withdraw. Unknown to him, however, three brigades of Americans passed in succession around the Mexican left flank, cutting the road north from Padierna.

During the night of August 19, Brigadier General Persifor F. Smith developed a plan for moving most of the American force on the San Ángel road to the rear of Valencia's position and attacking at dawn. His force, now about 40 percent of Scott's army, consisted of his own brigade and those of Brigadier General George Cadwalader and Colonel Bennet Riley for the assault, with the brigade of Colonel James Shields, which had joined Smith during the night, left to block any reinforcements from Santa Anna. Scott approved Smith's plan and ordered a supporting frontal attack.

At 6:00 a.m. on August 20, after a difficult approach in the dark and rain, Smith launched his attack on the Mexican rear. Completely surprised, the Mexican force collapsed quickly. Disorganized troops then attempted to retreat but found their way blocked by Shields's brigade on the road north.

The American force quickly moved to the San Ángel Road and prepared for a counterattack by Santa Anna. The brief Battle of Contreras led Santa Anna to withdraw his forward troops and develop a new defensive position along the Churubusco River. Casualties numbered some 300 killed or wounded on the American side; the Mexicans suffered far greater losses of some 700 dead, 1,225 wounded, and almost 850 captured, along with 22 guns.

PHILIP L. BOLTÉ

See also

Cadwalader, George; Churubusco, Battle of; Mexico City, Battle for; Mexico City Campaign; Pillow, Gideon Johnson; Riley, Bennett; Santa Anna, Antonio López de; Scott, Winfield; Shields, James; Smith, Persifor Frazer; Valencia, Gabriel.

References

Eisenhower, John S. D. *So Far from God: The U.S. War with Mexico, 1846–1848.* Norman: University of Oklahoma Press, 2000.

Johnson, Timothy D. *A Gallant Little Army: The Mexico City Campaign.* Lawrence: University Press of Kansas, 2007.

Conventions of 1832 and 1833

Held in San Felipe de Austin, the Conventions of 1832 and 1833 were gatherings of Texan colonial leaders who sought to bring about political reforms in the Mexican government that they hoped would provide further autonomy for Texas colonists. Growing out of the largely Anglo-Texan desire for greater self-governance in

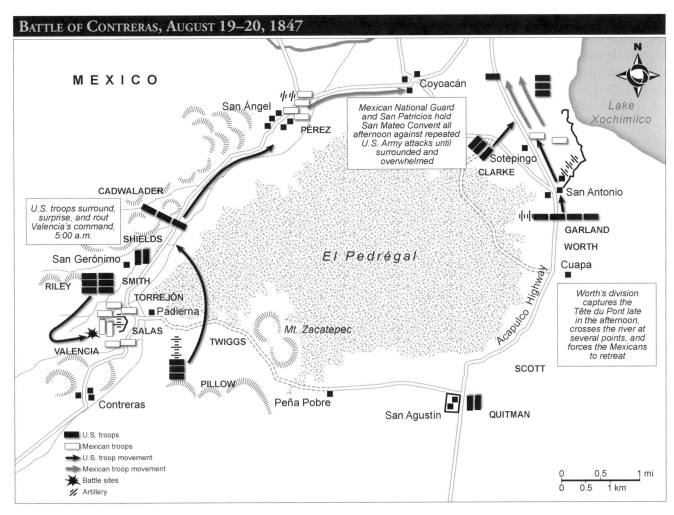

BATTLE OF CONTRERAS, AUGUST 19–20, 1847

MEXICO

Coyoacán

San Ángel

PÉREZ

Mexican National Guard
and San Patricios hold
San Mateo Convent all
afternoon against repeated
U.S. Army attacks until
surrounded and
overwhelmed

Lake
Xochimilco

Sotepingo

CLARKE

CADWALADER

U.S. troops surround,
surprise, and rout
Valencia's command,
5:00 a.m.

San Antonio

SHIELDS

San Gerónimo

El Pedrégal

GARLAND

WORTH

RILEY

SMITH

Cuapa

TORREJÓN

Padierna

SALAS

Mt. Zacatepec

VALENCIA

TWIGGS

Worth's division
captures the
Tête du Pont late
in the afternoon,
crosses the river at
several points, and
forces the Mexicans
to retreat

SCOTT

PILLOW

Contreras

Peña Pobre

San Agustín

QUITMAN

- U.S. troops
- Mexican troops
- U.S. troop movement
- Mexican troop movement
- Battle sites
- Artillery

0   0.5   1 mi
0   0.5   1 km

the province of Coahuila y Texas, and following the disturbances at Anáhuac and the Battle of Velasco in June 1832, the reform movement gathered momentum as the then liberal Mexican general Antonio López de Santa Anna fought with President Anastasio Bustamante for control of Mexico. Anglo-Texans and some Tejanos grew weary and then fearful of the centralizing tendencies and policies emanating from the Bustamante government as it attempted to extend greater control over Coahuila y Texas. At these conventions, the Texans voted for a series of political reforms that they insisted the Bustamante and later the Santa Anna administrations enact, demanding that the government act more in accordance with the federal Constitution of 1824.

Meeting during October 1–6, the Convention of 1832 was the first effort to address Texan grievances. Attended by 58 delegates from 16 districts—not including the heavily Tejano cities of San Antonio de Béxar and Victoria—the gathering was presided over by *empresario* Stephen F. Austin. Although he was interested in pursuing many of the reforms under discussion, Austin's tepid support for the convention and its long-term implications put him at odds with the more radical colonists led by William H. Wharton. Among the resolutions adopted by the convention were those extending Texan exemption from Mexican tariff policies, the easing of immigration restrictions for U.S. citizens, the donation of

government lands for public schools, the appointment of a land commissioner for east Texas, and a host of other local reforms.

The most controversial resolution called for the separation of Texas and Coahuila and the establishment of a separate Texas state. Before adjourning, the convention also established plans for the creation of committees of correspondence to help disseminate among the Texans news of political developments in the rest of Mexico, a move that hinted at the growing political restiveness among the Texan colonists. Authorizing Wharton and Tejano leader Rafael Manchola to deliver the resolutions to the Mexican congress, the Convention of 1832 came to naught as Ramón Músquiz, political chief of the province, refused to recognize the convention's legality. For a brief time, the more radical colonists were held at bay.

A new convention met from April 1 to April 13, 1833, and reflected the rapid resurgence of the less patient Texan colonists. In Austin's absence—he was traveling the region courting Tejano support for the proposed reforms of the earlier convention—this gathering was presided over by Wharton, with other aggressive colonists, including the recently arrived Sam Houston, holding prominent positions. The Convention of 1833 repeated the demands of the earlier gathering but this time also drafted a proposed state constitution for Texas, a move that assumed that the new federalist government under Santa Anna would approve separate Texas statehood. This time, the convention sent Austin, Tejano leader Juan Seguín, and Dr. James Miller to Mexico City to deliver the resolutions, but only Austin was able to make the trip.

Although Austin was not enthusiastic about the tone of the convention's resolutions, he apparently accepted this turn of events as inevitable and delivered the resolutions to the Mexican government in July 1833. The Mexican congress, somewhat suspicious of the proposed reforms, took action very slowly. The government eventually offered to repeal the restrictions on immigration and seemed to be willing to act on many of the other reforms but did not address the issue of separate statehood for Texas. After leaving Mexico City Austin continued to press for action on the proposals, and his persistence alienated the government of Santa Anna. He was arrested in Saltillo in January 1834 and spent the next three months in a prison in Mexico City. That year Santa Anna's regime finally enacted numerous reforms benefitting Texas, although not separate statehood, and relations between the province and the central government warmed briefly. Santa Anna, however, evolved into a much more authoritarian figure, and Texan demands continued apace, so the die seemed cast for a much larger conflict.

KELLY E. CRAGER

See also

Austin, Stephen Fuller; Bustamante y Oseguera, Anastasio; Coahuila y Texas; Congress, Mexican; Constitutions, Mexican; Empresarios; Houston, Samuel; Mexico; Santa Anna, Antonio López de; Texas; Texas Revolution; Velasco, Battle of.

References

Campbell, Randolph B. *Gone to Texas: A History of the Lone Star State.* New York: Oxford University Press, 2003.

Cantrell, Gregg. *Stephen F. Austin: Empressario of Texas.* New Haven, CT: Yale University Press, 1999.

Lack, Paul D. *The Texas Revolutionary Experience: A Political and Social History, 1835–1836.* College Station: Texas A&M University Press, 1995.

Cooke, Philip St. George

Birth Date: June 13, 1809
Death Date: March 20, 1895

U.S. Army officer. Philip St. George Cooke was born on June 13, 1809, in Leesburg, Virginia. Upon graduation from the U.S. Military Academy, West Point, in 1827 he was assigned to the 6th U.S. Infantry and served in the Black Hawk War of 1832. Advanced soon thereafter to second lieutenant, he was assigned to the 1st Dragoons and saw action against Native Americans in the West.

At the start of the Mexican-American War, Cooke was with Brigadier General Stephen W. Kearny's army as it marched toward New Mexico. As the force approached Santa Fe, Kearny sent Cooke ahead, accompanied by 12 soldiers, to negotiate with the Mexicans in hope of avoiding hostilities. Encountering no opposition, Cooke

proceeded to meet with local leaders, including Diego Archuleta. Within days, Kearny's army had occupied Santa Fe with virtually no resistance. Kearny brevetted Cooke a lieutenant colonel and gave him charge of the Mormon Battalion.

After drilling and training his charges relentlessly, Cooke marched his battalion west to California, leaving Santa Fe on October 19, 1846. Although the Mormon Battalion saw no active combat, it did accomplish its primary goal of constructing a wagon trail through the eastern mountains of California. Cooke arrived in San Diego on January 19, and the Mormon Battalion was disbanded soon thereafter. Cooke then rejoined Kearny's force.

After the war, Cooke fought against the Apaches in New Mexico in 1854 and the Sioux in Nebraska in 1855. In 1861, Cooke published a book titled *Cavalry Tactics*, which helped him to become known by many as the "Father of American Cavalry."

The Civil War, which began in April 1861, divided Cooke's family as well as the nation. His son, John R. Cooke, became a Confederate general; two of his daughters also sided with the South. One of those daughters was married to Confederate cavalry general J. E. B. Stuart. His other daughter was married to Union brigadier general Jacob Sharpe.

Cooke was promoted to brigadier general in the regular army in November 1861 and placed in command of cavalry forces in Washington, D.C. He participated in the March–August 1862 Peninsula Campaign and saw action in command of a cavalry division in the siege of Yorktown, the Battle of Williamsburg, and the Seven Days' Campaign.

Cooke's wartime leadership produced controversy. Early on, he was criticized for not pursuing aggressively enough his Confederate opponent and son-in-law, J. E. B. Stuart. Then he was humiliated when Stuart circled the entire Union Army in June 1862. Many speculated that Cooke feared losing a battle to Stuart.

Further controversy attended Cooke's actions during the Seven Days' Battles east of Richmond when he was criticized for advancing without orders and launching an ill-fated cavalry charge that attempted to save some cannon in danger of being captured but only resulted in heavy casualties among his men. Critics claimed he was too wedded to the idea of a saber charge to realize that such tactics were suicidal against entrenched infantry. On July 5, Cooke asked to be relieved of command, pending an investigation of his actions at Gaines' Mill.

Cooke never again served in the field during the Civil War and instead was limited to administrative duties. Until August 1863, he served on the courts-martial staff, after which he commanded the District of Baton Rouge until May 1864. From May 1864 to April 1865, he had charge of the Union's recruiting effort. Cooke was brevetted major general on March 13, 1865.

Following the Civil War, Cooke remained in the army and commanded the new Department of the Platte, which included Iowa, Nebraska, Utah, and part of Dakota and Montana Territories. In his final days in uniform, Cooke, ever the cavalry traditionalist, resisted efforts to eliminate the saber, even though it was not practical for fighting Native Americans in the West. Like many of his fellow army officers, he was often more sympathetic toward the Native Americans than he was toward the white settlers, believing that whites had corrupted the Native Americans with their introduction of alcohol, gambling, and the like. Cooke even learned to speak several Native American languages.

Cooke retired from active duty on October 29, 1873, after more than 45 years in the military and died in Detroit, Michigan, on March 20, 1895.

ALAN K. LAMM AND PAUL G. PIERPAOLI JR.

See also

Archuleta, Diego; Kearny, Stephen Watts; Mormon Battalion; New Mexico; Santa Fe.

References

Cooke, Philip St. George. *Cavalry Tactics.* Washington, DC: Government Printing Office, 1861.

Cook, Philip St. George. *The Conquest of New Mexico and California.* New York: G. P. Putnam's Sons, 1878.

Cooke, Philip St. George. *Scenes and Adventures in the Army, or, Romance of Military Life.* Philadelphia, PA: Lindsay & Blakiston, 1857.

Young, Otis E. *The West of Philip St. George Cooke.* Glendale, CA: Arthur H. Clark, 1955.

Cooke's March
Event Date: October 1846–January 1847

Epic march of the so-called Mormon Battalion led by Colonel Philip St. George Cooke. Cooke, born in 1809, graduated from the U.S. Military Academy at West Point in 1827 and joined the 6th Infantry on the Missouri frontier. In 1833, he was transferred to the recently organized dragoon regiment. When war erupted with Mexico in 1846, Cooke accompanied Brigadier General Stephen Watts Kearny's Army of the West, which departed on June 30, 1846, from Fort Leavenworth in Kansas for New Mexico.

Kearny entered Santa Fe unopposed in August 1846. He quickly divided his forces in anticipation of the next part of his mission—the conquest of California. Colonel Alexander W. Doniphan led the 1st Missouri Mounted Rifles on a storied march to Chihuahua, Mexico. Kearny, with 300 dragoons and a 14-man topographical unit under Lieutenant William Hemsley Emory, left the conquered Santa Fe for San Diego, California. Cooke's battalion of 300 Mormon volunteers followed a few days behind Kearny. The Mormon Battalion was not a combat unit but rather served as an engineering battalion, the mission of which was to create a wagon road through the northern Sonora Desert to California.

Cooke's expedition departed Santa Fe in October 1846, headed southwest across New Mexico into Sonora, and then reached the headwaters of the San Pedro River. From there, it moved west across present-day southern Arizona and arrived at Tucson in mid-December. The battalion continued north to the Gila River and then west. It crossed the Colorado River and rejoined Kearny in California in late January 1847.

Perhaps the most amazing aspect of Cooke's March is that he and his men covered 1,125 miles in only 102 days under hazardous and grueling conditions. At one point, a herd of wild cattle attacked the battalion, resulting in the so-called Battle of the Bulls. Perhaps most important, Cooke's wagon road became a major trail for pioneers heading west. Cooke went on to become a brigadier general during the Civil War and played a pivotal role in shaping the U.S. Cavalry, becoming the best U.S. authority on cavalry tactics.

DEBRA J. SHEFFER

See also

Cooke, Phillip St. George; Doniphan, Alexander William; Doniphan's March; Emory, William Hemsley; Kearny, Stephen Watts; Mormon Battalion.

References

Cooke, Philip St. George. *The Conquest of New Mexico and California.* New York: G. P. Putnam's Sons, 1878.

Cooke, Philip St. George. *Scenes and Adventures in the Army, or, Romance of Military Life.* Philadelphia, PA: Lindsay & Blakiston, 1857.

Fleek, Sherman L. *History May Be Searched in Vain: A Military History of the Mormon Battalion.* Spokane, WA: Arthur H. Clark, 2006.

Goetzmann, William H. *Army Exploration in the American West, 1803–1863.* New Haven, CT: Yale University Press, 1959.

Goetzmann, William H. *Exploration and Empire: The Explorer and the Scientist in the Winning of the American West.* New York: Alfred A. Knopf, 1971.

Ricketts, Norma Baldwin. *The Mormon Battalion: U.S. Army of the West.* Logan: Utah State University Press, 1997.

Young, Otis E. *The West of Philip St. George, 1809–1895.* Cleveland, OH: Arthur H. Clarke, 1955.

Cooper, James Fenimore
Birth Date: September 15, 1789
Death Date: September 14, 1851

Influential U.S. writer and the first American to support himself entirely by writing novels. Cooper helped both to create a unique genre of American literature and to advance the notion of Manifest Destiny, capturing the influences of nature and the frontier experience in his stories. James Fenimore Cooper was born on September 15, 1789, in Burlington, New Jersey. He moved with his family to upstate New York in 1790, first to Cooperstown and then to a village on the edge of the wilderness, where he often played in the forest and dreamed of earlier days. Cooper was not a good student and often got into trouble. He was expelled from Yale when he was 16 for blowing up another student's door.

Cooper's father then arranged for him to go to sea, preparatory to entering the U.S. Navy. The experience gave Cooper a love of the sea as a place of freedom and adventure. After commissioning as a midshipman on January 1, 1808, Cooper was assigned to the brig

Wasp as a recruiting officer. When his father died in 1809, Cooper inherited $50,000 and resigned his commission on May 6, 1811. Within 10 years, however, Cooper had gone through his inheritance and faced financial ruin. In desperation, he then turned to writing as a career.

Cooper's first novels were published anonymously. The second one, titled *The Spy* (1821), was a patriotic historical novel about the American Revolutionary War. It was one of the first novels written by an American with an American setting and characters. *The Spy* was hugely popular and went through three editions in quick order. His next novel was autobiographical. Called *The Pioneers* (1823), it dealt with the founding of Cooperstown. A prevalent theme in *The Pioneers* was the conflict between taming the wilderness and preserving it. Cooper introduced his most memorable character in *The Pioneers,* Natty Bumpo, an aged hunter. Bumpo became the symbol of the American frontiersman, based on Daniel Boone and other scouts and explorers who lived in the area between civilization and unknown territory. He appeared in four other novels by Cooper, including *The Last of the Mohicans* (1826), Cooper's most famous novel. The five are known as the Leatherstocking novels.

Cooper's works were widely read by both Americans and Europeans, and his descriptions of the frontier and its effect on the American character were quite influential. His depiction of American expansion as inevitable and preordained conformed with the ideology of Manifest Destiny that many Americans at the time believed in.

During the 1830s Cooper's popularity declined because his elitist temperament alienated many. He disliked the tyranny of popular democracy and favored a republic controlled by the elite, and his later writings were often permeated with polemics against the vulgar crowd. Cooper became known for his many libel suits against publishers critical of his ideas and writings.

Cooper supported the Mexican-American War, believing that the United States had a mission to spread liberty around the world, and he thought the Mexican people would benefit by fair and honest rule in the U.S. model. He wrote one novel set during the war, titled *Jack Tar, or, The Florida Reef.* One of the novel's most important themes was that a benevolent U.S. government rescued Mexico from ambitious and dishonest rulers. Cooper also wrote an excellent study of the early U.S. Navy, *History of the Navy of the United States of America.*

Cooper's health declined in the spring of 1851, and he died at Cooperstown on September 14, 1851.

TIM WATTS

See also

Expansionism and Imperialism; Literature; Manifest Destiny.

References

Dekker, George, and John P. McWilliams, eds. *James Fenimore Cooper: The Critical Heritage.* London: Routledge & Kegan Paul, 1973.

McWilliams, John. *Political Justice in a Republic: James Fenimore Cooper's America.* Berkeley: University of California Press, 1972.

Corpus Christi

Small trading center located at the mouth of the Nueces River on the lower Gulf Coast of Texas used as a camp and staging area for Brigadier General Zachary Taylor's Army of Occupation during 1845–1846. At the time of the Mexican-American War, Corpus Christi was known as Kinney's Ranch, named for its founder Henry Lawrence Kinney, a speculator, rancher, and trader. Corpus Christi means "Body of Christ" in Latin, and derives its name from Corpus Christi Bay on which it is located.

In 1832 Kinney arrived in the area, one of many Anglos who settled in Mexican-held Texas. By 1839, Kinney had established a permanent settlement in the area and had been engaged in a prosperous trade with Mexicans in Matamoros. He also sold goods to a Mexican army contingent located about 25 miles west of Corpus Christi. By the mid-1840s, Kinney's Ranch, now also known as Corpus Christi, had attracted about 100 inhabitants. The settlement included Kinney's extensive holdings just inland and some 30 homes.

In the late spring of 1845, President James K. Polk ordered Taylor's Army of Occupation to take up a position deep in Texas, within striking distance of the Rio Grande, in anticipation of a conflict with Mexico. Taylor decided to use Corpus Christi as a staging area and camp, where he would wait out the autumn and winter before receiving further instructions. He chose the area because of its location on the Gulf Coast, which made it easy for the transportation of troops and supplies there by sea, and because of its relative proximity to the Rio Grande, which lay to the south. It was, nevertheless, on the north bank of the Nueces and thus outside of the disputed Nueces Strip, a region claimed by both the United States and Mexico. The first troop deployments, arriving by steamboat, began filing into Corpus Christi in mid-July 1845.

Kinney was initially annoyed by the usurpation of his land, but eventually he found ways to enrich himself. By the end of the month, approximately 4,000 troops had set up a huge tent camp. Told that they were likely to remain in Corpus Christi at least through the end of the year, the soldiers made arrangements for their own entertainment, which included the creation of a theater. Indeed, there Captain (and future army general and president) Ulysses S. Grant portrayed Desdemona in William Shakespeare's *Othello.* Many soldiers fished in the nearby Gulf of Mexico, and Kinney, ever the businessman, began publishing a newspaper that he sold to the troops.

The problems of housing such a large contingent at Corpus Christi soon became manifest, especially during the winter months. The winter of 1845–1846 was unusually cold and rainy, rendering most of the troops miserable, forced as they were to live in leaky tents. A scarcity of firewood meant that camp fires were few and far between. Many nights, soldiers had to sleep in leaking tents in wet blankets on the cold, damp ground. The fresh drinking water supply was quickly overwhelmed, so that by the end of 1845 many troops were forced to drink contaminated or brackish

The 1845 Corpus Christi, Texas, campsite of the U.S. Army of Occupation, commanded by Brigadier General Zachary Taylor. (Library of Congress)

water. Not surprisingly, many men became sick, especially with dysentery. By January 1846, an estimated 25 percent of Taylor's force was ill.

Boredom also proved to be a significant problem. Fighting, heavy drinking, gambling, larceny, and even desertion became commonplace. Entrepreneurs flooded the area, sensing a golden business opportunity. Some offered legitimate services, such as food and clothing, while others established saloons and brothels, much to Taylor's chagrin. By February 1846, the nonmilitary population of Corpus Christi had ballooned to more than 2,000 people. One soldier wrote of his time there, stating that Corpus Christi was the "most murderous, thieving, gambling, cutthroat, God-forsaken hole in the Lone Star State."

Upon receiving orders to move toward the Rio Grande, Taylor ordered the massive camp disassembled. On March 9, 1846, his men gladly struck camp and began the march to the south. After the Mexican-American War, Corpus Christi grew slowly but steadily and was the site of an army depot until 1855. In 1852, it was officially incorporated as a city. In the 20th century, Corpus Christi became a prosperous commercial, transportation, and trade hub. Cattle from inland areas were shipped into the area for transport via ship or railroad. The oil business also became a big enterprise, particularly with the discovery of large petroleum deposits in the Gulf of Mexico. The port of Corpus Christi opened in 1926; today it is the sixth-largest port in the United States and the deepest port facility along the Gulf Coast.

Paul G. Pierpaoli Jr.

See also

Kinney, Henry Lawrence; Polk, James Knox; Rio Grande; Taylor, Zachary; Texas.

References

Lea, Tom, with Richard King. *The King Ranch.* Boston, MA: Little, Brown, 1957.

Smith, George W., and Charles Judah. *Chronicles of the Gringos: The U.S. Army in the Mexican War, 1846–1848.* Albuquerque: University of New Mexico Press, 1968.

Cortina, José Gómez de la
Birth Date: 1799
Death Date: 1860

Mexican writer, scholar, and politician. José Gómez de la Cortina was born in Mexico City, the son of a wealthy and well-known Spanish family. He inherited from his father the title of Conde de la Cortina, and went on to become a respected man of letters in 19th-century Mexico. A member of several scientific and literary societies, Cortina authored works of fiction, wrote for newspapers, and in 1833 cofounded the Mexican Geographic and Statistical Society, Latin America's first such organization.

Cortina, whose views leaned to the conservative and *moderado* (moderate liberal) camp, also played a prominent role in the politics of the early republic. He served as governor of the Federal District in 1835, as minister of finance between December 1838 and

March 1839, and as head of a group that favored the establishment of a monarchy in 1840. His daughter was married to José María Gutiérrez Estrada, who at the time published a controversial pamphlet supporting that form of government. Cortina subsequently was a member of the Assembly of Notables, which drafted the 1843 charter known as the Bases Orgánicas, and of the senate that spearheaded the *moderado*-led December 6, 1844, revolt.

Cortina played a key role in public affairs during the war with the United States, particularly during his tenure as governor of the Federal District (August–October 1846). In that capacity Cortina tried, in early October, to curtail the political ascendancy of the *puros,* the pro-war faction that had taken power two months earlier thanks to the *pronunciamiento* (rebellion) of the Ciudadela. He first apprehended *puro* (radical liberal) partisan Francisco Próspero Pérez on the grounds that he had threatened domestic tranquility, and next tried to disband a *puro*-led National Guard battalion. A wealthy merchant group then elected Cortina as colonel of a militia unit to protect *moderado* interests, and Cortina also tried to organize the Cuerpo de Seguridad Mutua, an armed force designed to protect private property.

By mid-October, as these and other issues divided *puros* and *moderados,* Mexico City came to the brink of civil war. Cortina then traversed the capital in an effort to calm the contending groups and their supporters and prevent an outbreak of violence. He also went to the National Palace, where he met the commandant general of Mexico, General Pedro Lemus, a *puro* supporter. Shortly thereafter, both men walked out to the city's main square, the Zócalo, where they embraced each other in front of anxious bystanders, who doubtlessly feared the outbreak of another rebellion.

Notwithstanding this conciliatory measure, political divisions endured and forced Cortina to resign his post. He then continued to plot against the *puros.* Not only did he help organize the February 1847 Polkos Revolt, but he also took command, in the early stages of that insurrection, of one of the three principal columns of rebel troops. Cortina later served as a councilman in the Mexico City *ayuntamiento* (town council) during the civil conflict known as the War of the Reform (1858–1861). Cortina died a pauper in the Mexican capital in 1860.

PEDRO SANTONI

See also

Mexico City; *Moderados*; Polkos Rebellion; *Puros.*

References

Bustamante, Carlos María. *El nuevo Bernal Díaz del Castillo, o sea, historia de la invasión de los anglo-americanos en México.* 2 vols. 1847. Reprint, Mexico City: Instituto Nacional de Estudios de la Revolución Mexicana, 1987.

Haworth, Daniel S. "Civilians and Civil War in Nineteenth-Century Mexico: Mexico City and the War of the Reform, 1858–1861." In *Daily Lives of Civilians in Wartime Latin America: From the Wars of Independence to the Central American Civil Wars,* edited by Pedro Santini, 91–122. Westport, CT: Greenwood Press, 2008.

Santoni, Pedro. *Mexicans at Arms: Puro Federalists and the Politics of War, 1845–1848.* Fort Worth: Texas Christian University Press, 1996.

Cortina, Juan Nepumeceno
Birth Date: May 16, 1824
Death Date: October 30, 1894

Mexican soldier, rancher, and guerrilla. Born in the city of Camargo, Tamaulipas, on May 16, 1824 and descended from the founding family of that place, Juan Nepumeceno Cortina's role as a cavalryman in the war between the United States and Mexico proved far less significant than the roles he played in the decades following the conflict. Cortina's military service began in 1844, when he joined the Defensores de la Patria (Defenders of the Homeland). This unit of the National Guard of Tamaulipas was responsible for defending the Tamaulipan section of Mexico's northern frontier. He rose to the rank of corporal by the eve of the Mexican-American War.

As war with the United States approached in 1846, General Pedro de Ampudia utilized Cortina and other members of his unit as mounted scouts. He served in that capacity during the conflict's first two engagements, the Battles of Palo Alto and Resaca de la Palma, and soon received promotion to sergeant. Cortina fought again at the Battle of Monterrey, but his combat record from the end of that battle until the conclusion of the war cannot be verified. Historians have speculated that he fought with Mexican guerrillas who harassed American supply lines.

After the war, Cortina crossed into Texas to settle at the Rancho del Carmen, at the center of the 44,000-acre hereditary land grant deeded to his second wife's mother, Estefana Cortéz. Greatly angered by the violent and inequitable treatment that former Mexicans living in the Rio Grande Valley received at the hands of the governments of Texas and the United States, Cortina led a revolt that began on July 13, 1859. On that day he led about a dozen men into Brownsville and shot the town marshal, Robert Shears, in retaliation for Shears's pistol-whipping of one of Cortina's former ranch hands. He then proclaimed a revolt and in the following months waged a mounted guerrilla war. Although his forces totaled more than several hundred men, his burnings of Anglo-American property and the ethnic retaliation launched against Mexican Americans reduced most ranches from Brownsville to Rio Grande City to ashes. Following twin losses to a combined force of U.S. Army regulars, Texas Rangers, and local militia on December 21 and December 27, 1859, Cortina crossed into Mexico with his remaining forces. The commander of the U.S. force, Major Samuel P. Heintzelman, halted his pursuit at the river.

Although temporarily defeated, Cortina refused to abandon his struggle and took full advantage of the U.S. Civil War to continue raiding across the Mexican-U.S. border. However, civil conflicts in Mexico soon took him away from the border. During the War of the Reform (1858–1861), Cortina fought with the victorious liberal armies of President Benito Juárez. Defeated Mexican conservatives soon united with the forces of French emperor Napoléon II to wage the War of the French Intervention (1862–1867) against the victors.

Juan Nepomuceno Cortina fought in the Mexican Army in the war against the United States. After the war, he settled in Texas and, angered by the treatment accorded Mexicans there, led a revolt in 1859. (Library of Congress)

On November 6, 1863, Cortina, by now a general in the liberal army, interrupted his war with the French to lead the violent overthrow of the governor of the state of Tamaulipas, Manuel Ruiz. From his base in Matamoros, Cortina assumed duties as the state's governor. Until 1865, he manipulated Union and Confederate leaders for political and commercial advantages. Although Cortina momentarily switched sides as Franco-Mexican forces approached Matamoros, he escaped the punishment that usually accompanies such treason when a fellow general, Porfirio Díaz, prevented his execution.

After the war, Cortina resumed cross-border raiding on an enormous scale, stealing tens of thousands of cattle. This practice came to an end soon after Díaz became president of Mexico in 1876, however. As part of a successful effort to attract U.S. technology and investment, Díaz agreed to end Cortina's operations. He convinced Cortina to cease and desist by offering him an ample pension and a mansion in the Mexico City suburb of Atcapotzalco. Cortina then entered a peaceful retirement that continued until his death on October 30, 1894, at Atcapotzalco.

Cortina's decision to interrupt his fight against the French invaders to pursue personal gain prompted many Mexican historians to lower their opinion of him. He remains, nonetheless, a popular historical figure along both sides of the border in the Rio Grande Valley.

IRVING W. LEVINSON

See also

Ampudia, Pedro de; Guerrilla Warfare; Juárez, Benito; Monterrey, Battle of; Palo Alto, Battle of; Resaca de la Palma, Battle of; Tamaulipas; Texas

References

Leon-Portilla, Miguel, ed. *Diccionario porrúa de historia, biografía, y geografía de México.* Mexico City: Editorial Porrúa, 1997.

Thompson, Jerry. *Cortina: Defending the Mexican Name in Texas.* College Station: Texas A&M University Press, 2007.

Thompson, Jerry. *Juan Cortina and the Texas-Mexico Frontier, 1859–1877.* El Paso: Texas Western Press, 1994.

Corwin, Thomas
Birth Date: July 29, 1794
Death Date: December 18, 1865

U.S. politician, U.S. senator (1845–1850), secretary of the treasury (1850–1853), and staunch opponent of the Mexican-American War. Thomas Corwin was born on July 29, 1794, in Bourbon County, Kentucky. His father was active in local and state politics and served in several public positions, most notably as a judge.

Corwin began his career as a lawyer in western Ohio and, following several terms in the state legislature, he was elected a U.S. representative in 1830 and went on to serve five consecutive terms as a Whig. He soon earned the reputation as one of the best orators of his generation. As a moderate Whig, Corwin opposed the sectional divisiveness in his own party as well as in the nation.

In 1840 Corwin was elected governor of Ohio, but he lost his reelection bid in 1842. Two years later, he was elected to the U.S. Senate, taking office in 1845. His best-known service in the U.S. Senate occurred during the administration of James K. Polk, where his opposition to the Mexican-American War garnered much notice. Most Whigs opposed the war but strove to support the troops prosecuting it. Accordingly, Corwin voted in favor of an initial appropriations bill for the army and spoke in favor of a bill to provide land grants to soldiers who served during the war. But, as the fighting moved deeper into Mexican territory, Corwin's opposition to the conflict hardened.

Corwin's most famous speech, titled "On the Mexican War," denounced the war as unjust and accused the president of provoking Mexico and initiating the conflict, thus contravening Congress's constitutional prerogative to make war. Attacking the Polk administration's contention that territorial and financial benefits would result from the war, he argued that this assertion belied the administration's argument that it was not the aggressor in the war. He noted deceptive statements and reasons issued by the administration for going to war, and he insisted that the United States was acting in bad faith by invading another republic. Unlike many other opponents of the conflict, Corwin declared that he would vote against all future war appropriations. Corwin concluded by presciently observing that any territorial gains would only exacerbate the domestic tension caused by the question of slavery. Corwin's principled stand brought him much attention, including support from many across the nation and condemnation from many others.

While the Polk administration's prosecution of the war was not hampered by Corwin's actions, in retrospect Corwin's contrarian position proved highly perceptive. Historians have more favorably judged his interpretation of the events leading up to the war and his assessment of the relative responsibility for bringing about the conflict than his contemporaries. As Corwin predicted, the sectionalism present in 1846 was only made worse by the acquisition of new territory. His attempts to balance respect for those serving in the military with opposition to how they were employed, as well as the nature of his objections to the policies of President Polk, resonate even today.

Upon the death of President Zachary Taylor in 1850, his successor Millard Fillmore named Corwin secretary of the treasury, a post in which he served until the end of Fillmore's term in 1853. Corwin then retired to private life and resumed the practice of law. He returned to public service in 1859 as a Republican member of the House of Representatives. Elected to a second term in 1860, he was appointed by President Abraham Lincoln as minister to Mexico in March 1861. Returning to the United States in 1864, Corwin resigned his position and again took up law before his sudden death in Washington, D.C., on December 18, 1865.

JOSHUA B. MICHAEL

See also

Fillmore, Millard; Mexican Cession; Opposition to the Mexican-American War, U.S.; Polk, James Knox; Slavery; Taylor, Zachary; Whigs.

References

Carroll, Stephen Graham. *Thomas Corwin and the Agonies of the Whig Party.* Boulder: University of Colorado Press, 1970.

Morrow, Josiah, ed. *Life and Speeches of Thomas Corwin: Orator, Lawyer, and Statesman.* Cincinnati, OH: W. H. Anderson, 1896.

Cos, Martín Perfecto de
Birth Date: October 1, 1800
Death Date: October 1, 1854

Mexican army officer. Martín Perfecto de Cos was born in Veracruz on October 1, 1800, the son of an attorney. He entered the Mexican army as a cadet in 1820, and the following year he achieved the rank of lieutenant. In 1823, he supported the uprising against Emperor Agustín de Iturbide led by Antonio López de Santa Anna and subsequently rose steadily through the ranks. He became a brigadier general in 1833 and attained the rank of general by 1835. That same year he campaigned against federalist insurrectionists in Zacatecas. Cos was married to one of Santa Anna's sisters, Lucinda López.

In July 1835 Cos was appointed commander of military forces in Texas, and that September then president Santa Anna dispatched him to put down a growing revolt among the Texan colonists, who referred to themselves as Texians. General Cos dispersed the legislature of Coahuila y Texas, then in session at Monclova, and subsequently took a force of 300 men to Matagorda Bay, arriving in Texas on September 21, 1835.

Reaching the town of Goliad on October 1, Cos moved on to San Antonio where he set up his headquarters at the Alamo. There he planned to arrest troublemakers and crush the growing rebellion. Emboldened by a victory at Gonzales, however, Texan rebels under Stephen F. Austin and Edward Burleson marched to San Antonio. The Texians laid siege to San Antonio and General Cos's headquarters for more than a month. The siege depleted Cos's supplies and starved his men and animals. In December 1835, pitched house-to-house fighting at the center of San Antonio prompted Cos to surrender to the rebels. Under the terms of the capitulation, Cos agreed to withdraw his force to the Mexican interior. Under parole of honor, he and his men were allowed passage home, having promised never again to invade Texas under arms. On his way south Cos met Santa Anna's forces marching north to put down the rebellion, and he returned with them to San Antonio on February 23, 1836. Santa Anna's troops then laid siege to the Alamo, and on March 6, the day of the final assault on the former mission, Cos led a column of 300 soldiers against the northwest corner of the Alamo.

Following the Mexican victory at the Alamo, Cos met Texas's forces one final time at the Battle of San Jacinto on April 21, 1836, where he had arrived with more than 500 reinforcements for Santa Anna shortly before the battle. He was taken prisoner—1 of the 730 Mexicans who suffered that fate—on April 24 after his battalion was smashed and routed by an attack of Texas volunteers.

General Cos was released soon thereafter and eventually returned to Mexico. During the Mexican War he commanded an obscure military post in Tuxpan, Veracruz, but in the Battle of Tuxpan on April 18, 1847, was unable to halt the U.S. advance. Cos died in Minatitlán, Veracruz, on October 1, 1854, while serving as commandant general and political chief of the Tehuantepec territory in Mexico.

STEPHEN R. ORTMAN

See also

Alamo, Battle of the; Austin, Stephen Fuller; Béxar, Siege of; Burleson, Edward; Coahuila y Texas; San Antonio; San Jacinto, Battle of; Santa Anna, Antonio López de; Texas Revolution; Tuxpan; Tuxpan, Battle of.

References

Barr, Alwyn. *Texans in Revolt: The Battle for San Antonio, 1835.* Austin: University of Texas Press, 1990.

Davis, William C. *Lone Star Rising: The Revolutionary Birth of the Texas Republic.* New York: Free Press, 2004.

Roberts, Randy, and James S. Olson. *A Line in the Sand: The Alamo in Blood and Memory.* New York: Simon & Schuster, 2002.

Cotton Gin

Device developed and perfected by Eli Whitney in 1793. The cotton gin easily and quickly separated the cotton fibers from the seeds and other unwanted products, making the large-scale cultivation and marketing of short-staple cotton profitable. By making cotton a commercial success, Whitney helped to perpetuate the institution of slavery and further entrenched cotton as the bedrock of the southern economy. A need for more land for cotton cultivation also led to the forced removal of Native Americans from their lands east of the Mississippi River. The expansion of slavery led to greater tensions between northern abolitionists and southern planters, who depended on slave labor for their economic survival.

By the late 18th century, several inventors had turned to the problem of how to get seeds and other debris from cotton, as the seeds were barbed and difficult to remove. The only method available was to remove them by hand, with a comblike device. The process was slow, with one worker being able to clean only about one pound of cotton per day. Joseph Eve, a Philadelphia inventor, created a primitive cotton gin in the 1780s that was used by British planters in the West Indies. Eve's gin (short for engine) was the first to substitute mechanical energy for human energy, but it was inefficient.

The breakthrough came in 1793, when recent Yale graduate Eli Whitney was touring the South. He became acquainted with Catherine Littlefield Greene, widow of Revolutionary War major general Nathanael Greene, who told him about the need for a machine to clean cotton. Whitney decided to apply his energies to the problem. Greene offered the use of her basement and provided slaves to demonstrate how the work was done and to assist him. Within six months, Whitney had a workable model of an efficient cotton gin.

Whitney's invention consisted of a wooden cylinder with rows of spikes. The spikes meshed with a wire grid and pulled cotton fibers through the grid. The wires were too close for the cotton seeds to pass through, so they remained behind. A brush cleaned the cotton off the spikes, so it could be collected and packed into bales. The bales could then be shipped to factories that produced textiles. The process was simple once Whitney had shown the way.

Whitney was later forced to defend his patent in the courts, but blacksmiths were able to turn out copies of his gin without regard to patent laws. His hand-cranked invention could process up to 50 pounds of cotton a day. Suddenly, planters could produce marketable cotton at a rate previously unknown. The invention became a great commercial success. Before Whitney developed his cotton gin, the United States had exported 500,000 pounds of cotton per year. Ten years later, in 1803, more than 40 million pounds of cotton were exported to factories in Europe.

The increasing demand for cotton resulted in a greater demand for agricultural land on which to grow it. Southern planters coveted the lands held by the Creeks, Choctaws, Chickasaws, Cherokees, and Seminoles—the five so-called civilized tribes of the lower South—and used political and military pressure to force the Native Americans to cede parts of their territory for

The cotton gin, invented by Eli Whitney in 1793 to remove seeds from cotton. The cotton gin could clean the seeds from 50 pounds of cotton a day, a vast improvement over the single pound possible by hand. It made cotton production a great commercial success and helped perpetuate the institution of slavery. (Hulton Archive/Getty Images)

white settlement. Eventually, the Native Americans were forcibly removed to new lands west of the Mississippi River.

The growth of a cotton economy also led to more demand for slaves. Prior to 1793, slavery had seemed to be a dying institution. Without an economic need for slave labor, abolitionists hoped that it would disappear. Instead, the increase in cotton production required more slaves, and the more efficient gin could process all the cotton that slaves could harvest. Southern politicians soon advocated the spread of slavery into other territories where cotton could be grown, while abolitionists and other groups opposed it.

When the Mexican-American War began in 1846, some critics condemned it as an attempt to obtain additional territory in which to spread slavery and cotton production. The issue became sharply focused with the August 1846 introduction of the Wilmot Proviso. This piece of legislation, introduced by Representative David Wilmot, a Democrat from Pennsylvania, was added to an appropriations bill and stipulated that slavery would not be allowed to exist in any territory obtained from Mexico. Southern senators vigorously opposed the proviso, even though they had already realized that most of the territory that would likely be taken from Mexico was unsuitable for cotton cultivation. The Wilmot Proviso was defeated in the Senate in 1847 after a hard-fought battle, but was nevertheless a major step toward southern secession and the Civil War.

Tim Watts

See also

Abolitionism; Expansionism and Imperialism; Opposition to the Mexican-American War, U.S.; Slavery; Wilmot, David; Wilmot Proviso.

References

Green, Constance McL. *Eli Whitney and the Birth of American Technology*. Old Tappan, NJ: Longman, 1997.

Lakwete, Angela. *Inventing the Cotton Gin: Machine and Myth in Antebellum America*. Baltimore, MD: Johns Hopkins University Press, 2005.

Couch, Darius Nash

Birth Date: July 23, 1822
Death Date: February 12, 1897

U.S. Army officer. Darius Nash Couch was born on July 23, 1822, in Putnam County, New York. He graduated from the U.S. Military Academy, West Point, in 1846. His classmates included Civil War leaders George B. McClellan and Thomas J. "Stonewall" Jackson. Upon graduation, Couch was commissioned a second lieutenant in the 4th U.S. Artillery Regiment.

Often in precarious health, Couch could be very demanding of the men under his command. During the opening months of the Mexican-American War he was frequently bedridden, suffering from high fevers. Yet he performed admirably on February 23, 1847, during the Battle of Buena Vista, handling his own guns as well as several batteries of those under Captain John M. Washington's command. Couch went on to serve in Major General Winfield Scott's Mexico City Campaign, during which he carried his duties with considerable efficiency. In December 1847 he was brevetted first lieutenant.

In 1853, after fighting in the Second Seminole War in 1849–1850, Couch, a self-taught naturalist, took a leave of absence from the army and embarked on an expedition to Mexico, sponsored by the Smithsonian Institution. He helped gather many samples of flora, fauna, and geological specimens. Couch resigned from the army two years later and joined a copper goods manufacturing concern.

In June 1861, not long after the Civil War began, Couch became the colonel of the 7th Massachusetts Infantry. By August, he had been promoted to brigadier general. He ably led a division in IV Corps during the March–August 1862 Peninsula Campaign and was advanced to major general in July 1862. Continuing to head a division, Couch saw action during the Second Battle of Bull Run (August 29–30, 1862) and the Antietam Campaign during September 4–22, 1862. He commanded the II Corps during the Battle of Chancellorsville on May 1–4.

Frustrated with Major General Joseph Hooker's leadership of the Army of the Potomac, Couch requested a transfer, becoming commander of the newly created Department of the Susquehanna in June 1863. As such, he was in charge of Pennsylvania home guard troops who resisted Confederate general Robert E. Lee's incursion into Pennsylvania. Transferred to the west in response to General John Bell Hood's ill-starred Tennessee Campaign of 1864, Couch led a division of XXIII Corps in the Battle of Nashville

on December 15–16, 1864. He subsequently commanded operations in North Carolina.

On May 26, 1865, Couch resigned his commission, thereafter residing in Massachusetts for a time. He served briefly as head of a West Virginia mining company before moving permanently to Connecticut, where he was active in that state's militia. Couch died in Norwalk, Connecticut, on February 12, 1897.

PAUL G. PIERPAOLI JR.

See also

Buena Vista, Battle of; Mexico City Campaign; Scott, Winfield.

References

Gambone, A. M. *Major General Darius Nash Couch: Enigmatic Valor*. Baltimore, MD: Butternut & Blue, 2000.

Lavender, David. *Climax at Buena Vista: The American Campaigns in Northeastern Mexico*. New York: J. B. Lippincott, 1966.

Couto y Pérez, José Bernardo

Birth Date: December 29, 1803
Death Date: November 11, 1862

Mexican intellectual and politician, one of three Mexican representatives who signed the Treaty of Guadalupe Hidalgo on February 2, 1848, which officially ended the Mexican-American War. Born on December 29, 1803, in Orizaba, Veracruz, Mexico, José Bernardo Couto y Pérez moved to Mexico City in 1817 to study at the Colegio de San Ildefonso. He graduated with a law degree in 1827 and briefly served as a representative in the Mexican congress in 1828. That same year, he was appointed a professor of law at the Colegio de San Ildefonso, where he published several books on art, poetry, and literature. Couto was briefly minister of justice in 1845.

In August 1847, after the Battles of Contreras and Churubusco had been won by the United States, American troops led by Major General Winfield Scott arrived at the gates of Mexico City. On August 24, 1847, a truce (the Armistice of Tacubaya) went into effect, and U.S. special envoy Nicholas Trist met with four Mexican commissioners—General José Joaquín Herrera, Ignacio Mora y Villamil, Miguel Atristain Barroeta, and Couto—to discuss the terms of a peace treaty. General Antonio López de Santa Anna, who was still president, however, disagreed with the proposed terms, specifically the cession of the New Mexico Territory.

As a result, the Mexican-American War resumed on September 6, 1847, and Scott's subsequent capture of Mexico City led to Santa Anna's ouster from power. In November 1847 the new Mexican government, now led by *moderado* (moderate) president Manuel Peña y Peña, decided to reopen negotiations with Trist. Notwithstanding the fact that President James K. Polk had issued an order for him to leave Mexico, Trist remained to renew discussions for a peace treaty. Couto was among those who urged Trist to ignore Polk's order and continue the negotiations, which were conducted in the town of Guadalupe Hidalgo on the outskirts of Mexico City.

The Mexicans were represented in the negotiations by Couto, Atristain, and former minister of foreign relations Luis Gonzaga Cuevas. The Mexican commissioners were willing to agree to all of the American demands, save for the cession of Baja California. Although many Mexicans were furious that the commission granted so many territorial concessions to the Americans, Couto argued that giving way was necessary to prevent the United States from annexing all Mexico (the "All of Mexico" movement), and that the Treaty of Guadalupe Hidalgo should be viewed as a treaty of recovery rather than a treaty of alienation. Couto contended that Mexico would still retain considerable territory occupied by the Americans and only cede territories that were virtually uninhabited and uncultivated. On February 2, 1848, therefore, Trist, Couto, Atristain, and Cuevas signed the treaty and sent it off to their respective governments for ratification. On May 30, 1848, the United States, represented by Nathan Clifford, and Mexico, represented by Luis de la Rosa, exchanged ratifications of the Treaty of Guadalupe Hidalgo.

Couto then returned to his academic career, and in 1853 the Mexican government (then headed by Santa Anna in what would be his last term as president) selected him and two others as jurors charged with selecting the words for the Mexican national anthem. The next year the committee chose the entry submitted by Francisco González Bocanegra, which alluded to Mexican victories in battle and the defense of the homeland. Couto continued his scholarly activities until his death in Mexico City on November 11, 1862.

MICHAEL R. HALL

See also
All of Mexico Movement; Churubusco, Battle of; Clifford, Nathan; Contreras, Battle of; Cuevas, Luis Gonzago; Herrera, José Joaquín de; Guadalupe Hidalgo, Treaty of; Mexico City, Battle of; Mora y Villamil, Igacio de; Polk, James Knox; Peña y Peña, Manuel de la; Rosa Oteiza, Luis de la; Santa Anna, Antonio López de; Scott, Winfield; Tacubaya, Armistice of; Trist, Nicholas Philip.

References
Costeloe, Michael P. *The Central Republic in Mexico, 1835–1846: Hombres de Bien in the Age of Santa Anna.* Cambridge, UK: Cambridge University Press, 2002.
Griswold del Castillo, Richard. *The Treaty of Guadalupe-Hidalgo: A Legacy of Conflict.* Norman: University of Oklahoma, 1992.

Crabb, Henry Alexander
Birth Date: ca. 1823
Death Date: April 7, 1857

U.S. attorney, politician, journalist, and filibusterer. Henry Alexander Crabb was born near Nashville, Tennessee, circa 1823, to a prominent and well-to-do family. His father, Henry Crabb Sr., was a Tennessee State Supreme Court justice. Not much is known about Crabb's early years, but by 1845 he had been admitted to the bar in Mississippi and had opened a law practice that same year in Vicksburg. In 1848 he was charged with killing a political opponent, although a jury later found him not guilty.

In 1849, Crabb decided to leave his troubled past and seek his fortunes in California. He soon became the editor of the *Stockton Argus* and by 1853 was sufficiently well known to be elected to the California state senate, where he served until 1854. In 1855 and again in 1856, Crabb ran unsuccessfully for a seat in the U.S. Senate as a candidate of the Know-Nothing Party. As a youth, Crabb had known the noted filibuster William Walker and had hoped to join one of his expeditions, but Walker had refused Crabb's offers. Nevertheless, Crabb sought to emulate his old friend, as both men believed that a filibustering expedition into Mexico might well succeed given the weakness and instability of Mexico's government.

In the meantime, Crabb had wisely married into an elite Californio family with tight political connections with the northwestern Mexican state of Sonora. Indeed, his father-in-law was a close friend of Ignacio Pesqueira, the leader of one of Sonora's chief political factions. Crabb cultivated a relationship with Pesqueira, and, after understanding that Pesqueira would welcome an expedition of American colonizers into Sonora, began mobilizing a filibustering force in Southern California and Arizona. Some scholars have posited that Pesqueira may have offered Crabb an extensive land grant in northern Sonora in exchange for his political support while others believe that Pesqueira had not authorized a colonization venture in Sonora, but that Crabb may have understood otherwise.

Crabb formed the Arizona Colonization Company in 1856, but by the end of the year, enjoying uncontested power in Sonoran politics, Pesqueira disavowed any links with Crabb's colonization efforts. Even without Pesqueira's support, Crabb gathered a force of about 100 men in Los Angeles in January 1857 and was poised to enter Sonora. By the time his force had reached the U.S.-Mexican border, Crabb had received word that Pesqueira would resist the filibustering expedition by force of arms.

Undeterred, Crabb continued on and entered northern Sonora late that winter. A local militia unit intercepted Crabb's party near Hermosillo on April 6 and captured most of the Americans, including Crabb. All captives were summarily executed the next day. Crabb's head was severed, placed in a jar filled with mescal, and put on display at the town hall, a grim reminder to other Americans who might harbor filibustering sentiments.

PAUL G. PIERPAOLI JR.

See also
California; Filibusters; Know-Nothing Party; Sonora y Sinaloa; Walker, William.

References
Forbes, Robert H. *Crabb's Filibustering Expedition into Sonora, 1857.* Tucson: Arizona Silhouettes, 1952.
Stout, Joseph A. *The Liberators: Filibustering Expeditions into Mexico, 1848–1862, and the Last Thrust of Manifest Destiny.* Los Angeles: Westernlore Press, 1973.

Criolla, Destruction of the
Event Date: November 26, 1846

Taking advantage of the fact that most of the blockading U.S. Home Squadron was off station at Tampico with only the brig *Somers* (16 guns) maintaining the American blockade there, the captain of the Mexican schooner *Criolla* sailed into Veracruz, anchoring under the guns of the San Juan de Ulúa fortress.

With the members of his crew upset over this event, the commander of the *Somers,* Lieutenant Raphael Semmes, authorized an attempt to cut out the Mexican schooner. On the night of November 26, he sent in a boat with eight volunteers led by Lieutenant James L. Parker. The American boarding party had no problem capturing the *Criolla* and its crew shortly before midnight, but the noise alerted one of the sentinels at San Juan de Ulúa, who called out to ask what was transpiring. Parker, pretending to be the Mexican captain, replied in excellent Spanish that the men had become drunk and he was having them placed in irons.

Unfortunately for the Americans, when they were ready to sail the schooner out to the *Somers,* there was no wind. Parker was therefore forced to set the schooner on fire, destroying it. The Americans escaped to the *Somers* under a hail of fire from San Juan de Ulúa, bringing with them seven Mexican prisoners. Unfortunately, it was later learned that the *Criolla* was a spy ship, which had sailed to Veracruz with the blessing of the U.S. Home Squadron commander Commodore David Conner.

SPENCER C. TUCKER

See also

Conner, David; Semmes, Raphael; *Somers,* U.S. Navy Brig; Tampico and Victoria, Occupation of.

References

Bauer, K. Jack. *Surfboats and Horse Marines: U.S. Naval Operations in the Mexican War, 1846–48.* Annapolis, MD: United States Naval Institute, 1969.

Semmes, Raphael. *Service Afloat and Ashore during the Mexican War.* Cincinnati, OH: W. H. Moore, 1851.

Crockett, David
Birth Date: August 17, 1786
Death Date: 1836

Soldier, frontiersman, politician, and one of the best-known frontier folk heroes of the 19th century. David (Davy) Crockett was born into a poor frontier family on August 17, 1786, in Greene County in eastern Tennessee. He rarely attended school and was hired out by his father in 1798 to help on a cattle drive to Virginia. Crockett ran away when his employer tried to keep him against his will. He made his way back to Tennessee but soon was off again on his own.

Crockett married in August 1806 and moved to middle Tennessee in 1811. He moved his family to his first home outside the mountains in Franklin County in south central Tennessee. Crockett proved to be a poor farmer, but he was an excellent hunter. In 1813, he joined the Tennessee militia units headed to Alabama following the massacre at Fort Mims and participated in Major General Andrew Jackson's campaign against the Red Stick faction of the Creeks. He apparently served primarily as a scout and guard for the horse herds. After his first enlistment expired, he returned home but reenlisted in the late summer of 1814, spending the fall of that year at Pensacola.

After the war, Crockett was elected a lieutenant in the 32nd Militia Regiment of Franklin County. His wife died that summer, and Crockett married a widow with two children the following year. In 1817 they moved to Lawrence County, Tennessee. Crockett soon established himself there and was appointed justice of the peace. He apparently used stories about his exploits in the war against the Creeks to enhance his reputation. He was elected colonel of the 57th Militia Regiment in 1818 and three years later was elected to the state legislature. He won reelection in 1823 but was defeated in 1825. Although Crockett lacked formal schooling, he was not as illiterate as the public image that he had created, and he established himself as a supporter of settlers' rights on public lands.

In 1827 Crockett was elected to the U.S. House of Representatives. He campaigned as an honest country boy who was an

Frontiersman, soldier, and political figure David ("Davy") Crockett became a mythic American figure as a coinsequence of the Battle of the Alamo on March 6, 1836. (Library of Congress)

outstanding hunter and "straight shooter" in every sense of the phrase. Crockett soon became a noted member of the House thanks to his backwoods persona. Strangers called him "Davy," a name appropriate to that image.

Crockett's support for settlers' rights, for the Bank of the United States, and against Native American removal brought him into conflict with President Andrew Jackson. The anti-Jackson faction, later to become the Whig Party, took interest in Crockett as a potential national candidate. He was reelected to the House in 1829 but defeated in 1831. With the Whigs' support, Crockett won reelection in 1833.

In 1833 a book of frontier stories, titled *Sketches and Eccentricities of Colonel David Crockett of West Tennessee,* made its appearance. Supposedly written by Crockett, it was in fact ghosted by an anonymous Whig and was enormously popular. The book made Crockett into a folk hero among eastern readers. Although Crockett probably supplied many of the stories, he was apparently embarrassed by the extent to which the truth was bent. He then wrote, with help, his own autobiography, titled *A Narrative of the Life of David Crockett of the State of Tennessee.* Published in 1834, the book could be viewed as a campaign biography for a future run for the presidency. Crockett spent a month traveling through the Northeast to promote the book and to make himself known to voters. In his autobiography, Crockett again portrayed himself as a simple frontiersman, honest and straightforward, who stood up for the ordinary man, rather than a politician.

Nonetheless, Crockett's opposition to Jackson led ultimately to his political demise, and he was defeated in the election of August 1835. That November he and a small party left for Texas to seek their fortunes, and in early February 1836 he arrived in San Antonio, where he joined the garrison of the Alamo. He died there on March 6, 1836, when the fortress was overwhelmed by Mexican forces under General Antonio López de Santa Anna. All that is certain is that he died at the Alamo that day, but the exact manner remains in dispute. José Enrique de la Peña's diary states that a handful of the defenders, including Crockett, were taken prisoner, but that an incensed Santa Anna ordered their execution. However, Ben, a former African American slave and cook for one of the Mexican officers, recounted that Crockett's body was found in the barracks surrounded by no fewer than 16 Mexican corpses and that Crockett's knife was found buried in one of them. Regardless of how he died, Crockett's frontiersman reputation long survived him; he remains part of American legend to this day.

TIM WATTS

See also
Alamo, Battle of the; de la Peña, José Enrique; Santa Anna, Antonio López de; Texas; Texas Revolution; Whigs.

References
Davis, William C. *Three Roads to the Alamo: The Lives and Fortunes of David Crockett, James Bowie, and William Barret Travis.* New York: HarperCollins, 1998.
Kilgore, Dan. *How Did Davy Die?* College Station: Texas A&M University Press, 2010.
Lofaro, Michael A. *Davy Crockett: The Man, the Legend, the Legacy.* Knoxville: University of Tennessee Press, 1985.
Long, Jeff. *Duel of Eagles: The Mexican and U.S. Fight for the Alamo.* New York: William Morrow, 1990.

Cross, Trueman
Birth Date: ca. 1795
Death Date: 1846

U.S. Army officer. Trueman Cross was born in Prince George's County, Maryland, circa 1795. Little is known of his youth. In April 1814 he joined the 42nd Infantry Regiment as an ensign but was probably not involved directly in any actions during the closing months of the War of 1812. Cross was reportedly a fine soldier with an eye for detail and keen organizational abilities. By 1818, at the rank of captain, he had become assistant deputy quartermaster general. In 1826, he was advanced to major, and in 1838 he became assistant quartermaster general with the rank of colonel. In 1825, Cross published *Military Laws of the United States,* a compendium of legal and procedural guidelines for U.S. soldiers and marines.

When the Mexican-American War began in 1846, Cross was serving as Brigadier General Zachary Taylor's chief quartermaster in charge of all logistics for the Army of Occupation, a post he had held since the previous October. Cross, in fact, had been stationed with the army at Corpus Christi since his arrival. In March 1846 President James K. Polk ordered Taylor's force to move south and take up positions along the Rio Grande, and by the month's end Corpus Christi had been all but abandoned while a new camp had been erected along the river.

On April 10, 1846, Cross left the camp on a leisurely horseback ride along the riverbank. Several hours later, it was noted that he had failed to return to camp. Concerned that Cross was lost, Taylor ordered his men to fire a cannon so that Cross might reorient himself, but Cross never returned. About a week later, a scouting party came across Cross's coat in some scrub vegetation. A week after that, on April 21, a Mexican farmer found Cross's remains. His skull had been bashed in and his clothes stripped from his body, but it was impossible to tell how long he had been dead. It is widely posited that Cross died at the hands of Mexican *banditti* (bandits) who operated in the Rio Grande Valley. Some have attributed the killing to the bandit Rámon Falcón.

Cross's body was taken to Fort Texas for burial on April 24, where he was accorded full military honors, including a caisson with six horses. Hundreds of Mexicans viewed the ceremony from across the Rio Grande. Cross is considered to be the first U.S. casualty of the Mexican-American War.

PAUL G. PIERPAOLI JR.

See also
Banditry; Corpus Christi; Falcón, Rámon; Polk, James Knox; Rio Grande; Taylor, Zachary.

References
Henry, Robert Selph. *The Story of the Mexican War.* Indianapolis: Bobbs-Merrill, 1951.
Weems, John Edward. *To Conquer a Peace: The War Between the United States and Mexico.* College Station: Texas A&M University Press, 1988.

Cuba

Island archipelago located in the West Indies surrounded by the Gulf of Mexico and the Caribbean Sea. Cuba is part of the Greater Antilles, lies just 90 miles south of the Florida coast, and at the time of the Mexican-American War was a Spanish colonial possession. Mainland Cuba and Isla de la Juventud are the two of the most significant islands, with more than 4,000 smaller islands, islets, and cays in the surrounding bays and waters. Cuba's territory covers 42,804 square miles. The main island is 708 miles long and 135 miles wide and has a coastline approximately 2,100 miles long. Havana has been the Cuban capital since colonial times.

During the 1840s Cuba's estimated population was about 1 million people, with slaves comprising about 40 percent of that figure. Reflecting its Spanish heritage, Catholicism was the official religion at the time. Presently, about 11.45 million persons inhabit the island, about 65 percent of European descent, 24 percent mestizo or mixed race, 10 percent African, and 1 percent Asian, with Spanish as the official language. There is currently no official religion, although Catholicism remains an integral part of many Cubans' lives.

Initially, various Native American groups, including the Taino and the Ciboney, inhabited the island. Spanish settlers arrived after Christopher Columbus claimed the land during his first voyage of exploration in 1492. For most of the colonial period Cuba was a relatively minor Spanish colony, but it became far more important after Spain's other American colonies gained their independence between 1815 and 1826. Indeed, Cuba remained Spain's last colony in the Western Hemisphere until 1898, at which point it became nominally independent as a consequence of the Spanish-American War.

Most Latin American officials saw Spanish-held Cuba as a potential threat to their nations' interests. Mexicans were especially leery, particularly after the Spanish invaded Tampico in 1829 with an expedition that was launched from Havana. At the same time, Cuba became a favored place where exiled Mexicans, like Antonio López de Santa Anna, went for asylum or planned political comebacks. Indeed, Santa Anna, exiled to Cuba in 1845, offered to aid Mexico's war efforts while at the same time negotiating an agreement with the United States to end hostilities and transfer Alta California and Nuevo Mexico to the Americans if they allowed him passage through the naval blockade. Despite having provided safe passage for Santa Anna, the Americans received neither the land nor an end to the war, as the general subsequently led Mexican troops against U.S. forces. Brigadier General William Jenkins Worth, commander of the U.S. 1st Division during the Mexican-American War, agreed to lead an invasion of Cuba by Mexican-American War veterans shortly after the war ended in 1848, but he was transferred and then died in 1849.

In the aftermath of the Mexican-American War, Spain continued to govern Cuba; and the United States, which had been interested in acquiring Cuba during much of its early history, an interest that principally manifested itself through attempted negotiations or filibustering expeditions (neither of which proved successful), continued to eye the island covetously.

In 1854, U.S. minister to Spain Pierre Soule urged U.S. secretary of state William L. Marcy to push for the purchase of Cuba from the Spanish. The resulting Ostend Manifesto (so named after the city in Belgium where it was signed) called for the peaceful acquisition of Cuba for $130 million. Should that proposal fail, the manifesto recommended that the United States invoke the 1823 Monroe Doctrine and invade Cuba. Marcy ultimately rejected the proposal, realizing that building sectional tensions would have made it virtually impossible for the United States to seize Cuba without serious domestic political repercussions.

During the next half century Cubans themselves began agitating for independence from Spain, but despite several revolts, Spain maintained its hold over the island until 1898, when U.S. troops and Cuban revolutionary forces defeated Spain. At first American forces occupied and governed the island for approximately three years, and on May 20, 1902, Cubans finally took control over their own affairs. However, the United States retained the right to intervene in Cuba's internal affairs (through the Platt Amendment, which was finally abrogated in 1934) and acquired a long-term lease over territory at Guantanamo Bay, which the United States still maintains as a naval base and, since 2001, as a prison camp for terror suspects.

WYNDHAM E. WHYNOT

See also
Mexico; Santa Anna, Antonio López de; Tampico; Worth, William Jenkins.

References
Cluster, Dick, and Rafael Hernandez. *The History of Havana.* New York: Palgrave Macmillan, 2006.
Henken, Ted A. *Cuba: A Global Studies Handbook.* Santa Barbara, CA: ABC-CLIO, 2007.
Staten, Clifford L. *The History of Cuba.* New York: Palgrave Macmillan, 2005.

Cuevas, Luis Gonzaga

Birth Date: 1800
Death Date: 1867

Important Mexican diplomat and influential conservative writer. Luis Gonzaga Cuevas was born to an affluent family in the town of Lerma in the state of Mexico. He received his law degree from Mexico City's finest school, the Colegio de San Ildefonso. At age 35, Cuevas began his political and administrative career at the secretariat of the prefecture of Mexico. Only a year later, in 1836, he was named minister of foreign affairs, a post he held for less than a year.

While traveling in Europe on state business, Cuevas met and befriended the deposed centralist politician and ex-Mexican president Anastasio Bustamante. When Bustamante returned to power in 1837, after General Antonio López de Santa Anna's defeat in Texas, he appointed Cuevas foreign minister (ex officio prime minister), a post he held for one year. Bustamante also appointed Cuevas minister plenipotentiary to France during the first French intervention in Mexico, known as the Pastry War (1838–1839). Before leaving public service in 1839, Cuevas wrote a report that sharply denounced the expansionist policies of Texas and the United States.

Just prior to the Mexican-American War, Cuevas served as foreign minister in the administration of President José Joaquín Herrera, a *moderado* federalist who was overthrown in December 1845 by centralist general Mariano Paredes y Arrillaga. As such, Cuevas struck a cautious note on the prospect of a war with the United States, inflaming *puro* nationalists who already distrusted Cuevas for his conservatism. At the end of the war, Cuevas played an important role in the crafting of the Treaty of Guadalupe Hidalgo as one of three official Mexican agents who negotiated the agreement with Nicholas Trist. In the Mexican congress, Cuevas defended the treaty against the opposition of notable leaders such as Melchor Ocampo, Manuel Crecencio Rejón, Benito Juárez, and his own brother, José María Cuevas.

Cuevas again served as foreign secretary under President Herrera (1848–1849), and General Félix Zuloaga (1858). But even more important, in 1851 Cuevas published a landmark work of conservative historiography, *The Future of Mexico: An Assessment of Its Political State in 1821 and 1851* (1851), which celebrated religion as a foundational, spiritual guarantor of peace, prosperity, and progress. Contrary to his liberal contemporaries, whose nationalist vision of the era of independence was based on the celebration of Miguel Hidalgo y Costilla, Cuevas's book celebrated the example of Emperor Agustín de Iturbide. The work also pointed out the shortfalls of Mexico, which had led to its defeat to the United States and other crises.

Cuevas's sterling credentials as a conservative and his extensive diplomatic experience attracted the attention of Emperor Maximilian I and his supporters during the second French intervention (1864–1867). Nevertheless, the aged Cuevas, deeply disillusioned by the foreign occupation of his country, refused to serve as a member of Maximilian's Junta of Notables, or his Imperial Council. Cuevas died in 1867 in Mexico City.

CHRISTOPHER CONWAY

See also

Bustamante y Oseguera, Anastasio; Guadalupe Hidalgo, Treaty of; Herrera, José Joaquín de; Juárez, Benito; Mexico, 1821–1854; *Moderados*; Ocampo, Melchor; Paredes y Arrillaga, Mariano; Pastry War; Politics, Mexican; *Puros*; Rejón, Manuel Crecencio; Trist, Nicholas Philip.

References

Cuevas, Luis Gonzaga. *Porvenir de México: Juicio sobre su Estado Político en 1821 y 1851.* Mexico City: Imprenta de Ignacio Cumplido, 1851.
Diccionario Porrúa de historia, biografía y geografía de México. Mexico City: Editorial Porrúa, 1964.
Pérez Rosales, Laura. *Luis Gonzaga Cuevas.* Mexico City: Patrimonio Cultural y Artístico del Estado de México, 1979.

Cult of Domesticity

During the years between the War of 1812 and the Civil War, a movement later labeled the cult of domesticity helped shape and define the private and public roles of white women and men in the United States. According to this viewpoint, women were required to remain within the confines of the home to establish and uphold a private and safe sphere of influence as nurturing mothers, domesticated homemakers, and virtuous wives. Men were expected to work outside the home in the public domain of the marketplace or other career choice and to serve in the military if need be.

The publicized expectations of women could be readily found within the pages of contemporary newspapers and periodicals throughout the United States, including women's magazines, popular fiction novels, and religious handbooks. These materials identified the American woman as a compassionate mother who established the home as a safe haven for her children and as a sexually submissive wife who provided the domestic comforts for her husband upon his return from the rough and dangerous world of the workplace or the violent arena of the war front.

Within the home, women were expected to raise children who would epitomize the American ideals of good character, patriotic citizenship, and Christian morals. During the nineteenth century, women were often understood as embodying moral superiority compared to men, thus requiring wives to maintain a virtuous environment in order to keep their husbands interested in religion and pious activity. As a result, women were understood to have been created for work in the private realm of the home as mothers and wives who avoided politics and the business world in order to invest their energies and sympathies for the care and uplifting of their children and support of their husbands. To be sure, American women during the Mexican-American War exemplified the cult of domesticity and almost always clung to their prescribed social, cultural, and sexual roles.

CHRISTOPHER J. ANDERSON

See also
Women, Mexican; Women, U.S.

References
Clinton, Catherine. *The Other Civil War: American Women in the Nineteenth Century.* Rev. ed. New York: Hill & Wang, 1999.
Matthews, Glenna. *"Just a Housewife": The Rise and Fall of Domesticity in America.* New York: Oxford University Press, 1987.
Welter, Barbara. "The Cult of True Womanhood: 1820–1860." *American Quarterly* 18, no. 2 (Summer 1966): 151–174.

Currier, Nathaniel
Birth Date: March 27, 1813
Death Date: November 20, 1888

Noted American lithographer who depicted the Mexican-American War in numerous lithographs, and with his partner James Ives, the Civil War, the American Revolutionary War, and other subjects, including portraits and landscapes. Born in Roxbury, Massachusetts, on March 27, 1813, Nathaniel Currier began his career as an apprentice in 1828 and went on to establish his reputation in the late 1830s and 1840s as a leading lithographer of American scenes, history, and current events. He described these as "Colored Engravings for the People." One such event was the dramatic fire that destroyed Planters Hotel in New Orleans and killed 10 persons, the print of which appeared in 1835. In 1852, Currier entered a partnership with James Merritt Ives to form the celebrated lithographic publishing company of Currier and Ives. Currier is credited with developing new lithographic techniques in the creation of prints, standardizing the process of production, developing new lithographic crayons for colorization, and above all greatly improving the marketing and distribution of prints.

The outbreak of war with Mexico in 1846 provided an ideal outlet for prints depicting a contemporary event. During this conflict, lithographic publishers were eager to produce prints of the battles and portraits of the leading commanders that would find a ready market among the art-buying public and provide reassurance. Currier along with his rivals, Napoleon Sarony, Henry B. Major, James S. Baillie, and David W. Kellogg, emerged as leading purveyors of lithographic prints during this period.

Currier, more than his competitors, single-handedly created a market for prints of the Mexican-American War. He published a total of 70 lithographs depicting scenes of the war, many of which appeared shortly after the actual events. These prints, therefore, were remarkable for their currency. The fact that so many were published suggests that there was a ready market for such iconography. He employed a large pool of talented artists, but their names were not included on the finished prints with one exception, that of John Cameron who in fact was not the artist but the lithographer.

The artists would take eyewitness descriptions of the battles published in the New York press such as the *Herald* and work them up into dramatic and spirited scenes. The finished prints sometimes included an extract from the press account. In the 1847 print titled *Landing of the American Forces under Genl. Scott at Verza Cruz, March 9th 1847,* the caption was followed by a quote describing the landing and the planting of the colors.

Some of the craftsmen who worked for Currier went on to develop their own lithographic businesses, although they often deferred to his marketing savvy to distribute their own prints and in some cases used designs by Currier. A print published by Sarony and Major in 1846 titled *Repulsion of the Mexicans, and Bombardment of Matamoras . . .* is the same plate published by Currier under the title *The Bombardment of Matamoras, May, 1847, by the U.S. Troops under Major Brown.* Prints showing individual deeds of valor were a popular subject, such as the Capture of Mexican general Rómulo Díaz de la Vega, and the deaths of Colonel Pierce M. Butler, Lieutenant Colonel Henry Clay, and Major Samuel Ringgold. Currier also published two naval scenes, one showing the bombardment of Veracruz, the other an attack by U.S. gunboats on the city of San Juan de Ulúa.

While Currier is remembered chiefly for his collaboration with Ives and the numerous lithographs that their company produced from the 1850s onward, especially 80 scenes of the Civil War, the prints he published during the war with Mexico are worthy of study. While the majority of these popular lithographs were highly inaccurate representations of the major battles, with the exception of the portraits of the leading commanders such as Winfield Scott and Zachary Taylor, they were based on newspaper accounts and tried to present a realistic impression of the events but often in the heroic and glorious style common to the period. Beyond this, they offered little reliable information.

It is also interesting to note that the Mexican soldiers were depicted fighting valiantly, a reflection of actuality. Many of the scenes contain close-up hand-to-hand fighting offering excitement. As such, they provided a misleading idea of war to a populace at home.

Currier continued his work with Currier and Ives until his death on November 20, 1888, at Amesbury, Massachusetts.

PETER HARRINGTON

See also
Art.

References
Sandweiss, Martha A., Rick Stewart, and Ben W. Huseman. *Eyewitness to War. Prints and Daguerreotypes of the Mexican War, 1846–1848.* Fort Worth, TX: Amon Carter Museum, 1989.
Tyler, Ronnie C. *The Mexican War. A Lithographic Record.* Austin: Texas State Historical Association, 1973.

Pratt, John Lowell, ed. *Currier & Ives Chronicles of America*. Maplewood, NJ: Hammond, 1968.

Cushing, Caleb
Birth Date: January 17, 1800
Death Date: January 2, 1879

American politician, lawyer, and diplomat who represented Massachusetts in the U.S. House of Representatives (1835–1843) and served as attorney general in the Franklin Pierce administration (1853–1857). During the Mexican War, he privately raised funds to support a regiment of soldiers from Massachusetts. He commanded them as a colonel and was later a brigadier general. Caleb Cushing was born in Salisbury, Massachusetts, on January 17, 1800, the son of a wealthy merchant and shipbuilder. His mother died when he was 10. Intellectually precocious and well read, he entered Harvard College at the age of 13 and graduated in 1817. In December 1821 he was admitted to practice in the court of common pleas and three years later began a private practice in Newburyport, Massachusetts. Inclined toward politics, he served as a Democratic-Republican member of the Massachusetts House of Representatives in 1825 and the state senate a year later. Cushing then spent two years in Europe (1829–1831), and he returned to the state legislature until he gained election to the U.S. House of Representatives in 1834.

Cushing remained in the House as a member of the Whig Party until 1843, not having been renominated in 1842. On May 8, 1843, President John Tyler appointed him minister plenipotentiary to China as well as commissioner. In his new capacity, he negotiated the Treaty of Wanghia, the first diplomatic agreement between China and the United States and the first one to deal with trade issues between the two governments. Cushing was also given authority to negotiate a treaty of navigation and commerce with Japan.

Returning to the Massachusetts state legislature in 1847, he supported President James K. Polk's war against Mexico. Although loyal to his Whig leaders, Cushing introduced a bill in the state legislature appropriating money for the equipment of a regiment to serve in the Mexican-American War. The bill was defeated by antiwar Whigs in his state party and the general feeling among many New Englanders that Polk's imperial ambitions would only lead to the expansion of slavery further westward. Not to be deterred, he raised the necessary funds privately and served as the colonel of a Massachusetts regiment that marched into Mexico. Polk subsequently appointed him a brigadier general. Cushing did not see any action during the war, and the reserve unit he led entered Mexico City only after it had been secured.

Cushing ran unsuccessfully as the Democratic candidate for governor in 1847 and again in 1848; again elected to the state house of representatives in 1850, he was the mayor of Newburyport, Massachusetts, during 1851–1852 and was appointed an associate justice of the Massachusetts Supreme Court in 1852.

From March 7, 1853, to March 3, 1857, Cushing served in the Franklin Pierce administration as the 23rd attorney general of the United States. During the Civil War, he again served in the Massachusetts legislature. From 1866 to 1870, he was a commissioner appointed by President Andrew Johnson to codify the laws of the United States. In 1868, he was instructed to negotiate a treaty with the minister resident to Colombia for a ship canal across the Panamanian Isthmus. In 1872, President Ulysses S. Grant selected Cushing consul for the United States before the Geneva Tribunal of Arbitration on the *Alabama* claims. Although his appointment to become chief justice of the U.S. Supreme Court was blocked in 1874, Cushing continued serving his nation as minister to Spain from January 6, 1874 to April 9, 1877. His efforts helped defuse the *Virginius* Affair, a diplomatic dispute between the United States and Great Britain arising from the involvement of an American-flagged vessel in delivering arms to Cuban insurgents in violation of the international laws of neutrality.

Patrician in background and purpose, Cushing also authored a number of books including the *Life and Public Services of William H. Harrison* (1840) and *The Treaty of Washington* (1873). He died on January 2, 1879, at Newburyport, Massachusetts, his place of residence.

CHARLES F. HOWLETT

See also
Mexico City, Battle for; Mexico City Campaign; Whigs.

References
Belohlavek, John M. *Broken Glass: Caleb Cushing and the Shattering of the Union*. Kent, OH: Kent State University Press, 2005.
Fuess, Claude M. *The Life of Caleb Cushing*. 2 vols. New York: Harcourt, Brace, 1923.
Kuo, Ping Chia. "Caleb Cushing and the Treaty of Wanghia, 1844." *Journal of Modern History* 5, no. 1 (1933): 34–54.
Smith, Justin. *The War with Mexico*, 2 vols. New York: Macmillan, 1919.

D

Daguerreotypes

Daguerreotypes were the first large-scale, commercially viable photographs. Modern photography began as an attempt by artists to record an image of a subject that they could then use as a reference as they painted. What was intended as an artist's aid soon became an art form itself.

The man most credited with developing modern photography was the Frenchman Louis-Jacques-Mandé Daguerre, who lived from 1787 to 1851. A chemist and an artist, Daguerre discovered that a copper plate bathed in iodine fumes would enable a positive image to form on the plate when exposed to light. Being a positive image (meaning that no negative was made) meant that each exposure produced a unique picture. News of Daguerre's discovery became public in January 1839. From Paris, the process quickly spread to the rest of Europe and to North America. Photographs produced by this method became known as daguerreotypes in recognition of Daguerre.

The American inventor Samuel F. Morse, who is perhaps best known for developing and patenting the telegraph, also holds the title of the "Father of American Photography." An artist of considerable repute himself, Morse had also experimented with capturing images, and in early 1839 he happened to be in Paris and met Daguerre. The two men engaged in a lengthy discussion about early photographic processes. Upon returning to the United States, Morse and a partner opened a daguerreotype studio in New York City around 1840. Soon many cities and towns boasted of their own photographic "parlors." In addition, itinerant daguerreotypists loaded their new cameras into wagons, introducing Americans throughout the countryside to the wonders of photography.

Photography also helped advance democracy. Prior to photography, only the wealthy or famous sat for artists, who were paid

U.S. Army captain James Duncan of Illinois received three brevets—major, lieutenant colonel, and colonel—for his actions in the Mexican-American War. This daguerrotype of him as a colonel was made sometime between late 1846 and 1849 and produced by Mathew Brady's studio. (Library of Congress)

considerable sums of money to paint their portraits. Common people were rarely represented in art unless an artist chose specifically to paint them. The images of most of mankind, then, went unrecorded. Although photography began as an expensive process available only to the wealthy and famous, it followed the course of technology in general until the price became affordable to the general population. Thus, photography, first through the daguerreotype then through subsequent methods, made it possible for the small farmer, laborer, mill worker, and enlisted soldier to preserve their likenesses for their contemporaries and ultimately for future generations to view.

The development of the daguerreotype came just at the right time for the officers and men who participated in the Mexican-American War. Men departing for the front often had their pictures taken for their friends and families before they left home. Additionally, numerous daguerreotypists traveled to Mexico to offer their services to soldiers in the field. Although the process was not able to capture shots on the battlefield, shutter speeds being much too slow to capture action, a number of officers and soldiers had their pictures taken at temporary daguerreotype parlors set up in occupied towns in Mexico.

When the image was captured, the metal plate on which the image appeared was placed in a small leather and wooden case which was covered for safekeeping. A piece of glass was placed over the metal plate because moisture or hand oils would damage the picture. Unfortunately, only a small number of Mexican-American War daguerreotypes have been located by museums and private collectors. Although Mexico had its own daguerreotypists, hardly any of their work seems to exist. The crystal clear image of existing daguerreotypes, however, gives historians and students of history an important graphic reference that literally shows the human face of warfare. Beginning in the 1850s, ambrotypes, which were much less costly and easier to produce, began to supersede daguerreotypes in popularity, and by the early 1860s hardly anyone produced daguerreotypes.

BRUCE WINDERS

See also
Art; Lithographs; Morse, Samuel Finley Breese.

References
Barger, M. Susan, and William B. White. *The Daguerreotype: Nineteenth-Century Technology and Modern Science.* Baltimore, MD: Johns Hopkins University Press, 2000.
Sandweiss, Martha A., Rick Stewart, and Ben W. Huseman. *Eyewitness to War: Prints and Daguerreotypes of the Mexican War, 1846–1848.* Fort Worth, TX: Amon Carter Museum, 1989.

Dallas, George Mifflin
Birth Date: July 10, 1792
Death Date: December 31, 1864

Attorney and Democratic politician who served as U.S. senator from Pennsylvania (1831–1833) and vice president of the United

States during the administration of James K. Polk (1845–1849). Born on July 10, 1792, in Philadelphia, Pennsylvania, George Mifflin Dallas graduated from Princeton University in 1810 and was admitted to the Pennsylvania bar three years later. He served as the mayor of Philadelphia from 1828 to 1829 and as district attorney for the eastern district of Pennsylvania from 1829 to 1831.

In December 1831 Dallas was selected to fill the vacancy in the U.S. Senate created by Isaac D. Bernard's resignation. Dallas left the Senate in March 1833, and for the next two years he was the attorney general of Pennsylvania. He subsequently served as Martin Van Buren's minister to Russia from 1837 to 1839.

Dallas became the vice-presidential running mate of James K. Polk in the presidential election of 1844. In an effort to appease Van Buren supporters, Democratic leaders had offered to make pro–Van Buren New York senator Silas Wright the vice-presidential candidate, but Wright did not accept the nomination. Dallas's support of protective tariffs appealed to northeastern commercial interests and offset Polk's ambiguous position on the sensitive issue, and his pro-Texas annexation stance also bolstered his political fortunes. The party leaders selected Dallas, who served as the 11th vice president of the United States from March 4, 1845, to March 4, 1849.

As vice president, Dallas supported Polk's war plans, but when Dallas cast the tie-breaking vote in the U.S. Senate on July 28, 1846, for the Walker Tariff, which lowered the protective tariff, he alienated much of his power base in Pennsylvania. Relations between Polk and Dallas, who met for the first time in February 1846, were never friendly, and the president rarely consulted his vice president on matters of policy. By 1848, they barely spoke to each other. The Democrats rejected Dallas as a possible presidential candidate in the 1848 presidential election. After leaving office, Dallas returned to Pennsylvania and the practice of law. In 1856, President Franklin Pierce appointed Dallas U.S. minister to Great Britain, where he served until 1861. Dallas died in Philadelphia on December 31, 1864.

MICHAEL R. HALL

See also
Democratic Party; Pierce, Franklin; Polk, James Knox; Van Buren, Martin.

References
Belohlavek, John M. *George Mifflin Dallas: Jacksonian Patrician.* State College: Pennsylvania State University Press, 1977.
Borneman, Walter R. *Polk: The Man Who Transformed the Presidency and America.* New York: Random House, 2008.

Dalton, Patrick
Birth Date: ca. 1824
Death Date: September 10, 1847

Irish-born U.S. soldier who deserted during the Mexican-American War, took a commission in the Mexican army, and fought with the Batallón de San Patricio (San Patricio [Saint Patrick's] Battalion). Patrick Dalton was born around 1824 in Ireland and immigrated to the United States probably in 1844.

Dalton enlisted in the 2nd U.S. Infantry Regiment in 1846. That unit was a part of Major General Zachary Taylor's Army of Occupation, which set up a base at Camargo in northern Mexico during the summer of 1846. Then, on October 23, 1846, Dalton, along with several others whom he likely talked into joining him, fled Camargo to join the Mexican army.

Dalton was immediately commissioned as a first lieutenant. He then joined and fought with the San Patricio Battalion, being promoted to captain and second in command. The battalion included about 200 men, most of whom were European immigrants, expatriates, or U.S. deserters. The battalion was known for its fierce and fearless combat and was understandably despised by most U.S. soldiers. By all accounts, Dalton was a capable officer who performed admirably in his duties.

On August 20, 1847, during hand-to-hand combat in the Battle of Churubusco, Dalton and a number of other San Patricios were taken prisoner by American forces. Dalton and 71 others of his battalion were immediately charged with treason and/or desertion and were subjected to immediate courts-martial.

According to U.S. military law, and by orders of the commanding general, Major General Winfield Scott, all those found guilty were to be executed. Dalton's trial took place on August 23 at San Ángel; in all, 20 men, including Dalton, were found guilty and sentenced to death by hanging at San Ángel's San Jacinto Plaza.

His captors reportedly treated Dalton with great derision because he had become an officer in the San Patricio Battalion, and also because he had allegedly coerced or intimidated other U.S. soldiers to desert and join the Mexican cause. In his own defense, Dalton explained, improbably, that he had been captured by Mexican bandits, taken to General Antonio López de Santa Anna, and forced to join the Mexican army. The court-martial did not accept the story. During the trial, it became evident that Dalton had most likely forced others to desert along with him. Dalton and 19 others were hanged on September 10, 1847, at San Ángel.

PAUL G. PIERPAOLI JR.

See also
Churubusco, Battle of; Desertion; San Patricio Battalion.

References
Hogan, Michael. *The Irish Soldiers of Mexico*. Guadalajara, Mexico: Fondo Editorial Universitario, 1997.
Miller, Robert G. *Shamrock and Sword: The Saint Patrick's Battalion in the Mexican-American War*. Norman: University of Oklahoma Press, 1989.
Stevens, Peter F. *The Rogue's March: John Riley and the St. Patrick's Battalion, 1846-48*. Washington, DC: Potomac Books, 2005.

Dana, Richard Henry
Birth Date: August 1, 1815
Death Date: January 7, 1882

American writer. Richard Henry Dana was born in Cambridge, Massachusetts, on August 1, 1815, to a prominent New England family. His early tutor was the celebrated author Ralph Waldo Emerson. After briefly attending Harvard College, Dana joined the sailing brig *Pilgrim* as a common sailor in 1834, rounding Cape Horn to California. His experience led him to write in 1840 the vivid and realistic account *Two Years before the Mast,* which became an instant bestseller and has remained popular ever since. It pictured California as a new Eden and heightened interest in the United States in acquiring this Mexican province.

Dana later graduated from Harvard and was admitted to the bar. In 1842 he attended the court of inquiry of Captain Alexander Slidell Mackenzie, who tried and executed three sailors in what became known as the *Somers* mutiny. Dana wrote in support of Mackenzie, who he believed had acted appropriately. Also in attendance was fellow author and naval historian James Fenimore Cooper, who criticized Mackenzie for heavy-handedness. The *Somers* mutiny was also a major source for Herman Melville's novella *Billy Budd*.

Dana was not a vocal opponent of the Mexican-American War until its conclusion in 1848, when the acquired territories threatened to result in the creation of more slave states. Consequently, Dana became one of the founders of the Free Soil Party and, later, the Republican Party.

In 1853, Dana served as counsel to defendants under the Fugitive Slave Law. After the Civil War (1861-1865), he was one of the counsels in the trial of Confederate president Jefferson Davis, and he served as a state representative in Massachusetts. Although he was appointed by President Ulysses S. Grant as ambassador to Great Britain, his enemies in the Senate prevented his confirmation. Dana died of influenza in Rome, Italy, on January 7, 1882.

CLAUDE G. BERUBE

See also
Cooper, James Fenimore; Emerson, Ralph Waldo; Free Soil Party; Mackenzie, Alexander Slidell; Republican Party; Slavery; *Somers*, U.S. Navy Brig.

References
Adams, Charles Francis. *Richard Henry Dana: A Biography*. Vols. 1 and 2. Cambridge, MA: Riverside Press, 1891.
Dana, Richard Henry. *Two Years before the Mast*. New York: Harper and Brothers, 1846.
Lucid, Robert F., ed. *The Journal of Richard Henry Dana, Jr.* Vols. 1-3. Cambridge, MA: Belknap Press, 1968.

Davis, Jefferson Finis
Birth Date: 1808
Death Date: December 6, 1889

U.S. Army officer, politician, secretary of war (1853-1857), and president of the Confederate States of America (1861-1865). Born in Christian County, Kentucky, Jefferson Finis Davis was the youngest in a family of 10 children. He attended Transylvania University in Lexington, Kentucky, and then entered the U.S. Military

Colonel Jefferson Davis of Mississippi commanded a volunteer regiment in the Mexican-American War and played an important role in the Battle of Buena Vista. In Ferbruary 1861, Davis was elected president of the Confederate States of America. (Library of Congress)

Academy at West Point, from which he graduated in 1828. Commissioned a second lieutenant in the 1st U.S. Infantry Regiment, Davis was assigned to the northwestern frontier.

In 1832 Davis served very briefly in the Black Hawk War. He subsequently courted and won the hand of Zachary Taylor's daughter, who as his commanding officer opposed their marriage. Davis resigned his commission in 1835 and arrived in Mississippi and retired to Brierfield, a plantation on the banks of the Mississippi River north of Natchez, which his older brother Joseph had given him.

After his young wife died, Davis secluded himself for several years before returning to public life. In 1844 Davis campaigned for James K. Polk in the latter's successful presidential bid and ran successfully for a seat in the U.S. House of Representatives.

With the beginning of the war with Mexico in 1846, Davis resigned his seat in Congress to accept the colonelcy of the 1st Mississippi Rifle Regiment. He soon found himself under the command of his once reluctant father-in-law, Major General Zachary Taylor, who welcomed him into his military family. Upon arriving on the Rio Grande, Davis immediately set about training and organizing his unit. As a former regular officer, he drilled his men diligently and often, and his political connections enabled him to arm them with percussion rifles. Although the unit was arguably one of the best-trained volunteer regiments in Taylor's command, many suspected that Davis's special relationship with the general affected Taylor's decision to include the 1st Mississippi Rifles in his march into northern Mexico as summer drew to a close.

At the Battle of Monterrey on September 21, 1846, Davis performed exceptionally well, staging a daring and successful assault on Fort Tenería. Davis and his men rooted out Mexican forces from surrounding redoubts, earning high accolades from Taylor. Taylor selected Davis and Colonel Albert Sidney Johnston as his negotiators in the truce that ended the battle and arranged a six-weeks' armistice with the Mexican army, an arrangement that was subsequently abrogated by President Polk. In the Battle of Buena Vista on February 23, 1847, Davis's men again played a pivotal role when they blunted a charge by Mexican lancers. The colonel arranged his companies in what he later called an "inverted V" formation that caught Mexican cavalry in a crossfire and, according to many of Davis's critics, inflated his opinion of his tactical genius beyond its true estimate. Davis and his men repulsed the assault but sustained high casualties, including Davis, who was struck in the ankle by a musket ball. Although badly wounded, he refused to leave the battlefield, remaining mounted the rest of the day. Spent by hours of battle and diminished by casualties, Davis's regiment again played a critical role late in the afternoon, helping to stop the last Mexican charge of the battle. Taylor gave Davis much of the credit for the American victory and offered to secure Davis's appointment as brigadier general. When it came, Davis and his regiment were already back in Mississippi, and the popular war hero, who was recovering from his wound, declined an army career in favor of election to the U.S. Senate.

Davis served in the Senate from August 1847 until September 1851. In 1853, President Franklin Pierce appointed him secretary of war. In that office Davis lent strong support to the army's ongoing modernization program, including adoption of the new Springfield rifled musket and the formation of the army's first two cavalry regiments. He also supported the building of a transcontinental railroad along a southern route. As one of the most influential members of Pierce's cabinet, he took a leading role in securing the president's approval for the 1854 Kansas-Nebraska Act, which reopened the sectional turmoil that led to the Civil War. Upon leaving his post in 1857, Davis returned to the U.S. Senate.

In response to the 1860 elections, seven states in the Deep South, including Mississippi, declared themselves out of the Union. Davis strongly approved, despite his earlier statements against secession, and resigned his Senate seat. In February 1861, the Montgomery Convention named Davis president of the Confederate States of America. On the whole, Davis performed effectively as president, although critics claimed that his military experience caused him to interfere in army operations instead of leaving decisions to his generals. Even his supporters admitted that he made some very poor strategic and personnel decisions that hastened the South's defeat. At war's end, Davis fled Richmond, but Union cavalry apprehended him near Irwinville, Georgia. He was imprisoned for two years.

Following his release, Davis served as president of an insurance company. In 1877 he moved to the Beauvoir estate near

Biloxi, Mississippi, as a guest of its owner. He inherited it in 1879. There he wrote his two-volume memoir *The Rise and Fall of the Confederate Government.* Davis died in New Orleans on December 6, 1889.

ETHAN S. RAFUSE

See also

Buena Vista, Battle of; Fort Tenería; Monterrey, Battle of; Polk, James Knox; Rio Grande; Slavery; Taylor, Zachary.

References

Carleton, James Henry. *The Battle of Buena Vista.* New York: Harper & Brothers, 1848.

Cooper, William J., Jr. *Jefferson Davis: American.* New York: Vintage, 2001.

Davis, William C. *Jefferson Davis: The Man and His Hour.* New York: Harper/Perennial, 1992.

McIntosh, James T., Lynda L. Crist, and Mary S. Dix, eds. *The Papers of Jefferson Davis.* Vol. 3, *July 1846–December 1848.* Baton Rouge: Louisiana State University Press, 1981.

Thorpe, Thomas Bangs. *Our Army at Monterey.* Philadelphia: Carey & Hart, 1847.

Davis, John
Birth Date: January 13, 1787
Death Date: April 19, 1854

American businessman, lawyer, and politician who was vociferously opposed to the expansion of slavery and to the Mexican-American War. Born on January 13, 1787, in Northborough, Massachusetts, John Davis attended the Leicester Academy before matriculating at Yale College, from which he graduated in 1812. His family was prominent and well connected, and he was the great-great-grandfather of Henry Cabot Lodge Jr. Davis wed Eliza Bancroft, daughter of a Revolutionary War hero and Unitarian minister and sister of the historian George Bancroft.

Davis read for the law, passed the bar examination, and began his legal practice in Worcester in 1815. Running as an anti-Jacksonian, he gained a seat in the U.S. House of Representatives. He began serving his first term in March 1825 and continued in that post until January 1834. He was the governor of Massachusetts during 1834–1835. Davis served in the U.S. Senate from 1835 until 1841, at which time he resigned his seat.

From 1841 to 1843, Davis again served as governor of Massachusetts before returning to the U.S. Senate as a Whig in 1845, replacing Senator Isaac C. Bates, who had died in office. Reelected in 1847, Davis served in the Senate for six more years. A few years earlier, in 1844, Davis and several of his nephews established the State Mutual Life Company of Worcester, then one of only five insurance companies in the United States.

Davis earned much derision from his colleagues when he cast one of only two Senate votes that opposed the war declaration against Mexico in May 1846. Later that same year, on August 12, he gave a marathon speech denouncing the war, which effectively scuttled the Senate's attempt to pass President James K. Polk's $2 million war appropriations bill and the Wilmot Proviso, which had been attached to it. The senator was roundly criticized for his actions, even by some in his own party, but he nevertheless held his ground. Davis resigned from the Senate in 1853 and returned to private life. He died in Worcester, Massachusetts, on April 19, 1854.

PAUL G. PIERPAOLI JR.

See also

Congress, U.S.; Slavery; Whigs; Wilmot Proviso.

References

Clary, David A. *Eagles and Empire: The United States, Mexico, and the Struggle for a Continent.* New York: Bantam Books, 2009.

Eisenhower, John S. D. *So Far from God: The U.S. War with Mexico, 1846–1848.* New York: Anchor Books, 1990.

Dawson Massacre
Event Date: September 18, 1842

Responding to Mexican general Adrián Woll's invasion of south Texas and occupation of San Antonio de Béxar (present-day San Antonio) on September 11, 1842, Texas captain Nicholas M. Dawson raised a company of 53 men at La Grange. Dawson was moving from La Grange to join Captain Mathew Caldwell's men at Salado Creek north of San Antonio de Béxar when he and his men were intercepted by several hundred irregular Mexican cavalry supported by two field pieces. After a spirited but futile resistance in which half of their number fell victim to Mexican artillery fire, Dawson's men surrendered. Once they were all disarmed, however, the Mexicans again opened fire on them in what came to be known as the Dawson Massacre. Most Anglo-Texans blamed Colonel Juan Seguin, once a friend of Texas independence and an officer in the Texas revolutionary army, for giving the command to execute the prisoners, only 17 of whom survived. Two of them managed to escape; the other 15 were marched off to Perote Prison, near Mexico City. Of the latter, only 9 survived to return to Texas.

SPENCER C. TUCKER

See also

Perote Castle; Salado Creek, Battle of; San Antonio; Woll's Expedition.

References

Nance, Joseph Milton. *Attack and Counterattack: The Texas-Mexican Frontier, 1842.* Austin: University of Texas Press, 1964.

Sowell, Andrew Jackson. *Rangers and Pioneers of Texas.* San Antonio: Shepard, 1884. Reprint, New York: Argosy-Antiquarian, 1964.

Stapp, William Preston. *The Prisoners of Perote: A Journal.* Philadelphia: Zieber, 1845.

Tyler, Ron, Douglas E. Barnett, and Roy R. Barkley, eds. *The New Handbook of Texas.* Austin: Texas State Historical Association, 1996.

Dayton, Wreck of the
Event Date: September 13, 1845

Explosion aboard a civilian side-wheel steamer, the *Dayton,* in the Gulf of Mexico on September 13, 1845, that resulted in the deaths of eight U.S. Army officers and enlisted men and the injury of 17 others. On July 2, 1845, Brigadier General Zachary Taylor began implementing orders from Washington that he move his Army of Observation from Fort Jesup, Louisiana, to Corpus Christi, Texas, in anticipation of hostilities with Mexico resulting from the U.S. decision to annex the Republic of Texas. He sent his dragoons over land, but the bulk of his men sailed via steamer from New Orleans to Corpus Christi. At the time, the United States was ill-prepared to move thousands of troops, masses of supplies, and hundreds of animals over long distances, so the federal government temporarily requisitioned civilian ships for this purpose. The *Dayton,* described at the time as a "small steamer," was an aging vessel that many deemed unfit for long-distance transport, but, given the shortage of naval vessels, the War Department had little choice but to use it to transport U.S. soldiers to Texas.

At about 20 minutes after midnight on September 13, 1845, as the *Dayton* neared McCloins Bluff with Corpus Christi in sight, the steamer's boiler exploded. Several men were killed instantly, while others were blown about the deck or into the water. Some men were catapulted into the water up to 60 yards distant from the ship, and others were scalded by the boiler's hot water and steam. Some, miraculously, survived with only minor injuries. The explosion was so intense that it was felt by men in camp at Corpus Christi, who awoke to see the sky aglow.

The dead were buried in a cemetery near Corpus Christi. The *Dayton* was a complete wreck.

Paul G. Pierpaoli Jr.

See also

Corpus Christi; Fort Jesup; Taylor, Zachary.

References

Henry, W. S. *Campaign Sketches of the War with Mexico.* New York: Harper & Brothers, 1847.

Smith, E. Kirby. *To Mexico with Scott: Letters of Ephraim Kirby Smith to His Wife.* Cambridge, MA: Harvard University Press, 1917.

Decree of 1830

Law enacted by the Mexican legislature on April 6, 1830, that directly affected Texas. The legislation prohibited the further introduction of slaves into Mexico, including Texas; established customhouses and garrisons at key entry points to Texas; halted immigration of Americans into Texas; canceled unfilled *empresario* land-grant contracts; and established tariffs on goods arriving through Texan ports. The Decree of 1830 (also known as the Law of 1830) was intended to increase Mexico City's control over Texas and to increase tax revenues from this rapidly developing province. Instead, it outraged many Anglo-Texans and helped precipitate the war for independence in 1836. Indeed, a number of historians have argued that the decree acted as a trigger mechanism for the Texas Revolution, much as the Stamp Act of 1765 served as a potent catalyst for the American Revolutionary War.

In 1820, to increase the population of the province of Texas (Coahuila y Texas) and to promote economic activity there, the Spanish colonial government passed a law that granted land to foreigners willing to settle in Texas. After gaining its independence in 1821, the new Mexican government continued these immigration policies. *Empresarios* authorized by the Republic of Mexico—Stephen F. Austin most prominent among them—recruited colonists and led them into the unsettled portion of the Mexican province between the Sabine River and San Antonio. As a result, several thousand people, mostly Americans, had settled in Texas by 1830. Most of the Americans came from the southern states, often bringing their slaves with them. According to the *empresarial* contracts, the new settlers were required to learn Spanish and convert to Catholicism. Most of the Americans, however, did neither, and they retained as well their allegiance to American institutions.

In the late 1820s the Mexican government became increasingly concerned about the immigration of Americans into Texas and attempted to increase its control over that province. In 1827, Mexican general José Manuel Rafael Simeón de Mier y Terán led an expedition across Texas to verify the northeastern border between Mexico and the United States and study the American settlers. He noted that the population of Texas had a large number of wealthy and independent-minded Americans and realized that Mexico might soon lose control of this very valuable province. As a result, Mier y Terán presented the Mexican legislature with several suggestions designed to establish tighter control over Texas, which were eventually incorporated into the Decree (Law) of April 6, 1830.

Many of the American settlers in Texas were furious at the passage of the law. Some colonists called for separate statehood for Texas (under Mexican control), while others clamored for revolution and an independent Texas republic. Others feared that they would lose their land, although the colonies of Stephen B. Austin and James McGloin were unaffected by the decree. The establishment of customhouses caused some problems, mainly because of poor choices for custom officers. The establishment of garrisons and the building of fortifications caused a major problem, however, especially when colonists learned that they would be garrisoned by inmates from Mexican prisons.

In June 1832, Colonel Juan Davis Bradburn, commanding the garrison at Anahuac on Galveston Bay, arrested three illegal aliens from the United States and charged them with illegally entering Mexico under the Law of April 6 and practicing law in Mexico without a license. He held them for military trial at Anahuac. After angry Texans skirmished with Mexican soldiers, Bradburn withdrew into an unfinished brick fortification. The Texans sent for reinforcements and cannon, leading to the Texan victory in the

Battle of Velasco, after which the Mexican forces were withdrawn and little official Mexican presence remained in Texas.

In summer 1833 Austin went to Mexico City to lobby for repeal of the law but secretly negotiated for separate statehood for Texas. Despite the political turmoil in Mexico at the time, the Mexican legislature officially repealed the law on December 7, 1833. Tariff collections were also suspended in Texas, and most Mexican troops were withdrawn. Three years later, however, Austin would lead another militia into San Antonio de Béxar at the start of what became the Texas Revolution.

ROBERT B. KANE

See also

Austin, Stephen Fuller; Bradburn, Juan Davis; Coahuila y Texas; Empresarios; Land Grants; Land Speculation, Texas; Mier y Terán, José Manuel Rafael Simeón de; Texas; Texas Revolution; Velasco, Battle of.

References
Benson, Nettie Lee. "Territorial Integrity in Mexican Politics, 1821–1833." In *The Independence of Mexico and the Creation of the New Nation,* edited by Jaime E. Rodríguez, 275–307. Los Angeles: UCLA Latin American Center, 1989.
Fehrenbach, T. R. *Lone Star: A History of Texas.* New York: Macmillan, 1968.
Hardin, Stephen L. *Texian Iliad: A Military History of the Texas Revolution, 1835–1836.* Austin: University of Texas Press, 1994.
Henson, Margaret. *Juan Bradburn: A Reappraisal of the Mexican Commander of Anahuac.* College Station: Texas A&M University Press, 1982.

de la Peña, José Enrique
Birth Date: 1807
Death Date: 1842

Mexican army officer who fought with General Antonio López de Santa Anna in his campaigns in Texas. José Enrique de la Peña was born in Jalisco, Mexico, in 1807. Little is known about de la Peña's upbringing or education. Although he trained as a mining engineer, he joined the Mexican navy in 1825; then, several years afterward, he joined the army. As an army captain, he secured a field commission as a lieutenant colonel at the onset of the Texas Revolution of 1835–1836.

De la Peña kept a field diary documenting his experiences and observations. Present at the Battle of the Alamo (February 23–March 6, 1836), he provided a firsthand account of the deaths of William Barret Travis and frontiersman David "Davy" Crockett. In addition, de la Peña's diary provides accounts of both the Battle at Coleto Creek (March 19–20, 1836) and the Battle of San Jacinto (April 21, 1836).

Over the years, scholars have disagreed over de la Peña's rendition of the events, particularly over his description of the death of Davy Crockett. According to de la Peña, Crockett was one of only seven survivors who surrendered, and he was executed on Santa

Anna's direct orders in his presence, casting doubt on the idea that Crockett died while fighting at the Alamo. In 1975, the first English version of his diary, *With Santa Anna in Texas: A Personal Narrative of the Revolution,* translated by Carmen Perry, received much attention. For decades, historians have debated its true publication date and its authenticity. Still, de la Peña's account, which sold for almost $400,000 in auction in 1998, setting a world record for a price paid for a diary, remains an important primary source about the Texas Revolution.

The diary also criticized Santa Anna's leadership and documented various arguments that the Mexican commander had with his subordinate officers. When, for example, Santa Anna ordered the withdrawal of Mexican forces from Texas after his defeat in the Battle of San Jacinto, General José Urrea, who had defeated James Fannin and Texan forces at the Battle of Coleto Creek, actively opposed the move.

Subsequently, de la Peña sided with Urrea in opposition to the Mexican central government and spent much of the last years of his life in prison as a result of his support for Urrea and for federalism. The exact date of de la Peña's death is unknown, but he is believed to have died in 1842 from an illness he contracted while in prison.

ASHLEY R. ARMES

See also

Alamo, Battle of the; Coleto Creek, Battle of; Crockett, David; Fannin, James Walker; San Jacinto, Battle of; Santa Anna, Antonio López de; Texas Revolution; Travis, William Barret; Urrea y Elías Gonzales, José de.

References
Crisp, James E. *Sleuthing the Alamo: Davy Crockett's Last Stand and Other Mysteries of the Texas Revolution.* New York: Oxford University Press, 2005.
De la Peña, José Enrique. *With Santa Anna in Texas: A Personal Narrative of the Revolution.* Translated and edited by Carmen Perry. College Station: Texas A&M University Press, 1997.

Delawares (Lenni Lenapes)

Native American group of the Algonquian linguistic family located, at the time of first European contact, in modern-day Delaware, New Jersey, southeastern New York, and southeastern Pennsylvania. By the time of the Mexican-American War, most were located in Missouri and Kansas.

On his expedition to the West in the mid-1840s, Colonel John C. Frémont took 12 Delaware warriors who acted as scouts, guides, interpreters, and emissaries to other Native American tribes. The Delaware scouts were also largely responsible for feeding the 60-man expedition, engaging in frequent buffalo and other game hunts.

When the Mexican-American War began in May 1846, Frémont diverted his expedition south to California, fighting a skirmish with the Modocs and Klamaths at Klamath Lake, which claimed the life of his favored Delaware Scout, Crane. Shortly thereafter,

Frémont helped establish the short-lived Bear Flag Republic. The Delaware scouts remained with him until early 1848.

During the 1860s, numerous Delaware bands were relocated to Indian Territory (Oklahoma). By this time, the Lenni Lenape were scattered about the United States and Canada, ranging from Massachusetts to Kansas.

ROGER M. CARPENTER

See also

Bear Flag Revolt; Frémont, John Charles; Klamaths; Native Americans.

References

Dunlay, Thomas W. *Wolves for the Blue Soldiers: Indian Scouts and Auxiliaries with the United States Army, 1860–90.* Lincoln: University of Nebraska Press, 1987.

Kraft, Herbert C. *The Lenape: Archaeology, History, Ethnography.* Newark: New Jersey Historical Society, 1986.

Weslager, Clinton A. *The Delaware Indians: A History.* New Brunswick, NJ: Rutgers University Press, 1972.

Democratic Party

The oldest political party in the United States, the Democratic Party traces its origins to the anti-Federalists of the 1790s. By the mid-19th century the Democratic Party had become one of the country's two major political parties (the other was the Whigs).

In the early 1790s the Democratic-Republican Party (the forerunner of the Democratic Party) came into being as a reaction to the Federalists, led by Alexander Hamilton. Hamilton and the Federalists believed in a strong central government, a national bank, and government support of business and industry. The anti-Federalists, best exemplified by Thomas Jefferson and James Madison, helped form what would ultimately become the Democratic Party in opposition to the Federalist agenda. The Democratic-Republicans wanted to keep the federal government small and unobtrusive. They believed that democracy was best served by a system in which the states and individual citizens held the majority of the economic and political power of the nation. They eschewed the buildup of industry in the United States and deplored governmental attempts to support it. For them, the model American citizens were the small, yeoman farmers and the local tradesmen and shopkeepers. This idealized concept, which never actually existed in any large sense, came to be known as "Jeffersonian Democracy" and would be the hallmark of Democratic Party ideology into the 20th century.

The Democrats ultimately became known as the party of states' rights by the early 1800s, which explains its great influence among southern planters who wanted as little interference as possible with their "peculiar institution" of slavery. The Democratic Party was powerful not just in the South but also in parts of the western Great Plains and Far West. It was weakest in the populous and industrialized northeastern states.

War hero Andrew Jackson, elected to the presidency in 1828, picked up the mantle of the old Democratic-Republican Party, which had splintered by the mid-1820s, and helped forge the modern Democratic Party. This inaugurated the era of "Jacksonian Democracy," with Jackson's belief in the sovereignty of the people above all else, a strong aversion to centralized banks and industrialists, and a healthy fear of the "moneyed elite" in the Northeast. Until the late 1840s, most Democrats were slave owners, farmers, tradesmen, small businessmen, and, increasingly, immigrants and laborers, whom the Democrats claimed to champion. Democratic Party priorities reflected its constituency, as witnessed by the opening of new lands in the West for farming and the expulsion of Native Americans from their ancestral lands.

Not surprisingly, Democrats, particularly in the southern states, enthusiastically supported the Mexican-American War. A significant minority of northerners in the party, however, opposed it, which initiated a sectional division among Democrats that reappeared and sharpened over the next 15 years. Northern Whigs generally were against the war, while their southern counterparts mostly embraced it. Southern men furnished the vast majority of volunteers who fought in the war, and southern congressmen provided the bulk of the political support. Thus, the war to some extent divided both national parties and foreshadowed the greater partisan realignment and sectional cleavage of the 1850s and 1860s.

President James K. Polk, a Democrat from Tennessee who had inherited the mantle of Andrew Jackson and was known to his admirers as "Young Hickory," was elected in 1844 on a platform that called for aggressive territorial expansion to the West. Democrats championed "Manifest Destiny" throughout the campaign (although the term was not coined until 1845, the ideas were prominent long before that). Once in office, Polk helped engineer a conflict over the disputed border of Texas (annexed after the election but before he was inaugurated), and Congress officially declared war on May 13, 1846, after fighting between Mexican and U.S. troops had broken out in late April. Nearly from the beginning, northerners, including many Democrats, voiced objections to the war. Some believed it was a clumsy and obvious attempt to add territory that potentially would expand slavery, which would benefit planters and strengthen the southern-oriented Democratic Party. Others argued that the United States—a former colony itself—had no business provoking a war against a weaker country simply to grab territory. Finally, many northern Democrats (and Whigs) were disappointed with Polk for compromising on the Oregon boundary dispute with Great Britain, while conversely pressing the Mexicans on Texas.

Perhaps the most dramatic measure of the war's divisiveness among Democrats was the Wilmot Proviso, certainly the most famous piece of legislation associated with the conflict. David Wilmot was a Democratic congressman from Pennsylvania who, on August 8, 1846, introduced a proviso (attached to a spending bill for the war and actually written by Jacob Brinkerhoff, an Ohio Democrat) stipulating that no territory gained in the war would

THE DEMOCRATIC FUNERAL OF 1848.

Political cartoon foreseeing political death for the Democrats in the national election of 1848. The artist imagines a funeral of the party's standard-bearers, with a procession of the faithful. Democratic senators (left to right) Sam Houston of Texas, Thomas Hart Benton of Missouri, and South Carolina's John Calhoun carry a litter bearing the bodies of Martin Van Buren, as a fox, and Lewis Cass, as a gas balloon (an unflattering play on his last name). (Library of Congress)

permit slavery. Wilmot himself had no interest in abolition and did not care about African Americans. Rather, like many other northern whites, he wanted western territory to be free of both planters and slaves and from "the disgrace which association with negro slavery brings upon free labor," as Wilmot expressed it. The Wilmot Proviso passed the House of Representatives with solid support from northeastern Democrats; southerners opposed it. The legislation failed in the Senate, however, where southerners had an equal number of votes. Eventually, the Wilmot Proviso became the basis for "free soil," the policy that slavery would not expand beyond its current limits.

Many northern Democrats—usually called Free Soil Democrats—left their party and joined the new Republican Party (including David Wilmot) when it was formed in the early 1850s. The Mexican-American War exposed a sharp sectional division among Democrats and helped lead to the complete rupture of the party in the late 1850s.

CHRISTOPHER OLSEN AND PAUL G. PIERPAOLI JR.

See also

Expansionism and Imperialism; Free Soil Party; Manifest Destiny; Politics, U.S.; Polk, James Knox; Republican Party; Slavery; Whigs; Wilmot, David; Wilmot Proviso.

References

Bauer, K. Jack. *The Mexican War: 1846–1848*. New York: Macmillan, 1974.

Fisher, Murray, ed. *Of the People: The 200-Year History of the Democratic Party*. Los Angeles: General Publishing Group, 1992.

Haynes, Sam. *James K. Polk and the Expansionist Impulse*. New York: Addison-Wesley, 1997.

Johannsen, Robert W. *To the Halls of the Montezumas: The Mexican War in the American Imagination*. New York: Oxford University Press, 1985.

Dent, Frederick Tracy
Birth Date: December 17, 1820
Death Date: December 23, 1892

U.S. Army officer and veteran of both the Mexican-American War and U.S. Civil War. Frederick Tracy Dent was born on December 17, 1820, outside Saint Louis, Missouri. He graduated from the U.S. Military Academy, West Point, in 1843. There he befriended his classmate Ulysses S. Grant. Dent introduced Grant to his sister, Julia, whom Grant later married.

Commissioned a second lieutenant in the 6th U.S. Infantry Regiment, Dent saw frontier duty in Indian Territory and was then posted to Baton Rouge, Louisiana. He saw significant action during the Mexican-American War, serving throughout much of Major General Winfield Scott's Mexico City Campaign. He was brevetted to first lieutenant for his actions at Veracruz as well as the Battles of Contreras and Churubusco. During the September 7, 1847, Battle of El Molino del Ray, he led a heroic frontal assault amid heavy fire and then participated in hand-to-hand combat. Dent was wounded seriously in the leg during the engagement and was brevetted colonel for his gallantry.

When the war ended, Dent remained in the army, serving in the West, on the Pacific coast, and in Florida during the Seminole removal. When the Civil War began in 1861, Dent was a captain with the 9th Infantry Regiment stationed in San Francisco. He remained there until March 1863, when he received promotion to major in the 4th Infantry Regiment and was ordered to the East. After seeing action at the Battles of Chancellorsville (May 1–4, 1863) and Gettysburg (July 1–3, 1863), he was transferred to New York City and appointed as a member of a military commission charged with trying prisoners of the state.

In the spring of 1864, Lieutenant General Grant, then commander of all Union forces, appointed Dent as his aide-de-camp with the rank of lieutenant colonel. He stayed with Grant for the duration of the war. On April 5, 1865, Dent was promoted to temporary brigadier general. After Richmond fell in April 1865, Dent served briefly as military governor of the city. He subsequently commanded the defenses of Washington, D.C. When Grant became president in 1869, Dent served as the president's military secretary until 1873, at which time he took command of Fort Trumbull, Connecticut. He held several other command posts before retiring in 1883 at the permanent rank of colonel. He resided in Washington, D.C., for a time before moving to Denver, Colorado, where he died on December 23, 1892.

PAUL G. PIERPAOLI JR.

See also

Churubusco, Battle of; Contreras, Battle of; El Molino del Rey, Battle of; Grant, Ulysses Simpson (Hiram Ulysses Grant); Mexico City Campaign; Veracruz, Landing at and Siege of.

References

Clary, David A. *Eagles and Empire: The United States, Mexico, and the Struggle for a Continent.* New York: Bantam Books, 2009.
Grant, U. S. *Personal Memoirs of U.S. Grant.* New York: Webster, 1885.

Desertion

Soldiers on both sides chose to abandon military service during the Mexican-American War, although the desertion rate for the Mexican army was considerably higher than that of the American army. Principal catalysts for desertion included boredom, fear, harsh military discipline, difficult living conditions, poor medical care, poor training, and reasons of conscience. On rare occasions, deserters joined the opposing army and fought their former comrades.

Military records indicate that about 9 percent of the U.S. Army's soldiers deserted during the war, with regulars deserting at twice the rate of volunteers. Approximately 9,000 soldiers deserted of the 104,556 who served in the conflict. Only 8 U.S. marines deserted of the 548 who served. Navy desertions are not documented. These rates of desertion were lower than comparable rates during the American Revolutionary War and the Civil War, although they were higher than the rate of desertion for later American wars on foreign soil. Additionally, they were lower than the peacetime rate of desertion for the regular army. Punishment for American deserters could include being branded with a *D*, corporal punishment such as flogging, and death. The success of the American war effort, the relatively short duration of the conflict with Mexico, and the voluntary nature of most of the forces all contributed to a relatively low rate of desertion.

Figures for the Mexican army are much harder to determine, but desertion in the Mexican army was significantly higher than the rate in the American army. The penalty for desertion in the Mexican army was almost invariably death. It is believed that as many as 10,000 Mexicans deserted during the war. One example demonstrates that the desertion rate may have been as high as 20–25 percent. In January 1847, during General Antonio López de Santa Anna's march from San Luis Potosí toward Saltillo (with an army of 20,000 men), between 4,000 and 5,000 soldiers deserted.

In addition to the usual reasons for desertion listed previously, soldiers in the Mexican army were usually impoverished, rural-based conscripts, often undersupplied, paid infrequently or not at all, poorly trained, and poorly led. They had little esprit de corps and lacked even the most basic medical care. Lack of success on the battlefield encouraged desertion, too.

The Mexican army made concerted efforts to induce Americans to desert, publishing notices and leaflets that offered money, land, clothing, and even commissions to deserters. The Mexican government frequently contracted with British agents who would try to entice Americans to desert by promising them land grants and cash payments. Foreign-born members of the American army may have been more disposed to desert because they were less assimilated, were often deserters from European armies, and, if Roman Catholic, may have wished to avoid waging war against fellow members of the same religion. To target Roman Catholics, the Mexicans distributed leaflets asserting that the U.S. war effort was an attack on the Roman Catholic Church. In all, it is estimated that fewer than 300 Americans defected to the Mexican side during the conflict.

Some American deserters fought for Mexico in the San Patricio Battalion, a unit composed primarily of Irish Catholic deserters from the United States army along with some foreign-born residents of Mexico. The battalion was formed as an artillery company and fought at Matamoros and Monterrey. Later it was reformed as a two-company battalion of infantry and fought during the Mexico City Campaign. At the Battle of Churubusco on August 20, 1847, the battalion was part of the Mexican force holding the fortress-convent of San Mateo and suffered heavy casualties, effectively finishing the battalion. Twenty captured members of the San Patricio Battalion were hanged in September 1847, while others were flogged and branded. Execution was not permitted as a punishment for those who deserted during peacetime, so some San Patricio members who had deserted before hostilities commenced escaped that punishment.

JOSHUA B. MICHAEL

See also

Churubusco, Battle of; Monterrey, Battle of; San Patricio Battalion.

References

Bauer, K. Jack. *The Mexican War, 1846–1848.* New York: Macmillan, 1974.

McCaffrey, James M. *Army of Manifest Destiny: The American Soldier in the Mexican War, 1846–1848.* New York: New York University Press, 1992.

Miller, Robert R. *Shamrock and Sword: The Saint Patrick's Battalion in the U.S.-Mexican War.* Norman: University of Oklahoma, 1989.

Winders, Richard B. *Mr. Polk's Army: The American Military Experience in the Mexican War.* College Station: Texas A&M University, 1997.

Díaz de la Vega, Rómulo
Birth Date: 1804
Death Date: October 3, 1877

Mexican military and political leader and interim president (1855) whose career became associated with national defense and the nation's conservative faction. Born in Mexico City in 1804, Rómulo Díaz de la Vega began his military career in 1825 as a sublieutenant of the Engineers after schooling as a cadet for three years. He moved steadily up the ranks and served under General Antonio López de Santa Anna as the head of a sapper company in the successful defense of Tampico during the Spanish invasion in 1829. Seven years later he participated in the Texas Campaign, earning the rank of lieutenant colonel for his role at the Battle of the Alamo. After battling the French at Veracruz in 1838 in the so-called Pastry War, Díaz returned to the northern frontier in 1839. His success against the Mier Expedition earned him the rank of brigadier general in 1843.

In January 1845 Díaz was named commander of the 4th Brigade of the Army of the North, headquartered at Monterrey. Soon thereafter, he joined General Francisco Mejía at Matamoros to prepare a defense against advancing U.S. troops. He acted as the spokesman for Mexico when U.S. troops arrived at the Rio Grande on March 28, 1846. In a brief conference with Brigadier General

The capture of Mexican general Rómulo Díaz de la Vega by Captain Charles May during the Battle of Resaca de la Palma. Fought on May 9, 1846, it was the second battle of the Mexican-American War. (Library of Congress)

William J. Worth, he expressed his indignation at seeing the American flag placed along the river. When war finally erupted, he commanded the Mexican 1st Brigade at the Battle of Palo Alto on May 8, 1846.

The next day, at the Battle of Resaca de la Palma, Díaz stood by his artillery as troops around him retreated. Taken prisoner during Captain Charles A. Mays's famed dragoon charge on the Mexican center, he was offered parole in exchange for a pledge to lay down his arms. He refused, citing his vow to defend his nation. The general then traveled to New Orleans, where his internment included housing in fine hotels, visits to the theater, and permission to travel. He remained in custody until December 1847, when he was exchanged for the captured crew of a U.S. Navy brig.

The newly liberated Díaz soon resumed his military service as second in command of Mexico's Army of the East. On April 18, 1847, during the Battle of Cerro Gordo, he fell captive once more, again refusing to retreat or surrender as General Antonio López de Santa Anna and others fled. He was interned in the city of Veracruz and was set free in December 1847.

Following the war, Díaz became military commander of Yucatán in 1851 and quelled the Maya-inspired Caste War there. He was rewarded with the governorship of Yucatán in 1853, and of Tamaulipas the following year; Díaz also became a general of division in 1854. He returned to the Federal District in 1855 to help defend Santa Anna against the liberal cabal formed under the Plan of Ayutla. When Santa Anna fled the capital in August 1855, Díaz himself supported the plan and briefly served as interim president of Mexico from September 12 to November 15, 1855. Soon after, he rebelled against the liberals and again cast his lot with the conservatives. Exiled in 1856, he returned in 1859 to serve President Miguel Miramón and the conservatives in the War of the Reform, during which he was wounded in a battle in Zacatecas in 1860.

In 1863 Díaz helped bring Emperor Maximilian I to Mexico and accepted both civil and military roles in the short-lived empire. When Republican forces triumphed the general was spared execution because of his previous defense of the nation, but he was forced to withdraw to civilian life. He died, penniless, in the city of Puebla on October 3, 1877.

DOUGLAS MURPHY

See also

Alamo, Battle of the; Cerro Gordo, Battle of; Mejía, Francisco; Mier Expedition; Palo Alto, Battle of; Pastry War; Politics, Mexican; Resaca de la Palma, Battle of; Santa Anna, Antonio López de; Worth, William Jenkins.

References

Clary, David A. *Eagles and Empire: The United States, Mexico, and the Struggle for an Empire.* New York: Bantam Books, 2009.

Johannsen, Robert. *To the Halls of the Montezumas: The Mexican War in the American Imagination.* New York: Oxford University Press, 1985.

Orozco Linares, Fernando. *Gobernantes de México.* México, DF: Panorama, 1985.

Smith, Justin. *The War with Mexico.* 2 vols. New York: Macmillan, 1919.

Digger Indians

A pejorative term first applied by Anglo-Americans to the desert Native American tribes of the Great Basin region, such as the Paiutes and Maidus. It has been used to identify Native Americans of the central plateau region, including Utah, Arizona, Nevada, Idaho, and Oregon, as well as California. Eventually this became a term preferred by many Anglos to describe all of California's Native American population. Labeling these Native Americans as "diggers" helped create a mind-set among Anglo-Americans that such tribes were subhuman. This, in turn, made it easier to pursue a blatant policy of genocide that decimated the California Indians in the years following the California Gold Rush, which began in 1848.

While the union of Spaniards and Indians created the mestizo or mixed-race peoples of Mexico, and the Spaniards had built a system of 21 missions in California to proselytize Native Americans, there had been less interest in assimilation of Native Americans during the Anglo-Americans' inexorable march westward. Indeed, Americans encountered hardscrabble Indians tribes in the desert approaches to California and interpreted their lack of overt sophistication as an indication of social and spiritual inferiority. Many of these Native Americans had experienced decades of demographic decline because of exposure to diseases such as smallpox. Pioneering Americans, accustomed to encountering vigorous Plains tribes such as the Sioux and Cheyennes, invariably portrayed these Native Americans as inferior and frequently described them as being animal-like. In his classic account, *The Oregon Trail,* historian Francis Parkman describes the Diggers as "a wretched tribe beyond the mountains" that turned grasshoppers "to good account by making of them a sort of soup, pronounced by certain unscrupulous trappers to be extremely rich." Mark Twain, in *Roughing It,* says that the Digger Indians possessed "no higher ambition than to kill and eat jackass rabbits, crickets, and grasshoppers, and embezzle carrion from the buzzards and coyotes."

European settlers had never been particularly impressed with the Native Americans of California, although their numbers were large (compared to the rest of what is now the United States) and their cultures were interesting, diverse, and long-standing. This stereotyping of California's native peoples was exacerbated by American encounters with desert and tribal Indians who scratched out a living in the harsh environs of the Great Basin region in Utah, Nevada, and California. Often living on grubs, roots, rats, and other sparse fare, the Native Americans of the Great Basin were remarkably adept at surviving some of the harshest environmental conditions on the planet. Encroaching on their tribal hunting grounds and resource base, outsiders often attacked impoverished Native Americans for real and perceived crimes, including the stealing of cattle. Indian children were often taken from their families and sold to ranchers as virtual slave labor in the 1850s in California.

Newspaper accounts through the 1870s described the killing of natives as "good hauls of diggers." By 1900 the Native American population of California had declined to approximately 10,000, a monumental demographic reduction from an estimated 300,000 Indians there in 1750. Several notorious massacres occurred in California in the 1850s and 1860s, and the state of California was actually reimbursed by the federal government for bounties paid at the rate of $5 per head and 50 cents per scalp.

The horrific mistreatment of the "diggers" helped revive a nascent Indian reform movement. Following the Gold Rush period, many social reformers attempted to help the survivors by establishing reservations for the remaining tribal groups and boarding schools for their youth. Ironically, Californians celebrated the discovery, in 1911, of the "Stone Age man" Ishi, whose Yahi tribe had been effectively wiped out in the campaign against the diggers.

RANDAL BEEMAN

See also

California; Gold Rush, California; Mestizos; Native Americans.

References

Cooke, Sherburne. *The Population of the California Indians, 1769–1970.* Berkeley: University of California Press, 1976.

Heizer, Robert F. *The Destruction of the California Indian.* Lincoln, NE: Bison Books, 1993.

Hurtado, Albert. *Indian Survival on the California Frontier.* New Haven, CT: Yale University Press, 1990.

Dimick, Justin
Birth Date: August 5, 1800
Death Date: October 13, 1871

U.S. Army officer who served with distinction under Major Generals Zachary Taylor and Winfield Scott. Justin Dimick was born near Hartford, Connecticut, on August 5, 1800. He graduated from the U.S. Military Academy, West Point, in 1819 and was assigned as a second lieutenant of light artillery. Following postings to several stations, he returned in 1822 to teach at West Point. Two years later he was promoted to first lieutenant, and in 1834 he was brevetted captain for 10 years' exemplary service in a single grade. The following year he was promoted to the permanent grade of captain.

Dimick saw action during the Second Seminole War of 1835–1836, for which he was brevetted major in 1836. Subsequently, he was stationed along the U.S.-Canadian border and participated in the quelling of a border disturbance in upstate New York during 1838–1839.

When the Mexican-American War began in 1846, Dimick was a brevet major in an artillery battalion in Taylor's Army of Occupation. He saw action at the Battles of Palo Alto and Resaca de la Palma in May 1846. The following year, with Winfield Scott's army, Dimick participated in the Battles of Contreras and Churubusco, service which brought him a brevet promotion to lieutenant colonel. For his gallantry at the Battle of Chapultepec, where he was wounded, he earned another brevet promotion to colonel.

After that, he commanded U.S. occupation troops at Veracruz during 1847–1848 and helped supervise the U.S. withdrawal from Mexico later in 1848.

During 1849–1850 and again during 1856–1857, Dimick again saw action against the Seminoles in Florida. He became a permanent lieutenant colonel in 1857 and commanded the artillery school at Fort Monroe during 1859–1861. Advanced to permanent colonel in October 1861, he commanded a Union prison depot in Massachusetts until 1864, at which point he retired from active service. From 1864 to 1868, he supervised the Soldiers' Home near Washington, D.C. In March 1865, Dimick was brevetted to brigadier general, retired, for his long service to the army. Dimick died in Philadelphia on October 13, 1871.

PAUL G. PIERPAOLI JR.

See also

Chapultepec, Battle of; Churubusco, Battle of; Contreras, Battle of; Palo Alto, Battle of; Resaca de la Palma, Battle of.

References

Bauer, J. Jack. *The Mexican-American War, 1846–1848.* New York: Macmillan, 1974.

Clary, David A. *Eagles and Empire: The United States, Mexico, and the Struggle for a Continent.* New York: Bantam Books, 2009.

Diplomacy, Mexican

In the decades following independence from Spain in 1821, the Mexican government faced myriad political, social, and economic problems as it struggled to mature. Those realities, in addition to the lack of support from foreign powers such as Spain and France, made it increasingly difficult for Mexican leaders to confront the dangers that U.S. expansionism posed to the country's territorial integrity.

Mexican diplomatic efforts in the early 19th century built on those of Spanish colonial authorities and largely focused on halting the U.S. westward advance. Because the United States had long coveted Texas, a desolate Spanish province in the early 1800s, both Spanish and Mexican officials moved to populate and settle that territory and allowed some American families to settle in Texas. They could not prevent, however, the influx of thousands of additional illegal immigrants from the United States, and by 1830 Anglo-Americans in Texas outnumbered Mexicans by a ratio of eight to one. The settlers' sensibilities also clashed with the Mexican government's efforts to outlaw slavery and restrict their trading rights. Tensions came to a head in 1835 when Mexican legislators abolished federalism and prepared to install a centralist regime. Settlers in Texas then rebelled, and Mexican president Antonio López de Santa Anna's unsuccessful attempt to quell the uprising resulted in the independence of Texas in 1836.

During the next nine years Mexican officials refused to recognize Texas as a sovereign nation and held out hope that they might be able to bring the former province back into the union. Early in

1843, for instance, then president Santa Anna became absorbed with the idea that Texas might accept reunification with Mexico under a bilateral arrangement that would preserve its local autonomy, as a similar agreement had been signed with Yucatán. The ensuing negotiations came to nothing, and the following spring Santa Anna's administration announced that it intended to organize a large military expedition to subdue the recalcitrant province, but that incursion never materialized.

It is not surprising, therefore, that the U.S. Congress's joint resolution annexing Texas to the United States late in February 1845 created a full-blown political crisis. Mexico's minister to the United States, Juan Nepomuceno Almonte, demanded his passport and returned home one month later, which for all practical purposes broke off diplomatic relations between the two nations. Although war seemed imminent at this point, a British proposal to have Texas authorities discuss a settlement with Mexico that assured its independence so long as it did not join the United States gained traction in Mexican diplomatic circles.

The July 15 decision by Texas to annex itself to the United States, however, dashed all hopes of a harmonious agreement, and the clamor for war revived with great intensity. Nonetheless, Mexican president José Joaquín de Herrera and his advisers, cognizant of the remote possibility of winning a war with their northern neighbor, tried to avert an armed confrontation. They agreed to receive a commissioner but were disappointed when U.S. diplomat John Slidell arrived in Mexico late in November 1845. Not only did Slidell have the title of minister plenipotentiary (which would have essentially reestablished full diplomatic relations with the United States) but he also had instructions to discuss the purchase of New Mexico and California. Mexican leaders could not receive Slidell under these circumstances and did not allow him to remain in the capital. The U.S. envoy withdrew to Jalapa, halfway between Mexico City and the coastal city of Veracruz, in hopes that he might have other opportunities to accomplish his mission.

Herrera's political enemies fiercely attacked him for even considering meeting with Slidell, and such pressure contributed to his overthrow late in December by General Mariano Paredes y Arrillaga. But Paredes's regime, its bellicose proclamations and reaffirmations to the contrary of Mexico's claim to Texas, also tried to avoid war with the United States. Slidell's continued presence in Mexico kept the door open to this possibility, but in the end the Mexican Council of State rebuffed him for the same reason it had done so in 1845: he lacked proper credentials. Slidell requested his passports on March 17 so he could return home, closing the door to diplomatic exchange and setting the stage for war. A skirmish known as the Thornton Affair (April 25–26, 1846), on the north bank of the Rio Grande, resulted in the deaths of 11 American soldiers and gave U.S. president James K. Polk the justification that he needed to call for a declaration of war on May 11, 1846.

Three months later, amid much fanfare, Santa Anna returned to Mexico from exile in Cuba to lead a military resistance against advancing U.S. forces. With the focus on war Mexican diplomatic efforts became of secondary importance, and serious negotiations to end the war did not resume until early June 1847. By that time U.S. brigadier general Winfield Scott had taken Veracruz, defeated Santa Anna at Cerro Gordo, and had occupied the city of Puebla. Santa Anna then proposed to Scott that discussions would begin should he and his army remain in Puebla. This entreaty proved to be another one of Santa Anna's well-known crafty tricks, so nothing happened. Another effort to settle the war transpired during the two-week armistice that followed the United States' twin August 20, 1847, victories at Contreras and Churubusco, but this time both sides could not reach a compromise. Historical judgment as to why diplomats could not find a middle ground remains divided. According to Timothy D. Johnson, the Mexicans "made demands that seemed unrealistic, coming from a vanquished foe," while Will Fowler has noted that Mexico rejected the proposal set forth by U.S. envoy Nicholas P. Trist because "neither Santa Anna nor his commission was going to agree to such an insulting treaty."

In any event, the fall of Mexico City to Scott's forces in mid-September 1847 insured that negotiations to end the conflict would begin shortly thereafter. These discussions culminated with the February 1848 Treaty of Guadalupe Hidalgo, whose terms some historians have characterized as among the harshest ever imposed on a losing side of an international conflict. In so doing, however, these scholars have not considered the influence of factors other than the U.S. desire for territorial aggrandizement on Mexican diplomacy. Recent research has suggested that as Mexican diplomats hammered out the terms of the peace treaty, members of the upper clergy sought peace and even advocated that the United States absorb Mexico so the church could keep its property. The British also wanted Mexico to sign the Treaty of Guadalupe Hidalgo because the anticipated monetary indemnity would facilitate the payment of debts to British bondholders outstanding since 1827.

Given these pressures, one can well argue that Mexican diplomats did the best job possible under difficult circumstances. Indeed, one must consider the fact that before the conflict U.S. statesmen like Secretary of State James Buchanan noted that the proper postwar boundary should be set at the 26th parallel, and such a border would have included the present-day Mexican states of Chihuahua and Sonora, as well as large parts of Baja California, Coahuila, Tamaulipas, and Nuevo León. The cession of more than 500,000 square miles of territory to the United States, however, left a bitter legacy that has soured relations between both nations to the present day.

MATTHEW J. KROGMAN AND PEDRO SANTONI

See also

Almonte, Juan Nepomuceno; Ampudia, Pedro de; Arista, Mariano; Bustamante y Oseguera, Anastasio; Cuevas, Luis Gonzaga; Diplomacy, U.S.; Gorostiza, Manuel Eduardo de; Herrera, José Joaquín de; Mexico; Paredes y Arillaga, Mariano; Peña y Peña, Manuel de la; Polk, James Knox; Santa Anna, Antonio López de; Slidell, John; Texas; Texas Declaration of Independence; Texas Revolution; Tornel y Mendivil, José María de; Tyler, John; United States, 1821–1854.

References

Brack, Gene M. *Mexico Views Manifest Destiny, 1821–1846: An Essay on the Origins of the Mexican War.* Albuquerque: University of New Mexico Press, 1975.

Gleijeses, Piero. "A Brush with Mexico." *Diplomatic History* 29, no. 2 (April 2005): 223–254.

Haynes, Sam W. "'But What Will England Say?'—Great Britain, the United States, and the War with Mexico." In *Dueling Eagles: Reinterpreting the U.S.-Mexican War, 1846–48,* edited by Richard Francaviglia and Douglas W. Richmond, 19–40. Fort Worth: Texas Christian University Press, 2000.

Henderson, Timothy J. *A Glorious Defeat: Mexico and Its War with the United States.* New York: Hill & Wang, 2007.

Lamar, Curt. "A Diplomatic Disaster: The Mexican Missions of Anthony Butler, 1829–1834." *The Americas* 49, no. 1 (July 1988): 1–17.

Pletcher, David M. *The Diplomacy of Annexation: Texas, Oregon, and the Mexican War.* Columbia: University of Missouri Press. 1975.

Santoni, Pedro. *Mexicans at Arms: Puro Federalists and the Politics of War, 1845–1848.* Fort Worth: Texas Christian University Press, 1996.

Soto, Miguel. *La conspiración mónarquica en México, 1845–1846.* Mexico City: EOSA, 1988.

Tenembaum, Barbara. "Neither a Borrower Nor a Lender Be: Financial Constraints and the Treaty of Guadalupe Hidalgo." In *The Mexican and Mexican American Experience in the 19th Century,* edited by Jamie E. Rodríguez O., 68–84. Tempe, AZ: Bilingual Press, 1989.

Diplomacy, U.S.

American expansion into what is now the southwestern and western United States was a concern to other countries since the turn of the 19th century. The United States wanted Spain to acknowledge that Texas was part of the 1803 Louisiana Purchase, but the United States gave up its claim to Texas in the 1819 Adams-Onís Treaty in return for a new boundary agreement with Mexico. Texas lobbied for statehood as soon as it became independent of Mexico in 1836, and although President Andrew Jackson warmly received representatives from the new republic, he did not support statehood. His successor, Martin Van Buren, was also circumspect on Texas. Van Buren and Secretary of State John Forsyth were concerned about the degree to which annexing Texas would damage Mexican-American relations. They nevertheless tried, but failed, to persuade Mexico that U.S. recognition of Texas's independence was not a gesture of disrespect toward Mexico.

America's westward growth exacerbated tensions with Mexico. The U.S. population was growing at an annualized rate of over 3 percent by the 1840s, and many people were migrating west. Not surprisingly, U.S. interest in Mexican territory, especially California, grew. Meanwhile, President John Tyler orchestrated an offer for Texas to become a U.S. state just before the end of his term in December 1844. This precipitated a diplomatic crisis, and Mexico withdrew its minister just after President James K. Polk's inauguration in March 1845. The Americans responded in kind. Polk was intensely nationalistic and, like most Democrats at the time, advocated territorial expansion.

The Oregon boundary dispute with Great Britain had commanded most of America's attention throughout the winter and spring of 1845, however, and the president improvised a policy toward Mexico that rested on both diplomatic initiatives and military maneuvers. Antiwar sentiment in the United States was strong—especially in New England—but the public supported the goal of acquiring more land, and Polk expected that he could accomplish his goals without hostilities. Secretary of State James Buchanan assured departing Mexican minister Juan N. Almonte that the United States wanted to settle its differences with its neighbor peacefully. Polk sent William S. Parrot to Mexico City to convince the Mexican government of the finality of the U.S. annexation of Texas to explore the possibility of resuming diplomatic relations. The Mexican government, well aware of the popular anger in Mexico over the U.S. annexation of Texas, was noncommittal.

Then, in November 1845, Polk sent John Slidell to Mexico City as an emissary. He was authorized to forgive millions of dollars of Mexican debt owed to Americans and offer as much as $40 million for Mexican acknowledgment of the Rio Grande boundary and for the Alta California and Santa Fe de Nuevo Mexico territories. The United States was unwilling to discuss other issues related to Texas, however. Mexican officials, maintaining that Texas should be the only topic of discourse, refused to even receive the diplomat.

Chastised, Slidell suggested that the United States require Mexico to withdraw the note by which it rejected him and advocated war because he believed that the Mexicans viewed American diplomatic overtures as a sign of timidity. Taking a hard line, Polk blamed Mexico for the failure of the diplomatic initiative and broadly suggested that he would resort to warfare if Mexico did not respond positively to Slidell's mission. Slidell handed Mexican officials such a note on March 1, 1846, indicating that they had to decide between peace and war. But he held out hope that war could be avoided because Mexico's failure to acquire sufficient loans had left its treasury depleted.

Ultimately, Slidell received a message from the Mexican government indicating that its position remained unchanged. He then declared that Mexico had announced its intention to fight by rejecting his efforts to negotiate and asked for his passports. He left the country on March 31, 1846, confident that Mexico had given the United States no choice but to declare war. Although Polk had not been in close contact with Slidell, the president approved all of Slidell's individual decisions as he received word of them.

Central to U.S. diplomacy in this crisis was Polk's determination to negotiate from a position of strength. To accomplish this, he took a bellicose stance. He promised Americans security against any Mexican attacks, ordered Brigadier General Zachary Taylor's 3,000-man Army of Observation from Fort Jesup, Louisiana, to Corpus Christi, Texas, on the north bank of the Nueces River, and positioned a naval squadron off the Mexican coast. Based on the questionable 1836 Treaty of Velasco, Texas and the United States had always claimed the Rio Grande as the boundary with Mexico, while the Mexicans claimed that the border was the Nueces, some 150 miles farther north. In January 1846, with the failure of Slidell's diplomatic mission, the president commanded Taylor's army, now known as the Army of Occupation, to the Rio Grande, with contingency orders for Taylor to respond if Mexicans crossed the Rio Grande. He further instructed Commodore John D. Sloat's squadron in the Pacific to seize San Francisco if war erupted. While some have argued that Polk believed that the show of strength would prevent the Mexicans from attacking and compel them to negotiate, others maintain that he lured Mexico into hostilities, knowing that the United States would prevail and gain territory.

Polk had wanted to delay resolving the Mexican issue because the Oregon boundary dispute was at a sensitive juncture, and reports had surfaced that there was emerging opposition to the new hard-line Mexican president, Mariano Paredes y Arrillaga. Polk's instruction to Slidell to draw out negotiations took three to four months to arrive and did not reach the diplomat before his departure from Mexico. Polk had decided to go to war by the end of April and soon after received word of the so-called Thornton Affair in which Mexican soldiers killed 11 U.S. soldiers at a farm some 20 miles northwest of modern-day Brownsville, Texas, on April 25, 1846. Polk met with his cabinet, which unanimously supported sending a war message to Congress. The president blamed Mexico for committing acts of aggression, and the U.S. Congress officially declared war against Mexico on May 13, 1846.

By the beginning of 1848, with their capital occupied by the invaders and over half of their national territory in U.S. hands, Mexican officials decided to sue for peace rather than risk having all of Mexico annexed by the Americans. After intense negotiations, the American diplomat Nicholas Trist managed to convince the newly elected Mexican president, Pedro María Anaya, and the Mexican peace commissioners to agree to the terms of the Treaty of Guadalupe Hidalgo, a peace agreement that accomplished nearly all of the Americans' objectives. It was signed on February 2, 1848, at the Cathedral of Guadalupe in Villa Hidalgo. The U.S. Senate ratified the accord on March 10, 1848, and the Mexican government did so on May 19. Mexico agreed to cede approximately 525,000 square miles of territory in return for a payment of $15 million. The U.S. government also agreed to assume $3.25 million of Mexican debt owed to U.S. citizens. The Mexican land cession resulted in the loss of over half of Mexico's entire land mass.

MATTHEW J. KROGMAN

See also

Adams-Onís Treaty; Almonte, Juan Nepomuceno; Buchanan, James; Diplomacy, Mexican; Guadalupe Hidalgo, Treaty of; Jackson, Andrew; Louisiana Purchase; Mexican Cession; Nueces River; Oregon Boundary Dispute; Paredes y Arrillaga, Mariano; Parrott, William S.; Polk, James Knox; Rio Grande; Santa Anna, Antonio López de; Slidell, John; Sloat, John Drake; Taylor, Zachary; Texas; Texas Declaration of Independence; Texas Revolution; Thornton Affair; Trans-Nueces; Trist, Nicholas Philip; Tyler, John; Van Buren, Martin; War Address, James K. Polk.

References

Haynes, Sam. *James K. Polk and the Expansionist Impulse*. New York: Longman, 1997.

Henderson, Timothy J. *A Glorious Defeat: Mexico and Its War with the United States*. New York: Hill & Wang, 2007.

Ohrt, Wallace. *Defiant Peacemaker: Nicholas Trist in the Mexican War*. College Station: Texas A&M University Press, 1997.

Pletcher, David M. *The Diplomacy of Annexation: Texas, Oregon, and the Mexican War*. Columbia: University of Missouri Press. 1975.

Varg, Paul. *United States Foreign Relations, 1820–1860*. East Lansing: Michigan State University Press, 1979.

Donelson, Andrew Jackson
Birth Date: August 25, 1799
Death Date: June 26, 1871

U.S. Army officer, lawyer, Democratic politician, and diplomat. Andrew Jackson Donelson was born in Davidson County, Tennessee, on August 25, 1799. His father died when he was a small boy, and at the age of five Donelson moved to the Hermitage, where he was reared mainly by his aunt, Rachel Donelson, and her husband, future president Andrew Jackson. Jackson took the young boy under his wing, treating him as an adoptive son.

Donelson graduated from the U.S. Military Academy at West Point in 1820 and was commissioned a second lieutenant. He remained in the army for two years, serving as his uncle's aide-de-camp during Jackson's tenure as military governor in Florida. Donelson then resigned his commission and studied law at Transylvania University. He began practicing law in Nashville in 1823.

Donelson played a major role in his uncle's 1824 and 1828 bids for the U.S. presidency. After Jackson was elected in 1828, he asked Donelson to serve as his personal secretary in 1829. Because Jackson's wife, Rachel, had died only weeks after the election, Donelson's wife acted as the official White House hostess and unofficial First Lady. Donelson remained in the White House throughout Jackson's two terms in office. He returned to Nashville in 1837, where he practiced law and remained influential in Democratic Party politics.

During the 1844 presidential campaign, Donelson helped James K. Polk secure the Democratic Party's nomination. That November he became U.S. minister to the Republic of Texas, where he was charged with cultivating good relations between the two governments in anticipation of Texas annexation. As such, he formally submitted the U.S. Congress's annexation resolution to the Texans, which would protect slavery in the state of Texas, permit Texas to retain its public land claims, and leave open the possibility of subdividing Texas into as many as five smaller states. Subject to the Compromise of 1820, however, slavery would not be permitted above the 36 degree 30 minute latitude. In July 1845, the Texas Congress accepted the annexation deal with a large margin of support, and the following January Donelson left Texas to return to the East.

Donelson served as U.S. minister to the Kingdom of Prussia from 1846 to 1849. He later became an editor for a Democratic newspaper, and in 1856 he was an unsuccessful candidate for the vice presidency, running with former president Millard Fillmore on the American Party ticket. Donelson then moved to Memphis, ultimately splitting his time between that city and his plantation in Mississippi. A fierce critic of Southern secession, he did not support the Confederate cause during the Civil War, although he maintained his southern residence and business concerns. Donelson died in Memphis on June 26, 1871.

PAUL G. PIERPAOLI JR.

See also

Congress, Texas; Polk, James Knox; Texas.

References

Middleton, Annie. "Donelson's Mission to Texas in Behalf of the Annexation." *Southwestern Historical Quarterly* 24 (1921): 279–291.

Meacham, John. *American Lion: Andrew Jackson in the White House.* New York: Random House, 2009.

Doniphan, Alexander William
Birth Date: July 9, 1808
Death Date: August 8, 1887

American lawyer and politician who successfully led a regiment of Missouri troops during the Mexican-American War. Alexander William Doniphan was born on July 9, 1808, in Mason County, Kentucky. After graduating from Augusta College (Kentucky), he sought a legal career and was admitted to the Kentucky bar in 1829. Soon thereafter he moved to Missouri and began practicing law in Lexington in 1830. After three years Doniphan moved to Liberty, Missouri, at the western edge of the state and there established a law practice.

Doniphan was well regarded as a lawyer and gained attention through his legal work on behalf of the Latter Day Saints (Mormons) in Missouri and his service as an officer in the state militia. By 1838, Doniphan held the rank of brigadier general. That year he was responsible for arresting Joseph Smith and other Mormon officials and escorting them out of the state. Despite orders that he kill Smith, Doniphan protected him and other Mormons from vigilante-style attacks until they had departed Missouri.

Doniphan became active in the Whig Party in Missouri and served three terms in the state assembly (1836, 1840, and 1854). Unlike Whigs nationally, Doniphan and many of his fellow Missouri Whigs were generally in favor of Texas annexation, and they willingly served in the Mexican-American War. When that conflict began, Doniphan enlisted as a private and raised a company of volunteers to serve in the 1st Missouri Mounted Volunteer Regiment. He was soon elected colonel of the regiment and commanded it through the remainder of the war.

After the regiment was incorporated into Brigadier General Stephen Kearny's Army of the West, it marched with the rest of that force along the Santa Fe Trail to New Mexico. After securing the surrender of New Mexico and establishing a civil government there, Kearny continued on to California, leaving Doniphan and his unit to control New Mexico. In that capacity, Doniphan drafted the New Mexico territorial constitution and negotiated several treaties with Native American tribes, including the Navajos, but as soon as Colonel Sterling Price's 2nd Missouri Mounted Rifles arrived in Santa Fe, he led his regiment south to rendezvous with Brigadier General John Wool's forces at Chihuahua. This began what became known as "Doniphan's March."

Departing from Valverde, New Mexico, on December 14, 1846, the Missouri troops first encountered opposition on December 25. After they had made camp, Doniphan's force was attacked at Brazito, Mexico (near modern-day El Paso, Texas) by a larger force of Mexican regulars and militiamen. The Missouri troops quickly routed the attackers with negligible losses to themselves.

After occupying and resting in the town of El Paso del Norte, Mexico, until artillery sent from New Mexico arrived, Doniphan departed toward the city of Chihuahua, Mexico, on February 3, 1847. The column encountered stiff resistance on the Sacramento River north of the city in the Battle of Río Sacramento on February 28, 1847. American artillery proved decisive, permitting the Missouri troops to assault the Mexican positions effectively from the flank. Again, Doniphan's forces suffered few casualties.

Colonel Alexander William Doniphan commanded a volunteer regiment from Missouri and led his men on a celebrated march to Chihuahua, Mexico, winning several battles along the way. (Library of Congress)

After occupying Chihuahua, Doniphan directed his energies toward securing the surrender of the state of Chihuahua from Mexican governor Angel Trías Alvarez and determining the location of Wool's forces in order to rendezvous with him. Receiving orders to march to Saltillo, Doniphan departed Chihuahua and arrived at Saltillo on May 21, 1847. From there, he marched his men to the coast and embarked them for a return to Saint Louis, Missouri, by ship. In little more than a year, Doniphan's men had traveled some 5,500 miles, 2,500 of these in very difficult overland conditions.

The achievements of Doniphan and his troops earned him much praise. After the war, he returned to law and political involvement in Missouri. He remained a moderate proslavery advocate, asserting that if emancipation were to occur, it should be gradual, but he argued against secession in the years prior to the Civil War. Doniphan sought to remain neutral during that conflict and continued serving as a lawyer and involved himself in state politics when it ended. He died on August 8, 1887, in Richmond, Missouri.

JOSHUA B. MICHAEL

See also

Brazito, Battle of; Chihuahua, State of; Doniphan's March; Kearny, Stephen Watts; New Mexico; Río Sacramento, Battle of; Saltillo; Santa Fe–Chihuahua Trail; Trías Alvarez, Angel; Whigs; Wool, John Ellis.

References

Dawson, Joseph G., III. *Doniphan's Epic March: The First Missouri Volunteers in the Mexican War.* Topeka: University of Kansas Press, 1999.

Hughes, John Taylor. *Doniphan's Expedition and the Conquest of New Mexico and California.* Reprint, College Station: Texas A&M University Press, 1997.

Launius, Roger D. *Alexander William Doniphan: Portrait of a Missouri Moderate.* Columbia: University of Missouri, 1997.

Doniphan's March
Event Dates: June 1846–May 1847

Epic military expedition of a U.S. volunteer regiment into Mexico during Mexican War. With the beginning of the Mexican-American War, in May 1846, Alexander W. Doniphan, a prominent lawyer with little military experience but an advocate of both Manifest Destiny and the expansion of slaveholding territories, organized for war service a volunteer regiment drawn from the western counties of Missouri. This regiment of 1,000 men became known as the 1st Regiment of Missouri Mounted Volunteers, and Doniphan was its colonel and commanding officer.

The new regiment passed under the authority of then Colonel Stephen W. Kearny and formed part of his new Army of the West. Following a brief period of training at Fort Leavenworth, Kearny departed on June 26, 1846, for Santa Fe in an effort to bring New Mexico under American control. The march was a difficult one,

with the men on half-rations and short of water for themselves and their horses. Despite these obstacles, on August 18 the regiment participated in Kearny's occupation of Santa Fe.

Kearny then ordered Doniphan and his men into the Rocky Mountains to meet with leaders of the Apache, Navajo, and Ute tribes in order to negotiate a peace settlement with them to prevent Indian hostility toward American settlers. Doniphan arranged a treaty with the Navajo, and he also created a framework of government for the newly conquered region. These laws allowed those Mexicans already living in the territory prior to its conquest to receive U.S. citizenship.

In November Kearny departed Santa Fe for California, leaving Doniphan and his regiment to garrison all of New Mexico. On December 14, however, Doniphan yielded command to Colonel Sterling Price, who had arrived in the New Mexico territory with a large force, and departed Santa Fe with 800 men of his regiment for El Paso del Norte (present-day Ciudad Juárez on the south bank of the Rio Grande, and El Paso, Texas, on the north side of the river), 250 miles distant, with the goal of reinforcing units under Brigadier General John Wool operating in the state of Chihuahua.

This was perhaps the most difficult stretch of the entire march, and Doniphan divided his force into two columns so the men could more easily find forage and sustenance. On December 25, some five miles north of their objective of El Paso del Norte, a force of 1,200 Mexicans led by Colonel Antonio Ponce de León caught Doniphan by surprise. Although heavily outnumbered, Doniphan rallied his men and halted a series of Mexican charges. The Battle of Brazito cost the Mexican army about 50 killed and 150 wounded, while the Americans suffered only 7 wounded. Doniphan captured El Paso del Norte two days later with no resistance.

After being reinforced by Major Meriwether Lewis Clark's two batteries of artillery on February 8, 1847, Doniphan continued his march south, moving deep into the state of Chihuahua. On February 28, at Sacramento, 15 miles north of Ciudad Chihuahua, Doniphan won another victory against overwhelming odds by executing a daring flanking maneuver against a Mexican force of 4,200 infantry and cavalry under Major General José Antonio de Heredia. The Mexicans suffered 169 killed, 300 wounded, and 79 prisoners. U.S. losses were 4 killed and 8 wounded. With the Mexicans driven from the field, the Missourians continued their march south and captured the provincial capital of Chihuahua City on March 2. In the vicinity of the city, the regiment skirmished with Apaches.

Doniphan's troops remained in Chihuahua City until April 23 when they received orders from Major General Zachary Taylor to join his command near Saltillo, 600 miles to the southeast. During this 750-mile march, the soldiers contended with natural forces as dangerous as any hostile military army, including windstorms, lack of water, food and forage, oppressive heat, and hostile Native Americans, with whom they fought one skirmish. The regiment arrived at Saltillo on May 21, two months after the Battle of Buena

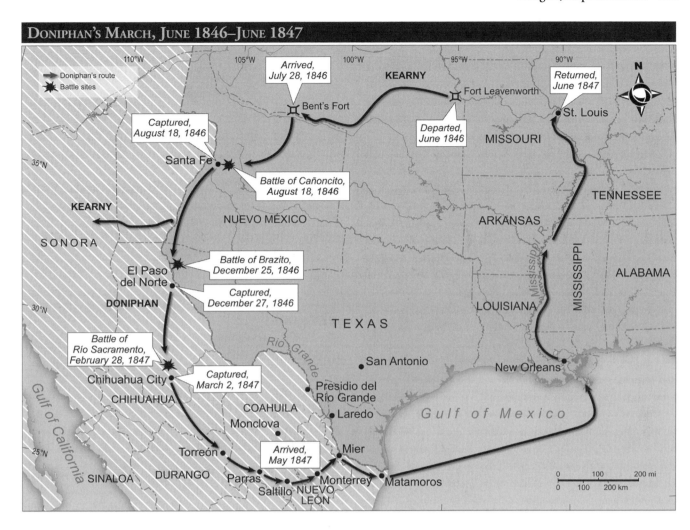

DONIPHAN'S MARCH, JUNE 1846–JUNE 1847

Vista. The regiment's enlistments were now up, and the men continued to Matamoros, where they boarded ships for passage to New Orleans. From there they proceeded up the Mississippi on steamers, arriving in Saint Louis early in June 1847. Doniphan's band of 800 inexperienced volunteers had traveled some 5,500 miles by land and water in slightly more than a year, including some 2,500 miles in very difficult conditions overland. At Brazito and Sacramento, they had defeated Mexican forces considerably larger than their own force with few American casualties. These victories were not unimportant. They stymied Mexican hopes of mounting an expedition to retake Santa Fe and adversely affected Mexican morale while raising that of the Americans.

BRADFORD A. WINEMAN

See also

Brazito, Battle of; Buena Vista, Battle of; Clark, Meriwether Lewis; Doniphan, Alexander William; Heredia, José Antonio de; Kearny, Stephen Watts; New Mexico; Price, Sterling; Río Sacramento, Battle of; Santa Fe; Wool, John Ellis.

References

Dawson, Joseph G., III. *Doniphan's Epic March: The First Missouri Volunteers in the Mexican War.* Lawrence: University of Kansas Press, 1999.

Hughes, John Taylor. *Doniphan's Expedition.* College Station: Texas A&M University Press, 1997.

Launius, Roger D. *Alexander William Doniphan: Portrait of a Missouri Moderate.* Columbia: University of Missouri Press, 1997.

Douglas, Stephen Arnold

Birth Date: April 23, 1813
Death Date: January 3, 1861

U.S. Democratic Party jurist, politician, and U.S. senator best known for a series of debates held with Abraham Lincoln on the subject of slavery in 1858. Stephen Arnold Douglas was born in Brandon, Vermont, on April 23, 1813, and apprenticed in a local law office until 1833. The following year, Douglas moved to Winchester, Illinois, where he was admitted to the bar.

Douglas entered politics as a state's attorney at the age of 21. In 1836, he was elected as a Democrat to the Illinois House of Representatives. By this time he was an ardent Jacksonian Democrat. After losing a bid for the U.S. House of Representatives in 1838, Douglas was appointed secretary of state for Illinois in 1840 and to the Illinois Supreme Court in 1841.

In 1843 Douglas was elected to the U.S. House of Representatives, a position he held until his election into the U.S. Senate in 1847. In the House, he was instrumental in securing passage of legislation giving federal jurisdiction over the Great Lakes. His eloquent defense of a bill to refund Andrew Jackson a fine paid for contempt of a New Orleans court some 20 years earlier led to his recognition as a rising figure in the Democratic Party.

Douglas was a staunch supporter of Manifest Destiny. His expansionist views, coupled with his role as chairman of the Committee on Territories, helped secure the annexation of Texas in December 1845 and U.S. territorial expansion as a result of the Mexican-American War. Douglas firmly sided with President James K. Polk's efforts to end British influence in Oregon, a matter that was resolved by the 1846 Treaty of Oregon. Douglas foresaw a greatly expanded United States that would eventually include the island of Cuba and much of Central America.

By 1847 Douglas had earned sufficient support in Illinois to win a U.S. Senate seat, from which he continued to support President Polk and the Mexican-American War. He also played an increasingly important role regarding the admission of new states and formation of territories and played a role in overseeing the formation of the transcontinental railroad.

Douglas's greatest national recognition came from his efforts to maintain a compromise on the expansion of slavery. Although he was never a slave owner himself, his wife had inherited a southern plantation with slaveholdings. Early on, he believed that the institution of slavery was a matter for the states and not the federal government. A strong supporter of the Compromise of 1850, Douglas first proposed popular sovereignty, the idea that each state or territory had the right to control its destiny. The manifestation of this idea was the Kansas-Nebraska Bill of 1854 that effectively ended the Missouri Compromise of 1820 and stipulated that states could enter the United States with or without slavery. This act, however, reinvigorated the tension that ultimately contributed to the Civil War.

In 1858 Abraham Lincoln challenged Douglas for his Senate seat. As part of the campaign, the two men held a series of seven debates that propelled Lincoln to the national spotlight and led to the alienation of Douglas from many of the southern states for his proposed Freeport Doctrine that allowed territories to exclude slavery.

Douglas received the Democratic nomination for the presidency in 1860; however, the party split when the southern delegates walked out of the convention over the issue of slavery and nominated their own candidate, John C. Breckenridge. Following Lincoln's victory in the 1860 presidential election, Douglas urged the southern states to accept the result. From the beginning of the Civil War, Douglas supported Lincoln's efforts to maintain the Union, no matter the cost.

Over the years, Stephen Douglas has been overshadowed by Abraham Lincoln. However, his service to country and compromising spirit helped maintain the peace in the difficult years prior to the Civil War. His last dying words to his sons were, "Tell them to obey the laws and support the Constitution of the United States." Douglas died in Chicago on January 3, 1861.

JACK COVARRUBIAS AND TOM LANSFORD

See also

Congress, U.S.; Democratic Party; Expansionism and Imperialism; Lincoln, Abraham; Manifest Destiny; Oregon, Treaty of; Polk, James Knox; Slavery.

References

Johannsen, Robert W. *The Frontier, the Union, and Stephen A. Douglas.* Urbana: University of Illinois Press, 1989.
Wells, Damon. *Stephen Douglas: The Last Years, 1857–1861.* Austin: University of Texas Press, 1971.

Dragoons
See Cavalry and Dragoons

Drum, Simon Henry
Birth Date: June 1807
Death Date: September 13, 1847

U.S. Army officer and elder brother of Brigadier General Richard Coulter Drum. Simon Henry Drum was born in Greensburg (Westmoreland County), Pennsylvania, in June 1807. He graduated from the U.S. Military Academy, West Point, in 1830. Commissioned a second lieutenant in the 4th United States Artillery, he taught artillery tactics at West Point during the next two years before seeing action in the 1832 Black Hawk War and the Second Seminole War of 1835–1842. He was promoted to captain in 1846.

Drum served effectively during the entirety of Major General Winfield Scott's Mexico City Campaign. During the Battle of Contreras on August 19–20, 1847, he recaptured two U.S. field pieces that had been taken by the Mexicans at the Battle of Buena Vista. On September 13, 1847, however, he was mortally wounded during the Battle of Mexico City as he entered the Belén Gate, felled while directing artillery fire from a 9-pounder that he and his men had captured earlier in the day. His remains were interred at Fern Cliff Cemetery, Springfield, Ohio.

PAUL G. PIERPAOLI JR.

See also

Buena Vista, Battle of; Contreras, Battle of; Mexico City, Battle for; Mexico City Campaign.

References

Bauer, K. Jack. *The Mexican War, 1846–1848.* New York: Macmillan, 1974.
Clary, David A. *Eagles and Empire: The United States, Mexico, and the Struggle for a Continent.* New York: Bantam Books, 2009.

Du Pont, Samuel Francis
Birth Date: September 27, 1803
Death Date: June 23, 1865

U.S. naval officer and reformer. Born in Bergen Point (today Bayonne), New Jersey, on September 27, 1803, Samuel Du Pont attended Mount Airy College in Pennsylvania beginning in 1812. He secured a warrant as a midshipman on December 19, 1815, but it was not until February 1817 that Du Pont received orders to the ship of the line *Franklin* in the Mediterranean Squadron. He next served in the sloop of war *Erie* (1817–1818). He returned home to resume his studies at Mount Airy and then served in the frigates *Constitution* (1821) and *Congress* (1822), the latter in the West Indies Squadron. He was promoted to lieutenant on April 26, 1826, while serving in the ship of the line *North Carolina* in the Mediterranean. He then served in the schooner *Porpoise*.

Du Pont was much interested in naval professionalism and reform and carried on an extensive correspondence toward that end with fellow officers, congressmen, and businessmen. He joined the U.S. Naval Lyceum, forerunner of the U.S. Naval Institute, and was a chief advocate for naval reform. He also attacked the navy's organizational structure and advocated a bureau system in place of the Board of Navy Commissioners. Promoted to commander on October 28, 1842, by 1845 Du Pont was in command of the frigate *Congress,* the flagship of Commodore Robert F. Stockton's Pacific Squadron.

In the early summer of 1846, the *Congress* sailed to Monterey, California, where Stockton took command of the Pacific Squadron, and U.S. forces secured the surrender of that small port town. Du Pont then commanded the sloop of war *Cyane* and transported the California Battalion south to San Diego, forcing its surrender. He then sailed south to San Blas, where he sent a small landing party ashore to spike Mexican artillery. Du Pont next proceeded to the Gulf of California, where he seized La Paz and launched an assault against Guaymas. In March 1847 he landed a small force at San José del Cabo, at the southern tip of the Baja Peninsula, which marched some three miles inland to rescue Americans being held prisoner there. Du Pont also played a key role in the blockading of the Baja coastline. Between 1846 and 1848, he was responsible for the capture or destruction of 30 Mexican vessels in the Gulf of California.

Du Pont was involved in the creation of both the U.S. Naval Academy (1845) and the Lighthouse Board (1852). Not known as a strict disciplinarian, he nonetheless supported the use of corporal punishment. Promoted to captain on September 14, 1855, he was instrumental in the formation of, and chaired, the Naval Efficiency Board (1855), which removed deadwood from the officer corps. Du Pont established his reputation as a reformer, but he also had a deserved reputation as an advocate of new technology in a service that was often reluctant to embrace change.

At the beginning of the Civil War in 1861, Captain Du Pont was already a veteran of 46 years of service. Secretary of the Navy Gideon Welles thought highly of him and named him the chair of

Lithograph of American naval officer Samuel Francis Du Pont. A naval reformer, he helped establish the Naval Academy in 1845. During the Mexican-American War, Commander Du Pont assisted in the capture of Mexican ports and ships along the Pacific coast and Gulf of California. (Bridgeman Art Library)

the Commission of Conference, popularly known as the Blockade Board, which was charged with establishing Union naval strategy. On September 18, 1861, Du Pont took command of the South Atlantic Blockading Squadron. Two months later, on November 7, he commanded the largest fleet in U.S. Navy history to that point in the capture of Port Royal, South Carolina, which became a major Union naval base. Du Pont then directed the Union capture of nearby Beaufort, as well as Cumberland Island and Saint Mary's; Fort Pulaski, Georgia; and Amelia Island, Fernandina, and Fort Clinch, Florida.

Promoted to rear admiral on July 16, 1862, and urged on by Welles and Assistant Secretary of the Navy Gustavus V. Fox, Du Pont directed the much more difficult Union effort to capture the city of Charleston. Taking the city with naval forces alone was in fact an impossible task, especially given the limitations of the slow-firing Union monitors. Du Pont was correct in his belief that a combined operation with land forces was the only way success would be achieved against the formidable Confederate forts guarding the city approaches.

The Union assault, finally launched on April 7, 1863, was a failure. Given the way Du Pont handled criticism of his actions and his continued pessimism regarding a new assault, Welles concluded that the admiral would have to be replaced. Rear Admiral John Dahlgren assumed command of the South Atlantic Blockading Squadron on July 6.

Du Pont refused Welles's offer of command of the Pacific Squadron, returning to his home near Wilmington, Delaware, in failing health. He then served on the board in Washington, D.C., formed to consider the promotion of those who had rendered outstanding service during the war. Du Pont never completely recovered his health and died on June 23, 1865, during a visit to Philadelphia.

RICHARD W. PEUSER AND SPENCER C. TUCKER

See also

Baja California; Blockades, Naval; California Battalion; Guaymas, Battle of; Gulf of California (Mar de Cortés); La Paz; Monterey, California; Stockton, Robert Field; United States Navy.

References

Bauer, K. Jack. "Samuel Francis Du Pont: Aristocratic Professional." In *Captains of the Old Steam Navy,* edited by James C. Bradford, 142–165. Annapolis, MD: Naval Institute Press, 1986.

Merrill, James M. *Du Pont: The Making of an Admiral: A Biography of Samuel Francis Du Pont.* New York: Dodd, Mead, 1986.

Durán, Augustín
Birth Date: Unknown
Death Date: Unknown

New Mexican trader who, along with coconspirators Diego Archuleta and Tomas Ortiz, plotted to topple the U.S. occupation government in New Mexico in late 1846. The scheme also called for the assassination of U.S. governor Charles Bent and Colonel Sterling Price, the U.S. military commander in Santa Fe. There is virtually no biographical information on Durán. He was likely born in New Mexico, perhaps in the early 1800s, and eventually settled in Santa Fe, where he became a successful trader. Numerous references to him have the deferential "Don" before his name, indicating that he was a man of financial means and well-respected in his community.

By the early autumn of 1846, Durán, along with Archuleta, Ortiz, and other native-born New Mexicans, had become furious with the American occupation that had begun just a few months before. When U.S. forces had first arrived the Americans claimed not to be interested in a wholesale occupation of New Mexico, but only in the disputed area from the Rio Grande east to Texas. By late September or so, however, it became clear to the New Mexicans that the United States planned on annexing all of New Mexico. At that point, Durán and his coconspirators began to formulate a plan to oust the U.S. occupation government and to recruit men from the Santa Fe and Taos areas to participate in the rebellion.

The conspirators hoped to launch the attack on Christmas day, taking the Americans by surprise. The insurrectionists were to hide in a church in Santa Fe. When the church bells tolled at midnight, signaling the start of the Christmas holiday, they would capture the artillery in the main square and then hunt down and assassinate Price and Bent. Meanwhile, messengers would inform rural residents of the rebellion.

The plan was never carried out, however, because in early December Price received word of the insurrection from an informant. He ordered the immediate arrest of Durán, Archuleta, and Ortiz, but the three escaped under cover of night, perhaps into the rugged New Mexican mountains, or south into the state of Chihuahua. The Taos Revolt, which began in January 1847, resulted in the murder of Bent, but the rebellion was soon quashed by American occupation forces. That plan had been based largely on the earlier failed scheme hatched by Durán and his fellow conspirators. The whereabouts of Durán after he fled Santa Fe in December 1846 are not known, and there is no information on the remainder of his life or his death.

PAUL G. PIERPAOLI JR.

See also

Archuleta, Diego; Armijo, Manuel; Bent, Charles; Kearny, Stephen Watts; Magoffin, James Wiley; Martinez, Antonio José; New Mexico; Ortiz, Tomás; Price, Sterling; Santa Fe; Taos Revolt.

References

Coldsmith, Don. *Trail from Taos.* New York: Bantam Books, 1990.

Crutchfield, James Andrew. *Tragedy at Taos: The Revolt of 1847.* Plano: Republic of Texas Press, 1995.

Twitchell, Ralph Emerson. *The History of the Military Occupation of the Territory of New Mexico.* New York: Arno Press, 1976.

Durango, State of

Officially known as the Free and Sovereign State of Durango, located in the northern part of the Republic of Mexico; under Spanish colonial rule, it was part of the viceroyalty of New Spain's province of Nueva Vizcaya. Durango is bordered by Chihuahua to the north, Sinaloa and Nayarit to the west, Zacatecas to the east and southeast, and Coahuila to the east and northeast. Durango's territory covers 47,560 square miles. The largest city and capital of the state is also called Durango, formerly called Victoria de Durango. Durango's major rivers include the Florido, Acaponeta, and the Nazas; the Sierra Madre Occidental mountain range runs through the western part of the state.

Although the fourth-largest Mexican state in size, Durango has historically been sparsely populated, with only 1.5 million people as of 2007. Durango's population during the late 1840s was approximately 163,000, with an estimated 22,000 living in the capital city. Ethnically, the inhabitants were mainly Europeans and Mestizos.

Prior to Spain's conquest of Mexico in the early 1500s, several Native American groups, including the Xiximes, Tepehuanes, and

Tarahumares, had inhabited the region. During the mid-1500s, Spanish conquistador Francisco de Ibarra led expeditions and established settlements in northern Mexico, including a region he named Nueva Vizcaya, which contained Durango. Despite resistance from the Native Americans, Spanish settlers gradually moved into the region, establishing ranches and farms and developing mines. The Royal Road of the Interior Land passed through Durango, allowing for goods and men to move fairly quickly between Mexico City and Santa Fe, New Mexico.

In the aftermath of the Mexican wars for independence, Nueva Vizcaya was divided into the states of Chihuahua and Durango. During the Mexican-American War, U.S. traders used the Royal Road to transport goods into Mexico. In February 1847, Colonel Alexander Doniphan, commander of the 1st Missouri Mounted Volunteers, attacked Mexican forces, which included the 2nd Durango Squadron from Durango, cavalry and infantry forces from Chihuahua, and other Mexican military units commanded by Major General José Antonio de Heredia, at the Battle of Río Sacramento, although American forces never occupied Durango.

Durango faced a series of conflicts and occupations after the Mexican-American War, including the French occupation during the Franco-Mexican War (1861–1867), the Mexican Revolution (1910–1920), and the Cristero War (1926–1929). Since the end of the Cristero War, Durango has enjoyed many internal improvements. Traditionally, its major industries have been agriculture, livestock, and mining (especially silver); however, it has especially benefited from the 1994 North American Free Trade Agreement (NAFTA), which has resulted in many manufacturing plants being located in the state.

WYNDHAM E. WHYNOT

See also

Chihuahua, State of; Coahuila y Texas; Doniphan, Alexander William; Heredia, José Antonio de; Río Sacramento, Battle of.

References

Eisenhower, John S. D. *So Far from God: The U.S. War With Mexico, 1846–1848.* Norman: University of Oklahoma Press, 2000.

Moorhead, Max L. *New Mexico's Royal Road: Trade and Travel on the Chihuahua Trail.* Norman: University of Oklahoma Press, 1958.

Navarro Gallegos, César. "Una 'Santa Alianza': El gobierno duranguense y la jerarquía eclesiástica durante la intervención norteamericana." In *México en Guerra (1846–1848): Perspectivas regionales,* coordinated by Laura Herrera, 233–252. Mexico City: Consejo Nacional para la Cultura y las Artes, 1997.

Pacheco Rojas, José de la Cruz. "Durango entre dos guerras, 1846–1847." In *México al tiempo de su Guerra con los Estados Unidos (1846–1848).* Coordinated by Josefina Zoraida Vázquez, 189–212. Mexico City: Secretaría de Relaciones Exteriores, El Colegio de México, y Fondo de Cultura Económica, 1997.

E

El Bosque de San Domingo (Walnut Springs)

Wooded area to the northeast of Monterrey, Mexico, used as a campsite for Major General Zachary Taylor's army and as a staging area during U.S. operations in northern Mexico, including the Battle of Monterrey. As Taylor's force approached Monterrey in early September 1846, Taylor chose El Bosque de San Domingo (San Domingo's Wood) as a campsite because of its bountiful trees, which could provide shade and firewood, and because of the several springs that ran through the area. The woods abounded with live oak, ebony, and pecan trees, which some had mistakenly identified as walnut trees. Thereafter, the Americans referred to the camp as Walnut Springs.

By mid-September 1846, approximately 6,650 men made Walnut Springs home. Taylor lived on the site for the entirety of his stay in northern Mexico, as did Brigadier General John A. Quitman. El Bosque de San Domingo was also used as a cemetery for those officers and men who died during the Battle of Monterrey. While some of the dead who had been buried at Walnut Springs were later disinterred to be buried in the United States, many bodies remained. Several modern attempts to locate El Bosque de San Domingo and its cemetery ended in failure, however, as the city of Monterrey had long ago engulfed the area.

At Walnut Springs, artist William Carl Brown Jr. painted his well-known portrait of Taylor and his staff.

PAUL G. PIERPAOLI JR.

See also

Monterrey, Battle of; Quitman, John Anthony; Taylor, Zachary.

References

May, Robert E. *John A. Quitman: Old South Crusader.* Baton Rouge: Louisiana State University Press, 1985.

Election of 1844, U.S.

U.S. presidential election that served as a catalyst of the Mexican-American War. During the first six months of 1844, President John Tyler had made a determined effort to annex Texas to the United States. Although the U.S. Senate rejected annexation by a 2–1 margin, Tyler's policy ensured that the issue of Texas annexation would be at the forefront of the presidential election campaign that fall.

Hoping to keep the annexation issue out of the contest, both of the expected nominees, Democrat Martin Van Buren and Whig Party candidate Henry Clay, announced their opposition to acquiring Texas. But while Clay easily secured his party's nomination, Van Buren ran into difficulty at the Democratic convention in May 1844. Slaveholders eager to add Texas to the Union as a slave state and Democrats who favored territorial expansion refused to support Van Buren. Finally, after failing to select a nominee after eight ballots, endorsement of party hero and former president Andrew Jackson clinched the nomination for Tennessee governor James K. Polk.

Unlike Van Buren, Polk was an outspoken advocate of expansion. Running under the campaign slogan, "Fifty-Four Forty or Fight!" he inserted a plank into the Democratic platform by calling for the acquisition of both Texas and the whole of the Oregon Territory, where American and British claims conflicted. Polk's demands for annexation proved popular in the South and West. Fearing that he might lose the votes of southern Whigs over the Texas issue, Clay shifted his position, declaring that he would not object to the annexation of Texas if it could be accomplished honorably and without war.

Whatever benefits Clay derived in the South from his change of opinion were more than offset by losses in the North. Antislavery voters there believed Clay was pandering to slaveholders,

A Democratic Party campaign banner of 1844 featuring portraits of Democratic presidential candidate James K. Polk (left) and his running mate George Dallas (right). Polk, an outspoken supporter of U.S. territorial expansion, won election on the issue of the annexation of Texas. (Library of Congress)

and thousands abandoned him in favor of the abolitionist Liberty Party. That party had won support from only 7,000 voters in 1840 but amassed 62,000 votes in 1844. The shift of Whig votes to the Liberty Party cost Clay the election in New York State.

Polk strengthened his candidacy by adeptly handling other issues, such as the tariff. The Democratic platform called for low tariffs, which created concerns in Pennsylvania and other manufacturing states about foreign competition. Polk assured voters that while he opposed a protective tariff, he would keep duties sufficiently high to provide adequate funds for the federal government.

The campaign of 1844 was bitter; supporters of both candidates heaped insults on their opponent. Polk won by a margin of 38,000 votes out of 2.7 million cast. His success in the Deep South, West, and Northeast gave him a decisive victory in the Electoral College, 170 votes to Clay's 105.

Before Polk's term began, Tyler used a joint resolution of Congress to bypass Senate opposition and annex Texas in March 1845. After taking office, Polk reached a compromise with Great Britain over Oregon. With regard to Texas, however, Polk insisted that the

disputed territory between the Nueces River and the Rio Grande belonged to the United States and sent troops into the region, which resulted in the skirmish with Mexican forces that sparked the war with Mexico.

JIM PIECUCH

See also

Clay, Henry; Democratic Party; Expansionism and Imperialism; Manifest Destiny; Polk, James Knox; Slavery; Tariffs; Texas; Tyler, John; Van Buren, Martin; Whigs.

References

Haynes, Sam W. *James K. Polk and the Expansionist Impulse.* New York: Longman, 2002.

Remini, Robert V. *Henry Clay: Statesman for the Union.* New York: W. W. Norton, 1991.

El Embudo Pass, Skirmish at
Event Date: January 29, 1847

Military engagement in New Mexico between U.S. forces under the command of Colonel Sterling Price and a mixed force of Mexicans and Native American rebels. The clash occurred on January 27, 1847. The skirmish at El Embudo Pass was part of the U.S. attempt to quell the Taos Revolt, which had begun on January 19. The El Embudo Pass (or Canyon) is located in modern-day Dixon, New Mexico, in the extreme north central part of the state. Then as now, the area was sparsely populated and featured a strikingly beautiful and rugged high desert, about 6,000 feet above sea level.

Price and his command of about 350 men were determined to track down the rebels who had murdered New Mexican governor Charles Bent. On January 24, Price had defeated a rebel force at the Battle of La Cañada, but he continued to pursue disparate bands of insurrectionists, moving generally north-northwest through New Mexico. After that engagement, Price's command was reinforced to approximately 480 men; it also received several more artillery pieces. Rebel forces were estimated to be around 1,500.

Early on January 29, Price received a report that rebels had taken up position in El Embudo Canyon astride the wagon road that ran through the area. Wasting no time, Price sent his men into the pass, attacking on a broad front. The rebels panicked and quickly fled the scene, some ascending the surrounding mountains where the snow was deep and the temperatures bitterly cold. Some U.S. soldiers pursued them but were hampered by the weather; several returned to the main force suffering from frostbite. Price's forces suffered 1 dead and 1 wounded in the skirmish; rebel losses were estimated at 20 killed and 60 wounded.

Price's quick and relatively inexpensive victory buoyed the Americans and deeply demoralized the Taos rebels. The quickness with which they disintegrated and fled the scene suggested that the rebels were losing their cohesiveness; in fact, numerous

Mexicans and Native Americans simply disappeared, more than likely returning to their home villages.

PAUL G. PIERPAOLI JR.

See also

Bent, Charles; New Mexico; Price, Sterling; Taos Revolt.

References

Coldsmith, Don. *Trail from Taos.* New York: Bantam, 1990.

Crutchfield, James Andrew. *Tragedy at Taos: The Revolt of 1847.* Plano: Republic of Texas Press, 1995.

McNierney, Michael. *Taos 1847: The Revolt in Contemporary Accounts.* Boulder, CO: Johnson, 1980.

Elliot, Charles
Birth Date: 1801
Death Date: September 9, 1875

British naval officer and diplomat who served as British chargé d'affaires to the Republic of Texas from 1842 to 1845. Born in 1801 in Dresden, Saxony, where his father, Hugh Elliot, brother of the first Earl of Minto, was serving as British minister, Charles Elliot attended a British boarding school when his father was posted as British governor of Madras in 1814. Elliot joined the Royal Navy a year later and served in the Africa Squadron attempting to end the Atlantic slave trade, which Britain had outlawed in 1807.

Elliot retired from the navy in 1828 and joined the British colonial service. The Colonial Office sent him to Demerara, British Guiana, in 1830 to be the protector of slaves. Occupying the position for four years, Elliot became a committed abolitionist.

Elliot next served in Canton, China, beginning in 1834 as secretary to the British trade commissioner. One year later he was promoted to British trade superintendent in Canton. Elliot, therefore, was in charge of British trade relations with China at the moment when Chinese officials were attempting to end the illegal opium trade being conducted by British merchants. The dispute between the British and Chinese authorities culminated in the outbreak of the First Opium War in 1839. Then, in 1841, Elliot and the governor of Guangdong Province signed the Convention of Chuenpeh, an attempt to end the war. The treaty provided for the cession of Hong Kong to England but allowed the Chinese to continue to collect taxes in Hong Kong. The British government refused to ratify the treaty, however, and the war continued until 1842. Regardless, Elliot became the first British administrator of Hong Kong in January 1841. That August the British government removed Elliot from his post, alleging that he had not adequately represented British merchant interests. He was next assigned to the top British diplomatic post in the Republic of Texas.

Elliot arrived at the port of Galveston to assume his duties as the British chargé d'affaires on August 6, 1842. Elliot worked for the abolition of slavery in Texas, the establishment of free trade, and a lasting peace treaty with Mexico. Elliot became a close friend of Republic of Texas presidents Sam Houston and Anson Jones, and he secretly worked with the British minister in Mexico City to implement a workable peace treaty between Texas and Mexico. Because of the advantages to England of an independent Texas, Elliot actively campaigned against annexation by the United States. In 1845, with the support of Jones, Elliot traveled incognito to Mexico City to secure a treaty recognizing Texan independence, to be guaranteed by England. Elliot was assisted in his endeavor by Jean Peter Alphonse Dubois, the Count de Saligny, the French chargé d'affaires in Texas.

In June 1845, after Elliot returned to Texas with the treaty, Jones offered Texans two choices: accept the American offer of annexation or sign the treaty with Mexico and remain an independent nation. Notwithstanding Elliot's efforts, Texans voted for annexation and Elliot was recalled to England.

Elliot subsequently served as governor of Bermuda from 1846 to 1854, Trinidad from 1854 to 1856, and Saint Helena from 1863 to 1869. In 1856, he was knighted and returned to active duty in the British Navy, eventually rising to admiral. Elliot died at Witteycombe, Exeter, England, on September 9, 1875.

MICHAEL R. HALL

See also

Abolitionism; Great Britain; Houston, Samuel; Jones, Anson; Slavery; Texas.

References

Adams, Ephraim Douglass. *British Interests and Activities in Texas, 1836–1846.* Baltimore, MD: Johns Hopkins University Press, 1910.

Blake, Clagette. *Charles Elliot, R.N., 1801–1875: A Servant of Britain Overseas.* London: Cleaver-Hume Press, 1960.

Haynes, Sam W. "'But What Will England Say?'—Great Britain, the United States, and the War with Mexico." In *Dueling Eagles: Reinterpreting the U.S.-Mexican War, 1846–1848,* edited by Douglas W. Richmond and Richard Francaviglia, 19–40. Fort Worth: Texas Christian University Press, 2000.

Hoe, Susanna, and Derek Roebuck. *The Taking of Hong Kong: Charles and Clara Elliot in China Waters.* Richmond, Surrey, England: Curzon, 2000.

Pletcher, David. *The Diplomacy of Annexation: Texas, Oregon, and the Mexican War.* Columbia: University of Missouri Press, 1973.

El Molino del Rey, Battle of
Event Date: September 8, 1847

Battle that took place during Major General Winfield Scott's Mexico City Campaign. The encounter occurred on September 8, 1847, and was named for a series of low stone buildings located barely 1,000 yards from the castle of Chapultepec and two miles southwest of the gates to Mexico City. El Molino del Rey (the King's Mill) was a key element of Mexican general Antonio López de Santa Anna's plan for the defense of the city, and Mexican engineers had used the period of the August 24 armistice between the belligerents to turn the mill into a formidable stronghold. The buildings offered

BATTLE OF EL MOLINO DEL REY, SEPTEMBER 8, 1847

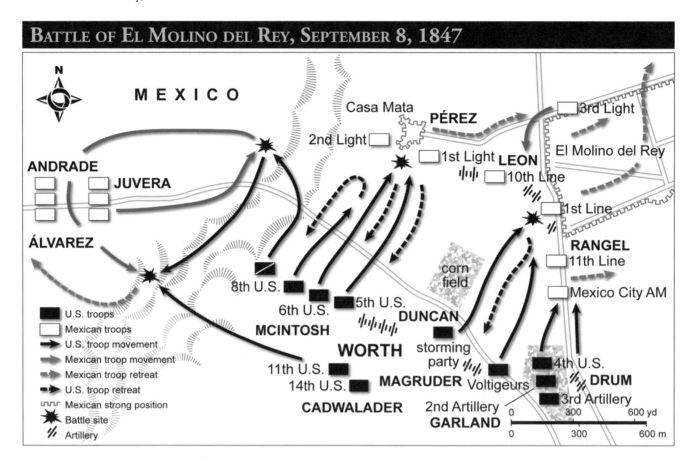

excellent defensive positions for the Mexican troops, but Brigadier General Antonio León initially chose to deploy his regiments and artillery in front of them rather than sheltering his forces within the structures.

Intelligence reports gathered from Mexican deserters and captured civilians had led Scott to believe that El Molino del Rey served as a foundry that cast heavy artillery for the defense of Mexico City. Accordingly, Scott had made its capture a priority en route to the capital city. He assigned Major General William J. Worth the task of driving off León's forces and capturing the supposed foundry. Worth's 3,400 troops included seven infantry regiments, two regiments of dragoons, and an assortment of artillery batteries. León's defenders numbered three light infantry regiments, three regiments of infantry regulars, and six artillery pieces manned by elements of the famed San Patricio Battalion.

The attack on El Molino del Rey was conducted with little reconnaissance and scant planning. Worth's division charged the Mexican positions, only to be met by a hail of artillery fire and volleys of musketry. The U.S. troops, who had not expected such strong resistance, recoiled from the assault with heavy losses. The three U.S. columns then re-formed outside effective musket range and prepared for a second assault. In the meantime, American dragoons drove off a Mexican cavalry force attempting to reinforce León's position. Worth ordered some of his divisional artillery to move into a flanking position, enfilading the entire left wing of León's defenses.

The second American assault drove the Mexican defenders back into El Molino del Rey. By maintaining contact, the attackers prevented the Mexican troops from moving into secure positions amid the buildings. Eventually, the defenders abandoned not only El Molino del Rey but also the earthworks protecting Casa Mata, an earthen fort some 2,000 yards to the west of Chapultepec Castle. The American forces swarmed into the buildings of El Molino del Rey, only to discover that they housed no cannon.

Although Worth had seized the objective, he had paid a heavy price. Of the 3,400 Americans engaged at El Molino del Rey, 800 were killed or wounded, a casualty rate of 23 percent. Worth was later severely criticized for his ill-conceived headlong assault on the Mexican positions. Clearly, his poor reconnaissance had failed to reveal the presence of Mexican artillery and underestimated the size of León's forces. For their part, León's

Battle of El Molino del Rey, September 8, 1847

	United States	Mexico
Total Mobilized	3,400	4,000
Casualties		
Killed	116	269
Wounded	665	500
Captured	0	852*
Missing	18	Unknown

* Includes some wounded

Print depicting the Battle of El Molino del Rey. This costly U.S. victory occurred on September 8, 1847, and was part of Major General Winfield Scott's Mexico City Campaign. (Library of Congress)

defenders suffered approximately 2,000 casualties in the battle. Many of these men fought heroically, and one of them, Lucas Balderas, colonel of the Mina National Guard Battalion, was subsequently enthroned in the pantheon of Mexican national heroes.

The significance of the Battle of El Molino del Rey came in the form of lessons learned by Scott. With the Mexican capital in sight, Scott knew that he faced the heart of Mexican defenses. If the fighting at El Molino del Rey were indicative of the cost to be paid for the capture of Mexico City, U.S. forces would be destroyed through attrition before breaching the city gates. Scott now dedicated considerably more time and resources to reconnaissance and planning. After conducting a feint against Mexico City from the south, the Americans advanced on the city's defenses in a direct line from El Molino del Rey. Just five days after the Battle of El Molino del Rey, American troops began bombarding Chapultepec Castle protecting the final approach to the city gates.

PAUL J. SPRINGER

See also

Chapultepec, Battle of; Mexico City, Battle for; Mexico City Campaign; Santa Anna, Antonio López de; Scott, Winfield; Worth, William Jenkins.

References

Bauer, K. Jack. *The Mexican War, 1846–1848.* New York: Macmillan, 1974.

Johnson, Timothy D. *A Gallant Little Army: The Mexico City Campaign.* Lawrence: University Press of Kansas, 2007.

Salas Cuesta, María Elena, ed. *Molino del Rey: Historia de un monumento.* Mexico City: Consejo Nacional para la Cultura y las Artes, 1997.

Santoni, Pedro. "Lucas Balderas: Popular Leader and Patriot." In *The Human Tradition in Mexico,* edited by Jeffrey M. Pilcher, 41–56. Wilmington, DE: Scholarly Resources, 2003.

El Rincón del Diablo

Mexican stronghold on the outskirts of Monterrey in northern Mexico. El Rincón del Diablo (Devil's Corner), along with a redoubt known as La Tenería, protected the eastern approaches of the city of Monterrey. To get into the city, portions of Major General Zachary Taylor's army would have to neutralize both defensive positions. Unlike La Tenería, which was a building constructed of stone with a parapet reinforced with sandbags, Devil's Corner was little more than an area of high ground surrounded by makeshift walls and sandbags.

At the beginning of the Battle of Monterrey, on September 21, 1846, Devil's Corner was garrisoned by approximately 200 Mexican soldiers supported by three cannon of undetermined size. Taylor's men attempted to take the redoubt several times that day, but each time they were pushed back by an accurate and continual fire by the Mexican artillery. Only after La Tenería had been captured early the next day, and after the Mexicans had withdrawn with their artillery from El Rincón del Diablo under cover of night on September 22, were U.S. troops able to occupy the stronghold.

PAUL G. PIERPAOLI JR.

See also
Monterrey, Battle of; Taylor, Zachary.

References
Feldman, Ruth Tenzer. *The Mexican-American War.* Minneapolis, MN: Lerner, 2004.

Ferrell, Robert H., ed. *Monterrey Is Ours! The Mexican War Letters of Lt. Dana, 1845–1847.* Lexington: University of Kentucky Press, 1990.

El Tomacito (Tomás Baca, Tomás Romero)
Birth Date: ca. 1805
Death Date: 1847

Pueblo Indian who played a key role in the Taos Revolt of January–February 1847 against U.S. occupation forces in New Mexico. El Tomacito, also known as Tomás Baca and Tomás Romero, was born in northern New Mexico, perhaps around 1805. Nothing of him is known beyond his birth and early years. He became a local Pueblo leader by the 1830s and made his home at Don Fernando de Taos (near modern-day Taos, New Mexico). Numerous Mexican nationals had been plotting to overthrow the American occupation government as early as the autumn of 1846, but a plot that included the assassination of Governor Charles Bent and U.S. military commander Colonel Sterling Price was foiled in December 1846, when Price learned of the scheme and arrested most of the conspirators. Nevertheless, a number of Mexicans—including Pueblos—were determined to end the American occupation and drive U.S. forces out of New Mexico. El Tomacito, along with Pablo Montoya and Pablo Chávez, continued to move forward with their planned insurrection, which they hoped to launch in mid-January 1847.

On January 19, 1847, El Tomacito and his coconspirators launched what came to be known as the Taos Revolt. Americans were attacked throughout Don Fernando de Taos, and Governor Bent was killed and scalped in front of his horrified family. Several other U.S. officials were also murdered. Mexican nationals and select Pueblos also committed acts of violence throughout the countryside, resulting in more deaths. Within days, Price was leading a detachment of soldiers, determined to quash the revolt and detain its instigators.

Realizing that the Americans were closing in, El Tomacito ordered most of his rebel force to take up defensive positions in a church at Don Fernando de Taos, which U.S. forces shelled with little effect. By February 9, however, the church and surrounding town had been cleared of rebels, some of whom were killed. Others, including El Tomacito, were captured by U.S. forces. Ultimately, 28 men, including El Tomacito, were charged, tried, and convicted of murder. On February 11, while El Tomacito sat in a cell awaiting trial, an impetuous U.S. dragoon was allowed entrance to the jail. Apparently in the presence of several other soldiers, the dragoon drew his pistol and shot El Tomacito at point-blank range, killing him instantly. The soldier who killed the Pueblo leader fled and was never brought to justice. By April 1847, 28 rebels had been executed for their roles in the Taos Revolt.

PAUL G. PIERPAOLI JR.

See also
Bent, Charles; New Mexico; Price, Sterling; Pueblo de Taos, Skirmish at; Pueblos; Taos Revolt.

References
Coldsmith, Don. *Trail from Taos.* New York: Bantam Books, 1990.

Crutchfield, James Andrew. *Tragedy at Taos: The Revolt of 1847.* Plano: Republic of Texas Press, 1995.

McNierney, Michael. *Taos 1847: The Revolt in Contemporary Accounts.* Boulder, CO: Johnson, 1980.

Emerson, Ralph Waldo
Birth Date: May 25, 1803
Death Date: April 27, 1882

American poet, philosopher, and writer who founded the transcendentalist movement and adamantly objected to the Mexican-American War. Ralph Waldo Emerson was born on May 25, 1803, in Boston, Massachusetts, to a prominent Boston family with strong ties to Unitarianism. He attended Harvard Divinity School, where he studied to become a Unitarian minister. Emerson accepted a pastoral position at a Boston church but resigned his post in 1832 after expressing doubts about institutional Christianity. He then became a lecturer in the lyceum movement of New England as well as a popular writer of literature and philosophy.

Emerson's essay *Nature* (1836) received considerable attention for its criticism of materialism and its lyrical depiction of the human relationship with the beauty and virtue of nature. Also in 1836 Emerson founded the Transcendental Club. His 1837 address to Harvard's Phi Beta Kappa Society, titled "The American Scholar," brought Emerson even more celebrity. In it he urged his audience to rely less on European intellectual traditions and to create a distinctively American way of thinking. Emerson's celebrity turned to controversy in 1838 when he delivered his famous Harvard Divinity School Address. In it, he renounced Christianity

Ralph Waldo Emerson, leader of the Transcendentalism movement, was one of the foremost American writers and thinkers of the 19th century. (Library of Congress)

in its historical form and elaborated on his transcendentalist philosophy.

During the 1840s, Emerson became the leading mind in the emerging transcendentalist movement of New England. He joined Margaret Fuller, Amos Bronson Alcott, and Henry David Thoreau, among others, in the publication of a small quarterly called *The Dial.* Also at this time, Emerson enhanced his status as an eminent lecturer and essayist. He compiled many of his early works in *Essays* (1841) and then expounded on his thoughts in *Essays: Second Series* (1844), *Representative Men* (1850), *Conduct of Life* (1860), *Society and Solitude* (1870), *Parnassus* (1874), and *Letters and Social Aims* (1876).

Emerson often turned his attention to issues of social reform, especially in relation to the cause of abolitionism. He commemorated the British emancipation of the West Indies in 1844, and he opposed the Mexican-American War because of its potential to augment the number of slave states. He also objected to the war because he believed it to be immoral and little more than a drive on the part of the James K. Polk administration to annex most or all of Mexico. More generally, Emerson opposed war in all its forms and promoted nonviolent means of resistance. He denounced the Fugitive Slave Law of 1850 and then referred to the radical abolitionist John Brown as a saint and a martyr after the 1859 raid at Harpers Ferry. Although initially unimpressed with Abraham Lincoln, Emerson welcomed his Emancipation Proclamation of

1862 and mourned for the president upon his assassination in April 1865.

Harvard College awarded Emerson a doctor of laws degree in 1866 and made him an overseer of the college in 1867. Emerson's home burned in 1872, after which he embarked on one last European tour before his death in Concord, Massachusetts, on April 27, 1882. Emerson's intellectual legacy contributed significantly to the advancement of uniquely American philosophical and literary endeavors for the remainder of the 19th century and well into the 20th century.

Michael Pasquier

See also

Abolitionism; Opposition to the Mexican-American War, U.S.; Slavery; Thoreau, Henry David; Transcendental Club.

References

Buell, Lawrence. *Emerson.* Cambridge, MA: Belknap Press of Harvard University Press, 2003.

Emerson, Ralph Waldo. *The Essential Writings of Ralph Waldo Emerson.* Edited by Brooks Atkinson. New York: Modern Library, 2000.

Sacks, Kenneth S. *Understanding Emerson: The American Scholar and His Struggle for Self-Reliance.* Princeton, NJ: Princeton University Press, 2003.

Emory, William Hemsley
Birth Date: September 7, 1811
Death Date: December 1, 1887

U.S. Army officer, engineer, and surveyor. Born in Queen Anne's County, Maryland, on September 7, 1811, William Hemsley Emory graduated from the U.S. Military Academy at West Point in 1831 and was commissioned a second lieutenant in the 4th Artillery Regiment, later joining the Topographical Engineers with the rank of first lieutenant. In 1836 he left the army to pursue a career as a civil engineer but rejoined the army two years later. From 1844 to 1846, Emory was part of the survey mission charged with demarcating the Canadian-American border in the Pacific Northwest.

When the Mexican-American War began in 1846, Emory served as chief engineer and acting assistant adjutant general in Brigadier General Stephen Kearny's Army of the West, which occupied New Mexico. He was then a lieutenant colonel of volunteers. Emory went on to California with Kearny and a detachment of some 300 men in September 1846, where he provided highly effective service at the Battles of San Pascual, San Gabriel River, and La Mesa, winning two brevets, the last one to brigadier general. He was briefly stationed in Washington, D.C., before going to Mexico where he was executive officer of a regiment of Maryland volunteers. After the war, from 1848 to 1855, Emory was on the team that surveyed the new U.S.-Mexican border and that also delineated the land boundaries of the 1853 Gadsden Purchase.

Between 1855 and 1861, Emory remained in the West, where he continued to conduct surveying missions and compiled a series of detailed maps of the American West. In 1861, when the Civil War began, Emory was a lieutenant colonel in the 3rd Cavalry Regiment. In March 1861, he was dispatched to Fort Smith, Arkansas, tasked with holding Indian Territory for the Union. Faced with overwhelming Confederate pressure, Emory withdrew the garrison there to Fort Leavenworth, Kansas, without losing a single man.

In March 1862, Emory was promoted to brigadier general of volunteers. He served under Major General George B. McClellan during the Peninsula Campaign and earned one of four wartime brevets for his intrepid action at the Battle of Hanover Courthouse, where he effectively split the Confederate Army in two. In 1863, Emory was sent to Louisiana where he assumed command of a division under Major General Nathaniel P. Banks's command. During the March–May 1864 Red River Campaign, he admirably led the XIX Corps. Although that operation ended in failure, Emory's firm stand in the face of Confederate opposition allowed Union forces to safely engage in an orderly retreat. Later that same year, Emory and his corps were transferred to Virginia, where they served under Major General Philip H. Sheridan during his campaign in the Shenandoah Valley.

Despite his excellent and long service, however, Emory was not promoted to major general of volunteers until after the Civil War had ended, in September 1865. Returned to duty in the regular army, Emory commanded the Departments of West Virginia, Washington, and the Gulf before he retired in July 1876 at the rank of brigadier general. Emory died in Washington, D.C., on December 1, 1887.

Paul G. Pierpaoli Jr.

See also

Gadsden Purchase; Kearny, Stephen Watts; La Mesa, Battle of; San Gabriel River, Battle of; San Pascual, Battle of.

References

Goetzmann, W. H. *Army Exploration in the American West, 1803–1863.* Austin: Texas State Historical Association, 1991.
Norris, L. David, James C. Milligan, and Odie B. Faulk, eds. *William H. Emory: Soldier-Scientist.* Tucson: University of Arizona Press, 1998.

Empresarios

Individuals empowered by the Mexican government to apportion land grants to settlers. *Empresarios* (from the Spanish, meaning "businessman" or "manager") played a major role in the settlement of Mexican-held Texas between 1821 and 1836, although *empresarios* did play a role in the settling of other areas within Mexico. In the early years of the 19th century, Spain hoped to encourage settlement in its long-neglected province of Texas. To do so, Spanish authorities made the process of land distribution easier and encouraged land speculators to transfer parcels of land to prospective settlers. The first *empresario* to receive a land grant in Texas was Moses Austin, an industrialist and businessman from Missouri. He was authorized to settle up to 300 families in Texas, beginning in January 1821.

As soon as Mexico gained its full independence in September of that year, leaders of the new nation sought to continue—and to expand—the Spanish settlement policies. Given that Moses Austin had died in June 1821, his land grant was passed on to his son, Stephen F. Austin, who was highly successful in his endeavor and proved to be the exemplar for other *empresarios* operating in Texas. From 1823 to 1836, 41 *empresario* deals were made with the Mexican government. The centerpiece of these agreements stipulated that the land grants be settled by 100 to 800 families (depending on the acreage) within a six-year period. A single family could purchase 177 acres (a *labor*) for farming, or 4,428.4 acres (a *sitio*) for ranching. The cost of each was almost absurdly low—a *labor* cost $3.50 while a *sitio* cost $30. Those amounts could be paid in installments over a six-year period. In the United States, 177 acres of land cost, on average, $221; 4,428.4 acres cost about $5,310.

The Mexican government allowed *empresarios* to keep for themselves five *labores* and five *sitios* for every 100 families they settled and bestowed on them full judicial authority to rule their colonies as they wished. Despite these lucrative incentives, only two *empresarios* fulfilled the entirety of their contracts—Green De Witt and Stephen Austin. Fourteen others partially fulfilled their commitments.

By 1834, the majority of the Texas population (24,700) had settled under the auspices of an *empresario*. Because *empresarios* were given wide latitude in governing their areas, and because most settlers chose to deal with their *empresario* rather than the Mexican government, Anglo settlers never learned Mexican laws and never became emotionally or politically attached to the Mexican regime. This bred antipathy among Anglos when Mexico City attempted to impose fiats on its Texan settlers and ultimately helped spawn the Texas Revolution and the formation of the Lone Star Republic. Rampant land speculation was also a by-product of the *empresario* system.

Paul G. Pierpaoli Jr.

See also

Austin, Stephen Fuller; Mexico; Texas; Texas Revolution.

References

Cantrell, Greg. *Stephen F. Austin: Empresario of Texas.* New Haven, CT: Yale University Press, 1999.
Recihstein, Andreas. *Rise of the Lone Star: The Making of Texas.* College Station: Texas A&M University Press, 1989.
Weber, David J. *The Mexican Frontier, 1821–1846: The American Southwest under Mexico.* Albuquerque: University of New Mexico Press, 1982.

Encarnación, Hacienda de

Large ranch/plantation located about 50 miles south of Saltillo, Mexico, astride the wagon road that connected San Luis Potosí and Saltillo. By mid-January 1847, U.S. major general William O. Butler's division of Major General Zachary Taylor's army was located at Saltillo. Hoping to follow up on persistent rumors that Mexican general Antonio López de Santa Anna's army was approaching the area, Butler sent several patrols to Hacienda de Encarnación to conduct reconnaissance. Major Solon Borland, with 50 troopers from the 1st Arkansas Volunteer Cavalry, joined Major John P. Gaines's detachment of 30 men from the 1st Kentucky Volunteer Cavalry as they moved south. On January 22, Borland and Gaines, defying their orders to halt at Encarnación, moved south of the hacienda. Encountering rain, however, they returned to Encarnación, where they camped for the night.

Neither Borland nor Gaines thought to post sentries during the night. When the men awoke the next morning, they were surrounded by some 3,000 Mexican troops under the command of General José Vincente Miñón. Gaines and Borland surrendered, and they and their detachments were taken prisoner. One man, Daniel Drake Henrie, managed to escape and informed Butler of the situation.

Meanwhile, the Americans continued to receive reports of Santa Anna's movements. On February 20, 1847, Major General Taylor, now at Saltillo (he had replaced Butler as commander), sent another scouting mission to Encarnación, this one under the command of Taylor's chief of scouts, Captain Ben McCulloch. When McCulloch and six of his men reached the hacienda after dark, they discovered Santa Anna's army camped close by. McCulloch disguised himself and sneaked into the Mexican camp to gather information. On his return, he immediately related the news of Santa Anna's presence and approximate Mexican strength. On February 22–23, 1847, the Americans engaged the Mexicans at the Battle of Buena Vista (La Angostura). While historians remain divided on the encounter's ultimate outcome, there is little doubt that McCulloch's actions at the Hacienda de Encarnación helped prevent an American defeat.

After that battle, Santa Anna's army withdrew through Encarnación, leaving hundreds of its wounded there. Thus, the hacienda acted as a field hospital for about six weeks as the soldiers recovered.

PAUL G. PIERPAOLI JR.

See also

Borland, Solon; Buena Vista, Battle of; Butler, William Orlando; Gaines, John Pollard; McCulloch, Ben; Miñón, José Vicente; Santa Anna, Antonio López de; Taylor, Zachary.

References

Bauer, K. Jack. *The Mexican War, 1846–1848.* New York: Macmillan, 1974.
Cutrer, Thomas W. *Ben McCulloch and the Frontier Military Tradition.* Chapel Hill: University of North Carolina Press, 1993.

Engineering, Military

Military engineers held a respected position within the army at the time of the Mexican-American War. In peacetime, engineers oversaw the construction of the large stone forts that guarded the nation's harbors, laid out roads, and opened waterways to navigation. In addition, the army relied on engineers to explore, survey, and map newly acquired territories. A military engineer's work was considered so important that he could only be assigned other duties by order of the president of the United States.

The U.S. Army did not begin its existence with a corps of engineers. Most engineers who served in the Revolutionary War were Europeans who offered their skills to the Americans. President Thomas Jefferson saw the need for engineers, however, and in 1802 Congress authorized the creation of the U.S. Military Academy at West Point, New York. There the cadets undertook a four-year-long course of study, which in addition to offering military subjects also devoted much attention to mathematics and engineering. Each West Point graduate received a commission or brevet as a second lieutenant and began his career in the army. Assignment to the various branches depended on one's class ranking, with those earning the highest grades becoming engineers.

The U.S. Army contained two categories of military engineers. The Corps of Engineers had responsibility for building and maintaining forts, roads, locks, and other structures, while the Topographic Engineers conducted explorations into the West. These officers supervised contract labor, or, during the war with Mexico, Company A, Corps of Engineers, performed the hard and dangerous work that was required for the construction projects they managed.

The onset of the Mexican-American War in 1846 meant a new role for the engineers. Their primary task shifted to what today is called combat engineering, and they often would lead the columns of U.S. soldiers into Mexico. Once there, the engineers would open roads for troop and supply movements, supervise construction of fortifications, and locate pathways through or around the Mexican army's lines.

On May 16, 1846, Congress authorized the creation of a unit of enlisted men, designated Company A, U.S. Engineers. The recruits were trained in the basics of military engineering and held a higher standing in the army than the average soldier. In the field, they not only performed work themselves but could oversee the work of other soldiers. Company A also participated in many of the battles that occurred in central Mexico.

Engineer officers won high praise for their deeds and were often noted for special commendation by their commanders. Colonel Joseph G. Totten, head of the U.S. Engineers, directed Major General Winfield Scott's siege that resulted in the capture of Veracruz in March 1847. One of his officers was future Confederate general Captain Robert E. Lee. The energetic Virginian, already highly regarded within the army prior to the war, played major roles in fighting at Veracruz, Cerro Gordo, and Contreras. Also prominent among Scott's engineers were First Lieutenant Pierre T. G. Beauregard; Second Lieutenant George B. McClellan, who was second in command of Company A, U.S. Engineers, under future Confederate general Gustavus Woodson Smith; and George G. Meade, a captain in the Topographic Engineers. Another topographic engineer,

Colonel Joseph E. Johnson, was appointed commander of the new Voltigeur Regiment.

Mexico also had military engineers known as *zapadores*. Following independence from Spain, Mexico had to combine old royalist and rebel factions into one national army. Some military institutions, like the medical department and engineers, had to be rebuilt almost from scratch. In 1833, Mexico established its own military academy at Chapultepec Castle outside Mexico City. Unfortunately for Mexico, the number of graduates was relatively small compared to its U.S. counterpart at West Point.

The importance of the West Point–trained engineers reached far beyond their service to the military, as the United States was ready to expand across the continent. An entire transportation network was thus needed, consisting of roads and railroads. Engineers who left the army routinely were hired to oversee building projects like these. Some even subsequently found work in Mexico, building bridges, laying track, and operating mines.

BRUCE WINDERS

See also

Beauregard, Pierre Gustave Toutant; Cerro Gordo, Battle of; Chapultepec, Battle of; Contreras, Battle of; Lee, Robert Edward; McClellan, George Brinton; Meade, George Gordon; Mexican Military Academy (Colegio Militar); Mexico, Army; Veracruz, Landing at and Siege of; United States Army; United States Military Academy, West Point.

References

Cutrer, Thomas W., ed. *The Mexican War Diary and Correspondence of George B. McClellan.* Baton Rouge: Louisiana State University Press, 2009.

DePalo, William, Jr. *The Mexican National Army, 1822–1852.* College Station: Texas A&M University Press, 1997.

Fowler, Will. *Military Political Identity and Reformism in Independent Mexico: An Analysis of the Memorias de Guerra (1821–1855).* London: Institute of Latin American Studies, 1996.

Mahan, Dennis H. *A Complete Treatise on Field Fortification.* New York: Wiley & Long, 1836.

Scott, H. L. *Military Dictionary.* New York: D. Van Norstrand, 1864.

Smith, Gustavus Woodson. *Company "A" Corps of Engineers, U.S.A., 1846–1848, in the Mexican War.* Edited by Leonne M. Smith. Kent, OH: Kent State University Press, 2001.

Traas, Adrian George. *From the Golden Gate to Mexico City: The U.S. Army Topographical Engineers in the Mexican War, 1846–1848.* Washington, DC: Office of History, Corps of Engineers, and Center of Military History, 1993.

Waugh, John C. *The Class of 1846: From West Point to Appomattox.* New York: Warner Books, 1993.

Winders, Richard Bruce. *Mr. Polk's Army: The American Military in the Mexican War.* College Station: Texas A&M University Press, 1997.

Espionage

Prior to the Mexican-American War, the United States maintained no formal intelligence organization at any level. National intelligence was normally collected by diplomats, special presidential agents, or by self-appointed agents who gathered information for personal adventure. This lack of an organized intelligence community constrained diplomatic operations prior to the war as well as operations during military campaigns. Likewise, no blueprint for collecting tactical intelligence existed in the U.S. War Department, which had developed no prior war plans against Mexico.

The U.S. War Department was not able to identify any intelligence gaps or properly focus intelligence collection. It even lacked adequate maps of Mexico. At the time, Zebulon Pike's journal of his travels in Texas and northern Mexico 30 years earlier was the best source of information about Mexico. Nor did American military commanders employ any staff officers with the full-time task of collecting or analyzing intelligence.

Under orders to advance into the disputed territory between the Nueces River and the Rio Grande, Brigadier General Zachary Taylor encamped at Corpus Christi from July 31, 1845, until March 11, 1846. Taylor's force faced several obstacles to effective intelligence collection. First and foremost, none of his troops spoke Spanish. They relied only on walk-in sources of dubious reliability. Taylor also did not attempt to establish an intelligence network. His troops collected no information on the terrain, possible approach routes, or Mexican forces. Taylor even refused to recruit Mexican spies and informers because he did not trust them. He relied primarily on advance scouting parties that reconnoitered the area between the U.S. lines and Mexican army fortifications.

One such party was Colonel John C. Hays's 1st Regiment, Texas Mounted Volunteers, organized in February 1845. As Texas Rangers, Hays's men had fought Native Americans and Mexicans since before Texas independence in 1836. The regiment was loosely organized, and the companies usually operated separately. The Rangers conducted reconnaissance and screening operations, flushing out Mexican ambushes and discovering their positions before Taylor's forces came under fire. They occasionally participated in regular attacks, such as at the Battle of Monterrey on September 23, 1846, when the Rangers joined the attack of Independence Hill, a strongly fortified and commanding Mexican position. Most of the more "unmilitary" Texas Rangers went home after Monterrey, but one company—Ben McCulloch's Company A—remained with Taylor until mustering out of federal service in June 1847. This company became Taylor's "Spy Company," and McCulloch was appointed as the general's chief of scouts. The unit performed vital reconnaissance service on the army's march to Monterrey and was responsible for the discovery of Santa Anna's presence at Encarnacíon on the eve of the battle of Buena Vista.

For his part, Major General Winfield Scott recognized the advantage of intelligence operations. He assigned cavalry and engineer officers, including Major Robert E. Lee and Captain Pierre Gustave Toutant Beauregard, to gather information on Mexican forces, and they provided valuable data that helped U.S. forces prevail at the Battles of Cerro Gordo and Contreras. Others who gained experience as intelligence officers included future Union generals George G. Meade and George B. McClellan. Additionally, Scott obtained accurate topographical information from Colonel Anthony Butler and Brigadier General J. T. Mason in Washington, D.C., both of whom had traveled extensively in northern and central Mexico.

Scott also appreciated the value of Mexican irregulars as scouts and spies, and one of his officers, Colonel Ethan Allen Hitchcock, organized an irregular intelligence unit later known as the Mexican Spy Company. Manuel Domínguez, commissioned a colonel by Hitchcock, commanded the company, which came to number more than 100 members. It scouted Mexican positions and reported Mexican movements. The Spy Company also provided security for the marching columns and their supply lines. Members of the Spy Company even infiltrated Mexico City during Scott's siege of Mexico City, which capitulated on September 14, 1847.

Mexico also employed intelligence agents and intelligence collection against the United States. Mexican liaison officer Colonel Alexander Atocha met President Polk in February 1846. He offered to cede territory to the United States for payment and support in returning the exiled general Antonio López de Santa Anna to the Mexican presidency. The Mexicans intercepted American dispatches. One such instance was a January 1847 communication from Scott to Taylor that detailed Scott's planned landing at Veracruz and directed Taylor to detach forces to support the operation. This information convinced Santa Anna to drive north against a weakened Taylor, culminating in the Battle of Buena Vista on February 23, 1847.

The Mexican-American War provided an effective training ground for military intelligence practices and techniques. After the conflict ended, however, the U.S. government did not establish any formal intelligence collection or analysis service. Through the end of the Civil War, therefore, cavalry and engineers continued to play a major role in the collection, analysis, and dissemination of tactical intelligence.

KEVIN SCOT GOULD

See also

Anaya, Pedro María de; Atocha, Alexander José; Beach, Moses Yale; Beauregard, Pierre Gustave Toutant; Buena Vista, Battle of; Butler, Anthony Wayne; Cazneau, Jane McManus Storms; Hays, John Coffee; Herrera, José Joaquín de; Hitchcock, Ethan Allen; Lee, Robert Edward; McClellan, George Brinton; McCulloch's Spy Company; Meade, George Gordon; Mexican Spy Company; Mexico City, Battle for; Monterrey, Battle of; Paredes y Arrillaga, Mariano; Parrott, William S.; Polk, James Knox; Santa Anna, Antonio López de; Scott, Winfield; Taylor, Zachary; Texas Rangers; Veracruz, Landing at and Siege of.

References

Ameringer, Charles D. *U.S. Foreign Intelligence: The Secret Side of American History.* Lexington, MA: Lexington Books, 1990.
Caruso, A. Brooke. *The Mexican Spy Company: United States Covert Operations in Mexico, 1845–1848.* Jefferson, NC: McFarland, 1991.
Clary, David A. *Eagles and Empire: The United States, Mexico, and the Struggle for a Continent.* New York: Bantam Books, 2009.
Cutrer, Thomas W. *Ben McCulloch and the Frontier Military Tradition.* Chapel Hill: University of North Carolina Press, 1993.
Cutrer, Thomas W., ed. *The Mexican War Diary and Correspondence of George B. McClellan.* Baton Rouge: Louisiana State University Press, 2009.
Eisenhower, John S. D. *So Far from God: The U.S. War with Mexico, 1846–1848.* New York: Anchor Books, 1990.
O'Toole, G. J. A. *Honorable Treachery: A History of U.S. Intelligence, Espionage, and Covert Action from the American Revolution to the CIA.* New York: Atlantic Monthly Press, 1991.

Ether, First Use of

Ether, discovered in 1275 by Spanish chemist Raymundus Lullis, was first used as an anesthetic on the battlefields of North America during the Mexican-American War. Ether is an organic compound that contains an ether group, consisting of an oxygen atom attached to two alkyl or aryl groups. The type of ether used for anesthetic purposes is diethyl ether, which also acts as a highly flammable common solvent. It is the fumes from diethyl ether that are used as an anesthetic.

In the United States, Crawford W. Long, a Georgia doctor, was the first physician to use ether successfully in his private practice on March 30, 1842. The greater recognition, however, has gone to Dr. William Thomas Green Morton, a Boston dentist, who on October 16, 1846, at Massachusetts General Hospital, publicly administered ether to relieve the pain of dental surgery. Dr. Edward Barton, however, first used anesthetic ether in war during an amputation on March 29, 1847. Unlike alcohol, which was commonly used to moderate the pain of surgical procedures before the use of ether, ether was inhaled, not ingested, and therefore prevented asphyxiation during surgery.

Initially during the Mexican-American War, anesthetics such as ether were frowned upon as they were believed to detract from a soldier's masculinity. Despite such negative connotations, the use of anesthesia continued to grow. During the war, ether was administered as a vapor by an ether dome, which was placed over the patient's nose and mouth. Although ether gained more acceptance, other anesthetics, such as chloroform, became more popular because they were fast acting and easier to transport. Nevertheless, the use of anesthetics such as ether during surgical procedures led to less traumatic treatment of war-related injuries, and the widespread use of ether as a general anesthetic meant that doctors were able to perform major surgeries with fewer complications. Most surgeries during the war, however, continued to be performed without the benefit of ether or other anesthetic agents.

LAZARUS O'SAKO

See also

Military Medicine.

American dentist William T. G. Morton (1819–1868), shown here giving the first public demonstration of inhaled ether as a surgical anesthetic at the Massachusetts General Hospital, Boston, on October 16, 1846. (Getty Images)

References

Duncan, Louis C. "Medical History of General Scott's Campaign to the City of Mexico in 1847." *Military Surgeon* 47 (1920): 436–470, 596–609.

Fenster, J. M. *Ether Day: The Strange Tale of America's Greatest Medical Discovery and the Haunted Men Who Made It.* New York: Harper Perennial, 2002.

Gillett, Mary. *The Army Medical Department: 1818–1865.* Washington, DC: Center of Military History, United States Army, 1987.

Moreno, Luis Gerardo Morales, et al., eds. *Echoes of the Mexican-American War.* Toronto, Canada: Groundwood Books, 2005.

Europe and the Mexican-American War

Although the governments and press of France and Great Britain in particular closely followed the Mexican-American War, Europe played no direct role in the conflict. The Mexican government's assumption that the major European powers, specifically Britain, would intervene to prevent a victory by the United States proved illusory. Not enough was at stake to trigger a European intervention.

At the beginning of the war in 1846, Mexican officials held out hope of possible British intervention. They believed that an alliance with Great Britain was possible because of British opposition to the U.S. annexation of Texas as well as the situation regarding Oregon, control of which was then contested by the Americans and British. In June 1846 the British government offered a compromise on the Oregon dispute, establishing the boundary at the 49th parallel and giving the United States control of the Columbia River and Puget Sound in exchange for British governance of Vancouver Island. Already embroiled in war with Mexico, President James K. Polk accepted the compromise rather than risk a two-front war. The Oregon Treaty, signed on June 15, 1846, was devastating news for the Mexican government, which had placed great hope in British intervention.

The British press was decidedly negative toward the United States when word arrived that hostilities had commenced. As with many Americans, the British tended to see the United States as the aggressor. The *Times* of London assumed that the United States would be unsuccessful in its invasion of Mexico, editorializing that "bluster does not win battles, though it may begin brawls." The British government offered to mediate the conflict, but the Polk administration replied on September 11, 1846, that, while the good offices of the British were appreciated, the United States had already offered the Mexicans on July 27 a generous and just peace. The British government could best serve the interests of peace, reasoned Polk, by convincing the Mexicans to accept these terms, which included surrendering to the United States both the California and New Mexico territories.

The rapid advance of American armies into Mexico rendered moot any thoughts of European intervention. The *Times* of London concluded that the British government could devote little time and attention to Mexico, a nation incapable of defending its own territorial integrity. British commercial interests were also pleased with the American occupation, which opened Mexican ports, lowered tariffs, and attempted to protect trade with the interior of the nation. Other reasons prompted European nations to follow Great Britain. Spain not only was estranged from its former colony, pledging itself to "strident neutrality" and failing to offer mediation, but it also tried to take advantage of the war to restore a monarchical regime in Mexico. King Frederick William IV of Prussia believed that the American invasion represented the forces of civilization against the instability and anarchy of Mexico. In France, however, *L'epoque,* often perceived as personal media organ for Premier François Guizot, called for a joint French-British intervention to block American territorial and financial gains in Mexico. Again, the military success of the United States in Mexico rendered such an initiative moot.

Finally, Europe gave little diplomatic support to Mexico because by 1848 its attention was focused on a spate of revolutions that had broken out all across the continent. That February a revolution swept French king Louis Philippe from power and inaugurated the short-lived Second Republic. In line with the maxim, "When France sneezes, Europe catches a cold," Europeans found themselves preoccupied with continental affairs. While the French newspaper *Le journal des débats* denounced American expansionism, it also concluded that the terms of the Treaty of Guadalupe Hidalgo ending the war were generous, for "assuredly this is sparing a foe who lies in the dust." The rapidity of the American military conquest in Mexico and the threat of revolution on the continent served to soften European criticism of the Mexican-American War.

RON BRILEY

See also
France; Great Britain; Guadalupe Hidalgo, Treaty of; Guizot, François; Oregon Boundary Dispute; Oregon Treaty; Polk, James Knox; Spain.

References
Bauer, K. Jack. *The Mexican War, 1846–1848.* New York: Macmillan, 1974.
Clary, David A. *Eagles and Empire: The United States, Mexico, and the Struggle for a Continent.* New York: Bantam Books, 2009.
Haynes, Sam W. "'But What Will England Say?': Great Britain, the United States, and the War with Mexico." In *Dueling Eagles: Reinterpreting the U.S.-Mexican War, 1846–1848,* edited by Douglas W. Richmond and Richard Francaviglia, 19–40. Fort Worth: Texas Christian University Press, 2000.
Pletcher, David M. *The Diplomacy of Annexation: Texas, Oregon, and the Mexican War.* Columbia: University of Missouri Press, 1973.
Smith, Justin H. *The War with Mexico.* Gloucester, MA: Peter Smith, 1963.
Soto, Miguel. *La conspiración monárquica en México, 1845–1846.* Mexico City: Editorial Offset, 1988.

Ewell, Richard Stoddert
Birth Date: February 8, 1817
Death Date: January 25, 1875

U.S. and Confederate Army officer. Richard Stoddert Ewell was born on February 8, 1817, in Georgetown, District of Columbia, although he was brought up in nearby Virginia from an early age. Ewell graduated from the U.S. Military Academy, West Point, in 1840 and was commissioned a second lieutenant in the 1st Dragoons that same year. From 1843 to 1845, he served on escort duty for pioneers along the Santa Fe and Oregon Trails. He was promoted to first lieutenant in 1845.

During the Mexican-American War, Ewell served with distinction in the Battle of Contreras, receiving a brevet promotion to captain for carrying out a reconnaissance mission along with Captain Robert E. Lee. He also distinguished himself at the Battle of Churubusco. On September 13, 1847, when American troops took Chapultepec Castle, Ewell, along with Captain Philip Kearny and a small force of dragoons, doggedly pursued fleeing Mexican troops as they neared the gates of Mexico City. Ewell had two horses shot from beneath him, and although forced to turn back, he still was among the first Americans to reach the city's defenses.

Following the war, Ewell was on duty first in Baltimore and then was assigned to the American Southwest. After the secession of Virginia from the Union, Ewell resigned his commission on May 7, 1861, and was appointed a colonel in the Confederate cavalry on May 9. He was wounded in fighting at Fairfax Court House on May 31. In June, Ewell received promotion to brigadier general.

Ewell commanded a brigade at the First Battle of Bull Run. In January 1862, he was promoted to major general and assumed command of a division in Major General Thomas J. "Stonewall" Jackson's corps. Ewell fought throughout the Shenandoah Valley Campaign until that June, when Jackson's Army of the Valley was recalled to Richmond to take part in the Peninsula Campaign. Ewell defeated Union forces at the Battle of Cedar Mountain on August 9, 1862. In the last week of August, he fought at the Second Battle of Bull Run. He was severely wounded at Groveton on August 28, resulting in the amputation of his left leg.

Fitted with a wooden leg, Ewell again took up active command. He fought in the Battle of Chancellorsville in May 1863, and upon the death of Jackson on May 10, took over command of his II Corps with the rank of lieutenant general. At the beginning of the Gettysburg Campaign, Ewell performed well at the Second Battle of Winchester, capturing the Union garrison.

Subsequently, Ewell took part in the Battle of Gettysburg but did not distinguish himself there, being criticized for want of aggressiveness. Ewell was once more wounded, at Kelly's Ford, Virginia, on March 17, 1864. He took part in the Battles of the Wilderness and Spotsylvania Court House, but Lee was highly critical of Ewell's lack of nerve and effectively commanded Ewell's corps himself. Ewell was then removed from corps command and placed in command of the garrison at Richmond. In April 1865, with Union forces closing in, Ewell was forced to retreat from Richmond. He was captured at the Battle of Sayler's Creek on April 6. He remained a prisoner until July 1865.

Upon his release, Ewell became a farmer on his wife's property at Spring Hill, Tennessee, and in time became an affluent planter. His later years were clouded, however, by ongoing controversy about whether the Confederate defeat at Gettysburg could be blamed on Ewell's failure to take Cemetery Hill. Ewell died on January 25, 1875, at Springhill, Tennessee.

RALPH M. BAKER

See also

Churubusco, Battle of; Contreras, Battle of; Kearny, Philip; Lee, Robert Edward; Mexico City Campaign.

References

Pfanz, Donald C. *Richard S. Ewell: A Soldier's Life.* Chapel Hill: University of North Carolina Press, 1998.

Expansionism and Imperialism

Expansionism is the process by which a nation increases the territory over which it exercises sovereignty or a lesser degree of influence. For the United States, this movement included both the territorial growth westward from the original borders of the 13 British colonies to Hawaii and the subsequent establishment of commercial and military spheres of influence in other areas. The Americans gained new lands by various means, including cash (as in President Thomas Jefferson's purchase of the Louisiana Territory from France in 1803) and force (such as the seizure from Mexico of the present-day states of Arizona, California, New Mexico, and Texas).

Often, expansionism served as a synonym for *Manifest Destiny*, a phrase first used in the 1840s to describe the United States' effort to extend its boundaries westward to the coasts of California, Oregon, and Washington. The main distinction between the two is that while *expansionism* remains a generic term applicable to the conduct of many nations, "Manifest Destiny" refers to U.S. expansionism. Several assumptions form its ideological basis.

First, both early colonists and future generations of Americans believed that they indeed did live in a new world and possessed the right and obligation to make that world over in their image. When John Winthrop spoke in 1630 of building "a city on a hill," he provided a metaphor that remains central to the United States' self-image. Part of that self-image included the nation of virtuous farmers envisioned by many of the nation's early leaders. Jefferson, George Washington, and Benjamin Franklin believed that agrarians working on their own land would form the most reliable and independent of citizens. By definition, a growing and primarily agrarian population would need new land, and

the economically accessible land would be found in frontier areas remote from previously settled communities. Many prominent early Americans, from Washington to Andrew Jackson, profited from purchasing large tracts of land and later selling that land to such settlers.

Immigration proved to be an additional base of American expansionism. The millions who came to the United States in the early and middle 19th century often found much of the best eastern land already populated and so moved westward. Arguably, the United States could so frequently double its population during the 19th century only because the western spaces were made available.

The final economic assumption underlying Manifest Destiny was that nations must have new markets. For an economy to continue growing, production had to increase. This would come about only if markets, furnished by territorial expansion, grew.

Ideological assumptions of a less benign nature also served as a foundation for expansionism. The dominant 19th-century theory of relations between nations held that competition between states was both natural and inevitable. Girded later in the century by the beliefs of social Darwinists, the duty of the strong to triumph over the weak seemed both natural and unavoidable.

Closely associated with this assumption were concepts of racial superiority. Proponents of such racism argued that Europeans, and in particular northern Europeans, stood above others in terms of intelligence and strength and consequently possessed the right and duty to conquer and dominate. Throughout the 19th century, many American officials spoke in disparaging racial stereotypes of the indigenous tribes and Mexicans who stood in their path.

"Imperialism" is a term even more generic than "expansionism" and, like expansionism, exists in many forms. For example, in the case of economic imperialism, one nation may influence or dominate the economy of another without actually claiming possession of the dominated state's territory. In some cases, economic imperialism arose when politically unstable states proved incapable of maintaining a reliable currency or financial system. In such cases, another nation would make capital and banking services available. As the providers of such services, the foreigners acquired significant influence in the less orderly nation and an imperialist relationship would be said to exist.

IRVING W. LEVINSON

See also

Immigration; Louisiana Purchase; Manifest Destiny; Racism.

References

Ferguson, Niall. *Empire: The Rise and Demise of the British World Order and the Lessons for Global Power.* London: Allan Lane, 2002.

Kennedy, Paul. *The Rise and Fall of Great Powers: Economic Change and Military Conflict from 1500 to 2000.* New York: Random House, 1987.

LaFeber, Walter. *The New Empire: An Interpretation of American Expansion, 1860–1898.* Ithaca, NY: Cornell University Press, 1963.

Weinberg, Albert K. *Manifest Destiny: A Study of Nationalist Expansion in American History.* Baltimore, MD: Johns Hopkins University Press, 1935.

F

Falcón, Rámon
Birth Date: Unknown
Death Date: December 19, 1847

Mexican soldier, bandit, and guerrilla who frequented the area along the Rio Grande separating Texas from Mexico. He is credited with causing the first U.S. casualty of the Mexican-American War in April 1846. Rámon Falcón was born in Mexico, perhaps in the first decade of the 19th century, but the exact circumstances of his birth and early years are not known.

By his early twenties Falcón had been clashing with Anglo-Texans for several years. In addition to acting on his own as a guerilla and scout, Falcón also held the rank of lieutenant in La Bahía Company of the Mexican Army of the North, headquartered at Matamoros. Eradicating him was, not surprisingly, a goal of the Texas Rangers.

When Brigadier General Zachary Taylor's Army of Occupation moved toward the Rio Grande in the early spring of 1846, Falcón reportedly warned an advance force sent forward by Taylor that the Americans should vacate Mexican territory at once. Taylor paid no heed to the threat, however, and his army came under constant surveillance by rancheros, Mexican cavalry patrols, and an assortment of bandits and guerillas.

On April 10, 1846, Taylor's chief quartermaster, Colonel Trueman Cross, left camp on a leisurely horseback ride. He never returned. His body was discovered three weeks later, on April 21. He had been savagely beaten and stripped of his clothing and personal possessions. Cross is considered to be the first American casualty of the Mexican-American War. Taylor immediately suspected Falcón of the killing, and after occupying Matamoros he sent a detachment of Texas Rangers on a scouting mission to locate Falcón and other suspected bandits. Falcón managed to elude American forces, however.

In early December 1847, at Rinconada Pass, Falcón reportedly killed three U.S. volunteer soldiers from Mississippi; a fourth was left for dead but survived. Several days later, at a dance in Saltillo, the soldier who survived the attack identified Falcón. Falcón was promptly arrested by U.S. officials, tried, and sentenced to death by hanging. On December 19, 1847, Falcón was hanged at the Grand Plaza in Saltillo. He reportedly showed no remorse, and coldly told his executioners that "I will see you again in hell."

Paul G. Pierpaoli Jr.

See also
Banditry; Cross, Trueman; Guerrilla Warfare; Taylor, Zachary; Texas Rangers.

References
Bauer, K. Jack. *The Mexican War, 1846–1848.* New York: Macmillan, 1974.
Henry, Robert Selph. *The Story of the Mexican War.* New York: Da Capo, 1989.
Weems, John Edward. *To Conquer a Peace: The War between the United States and Mexico.* New York: Doubleday, 1974.

Fannin, James Walker
Birth Date: January 4, 1804
Death Date: March 27, 1836

Texan volunteer military leader during the 1835–1836 Texas Revolution against Mexican rule. Fannin's command of more than 300 men was massacred at Goliad, Texas, on March 27, 1836. Born on January 4, 1804, James Walker Fannin was the illegitimate son of Morgan County, Georgia, plantation owner Isham Fannin. He was adopted by his maternal grandfather, James W. Walker, and grew up on a plantation near Macon, Georgia. In 1819 Fannin entered the U.S. Military Academy, West Point, but he failed to graduate because of poor grades and an altercation with another cadet. Returning to Georgia, he then worked as a merchant.

In 1834 Fannin moved his family to Velasco, Texas, where he was involved with the slave trade. He sympathized strongly with the Anglo-Texans, who were growing restive under Mexican rule. Fannin was soon selected by the Committee of Public Safety and Correspondence, which was seeking independence from Mexico, to solicit military and financial support from the United States. When fighting broke out between Mexico and the Texans on October 2, 1835, Fannin served as a captain of volunteers and saw action at the Battles of Gonzales (October 2, 1835) and Concepción (October 28, 1835).

Fannin was then elected colonel of the provisional regiment of volunteers at Goliad. Sam Houston, commanding general of the Texas armies, initially ordered Fannin to relieve the Texan forces besieged at the Alamo, but he countermanded the order when he learned of the garrison's fall on March 6, 1836. Houston instead directed Fannin to seek refuge at Victoria, but Fannin delayed his movement. As a result, he was soon surrounded by a superior Mexican force under the command of General José de Urrea at Goliad.

On March 20, Fannin surrendered under the condition that the lives of the Texas rebels be spared. However, Mexican leader General Antonio López de Santa Anna overruled Urrea's conditional terms. Fannin and most of his command were executed on March 27 at Goliad. The already wounded Fannin was shot separately. In addition to "Remember the Alamo," "Remember Goliad" became one of the rallying cries of the Texas Revolution.

RON BRILEY

See also

Alamo, Battle of the; Concepción, Battle of; Goliad Massacre; Gonzales, Battle of; Houston, Samuel; Santa Anna, Antonio López de; Urrea y Elías Gonzales, José de; Texas; Texas Revolution.

References

Brown, Gary. *Hesitant Martyr in the Texas Revolution: James Walker Fannin.* Plano: Republic of Texas Press, 2000.
Hardin, Stephen L. *Texian Iliad: A Military History of the Texas Revolution, 1835–1836.* Austin: University of Texas Press, 1994.
Roell, Craig H. *Remember Goliad!* Austin: Texas State Historical Association, 1994.

Filibusters

Adventurers and mercenaries from the United States who led or participated in private military expeditions, especially from the mid-1830s to 1860, against sovereign nations in the Western Hemisphere. Most of these expeditions were against nations not then at war with the United States. Filibustering expeditions, which at various times attacked Canada, Mexico, Nicaragua, Honduras, Ecuador, and Cuba, violated the U.S. Neutrality Act of 1818. Although the term *filibuster* did not become common usage until 1850 or so, the concept had existed since the late 18th century. The term is derived from the Spanish term *filibustero,* which was derived from an earlier Dutch term for freebooter (a pirate or plunderer).

Filibustering into Mexico became more commonplace following the war with the United States. After failed attempts to take Cuba and the Yucatán toward the end of the war, during 1850–1851 Joseph C. Morehead, a Mexican-American War veteran, led an abortive filibustering mission that sought the capture of Baja California. In 1852, Charles de Pindray, a Frenchman residing in California, attempted to declare himself head of a new nation, to be carved out of the Mexican state of Sonora. His mission failed, and he died a mysterious death. Between 1852 and 1854, another Frenchman, who called himself Count Raoussett de Boulboun, led two separate unsuccessful expeditions to seize Sonora. After declaring himself the "Sultan of Sonora," the count was tried and executed by Mexican authorities. Not soon after, William Walker led a filibustering expedition in an attempt to take Baja and Sonora, a mission that failed as well. Finally, in 1857, Californian Henry Crabb commanded an overland mission through Arizona in an attempt to seize Sonora. Crabb's expedition failed, and he and his coconspirators were executed.

Filibusters played a significant part in the sectional conflict that led to the Civil War and epitomized the spirit of Manifest Destiny that was prevalent in the United States throughout the 19th century. Yet although many U.S. leaders advocated territorial expansion, they did not overtly support filibustering expeditions, and the filibuster invasions of Latin America proved counterproductive to their stated goal of territorial expansion. These interventions, which enhanced sectional differences prior to the Civil War, also bred a legacy of anti-Americanism in Latin America, particularly so in Mexico, where they continued for some years, particularly from 1900 to 1921.

MICHAEL R. HALL AND PAUL G. PIERPAOLI JR.

See also

Expansionism and Imperialism; Manifest Destiny; Slavery; Walker, William.

References

Brown, Charles H. *Agents of Manifest Destiny: The Lives and Times of the Filibusters.* Chapel Hill: University of North Carolina Press, 1980.
May, Robert E. *Manifest Destiny's Underworld: Filibustering in Antebellum America.* Chapel Hill: University of North Carolina Press, 2002.
Stout, Joseph A., Jr. *Schemers and Dreamers: Filibustering in Mexico, 1848–1921.* Fort Worth: Texas Christian University Press, 2002.

REVOLTS AND INTERVENTIONS IN MEXICO, 1821–1857

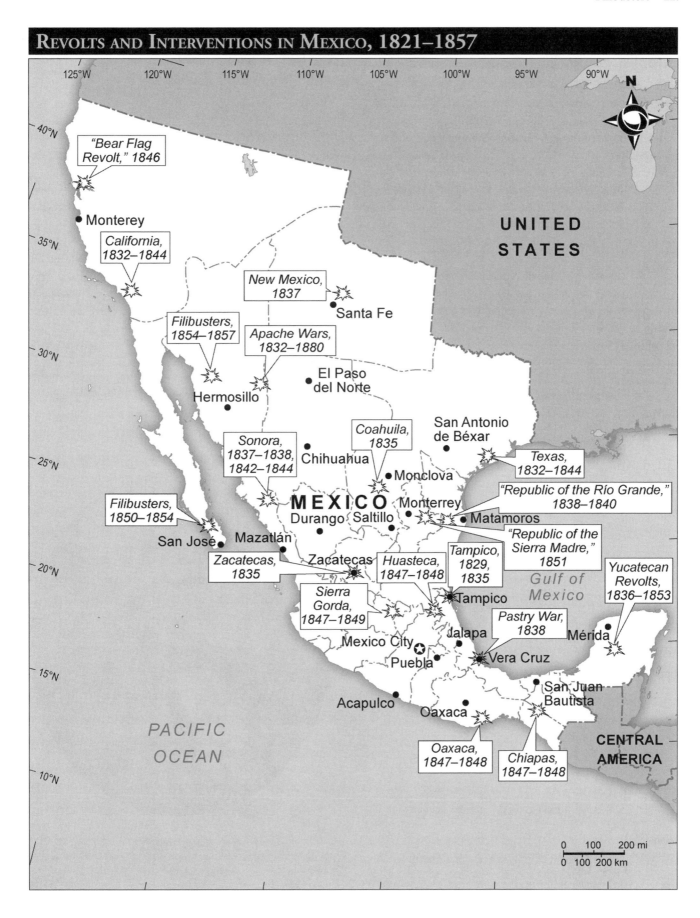

"Bear Flag Revolt," 1846

Monterey

California, 1832–1844

New Mexico, 1837

Santa Fe

Filibusters, 1854–1857

Apache Wars, 1832–1880

El Paso del Norte

UNITED STATES

Hermosillo

San Antonio de Béxar

Coahuila, 1835

Sonora, 1837–1838, 1842–1844

Chihuahua

Monclova

Texas, 1832–1844

Filibusters, 1850–1854

MEXICO

Monterrey

Matamoros

"Republic of the Río Grande," 1838–1840

San José

Mazatlán

Durango

Saltillo

"Republic of the Sierra Madre," 1851

Zacatecas, 1835

Zacatecas

Huasteca, 1847–1848

Tampico, 1829, 1835

Gulf of Mexico

Yucatecan Revolts, 1836–1853

Sierra Gorda, 1847–1849

Tampico

Pastry War, 1838

Mérida

Mexico City

Jalapa

Puebla

Vera Cruz

San Juan Bautista

Acapulco

Oaxaca

CENTRAL AMERICA

PACIFIC OCEAN

Oaxaca, 1847–1848

Chiapas, 1847–1848

0   100   200 mi
0   100 200 km

Filisola, Vicente

Birth Date: ca. 1785
Death Date: 1850

Italian-born soldier who served in the Spanish and then the Mexican army. Born Vincenzo Filisola in Naples, Italy, probably in 1785, Filisola joined the Spanish army as a young man and was dispatched to Mexico in 1811, at which time the Spanish were attempting to subdue the Mexican independence movement. During the late 1820s and early 1830s, after Mexico gained its independence, Filisola became a friend and confidant of General Antonio López de Santa Anna and held numerous high-profile posts in the Mexican army. Then, in 1833, Filisola was promoted to general of division.

Filisola saw action during the Texas Revolution in 1836 and was Santa Anna's second in command at the Battle of Jacinto where he was accused of cowardice and treachery. Filisola vigorously denied such accusations and wrote a lengthy memoir, published in 1848, in which he attempted to clear his name. After San Jacinto, Filisola led the Mexican retreat to Matamoros and by falling back beyond the Rio Grande lent credence to the Texans' claims that the Rio Grande was the official border between Mexico and Texas. Despite his blunders, Filisola remained a general officer.

In March 1847, during the Mexican-American War, Filisola was ordered to reoccupy the state of Chihuahua, but that became unnecessary after American forces under Colonel Alexander Doniphan abandoned the region. He was subsequently tasked with mounting attacks on U.S. troops occupying Monterrey and Saltillo. Filisola made ample preparations, but his campaign against the two cities failed by early August 1847 because of supply shortages, desertions, torrid heat, and illness among his soldiers.

Early in 1848 Mexican president Manuel de la Peña y Peña made Filisola commander of the Mexican army's Queretaro Division, then the largest of the three still-existing army divisions. Filisola was stymied in this position as well, however, as a result of supply problems and high desertion rates.

In the winter of 1850, only weeks after having been named president of the Supreme War Tribunal, Filisola died of cholera during the epidemic that swept Mexico City.

PAUL G. PIERPAOLI JR.

See also

Matamoros; Peña y Peña, Manuel de la; Rio Grande; Saltillo; San Jacinto, Battle of; Santa Anna, Antonio López de; Texas Revolution.

References

Eisenhower, John S. D. *So Far from God: The U.S. War with Mexico, 1846–1848.* New York: Anchor Books, 1990.
Filisola, Vicente. *Memoirs of the History of the War in Texas.* Translated by Wallace Woolsey. 2 vols. Austin, TX: Eakin Press, 1985.

Fillmore, Millard

Birth Date: January 7, 1800
Death Date: March 8, 1874

U.S. Whig politician, vice president (1849–1850), and president of the United States (1850–1853). Millard Fillmore was born in Locke, New York, on January 7, 1800, the son of a poor farming family. At age 14 he apprenticed with a local clothier in Sparta, New York, and remained self-educated until age 19, when he attended an academy in New Hope, New York. Fillmore moved to Buffalo, New York, in 1822, where he taught elementary school until passing the New York bar exam that same year.

In June 1828 Fillmore served as a delegate to the Erie County Convention of the short-lived, anti-Jackson National Republican Party. Eventually, Fillmore rose to state and national political prominence by identifying with the Anti-Mason and Whig political parties. After forging one of the most lucrative law partnerships in New York, Fillmore served two years as an Anti-Mason Party state representative between 1828 and 1830 and was elected to the U.S. House of Representatives as an Anti-Mason in 1832.

Sensing the political decline of the Anti-Mason Party, Fillmore publicly aligned himself with the Whig Party in 1834. Following a brief return to the private sector the following year, Fillmore was again elected to the U.S. House of Representatives in 1837 on the

Whig politician Millard Fillmore was elected vice president of the United States in 1848. On the death of President Zachary Taylor on July 10, 1850, Fillmore assumed the presidency. (Library of Congress)

Whig ticket and served two years as chairman of the powerful House Ways and Means Committee. Fillmore then served as comptroller of New York beginning in November 1847. Despite a failed bid for the governorship in 1844, Fillmore was considered by many Whig Party leaders as a potential nominee for president of the United States.

In 1848 Fillmore was selected as presidential candidate Zachary Taylor's running mate to balance the Whig ticket geographically and ideologically. Taylor won, and Fillmore served as vice president from March 1849 to July 1850. He assumed the presidency on July 10, 1850, after Taylor died suddenly.

For nearly three years, Fillmore presided over unprecedented national economic prosperity, including the expansion of markets abroad, exemplified by the opening of American commercial trade with Japan. However, the entire Fillmore presidency was overshadowed by growing sectional antagonism between North and South. Territory acquired from Mexico in the February 1848 Treaty of Guadalupe Hidalgo that ended the Mexican-American War assured that the issue of slavery in the territories would remain a continuing political dilemma. Fillmore is considered the first in a dynasty of so-called doughface presidents—northern men with southern principles—who included Franklin Pierce and James Buchanan. While personally opposed to slavery, Fillmore nonetheless signed into law the Fugitive Slave Act on September 18, 1850, which required that escaped slaves be captured and returned to their owners. He also supported, albeit reluctantly, the Compromise of 1850. In the final analysis, the brief Fillmore administration, like its predecessors, only postponed the growing crisis over slavery.

Fillmore remained active in civil affairs after leaving office. He accepted the anti-immigrant American (Know-Nothing) Party presidential nomination in the 1856 election but was defeated soundly by Democrat James Buchanan. After travels through Europe, Fillmore founded and served as the first president of Buffalo General Hospital. Fillmore died in Buffalo, New York, on March 8, 1874.

JASON GODIN

See also

Freemasonry; Guadalupe Hidalgo, Treaty of; Perry, Matthew Calbraith; Slavery; Taylor, Zachary; Whigs.

References

Grayson, Benson Lee. *The Unknown President: The Administration of President Millard Fillmore.* Washington, DC: University Press of America, 1981.

Rayback, Robert J. *Millard Fillmore: Biography of a President.* East Aurora, NY: Henry Steward, 1972.

Smith, Elbert B. *The Presidencies of Zachary Taylor and Millard Fillmore.* Lawrence: University Press of Kansas, 1988.

Film and the Mexican-American War

The war film has long served as a staple genre for Hollywood, yet the Mexican War has received scant attention from the American film industry. Perhaps a conflict in which the United States is perceived as the aggressor does not agree with the public perception of American exceptionalism and innocence. On the other hand, a national cinematic mythology has developed over the heroic defense of the Alamo (February 23–March 6, 1836) and the role played by Tennessee frontiersman and congressman David Crockett in the siege. The traditional Hollywood interpretation presents the Texans and Crockett as fighting for their natural rights against the tyranny of Mexico. With this reading of the events at the Alamo, it is easier to perceive the Mexican War as the legacy of defending American liberty against Mexican oppression.

Among the first films to perpetuate the Crockett myth was the silent feature *Martyrs of the Alamo* (1915), directed by D. W. Griffith. An indication of this film's cultural bias may be seen in the casting of Walter Long, the same actor who played the depraved and villainous Gus in Griffith's *Birth of a Nation,* as Mexican general Antonio López de Santa Anna. *Martyrs of the Alamo* was followed in 1926 by *Davy Crockett at the Fall of the Alamo,* directed by Robert North Bradbury, in which Crockett and the valiant Texans are massacred by the diabolical Santa Anna. To commemorate the centennial of the siege, in 1937 Hollywood released *Heroes of the Alamo,* directed by Harry L. Fraser, but the low-budget feature, with Lance Chandler as Crockett, fared poorly at the box office. The film's negative depiction of the Mexican government violated the film industry's commitment to Franklin Roosevelt's Good Neighbor Policy, which sought to ameliorate U.S.–Latin American relations. *The Alamo: Shrine of Texas Liberty,* directed by Stuart Paton and released the following year, fared no better.

Hollywood rediscovered the Alamo during the 1950s. *The Last Command* (1955) told the story of the Alamo from the perspective of James (Jim) Bowie (Sterling Hayden) as an entrepreneur whose plans for developing Texas were thwarted by a corrupt central government in Mexico City. In this film veteran character actor Arthur Hunnicut portrayed Crockett as an elder statesman who brought the benefit of his frontier experience to the struggle for Texas independence. Bowie was also the subject of the 1952 film *Iron Mistress,* starring Alan Ladd and Virginia Mayo and based on the popular novel by Paul I. Wellman.

Crockett, of course, was immortalized by Walt Disney's *King of the Wild Frontier* (1956), which premiered on ABC Television. Fess Parker in the title role brought a sense of individualism and nonconformity to Crockett's character, challenging the conservative consensus values of the 1950s. On the other hand, Disney's perception of Crockett at the Alamo as fighting for liberty fit well with the Cold War crusade against the Soviet Union. Disney's commercialization of Crockett also made the Alamo a household word for Americans during the 1950s.

The successful Disney version was followed by director John Wayne's *The Alamo* (1960) in which the veteran actor portrayed Crockett. Bowie was played by Richard Widmark and a foppish but iron-willed Travis by Lawrence Harvey. This ambitious epic,

Lawrence Harvey as Colonel William Barret Travis (in white hat) and Ken Curtis as Captain Almaron Dickinson, aide to Colonel Travis, in a scene from the 1961 film *The Alamo*. (AP/Wide World Photos)

which was also financed by Wayne, proved to be a little too serious and overly long for most viewers. By interpreting the meaning of the Alamo siege in such abstract terms as establishing a republic, Wayne, who was well known for his conservative political views, placed the battle for Texas independence within the global anti-communist struggle.

In 1976, for the American bicentennial, Vladimir Goetzelman directed *The Spirit of Independence,* an animated treatment of the siege and storming of the Alamo. Subsequent commercial television efforts to emulate Disney's achievement with the Alamo did not attract large audiences. In 1987 director Burt Kennedy produced *Thirteen Days to Glory,* based on the popular history of the same name by Leon Tinker, and in 1994 Richard Long adopted James A. Michener's *Texas* for the small screen. The failure of these television productions did not dissuade the Disney studio from resurrecting *The Alamo* in 2004, however. Censured by some critics as revisionist history, *The Alamo* plowed new ground for a feature film by recognizing the role played by slavery in the Texas revolt against Mexico as well as presenting a more nuanced

portrayal of Crockett (played by Billy Bob Thornton) and the Mexican side of the story. Nevertheless, director John Lee Hancock's more historically accurate film did poorly at the box office and failed to undermine the more mythical depictions of the siege.

An IMAX version of the siege, *Alamo: The Price of Freedom,* was filmed in 1988 and is screened on a continual basis at a theater near the old mission. Crockett is played by Merrill L. Connally.

Cinematic portrayals of the Texas Revolution have also focused on Sam Houston and the Battle of San Jacinto (April 21, 1836) in which the Texans achieved their independence. Biographical pictures from the 1930s and 1950s depict Houston as a national hero fighting for freedom against a tyrannical Mexican government. Richard Dix played Houston in *Man of Conquest* (1939), a film that offered a sympathetic treatment of Houston's association with the Cherokee Nation. *The First Texan* (1956) starred Joel McCrae as Houston, whose triumph at San Jacinto assures Texas liberty in a film with allegorical references to American values in the Cold War. In 1986 Sam Elliott portrayed Sam Houston in the made-for-TV biographical drama *Houston: The Legend of Texas* (later released on DVD as *Gone to Texas*). The Battle of San Jacinto is also the focus of a 1998 cable television film for Turner Network Television, director Rod Hardy's *Two for Texas*. Tom Skerritt portrays Houston, but most of the story centers on two fictional characters (Kris Kristofferson and Scott Bairstow) who escape from a Louisiana chain gang to join the Texas Revolution. The savagery of the Texans taking revenge for the Alamo on Mexican prisoners is well captured in this film as well as Hancock's *The Alamo*.

While the Texas struggle for independence has gained the attention of feature films, the Mexican-American War itself continued to be largely ignored by Mexican and Hollywood filmmakers. Two noteworthy exceptions are *El cementerio de las aguilas,* a 1939 production starring one of Mexican cinema's top box-office idols, Jorge Negrete; the film tells the story of the Niños Héroes who defended Chapultepec Castle against U.S. forces in September 1847. Sixty years later director Lance Hool filmed *One Man's Hero,* which tells the story of John Riley (Tom Berenger) and the San Patricio Battalion, a unit of the Mexican army formed in large part from Irish deserters from the U.S. Army. While a fascinating story, this sympathetic portrayal of military deserters failed to attract an audience.

Feature filmmakers may have practically ignored the Mexican War, but documentaries on the conflict have proliferated in recent years. *Seguin,* written and directed by Jesús Treviño for American Playhouse, was broadcast over PBS in 1982. Fourteen years later documentary filmmaker Mark Day produced *The San Patricios,* a positive account of Riley and the San Patricio Battalion. Based primarily on interviews with journalists, historians, and writers, the film has enjoyed only limited release in Ireland, Mexico, and the United States. Then, in 1998, public television stations aired *U.S.-Mexican War, 1846–1848.* Executive producer Sylvia Komatsu and coproducer/writer Rob Tranchino blended diary entries, letters, and photography to craft a production offering multiple perspectives of the conflict. The documentary also includes interviews with Mexican scholars who argued that the war was both an assault on Mexican culture and an expansionist military occupation.

A 1998 four-part documentary, *Mexico,* produced by the History Channel, echoed some of the perspectives contained in the PBS documentary. The second episode, titled "From Independence to the Alamo," suggests that the Alamo is overemphasized by historians and popular culture and should be perceived as just one example of Anglo incursions into Mexico. "Battle for North America," the third installment of the film, presents the Polk administration as the aggressor in the Mexican War. Eight years later, the History Channel produced another documentary on the conflict, *The Mexican-American War.* Narrated by boxing legend Oscar de la Hoya, the program generally cast U.S. actions in a negative light, and perhaps this led producers to release it with as little fanfare as possible.

These documentaries that are largely critical of American policy during the Mexican-American War have not attracted the audience achieved by many feature films on the Alamo, Davy Crockett, Sam Houston, and Texas independence. Nevertheless, a more jaundiced view of how modern presidents have manipulated the nation into war may encourage Hollywood and feature filmmakers to reexamine the Mexican-American War.

RON BRILEY

See also

Alamo, Battle of the; Bowie, James; Cherokees; Crockett, David; Houston, Samuel; Literature; Polk, James Knox; Riley, John; San Jacinto, Battle of; San Patricio Battalion; Santa Anna, Antonio López de; Texas; Texas Declaration of Independence; Texas Revolution.

References

Carnes, Mark C., ed. *Past Imperfect: History According to the Movies.* New York: Henry Holt, 1995.
Fraser, George MacDonald. *The Hollywood History of the World.* New York: Fawcett Columbine, 1988.
Johannsen, Robert W. *To the Halls of the Montezumas: The Mexican War in the American Imagination.* New York: Oxford University Press, 1985.
Lofaro, Michael, ed. *Davy Crockett: The Man, the Legend, the Legacy, 1786–1986.* Knoxville: University of Tennessee Press, 1985.
Roberts, Randy, and James S. Olson. *A Line in the Sand: The Alamo in Blood and Memory.* New York: Free Press, 2001.
Yates, James. "The Mexican-American War and the Spanish-American War." In *The Columbia Companion to American History on Film: How the Movies Have Portrayed the American Past,* edited by Peter Rollins, 86–92. New York: Columbia University Press, 2003, 86–92.

Finances, Mexican and U.S.

Financing the Mexican-American War proved to be a daunting task for both the Mexican and U.S. governments. The conflict proved far costlier than either side had envisioned, largely because it lasted far longer than planned. Because of the dismal state of the Mexican economy prior to and during the war, however, the Mexican government found it extremely difficult to raise funds for the conflict. The war only added to the country's economic and political woes, while it provided a sizable economic boom in the United States. At war's end in 1848 the Mexican economy teetered on the edge of bankruptcy, while the U.S. economy entered a period of sustained growth and prosperity.

Various factors had wracked the Mexican economy since the achievement of independence from Spain in 1821. First, the 11-year struggle against Spanish rule (1810–1821) crippled agriculture and mining, the two main pillars of the colonial economy, and led to the flight of capital as well. Then, following independence, Mexican governments could not overcome three major problems to secure a reliable and steady stream of revenue. First, elites proved reluctant to support any government with loans, even for short periods, and to pay new taxes. Second, government attempts to revamp the fiscal structure failed to generate sufficient revenue to offset expenses. And third, following defaults on foreign loans obtained in the early 1820s, many European financiers

Comparative Cost of America's Wars

War	Cost*
American Revolutionary War	$1.8 billion
War of 1812	$1.2 billion
Mexican-American War	$1.8 billion
Civil War (Union)	$45 billion
Civil War (Confederacy)	$15 billion
Spanish-American War	$6.8 billion
World War I	$253 billion
World War II	$4.1 trillion
Korean War	$320 billion
Vietnam War	$686 billion
Persian Gulf War	$96 billion
Wars in Iraq and Afghanistan (through fiscal year 2011)	$1.257 trillion

* Wars in Iraq and Afghanistan in 2011 dollars, all other wars in 2008 dollars

and governments concluded that loans and bonds extended to Mexico were simply too risky, a decision that closed off the possibility of large-scale foreign investment.

This situation had dismal consequences for Mexico, particularly in the area of foreign relations. In 1838, for example, the French government blockaded and then occupied Veracruz in what came to be called the Pastry War, an attempt to collect unpaid claims made by French citizens. The conflict cost the Mexican government more money. Mexico's financial crisis also hindered its ability to meet its financial obligations to the United States, a factor that heightened tensions with its northern neighbor by the early 1840s and helped set the stage for war.

In an attempt to solve the financial crisis, many regimes resorted to measures that not only proved ineffective but also contributed to their removal from office. In 1829, for example, the Vicente Guerrero administration proposed a progressive income tax on wealthy property owners and merchants; it also demanded a forced loan from state governments and called on high-level bureaucrats and military employees to accept a salary reduction. These measures proved unpopular and contributed to Guerrero's downfall. Likewise, in 1844, General Antonio López de Santa Anna's plan for a public contribution of 10,000,000 pesos, in addition to steadily increasing taxes and previous revenue-raising schemes, intensified public opposition against the regime and led to its demise.

Further aggravating Mexico's fiscal problems was the fact that even those well-conceived efforts to promote the country's economic recovery, like the creation in the early 1830s of the Banco del Avío (or Credit Bank), met with failure. The brainchild of Minister of Interior and Exterior Relations Lucas Alamán, this bank was intended to promote industrialization and give preference to the production of cotton, wool, and silk cloth. The bank, however, fell victim to the country's turbulent politics and was abolished in 1842.

To secure revenue, therefore, governments entered into deals with so-called private moneylenders known as *agiotistas,* who since the late 1820s regularly advanced money to the government at high interest rates (sometimes over 300 percent). Conventional wisdom has portrayed these individuals in a negative light, but

Barbara Tenenbaum, whose analysis of Mexico's 19th-century fiscal crisis remains unsurpassed, has argued that *agiotistas* "were careful to maintain good business relations with all [political groups . . . and] served as the invisible stability which helped Mexico survive."

In any case, on the eve of war with the United States, Mexican officials were deeply aware of their country's unfavorable financial situation. Late in 1845 Minister of Finance Pedro Fernandez del Castillo stated that the government's fiscal resources were "almost completely exhausted." Indeed, at that time 87 percent of Mexico's 16.5-million-peso annual revenue stream was earmarked for debt obligations. The situation did not improve early in 1846. President Mariano Paredes y Arrillaga solicited a loan from the Catholic Church in mid-May to help fund the war, but the attempt proved unsuccessful, while his decision to stop the payment of government salaries and debt repayments led to a backlash against the government. Meanwhile, the U.S. naval blockade of Mexico vastly reduced customs and tariffs duties, which were the government's main sources of income. By the fall of 1846, the Mexican treasury had a mere 1,800 pesos in its coffers. A grass-roots voluntary effort to raise money for the war effort raised that figure to 90,000 pesos, but that was still woefully inadequate.

Consequently, early in January 1847, *puro* leader and acting vice president Valentín Gómez Farías, with the help of his allies in Congress, issued a decree that authorized the government to raise 15 million pesos by mortgaging or selling church-owned property. This move angered both the clergy and *moderado* elements in Mexico and precipitated the so-called Polkos Revolt in late February. One month later Santa Anna removed Gómez Farías from office and reversed the earlier decree. He also asked the church for a 2-million-peso cash infusion and the right to access up to 20 million pesos in church property, should it become necessary. Still desperate for cash, Santa Anna levied broad-based war taxes and sold government bonds at discount, neither of which resulted in a reversal of Mexico's deteriorating financial situation. As a result, by the summer of 1847, the Mexican government resorted to the requisitioning of private property and the seizure of private citizens' cash assets.

By the time the Treaty of Guadalupe Hidalgo was signed in 1848, the Mexican economy was prostrate. In total, the conflict cost the Mexican government at least 100 million pesos, only a small fraction of which it had been able to cover with taxes, loans, and other revenue-enhancing devices. The terms of the treaty did offer some relief, however, as the Americans agreed to a cash payment of $15 million for the Mexican land cession and the assumption of $3 million in debt obligations to American citizens. Nevertheless, Mexican finances remained precarious in the postwar period. In December 1853 Santa Anna agreed to sell to the United States land in the southern portion of the present states of Arizona and New Mexico (the Gadsden Purchase) for $10 million, a move that many perceived as an unnecessary capitulation to the United States and contributed to his ouster from power two years later.

North of the border, the United States' economic situation was far better than Mexico's, but this does not imply that the James K. Polk administration easily financed the conflict. Indeed, on the eve of the war the American economy was in the doldrums. A severe depression had gripped the nation in 1837, and it did not ease until the mid-1840s. In 1843, federal revenues had dwindled to only $8.3 million, the lowest figure in a decade or more. Compounding this macroeconomic burden were inflation, slumping trade, and the U.S. government's inability to secure adequate foreign loans with affordable repayment terms.

A high tariff on imports, enacted in 1842, had served only to discourage importers from sending goods to the United States, which drastically reduced customs duties. At the time, customs duties were one of the government's chief means of raising money. Most states were also burdened with foreign debt, at least $200 million by 1845. This further discouraged foreign investors and governments from extending loans to the U.S. government. By the time the Mexican-American War began, the U.S. Treasury had a mere $7 million in its coffers.

President Polk recognized immediately the urgency of increasing revenue to pay for the war. Thus, he requested—and received—congressional approval for a $10 million war appropriation, which was attached to the war declaration in May 1846. That August, Congress enacted legislation to lower the 1842 tariff, but the new law would not take effect until December. The short-term result was disastrous, as importers all but stopped trade with the United States until the lower tariff was in place. The U.S. Treasury reported a $23 million budget deficit for 1846 alone, and so dire was the economic situation that in December Polk asked Congress for more resources to wage the war. As part of the so-called Ten Regiment Bill, Polk requested a $23 million loan from Congress to plug the deficit, but Congress approved only a $10 million loan. Then, in 1847, he requested and received a $3 million appropriation to pursue peace negotiations with the Mexicans.

By mid-1847, however, the U.S. financial picture had begun to brighten considerably. A string of military victories had increased financial support for the war, both from individuals and foreign governments. Meanwhile, a huge influx of Irish and German immigrants, fleeing a devastating famine in northern Europe, brought with it the infusion of some $25 million into the U.S. economy.

Meanwhile, American farmers benefited enormously from the famine, as many European nations were forced to purchase agricultural products from the United States. As in most wars, the U.S. economy began to experience the positive effects of government spending, which swelled the profits of steamship lines, railroads, arms makers, textile manufacturers, and the like. Meanwhile, reduced import tariffs had begun to stimulate foreign trade.

To reduce the budget shortfall, in the spring of 1848, Congress authorized another loan, in the amount of $16 million, shortly after the Treaty of Guadalupe Hidalgo had been signed.

In all, the conflict cost the U.S. government $98 million, which included damage claims, pensions, and payments for soldiers and veterans. On top of that figure, the United States paid Mexico $15 million for the land cession and agreed to absorb $3 million of Mexico's damage claims owed to American citizens. This brought the total cost of the war to $116 million.

Despite such costs, the conflict greatly stimulated the economy for several years. The discovery of large deposits of gold in California in 1848 also proved to be a financial boon to the U.S. economy. Gold production in the United States exploded from 43,000 ounces in 1847 to 1,935,000 ounces in 1849. By 1853, California alone was producing 3 million ounces of gold per year, valued at $65 million, or $4 million more than total government revenues that year. As well, the vast new tracts of land available for settlement as a result of the Mexican land cession also served as a powerful stimulus to the American economy.

PAUL G. PIERPAOLI JR. AND PEDRO SANTONI

See also

Catholic Church, Mexico; Congress, Mexican; Congress, U.S.; Europe and the Mexican-American War; Gadsden Purchase; Gómez Farías, Valentín; Gold Rush, California; Guadalupe Hidalgo, Treaty of; Mexican Cession; Mexico; Mexico, 1821–1854; Paredes y Arrillaga, Mariano; Pastry War; Politics, Mexican; Politics, U.S.; Polk, James Knox; Polkos Revolt; Public Opinion and the War; Santa Anna, Antonio López de; Ten Regiment Bill; Trade; United States, 1821–1854.

References

Clary, David A. *Eagles and Empire: The United States, Mexico, and the Struggle for a Continent.* New York: Bantam Books, 2009.

Costeloe, Michael P. *The Central Republic in Mexico, 1835–1846: Hombres de Bien in the Age of Santa Anna.* New York: Cambridge University Press, 1993.

Gordon, John Steele. *An Empire of Wealth: The Epic History of American Economic Power.* New York: Harper/Perennial, 2004.

Tenenbaum, Barbara A. *The Politics of Penury: Debt and Taxes in Mexico, 1821–1856.* Albuquerque: University of New Mexico Press, 1986.

Fisher, William S.
Birth Date: Unknown
Death Date: 1845

Texas soldier and, briefly, secretary of war for the Republic of Texas (December 1836–November 1837). It is not certain where or when William S. Fisher was born, but in 1834 he moved from Virginia to Texas, then Mexico, settling at Gonzales. The following year he represented Gonzales at a convention of Anglo-Texans, known as the Consultation, in preparation for Texas independence. When the Texas Revolution began, Fisher joined the Texas army in March 1836. Serving under General Sam Houston, he saw action at the Battle of San Jacinto that April 21. He left the army in June 1836, only to rejoin it several weeks later before mustering out for good in September 1836.

That December, Houston, then president of the Republic of Texas and impressed with Fisher's performance on the battlefield, appointed him secretary of war. Fisher took office on December

21, 1836, and remained in that post until November 13, 1837. His appointment, however, was never confirmed by the Texas Senate. In January 1837, Texas vice president Mirabeau Lamar commissioned Fisher colonel of a cavalry regiment operating along the frontier. On March 19, 1840, Fisher represented the republic in its negotiations with the Comanches in San Antonio, resulting in the disastrous Council House Fight. Later that same year, Fisher joined the leaders of the Republic of the Rio Grande, a separatist group seeking independence from Mexico.

Fisher recruited some 200 men for the cause, but the bid for independence by the Rio Grande Republic was quickly subdued. In 1842, Fisher joined the so-called Somervell Expedition, led by Alexander Somervell, and served as a captain. This filibustering expedition across the Rio Grande and into northern Mexico was authorized by Texas president Sam Houston. In December 1842 Somervell abandoned the mission because of supply problems, inclement weather, and desertions.

While some 300 of Somervell's men returned with him to Texas, a number decided to continue the operation and chose Fisher as their commanding officer. He led the small force to Ciudad Mier, just south of the Rio Grande, and on Christmas night 1842 Fisher and his men assaulted a detachment of the Mexican army. Despite initial success, Fisher's men were soon surrounded by a superior force of Mexican reinforcements. The ill-starred Mier Expedition came to an end with Fisher's surrender on December 26. The wounded Fisher and most of his men were taken prisoner and marched to Mexico City and then Perote Castle where they were incarcerated.

Although Fisher's second in command managed to escape, Fisher refused to follow suit, vowing that he would not leave his men behind. In late 1843, the Mexicans released Fisher and his men in a goodwill gesture that they hoped would ameliorate relations with the U.S. government. Fisher returned to Texas in 1844, where he died the following year at his home in Jackson County.

PAUL G. PIERPAOLI JR.

See also

Filibusters; Houston, Samuel; Lamar, Mirabeau Buonaparte; Mier Expedition; Perote Castle; Rio Grande, Republic of the; San Jacinto, Battle of; Texas; Texas Revolution.

References

Haynes, Sam M. *Soldiers of Misfortune: The Somervell and Mier Expeditions.* Austin: University of Texas Press, 1990.

Wooten, Dudley Goodall, ed. *A Comprehensive History of Texas.* 2 vols. Dallas, TX: Scarff, 1898. Reprint, Austin: Texas State Historical Association, 1986.

Flacco the Elder
Birth Date: Unknown
Death Date: Unknown

Lipan Apache chief who frequently allied with Anglo-Texans. Flacco the Elder and his son, Flacco the Younger, who was born circa 1818, often acted as scouts and guides for Texas settlers against the Mexicans and the Comanches. The younger Flacco participated in several Texas expeditions into Mexico, including the Somervell Expedition of 1842. Leaving that expedition early with a group of horses he had captured in Mexico, the younger Flacco was killed under peculiar circumstances near San Antonio in December 1842. Some believed he had been the victim of Mexican bandits; others suspected he was killed by a rival Native American tribe, perhaps the Comanches or Cherokees. Flacco the Elder, however, believed that his son had been murdered by two white Texans who had been part of the Somervell Expedition and had coveted his horses.

President Sam Houston, fearing an outbreak of retaliatory violence on the part of the aggrieved Apaches, insisted that Flacco the Younger's murder had been perpetrated by the Mexicans. Nevertheless, Houston presented gifts to Flacco and his family and vowed to uncover the circumstances surrounding Flacco the Younger's murder. He even sent the grieving chief a poem in honor of his fallen son. In early 1843, the disconsolate Flacco led a band of as many as 400 warriors into northern Mexico, where he joined forces with a contingent of Mescalero Apaches. From there the Apaches conducted raids against Mexican villages and Texan settlements as well. It is not known if Flacco actively encouraged the raids into Texas. Flacco dropped out of the historical record after 1843, and the remaining years of his life and the circumstances of his death are unknown. Some historians have suggested that Flacco the Younger's unsolved murder led to the nearly constant warfare between Texans and the Apaches during the 1840s and 1850s.

PAUL G. PIERPAOLI JR.

See also

Apaches; Cherokees; Comanches; Houston, Samuel; Mier Expedition.

References

Schilz, Thomas F. *Lipan Apaches in Texas.* Dallas, TX: Southern Methodist University Press, 1987.

Williams, Amelia W., and Eugene C. Barker, eds. *The Writings of Sam Houston, 1813–1863.* 8 vols. Austin: University of Texas Press, 1938–1943. Reprint, Austin: Pemberton Press, 1970.

Flags, Mexican

At the time of the Mexican-American War, the national flag of Mexico (*pabellón nacional*) consisted of equal-sized red, white, and green vertical bands with an eagle perched atop a cactus holding a snake in its beak at the center (*escudo de armas*). During the reign of Emperor Augustín de Iturbide, a crown sat atop the eagle's head. This flag had been adopted by a decree of November 2, 1821. When Iturbide was deposed in 1823 the crown was removed from the eagle's head, but all else remained unchanged. That flag continues to be the standard flag of the Mexican Republic to the present day.

The choice of a tricolor was inspired by the flag of France, introduced following the French Revolution of 1789 but later temporarily retired after Napoleon's defeat in June 1815. By then, the tricolor was hailed as a symbol of freedom and revolution by liberation movements and, by replacing blue with green and adding the eagle, the newly liberated nation of Mexico developed a distinct flag. Green represented hope for a better nation; white, the purity of the Catholic faith; and red, the blood shed in securing national independence. The depiction of the eagle and snake was borrowed from an ancient Aztec legend that held that an eagle on a cactus with a snake in its beak would signify the site of the Aztec capital. The design of the eagle varied, but it was generally shown full front with fully spread wings and was painted in natural colors. The national flag was hoisted on government buildings, forts, and ships.

Regular army units also carried the national banner, with the addition of unit designations above and/or below the central eagle. Infantry and artillery units had a slightly rectangular size with no fringe, while mounted units had square standards bordered with fringe. Each battalion was to have one color and each squadron a standard. Swallow-tailed guidons, suitable for light cavalry, were later added. The eagle and designations could be embroidered or painted. Militia units were ordered to have the same type of colors and standards, dating from August 1822. As in most armies of the period, designs and use of flags tended to follow practices of the French army. For instance, Mexican regimental companies might also have had small company flags that usually bore a company designation or badge, such as a number or a bugle.

In 1846 permanent infantry units carried a total of 22 colors, while *Activo* infantry corps carried 11 colors. Other regular infantry, cavalry, and artillery units, as well as state militia units, did not officially report having standards, guidons, or colors, but many did, because some were captured by the American units. Apart from specific military colors and flags, the national flag was sometimes deployed in battle. The most famous Mexican flag of the war was heroically defended during the American assault on Chapultepec Castle on September 13, 1847. Chapultepec served as the Mexican military academy, and a number of young cadets took part in its defense. About to be overwhelmed by U.S. troops, Cadet Juan Escutia supposedly wrapped the flag around himself and jumped to his death from the castle's wall, an act solemnly commemorated in Mexico ever since.

During the Mexican-American War and the 1836 Texas Revolution, numerous U.S. military units captured Mexican flags. Some were taken as official trophies while others were kept as mementos by the individuals who seized them. In 1950, as a gesture of goodwill, the U.S. government returned nearly 70 captured flags to the Mexican government, but a number of others remain privately held. Currently, the Texas State Archives has three Mexican flags in its possession, all taken during the Battle of San Jacinto.

René Chartrand

See also
Chapultepec, Battle of; Flags, Texan; Flags, U.S.; San Jacinto, Battle of; Texas Revolution.

References
Almonte, Juan Nepomuceno. *Memoria del Ministerio de estado y del despacho de guerra y marina del gobierno supremo de la República Mexicana, leída al augusto Congreso nacional el día 9 de diciembre de 1846 por el general Almonte.* Mexico City: Mexican Archives, 1846.

Dublán, Manuel, and José María Lozano, comps. *Legislación Mexicana, o colección complete de las disposiciones legislativas expedidas desde la independencia de la república.* Vol. 1. Mexico City: Imprenta del Comercio, 1876.

Flores, Romero Jesús. *Banderas Históricas Mexicanas.* Mexico City: Mexican Archives, 1958.

Flags, Texan

In the early days of its struggle for independence, Texas did not have an official national flag. However, a variety of flags, usually inspired by U.S. flags, were used. A "stand of general colors" and infantry regimental colors were ordered for the Texas army in November 1835, but their design is unknown. In January 1836 Mexico decreed that it did not recognize a flag consisting of red and white stripes with a blue canton bearing a single white star, a cross, and the date 1824 hoisted by Texas ships. The date was a reminder by Texans for Mexico to respect its own constitution, adopted that year.

The only flag that is known for certain to have flown over the Alamo was that of the New Orleans Grays, a volunteer battalion from Louisiana. It was a gray flag bearing the unit's name and an American eagle with a scroll in its beak proclaiming "God and Liberty." Another possible Alamo flag was a Mexican tricolor bearing two stars or the date 1824. A Texas national flag design was proposed in the spring of 1836, but nothing more is known of it. With the Texas army's stunning victory over Mexican troops at

The state flag of Texas—which is identical to the 1839 national flag of the Republic of Texas—was adopted when Texas achieved statehood in 1845. Its colors of red, white, and blue symbolize bravery, strength, and loyalty. (Corel)

San Jacinto in April 1836, the republic's flag was said to be a white field with a lone blue star bearing the motto, *Ubi Libertas Habitat Ibi Nostra Patria Est* (Where Liberty Dwells, There Is My Country), but this could also have been one of the colors carried by volunteer units. Several of these are known and their design varied greatly. Col. Sidney Sherman's regiment carried a white banner with a bare-breasted depiction of Lady Liberty, armed with a sword and bearing the motto "Liberty or Death." This banner, a gift from the ladies of Newport, Kentucky, now hangs (more discreetly clad) in the House chamber of the Texas capitol.

In December 1836, the Texas Congress adopted a blue flag with a single gold star at its center, but this "lone star" flag was not widely used or even known. At last, on January 25, 1839, the Texas Republic's flag was decreed to be a blue vertical band with a five-point white star with two horizontal bands of white (uppermost) and red for the two-thirds of the flag's fly. This flag became well known and remained the official Texas Republic national flag until its union with the United States on December 29, 1845, after which it became the Texas state flag.

The May 23, 1839, Texas army dress regulations included orders for cavalry standards and guidons. The regimental standard was to be "the same as the national color, with the number and name of the regiment in a scroll above the star" and it was to be 2 feet 4 inches (73 centimeters) on the lance and 2 feet 6 inches (79 centimeters) on the fly. The swallow-tailed guidons of the cavalry squadrons were of "blue silk with a white star in the centre, and the letter of the troop (in red) within the star." Texas units participating in the Mexican War probably still had their old regimental colors and guidons, although the national colors and standards may have been of the U.S. 1841 models.

RENÉ CHARTRAND

See also

Congress, Texan; Flags, Mexican; Flags, U.S.; Texas.

References

Fehrenbach, T. R. *Lone Star: A History of Texas and the Texans.* New York: Collier, 1968.

Gilbert, Charles E. *Flags of Texas.* Gretna, LA: Pelican, 1989.

Jenkins, John H. *The Papers of the Texas Revolution, 1835–1836.* Vols. 4 and 9. Austin: Jay A. Matthews, 1973.

Quaife, Milo M., Melvin J. Weig, and Roy E. Appleman. *The History of the United States Flag.* New York: Harper & Row, 1961.

Flags, U.S.

Since 1818 the "Stars and Stripes" national flag of the United States has had a field of 13 stripes—6 white and 7 red—and a blue canton with the number of white stars within indicating the number of states in the Union. Prior to the start of the Mexican-American War, as of July 4, 1845, the canton officially had 27 white stars. During the war, however, Texas and Iowa were officially admitted as states, and a star was officially added for each on July 4, 1846, and July 4, 1847, respectively. With so many changes in a few years' time, as well as the cost of replacing flags and the practice of doing so only when they were worn out, a variety of flags would have been seen during the war, including many 26-star flags that had been in use since 1837. The size, design, and placement of the stars and canton varied throughout the 19th century and were not fixed by law until 1912.

Regular U.S. Army infantry, dragoon, and artillery regiments carried a stand of two colors, each having 6 feet on the staff by 6 feet and 6 inches on the fly, edged with yellow fringe. The infantry colors were blue silk and featured a slight variation on the Great Seal of the United States: a large eagle with a sheaf of arrows and an olive branch clutched in its talons. Covering the eagle's breast was the American shield; its beak held a scroll with the motto *E Pluribus Unum* (Out of Many, One), with the appropriate number of stars above and a scroll with the regimental designation below. The field was blue for infantry and yellow for artillery. The artillery colors featured crossed cannon barrels in the center, with the letters "U.S." above it; below was the regiment's name in scroll. However, some regiments still carried the older national color of blue with an eagle and yellow with a scroll for the regimental color. Companies also had small, square camp flags, white for infantry and red for artillery.

Dragoon and mounted-rifle regiments had a smaller blue standard edged with yellow fringe bearing the eagle, stars, and designations, and each squadron also carried a guidon, half red (above) and half white (below), with "U.S." and the squadron's letter.

American state militia colors generally followed the styles used in the regular army, but with many variations. The blue regimental colors usually bore the state's coat of arms, but some, such as the Palmetto Regiment of South Carolina, had the eagle instead.

Among the best-remembered of the unofficial American flags is the California (Bear Flag) Republic flag, "to represent California Independence," according to a British observer, with its grizzly or golden bear, single red star, and bottom stripe, first hoisted in July 1846 by the men of the California battalion. California became the 31st state in 1850 and the "bear" flag was adopted as its official state flag in 1911.

RENÉ CHARTRAND

See also

Bear Flag Revolt; California; Flags, Mexican; Flags, Texan; Frémont, John Charles.

References

Horner, Harlan Hoyt. *The American Flag.* Albany: State of New York, 1910.

Johannsen, Robert. *To the Halls of the Montezumas: The Mexican War in the American Imagination.* Oxford, UK: Oxford University Press, 1985.

Katcher, Philip R. *The Mexican-American War, 1846–1848.* Oxford, UK: Osprey, 2003.

Quaife, Milo M., Melvin J. Weig, and Roy E. Appleman. *The History of the United States Flag.* New York: Harper & Row, 1961.

Flores, José María
Birth Date: 1818
Death Date: 1866

Mexican soldier and military governor of California during late 1846. José María Flores was born in Mexico (then New Spain) in 1818. When he was only 12 years old, he joined the Mexican army, worked his way up in rank, and by 1840 held a captain's commission. Two years later he was sent to Alta California, where he acted as secretary to Mexican governor Manuel Micheltorena. In 1845, after Micheltorena was ousted from office, Flores stayed in California, opting to join forces with the new Mexican military commander José Castro.

After the Mexican-American War commenced in 1846, U.S. forces under the command of Commodore Robert F. Stockton and Colonel John C. Frémont quickly secured much of California; by August, Los Angeles was under American control, and the Americans had encountered only token resistance. Although Flores and Castro had pledged not to wage war against occupying U.S. forces, Flores withdrew south of Los Angeles, where he assembled a force of some 500 Californios. By September Flores's force had laid siege to Los Angeles, which was lightly defended by only 60 U.S. soldiers. On September 29, the Americans capitulated, and Flores's troops occupied the town.

Less than a month later, on October 26, the Californios elected Flores as the military governor and commander in chief of California. Now resolute in his desire to rid California of its American occupiers, Flores unleashed an offensive all over central and Southern California, including San Luis Obispo, Santa Ines, Santa Barbara, and as far south as San Diego. Meanwhile, small guerilla units launched raids against white settlers and U.S. troops.

Flores was not without his detractors, however. Some Californios doubted his loyalty to the cause because he was a Mexican and not a Californio. Consequently, in late 1846, some of his followers imprisoned him. The short-lived incarceration, however, proved deadly to the Californios' morale and momentum in the war. Meanwhile, while Flores was imprisoned, Stockton and Brigadier General Stephen W. Kearny had departed San Diego with a U.S. force, determined to retake Los Angeles. Flores attempted to check the American advance with about 500 men, but he was defeated at the Battles of San Gabriel and La Mesa in early January 1847. On January 10 Kearny recaptured Los Angeles, effectively ending Flores's resistance.

Flores now fled south to Sonora, Mexico, with only a handful of followers. He tried to raise another resistance force there but was unsuccessful. His return to California was improbable, because Stockton had threatened to arrest and execute him for having broken his promise not to engage in warfare with the Americans. Flores saw action during the military campaigns in Mexico between 1847 and 1848, and by 1851 he had been appointed military commander of Sonora. Flores actively opposed the French military intervention in Mexico, which began in 1861, and successfully led Mexican troops in several clashes with the French. Detailed to Mazatlán, Flores died there in 1866.

PAUL G. PIERPAOLI JR.

See also

California; California Theater of War, Overview; Californios; Frémont, John Charles; Kearny, Stephen Watts; La Mesa, Battle of; Los Angeles; Micheltorena, Manuel; San Gabriel, Battle of; Stockton, Robert Field.

References

Harlow, Neal. *California Conquered: War and Peace on the Pacific, 1846–1850.* Berkeley: University of California Press, 1982.

Johannsen, Robert W. *To the Halls of the Montezumas: The Mexican War in American Imagination.* Oxford, UK: Oxford University Press, 1985.

Florida Battalion

A formation of two companies of volunteers from Florida who saw action during the latter stages of the Mexican-American War. Company A, commanded by William W. J. Kelly of Pensacola, Florida, was recruited in Tallahassee and Pensacola in the early months of 1847 and was originally mustered to garrison Fort Pickens off the Pensacola coast. Kelly was a state legislator and veteran of the Second Seminole War. He later served as an officer in both the U.S. Navy and then the Confederate States Navy and was the first lieutenant governor of Florida. Company C, commanded by Captain Robert G. Livingston of Newnansville, Florida, an attorney with no military experience beyond service in the local militia, was recruited in northern Florida from May to June 1847 and mustered in at Tallahassee.

Livingston's company trained in New Orleans before boarding ship and traveling to Pensacola to pick up Kelly's company. The Florida Battalion then sailed to Veracruz, Mexico. When the two companies joined, Kelly, as the senior officer, took command of the battalion, although he was never promoted to higher rank. The battalion served in Veracruz, Puebla, and Jalapa during the late stages of the war after Mexico City had been taken by U.S. troops in September 1847. The battalion saw many losses due to illness, one soldier died from a sniper's bullet, and Livingston was mortally wounded by a self-inflicted gunshot while hunting a wolf. The battalion left Mexico as separate companies during June and July 1848.

RUSSELL D. JAMES

See also

Jalapa; Mexico City Campaign; Puebla; Veracruz.

References

James, Russell D. *Pensacola's Other Statesman: William W. J. Kelly, a Life of Service.* Milton, FL: Cantadora Press, 2005.

James, Russell D. *Too Late for Blood: Florida Volunteers in the Mexican War.* Bowie, MD: Heritage Books, 2006.

Flying Artillery

A commonly used term for the U.S. Army's light or field artillery batteries during the Mexican-American War. Prior to the opening of hostilities, only five batteries were outfitted as light artillery; during the war, four additional batteries were added. A complete battery could include as many as 50 men.

Each of the original five batteries usually possessed a combination of bronze Model 1841 6-pounder guns (their main source of firepower) and bronze Model 1841 12-pounder howitzers. The Model 1841 artillery tubes were married with new carriages, which created lethal yet lightweight weapon systems. Flying artillery was capable of firing grapeshot, shells, or round shot.

In practice, the light batteries proved extremely mobile on the battlefield, hence the appellation "flying." The guns were usually mounted to two-wheeled carriages or caissons. The crew members rode into battle on either the horses pulling the caisson or on the caisson itself.

Increased mobility contributed to only part of the flying batteries' effectiveness. They were also blessed with outstanding leadership. The roll of artillery officers who served in the Mexican-American War included at least nine future Union Civil War generals and six who served the Confederacy. These included Robert Anderson, the defender of Fort Sumter; Braxton Bragg, commander of the Confederate Army of Tennessee; and the redoubtable Thomas J. "Stonewall" Jackson. Major Samuel Ringgold, credited as the father of the flying artillery, was mortally wounded in action at the Battle of Palo Alto, becoming one of the war's earliest national heroes.

Generally, crew training was of a high standard, which allowed, in some cases, a ratio of six to one shots versus their Mexican opponents. The combination of mobility, leadership, and training meant that the light artillery emerged as the U.S. Army's outstanding combat arm during the war. The flying artillery played a crucial role in most American victories, perhaps most notably at Palo Alto (May 8, 1846) and Buena Vista (February 22–23, 1847).

On the offense, the batteries often led an attack by firing into Mexican infantry and cavalry formations from outside effective musket range and suppressing concentrations of Mexican artillery. On the defense, flying batteries served as a mobile reserve of firepower and were often found wherever the fighting was hottest.

GREGORY S. HOSPODOR

See also

Artillery; Buena Vista, Battle of; Palo Alto, Battle of; Ringgold, Samuel; Weapons, Mexican; Weapons, U.S.

References

Birkhimer, William E. *Historical Sketch of the Organization, Administration, Material and Tactics of the Artillery, United States Army.* 1884. Reprint, New York: Greenwood Press, 1968.

Dillon, Lester R., Jr. *American Artillery in the Mexican War, 1846–1847.* Austin, TX: Presidial Press, 1975.

Foraging

Technically, the act of foraging usually involves a systematic gathering of food for livestock. Forage is usually hay, which is consumed by draft animals and cattle. The term "foraging" has also been used to describe a much wider and more indiscriminate gathering of food and supplies from the surrounding area, both for animal and human consumption. During the Mexican-American War, U.S. troops engaged in foraging for their animals and for themselves.

Soldiers sent on a foraging expedition went into the surrounding countryside equipped with reaping tools and cord or rope to bind together the gathered hay. When operating in enemy territory, a foraging squad was almost always accompanied by armed guards. During the war with Mexico, Major General Winfield Scott stipulated that U.S. troops were not to engage in indiscriminate foraging or marauding, out of fear that such activity would alienate Mexican civilians. Indeed, in the 1840s, the U.S. Army's Articles of War clearly forbade unauthorized foraging, under threat of court-martial or even execution. Indiscriminate foraging, however, was difficult to discourage, particularly because many officers condoned such behavior or looked the other way when it occurred.

During the Mexican campaigns, a large number of American soldiers expropriated produce, beef, and other items from Mexican ranches and farms. Many saw this activity as a welcome diversion from the boredom and stress of army life. They also were glad to augment their poor and often meager rations of hardtack, salt pork, dried beef, and coffee. Unaccustomed to having at their disposal fresh fruit, many U.S. soldiers plundered Mexican citrus groves. Those who participated in such activity saw no harm in it, while

A Camp Kitchen.

A scene from Brigadier General Zachary Taylor's camp near Walnut Springs, Texas, in 1846. Armies of the time relied on foraging to supplement army-issued rations. (Library of Congress)

others referred to it euphemistically as "capturing" supplies. Many officers who caught enlisted men found foraging illegally would request a portion of the take rather than turn in the guilty parties.

Foraging was an essential activity for the U.S. Army during the Mexican-American War. During a conflict that was waged several thousand miles from U.S. population centers, and at a time when railroads were still underdeveloped, American supply lines quickly proved inadequate. Foraging for supplies thus became a necessary evil. In addition to foraging, U.S. soldiers also purchased food and other supplies from camp vendors and Mexican markets.

During the Civil War, Union armies, most famously Major General William T. Sherman's as it moved from Atlanta to Savannah and then into the Carolinas, supplied themselves by extensive foraging.

PAUL G. PIERPAOLI JR.

See also
Army Life, Mexican and U.S.; Logistics, U.S.; Mexico, Occupation of; Scott, Winfield; United States Army.

References
Cuncliffe, Marcus. *Soldiers and Civilians: The Martial Spirit in America, 1775–1865.* 2nd ed. Boston: Little, Brown, 1968.
Winders, Richard Bruce. *Mr. Polk's Army: The American Military Experience in the Mexican War.* College Station: Texas A&M University Press, 1997.

Ford, John Salmon
Birth Date: May 26, 1815
Death Date: November 3, 1897

Soldier, journalist, and Texas politician. John Ford Salmon was born near Greenville, South Carolina, on May 26, 1815. As a youth, he moved with his family to Lincoln County, Tennessee, and studied medicine in Shelbyville when he was 16. In June 1836 he relocated to San Augustine in east Texas, where he established a medical practice. The Texas Revolution was under way, and Ford quickly became involved in the political and military matters of the fledgling Republic of Texas.

In 1844 Ford was elected to the Texas House of Representatives and for all practical purposes gave up medicine. The next year Ford moved to Austin, where he purchased a newspaper and renamed it the *Texas Democrat.* He also joined the Texas army with the rank of lieutenant. Ford advocated forcefully for Texas annexation in both the Texas House and in the pages of his newspaper.

When the Mexican-American War began in 1846, Ford became adjutant of Colonel John C. Hays's 2nd Regiment of the Texas Mounted Rifles during Major General Winfield Scott's Mexico City Campaign. As such, Ford participated in the grueling 1847 antiguerrilla campaigns near Mexico City and along the National Road, including the skirmishes at Galaxara, San Juan Teotihuacán, and Zacualtipán. Part of Ford's duties included writing to the

families of soldiers killed during the fighting. He thus earned the macabre sobriquet "RIP" because he ended all of the letters he wrote with "RIP," meaning "Rest in Peace." Ford also served with several Texas Ranger units in operations against hostile Native Americans, particularly the Comanches.

After the war, Ford returned to his political and journalistic career but retained his military commission. In 1849 he led an expedition from San Antonio to El Paso, mapping the area and writing a report on the region that helped establish a major wagon route through west Texas. That same year, he led a company of Texas Rangers in numerous skirmishes with Native Americans. In 1852 Ford was elected to the Texas State Senate and took over a major Austin newspaper, the *State Times,* which position he held until 1857. In the winter of 1858, he took a temporary commission as a colonel in the state militia and fought two pitched battles against Native Americans in the Texas Panhandle.

In 1861, Ford was a member of the Texas Secession Convention. He then helped negotiate a trade accord between the Confederate States and Mexico. From 1862 to 1865, Ford oversaw recruitment and training for Texas conscripts and fought several skirmishes along the Mexican border with Mexican bandits and hostile Native Americans. In May 1865, Ford, although he refused an official commission in the Confederate Army several times, had the distinction of leading Southern forces at the Battle of Palmito (or Palmetto) Ranch, the last land battle of the Civil War. After the Civil War, Ford returned to the Texas Senate for two additional terms and also served as the mayor of Brownsville during 1874. He later retired to San Antonio and wrote his memoirs. Ford died there on November 3, 1897.

PAUL G. PIERPAOLI JR.

See also
Comanches; Galaxara, Skirmish at; Guerrilla Warfare; Hays, John Coffee; Mexico City Campaign; Texas; Texas-Comanche Relations.

References
Collins, Michael L. *Texas Devils: Rangers and Regulars on the Lower Rio Grande, 1846–1861.* Norman: University of Oklahoma Press, 2008.
Ford, John S. *RIP Ford's Texas.* Edited by Steven Oates. Austin: University of Texas Press, 1963.
Hughes, William J. *Rebellious Ranger: RIP Ford and the Old Southwest.* Norman: University of Oklahoma Press, 1964.
Hunt, Jeffrey William. *The Last Battle of the Civil War: Palmetto Ranch.* Austin: University of Texas Press, 2002.

Forrest, French
Birth Date: 1796
Death Date: December 22, 1866

U.S. Navy officer. Born in Saint Mary's City, Maryland, in 1796, French Forrest secured a warrant as a midshipman in the U.S. Navy on June 9, 1811. During the War of 1812 he took part in the action between the U.S. Navy brig *Hornet* and the Royal Navy brig *Peacock* on February 24, 1813, and the Battle of Lake Erie on September 10, 1813. Forrest was promoted to lieutenant on March 5, 1817, to commander on February 9, 1837, and to captain on March 30, 1844.

During the Mexican-American War, Captain Forrest commanded the frigate *Cumberland.* He had charge of the 253-man landing force that captured Tabasco in October 1846. Because the *Cumberland* had grounded on Chopas Reef in July 1847 and needed docking, Forrest took command of the frigate *Raritan.* Earlier, in the amphibious operation against Veracruz in March 1847, Forrest had charge of the embarkation of the troops who departed Antón Lizardo and also charge of the landing operations at Collado Beach. By the time Major General Winfield Scott moved ashore, however, Commander Joshua Sands had replaced Forrest. Forrest subsequently took part in operations against Tuxpan that April.

Said to be completely fearless in battle, Forrest had little opportunity to demonstrate this quality during the Civil War. When Virginia seceded, Forrest resigned his commission on April 19, 1861, to become the first and only flag officer of the Virginia State Navy and assumed command of the Norfolk (Gosport) Navy Yard. He then joined the Confederate Navy and received a captain's commission on June 10 as the third most senior officer. Forrest remained in command of the Norfolk Yard from April 22, 1861, to May 15, 1862. Confederate secretary of the navy Stephen R. Mallory ordered Forrest to raise the scuttled U.S. steam frigate *Merrimack* and rebuild it as the ironclad *Virginia.* Forrest had expected to command the ironclad when it was completed, but that assignment went to Captain Franklin Buchanan. Mallory replaced Forrest at Norfolk several months after the epic clash between the USS *Monitor* and the *Virginia* because he believed that Forrest had been slow to repair the *Virginia.* Forrest then headed the Confederate Navy Office of Orders and Details (the senior navy bureau that dealt with personnel matters) until March 1863.

Forrest twice commanded the James River Squadron: during July 10, 1861–February 27, 1862, when he was succeeded by Captain Buchanan, and March 24, 1863–May 6, 1864, when he was succeeded by Captain John K. Mitchell. The squadron did not engage in any significant action during Forrest's tenure. Forrest then became acting assistant secretary of the navy.

Forrest died shortly after the war, in Georgetown, District of Columbia, on December 22, 1866.

SPENCER C. TUCKER

See also

Antón Lizardo; Collado Beach; Sands, Joshua Ratoon; Scott, Winfield; Tabasco River Expeditions; Tuxpan; Tuxpan, Battle of; Veracruz, Landing at and Siege of.

References

Callahan, Edward W., ed. *List of Officers of the Navy of the United States and of the Marine Corps from 1775 to 1900.* 1901. Reprint, New York: Haskell House, 1969.

Coski, John M. *Capital Navy: The Men, Ships and Operations of the James River Squadron.* Campbell, CA: Savas, 1996.

Thompson, Kenneth E. *Civil War Commodores and Admirals: A Biographical Directory of All Eighty-Eight Union and Confederate Navy Officers Who Attained Commissioned Flag Rank during the War.* Portland, ME: Thompson, 2001.

Fort Jesup

U.S. military post built in 1822 about 22 miles west of Natchitoches, Louisiana, near the present-day town of Many, Louisiana. It was constructed primarily to guard the U.S.-Mexican border after the Adams-Onís Treaty of 1819 fixed the border at the Sabine River and to bring order to the neutral zone in what is now Sabine Parish, Louisiana.

Between 1803 and 1819 Spain and the United States had been unable to agree on a border between Louisiana and Texas. Thus they created a neutral zone from the Sabine River to Arroyo Hondo, roughly the area that is now Sabine Parish. Within this zone, neither country was permitted to garrison troops or police forces or to enforce its own laws. While this temporary arrangement helped the two nations avoid conflict, it also resulted in a lawless region in which bandits, criminals, and other undesirables roamed with impunity.

By 1822, the U.S. government sought to garrison the region and bring law and order to the former neutral zone. Lieutenant Colonel Zachary Taylor helped establish Fort Jesup, which he named for Brigadier General Thomas Sidney Jesup, that same year. Taylor served as commander of the fort for its entire lifespan, until it was decommissioned in 1846. In little time, Taylor's force had asserted U.S. control over the neutral zone. The fort also served as a base of operation for Indian agents, helped local plantation owners avoid slave uprisings, and reassured new settlers in the area that U.S. forces would protect them from hostile Native Americans. Also, Taylor's men helped construct roads in the area.

By 1843, Fort Jesup was the strongest fortification in Louisiana, with a redoubt that enclosed as many as 82 structures including officers' quarters and barracks for enlisted men, clustered around a central parade ground. Many of the buildings were constructed of cypress, which is well suited to Louisiana's damp and humid climate and abounded nearby.

In 1846, on the eve of the war with Mexico, Taylor used Fort Jesup as a staging area for his Army of Observation's march to Texas. By the end of that year, the U.S. Army deemed the fort unnecessary and abandoned it. It deteriorated for many years, and not until the 1930s did local citizens band together to preserve what was left, which at that point was only the cook house. In 1956, the state of Louisiana turned the site into a state park, and in 1961 it was declared a National Historic Landmark. Since then, the cook house has been refurbished, and several reconstructed buildings have been added.

PAUL G. PIERPAOLI JR.

See also

Adams-Onís Treaty; Forts; Louisiana Purchase; Sabine River; Taylor, Zachary; Texas; United States Army of Observation.

References

Eisenhower, John S. D. *Zachary Taylor*. New York: Times Books, 2008.

Katcher, Philip. *The Mexican-American War, 1846–1848*. University Park, IL: Osprey, 1989.

Fort Leavenworth

The oldest U.S. fort west of the Mississippi River. Located in the northeastern portion of modern-day Kansas on the bank of the Missouri River, during the 1840s and 1850s Fort Leavenworth served as the starting point for traders and immigrants heading to Santa Fe, Oregon, and California. During the Mexican-American War, the fort was an important training and staging area for U.S. troops. Indeed, three forces that secured California in 1846 originated at Fort Leavenworth.

Before 1821 Mexico was a closed economy, unable to trade with the United States, but following independence from Spain that year U.S. traders quickly opened a trading route to Santa Fe. Each year, more and more Americans and their herds of pack mules laden with American manufactured goods would cross the Arkansas River and follow the Santa Fe Trail into Mexican territory, returning with Mexican silver. These smaller groups, however, increasingly came under attack by Native Americans angered by the trespassing on their lands.

To protect the trade on the Santa Fe Trail, Missouri senator Thomas Hart Benton proposed that an army post be constructed. After rejecting a site on the Arkansas River, Congress approved funds for a fort on the Missouri River. In April 1827, Colonel Henry Leavenworth and four companies of the 3rd United States Infantry left Saint Louis and traveled up the Missouri. Leavenworth rejected the original site for one on higher ground on the west bank of the Missouri. Temporary accommodations for the 188 men were soon built, and the post was named "Cantonment Leavenworth" on September 19, 1827. Leavenworth soon returned to Saint Louis, but his name remained. On February 8, 1832, the cantonment was renamed Fort Leavenworth.

Leavenworth provided an important base for trading and exploration expeditions heading west. Steamboats were able to sail up the Missouri to its location, carrying supplies and passengers. Overland trails originating at or near Fort Leavenworth included both the Santa Fe Trail and the Oregon Trail. Thousands of immigrants passed through the area between 1841 and 1858, heading for Oregon and California, while soldiers from the fort provided escorts for travelers and kept the local peace between Native Americans and increasing numbers of white settlers.

When the Mexican-American War began in May 1846, Fort Leavenworth was a natural staging area for forces heading west and south. It also provided training grounds for thousands of the volunteers who fought in the war. U.S. strategy called for the occupation of New Mexico and California, and Colonel (soon promoted to brigadier general) Stephen W. Kearny organized the Army of the West at Fort Leavenworth to undertake that operation. The Army of the West was comprised of approximately 1,700 soldiers, including 300 regulars from the 1st Dragoon Regiment; the 1st Missouri Mounted Rifles, a volunteer regiment commanded by Colonel Alexander Doniphan; and the so-called Mormon Battalion. After training and equipping his army at Fort Leavenworth, Kearny departed on June 26, 1846, accompanied by a train of more than 100 wagons, 500 pack mules, and a large herd of cattle. The Army of the West traveled down the Santa Fe Trail, capturing Santa Fe without a fight. Kearny and his dragoons then proceeded to California, where Kearny quickly secured Los Angeles. Kearny returned to the fort on August 22, 1847. Doniphan's mounted rifle regiment captured Saltillo and Chihuahua after leaving Kearny's command at Santa Fe. The Mormon Battalion, serving as combat engineers, opened a wagon road from Santa Fe to San Diego.

Also organized at Fort Leavenworth was Colonel Sterling Price's 2nd Missouri Mounted Rifles, which was charged with garrisoning New Mexico after Kearny's and Doniphan's departures.

Following the war, Fort Leavenworth remained an important outpost and gateway to the west. When war with the Mormons threatened in 1857, an army under Albert Sidney Johnston massed at the fort before leaving for Utah. Later, federal troops at Fort Leavenworth secured Kansas for the Union at the start of the Civil War. Today, Fort Leavenworth is the site of the U.S. Army's Command and General Staff College.

TIM WATTS

See also

Army of the West, United States; Benton, Thomas Hart; Chihuahua, State of; Doniphan, Alexander William; Forts; Kearny, Stephen Watts; Mormon Battalion; Price, Sterling; Saltillo; Santa Fe–Chihuahua Trail.

References

Hughes, J. Patrick. *Fort Leavenworth: Gateway to the West*. Topeka: Kansas State Historical Society, 2000.

Partin, John W., ed. *A Brief History of Fort Leavenworth, 1827–1983*. Fort Leavenworth, KS: Combat Studies Institute, U.S. Army Command and General Staff College, 1983.

Walton, George H. *Sentinel of the Plains: Fort Leavenworth and the American West*. Englewood Cliffs, NJ: Prentice-Hall, 1973.

Fort Lipantitlán, Battle of
Event Date: July 7, 1842

In the summer of 1842, Mexican army colonel Antonio Canales Rosillo invaded southern Texas with 700 troops and attacked Fort Lipantitlán on July 7, 1842. The fort had been constructed by the Mexicans and was the scene of another battle during the Texas Revolution. It was located at a campground of the Lipan Apache Indians on the west bank of the Nueces River, about three miles upstream from the old town of San Patricio on the east side of the river.

In July 1842 Fort Lipantitlán was held by 192 Texans under James Davis, adjutant general of the Texas army. The Texans managed to hold off the Mexicans and force their withdrawal. Rosillo's raid was one of three by the Mexican army into south Texas that year, and all three prompted the reprisal of the Somervell Expedition during November and December 1842.

SPENCER C. TUCKER

See also

Somervell Expedition; Vasquez Expedition; Woll's Expedition.

References

Huson, Hobart. *Refugio: A Comprehensive History of Refugio County from Aboriginal Times to 1953.* 2 vols. Woodsboro, TX: Rooke Foundation, 1953, 1955.

Nance, J. Milton. *Attack and Counter Attack: The Texas-Mexican Frontier, 1842.* Austin: University of Texas Press, 1964.

Fort Marcy

Adobe fort built by the U.S. Army during 1846–1847 on a small rise just north of Santa Fe, New Mexico. Fort Marcy was designed to provide protection for the capital of the New Mexico Territory and emerging American interests near the Santa Fe Trail from an invading Mexican army. The redoubt was named in 1846 by Brigadier General Stephen W. Kearny in honor of Secretary of War William L. Marcy and was completed in the spring of 1847. During the Mexican-American War, Kearny and his Army of the West swept through the Southwest Territories on their way to California. The army's presence established U.S. control over New Mexico Territory and provided protection for American traders and settlers in the area.

Kearny's force of some 1,700 men set out from Fort Leavenworth, Kansas, in June 1846. On August 18, the Army of the West arrived on the outskirts of Santa Fe, only to find the city leaders willing to surrender. Kearny then sent his two engineers—Lieutenants William H. Emory and Jeremy F. Gilmer—to scout for a suitable location on which to build a fortification near the city. The resulting fort became the first American post built on seized Mexican territory.

Fort Marcy was an irregular-shaped hexagonal polygon, with adobe walls measuring 9 feet high and 5 feet thick, with numerous gun placements on all sides. The redoubt was originally designed to house a garrison of 1,000 men, but because the need to defend the fort from a hostile Mexican army never materialized, the fort was only partially built. The garrison was housed in makeshift barracks near the Santa Fe Plaza.

Within a few weeks of Santa Fe's capitulation, General Kearny had established American authority over the territory and enacted laws of governance for the New Mexico Territory. When Kearny moved on toward California, Charles Bent became the first provisional

Fort Marcy and La Parroquia Church at Santa Fe in New Mexico, February 9, 1848, by Lieutenant Colonel W. H. Emory, a member of the U.S. Army of the West dispatched to California. (Beinecke Rare Book & Manuscript Library)

governor, with Colonel Sterling Price superseding Kearny as military commander based at Fort Marcy.

After the war, other American posts in the Southwest, such as Fort Bliss in El Paso, Texas, became more important in the 1850s, and as a result the fort fell into disrepair, seeing only limited use until the Civil War. The U.S. governor of New Mexico abandoned Santa Fe on March 4, 1862, and a brigade of Confederate troops led by Brigadier General Henry H. Sibley captured the city and seized Fort Marcy. By April 1862, the Confederates were forced to vacate the fort as Union forces staged a counterattack from Fort Union (Las Vegas). In 1868, the fort ceased to function as a military outpost when President Andrew Johnson deemed it unnecessary for the protection of Santa Fe. An army hospital at the site remained in use until 1892, however, and the post also served as a weather observation station from 1849 to 1892. Today only a few mounds of earth and a historical marker remain where the walls once stood.

CALEB KLINGLER

See also

Bent, Charles; Emory, William Hemsley; Fort Leavenworth; Forts; Frémont, John Charles; Kearny, Stephen Watts; Marcy, William Learned; New Mexico; Price, Sterling; Santa Fe; Santa Fe–Chihuahua Trail

References

Clark, Dwight L. *Stephen Watts Kearny: Soldier of the West.* Norman: University of Oklahoma Press, 1961.

Dawson, Joseph G., III. *Doniphan's Epic March: The First Missouri Volunteers in the Mexican War.* Topeka: University of Kansas Press, 1999.

Emory, William H. *Notes of a Military Reconnaissance, from Fort Leavenworth, in Missouri, to San Diego, in California.* 1848. Reprint, Albuquerque: University of New Mexico Press, 1951.

Fort Polk

U.S. military post constructed at Point Isabel, on the north end of Brazos Island, in modern-day Cameron County, Texas. Fork Polk (also known as Fort Brazos Santiago) was built as a military depot on the order of Brigadier General Zachary Taylor on March 26, 1846. The site is located approximately six miles north of the Rio Grande. Taylor selected the location in order to control navigation between Padre and Brazos Islands and to establish a U.S. military presence south of the Nueces River. As early as 1840, in fact, Republic of Texas officials had planned to erect a military post on Brazos Island, but such plans never came to fruition.

Initially, Major John Munroe of the 2nd U.S. Artillery garrisoned the post with a small detachment while Taylor and his army marched south to the Rio Grande. Little is known about the fort's physical characteristics, and no remains are extant. The rampart, however, is believed to have been earthen-walled.

During the Mexican-American War, Fort Polk was used primarily as a supply depot and a hospital. An unknown number of soldiers are buried outside the fort's walls. Men of the 4th U.S. Infantry, commanded by Captain F. C. Hunt, garrisoned the depot from 1848 to 1850. As early as January 1849, some buildings had been dismantled and relocated to different spots along the Rio Grande, and in February 1850 Fort Polk was officially abandoned. In 1852 the site was used as a transit point for materials arriving in the area to be used at Fort Brown. In February 1861, what remained of the post was seized by a Confederate artillery company based at Galveston. In the 20th century, the site of Fort Polk disappeared entirely after the U.S. Army Corps of Engineers straightened the waterway between Brazos and Padre Islands.

PAUL G. PIERPAOLI JR.

See also

Forts; Nueces River; Rio Grande; Taylor, Zachary.

References

Bauer, K. Jack. *The Mexican War, 1846–1848.* New York: Macmillan, 1974.

Pierce, Gerald S. *Texas under Arms: The Camps, Posts, Forts, and Military Towns of the Republic of Texas.* Austin, TX: Encino, 1969.

Forts

Projecting a military presence had been a critical part of the United States' westward expansion, both for the purpose of protecting settlers and displaying American sovereignty. Housing and supplying troops necessitated the establishment of a successive line of forts, which occurred in three phases in the 19th century. The first phase provided a military buffer between settlers and hostile Indians, with a line of posts built in advance of settlement. By 1845, the United States had 12 permanent posts, 11 forts, and the Jefferson Barracks located west of the Mississippi River. These posts represented the western line of military defense prior to the Mexican-American War. Confusion existed concerning names and functions of posts, camps, cantonments, depots, and presidios, so on February 6, 1832, Adjutant General Roger James issued General Order No. 11, designating that all be called forts and that the War Department name all new forts. By the end of 1832, all permanent posts west of the Mississippi River were identified as forts, except for the Jefferson Barracks.

These forts were seldom attacked. Their importance lay in the troop presence, a symbol of American authority in the region. They also served as bases of operation during campaigns against Indians, and they sometimes served as centers of trade and diplomacy with Native American tribes. With increased westward expansion, defense needs changed from regional to overall defense of the West, resulting in the establishment in 1826 of Jefferson Barracks south of Saint Louis on the Mississippi River; and Fort Leavenworth, in Kansas, just west of the Missouri border on the Missouri River, in 1827. These two forts served as the administrative components of the western defense system and as bases for western expeditions, especially in the years just prior to the beginning of the Mexican-American War.

The removal in the 1830s of several large eastern Indian tribes to the trans-Mississippi West and increased movement of settlers signaled the need for the War Department to plan for western frontier defense, which meant more mounted troops and forts to house and supply them. All proposed plans recommended a cordon of forts and their locations, from Fort Brady or Fort Snelling in the north down through Fort Leavenworth and Fort Gibson, to Fort Towson or Fort Jesup in the south. In 1836, Secretary of War Lewis Cass's plan proposed a military road along the frontier connecting the line of forts, beginning at the Red River near Fort Towson and ending at the Mississippi between the Des Moines and Minnesota Rivers. Joel R. Poinsett, Cass's successor, objected to this plan, however. Poinsett recommended a line of forts along the newly surveyed wagon road from San Antonio to Presidio Rio Grande. Before 1850, his suggestions had resulted in the establishment of the inner ring of forts in western Texas.

Ongoing events in the Southwest proved the wisdom of the establishment of these forts. The 1836 Texas Revolution had upset the peace in the region, and the Mexican government refused to recognize Texan independence. Nine years later Texas sought annexation by the United States, an effort that increased tensions between Mexico and the United States. Indeed, the Mexican-American War disrupted and refocused frontier defense plans, drawing attention away from the Canadian border and the ongoing Seminole Wars in Florida. The recently established line of forts in the Southwest provided bases of operation, supply depots, troop housing, and American military presence during the Mexican-American War.

Fort Leavenworth had served as a base for western expeditions in 1835, 1839, and 1845; it also served as a base for actions in New Mexico and California in 1845 and in 1846 during the Mexican-American War. Jefferson Barracks was an important reserve post, housing large numbers of mounted troops deployable to remote areas of the frontier as well as Mexico.

From a design perspective, both the American and Mexican engineers supervising fort construction took their cues from classic European concepts, chiefly those proposed by the noted French engineer Sébastien Le Prestre de Vauban. These included detailed terrain analyses, the incorporation of unique terrain features into the overall design of the fort, geometrically complex fortifications that aided and amplified firing power, and interlocking fire patterns and outer works. During the Mexican-American War itself, which was fought almost exclusively on Mexican soil, the Americans did not have the luxury of depending on previously built forts and redoubts. Instead, they had to build their own, which usually consisted of earthen field works, temporary strongholds using locally available stone and timber, and trenches, including the 9,000 yards of trenches dug around Veracruz during the siege of that city in March 1847. The U.S. Army had at its disposal a large number of highly trained engineers, most of whom were graduates of the U.S. Military Academy at West Point. These men did an admirable job of erecting forts and redoubts during the war.

Perhaps the most famous—and durable—U.S. fort built for the war was Fort Texas (Fort Brown), built by engineers under Brigadier Zachary Taylor's command in early 1846 beside the Rio Grande opposite Matamoros, Mexico. A classic "star" design in the Vauban tradition, Fort Texas allowed some 400 men manning four 18-pounder and three 6-pounder cannon and one mortar to successfully hold off a weeklong Mexican artillery barrage that hurled nearly 2,800 shells at the fort in May 1846.

On the Mexican side, forts played a central role in the defense of the nation, and Mexican engineers effectively utilized local terrain and existing Spanish colonial structures, some of which included convents, churches, and even the ruins of a cathedral, to erect stout and formidable defensive works to impede an enemy advance. Well-placed and designed forts encircling Monterrey proved a daunting obstacle for Major General Zachary Taylor's forces in September 1846. These included two stone forts atop hills—Fort Libertad and El Soldado—and the Bishop's Palace, a former episcopal residence that the Mexicans had expertly fortified. Guarding the northern approach to Monterrey was an unfinished cathedral known as the Citadel, which featured four arrow-shaped protruding bastions. To the south, smaller redoubts, including El Diablo and La Tenería, proved to be additional obstacles to the U.S. advance on the city. In preparation for the battle there, Mexican troops also barricaded streets and placed sandbags atop roofs, turning them into deadly firing positions. The forts protecting Veracruz were also impressive.

Forts and redoubts also played a major role in the battles for Mexico City in the late summer of 1847. To protect the nation's largest and most important city, the Mexicans had devised a serpentine and layered series of defenses, some permanent, some temporary, and some fieldworks located on the outskirts of the city. These included fortifications at Churubusco, some four miles from the city. Churubusco's Convent of San Mateo featured thick walls, parapets, square bastions, and frontal earthworks. A massive earthwork lay just beyond it, housing three heavy guns near the Río Churubusco. Two miles closer to Mexico City was El Molino del Rey, a stoutly built stone redoubt that commanded the approaches to Chapultepec. Chapultepec, home to the Colegio Militar, was a massive, castle-like structure that featured angled walls 4-feet-thick built on a high terrace some 200 feet high. It defended the two causeways leading into Mexico City's western gates.

Beyond Chapultepec lay the fortified *garitas* (gates) of Belén and San Cosme, which offered another layer of defense in addition to the Ciudadela (the armory in the capital), which lay within the city itself. That installation was also protected by advance artillery batteries and a series of stout earthen redoubts. The Mexicans' intricate, well-designed, and well-placed defenses around their capital city certainly prolonged the war and resulted in high casualties as the Americans made their way through them.

Debra J. Sheffer and Paul G. Pierpaoli Jr.

See also

Bishop's Palace, Monterrey, Action at; Chapultepec, Battle of; Citadel, Monterrey; El Molino del Rey, Battle of; Engineering, Military; Fort Tenería; Fort Texas (Fort Brown); Monterrey, Battle of; Mexico City, Battle for; Missions; Presidios; Veracruz, Landing at and Siege of; Wool, John Ellis.

References

Frazer, Robert W. *Forts of the West: Military Forts and Presidios and Posts Commonly Called Forts West of the Mississippi River to 1898.* Norman: University of Oklahoma Press, 1972.

Goetzmann, William H. *Army Exploration in the American West, 1803–1863.* Austin: Texas State Historical Association, 1991.

Hogg, Ian V. *Fortress: A History of Military Defence.* New York: St. Martin's Press, 1977.

Fort Tenería

Makeshift Mexican redoubt built along a river bank that protected the eastern approaches to Monterrey, Mexico. A commercial tannery before the Mexican-American War began, the stone building was fortified in 1846 with a parapet of cotton-cloth sandbags and surrounded by hastily constructed earthen walls. Fort Tenería could accommodate a garrison of 200 men.

On September 21, 1846 Major General Zachary Taylor ordered several infantry charges against the Tenería. The attackers were repulsed with heavy losses by the three large artillery pieces in the fort. The Mexicans then abandoned Tenería, opting to move into fortified positions within Monterrey itself. Taylor's force secured the redoubt the night of September 21. The fort had been won at a very high cost. Indeed, the U.S. 4th Infantry reportedly lost almost a third of its men in the effort to capture Tenería.

PAUL G. PIERPAOLI JR.

See also

Monterrey, Battle of; Rincón del Diablo; Taylor, Zachary.

References

Bauer, K. Jack. *The Mexican War, 1846–1848.* Lincoln: University of Nebraska Press, 1974.

Eisenhower, John S. D. *So Far from God: The U.S. War with Mexico, 1846–1848.* New York: Random House, 1989.

Wheelan, Joseph. *Invading Mexico: America's Continental Dream and the Mexican War, 1846–1848.* New York: Carroll & Graf, 2007.

Fort Texas (Fort Brown)

U.S. redoubt constructed by Brigadier General Zachary Taylor's Army of Occupation in the early spring of 1846. The fort was located on the north bank of the Rio Grande across from the Mexican village of Matamoros, near modern-day Brownsville, Texas. Fort Texas (later renamed Fort Brown) endured a weeklong siege and artillery bombardment by Mexican forces in May 1846 during the opening days of the Mexican-American War.

In February 1846 President James K. Polk ordered Taylor to occupy the territory claimed by Texas south of the Nueces River as far as the Rio Grande. In complying with this order, Taylor established a supply base at Point Isabel, near the mouth of the Rio Grande on the Gulf Coast. He then moved his command 27 miles southwest, to a point directly across from Matamoros, where his men constructed Fort Texas. The new fort dominated the river in both directions, with three of its six redans (V-shaped salients oriented toward potential attackers) commanding Matamoros to its front. The fort's 9-foot walls were at least 15 feet thick at the base, and the fort's entire 800-yard perimeter was protected by an 8-foot-wide trench. Designed by Captain Joseph K. F. Mansfield, Fort Texas was made entirely of earth, but it was nevertheless considered secure against fire from 12-pounders, the largest artillery pieces fielded by the Mexican army.

On May 1, 1846, Mexican general Mariano Arista crossed the Rio Grande, hoping to place his own force between Taylor's army at Fort Texas and the American supply base at Point Isabel. With solid intelligence that his enemy was indeed across the river in force, Taylor rushed back to the coast to secure his supply line. To hold Fort Texas, he left the 7th Infantry, Company I of the 2nd Artillery under Captain Allen Lowd, Company E of the 3rd Artillery under First Lieutenant Braxton Bragg, as well as a number of camp followers including, reputedly, the redoubtable Sarah Borginnis, and the men of the sick list, all under the command of Major Jacob Brown, a 34-year army veteran.

Having missed Taylor, Arista halted his army astride the river road to await Taylor's return. Hoping to hurry his quarry along, he dispatched a force under General Pedro de Ampudia to lay siege to Fort Texas.

At dawn on May 3, the Mexican batteries opened fire on Fort Texas. The Mexican artillery reportedly fired some 1,500 rounds against the fort in the first 24 hours and 3,000 during the course of a week. The fort's defenders quickly realized that the bastion would hold, but the noise and resulting lack of sleep nevertheless taxed their endurance. Major Brown was one of the very few serious casualties of the siege. Hit by a shell on May 6 while directing repairs to the beleaguered fort, his right leg was horribly mangled.

Meanwhile, having secured his supply base on the coast, Taylor and 2,228 men departed Point Isabel on May 7 with more than 200 wagons loaded with essential supplies. Taylor's men fought their way back to Fort Texas and lifted the siege, defeating Arista's forces on consecutive days at Palo Alto (May 8) and Resaca de la Palma (May 9).

Although the unit surgeon amputated Brown's leg, the fort's commander succumbed to his wounds on May 9, just hours before Taylor's triumphant arrival. On May 17, 1846, Taylor issued General Order No. 62, decreeing that Fort Texas would henceforth be named Fort Brown. As Mexican forces withdrew from Matamoros into the Mexican interior, the threat to Fort Brown evaporated, but the post nevertheless continued to play a vital role in the larger war effort, its garrison performing crucial quartermaster functions for

Taylor's Army of Invasion, which went on to victory against the Mexican army at Monterrey.

Fort Brown remained an active military facility through the U.S. Civil War and into the 20th century. The U.S. Army finally abandoned the post in 1944. Fort Brown is today a National Historic Landmark. Several buildings at the site remain, but none of them are from the Mexican-American War period.

DAVID R. SNYDER

See also

Ampudia, Pedro de; Arista, Mariano; Borginnis, Sarah; Bragg, Braxton; Brown, Jacob; Matamoros; Palo Alto, Battle of; Point Isabel; Resaca de la Palma, Battle of; Taylor, Zachary.

References

Eisenhower, John S. D. *So Far from God: The U.S. War with Mexico, 1846–1848*. Norman: University of Oklahoma Press, 1989.

Weems, John E. *To Conquer Peace: The War between the United States and Mexico*. College Station: Texas A&M University Press, 1988.

Foster, John Gray

Birth Date: May 27, 1823
Death Date: September 22, 1874

U.S. Army officer. John Gray Foster was born in Whitefield, New Hampshire, on May 27, 1823. He graduated fourth in his class from the U.S. Military Academy at West Point in 1846, two below classmate George B. McClellan, and was commissioned a second lieutenant in the Topographical Engineers. Following the death of Captain Alexander Joseph Swift on April 24, 1846, Second Lieutenant Gustavas Woodson Smith moved up to command of the prestigious Company A, Engineer Troops; McClellan replaced Smith as second in command; and Foster was appointed as the company's third officer. As such, Foster participated in several battles, including Veracruz, Contreras, and Churubusco, for which he was brevetted first lieutenant.

In the late summer of 1847, Major General Winfield Scott learned of the existence of a foundry located in El Molino del Rey, which General Antonio López de Santa Anna was reportedly using for cannon manufacture. Scott regarded destruction of the foundry as a major objective, and he dispatched Brigadier General William J. Worth to defeat Mexican forces there and destroy the foundry. Nearby was the citadel of Casa Mata, a large stone building, well fortified and heavily defended. Foster helped lead a contingent of soldiers in the assault on the Casa Mata at 3:00 a.m. on September 8, 1847. Greatly outnumbered, the Americans suffered heavy casualties in a hard-fought engagement. Foster was severely wounded during the assault, and the surgeon recommended the amputation of his injured leg. Foster refused, however, gradually recovered, and returned to duty before the war ended. For his "gallant and meretricious conduct" at El Molino del Rey he was brevetted captain.

After the war, Foster was assigned to the Corps of Engineers and was posted as an assistant professor of engineering at West Point from 1855 to 1857. At the start of the Civil War in April 1861, Foster was serving as chief engineer at Fort Sumter in Charleston harbor.

After the surrender of that post, he was commissioned a brigadier general of volunteers in October 1861. He performed effectively in the Battles of Roanoke Island (February 8, 1862) and New Berne, North Carolina (March 14). He then served as military governor of New Berne, and on July 6, 1862, assumed command of the Department of North Carolina. That same month he was promoted to major general of volunteers. He left North Carolina in November 1863 and saw service during the Knoxville Campaign during November–December 1863. He then replaced Major General Ambrose Burnside as commander of the Army of the Ohio, which post he held until February 1864, when he was badly injured from a fall from a horse.

In May 1864, fully recovered, Foster headed the Department of the South and took part in Major General William T. Sherman's operations against Savannah and Charleston. In February 1865, Foster received Charleston's surrender. He spent the remaining weeks of the war in Florida. After the war, Foster remained on active duty as an engineer. He wrote *Submarine Blasting in Boston Harbor, Massachusetts: Removal of Tower and Corwin Rocks* in 1869, a manual on underwater demolition. He died at his home in Nashua, New Hampshire, on September 22, 1874.

DEBRA J. SHEFFER AND PAUL G. PIERPAOLI JR.

See also

Churubusco, Battle of; Contreras, Battle of; El Molino del Rey, Battle of; McClellan, George Brinton; Mexico City Campaign; Veracruz, Landing at and Siege of.

References

Bauer, K. Jack. *The Mexican-American War, 1846–1848*. Lincoln: University of Nebraska Press, 1992.

Cutrer, Thomas W., ed. *The Mexican War Diary and Correspondence of George B. McClellan*. Baton Rouge: Louisiana State University Press, 2009.

Warner, Ezra. *Generals in Blue*. Baton Rouge: Louisiana State University Press, 1964.

France

The western European nation of France is bordered by Spain to the southwest; the Bay of Biscay to the west; the English Channel and North Sea to the north; Belgium, Luxembourg, Germany, Switzerland, and Italy to the east; and Monaco and the Mediterranean Sea to the south. With 643,427 square miles, France is western Europe's largest country.

Bourbon King Louis XVIII assumed power in 1814 upon the abdication of Emperor Napoléon I, and the Bourbon dynasty ruled France until 1830 (with the exception of the Hundred Days in 1815 when Napoleon Bonaparte briefly returned to power), when a revolution established a more liberal constitutional monarchy, leading to the accession of Louis-Philippe, the Duke of Orléans, as king, a position he held until the Revolution of 1848 established the Second French Republic. Louis Napoléon Bonaparte was elected as president of the Second Republic, but he later seized power, becoming the emperor of the Second French Empire as Napoléon III from 1852 until 1870.

Franco-Mexican relations after Mexican independence in 1821 were often strained. During the reign of Louis XVIII (1815–1824), France refused to recognize Mexico's independence and had limited diplomatic relations to the consular level because of its strong ties to the Bourbon court in Spain. Although Mexico and France had signed a trade agreement, neither party seemed willing to abide by its rules, except when they favored them. Nevertheless, French citizens represented one of the largest foreign populations—between 4,000 and 6,000—in Mexico during the postindependence era; most lived in urban areas and were primarily merchants, craftsmen, or professionals.

During Mexico's civil unrest in the late 1820s, French residents saw their property damaged by both government and rebel forces, but repeated French requests for compensation were rejected by Mexican governments. French officials did not pursue the matter immediately, but these claims became one cause of the so-called Pastry War in 1838. That conflict was also grounded in the forced loans that Mexico imposed in 1836 to raise funds to wage a war to reclaim Texas, loans that targeted both Mexicans and foreigners. Consequently, the French government presented an ultimatum to Mexico that called for the immediate payment of 600,000 pesos to French businessmen, including one pastry chef whose shop had been damaged by rioting Mexicans. Tensions resulting from this demand culminated on November 28, 1838, with the first French armed intervention in Mexico. In the French bombardment of Veracruz, General Antonio López de Santa Anna lost a leg, which he buried three years later with full military honors. The Pastry War ended on March 9, 1839, when the Mexicans agreed to pay the 600,000-peso indemnity.

Relations between the two countries, nevertheless, remained strained. French opposition to U.S. expansion into Mexican territory won support from some Mexican government officials but failed to significantly ameliorate Franco-Mexican relations.

In February 1848, Louis-Philippe was swept from power in a revolution that was part of a larger revolutionary movement across much of Europe. Interest in the Mexican-American War thus waned, and the French remained officially neutral, able only to watch as the United States acquired some 55 percent of Mexico's territory in the 1848 Treaty of Guadalupe Hidalgo.

French interest in Mexico grew dramatically after 1852 under Emperor Napoléon III, who wholeheartedly supported the desire of Mexican conservatives to reestablish a monarchy. The French Intervention, an attempt to place Archduke Ferdinand Maximilian Joseph of Austria on the throne as the emperor of Mexico, began on December 8, 1861. The United States, involved in its own civil war, was in no position to enforce its Monroe Doctrine, forbidding

French troops battle Mexican rebels near Veracruz in February 1862. Despite an unexpected defeat at Puebla on May 5 (still celebrated as Cinco de Mayo), French troops came to control most of Mexico, and in 1864 Austrian archduke Ferdinand Maximilian Joseph was installed as emperor of Mexico. (Library of Congress)

foreign interference in the Western Hemisphere. Although initially assured of Mexican support, the French were taken by surprise by the resistance they faced, including a Mexican victory at the Battle of Puebla on May 5, 1862. The French army recovered from that defeat and came to control a large part of Mexico, including the capital. In May 1864 the French managed to install Archduke Ferdinand as emperor. The self-styled Maximilian I never fully governed the country, however, and was maintained in power only by the French army. A series of Mexican victories, coupled with the end of the U.S. Civil War, and the looming threat of a militant Prussia led the French to withdraw its troops early in 1867. Maximilian refused to flee and was captured and executed on June 19, 1867.

WYNDHAM E. WHYNOT

See also

Europe and the Mexican-American War; Great Britain; Guadalupe Hidalgo, Treaty of; Mexico; Pastry War; Spain; Texas; Texas Revolution.

References

Barker, Nancy Nichols. *The French Experience in Mexico, 1821–1861: A History of Constant Misunderstanding.* Chapel Hill: University of North Carolina Press, 1979.

Cunningham, Michele. *Mexico and the Foreign Policy of Napoleon III.* New York: Palgrave Macmillan, 2001.

Jones, Colin. *The Cambridge Illustrated History of France.* Cambridge, UK: Cambridge University Press, 1999.

Pletcher, David. *The Diplomacy of Annexation: Texas, Oregon, and the Mexican War.* Columbia: University of Missouri Press, 1973.

Freaner, James L.
Birth Date: Unknown
Death Date: August 1852

Reporter and war correspondent for the *New Orleans Delta* newspaper during the Mexican-American War, also known by his pseudonym, "Mustang." Born and raised in Hagerstown, Maryland, James L. Freaner served as a printer's apprentice in Tallahassee, Florida; from there he moved to New Orleans around 1845 and began working as an assistant editor for the *New Orleans Delta.*

Freaner was among the first to enlist as a volunteer in Brigadier (later major) General Zachary Taylor's army. His first war reports appeared under the pseudonym "Corporal" and "Lancer"; only after the September 21–23, 1846, Battle of Monterrey did he begin to use the nom de plume "Mustang." Freaner subsequently moved from Taylor's army to the expeditionary force headed by Major General Winfield Scott. Although his first published pieces were dated May 20, 1846, those he wrote in 1847 during the march from Veracruz to Mexico City were perhaps the most important in the American press.

On several occasions Freaner was entrusted to carry official documents, such as the dispatches that Major General Winfield Scott sent to Washington in November 1847 and the Treaty of Guadalupe Hidalgo, which Nicholas P. Trist sent to President James K. Polk in February 1848. Freaner made his final trip to the American capital in a record time of only 17 days. Interestingly, during the peace negotiations, Freaner helped persuade his friend Trist to remain in Mexico City after he had been recalled to Washington on November 16, 1847, because he had strayed too far from the administration's instructions. Trist did stay and, although he disregarded his official instructions, ultimately concluded the peace treaty on February 2, 1848.

After the war, Freaner reported on the California Gold Rush, which began in 1848, for the venerable *New Orleans Picayune,* a rival of the *New Orleans Delta.* Freaner died in August 1852.

FABIOLA GARCÍA RUBIO

See also

Associated Press; Gold Rush, California; Guadalupe Hidalgo, Treaty of; Kendall, George Wilkins; Mexico City Campaign; New Orleans; Taylor, Zachary; Trist, Nicholas Philip; War Correspondents.

References

Copeland, Fayette. *Kendall of the Picayune Being His Adventures in New Orleans, on the Texan Santa Fe Expedition, in the Mexican War, and in the Colonization of the Texas Frontier.* Norman: University of Oklahoma Press, 1997.

Ohrt, Wallace Ohrt. *Defiant Peacemaker: Nicholas Trist in the Mexican War.* College Station: Texas A&M University Press, 1998.

Reilly, Thomas William. "American Reporters and the Mexican War, 1846–1848." PhD Diss., University of Minnesota, 1975.

Reilly, Thomas William. "The War Press of New Orleans." *Journalism History* 13 (Autumn–Winter 1986): 86–95.

Fredonia Rebellion
Event Dates: 1826–1827

Brief, unsuccessful revolt against the Mexican government fomented in east Texas by Hayden Edwards, a Texas *empresario,* and his brother, Benjamin Edwards. In April 1825, Hayden Edwards was given an empresarial land grant by the Mexican government. As with most such grants, Edwards was authorized to recruit and settle up to 800 families from the United States in Nacogdoches and the surrounding area of far eastern Texas. He was also bound to honor previous land grants in the area, some of which dated to the late 18th century. Eager to begin his new venture, Edwards arrived in Nacogdoches in September 1825. He immediately informed all current settlers in the area that they would have to present him with solid proof of ownership or risk losing their land to incoming settlers. Many of the existing settlers were unable to do so and, not surprisingly, this alienated many from the Edwards regime.

While the number of questionable prior land grants within Edwards's empresarial domain was not that great, his heavy-handed tactics alarmed the Mexican government. In December 1825, an election was held to select an *alcalde,* the official who would act as the local agent of the Mexican government for Nacogdoches and the Edwards land grant. The existing settlers backed their own candidate, while Edwards's son-in-law represented Edwards's interests and those of his new settlers. When the contest ended, Edwards proclaimed his son-in-law as the new *alcalde*. The old settlers vociferously opposed the outcome of the election, accusing Edwards of having rigged the results. The existing settlers appealed the election result to José Antonio Saucedo, Mexico City's political chief in San Antonio, who overturned the election results in March 1826 and backed the old settlers' candidate. Saucedo's ruling incensed Edwards, who declined to abide by the decision and refused to adhere to the agreements contained in his empresarial contract.

Edwards then left for the United States on a recruiting mission. In his absence, he had empowered his brother, Benjamin, to handle his Texas business dealings, a man who proved to be even more difficult than Edwards. He immediately began proceedings to oust existing settlers from their lands and wrote increasingly shrill letters to Saucedo, some of which contained veiled threats of violence. When word of Edwards's bad faith reached Mexico City, the government summarily revoked Edwards's empresarial grant. Alarmed by the growing crisis, Mexican officials dispatched troops to the area in December 1826.

That December 21, Hayden Edwards, who feared losing his grant and some $50,000 he had already invested in his Texas colony, declared the independent Republic of Fredonia, which encompassed the area around Nacogdoches. Hayden Edwards also made his brother commander in chief of the upstart republic and appealed to the U.S. government for help. American officials, however, remained silent, and another American settler in Texas, Stephen Austin, refused to back Edwards's independence bid. By the time the Mexican army and militia forces reached Nacogdoches on January 31, 1827, Edwards and his followers had already left the area. The Republic of Fredonia was no longer.

Although the events of 1826 and early 1827 never amounted to a bona fide independence movement among Anglo settlers in Texas, some scholars have argued that Edwards's actions presaged the better-organized Anglo revolts in the 1830s, which led to the Texas Revolution of 1836. In any case, Edwards's adventure served as a cautionary note for the Mexican government, and from that point forward relations between new American settlers and the Mexican regime remained tense.

PAUL G. PIERPAOLI JR.

See also

Austin, Stephen Fuller; Empresarios; Texas; Texas Revolution.

References

McDonald, Archie P. "The Fredonia Rebellion." In *Nacogdoches: Wilderness Outpost to Modern City, 1779–1979,* edited by Archie P. McDonald, 37–44. Austin, TX: Eakin Press, 1980.

Partin, James G., Carolyn Reeves, Joe Ericson, and Archie P. McDonald. *Nacogdoches: The History of Texas' Oldest City.* Lufkin: Best of East Texas, 1995.

Freemasonry

Highly secretive organizations that played a major role in political affairs during the early years of the Mexican republic. Freemasonry, which today remains a worldwide group with perhaps as many as 6 million members, emerged in Europe (probably first in Scotland) as early as the late 16th century. As its name and symbols suggest, it was probably a guild or organization first developed by stonemasons. Members describe their organization as a system of morality embracing a specific code of conduct cloaked in allegory and symbolism. Freemasonry is organized into Grand Lodges or Grand Orients that have jurisdiction over specific geographic areas; while local lodges have a hierarchical organization, there is no overarching organizational structure, and each lodge acts independently of the others, although certain lodges do coassociate. Lodges are often organized by Masons sharing similar professions, avocations, or interests. There are also numerous different "rites" within Freemasonry, which vary according to locale and membership makeup. While members are expected to believe in a "Supreme Being," Freemasonry is not a religious organization.

Two Masonic organizations exercised considerable influence over Mexican politics in the mid-1820s and gave the young nation its early manifestations of a political system. Scottish Rite lodges, first established in 1813 by Spanish officers sent to fight the insurgents, dominated public affairs until 1825. *Escoceses,* as their members came to be known, were sympathetic to the colonial experience. Most Scottish Rite Masons belonged to society's upper crust and favored a centralist form of government that would not disturb the existing social and economic order. *Escoceses* wielded much clout in the Guadalupe Victoria administration (1824–1828). Important *escoceses* included Victoria's vice president, General Nicolás Bravo, and cabinet ministers Pablo de la Llave and Sebastián Camacho.

To offset such influence, a number of radical politicians, eager to gain greater leverage in the government, established the York Rite Lodge in September 1825. The new organization attracted influential politicians like José Ignacio Esteva and Miguel Ramos Arizpe (who also served in Victoria's cabinet), Lorenzo de Zavala, as well as Joel Poinsett, the U.S. minister to Mexico. By the end of the year these men and their accomplices (who came to be identified as *yorkinos*) had begun to mobilize Mexico City's urban masses in the pursuit of political power and electoral victory at the national, state, and local levels. To elicit popular support they demanded the expulsion of the Spaniards, who provided a visible reminder of the former colonial order, were thought to be exploiters of Mexico's wealth, and seemed a potential threat to the country's independence. The *yorkinos*' tactics worked, and they swept the 1826 elections for national and state congresses.

The *yorkinos*' success at the polls, coupled with the fact that the *escoceses* lost much public credibility through their support of the Spaniards through 1827, led to open warfare at the end of that year. Some *escoceses* apparently panicked and came to the conclusion that only an armed revolt could halt their declining influence. The so-called Montaño Revolt erupted on December 27 in northeast Mexico State, but within two weeks Vicente Guerrero had captured General Bravo and other key rebel leaders. Many Scottish Rite members, including Bravo, were subsequently expelled from Mexico, and their departure dealt the movement a blow from which it never recovered.

Despite their electoral triumphs and military victories, the December 4, 1828, Parián riot, commonly known as the *motín de la Acordada,* insured the *yorkinos'* eventual demise. On that date a crowd of approximately 5,000 pillaged shops and stores in the Parián building in Mexico City's central square (the Zócalo). The riot, which allowed Guerrero to ascend to the presidency following his defeat in the recent elections, cast a pall over the democratic idealism of the early independent republic as elites came to fear that mass mobilization would lead to class warfare. The *yorkino* movement consequently broke into two separate factions (a moderate and a radical bloc), and Freemasonry, as an organizational vehicle, lost much of its primacy in Mexican political life.

PAUL G. PIERPAOLI JR. AND PEDRO SANTONI

See also

Bustamante y Oseguera, Anastasio; Gómez Farías, Valentín; Guerrero, Vicente; Mexico; Santa Anna, Antonio López de; Victoria, Guadalupe.

References

Green, Stanley C. *The Mexican Republic: The First Decade, 1823–1832.* Pittsburgh: University of Pittsburgh Press, 1987.

Jacob, Margaret C. *The Origins of Freemasonry: Facts and Fictions.* Philadelphia: University of Pennsylvania Press, 2005.

Sims, Harold Dana. *The Expulsion of Mexico's Spaniards, 1821–1836.* Pittsburgh: University of Pittsburgh Press, 1990.

Vázquez Semadeni, María Eugenia. *La formación de una cultura republicana: El debate público sobre la masonería, México, 1821–1830.* México: El Colegio de Michoacán and Universidad Nacional Autónoma de México, 2010.

Vázquez Semadeni, María Eugenia. "Masonería, papeles públicos y cultura política en el primer México independiente, 1821–1828." *Estudios de historia moderna y contemporánea de México* 38 (July–December 2009): 35–83.

Warren, Richard Andrew. *Vagrants and Citizens: Politics and the Masses in Mexico City from Colony to Republic.* Wilmington, DE: Scholarly Resources, 2001.

Free Soil Party

Alternative political party existing in the United States from 1848 to 1854, which primarily focused on preventing the spread of slavery into U.S. territories. The Free Soil Party began to coalesce in 1846 as a small political movement in New York State, when dissent arose over the Whig and Democratic Party nominees for state offices. Although it had little immediate impact, the concept of a Free Soil Party at the national level gained momentum as a result of the Mexican-American War.

In August 1846 Pennsylvania's Democratic U.S. representative David Wilmot proposed an amendment to a war appropriations bill, known as the Wilmot Proviso. The amendment would have prohibited the establishment of slavery in any territory gained as a result of the war. The U.S. House of Representatives passed the proviso, but it was not approved by the U.S. Senate and thus never became law. The Free Soil Party was officially formed in Buffalo, New York, in August 1848 and essentially adopted the Free Soil concept proposed by Wilmot as a major part of its political platform. The party's slogan was "Free soil, free speech, free labor, and free men." Its most passionate adherents were abolitionists Henry B. Stanton, Gamaliel Bailey, and former Liberty Party politician Salmon P. Chase, who was elected to the U.S. Senate from Ohio in 1848.

Free Soil Party members were mainly antislavery ("Conscience") Whigs, radical New York Democrats ("Barnburners"), and former members of the Liberty Party. Although calling for free labor and restrictions on the expansion of slavery, few party supporters were strict abolitionists per se, and most did not necessarily call for the elimination of slavery. The Free Soilers' platform also advocated reduced postage rates, the reduction of the number of political offices and employees, free homesteads, internal improvements, and tariff reform.

The majority of the Free Soil Party's support came from Ohio, Massachusetts, and New York. Although the Free Soil Party successfully elected some of their candidates to offices at the national level (including 12 congressmen in 1848 and four senators between 1848 and 1852), the party's officeholders did not play a significant role in the legislative process. Their two presidential candidates were former president Martin Van Buren in 1848 and John Parker Hale in the 1852 election. Neither candidate won any electoral votes, with Van Buren receiving 10 percent and Hale receiving only 5 percent of the popular vote. Arguably, Van Buren was considered to be a spoiler during the 1848 election, as neither the Whig nor the Democratic candidate received 50 percent of the vote.

By 1854, the remnants of the Free Soil Party merged with other parties, including the American (Know-Nothing Party) and the newly established Republican Party. A number of Free Soilers successfully ran as Republican candidates. The passage of the Kansas-Nebraska Act of 1854 and Illinois Democratic senator Stephen Douglas's call for popular sovereignty helped ensure the failure of the Free Soil Party to achieve its principal goal of preventing the spread of slavery into new areas.

WYNDHAM E. WHYNOT

See also

Abolitionism; Democratic Party; Douglas, Stephen Arnold; Know-Nothing Party; Liberty Party; Politics, U.S.; Popular Sovereignty; Republican Party; Slavery; Van Buren, Martin; Whigs; Wilmot Proviso.

References

Earle, Jonathan H. *Jacksonian Antislavery and the Politics of Free Soil, 1824–1854.* Chapel Hill: University of North Carolina Press, 2003.

Foner, Eric. *Free Soil, Free Labor, Free Men: The Ideology of the Republican Party before the Civil War.* New York: Oxford University Press, 1995.

Niven, John. *Salmon P. Chase: A Biography.* New York: Oxford University Press, 1995.

Frémont, John Charles
Birth Date: January 21, 1813
Death Date: July 13, 1890

U.S. Army officer, politician, and explorer who played an important role in promoting settlement of the American West. John Charles Frémont was born John Charles Fremon in Savannah, Georgia, on January 21, 1813, the illegitimate son of a Virginia socialite and an impecunious French refugee. In 1837 he entered the U.S. Army's Corps of Topographical Engineers as a protégé of Secretary of War Joel Poinsett. The following year, he became an enthusiastic supporter of Missouri senator Thomas Hart Benton and Benton's vision for the westward expansion of the United States. Benton was not only one of the most powerful men in the Senate but also a close friend and political ally of Andrew Jackson, who, although no longer president, still loomed large on the political landscape of the era. It was therefore particularly reckless of Frémont to provoke Benton's fury by eloping with the senator's daughter, Jessie. Once the deed was done, however, Frémont and his new bride succeeded in assuaging the unhappy father and winning him back as a patron for Frémont's army career.

As a member of the Corps of Topographical Engineers, Frémont participated in and later led exploratory expeditions into the western territories of the United States and sometimes Canada and Mexico. In the late 1830s these explorations led him into what later became Iowa, and in the early 1840s he led more dramatic explorations along the Oregon Trail and into the Sierra Nevada. Guided by renowned mountain man Christopher Houston "Kit" Carson, Frémont made a number of geographic discoveries in the West and won the nickname "the Pathfinder." His explorations, which included considerable hardship and danger, and the publicity surrounding them (Frémont's wife, Jessie Benton Frémont, was a highly skilled writer and publicist and a tireless promoter of her husband's career) helped encourage American migration into western areas, much to Benton's satisfaction.

On June 1, 1845, Frémont, then a brevet captain of engineers, set out with 55 men from Saint Louis, with Kit Carson as guide, on a third expedition. The stated goal of the expedition was to "map the source of the Arkansas River" on the east side of the Rocky Mountains, but there is little doubt that its real and secret intention was to prime a revolt in sparsely populated Alta (Upper) California against Mexico. Arriving in the Sacramento Valley at the beginning of 1846, Frémont proceeded to stir up sentiment for revolt among the American settlers there, promising them that in the event of war with Mexico his small force would provide them protection.

John C. Frémont (1813–1890), known as "the Pathfinder." An officer in the U.S. Topographical Corps, Frémont was in California at the start of the Bear Flag Revolt and took part in the subsequent U.S. conquest of California. (Library of Congress)

When approaching Monterey in early March 1846, Frémont was ordered by Mexican authorities to quit California. After a four day standoff with numerically superior Mexican forces, he withdrew north toward Oregon. Following a May 9 attack on his party by Modoc Indians, Frémont retaliated the next day by attacking and massacring the inhabitants of a Klamath Indian fishing village situated at the junction of the Williamson River and Klamath Lake, even though its inhabitants were not involved in the May 9 attack.

Some weeks later, and without authorization, Frémont led his small band back into California and assisted American settlers in the region in the establishment of the independent Bear Flag Republic. At the end of December, Frémont, now a brevet lieutenant colonel, led 300 men in the capture of Santa Barbara.

On January 13, 1847, after sporadic fighting, California's Mexican governor capitulated, turning the state over to Commodore Robert F. Stockton; Frémont himself accepted the surrender. Soon thereafter, Frémont stated that Stockton had appointed him interim military governor of California. Brigadier General Stephen Watts Kearny, however, claimed that Stockton could not have made such an appointment; further, he argued that he outranked Frémont and therefore should be governor himself. Kearny brought the matter to the attention of the War Department, which backed the general's assertions. Frémont was later charged with insubordination and convicted in a court-martial proceeding that recommended he receive a dishonorable discharge. At the instigation of the powerful Benton faction, President Polk commuted Frémont's sentence for the services he had rendered to the nation, but in a fit of pique, Frémont resigned from the army. His tenure as governor had lasted barely three months.

As a civilian, in 1848, Frémont led another western expedition, but without Carson and other key guides, he lost his way in the snows of the mountains. Several members of the party died, and Frémont and the others narrowly escaped. His popularity remained undiminished, however, and Frémont was elected a U.S. senator from California, serving from 1850 to 1851. Meanwhile, gold discovered on his land in California made him a rich man.

In 1856, Frémont became the first presidential candidate of the newly organized Republican Party. He made a respectable showing in the general election, although he failed to carry his own state of California and lost the electoral vote to Democratic candidate James Buchanan.

During the Civil War, Frémont served as a major general, first in Missouri, where he embarrassed the Lincoln administration by issuing a harsh and premature proclamation of martial law and emancipation (which the president revoked), and later in what was soon to become West Virginia. There too he proved a dismal failure. In the spring of 1862 he blundered militarily and helped to make possible the spectacular success of Confederate major general Thomas J. "Stonewall" Jackson's Shenandoah Valley Campaign.

After the war, President Rutherford Hayes appointed Frémont governor of the Arizona Territory, where he served from 1878 to 1881. He died in New York City on July 13, 1890.

ETHAN S. RAFUSE

See also
Bear Flag Republic; Benton, Thomas Hart; Buchanan, James; California; California Theater of War, Overview; Carson, Christopher Houston "Kit"; Kearny, Stephen Watts; Poinsett, Joel Roberts; Republican Party; Stockton, Robert Field.

References
Chaffin, Tom. *Pathfinder: John Charles Frémont and the Course of American Empire.* New York: Hill and Wang, 2002.
Roberts, David. *A Newer World: Kit Carson, John C. Frémont, and the Claiming of the American West.* New York: Touchstone, 2001.

French, Samuel Gibbs
Birth Date: November 22, 1818
Death Date: April 20, 1910

U.S. and Confederate Army officer. Born in Mullica Hill, New Jersey, on November 22, 1818, Samuel Gibbs French graduated from the U.S. Military Academy at West Point in 1843. Commissioned as a second lieutenant, he was assigned to Company F of the 3rd

Artillery Regiment. He joined Brigadier General Zachary Taylor's Army of Observation in Texas in 1845, participating in its four major battles: Palo Alto (May 8, 1846), Resaca de la Palma (May 9, 1846), Monterrey (September 21–23, 1846), and Buena Vista (February 22–23, 1847). On September 23, 1846, he was brevetted first lieutenant for his performance at Monterrey. At the Battle of Buena Vista, French was shot in his right thigh while preparing to mount his horse but continued directing his men through the battle. At a field hospital after the battle, he became friends with the man on the litter next to him, Colonel Jefferson Davis, later U.S. secretary of war and then president of the Confederacy. The two men continued their friendship for many years. French's wound kept him out of action for the remainder of the war, and he was eventually sent to Washington, D.C., for recuperation. By January 1848, French had been promoted to captain and had received appointment as assistant quartermaster in the general staff of the army.

French remained in the army until 1856, when he resigned his commission and retired to his plantation near Greenville, Mississippi. When the Civil War began in 1861, he accepted an appointment from the governor of Mississippi as a lieutenant colonel of militia, and in October 1861 Confederate president Jefferson Davis appointed him a brigadier general. Between July 1862 and June 1863, French helped construct fortifications at Fort Fisher, North Carolina, and around Petersburg, Virginia. He also saw action during the Second Battle of Bull Run (Second Manassas) and was promoted to major general in August 1862. After further service in North Carolina, he requested a transfer west and served with General Joseph E. Johnston's army in Mississippi and then in Lieutenant General John B. Hood's army, where he saw considerable action during the Franklin and Nashville Campaign. After that, he was detailed to Mobile, Alabama, where he was taken prisoner upon its surrender on April 12, 1865.

In the years following the Civil War, French was the Mississippi state levee commissioner. He later invested in orange groves in Florida. French also wrote a memoir of his time in the U.S. and Confederate armies, which was first published in 1901 in the periodical *Confederate Veteran.* French died on April 20, 1910 at Florala, Florida.

JAMES SCYTHES

See also
Buena Vista, Battle of; Davis, Jefferson Finis; Flying Artillery; Monterrey, Battle of; Palo Alto, Battle of; Resaca de la Palma, Battle of; Ringgold, Samuel.

References
Davis, William C., and Julie Hoffman, eds. *The Confederate General.* Vol. 2. Harrisburg, PA: National Historical Society, 1991.
French, Samuel G. *Two Wars, an Autobiography.* Nashville, TN: Confederate Veteran Publications, 1901. Reprint, Huntington, WV: Blue Acorn Press, 1999.
Weems, John Edward. *To Conquer a Peace: The War between the United States and Mexico.* New York: Doubleday, 1974.

Frontera, José
Birth Date: 1798
Death Date: August 19, 1847

Mexican army officer. José Frontera was born in Jalapa, Veracruz, in 1798. In August 1814, at the age of 16, Frontera joined a militia company in Jalapa as a cadet, beginning a lifelong career in the military. During the Wars for Independence, Frontera fought on the royalist side until 1821, when he defected to the independence movement. After that, he held numerous positions, including commands with the Puebla Dragoons and the 7th Cavalry Regiment.

Frontera subsequently served as aide-de-camp to division generals Manuel Rincón and José Rincón and then helped organize the Comercio Cavalry Regiment. Sometime thereafter he played a key role in the establishment of two squadrons of the Querétaro Cavalry Regiment. Sometime in the early to mid-1840s Frontera was advanced to general of brigade, the rank equivalent to U.S. brigadier general.

Frontera, like many other Mexican generals, took an active part in national politics. During the July 15, 1840, federalist insurrection, a revolt that attempted to overthrow President Anastasio Bustamante's regime, Frontera supported the president. One year later, however, he abandoned Bustamante in favor of General of Division Mariano Paredes y Arrillaga's bid to oust Bustamante, an endeavor that succeeded in October.

Frontera remained in Mexico City during the early stages of the Mexican-American War and was attached to the Army of the North in mid-1847. He commanded the 2nd Cavalry Regiment, apparently as a brigadier general, under the overall command of General Anastasio Torrejón. During the Battle of Contreras on August 19, 1847, Frontera mounted a counterattack against American forces that were trying to turn the Mexican left flank, but he was mortally wounded by musket fire and died on the field of battle.

Mexican statesmen paid homage to Frontera one year after his death. Then, in an attempt to rally national spirit, government leaders organized several memorial services to honor a number of patriots who died defending the Mexican capital. In one such ceremony, held on September 17, Frontera's cadaver, as well as those of three other regular army officers, was disinterred and reburied at the Santa Paula cemetery.

PAUL G. PIERPAOLI JR.

See also

Bustamante y Oseguera, Anastasio; Contreras, Battle of; Paredes y Arrillaga, Mariano; Rincón, Manuel E.; Torrejón, Anastasio.

References

DePalo, William A., Jr. *The Mexican National Army, 1822–1852*. College Station: Texas A&M University Press, 1997.

Smith, Justin H. *The War with Mexico*. 2 vols. New York: Macmillan, 1919.

Vázquez Mantecón, María del Carmen. "Las reliquias y sus héroes." *Estudios de historia moderna y contemporánea de México* 30 (July–December 2005): 47–109.

Fueros

Special legal immunities extended to Mexican institutions such as the Roman Catholic Church and the military. These privileges were more readily available to clerics than to soldiers for much of the Spanish colonial era. Both clergymen and soldiers were exempt from civil and criminal litigation, but clerics also enjoyed benefits like tax exemption on income, property, and inheritance.

During the late 1700s Spain's Bourbon monarchs sought to reassert control over their colonial possessions, and the measures they instituted in pursuit of this goal had different effects on the military and ecclesiastical *fueros*. Bourbon rulers moved to restrict the personal immunity of clergy in civil and criminal cases. At the same time, however, they extended *fueros* to all militia categories in an attempt to bolster recruitment efforts and build an effective professional military.

Independence did not eviscerate the system of *fueros*. Instead, the military and ecclesiastical privileges were enshrined in Article 154 of the 1824 Constitution, issued three years after Mexico threw off Spanish rule. Members of the civic militia (also known as the National Guard), a military force formally established in 1827 to protect states' rights, could also claim the *fuero*, but only when they came under the authority of the national government. According to some historians, the survival of this aspect of the corporatist colonial legal culture allowed military courts in the 1820s to issue harsher penalties to defendants who did not support the political faction in power at the time. By the 1830s, consequently, Mexican liberal thinker José María Luis Mora was calling for the abolition of the aforementioned Article 154. To him it symbolized, as the late Charles A. Hale noted, "the gulf between Mexican social reality and a liberal and republican juridical order."

Nonetheless, efforts to overturn these symbols of corporate power in early republican Mexico proved difficult. In 1833–1834, for instance, *puro* leader and acting president Valentín Gómez Farías, with the help of his allies in Congress, unleashed a powerful attack that sought to overturn the privileged status of the church and the army. That assault, however, resulted in a military reaction that helped bring down the federal republic. Not until the Mexican *Reforma* of the mid-1850s did liberals manage to curtail, and then to eliminate, these privileges. The Juárez Law, issued in November 1855, restricted both the clerical and military *fuero*, while the 1859 Reform Laws completely abolished the latter.

Recent research on the Mexican army, however, suggests that the special privileges inherent in the *fuero* did not allow the military to act with impunity. According to Linda Arnold, judges in military courts "applied jurisprudence not corporate biases when they decided guilt or innocence, determined liability, and issued definitive sentences." Many different individuals and actors, therefore, found this aspect of colonial legal culture to be a fair and "actively asserted agency," a key factor in insuring that *fueros* would survive until the mid-1850s.

PEDRO SANTONI

See also

Catholic Church, Mexico; Mexico; Mexico, Army.

References

Arnold, Linda. "Privileged Justice? The *Fuero Militar* in Early National Mexico." In *Judicial Institutions in Nineteenth-Century Latin America*, edited by Eduardo Zimmermann, 49–64. London: Institute for Latin American Studies, 1999.

DePalo, William A., Jr. *The Mexican National Army, 1822–1852*. College Station: Texas A&M University Press, 1997.

Hale, Charles A. *Mexican Liberalism in the Age of Mora, 1821–53*. New Haven: Yale University Press, 1968.

Sinkin, Richard N. *The Mexican Reform, 1855–1876: A Study in Liberal Nation-Building*. Austin: University of Texas Press, 1979.

G

Gadsden Purchase
Event Date: December 30, 1853

Agreement between the United States and Mexico, finalized on December 30, 1853, that allowed the U.S. government to purchase Mexican territory in the Southwest, today comprising the southern third of Arizona and a small piece of far southwestern New Mexico. After President Franklin Pierce was inaugurated in March 1853, he attempted to appease southern expansionists by planning to annex extensive Mexican territory south of the Rio Grande. When Nicholas Trist, who was chief clerk of the State Department, negotiated the Treaty of Guadalupe Hidalgo to conclude the Mexican-American War in 1848, he had left most of the area south of the Gila River in Mexican possession. This included the Baja Peninsula of California, and the states of Coahuila, Sonora, and Chihuahua. By 1853, the Pierce administration had come to believe that these lands contained valuable mineral deposits. Secretary of War Jefferson Davis and other southern officials also coveted the area because the flat terrain was suitable for the site of a proposed southern route of the transcontinental railroad. That route would have extended from Houston, Texas, through the Mesilla Valley to Los Angeles, California.

While the Pierce administration was determined to obtain the Mesilla Valley area and conclude the unsettled border dispute between the United States and Mexico, the president favored diplomatic tactics to force. Thus, Pierce instructed U.S. minister to Mexico James Gadsden to travel to Mexico City in an effort to gain as much land as the Mexican government was willing to sell. Upon his arrival in mid-August 1853, Gadsden learned that Antonio López de Santa Anna had returned to power. After several months of delays and intrigues, Gadsden and Santa Anna drew up a formal treaty on December 30, 1853, which approved the sale of a strip of land south of the Gila River.

President Santa Anna agreed to these terms because he believed that the cession was the only way to avoid another conflict with the United States. As a result of the treaty, Santa Anna agreed to sell to the United States a 29,640-square mile area of the land south of the Gila River and west of the Rio Grande for $10 million. This acquisition by the United States eventually became known as the Gadsden Purchase. However, the loss of additional land so soon

Land Acquired from Mexico after the Mexican-American War (in acres)

Acquisition	Date	Total Area	Land	Island Water	Cost	Price per Acre
Mexican Cession[1]	1848	338,681,000	334,479,000	4,202,000	$16,295,000	$0.05
Purchase from Texas	1850	78,927,000	78,843,000	84,000	$15,496,000	$0.20
Gadsden Purchase	1853	18,989,000	18,962,000	27,000	$10,000,000	$0.53

Note: All areas are as computed in 1912 and have not been adjusted for subsequent recomputation of the area of the United States.
[1] Includes 33,920 acres subsequently recognized as part of the State of Texas

GADSDEN PURCHASE, 1853

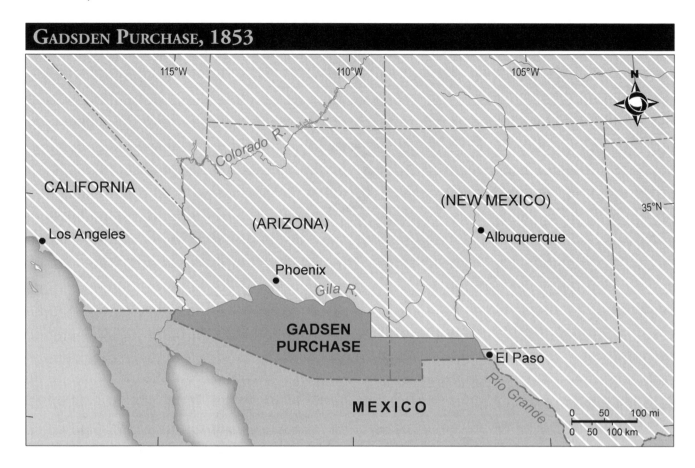

after the Mexican-American War caused the Mexican population, particularly liberal leaders, to turn against Santa Anna, who was forced into exile for the next 20 years.

Although Congress balked at the price the United States paid for the territory, the Senate narrowly ratified the treaty in 1854. Many antislavery senators, however, were not keen about adding more territory in the Southwest, which they feared might lead to the further expansion of slavery. The saving grace in this case may have been the fact that most of the territory was either mountainous or arid (receiving only 7–12 inches of rain per year). Such topography and climate were not conducive to agriculture and a slave-based planting economy.

The Gadsden Purchase, however, proved to be a disappointment for both countries. Americans were unable to gain control of the entire Mesilla Valley, while the treaty forced the Mexican government to relinquish additional lands to the United States. Nevertheless, the treaty ended the controversy surrounding Article XI of the Treaty of Guadalupe Hidalgo, which had made the United States responsible for Native American raids into Mexico.

KEVIN M. BRADY

See also

Baja California; Guadalupe Hidalgo, Treaty of; Mesilla Valley; Mexico; Pierce, Franklin; Santa Anna, Antonio López de; Slavery; Trist, Nicholas Philip.

References

Fowler, Will. *Santa Anna of Mexico.* Lincoln: University of Nebraska Press, 2007.

Goetzmann, William H. *Army Exploration in the American West, 1803–1863.* New Haven, CT: Yale University Press, 1959.

Martinez, Oscar J., ed. *U.S.-Mexico Borderlands: Historical and Contemporary Perspectives.* Wilmington, DE: Scholarly Resources Books, 1996.

Olliff, Donathon C. *Reforma Mexico and the United States: A Search for Alternatives to Annexation, 1854–1861.* University: University of Alabama Press, 1981.

Winders, Richard Bruce. *Crisis in the Southwest: The United States, Mexico, and the Struggle over Texas.* Wilmington, DE: Scholarly Resources Books, 2002.

Gaines, Edmund Pendleton

Birth Date: March 20, 1777
Death Date: June 6, 1849

U.S. Army officer. Born in Culpepper County, Virginia, on March 20, 1777, Edmund Pendleton Gaines moved with his family to the frontier of North Carolina and Tennessee, where at age 18 he served as a lieutenant of a volunteer company fighting Native

Americans. In 1797 he joined the U.S. Army as an ensign and was quickly promoted to lieutenant. Assigned to the Old Southwest, Gaines surveyed the Natchez Trace from 1801 to 1804, served as military collector in Mobile, Alabama, and commanded Fort Stoddert.

Promoted to captain in 1807, Gaines led the troops that apprehended Aaron Burr following the failed Burr Conspiracy and provided testimony at Burr's trial. After an extended leave in which he studied law and began practicing law in the Mississippi Territory, Gaines returned to active service as a major upon the outbreak of the War of 1812; he was advanced to colonel the following year. Gaines established his military reputation while covering the American retreat after the Battle of Chrysler's Farm on November 11, 1813, after which he was promoted to brigadier general. His defense of Fort Erie during August–September 1814, where he was wounded and promoted, earned him a brevet to major general.

After recovering from his wound, Gaines returned to duty under Major General Andrew Jackson's Southern Command. Dispatched to southwestern Georgia in 1817 to protect settlers against the Seminoles, Gaines constructed Fort Scott on the Flint River and helped precipitate the First Seminole War when he sent troops to attack Negro Fort, a former British outpost on Prospect Bluff on the Apalachicola River that runaway slaves had refortified. On July 17, 1817, American gunboats opened fire, striking the fort's powder magazine with heated shot, causing an explosion that killed 270 runaways. After the Seminoles launched retaliatory raids, and Chief Neamathla of Fowltown rejected Gaines's demands that those responsible be turned over, Gaines ordered Major David E. Twiggs to attack Fowltown on November 12. Following the First Seminole War, Gaines was named commander of the new Western Department in 1821 and took the field during Black Hawk's War in 1832 without seeing significant action.

Upon the outbreak of the Second Seminole War in 1835, Gaines led some 1,100 men to the vicinity of Tampa, Florida, where he was besieged by Seminoles, wounded, and ended up quarreling with Major General Winfield Scott, comparing him to Benedict Arnold. After his failed Tampa Campaign, Gaines returned to Louisiana where he led a force across the Sabine River and held Nacogdoches during the Texas Revolution of 1835–1836.

The ongoing conflict between Gaines and Scott worked more to the detriment of Gaines than it did Scott, even though an official court of inquiry in 1837 criticized both commanders. When the War Department rejected Gaines's recommendations for using floating batteries and railroads to improve western defenses, Gaines believed that he had been foiled by Scott. Consequently, in 1840, he bypassed the War Department and sent his recommendations directly to Congress. This may have played a role in his court-martial in late 1846 for raising Louisiana volunteers for Brigadier General Zachary Taylor without the express approval of the War Department. At the time, Gaines was in command of the army's Western Division. Gaines was acquitted on the grounds that his actions were excusable because Taylor was his subordinate and had been authorized to raise volunteers. Nevertheless, Gaines remained bitter toward Scott, who had spearheaded the charges against Gaines. In the meanwhile, Taylor and Scott had their own personality clashes during the Mexican-American War. Gaines died in New Orleans on June 6, 1849, without having seen action in the Mexican War.

JUSTIN D. MURPHY

Major General Edmund P. Gaines distinguished himself in the War of 1812 and the First and Second Seminole Wars. His celebrated long-standing feud with fellow officer Winfield Scott worked to his detriment, however. Gainesville, Florida, is named in his honor. (Frick Art Reference Library)

See also

Jackson, Andrew; Scott, Winfield; Taylor, Zachary; Texas Revolution; Twiggs, David Emanuel.

References

Mahon, John K. *History of the Second Seminole War.* Gainesville: University of Florida Press, 1967.

Prucha, Francis P. *The Sword of the Republic: The United States Army on the Frontier.* New York: Macmillan, 1969.

Silver, James W. *Edmund Pendleton Gaines, Frontier General.* Baton Rouge: Louisiana State University Press, 1989.

Gaines, John Pollard
Birth Date: September 22, 1795
Death Date: December 9, 1857

Attorney, soldier, politician, and volunteer cavalryman during the Mexican-American War. John Pollard Gaines was born in Augusta County, Virginia, on September 22, 1795. At the age of 17, he began serving as a volunteer private in the War of 1812. When that conflict ended, he read for the law, moved to Boone County, Kentucky, and began to practice law. He also served in the Kentucky state legislature for several terms.

When the Mexican-American War began, Gaines volunteered to serve. He was commissioned a major in a Kentucky cavalry brigade and sent to join Brigadier General Zachary Taylor's Army of Occupation along the Rio Grande. In mid-January 1847, Taylor dispatched a reconnaissance force of some 80 men, under Captain Cassius M. Clay, to ascertain the position of General Antonio López de Santa Anna's army. Gaines joined the scouting party late but caught up with it after several hours. On January 22, 1847, Clay and Gaines decided to encamp at an abandoned hacienda known as La Encarnación. Foolishly, neither officer thought to post sentries. When the reconnaissance team awoke the following morning, they found themselves surrounded by Mexican troops, who promptly captured them and incarcerated them in Mexico City. Gaines managed to escape en route to Mexico City and rejoined U.S. forces in Mexico. The remainder of the group was released in August 1847.

Following his escape, Gaines became aide-de-camp to Major General Winfield Scott during his Mexico City Campaign. Gaines saw action during several engagements, including the Battle of El Molino del Rey on September 7, 1847, where he performed admirably. While he was still in the army, he had his name placed on the Whig Party ballot in his home district for a special 1847 election for the U.S. House of Representatives. He won the election and served less than one full term, until 1849, having lost his reelection bid.

That same year, after Abraham Lincoln turned down the appointment, President Zachary Taylor, a Whig, appointed Gaines to the governorship of the Oregon Territory. Gaines held this position until 1853. His tenure in office was a rather tumultuous one, marked by a series of stalled negotiations with Native Americans and acrimonious relations with the Democratically controlled territorial legislature and the local press. Despite his troubled governorship, Gaines remained in Oregon after stepping down. There he purchased a farm near Salem. In 1855, he ran unsuccessfully for the U.S. House as a representative of the district encompassing Salem. Gaines died on December 9, 1857, near Salem, Oregon.

Paul G. Pierpaoli Jr.

See also
Clay, Cassius Marcellus; El Molino del Rey, Battle of; Encarnación, Hacienda de; Mexico City Campaign; Scott, Winfield; Taylor, Zachary.

References
Bauer, K. Jack. *The Mexican War, 1846–1848.*
Lansing, Ronald B. *Nimrod: Courts, Claims, and Killing on the Oregon Frontier.* Pullman: Washington State University Press, 2005.
McQueen, Kevin. *Cassius M. Clay: Freedom's Champion.* Whitehall, KY: Turner, 2001.

Galaxara, Skirmish at
Event Date: November 24, 1847

Brief military engagement between U.S. forces under the command of Brigadier General Joseph Lane and Mexican guerrillas and lancers led by Mexican general Joaquín Rea. Galaxara was located not far from Izúcar de Matamoros in present-day Puebla State, between Mexico City and the port city of Veracruz in southeastern Mexico. On the day prior to the action at Galaxara Pass, Lane's force of 160 men had blunted a Mexican guerrilla offensive at Izúcar de Matamoros. Then, on November 24, Lane's men began to march toward the city of Puebla. As they approached the relatively narrow pass at Galaxara, Lane sent forward an advance force of about 30 soldiers, including Texas Rangers, instructed to be on the lookout for Mexican soldiers and report back their position if encountered.

The advance force, led by Ranger colonel John C. Hays, came under sudden attack by Mexican guerrillas and lancers just as it entered the pass at Galaxara. Hays performed heroically, managing to shoot two of the Mexicans dead while he and several Rangers covered the retreat of the remainder of his force. These actions bought just enough time for Lane to rush forward reinforcements. The main body of Lane's force then arrived on the scene, and the fighting continued but with the Mexicans incurring heavy casualties. In only a few hours of fighting, the Mexicans suffered 50 dead or wounded; the U.S. force sustained only two dead and two wounded.

Lane was highly laudatory of Hays's action, and the engagement at Galaxara was just one of several skirmishes that Hays spearheaded on the road from Veracruz to Mexico City. In some instances Hays resorted to assaulting and burning private homes to force Mexican guerrillas from their strongholds. After the action at Galaxara, Lane's men marched to Puebla with no further harassment.

Paul G. Pierpaoli Jr.

See also
Guerrilla Warfare; Hays, John Coffee; Lane, Joseph; Mexico City; Rea, Joaquín; Texas Rangers; Veracruz.

References
Collins, Michael L. *Texas Devils: Rangers and Regulars on the Lower Rio Grande, 1846–1861.* Norman: University of Oklahoma Press, 2009.
Greer, James K. *Colonel Jack Hays: Texas Frontier Leader and California Builder.* College Station: Texas A&M University Press, 1987.
Lane, Walter P. *Adventures and Recollections*, 1887. Austin, TX: Pemberton Press, 1970.
Webb, Walter P. *The Texas Rangers: A Century of Frontier Defense.* Austin: University of Texas Press, 1965.

Gaona, Antonio
Birth Date: 1793
Death Date: 1848

Mexican army general. Born in Havana, Cuba, in 1793, Antonio Gaona entered military service in 1801 as an underage cadet in the Regiment of New Spain. Fighting initially under the royalist banner during the Mexican Wars of Independence, he switched allegiance upon the issuance of the Plan de Iguala in 1821, joining the Army of the Three Guarantees. Serving in the imperial forces of Emperor Agustín de Iturbide, he turned against Iturbide in 1823 when he seconded the Plan of Casa Mata, which gave rise to a revolt ultimately forcing Iturbide's abdication. Subsequently, Gaona served in a variety of positions of increasing importance and authority, culminating in his promotion in 1832 to brigadier general.

During the campaign to quell the Texas Revolution of 1835–1836, Gaona was appointed to command the 1st Infantry Brigade in General Antonio López de Santa Anna's Army of Operations. General Gaona participated in the siege of and assault on the Alamo on March 6, 1836, and was then ordered by Santa Anna on March 11 to advance northeast to Bastrop with several hundred troops and from there move to Nacogdoches in an attempt to flank Major General Sam Houston's Provisional Army of Texas. Following Santa Anna's defeat at the Battle of San Jacinto on April 21, 1836, he was ordered to withdraw from Texas before he could reach his final objective.

During the French incursion of November 1838–March 1839, popularly known as the Pastry War, Gaona commanded San Juan de Ulúa, the island fortress that defended Veracruz, which he surrendered to French admiral Charles Baudin following a brief naval bombardment. The commander of Veracruz and Gaona were both subsequently relieved of command, and Gaona was court-martialed for what was regarded as his weak defense of the fortress. In the end, however, the tribunal cleared him of all culpability in its surrender.

When the Mexican-American War broke out in 1846, Gaona was serving as commandant general of Puebla and governor of the infamous Perote Castle, where the Texan prisoners of the Mier Expedition, the Battle of Salado, and those captured at San Antonio in 1842 had been imprisoned. During the later stages of the Mexico City Campaign, in August 1847, Gaona was reassigned as second in command of the Army of the Center, under Division General Nicolás Bravo Rueda. Gaona's troops initially took up position at Mexicalzingo to protect the southern approaches to Mexico City from Major General Winfield Scott's American forces, but Santa Anna ordered Gaona to redeploy his men to Candelaria Gate following Scott's victory at Churubusco. Gaono saw little action during the remainder of the war. He died in Mexico City in 1848, during the American occupation.

JEFFREY D. PEPPERS

See also
Alamo, Battle of the; Bravo Rueda, Nicolás; Churubusco, Battle of; Houston, Samuel; Mexico City, Battle for; Mexico City Campaign; Mier Expedition; Pastry War; Perote Castle; San Jacinto, Battle of; San Juan de Ulúa; Santa Anna, Antonio López de; Texas Revolution; Veracruz.

References
Bancroft, Hubert Howe. *History of the North Mexican States and Texas.* San Francisco: History Company, 1886.
Henderson, Timothy J. *A Glorious Defeat: Mexico and Its War with the United States.* New York: Hill and Wang, 2007.
Rives, George L. *The United States and Mexico, 1821–1848: A History of Relations between the Two Countries from the Independence of Mexico to the Close of the War with the United States.* Vol. 1. New York: C. Scribner's Sons, 1913.
Roberts, Randy, and James S. Olson. *A Line in the Sand.* New York: Free Press, 2001.

Garay, Francisco de
Birth Date: 1796
Death Date: 1865

Mexican army officer and diplomat. Francisco de Garay was born in Jalapa, Veracruz, in 1796. Little is known about his early years and military career, but he did serve as one of Mexico's first foreign diplomats when he was posted to Gibraltar as a consul from 1824 to 1828. Garay's first major military campaign came during the Texas Revolution of 1835–1836. He entered Texas as a senior officer under the command of General José de Urrea, who had been charged with clearing the area surrounding the town of Goliad of rebels and opening the southern doorway to the Mexican reoccupation of Texas. In late February and early March 1836, Urrea routed several isolated groups of rebels at San Patricio, Refugio, and Agua Dulce, located south of Goliad. On March 19, rebel commander Colonel James W. Fannin evacuated Fort Defiance (Presidio La Bahía) and headed for the town of Victoria. Urrea and his men soon caught up with and surrounded Fannin on open ground near Coleto Creek. Although Fannin's command consisted of almost 400 men, he was forced to surrender the following day. Fannin and his men were taken back to Presidio La Bahía and kept under armed guard while their fate was decided.

Late on March 26, orders arrived at Presidio La Bahía from General Antonio López de Santa Anna for Fannin and his men to be executed as pirates. Several of the Mexican officers, including Garay, took issue with the order. Garay and his consort, Francisca Alvarez, were able to rescue a small number of Fannin's men by hiding them in tents and a nearby building. For her effort, Alvarez became known as the "Angel of Goliad." Survivors of the ensuing Goliad Massacre singled out Garay's act of compassion as the exception to the overall treatment they received while in captivity.

Garay left Texas when the Mexican army withdrew to Matamoros in the months immediately following Santa Anna's defeat and capture at San Jacinto. In 1841, Garay was promoted to general.

Upon the outbreak of the Mexican-American War in 1846, Garay commanded some 800 troops, mostly national guardsmen, some 120 miles inland from Tampico. He was involved in an attempt to exchange several hundred American prisoners of war for Mexican soldiers captured at the Battle of Cerro Gordo on April 17–18, 1847. The exchange did not go as planned, however, and the Americans occupying Tampico organized a rescue plan, to be implemented in June 1847. Posted along the Río Calabozo in the vicinity of Huejutla, Garay and his force of about 500 men stopped the American advance on June 12 and then doggedly pursued the retreating Americans. Garay was lauded for his action, but he did not have the opportunity to take part in any of the major battles of the war.

Following the Mexican War, Garay held a consular post in New York City, beginning in 1859, and supported the government of Benito Juárez during the French intervention of the 1860s. To reward him for his service, Juárez named Garay Mexican consul at New Orleans. Garay died there in 1865.

BRUCE WINDERS

See also

Cerro Gordo, Battle of; Coleto Creek, Battle of; Fannin, James Walker; Goliad Massacre; Juárez, Benito; Santa Anna, Antonio López de; Tampico; Tampico and Victoria, Occupation of; Texas; Texas Revolution; Urrea y Elías Gonzales, José de.

References

Barnard, Dr. J. H. *Dr. J. H. Barnard's Journal from December, 1835, to March 27, 1836, Giving an Account of Fannin Massacre.* Aransas Pass, TX: Biography Press, 1983.

Hardin, Stephen L. *Texian Iliad: A Military History of the Texas Revolution.* Austin: University of Texas Press, 1993.

Roa Bárcena, José María. *Recuerdos de la invasión norte-americanam (1846–1848).* Edited by Antonio Castro Leal. 3 vols. Mexico City: Editorial Porrúa, 1947.

García Conde, Pedro
Birth Date: February 8, 1806
Death Date: December 19, 1851

Mexican soldier and politician who served as commissioner of the Mexican boundary survey team that worked in tandem with the American boundary survey team to establish the boundary between the United States and Mexico after the Mexican-American War. Born on February 8, 1806, in Arispe, Sonora, to a prominent Spanish political and military family, Pedro García Conde joined the military in 1818 and supported Mexican independence in 1821. He studied engineering at the Colegio de Minería in Mexico City from 1822 to 1825. García Conde became a member of the Corps of Engineers in 1828 and was promoted to captain. Stationed in Chihuahua, he conducted numerous topographical surveys throughout Mexico. In 1836 García Conde was appointed commander of the Military Academy. He was promoted to colonel in 1837 (retroactive to 1835) and appointed general in 1841.

After being elected to the Mexican Senate in 1843, García Conde supported the revolution that overthrew Antonio López de Santa Anna in December 1844. General José Joaquín de Herrera, the new Mexican president, convinced García Conde to resign the directorship of the Military College and serve as minister of war from December 1844 to August 1845. Following Herrera's overthrow in December 1845, García Conde, prohibited from resuming his duties at the Military Academy, returned to Chihuahua.

At the outset of the Mexican-American War, García Conde was ordered to help defend Chihuahua from an American attack, but he saw little action during the war. In 1847, he was reelected to the Mexican Senate. After the Mexican government signed the 1848 Treaty of Guadalupe Hidalgo, which stipulated that each country appoint a commission to survey the new boundary and jointly agree to its location, it appointed García Conde the commissioner of a Mexican survey team supported by a staff consisting of one surveyor and four engineers. With limited funding, in July 1849, García Conde's team began surveying the new boundary from a point on the Pacific coast one marine league below the southernmost point of San Diego Bay. The Mexicans worked in concert with an American team led by John B. Weller and John Russell Bartlett. By the time of his death on December 19, 1851, in Arispe, García Conde's team had successfully surveyed the boundary from the Pacific coast to New Mexico. The boundary between the United States and Mexico was not completely marked until 1855 because of the 1853 Gadsden Purchase, however.

MICHAEL R. HALL

See also

Bartlett, John Russell; Bartlett-Conde Agreement; Boundary Disputes, U.S. and Mexican; Chihuahua, State of; Gadsden Purchase; Guadalupe Hidalgo, Treaty of; Herrera, José Joaquín de; Santa Anna, Antonio López de.

References

Clary, David A. *Eagles and Empire: The United States, Mexico, and the Struggle for a Continent.* New York: Bantam Books, 2009.

Faulk, Odie B. *Too Far North, Too Far South.* Los Angeles, CA: Westernlore Press, 1967.

Hewitt, Harry P. "The Mexican Boundary Survey Team: Pedro García Conde in California." *Western Historical Quarterly* 21, no. 2 (May 1990): 171–196.

Werne, Joseph. *The Imaginary Line: A History of the U.S.-Mexican Boundary Survey, 1848–1857.* Fort Worth: Texas Christian University Press, 2007.

Garrison, William Lloyd
Birth Date: December 10, 1805
Death Date: May 24, 1879

American writer, newspaper editor, reformer, and noted abolitionist. William Lloyd Garrison was born in Newburyport, Massachusetts, on December 10, 1805. At the age of 13, he began a seven-year apprenticeship to Ephraim W. Allen, editor of the

Influential abolitionist journalist William Lloyd Garrison was an outspoken opponent of the Mexican-American War. He saw it as a conspiracy on the part of slave owners to expand slavery into new territories. (Library of Congress)

Newburyport *Herald.* There he learned the newspaper trade, developed a talent for writing, and became convinced of the power of words to effect change in society. In 1826 Garrison became editor of a local newspaper, the *Free Press.* Two years later he and Nathaniel H. White coedited the *National Philanthropist,* which was devoted to speaking out against societal vice and war.

As the slavery issue began to dominate the national scene, Garrison joined the American Colonization Society, which pushed for colonizing slaves outside the United States. In 1829 abolitionist Quaker Benjamin Lundy recruited Garrison to join him in Baltimore and help edit his newspaper, the *Genius of Universal Emancipation.* From 1829 on, Garrison continued to protest injustice in general, but opposition to slavery became the major focus of his work. He not only coedited the *Genius of Universal Emancipation* with Lundy but began making public speeches against slavery, and he made several trips to Great Britain for the cause of emancipation.

Unlike many abolitionists of his day who supported gradual compensated emancipation, Garrison believed that the only way to deal with the slavery dilemma was immediate and complete emancipation. Garrison had no plan for how the liberated slaves would fit into society, however. He simply denounced the institution of slavery at every opportunity, and his words became increasingly inflammatory. Garrison became so uncompromising

that he sometimes alienated even his closest allies. He eventually left the American Colonization Society and denounced it.

In 1829, when Garrison accused Francis Todd, a shipowner, of engaging in domestic slave trading, Todd sued Garrison for libel and won. Unable to pay the fine, Garrison was sentenced to six months in jail. He served only seven weeks of his sentence, however, because Arthur Tappan, a wealthy philanthropist, paid the fine. With this unpleasantness behind him, Garrison believed it was time for him to move on, and he parted ways with Lundy in 1830. Before long, Garrison enlisted the help of Isaac Knapp and began publishing the *Liberator,* which became Garrison's antislavery vehicle for the next 35 years.

In the *Liberator,* Garrison expounded on his antislavery philosophy of nonviolent resistance. He believed that moral arguments alone should be enough to exact reform. In a blatant contradiction to his philosophy, however, Garrison called John Brown, who led a violent 1859 attack on Harpers Ferry in the name of destroying slavery, a just martyr. As a rule, Garrison continued to use words instead of swords as weapons. His words were so harsh, in fact, that he sometimes received threats of bodily harm. He also attacked both North and South with equal zeal. In his opinion, the U.S. Constitution should have been replaced because it tacitly protected the institution of slavery. At one point, the state of Georgia found Garrison's words so offensive that it set a reward for his arrest.

In spite of these dangers, Garrison did not retreat. To organize the antislavery movement more effectively, in 1831 he contributed to the creation of the New England Anti-Slavery Society. After 1833, however, Garrison's influence in the movement began to diminish because he was regarded as too radical. His attempt to include women's rights in the society's agenda, for example, met with widespread disapproval and splintered the organization. In 1835, had Boston's mayor Theodore Lyman not intervened, Garrison would have become a martyr to his cause when an angry mob threatened to hang him. In 1841 Garrison endorsed secession as a way of removing slavery from the country, and in 1854 he publicly burned a copy of the U.S. Constitution.

Garrison was also a vociferous and vocal opponent of the Mexican-American War, terming it a conspiracy on the part of slave owners to expand slavery into new territories. During the conflict, which he believed to be morally reprehensible, he wrote letters and editorials and gave speeches in which he denounced the war at every turn.

During the Civil War, the 1863 Emancipation Proclamation, which freed slaves in the rebelling states, encouraged the American Anti-Slavery Society groups to reunite and Garrison to support the Union. After the passage of the Thirteenth Amendment, which abolished slavery, Garrison resigned from the society and closed down the *Liberator* in 1865. During Reconstruction, Garrison continued to write editorials in the *Independent* in support of the Fourteenth and Fifteenth Amendments, and he continued to support various reform movements. Garrison died in New York on May 24, 1879.

Rolando Avila

See also
Abolitionism; Opposition to the Mexican-War, U.S.; Slavery.

References
Mayer, Henry. *All on Fire: William Lloyd Garrison and the Abolition of Slavery.* New York: St. Martin's Press, 1998.
Stewart, James Brewer. *William Lloyd Garrison and the Challenge of Emancipation.* Arlington Heights, IL: Harlan Davidson, 1992.

Garza, Carlos de la
Birth Date: 1807
Death Date: March 5, 1882

Texan rancher who remained loyal to Mexico during the Texas Revolution of 1835–1836 and who contributed to General José de Urrea's victory at the Battle of Coleto Creek (March 19, 1836). That engagement subsequently led to the so-called Goliad Massacre. Notably, Garza intervened on behalf of his Anglo neighbors, who were exempted from the mass execution.

Carlos de la Garza was born into a third-generation Hispanic Texan ranching family in 1807 in Bahia, Texas. Garza's father, Antonio, was a rancher and soldier stationed at Goliad, Texas. As a young man, Garza served in the Mexican army before marrying in 1829 and moving to his family's ranch at Carlos Crossing on the San Antonio River. The family's property was located on the road between Victoria and Refugio, about 12 miles south of Goliad.

A small community called Carlos Rancho, in honor of Garza, was established on the northern side of the San Antonio River in 1830. Garza operated a commissary in the village and a ferry across the river, and he supervised the family's extensive livestock holdings. When the Texas Revolution erupted in late 1835, Garza, although a sincere republican, chose to remain loyal to Mexico.

When armed conflict broke out, Garza organized some 80 of his rancher neighbors into a military unit known as the Guardia de Victoria, which served as a scouting unit and advance cavalry for General Urrea's advancing Mexican troops. Garza gave sanctuary to Mexican citizens who had fled Goliad after the town was captured by Texan forces led by Colonel James Fannin in February 1836. Early the following March, Garza's men, quite familiar with their surroundings, raided Refugio, which caused Fannin to send Captain Amon Butler King and 28 men to help evacuate the families loyal to the independence struggle remaining in Refugio. King and his troops encountered Garza and his men on March 12, 1836, in the Battle of Refugio and were forced to retreat.

Upon learning of the setback, Fannin dispatched Lieutenant Colonel William Ward and 120 men of the Georgia Battalion to reinforce King's troops. On March 14, 1836, Garza and his men kept Ward's troops under fire until 300 of Urrea's troops could arrive to defeat the revolutionaries. Meanwhile, General Sam Houston ordered Fannin to abandon Goliad. Fannin's troops, however, were caught by Urrea's men and obliged to do battle at Coleto Creek on March 19, 1836. When Fannin was forced to surrender, he and his men were marched back to Goliad and imprisoned.

Meanwhile, General Antonio López de Santa Anna ordered that the rebel prisoners be summarily executed. Garza argued for clemency for several of his neighbors who had fought with Fannin's men. Among the 28 men spared from the mass execution of Texan revolutionaries on March 27, 1836, known as the Goliad Massacre, were Garza's neighbors James Byrne, John Fagan, Nicholas Fagan, Edward Perry, Anthony Sydick, and John Sydick. Fannin was among those shot to death, however.

After the Goliad Campaign, Garza retired to private life on his ranch. Although resented by some for his aid to the Mexican side in the war, Garza was not harassed by the Texans once they had achieved independence, undoubtedly because of the assistance he had rendered to his Anglo neighbors. Garza returned to ranching and supported the annexation of Texas to the United States in 1845.

During the Mexican-American War, Brigadier General Albert Sidney Johnston used Garza's ranch at his headquarters while he was establishing the 1st Texas Rifle Volunteers. Garza sold cattle to the U.S. Army and provided mules and ox carts for the transportation of supplies to the army in Mexico. He died at his ranch on March 5, 1882.

MICHAEL R. HALL

See also
Coleto Creek, Battle of; Fannin, James Walker; Goliad Massacre; Johnston, Albert Sidney; Texas Revolution; Urrea y Elías Gonzales, José de.

References
Huson, Hobart. *Refugio: A Comprehensive History of Refugio County from Aboriginal Times to 1953.* Woodsboro, TX: Rooke Foundation, 1955.
Stout, Jay A. *Slaughter at Goliad: The Mexican Massacre of 400 Texas Volunteers.* Annapolis, MD: Naval Institute Press, 2008.

Gillespie, Archibald H.
Birth Date: August 14, 1810
Death Date: August 16, 1873

U.S. Marine Corps officer. Archibald H. Gillespie was born in New York City on August 14, 1810. Commissioned a second lieutenant in the marines in 1832, he commanded the marine detachments aboard several U.S. Navy warships, including the sloop *Fairfield,* sloop *Vincennes,* ship of the line *North Carolina,* and the frigate *Brandywine.* In mid-October 1845, Gillespie was selected to engage in a clandestine mission to California, where he would relay information and secret papers to the U.S. consul, Thomas O. Larkin, and to U.S. Army captain John C. Frémont. Then a first lieutenant, Gillespie attended a meeting on October 30, 1845, at the White House, with President James K. Polk in attendance. Polk personally instructed the young marine as to the nature of his mission. Already preparing for war with Mexico and hoping to seize California at the earliest practical opportunity, Polk instructed Gillespie to carry secret documents from the U.S. State Department to Larkin (who was then in Monterey, California) and to Frémont, who was already in southern Oregon, not far from the California border.

In early November, Gillespie, disguised as a civilian British merchant, left Washington, D.C., for the arduous journey to the West Coast. He arrived in Monterey in April 1846. So as not to raise Mexican suspicions, Gillespie had sailed to Veracruz, Mexico, crossed the entirety of Mexico to Mazatlán, and then sailed north along the coast in the U.S. Navy sloop *Cyane* to meet Larkin in Monterey. Fearful that his documents might fall into the wrong hands, Gillespie memorized some of the State Department correspondence and then burned the original copies. He met with Larkin on April 17, informing him that he should support any Californio rebellions against the Mexican government and resist any attempt by the British to seize California.

Gillespie then rushed to meet Frémont in Oregon, finding him encamped along Klamath Lake on May 9. He informed Frémont of the preparations being made for war and reported on Mexican military activities he had witnessed while passing through Mexico. Gillespie's report convinced Frémont that he should head south into California immediately. Gillespie joined Frémont, who arrived near Sacramento the next month and played a key role in the Bear Flag Revolt. Upon hearing the news of the official declaration of war with Mexico, Frémont formed the California Battalion, which Gillespie joined. The battalion of American volunteers soon conquered virtually all of California with only token resistance. Late in the summer of 1846, Frémont placed Gillespie in charge of the small garrison at Los Angeles. His heavy-handed tactics and mistreatment of local citizens, however, led to a revolt among Californios, who seized control of the town before U.S. reinforcements could arrive. Gillespie was compelled to surrender his garrison in September 1846, and the Americans did not retake Los Angeles until the following January.

Although the above incident badly tarnished Gillespie's reputation, he remained in California and in December 1846 provided ammunition and supplies to Brigadier Stephen Watts Kearny's army, which was moving west from New Mexico to San Diego. Gillespie also saw action during the Battle of San Pasgual (San Pascual), where he was slightly wounded. When Kearny and Commodore Robert F. Stockton retook Los Angeles on January 10, 1847, Gillespie was among the first Americans to reenter the city.

In August 1847, Gillespie departed California, taking the overland route. He arrived in Washington, D.C., that autumn. Gillespie was forced to testify during Frémont's famous court-martial for insubordination and mutiny arising from a dispute with General Kearny. Gillespie was stationed in Washington, D.C., for a time and then at Pensacola, Florida. On October 14, 1854, he resigned

U.S. Marine Corps first lieutenant Archibald H. Gillespie carried secret documents from President James K. Polk to U.S. officials in California before the start of the Mexican-American War. (U.S. Marine Corps Art Collection)

his commission with the rank of brevet major (permanent captain), ending a 22-year career with the marines. Thereafter, he engaged in private business concerns. Gillespie died in San Francisco on August 16, 1873.

Paul G. Pierpaoli Jr.

See also

Bear Flag Revolt; California; California Battalion; California Theater of War, Overview; Californios; Frémont, John Charles; Kearny, Stephen Watts; Larkin, Thomas Oliver; Polk, James Knox; San Pasqual, Battle of; Stockton, Robert Field.

References

Callahan, Edward W., ed. *List of Officers of the Navy of the United States and of the Marine Corps from 1775 to 1900.* 1901. Reprint, New York: Haskell House, 1969.

Harlow, Neal. *California Conquered: War and Peace on the Pacific, 1846–1850.* Berkeley: University of California Press, 1982.

Marti, Werner H. *Messenger of Destiny: The California Adventures, 1846–1847, of Archibald H. Gillespie, U.S. Marine Corps.* San Francisco: J. Howell Books, 1960.

Gillespie, Robert Addison

Birth Date: June 12, 1815
Death Date: September 23, 1846

Indian fighter, Texas Ranger, merchant, and soldier in the Mexican-American War. Born on June 12, 1815, in Blount County, Tennessee, Robert Addison Gillespie departed for Texas after the province won its independence from Mexico in 1836. Arriving on the Texas Gulf Coast in 1837, Gillespie and his two brothers, Matthew and James, established a mercantile and land business in Matagorda. Two years later, the brothers moved to the east central Texas town of LaGrange, where they established a similar business enterprise.

Beginning in 1840, Gillespie served the Republic of Texas as a member of a number of volunteer military forces. He was a member of John Henry Moore's expedition against the Comanches on the upper Colorado River in October 1840, and he participated in the Battle of Salado Creek in September 1842, when some 215 Texan volunteers defeated the Mexican forces that had taken control of the city of San Antonio earlier that month. Two months later Gillespie joined the controversial Sommervell Expedition, a half-hearted attempt ordered by President Sam Houston to exact revenge against Mexico for its continued invasions of Texas and occupation of Texan territory. In 1843, Gillespie joined the famed Indian fighter Captain John Coffee Hays's Texas Ranger company, engaging Native Americans in numerous skirmishes. Gillespie was severely wounded at the Battle of Walker's Creek in 1844 but served with Hays's Rangers until 1845.

As tensions grew between the United States and Mexico in 1845, President James K. Polk ordered Brigadier General Zachary Taylor to the Texan-Mexican border. In 1845 Gillespie raised and was elected captain of a volunteer company in Hays's 1st Regiment of Texas Mounted Riflemen.

As part of Taylor's army, Gillespie's company saw heavy action during the Battle of Monterrey. On September 21, 1846, he was among the soldiers who assaulted El Soldado, a fortification atop Federation Hill, which commanded the western approach to Monterrey. He reportedly was the first American soldier to enter the redoubt. Gillespie was gravely wounded in the attack on the heavily fortified Bishop's Palace the next day as he and his men scaled the western slope of Independence Hill. He died from his wounds on September 23, 1846.

KELLY E. CRAGER

See also

Bishop's Palace, Monterrey, Action at; Hays, John Coffee; Houston, Samuel; Mier Expedition; Monterrey, Battle of; Texas Rangers; Texas Revolution.

References

Campbell, Randolph B. *Gone to Texas: A History of the Lone Star State.* New York: Oxford University Press, 2003.

Haynes, Sam W. *Soldiers of Misfortune: The Somervell and Mier Expeditions.* Austin, TX: University of Texas Press, 1990.

Wilkins, Frederick. *The Legend Begins: The Texas Rangers, 1823–1845.* Austin, TX: State House Press, 1996.

Gold Rush, California

Large influx of prospectors who flocked to California beginning in 1848 after the discovery of significant gold deposits there. Ten days prior to the February 2, 1848, signing of the Treaty of Guadalupe Hidalgo, which formally ended the Mexican-American War, James W. Marshall discovered gold in California. Although this event had no influence on the negotiations for or ratification of the treaty, it did have a major impact on California and the United States.

With the end of hostilities in California in January 1847, Anglos and other European elements in Northern California turned to speculation, mostly in land. Approximately 1,000 Anglo immigrants had arrived in the region during 1846. With the expectation that immigration over the next few years would be at least as large, speculators anticipated an increase in the demand for land. One such speculator was John Sutter, already the owner of 48,827 acres at the junction of the Sacramento and American Rivers known as New Helvetia, including Sutter's Fort. Besides laying out a town near the fort, Sutter decided he could make money by harvesting trees and selling lumber to the buyers of his lots and anyone else who needed lumber during the expected building boom. What he needed for this, of course, was a saw mill.

Because a number of enterprises absorbed most of Sutter's time, he decided a partner could do most of the work on the saw mill project, to be paid with a portion of the production. This man turned out to be James W. Marshall. Finding a suitable spot on the American River, Marshall began construction of the saw mill with a crew of Latter-Day Saints, recently discharged from Stephen Watts Kearny's Mormon Battalion. By January 1848, most of the building was completed and several thousand yards of dirt for the dam and channel above the mill to power it had been dug. Running out of time, Marshall decided to let the water cut the channel

THE WAY THEY GO TO CALIFORNIA.

Illustrator Nathan Currier (of Currier & Ives fame) drew this editorial cartoon in 1849 to illustrate how eager Americans were to reach California in search of gold. (Library of Congress)

below the mill when the men were not working on the mill itself. Shutting the water source each morning, Marshall would walk the lower channel to inspect how well the channel was being cut. On the morning of January 24, 1848, Marshall saw shiny yellow specks in a pool of water. Finding a couple of nuggets, he returned to camp and tested the material. Convinced that he had gold, Marshall took the samples to Sutter a few days later. Sutter and Marshall agreed to keep the discovery quiet, although Marshall allowed the workers to look for gold in their off hours.

When Sam Brannan, a Mormon and editor of the *California Star* newspaper visited the site in March, he reported the discovery, but his revelation produced no immediate excitement. In May, however, he returned with enough evidence to stir the population. The Gold Rush was on.

The impact of the Gold Rush on California was dramatic, especially in Northern California. Although many sailors had jumped ship in California before, captains could no longer man their ships. Day laborers left for the gold mines as well. Shop owners and almost everyone else joined the Gold Rush in hopes of becoming rich. Cities like San Francisco witnessed a population explosion, but the influx of so many prospectors and settlers greatly disrupted the area's Native American tribes, which never completely recovered from the onslaught.

In the early days, a placer miner panned for gold using a pick, shovel, pan, and a lot of water to separate the alluvial deposits from the gold. Soon, sluice boxes were built through which to run water, into which the loose material would be dropped. A sluice box uses a series of short obstructions to catch the heaviest pieces that drop to the bottom while the water washes away the lighter material. Later during the Gold Rush, miners dug prospect holes and mine shafts, following veins of gold ore deep into the mountains. By 1853, hydraulic mining was the main method employed in the mining process. Hydraulic mining involved forcing water through a nozzle under high pressure. This stream of water washed away the hillside to get to the gold. Quite obviously, such techniques wrought terrible environmental damage, producing severe soil erosion and flooding.

By August 1848, news of the gold discovery had reached the East Coast, and that December 5 President James K. Polk made the discovery official. At a time in which the typical day laborer made just $2 a day, the average prospector was taking in $50 per day in the goldfields. With predictable speed, gold fever swept the entire country. Some men abandoned their homes and families and started up the Oregon Trail with only what they could carry. Many who headed for California during the Gold Rush never returned home or even asked for their families to join them. By

1855, hundreds of thousands of people had migrated to California, the largest migration of its kind to that point in U.S. history.

The huge population influx brought many problems that the new California government was unable to handle. Prices skyrocketed, and a lawless element appeared. Indeed, the vigilante movement helped bring forth cries for official law and order.

As for John Sutter, the discovery of gold on his land was the beginning of the end. His workers deserted him, immigrants squatted on his lands, and gold seekers took his equipment and killed his livestock. In 1849, Sutter helped frame the California State Constitution, but the new government refused to recognize his land grant, and Sutter died, nearly impoverished, on June 18, 1880. Sutter's bad luck notwithstanding, the Mexican-American War and the huge U.S. land grab that resulted from it ensured that the newfound California wealth would accrue to the United States rather than Mexico.

RICHARD GRISET

See also

California; Guadalupe Hidalgo, Treaty of; Polk, James Knox; Sutter, John Augustus; Sutter's Fort.

References

Brands, H. W. *Age of Gold*. New York: Doubleday, 2002.
De Voto, Bernard. *The Year of Decision: 1846*. Boston, MA: Little, Brown, 1943.
Rohrbough, Malcolm J. *Days of Gold: The California Gold Rush and the American Nation*. Berkeley: University of California Press, 1998.

Goliad Massacre
Event Date: March 27, 1836

The termination of the Goliad Campaign of 1836 during the Texas Revolution in which Mexican forces summarily executed a large number of Texan prisoners on March 27, 1836. The Goliad Massacre is one of the most important events of the Texas Revolution.

On November 15, 1835, federalist general José Antonio Mexía, who opposed General Antonio López de Santa Anna's assumption of dictatorial powers, attacked Tampico with three companies of men enlisted at New Orleans. A number of Mexía's men were captured that day and the next by forces loyal to Santa Anna. In large measure to discourage Americans from aiding revolutionaries in Texas, Santa Anna approved the execution of 28 of the prisoners, whom he characterized as "pirates." The men were shot on December 14. On December 30, the Mexican Congress retroactively legalized his action by passing a decree that ordered all foreigners who took up arms against Mexico be executed for piracy. As a consequence of this decree, Santa Anna's forces took no prisoners.

On February 27, 1836, General José de Urrea, commander of the right wing of Santa Anna's army, took 28 Texans prisoner near San Patricio, and three days later, on March 2, 1836, he captured an additional six in the Battle of Agua Dulce Creek. Although

ordered by Santa Anna to execute them under the law of December 30, he instead sent the prisoners to Matamoros, thereby avoiding responsibility for their fate.

On March 15, Urrea took 33 additional Texans prisoner at Refugio where Texan rebels had burned a number of local ranchos and shot eight Mexicans at a campfire. These actions prompted Urrea to order the execution of Captain Amon B. King and 14 of his men. The other prisoners, whom Urrea characterized as "colonists or Mexicans," he set free.

Urrea found himself facing a much more difficult situation on March 20 in negotiating the surrender of Colonel James Walker Fannin and his command following the Battle of Coleto Creek. Urrea was aware that the Mexican policy calling for the execution of prisoners, in effect, forced the Texans to fight to the death. Fannin's force was well armed, with some 1,000 muskets and nine cannon, and were thus in position to sell their lives at a high price to their attackers.

Fannin's situation was militarily hopeless, however. His men drew up surrender terms in writing that would have the Texans give up their arms to become prisoners of war "according to the practices of civilized nations" and, as soon as possible, to be paroled and returned to the United States.

Urrea could not agree to these terms and instead offered written terms whereupon the Texans would surrender their weapons and become prisoners of war "at the disposal of the Supreme Mexican Government." Urrea maintained that no prisoner of war "at the disposal" of Mexico had ever been executed. Moreover, he promised to recommend to Santa Anna that these terms be honored and expressed confidence that Fannin's men would be paroled and repatriated to the United States within eight days.

Fannin had little choice but to accept. Urrea had been reinforced by additional infantry and artillery during the night, Fannin's position was largely exposed, and his men were short of water and supplies. Additionally, Fannin's command was burdened by a growing list of wounded for whom they had no transportation. Yet he did not inform his men of the conditional nature of the agreed-on terms.

The some 230–240 uninjured and slightly wounded Texans were marched back to Goliad, where they were imprisoned in the chapel of Neuestra Señors de Loredo Presidio at La Bahía, the fortress they had previously occupied as Fort Defiance. They were joined there during the course of the next several days by some 50 or more wounded from the battle, including Fannin. On March 25 another 80 Texans who been defeated in the earlier Battle of Refugio surrendered near Dimitri's Landing on the basis of the same terms accorded to Fannin.

Urrea then reported to Santa Anna the presence of the prisoners and recommended that their lives be spared; however, he failed to apprise Santa Anna of the exact terms of the surrender he had arranged with Fannin. On March 23, Santa Anna, knowing that the prisoners were "at the disposal of the Supreme Mexican Government," ordered them to be executed. Then, on March 26, he sent a direct order to Goliad's commanding officer, Mexican colonel José Nicolás de la Portilla, to execute the prisoners. Also on March 26, Portilla received an order from Urrea "to treat the prisoners with consideration, and especially their leader, Fannin," and ordered that the prisoners be employed in the reconstruction of the town. Urrea certainly knew that Portilla would not be able to comply with his order.

After contemplating the conflicting orders through the night, Portilla decided that Santa Anna's order superseded that of Urrea. On Palm Sunday, March 27, 1836, the prisoners were called into three formations and marched toward the San Antonio River. One group was told that they were going to gather wood, another group was informed that they were being sent to freedom in New Orleans, and the last group was advised that they were going to herd cattle.

At selected spots on the three roads, the Mexican soldiers opened fire on the prisoners at close range. Twenty-eight of the prisoners in the three groups managed to escape. The wounded prisoners unable to make the march were executed at the presidio. Fannin was executed last. He asked that his belongings be sent to his family and that he not be shot in the face; nonetheless, he was blindfolded, put in a chair, and shot in the face, and his belongings were distributed among the executioners.

Estimates of the number of Texans executed vary from 342 to as many as 445, but most Texan sources agree on 407. Mexican colonel Francisco Garay and Francita Alavez (who became known as the "Angel of Goliad") saved 20 from execution—men identified as doctors, orderlies, interpreters, and mechanics. The bodies of those executed were burned, and the remains were left along the river.

The Goliad Massacre had profound impact. Although he had operated within the boundaries of Mexican law, Santa Anna, previously known only as a crafty foe, was now branded as a cruel and brutal commander. It greatly increased support for the cause of the Texas Revolution both from within Texas and in the United States, which was critical for Texas independence. The words "Remember the Alamo" and "Remember Goliad" inspired Texans during the Battle of San Jacinto, the decisive battle of the revolution.

On June 3, 1836, 12 days after San Jacinto, Texas general Thomas J. Rusk discovered the remains and buried them in a common grave with military honors. The grave, however, was left unmarked until 1858 when a resident of Goliad commemorated it with a pile of rocks, which served as the only reminder of the location until the 1930s when a group of Boy Scouts discovered human bones. An anthropologist from the University of Texas investigated the site and, with the assistance of historians, determined it to be the site of the mass execution. A monument was dedicated to the victims of the Goliad Massacre on June 4, 1938.

PHILIP J. MACFARLANE AND SPENCER C. TUCKER

See also

Alamo, Battle of the; Coleto Creek, Battle of; Fannin, James Walker; Mexía, José Antonio; Refugio, Battle of; Rusk, Thomas Jefferson; San Jacinto, Battle of; Santa Anna, Antonio López de; Texas Revolution; Urrea y Elías Gonzales, José de.

References

Hardin, Stephen L. *Texian Iliad: A Military History of the Texas Revolution, 1835–1836.* Austin: University of Texas Press, 1994.
Hopewell, Clifford. *Remember Goliad: Their Silent Tents.* Austin, TX: Eakin Press, 1998.
Pruett, Jakie L., and Everett B. Cole. *Goliad Massacre: A Tragedy of the Texas Revolution.* Austin, TX: Eakin Press, 1985.
Roell, Craig H. *Remember Goliad!* Austin: Texas State Historical Association, 1994.

Gómez Farías, Valentín
Birth Date: February 14, 1781
Death Date: July 5, 1858

Mexican *puro* politician and acting president of Mexico (1833–1835, 1846–1847). Born in Guadalajara, Jalisco, Mexico, on February 14, 1781, to a middle-class family, Valentín Gómez Farías studied medicine and entered practice in 1807. From 1820 onward, however, he devoted himself to politics and became the leading figure in the radical liberal faction known as the *puros*. The *puros* sparred not only with conservatives but also with the moderate wing of the liberal movement, often referred to as *moderados*. *Puros* believed that the wealth and power of the Roman Catholic Church should be severely curtailed, that power should be decentralized among the various states, that all citizens should be legally equal, that basic civil rights should be protected, that the power of the military should be checked, and that U.S. expansionism should be confronted forcefully.

Gómez Farías first served on the municipal council of Aguascalientes before serving in the national assembly. He served as vice president of Mexico under Antonio López de Santa Anna in 1833 and 1834. During the early part of his presidency, Santa Anna resided on his hacienda in the state of Veracruz, allowing Goméz Farías to pursue his liberal agenda as acting president. Gómez Farías carried out vindictive policies against his political adversaries while attacking the wealth and influence of the Catholic Church. In the process, he antagonized many powerful interests, who in 1835 persuaded Santa Anna to dismiss his vice president and institute a conservative, authoritarian, and highly centralized regime.

Exiled by Santa Anna, Gómez Farías spent approximately three years in New Orleans before returning to Mexico in February 1838. Two years later, in July 1840, he led an exceedingly violent but failed effort to overthrow the conservative government of President Anastasio Bustamante and restore federalism. Forced into exile a second time, Gómez Farías ended up in Yucatán before moving to New Orleans in the spring of 1843. By this time, given the autocratic nature of General Santa Anna's 1841–1844 regime, as well as because of the financial hardships that he and his family were subject to, he had come to the conclusion that his political goals could only be achieved through force of arms.

Therefore, when crisis erupted in Mexico over the U.S. annexation of Texas early in 1845, Gómez Farías was convinced that the country's salvation lay not only in the immediate restoration of the federalist Constitution of 1824 but also in taking aggressive measures to reclaim the lost province for Mexico. In pursuit of these goals, Gómez Farías became one of Mexico's most enthusiastic advocates of war against the United States as well as a political agitator who organized numerous plots to overthrow the regimes of Generals José Joaquín Herrera (1844–1845) and Mariano Paredes y Arrillaga (1846). His efforts did not meet with success until he struck an alliance with the *moderados* and Santa Anna's supporters in the spring of 1846, and that August the unwieldy coalition toppled the Paredes y Arrillaga regime.

By year's end, as in 1833–1834, Gómez Farías had been elected vice president, and he wielded executive authority while Santa Anna devoted himself to the war effort. Gómez Farías's attempts to raise funds to prosecute the war effort through a January 11, 1847, decree that called on the church to mortgage or sell some of its property, however, once again stirred controversy. In response, moderate and conservative opponents, backed by the church, launched the so-called Polkos Revolt in late February 1847. Santa Anna returned to Mexico City following the Battle of Buena Vista and that March persuaded Congress to abolish the office of vice president, thus once again putting an end to Gómez Farías's experiments in radical reform.

From this time until the formal end of hostilities in the late spring of 1848 Gómez Farías pursued two goals with considerable energy: one, he bitterly denounced the 1848 Treaty of Guadalupe Hidalgo, which ended the war, and, two, he advocated continuing hostilities against the United States. By the early 1850s, disillusioned and in failing health, he retired to private life. He lived just long enough to witness the enactment of a liberal constitution in 1857 that incorporated many of the ideas for which he had fought. Gómez Farías died in Mexico City on July 5, 1858.

TIMOTHY J. HENDERSON AND PEDRO SANTONI

See also

Bustamante y Oseguera, Anastasio; Guadalupe Hidalgo, Treaty of; *Moderados*; Paredes y Arrillaga, Mariano; Politics, Mexican; Polkos Revolt; *Puros*; Salas, José Mariano; Santa Anna, Antonio López de; Texas Revolution.

References

Costeloe, Michael P. *The Central Republic in Mexico, 1835–1846: Hombres de Bien in the Age of Santa Anna.* Cambridge: Cambridge University Press, 1993.

Fowler, Will. *Mexico in the Age of Proposals, 1821–1853.* Westport: Greenwood Press, 1998.

Pletcher, David M. *The Diplomacy of Annexation: Texas, Oregon, and the Mexican War.* Columbia: University of Missouri Press, 1973.

Santoni, Pedro. *Mexicans at Arms: Puro Federalists and the Politics of War, 1845–1848.* Fort Worth: Texas Christian University Press, 1996.

Gómez Pedraza, Manuel

Birth Date: April 22, 1789
Death Date: May 14, 1851

Mexican general, statesman, and president (1832–1833). Born in Querétaro, Mexico, on April 22, 1789, to a notable family, in 1810, Manuel Gómez Pedraza joined the Loyalists of Potosí Regiment that fought on behalf of Spain against the movement for Mexican independence. He participated in the capture of José María Morelos, perhaps the greatest of the insurgent leaders. Elected to serve as a deputy to the Spanish Parliament in 1820, Gómez Pedraza returned to Mexico in 1821 and joined forces with Agustín de Iturbide, who after declaring Mexico's independence and taking power that September named him general and commander of the garrison at Mexico City. Three years later Gómez Pedraza served as governor and military commander of the state of Puebla, and in 1825 he became minister of war.

In 1828, supported by disaffected *yorkinos* and former Scottish Rite Masons, Gómez Pedraza ran for the presidency and was elected by a majority of the state legislatures in accordance with the indirect voting method in force at the time. Radical supporters of General Vicente Guerrero, however, refused to accept his election and rebelled, forcing Gómez Pedraza into exile. The rebellion put an end to constitutional government in Mexico for the next two decades. Not until 1848 would a Mexican president serve a full term in office and surrender power to a legally elected successor. Gómez Pedraza eventually returned from exile—first in Paris, France, and New Orleans, Louisiana—to serve out the remainder of his constitutional term, from December 27, 1832, to April 1, 1833.

Gómez Pedraza occupied a number of high government offices in the years that preceded the U.S.-Mexican War. He served as minister of foreign relations in 1838, and again in late 1841. Gómez Pedraza also was a member of the Senate that helped bring down General Antonio López de Santa Anna's regime late in 1844. He consequently came to exert considerable influence in public affairs, and by the mid-1840s he had emerged as the leader of the *moderado* political bloc.

In that capacity, and likely influenced by the bitter skirmishes that had characterized Mexican politics during the early republic, several times in 1846 and 1847 Gómez Pedraza refused to cooperate with the efforts of *puro* chieftain Valentín Gómez Farías to achieve national unity so the country could fend off the U.S. invasion. In late 1847 and early 1848, following the cessation of hostilities, the government had moved from Mexico City to Querétaro, and there Gómez Pedraza served as president of the Mexican Senate. Renowned for his oratorical skills, he repeatedly urged his colleagues to approve the 1848 Treaty of Guadalupe Hidalgo, believing it to be the best course for Mexico.

In 1850, two years after the war ended, Gómez Pedraza ran a lackluster campaign for the presidency in what has been described as the first genuinely contested such campaign in Mexican history.

Although he lost that contest to General Mariano Arista, Gómez Pedraza remained involved in public affairs. He was serving as director of the Monte de Piedad, the national pawnshop in Mexico City, at the time of his death on May 14, 1851.

TIMOTHY J. HENDERSON AND PEDRO SANTONI

See also

Arista, Mariano; Bustamante y Oseguera, Anastasio; Guadalupe Hidalgo, Treaty of; Guerrero, Vicente; *Moderados*; Politics, Mexican; *Puros*; Santa Anna, Antonio López de.

References

Costeloe, Michael P. *The Central Republic in Mexico, 1835–1846: Hombres de Bien in the Age of Santa Anna.* New York: Cambridge University Press, 1993.

Green, Stanley C. *The Mexican Republic: The First Decade, 1823–1832.* Pittsburgh: University of Pittsburgh Press, 1987.

Santoni, Pedro. *Mexicans at Arms:* Puro *Federalists and the Politics of War, 1845–1848.* Fort Worth: Texas Christian University Press, 1996.

Solares Robles, Laura. *Una revolución pacífica: Biografía política de Manuel Gómez Pedraza, 1789–1851.* Mexico City: Instituto José María Luis Mora, 1996.

Gonzales, Battle of
Event Date: October 2, 1835

The first military engagement of the Texas Revolution, often referred to as "the Lexington of the Texas Revolution," which took place on October 2, 1835, along the banks of the Guadalupe River near the town of Gonzales in southeastern Texas. A minor skirmish between Texan settlers and Mexican regular forces, the Battle of Gonzales marked the beginning of hostile activities between the two sides that led to Texas independence the following year.

As tensions between Anglo settlers in Mexican Texas and the Mexican government increased in 1835, General Antonio López de Santa Anna, then the ruler of Mexico, pursued a policy designed to rein in the independently minded settlers. Toward this end, Colonel Domingo de Ugartechea, the Mexican military commander in Texas, demanded that the Anglo settlers of Gonzales surrender a small cannon given to them by the Mexican government for defense against Native Americans. The Gonzales colonists refused the request, prompting Ugartechea to send a force of 100 dragoons led by Lieutenant Francisco de Castaneda to Gonzales to again request the surrender of the cannon.

Upon reaching the swollen Guadalupe River near Gonzales on September 29, Castaneda informed the town's settlers of his intention to speak with Gonzales's *alcalde* (mayor), Andrew Ponton, and to request the surren*der* of the cannon. Ponton was not present in Gonzales, and Castaneda announced that he and his force would remain on the west side of the Guadalupe until the *alcalde*'s return. In the meantime, the Gonzales militia gathered and received reinforcements from local settlers, forming a force of more than 100 men who threatened the smaller Mexican force.

Informed of these developments, Castaneda and his men abandoned the campsite and moved upriver seven miles, where they set up a new camp.

On the night of October 1, the Texans crossed the Guadalupe and moved upriver to the new Mexican campsite. The next morning, the Texans attacked the Mexican force, forcing Castaneda's forces to fall back. John Henry Moore, commander of the Texans, explained to Castaneda that his troops initiated the attack out of their belief that Santa Anna's government had violated the Mexican Constitution of 1824, and that Castaneda's attempt to take the cannon was yet another effort to rob the Texans of their rights under the constitution. Moore then demanded that the Mexican force surrender and join the Texans.

Castaneda replied that he was also opposed to the policies of the Santa Anna government, but that as a military officer he was obliged to follow orders. Fighting resumed shortly after this meeting, with the Texans deploying the disputed cannon while flying a flag—made by local blacksmith Noah Smithwick from the wedding dress of Naomi DeWitt, daughter of empresario Green DeWitt—emblazoned with the image of the cannon and the words "Come and Take It." The outnumbered and outgunned Mexican force quickly fell back toward San Antonio de Béxar. The battle resulted in no deaths and few casualties for either side, but it marked the breaking point between the Mexican government and the Texan settlers as both sides took up arms. From that point, the Texas Revolution gathered momentum, and by the summer of 1836, the Texans had managed to declare their own sovereign republic.

KELLY E. CRAGER

See also

Constitutions, Mexican; Mexico; Santa Anna, Antonio López de; Texas; Texas Revolution; Ugartechea, Domingo de.

References

Brands, H. W. *Lone Star Nation: How a Ragged Army of Volunteers Won the Battle for Texas Independence—and Changed America.* New York: Doubleday, 2004.

Campbell, Randolph B. *Gone to Texas: A History of the Lone Star State.* New York: Oxford University Press, 2003.

Hardin, Stephen. *Texian Iliad: A Military History of the Texas Revolution.* Austin: University of Texas Press, 1996.

González Cosío, Manuel
Birth Date: 1790
Death Date: 1849

Mexican *puro* politician. Manuel González Cosío was born in Mexico City in 1790 but was educated in Zacatecas. In the 1820s, he joined what later became known as the Liberal Party and entered politics at the state level. His first brief stint as governor of Zacatecas (January–May 1835) coincided with an attempt by conservative and *moderado* leaders to overturn federalism and turn Mexico into a centralist republic. One key initiative in this transition was a March 1835 decree that sought to restrict state sovereignty through a drastic reduction in the size of state militias. González Cosío mustered his forces—4,000 strong—to resist the measure, but General Antonio López de Santa Anna marched north from Mexico City and crushed Zacatecas's militiamen in May 1835.

Ten years later, as the specter of war with the United States loomed over Mexico, González Cosío actively supported *puro* leader Valentín Gómez Farías and counseled him on the issues of the day. He shared with Gómez Farías his frustrations with the domestic and foreign policies of General José Joaquín Herrera's government (1844–1845), his hopes and concerns regarding the consequences of an alliance with Santa Anna, and his insights on the best way to organize the National Guard to protect states' rights and assist in the war effort.

González Cosío's second stint as governor of Zacatecas came on the heels of the *puros'* ascendancy after the August 1846 *pronunciamiento* of the Ciudadela, and it has evoked debate among historians. To some, his manipulation of state electoral processes to insure a *puro* majority in national and state congresses, and his efforts to implement the January 11, 1847, decree intended to help finance the war against the United States through the mortgaging or selling of ecclesiastical property, precluded *puro-moderado* reconciliation and impeded national unity. Historians have also chastised González Cosío for failing to mobilize the National Guard and for not providing Santa Anna with enough men and war matériel that might have allowed him to defeat U.S. forces. Such arguments, however, have failed to consider how the *moderados'* political maneuverings also contributed to national discord, as well as the reasons that motivated Gónzalez Cosío's reluctance to assist Santa Anna in the fall and winter of 1846—one, the devastation that the events of 1835 had brought to the state; and two, Zacatecas's need to use existing military resources to protect itself from devastating attacks by Comanche Indians. The Comanches were then laying waste to nearby Durango, and their raids were threatening to spill over into Zacatecas.

After U.S. forces captured Mexico City in September 1847, González Cosío pledged to support *moderado* president Manuel de la Peña y Peña. However, once *moderado* leaders made it clear that they did not intend to further prosecute the war, González Cosío, like other *puros* who believed that national honor was at stake, protested against the peace negotiations and the Treaty of Guadalupe Hidalgo. He also plotted to overthrow the *moderado* governments so that hostilities might continue. González Cosío was elected in December 1848 to a third term as state governor and held that post at the time of his death in 1849 in Zacatecas.

PEDRO SANTONI

See also
Comanches; Gómez Farías, Valentín; Guadalupe Hidalgo, Treaty of; Herrera, José Joaquín de; *Moderados*; Peña y Peña, Manuel de la; Politics, Mexican; *Puros*; Santa Anna, Antonio López de; Zacatecas.

References
De Vega, Mercedes. "Puros y moderados: Un obstáculo para la defense nacional; Zacatecas, 1846–1848." In *México al tiempo de su guerra con Estados Unidos (1846–1848),* coordinated by Josefina Zoraida Vázquez, 616–644. Mexico City: Secretara de Relaciones Exteriores, El Colegio de México, and Fondo de Cultura Económica, 1997.
DeLay Brian. *War of a Thousand Deserts: Indian Raids and the U.S.-Mexican War.* New Haven: Yale University Press, 2008.
Santoni, Pedro. *Mexicans at Arms: Puro Federalists and the Politics of War, 1845–1848.* Fort Worth: Texas Christian University Press, 1996.

Gorostiza, Manuel Eduardo de
Birth Date: October 13, 1789
Death Date: October 23, 1851

Noted Mexican dramatist and diplomat. Manuel Eduardo de Gorostiza was born in Veracruz, Mexico, on October 13, 1789; his father, a brigadier general in the Spanish army, served as governor of Veracruz. After his father's death when he was still young, he moved to Spain with his mother and undertook studies there. He eventually became known for his liberal views and began writing and staging plays, a number of which were critically acclaimed and were performed throughout Europe and in Mexico. Initially, his work was characterized as neoclassical, but as his writing career matured he came to embrace Romanticism, which was gaining popularity in the literary world at the time. In 1823, he left Spain for political reasons and settled in Mexico. He continued to write (his career included 11 plays and four books) and went on to help found Mexico's national theater in Mexico City (Gran Teatro Nacional).

Gorostiza also became involved in the Mexican diplomatic corps, serving as an ambassador to the Netherlands, Belgium, Great Britain, France, and the United States during the 1830s and 1840s. While posted to London, he wrote several articles in the *Times* warning of Texan and American expansionism. Posted to Washington, D.C., near the end of the 1836 Texas Revolution, Gorostiza sent repeated dispatches to Mexico City in which he notified his government that despite U.S. neutrality, he had reason to suspect that the Texans were being aided and abetted by the Americans. After the Mexican-American War began in 1846, Gorostiza returned to Mexico to help defend his homeland. He commanded the elite Bravos, a National Guard battalion, and in that capacity led his men against U.S. forces in the Battle of Churubusco on August 20, 1847.

Early in 1849 Gorostiza urged the government of José Joaquín Herrera to erect a monument that venerated the National Guard for its bravery at the Battle of Churubusco. While Herrera's regime agreed to provide him with 14 to 16 marble stones to build such a memorial and even enlisted the help of the governor of the Federal District, the shrine did not get constructed for reasons that at present remain unknown. Gorostiza died at Tacubaya, just outside Mexico City, on October 23, 1851.

PAUL G. PIERPAOLI JR.

See also

Churubusco, Battle of; Diplomacy, Mexican; Romanticism; Texas Revolution.

References

Campos, Armando de María y. *Manuel Eduardo de Gorostiza y su tiempo: su vida, su obra.* Mexico City: Talleres Graficos Nacion, 1959.

Varg, Paul. *United States Foreign Relations, 1820–1860.* East Lansing: Michigan State University Press, 1979.

Wasserman, Mark. *Everyday Life and Politics in Nineteenth Century Mexico: Men, Women, and War.* Albuquerque: University of New Mexico Press, 2000.

Graham, Richard H.
Birth Date: ca. 1817
Death Date: October 12, 1846

U.S. Army officer mortally wounded in action during the September 21–24, 1846, Battle of Monterrey. Richard H. Graham was born in Kentucky, probably in 1817. In 1834 he enrolled at the U.S. Military Academy, West Point, graduating in 1838. He was commissioned a second lieutenant in the 2nd Dragoons Regiment before being transferred shortly thereafter to the 4th Infantry Regiment. During the forcible removal of the Cherokees to Indian Territory during the late 1830s, Graham was charged with supervising the relocation and defense of the Native Americans. After that, he served in several posts along the western frontier.

In 1845, Graham, then a first lieutenant, was attached to Brigadier General Zachary Taylor's Army of Observation, headquartered at Corpus Christi, Texas. When the Mexican-American War began in the spring of 1846, Graham saw action during the Battles of Palo Alto and Resaca de la Palma. From Resaca de la Palma, Taylor sought to move his army to Matamoros, which lay across the Rio Grande. He was hindered in this effort, however, by a lack of small craft and pontoon boats. Graham and several others suggested that they swim across the river to procure Mexican boats, which they would then transfer to the river's north bank. Taylor approved the daring mission, which was threatened by the presence of Mexican snipers. Despite the risks, Graham and his cohort secured numerous boats, which helped Taylor's army cross the Rio Grande. Taylor successfully occupied Matamoros by May 18.

On September 22, during the Battle of Monterrey, Graham led a charge that was repelled by Mexican troops, and he was seriously wounded. Graham lingered near death for nearly three weeks in a field hospital before dying on October 12. He was among 120 U.S. Americans killed in the Battle of Monterrey. Fort Graham, Texas, is named in his honor.

PAUL G. PIERPAOLI JR.

See also

Matamoros; Monterrey, Battle of; Palo Alto, Battle of; Resaca de la Palma, Battle of; Rio Grande; Taylor, Zachary.

References

Bauer, K. Jack. *The Mexican War, 1846–1848.* Lincoln: University of Nebraska Press, 1974.

Eisenhower, John S. D. *So Far from God: The U.S. War with Mexico, 1846–1848.* New York: Random House, 1989.

Henry, Robert S. *The Story of the Mexican War.* Indianapolis, IN: Bobbs-Merrill, 1950.

Grant, Ulysses Simpson
Birth Date: April 27, 1822
Death Date: July 23, 1885

U.S. Army officer and president of the United States (1869–1877). Born in Point Pleasant, Ohio, on April 27, 1822, Hiram Ulysses Grant grew up on his father's farm. Securing appointment to the U.S. Military Academy, West Point, Grant discovered that his name had been changed to Ulysses Simpson (his mother's maiden name) Grant, which he kept. At West Point, Grant excelled only in horsemanship, graduating 21st of 39 cadets in the class of 1843.

Grant served with distinction in the Mexican War (1846–1848), first as a second lieutenant in the 4th U.S. Infantry Regiment. Later serving as regimental quartermaster with the rank of first lieutenant, he saw action under Major General Zachary Taylor in northern Mexico in the Battles of Palo Alto, Resaca de la Palma, and Monterrey. Transferred to Major General Winfield Scott's command in March 1847, he fought in the Battles of Cerro Gordo, Churubusco, and El Molino del Rey. After the latter battle he was brevetted first lieutenant. Grant received a second brevet, to captain, following the Battle of Chapultepec. Ironically, perhaps, Grant strongly opposed the Mexican-American War, a stance he made quite clear in his memoirs, where he characterized the conflict as "the most unjust war ever waged by a stronger nation against a weaker nation."

After the war, Grant was on duty in California, where he was promoted to captain in August 1853. Bored and upset at being separated from his wife, Grant drank heavily and was forced to resign from the army in July 1854, reportedly to avoid a court-martial. He returned to his family in Missouri but was unsuccessful as a farmer and in selling real estate. In 1860 his father gave him a position as a clerk in the family leather store in Galena, Illinois.

In June 1861, a month after the outbreak of the Civil War, Grant secured command of the 21st Illinois Regiment with the rank of colonel. Promoted to brigadier general of volunteers, he received command of the Southwest Missouri Military District that August. He distinguished himself in the early fighting in Kentucky (where he took Paducah without waiting for authorization that September) and in Missouri, in the Battle of Belmont on November 7.

Ulysses S. Grant distinguished himself during the Mexican-American War. Grant actually opposed the war, calling it "the most unjust war ever waged by a stronger nation against a weaker nation." This image of Grant is from around the time of his graduation from West Point in 1843. (Nathaniel W. Stephenson, *Texas and the Mexican War,* 1921)

In the subsequent Union campaigns, Grant performed well, winning significant victories at Forts Henry and Donelson early in 1862. Now known as "Unconditional Surrender Grant," on President Abraham Lincoln's insistence he received promotion to major general of volunteers and command of the Army of Tennessee.

Grant was preparing to attack Corinth, Mississippi, when he was surprised by Confederate forces at Shiloh on April 6, 1862. In the ensuing hard-fought battle, Grant rallied his men and managed to win a victory.

Grant was then ordered to capture the Confederate stronghold of Vicksburg on the Mississippi River. After the Confederates rebuffed his efforts to take the city from the north, Grant struck from the south. After initial assaults failed, he laid siege to Vicksburg, taking the city on July 4, 1863.

Promoted to major general in the regular army and given command of the Military District of the Mississippi on October 4, 1863, Grant directed the relief of the besieged Army of the Cumberland at Chattanooga, Tennessee, and drove the Confederates from Lookout Mountain and Missionary Ridge on November 24–25.

Named commanding general of the armies of the United States, with the revived rank of lieutenant general in April 1864, Grant opened a multipronged offensive against the Confederates with the main effort coming in Virginia against Confederate general Robert E. Lee's Army of Northern Virginia in the so-called Overland Campaign, beginning in May. A series of bloody rebuffs followed, but Grant kept pressing the attack. Following costly engagements in the Wilderness, at Spotsylvania Court House, and Cold Harbor, Grant attempted to get in behind Lee at Petersburg but failed. In August 1864, Grant laid siege to Petersburg, beginning the longest such operation of the war. His victory at Five Forks in late March sealed the fate of Richmond and Petersburg. With his forces being starved into submission, Lee broke free and headed west but was forced to surrender at Appomattox Court House on April 9, 1865.

Following the war, Grant continued as commanding general of the army and was advanced to full general by act of Congress in January 1866. Grant has been regarded as a controversial figure for his supposed failure as president. Elected in November 1868 as a Republican to the first of his two terms in office (1869–1877), he was personally honest but his administration was wracked by scandal. Grant remained popular, however. Becoming bankrupt after leaving the presidency when a brokerage firm failed, Grant developed throat cancer but struggled, with the able assistance of his friend Mark Twain, to complete his memoirs in order to provide for his family financially. He completed the task only two days before his death at Mount McGregor, New York, on July 23, 1885. His *Memoirs* (1885) proved a great literary success and reveal the depth of his intelligence and character. A bold, aggressive commander who avoided hunting because he hated killing things, Grant eschewed military ceremony and dress. A highly effective strategist, he could see the overall situation clearly and determine the correct course of action.

SPENCER C. TUCKER

See also

Cerro Gordo, Battle of; Chapultepec, Battle of; Churubusco, Battle of; El Molino del Rey, Battle of; Monterrey, Battle of; Palo Alto, Battle of; Resaca de la Palma, Battle of; Scott, Winfield; Taylor, Zachary.

References

Dugard, Martin. *The Training Ground: Grant, Lee, Sherman, and Davis in the Mexican War, 1846–1848.* New York: Little, Brown, 2008.

Grant, Ulysses S. *The Personal Memoirs of Ulysses S. Grant.* 1885. Reprinted with an introduction by Brooks D. Simpson. Lincoln: University of Nebraska Press, 1996.

McFeely, William S. *Grant: A Biography.* New York: W. W. Norton, 1981.

Perret, Geoffrey. *Ulysses S. Grant: Soldier and President.* New York: Random House, 1997.

Gray, Andrew Belcher
Birth Date: July 6, 1820
Death Date: April 16, 1862

First chief surveyor of the joint U.S.-Mexican boundary commission charged with establishing the border between the United States and Mexico after the 1848 Treaty of Guadalupe Hidalgo. Born on July 6, 1820, in Norfolk, Virginia, Andrew Belcher Gray, the son of the British consul in Norfolk, was apprenticed to American surveyor Andrew Talcott, assisting him in his survey of the Mississippi River Delta in 1839. From 1839 to 1840, Gray worked for Memucan Hunt, the Texan representative on the joint U.S.-Texan boundary commission. Gray also surveyed Lake Superior and parts of Southern California, including the San Diego area.

After the Mexican-American War, Gray was appointed the chief surveyor of the joint U.S.-Mexican commission charged with establishing the border between the United States and Mexico. Gray, however, argued that the map being used by U.S. boundary commissioner John B. Weller to determine the border was faulty, contending that it would deny the United States the only practical southern railroad route to the Pacific Ocean. Gray's complaints continued after John R. Bartlett replaced Weller, which led to William H. Emory replacing Gray as chief surveyor. Gray's concerns were eventually addressed in the 1853 Gadsden Purchase, which included a 29,670-square-mile area encompassing the southern third of Arizona and a small section of southwestern New Mexico.

In 1852 the Texas Western Railroad contracted Gray to survey a possible rail route from San Antonio, Texas, to California's Pacific coast. During the Civil War, Gray entered the Confederate Army as a captain and served as chief engineer of fortifications along the Mississippi River for the Confederacy. He died in an accident on April 16, 1862, at Fort Pillow, Tennessee.

MICHAEL R. HALL

See also
Bartlett, John Russell; Emory, William Hemsley; Gadsden Purchase; Guadalupe Hidalgo, Treaty of.

References
Goetzmann, William H. *Army Exploration in the American West, 1803–1863*. New Haven, CT: Yale University Press, 1959.
Griswold del Castillo, Richard. *The Treaty of Guadalupe Hidalgo: A Legacy of Conflict*. Norman: University of Oklahoma Press, 1992.

Gray, Mabry B.
Birth Date: 1817
Death Date: 1848

Texas frontier ruffian and soldier. Mabry B. "Mustang" Gray was born in 1817 near Spartanburg, South Carolina. Nothing is known of his early life. In 1835, at the age of 18, he moved to Texas and was given a parcel of land as part of Texas *empresario* Stephen F. Austin's fifth colony. Gray also became involved in the incipient Texas Revolution. By the time he joined the Texas army as an enlisted man in 1836, Gray had earned the sobriquet "Mustang" for an exploit he had performed during a buffalo hunt, at which time he became separated from the rest of the party and lost his mount. He allegedly killed a longhorn and fashioned a lariat from the carcass, which he dropped from a tree onto a wild mustang. He

then supposedly tamed the horse sufficiently to ride it back to civilization. During the Texas Revolution, he saw action at the Battle of San Jacinto. After the Republic of Texas was established, Gray was given a parcel of land in San Patricio County.

Gray soon became infamous for his sometimes barbaric raids in the Nueces Strip between the Nueces River and the Rio Grande, during which Mexicans were routinely brutalized and even murdered. Gray also engaged in cattle poaching in northern Mexico and was even known to burglarize Mexican homes. It is strongly suspected that he was deeply involved in a massacre that occurred between Camargo and Refugio when a group of Mexican traders was attacked, robbed, and left for dead. Only one trader survived, and he later placed Gray at the scene of the assault.

When the Mexican War began in 1846, Gray joined Colonel John Coffee Hays's 1st Texas Mounted Volunteer Riflemen. When the regiment was disbanded in September 1846, Gray was determined to remain in Mexico, leading a ragtag band of former Rangers known as the "Mustangers." Not sure what to do with Gray's irregular company, the U.S. Army instructed it to keep the roads around Monterrey clear of Mexican guerillas and bandits. In the process, Gray's unit was thought to have perpetrated a grisly massacre at Guadalupe Rancho, where nearly the entire male population of the village was summarily shot. The town was then plundered of all items of value.

Some accounts suggest that Gray was taken prisoner during the Battle of Monterrey, but no solid evidence confirms this, and he was not among the prisoners exchanged after Major General Zachary Taylor finalized the Armistice of Monterrey. On July 21, 1847, Gray's Corpus Christi Rangers were mustered out of service, but Gray remained in Mexico, where he settled for a time in Camargo. There he may have become involved with a Mexican woman. He apparently contracted yellow fever or cholera and died in Camargo sometime in 1848. Gray's body was interred in an unmarked grave in the vicinity of that city. After his death, legends about his alleged exploits and proven brutality abounded, making it hard to separate fact from hyperbole. One thing is certain: Mexicans feared and despised him because of his savagery, and they likely expressed no regret at his passing.

PAUL G. PIERPAOLI JR.

See also
Austin, Stephen Fuller; Camargo; Monterrey, Battle of; San Jacinto, Battle of; Texas; Texas Rangers; Texas Revolution.

References
Bauer, K. Jack. *The Mexican War, 1846–1848*. Lincoln: University of Nebraska Press, 1974.
Chamberlain, Samuel E. *My Confession: The Recollections of a Rogue*. New York: Harper & Brothers, 1956.
Collins, Michael L. *Texas Devils: Rangers and Regulars on the Lower Rio Grande, 1846–1861*. Norman: University of Oklahoma Press, 2008.
Dobie, J. Frank. *Mustang Gray: Fact, Tradition, and Song*. Austin: Texas Folklore Society, 1932.
Eisenhower, John S. D. *So Far from God: The U.S. War with Mexico, 1846–1848*. New York: Random House, 1989.

Great Britain

Island nation located off the northwestern coast of Europe, encompassing some 80,100 square miles. Great Britain is surrounded by the Irish Sea, English Channel, the North Sea, and the Atlantic Ocean. Great Britain included England, Scotland, and Wales in Great Britain and Ireland. In 1861 it had a population of approximately 28 million. It also possessed numerous overseas territories, including those in the Caribbean, the island chain of Bermuda, and Canada. Great Britain—then as now—is a constitutional, parliamentary democracy in which much of the day-to-day governing power is vested in a prime minister drawn from Parliament and served by a cabinet, also drawn from Parliament. In the 19th century, the crown generally exercised more power than modern-day kings and queens, but in the main the sovereign deferred to the political process and the prime minister. Although it lay an ocean away from North America, London displayed considerable interest in North America during the last half of the 19th century, no doubt because of its holdings in Canada, but also because it had a vested interest in keeping its principal rivals—which now included the United States—from becoming too powerful.

Britain was quick to recognize the Lone Star Republic and went to significant effort to prevent its annexation to the United States. Believing, as Lord Palmerston wrote, that "it was in the interest of the community of nations that no nation should acquire such a preponderance as to endanger the security of the rest," British diplomats wished to play Texas and the United States against each other in a continuation of its diplomatic strategy of maintaining a balance of power among its potential rivals. Thus, Her Majesty's government played a significant role in convincing Mexico to accept Texan independence.

The years surrounding the Mexican-American War of 1846–1848 were ones of considerable strain in Anglo-American relations and were punctuated by numerous diplomatic crises. In 1839, the so-called Aroostook War erupted between lumberjacks of British-held New Brunswick and Maine, eventually escalating to military preparation on both sides of the border. Formal conflict between the two nations was ultimately averted by hasty diplomatic efforts.

This same region again proved a flashpoint in 1840, when some 100 Americans and a handful of French Canadians gathered north of the Aroostook River to cast their ballots in the American presidential election. The Canadian provincial justice of the peace who arrived on the scene to disperse the meeting was carried away by force by the Americans, leading to an official British protest of encroachment on its dominions. The matter was finally settled only after British prime minister Sir Robert Peel dispatched Privy Counselor Alexander Baring, Lord Ashburton (who was married to an American), as a special envoy to the United States, where he negotiated the 1842 Webster-Ashburton Treaty with U.S. secretary of state Daniel Webster. The treaty adjusted the border between Maine and New Brunswick to three-quarters of a mile north of the 45th parallel, with the rest of the boundary between British North America and the United States set at the 49th parallel (as far west as the Rocky Mountains). Britain also abandoned its right to search American maritime vessels while the United States granted Britain the Halifax-Québec sea route.

Despite the Webster-Ashburton Treaty, tensions between Great Britain and the United States still ran high, and on the West Coast of the Americas an even more serious confrontation occurred. Although the U.S. border was now settled on the East Coast, the vast area of land between the Rockies and the Pacific known as the Oregon Territory was covered by a convention dating to 1818 whereby subjects of both states had been given access to the land.

In 1845, the belligerent and expansionist James K. Polk took office as president, having campaigned on a platform of "Fifty-Four Forty or Fight." This referred to the parallel in the Pacific Northwest at which Polk believed the Anglo-American border should be set. In his inaugural address, Polk declared that the American "right" to the Oregon Territory was "clear and unquestionable," and that force would be used to maintain America's claim to it if necessary. Again, Great Britain was able to disarm the situation with the June 1846 Treaty of Oregon settlement, which set the border at the 49th parallel, consistent with the border east of the Rockies. Nevertheless, tensions persisted, and as late as October 1851 President Zachary Taylor feared a renewal of hostilities between the two nations over fishing rights in the Atlantic.

Notwithstanding this atmosphere of mutual antagonism and distrust, the American conquest of Mexico was made easier by British benevolence. British foreign secretary Henry Temple, Lord Palmerston, adopted a policy of realpolitik concerning the matter. He believed that the United States was a greater power, greater threat, and potentially a greater ally than Mexico; thus, Mexican interests could be sacrificed. The British government, therefore, recognized the American blockade of Mexico's eastern coast at the beginning of the Mexican War, allowed the British consul in Mexico to act as a liaison between Washington and American diplomatic representatives in Mexico, and raised no objection to the U.S. occupation for military purposes of British property in Mexico. In return, British mail packets were permitted by the U.S. Navy to pass through the blockade, and in the few Mexican ports that remained open, favorable tariffs were given to British goods.

There were other signs during the era of the Mexican-American War that Anglo-American relations, despite noticeable strains, were improving. In 1846, the British Parliament at Westminster repealed the Corn Laws, which had protected the British production of wheat through the use of a sliding scale of import duties whereby duties would go down as domestic prices rose and vice versa. Since the colonies were also given tariff preferences under this system, its repeal had a great effect on the agricultural communities of the Canadian provinces, so much so that in 1849 (the year the repeal took effect) a movement spread in Montreal that called for the American annexation of the provinces. Montreal believed that it could profit under the Corn Laws by shipping American grains to Great Britain; with their repeal, Montreal determined that a union with the United States was preferable to a weakened tie with Britain. The United States, however, benefited greatly from the repeal of the Corn Laws and thus spurned the Canadians' advances. British North America would remain British, and in this respect, a key component of American Manifest Destiny was abandoned.

The British government's acceptance of the U.S. position in the Mexican-American War and the repeal of the Corn Laws, however, were exceptions rather than the rule in Anglo-American relations. The British remained suspicious of the United States, particularly its expansionist desires in the Caribbean, and Lord Palmerston maintained a lifelong animosity toward American statesmen. This was manifested most clearly during the American Civil War when Palmerston, as prime minister, at first declared neutrality and then recognized the Confederate States of America as a legitimate belligerent power under international law. Nevertheless, the Mexican-American War was an early indicator that amicable relations between Great Britain and the United States were possible, but it would be many decades (until World War I) before the relationship between the two countries could be said to be friendly.

BENJAMIN J. GROB-FITZGIBBON

See also

Europe and the Mexican-American War; France; Manifest Destiny; Oregon Boundary Dispute; Oregon Treaty; Polk, James Knox; Taylor, Zachary; Temple, Henry, John, 3rd Viscount Palmerston; Webster, Daniel.

References

Bourne, Kenneth. *Britain and the Balance of Power in North America, 1815–1908.* Berkeley: University of California Press, 1967.

Crawford, Martin. *The Anglo-American Crisis of the Mid-Nineteenth Century: The* Times *and America, 1850–1862.* Athens: University of Georgia Press, 1987.

Jones, Howard, and Donald A. Rakestraw. *Prologue to Manifest Destiny: Anglo-American Relations in the 1840s.* Wilmington, DE: Scholarly Resources, 1997.

Stuart, Reginald. *United States Expansionism and British North America, 1775–1871.* Chapel Hill: University of North Carolina Press, 1988.

Greeley, Horace
Birth Date: February 3, 1811
Death Date: November 29, 1872

Polemicist, newspaper editor and publisher, writer, politician, and staunch opponent of the Mexican-American War. Born in Amherst, New Hampshire, on February 3, 1811, Horace Greeley came from an impoverished farming family forced to move frequently to evade bankruptcy. Largely self-educated, he early gravitated toward a journalistic career. First employed as an apprentice printer in Vermont, he moved to New York City in 1831 and worked on various penny dailies. In 1834, he and Jonas Winchester founded the *New-Yorker,* a literary weekly; six years later Greeley launched the *Log Cabin,* a paper that endorsed the Whig Party led by William Henry Harrison and favored Henry Clay's policy of a gradual reduction in protectionist tariffs. Concurrently, Greeley espoused social reform, arguing for the elimination of slavery and capital punishment and stricter controls on alcohol and prostitution. Particularly after the Civil War, he promoted western settlement, giving currency to the slogan "Go west, young man, go west."

Several years after his marriage in 1836, Greeley and his business partner Thomas McElrath merged the *New-Yorker* and the *Log Cabin* to found the *New York Tribune* (1841), a Whig daily that became New York's major newspaper. A galaxy of prominent contributors included Charles Dana, Margaret Fuller, and during the 1850s, even Karl Marx as a European correspondent. Committed to the principle of a free press, Greeley actively opposed the Mexican War and the extension of slavery into the new territories. Likewise, he condemned the Compromise of 1850 and the Fugitive Slave Act and, in 1854, opposed the Kansas-Nebraska Act, which gave settlers freedom to choose whether to extend slavery to the area.

Elected to the House of Representatives, he sat as a Whig member from 1848 to 1849. In 1854, he and other prominent northern Whigs founded the Republican Party. In spite of his initial opposition, Greeley supported Abraham Lincoln's nomination as presidential candidate in 1860. As the secession crisis mounted, he initially argued that the Union should let the "erring sisters" go, provided that their withdrawal was based on a true democratic majority among southern citizens. Even after the outbreak of hostilities, he continued to push for a peaceful solution, a hope that led him to participate in an abortive meeting with southern "peace commissioners" in Niagara Falls, Canada, in 1864. While it is doubtful that Greeley alone spurred Lincoln's emancipation policy, editorials in the *Tribune* served as powerful calls for the liberation of slaves. During the 1863 New York City Draft Riots, Greeley showed great courage in refusing to vacate the *Tribune* offices and braving a racist mob that had gathered outside the building. His two-volume history of the Civil War, *The American Conflict* (1864 and 1866), although biased, remains one of the most readable contemporary accounts of the conflict.

During the Reconstruction years (1865–1877), Greeley distinguished himself as a moderate voice calling for reconciliation; in 1867, his paper lost many subscribers when he guaranteed bail for former Confederate president Jefferson Davis. Initially a supporter of Ulysses S. Grant in the 1868 presidential election, he was soon disillusioned by what he viewed as Grant's vindictive southern policies and massive government corruption. He thus broke with the Radical Republicans and helped form a new Liberal Republican Party, which nominated him as presidential candidate to run against Grant in the scandal-ridden campaign of 1872. Greeley was soundly defeated, largely because his conciliatory southern policies gained him little support in the populous North. Bankrupt, exhausted, and devastated by the recent death of his wife, he died in Pleasantville, New York, shortly after the election, on November 29, 1872.

ANNA M. WITTMANN

See also
Abolitionism; Davis, Jefferson Finis; Grant, Ulysses Simpson (Hiram Ulysses Grant); Lincoln, Abraham; Opposition to the Mexican-American War, U.S.; Republican Party; Slavery; Whigs.

References
Lunde, Erik S. *Horace Greeley*. New York: Twayne, 1981.
Williams, Robert C. *Horace Greeley: Champion of American Freedom*. New York: New York University Press, 2006.

Green, Duff

Birth Date: August 15, 1791
Death Date: June 10, 1875

American journalist, politician, and diplomat who was a key figure in the popularization of Manifest Destiny and the annexation of Texas. Born on August 15, 1791, in Woodford County, Kentucky, Duff Green served in the Kentucky militia during the War of 1812. After the war, he studied medicine for a time and then moved to Missouri, where he was elected to the state House of Representatives in 1820 and the state senate in 1822. In 1825, he moved to Washington, D.C., and purchased the *United States Telegraph,* which he edited until 1835. Initially a mouthpiece for the policies of Andrew Jackson, in 1831 Green supported John C. Calhoun in his quarrel with Jackson over the issue of states' rights. Between 1835 and 1838, Green, who had become a vocal supporter of the

American diplomat Duff Green helped to negotiate how sums owed Mexico by the United States under the terms of the Treaty of Guadalupe Hidalgo were to be paid. (Library of Congress)

newly formed Whig Party, was the editor of the *Reformation,* a publication that championed Manifest Destiny, the annexation of Texas, free trade, and states' rights.

In September 1844, Secretary of State Calhoun, interested in the annexation of Texas, sent Green to Galveston, Texas, as U.S. consul to monitor the political situation between Mexico and Texas. Green reported that conditions were conducive to the annexation of Texas, writing that "war with Mexico will cost us nothing and [will] reinstate us in the estimation of other nations." He also reported to Calhoun that the Mexicans were adamantly opposed to selling California and New Mexico to the United States. Green even advocated the use of Native Americans and Texan forces to foment an insurrection in Mexico's northern provinces, thereby forcing Mexico to cede that territory to Texas or the United States. Neither Texan nor U.S. policy makers thought much of the scheme, however.

Green further alienated himself from Texan leaders when he suggested that he would begin a revolution to overthrow Texan leaders who did not champion the annexation of northern Mexico. He later apologized for that suggestion, but he continued to plot an insurrection after becoming a citizen of Texas in 1845.

After the Mexican-American War, President Zachary Taylor sent Green to Mexico City to negotiate how the money promised Mexico in the Treaty of Guadalupe Hidalgo would be paid. Green also saved his country a considerable sum of money by working out an arrangement whereby much of the payment would be made by the exchange of goods rather than by cash. Green subsequently played a major role in the transportation revolution as a developer of canal and railroad projects in Georgia and Alabama. When the Civil War broke out in 1861, Green was involved in developing iron works for the Confederacy and was an informal adviser to President Jefferson Davis on foreign policy. After that conflict ended, he was influential in southern Reconstruction. Green died on June 10, 1875, in Dalton, Georgia.

MICHAEL R. HALL

See also
Calhoun, John Caldwell; Guadalupe Hildalgo, Treaty of; Jackson, Andrew; Manifest Destiny; Taylor, Zachary; Texas; Texas Revolution; Tyler, John.

References
Belko, W. Stephen. *The Invincible Duff Green: Whig of the West.* Columbia: University of Missouri Press, 2006.
Caruso, A. Brooke. *The Mexican Spy Company: United States Covert Operations in Mexico, 1845–1848.* Jefferson, NC: McFarland, 1991.

Green, Thomas Jefferson

Birth Date: February 14, 1802
Death Date: December 12, 1863

Texas military officer and political figure who served as second in command to William S. Fisher, who led the remaining 308 men of the Somervell Expedition after Alexander Somervell ordered the disbandment of the expedition on December 19, 1842. Born on February 14, 1802, in Warren County, North Carolina, Thomas Jefferson Green briefly attended the U.S. Military Academy at West Point and was elected to the North Carolina legislature in 1823. After serving one term, he moved to Florida, where he was elected to serve in the territorial legislature. In 1836 Green moved to Bexar County, Texas, where he was commissioned a brigadier general in the Texas army and elected to serve in the Texas House of Representatives. Green traveled throughout the United States recruiting volunteers for the Texas army. In 1837, Green briefly served in the Texas senate.

On October 3, 1842, following a series of Mexican raids in Texas, Green and nearly 700 volunteers joined a punitive expedition against Mexico. After successful military engagements at Laredo and Guerrero, the majority of the expedition forces returned to Texas. When Alexander Somervell ordered the disbandment of the expedition, Green joined the group of men that eventually became known as the Mier Expedition. On December 26, 1842, after two days of battle in Mier, Mexican general Pedro de Ampudia's forces captured the survivors, who were jailed in Perote Castle.

After escaping from the prison on July 2, 1843, Green made his way back to Texas, was reelected to the Texas legislature, and introduced a bill that declared the Rio Grande to be the official southern boundary of Texas. Green subsequently moved to California in 1849 and was elected to the California senate in 1850, thus serving in four different state legislatures. There he sponsored the bill that created the University of California. He eventually returned to Warren County, North Carolina, where he died on December 12, 1863, after serving in the Confederate Army.

MICHAEL R. HALL

See also

Ampudia, Pedro de; Congress, Texan; Fisher, William S.; Mier Expedition; Perote Castle; Texas.

References

Green, William J. *Journal of the Texian Expedition against Mier.* New York: Harper and Brothers, 1845.

Texas House of Representatives. *Biographical Directory of the Texan Conventions and Congresses, 1832–1845.* Austin, TX: Book Exchange, 1941.

Gregg, Josiah
Birth Date: July 19, 1806
Death Date: February 5, 1850

Trader, explorer, chronicler of events along the Santa Fe Trail, and a correspondent during the Mexican-American War. Josiah Gregg was born on July 19, 1806, in Overton County, Tennessee. As a child, Gregg moved west with the other members of his family, settling near Independence, Missouri. Gregg tried teaching and studying law and medicine but realized that none of these enterprises suited him. When doctors recommended a trip to the prairies to ease symptoms of tuberculosis, Gregg joined a group of merchants traveling on the Santa Fe Trail in 1831. He became a trader along the trail, traversing its entire length four times between 1831 and 1840. Gregg continued his journeys into Arkansas and Texas, keeping notes as he also did on his trips to Santa Fe. In 1844, his book *Commerce of the Prairies* was published, detailing his travels on the Santa Fe Trail. Gregg's writings are rich in the descriptions of the botany, geology, geography, and cultural makeup of the places he visited.

When war commenced between the United States and Mexico in 1846, Gregg joined the Arkansas volunteers who were traveling to Chihuahua, Mexico, to reinforce Brigadier General John E. Wool's force. Gregg's official position in the military is unclear. He claimed that he was promised the commission of major, although he later refused to accept his pay, with the statement that his appointment had never been made official. Gregg's unofficial position was that of correspondent, and it was in this capacity that he probably made his most valuable contributions. He wrote about his observations at the Battle of Buena Vista on February 23, 1847, and about his experiences with Colonel Alexander William Doniphan's Missouri volunteers. Many of his stories were printed in the United States and served to inform U.S. citizens of various aspects of the war. Gregg also acted as a guide and interpreter.

In his writings, Gregg provided valuable insights into U.S. and Mexican successes and failures. In a few instances, he criticized the U.S. Army's treatment of Mexican citizens. For example, Gregg was upset that American officers took over Mexican homes for lodging without compensating the owners. More than likely, his earlier travels into Mexico had given Gregg a degree of sympathy for Mexican citizens that the officers lacked.

Following the Battle of Buena Vista, Gregg traveled with Brigadier General Wool's men to Saltillo and then left for Chihuahua to meet with a merchant's caravan carrying goods for Gregg. Colonel Doniphan's Missouri volunteers had recently taken Chihuahua, and the caravan followed the American troops into the city. Once Gregg arrived, Doniphan marched his men, accompanied by a group of merchants that included James and Susan Shelby Magoffin, another chronicler of the Santa Fe Trail and the Mexican War, to Saltillo.

Gregg briefly returned to the United States but went back to Saltillo as a physician in 1847. He continued to travel throughout Mexico and the American Southwest until he died on February 25, 1850, the result of complications from a fall from his horse near Clearlake, California.

AMY MESCHKE PORTER

See also

Buena Vista, Battle of; Doniphan, Alexander William; Santa Fe–Chihuahua Trail; Magoffin, James Wiley; Magoffin, Susan Shelby; Saltillo; War Correspondents; Wool, John Ellis.

References

Gregg, Josiah. *Commerce of the Prairies.* Edited by Max L. Moorhead. Norman: University of Oklahoma Press, 1954.

Gregg, Josiah. *Diaries and Letters of Josiah Gregg: Excursions into Mexico and California, 1847–1850.* Edited by Garland Fulton. Norman: University of Oklahoma Press, 1944.

Horgan, Paul. *Josiah Gregg and His Vision of the Early West.* New York: Farrar, Straus & Giroux, 1979.

Gregory, Francis Hoyt
Birth Date: October 9, 1789
Death Date: October 4, 1866

U.S. naval officer. Born in Norwalk, Connecticut, on October 9, 1789, Francis Hoyt Gregory received a midshipman's warrant on January 26, 1809. He was promoted to lieutenant on June 14, 1814, to master commandant on April 28, 1828, and to captain on January 18, 1838.

Gregory assumed command of the frigate *Raritan,* assigned to the Brazil Squadron in 1844. In May 1846 the *Raritan* was part of Commodore David Conner's Home Squadron in the Gulf of Mexico. Convinced that hostilities with Mexico were imminent, Conner moved part of his squadron from Veracruz to a position off the mouth of the Brazos River, where the ships might be able to support U.S. troops under Brigadier General Zachary Taylor. On May 8, 1846, Major John Monroe, commander of Fort Polk, the American supply base at Port Isabel, aware of actual fighting between U.S. and Mexican forces, asked Conner for assistance in defending the fort. Conner sent to his aid 500 sailors and marines under Gregory's command. Believing from a false report that Taylor had been defeated in battle, Gregory requested permission to go to Taylor's rescue. Knowing that the sailors and marines were not trained for land combat, Conner refused. In any event, the report of a defeat turned out to be false, for Taylor had won the Battle of Palo Alto on May 8. With the Mexican withdrawal across the Rio Grande, Gregory's force returned to their ships on May 13.

The *Raritan* then took part in the blockade of the Mexican port of Veracruz and the capture of Tampico on November 14. The following month, because the enlistments of Gregory's crew were about to expire and the frigate *Cumberland* in need of repair, Conner ordered Gregory and Captain French Forrest of the *Cumberland* and their crews to switch places, and Gregory then sailed that frigate to the Norfolk (Gosport) Navy Yard.

During 1848–1851, Gregory commanded the African Squadron. At the beginning of 1861, Gregory had been in the navy for 52 years: almost 20 years in sea service, 14 years ashore, and 18 years awaiting orders in a navy that had too many officers for assignments. Gregory was placed on the retired list on December 21, 1861, by reason of his age. During the Civil War, however, he supervised the construction of gunboats in private shipyards for the U.S. Navy. He was commissioned a rear admiral on the retired list with the effective date of July 16, 1862. Having served 57 years

in the navy, Gregory died in Brooklyn, New York, on October 4, 1866. Three of his sons were also naval officers.

SPENCER C. TUCKER

See also

Blockade, Naval; Conner, David; Forrest, French; Fort Polk; Palo Alto, Battle of; Tampico; Taylor, Zachary; United States Navy; Veracruz; Victoria and Tampico, Occupation of.

References

Bauer, K. Jack. *Surfboats and Horse Marines: U.S. Naval Operations in the Mexican War, 1846–48.* Annapolis, MD: United States Naval Institute, 1969.

Callahan, Edward W., ed. *List of Officers of the Navy of the United States and of the Marine Corps from 1775 to 1900.* 1901. Reprint, New York: Haskell House, 1969.

Thompson, Kenneth E. *Civil War Commodores and Admirals: A Biographical Directory of All Eighty-Eight Union and Confederate Navy Officers Who Attained Commissioned Flag Rank during the War.* Portland, ME: Thompson, 2001.

Guadalupe Hidalgo, Treaty of
Event Date: February 2, 1848

Diplomatic agreement formally ending hostilities between the United States and Mexico signed on February 2, 1848, in a village outside Mexico City called La Villa de Guadalupe Hidalgo. In addition to bringing the Mexican-American War to an official close, the Treaty of Guadalupe Hidalgo established the majority of the new U.S.-Mexican border.

Treaty negotiations to end the Mexican-American War commenced during the final months of the fighting, after Antonio López de Santa Anna, commanding general of the Mexican army and president of Mexico, agreed to a mutual cease-fire—the Armistice of Tacubaya—with U.S. major general Winfield Scott on August 22, 1847. The first round of talks began 10 days later, on September 1, when a four-man Mexican delegation composed of José Bernardo Couto, Miguel Atristain, General Ignacio Mora y Villamil, and former president José Joaquín Herrera met with the principal U.S. negotiator, Nicholas P. Trist. Although the armistice broke down and was abrogated on September 6, these initial meetings established talking points for future treaty negotiations. The points included U.S. annexation of Southern California, Arizona, and New Mexico; the status of Mexican peoples in newly acquired American territories; the location of the Texas-Mexico border; and the state of American citizens' land claims against the Mexican government. Disagreements regarding the Texas-Mexico border ended the first round of talks. Mexican leaders refused to recognize the Rio Grande as the border between Texas and Mexico, instead claiming the Nueces River farther north.

The cease-fire lasted for less than a month. In an effort to pressure Mexican leaders back into negotiations, Scott lifted the cease-fire and advanced American military forces into

The Treaty of Guadalupe Hidalgo, shown here and signed on February 2, 1848, ended the Mexican-American War and settled the majority of the U.S.-Mexican border. Territory received from Mexico became all or part of 10 U.S. states, with the United States paying Mexico $15 million. (Library of Congress)

Mexico City on September 13, 1847. Escaping the city, Santa Anna resigned the presidency in disgrace on September 16 and named Manuel de la Peña y Peña as his successor. Regional chaos ensued as rural insurgents and irregular troops carried out insurgency operations against the American occupation forces. The fighting proved especially violent and bloody as insurgents struck U.S. Army supply trains and escort units traveling between Veracruz and Mexico City.

In light of popular uprisings around Mexico City, both American and Mexican diplomats sought to end the war with all due haste. The heavy cost of the war, mounting political opposition to the fighting, and adverse publicity all helped push Washington back to the negotiating table. By late 1847, the cost for the American government to continue combat operations in Mexico was running $22 million a year. President James K. Polk also faced rising congressional hostility to the war among a bipartisan coalition of Whigs and conservative Democrats.

A government shutdown prevented Mexican leaders from reopening treaty talks until late November 1847. Peña y Peña was president in title only, unable to establish a congressional quorum at the temporary national capital of Querétaro, 100 miles north of Mexico City. Mexican legislators remained starkly divided over whether to continue the war against American military forces or to secure a treaty. Finally, on November 11, 1847, the Mexican Congress elected General Pedro María Anaya as interim president. General Anaya appointed Peña y Peña as minister of foreign relations and named Couto, Atristain, and Luis Gonzago Cuevas as peace commissioners. Treaty negotiations now appeared ready to reopen.

In Washington, however, Polk had grown increasingly disgusted with the stalled diplomatic talks. The president had received no word of the initial Santa Anna–Scott cease-fire settlement between October and early November 1847. Consequently, Polk dispatched a series of letters through U.S. secretary of state James Buchanan to Trist that recalled the chief U.S. negotiator to Washington and replaced Scott with Major General William O. Butler. On November 24, immediately after reading the letters, Trist notified the Mexican government that he had been recalled, and that preparations were under way for him to leave the Mexican capital.

Trist, however, ignored the presidential recall to Washington. Receiving assurances from Peña y Peña and the Mexican government that U.S. territorial demands would be met, Trist reopened treaty negotiations on January 2, 1848. U.S. and Mexican diplomats met for one month and reached agreement in principle over a series of provisions that eventually found expression in the final treaty.

The Mexican government agreed to the United States' annexation of lower portions of present-day California, Nevada, New Mexico, Arizona, Colorado, Wyoming, and Utah. In turn, the U.S. government agreed to pay $3.25 million to assume all insurance claims levied by American citizens against the Mexican government and to pay $15 million to the Mexican government in war damages.

Debates concerning the political border between the United States and Mexico ended when Article V established the Rio Grande as the boundary between Texas and the northern Mexican provinces. Additionally, Mexicans who remained in the territories gained by the United States during the war became immediately eligible for American citizenship and retained religious liberty as well as personal property security.

On February 2, 1848, Mexican negotiators and Nicholas Trist signed the treaty in the village of Guadalupe Hidalgo. Trist then dispatched James L. Freaner, his longtime friend and a war correspondent for the *New Orleans Delta,* to deliver the treaty to Secretary of State Buchanan. Freaner arrived in Washington late in the evening of February 19. After debating and amending its articles and provisions, the U.S. Senate ratified the Treaty of Guadalupe Hidalgo by a vote of 38–14 on March 10, 1848. Opposition over U.S. Senate amendments made to civil and property rights for former Mexican citizens, however, postponed Mexican congressional ratification until late May 1848. The Mexican Chamber of Deputies eventually voted 51–35 in favor of its ratification on May 19, 1848, and the Mexican Senate ratified the treaty with a vote of 33–4 on May 30, 1848.

In its final form, the Treaty of Guadalupe Hidalgo exemplified both the diplomatic triumphs and the increasing political turmoil that American leaders confronted throughout the 19th century. Following the Mexican-American War, the United States appeared to have fulfilled much of its Manifest Destiny policy by annexing large tracts of land across the North American Southwest and along the Pacific Ocean. Indeed, the dream of a nation stretching from the Atlantic to the Pacific had finally been realized.

Movement into these newly acquired territories, however, shattered close to 30 years of domestic political peace by reopening the heated sectional debate about whether to allow slavery in new territories. In light of its ratification on both sides of the Rio Grande, the ambiguous wording that remained in the Treaty of Guadalupe Hidalgo provoked numerous border disputes that ultimately led to the Gadsden Purchase in 1853, which once and for all settled border questions in the Southwest.

For Mexico, the Treaty of Guadalupe Hidalgo was a devastating psychological blow. The military defeats of the war and the loss of territories enshrined in the treaty constituted nothing less than a national trauma. This was especially true for the elites, as political and military leaders challenged one another on the best way to revive their country. Mexico itself fell into a long period of turmoil, civil war, and foreign intervention. New leaders eventually came to the fore, however. They drove out the foreign invaders, united their country, and established the foundations of a modern state.

JASON GODIN

See also

Anaya, Pedro María de; Arizona; Buchanan, James; Butler, William Orlando; California; Colorado; Congress, Mexican; Congress, U.S.; Couto, José Bernardo; Cuevas, Luis Gonzaga; Freaner, James L.; Frémont, John Charles; Gadsden Purchase; Herrera, José Joaquín de; Manifest Destiny; Mexican Cession; Mexico, Occupation of; Mora y Villamil, Ignacio; Nevada; New Mexico; Peña y Peña, Manuel de la; Politics, Mexican; Politics, U.S.; Polk, James K.; Rio Grande; Santa Anna, Antonio López de; Scott, Winfield; Slavery; Texas; Trist, Nicholas Philip; Tacubaya; Utah; Veracruz.

References

Bauer, K. Jack. *The Mexican War, 1846–1848.* New York: Macmillan, 1974.

Clary, David A. *Eagles and Empire: The United States, Mexico, and the Struggle for a Continent.* New York: Bantam Books, 2009.

Griswold del Castillo, Richard. *The Treaty of Guadalupe Hidalgo: A Legacy of Conflict.* Norman: University of Oklahoma Press, 1990.

Ohrt, Wallace. *Defiant Peacemaker: Nicholas Trist in the Mexican War.* College Station: Texas A&M University Press, 1997.

Tenenbaum, Barbara. "Neither a Borrower Nor a Lender Be: Financial Constraints and the Treaty of Guadalupe Hidalgo." In *The Mexican and Mexican American Experience in the 19th Century,* edited by Jaime E. Rodríguez O., 68–84. Tempe, AZ: Bilingual Press, 1989.

Guaymas, Battle of
Event Date: October 19–20, 1847

U.S. naval/amphibious operation conducted at Guaymas, Mexico, on October 19–20, 1847. Guaymas is a major Mexican port city on the Gulf of California (Sea of Cortez) in the state of Sonora. During the Mexican-American War it was blockaded and occupied by ships of the U.S. Navy's Pacific Squadron. At the beginning of the war, U.S. ships and their crews commanded by Commodore Robert F. Stockton and troops commanded by Brigadier General Stephen W. Kearny battled Mexican forces for possession of (Alta) California.

As a part of these operations, Captain Samuel F. Du Pont of the sloop *Cyane* arrived off Guaymas on October 6, 1846, and demanded that ships anchored in the port be surrendered. The Mexican commandant, Colonel Antonio Campuzano, refused. The following day, Du Pont dispatched a boarding party to seize and burn the Mexican brig *Condor* and two gunboats. Thereafter, the port was blockaded.

By January 1847, Mexican forces in Alta California had been defeated, but the U.S. Navy's campaign in the Gulf of California continued. On March 2, Commodore James Biddle replaced Stockton as commander of the Pacific Squadron and was in turn superseded on July 19 by Commodore W. Branford Shubrick. On October 17, 1847, Shubrick launched a major amphibious operation against Guaymas, under the command of Captain Elie A. F. Lavallette in the frigate *Congress,* accompanied by Commander John B. Montgomery in the sloop *Portsmouth* and the former Chilean brigantine blockade runner *Argo,* seized by the *Portsmouth* earlier. The three ships arrived off Guaymas on October 17.

The next day, on October 18, Lavallette sent ashore a demand for the surrender of the town, which Colonel Campuzano, commanding a garrison of some 400 men, rejected. Lavallette then landed a 32-pounder from the Congress on Isle Almagre, placing it in position to control the harbor, and undertook other preparations to shell Guyamas. On October 18, at noon, all preparations having been completed, Lavallette sent ashore a formal surrender demand. It too was rejected, whereupon Lavallette notified Campuzano that the American ships would commence a bombardment of the city after a delay of two hours to allow women and children to be evacuated. When Campuzano asked for five hours, Lavallette agreed. At the expiration of this period, however, it was almost dark, and so Lavallette delayed his fire until the following morning, October 20. During the night, Campuzano withdrew his garrison to Bocachicacampo, four miles up the coast.

On the morning of October 20, the American ships shelled Guaymas for an hour, doing considerable property damage and killing one person, ironically an Englishman. After the town surrendered, U.S. Marines went ashore and occupied it. The following day, they destroyed Mexican fortifications and collected arms and ammunition from the city's inhabitants. Lavallette, lacking the men to garrison the town securely, charged Commander Thomas

O. Selfridge, captain of the sloop *Dale,* which had arrived at Guaymas on November 8, to anchor in the roadstead and maintain order. Campuzano's men harassed the Americans in the next few weeks, and on the night of November 16–17, 350 of them moved back into Guaymas.

On November 17 Selfridge led ashore a landing party of 50 sailors and 17 marines, with one 6-pounder boat gun, against the Mexicans at Guaymas, but they were pinned down until the *Dale* provided fire support and its guns drove the Mexican forces from the town. Between November 1847 and April 1848, landing parties from the *Dale* harassed Campuzano's men near Guaymas until the latter were thoroughly weakened and demoralized. Reportedly, by the end of the war, every building in Guaymas had been damaged in the fighting.

Paul David Nelson

See also

Bocachicacampo, Skirmish at; Campuzano, Antonio; Du Pont, Samuel Francis; Lavallette, Elie Augustus Frederick; Shubrick, William Branford; Sonora y Sinaloa; United States Navy.

References

Bauer, K. Jack. *The Mexican War, 1846–1848.* New York: Macmillan, 1974.

Bauer, K. Jack. *Surfboats and Horse Marines: U.S. Naval Operations in the Mexican War.* Annapolis, MD: U.S. Naval Institute, 1969.

Connor, Seymour V., and Odie B. Faulk. *North America Divided: The Mexican War, 1846–1848.* New York: Oxford University Press, 1971.

Craven, Tunis A. M. *A Naval Campaign in the Californias—1846–1848: The Journal of Lieutenant Tunis Augustus Macdonough Craven, U.S.N., United States Sloop of War* Dale. San Francisco: Book Club of California, 1973.

Ripley, Roswell Sabine. *War with Mexico.* Vol. 2. New York: Harper and Brothers, 1899.

Guerrero, Vicente
Birth Date: August 10, 1783
Death Date: February 14, 1831

Leading revolutionary general of the Mexican Wars of Independence (1810–1821) and president of Mexico (1829). Vicente Guerrero was born on August 10, 1783, in Tuxtla in modern-day Guerrero. Guerrero's parents were peasants, and he was largely uneducated, spending much of his youth as a manual laborer and muleteer. In New Spain, European-born Spaniards considered themselves superior to racially mixed Mexicans and closely guarded their wealth, power, and social status. Possessing African, indigenous, and Spanish ancestry, Guerrero was thus committed to ending New Spain's discriminatory racial hierarchy and officially defined caste distinctions. He also came to champion the abolition of slavery.

Miguel Hidalgo de Costilla helped initiate the Mexican War of Independence in 1810. Hidalgo soon commissioned José María Morelos y Pavón to raise an insurgent army in southern Mexico.

Excited that Hidalgo and Morelos were proposing sweeping social and political changes to redress the grievances of the peasants, Guerrero enlisted in Morelos's army in December 1810. A courageous and resourceful leader, Guerrero rose through the ranks and became a general in March 1816. He was particularly adept at waging guerrilla operations against Spanish colonial forces and was quite successful in recruiting many Indians to the cause.

In November 1820, the viceroy of New Spain ordered Colonel Agustín de Iturbide to subdue Guerrero, who was then leading insurgent forces in Oaxaca. Iturbide's royalist troops failed to quell Guerrero's insurgents, however, and in January 1821 Guerrero urged Iturbide to support independence from Spain. The following month, Guerrero and Iturbide formally agreed to the Plan of Iguala, which stipulated that the new independent nation of Mexico would be ruled by a constitutional monarchy and officially Roman Catholic. The plan also guaranteed equal treatment under the law for all citizens, without regard to their ancestral heritage. In September 1821, Iturbide and Guerrero marched triumphantly into Mexico City.

Two years later, however, Guerrero joined the rebellion that toppled Iturbide, who in May 1822 had declared himself emperor. In the summer of 1823 Guerrero served in the interim government (the supreme executive power), and he acted as regional military commander during the presidency of Guadalupe Victoria (1824–1828).

Sometime in mid-1825 Guerrero joined the York Rite Freemasons (he later became their grand master), and three years later Guerrero ran for the presidency against his rival Manuel Gómez Pedraza, around whom former Scottish Rite Masons had rallied. Gómez Pedraza carried 11 states and Guerrero carried 9, so by law Gómez Pedraza won the presidency, but Guerrero and his fellow Yorkists refused to accept the election results and accused Gómez Pedraza of electoral fraud. General Antonio López de Santa Anna and other Guerrero supporters then led a successful revolt against Gómez Pedraza, who subsequently fled the country.

Guerrero took office on April 1, 1829, under dire conditions. Not only did he inherit a bankrupt government, but that July Spain landed forces at Tampico in an attempt to retake its former colony. Santa Anna led the Guerrero administration's defense against the Spanish and forced the withdrawal of their army in September. That same month Guerrero angered many American and European settlers in Texas by decreeing the end of slavery throughout Mexico. Guerrero had hoped to discourage slave-owning settlers from remaining in Texas, but fear of rebellion by settlers kept local authorities in Texas from enforcing the decree.

Meanwhile, Guerrero's opponents were succeeding in forcing his supporters, including Lorenzo de Zavala (his finance minister), out of government. In December 1829, backers of Mexican vice president Anastasio Bustamante took control of the nation, and on January 1, 1830, the Mexican Congress declared Bustamante president of Mexico. Guerrero then fled south, where a guerrilla war against Bustamante soon broke out. In February 1831, however, an Italian merchant employed by the government captured Guer-rero and turned him over to authorities, who summarily court-martialed and executed him that February 14.

DAVID M. CARLETTA AND PEDRO SANTONI

See also

Bustamante y Oseguera, Anastasio; Castes; Freemasonry; Gómez Pedraza, Manuel; Mexico; Mexico, 1821–1854; Santa Anna, Antonio López de; Slavery; Texas; Texas Revolution.

References

Green, Stanley C. *The Mexican Republic: The First Decade 1823–1832.* Pittsburgh: University of Pittsburgh Press, 1987.

Sims, Harold. *The Expulsion of Mexico's Spaniards, 1821–1836.* Pittsburgh: University of Pittsburgh Press, 1990.

Vincent, Theodore G. *The Legacy of Vicente Guerrero, Mexico's First Black Indian President.* Gainesville: University of Florida Press, 2001.

Guerrilla Warfare

Irregular military operations waged by independently function-ing forces that are sometimes part of a regular army. Guerrilla or partisan warfare emphasizes small-unit tactics characterized by hit-and-run raids, ambushes, sabotage, and, in some cases, terrorism perpetrated by mobile forces. In its initial phase, such warfare usually focuses on an enemy's supplies and lines of com-munication rather than on main combat formations. During the war with the United States, Mexico relied on guerrilla warfare for four reasons. First, the cavalry arm of the Mexican army tradition-ally had been the best branch of that service, and mounted troops are well-suited to the high level of mobility required of guerrillas. Second, a substantial percentage of the fighting during Mexico's War of Independence (1810–1821) and during the interwar years (1821–1846) had been waged by guerrillas, so Mexicans had much experience in irregular warfare. Third, the destruction of much of the Mexican army in fixed battles with the Americans left the nation with little alternative than to turn to this method of warfare. Finally, American lines of supply and communication, necessar-ily attenuated by operations deep in the Mexican heartland, made tempting targets for interdiction.

During the Mexican-American War, two major guerrilla forces operated against American forces. In northern Mexico, General José de Urrea led Mexican cavalry units in repeated attacks on the supply lines of U.S. major general Zachary Taylor's forces that ran between the port of Camargo and Taylor's base at Monterrey. His efforts forced the Americans to send substantial escorts with each convoy.

Urrea showed little mercy in his campaign and is best remem-bered for the Ramos Massacre. In this February 1847 encounter,

A Mexican guerrillero (guerrilla) of the Mexican-American War. A Currier & Ives lithograph from 1848. (Library of Congress)

his forces executed 50 American teamsters after having defeated the forces escorting them. Although he controlled a considerable amount of territory, Urrea never possessed the strength to attack Taylor's main forces at Monterrey.

In central Mexico, the primary focus of guerrilla activity was Major General Winfield Scott's supply route running from the port of Veracruz west to Mexico City. Here, volunteer guerrilla bands authorized by substitute president Pedro María Anaya in April 1847 continually harassed U.S. supply convoys. From June of that year until the signing of the Treaty of Guadalupe Hidalgo on February 2, 1848, each U.S. convoy required a minimum escort of 1,200 men, which cost the U.S. Army many men who could have otherwise been utilized in direct combat roles. In October 1847, Scott assigned additional forces to counterguerrilla duties. This included garrisons of 750 men each at Perote, Puente Nacional, Río Frío, and San Juan de Ulúa as well as a 2,200-man force at Puebla. When those numbers are added to those of the escort forces, the number of U.S. troops in central Mexico assigned to counterguerrilla duties amounted to almost a quarter of Scott's entire force. In spite of such efforts and the subsequent U.S. decision to form a mounted counterguerrilla unit composed of both regular dragoons and Texas Rangers, the route remained a dangerous one throughout the war.

In both northern and central Mexico, Mexican guerrilla force commanders never attempted to fully involve the main body of the civilian population in their activities. Previous efforts to do so during both Mexico's War of Independence and in subsequent conflicts had demonstrated that armed civilians soon used their newly acquired weapons and training to turn against the existing socioeconomic order. Furthermore, the emergence of armed groups of indigenous peasants who resisted the Mexican state in their efforts to protect both their autonomy and their lands forced Mexican authorities to abandon any hopes for a protracted struggle against the U.S. Army and to refocus their military efforts on crushing the guerrillas.

IRVING W. LEVINSON

See also

Álvarez, Juan; Anaya, Pedro María de; Camargo; Cavalry and Dragoons; Mexico; Mexico, Army; Mexico City; Mexico City Campaign; Northern Mexico Theater of War, Overview; Puebla; Scott, Winfield; Taylor, Zachary; Texas Rangers; United States Army; Urrea y Elías Gonzales, José de; Veracruz.

References

Chambers, John Whiteclay, II. *The Oxford Companion to American Military History.* New York: Oxford University Press, 1999.

Johannsen, Robert W. *To the Halls of the Montezumas: The Mexican War in the American Imagination.* Oxford, UK: Oxford University Press, 1985.

Levinson, Irving W. *Wars within Wars: Mexican Guerillas, Mexican Elites, and the United States of American, 1846–1848.* Fort Worth: Texas Christian University Press, 2005.

Guizot, François
Birth Date: October 4, 1787
Death Date: September 12, 1874

French statesman and historian. Born in Nîmes, France, on October 4, 1787, François Guizot was the son of a prosperous Protestant lawyer and advocate of federalism. The elder Guizot was executed during the French Revolution of 1789, and his property was confiscated. Educated in Geneva, François Guizot was influenced by English political thought. From 1812 he was professor of modern history at the University of Paris. He held government posts after the restoration, but his moderate views offended ultraroyalists, and he soon lost the posts and his teaching position. Guizot then turned to writing and in the 1820s produced important books treating English history and European and French civilization. An advocate of reform, in 1830 he won election to the Chamber of Deputies.

In the July 1830 Revolution, Guizot supported the Duc d'Orleans for the throne and then held ministerial posts for 13 of the 18 years of King Louis Philippe's reign. As minister of public instruction, in 1833 he secured passage of France's first basic law on primary education. From 1840 to 1848, he was minister of foreign affairs and de facto head of the ministry. Guizot advocated conservative policies designed to maintain peace abroad and order at home and to restrict political rights to the wealthy. He was an adroit practitioner of parliamentary corruption and refused to end this or to expand political rights. He also helped foster a tenuous entente with the British, which some of his detractors alleged amounted to subservience to British interests.

Under Guizot's influence, a new French concept of colonialism evolved. Colonies received new military and commercial significance. In the Far East, this began to supplant French traditional interest in missionary activities. More concerned with restoration of France's position in Europe than expansion in Asia, Guizot initially resisted suggestions that he send a naval squadron to the Far East. Following the 1841 British acquisition of Hong Kong as a consequence of the Opium War, however, Guizot changed his mind. Two years later, he sent sizable French naval forces under the command of Admiral Cécille and Captain Léonard Charner to Asian waters. Guizot instructed his naval commanders to acquire positions equal to those the British enjoyed in Hong Kong and Singapore and the Portuguese in Macao and Manila. But he also wanted the French to avoid operations along the coast of Vietnam. He thought the country too unhealthy and coastal positions there too difficult to defend.

Guizot's reaction to the 1846–1848 Mexican-American War was studiously indifferent, and he refused to lend anything more than occasional verbal support to British attempts to mediate a settlement or prevent the annexation of Mexican territory. Indeed, Guizot believed that cordial Franco-American relations were far more important than aiding an inherently unstable Mexico. He also argued that France's interests in North America were too slight to warrant any kind of intervention in the conflict. His indifference, however, led both the Americans and British to question his motives.

Louis Philippe resisted pressure to dismiss his favorite minister until early 1848, too late to save his throne. Guizot retired to write. He died at Val Richer in Normandy on September 12, 1874.

SPENCER C. TUCKER

See also

Europe and the Mexican-American War; France; Great Britain.

References

Barker, Nancy Nichols. *The French Experience in Mexico, 1821–1861: A History of Constant Misunderstanding.* Chapel Hill: University of North Carolina Press, 1979.

Guizot, François. *Mémoires pour servir à l'histoire de mon temps.* 8 vols. Paris: Nichel Levy Frères, 1872.

Newman, Edgar L. *Historical Dictionary of France from the 1815 Restoration to the Second Empire.* New York: Greenwood Press, 1987.

Woodward, Ernest L. *Three Studies in European Conservatism: Metternich, Guizot, the Catholic Church in the Nineteenth Century.* Hamden, CT: Archon Books, 1963.

Gulf of California (Mar de Cortés)

Large body of salt water separating the Baja Peninsula (Baja California) from the mainland of Mexico. The Gulf of California (Mar de Cortés, Sea of Cortez, or Vermilion Sea) is bordered by the Mexican states of Baja California, Baja California Sur, Sonora, and Sinaloa. The southern end of the Gulf joins the Pacific Ocean. The Gulf of California covers approximately 62,000 square miles and has a total shoreline that stretches some 2,500 miles. It is about 750 miles long and its average width is some 95 miles. The waterway is fed by several large rivers, including the Colorado, Fuerte, Mayo, Sinaloa, Sonora, and Yaqui. Much of the Gulf is home to a series of rich fisheries and fishing grounds; anchovies and sardines are especially plentiful and were a major Mexican export for many years. Significant port cities along the periphery of the waterway include Mazatlán, Cabo San Lucas, San Carlos, San Felipe, La Paz, Loreto, Guaymas, Puerto Peñasco, and Mulegé.

In 1532, Spanish conquistador Hernán Cortés sponsored an expedition commanded by Nuñez de Guzmán to the region of the Gulf, but he did not realize that the body of water was indeed a gulf. In 1535, Cortés himself led an exploratory expedition across the Gulf from mainland Mexico to the Baja Peninsula, which at that time was thought to be an island. Four years later, Spanish explorer Francisco de Ulloa determined that Baja California was a peninsula, not an island.

Much of the region bordering the Gulf of California is arid. The climate ranges from arid subtropical to moderately arid tropical. The Gulf is studded with white sandy beaches, coral lagoons, palm oases, rocky coves, and coral reefs. Several islands are located in the Gulf, including Isla Ángel de la Guarda, in the northwestern section of the Gulf; Isla Tiburón, in the northeastern portion; and

Isla Espíritu Santo and Isla Partida in the west, which are joined by an isthmus. The northern quarter of the Gulf is relatively shallow, averaging 600 feet in depth; the southern portion is far deeper and in some areas there are massive drop-offs, with depths from 5,000 to 10,000 feet.

During the Mexican-American War, U.S. naval forces enforced a blockade against Mexican ports along the Gulf of California, including Guaymas and Mazatlán. Although no major land offensives were launched via the Gulf of California, the Americans did land small-scale forces to effect the blockade, to occupy seaside towns, and to fight Mexican guerrillas. These included actions at Mulujé and Loreto in 1847.

PAUL G. PIERPAOLI JR.

See also

Baja California; Guaymas, Battle of; Guerrilla Warfare; Loreto; Mazatlán; Mulujé, Skirmish at; San Antonio, Skirmish at; Sonora y Sinaloa.

References

Bauer, K. Jack. *Surfboats and Horse Marines: U.S. Naval Operations in the Mexican War.* Annapolis, MD: U.S. Naval Institute, 1969.

Kemble, John Haskell, ed. "Amphibious Operations in the Gulf of California." *American Neptune* 5 (1945): 122–125.

Steinbeck, John, and E. F. Ricketts. *Sea of Cortez: A Leisurely Journal of Travel and Research.* New York: Viking Press, 1941.

Gulf of Mexico

Large body of salt water, a subset of the Atlantic Ocean, covering 615,000 square miles. Roughly oval in shape, the Gulf of Mexico is 810 nautical miles across at its widest point. Almost half of the Gulf of Mexico consists of shallow, intertidal waters. Much of the U.S. Gulf Coast, particularly from Texas to Florida, has very shallow waters, making the region susceptible to devastating tidal surges during severe storms and hurricanes. The Gulf of Mexico is bounded on the northwest, north, and northeast by the U.S. Gulf Coast (Texas to Florida); on the south and southwest by Mexico; and on the southeast by Cuba. The deepest part of the Gulf of Mexico is known as the Sigsbee Deep, located about 200 miles southeast of Brownsville, Texas. Part of an underwater trough, Sigsbee Deep is 14,880 feet deep.

The first European to explore the Gulf of Mexico was Amerigo Vespucci in 1497. A decade later, Hernán Cortés helped conquer Cuba and Hispaniola, and in 1518 he began his conquest of Mexico via the Gulf. In 1526, Pánfilo Narvaéz laid claim to much of the area that would eventually become the U.S. Gulf Coast. Later, the French, along with the Spanish, would lay claim to most of the Gulf Coast, although the area would not be settled in large numbers by Europeans until the early 19th century.

Thirty-three major U.S. river systems, draining 31 states, empty into the Gulf of Mexico, including the Mississippi, the most important river of the United States. It flows into the Gulf downriver from New Orleans, Louisiana. Control of the Gulf Coast

U.S. troops coming ashore at Veracruz on the Gulf of Mexico on March 9, 1847, in what was the largest U.S. amphibious landing until World War II. (North Wind Pictures)

was thus critical to controlling shipping on the Mississippi River and cities such as New Orleans; Mobile, Alabama; and Pensacola, Florida. The Straits of Florida were likewise crucial in controlling access to the Gulf itself. The Gulf Stream originates in the eastern Gulf of Mexico, bringing with it a powerful current of warm water that parallels the East Coast of North America. In the summer months, the Gulf's relatively shallow waters result in high sea temperatures, which periodically fuel large hurricanes that have, over the years, wrecked many areas along the Gulf Coast from Texas to Florida.

The Gulf of Mexico figured prominently in the Mexican-American War. The U.S. Navy conducted numerous operations there and instituted a blockade of major Mexican ports along the Gulf Coast. New Orleans, the second-largest port of the United States in 1846, is located just upriver from where the Mississippi River empties into the Gulf of Mexico. Thousands of American troops sailed from that place to the war front in Mexico, and the vast majority of supplies and war matériel used by the American military went through the port of New Orleans, into the western Gulf of Mexico, and then to Mexico. Major General Winfield Scott chose Veracruz, along Mexico's Gulf Coast, as the principal landing point for his campaign that ended triumphantly in Mexico City in September 1847. Veracruz was Mexico's deepest and busiest Gulf Coast port, and Scott's force occupied the city until after the end of hostilities.

PAUL G. PIERPAOLI JR.

See also

Blockade, Naval; Mexico City Campaign; Scott, Winfield; Veracruz; Veracruz, Landing at and Siege of.

References

Bauer, K. Jack. *Surfboats and Horse Marines: U.S. Naval Operations in the Mexican War, 1846–48*. Annapolis: U.S. Naval Institute, 1969.
Gore, Robert H. *The Gulf of Mexico: A Treasury of Resources in the American Mediterranean*. Sarasota, FL: Pineapple Press, 1992.

Gutiérrez-Magee Expedition
Event Dates: August 8, 1812–February 1813

Joint Mexican-American filibustering expedition that took place in Spanish-controlled Texas during 1812–1813 in the early stages of Mexico's war for independence. Insurrectionist sentiments began in Texas as early as January 1811, when Juan Bautista de las Casas led a failed coup against royalists at San Antonio. That December, José Bernardo Gutiérrez de Lara, a Mexican rebel, traveled to Washington, D.C., in hopes of securing support from Americans for another rebellion in Texas. With war against Britain looming, U.S. leaders refused to officially sanction the effort, but Gutiérrez was reasonably certain that the Americans would not stymie the rebellion once it began.

After securing a letter of introduction from Governor William C. C. Claiborne of Louisiana, Gutiérrez met with William Shaler, an American diplomat sent to observe the situation in Texas, who soon became the filibustering expedition's chief adviser. The expedition began mobilizing at Natchitoches, Louisiana, in the summer of 1812. Many soldiers of fortune joined the effort, including a number of Americans who dreamed of seizing Texas for the United States. Shaler convinced Augustus W. Magee, a frustrated former U.S. Army officer, to work with Gutiérrez and lead the military portion of the expedition, which came to be called the Gutiérrez-Magee Expedition.

On August 8, 1812, leading some 130 men, Magee crossed the Sabine River into Texas and dispersed the royalist forces guarding the frontier. Four days later he entered Nacogdoches, regrouped, recruited more men so that his force numbered some 300, and marched farther south and west. The Spanish governor of Texas, Manuel María de Salcedo, mobilized his troops along the Guadalupe River to protect San Antonio. Magee decided to avoid a clash there and instead seized La Bahía (Goliad) on November 7, unopposed. Salcedo laid siege to the filibusters, who defended a former mission converted to a fortress, but was unable to force their surrender. Magee died on February 6, 1813, and Samuel Kemper took command of the expedition.

On February 10 and 13, Kemper repelled two Spanish assaults on the Goliad mission before pressing on toward San Antonio on February 19. By then commanding some 800 men, Kemper defeated a larger royalist force at the Battle of Rosillo on March 29, and on March 1 Salcedo surrendered San Antonio to the rebels. After the rebels captured San Antonio, Gutiérrez, who had taken a somewhat peripheral role in the expedition, reasserted his authority and reportedly allowed Salcedo and several other Spanish officials to be executed. This brutal action alienated a number of rebels, especially the Americans, more than 100 of whom abandoned the campaign and departed for Louisiana under Kemper's leadership.

Thereafter, the expedition became increasingly ineffectual and suffered numerous turnovers in leadership. On August 18, 1813, the expeditionary force of 1,400 men, now led by General José Álvarez de Toledo y Dubois, blundered into an ambush set by Spanish royalist general Joaquín de Arrendondo, commandant general of the Provincias Internas with 1,830 men. The ensuing four-hour Battle of Median was the bloodiest engagement ever to occur in Texas. The expeditionary force was virtually annihilated, suffering some 1,300 killed. Only some 100 men escaped, and a number of those were subsequently captured and executed as traitors. Royalist forces lost only 55 killed in action. Antonio López de Santa Anna, a young lieutenant in the Spanish army, was cited for gallantry during the battle.

Thereafter, Spanish officials employed harsh tactics to insure Texas's submission to the central government. Although it failed, the expedition showcased how filibusters sought to take advantage of the expansionist fervor manifested in the War of 1812, and it focused attention on Texas. Although the first Texas republic had died stillborn, the Gutiérrez-Magee Expedition led to further attempts by American filibusters to seize Texas, and it served as an example for Texas revolutionaries a quarter century later.

JOHN H. BARNHILL AND PAUL G. PIERPAOLI JR.

See also

Santa Anna, Antonio López de; Texas Revolution.

References

Almaráz, Félix D. *Tragic Cavalier: Governor Manuel Salcedo of Texas, 1808–1813.* Austin: University of Texas Press, 1971.

Garrett, Julia Kathryn. *Green Flag over Texas: A Story of the Last Years of Spain in Texas.* Austin, TX: Pemberton Press, 1939.

Walker, Henry P., ed. "William McLane's Narrative of the Magee-Gutiérrez Expedition, 1812–1813." *Southwestern Historical Quarterly* 66 (January 1963): 457–479.

H

Hall, Willard Preble

Birth Date: May 9, 1820
Death Date: November 2, 1882

U.S. lawyer, soldier, and politician. Willard Preble Hall was born in Harpers Ferry, Virginia (now West Virginia), on May 9, 1820, into a family of some means. After attending a private boarding school in Baltimore, he entered Yale College, graduating in 1839. The next year he went to Missouri with his father and read for the law and in 1841 was admitted to the local bar. Hall practiced law in Sparta, Missouri, in 1842 before becoming a circuit attorney in Saint Joseph in 1843, a post he held for several years. A Democrat, Hall served as one of that party's presidential electors during the 1844 election.

At the start of the Mexican War in 1846, Hall joined the 1st Missouri Mounted Rifles as a private. At the urging of Colonel Alexander Doniphan, the regiment's commanding officer, and Brigadier General Stephen W. Kearny, commander of the Army of the West, Hall was promoted to first lieutenant. Hall remained with Doniphan and Kearny as they marched to New Mexico, arriving in Santa Fe in August 1846. Because of Hall's legal background, Kearny and Doniphan asked him to help draw a set of civil laws sometimes known as "Kearny's Code" by which to govern the new Territory of New Mexico. The codes were written in both Spanish and English and remained official until 1891, certainly a testament to Hall's good work.

Hall remained in New Mexico until October 1846, at which time he joined the Mormon Battalion then on its way to California. That November Hall was elected to the U.S. House of Representatives, and consequently he was discharged from the army in early 1847

so that he could take his seat in Congress that March. Hall served as a congressman until 1853. He settled in Saint Joseph, Missouri, one year later, where he again practiced law, and ran unsuccessfully for a U.S. Senate seat in 1856.

In 1861, Hall joined the Missouri convention that affirmed that state's policy of armed neutrality during the Civil War. This meant that while Missouri would not secede from the Union, it would not supply troops or war matériel to either side of the conflict. In 1864, when Missouri's unelected provisional governor Hamilton Rowan Gamble died of pneumonia, Hall, who had been provisional lieutenant governor (unelected) since 1861, became provisional governor. He held that office until the end of the Civil War in April 1865. Hall also held a commission as brigadier general of the Missouri militia, a pro-Union group. He commanded the Northwestern Missouri District from 1861 to 1863. After the Civil War, Hall returned to his law practice. He died in Saint Joseph on November 2, 1882.

PAUL G. PIERPAOLI JR.

See also
Doniphan, Alexander William; Doniphan's March; Kearny, Stephen Watts; Mormon Battalion; New Mexico.

References
Dawson, Joseph G., III. *Doniphan's Epic March: The 1st Missouri Volunteers in the Mexican War.* Lawrence: University of Kansas Press, 1999.

Hughes, John Taylor. *Doniphan's Expedition.* Cincinnati, OH: 1848. Reprinted with an introduction by Joseph G. Dawson III. College Station: Texas A&M University Press, 1997.

Parrish, William E. *A History of Missouri.* Vol. 3, *1860–1875.* Columbia, University of Missouri Press, 2001.

Halleck, Henry Wager
Birth Date: January 15, 1815
Death Date: January 9, 1872

U.S. Army officer. Born in Westernville, New York, on January 15, 1815, Henry Wager Halleck graduated from the U.S. Military Academy at West Point in 1839 and was assigned to the Corps of Engineers. His report on the coastal defenses of the United States won him the favorable attention of army commander Major General Winfield Scott, who assigned Halleck to travel to Europe in 1844 to study foreign military practices. On his return, Halleck gave a series of lectures at the Lowell Institute, later published as *Elements of Military Art and Science.* This helped win Halleck a reputation as a military intellectual.

In the Mexican War (1846–1848) Halleck, a first lieutenant, was sent to California, where he held several administrative posts. He also helped design U.S. fortifications at Mazatlán during the American naval occupation there. For a brief time, he served as lieutenant governor of Mazatlán in the autumn of 1847 and was brevetted captain for his wartime service. After the war he remained in California. As military secretary for the territory, he attended the state constitutional convention and played an active role in drafting that document. Retaining his military commission, he became an active partner in a California law firm, resigning from the army only in 1854 when the firm was well established. In the years that followed, Halleck expanded his efforts into the real estate and mining businesses and grew wealthy.

When the Civil War began, Halleck returned to the East and offered his services to the U.S. government. On Scott's recommendation, Lincoln nominated him as a major general and one of the highest-ranking officers in the army. Halleck's first assignment, received on November 9, 1861, was to command the Department of Missouri, where he used his considerable administrative skill to clean up the mess left by his predecessor, John C. Frémont. Halleck was not, however, disposed to advance against the Confederates as Lincoln wanted or to cooperate with the department commander to the east, Brigadier General Don Carlos Buell.

In February 1862, Halleck finally gave reluctant permission to his subordinates Brigadier General Ulysses S. Grant and Flag Officer Andrew H. Foote to advance against Confederate Fort Henry on the Tennessee River. Grant proceeded aggressively and captured not only Fort Henry but also nearby Fort Donelson.

Halleck demanded and received from Lincoln, on March 11, 1862, as a reward for the victories Grant had won, command over all the Union's western armies, including that of his rival Buell. Although he used Grant's victories for his personal advancement, he was both jealous of Grant's success and unnerved by Grant's aggressiveness. Halleck needlessly reprimanded Grant for failing to communicate frequently enough, and he reported to the army's new commanding general in Washington, Major General George B. McClellan, that Grant was frequently intoxicated, a report he knew to be false. Halleck removed Grant from command before

Grant's congressman, Elihu B. Washburne, prompted Lincoln to support Grant and force Halleck to restore him.

Halleck had planned on advancing via the Tennessee and Cumberland Rivers, the obvious routes into the Confederate heartland, but he had wanted to wait until every possible preparation was in place.

Following Grant's near run but strategically important victory at Shiloh in April, Halleck took the field for the only time in his career, pulling together all three field armies within his department and placing Grant in a meaningless second in command slot. With his massed forces, some 100,000 men, Halleck advanced with glacial slowness against the Confederate rail hub at Corinth, Mississippi, covering 20 miles in a month. He took Corinth but let the Confederate Army, under General P. G. T. Beauregard, escape.

Despite such a lackluster result, Lincoln, who was desperately seeking a general to mastermind and coordinate the movement of all the Union armies, selected Halleck for that task. Halleck went to Washington in the summer of 1862, but his efforts to direct the movements of such inadequate commanders as Major Generals John Pope and George B. McClellan during the dismal campaign in Virginia that summer were a failure. By its close, Halleck, who had never been comfortable actually directing operations in the field, all but refused to give further orders to his subordinate generals. Thereafter he made it an article of military faith that the general on the spot should be left to make the decisions with nothing more than advice—albeit sometimes persistent, almost nagging advice—from Halleck in Washington. A frustrated Lincoln complained that Halleck amounted to little more than "a first-rate clerk."

In this capacity, however, Halleck performed useful service not only as an adviser to the field commanders but also as a mediator between them and the administration. When Grant was appointed to supersede Halleck as general in chief, he retained Halleck in the de facto role he had already been filling, that of chief of staff. In that capacity Halleck continued to advise generals in the field, including Grant. Despite his early shortcomings, Halleck made an important contribution to Union victory.

After the Confederates' April 1865 surrender, Halleck commanded the Military District of the James. That August, he took command of the Division of the Pacific; in 1869, he took control of the Division of the South. Halleck died in Louisville, Kentucky, on January 9, 1872.

STEVEN E. WOODWORTH

See also
California Theater of War, Overview; Mazatlán; Scott, Winfield.

References
Ambrose, Stephen E. *Halleck: Lincoln's Chief of Staff.* Baton Rouge: Louisiana State University Press, 1962.
Marszalek, John F. *Commander of All Lincoln's Armies: A Life of General Henry W. Halleck.* Cambridge, MA: Harvard University Press, 2004.
Woodworth, Steven E., ed. *Grant's Lieutenants: From Chattanooga to Appomattox.* Lawrence: University Press of Kansas, 2008.

Halls of the Montezuma, Mexico City

American nickname for Chapultepec Castle located on a large hill on the outskirts of Mexico City that was the site of Mexico's Military College (Colegio Militar) during the Mexican-American War. The site had once been occupied by Aztec emperors, including the famed Moctezuma II (Montezuma). Others have claimed that the term "Halls of Montezuma" refers to the National Palace, where the office of Mexican presidents is located on the site of the former palace of the Aztec emperors. Following the U.S. conquest of Mexico City, the words "Halls of Montezuma" were added to the motto on the U.S. Marine Corps flag, and the anonymously authored "Marines' Hymn" included in the first verse, "From the halls of Montezuma to the shores of Tripoli."

As U.S. Army major general Winfield Scott prepared to assault Mexico City from the west in September 1847, he recognized the tactical importance of seizing Chapultepec Castle, which from its ridge-top position dominated two causeways leading to important city gates. The castle was then defended by 832 Mexican soldiers, including 100 cadets of the Colegio Militar, which the castle housed.

Maj. Levi Twiggs's marine battalion of 357 men was chosen to participate in the assault on Mexico City and played a prominent role, alongside the army, in storming Chapultepec Castle on September 13, 1847. In the confused and savage fighting, Twiggs was killed and an additional 23 marines were killed and wounded. A Mexican general and 10 colonels were among the 550 prisoners taken. Seven Mexican artillery pieces and approximately 1,000 muskets were also seized in the fighting. To Mexicans, the battle is best remembered for the death of six cadets (Los Niños Héroes, or the Boy Heroes), including Juan Escutia, who reportedly wrapped himself in a Mexican flag and leapt from the castle ramparts rather than surrender the banner.

The marines suffered an additional 15 casualties as they participated in the offensive along both causeways toward the city gates until darkness fell. During the night, the Mexican army evacuated the city, and the next morning the marines occupied the National Palace on the central city square (zócalo), providing security on surrounding streets as General Scott and his men arrived. In 1849 the U.S. Marine Corps uniform was modified to include the scarlet stripe on the outside seam of the dress uniform trousers—the so-called blood stripe—in honor of the disproportionately high number of marine officer and noncommissioned officer casualties sustained in the storming of Chapultepec.

GLENN E. HELM

See also

Chapultepec, Battle of; Los Niños Héroes; Mexican Military Academy (Colegio Militar); Mexico City Campaign; Scott, Winfield; United States Marines.

References

Clary, David A. *Eagles and Empire: The United States, Mexico, and the Struggle for a Continent.* New York: Bantam Books, 2009.
Johannsen, Robert W. *To the Halls of the Montezumas: The Mexican War in the American Imagination.* Oxford, UK: Oxford University Press, 1985.
Millett, Allen R. *Semper Fidelis: The History of the United States Marine Corps.* Rev. ed. New York: Free Press, 1991.
Santelli, Gabrielle M. Neufeld. *Marines in the Mexican War.* Washington, DC: History and Museums Division, Headquarters, U.S. Marine Corps, 1991.

Hamer, Thomas Lyon

Birth Date: July 1800
Death Date: December 2, 1846

Lawyer, politician, and volunteer army officer during the Mexican-American War. Thomas Lyon Hamer was born in July 1800 in Northumberland County, Pennsylvania. He moved to Ohio in 1817, where he briefly taught school. Hamer then read for the law and was admitted to the Ohio bar in 1821. That same year, he established a law practice in Georgetown, Ohio.

Hamer served in the Ohio House of Representatives in 1825 and again during 1828–1829. During 1829 he was also Speaker of the House. Three years later he was elected to the U.S. House of Representatives as a Jacksonian Democrat, serving until 1839.

Shortly after the Mexican-American War began in the late spring of 1846, Hamer enlisted as a private in a volunteer Ohio infantry regiment. That July, however, President James K. Polk, a fellow Democrat, offered Hamer a commission as a brigadier general of volunteers. Although he had no prior military experience, Hamer eagerly accepted the offer and was given command of the

U.S. representative Thomas Lyon Hamer, a strong supporter of the Mexican-American War, accepted a commission as a brigadier general. He distinguished himself in the fighting in northern Mexico but died there of yellow fever in December 1846. (North Wind Picture Archives)

1st Brigade of Major General William O. Butler's division in Major General Zachary Taylor's army, then advancing from Matamoros toward Monterrey.

Hamer performed remarkably well, given his limited military expertise. He ably led his men during the September 21–23, 1846, Battle of Monterrey and successfully held Fort Tenería after the Mexicans withdrew. When General Butler fell wounded during the engagement, Hamer was made temporary division commander.

While still at Monterrey, Hamer became ill, perhaps with yellow fever. In November, he was elected to another term in the U.S. House of Representatives, but his malady steadily worsened, and he died at Monterrey on December 2, 1846. Then lieutenant (and future U.S. president) Ulysses S. Grant was said to have remarked that the "United States has lost a future president." General Taylor felt the loss even more acutely, writing, "I have lost the balance wheel of my volunteer army."

PAUL G. PIERPAOLI JR.

See also

Butler, William Orlando; Fort Tenería; Grant, Ulysses Simpson (Hiram Ulysses Grant); Monterrey, Battle of; Taylor, Zachary.

References

Bauer, K. Jack. *The Mexican-American War, 1846–1848.* Lincoln: University of Nebraska Press, 1992.

Winders, R. Bruce. *Mr. Polk's Army: The American Military Experience in the Mexican War.* College Station: Texas A&M University Press, 1997.

Hamilton-Gordon, George, 4th Earl of Aberdeen

Birth Date: January 28, 1784
Death Date: December 14, 1860

British politician, foreign secretary (1828–1830, 1841–1846), and prime minister (1852–1855). George Hamilton-Gordon was born in Edinburgh, Scotland, on January 28, 1784. Orphaned at a young age, Hamilton-Gordon was reared by his legal guardians, William Pitt the Younger and Henry Dundas. In 1801, he inherited the earldom of Aberdeen from his grandfather, and three years later he graduated from St. John's College, Cambridge. A conservative traditionalist in outlook, he took his seat in the House of Lords in 1805.

In 1812, after his wife died, Hamilton-Gordon joined the British Foreign Service. He was appointed ambassador to Austria, and on October 9, 1813, he signed the Treaty of Töplitz between London and Vienna. He went back to Britain in 1814 and was granted a peerage as Viscount Gordon; at about the same time he also became a member of the Privy Council. Between 1815, when he remarried, and 1828, Hamilton-Gordon remained in the House of Lords but otherwise kept a low political profile.

From 1828 to 1830, Hamilton-Gordon was foreign secretary, and during 1834–1835 he served as secretary of state for war and

the colonies. In 1841 he was again appointed as foreign secretary, this time in the government of Sir Robert Peel. His five-year tenure proved to be a busy one. Among other things, he worked to improve Franco-British relations and negotiated with the Mexican, Texan, and U.S. governments in the months leading to and during the Mexican-American War.

In 1842, Hamilton-Gordon's work helped produce the Webster-Ashburton Treaty, which settled several border disputes between British-controlled Canada and the United States. He also helped broker the 1846 Oregon Treaty, thereby averting potential armed conflict between the United States and Great Britain over the border dispute between American-held Oregon and British-controlled Canada. It was Gordon who suggested the 49th parallel as the official boundary, which represented a sensible compromise to the James K. Polk administration. This treaty significantly ameliorated relations between London and Washington.

During 1842–1843, Hamilton-Gordon also tried to maintain Texas independence by brokering a peace between the Texas Republic and the Mexican government. One of his suggestions included the abolition of slavery in Texas, which the Texans dismissed out of hand. In 1844, he devised a plan by which the British and French would guarantee the independence of Texas and would negotiate the ongoing Texas-Mexico border dispute. In so doing, Hamilton-Gordon hoped to avoid the annexation of Texas by the United States and strengthen Franco-British ties. The French initially agreed to the idea but abandoned it once they realized that such a deal might compromise their relationship with Washington. Undeterred, Hamilton-Gordon again tried to broker a deal between Mexico and Texas, but his efforts ran afoul of the Polk administration's apparent intention to annex Texas in 1845. The foreign secretary was suspicious of American motives toward Texas and believed that American policy toward Mexico was overly aggressive. With those problems in mind, he refused to permit the British government to enter into any negotiations between the United States and Mexico over the Texas question.

Hamilton-Gordon indeed walked a diplomatic tightrope, hoping to convince the Texans (and Americans) that annexation was not a good idea, while at the same time trying to engage the United States in the Oregon boundary negotiations. When the Mexican-American War officially broke out in May 1846, Hamilton-Gordon offered to mediate a settlement of the conflict, but he was recalled the following month. Throughout the conflict, the British remained neutral.

In December 1852, Hamilton-Gordon was asked to form a coalition government as prime minister. His four-year tenure is remembered mainly for his decision to enter the Crimean War against the Russian Empire, a move he would soon regret. Pushed into an aggressive stance in the conflict, mainly by Lord Palmerston, he was soon overwhelmed by accusations that his government had badly mismanaged the war effort. He resigned in 1855 and retired to private life. Hamilton-Gordon died in London on December 14, 1860.

PAUL G. PIERPAOLI JR.

See also

Great Britain; Oregon Boundary Dispute; Oregon Treaty; Polk, James Knox; Texas.

References

Chamberlain, Muriel. *Lord Aberdeen: A Political Biography*. London: Longman, 1983.

Haynes, Sam W. "'But What Will England Say?': Great Britain, the United States, and the War with Mexico." In *Dueling Eagles: Reinterpreting the U.S.-Mexican War, 1846–1848*, edited by Richard Francaviglia and Douglas W. Richmond, 19–40. Fort Worth: Texas Christian University Press, 2000.

Iremonger, Lucille. *Lord Aberdeen: A Biography of the 4th Earl of Aberdeen*. London: Collins, 1978.

Pletcher, David. *The Diplomacy of Annexation: Texas, Oregon, and the Mexican War*. Columbia: University of Missouri Press, 1973.

Hannegan, Edward Allen

Birth Date: June 25, 1807
Death Date: February 25, 1859

Attorney, Democratic Party politician, and avid U.S. expansionist. Edward Allen Hannegan was born in Hamilton County, Ohio, on June 25, 1807. When he was still very young, Hannegan moved with his family to Bourbon County, Kentucky. Attending local schools, Hannegan worked as a farmhand, taught school, and read for the law. He was admitted to the bar in 1827 and moved to Indiana, where he lived in Terre Haute and Vincennes before settling down in Covington and opening a law practice.

Entering state Democratic politics, Hannegan served in the Indiana House of Representatives during 1832–1833 and 1841–1842. Elected to the U.S. House of Representatives in 1832, Hannegan served during 1833–1837. In 1836, he chose not to seek another term in the House and returned to his law practice in 1837.

In 1842, Hannegan ran successfully for a U.S. Senate seat. He served from 1843 to 1849, having lost a renomination bid in 1848. A staunch supporter of President James K. Polk and his expansionist agenda, Hannegan, a noted orator, pushed hard for a war declaration against Great Britain to ensure the annexation of all of Oregon. He also supported the Mexican-American War and for a time espoused the tenets of the All of Mexico movement, which sought to annex the entire Mexican Republic. Nevertheless, Hannegan was less than enthusiastic about permitting millions of Mexicans U.S. citizenship, famously stating, "The Mexicans are utterly unfit for the blessings and restraints of rational liberty."

After leaving the Senate in 1849, Hannegan was the U.S. minister to Prussia (1849–1850). Upon his return to the United States,

he recommended his law practice in Covington, Indiana. In 1857, he moved to Saint Louis, where he continued to practice law. Hannegan died in Saint Louis on February 25, 1859.

PAUL G. PIERPAOLI JR.

See also

All of Mexico Movement; Congress, U.S.; Democratic Party; Expansionism and Imperialism; Oregon Boundary Dispute; Polk, James Knox; Public Opinion and the War, U.S.

References

Curry, David P. *The Constitution in Congress: Democrats and Whigs, 1829–1861*. Chicago: University of Chicago Press, 2005.

Feldman, Ruth Tenzer. *The Mexican-American War*. Minneapolis, MN: Lerner, 2004.

Meed, Douglas V. *The Mexican-War, 1846–1848*. Oxford, UK: Osprey, 2003.

Hardee, William Joseph

Birth Date: November 10, 1815
Death Date: November 6, 1873

U.S. and Confederate Army officer and author of *Rifle and Light Infantry Tactics,* popularly known as "Hardee's Tactics," a well-regarded manual on infantry tactics. William Joseph Hardee was born in Savannah, Georgia, on November 10, 1815. He graduated from the U.S. Military Academy, West Point, in 1838. Commissioned a second lieutenant, he was sent to Europe to study cavalry tactics.

A captain at the beginning of the Mexican-American War, Hardee first served with Major General Zachary Taylor's army and was among the first Americans taken prisoner. His capture occurred during a reconnaissance mission on April 25, 1846, at Carricitos Ranch, where he and Captain Seth B. Thornton were taken by surprise by the Mexican cavalry. This incident came to be known as the Thornton Affair and served as one of the immediate catalysts of the conflict. Within weeks, however, Hardee was released in a prisoner exchange. He was then taken ill with dysentery and was largely bedridden during July and August, but in September 1846 he saw action at the Battle of Monterrey. He also participated in Major General Winfield Scott's Mexico City Campaign. By war's end, he had been brevetted to lieutenant colonel.

After the war, Hardee served in the 2nd U.S. Cavalry in the West under Colonel Albert S. Johnston and Lieutenant Colonel Robert E. Lee. In 1855, Hardee authored the *Rifle and Light Infantry Tactics for the Exercise and Maneuvers of Troops When Acting as Light Infantry or Riflemen,* a manual of infantry tactics that became the standard reference guide for infantrymen in both the Union and Confederate armies during the Civil War. Hardee was commandant of cadets at West Point from 1856 to 1861. He resigned his army commission as a lieutenant colonel after his home state of

Georgia seceded from the Union. Entering the Confederate army as a colonel, he was promoted to brigadier general by June 1861. That October, he was advanced to major general, and in October 1862 he became a lieutenant general.

Hardee spent most of the war as a corps commander in the Confederate Army of Tennessee. A thorough trainer, he was much admired by his men who called him "Old Reliable." Hardee's first assignment was to organize an Arkansas brigade. He commanded a corps at Shiloh (April 6–7, 1862) and was wounded in the arm during that battle. When General Braxton Bragg superseded P. G. T. Beauregard as commander of the Army of Tennessee, Hardee was not impressed with his new commander but nevertheless commanded the II Corps of Bragg's army in the Battles of Perryville and Stones River in which he led a major surprise attack that almost defeated Union forces. He briefly commanded the Confederate Department of Mississippi and East Louisiana, then returned to Bragg's command to take over command of Lieutenant General Leonidas Polk's corps besieging Chattanooga, Tennessee. Hardee's corps was forced to withdraw when Union troops assaulted Missionary Ridge on November 25, 1863. Hardee was one of a group of Confederate officers who finally convinced Confederate president Jefferson Davis to remove Bragg from command.

Hardee continued in command of his corps under General Joseph E. Johnston during the campaign from Chattanooga to Atlanta, and under Lieutenant General John Bell Hood through the Atlanta Campaign. Lacking confidence in the hapless Hood, Hardee requested a transfer and from October 1864 to February 1865 commanded the Department of South Carolina, Georgia, and Florida. Although unable to stop Union major general William T. Sherman's March to the Sea, Hardee was able to evacuate Confederate troops from Savannah before the Union occupation of the city. Hardee's troops then withdrew into North Carolina. Once again under the command of Joseph E. Johnston, his last battle was at Bentonville, North Carolina, on March 19–21, 1865, where his only son was killed in battle. Hardee surrendered with the remnant of the Army of Tennessee on April 26, 1865.

Following the war, Hardee retired to his wife's Alabama plantation. He then moved his family to Selma, where he was in the warehousing and insurance business and later became president of the Selma and Meridian Railroad. He also wrote *The Irish in America,* which was published in 1868. Hardee died in Wytheville, Virginia, on November 6, 1873.

MICHAEL R. HALL AND SPENCER C. TUCKER

See also
Mexico City Campaign; Monterrey, Battle of; Scott, Winfield; Taylor, Zachary; Thornton, Seth Barton; Thornton Affair.

References
Hardee, William J. *Rifle and Light Infantry Tactics for the Exercise and Maneuvers of Troops When Acting as Light Infantry or Riflemen.* 1855. Reprint, Westport, CT: Greenwood Press, 1971.
Hughes, Nathaniel C., Jr. *General William J. Hardee: Old Reliable.* Baton Rouge: Louisiana State University Press, 1965.

Hardin, John J.
Birth Date: January 6, 1810
Death Date: February 23, 1847

Lawyer, militia officer, Whig Party politician, and volunteer army officer during the Mexican-American War. John J. Hardin was born on January 6, 1810, in Frankfort, Kentucky. Hardon graduated from Transylvania University (Lexington, Kentucky) and subsequently read for the law. He was admitted to the Kentucky bar in 1831 and then moved to Jacksonville (Morgan County), Illinois, where he began a law practice. The following year, when the Black Hawk War began, he saw action in several engagements as a member of the Illinois militia.

From 1832 to 1836, Hardin was the prosecuting attorney for Morgan County. Entering elective politics as a Whig in 1836, he won a seat in the Illinois State House of Representatives, serving from 1836 to 1842. During this time Hardin befriended fellow Whig Abraham Lincoln, and by the early 1840s the two men were considered the most prominent Whigs in Illinois. During an uprising in Illinois in 1844 over the presence of Mormons in Hancock County, Hardin led the militia as a brigadier general. He would later become a major general.

At the start of the Mexican-American War, Hardin helped recruit the 1st Illinois Volunteer Infantry. He was immediately elected its colonel. Hardin's regiment joined Brigadier General John E. Wool's Army of the Center, headquartered at San Antonio, and marched with it south, where it joined Major General Zachary Taylor's Army of Occupation at Saltillo.

At the Battle of Buena Vista on February 23, 1847, Hardin's regiment held the left flank of the U.S. line with other volunteer units from Indiana and Kentucky. Hoping to catch the Mexicans off guard, Hardin ordered his men to charge; however, unbeknownst to him, a large number of Mexican infantrymen were hiding in a nearby ravine. Brutal hand-to-hand combat ensued, and Hardin was wounded in the melee. He refused to leave the battlefield, however, until the remainder of his men safely withdrew. Hardin and several other wounded officers died that day, probably killed by Mexican soldiers after being left behind by their retreating comrades.

Hardin's son, Martin Davis Hardin, born in 1837, became a brigadier general in the Union Army during the Civil War.

PAUL PIERPAOLI JR.

See also
Buena Vista, Battle of; Saltillo; Taylor, Zachary; Whigs; Wool, John Ellis.

References
Engelmann, Otto B. "The Second Illinois in the Mexican War, Mexican War Letters of Adolph Engelmann, 1846–1847." *Journal of the Illinois Historical Society* 26 (January 1934): 357–452.
Lavender, David. *Climax at Buena Vista: The American Campaigns in Northeastern Mexico, 1846–47.* Philadelphia, PA: Lippincott, 1966.
Winders, Richard Bruce. *Mr. Polk's Army: The American Military Experience in the Mexican War.* College Station: Texas A&M University Press, 1997.

Colonel John J. Hardin commanded the 1st Illinois Volunteer Infantry Regiment during the Mexican-American War. This illustration depicts Hardin's death during the Battle of Buena Vista on February 23, 1847. (Library of Congress)

Harney, William Selby

Birth Date: August 27, 1800

Death Date: May 9, 1889

U.S. Army officer whose military career spanned nearly 50 years, from 1818 to 1862. William Selby Harney was born on August 27, 1800, in Haysboro, Tennessee, and was commissioned in 1818 by direct appointment to second lieutenant in the 1st Infantry Regiment. Physically impressive at more than 6 feet 3 inches in height, he was also ambitious, a disciplinarian, argumentative, and highly temperamental.

Harney's initial military service involved mostly regimental garrison duties, primarily at Baton Rouge, Louisiana, with breaks for recruiting duty and a short period as aide to Major General Andrew Jackson. Harney then served almost exclusively in the upper Midwest until 1832. Accompanying an expedition aimed at resolving disputes regarding Native Americans and the fur trade on the upper Missouri River, he was exposed to the political-military problems of negotiating with Native Americans. His service included a minor role in the Black Hawk War, as part of a force under Colonel Zachary Taylor.

After several years as a paymaster that included promotion to major, Harney gained appointment as lieutenant colonel of the 2nd Dragoons, a regiment authorized by Congress in 1836. By

December, 300 men had been recruited and five companies were sent dismounted to Florida to join the military effort to force the Seminoles to move to Arkansas (Second Seminole War). During the war, Harney emerged as one of the army's most skilled and best-known Indian fighters.

The start of the war with Mexico in May 1846 found the 2nd Dragoons mounted and serving in Texas. One month later Harney was appointed commander of the regiment and promoted to colonel. Without authorization, he embarked on an expedition to the Presidio del Río Grande, and when Brigadier General John E. Wool received word of the foray he ordered Harney arrested. When he returned, however, Wool quickly released him from custody. Major General Winfield Scott later used the incident to remove Harney from command, just prior to the landing at Veracruz and the start of the Mexico City Campaign. President James K. Polk was highly annoyed by Scott's action, which he believed was politically motivated. Harney was an avowed Democrat and Scott a long-standing Whig. A court of inquiry eventually reinstated Harney, but only after he had apologized to Scott and received an official reprimand from the War Department.

During the operations to capture Mexico City, Harney commanded all of Scott's mounted troops, providing effective service throughout the campaign. He led an intrepid charge at the Battle of Cerro Gordo, which brought him a brevet promotion to brigadier general, and he performed admirably at the Battles of Contreras and Churubusco. On September 13, 1847, as U.S. troops entered Mexico City, Harney supervised the executions of 30 members of the San Patricio Battalion, who had been tried at Tacubaya.

Harney and his 2nd Dragoons were next ordered to Texas to guard frontier settlements. Harney was placed in charge of a line of posts along the westernmost region of Texas. In 1854 he saw action against the Brule Sioux on the North Plains, and in early 1856 further Seminole resistance to displacement took Harney to Florida in command of the Department of Florida. There he demonstrated considerable talent in unconventional warfare and amphibious tactics.

In 1857, Harney was appointed to command Federal forces in strife-torn Kansas, a mission including support of civil authority. He was then appointed to command the Utah Department and soon promoted to regular brigadier general; but before he arrived in Utah, the Mormon problems were resolved there and he went to Saint Louis instead to command the Department of the West.

In 1858, Harney was appointed commander of the new Department of Oregon, primarily to solve conflicts between Native Americans and whites. In 1860, Harney was ordered to Saint Louis to command the Department of the West for a second time. Although cautious in his actions as war approached, his ambiguous loyalty to the Union and southern background caused suspicion, and in May 1861 he was relieved and retired in 1862.

With the end of the Civil War in 1865, efforts to solve the situation with the western tribes were renewed. Thus, during 1866–1870, Harney, much respected by the Native Americans themselves, served the government both officially as a commissioner and unofficially as an adviser on Indian affairs until his death on May 9, 1889, at his home in Orlando, Florida.

PHILIP L. BOLTÉ

See also
Cerro Gordo, Battle of; Churubusco, Battle of; Contreras, Battle of; Mexico City Campaign; Polk, James Knox; San Patricio Battalion; Scott, Winfield; Taylor, Zachary; Wool, John Ellis.

References
Adams, George Rollie. *General William S. Harney: Prince of Dragoons.* Lincoln: University of Nebraska Press, 2000.
Bauer, K. Jack. *The Mexican War, 1846–1848.* New York: Macmillan, 1974.

Hawkins, Charles Edward
Birth Date: 1802
Death Date: February 12, 1837

Officer in the navies of the United States, Mexico, and Texas. Charles Edward Hawkins was born in 1802 in Kingston, New York. On March 4, 1818, he secured a warrant as a midshipman in the

U.S. Navy and served aboard the frigate *Guerriere,* ship of the line *Washington,* and frigate *Constellation.* In 1825, following service in the Mediterranean Squadron, he joined the newly established West Indian Squadron under Commodore David Porter.

On October 17, 1826, Hawkins resigned his commission when he was offered a position to head the new Mexican navy. He commanded the schooner *Hermon* for a time and saw action against Spanish ships operating in the Caribbean and Gulf of Mexico. In 1828, he resigned from the Mexican navy and worked as a riverboat captain.

By 1835 Hawkins had become involved in General José Antonio Mexía's filibustering expedition against Tampico, Mexico. Mexía, who had been banished from Mexico, hoped to return triumphant and seize power in Mexico City. The expedition was ultimately called off before it ever reached the Mexican capital. The next year, in 1836, Hawkins offered his services to the fledgling Texas navy. Commissioned as a commodore (Texas's first), he was given command of the *Independence,* an old U.S. revenue cutter.

Hawkins plied the waters in the Gulf of Mexico between Galveston and Tampico, engaging several small ships that had been perceived as threats to the Texas independence movement. He also attempted to disrupt trade between the United States and Mexico and transported supplies and troops for the Texan cause. After the Texan victory at the Battle of San Jacinto, Hawkins ordered his tiny squadron to blockade Matamoros, Mexico, an action that was largely stymied because most of his vessels, including the *Independence,* were in need of repair and resupply. In the early winter of 1837, he sailed to New Orleans for refitting and fell ill with smallpox. Hawkins died there on February 12, 1837.

PAUL G. PIERPAOLI JR.

See also
Mexía, José Antonio; Mexico, Navy; San Jacinto, Battle of; Texas; Texas Revolution; United States Navy.

References
Denham, James M. "Charles E. Hawkins: Sailor of Three Republics." *Gulf Coast Historical Review* 5 (Spring 1990): 92–103.
Douglas, C. L. *Thunder on the Gulf: The Story of the Texas Navy.* Fort Collins, CO: Old Army Press, 1973.
Jordan, Jonathan W. *Lone Star Navy: Texas, the Fight for the Gulf of Mexico, and the Shaping of the American West.* Washington, DC: Potomac Books, 2006.
Wells, Tom Henderson. *Commodore Moore and the Texas Navy.* Austin: University of Texas Press, 1960.

Hawk's Peak Affair

Hawk's Peak, more commonly known as Fremont Peak, Gabilan Peak, or Gavilan Peak (*gavilán* being Spanish for sparrow hawk), is the highest peak in the Gabilan Mountains on the border between Monterey County and San Benito Counties in central California. Today, the site is located in Fremont Peak State Park. The site was the location of what is known as the Hawk's Peak Affair, which occurred in March 1846. The incident itself is relatively unimportant, but in the long run it heightened tensions and distrust between the Mexicans and the Americans living in the area at the time of the war with Mexico.

On June 20, 1845, Captain John Charles Frémont of the U.S. Corps of Topographical Engineers departed from Saint Louis, Missouri, on his third expedition across the Rocky Mountains to determine the best route from the Mississippi River to the Pacific Ocean. The mission might have included Frémont's plans for further exploration into California, which was Mexican territory, even though exploration of California was not a part of Frémont's orders from Washington. Sixty-two men, including six Delaware scouts and seasoned explorer, trapper, and guide Joseph Reddeford Walker, accompanied Frémont.

In late November 1845, at Walker Lake in the Humboldt River Mountains, the group split; Frémont led one contingent across the mountains via Donner Pass and Walker took the other group south to Walker Pass to meet at the Tulares Lakes. Frémont arrived at the rendezvous first and awaited the Walker party at Sutter's Fort. In January 1846, Frémont made an official call on Mexican general Don José María Castro and the former governor of Monterey, informing them that his expedition was scientific and commercial, not military. Castro granted Frémont permission to resupply and to winter in the province, provided that the Americans stay away from the coastal settlements.

In mid-February 1846, the Mexicans decided that Frémont had violated the agreement about the coastal settlements and demanded that he leave immediately or face consequences. Frémont left on a route up the Salinas Valley, when he learned that the Mexicans had issued orders for the Americans' detention. On March 6, 1846, Frémont moved his party to Hawk's Peak, constructed earthworks, and raised an American flag over the impromptu fort. Frémont held the fortification for four days, awaiting an attack from a large Mexican force under General Castro. When the attack did not materialize, Frémont returned to Sutter's Fort, leaving the earthworks intact and camp fires still burning. Marine lieutenant Archibald Gillespie overtook Frémont on his march north, with orders from Washington for Frémont to serve in the war with Mexico as a lieutenant colonel in the Mounted Rifles.

The Hawk's Peak Affair was not very significant in itself, but the serious distrust and antipathy between the Americans and the Mexicans ultimately took form in increasingly negative diplomatic relations between the United States and Mexico, fueling the fires of war.

DEBRA J. SHEFFER

See also

California; Californios; Castro, José María; Frémont, John Charles; Gillespie, Archibald H.; Sutter's Fort.

References

Cleland, Robert Glass. *A History of California: The American Period.* New York: Macmillan, 1922.

Goetzmann, William H. *Army Exploration in the American West, 1803–1863.* Austin: Texas State Historical Association, 1991.

Harlow, Neal. *California Conquered: War and Peace on the Pacific, 1846–1850.* Berkeley: University of California Press, 1982.

Hays, John Coffee
Birth Date: January 28, 1817
Death Date: April 21, 1883

Noted Texas Ranger. John Coffee Hays was born in Little Cedar Lick (Wilson County), Tennessee, on January 28, 1817. His father was a War of 1812 veteran and a personal friend of both Andrew Jackson and Sam Houston. In 1832, Hays moved to Mississippi and four years later to Texas, although he did not participate in the 1836 Texas Revolution.

Upon the intercession of Sam Houston, Hays received a commission in the Army of the Republic of Texas; he was detailed to the Rangers and by 1840 had been elevated to the rank of captain. With fellow Ranger Captain Samuel H. Walker, Hays introduced the Colt revolver to those living along the western frontier. Hays saw action against Mexican bandits and Comanches and was a leader in the recapture of San Antonio from a Mexican expedition against the town in 1842. That same year, he was promoted to major. Also in 1842, Hays's Ranger detachment accompanied

Texas Ranger John Coffee Hays led two regiments of Texas volunteers during the Mexican-American War. Both units were accused of having committed atrocities against Mexican civilians. (Library of Congress)

the aborted Somervell Expedition to Mexico but left it prior to its surrender at Mier in December.

When the Mexican-American War began in the spring of 1846, Hays organized and became the colonel of the 1st Regiment, Texas Mounted Riflemen, which joined Major General Zachary Taylor's army in May 1846. The regiment served mainly as a guard and scout detail while Taylor's force marched into northern Mexico. At the Battle of Monterrey, Hays's regiment helped secure the American victory. Attached to Brigadier General William J. Worth's division, Hays's regiment played a key role in interdicting the road to Saltillo and in storming El Soldato on Federation Hill and Bishop's Palace on Independence Hill. As effective as Hays's regiment was, however, it was guilty of having committed atrocities against civilians on the march to Monterrey and in the city itself. In mid-October 1846, the regiment disbanded because the service commitment of most of its men had expired. Hays himself returned to Texas, marrying there in April 1847.

Eager to rejoin the U.S. war effort, in July 1847 Hays recruited a new 400-man mounted rifle regiment, which was assigned the task of fighting Mexican guerrillas who were then threatening Winfield Scott's supply line between Veracruz and Mexico City. Hays and his men arrived at Veracruz on October 17 and were attached to Brigadier General Joseph Lane's brigade. In November, Hays's regiment performed well during skirmishes at Izúcar de Matamoros and Galaxara. On December 6, Hays's force entered Mexico City. However, some of his men were accused of having perpetrated atrocities against Mexican civilians, which forced General Taylor to banish the unit from the city. On January 10, 1848, Taylor ordered Hays to pursue a group of Mexican guerrillas, and six weeks later, on February 25, Hay's regiment caught a group of guerrillas and rancheros unaware, in the process killing at least 150 of them. This action is considered to be the last of the Mexican-American War.

On April 30, 1848, Hays and his regiment mustered out of service and left Veracruz via boat for the United States. Hays went to San Antonio for a short while before heading west at the start of the California Gold Rush. From 1850 to 1853, he served as sheriff for San Francisco County. In 1853 President Franklin Pierce appointed Hays as the U.S. surveyor general for California. Hays subsequently became involved in numerous business activities, including banking, utilities, ranching, and real estate. He was one of the founders and developers of Oakland, California. He remained active in California politics and was a delegate to the 1876 Democratic National Convention. Hays died on April 21, 1883, at Piedmont, California.

Paul G. Pierpaoli Jr.

See also

Comanches; Houston, Samuel; Galaxara, Skirmish at; Guerrilla Warfare; Lane, Joseph; Mier Expedition; Monterrey, Battle of; Rancheros; Revolvers; Saltillo; Texas Rangers; Taylor, Zachary; Walker, Samuel Hamilton; Worth, William Jenkins.

References

Collins, Michael L. *Texas Devils: Rangers and Regulars on the Lower Rio Grande, 1846–1861.* Norman: University of Oklahoma Press, 2008.

Cutrer, Thomas W. *Ben McCulloch and the Frontier Military Tradition.* Chapel Hill: University of North Carolina Press, 1993.

Greer, James K. *Colonel Jack Hays: Texas Frontier Leader and California Builder.* New York: Dutton, 1952. Reprint, College Station: Texas A&M University Press, 1987.

Webb, Walter Prescott. *The Texas Rangers in the Mexican War.* Austin: Jenkins Garrett Press, 1975.

Hébert, Paul Octave

Birth Date: December 12, 1818
Death Date: August 29, 1880

U.S. and Confederate Army officer and governor of Louisiana (1853–1856). Paul Octave Hébert was born on December 12, 1818, in Iberville Parish, Louisiana. In 1836, he graduated first in his class from Jefferson College in Saint James Parish and immediately entered the U.S. Military Academy at West Point, graduating first in his class there as well in 1840 and receiving a commission as a second lieutenant in the Corps of Engineers.

After teaching engineering at West Point during 1841–1842, Hébert left the army on March 31, 1845, to become state engineer for Louisiana. However, as hostilities increased in Mexico, he reentered the army on March 3, 1847, and was commissioned lieutenant colonel of the 3rd U.S. Infantry. He distinguished himself at the Battles of Contreras and at Churubusco. Brigadier General Franklin Pierce's battle reports noted Hébert's heroism on the field. Hébert was then assigned to the 14th U.S. Infantry and served with that regiment for the remainder of the war. On September 8, 1847, Major General Winfield Scott brevetted Hébert to colonel for gallantry during the Battle of El Molino del Rey. Hébert also took part in the storming of Chapultepec and Mexico City.

Following the war, Hébert returned to Louisiana to manage his sugar plantation. In 1849, he ran for a state senate seat as a Democrat but lost the election by nine votes. Three years later, Hébert was elected governor of his state, an office he held from 1853 to 1856.

When Louisiana seceded from the Union on January 26, 1861, Hébert was commissioned a brigadier generalship by Governor Thomas Overton Moore and was assigned to the command of the state's volunteer militia. On February 5, 1861, the Confederate provisional congress commissioned Hébert colonel of the 1st Louisiana Volunteer Artillery Regiment in the Confederate Army. Promoted to brigadier general on August 17, 1861, Hébert was assigned to the Department of Texas, charged with evaluating coastal defenses at Galveston. On May 26, 1862, he was awarded temporary command of the Trans-Mississippi Department until being replaced by Major General John B. Magruder on June 20. Hébert then moved back to his home state to command the

Subdistrict of North Louisiana. Hébert's only combat action came during the Battle of Milliken's Bend, Louisiana, on June 7, 1863. In January 1865, Hébert was assigned to command the District of Texas, New Mexico, and Arizona.

Following the war, Hébert received a pardon from President Andrew Johnson, which freed him from the political restrictions placed on most former Confederate officers. He then returned to his plantation and immersed himself in politics. Although he never again sought office for himself, Hébert led a faction of the Louisiana Democratic Party that backed liberal Republican Horace Greeley's presidential campaign of 1872. The following year, Republican carpetbagger Governor William Pitt Kellogg favored Hébert with a seat on the Louisiana Board of Engineers.

Hébert was appointed to the U.S. Board of Engineers' Mississippi River Commission in 1874 to direct the building of a levee system. From 1877 to the end of his life, he was an active member of his state's Democratic Party. Hébert died on August 29, 1880, while in New Orleans.

ANGELA D. TOOLEY AND JIM PIECUCH

See also

Churubusco, Battle of; Contreras, Battle of; El Molino del Ray, Battle of; Pierce, Franklin; Scott, Winfield.

References

Frazier, Donald S., ed. *The United States and Mexico at War: Nineteenth-Century Expansionism and Conflict.* New York: Simon and Schuster, 1998.

Warner, Ezra J. *Generals in Gray: Lives of the Confederate Commanders.* Baton Rouge: Louisiana State University Press, 1959.

Henderson, Archibald
Birth Date: January 21, 1783
Death Date: January 6, 1859

U.S. Marine Corps commandant, often referred to as the "Grand Old Man of the Marine Corps," having served for nearly 53 years. Archibald Henderson was born near the village of Dumfries, Virginia, on January 21, 1783. After working in his father's ironworks for a time, he secured a commission as a second lieutenant in the Marine Corps on June 4, 1806. He was promoted to first lieutenant on March 6, 1807, and to captain on April 1, 1811.

Henderson commanded the marine detachment in the frigate *President* during 1811–1812 and was assigned to the Charleston Navy Yard at the beginning of the War of 1812 during 1812–1813. In June 1814, he took command of the marine detachment in the frigate *Constitution,* and he took part in the engagement with and capture of the British frigate *Cyane* and sloop *Levant.* In 1816 he was brevetted major to date from August 1814.

From September 16, 1818 to March 2, 1819, Henderson was acting Marine Corps commandant. On October 17, 1820, following the cashiering of Lieutenant Colonel Commandant Anthony Gale,

Lieutenant Colonel Henderson was appointed the fifth commandant of the corps. He served in this position for almost 39 years, the longest tenure in that position in history. On July 1, 1834, he was promoted to colonel commandant.

As commandant, Henderson not only restored the reputation of the Marine Corps, but is generally credited with preserving the corps, thwarting an attempt by President Andrew Jackson in 1829 to combine it with the army. Instead, in 1834 Congress passed the Act for the Better Organization of the Marine Corps, ensuring that the marines would remain part of the Navy Department. Henderson proved to be an able administrator who established the rigid, Spartan training regimen for which the marines became famous, and he secured better facilities for the men. He also made standard the carrying of the Mameluke pattern sword by marine officers. He was also able to expand the Marine Corps' role beyond mere ship service and naval yard security. Taking advantage of the Indian Wars, he developed select marine battalions that could serve in the field in conjunction with the army.

Indeed, Henderson took to the field himself while commandant. In 1836 Jackson ordered Henderson to send marines to assist in fighting during the Creek War. Henderson personally led two battalions of marines, more than half of the corps, in fighting in Alabama and Georgia. On the conclusion of the Creek War that

Colonel Commandant Archibald Henderson served 52 years as a U.S. Marine Corps officer. His 38-year tenure as commandant saw great expansion in numbers and increased professionalism. (National Archives)

summer, the marines transferred to Florida, where they fought in the Second Seminole War (1835–1842). Henderson was brevetted brigadier general on January 27, 1837, for his role in the fighting.

Henderson lobbied unceasingly for an expansion in the size of the corps, but he achieved this as a consequence of the Mexican-American War, although the battalion he organized to take part in amphibious operations with the navy did not arrive in Mexico until three months after the fall of Veracruz. (Some 180 marines from the ships of the Home Squadron did take part in the landings, however.) Attached to Major General John A. Quitman's division, the marine battalion gained laurels in the assault of Chapultepec Castle on September 13, 1847.

Henderson was a strong advocate for the marines acquiring their own artillery units, and he secured authorization for artillery training in 1857. This helped ensure the future role of the corps in amphibious warfare. In June 1857 Henderson played an important role in suppressing rioters supporting the Know-Nothing Party in Washington, D.C. Henderson died suddenly in Washington, D.C., on January 6, 1859.

SPENCER C. TUCKER

See also

Mexico City, Battle for; Quitman, John Anthony; United States Marine Corps; Veracruz, Landing at and Siege of.

References

Dawson, Joseph G. "With Fidelity and Effectiveness: Archibald Henderson's Lasting Legacy to the U.S. Marine Corps." *Journal of Military History* 62, no. 4 (October 1998): 727–753.

Millett, Allan R. *Semper Fidelis: The History of the United States Marine Corps.* New York: Macmillan, 1980.

Henderson, James Pinckney
Birth Date: March 31, 1808
Death Date: June 4, 1858

Attorney, soldier, Texas politician, and U.S. senator. James Pinckney Henderson was born on March 31, 1808, in Lincolnton, North Carolina. He attended the University of North Carolina, read for the law, and was admitted to the bar in 1828. He then commenced a law practice in Lincolnton. In 1835 he moved to Canton, Mississippi, where he took up the practice of law. The following year, at the start of the Texas Revolution, he raised a group of volunteers to fight in that struggle, the cost of which he incurred himself. Although he arrived in Texas after independence had been won at San Jacinto, he was commissioned a brigadier general in the Texas army. Later in 1836, he served in Texas president Sam Houston's cabinet as attorney general before becoming secretary of state in January 1837, succeeding Stephen F. Austin, who had died in office.

The following year, Henderson toured Great Britain and Western Europe as Texas's official representative in an attempt to garner financial support for the fledgling Texas Republic. In 1844, he went to Washington, D.C., to effect Texas annexation. It was Henderson who proposed the use of a joint congressional resolution as a means to secure the annexation of Texas. Henderson also served as a delegate to the Texas State Constitutional Convention.

After Texas was admitted to the Union in December 1845, Texans elected Henderson as their first governor in 1846. When the Mexican-American War began in May 1846, Henderson was granted permission by the Texas legislature to lead a division of Texas mounted volunteers. He was commissioned a major general of volunteers and joined Major General Zachary Taylor's Army of Occupation in southern Texas. His division saw action at the Battle of Monterrey, after which it was disbanded. With Jefferson Davis and Albert Sidney Johnston, Henderson briefly served on the commission that produced the Armistice of Monterrey. He subsequently returned to Texas and resumed his gubernatorial duties.

He declined to seek a second term in office and retired to private life. In October 1857, the Texas legislature elected Henderson to a U.S. Senate seat, which had been recently vacated by the death of Senator Thomas J. Rusk. In rapidly declining health, Henderson served in the Senate from November 9, 1857, until his death in Washington, D.C., on June 4, 1858.

PAUL G. PIERPAOLI JR.

James Pinckney Henderson was the first governor of the state of Texas. He served during 1846–1847 and was later a U.S. senator. (Texas State Library & Archives Commission)

Eisenhower, John S. D. *So Far from God: The U.S. War with Mexico, 1846–1848.* Norman: University of Oklahoma Press, 1989.

Herrera, José Joaquín de
Birth Date: February 23, 1792
Death Date: February 10, 1854

Mexican army officer who served twice as president of Mexico, just prior to and after the war with the United States. José Joaquín de Herrera was born on February 23, 1792, at Jalapa, Veracruz. He joined the Spanish army at a young age and fought on the royalist side during Mexico's War of Independence. He saw action in a number of skirmishes before retiring in 1820 as a lieutenant colonel. Herrera then briefly operated a drugstore before rejoining the army once Agustín de Iturbide called for independence under the Plan of Iguala in 1821.

Herrera rose to the rank of brigadier general before joining the movement that deposed Iturbide in 1823. He held a variety of important government and military positions during the next two decades. Herrera served as minister of war, as a member of Congress, and as governor of the Federal District (Mexico City). Most public-spirited Mexicans regarded him as a humane and honest man, as well as a moderate liberal federalist.

Herrera came to the presidency during a difficult time in Mexico's history. On December 6, 1844, opponents of General Antonio López de Santa Anna staged a coup that toppled his regime. Given that Herrera then served as president of the Council of Government, the presidency fell to Herrera; elections held the following summer formally conferred that post to him in September.

Herrera faced numerous problems when he took office late in 1844, but the most serious issue that troubled his administration was the question of Texas, the independence of which Mexican governments had refused to acknowledge since 1836. During the next decade periodical raids by both Texans and Mexicans over the disputed border frequently broke an uneasy peace, and Mexican hard-liners would not support any government that accepted an independent Texas. The situation worsened early in 1845 when the U.S. government indicated that it was prepared to annex Texas into the Union. What had been considered an internal Mexican problem now included a powerful foreign aggressor.

As a realist and a general, Herrera realized that Mexico could not hope to win a war with the United States, and in the fall of 1845 he agreed to accept John Slidell as a representative of the U.S. government in an effort to settle the dispute peacefully. Herrera was criticized by hard-liners for allowing Slidell, whose mission was supposed to remain secret, into the country, and some feared he would not stand up to the United States should that prove necessary. Herrera's apparent indecisiveness provided General Mariano Paredes y Arrillaga with a pretext to rise against him in mid-December 1845, and that December 30 Paredes forced Herrera to resign.

See also
Austin, Stephen Fuller; Houston, Samuel; Monterrey, Armistice of; Monterrey, Battle of; Taylor, Zachary; Texas; Texas Revolution.

References
Texas House of Representatives. *Biographical Directory of the Texan Conventions and Congresses, 1832–1845.* Austin, TX: Book Exchange, 1941.
Winchester, Robert. *James Pinckney Henderson, Texas' First Governor.* San Antonio, TX: Naylor, 1971.

Heredia, José Antonio de
Birth Date: ca. 1800
Death Date: 1870

Mexican army general. José Antonio de Heredia was born in Chilpancingo (state of Guerrero) in southern Mexico in 1800. Nothing more is known about the circumstances of his birth or early years. Heredia entered military service with the Spanish colonial army around 1815 and fought on the royalist side in the war for independence before embracing Colonel Agustín de Iturbide's Plan of Iguala in 1821. After Mexican independence was secured that same year, he held a series of commands in the Mexican army, and by 1844 he had risen to the rank of general of brigade. During 1844 and early 1845, he served as military commander and governor of the state of Durango.

When the Mexican-American War began in the spring of 1846, Heredia was dispatched to Chihuahua, where he was ordered to repulse a U.S. force bound for Chihuahua under the command of Colonel Alexander Doniphan. On February 28, 1847, Heredia, along with General Pedro García Conde and Governor Ángel Trías Álvarez, led more than 2,500 Mexican troops unsuccessfully against Doniphan's men at the Battle of Río Sacramento. Mexican losses totaled more than 500 killed, wounded, or captured compared to only 9 killed or wounded on the American side.

After the battle, Heredia's military superiors ordered a court of inquiry against him amid charges of military misconduct and incompetence, but he was eventually cleared of all charges. When the Mexican-American War ended in 1848, Heredia stayed in Durango and saw sporadic action against hostile Indians. As governor of Durango, he was credited with establishing several public institutions, the most notable of which was the state's first public library system. During the French intervention in the 1860s, Heredia supported the French-installed puppet emperor Maximilian I but was imprisoned for nearly two years after that regime failed in 1867. Heredia died in Mexico City in 1870.

PAUL G. PIERPAOLI JR.

See also
Doniphan, Alexander William; Durango, State of; García Conde, Pedro; Río Sacramento, Battle of; Trías Álvarez, Ángel.

References
Dawson, Joseph G. *Doniphan's Epic March: The 1st Missouri Volunteers in the Mexican War.* Lawrence: University Press of Kansas, 1999.

Presidents of Mexico, 1835–1851

Name	Party	Start Date	End Date
Miguel Barragán	Liberal	January 28, 1835	February 27, 1836
José Justo Corro	Conservative	March 2, 1836	April 19, 1837
Anastasio Bustamante	Conservative	April 19, 1837	March 20, 1839
Antonio López de Santa Anna	Liberal-Conservative	March 20, 1839	July 10, 1839
Nicolás Bravo	Conservative	July 10, 1839	July 19, 1839
Anastasio Bustamante	Conservative	July 19, 1839	September 22, 1841
Francisco Javier Echeverría	Conservative	September 22, 1841	October 10, 1841
Antonio López de Santa Anna	Liberal-Conservative	October 10, 1841	October 26, 1842
Nicolás Bravo	Conservative	October 26, 1842	March 4, 1843
Antonio López de Santa Anna	Liberal-Conservative	March 4, 1843	October 4, 1843
Valentín Canalizo	Conservative	October 4, 1843	June 4, 1844
Antonio López de Santa Anna	Liberal-Conservative	June 4, 1844	September 12, 1844
José Joaquín de Herrera	Liberal	September 12, 1844	September 21, 1844
Valentín Canalizo	Conservative	September 21, 1844	December 6, 1844
José Joaquín de Herrera	Liberal	December 7, 1844	December 30, 1845
Gabriel Valencia	Liberal	December 30, 1845	January 2, 1846
Mariano Paredes	Conservative	January 4, 1846	July 28, 1846
José Mariano Salas	Conservative	August 5, 1846	December 23, 1846
Valentín Gómez Farías	Liberal	December 24, 1846	March 21, 1847
Antonio López de Santa Anna	Liberal-Conservative	March 21, 1847	April 2, 1847
Pedro María de Anaya	Liberal	April 2, 1847	May 20, 1847
Antonio López de Santa Anna	Liberal-Conservative	May 20, 1847	September 15, 1847
Manuel de la Peña y Peña	Liberal	September 26, 1847	November 13, 1847
Pedro María de Anaya	Liberal	November 13, 1847	January 8, 1848
Manuel de la Peña y Peña	Liberal	January 8, 1848	June 3, 1848
José Joaquín de Herrera	Liberal	June 3, 1848	January 15, 1851

Herrera remained active in national affairs following his ouster from office. He served as commander general of Mexico City and as a deputy to the constituent Congress that assembled in December 1846; in the latter capacity he issued a report that insured the joint election of Santa Anna and Valentín Gómez Farías as president and vice president. He briefly shared the presidency with Manuel de la Peña y Peña following the U.S. occupation of Mexico City in mid-September 1847, and he again took sole possession of the presidential office on June 3, 1848.

Perhaps the most noteworthy aspect of Herrera's second term in office (he served until January 15, 1851, and thus became the second man in Mexican history to that date who completed his full term as president) was the attempt to carry out far-reaching reforms intended to turn the army into a more professional institution. In the end, however, lack of funds limited their effectiveness. After leaving the presidency he operated the national pawn shop, the Monte de Piedad, and then retired in 1853. Herrera died in poverty in Tacubaya on February 10, 1854.

TIM WATTS AND PEDRO SANTONI

See also

Canalizo, Valentín; Mexico; *Moderados*; Paredes y Arrillaga, Mariano; Politics, Mexican; Santa Anna, Antonio López de; Texas; Texas Revolution.

References

Costeloe, Michael P. *The Central Republic in Mexico, 1835–1846: Hombres de Bien in the Age of Santa Anna.* New York: Cambridge University Press, 1993.
Cotner, Thomas Ewing. *The Military and Political Career of José Joaquin de Herrera, 1792–1854.* Whitefish, MT: Kessinger, 2008.
DePalo, William A., Jr. *The Mexican National Army, 1822–1852.* College Station: Texas A&M University Press, 1997.
Fowler, Will. *Mexico in the Age of Proposals, 1821–1853.* Westport, CT: Greenwood Press, 1998.

Hill, Daniel Harvey
Birth Date: July 12, 1821
Death Date: September 24, 1889

U.S. and Confederate Army officer, educator, writer, and publisher. Daniel Harvey (D. H.) Hill, a descendant of American Revolutionary War patriots, was born on July 12, 1821, at Hill's Iron Works in York County, South Carolina. His father died when he was only four, and he grew up the youngest of 11 children in genteel poverty. Hill entered the U.S. Military Academy in 1838 and graduated in 1842 as a brevet second lieutenant of artillery. Hill served with the 1st and 3rd Artillery Regiments for three years before deploying to Texas in 1845 as part of the Army of Occupation under Brigadier General Zachary Taylor.

Hill was transferred to the 4th Artillery in January 1846 and distinguished himself in the Battle of Monterrey in September 1846. The following March, as a new first lieutenant, he took part in the siege of Veracruz, followed by the Battle of Cerro Gordo in April. Hill led one group of attackers in the Battle of Contreras in

August, and in September he volunteered to help lead the assault on the fortress of Chapultepec. For his gallantry at Contreras and Chapultepec, Hill received brevet promotions to captain and major, respectively.

Hill distinguished himself throughout the Mexican-American War, but also anonymously published several critical newspaper articles about the inefficiency of the War Department and the poorly disciplined volunteer regiments. Something of a perfectionist and disillusioned by the wartime politics within the army, he resigned his commission in February 1849.

From 1849 to 1859 Hill taught mathematics at Washington College in Virginia and Davidson College in North Carolina. During that time he published a book on algebra and two religious texts. In 1859, he became superintendent of the North Carolina Military Institute in Charlotte. In April 1861, Hill, a strong believer in state sovereignty, joined the Confederate cause as a colonel of North Carolina volunteers. He commanded a regiment in the Confederate victory at Big Bethel, Virginia, in June 1861, earning him promotion to brigadier general. Promoted to major general in March 1862, he commanded a division during the Peninsula and Maryland Campaigns and at the Battle of Fredericksburg. Although he performed well in all of these engagements, personal conflict with

Daniel Harvey Hill served as an artillery officer under generals Zachary Taylor and Winfield Scott during the Mexican-American War and was twice brevetted for gallantry. Hill was later a Confederate Army general. (Library of Congress)

General Robert E. Lee removed him from consideration for higher command in the Army of Northern Virginia, and he remained in Richmond during the Gettysburg Campaign. Deeply religious, yet highly opinionated and fiercely protective of his reputation, Hill often clashed with fellow officers and politicians. These conflicts tended to overshadow his considerable tactical skill.

Transferred to the Army of Tennessee with the provisional rank of lieutenant general, Hill took command of one of Gen. Braxton Bragg's corps at the beginning of the Chickamauga Campaign, but his withering criticism of Bragg's perceived failures at Chickamauga cost him his command and his promotion was never confirmed by the Confederate Congress. Thereafter, Hill saw sporadic action, commanding a division under Joseph E. Johnston at Bentonville, the last battle of the Army of Tennessee, but never achieved his early promise.

After the war, Hill edited and published two periodicals, the *Land We Love* (1854–1869) and the *Southern Home* (1870–1877), which featured local news, articles on the Confederacy's military history, southern literature, and critiques of Reconstruction. He returned to academia in 1877, first as the president of the Arkansas Industrial University (later the University of Arkansas), and then as president of Middle Georgia Military and Agricultural College (now the Georgia Military College). Hill died on September 24, 1889, in Charlotte, North Carolina.

Brit K. Erslev

See also

Cerro Gordo, Battle of; Chapultepec, Battle of; Contreras, Battle of; Monterrey, Battle of; Taylor, Zachary; Veracruz, Landing at and Siege of.

References

Bridges, Hal. *Lee's Maverick General: Daniel Harvey Hill.* Lincoln: University of Nebraska Press, 1991.

Cullum, George Washington, comp. *Biographical Register of the Officers and Graduates of the U.S. Military Academy.* Vol. 2. West Point, NY: Association of Graduates, U.S. Military Academy, 1891.

Hughes, Nathaniel Cheairs, Jr., and Timothy D. Johnson, eds. *A Fighter from Way Back: The Mexican War Diary of Lt. Daniel Harvey Hill, 4th Artillery, USA.* Kent, OH: Kent State University Press, 2002.

Historiography of the Mexican-American War

A brief survey of historical works about the Mexican-American War written since the late 1840s reveals that historians' perceptions and interpretations have often been influenced by their own lives and times. Thus, American and Mexican historians have written about the same war from two very different perspectives and, consequently, have usually come to very different conclusions. Their systematic approach to understanding and explaining the past has produced various schools of thought regarding the causes, conduct, and effects of the war.

Participants who sought to record their personal accounts documented the conduct of the war. Soldiers from all branches of the service wrote journals, diaries, letters, and memoirs, many of which have been published, that provided firsthand accounts of battles and the daily routine of military life. For the most part, these accounts from the rank and file were limited in scope. Captain William Seaton Henry's *Campaign Sketches of the War with Mexico* (1847), for example, was one of the first officer accounts published. George Ballentine's *Autobiography of an English Soldier in the United States Army* (1853) is just one of many works that represented the experiences of enlisted men, and George C. Furber's *The Twelve Months Volunteer* (1848) is typical of scores of volunteer accounts.

Because many of the soldiers who served in the Mexican-American War also served in the American Civil War (1861–1865) and sought to document their military careers during both conflicts, more primary sources of this type were published after the Civil War. High-profile examples included an account by George B. McClellan, who rose to prominence during the Civil War. Years later, *The Mexican War Diary of General George B. McClellan* (1917) was published by Princeton University Press, and a revised and expanded edition, which included McClellan's wartime correspondence, was published by the Louisiana State University Press in 2009 as *The Mexican War Diary and Correspondence of George B. McClellan.* Also, Ulysses S. Grant, who served as a lieutenant in the Mexican War, general in chief of the U.S. Army during the Civil War, and as president of the United States published his *Personal Memoirs of U.S. Grant* (1885), which included accounts of the fighting in Mexico. As new primary sources have been discovered and edited by scholars, the publication of firsthand accounts of both obscure and famous individuals has continued unabated.

The two-year war that gained for the United States about one-half of Mexico's territory and settled the Texas question left Mexican intellectuals in a state of shock. Various authors were stunned and overwhelmed with anger over Mexico's loss. No Mexican historian doubted that the United States had been the aggressor, but many also blamed Mexican leadership for the fiasco. Mariano Otero's *Consideraciones sobre la situación política y social de la república mexicana en el año 1847,* published in 1848, argued that the national government had failed to cultivate a sense of nationhood in its people. Carlos María Bustamante's 1847 work, *El nuevo Bernal Díaz del Castillo, o sea, historia de la invasión de los anglo-americanos en México,* placed the blame for the defeat squarely on General Antonio López de Santa Anna's shoulders. Another contemporary account that tried to explain the military defeat, the joint effort of 15 men headed by Ramón Alcaraz, *Apuntes para la historia de la guerra entre México y los Estados Unidos* (1848), edited and republished in 1850 by Albert C. Ramsey as *The Other Side, or, Notes for the History of the War between Mexico and the United States,* indicted the United States as the aggressor and identified U.S. expansionism as a cause of the war.

Meanwhile, American critics of the war pinned the blame on President James K. Polk for beginning the conflict. According to the Whig thesis, Polk pushed for war with Mexico to please his slave-owning constituents in the Deep South, because war with Mexico would mean more southern territory added to the Union, which might mean the expansion of slavery. Polk tried to purchase land from Mexico, but, when Mexico refused to sell, he schemed to create a situation in which Mexico would appear to be the aggressor in a war that would achieve his quest for more slaveholding territory. The classic work on the Whig thesis was William Jay's *A Review of the Causes and Consequences of the Mexican War* (1849), a thesis given a modern and more scholarly statement in Glen W. Price's *Origins of the War with Mexico: The Polk-Stockton Intrigue* (1967).

In the late 1800s and early 1900s, the United States went through a period of overseas conquest and colonization, and American historians began to see the Mexican-American War as part of a larger expansionist trend. So, some historians took slavery out of the equation and replaced it with the idea that the war was caused by a desire to expand American boundaries. The reasons for this varied from economic to cultural and racial imperatives. However, influential works redirecting scholarship back to the Whig thesis have continued to appear. These include David Brion Davis's *The Slave Power and the Paranoid Style* (1969) and Leonard L. Richards's *The Slave Power: The Free North and Southern Domination, 1780–1860* (2000).

The earliest general American histories written shortly after the Mexican-American War sought to explain the causes of the war. Not surprisingly, while patriotic Mexican writers blamed the United States for starting the war, American historians in tune with the so-called democratic thesis blamed Mexico for the conflict. John S. Jenkins, an American lawyer, wrote the first scholarly account of the war. In his *History of the War between the United States and Mexico* (1850), he rationalized that, because Texas had successfully maintained itself in rebellion from Mexico for 10 years, it deserved to be recognized as an independent nation with the right to enter into annexation talks with the United States. According to Jenkins, Mexico was to blame for the war because of its refusal to negotiate over Texas, a diplomatic stance that invited hostilities. In essence, Mexico's stubbornness had left the Americans no choice but to fight for what was right.

Many U.S. authors were influenced by Jenkins and wrote along the same lines. Nahum Capen took the idea of "right" to an ultimate level. In *The Republic of the United States of America: Its Duties to Itself, and Its Responsible Relations to Other Countries; Embracing Also a Review of the Late War between the United States and Mexico: Its Causes and Results* (1848), Capen justified the war by claiming the providence of God. In Capan's Puritan philosophy of history, the United States had shown Mexico kindness and patience, but, by refusing to communicate, cooperate, or pay its debts, Mexico had shown itself to be ungodly. Consequently, because God was always on the side of right, God had chosen to side with the United States and exercise judgment on Mexico. In Capan's opinion, the U.S. victory was proof positive of this fact. According to Capan's view, the causes and effects of the war had been God's will.

Mexican scholarly literature on the war largely disappeared after 1890 and did not reemerge until the 1940s. Perhaps the Mexican Revolution of 1910 changed the focus of historians for five decades until the centennial of the Mexican-American War revived interest in it, or maybe the newly enjoyed friendship with its American ally during World War II spurred Mexican historians to reassess its past relationship with its powerful northern neighbor. In any case, in the 1940s Mexican writers produced the most fair and balanced accounts of the war to that point in time. Two important objective works of this type, both published in 1947, were Vicente Fuentes Díaz's *La intervención norteamericana en México* and José Valadés's *Breve historia de la guerra con los Estados Unidos.*

The Vietnam War era brought renewed interest in the conflict of the 1840s. Revolutions in Cuba and Latin America gave Mexican historians a different perspective on the Mexican-American War. In their view, American imperialistic policies being played out in South and Central America in the 1960s were a continuation of the imperialist philosophy that had triggered the North American invasion of Mexico in 1846. Consequently, most Mexican historians disagreed with U.S. involvement in Vietnam, and histories written during the 1960s and 1970s tended to be highly critical of U.S. foreign policy. Two works that appeared in 1971, Agustín Cue Cánovas's *Los Estados Unidos y el México olvidado* and Gastón Garcia Cantu's *Las invasiones norteamericanas en México,* are representative of this type of literature. Midway through the decade Jesús Velasco Márquez and Gene M. Brack published books that offered a solid overview of the origins and nature of Mexican attitudes toward the United States—*La guerra del 47 y la opinión pública (1845–1848)* and *Mexico Views Manifest Destiny, 1821–1846: An Essay on the Origins of the Mexican War.*

The 1980s saw a return of a more positive Mexican historiography, and Mexican historians concentrated more on what had been gained from the war rather than on what had been lost. For example, César Sepúlveda's *La frontera norte de México: Historia, conflictos, 1762–1982* (second revised edition, 1983) praised the Mexican diplomats who adroitly negotiated the Treaty of Guadalupe Hidalgo that formally ended the war in 1848. Provisions gained by Mexico included a $15 million payment and the right of Mexicans to remain on their land if they chose to stay in newly acquired American territory.

Surprisingly, in the anniversary-conscious United States, the 1940s saw no revival of interest in the U.S.-Mexican War. Although important general histories of the war have been written since the 1980s, such as John S. D. Eisenhower's *So Far from God* (1989), one recent trend in historiography by both American and Mexican historians has been to write biographies of war participants. These works include K. Jack Bauer's *Zachary Taylor: Soldier, Planter, and Statesman of the Old South* (1985), John S. D. Eisenhower's *Winfield Scott: Agent of Destiny* (1997), Timothy D. Johnson's *Winfield Scott: The Quest for Military Glory* (1998), Mark E. Byrnes's *James K. Polk: A Biographical Companion* (2001), and Will Fowler's *Santa Anna of Mexico* (2007).

The military has been another area that has become the subject of increased study. James M. McCaffrey's *Army of Manifest Destiny: The American Soldier in the Mexican War, 1846–1848* (1992) was the first book to examine the detailed workings of the U.S. Army during the war. Then, in 1997 Richard Bruce Winders examined the effects of U.S. politics on the army in *Mr. Polk's Army: The American Military Experience in the Mexican War.* That same year William A. DePalo Jr. published *The Mexican National Army, 1822–1852,* which looked at the institutional development of Mexico's military establishment as a national force.

Historians have also recently addressed other heretofore neglected aspects of the war. Two collections of essays—Laura Herrera Serna's (coordinator) *México en guerra (1846–1848): Perspectivas regionales* (1997) and Josefina Zoraida Vázquez's *México al tiempo de su guerra con Estados Unidos (1846–1848)* (1997)—scrutinized how the conflict affected the country's various regions. Irving W. Levinson's *Wars within War: Mexican Guerrillas, Domestic Elites, and the United States of America, 1846–1848* (2005) illuminated the activities of many of the nameless guerrillas who roamed the Mexican countryside and resisted U.S. forces, while Luis Fernando Granados's *Sueñan las piedras: Alzamiento ocurrido en la ciudad de México, 14, 15 y 16 de septiembre de 1847* (2003) explains the reasons that led the capital's urban poor to attack the U.S. soldiers who occupied the Mexican capital with stones, bottles, rocks, and assorted loose objects.

Three recent articles by historians of Mexico have shed light on the war's cultural dimensions. Laura Herrera Serna studied the vision of the conflict generated by popular *calendarios* (almanacs), one of the vehicles that helped build a sense of national identity in nineteenth-century Mexico, in "La guerra entre México y Estados Unidos en los calendarios de mediados del siglo XIX" (2000). Scholars have also probed the ways in which Mexican statesmen manufactured heroic symbols and figures and subsequently negotiated their public memory to bolster the country's self-esteem and national spirit in the aftermath of war. Enrique Plasencia de la Parra separates myth from truth about the six cadets from the national military academy who fought to their deaths at the Battle of Chapultepec in "Conmemoración de la hazaña épica de los Niños Héroes: Su origen, desarrollo y simbolismos" (1995), and Pedro Santoni analyzes the public ceremonies staged in Mexico City to honor the elite national guardsmen who died defending the capital during the war with the United States in "Where Did the Other Heroes Go? Exalting the *Polko* National Guard Battalions in Nineteenth-Century Mexico" (2002).

Finally, two finely crafted scholarly volumes offer novel insights on the history of the present-day southwestern United States during the era of Mexican rule (1821–1846) and break new ground about the region and the factors that led to the U.S. war with Mexico. In *Changing Identities at the Frontier: Texas and New Mexico, 1800–1850* (2005) Andrés Reséndez examines the momentous collision between the nation-building project of the Mexican state and the shift of the frontier economy toward U.S.

markets, while Brian DeLay's *War of a Thousand Deserts: Indian Raids and the U.S.-Mexican War* (2008) explores the incursions that three societies of plains Indians (Kiowas, Kiowa Apaches, and Comanches) carried out across eight northern Mexican states during the 1830s and 1840s and shows how the ensuing havoc both undermined Mexico's ability to resist the U.S. advance in the mid-1840s and fueled the latter's expansionist agenda.

In conclusion, then, historians have continued to examine a variety of aspects of the Mexican-American War, and as their focus has diversified, so too, one hopes, will the public's interest in learning more about this seminal event in the history of both nations.

ROLANDO AVILA AND PEDRO SANTONI

See also
Bibliography.

References
Benjamin, Thomas. "Recent Historiography of the Origins of the Mexican War." *New Mexico Historical Review* 54 (1979): 169–181.

Brack, Gene M. *Mexico Views Manifest Destiny, 1821–1846: An Essay on the Origins of the Mexican War.* Albuquerque: University of New Mexico Press, 1975.

Harstad, Peter T., and Richard W. Resh. "The Causes of the Mexican War: A Note on Changing Interpretations." *Arizona and the West* 6 (1964): 289–302.

Johannsen, Robert W. *To the Halls of the Montezumas: The Mexican War in the American Imagination.* New York: Oxford University Press, 1985.

Robinson, Cecil, ed. *The View from Chapultepec: Mexican Writers on the Mexican-American War.* Tucson: University of Arizona Press, 1989.

Santoni, Pedro, and Richard Bruce Winders. "Historiography." In *The United States and Mexico at War: Nineteenth-Century Expansionism and Conflict*, edited by Donald S. Frazier, 193–197. New York: Simon & Schuster, 1998.

Van Horn, James. "Trends in Historical Interpretation: James K. Polk." *North Carolina Historical Review* 42 (1965): 454–464.

Vázquez, Josefina Zoraida. *Mexicanos y norteamericanos ante la Guerra del 47.* Mexico City: Ediciones Ateneo, 1977.

Hitchcock, Ethan Allen
Birth Date: May 18, 1798
Death Date: August 5, 1870

U.S. military officer and author. Born on May 18, 1798, in Vergennes, Vermont, Ethan Allen Hitchcock was a descendant of a prominent New England family. His father was a U.S. Circuit Court judge and his mother was a daughter of Ethan Allen, the American Revolutionary War hero. After graduating from the U.S. Military Academy, West Point, in 1817 and being commissioned a second lieutenant in the Corps of Artillery, Hitchcock served on garrison duty in Alabama and Louisiana before being appointed to the faculty of West Point in 1824.

An administrative quarrel at the academy led to Hitchcock's dismissal; he was subsequently ordered to garrison duty in

Minnesota in 1827. He returned to West Point in 1829 and served as commandant of cadets for three years, from 1830 to 1833.

In 1833, Hitchcock left West Point to join his company in Wisconsin. He then was assigned to duty in Florida as acting inspector general during the Second Seminole War (1835–1842). Hitchcock denounced that conflict as being the result of the U.S. government's unreasonable and deceitful policies toward the Seminoles.

From 1837 to 1842, Hitchcock resided in Saint Louis, Missouri, serving as a diligent and principled disbursing officer for Indian funds. In 1842, as a lieutenant colonel, he received command of the 3rd U.S. Infantry, which he transformed into one of the army's best fighting regiments. When the Mexican-American War began in 1846, Hitchcock was on duty with Brigadier General Zachary Taylor's forces in Texas. He opposed the war as immoral but nevertheless felt duty-bound to follow orders.

Major General Winfield Scott, preparing to launch an amphibious attack on the city of Veracruz, requested and received $30,000 from the War Department for covert activities. Scott also requested that Hitchcock be on his staff and put him in charge of covert operations, including the so-called Mexican Spy Agency. Hitchcock successfully managed the company's paid spies, couriers, and scouts, who remained loyal despite inducements from the Mexicans to betray American forces. In addition to his espionage

Ethan A. Hitchcock was a U.S. Army officer who led some of the army's best-trained regiments. He denounced U.S. Native American policies during the Second Seminole War. Hitchcock thought the Mexican-American War was immoral but nonetheless played an important role in the U.S. victory. Hitchcock also served during the Civil War, retiring in 1867 as a major general. (Library of Congress)

activities, Hitchcock served as an adviser to Scott on a variety of issues and helped plan for the eventual occupation of Mexico City. Hitchcock was twice brevetted during the war—once to colonel and then to brigadier general.

As commander of the Military Division of the Pacific in San Francisco, California, following the Mexican-American War, Hitchcock ordered the seizure of William Walker's ship, thereby thwarting the U.S. adventurer's plans to take over Mexican territory in Baja California and use it as a base from which to extend slavery. In 1855, after being denied a leave of absence for health reasons, Hitchcock resigned his commission and lived in Saint Louis, devoting himself to philosophical and literary pursuits.

Reentering the army during the U.S. Civil War, Hitchcock received a commission as a major general of volunteers in February 1862, but only upon the direct intercession of his old commander, Winfield Scott. Stationed in Washington, D.C., Hitchcock was dumbfounded when Secretary of War Edwin M. Stanton offered to give him command of the Army of the Potomac, in place of the unsteady Major General George B. McClellan. Hitchcock told Stanton that his advanced age (he was then 64), precarious health, and military experience rendered him unsuitable for such a command.

Hitchcock nonetheless remained in Washington and became a friend and adviser to U.S. president Abraham Lincoln while serving as commissioner for the exchange of prisoners, beginning in November 1862, and president of the board of officers that revised the U.S. military code. Hitchcock ably handled the intricate negotiations and plethora of paperwork involved in prisoner exchanges. He held no active command during the war and saw no direct military action but did serve in several court-martial proceedings, including the one against Major General Fitz John Porter during 1862–1863. Some have said that Hitchcock's best service during the war occurred when he realized his own limitations and rejected Stanton's flattering overture in 1862. Hitchcock mustered out in 1867. He died on August 5, 1870, in Sparta, Georgia.

DAVID M. CARLETTA

See also

Espionage; Mexican Spy Company; Mexico, Occupation of; Polk, James Knox; Santa Anna, Antonio López de; Scott, Winfield; Taylor, Zachary; Veracruz; Veracruz, Landing at and Siege of.

References

Baker, George, trans. *México ante los ojos del ejército invasor de 1847 (Diario del coronel Ethan Allen Hitchcock)*. 1st Spanish ed. Mexico City: Universidad Nacional Autónoma de México, 1978.

Caruso, A. Brooke. *The Mexican Spy Company: United States Covert Operations in Mexico, 1845–1848*. Jefferson, NC: McFarland, 1991.

Croffut, W. A., ed. *Fifty Years in Camp and Field: Diary of Ethan Allen Hitchcock, Major-General, U.S.A.* New York: G. P. Putnam's Sons, 1909.

Foreman, Grant. *A Traveler in Indian Territory: The Journal of Ethan Allen Hitchcock, Late Major-General in the United States Army*. 1930. Reprint, Norman: University of Oklahoma Press, 1996.

Holzinger, José Sebastían

Birth Date: 1821
Death Date: Unknown

German-born Mexican naval officer. Little is known about José Sebastían Holzinger's early life, although there are references to his birth in Germany in 1821 and his residence in Veracruz in 1842, where he applied for service in the Secretariat of War and Navy. He was commissioned on February 10, 1842, as an "enabled" second lieutenant. That same day he was detailed to the *Regenerador,* a Mexican navy steam warship. One month later, Holzinger was transferred to another Mexican navy schooner, the *Áquila.*

Meanwhile, in 1842 Yucatán had declared its independence from Mexico and had also acquired the brig of war *El Yucateco,* with a crew of 70. The commander of the naval district of Veracruz developed a plan for cutting out the *El Yucateco* while it was at anchor under the guns of the fortress at Campeche. A boarding party from the Mexican pilot boat *Margarita,* which included Holzinger, captured *El Yucateco* on July 7. The vessel, renamed *Mexicano,* arrived in Veracruz on July 11 with its former crew as prisoners. In recognition of his role in the capture, Holzinger was confirmed as a second lieutenant.

Holzinger enhanced his naval reputation in subsequent engagements against Yucatán rebels and the Texas navy. He participated in the 1843 amphibious landings at Campeche, blockade of Yucatán, and the May 16 engagement that pitted the Mexican navy ships *Guadalupe, Regenerado,* and the *Moctezuma* against the Yucatán-Texan Squadron, composed of the Texan brig *Austin* and schooner *Wharton* and seven Yucatan naval vessels. After a fierce running battle, the *Austin* and *Wharton* put into Campeche and the Mexican vessels withdrew to sea. Although the engagement was, at best, a draw, Holzinger was awarded the Cross of Honor for his participation in the action, and, on February 21, 1844, he was advanced to first lieutenant.

During the Mexican-American War, Holzinger played a major role in defending Veracruz from U.S. forces; he provided highly effective service as he commanded a battery of guns at Fort Santa Bárbara in March 1847. A shortage of ammunition forced Holzinger to gather and utilized expended American shot.

During the exchange of fire, an American round took down the Mexican standard with a hit on the halyard. Holzinger attempted to reraise the flag, but a second round struck the rampart on which he had climbed, throwing him off the wall. He again climbed the rampart and replaced the colors. The fire from Holzinger's battery was so effective that it drew mention in a dispatch of Captain John H. Aulick of the frigate *Potomac.* The U.S. officers even inquired whether Holzinger's guns were manned by foreigners.

Holzinger saw no further service during the war. On September 14, 1848, he requested and was granted a discharge from service. He rejoined the navy five years later and in 1854 received orders to take command of the fortress protecting the approaches to Acapulco on Mexico's west coast. On March 27, 1855, he was promoted to commander for past services and merit, but he was discharged in November.

Holzinger again returned to active duty on March 24, 1858, at the rank of commander and was ordered to Tampico to supervise the conversion of two merchant ships into warships. He was promoted to captain at that time.

Upon the occupation of Tampico by constitutionalists on September 10, 1858, Holzinger was directed to leave Mexico. There is no account of his further undertakings or death. He is enshrined in the secretary of the marine/navy listing of "Illustrious Sailors" in the Mexican Naval Museum in Mexico City.

JEFFREY D. PEPPERS

See also

Mexico, Navy; Veracruz, Landing at and Siege of; Yucatán; Yucatán Revolt.

References

Bauer, K. Jack. *The Mexican War, 1846–1848.* New York: Macmillan, 1974.

Henderson, Timothy J. *A Glorious Defeat: Mexico and Its War with the United States.* New York: Hill and Wang, 2007.

Jordan, Jonathon W. *Lone Star Navy: Texas, the Fight for the Gulf of Mexico, and the Shaping of the American West.* Dulles, VA: Potomac Books, 2006.

Parker, William Harwar. *Recollections of a Naval Officer, 1841–1865.* Annapolis, MD: U.S. Naval Institute Press, 2010.

Houston, Samuel

Birth Date: March 2, 1793
Death Date: July 26, 1863

Soldier, frontiersman, and politician who led Texan forces during the struggle for independence from Mexico and subsequently became president of the Texas Republic. Samuel (Sam) Houston was born on March 2, 1793, in Rockbridge County, Virginia, but moved to Tennessee as a boy. A rebellious youth, Houston left the family farm at age 16 and lived with the Cherokees, by whom he was given the Native American name "Raven." He remained with the Cherokees for two years before he returned and established a school for frontier children.

One year after the outbreak of the War of 1812 Houston enlisted in the army as a private, but his leadership skills were quickly recognized and he was commissioned an ensign four months later. During the war, he served with Major General Andrew Jackson in the campaign against the Creeks, including the Battle of Horseshoe Bend, where he was wounded three times. His heroism and leadership caught the attention of Jackson, who subsequently helped Houston at several points during his career.

Houston remained in the army after the war and was promoted to second lieutenant. In 1817, he was assigned to participate in the removal of the Cherokees from their lands to the Oklahoma Territory. Houston resigned from the army the

following year after he was given an official reprimand by Secretary of War John C. Calhoun for appearing before the secretary in Cherokee garb.

Houston then studied law, passed the bar, and established a practice in Lebanon, Tennessee. On Jackson's recommendation, Houston was appointed a colonel and then elected major general of the state militia. Houston also became active in politics and was elected first as attorney general for Nashville and then to the U.S. House of Representatives in 1823. In Congress, Houston worked to support Jackson's candidacy for the presidency following the election of 1824. In 1827, he left the House and became governor of Tennessee. Although he was reelected in 1829, Houston left politics and Tennessee after a brief, failed marriage.

Houston then returned to live among the Cherokees, this time in Oklahoma, for a three-year period. During this time he met and married a woman of mixed Cherokee and European ancestry, and the couple established a trading post on the Neosho River. In 1832, Jackson, then president, dispatched Houston to Texas to negotiate with tribes in the region.

Houston became involved in regional politics in Texas and emerged as one of the foremost proponents of independence from Mexico. He attended the San Felipe Convention in 1833 that drew up a constitution for the territory and a petition to the Mexican government that requested the area be made a state. In 1835, he

Sam Houston led Texas forces in securing independence from Mexico. He then served as president of the Republic of Texas. His opposition to secession in 1861 ended his political career. (National Archives)

was appointed commander of the Army of Texas with the rank of major general. The following year, Houston was a delegate when the Texas Assembly declared independence. Although Mexican forces initially enjoyed military success against the rebellious Texans, Houston won a major victory at the Battle of San Jacinto on April 21, 1836. During the engagement, Houston was wounded and had his horse shot out from under him. The day after the battle, the Mexican commander General Antonio López de Santa Anna was captured. The battle confirmed Texan independence, although Mexico refused to accept the loss of Texas until after the Mexican-American War.

Houston's popularity led to his election as president of Texas in 1836. He worked hard to convince the United States to annex Texas as a new state and to improve relations between white settlers and Native Americans. After his first term as president ended in 1838, Houston served in the Texas House of Representatives and was reelected president in 1841. After Texas joined the Union in 1845, Houston served two terms in the U.S. Senate, where he supported the Mexican-American War.

In the Senate, Houston supported efforts to compromise on the issue of slavery and became well known as a staunch unionist Democrat. His support for the Union and his efforts on behalf of Native Americans eroded his popularity in Texas, however. He ran unsuccessfully for governor of Texas in 1857 and left the Senate in 1859. He again ran for governor that same year and won in his second attempt. Once in office, Houston favored the use of force to establish a protectorate over Mexico and other areas of Central America as a way to divert attention from the growing sectional strife in the Union.

Following the election of Abraham Lincoln in 1860, Houston called a special session of the Texas legislature to debate secession. He opposed secession, but the convention voted overwhelmingly to leave the Union. He oversaw the initial steps to sever ties with the Union but refused to take the oath of allegiance to the Confederacy. On March 16, 1861, the legislature removed him from office. Houston and his family moved to Huntsville, Texas, where he died on July 26, 1863.

JACK COVARRUBIAS AND TOM LANSFORD

See also
Alamo, Battle of the; Calhoun, John Caldwell; Cherokees; Congress, Texan; Congress, U.S.; Politics, Texan; San Jacinto, Battle of; Santa Anna, Antonio López de; Slavery; Texas; Texas Revolution.

References
Braider, Donald. *Solitary Star: A Biography of Sam Houston.* New York: Putnam, 1974.
Bruhl, Marshall de. *Sword of San Jacinto: A Life of Sam Houston.* New York: Random House, 1993.
Campbell, Randolph B. *Sam Houston and the American Southwest.* New York: Addison-Wesley, 1993.
Day, Donald, and Harry Herbert Ullom, eds. *The Autobiography of Sam Houston.* Norman: University of Oklahoma Press, 1954.
Williams, John Holt. *Sam Houston: A Biography of the Father of Texas.* New York: Simon and Schuster, 1993.

Huamantla, Battle of
Event Date: October 9, 1847

The last significant military engagement of the Mexican-American War. It took place on October 9, 1847, in and around the town of Huamantla, in modern-day Tlaxcala State. The Battle of Huamantla was perhaps the most tragic encounter of the war, as it resulted in the death of an American hero and the sacking of Huamantla in retaliation.

Only hours before Major General Winfield Scott's troops entered Mexico City on September 14, 1847, General Antonio López de Santa Anna led the remnants of his army out of the Mexican capital. The Americans may have seized the "Halls of the Montezumas," but Santa Anna was not ready to concede defeat.

Scott had spent the summer of 1847 in Puebla training his army and waiting for reinforcements before beginning his advance on Mexico City. He was, however, forced to leave nearly 2,000 American soldiers who were too sick to travel. He left a small garrison to guard them, counting on the arrival of more troops to bolster their numbers. Shortly after Scott departed for Mexico City, on September 13, 1847, Puebla fell under siege by Mexican irregulars under the command of General Joaquín Rea. The Americans claimed their besiegers threatened to turn the city into a "second Alamo" if they did not surrender.

Following his departure from Mexico City, Santa Anna and the remains of his command marched to Puebla and there joined Rea's forces who seemed to have the Americans trapped. Santa Anna knew that if he could capture Puebla, Scott's position in Mexico City would be much more difficult to sustain.

The American garrison held out despite the dire circumstances. Meanwhile, Brigadier General Joseph Lane was leading a relief column from Veracruz to Puebla. Learning of Lane's approach, Santa Anna proceeded with his troops to Huamantla, where he planned to attack Lane's force before it could relieve the American garrison at Puebla.

On October 8, 1847, Lane received word of Santa Anna's plan, and Company C of the U.S. Mounted Rifles, commanded by the well-known former Texas Ranger captain Samuel Hamilton Walker, dashed ahead to Huamantla in an attempt to pin Santa Anna until Lane's main force arrived. About midday, the Mounted Rifles rode through the town, driving out the Mexican troops. Riding back to the main plaza, Walker was shot and killed by a Mexican in hiding.

Walker had been one of the most popular and celebrated officers in the army, and, angered by his death, his soldiers broke into public buildings and private houses, looting and assaulting

Battle of Huamantla, October 9, 1847

	United States	Mexico
Killed	13	100
Wounded	11	300

The death of Captain Samuel Hamilton Walker at Huamantla, Mexico. This engagement, fought on October 9, 1847, was the last significant battle of the Mexican-American War. (Library of Congress)

the residents. Lane finally restored order and resumed his march toward Puebla, but not before some 50–100 Mexicans, including some civilians, had died. Lane reported his own casualties at 13 killed (including Walker) and 11 wounded. Meanwhile, Santa Anna escaped, although by that time he no longer wielded any military or political power.

On October 12, Lane's column reached Puebla and lifted the siege. Although the road to Mexico City continued to be rendered dangerous by guerrillas and bandits, the Battle of Huamantla and the raising of the siege of Puebla ended serious organized resistance in Mexico.

BRUCE WINDERS

See also

Guerrilla Warfare; Lane, Joseph; Mexico City; Mexico City, Battle for; Mexico City Campaign; Puebla; Puebla, Siege of; Rea, Joaquín; Santa Anna, Antonio López de; Scott, Winfield; Walker, Samuel Hamilton.

References

Carney, Stephen A. *The Occupation of Mexico, May 1846-July 1848.* Washington, DC: U.S. Army Center of Military History, 2006.
Oswandel, J. Jacob. *Notes of the Mexican War, 1846–47–48.* Philadelphia: n.p., 1885.
Winders, Richard Bruce. "Puebla's Forgotten Heroes." *Military History of the West* (Spring 1994): 1–23.

Huasteca Revolts
Event Dates: 1521–1849

Intermittent revolts that occurred between the time of the Spanish conquest and the late 1840s by natives of the Huasteca region of Mexico. The Huasteca territory is the region of northeastern Mexico, centered on the drainage basin of the Pánuco River. It includes portions of the modern-day Mexican states of Veracruz, Tamaulipas, Puebla, Querétaro, San Luis Potosí, and Hidalgo.

The Huasteca was one of three important pre-Columbian civilizations that had developed in this region of Mexico. After taking control of Tenochtitlán (site of present-day Mexico City) in August 1521, Hernán Cortés marched a large force toward the Huasteca territory. After considerable resistance during 1522, he defeated the Huastecos. Later, in October–December 1523 and during 1525–1526, the Spaniards cruelly put down other Huasteca revolts.

Between 1750 and 1810 the region experienced at least 14 riots in native towns, primarily, but not exclusively, in reaction to increasing taxes and the imposition of new monopolies by the Spanish colonial government, which sought to exert its authority by increasingly intervening into local affairs. While dissidents never sought to challenge the legitimacy of the monarchy or the church and framed their arguments within established Spanish law, the encroaching power of the colonial state exacerbated relations among local factions.

When Father Miguel Hidalgo y Costilla began the war for independence on September 15, 1810, large numbers of Huasteca villagers rose up to support his movement. Their rebellion demonstrated their continuing grievances with administrators in Mexico City, and the insurrection quickly spread throughout the region. Through their actions and pronouncements, these villagers presented a growing consciousness that demonstrated the transition from colonial riots to national rebellion. By 1820, following the re-adoption of the 1812 Constitution of Cadiz, the local insurrections temporarily ended through a series of negotiated settlements. Many former insurgents, however, joined the independence movement of Agustín de Iturbide after the proclamation of the Plan of Iguala on February 24, 1821. The Huasteca insurgency aided Iturbide's entrance into Mexico City on September 27, 1821, effectively ending the war for independence.

Following Iturbide's short-lived empire (1822–1823), Mexican leaders enacted the Constitution of 1824, which established a federal republic. The charter also encouraged the creation of town councils in towns with at least 1,000 inhabitants and granted citizenship to all males. The federal constitution, however, gave the states the authority to decide their own internal political structure and some, including several in the Huasteca region, set the minimum number of inhabitants required to form a town council at 2,000, 3,000, or 4,000. As a result, new town governments, dominated by non-Indians, competed with the traditional *repúblicas de indios* composed of Indians in outlying villages and hamlets. These competing local governments decided who controlled the land and labor resources.

At the national level, armed movements organized around a political "plan" (*pronunciamento*) became the most common method for changing presidents, ministers, and policies. Their leaders sought the support of municipal governments for their faction, and *pronunciamentos* in the Huasteca became increasingly violent as local inhabitants became polarized over national political issues during the 1830s and 1840s.

Then, beginning in November 1846, a powerful insurrection that involved a wide range of pueblos and individuals swept through the Huasteca. As the movement gained momentum, it became a region-wide protest against the local government and encompassed not only Indians but also mestizos, blacks, ranchers, and tenant farmers. This crisis was sparked by the collapse of the centralist experiment of General Antonio López de Santa Anna and invasion by U.S. forces under Major General Zachary Taylor. Rebels burned haciendas and killed government officials, and federal troops carried out brutal reprisals, often with only mixed success. Although most of the rebellion had been put down by early 1847, the rebels renewed their struggle in March and, by November, had enveloped the area around Tampico. The violence continued to spread, and Mexico City was hard-pressed to control

it while also attempting to fend off the American invasion and occupation. Some governors claimed that the Huasteca revolts were being aided and abetted by the Americans, although it seems clear that the major motivation was rural and Indian dissatisfaction with the central government and its policies.

With the signing of the Treaty of Guadalupe Hidalgo in 1848, the central government was able to commit additional troops to crushing the rebellion. The insurrection collapsed during July–August 1849 when the army defeated the principal rebel force and captured major rebel leaders near Tamiahua. The individual states then granted general amnesties to the remaining rebels.

Over the centuries, the Huastecos have survived and have maintained many aspects of their traditional culture and language. Today, the region has about 80,000 speakers of the Huastec (Wastek) language and about 1 million speakers of the Huasteca Nahuatl dialects.

Robert B. Kane

See also

Mestizos; Mexico; Mexico, 1821–1854; Rancheros; Santa Anna, Antonio López de.

References

Ducey, Michael T. *A Nation of Villages: Riot and Rebellion in the Mexican Huasteca, 1750–1850.* Tucson: University of Arizona Press, 2004.
Ducey, Michael T. "Indian Communities and *Ayuntamientos* in the Mexican Huasteca: *Sujeto* Revolts, *Pronunciamientos* and Caste War." *The Americas* 57 (April 2001): 525–550.
Ducey, Michael T. "Municipalities, Prefects, and Pronunciamientos: Power and Political Mobilizations in the Huasteca during the First Federal Republic." In *Forceful Negotiations: The Origins of the Pronunciamiento in Nineteenth-Century Mexico,* edited by Will Fowler, 74–100. Lincoln: University of Nebraska Press, 2010.
Guardino, Peter. *Peasants, Politics, and the Formation of Mexico's National State: Guerrero, 1800–1857.* Stanford, CA: Stanford University Press, 1996.

Huejutla Expedition
Event Dates: July 7–15, 1847

Expedition dispatched by Colonel William Gates in July 1847 to rescue some 200 U.S. prisoners captured that February 1847 at Hacienda de Encarnación and held at Huejutla, Mexico, since May. Huejutla (also known as Huejutla de Reyes) is located in the state of Hidalgo in east central Mexico about 120 miles inland (west) from Tampico. Mexican authorites had planned to exchange the Americans for captured Mexican soldiers. However, the local commander at Huejutla decided to detain them there, presumably indefinitely. Six of the prisoners had escaped soon after arriving at Huejutla and, making their way to Tampico, informed Colonel Gates of the prisoners' whereabouts and of their poor treatment and living conditions.

In early July, Gates decided to mount an expedition to free them. The mission comprised 120 men, some from a Louisiana infantry regiment, some from the 3rd Artillery (with one cannon), and others from a dragoon detachment. The men were instructed to move inland on the Rió Pánuco (Pánuco River) by steamboat; from there they were to march to Huejutla. The task force, led by Colonel Lewis G. DeRussy, left Tampico on July 7 and by July 12 was within seven miles of their objective.

Just as the men were preparing to ford a river, a Mexican force ambushed them. Several members of the expedition were cut down by small-arms fire before the force could stage a safe withdrawal. The Americans fought steadily as they retreated toward Tampico. DeRussy repelled a Mexican force of some 1,000 men at Tantoyuca on July 14 and then ordered his men to occupy and destroy the town. Sensing that more Mexican soldiers were on the way, DeRussy departed Tantoyuca in the early morning hours of July 15 in a driving rainstorm and continued toward Tampico.

By now, the expedition was all but over, and the American prisoners had not been rescued. A 160-man relief force that Gates sent to DeRussy's assistance met the retreating column on the Pánuco River, where they boarded a steamboat which took them to safety at Tampico. Contemporary press accounts placed U.S. casualties in the expedition at between 9 and 30; the Mexicans allegedly suffered 150 casualties. The U.S. prisoners at Huejutla were paroled before the end of the war.

PAUL G. PIERPAOLI JR.

See also

Encarnación, Hacienda de; Prisoners of War, U.S.; Tampico; Victoria and Tampico, Occupation of.

References

Bauer, K. Jack. *The Mexican War, 1846–1848.* New York: Macmillan, 1974.

Cutrer, Thomas W. *Ben McCulloch and the Frontier Military Tradition.* Chapel Hill: University of North Carolina Press, 1993.

Huger, Benjamin
Birth Date: November 22, 1805
Death Date: December 7, 1877

U.S. Army officer who served as chief of ordnance for Major General Winfield Scott during the Mexican-American War and who later went on to serve, controversially, as a Confederate Army general. Born on November 22, 1805, in Charleston, South Carolina, Benjamin Huger was the grandson of noted South Carolina politician Thomas Pinckney. Huger graduated from the U.S. Military Academy, West Point, in 1825 and was assigned to the 3rd U.S. Artillery as a second lieutenant. After serving as a topographical engineer for three years, he took a two-year leave of absence to tour Europe and study continental warfare practices. In 1832 Huger was promoted to captain, transferred to the U.S. Army Ordnance Department, and took command of the arsenal at Fort Monroe, Hampton, Virginia. He remained at that post until the outset of the Mexican-American War in 1846, with one interruption from 1840 to 1841, when he was temporarily assigned as a military observer in Europe.

Huger served as Scott's chief of ordnance during 1846–1848. He was brevetted to major following the siege of Veracruz (March 9–29, 1847), where he supervised the placement and firing of artillery batteries; brevetted to lieutenant colonel following the Battle of Molino del Rey (September 8, 1847); and brevetted to colonel after the Battle of Chapultepec (September 13, 1847). By the time Mexico City had fallen, however, Huger was bedridden, perhaps with yellow fever. After the war, he returned to command the Fort Monroe arsenal until 1851 when he was transferred to command the Harpers Ferry arsenal. He was promoted to major in 1855 while serving as commander of the arsenal at Pikesville, Maryland (1854–1860). Posted to command the Charleston Arsenal in 1860, he resigned his commission on April 22, 1861, to join the Confederate Army.

Commissioned a brigadier general in June 1861 and major general just four months later, Huger first took command of the Department of Norfolk. He immediately warned that his district would not be able to withstand a Union assault but took no meaningful measures to fortify the area. After Federal forces compelled a Confederate surrender at Roanoke Island, North Carolina, on February 8, 1862, Huger's failure to strengthen the Confederate defenses there prompted an investigation by the Confederate Congress.

In May 1862, when Federal forces threatened eastern Tidewater, Virginia, Huger ordered the dismantlement of the Confederate defensive works there and the torching of the Norfolk Navy Yard, which led to the scuttling of the ironclad CSS *Virginia*. He also evacuated all Confederate forces from Norfolk and nearby Portsmouth. His actions were understandably controversial; nevertheless, President Jefferson Davis placed Huger in charge of a division under the command of General Joseph E. Johnston. Huger saw action at the Battle of Seven Pines and, after Johnston was severely wounded and replaced by General Robert E. Lee, in the Seven Days' Battles, but his performance left much to be desired. He was relieved of active command in July 1862 and returned to artillery and ordnance duties. In this capacity he served with efficiency in the Western Theater and, beginning in mid-1863, in the Trans-Mississippi Department. In failing health by the end of the war, Huger retired to North Carolina and Virginia before settling in Charleston, South Carolina, where he died on December 7, 1877.

MICHAEL R. HALL

See also

Artillery; Chapultepec, Battle of; El Molino del Rey, Battle of; Flying Artillery; Scott, Winfield; Veracruz, Landing at and Siege of.

References

Rhoades, Jeffrey L. *Scapegoat General: The Story of General Benjamin Huger, C.S.A.* Hamden, CT: Archon Books, 1986.

Johannsen, Robert W. *To the Halls of the Montezumas: The Mexican War in the American Imagination.* New York: Oxford University Press, 1985.

Hughes, John Joseph
Birth Date: June 24, 1797
Death Date: January 3, 1864

Roman Catholic bishop and the first archbishop of the Archdiocese of New York. John Joseph Hughes was born in County Tyrone, Ireland, on June 24, 1797. After his parents immigrated to the United States, Hughes followed them in 1817. He settled in Chambersburg, Pennsylvania, with his family and then took a job as a gardener at Mount St. Mary's College in Emmitsburg, Maryland. There he came under the tutelage of a Catholic priest who taught at the college. Hughes eventually enrolled and studied religion. He was ordained a priest in 1826.

In 1838, Hughes became a titular bishop (not presiding over a specific diocese). Four years later, he became the fourth bishop of the Diocese of New York. In 1850, he became the first archbishop of New York when that diocese was elevated to an archdiocese. A powerful speaker, Hughes was a strong advocate for Irish émigrés. He also lobbied unsuccessfully for government funding of parochial schools in New York. Undeterred, he founded an independent Catholic school system in New York that became the model of dioceses around the nation. Beyond secondary

John Joseph Hughes was the first Roman Catholic archbishop of New York. The parochial schools he founded served as a model for the rest of the nation. Hughes also championed abolition. (Hayward Cirker and Blanche Cirker, eds. *Dictionary of American Portraits,* 1967)

Catholic education, Hughes played a significant role in founding several noteworthy Catholic colleges and universities, including St. John's College (modern-day Fordham University), Marymount College, and Manhattan College. Hughes also supervised the beginning construction of modern-day St. Patrick's Cathedral in New York City.

In 1846, at the start of the Mexican-American War, Hughes was summoned to the White House to meet with President James K. Polk, who sought his advice on Catholicism in Mexico and about the use of Catholic chaplains in the U.S. Army. Hughes asked the president to appoint him as an envoy to the Mexican government in an attempt to allay fears in Mexico that the Americans were out to impose Protestantism on its population. Polk refused to consider Hughes's request. Hughes did, however, suggest to Polk that he confer with Father Peter Verhaegen of Georgetown College, who would be able to make specific recommendations concerning Catholic chaplains. As a result, two priests at the college—Fathers John McElroy and Antony Rey—became chaplains in Major General Zachary Taylor's Army of Occupation.

During the 1850s and into the early 1860s, Hughes spearheaded famine relief efforts, championed abolitionism, and sought municipal relief for poor immigrants in New York. During the Civil War, Hughes conferred frequently with President Abraham Lincoln and acted as the president's personal emissary in Europe. Hughes died in New York City on January 3, 1864.

Paul G. Pierpaoli Jr.

See also
Catholic Church, Mexico; Polk, James Knox; Religion.

References
Hassard, John. *The Life of Reverend John Hughes, First Archbishop of New York.* 1866. Reprint, New York: Cosimo Classics, 2008.

Hunt, Henry Jackson
Birth Date: September 14, 1819
Death Date: February 11, 1889

U.S. artillery officer. Henry Jackson Hunt was born on September 14, 1819, in Detroit, Michigan. Upon graduation from the U.S. Military Academy at West Point in 1839, he was assigned to the 2nd Artillery. He served ably under Major General Winfield Scott during the Mexico City Campaign of 1847, seeing action in the Battles of Churubusco and Chapultepec. During the latter engagement, Hunt provided highly effective artillery assistance at the San Cosme *garita* (gate) but lost five of the eight gunners in his badly exposed two-gun section. Hunt was wounded twice by musket fire at Chapultepec and was brevetted twice during the course of the war.

After the war, he served on an artillery board and helped shape modern artillery doctrine during the 1850s. Considered an authority on artillery, Hunt, with William H. French and William F. Berry, wrote *Instructions for Field Artillery* in 1861. Hunt, who was promoted to major, asserted that artillery batteries formerly assigned to individual divisions should be placed in an artillery reserve so they could be assigned more efficiently as needed. He also contended that artillery fire should be slow and deliberate.

During the First Battle of Bull Run (First Manassas) on July 21, 1861, Hunt employed his artillery to turn back a Confederate assault on the Union left. When Major General George McClellan assumed command of the Army of the Potomac, he secured promotion to colonel for Hunt and ordered him to organize and train the army's artillerists. From July to September 1861, Hunt oversaw the artillery defending Washington, D.C.

During the Peninsula Campaign of March–August 1862, Hunt skillfully handled the Army of the Potomac's artillery, especially in the Battle of Malvern Hill on July 1, 1862, where Hunt's gunners effectively silenced Confederate general Robert E. Lee's artillery and then helped to break up the Confederate infantry assaults. On September 15, 1862, Hunt was promoted to brigadier general and made chief of artillery in the Army of the Potomac. He employed his guns with great success in the Battle of Antietam (or Sharpsburg) on September 17, 1862. At Fredericksburg, Virginia, that December, Hunt's guns helped secure the town but could not silence the Confederates on Marye's Heights (December 13, 1862). New Army of the Potomac commander Major General Joseph Hooker weakened Hunt's authority over the army's artillery with resulting detrimental effects in the Battle of Chancellorsville (May 1–4, 1863). Restored to full authority by Hooker's successor, Major General George Gordon Meade, Hunt played an important role in the Battle of Gettysburg (July 1–3, 1863). His skillful placement of his artillery batteries and conservative use of firepower ensured the repulse of Pickett's Charge on July 3, 1863. Hunt also organized the artillery in the siege of Petersburg from June 15, 1864, to April 2, 1865.

Following the Civil War, Hunt continued in the army until retiring in 1883 to become governor of the Soldiers' Home in Washington, D.C., where he died on February 11, 1889.

MICHAEL R. HALL AND SPENCER C. TUCKER

See also

Artillery; Chapultepec, Battle of; Churubusco, Battle of; Mexico City Campaign.

References

Dillon, Lester R., Jr. *American Artillery in the Mexican War, 1846–1848.* Austin, TX: Presidial Press, 1975.
Longacre, Edward G. *The Man Behind the Guns: A Military Biography of General Henry J. Hunt, Chief of Artillery, Army of the Potomac.* Cranbury, NJ: A. S. Barenes, 1997.

Hunter, Charles G.
Birth Date: 1813
Death Date: 1873

U.S. naval officer. Born in Trenton, New Jersey, Charles G. Hunter joined the U.S. Navy as a midshipman on November 16, 1824. He

was advanced to passed midshipman on February 20, 1830, and to lieutenant on June 24, 1834.

During the Mexican-American War, Hunter commanded the twin-screw steamer *Scourge* (rated at 21 guns) as part of Commodore Matthew C. Perry's squadron in the Gulf of Mexico. Immediately after the capture of Veracruz on March 29, 1847, Major General Winfield Scott ordered Brigadier General John A. Quitman to proceed with his 2,500-man brigade to seize the port of Alvarado in conjunction with the navy. Scott hoped Alvarado might be a source of supplies, especially horses, for his march on Mexico City. Since the unsuccessful U.S. attack on Alvarado in October 1846, the Mexicans had strengthened their seaward defenses, adding two additional river forts for a total of eight, but the port was judged vulnerable to attack from the rear or land side. Quitman departed Veracruz with his brigade on March 30. The men spent that night camped at the mouth of the Madelin River, planning to make the crossing the next day in boats from the American naval squadron offshore.

Commodore Perry had ordered Hunter to proceed with the *Scourge* to Alvarado to support Quitman by blockading access to the Madelin River. Hunter arrived at the mouth of the Madelin shortly before dusk on March 30 and lobbed a few shells from his ship's largest gun, a 32-pounder, at Fort La Vigia at the mouth of the river. The onset of bad weather forced him to withdraw, and Hunter spent the night steaming back and forth across the river's mouth. The next morning Hunter again stood in the river and fired another shot at Fort La Vigia, which then promptly hoisted a white flag. A boat put out and the captain of the port informed Hunter that the Mexican garrison at Alvarado had departed during the night, that all military shipping there had been burned, and that the Americans were free to enter the town.

Hunter lost no time in taking advantage of the situation. Before noon, he had crossed the bar and anchored at the town of Alvarado, hoisted the American flag, fired a 21-gun salute, and landed six men to hold the town. Informed that some Mexican vessels had fled upriver with munitions, Hunter set out in pursuit. He found a schooner aground but, unable to refloat it, burned it. He then took three other vessels. Before dawn on April 1, he arrived at Tlacotalpán and took its surrender as well.

Meanwhile, Perry had set out to support Quitman in his capture of Alvarado. Not knowing what had happened, he sent in a message demanding the town's surrender and then dispatched gunboats over the bar. Learning that Hunter had already taken Alvarado, Perry ordered marines ashore to hold the town in force and relieve Hunter's garrison. Quitman's men arrived shortly thereafter, as did the *Scourge* with one of its prizes.

Hunter's success had, however, completely upset his superior's plans, for it had resulted in the destruction of the military shipping at Alvarado and had led the Mexicans to drive off the horses that Scott hoped Quitman might secure. A furious Perry ordered Hunter placed under arrest, and a court-martial convened aboard the flagship *Mississippi*. Hunter argued that he had been on detached duty and had discretionary power, thus his capture of Alvarado and the surrounding towns was permissible. Regardless, Hunter was found guilty of insubordination and disobeying orders of a superior officer and was sentenced to a reprimand and immediate dismissal from the squadron but not from the navy.

Many believed the sentence was unduly harsh. Indeed, the American press took up the lieutenant's cause, making a hero of "Alvarado" Hunter. In fact, the real effect of the court-martial proceeding was to tarnish the reputation of Perry in the eyes of the American public.

Hunter returned home to New Jersey and was honored at the Fourth of July celebration in Trenton in 1847. The town presented him with a silver water pitcher on which was inscribed a commemoration of his victories at Alvarado and Tlacotalpán. Later in the war, Hunter was assigned to command the revenue cutter *Taney* as part of a small squadron stationed at Gibraltar following the capture of an American merchant ship by a Spanish felucca with a Mexican privateer commission.

Hunter was dismissed from the U.S. Navy on January 29, 1855. During the Civil War, Hunter briefly had command of the Union steamer *Montgomery,* but he was again dismissed from the navy after he pursued a blockade runner into Cuban waters without permission. He then retired to Rhode Island. Hunter died in a shipwreck in 1873.

RUSSELL D. JAMES AND SPENCER C. TUCKER

See also

Alvarado Expeditions; Perry, Matthew Calbraith; Quitman, John Anthony; Scott, Winfield; United States Navy; Veracruz.

References

Bauer, K. Jack. *Surfboats and Horse Marines: U.S. Naval Operations in the Mexican War, 1846–1848.* Annapolis, MD: Naval Institute Press, 1969.

Morison, Samuel Eliot. *"Old Bruin": Commodore Matthew C. Perry, 1794–1858.* Boston: Little, Brown, 1967.

Nardo, Don. *The Mexican-American War.* San Diego, CA: Lucent Books, 1991.

Huston, Felix
Birth Date: 1800
Death Date: 1857

Lawyer, soldier, and general in chief of the Army of the Republic of Texas. Felix Huston was born in Kentucky sometime in 1800 and moved to Mississippi as a young man. He settled in Natchez, read for the law, was admitted to the bar, and began a legal practice. Huston was also involved in the slave trade and operated a plantation. Upon learning of the Texas Revolution in 1836, he began soliciting monetary support to help the Texans achieve independence. He also raised a volunteer mounted regiment of some 500 men, reportedly incurring a personal debt of $40,000 to outfit and supply it, and then led the contingent from Natchez on May 5, 1836. However, by the time his force had arrived in Texas in July, the fighting was all but over and he saw no action in the revolution. Huston then became involved in the Texas volunteer army.

Huston soon found himself on a committee to determine who would command the Republic of Texas army. This was the result of a power struggle among Sam Houston, David G. Burnet, Mirabeau B. Lamar, and Thomas Jefferson Rusk. When Rusk was compelled by Houston to relinquish control of the army and accept a position in his cabinet, now president Houston appointed Huston as a brigadier general and temporary general in chief of the army on December 20, 1836.

Almost immediately, the impetuous and hot-tempered Huston caused considerable controversy in his new role. In addition to his aggressive stance toward the Mexicans and desire to move troops into contested areas, Huston engaged Brigadier General Albert Sidney Johnston in a duel in February 1847, after Houston had named Johnston as the army's permanent general in chief. Johnston was seriously wounded.

Meanwhile, Huston continued to agitate for a Texas invasion of northern Mexico, much to President Houston's annoyance. In May 1847, Houston furloughed most of the volunteer units of the Texas army so that Huston would not be able to use them to mount a Mexican offensive. Huston then proposed to Houston that he be allowed to raise, equip, and command a large force of private soldiers that would seize and occupy Matamoros, Mexico. Houston denied the request.

In the summer of 1840, Huston led a contingent of Texas soldiers against the Comanches, who had been raiding and harassing Texans in southeastern Texas. At the August 12, 1840, Battle of Plum Creek, Huston's men defeated a Comanche contingent. Later that same year, Huston abandoned Texas and took up a law practice in New Orleans. He became an ardent supporter of Texas annexation and an early supporter of southern secession. In 1844, he campaigned vigorously for Democrat James K. Polk, and in 1851 he spoke at a political rally in support of Cuban independence from Spain. In the years just prior to his death, he had become a leader in the southern secession movement. Huston died in 1857 in Natchez, Mississippi.

PAUL G. PIERPAOLI JR.

See also

Comanches; Houston, Samuel; Johnston, Albert Sidney; Lamar, Mirabeau Buonaparte; Rusk, Thomas Jefferson; Texas; Texas Revolution; Texas-Comanche Relations.

References

Linn, John J. *Reminiscences of Fifty Years in Texas.* Reprint. Austin, TX: State House, 1986.

Williams, Amelia W., and Eugene C. Barker, eds. *The Writings of Sam Houston, 1813–1863.* 8 vols. 1938–1943. Reprint, Austin, TX: Pemberton Press, 1970.

Wooten, Dudley Goodall, ed. *A Comprehensive History of Texas.* 2 vols. Reprint, Austin: Texas State Historical Association, 1986.

I

Ide, William Brown

Birth Date: March 28, 1796
Death Date: December 19, 1852

Rancher, teacher, pioneer, and leader of the short-lived Bear Flag Republic in California. William Brown Ide was born in Rutland, Vermont, on March 28, 1796. After working as a carpenter and marrying, he lived for a time in Massachusetts before moving to Kentucky and Ohio. He then converted to Mormonism and relocated to central Illinois, where he farmed and taught school to augment his income.

In 1844, Ide was a delegate to the Mormon presidential convention. The next year, he decided to move his family to Oregon and joined a wagon train departing from Independence, Missouri. Along the way and after speaking with other western pioneers, he decided to split off from the wagon train and head to California. There he and his family settled at Barranca Colorada, a ranch supervised by Josiah Belden in the upper Sacramento River Valley.

In the spring of 1846, when reports reached Northern California that the Mexican government planned to expel all non-Mexican settlers from California, Anglo settlers began to organize a revolt, and Ide became one of its leaders. On June 14, 1846, he took part in the taking of the Mexican pueblo at Sonoma. Ide then took charge, drafted an independence declaration, and read it aloud the following day, proclaiming the Bear Flag Republic, named for the crude flag the rebels raised over the fort that pictured a grizzly bear and a single star.

Ide moved immediately to reinforce the redoubt in anticipation of a Mexican assault, but no such move occurred. Ide's republic was short-lived, and by July 9, U.S. forces had secured the area; the American flag was hoisted above Sonoma that very day. Anxious to participate in other offensives against the Mexicans, Ide enlisted as a private with Captain Granville P. Swift's company in the so-called California Battalion, although he saw only limited action.

In 1847, Ide coauthored a lengthy report on the Bear Flag Revolt under the title "The Revolution in California," which was published in several contemporary serial publications. Later that same year, Ide became chief land surveyor for the Northern Department of California. In the meantime, Ide returned to his farming and ranching interests, buying out Josiah Belden in 1849 and making a small fortune during the California Gold Rush.

Beginning in 1851, Ide held a series of positions in Colusa County, California, including judge, justice of the peace, and county auditor. Ide died from smallpox in Monroeville, California, on December 19, 1852.

Paul G. Pierpaoli Jr.

See also
Bear Flag Revolt; California; California Battalion; California Theater of War, Overview.

References
Kirov, George. *William B. Ide: President of California.* Fairfield, CA: James D. Stevenson, 1994.

Walker, Dale L. *Bear Flag Rising: The Conquest of California, 1846.* New York: Forge, 1999.

Warner, Barbara. *The Men of the California Bear Flag Revolt and Their Heritage.* Spokane, WA: Arthur H. Clark, 1996.

Immigration

Between 1841 and 1850, the bulk of immigrants to the United States came from three areas: Ireland (45.6 percent); the German states (25.3 percent); and Britain (6.5 percent). The total number of identified immigrants during the decade was 1,713,251, or three times the number to arrive on U.S. shores from 1831 to 1840. Indeed, the decade of the 1840s marked the beginning of a massive wave of immigration that would not taper off until 1920. This immigration movement may be broken down into two parts: the first, from 1840 to 1880, was made up largely of immigrants from northern and western Europe (Ireland, Scotland, Germany, and Scandinavia); the second, from 1880 to 1920, was made up principally by individuals from southern and eastern Europe (Italy, Greece, Russia, and the Balkans).

Immigrants came to the United States in the 1840s for a variety of reasons. The Industrial Revolution's growing impact, in the northeastern United States especially, resulted in the need for cheap, plentiful labor, which attracted foreign workers. These individuals found work in canal and railroad construction, mining, and the many factories that were being built at the time. Also, the availability of inexpensive land in the newly opened Midwest and Great Plains fueled migration to the United States.

Events in Europe also motivated migration to the United States. The biggest single contributor during the decade may have been the potato blight that struck Ireland beginning in 1845. The blight, which lingered until 1847, destroyed at least half the potato crop, the main staple in the Irish diet. A combination of starvation, loss of land, and disease drove 2.5 million Irish from their homeland between 1840 and 1860 and caused the deaths of another 2 million. About 1.8 million Irish came to the United States and Canada. Crop failures in 1846 in the Netherlands and German states compelled thousands of Dutch and German immigrants to seek passage to the United States.

Political unrest in Europe also contributed to migration. In 1847–1849, a series of revolutions swept continental Europe, including France, the German and Italian states, and Austria-Hungary. These uprisings temporarily reversed the political and social order, but the conservatives and reactionaries soon regained power. For many, especially the central Europeans, the United States became a refuge, dubbed "the Land of Freedom" by Germans. A reduction in customs duties in most German states in the 1840s made it easier for Germans to migrate to port cities like Hamburg, which was a major departure point for American emigration.

The end of the Mexican-American War also encouraged migration to and from the new American territories. The 1848 Treaty of Guadalupe Hidalgo presented both nations with a potential immigration concern. With the stroke of a pen, 80,000 Mexicans living in what was now the United States became Americans. The treaty gave them the choice of remaining in the United States or emigrating to Mexico. Only about 3,000 left. The remainder could choose between seeking American citizenship or retaining their Mexican citizenship.

This wave of immigration in the 1840s was met in the United States with increasing resistance. So-called nativists, anti-immigrant proponents who feared the consequences of increased immigration, steadily gained political power in the 1840s. Generated in part by an intense fear of increasing Catholic influence in the United States, nativists were particularly opposed to immigration by the Irish and other Catholics. Rapidly changing immigration patterns increased the number of Catholics in the United States from 318,000 in 1830 to more than 3 million in 1860. Nativists channeled their anti-immigration efforts into the American Republican Party (not to be confused with the Republican Party, which did not come into being until the 1850s). Founded in 1845, the party, later called the Know-Nothing Party, pressed for banning Catholic immigrants and stopping Catholics and noncitizens from voting and running for political office. The party, however, had little impact on limiting immigration.

Immigration radically changed the social, political, and cultural makeup of the United States. Numerous immigrants, particularly the newly arriving Irish, served in the American military, and as other immigrants had done, they used the experience to gain important insights into their adoptive homeland and to gain acceptance among the native-born.

STEVE POTTS

Illustrated sheet music glorifying the nativist cause, produced shortly after bloody anti-Catholic riots in Kensington, Philadelphia, in May 1844. Allegedly mutilated by Irish rioters during the tumult, the flag symbolized the threat that nativists believed Catholic immigrants posed to America. (Library of Congress)

See also
Army Life, Mexican and U.S.; Guadalupe Hidalgo, Treaty of; United States Army.

References
Bodnar, John. *The Transplanted: A History of Immigrants in Urban America.* Bloomington: Indiana University Press, 1985.
Daniels, Roger. *Coming to America: A History of Immigration and Ethnicity in American Life.* 2nd ed. New York: Harper Collins, 2002.
Gutman, Herbert. *Work, Culture and Society in Industrializing America.* New York: Random House, 1977.
Kite, Jodella D. "A Social History of the Anglo-American Colonies in Mexican Texas." PhD diss., Texas Tech University, 1990.

Immortal Fourteen

Group of 14 Whig U.S. congressmen that was resolutely opposed to the Mexican-American War. The men were so named when they voted against the May 11, 1846, War Bill then before the House of Representatives. That bill had acknowledged that a state of war was already in existence and that additional supplies and volunteer forces would be necessary to prosecute the war.

While Whigs in general were not supportive of the war and were in fact quite critical of Democratic president James K. Polk's prosecution of it, once the conflict began they voted in favor of war appropriations. They did so out of patriotism and the belief that U.S. soldiers in the field should not be endangered by political squabbling on the home front. The Immortal Fourteen, however, refused to vote for any war appropriation measure and believed that they were demonstrating their patriotism by refusing to support a war that they believed to be morally unjustified, even if that meant losing political power.

The Immortal Fourteen represented congressional districts in the Northeast; indeed they were all from Pennsylvania, Ohio, New York, Massachusetts, Rhode Island, and Maine. Among the more high-profile congressmen were Joshua Reed Giddings (Ohio) and the venerable statesman John Quincy Adams (Massachusetts). Adams, the son of founding father John Adams, was 78 years old in 1846 and had served as president of the United States, secretary of state, U.S. senator, and ambassador to Great Britain, the Netherlands, Prussia, and Russia. Although the Immortal Fourteen were in the distinct minority, Adams certainly added gravitas to the message that they were trying to send to the American people.

These 14 men had been virulent antislavery Whigs, and that ideology suffused their antiwar stance. They believed that President Polk, a southern Democrat, had manufactured the Mexican-American War in order to ensure the institution of slavery in Texas and to spread slavery into territories newly wrested from Mexico. They also saw the war as part of a larger political struggle by which southern slave owners would gain additional political influence, perhaps even eclipsing the power of northern businessmen and small landowners. The Immortal Fourteen also saw the Mexican-American War as a not-too-well-concealed move to annex California and New Mexico, a development they believed would imperil the delicate balance between free and slave states.

While it is fair to say that the Immortal Fourteen did not adversely impact the prosecution of the war, it is also fair to conclude that their effect on the political discourse was considerable. Indeed, by linking the conflict to the incendiary issue of slavery from the beginning, the group informed the thinking of others who did not support the war and helped solidify the abolitionist movement.

PAUL G. PIERPAOLI JR.

See also
Abolitionism; Adams, John Quincy; Congress, U.S.; Democratic Party; Polk, James Knox; Public Opinion and the War, U.S.; Slavery; Whigs.

References
Richards, Leonard L. *The Life and Times of Congressman John Quincy Adams.* New York: Oxford University Press, 1986.
Stewart, James Brewer. *Joshua R. Giddings and the Tactics of Radical Politics.* Cleveland, OH: Press of Case Western Reserve, 1970.

Indian Policy, Mexican, Texan, and U.S.

The governments of Mexico, Texas, and the United States all struggled during the period of the Mexican War to reconcile their official Indian policy with actions taken by the frontier settlers who dealt with Native Americans on an everyday basis. While the posture of all three governments at times appeared benign, the reality of the frontier often proved brutal and violent.

The southwestern portion of North America underwent extensive and rapid change in the three decades prior to the Mexican War. The departure of the Spanish, the creation of the Republic of Mexico, and the settlement of Texas and its subsequent annexation to the United States combined to forge a chaotic environment. This made virtually impossible the development of stable relationships with regional Native Americans. Indeed, tribes such as the Apaches, Comanches, Navajos, and later the Cherokees struggled to adapt to these rapidly fluctuating circumstances. To understand the Indian policy of these three governments during the Mexican War, a conflict that lasted only two years, it is necessary to explore how their respective approaches had evolved during the preceding decades.

Mexico's policy toward the Native Americans during this period reflected the complexities inherent in developing a coherent approach to dealing with indigenous tribes while simultaneously wrestling with Texas and the United States over territorial claims. This process would be further complicated by the frequent regime changes that plagued the comparatively new country. The Plan of Iguala, adopted in February 1821 as the blueprint for independence from Spain, promised citizenship to all inhabitants of Mexican territory regardless of race, caste, or class. These sentiments reappeared in the language of the federal Constitution of 1824 and its subsequent state counterparts. The government sought also to offer its Amerindian populations the opportunity to obtain private property, as opposed to the communal system of land ownership that the Spanish Empire had allowed several tribes to maintain. These principles, some historians have argued, capturing the spirit of the European Enlightenment, represented a clear departure from earlier Spanish imperial policy.

To some extent, however, Mexico's heritage as part of the Spanish Empire shaped its policy toward Native Americans. Over years of brutal conquest and enslavement, the Spanish developed in the late 18th and early 19th centuries an approach toward the indigenous tribes that envisioned only a few, albeit crucial, barriers to their full-fledged incorporation into the empire as subjects. To achieve this status, tribes such as the Comanches and the Apaches needed first to abandon their nomadic ways of life for a more sedentary pattern of existence based on agriculture. The Spanish also expected that Native Americans seeking something more than mere coexistence with the empire would convert to Catholicism. Mexico, having achieved independence from Spain in 1821, in essence continued these policies.

Before granting citizenship to Native Americans, however, the new country also required that they swear allegiance to the Mexican government. Further reflecting the influence of the Spanish, Mexico strove to establish civic celebrations to extend a sense of national identity to the frontier settlers and native populations on the margins of mainstream society. Thus, while Mexico required of the Native Americans many of the same cultural changes that the United States would eventually demand, the government envisioned a policy in which indigenous peoples would be acculturated through national incorporation rather than gradually via the reservation system.

To be sure, those tribes that refused to abandon their nomadic way of life constituted a threat with which the Mexican government would not hesitate to deal. Following Mexico's successful bid for independence in 1821, habitual ties of gift-giving and support between the settlers and peaceful Apaches broke down in the state of Chihuahua. As the Mexican military presence dwindled, along with its ability to support the Native American communities that surrounded their northern posts, necessity compelled the Apaches to find alternative sources of food. This scenario dictated their return to the cattle raiding that had been the cause of so much violence between the nomadic tribes and the Spanish Empire. The Mexican government, frustrated with the expenses incurred by continued Apache dependence on the state, terminated any federal effort to provide them with rations in 1831. The Apaches subsequently placed themselves on a war footing with Mexico, abandoning their peace establishments in exchange for intensified raids. War between these two belligerents would ebb and flow for much of the next two decades.

Despite a seemingly benevolent official policy toward settled tribes, however, Mexican practice along its northern borders also proved inconsistent with the approach's tenets. The government's efforts to optimize the economic potential of the frontier, in part

sparked by the development of a vital trading route known as the Santa Fe–Chihuahua Trail, had considerable impact on relations with Native Americans. In the 1820s, Comanches in Texas and New Mexico inserted themselves as a vital link in the trade between the eastern and western portions of Mexico's northern territories. Acquiring goods and livestock from raids on northern Mexico and Texas, they became the principal supplier of these valuable commodities to the west. Consequently, the Mexican government sought to impose along its borders a policy long practiced by the Spanish of creating hardy frontier settlements that might serve as barriers between civilization and those tribes beyond redemption. Thus, when Moses Austin approached the Mexican government with a proposal in which Mexico would allow Catholic Anglo-Americans to settle portions of eastern Texas, the young country quickly warmed to the idea of an Anglo-American buffer zone between the dreaded Comanches and their Kiowa allies and the states of Coahuila, Tamaulipas, and Nuevo León.

The Anglo-American settlement of Texas, however, provided Mexico scant comfort. Although it emerged as the intended buffer between the state center and the Indian periphery, Texas achieved its own independence in 1836. Under the direction of Sam Houston, the newly founded republic initially advocated a benevolent policy toward the Native Americans. Houston, once naturalized as a member of the Cherokee tribe, sought peaceful commercial alliances with the indigenous peoples rather than continued war. Once again, however, a nation's official policy squared little with practice on the borders. Even though Texans had minimal interest in the western lands occupied by the Comanches, continuous raids occurred between frontier settlers and their Indian neighbors. Houston endured constant pressure to adopt a harsher policy toward Native Americans in response to this persistent border violence but remained faithful to his conciliatory approach.

Mirabeau B. Lamar, elected president of Texas in 1838, however, dropped Houston's policy in favor of an aggressive approach much more in line with that advocated by settlers on the western frontier. Lamar accelerated and enlarged the recruitment of volunteer militia units with which to pursue a war against neighboring Native American tribes. His efforts forced the Cherokees in the northeast, recent victims of U.S. removal policy, off Texas land and likewise threatened the Shawnees in the east. Militia companies, along with the Texas Rangers, also intensified violence against their Comanche neighbors to the west. By 1840, the Comanches grew tired of the fighting and proved willing to discuss peace. The two sides met at the council house in San Antonio on March 19, 1840, but, following a heated argument over the repatriation of Comanche captives, a fight broke out. The violence quickly escalated out of control. By the end of the struggle, the Texans had killed 35 Comanches and had taken the rest of the Comanche delegates prisoner. In retaliation, the Native Americans launched extensive raids along the western frontier of Texas, with one spectacular thrust reaching all the way to the Gulf port of Linnville.

Official Texas Indian policy underwent further change with the election of Sam Houston as president of Texas once again in 1841. Houston strove to do away with the violent policies of Lamar but could do little to mollify the frontier hatred stoked by years of bitter hostility. Consequently, in 1843 Texas adopted a removal plan. To more clearly delineate the boundary between Native American and white territory and to further regulate trade with the indigenous tribes, Texas advanced a policy that called for the construction of a line of trading posts. These posts would mark the border between Texas and Indian country while also serving as centers for commercial exchange. Native American penetration of this line would not be tolerated. The United States' annexation of Texas in 1845, however, cut short efforts to implement the new strategy, which had as yet produced only one post.

Presumably, once Texas entered into the Union, its Indian policy would have been subordinated to the larger program advanced by the U.S. government. Texas, however, retained considerable authority over its own public domain. Consequently, although the United States negotiated a treaty with the Native Americans of Texas that promised federal protection and regulated commerce, its agents had little faith that these assurances carried weight within the state's borders.

There is some dispute among historians as to which direction the American approach toward Native Americans seemed to be headed in the mid-19th century. Some, like Francis Paul Prucha, argued that U.S. Indian policy in the 1840s reflected the spirit of reform that swept across much of America as part of the religious movement known as the Second Great Awakening. To be sure, as with both Mexico and Texas, there existed a significant disconnect between policy as conceived at the highest levels of government and implementation on the ground by frontier settlers, Indian Bureau agents, and the U.S. Army. Other scholars, such as Reginald Horsman, claim that a focus on the reform elements of official policy masked the development of scientific justifications for racism that would be embraced by many Americans outside of government, including much of the slaveholding South.

Nevertheless, in the years leading up to the Mexican War, the American approach to relations with the Native Americans consisted of removal, temperance, religion, and education. Removal to remote parts of the country isolated from white settlement, it was believed, would afford the Native Americans the opportunity to attain "civilization." Indeed, many in government viewed removal as the only method by which to protect the Native Americans from the dire fate sure to follow white encroachment on their lands.

Proponents of removal held that tribes, once in the comparative isolation of the West, could reform their societies, adopting settled agriculture in exchange for hunting and nomadic ways of life, embracing Christianity, and developing a system of education that would perpetuate these changes. To facilitate the tribes' efforts, and to further protect them from corrupt traders and merchants, Congress passed laws in March 1847 that ensured that annuity payments made to the Native Americans would be distributed among the heads of families rather than to tribal chiefs, who had been squandering these monies on useless merchandise and alcohol. These laws also stipulated that no payments could be made to Native Americans intoxicated from liquor or to those who could easily acquire alcohol, reinforcing the governmental policy that the Native Americans should embrace temperance. The program enjoyed only modest success. The Indian Bureau's efforts to develop education for Native Americans, however, proved much more successful. Many Americans believed that through schooling, Native Americans could elevate themselves from an inferior status.

The 1848 Treaty of Guadalupe Hidalgo, concluding the war between the United States and Mexico, did little to soothe Native American concerns about white encroachment on their lands. The U.S. acquired vast swaths of territory, including land on which nearly 150,000 Amerindians lived. Article XI of the treaty obligated the United States to prevent Native Americans raids into Mexico originating from American territory. Furthermore, the treaty required that the United States punish tribes for any successful raid conducted into Mexico. The treaty, to be sure, touched on more than merely the Native Americans' ability to raid south of the border. While under Mexican rule, Native Americans enjoyed rights as citizens provided that they follow through with the proper legal requirements. Transfer to U.S. sovereignty, however, denied indigenous peoples the right to seek citizenship.

James K. Perrin Jr.

See also

Apaches; Austin, Stephen Fuller; Catholic Church, Mexico; Cherokees; Comanches; Guadalupe Hidalgo, Treaty of; Houston, Samuel; Lamar, Mirabeau Buonaparte; Mexico; Native Americans; Navajos; New Mexico; Santa Fe–Chihuahua Trail; Second Great Awakening; Texas; Texas Rangers; United States, 1821–1854.

References

DeLay, Brian. *War of a Thousand Deserts: Indian Raids and the U.S.-Mexican War.* New Haven, CT: Yale University Press, 2008.

Del Castillo, Richard Griswold. *The Treaty of Guadalupe Hidalgo: A Legacy of Conflict.* Norman: University of Oklahoma Press, 1990.

Harmon, George D. "The United States Indian Policy in Texas, 1845–1860." *Mississippi Valley Historical Review* 17, no. 3 (December 1930): 377–403.

Himmel, Kelly F. *The Conquest of the Karankawas and the Tonkawas, 1821–1859.* College Station: Texas A&M Press, 1999.

Horsman, Reginald. "Scientific Racism and the American Indian in the Mid-Nineteenth Century." *American Quarterly* 27, no. 2 (May 1975): 152–168.

Pace, Robert F., and Donald S. Frazier. *Frontier Texas: History of a Borderland to 1880.* Abilene, TX: State House Press, 2004.

Prucha, Francis Paul. *Indian Policy in the United States: Historical Essays.* Lincoln: University of Nebraska Press, 1981.

Reséndez, Andrés. "National Identity on a Shifting Border: Texas and New Mexico in the Age of Transition, 1821–1848." *Journal of American History* 86, no. 2 (September 1999): 668–688.

Vandervort, Bruce. *Indian Wars of Mexico, Canada and the United States, 1812–1900.* New York: Routledge, 2006.

Industrial Revolution

The Industrial Revolution may be narrowly defined as the substitution of machine power for human and animal power. Although by the time of the Mexican-American War the United States trailed Great Britain by about a decade in the Industrial Revolution, that process was well under way and made a critical difference in the war effort, as Mexico still remained largely unindustrialized.

Early steam-driven vessels, designed by John Fitch, appeared in the 1790s, but it was not until Robert Fulton's *Clermont* (1807), the first commercially successful steamboat that plied the Hudson River, that waterways were opened to steam-powered ships. It was Fulton's attention to the economics of shipping that caused him to be known as the "father of steam navigation." By the 1820s, steam vessels had solved the problem of the vagaries of wind on interior rivers, and by the 1840s most western rivers were opened to them. These waterways proved immensely important in ferrying troops and war matériel to the battlefields in Texas and Mexico.

At the same time, Eli Whitney's revolution in manufacturing, known as the "American System," which included simple design, standardized parts, and mass production, began to spread throughout the United States and, then, back to England. Gun manufacturing drew heavily on the private sector, including clock makers and other small machinery makers, and innovations spread to government armories. Whitney's musket-manufacturing facility spawned other inventors, including Samuel Colt and John Deere, whose steel plow plant opened in 1846. Cyrus McCormick's mass-produced reaper went on sale in 1840, and by 1856 his company produced 4,000 of these huge machines a year. Iron manufacturing, already growing since the Revolutionary War, took off under a series of protective tariffs that increased the price of imported iron. Anthracite coal, introduced as a primary fuel for pig iron smelting in 1839, laid the groundwork for iron producers to make iron faster and cheaper. When combined with the British-invented "hot blast" furnace method, this expanded production fourfold over the old cold-blast furnaces.

Inexpensive iron made possible the rapid spread of the railroads, which first appeared in America in the 1830s. Within 20 years, railroads crisscrossed the nation, linking interior areas to the rivers and cities. Likewise, textile manufacturing, which had begun with Samuel Slater and was supplied with great quantities of inexpensive slave-grown cotton from the South, had grown into a vibrant industry in Lowell and Waltham, Massachusetts. The number of chartered banks in the United States, most of which were concentrated in the Northeast, rose from 500 in 1834 to 824 in 1850, further facilitated growth by providing credit and generally stable currencies. The federal government and states kept taxes low; land ownership was a possibility for virtually anyone; and there was little turmoil in the form of foreign invasions to upset markets.

Whitney's invention of the cotton gin in 1793, meanwhile, had generated an explosion in cotton production. This discovery brought prosperity to the South, where property values soared and the number of slaves increased sharply despite the ban on further importation of slaves. In 1800 there were 894,000 slaves in America, but by 1860 there were 3.95 million. The desire to add more slave territory helped drive the annexation of Texas in 1845 and the massive Mexican land cession in 1848. Even though returns on manufacturing in the South ran as high as 22 percent, slavery remained quite profitable (13 percent returns) and, when combined with the social and cultural structure, proved an immovable object short of war.

By the 1840s, then, the Industrial Revolution was having a major impact on the United States. Iron manufacturing, book publishing, the chemical and metallurgical industry, railroads, steamboats, and steam-powered mills of all sorts were supported and facilitated by cutting-edge infrastructure, legal statutes, a large network of banks, and an easy regulatory climate.

All that was lacking was a cheap labor force, and despite trying several approaches (headright, indentured servitude, and even slavery) the United States remained locked in a labor "feedback loop." This feedback loop worked as follows: the availability of cheap land meant that labor was scarce, hence expensive. American employers, therefore, constantly sought to substitute machinery for labor, embracing the most recent and revolutionary designs. These machines, however, required highly skilled and often well-educated laborers, which meant that labor costs were driven up again. Then the cycle started all over. This put the United States on a "high-tech" path from early in its history, one from which it never looked back.

Transportation and production costs fell, especially for upstream traffic and, after the railroads, over land. Some 3,000 miles of railroads in 1850 expanded to 9,000 miles in 1850 and 30,000 miles in 1860. As larger railroad networks grew, managerial changes occurred that made American businesses even more productive. Labeled the "managerial revolution," it began when firms grew too large and complicated, or covered too much territory, for a single owner to manage the company. As railroads sold stock to increase capital, the large number of owners required that a single hierarchy of managers be hired, and increasingly these men came from the ranks of professionals. By the early 1850s, the "managerial revolution" was well in place.

Communication, which was largely by letters delivered by riders or stagecoaches, stood on the verge of a similar revolution when Congress authorized $30,000 for Samuel F. B. Morse to test his new telegraph on a line from Baltimore to Washington. The line was completed in 1844 with the message "What hath God wrought!" Although the telegraph was still in its infancy during the Mexican-American War, it undoubtedly facilitated faster communications between U.S. commanders in the field and government officials in Washington, D.C., as well as delivering war news to the nation's burgeoning press at an unprecedented speed.

American law also facilitated the Industrial Revolution through the Mill Acts, which ruled in favor of development over pristine property rights, and several U.S. Supreme Court decisions (*Dartmouth College, Bank of Augusta v. Earle, Charles River Bridge,* and *Gibbons v. Ogden*) established a framework of rules and regulations that rewarded competition, interstate cooperation, production, and contracts. In short, both lower and higher courts accelerated the Industrial Revolution by pro-business rulings.

The ease of acquiring capital, the patent system, and overall opportunity encouraged invention and innovation, as with Elias Howe's sewing machine, Deere's plow, and McCormick's reaper, matched only in England and seldom exceeded. Although the real age of military breakthroughs did not occur until the Civil War, Samuel Colt had already patented his revolver (and saw his factory fail for want of sales in 1840). Sales slowly recovered after the adoption of the Patterson and then the Walker Colt by the Texas Rangers, and the War Department eventually accepted his weapon. Grapeshot was discarded in the 1840s by American artillerists in favor of canister. Advances in cannon making also occurred, with lighter tubes making possible the highly effective "flying artillery." The Industrial Revolution in America had gained such momentum that soon the United States would overtake all of its continental rivals in industrial output.

Although there were logistical and supply problems during the Mexican-American War, the United States was able to use its well-oiled industrial capacity, efficient transportation network, and rapidly advancing communication infrastructure to wage a war against Mexico that the Mexicans could not hope to win. U.S. weapons were far newer, more accurate, and in much greater supply than Mexican weapons. And although the war was fought almost exclusively on Mexican soil, the Mexicans lacked modern transportation and communications infrastructure, which impeded their ability to implement an effective war strategy. Thus, the Industrial Revolution, without a doubt, helped win the war for the Americans.

LARRY SCHWEIKART

See also

Colt, Samuel; Cotton Gin; Logistics, Mexican; Logistics, U.S.; Morse, Samuel Finley Breese; Railroads; Slavery; Telegraph; Weapons, Mexican; Weapons, U.S.

References

Atack, Jeremy, and Fred Bateman. *To Their Own Soil: Agriculture in the Antebellum North.* Ames: Iowa State University Press, 1987.

Atack, Jeremy, and Peter Passell. *A New Economic View of American History.* 2nd ed. New York: Norton, 1994.

Chandler, Alfred. *The Visible Hand: The Managerial Revolution in American Business.* Cambridge, MA: Belknap Press, 1977.

Gordon, John Steele. *An Empire of Wealth: The Epic History of American Economic Power.* New York: Harper Perennial, 2004.

Schweikart, Larry. *The Entrepreneurial Adventure: A History of Business in the United States.* Fort Worth, TX: Harcourt, 2000.

Smith, Merritt Roe, ed. *Military Enterprise and Technological Change: Perspectives on the American Experience.* Cambridge, MA: MIT Press, 1985.

Temin, Peter. *Iron and Steel in Nineteenth Century America: An Economic Inquiry.* Cambridge, MA: MIT Press, 1964.

Ingraham, Duncan Nathaniel
Birth Date: December 6, 1802
Death Date: October 16, 1891

U.S. and Confederate Navy officer. Duncan Nathaniel Ingraham was born in Charleston, South Carolina, on December 6, 1802. He received a midshipman's warrant on June 18, 1812, saw service during the War of 1812, and was advanced to lieutenant on January 13, 1825, and to commander on September 8, 1841.

During the Mexican-American War, Ingraham commanded the brig *Somers* in the Home Squadron in the Gulf of Mexico. His ship participated in blockading duties along the Mexican coast, especially off Tabasco and Alvarado. Ingraham also took part in the capture of Tampico in November 1846, where he and Commander Joseph Tattnall negotiated that port city's surrender with local officials. Subsequently, Ingraham commanded naval expeditions up the Tabasco and Alvarado Rivers during the spring and summer of 1847.

In 1853, Ingraham was commanding the sloop *St. Louis* in the Mediterranean Squadron when he was informed that a Hungarian named Martin Koszata, who had lived in New York City for two years and had declared his intention to become an American citizen, had been arrested at Smyrna by Austrian authorities and was being held on the Austrian ship *Hussar.* On July 2, 1853, Ingraham demanded that Koszata be released within eight hours or he would attack the *Hussar,* even though the Austrian warship was larger and more heavily gunned than his own ship. The Austrian captain

U.S. Navy officer Duncan N. Ingraham. During the Mexican-American War, Commander Ingraham was the captain of the brig *Somers* in the Home Squadron in the Gulf of Mexico. (Library of Congress)

agreed to release Koszata to the French consul and the Hungarian was subsequently freed. For this action, the U.S. Congress voted Ingraham a Gold Medal. Ingraham was promoted to captain on September 14, 1855.

In 1856, Ingraham was appointed chief of the Bureau of Ordnance and Hydrography. In this post he frequently clashed with Commander John A. Dahlgren who was seeking to develop a new ordnance system for the navy at the Washington Navy Yard. In 1860, Ingraham took command of the screw sloop *Richmond* in the Mediterranean Squadron.

Upon learning that South Carolina had seceded from the Union, Ingraham resigned his commission on February 4, 1861. He joined the Confederate Navy as a captain on March 26, 1861. After service on a board appointed by Secretary of the Navy Stephen R. Mallory to develop naval policy, he commanded the Pensacola, Florida, Navy Yard. On November 16, 1861, he was assigned command of the Charleston, South Carolina, Naval Station. There he oversaw construction of the ironclad Confederate ram *Palmetto State*. On January 31, 1863, Ingraham commanded the *Palmetto State* when it and the Confederate ironclad *Chicora* attacked the wooden U.S. Navy blockaders off Charleston. Although Ingraham

and Confederate commander at Charleston, General P. G. T. Beauregard, announced that the Union blockade had been broken and was now no longer valid, U.S. officials disagreed, claiming correctly that the attackers had been driven off.

Relieved of sea duty in March 1863 by reason of his age, Ingraham continued in command of Confederate Navy shore installations at Charleston until the city fell to Union forces in 1865. After the war Ingraham resided in Charleston. He died there on October 16, 1891.

Spencer C. Tucker

See also

Alvarado Expeditions; *Somers*, U.S. Navy Brig; Tabasco River Expeditions; Tampico; Tampico and Victoria, Occupation of; Tattnall, Josiah; United States Navy.

References

Bauer, K. Jack. *Surfboats and Horse Marines: U.S. Naval Operations in the Mexican War.* Annapolis, MD: U.S. Naval Institute, 1969.

Callahan, Edward W., ed. *List of Officers of the Navy of the United States and of the Marine Corps from 1775 to 1900.* 1901. Reprint, New York: Haskell House, 1969.

Tucker, Spencer C. *Blue and Gray Navies: The Civil War Afloat.* Annapolis, MD: Naval Institute Press, 2006.

J

Jackson, Andrew

Birth Date: March 15, 1767
Death Date: June 8, 1845

U.S. general and president (1829–1837). Born the son of Scotch-Irish poor immigrant parents in the Waxhaws Settlement on the South Carolina frontier on March 15, 1767, Andrew Jackson received little formal education. During the American Revolutionary War he fought in guerrilla operations against the British in the Carolinas in 1780–1781 and was captured there in 1781. A drunken British officer slashed Jackson's face with a saber and he contracted smallpox while a prisoner. His mother and both older brothers also died in the war, and these events no doubt influenced Jackson's subsequent strong Anglophobia.

Following the war, Jackson first read for and then practiced law in North Carolina and then in Tennessee in 1788, where he was highly successful. He became state prosecuting attorney in 1788, and he was a delegate in the state constitutional convention of 1796 and Tennessee's first representative in the U.S. House of Representatives during 1796–1797. Appointed U.S. senator in 1797, Jackson resigned the next year because of financial problems. He then served as a superior court judge during 1798–1804 but again resigned because of financial difficulties.

Jackson found his calling when he was elected major general of the Tennessee militia in 1802. Jackson and his men entered federal service at the beginning of war with Britain in June 1812. Jackson led his men to Natchez, Mississippi, in preparation for an invasion of Florida, which was canceled by decision of Congress. He then marched his men back to Tennessee, earning the nickname of "Old Hickory" for his toughness.

When the Creeks of Alabama and Mississippi allied with the British and went on the warpath in the autumn of 1813, Jackson led his men against them. A strict disciplinarian, he drilled his men thoroughly, believing that militia, if well trained and adequately supplied, could prove an effective fighting force. After carefully stockpiling supplies, he began a campaign against the Creeks that November when their own food supplies were low. Part of his force defeated the Creeks at Tallasahatchee, Alabama, on November 3, while Jackson himself won a lesser victory at Talladega six days later. After reorganizing his forces, Jackson invaded the Creek heartland in March 1814, taking the main Creek encampment in the Battle of Horseshoe Bend/Tohopeka on March 27, 1814. In this engagement one of his junior officers, Sam Houston, who was to become Jackson's protégé, was severely wounded.

Appointed major general in the regular army in May 1814, Jackson assumed command of the Seventh Military District. He improved the defenses of Mobile, Alabama, and defended it against a British naval attack on September 15, 1814. He then marched into Florida without official authorization. Taking Pensacola on November 7, he destroyed its fortifications and then hastened to New Orleans to defend the city against a British attack in December. Jackson assembled a force of regulars and hastily assembled militia and volunteers that repulsed a British assault on January 7, 1815, making him a national hero.

Following the end of the war, Jackson assumed command of the Southern Division of the army at New Orleans. Using the outbreak of the First Seminole War (1817–1818) as a pretext, he invaded Florida. Exceeding his authority, he not only seized Pensacola on May 24, 1818, but also created an international incident that April by hanging two British nationals for allegedly supplying the Seminoles with arms. The James Monroe administration used Jackson's actions to induce Spain to sell Florida to the United States in 1819.

Resigning his commission in June 1821, Jackson served briefly as military governor of Florida during March–October 1821 before returning to his plantation home, the Hermitage, near Nashville. Elected to the U.S. Senate from Tennessee in 1823, he resigned after one session to run for president. In the election of November 1824, he won a plurality of the popular vote and electoral votes but lost the election in the House of Representatives to John Quincy Adams. His supporters worked to bring about electoral changes that then led to his election to the presidency by wide margins in both 1828 and 1832.

As president, Jackson maintained U.S. neutrality but strongly encouraged his friend Sam Houston in the Texas Revolution of 1835–1836. An ardent expansionist, Jackson tried numerous times to purchase Mexican territory. He believed annexing Texas was essential to keeping British influence out of the Southwest and West. Jackson secured congressional approval for the Indian Removal Bill that forced many Native Americans, especially the Cherokees, to move west of the Mississippi River. This act led to both the Black Hawk War (1832) in Illinois and the Second Seminole War (1835–1842) in Florida. Among other events during his presidency were the South Carolina Nullification Crisis, the end of the First Bank of the United States, and the Panic of 1837. On the completion of his second term in 1837, Jackson returned to Nashville. Even out of office, Jackson's shadow loomed large over the American political scene. Jackson lobbied hard for the annexation of Texas, which occurred only months after his death, and at the 1844 Democratic Convention he played a key role in securing the presidential nomination for fellow Tennessean James K. Polk, "Young Hickory," despite his rapidly failing health and tuberculosis.

Jackson died at the Hermitage on June 8, 1845.

SPENCER C. TUCKER

See also

Expansionism and Imperialism; Houston, Samuel; Politics, U.S.; Polk, James Knox; Texas; Texas Revolution.

References

Meacham, Jon. *American Lion: Andrew Jackson in the White House.* New York: Random House, 2008.

Remini, Robert V. *Andrew Jackson and the Course of American Empire, 1767–1821.* New York: Harper & Row, 1977.

Remini, Robert V. *Andrew Jackson and the Course of American Freedom, 1822–1832.* New York: Harper & Row, 1981.

Jackson, Samuel
Event Date: September 17, 1847

U.S. sailor hanged for having struck a commanding officer in 1847. Little is known about Samuel Jackson's life, including the circumstances of his birth or early years. Two facts seem fairly indisputable, however: he was of Irish ancestry and enlisted in the U.S. Navy under an assumed name.

By 1846, Jackson was a seaman serving in the sloop of war *St. Mary's.* That summer the ship was part of Commodore David Conner's Home Squadron, assigned to blockade the east coast of Mexico. Blockade duty was an onerous and often boring task, consisting of long periods of patrolling large stretches of water and coast. The area itself was barren and unhealthy. Consequently, morale was low in the Home Squadron generally, and onboard the *St. Mary's* in particular. Its crew had become sullen and difficult to manage, and Commodore Conner was concerned about discipline within his command. To remedy this deteriorating situation, he decided to make an example of a crew member at the first opportunity.

Naval discipline in the U.S. Navy at the time seems severe by modern standards, yet it was less barbarous than in the British and French navies. Punishment such as "keelhauling," wherein the accused was dragged underwater against the barnacles on the ship's hull, was never practiced in the U.S. Navy. Another punishment, known as "flogging 'round the fleet"—a sentence tantamount to the death penalty—had only been inflicted about 20 times in the preceding 75 years. When a death sentence was the result of a court-martial, the method of execution was generally hanging for seamen and shooting for marines. Between 1799 and 1861, only six seamen are known with certainty to have been hanged. Samuel Jackson was one of those six.

On August 14, 1846, some articles of crew clothing were collected about the *St. Mary's* booms. These were brought to the officer of the deck, Lieutenant William Rodgers Taylor, and he distributed them to their owners among the crew. However, a pair of wet and worn shoes was thrown overboard. Jackson was at the time standing to the side of Taylor between two guns. According to Jackson's court-martial transcript, when the shoes were thrown overboard, he remarked, "There goes a good pair of shoes overboard. If there ain't, I'm damned." Taylor asked Jackson if it were any concern of his, to which he replied in the negative. Taylor then reported Jackson's comment to his superior officer. Jackson later disavowed any disrespectful intent upon making the remark.

Later that day, Taylor was in conversation with some members of a gun crew when Jackson stepped up to him and asked him to forgive him for his earlier outburst. Taylor replied that it was out of his hands, because he believed it was his duty to report it to his superior officer. Jackson asked Taylor if he thought he would be punished. Taylor replied that he did not know, but thought it likely. Jackson then hit Taylor several times, causing him to fall to the deck.

Jackson was quickly charged with raising a weapon against his superior, striking his superior, treating his superior with contempt, and uttering seditious and mutinous words. A court-martial found him guilty of the second, third, and fourth charges and sentenced him to be hanged. On September 17, 1846, Seaman Samuel Jackson was hanged from the fore yardarm of the *St.*

Mary's at the fleet anchorage at Antón Lizardo in full view of the entire Home Squadron. The swift and severe punishment reportedly shocked sailors as well as their officers. No other such incident took place in the U.S. Navy during the war.

HAROLD N. BOYER SR.

See also

Antón Lizardo; Blockade, Naval; Conner, David; United States Navy.

References

Taylor, Fitch W. *The Broad Pennant; or, A Cruise in the United States Flag Ship of the Gulf Squadron during the Mexican Difficulties.* New York: Leavitt, Trow, 1848.

Valle, James E. *Rocks and Shoals: Order and Discipline in the Old Navy, 1800–1861.* Annapolis, MD: United States Naval Institute Press, 1980.

Jalapa

Capital city of the Mexican state of Veracruz that served as a staging area for Mexico's Army of the East in March 1847 and which American troops occupied beginning in April 1847. At the time of the Mexican-American War, Jalapa (also known as Xalapa) had a population of about 7,500 people. Located some 75 miles west of Mexico's Gulf Coast and some 100 east of Mexico City, Jalapa is frequently shrouded in mist and fog owing to its altitude of 4,680 feet above sea level. Moisture from the nearby Gulf of Mexico is often funneled up into the area, which has historically made it a rich agricultural region. Indeed, during the 19th century, Jalapa was surrounded by farms and ranches where citrus, avocados, coffee, and jalapeño peppers grew in great abundance.

During the war, Jalapa was a prosperous town and abounded with textile mills, shops, hotels, and eating establishments. After Major General Winfield Scott's army landed at Veracruz in March 1847, Mexican general Antonio López de Santa Anna instructed Major General Valentín Canalizo to cobble together a military force, which was to be based at Jalapa, to stop the Americans' inland advance. Dubbed the Army of the East, Canalizo's hastily mustered force joined Santa Anna's force at Cerro Gordo, where they hoped to defeat the Americans and turn them back toward the sea. The Mexicans lost the Battle of Cerro Gordo, however, and the day after the engagement, on April 19, Scott's army moved into Jalapa, beginning an occupation that endured until war's end. Second Lieutenant George B. McClellan called Jalapa "the most beautiful place I ever beheld" and declared the surrounding country to be "a perfect Paradise."

To cultivate good relations with the locals, Scott issued orders strictly forbidding U.S. troops from harassing or stealing from the residents of Jalapa. Regular U.S. troops were encamped within the town limits while volunteer forces set up camp in the surrounding countryside. U.S. soldiers reported that they were treated well by the townspeople, although it is unclear if Jalapa's residents actively collaborated with their occupiers or simply chose not to provoke them.

Jalapa, Mexico, during the Mexican-American War. The capital city of the state of Veracruz, Jalapa was occupied by U.S. forces beginning in April 1847. (N. C. Brooks, *A Complete History of the Mexican War,* 1849)

Meanwhile, in the areas surrounding the town, Mexican guerrillas continued to operate, harassing both U.S. forces and Mexicans whom they deemed too friendly to the enemy. In early July, Scott ordered most of his force to march toward Puebla, leaving behind a small occupation force of some 1,000 men. Scott's army moved out on July 12; however, before departing he appointed Lieutenant Colonel Thomas Childs as Jalapa's military governor.

The town was occupied until the end of 1848, and although there was little friction during this period, two Mexican guerrillas were executed in the town square in November 1847. The following month U.S. troops executed two American teamsters who had been convicted of murdering a Mexican boy. Clearly, Scott wished to send a message that he would not tolerate depredations perpetrated by U.S. occupiers.

Today, Jalapa is a large and thriving city, with a population approaching 400,000 people. It is the second-largest city, after only Veracruz, in the state of Veracruz. Jalapa is also a major educational and cultural center. Three major universities are located there.

PAUL G. PIERPAOLI JR.

See also

Canalizo, Valentín; Cerro Gordo, Battle of; Childs, Thomas; Guerrilla Warfare; Santa Anna, Antonio López de; Scott, Winfield; Veracruz.

References

Eisenhower, John S. D. *So Far from God: The U.S. War with Mexico, 1846–1848.* New York: Random House, 1989.

Siemans, A. H. *Between the Summit and the Sea: Central Veracruz in the Nineteenth Century.* Vancouver: University of British Columbia, 1990.

Jarauta, Celedonio Domeco de
Birth Date: March 3, 1814
Death Date: July 19, 1848

Spanish-born Catholic priest who commanded a substantial partisan/guerrilla force that fought U.S. occupying forces between the port of Veracruz and the city of Jalapa during and after the Mexican-American War. Born on March 3, 1814, in Zaragosa, Spain, Celedonio Domeco de Jarauta first became involved in military matters as a supporter of Spain's conservative Carlista guerrilla movement. Subsequently ordained a priest in the Order of St. Francis, he traveled to Havana, Cuba, then a Spanish colony. In 1844, he settled in Veracruz, Mexico, and took up duties as a parish priest. When U.S. forces invaded central Mexico in March 1847, Jarauta was named chaplain of the Mexican army's 2nd Infantry Regiment.

In response to substitute president Pedro María Anaya's April 1847 proclamation calling for commanders to wage partisan warfare against the U.S. Army, Jarauta applied for and received authorization to lead such a group. He then played a leading role in the attack on a U.S. Army supply convoy at La Hoya on June 20, 1847. Jarauta's skills in attacking U.S. convoys and picking off American

stragglers prompted Major General Winfield Scott to create a command tasked with stopping him. Major General Joseph Lane commanded the resulting cavalry force, which consisted of both U.S. Army troopers and a force of Texas Rangers led by Major Samuel H. Walker. This force was in pursuit of Jarauta and his men when American and Mexican negotiators signed the Treaty of Guadalupe Hidalgo on February 2, 1848.

Jarauta refused to acknowledge the validity of the peace treaty ending the war, however. He denounced as traitors the Mexican officials who signed it and vowed to continue fighting. On February 25, 1848, Lane's force surprised Jarauta and his men at Sequalteplan. In the ensuing clash, the Americans killed hundreds of Jarauta's men, but Jarauta escaped.

Three days later Jarauta and the remaining 350 men in his command entered the town of Zacualtipan and seized 500,000 pesos to support their military operations. Jarauta also forged an alliance with General Mariano Paredes y Arrillaga, the former president who shared Jarauta's determination to resist both the Treaty of Guadalupe Hidalgo and the March 16, 1848, truce agreement.

The high tide of Jarauta's subsequent campaign occurred on July 15, 1848, when he seized the city of Guanajuato. This success was short-lived, however. Three days later, while leading a force of 50 men on reconnaissance between Mellado and Valencia, he was surprised and captured by units of the Mexican army. The commander of these units, General Anastasio Bustamante, possessed a well-deserved reputation for harshly suppressing rebels of various sorts. He thus gave Father Jarauta 24 hours to confess his sins and to write a letter to his mother in Spain. Jarauta refused to comply, and on July 19, 1848, he was executed by a firing squad in Valencia.

IRVING W. LEVINSON

See also

Anaya, Pedro María de; Bustamante y Oseguera, Anastasio; Guadalupe Hidalgo, Treaty of; Guerrilla Warfare; La Hoya, Skirmish at; Lane, Joseph; Paredes y Arrillaga, Mariano; Sequalteplán, Skirmish at; Texas Rangers; Walker, Samuel Hamilton.

References

Alvarez, Daniel Molina. *La pasión del Padre Jarauta.* Mexico, DF: Gobierno de la Ciudad de México, 1999.

Field, Ron. *Mexican-American War, 1846–1848.* London: Brassey's, 1997.

Jarero, José María
Birth Date: 1801
Death Date: 1867

Mexican army officer. José María Jarero was born in Jalapa, in the state of Veracruz, in 1801. In 1816, at age 15, he entered Spanish colonial military service with the Urban Infantry Regiment of Jalapa. He fought on the royalist side during the wars for independence until 1821, at which time he switched sides and embraced the proposal for independence set forth by Agustín de Iturbide. Jarero remained in the army and in 1832 was promoted to general of brigade. The following year he was court-martialed for dereliction of duty because in November government forces under his command were defeated by rebels at Chilpancingo.

After a brief period in prison, Jarero managed to ingratiate himself with different political factions, and his malleability allowed him to rehabilite his military career. In 1839, following the brief Pastry War with France, he was commander at San Juan de Ulúa, Veracruz. Jarero then held a series of notable posts, including those of commandant general at Aguascalientes in 1841, Jalisco in 1842, Sonora in 1846, and Mexico in 1847.

Jarero's most notable Mexican-American War contribution came during the April 17–18, 1847, Battle of Cerro Gordo. During that engagement Jarero's brigade comprised the right flank of General Antonio López de Santa Anna's main force. Much of the fighting occurred along the Mexican left flank, but Jarero's men nevertheless helped push back Brigadier General Gideon Pillow's ill-advised assault on the right on April 18 with withering small-arms and artillery fire. Later that day, however, with the fall of El Telégrafo, Jarero's position became untenable and he was forced to surrender. Santa Anna was reportedly furious at Jarero's capitulation, and for the remainder of the war Jarero held only obscure commands removed from major action.

After the war, in 1848, Jarero served as commandant general of Querétaro. The following year he began serving in the same position in Puebla and held that post until he retired in 1857 at the rank of general of division. Jarero died in Mexico City in 1867.

PAUL G. PIERPAOLI JR.

See also
Cerro Gordo, Battle of; Jalapa; Mexico, Army; Mexico City Campaign; Pastry War; Pillow, Gideon Johnson; San Juan de Ulúa; Santa Anna, Antonio López de; Veracruz.

References
DePalo, William A. *The Mexican National Army, 1822–1852.* College Station: Texas A&M University Press, 1997.
Eisenhower, John S. D. *So Far from God: The U.S. War with Mexico, 1846–1848.* New York: Random House, 1989.

Jesup, Thomas Sidney
Birth Date: December 16, 1788
Death Date: June 10, 1860

U.S. Army officer and quartermaster general of the army from 1818 to 1860. Thomas Sidney Jesup was born in Berkeley County, Virginia (now West Virginia) on December 16, 1788, the son of a well-regarded American Revolutionary War officer. Jesup entered army service in 1808 as a second lieutenant in the 7th Infantry. He saw action during the War of 1812, by which time he was the major of the 19th Infantry. Jesup was taken prisoner at Detroit when Brigadier General William Hull surrendered that place in

August 1812. Later exchanged, he subsequently served most effectively, including during the Battle of Chippewa (Chippawa) in July 1814. That same month, he was brevetted lieutenant colonel for his performance in the Battle of Lundy's Lane, where he was badly wounded.

Jesup continued in the army after the war and, in 1818, President James Monroe appointed him quartermaster general, at the rank of brigadier general, a post he would hold for 42 years until his death in 1860. Jesup is considered the father of the modern quartermaster corps.

Jesup immediately set about creating efficient, effective quartermaster procedures designed to provide adequate supplies of quality products, flexible and mobile delivery systems, and strict accountability on the part of suppliers and officers tasked with producing, requisitioning, and paying for military items. This marked the first time in which supplying the U.S. Army became a well-organized endeavor based on modern business techniques. Most of Jesup's improvements made their way into *Army Regulations*, and many of the procedures he pioneered remain in use today.

Jesup also held field commands. During the 1835–1842 Second Seminole War, he took over command from Brigadier General Winfield Scott, whom he had severely criticized for his performance in Florida. But Jesup stirred up controversy when he violated the terms of a truce and illegally incarcerated Indian leaders, including Chief Osceola, in 1837. Brigadier General Zachary Taylor replaced Jesup as commander in Florida in May 1838, and Jesup resumed his quartermaster duties. During his time in Florida, however, Jesup fine-tuned his system of employing base supply camps and advance depots that greatly aided the U.S. Army in the prosecution of the war. He would use these same procedures, with considerable success, during the Mexican-American War.

A major general by the time the Mexican-American War began in 1846, Jesup was first charged with setting up a supply center along the Rio Grande opposite Matamoros, Mexico, for Brigadier General Zachary Taylor's force. Supplying an army so far from U.S. population centers proved to be a severe challenge, and during the early days, Taylor's army lacked sufficient quantities of such necessary items as tents, horses, pack animals, boats, and barges. Jesup soon implemented a policy by which supplies would be carried by pack animals instead of by traditional baggage trains, a change that was well-suited to the rugged landscape and poor roads of northern Mexico. He also prescribed specific weight limits for pack animals. Still, Jesup was faced by less than cooperative field commanders, thin supply reserves, and little money. Some suppliers in the United States proved less than scrupulous, meaning Jesup had to keep a watchful eye on product quality and costs. These various challenges compelled Jesup to be highly resourceful, as when he bought plain muslin to be used as shelter for soldiers when traditional tents were in short supply.

In 1847, Jesup was tasked with supplying Major General Winfield Scott's army during its assault on Veracruz and subsequent Mexico City Campaign. Planning for this operation, the largest amphibious landing undertaken by the U.S. Army to that point in time, began in late 1846. Jesup arranged for and supervised the construction of landing craft, known as surfboats. These were later credited with ensuring a safe and smooth landing for thousands of U.S. troops at Veracruz.

During the war, numerous commanders, including Taylor and Scott, criticized Jesup for supply shortages, but overall he performed admirably, given the distinct limitations under which he labored. Compared to the Mexicans' logistical operation, Jesup's system was a model of efficiency. After the war ended, Jesup retained his post, fighting to keep his systems functional during draconian budget cuts that occurred in the 1850s. Jesup died at his home in Washington, D.C., on June 10, 1860, still on active duty and the longest-serving quartermaster general in U.S. Army history.

PAUL G. PIERPAOLI JR.

See also

Logistics, Mexican; Logistics, U.S.; Mexico City Campaign; Northern Mexico Theater of War, Overview; Quartermaster Services, U.S. and Mexican; Scott, Winfield; Surfboats; Taylor, Zachary; Veracruz, Landing at and Siege of.

References

Kieffer, Chester L. *Maligned General: A Biography of Thomas S. Jesup.* Novato, CA: Presidio Press, 1979.

Winders, R. Bruce. *Mr. Polk's Army: The American Military Experience in the Mexican War.* College Station: Texas A&M University Press, 1997.

Johnston, Albert Sidney

Birth Date: February 2, 1803
Death Date: April 6, 1862

Republic of Texas, U.S., and Confederate Army officer. Born in Washington, Kentucky, on February 2, 1803, Albert Sidney Johnston attended Transylvania University before entering the U.S. Military Academy at West Point, graduating in 1826. He served in the Black Hawk War but resigned his commission and returned to Kentucky in 1834 to care for his wife, Henrietta, who was dying of tuberculosis. They moved to Texas, where Johnston took up farming, but Henrietta passed away in 1836. Johnston enlisted as a private in the Texas army when the Texas Revolution began, and by January 1837 he was senior brigadier general commanding the army of Texas. He had held the job for scarcely a week, however, when Brigadier General Felix Huston, slighted by Johnston's promotion, challenged him to a duel. Johnston refused to fire on Huston, who shot him in the pelvis, putting him out of action and out of the job. Johnston subsequently served as Texas's secretary of war (1838–1840) before resigning and returning to farming.

In the Mexican-American War, Johnston commanded a regiment of Texas volunteers—the 1st Foot Riflemen of Texas. Johnston drilled and trained his men so thoroughly that Major General Zachary Taylor appointed Johnston commander of the U.S. staging area at Camargo. Arriving there in August 1846 with

a detachment of his men, illness and disease decimated his command, leading to the disbandment of the unit. Later that month, Johnston became inspector general for Major General William O. Butler's division. Johnston performed admirably at the Battle of Monterrey (September 21–23, 1846), where his actions may well have staved off a U.S. defeat. With his friend and fellow Kentuckian Jefferson Davis, he served on the commission that negotiated the armistice that ended the Battle of Monterrey. Although he was subsequently recommended for a regular army commission, none was forthcoming, and he finished the war as a volunteer colonel.

In 1849, Johnston returned to the regular U.S. Army as a major. In 1855, with his old West Point friend Jefferson Davis serving as secretary of war, Johnston was appointed colonel of the newly formed 2nd U.S. Cavalry. In 1857 Johnston commanded U.S. forces in the confrontation known as the Mormon War, for which he received a brevet to brigadier general. In 1860 he received appointment to command the Department of the Pacific, headquartered in California.

In April 1861, Johnston learned of the secession of Texas and resigned from the U.S. Army. In September, Confederate president Jefferson Davis commissioned him a full general and assigned him to direct all northward-facing defenses west of the Appalachian Mountains.

Johnston took over a difficult situation. His department was short of troops and even more short of weapons. He deployed his available forces in southern Kentucky in hopes of protecting Tennessee. Between Columbus and Bowling Green, Forts Henry and Donelson guarded access to the Tennessee and Cumberland Rivers.

In the early months of 1862, Johnston's defensive perimeter was tested and collapsed. On February 6, Fort Henry on the Tennessee River surrendered to a joint Union army and navy force. This action opened the Tennessee River to Union penetration all the way to northern Alabama, rendering Bowling Green and Columbus untenable. Johnston unwisely reinforced Fort Donelson on the Cumberland River with too few men to make a successful defense. When the fortress was forced to surrender its 15,000-man garrison on February 16, Johnston's army was seriously depleted in the face of superior Union numbers under the aggressive leadership of Brigadier General Ulysses S. Grant.

Assisted by General P. G. T. Beauregard, whom Jefferson Davis sent West to lend assistance to the demoralized commander, Johnston reunited all the forces in his department (save those west of the Mississippi who could not get there in time) at the important northern Mississippi rail junction of Corinth, only 20 miles from Grant's new encampment at Pittsburg Landing on the west bank of the Tennessee River. Johnston's plan was to strike Grant before he could be joined by the Union army of Major General Don Carlos Buell, marching overland from Nashville.

Learning on April 1 of Buell's approach, Johnston moved toward Grant's camp. Rain and inexperienced troops delayed the attack until the morning of April 6, beginning the Battle of Shiloh.

Confederate attacks were initially successful, and by midmorning Johnston believed, mistakenly, that he had succeeded in tearing Grant's left loose from the Tennessee River and that his advancing regiments would soon push the Federals into a pocket formed by the river and impenetrable swamps. Leading an assault aimed at accomplishing that purpose that afternoon, Johnston received a mortal wound.

STEVEN E. WOODWORTH

See also

Butler, William Orlando; Camargo; Huston, Felix; Monterrey, Battle of; Taylor, Zachary; Texas Revolution.

References

Roland, Charles P. *Albert Sidney Johnston: Soldier of Three Republics.* Austin: University of Texas Press, 1964.

Woodworth, Steven E. *Jefferson Davis and His Generals: The Failure of Confederate Command in the West.* Lawrence: University Press of Kansas, 1990.

Jones, Anson
Birth Date: January 20, 1798
Death Date: January 9, 1858

Texas revolutionary, politician, and last president of the Republic of Texas. Born in Seekonkville, Great Barrington, Massachusetts, on January 20, 1798, Anson Jones received a medical license from the Oneida, New York, Medical Society in 1820. After traveling throughout the Northeast and practicing medicine for two years in Venezuela, Jones earned an MD degree from the Jefferson Medical College (Philadelphia) in 1827. He migrated to New Orleans in 1832, where financial failure induced him to settle in Brazoria, Texas, the following year.

As confrontations between Texas colonists and the Mexican government escalated, Jones initially urged caution, but in 1835 he authored resolutions calling for Texas independence. During the Texas Revolution, Jones served as judge advocate and surgeon of the Texas 2nd Regiment at the Battle of San Jacinto on April 21, 1836. Following independence, Jones won election to the Second Congress of the Republic of Texas, and in 1838 President Sam Houston appointed Jones minister to the United States. Recalled in 1839 by Houston's successor, President Mirabeau Lamar, Jones then served in the Texas Senate and in 1841 a reelected President Houston appointed him secretary of state.

Jones became a key element in Houston's attempts to secure annexation to the United States or recognition of Texas independence from the Mexican government. In 1844, Jones won election to succeed Houston as president, and in 1845 he oversaw the final negotiations for annexation by the United States. In his remaining years, Jones wrote his autobiography, *Republic of Texas,* which was published posthumously in 1859. Jones took his own life in Houston, Texas, on January 9, 1858.

STEVEN NATHANIEL DOSSMAN

Physician Anson Jones fought during the Texas War of Independence and was the last president of the Republic of Texas before it was annexed by the United States in 1845. (Texas State Library)

See also

Congress, Texan; Houston, Samuel; Lamar, Mirabeau Buonaparte; San Jacinto, Battle of; Texas; Texas Revolution.

References

Davis, William C. *Lone Star Rising: The Revolutionary Birth of the Texas Republic.* College Station: Texas A&M University Press, 2006.

Gambrell, Herbert Pickens. *Anson Jones: The Last President of Texas.* Garden City, NY: Doubleday, 1948.

Jones, Anson. *Memoranda and Official Correspondence Relating to the Republic of Texas, Its History and Annexation.* 1859. Chicago: Rio Grande Press, 1966.

Jones, Thomas ap Catesby
Birth Date: April 24, 1790
Death Date: May 30, 1858

U.S. naval officer. Thomas Jones was born on April 24, 1790, on a plantation in Westmoreland County, Virginia. The "ap" in his name is Welsh for "son of." He was thus Thomas, the son of Catesby Jones. Orphaned at an early age, on November 22, 1805, Jones secured an appointment as a midshipman in the U.S. Navy and participated in the suppression of the slave trade in the Gulf of Mexico from 1808 to 1812. Promoted to lieutenant at the New

Orleans station on May 24, 1812, he won acclaim for his role in the seizure and destruction of pirate Jean Lafitte's stronghold on Barataria Island near New Orleans on September 14, 1814. Jones then commanded a squadron of five gunboats, with a total of 21 guns, on Lake Borgne that attempted to prevent British troops from reaching New Orleans. The gunboats were defeated that December 14 by sheer force of 40 British barges with 41 guns. Jones was among the U.S. wounded and captured but received commendation for delaying the British advance that culminated in the Battle of New Orleans (January 8, 1815).

Following the war, Jones continued his naval career and served in a variety of postings. During 1819–1822 he was assigned to ordnance duties at the Washington Navy Yard. Promoted to commander on March 28, 1820, from 1822 to 1824 Jones served as inspector and superintendent of ordnance at the Washington Yard, and during 1824–1825 he was inspector and superintendent of ordnance for the U.S. Navy. In 1826 he was the first U.S. Navy officer to visit Tahiti, and on December 23 of that year he concluded a treaty with King Kamehameha III of the Sandwich Islands (Hawaii), which protected American interests on the islands. Jones was promoted to captain on March 11, 1829. Jones was named commander of the South Pacific Exploring Expedition in 1836, but sickness the next year led to his replacement.

Jones was named commander of the U.S. Pacific Squadron in September 1841; he held that assignment until May 1844 and again from October 1847 to December 1850. When his squadron was at Callao, Peru, he received the mistaken impression via a newspaper account that the United States and Mexico were at war. Fearful that the British or French would take advantage of the situation to conquer California, Jones sailed his ships to Monterey, California, on October 19, 1842, and demanded of the astonished Mexicans that they surrender to the United States.

Because Governor Juan Bautista Alvarado had recently been replaced by Manuel Micheltorena, who was still in Los Angeles, Alvarado refused to discuss the capitulation of Monterey with Jones. A group of Monterey's prominent citizens, led by José Abrego and Pedro Narvaez, therefore negotiated the surrender of Monterey (but not California) the following day. After occupying Monterey for one day, on October 21 Jones realized that Mexico and the United States were indeed not at war. Apologizing for his mistake, he lowered the American flag and sailed away. The incident further soured Mexican-U.S. relations.

The U.S. government eventually censured Jones for his occupation of Monterey and relieved him of his command to appease the Mexican government. John Drake Sloat, who would capture Monterey in July 1846, replaced Jones as commander of the U.S. Pacific Squadron.

Jones's naval career was not yet at an end. Many senior U.S. officials, believing that Jones's decision to intervene was in the national interest, argued that he had acted correctly. Given the poor state of U.S.-Mexican relations at the time, few U.S. policy makers were concerned by his infringement on Mexican national

honor. Therefore, in October 1847 Jones was again appointed to command of the Pacific Squadron. He then oversaw the evacuation of Mexicans from Lower California who had been loyal to the United States and were to be resettled in Alta California. Jones held the Pacific Squadron command until December 1850.

Controversy, nevertheless, continued to surround Jones. In 1843 he had met the novelist Herman Melville, who used him as the basis for the abusive commodore character in *White-Jacket* (1850). Melville's writing and Jones's own reports to the Navy Department all gave the impression of an officer who was both contentious and rash. In December 1850 a well-publicized court-martial found Jones guilty of misappropriation of funds and suspended him for five years. President Millard Fillmore remitted the sentence in February 1853, but Jones was then awaiting orders until placed on the reserve list in September 1855. Jones died at his home, Sharon, in Fairfax County, Virginia, on May 30, 1858.

MICHAEL R. HALL AND SPENCER C. TUCKER

See also
California; Micheltorena, Manuel; Monterey, California.

References
Gapp, Frank W. *The Commodore and the Whale: The Lost Victories of Thomas ap Catesby Jones*. New York: Vantage Press, 1996.
Smith, Gene A. *Thomas ap Catesby Jones: Commodore of Manifest Destiny*. Annapolis, MD: Naval Institute Press, 2000.

Jordan, Samuel W.
Birth Date: ca. 1810
Death Date: June 22, 1841

U.S. soldier of fortune and renegade Texas adventurer. Samuel W. Jordan was born circa 1810. Nothing more is known about the circumstances of his birth or of his early years. Indeed, Texas politician Sam Houston referred to Jordan because of his inscrutable past as the "abandoned man." Jordan did not enter the historical record until 1836, when he arrived in Texas to participate in the Texas Revolution. He appeared too late to see any military action, but he subsequently joined the Texas army, rising to the rank of captain by 1838. In May 1839 Jordan was dispatched to East Texas where he saw action against the Cherokees. That September 2 Jordan resigned his commission and then joined Mexican general Antonio Rosillo Canales's federalist bid to create the Republic of the Rio Grande.

Now with the rank of colonel, Jordan, along with Texas Ranger captain Reuben Ross, led a force of about 200 Texans and other adventure seekers into northern Mexico. On October 3–4, 1839, Jordan's force saw action at the Battle of Alcantra, some 12 miles distance from Mier in the department of Nuevo León. After the encounter Jordan's men secured towns on either side of the Rio Grande, although they withdrew into the Texas border towns for the winter.

In June 1840, Jordan, operating with Canales, again occupied Mexican border towns. He then moved into the Mexican interior, taking the city of Victoria, Tamaulipas. His next objective was San Luis Potosí, but by then he came to realize that Canales no longer supported his mission and may in fact have betrayed him by indicating his movements to Mexican centralist authorities. At Saltillo, on October 25, 1840, Jordan's contingent barely repelled a Mexican force under General Raphael Vásquez before withdrawing to the Rio Grande. Within weeks, Jordan had abandoned the federalist cause and dissolved his command. Jordan arrived in Austin, Texas, that December, where he became engaged in a vituperative disagreement with Sam Houston; in the process, Houston was nearly killed when Jordan swung at him with an axe.

No longer welcome in Texas, Jordan went to New Orleans in the summer of 1841. There he enlisted in General Mariano Arista's abortive effort to gain control of the Yucatán. He somehow missed the boat bound for the Yucatán, and in a fit of despair committed suicide on June 22, 1841.

PAUL G. PIERPAOLI JR.

See also
Arista, Mariano; Canales Rosillo, Antonio; Texas; Texas Revolution.

References
Bancroft, Hubert Howe. *History of the North Mexican States and Texas.* 2 vols. San Francisco: History Company, 1886, 1889.
Pierce, Gerald S. "The Texas Army Career of Samuel W. Jordan." *Texas Military History* 5 (Summer 1965): 8–14.

Jornada del Muerto

A segment of what was once the longest road in North America, the 1,800-mile El Camino Real de Tierra Adentro (Royal Road of the Interior Lands), which connected Mexico City with northern New Mexico. The roughest and deadliest part of the road, called Jornada del Muerto, Spanish for "Journey of the Dead," comprised almost 100 miles between Las Cruces and San Marcial. It was so named after a German immigrant who died on that stretch attempting to escape a charge of witchcraft in the late 1600s. Lying between the Caballo Mountains and Fra Cristobal Range to the west and the San Andres Mountains to the east, the Jornada is a desert, virtually without wood for fuel or surface water. Although challenging for any traveler, the route was shorter than the alternate path along the Rio Grande, which ran through steep canyons and was almost impassable for wagons and artillery. Thus, it was the Jornada del Muerto over which Colonel Alexander Doniphan marched from Santa Fe in December 1846 during the Mexican-American War.

Following the capture of Santa Fe in August, Brigadier General Stephen W. Kearny ordered Doniphan to rendezvous with a 3,000-man column from San Antonio under Brigadier General John E. Wool. In Doniphan's command were the volunteers of his own 1st Missouri Mounted Rifles, a portion of the 2nd Missouri Mounted

Rifles, an independent mounted company known as the St. Louis LeClede Rangers, and an artillery battalion. In addition, the command included a large contingent of supply wagons and wagon-mounted civilian merchants. Kearny had also provided Doniphan, a volunteer, with three regular army officers as advisers.

Leaving Santa Fe in early December, Doniphan divided his column because of the shortage of wood and water and entered the inhospitable Jornada del Muerto. He maintained a moderate pace for 16 hours per day to traverse the Jornada as rapidly as possible without wearing out the expedition's animals. The troops would face other challenges of difficult desert terrain, but none worse than the Jornada.

The command successfully passed through the Jornada del Muerto in three days without Mexican army contact, reaching the Rio Grande about 60 miles from El Paso, Texas. After a rest of several days, Doniphan continued his march in two segments, finally encountering Mexican resistance about 25 miles north of his objective. There, at a place called Brazito (Little Arm), he fought his first battle, sometimes known as the Battle of Temascalitos.

PHILIP L. BOLTÉ

See also
Chihuahua, State of; Doniphan, Alexander William; Brazito, Battle of; Kearny, Stephen Watts; New Mexico; Santa Fe; Santa Fe–Chihuahua Trail; Wool, John Ellis.

References
Dawson, Joseph G. *Doniphan's Epic March.* Lawrence: University Press of Kansas, 1999.
Peterson, Douglas, and José Antonio Esquibel. *The Royal Road: El Camino Royal from Mexico City to Santa Fe.* Albuquerque: University of New Mexico Press, 1998.

Juárez, Benito
Birth Date: 1806
Death Date: July 18, 1872

Mexican politician. Considered one of the monumental figures in Mexican history, Benito Juárez was born in 1806 to a poor Zapotec family in San Pablo Guelatao, located in the present-day state of Oaxaca. His parents died when he was 4 years old, and Juárez worked as a field hand and a shepherd until age 12. When he arrived in Oaxaca City in 1818, Juárez could not read or write Spanish. He was taken in as a domestic servant by the Maza family, for whom his older sister had also worked as a servant. The Mazas took an interest in the young boy early on, and a friend of the family, Antonio Saleneuva, a lay member of the Franciscan order, educated him. Juárez was then sent to the seminary with the expectation that he might become a Catholic priest.

In 1828, however, Juárez withdrew from the seminary and enrolled in Oaxaca's Institute of Science and Art, a secular college of higher education, from where he graduated with a law degree in 1834. Juárez, meanwhile, began to dabble in public affairs. As a

Benito Juárez, president of Mexico during 1858–1872, was one of the greatest Mexican political leaders. Despite the limited effectiveness of his reforms, he remains the hero of Mexican nationalism, a leader who restored constitutional order and maintained Mexican sovereignty. (Perry-Castaneda Library)

city councilman in Oaxaca between 1831 and 1833, he developed a reputation as a staunch defender of indigenous rights, and in 1841 he became a civil judge.

Juárez made the transition from provincial to national politics in August 1846 following the restoration of the 1824 federal constitution. By that time he was known as a true liberal and federalist (the state governor so characterized him in a letter of introduction to *puro* politician Valentín Gómez Farías), and Juárez lived up to that reputation as one of Oaxaca's 10 deputies to the national legislature. He belonged to a congressional committee that gave shape to the controversial January 11, 1847, law—designed to finance the war with the U.S.—that authorized the government to raise 15 million pesos by mortgaging or selling ecclesiastical property. That April he and other *puro* deputies tried to derail *moderado* efforts to pass the so-called Acta de Reformas, a bill that aimed to sanction some minor modifications to the 1824 charter.

After returning to Oaxaca, Juárez served as state governor from late October 1847 until August 1852. In 1848 he prohibited General Antonio López de Santa Anna, who was hoping to continue the struggle against the United States, from entering Oaxaca because he feared that Santa Anna's presence in the state might provoke a rebellion. Juárez paid a heavy price for this decision in 1853 when Santa Anna, shortly after assuming power for the last time, forced him into exile in New Orleans.

Juárez returned to Mexico in 1855 and joined the movement to overthrow Santa Anna, the so-called Revolution of Ayutla. Following Santa Anna's ouster, Juárez became minister of justice, and in that position he wrote the 1855 Juárez Law, which abolished clerical immunity from prosecution in civil courts and curtailed the privileges of the Catholic Church in Mexico. In November 1857 Juárez was named minister of the interior, and the following month he became chief justice of the Supreme Court.

The next decade cemented Juárez's place as one of Mexico's greatest political figures. He became president in January 1858 (due to his status as chief Supreme Court justice) following a military coup against the liberal government and remained in that post until his death in mid-1872. Juárez then led Mexican liberals against their foreign and domestic enemies in the War of the Reform (1858–1861) and the French intervention (1862–1867), and in so doing he achieved near-mythic status as the person responsible for restoring constitutional order and preserving Mexico's sovereignty. Juárez died of a heart attack on July 18, 1872, while at his desk in the National Palace in Mexico City.

DANIEL W. KUTHY AND PEDRO SANTONI

See also

Catholic Church, Mexico; Guadalupe Hidalgo, Treaty of; Lincoln, Abraham; Monroe Doctrine; Politics, Mexican; Santa Anna, Antonio López de.

References

Cadenhead, Ivie E. *Benito Juárez.* New York: Twayne, 1973.

Hamnett, Brian. *Juárez.* London: Longman, 1994.

Ridley, Jasper Godwin. *Maximilam and Juárez.* New York: Ticknor & Fields, 1992.

Sordo Cedeño, Reynaldo. "El congreso y la guerra con Estados Unidos de América, 1846–1848." In *México al tiempo de su Guerra con Estados Unidos (1846–1848),* coordinated by Josefina Zoraida Vázquez, 47–103. Mexico City: Secretaría de Relaciones Exteriores, El Colegio de México, and Fondo de Cultura Económica, 1997.

Weeks, Charles A. *The Juárez Myth in Mexico.* Tuscaloosa: University of Alabama Press, 1987.

Juvera, Julián
Birth Date: 1784
Death Date: 1860

Mexican army general and cavalry leader during the Mexican-American War. Julián Juvera was born in 1784 in Atitaliquia (modern-day Hidalgo) in south central Mexico. As a youth, he entered military service with the Spanish colonial army and fought on the royalist side during Mexico's wars for independence. In 1821, like many other prominent military figures, he joined Agustín de Iturbide's proposal for independence as embodied in the Plan of Iguala. He remained in the army thereafter, rising steadily through the ranks and attaining the rank of general of brigade by the 1830s. Juvera became known for his leadership of cavalry units, and it was in that capacity that he participated in the Mexican-American War.

When General Antonio López de Santa Anna's main force, the Army of the North, marched from San Luis Potosí to La Angostura in February 1847, Juvera's men served as an advance scouting and screening force in an attempt to slow down and distract the American forces under Major General Zachary Taylor and Brigadier General John E. Wool. Juvera had at his disposal 39 cavalry squadrons in all—some 3,000 men—that included the 3rd, 4th, 5th, 7th, 8th, and 9th cavalry regiments. During the Battle of Buena Vista on February 22–23, Juvera's brigade anchored the Mexican right flank. Although Juvera conducted himself competently during the encounter, Santa Anna's decision not to continue the battle and withdraw his forces has prompted many historians to deem the engagement a Mexican defeat.

Following Buena Vista, Juvera's cavalry formation became part of the Army of the East, and Juvera's next major action came late that summer during the battles for Mexico City. On the morning of September 8, 1847, Brigadier General William Worth's division attacked El Molino del Rey, a complex of two stone buildings. He began with a brief but heavy artillery barrage, and immediately followed that with an infantry advance. Mexican military plans, having anticipated the engagement, called for some 4,000 cavalry troops under General Juan Álvarez, bivouacked nearby, to go on the offensive and hit Worth's vulnerable left flank. The Mexican cavalry took too long to accomplish this, however, and the opportunity to inflict serious damage on American forces was lost. Faced with withering artillery fire, most of the cavalrymen withdrew in confusion, and the battle was ultimately lost. The Americans were now poised to advance on Mexico City. Álvarez never explained the reasons for his hesitation, but he did complain that his subordinates, including Juvera, had failed to react quickly enough to his commands.

Juvera remained in the military after the war, serving as military commander at Querétaro and then governor. He died at Querétaro in 1860.

PAUL G. PIERPAOLI JR.

See also

Álvarez, Juan; Buena Vista, Battle of; Cavalry and Dragoons; El Molino del Rey, Battle of; Northern Mexico Theater of War, Overview; Santa Anna, Antonio López de; Taylor, Zachary; Wool, John Ellis; Worth, William Jenkins.

References

Francaviglia, Richard V., and Douglas W. Richmond, eds. *Dueling Eagles: Reinterpreting the U.S.-Mexican War, 1846–1848.* Fort Worth: Texas Christian University Press, 2000.

Lavender, David. *Climax at Buena Vista: The American Campaigns in Northeastern Mexico, 1846–47.* Philadelphia, PA: Lippincott, 1966.

Wheelan, Joseph. *Invading Mexico: America's Continental Dream and the Mexican War, 1846–1848.* New York: Carroll & Graf, 2007.

Kearny, Philip

Birth Date: June 2, 1815
Death Date: September 1, 1862

U.S. Army officer. Philip Kearny was born into a wealthy New York City family on June 2, 1815. His parents died when he was young and Kearny was raised by his maternal grandfather, one of the wealthiest residents of New York City. Kearny wanted to pursue a military career, but his grandfather insisted that he study law at Columbia College (since 1896, Columbia University), where he earned a degree in 1833. His grandfather died three years later, and Kearny then inherited a fortune of more than $1 million.

In 1837, Kearny secured a commission as a second lieutenant in the U.S. Army and was assigned to the 1st Dragoons in the West, commanded by his uncle, Colonel Stephen W. Kearny. Two years later the army sent him to study at the French Cavalry School at Saumur. Kearny then participated in several cavalry actions with the Chasseurs d'Afrique in Algeria, where he became known as "Kearny le Magnifique."

Returning to the United States in 1840, Kearny prepared a cavalry manual based on his experiences. The death of his father gave him a second fortune. Kearny then served successively as aide-de-camp to Major Generals Alexander Macomb and Winfield Scott. Disappointed with the lack of military action, Kearny resigned his commission in 1846.

Kearny returned to the army a month later for the Mexican-American War (1846–1848), commanding a volunteer cavalry company that he raised and equipped at his own expense. Captain Kearny accompanied Scott on his Mexico City Campaign. Leading a charge at the Battle of Churubusco in 1847, he was severely wounded in the left arm, which had to be amputated. He soon returned to duty and was recognized as the first American soldier to enter Mexico City. Kearny was brevetted to major for his action at Churubusco and continued on active duty until 1851, when the frustrations of the peacetime military led him again to resign his commission.

Kearny then traveled extensively, spending much of his time in France. He took advantage of the war between France and Piedmont-Sardinia Austria to join the French cavalry and saw combat at the Battle of Solferino (June 24, 1859), where he led a charge against the center of the Austrian line. For this action he was awarded the Legion of Honor.

The approach of the Civil War prompted Kearny to return to the United States in late April 1861. Despite his combat record, Kearny found it difficult to secure a military command. Even a command in the New York Volunteers fell through, in part because of his physical disability but also because of his divorce from his wife and stories of his unconventional relationship with Agnes Maxwell, with whom he had lived for some years before he was able to secure a divorce and marry her in 1858. In late 1861, Kearny finally obtained command of a brigade of New Jersey volunteers as a brigadier general.

Kearny trained his unit well and then led it in minor actions in northern Virginia in early 1862. In late April 1862, during the Peninsula Campaign, Kearny received command of the 3rd Division of III Corps in the Army of the Potomac. At the Battle of Williamsburg (May 5, 1862) and during the subsequent Battle of Seven Pines (May 31–June 1, 1862), Kearny emerged as an aggressive commander who led his troops from the front. He also became a vocal critic of the cautious strategy of army commander Major General George B. McClellan. Following the Battle of Malvern Hill (July 1, 1862), Kearny urged McClellan in vain to take the offensive. Kearny is also credited with designing the first insignia patches for the army, used by his division. This device was later copied throughout the army.

In August 1862, Kearny's division joined the newly formed Army of Virginia south of Washington, commanded by Major General John Pope. Kearny fought valiantly in the Union defeat of the Second Battle of Bull Run (August 28–30, 1862). With his division serving as a rear guard for the retreating Union forces in the Battle of Chantilly on September 1, 1862, Kearny rode into a Confederate unit. Ignoring calls to surrender, he was shot dead.

NEIL M. HEYMAN AND SPENCER C. TUCKER

See also

Churubusco, Battle of; Kearny, Stephen Watts; Mexico City Campaign; Scott, Winfield.

References

Clary, David A. *Eagles and Empire: The United States, Mexico, and the Struggle for a Continent*. New York: Bantam Books, 2009.

Werstein, Irving. *Kearny the Magnificent: The Story of General Philip Kearny, 1815–1862*. New York: John Day, 1962.

Kearny, Stephen Watts
Birth Date: August 30, 1794
Death Date: October 31, 1848

Career U.S. Army officer and commander of the Army of the West during the Mexican-American War, the culmination of a 36-year military career. Stephen Watts Kearny was born on August 30, 1794, in Newark, New Jersey, 1 of 15 children. His father was a prosperous merchant, but much of his wealth was confiscated as a result of his Loyalist sympathies during the American Revolutionary War. Kearny attended school in Newark and was admitted to Columbia College in 1811.

The coming of the War of 1812 cut Kearny's college career short, as he joined the army in March 1812. He demonstrated great bravery in the Battle of Queenston Heights on October 13, 1812, and, although captured, was later released in a prisoner exchange with the British. Beginning in 1819, Kearny served almost exclusively on the western frontier and rose rapidly in rank. In 1820 Kearny made an exploratory march through the upper Midwest, during which he kept a detailed diary. He achieved literary fame posthumously when the diary was published in book form 88 years later.

During the late 1820s and early 1830s, Kearny was responsible for establishing numerous forts throughout the west, including Fort Des Moines and what would later be called Fort Kearny in present-day Nebraska. In 1825, he led an expedition to the edge of Yellowstone, and three years later he assumed command of Fort Crawford in present-day Wisconsin. In 1829, he was promoted to major and in 1833 he was made lieutenant colonel. Then, in 1836 he was transferred to Fort Leavenworth, Kansas, and promoted to colonel.

At the beginning of the Mexican-American War, Kearny received command of the so-called Army of the West. In June 1846,

he led a force of 1,660 men from Fort Leavenworth, with the goal of assisting in the conquest of California. On the march down the Santa Fe Trail, Kearny received word of his promotion to brigadier general. Kearny's force took Santa Fe, New Mexico, virtually unopposed, on August 18, 1846. President James K. Polk then ordered him to proceed on to California to augment U.S. forces there.

Leaving part of his force to garrison New Mexico and sending Alexander Doniphan's 1st Missouri Mounted Rifles down the Rio Grande toward Chihuahua, Kearny set out on September 25 with some 300 men of his regiment, the 1st U.S. Dragoons. On October 6, Kearny encountered Lieutenant Christopher "Kit" Carson, who informed Kearny, incorrectly, that California had already been secured for the United States. As a result of this misinformation, Kearny sent two-thirds of his men back to Santa Fe and continued on with only 121 men.

Shortly after his arrival in California, on December 6, 1846, Kearny attacked a force of Californios (Spanish-speaking inhabitants of California) commanded by Don Andres Pico northeast of San Diego, but in the ensuing Battle of San Pascual the Californios inflicted heavy losses on Kearny's force. Kearny himself was badly wounded in the fighting, suffering two lance wounds.

His escape route blocked, Kearny fortified Mule Hill and dispatched Carson and Edward Beale to San Diego for assistance. A relief column of sailors and marines was quickly dispatched by

U.S. Army colonel (later brigadier general) Stephen Watts Kearny commanded the Army of the West during the Mexican-American War. Kearny played an important role in the U.S. victory in and acquisition of California and served for a time as military governor of the newly acquired territory. (Library of Congress)

Commodore Robert F. Stockton, and Kearny and his men continued to San Diego. There he joined forces with Stockton's new Pacific Squadron, and the united command proceeded on to Los Angeles, winning two victories on the way, the Battle of San Gabriel on January 8 and the Battle of La Mesa on January 9. On January 13, 1847, the Mexican governor surrendered California.

The question of who was in charge of California immediately arose: Kearny or Lieutenant Colonel John C. Frémont of the U.S. Mounted Rifles, who had accepted the surrender and who claimed that Stockton had made him California's military governor. Kearny, however, who outranked Frémont, sent word to Washington, D.C., about the impasse. President Polk backed Kearny, and Frémont was subsequently tried and convicted of insubordination. Kearny served as military governor for three months before turning over authority to Colonel Richard Barnes Mason.

In 1847, Kearny became civil governor of Veracruz, Mexico, and, for a time, governor of Mexico City. In September 1848, Kearny received a brevet to major general. While in Veracruz, however, he caught a fever—most likely malaria—and, after returning to Saint Louis, died there on October 31, 1848.

CRAIG CHOISSER

See also

California; California Theater of War, Overview; Californios; Carson, Christopher Houston "Kit"; Frémont, John Charles; La Mesa, Battle of; Mason, Richard Barnes; New Mexico; Pico, Andrés; San Gabriel River, Battle of; San Pascual, Battle of; Santa Fe; Stockton, Robert Field; Veracruz.

References

Clarke, Dwight D. *Stephen Watts Kearny: Soldier of the West.* Norman: University of Oklahoma Press, 1961.

Von Sachsen Altenberg, Hans, and Laura Gabiger. *Winning the West: Stephen Watts Kearny's Letter Book, 1846–1847.* Boonville, MO: Pekitanoui, 1998.

Kendall, George Wilkins
Birth Date: August 22, 1809
Death Date: October 21, 1867

Writer, journalist, and soldier. Born on August 22, 1809, at Mont Vernon near Amherst, New Hampshire, George Wilkins Kendall is often held to be the first U.S. war correspondent because of his firsthand accounts of military activities during the war with Mexico, which he published in 1851. He learned printing as a youth and then practiced this profession first in Washington and then in New York, where he worked for Horace Greeley. Kendall then worked a year in Mobile, Alabama, for the *Alabama Register* and moved to New Orleans.

In 1837 Kendall helped establish the *Picayune,* the first inexpensive daily newspaper in New Orleans. The paper, which proved successful in large part because of Kendall's humorous articles, also became a strong voice for Texas annexation.

In the spring of 1841 Kendall joined the Santa Fe Expedition, an ill-fated attempt ordered by Republic of Texas president Mirabeau B. Lamar to establish jurisdiction over the busy trading region surrounding Santa Fe, New Mexico. The 320 men who began the trek on June 19, 1841, fought several engagements with the Mexican army, and Kendall, among others, was taken prisoner and marched to Mexico City. The *Picayune* published many of his letters during his imprisonment. Released in May 1842, Kendall returned to New Orleans, and in 1844 he published *Narrative of the Texan Santa Fe Expedition,* which sold an astounding 40,000 copies in its first few years in print.

Long a proponent of war with Mexico to secure land cessions for the United States, with the beginning of the Mexican-American War in 1846, Kendall volunteered for Captain Ben McCulloch's company of Rangers that became Company A of Colonel John C. Hays's 1st Texas Mounted Rifles, which was attached to Major General Zachary Taylor's forces on the Rio Grande. During his military service, Kendall documented the Rangers' activities, including the Battle of Monterrey. After Hays's regiment disbanded, Kendall embedded himself with Major General Winfield Scott's army, taking part in the landing at Veracruz, Mexico. For a brief time, he also served as an aide to Major General William J. Worth.

In the 1850s, Kendall devoted himself to raising sheep in the Texas Hill Country, ultimately possessing a herd of some 5,000 animals. He is considered the father of the state's sheep industry. Kendall died in Boerne, Texas, on October 21, 1867.

ASHLEY R. ARMES

See also

Lamar, Mirabeau Buonaparte; McCulloch, Ben; Monterrey, Battle of; Scott, Winfield; Taylor, Zachary; Texas Rangers; Veracruz, Landing at and Siege of; War Correspondents; Worth, William Jenkins.

References

Copeland, Fayette. *Kendall of the* Picayune. Norman: University of Oklahoma Press, 1943.

Cutrer, Thomas W. *Ben McCulloch and the Frontier Military Tradition.* Chapel Hill: University of North Carolina Press, 1993.

Kendall, George Wilkins. *Dispatches from the Mexican War.* Edited and with an introduction by Lawrence Delbert Cress. Norman: University of Oklahoma Press, 1999.

Kinney, Henry Lawrence
Birth Date: June 3, 1814
Death Date: March 3, 1862

Texas rancher, politician, land speculator, and one of the founders of Corpus Christi, Texas. Henry Lawrence Kinney was born on June 3, 1814, near Shesequin, Pennsylvania. In 1835 he moved to Indiantown, Illinois, where he began speculating in land with his brother. Driven to the brink of bankruptcy by a sharp economic downturn in 1837–1838, Kinney and his brother fled their creditors in Illinois.

Henry Lawrence Kinney was a prominent rancher and resident of the Corpus Christi area in Texas. He greatly profited from the Mexican-American War selling beef and other supplies to the U.S. Army. (Library of Congress)

Kinney went to Texas and settled near modern-day Brownsville and mysteriously began referring to himself as "colonel," a rank he claims to have earned during the Second Seminole War. There is no evidence to suggest, however, that he had ever served in that conflict or held any position in the U.S. military.

By 1841, Kinney had entered a business partnership with William B. Aubrey and moved to the area that is now Corpus Christi, Texas, a city he helped found. There he engaged in ranching and a lucrative trade with Mexicans at Matamoros. At the time, the area that became Corpus Christi was known as Kinney's Ranch. Kinney engaged in certain business practices that raised the ire of other local businessmen. They included illegal trade with Mexico and buying out other ranchers and traders at prices lower than the market would bear.

Kinney had to contend with sporadic Comanche raids, which finally compelled him to maintain a 40-man security force to patrol his holdings. When a rival rancher, Philip Dimmitt, and several others were taken captive by Mexican bandits and taken to Mexico, Kinney was accused of having collaborated with the Mexicans and was charged with treason. He was later exonerated but nevertheless remained a thorn in the side of his fellow traders and ranchers.

Kinney entered Texas politics in 1845 when he was elected to the Texas senate. He was also a delegate to the Texas Convention of 1845, which prepared the way for Texas annexation and statehood. That summer Brigadier General Zachary Taylor's Army of Occupation encamped in the area around Kinney's Ranch. At first uncomfortable with the idea of having 4,000 largely idle men invade his ranch, Kinney soon found himself engaged in an extremely lucrative trade with Taylor's army, which he later embraced with open arms.

In 1846, Major General James Pinckney Henderson appointed Kinney as a staff member, which allowed him to travel with the army. He served as Henderson's quartermaster, procuring foodstuffs, beef cattle, mules, wagons, and other supplies, using his extensive contacts among Mexican and Texan traders. Kinney had no trouble securing the needs of the army and no doubt profited handsomely in the process. In 1847 he worked directly for Major General Winfield Scott, securing beef contracts in Veracruz. Kinney even procured horses, cattle, and mules from General Antonio López de Santa Anna's own procurement agent, although their delivery was impeded by guerrilla operations.

When the war ended in 1848, Kinney returned to his Corpus Christi empire, significantly more prosperous than when he had left. He was soon engaged in trade with numerous nations in South and Central America, and he founded a freight-hauling company that moved goods from Corpus Christi into the interior of Texas using prairie schooners. He served in the Texas state legislature for several terms, purchased large tracts of land, and attempted to settle immigrants on them. Kinney may have overextended himself, however, and by the mid-1850s the businesses began to lose money. In 1854, he tried to establish an American colony in Nicaragua, contracting to buy 30 million acres of land along the Mosquito Coast. He had lined up a number of New York financiers, who agreed to bankroll the venture, but the U.S. government opposed the scheme, and when his primary financial backer pulled out, the plan fell apart.

The failure of the Nicaragua venture caused Kinney much financial and emotional turmoil, but he nevertheless served again in the Texas legislature. Kinney did not support the southern secession movement in the years leading up to the Civil War. In 1861, when Texas seceded from the Union, he moved to Matamoros, Mexico. Kinney was killed when he was caught in a gunfight in Matamoros on March 3, 1862.

PAUL G. PIERPAOLI JR.

See also

Corpus Christi; Henderson, James Pinckney; Scott, Winfield; Taylor, Zachary; Texas.

References

Caruso, A. Brooke. *The Mexican Spy Company: United States Covert Operations in Mexico, 1845–1848.* Jefferson, NC: McFarland, 1991.
Lea, Tom. *The King Ranch.* New York: Little, Brown, 1957.
McCampbell, Coleman. *Saga of a Frontier Seaport.* Dallas, TX: South-West, 1934.

Kinney's Ranch

See Corpus Christi

Kirker, James Santiago

Birth Date: December 2, 1793
Death Date: 1853

Bounty hunter, Indian fighter, and frontiersman. James Santiago Kirker was born in the small village of Kilcross, near Belfast, Ireland, on December 2, 1793. To escape having to serve in the British army, Kirker immigrated to New York City in 1810, arriving on June 10. He served during the War of 1812 on the privateer *Black Joke* and was captured but later exchanged for British captives.

Returning to New York City, Kirker married and became a major in the U.S. Army. In 1817, he left his family to travel west. That December, he worked for the leading mercantile business in Saint Louis, McKnight and Brady, and later opened his own mercantile business.

By 1822 Kirker was in the West, where he traveled up the Missouri River as a member of the Rocky Mountain Fur Company trapping expedition. In 1824, he began trading in Santa Fe, New Mexico, and for the next 10 years he was a trapper in the southern Rockies and along the Gila River. In 1826, disappointed with trapping, he began working for the Santa Rita Copper Mine, escorting copper trains through Apache territory to the mint in Chihuahua City. Kirker and his guards fought off numerous Apache attacks. His reputation as an Indian fighter allowed him to establish his own escort and security service.

In 1833, without divorcing his first wife, Kirker married Rita Garcia; the couple had three children. That same year, he became a Mexican citizen. In 1835, he received a license to trade with the Apaches, which caused him to be charged with dealing in contraband and declared an outlaw. He fled to Colorado. Two years later he hunted Apaches, Comanches, and Navajos under contract with the governor of Chihuahua. Kirker's men were offered $40 for every male scalp and $20 for the scalps of women and children. When the Chihuahuan government could no longer pay for the scalps, it offered Kirker the rank of colonel in the Mexican army. He refused and, with a price on his own head as an enemy of the state, fled Chihuahua.

In December 1846, Kirker joined Colonel Alexander Doniphan's 1st Regiment of Missouri Mounted Volunteers in the occupation of El Paso, Texas. Doniphan hired him as a guide, scout, and interpreter during his campaign in northern Mexico. At Doniphan's direct request, Kirker scouted the Mexican position at Río Sacramento and later participated in the battle there on February 28, 1847. His intimate knowledge of the Mexican countryside and Mexicans proved invaluable.

In 1848, following the war, Kirker served with Major William W. Reynolds as a spy, guide, and interpreter against the Apaches and Utes. The next year, he guided a wagon train across the plains to New Mexico, and in 1850 he reached California and settled in Contra Costa County. Although known for his fearlessness, enterprise, and vision, by this time his reputation was tarnished. He was portrayed as a villain in Thomas Mayne Reid's *The Scalp Hunters* (1851), a popular novel. Kirker died at Oak Springs, California, in 1853.

GARY KERLEY

See also

Apaches; Chihuahua, State of; Comanches; Doniphan, Alexander William; Navajos; Río Sacramento, Battle of; Santa Fe.

References

McGaw, William Cochran. *Savage Scene: The Life and Times of James Kirker, Frontier King.* New York: Hastings House, 1972.

Smith, Ralph Adam. *Borderlander: The Life of James Kirker, 1793–1852.* Norman: University of Oklahoma Press, 1999.

Klamaths

Native American tribe that was culturally similar to the Modocs and to other Northern California Indian peoples. By the early 19th century, the Klamath people lived on some 20 million acres in south central Oregon and northeastern California. Traditionally, the Klamaths were organized into four to seven autonomous subdivisions or tribelets. Tribelets may have consisted of about 10 winter hamlets. Each had a chief, but shamans probably wielded more authority. The Klamaths were probably spared direct contact with non-natives until the arrival in 1829 of Peter Skene Ogden.

Just prior to the beginning of the Mexican-American War, when Lieutenant Colonel John C. Frémont's expedition entered southern Oregon, Frémont and 12 men, including Christopher "Kit" Carson, set up camp on the shore of Klamath Lake, deep in Klamath territory on May 9, 1846. Frémont neglected to post sentries for the night, however, and his party came under attack by a band of 15 to 20 Klamath warriors, who stole into camp under cover of darkness and killed two men. Carson, who was acting as a civilian guide and hunter, alerted the other men, but not before a third man, one of Frémont's Delaware scouts, was also killed. A fourth man was wounded.

The following morning, Frémont's small force left its temporary campsite, but his surviving Delaware scouts sought revenge against the Klamaths, and so they returned to the camp and waited for the Klamaths to approach. Within a few hours, several Klamath warriors entered the campsite, where the scouts ambushed and killed them. Later, when Frémont reached a Klamath village, he ordered his men to attack. In that melee, 14 Klamaths died; Frémont's force suffered no losses. Before leaving, Frémont ordered all of the Klamaths' housing torched and their food supplies destroyed.

The large influx of white Americans in the 1850s brought disease and scattered the game, destroying traditional Klamath subsistence patterns. In an 1864 treaty, the Klamath and Modoc people ceded more than 13 million acres of land for a 1.1-million-acre reservation on former Klamath lands in southern Oregon.

Some Modocs left the reservation in 1870 because of friction between themselves and the Klamaths. The latter did not directly participate in the 1872–1873 Modoc War. By the end of the 19th century, all Indians on the Klamath Reservation were known as the Klamath tribe. In 1901, the government agreed to pay the tribe $537,000 for misappropriated lands. Other land claims settlements, for millions of dollars, followed during the course of the century.

In 1958 the U.S. government terminated the Klamath Reservation. The government had long coveted the timber-rich reservation, but many Klamaths opposed termination. In 1958, however, 77 percent of the tribe voted to withdraw from the collective entity and take individual shares of the land proceeds. In 1974, the remaining 23 percent agreed to sell the rest of the reservation for per capita shares. Termination has had a profoundly negative effect on members of the tribe.

BARRY M. PRITZKER AND PAUL G. PIERPAOLI JR.

See also

Carson, Christopher Houston "Kit"; Delawares (Lenni Lenapes); Frémont, John Charles; Oregon.

References

Fixico, Donald Lee. *The Invasion of Indian Country in the Twentieth Century*. Niwot: University Press of Colorado, 1998.
Sturtevant, William C., ed. *Handbook of North American Indians*. Vol. 12, *Plateau*. Washington, DC: Smithsonian Institution, 1998.

Knight, Sarah

See Borginnis, Sarah

Knights of the Golden Circle

A secret antebellum organization founded in 1854 in Cincinnati, Ohio, by Virginia-born physician and editor George W. L. Bickley, which attempted to create a slaveholding empire in the southern United States, Mexico, and the Caribbean. Bickley's main objective, however, was to annex Mexico. The acquisition of new territories following the conclusion of the Mexican-American War prompted a number of proslavery expansionists to seek additional territories. The objective of the secret organization was to expand the slaveholding society of the American South to encompass an area that approximated a "Golden Circle" of some 2,400 miles, to include the West Indies, Mexico, and part of Central America, in order to control its commerce and secure a complete monopoly of the world's supply of tobacco. The organization hoped thereby to restore the balance of power between the industrial North and slaveholding South by establishing a ring of colonies that would eventually evolve into new slave states.

The organization grew slowly, at least until 1859, and eventually reached its zenith about 1860. The membership was widely scattered from New York to the West Coast but was never very large. It was also poorly financed and lacked effective leadership.

During the turbulent late 1850s, American adventurers referred to as filibusters were involved in numerous illegal military expeditions aimed at liberating Cuba or acquiring land in Mexico or Central America. Bickley left Cincinnati and moved about throughout the East and South, promoting one such campaign to seize Mexico. He found the greatest support in Texas, where he organized 32 chapters in various cities, including Houston, Austin, and San Antonio. In the spring of 1860 the Knights attempted to invade Mexico from Texas. A small band reached the Rio Grande, but Bickley was unable to gather the large force he claimed he was assembling in New Orleans, and the campaign quickly ended. Later that year he attempted to mount a second expedition to Mexico, but Abraham Lincoln's election forced him and his followers to turn their attention to the secessionist movement. Bickley, then living in Tennessee, devoted his efforts to secessionism and transformed his Knights into a secret society dedicated to establishing Confederate rule in Kentucky.

During the Civil War the organization was renamed the Order of the American Knights, and in 1864 it became the Sons of Liberty. Total membership of the order was between 250,000 and 300,000 people, principally in Ohio, Indiana, Illinois, Iowa, Wisconsin, Kentucky, and southwestern Pennsylvania. Among its leaders were Fernando Wood and Clement L. Vallandigham. Its primary objective now was to oust the Lincoln government in the elections of 1864 and give Democrats control of the state and federal governments to make peace and invite the southern states back into the Union on antebellum footing. Their efforts were foiled, however, with the arrests of various leaders and numerous confiscations of arms by U.S. authorities.

The Knights essentially dissolved because of the arrests of some of its members and the seizure of weapons. Its original founder, Bickley, who had served for a time as a Confederate surgeon, was arrested for spying in Indiana in July 1863. Although never tried, he remained under arrest until October 1865 and reportedly died, disillusioned and dispirited, in Baltimore on August 3, 1867.

CHARLES F. HOWLETT

See also

Expansionism and Imperialism; Slavery; Texas.

References

Crenshaw, Ollinger. "The Knights of the Golden Circle: The Career of George Bickley." *American Historical Review* 47, no. 1 (October 1941): 23–50.
Curry, Richard O. *A House Divided*. Pittsburgh: University of Pittsburgh Press, 1964.

Frazier, Donald S., and Shaw Frazier. *Blood and Treasure: Confederate Empire in the Southwest.* College Station: Texas A&M University Press, 1995.

Getler, Warren. *Shadow of the Sentinel: One Man's Quest to Find the Hidden Treasure of the Confederacy.* New York: Simon & Schuster, 2003.

Klement, Frank L. *Dark Lanterns: Secret Political Societies, Conspiracies, and Treason Trials in the Civil War.* Baton Rouge: Louisiana State University Press, 1984.

May, Robert E. *The Southern Dream of a Caribbean Empire, 1854–1861.* Baton Rouge: Louisiana State University Press, 1973.

Campaign banner of the Know-Nothing Party for the election of 1856. The Know-Nothings were anti-Catholic and anti-immigrant. Millard Fillmore was the party nominee in 1856, but lost to Democrat James Buchanan. (Library of Congress)

Know-Nothing Party

More a political movement than a traditional political party, the Know-Nothing Party was also known as the American Republican Party and the American Party. It was a political force from the mid-1840s until about 1860 and was composed chiefly of native-born working-class and middle-class whites. The party was most prominent in the urban centers of the Northeast and Midwest, and was rather one-dimensional in its focus. The Know-Nothing Party was chiefly anti-immigrant and anti-Catholic. It arose in response to the large influx of Irish and German Catholic immigrants who had begun to arrive in the United States during the early 1840s.

Adherents of the Know-Nothing Party feared that the largely Anglo-Saxon, Protestant United States would soon be overrun by Catholics. Many feared that these immigrants would not be loyal U.S. citizens, instead giving their allegiance to the Pope in Rome. Some even believed that Catholics intended to take over the United States, hoping to place it under the auspices of the church itself. This nativism was soon transformed into a more concrete political platform that sought to limit or forbid further immigration among Catholics, to prevent Catholics from being elected to public office, and to preclude Catholics from being hired in the private sector. This platform was part of a larger trend of nativist sentiment in the United States that resulted in much discrimination against foreigners and Catholics, especially Irish Catholics, who came predominantly from poor and lower-class backgrounds. Many of the newer immigrants were settling in the cities of the Northeast and Midwest, which explains why the movement was strongest there. Many Americans who subscribed to the Know-Nothing platform feared that continued large influxes of poor immigrants would result in the loss of jobs for native-born Americans, as immigrants were able and willing to work for far less than their native-born compatriots.

Because the Know-Nothing Party was highly decentralized, and its workings were largely kept hidden from the public eye, it was dubbed the "Know-Nothing" Party because its adherents often refused to answer questions about their political philosophy, simply responding, "I know nothing." The party became so popular in Massachusetts that its members briefly controlled that state's legislature in 1854. The following year, the city of Chicago elected a Know-Nothing mayor, who promptly barred all immigrants from holding jobs with the city government. Also in 1855, the party gained momentum in Ohio, successfully running candidates in several municipal and statewide elections.

In 1856, the Know-Nothing Party, then running under the banner of the American Party, nominated Millard Fillmore as its presidential candidate. Fillmore, a former Whig who had served as president from 1850 to 1853, did not come close to winning the 1856 contest, but he captured nearly 900,000 votes, or nearly 25 percent of the ballots cast. Because the Know-Nothing Party never addressed the issue of slavery, which by the late 1850s had become the most important political and social issue of the era, it quickly lost ground to the emergent Republican Party. The American Party declined to nominate a candidate for the 1860 presidential election, which spelled the practical end of the movement. Many former adherents of the Know-Nothing platform in fact had joined ranks with the Republicans. The movement was simply unable to transcend local or regional politics in a coherent manner because of the clandestine nature of its organization and the fact that adherents to its philosophy differed considerably. For example, southerners tended to be more concerned with unionism than true nativism.

Regardless of its long-term political efficacy, the Know-Nothing Party clearly reflected the prejudices of the era. Thus, it helps explain why a southern, proslavery politician like John C. Calhoun refused to support the Mexican-American War and the annexation of vast new territory where slavery might theoretically thrive. Indeed, he believed that Mexicans, who were Catholics and non-Anglos, would prove to be unsuitable American citizens. In his mind, the absorption of millions of nonwhite, Catholic citizens would prove to be the undoing of the American polity. The Know-Nothing movement also explains why some immigrants, pressed into U.S. military service and who there faced overwhelming discrimination and ill treatment, deserted and joined ranks with the Mexicans. The primary example of this, of course, was the San Patricio Battalion.

PAUL G. PIERPAOLI JR.

See also

Calhoun, John Caldwell; Democratic Party; Fillmore, Millard; Free Soil Party; Politics, U.S.; Republican Party; San Patricio Battalion; Slavery; United States, 1821–1854.

References

Anbinder, Tyler Gregory. *Nativism and Slavery: The Northern Know Nothings and the Politics of the 1850s.* New York: Oxford University Press, 1992.

Voss-Hubbard, Mark. *Beyond Party: Cultures of Antipartisanship in Northern Politics Before the Civil War.* Baltimore, MD: Johns Hopkins University Press, 2002.

L

La Cañada, Battle of
Event Date: January 24, 1847

First battle of the Taos Revolt, pitting New Mexican forces against a U.S. Army force under the command of Colonel Sterling Price. The engagement took place on January 24, 1847, at Santa Cruz de la Cañada, some 20 miles north of Santa Fe.

Learning of the murder of Charles Bent, U.S. military governor of New Mexico, along with other Americans, Price assembled a force of more than 280 soldiers, some 65 militiamen, and 4 howitzers to pursue and defeat the Native Americans and New Mexicans responsible for the violence. He departed Santa Fe for Taos on January 23, 1847. Among the militiamen were a few New Mexican volunteers, organized by Ceran St. Vrain, one of Bent's business partners.

On January 24, Price encountered nearly 4,000 New Mexican rebels, including Mexicans and Native Americans, near the presidio town of Santa Cruz de la Cañada. This force was commanded by Jesús Tafoya, Pablo Chavez, and Pablo Montoya (one of the leaders of the men responsible for the death of Governor Bent). Upon the army's arrival, the rebels withdrew into adobe houses and to positions in the hills surrounding the town. Price then launched an attack while the insurgents attempted a flanking attack of their own. The Americans successfully drove back the insurrectionists while scattering the opposing forces entrenched in the hills. Rebel losses were some 36 killed, among them Jesús Tafoya, and 45 captured. American casualties were 2 killed and 7 wounded.

Price remained at La Cañada for two days, reinforced by a second company of the 2nd Missouri Mounted Rifles. With a force now numbering approximately 480 men, he marched for Taos on February 2, 1847, again defeating the insurgents in a skirmish at Embudo Pass, the strategic location to which they had fallen back following their defeat at La Cañada. This drove the rebels back into the fortified adobe church at Pueblo de Taos. During an engagement there, on February 4, more than 150 rebels were killed and 400 others were captured.

Convening courts-martial to try the insurgents following the capture of Taos, Price had to select judges and jury members from among a much-reduced Anglo-American community. Among those chosen as judges were Joab Houghton, a close friend and business associate of Charles Bent, and Charles Beaubien, the father of one of those slain on January 19 in Taos. The jury foreman was Governor Bent's brother, George, and jury members included the brother-in-law of one of those slain in Taos, as well as several of Governor Bent's friends. Ceran St. Vrain served as court interpreter.

The jury met for 15 days and returned a guilty verdict of treason and murder against 15 men and sentenced them to death. On April 9, 1847, the sentence was carried out against 6 of the condemned men; another 5 followed them in two weeks. In all, 28 individuals were executed for their role in the Taos Revolt.

JEFFREY D. PEPPERS

See also

Beaubien, Carlos (Charles); Bent, Charles; El Embudo Pass, Skirmish at; Mora, Skirmish at; New Mexico; Price, Sterling; Pueblo de Taos, Skirmish at; Taos Revolt.

References

Bauer, K. Jack. *The Mexican War, 1846–1848.* New York: Macmillan, 1974.

Crutchfield, James Andrew. *The Revolt of 1847.* Plano: Republic of Texas Press, 1995.

Durand, John. *The Taos Massacres.* Elkhorn, WI: Puzzlebox Press, 2004.

McNierney, Michael, ed. *Taos 1847: The Revolt in Contemporary Accounts.* Boulder, CO: Johnson, 1980.

Lafragua, José María
Birth Date: April 2, 1813
Death Date: November 15, 1875

Mexican journalist, writer, and *moderado* liberal politician. José María Lafragua was born in the city of Puebla on April 2, 1813, and studied law at the local university, graduating in 1835. He then opened a legal practice in that city and became involved in politics as secretary of the local branch of a York lodge Masonic society known as the Anfictiones. Lafragua opted not to support *puro* leader Valentín Gómez Farías's July 15, 1840, coup to overthrow then president Anastasio Bustamante. The next year he became a contributor to *El siglo XIX*, and in 1842 he served as a deputy in the Constituent Congress. Lafragua also played a key role in bringing the presidency of General Antonio López de Santa Anna to an end late in 1844.

Early in 1845 Lafragua joined the *puros* in calling for the convocation of a special Congress to reform the 1824 Constitution, for the re-creation of the National Guard, and for the inauguration of a military campaign to recover Texas. The following year he assisted the *puros* in their efforts to depose General Mariano Paredes y Arrillaga. He then served as minister of foreign relations from October 21 until December 23, 1846.

On the heels of the January 11, 1847, decree that authorized the government, then led by acting president Gómez Farías, to finance the war by mortgaging or selling church property, Lafragua joined other *moderados* in planning the February 1847 "rebellion of the *polkos*" and then spearheaded the movement to oust Gómez Farías by endorsing Santa Anna's return to power.

After the Mexican-American War Lafragua held a number of key government positions. He served as a senator until 1853, when Santa Anna dissolved Congress, and then had to go into exile. Lafragua had returned to Mexico by 1855, and he served as minister of the interior under President Ignacio Comonfort (December 13, 1855–January 31, 1857). Lafragua also served on the constitutional congress that gave Mexico its 1857 Constitution. Lafragua also served as Mexico's diplomatic representative to Spain (1857–1860), and in the late 1860s he was both magistrate to the Supreme Court and director of the National Library. Lafragua died on November 15, 1875, in Mexico City.

FABIOLA GARCÍA RUBIO AND PEDRO SANTONI

See also

Moderados; Politics, Mexican; Salas, José Mariano; Santa Anna, Antonio López de.

References

Costeloe, Michael P. *The Central Republic in Mexico, 1835–1846: Hombres de Bien in the Age of Santa Anna*. New York: Cambridge University Press, 1993.

García García, Raymundo. *José María Lafragua: Político poblano*. Puebla: Gobierno del Estado de Puebla, Benemérita Universidad Autónoma de Puebla, 2002.

Sánchez Flores, Ramón. *José María Lafragua: Vida y obra*. Puebla: Gobierno del Estado de Puebla, Benemérita Universidad Autónoma de Puebla, 2002.

Santoni, Pedro. *Mexicans at Arms: Puro Federalists and the Politics of War, 1845–1848*. Fort Worth: Texas Christian University Press, 1996.

Sinkin, Richard N. *The Mexican Reform, 1855–1876: A Study in Liberal Nation Building*. Austin: University of Texas Press, 1979.

La Hoya, Skirmish at
Event Date: June 20, 1847

Fight between Mexican guerrillas and elements of Major General Winfield Scott's army in La Hoya Pass, a strong defensive position about 10 miles west of Jalapa on the road from Veracruz to Mexico City. On May 15, 1847, Brigadier General William J. Worth's army of 4,200 men occupied Puebla to the west of La Hoya Pass, and the remainder of Scott's army arrived about a week later. At Puebla, Scott halted his advance toward Mexico City to await the arrival of reinforcements and a cash infusion on its way from Veracruz. On June 16, a five-mile-long column of 1,200 men and wagons carrying $350,000 and army supplies and commanded by Brigadier General George Cadwalader reached Jalapa after being threatened by guerrillas along the way.

A guerrilla leader at Las Vigas, Celestino Domeco de Jarauta, learned of the money being carried by the convoy. Determined to seize it, he ordered his 700 men to prepare an ambush in La Hoya Pass, where Cadwalader's hard-to-defend wagons would be most vulnerable. Colonel Francis M. Wynkoop, commander of the American garrison at Perote not far to the west of La Hoya Pass, learned of Jarauta's plans. He immediately warned Cadwalader of the threat and dispatched Texas Ranger captain Samuel Walker with about 30 mounted men to attack the guerrilla base at Las Vigas.

On June 20, Walker surprised Jarauta's force and destroyed his camp. Later that day, reinforced by Wynkoop with five Pennsylvania volunteer companies from Perote, he continued to harass the Mexicans, who were driven from their ambush sites in La Hoya Pass. Fifty Mexicans were killed or wounded in the fighting, and a number of guerrilla flags were captured; American officers reported no losses. Shortly thereafter, Cadwalader marched his column unhindered through La Hoya Pass. He joined General Scott at Puebla on August 8, 1847.

PAUL DAVID NELSON

See also

Cadwalader, George; Guerrilla Warfare; Jarauta, Celestino Domeco de; Puebla; Scott, Winfield; Walker, Samuel Hamilton; Worth, William Jenkins.

References

Bauer, K. Jack. *The Mexican War, 1846–1848*. New York: Macmillan, 1974.

Jenkins, John S. *History of the War between the United States and Mexico: From the Commencement of Hostilities to the Ratification of the Treaty of Peace.* Auburn, NY: Daerby and Miller, 1851.

Oswandel, J. Jacob. *Notes of the Mexican War, 1846–1848.* Edited by Timothy D. Johnson and Nathaniel Cheairs Hughes Jr. Knoxville: University of Tennessee Press, 2010.

Spurlin, Charles, "Ranger Walker in the Mexican War." *Military History of Texas and the Southwest* 9 (1971): 159–179.

Lamar, Mirabeau Buonaparte
Birth Date: August 16, 1798
Death Date: December 19, 1859

Politician, soldier, and second president of the Republic of Texas (1838–1841). Mirabeau Buonaparte Lamar was born near Louisville, Georgia, on August 16, 1798, and grew up around Milledgeville. He attended local academies, served as a newspaper publisher, was elected state senator in 1829, and ran unsuccessfully for the U.S. Congress in 1832 and again in 1834.

Lamar made his way to Texas in 1835 to conduct studies of the area and to witness the burgeoning independence movement there, but he decided to stay and volunteered to serve with forces fighting for Texas independence. After rendering highly effective service in the Battle of San Jacinto on April 21, 1836, he was commissioned a colonel and then enjoyed a meteoric political rise, including winning election as vice president of the Republic of Texas in 1836 and as the second president of Texas in 1838.

Lamar was a true Texas nationalist, envisioning an empire extending from the Sabine River west to the Pacific Ocean. As such, he vehemently opposed annexation by the United States. This nationalism included pursuing aggressive policies against Texas Indians, as opposed to the more conciliatory policies followed by his predecessor, Sam Houston, with whom he disagreed on most issues. Lamar argued that Texas Cherokees did not have legitimate land titles from Mexico or Texas and had to be eradicated to open their lands to new white settlers.

In due course, on Lamar's orders, the new republic sent military forces against the Cherokees and their Native American allies. On July 15–16, 1839, Texas forces destroyed the Cherokees and their allies in battle in Van Zandt County, Texas. Survivors were forcefully driven out of Texas to Arkansas.

Further campaigns occurred against Comanche forces throughout Texas. During August 1840, Comanche raiders drove all the way to the Gulf port of Linnville, which they looted and burned. Texan forces retaliated and won a victory in the Battle of Plum Creek, near Lockhart, on August 12, 1840. The following year saw Lamar's administration launch an offensive against north Texas Wichita Indians, destroying several Wichita towns on the Trinity River in Tarrant County. Despite these successes, however, peace with the Comanches would be fleeting.

As president, Lamar used the United States and Great Britain in unsuccessful attempts to make peace with Mexico and then leased the Texas navy to Yucatán rebels. His administration also sought to retaliate against Mexico by sending an expedition to Santa Fe, a city claimed by the Texas Republic under the terms of the 1836 Treaty of Velasco. The expedition proved disastrous. Its participants had inaccurate maps, endured intense summer heat with insufficient provisions, and ultimately surrendered to waiting Mexican authorities on October 5, 1841. These Texans were sent on a brutal forced march to Mexico City and then imprisoned in the notorious Perote prison.

Lamar's presidency left Texas virtually bankrupt, and he retired from politics altogether when his term ended in 1841. Lamar did fight in the Mexican-American War (1846–1848), winning a citation for bravery for participation in the Battle of Monterrey (September 20–24, 1846). Promoted to lieutenant colonel, Lamar organized the Laredo Guards, a Texas volunteer outfit that patrolled the border between Texas and Mexico for raiding Comanches.

Following the Mexican-American War, Lamar retired to his plantation at Richmond, Texas. In 1857, President James Buchanan appointed him U.S. minister to Nicaragua and Costa Rica. In that position, Lamar worked to prevent the granting of a contract to the French to build an Isthmian canal. In poor health on his return to Texas in 1859, he died on his plantation at Richmond on December 19, 1859. Lamar is best remembered as a charming but impulsive leader who sought to achieve power for Texas without the requisite resources with which to achieve it. Perhaps Lamar's most enduring legacy was his support of education in Texas; he is known as the "father of Texas education."

BERT CHAPMAN

See also
Cherokees; Comanches; Houston, Samuel; Monterrey, Battle of; San Jacinto, Battle of; Santa Fe; Texas; Texas Revolution; Texas-Comanche Relations.

References
Campbell, Randolph. *Gone to Texas: A History of the Lone Star State.* New York: Oxford University Press, 2003.

Ramsey, Jack C. *Thunder beyond the Brazos: Mirabeau B. Lamar, a Biography.* Austin, TX: Eakin Press, 1984.

La Mesa, Battle of
Event Date: January 9, 1847

Engagement between Californios and U.S. forces on January 9, 1847. The battle took place on the outskirts of Los Angeles, California. This U.S. Army victory secured California territory from Mexican control.

BATTLE OF LA MESA, JANUARY 9, 1847

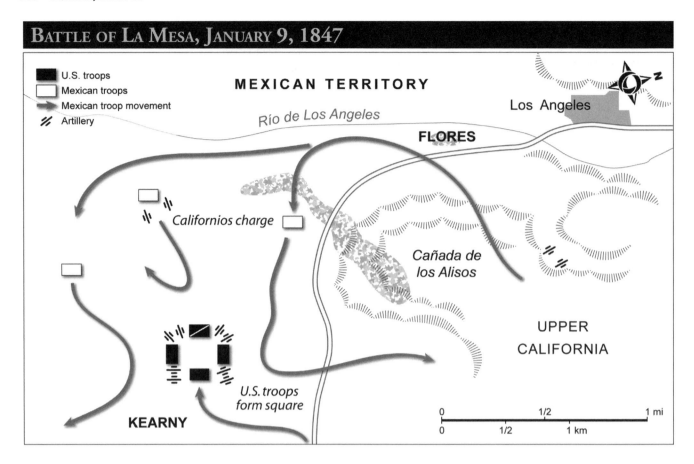

An American force of nearly 600 soldiers, marines, sailors, militia, and dragoons, with six artillery pieces and led by Commodore Robert F. Stockton and Brigadier General Stephen W. Kearny, marched toward Los Angeles on December 29, 1846, to recapture the town from the control of the California militia led by General José Mariá Flores. The two American commanders disputed who should have final authority. Kearny had orders from Washington, but Stockton had the larger number of men and was more familiar with the local terrain. Kearny temporarily conceded command but maintained control over his own 60 dragoons.

The Americans encountered no resistance on their march until they reached the outskirts of Los Angeles, where about 200 of Flores's troops defended the heights above the eastern bank of the San Gabriel River. Stockton's sailors and marines charged the Mexican positions without artillery support, screaming, "New Orleans!" to honor the battle that had taken place that day in 1815. The Americans advanced in a square formation to protect their flanks. The American assault succeeded, and the Californios withdrew from their defensive positions on the river. Both sides sustained about a dozen casualties.

After spending the night on the battlefield, the next morning, January 9, Stockton and Kearny resumed their march toward Los Angeles. Their scouts spotted the Mexicans repositioned six miles down the road along a ravine known as La Mesa. As the Americans came within artillery range, Flores opened an ineffective fire,

hampered by his limited and unreliable ordnance. American guns returned fire and quickly drove the enemy gunners from their positions. In an act of desperation, Flores ordered his cavalry to assault Stockton's left flank, but the charge was haphazard. Armed only with pikes, the Mexican horsemen withered under aimed American rifle fire and withdrew in disorder. The remainder of Flores's troops retreated, leaving the field and the road to Los Angeles open to their adversaries.

The engagement, much like one the previous day at Rio San Gabriel, lasted just over an hour and saw minimal losses on both sides. Each side claimed one killed and about a half dozen wounded.

The Battle of La Mesa signaled the end of armed Californian resistance to the American invasion. The few remaining organized Californian units in the region dispersed after the engagement while their commander General Flores fled to Mexico. Stockton camped three miles outside of Los Angeles the night of the battle and entered the city in triumph the following morning. On January 14, the remaining Mexican resistance met with Lieutenant Colonel John C. Frémont and signed the Treaty of Cahuenga, officially ending the hostilities in California and allowing all those who fought for the Mexicans to return home. Although U.S. forces had officially secured Southern California for the United States, Stockton, Frémont, and Kearny continued to squabble over command and the territorial governorship of California.

BRADFORD A. WINEMAN

Battle of La Mesa, California, by William H. Meyers in 1847. Assuming a hollow square formation, American forces under Brigadier General Stephen W. Kearny were able to repel a mounted Mexican assault on January 9, 1847. (Franklin D. Roosevelt Presidential Library)

See also

Cahuenga, Treaty of; California; Californios; California Theater of War, Overview; Flores, José María; Frémont, John Charles; Kearny, Stephen Watts; Los Angeles; San Gabriel River, Battle of; Stockton, Robert Field.

References

Clarke, Dwight L. *Stephen Watts Kearny: Soldier of the West.* Norman: University of Oklahoma Press, 1961.

Harlow, Neal. *California Conquered: War and Peace on the Pacific, 1846–1850.* Berkeley: University of California Press, 1982.

Moyano Pahissa, Angela. *La resistencia de las Californias a la invasión norteamericana, 1846–1848.* Mexico City: Consejo Nacional para la Cultura y las Artes, 1992.

La Mesilla, Treaty of

See Gadsden Purchase

Lamy, Jean Baptiste

Birth Date: October 11, 1814
Death Date: February 13, 1888

Controversial French-born Roman Catholic clergyman and the first bishop of the Diocese of New Mexico, created after that province's annexation to the United States in 1848. Jean Baptiste Lamy was born on October 11, 1814, in Lempdes, in the Auvergne region of France. After attending a Jesuit seminary in Billom for nine years, he decided at age 18 to become a priest. He studied first in the seminary at Clermont, then at the grand seminary at Mont-Ferrand. In December 1838, he was ordained a priest and was assigned to a parish in Chapdes in the diocese of Clermont.

A year later, Lamy was given permission to become a missionary in America under the tutelage of Bishop Jean Baptiste Purcell of Cincinnati, Ohio. He served eight years in Danville, Ohio, and in 1847 was moved to Covington, Kentucky.

Lamy was surprised when in 1850 he was appointed apostolic vicar of New Mexico. As such, he was charged with reorganizing the Catholic Church there, as U.S. Catholic prelates hoped to bring it in line with U.S. diocesan practices. In June 1851 he reached Santa Fe after an arduous journey from Ohio.

Perceived as despotic and unyielding by his flock and fellow clergymen, Lamy refused to permit pre-1848 Catholic practices to continue in New Mexico. Indeed, he insisted on the orthodox practice of Catholicism and was especially insistent on the need for tithing. Many New Mexico citizens came to resent him for this, and some even argued that his view of Catholicism demonstrated a blatant disregard of freedom of religion. Lamy also alienated many of his own clergy. In 1854 he became the first bishop of the New Mexico Diocese, which covered a huge area in what is now New Mexico, Arizona, and parts of Colorado and

Jean Baptiste Lamy was a controversial Roman Catholic priest and first bishop of the Diocese of New Mexico after that territory became part of the United States. (Hayward Cirker and Blanche Cirker, eds., *Dictionary of American Portraits,* 1967)

Utah. Refusing to bend to the will of others, Lamy simply excommunicated the most obstreperous of his detractors, including priests.

In spite of his unyielding ways, Lamy also accomplished much, including the establishment of Catholic schools and the construction of churches such as St. Francis Cathedral in Santa Fe. When his diocese was elevated to an archdiocese in 1875, Lamy was appointed archbishop. Lamy died of pneumonia on February 13, 1888, at Sante Fe and was buried in St. Francis Cathedral. Willa Cather's 1927 novel, *Death Comes for the Archbishop,* was based on Lamy's experiences in New Mexico.

PAUL DAVID NELSON

See also
Catholic Church, Mexico; New Mexico; Santa Fe.

References

Horgan, Paul. *Lamy of Santa Fe: His Life and Times.* New York: Farrar, Straus and Giroux, 1975.
Lamy, John Baptiste. *Archbishop Lamy: In His Own Words.* Edited by Thomas J. Steele. Albuquerque, NM: LPD Press, 2000.
Warner, Louis H. *Archbishop Lamy: An Epoch Maker.* Santa Fe: Santa Fe New Mexican Publishing, 1936.

Lancers

Lancers were the elite units of the Mexican cavalry. Armed with a lance, a long pole with a sharp tip, these horsemen were trained to impale and/or knock opposing cavalrymen from their horses. This tactic differed markedly from the American emphasis on dragoons (mounted infantry armed with firearms and trained to fight on foot) or light cavalry.

At the Battle of Monterrey, Captain Ben McCulloch's company of Texas mounted rifles met the charge of a regiment of Mexican lancers commanded by Lieutenant Colonel Juan Najera. Although the Rangers broke the lancers' charge with fire from sawed-off shotguns and Colt revolvers, the charge was conducted with what the Clarksville, Texas, *Northern Standard* described as "a fierce desperation almost unparalleled amongst the Mexicans."

In addition to their use by regular cavalry, lances were employed by Mexican irregulars, or "rancheros," especially in California. There many native Californios (those of Mexican/mestizo descent living in Alta California [Upper California]) fought a partisan resistance against American military occupation. While also used with weapons such as lariats and firearms, lances were a crucial cavalry weapon for Californios during the war.

Californio lancers under the governor of Alta California, Andrés Pico, achieved a significant victory at the Battle of San Pascual (December 6–11, 1846), aided by wet weather that had earlier ruined the Americans' gunpowder. One month later, however, at a skirmish at Río San Gabriel (Battle of San Gabriel) on January 8, 1847, Mexican lancers failed to break an American force arrayed in a square defensive formation. Casualties here amounted to about a dozen on each side. The Battle of La Mesa occurred the following day. Here Mexican and American artillery fought a duel that diminished Mexican powder reserves, but a charge by lancers was checked by American gunfire. The fighting at La Mesa resulted in only two combat deaths, but the combat at Río San Gabriel and at La Mesa nevertheless brought Californio resistance and the use of lancers in the west to a virtual close.

The lance was an effective close-combat weapon in the hands of Californio riders, who were experienced in using the tool for cattle ranching. Lancers were, of course, much less effective against determined, concentrated gunfire. Thus, in the later battles waged in Mexico, Mexican lancers were no match for American infantrymen or horsemen who were well armed, especially after U.S. cavalrymen began carrying revolving pistols. Lancers nevertheless remained an elite and integral part of the Mexican army until the end of the 19th century.

NICHOLAS M. SAMBALUK

See also
California; California Theater of War, Overview; Californios; Cavalry and Dragoons; La Mesa, Battle of; Mexico, Army; Pico, Andrés; San Gabriel River, Battle of; San Pascual, Battle of; Weapons, Mexican.

References

Bauer, K. Jack. *The Mexican War, 1846–1848.* New York: Macmillan, 1974.

Smith, George Winston, and Charles Judah. *Chronicles of the Gringos: The U.S. Army in the Mexican War, 1846–1848.* Albuquerque: University of New Mexico Press, 1968.

Landero Bauza, José Juan

Birth Date: 1802
Death Date: 1869

Mexican army officer. José Juan Landero Bauza was born in 1802 in Veracruz, state of Veracruz. As a teenager, he undertook seminary studies in Veracruz before deciding to join the Mexican army, probably in 1822 or 1823. Little is known of Landero Bauza's early career except that he became an important political and military figure in his home state. In 1838, when the French blockaded and then attempted to capture Veracruz because of unpaid French claims against the Mexican government, he mounted a spirited defense. Working closely with General Antonio López de Santa Anna, Landero Bauza helped repel the French in what came to be known as the Pastry War, making him a local hero. In 1843, Santa Anna rewarded Landero Bauza for his loyalty and efficient service by promoting him to general of brigade.

Long an admirer of Santa Anna, Landero Bauza was pleased when the exiled general returned to Mexico in August 1846, following a string of stinging Mexican military defeats at the hands of the Americans in northern Mexico. Early the next year, Santa Anna sent Landero Bauza to Veracruz to defend the strategic port city from an anticipated amphibious assault by U.S. forces under Major General Winfield Scott, instructing him to keep the city out of American hands at any cost. The American landings began on March 9, 1847, and Landero Bauza put up a stout defense, resulting in a monthlong siege of Veracruz that did not end until March 29.

Santa Anna, nevertheless, was dissatisfied with his general's performance and ordered him arrested shortly after the capitulation. Landero Bauza was detained at Perote Castle, Veracruz (long a favored prison for political prisoners and others who had run afoul of the government) until he was released by American troops on April 22, 1847. Landero Bauza agreed not to take up arms again as the primary condition of his release.

After the war, Landero Bauza held numerous army posts, mostly in his home state. He saw action fighting pro-French forces during the French intervention of the 1860s and retired from service in 1867 at the end of the French intervention. Landero Bauza died in 1869 at Veracruz.

PAUL G. PIERPAOLI JR.

See also

Pastry War; Perote Castle; Santa Anna, Antonio López de; Scott, Winfield; Veracruz; Veracruz, Landing at and Siege of.

References

Diccionario Porrúa de historia, biografía, y geografía de México. 6th ed. Mexico City: Editorial Porrúa, 1995.

Eisenhower, John S. D. *So Far from God: The U.S. War with Mexico, 1846–1848.* New York: Random House, 1989.

Smith, George W., and Charles Judah. *Chronicles of the Gringos: The U.S. Army in the Mexican War, 1846–1848.* Albuquerque: University of New Mexico Press, 1968.

Land Grants

Tracts of land issued to *empresarios* or individuals by the governments of Spain, Mexico, and the Republic of Texas. From 1791 to 1819, Spain granted these men between 10 million and 20 million acres of land in Texas; the primary stipulation was that the land be settled and improved. In 1820, with the hope of attracting North Americans, Texas was opened to foreign settlers. Given that land was the only commodity with inherent worth in Texas, land grants were issued to foreigners, chiefly through *empresarios*, although some was distributed directly to individuals.

Texas land grants proved highly desirable among Americans because the land was so inexpensive. Farm and ranch land in Texas during the 1820s and 1830s averaged just $0.02 per acre, while comparable land in the United States sold for an average of $1.26 per acre. Not surprisingly, many Americans engaged in rampant land speculation in Texas, but such activity did little to drive up the cost of land there because acreage was plentiful and the Mexican government (after 1821) and local governments issued land grants for approximately 26.28 million acres.

The Republic of Texas, beginning in the immediate aftermath of the Texas Revolution, also relied on land grants to lure settlers to Texas. Because the republic's government had virtually no money, it also used land grants as a way to reward military service. A provision of the 1836 Texas Constitution stipulated that anyone who had been domiciled in Texas on March 4, 1836, the day Texas declared its independence, automatically received 4,605.4 acres of land (as a head of a household); individuals received one-third as much. Anyone who emigrated to Texas after March 4, 1836, was entitled to 1,280 acres (head of household), or 640 acres (individual). As of October 1, 1837, however, the size of such land grants was sharply diminished to just 640 acres for a head of household or 320 acres for an individual. The Republic of Texas gave away a cumulative total of 36,876,492 acres of land between 1836 and 1845, at which time Texas was annexed by the United States.

The Republic of Texas frequently issued land grants in exchange for military service because it could not afford to pay its soldiers in currency. The state of Texas continued this policy after 1845. For those who saw action at the April 1836 Battle of San Jacinto, the republic automatically offered 640 acres of land; anyone who saw service during any previous battle of the Texas Revolution also received 640 acres of land. The Republic of Texas and, later, the state of Texas issued 3,149,234 acres of land in return for military service; included within that total were land donations to disabled veterans of the Civil War (1861–1865).

In 1844 the Republic of Texas stopped issuing land grants via *empresarios*, as the government was concerned about the excesses of some *empresarios* and hoped to exercise more control over the disposition of land. Nevertheless, previous land grants issued to them caused considerable confusion and conflicting claims to the same land. Further complicating matters was the fact that many settlers had been swindled into buying useless or already-occupied lands in Texas. Despite these problems, however, land grants remained the primary vehicle for the settlement and development of Texas.

PAUL G. PIERPAOLI JR.

See also

Constitution, Texan; *Empresarios*; Land Speculation, Texas; San Jacinto, Battle of; Texas; Texas Revolution.

References

Lack, Paul D. *The Texas Revolutionary Experience: A Political and Social History, 1835–1836.* College Station: Texas A&M University Press, 1999.

Reichstein, Andreas. *Rise of the Lone Star: The Making of Texas.* College Station: Texas A&M University Press, 1989.

Weber, David J. *The Mexican Frontier, 1821–1846: The American Southwest under Mexico.* Albuquerque: University of New Mexico Press, 1982.

Land Speculation, Texas

Land speculation in Texas brought with it potential peril as well as the promise of economic development. Land speculation in Texas, driven largely by Americans, began in earnest in 1820, stimulated in part by ratification of the 1819 Adams-Onís Treaty. The pact held that the U.S. government would honor all existing land claims in lands previously held by Spain, and many Americans believed that part or all of Texas belonged to the United States by virtue of the 1803 Louisiana Purchase. Therefore, land speculators hoping to seize opportunities in Texas concluded—erroneously—that their claims there would be protected. As a result, beginning in the early 1820s, a number of land development companies formed in the United States. American-based land speculators were predominant in Texas, but Mexicans and Europeans also participated in the speculation frenzy.

The Texas Association, formed in 1822 by a group of investors from Tennessee and Kentucky, was the first U.S.-based speculation endeavor. The Mexican government granted Robert Leftwich, the official agent of the association, an empresarial land grant in 1825 in east Texas, just north of a grant already issued to Stephen F. Austin. Leftwich was allowed to settle as many as 800 families with his grant, but he never fulfilled his contract. The grant was subsequently issued to Austin. The Mexican government also issued a land grant to Haden Edwards around 1825; he too was empowered to settle 800 families. However, after his brother Benjamin fomented an armed insurrection against Mexican authorities in 1826, Mexico City revoked the grant and divided it among

three Texas speculators: Joseph Vehlein, David G. Burnet, and Lorenzo de Zavala. In 1830, they combined their holdings to form the Galveston Bay and Texas Land Company, which would become the most successful landholding company in Texas.

Other land speculation ventures were also formed, many of them based on empresarial contracts. New Yorker James Prentiss used his *empresario* status to become the most successful individual land speculator in Texas history. Rampant land speculation in 1835, which some scholars assert may have helped trigger the Texas Revolution, had its origin among local representatives to the Coahuila y Texas legislature. These representatives were instrumental in passing a law at the state level that allowed the purchase of up to 400 leagues of land from $50 to $100 per league by any individual who could pay cash. Some 1,600 leagues were sold as a result, the cash from which was to be used to defend Coahuila y Texas from a potential attack by Mexican president Antonio López de Santa Anna. Santa Anna did indeed send his army into Texas, sparking the Texas Revolution.

Between 1821 and 1836, when Texas won its independence from Mexico, innumerable land schemes were designed to effect the transfer of Texas to the United States. Indeed, Anthony Butler, the American chargé d'affaires in Mexico City, used his position to leverage land deals for James Prentiss, while another U.S. government official, James T. Mason, used his position to enrich the Galveston Bay and Texas Land Company. After independence, Texas land speculators continued to make large profits, and the new government upheld most of the prior land grants.

After the Mexican-American War ended, a commission created by the federal government to settle old land claims ultimately enriched many land speculators, some of whom, like James Prentiss, received thousands of dollars in compensation for land they never controlled.

PAUL G. PIERPAOLI JR.

See also

Austin, Stephen Fuller; Butler, Anthony Wayne; *Empresarios*; Land Grants; Texas; Texas Revolution.

References

Barker, Eugene Campbell. "Land Speculation as a Cause of the Texas Revolution." *Southwestern Historical Quarterly* 10 (1906): 76–95.

Lack, Paul D. *The Texas Revolutionary Experience: A Political and Social History, 1835–1836.* College Station: Texas A&M University Press, 1999.

Reichstein, Andreas. *Rise of the Lone Star: The Making of Texas.* College Station: Texas A&M University Press, 1989.

Weber, David J. *The Mexican Frontier, 1821–1846: The American Southwest under Mexico.* Albuquerque: University of New Mexico Press, 1982.

Lane, Joseph

Birth Date: December 14, 1801
Death Date: April 19, 1881

U.S. politician and army officer during the Mexican-American War. Joseph Lane was born on December 14, 1801, in Buncombe

Joseph Lane, a U.S. brigadier general of volunteers, distinguished himself in fighting Mexican guerrillas along the National Road during the 1847 campaign from Veracruz to Mexico City. (Dictionary of American Portraits)

County, North Carolina. As a youth, he moved with his family to Kentucky. Lane left home at age 15 and then settled in Indiana, where he engaged in farming and was elected to the state legislature at age 21.

Lane resigned his seat as a member of the Indiana senate when the Mexican War began in 1846. Enlisting in the 2nd Indiana Infantry, Lane was elected its colonel. President James K. Polk subsequently appointed Lane, a staunch Democrat, a brigadier general of volunteers.

Lane was assigned to the army of Major General Zachary Taylor in northern Mexico, where Brigadier General John Wool directed him to investigate the killing of Mexican citizens by American volunteers from Arkansas. On February 9, 1847, certain individuals had entered an American camp and killed a private from Arkansas. Approximately 100 of the soldier's comrades searched for those responsible and came upon a group of Mexican refugees. Finding a weapon sling they identified as belonging to the dead soldier, the group then killed a number of the Mexicans. Although Lane's investigation failed to identify the individuals responsible, he was able to identify the two Arkansas companies involved in the incident, and Taylor ordered both of them home.

Lane fought in the Battle of Buena Vista on February 23, 1847, his first engagement as commander of the brigade composed of the 2nd and 3rd Regiments of Indiana volunteers. Mexican general Antonio López de Santa Anna's main assault during the battle was against the American left flank, which included the 2nd Indiana. The 3rd Indiana was in reserve. Lane ordered the 2nd Indiana and an artillery battery forward, but the commander of the 2nd Indiana evidently misunderstood the directive and ordered a retreat. Without infantry support, the artillery battery had to beat a hasty withdrawal and was forced to abandon one of its cannon.

Soldiers from the 2nd Indiana ended up at various locations on the battlefield. Many of them joined in the stout defense of a hacienda that blocked the advance of Mexican cavalry attempting to turn the American left flank. The 3rd Indiana, meanwhile, moved forward to assist a Mississippi regiment in halting a Mexican unit advancing against the American left. Many historians consider the battle an American victory, but the encounter led to doubts regarding Lane's leadership.

Lane is best known for his operations west of Veracruz after the capture of Mexico City in September 1848. While his military leadership in these actions won him praise from superiors, he was also responsible for an incident that was possibly the worst single American atrocity during the war. On September 13, 1847, the Mexican army began the siege of the small American garrison at Puebla on the supply route between Mexico City and Veracruz. Lane marched west from Veracruz with an American force to relieve the garrison. General Santa Anna arrived to assume personal command of Mexican forces in the area, and he then withdrew most of the besiegers to ambush Lane's column at the Paso del Pintal. Lane, aware of the Mexican forces encamped at Huamantla, left his baggage with guards and marched toward the town. On October 7, an American advance party of cavalry surprised nearly 2,000 Mexican cavalry and forced them to withdraw into Huamantla. A Mexican counterattack caught the Americans off guard, however, and led to a stiff fight until American infantry arrived, which then drove the Mexican troops out of town. The commander of the American cavalry unit, Major Samuel Walker, was killed in the engagement. Lane reportedly allowed American troops to commit wholesale property destruction, looting, and rape in retaliation for Walker's death. Lane's column then continued west and relieved Puebla on October 12, 1847.

Throughout the remainder of 1847 and into 1848, Lane proved highly effective in countering Mexican guerrillas between Mexico City and Veracruz. At the end of October 1847, Lane led a successful attack on guerrillas based at Tlaxcala. In November, he hit the guerrillas at Izucar de Matamoros, liberating American prisoners and seizing two guns and a large supply of ammunition. In January 1848, Lane mounted an unsuccessful raid to capture General Santa Anna. His antiguerrilla campaigns continued into the next month and earned him a brevet to major general.

After the war, in August 1848, President Polk appointed Lane governor of Oregon Territory. He later served in the U.S. House of

Representatives (1851–1859) and in the U.S. Senate (1859–1861). In 1860, Lane was the vice-presidential nominee for the proslavery faction of the Democratic Party. His position regarding slavery ended his political career, and he retired to Oregon. Lane died on April 19, 1881, in Roseburg, Oregon.

TERRY M. MAYS

See also

Atrocities; Buena Vista, Battle of; Guerrilla Warfare; Huamantla, Battle of; Mexico City, Battle for; Mexico City Campaign; Puebla, Siege of; Santa Anna, Antonio López de; Scott, Winfield; Taylor, Zachary; Walker, Samuel Hamilton; Wool, John Ellis.

References

Bauer, K. Jack. *The Mexican War, 1846–1848.* New York: Macmillan, 1974.

Brackett, Albert G. *General Lane's Brigade in Central Mexico.* New York: J. C. Derby, 1854.

Heidler, David, and Jeanne Heidler. *The Mexican War.* Westport, CT: Greenwood Press, 2005.

Johnson, Timothy D. *A Gallant Little Army: The Mexico City Campaign.* Lawrence: University Press of Kansas, 2007.

La Paz

City located in the southeastern portion of the Baja Peninsula on the Gulf of California (Sea of Cortez). Since the early 1800s, La Paz has served as the capital of the Mexican state of Baja California Sur. During the Mexican-American War, La Paz was a small fishing village with a population of some 500 people. Blessed by a warm, dry climate virtually year-round, La Paz is easily accessed by the commodious Bahia de La Paz (La Paz Bay).

On September 14, 1846, Commander Samuel F. Du Pont arrived at La Paz in the sloop of war *Cyane* to seize the port as part of a larger plan to exert control over the entire Gulf of California. Upon his arrival, Du Pont engaged in negotiations with officials of the state government to effect a peaceful capitulation; he also ordered nine small Mexican vessels seized. Du Pont was ordered to move to Guaymas and other Mexican ports, however, and the talks proved inconclusive. The Americans tried to blockade the port at La Paz but did not occupy the town.

In April 1847, the Americans attempted to reinforce the blockade and force a formal surrender from local officials at La Paz. On April 13, the U.S. sloop *Portsmouth* arrived off the port, and its captain, Commander John B. Montgomery, sent Lieutenant John S. Missroon ashore to demand the town's surrender. Collaborationist colonel Francisco Palacios Miranda, the governor of the state, complied. The civil government remained in place and local citizens were granted rights as U.S. citizens. This ready capitulation outraged local Mexican patriots, however, who now formed a guerrilla group under the command of Captain Manuel Pineda.

The following month, Brigadier General Stephen W. Kearny ordered Lieutenant Colonel Henry S. Burton to lead two companies of New York infantry volunteers to La Paz in order to institute a full occupation of the city. They set sail on the storeship *Lexington,* arrived at La Paz Bay on July 21, 1847, and waded ashore encountering no resistance from the locals. Burton and his men then proceeded to erect a small redoubt on a hill with unobstructed views of the town and bay. His men also patrolled the local streets.

On November 11, 1847, Pineda and a group of 120 fellow rebels assaulted the U.S. fort and town; they were repulsed by American artillery. On November 17, a second assault by Pineda was also rebuffed. Burton's contingent suffered 1 killed and 2 wounded in the attacks; the Mexicans suffered 10 killed and 10 wounded. Pineda now regrouped and augmented his force, which stood at about 350 men. On November 27, Pineda's guerrillas again assaulted La Paz, this time laying siege to it until December 8. Pineda's force was scattered on December 8 after the arrival of the *Cyane.* Pineda reportedly suffered 17 killed and wounded. No U.S. casualties were reported.

From La Paz, Burton launched raids against nearby Mexican guerrilla camps at San Antonio and Todos Santos during February and March 1848. In spite of these actions, guerrilla activity continued in the area, and Burton proved unsuccessful in hunting down Pineda. U.S. troops continued to occupy and patrol La Paz until September 1848, when they were withdrawn. When the American force left, some 300 local residents also departed, fearful of retaliation because of their collaboration with U.S. forces.

PAUL G. PIERPAOLI JR.

See also

Baja California; Du Pont, Samuel Francis; Guaymas, Battle of; Guerrilla Warfare; Kearny, Stephen Watts.

References

Bauer, K. Jack. *Surfboats and Horse Marines: U.S. Naval Operations in the Mexican War.* Annapolis, MD: U.S. Naval Institute, 1969.

Meadows, Don. *The American Occupation of La Paz.* Los Angeles: Glen Dawson, 1955.

Laredo

Town founded by Spanish settlers in 1755 astride the Rio Grande in modern-day southern Texas (Webb County). The city is situated at the western end of the Rio Grande Plains; the topography is generally flat, with some small hills in the surrounding countryside. It is surrounded by flora that is typical for south Texas: extensive grasslands, brush, oak, and mesquite trees. The city is arid, receiving only about 20 inches of rain per year. Temperatures in the summer are quite hot, routinely reaching or exceeding 100 degrees. The area is subject to sudden and ferocious thunderstorms, including tornadoes. Temperatures in the winter are cool for the standards of south Texas, owing to Laredo's distance from the Gulf of Mexico; snow is rare but not unheard of. The population of Laredo circa 1845 was about 2,000.

Laredo served as General Antonio López de Santa Anna's staging area for his invasion of Texas in 1836. Following Santa Anna's defeat at San Jacinto and the Texas Declaration of Independence from Mexico, Laredo should have come under the control of the new Republic of Texas under the terms of the Treaty of Velasco. The Texas government, however, never made a serious attempt to assert control over the city. Indeed, the citizens of the town went on as before and remained loyal to the state government of Tamaulipas and the central government in Mexico City.

In 1840, when federalist generals Antonio Zapata and Antonio Canales Rosillo declared the Republic of the Rio Grande, they made Laredo the capital of the upstart republic. Centralist forces under Santa Anna, however, promptly quashed the rebellion, and Laredo remained little more than a small city in Mexico. Laredo, nonetheless, remained near the epicenter of the enduring border conflict between the Mexicans and Texans. In 1842, during the Somervell Expedition, Texas army brigadier general Alexander Somervell ordered Laredo sacked, but oddly the Texas government failed to place it under its own jurisdiction. Captain Richard A. Gillespie led a company of Texas Rangers into Laredo and formally claimed it for the United States in March 1846, just prior to the formal declaration of war between the United States and Mexico. Later that same year, a Texas militia force under Captain Mirabeau B. Lamar also laid claim to the area, leaving a small garrison there.

After the Mexican-American War ended in 1848, Laredo became the seat of Webb County, Texas. This event, however, badly splintered the city's population, many of whom wished to remain Mexican citizens. Those refusing U.S. citizenship thus relocated to an area across the Rio Grande, where they founded the Mexican city of Nuevo Laredo, Tamaulipas. In 1849, the U.S. Army erected Fort McIntosh a mile west of Laredo to guard the area from potential Mexican and Native American attack. Today, Laredo is a thriving city of some 240,000 people; its metropolitan area boasts a population of 720,000 people.

PAUL G. PIERPAOLI JR.

See also
Canales Rosillo, Antonio; Gillespie, Robert Addison; Lamar, Mirabeau Buonaparte; Rio Grande; Santa Anna, Antonio López de; Texas; Texas Revolution.

References
Green, Stanley C., ed. *A Changing of the Flags: Mirabeau B. Lamar at Laredo.* Laredo, TX: Border Studies, 1990.
Hinojosa, Gilberto Miguel. *A Borderlands Town in Transition: Laredo, 1755–1870.* College Station: Texas A&M University Press, 1983.

Larkin, Thomas Oliver
Birth Date: September 16, 1802
Death Date: October 27, 1858

Early American emigrant to Mexico who became the first and only American consul to California. Thomas Oliver Larkin was born in Charlestown, Massachusetts, on September 16, 1802. At age 15, he went to Boston to apprentice as a bookbinder. From 1821 to 1830, he worked in North Carolina, lost his business, and returned to Massachusetts destitute. In September 1830, Larkin left Boston to help his half brother, John Bautista Rogers Cooper, in California; he arrived in San Francisco in April 1832.

En route to California, Larkin developed an intimate relationship with Mrs. Rachel Hobson Holmes, who was on her way to California to join her husband. After she discovered that she was pregnant with Larkin's child, she moved to Santa Barbara, California, and gave birth. After learning that her husband had died on a voyage to Lima, Peru, she married Larkin on June 10, 1833.

Larkin worked for his half brother for about a year, started a store of his own in early 1833, and became a prominent merchant. In 1835, he built a house in Monterey, the provincial capital of California, and was commissioned to rebuild the Monterey customhouse. He never became a Mexican citizen, however, because he would have had to convert to Catholicism, but he renewed his visa annually to maintain his legal status.

In October 1842, U.S. Navy commodore Thomas ap Catesby Jones, convinced that war had broken out between the United States and Mexico, occupied Monterey. Larkin and William Hartnell smoothed the resulting tensions. As a result, President John

Thomas Oliver Larkin, an American who had settled in California, served as the first (and only) U.S. consul to California at Monterey from 1843 to 1848. He played an important role in the Mexican-American War. (Dictionary of American Portraits)

Tyler in 1843 appointed Larkin as the first (and last) American consul to California.

Early in 1846, Secretary of State James Buchanan sent Larkin instructions to covertly assure Americans in California that the United States would support any secession attempt. As he was negotiating with General Mariano Guadalupe Vallejo to arrange for the peaceful annexation of California, the Bear Flag Revolt occurred on June 14, 1846. A few weeks later, Captain John C. Frémont and his 60-man Corps of Topographical Engineers arrived in Monterey and took control of the Bear Flag Revolt.

As these events unfolded, early that same June U.S. Marine lieutenant Archibald Gillespie arrived at Monterey with secret messages from President James Polk for Larkin, and Commodore John D. Sloat, commander of the U.S. Pacific Squadron, and Frémont. On July 7, 1846, Sloat's marines and sailors occupied Monterey. A week later, Commodore Robert F. Stockton replaced Sloat as commander of the Pacific Squadron. Stockton appointed Frémont as the commander of the California Battalion, formed from Frémont's 60 U.S. Army soldiers and the Bear Flag rebels. Larkin then joined a 160-man contingent that Stockton sent to occupy San Diego and Los Angeles. By August 13, the Americans had peacefully occupied the two towns. Stockton then appointed Larkin as naval agent, and Larkin returned to Monterey.

Soon, the Californios (Californians of Hispanic ancestry) in Los Angeles revolted against the Americans and drove them out. Larkin moved his family to Yerba Buena (San Francisco) but was captured while trying to bring his deathly ill daughter out of Monterey. He was imprisoned in Los Angeles and was not reunited with his family until after the signing of the Treaty of Cahuenga on January 13, 1847. By that time, his daughter had died.

After the establishment of peace in Alta California, Larkin helped established a town at the Carquinez Straits, which became Benicia. Several years later, he returned to San Francisco where he had firmly established himself by the time of the California Gold Rush. In 1849, San Franciscans selected Larkin as their representative to the California Constitutional Convention held in Monterey. In late 1850, he returned to New York and remained there until 1853. While in Colusa, California, Larkin contracted typhoid fever and died on October 27, 1858.

ROBERT B. KANE

See also

Bear Flag Revolt; Buchanan, James; Cahuenga, Treaty of; California; California Battalion; California Theater of War, Overview; Frémont, John Charles; Jones, Thomas ap Catesby; Monterey, California; Sloat, John Drake; Stockton, Robert Field; Vallejo, Mariano Guadalupe.

References

Bean, Walton. *California: An Interpretive History.* New York: McGraw-Hill, 1968.
Haque, Harlan, and David J. Langum. *Thomas O. Larkin: A Life of Patriotism and Profit.* Norman: University of Oklahoma Press, 1990.
Rosenus, Alan. *General M. G. Vallejo and the Advent of the Americans.* Albuquerque: University of New Mexico Press, 1994.
Walker, Dale L. *Bear Flag Rising: The Conquest of California.* 1946. New York: Forge, 1999.

Lavallette, Elie Augustus Frederick
Birth Date: May 3, 1790
Death Date: November 18, 1862

U.S. Navy officer. Born in Alexandria, Virginia, into a family of French origin on May 3, 1790, Elie Augustus Frederick Lavallette was the son of a U.S. Navy chaplain. He sailed with his father at age 10 on a cruise in the frigate *Constitution.* Following several merchant marine cruises, Lavallette received an appointment as a sailing master in the navy on June 25, 1812. Lavallette distinguished himself during the War of 1812 as acting lieutenant in the sloop *Saratoga,* Commodore Thomas Macdonough's flagship, during the Battle of Lake Champlain (September 11, 1814). Promoted to lieutenant on December 9, 1814, he assumed command of the schooner *Dispatch* in the U.S. Coast Survey.

Following other assignments, during 1824–1828 Lavallette was in the frigate *Constitution* and on several occasions exercised command of that ship. In 1830, he changed the spelling of his name from La Vallette to the more Americanized Lavallette. He was promoted to master commandant on March 3, 1831, and in 1833 he commanded the sloop *Fairfield* off Ecuador. Lavallette was promoted to captain on February 23, 1840.

At the beginning of the Mexican-American War, Lavallette commanded the razee frigate *Independence.* He sailed from Boston on August 22, 1846, to join Commodore John D. Sloat's Pacific Squadron. In August 1847, in command of the frigate *Congress,* he was ordered to proceed to Cabo San Lucas, Mexico, with his own ship and the sloops *Portsmouth* and *Dale* assigned to the mission of commerce destruction. Lavallette took possession of the Mexican port of Guaymas on October 20. On November 11, he led the American delegation that secured the surrender of Mazatlán, the most important Mexican port on the Pacific. Commodore William Bradford Shubrick then appointed Lavallette military governor of Mazatlán and gave him command of a 400-man garrison consisting of the crew of the *Congress.* By February 1848, he and his men had completed fortifications at Mazatlán that would enable them to withstand any attack the Mexicans could launch. With the end of the war, Lavallette returned control of Mazatlán to the Mexican government on June 17, 1848.

Lavallette commanded the Africa Squadron in 1851, and he subsequently commanded the East India Squadron and the Mediterranean Squadron. At the outbreak of the Civil War, Lavallette had served in the navy for 48 years: some 19 years of service at sea, 12 years in assignments ashore, and 16 years waiting orders in a navy that had too many officers for billets available.

In early 1861, Lavallette was assigned command of the naval station at Sackets Harbor, New York, and he remained there into

1862. He also served on board duty until August 1862. On July 16, 1862, Lavallette was commissioned a rear admiral on the retired list. Lavallette died in Philadelphia on November 18, 1862. Lavallette, New Jersey, is named in his honor. Two U.S. destroyers subsequently named for him retained the French spelling of his name.

Spencer C. Tucker

See also

Guaymas, Battle of; Mazatlán; Shubrick, William Branford; Sloat, John Drake.

References

Bauer, K. Jack. *Surfboats and Horse Marines: U.S. Naval Operations in the Mexican War, 1846–48.* Annapolis, MD: United States Naval Institute, 1969.

Callahan, Edward W., ed. *List of Officers of the Navy of the United States and of the Marine Corps from 1775 to 1900.* 1901. Reprint, New York: Haskell House, 1969.

Thompson, Kenneth E. *Civil War Commodores and Admirals: A Biographical Directory of All Eighty-Eight Union and Confederate Navy Officers Who Attained Commissioned Flag Rank during the War.* Portland, ME: Thompson, 2001.

Lawson, Thomas
Birth Date: 1781?
Death Date: May 15, 1861

U.S. surgeon general during the Mexican-American War and second surgeon general of the United States. Thomas Lawson was born in Virginia, although the date of his birth and details of his early life are vague. He was appointed an assistant surgeon in the navy on March 1, 1809, but resigned on January 12, 1811, to join the army as surgeon to the 6th U.S. Infantry. Lawson aspired to line command as well as medical duties and served as lieutenant colonel of a combat battalion of New York and Pennsylvania volunteers during the Seminole War. In his role as military surgeon he was in the field in every American conflict save the Black Hawk War from his entry into the Army Medical Corps until his death.

Lawson was a difficult subordinate with a dour and quarrelsome personality that frequently brought him into conflict with both his associates and his superiors. He once brought charges against a lieutenant who severely beat him in a fist fight and who subsequently filed his own charges against Lawson for insubordination. Both accusations were later dropped.

Lawson rose to senior surgeon of the Medical Corps in 1821 and was appointed surgeon general in 1836, succeeding Joseph Lovell who had been the first to hold that office. Although he was not as efficient an administrator as his predecessor, Lawson did prove to be a better superior than subordinate. He spent much time endeavoring to improve the status and prerogatives of his surgeons. Lawson managed to get formal rank for them for the first time along with the right to wear epaulets, to be saluted by soldiers, and to serve on military boards and commissions. He

also got permission for his surgeons to augment their income with private practice while on active duty, and he organized a formal training program for hospital stewards, although that program was allowed to lapse.

Lawson was a close personal friend of Major General Winfield Scott, and he accompanied Scott on his Mexican campaign. While in Mexico, Lawson retained his position as surgeon general and declined to replace Scott's medical director; instead he worked alongside the other surgeons treating the sick and wounded. His presence in Mexico led to organizational confusion, and his absence from Washington resulted in administrative failures that contributed to the generally dismal performance of the Medical Corps during the war.

Lawson made the unfortunate decision that ether was too volatile and the equipment too delicate for anesthesia to be useful on the battlefield. He also believed (incorrectly) that the anesthetic increased the risk of hemorrhage and gangrene. Lawson did receive a brevet appointment as brigadier general for gallantry, and he successfully campaigned for expansion of both the medical corps and the contingent of hospital stewards and attendants after the war.

Lawson continued as surgeon general until May 15, 1861, when he died of apoplexy while on leave in Norfolk, Virginia.

Jack McCallum

See also

Mexico City Campaign; Scott, Winfield.

References

Ashburn, Percy. *A History of the Medical Department of the United States Army.* Boston: Houghton Mifflin Company, 1929.

Gillett, Mary C. *The Army Medical Department, 1818–1865.* Washington, DC: Center of Military History, United States Army, 1987.

Packard, Francis R. *History of Medicine in the United States.* New York: Paul B. Hoeber, 1931.

Lee, Robert Edward
Birth Date: January 19, 1807
Death Date: October 12, 1870

U.S. and Confederate Army officer. Robert Edward Lee was born on January 19, 1807, in Stratford, Virginia. He graduated from the U.S. Military Academy, West Point, in 1829 and was commissioned in the Corps of Engineers. Lee rose to the rank of captain in 1838 and distinguished himself in a variety of engineering assignments along the Mississippi River.

During the Mexican-American War, Lee was first assigned to forces under Brigadier General John E. Wool at San Antonio de Béxar. As a member of the Topographical Engineers, Captain Lee conducted noteworthy reconnaissance missions for Wool as that force moved south. Wool thought highly of Lee's work and appointed him acting inspector general, a position he held in addition to his engineering work.

Portrait of Robert E. Lee, ca. 1848. Lee was a captain of topographical engineers during the Mexican-American War. His reconnaissance missions were of vital importance during the campaign from Veracruz to Mexico City. By the end of the war, he had received three brevets: to major, lieutenant colonel, and colonel. (Nathaniel W. Stephenson, *Texas and the Mexican War,* 1921)

Transferred to Major General Winfield Scott's army as it prepared to land at Veracruz in March, Lee became a member of Scott's engineering staff, which also included P. G. T. Beauregard, George B. McClellan, and Gustavus Woodson Smith. Lee rendered invaluable service in the Mexico City Campaign. He was largely responsible for the placement of the heavy batteries that reduced Veracruz, and he located the route by which American forces turned Santa Anna's supposedly invulnerable left flank at the Battle of Cerro Gordo (April 17–18, 1847). On August 18, 1847, Lee conducted what was probably the most daring reconnaissance of the war, locating and enlarging passageways through the evidently impenetrable *pedregal* (lava fields), which permitted U.S. forces to turn the flank of General of Division Gabriel Valencia's Army of the North, leading to the decisive American victory at the Battle of Contreras. At the Battle of Churubusco (August 20, 1847), where he was slightly wounded, he aided in the placement of artillery batteries while under withering enemy fire. By war's end, Lee had been brevetted three times for gallantry, the last one to colonel. Upon Colonel Joseph G. Totten's return to the United States following the capture of Mexico City, Lee was appointed Scott's chief of engineers, a position he held until the end of the war.

In 1852, Lee became superintendent at West Point, revitalizing its curriculum. In 1855, he left the academy to become lieutenant colonel of the 2nd U.S. Cavalry. In 1859, Lee was called on to suppress abolitionist John Brown's uprising at Harpers Ferry.

Lee then advanced to colonel of the 1st U.S. Cavalry and was commanding the Department of Texas by 1860.

Lee supported neither secession nor slavery, but he felt deeply obliged to support his native state of Virginia in the Civil War. He tendered his resignation in April 1861, and by May he was a lieutenant general in the Confederate Army. In August he became a full general. Lee, however, bungled his initial assignment to subdue the western counties of Virginia, mostly because of uncooperative subordinates. Confederate president Jefferson Davis, however, assigned him to improve the defenses of the south Atlantic coast. Lee was soon back in Richmond as Davis's military adviser, without command responsibilities. In this capacity, Lee suggested to Davis that Union pressure on Richmond might be relieved by reinforcing Major General Thomas J. Jackson in the Shenandoah Valley, which resulted in a brilliant success in the spring of 1862.

Lee's fortunes, and those of the Confederacy, changed dramatically when he assumed command of the Army of Northern Virginia after General Joseph E. Johnston was severely wounded in May 1862. Lee immediately launched what became his tactical trademark—a relentless series of hard-hitting and punishing attacks. This offensive, known as the Seven Days' Campaign, pushed Union forces away from Richmond. In August 1862, following the Peninsula Campaign, Lee soundly defeated the Federals in the Second Battle of Bull Run.

Having gained the strategic initiative, Lee then carried the war north into Maryland, and on September 17, 1862, he fought McClellan again in the Battle of Antietam, which was a strategic defeat for the South. Nevertheless, when Union Major General George McClellan failed to pursue, Lincoln replaced him with Major General Ambrose Burnside.

Burnside attacked Lee in another poorly orchestrated Union effort at Fredericksburg on December 17, 1862. The battle was Lee's most lopsided victory. The year ended with the Army of Northern Virginia enjoying high morale and an aura of invincibility.

In the spring of 1863, a new commander of the Army of the Potomac, Major General Joseph Hooker, again attacked Lee, at Chancellorsville, during May 1–4. It was Lee's most brilliant victory but was a costly one for the South in terms of casualties.

In June 1863, Lee again led his army north, into Pennsylvania. Major General George Gordon Meade took command of the Army of the Potomac on the eve of battle, with the contending armies colliding at Gettysburg during July 1–3, 1863. Suffering heavy losses, Lee retreated back to Virginia beginning on the night of July 4.

In the spring of 1864, Lee was confronted by a new adversary, Lieutenant General Ulysses S. Grant, the Union general in chief, who accompanied the Army of the Potomac in the field. Lee was now outnumbered two to one. When Grant advanced on Richmond in his Overland Campaign, Lee fought a series of battles with him. Although Grant sustained casualties equivalent to the size of Lee's entire army, he continued to pursue and hit Lee hard. Grant tried to get in behind Lee at Petersburg, but this effort failed and ended in a long siege.

For nearly a year, Lee maintained his dwindling army in the trenches before Richmond and Petersburg. In February 1865, Lee was appointed general in chief of all Confederate forces, but by then the Southern cause was lost. The impasse ended on March 31, 1865, when Major General Philip H. Sheridan broke through Confederate lines at Five Forks. His position untenable, Lee abandoned Richmond and headed west. Grant, however, pursued vigorously and the Army of Northern Virginia was cut off by Union cavalry at Appomattox Court House. Lee surrendered there with great dignity on April 9, 1865.

Following the war, Lee served as president of Washington College (now Washington and Lee University) in Lexington, Virginia. He transformed the curriculum and created the nation's first departments of journalism and commerce. Lee also urged southerners to put the war behind them and become loyal citizens of the United States. Lee died in Lexington on October 12, 1870.

SPENCER C. TUCKER

See also

Buena Vista, Battle of; Cerro Gordo, Battle of; Churubusco, Battle of; Contreras, Battle of; Mexico City Campaign; *Pedregal*; Scott, Winfield.

References

Freeman, Douglas Southall. *R. E. Lee: A Biography.* 4 vols. New York: Charles Scribner's Sons, 1934, 1935, 1936.

Gallagher, Gary W., ed. *Lee the Soldier.* Lincoln: University of Nebraska Press, 1996.

Thomas, Emory M. *Robert E. Lee: A Biography.* New York: W. W. Norton, 1995.

Legacy of the Mexican-American War

The Mexican-American War ended in clear-cut victory for the United States and major defeat for Mexico. It helped secure for the United States its western and southwestern geographical boundaries as well as the acquisition of vast new territories that eventually became the states of Arizona, New Mexico, Nevada, Utah, Wyoming, California, and parts of Colorado. It also brought to fruition the concept of Manifest Destiny, or the belief that the United States had a divinely ordained right to expand from the Atlantic to the Pacific Oceans. For Mexico, this meant the loss of more than 500,000 square miles, or over half its pre-war territory, and greater political, economic, and social instability in the decades after the war.

The western territories acquired through the war with Mexico proved a bonanza to a burgeoning American population in need of both land and resources. One resource, gold, proved immensely valuable when it was discovered in California on January 24, 1848, only nine days before the signing of the Treaty of Guadalupe Hidalgo on February 2. The acquisition of new territories also brought many Native American populations under the umbrella of a white, Anglo-Saxon culture. This forced many Native Americans

on the defensive, resulting in frequent clashes between white western settlers and the U.S. Army and Indian tribes trying desperately to stave off encroachment on their ancestral lands. Many Native Americans were forced onto reservations and into white schools and to accept Christianity and white culture. Treaties, often negotiated illegally, closed the American frontier, since the nation's Manifest Destiny was finally realized. Thereafter, the United States turned its sights beyond its geographical boundaries and began looking for new markets and colonies abroad.

The Mexican-American War proved once again that the U.S. military was unprepared for conflict when the hostilities began. Like the wars it had fought before and would fight subsequently, inadequate leadership, obsolete weapons, poor logistics, lack of hygiene, substandard medical care, and camp diseases wrought havoc on the military, killing many more soldiers than actual combat wounds. Nonetheless, the new U.S. Army's lighter and more mobile flying artillery batteries proved their worth in battle as far superior to Mexico's aging and slower-to-move guns. In terms of military organization, U.S. command and control was also far superior to that of the Mexican army.

The war also produced future U.S. political and military leaders. Major General Zachary Taylor, a soldier's soldier who rarely ever wore the prescribed uniform and never wanted to be president, nevertheless won election to the highest office in 1848 as a "war hero." By contrast, Major General Winfield Scott, nicknamed "Old Fuss and Feathers" for his meticulous attention to military organization and form, and who wanted desperately to be president, was defeated in the general election in 1852.

The Mexican-American War proved the worth of the training received by many junior officers at the U.S. Military Academy, West Point, especially engineers, who proved their worth in extended combat operations. Indeed, the conflict with Mexico served as a training ground for the American generals who fought on both sides of the American Civil War. Generals like Robert E. Lee, U. S. Grant, Thomas J. Jackson, George B. McClellan, Joseph E. Johnston, and Albert Sidney Johnston, among a host of others, were comrades and friends during the Mexican War, and for some this proved a great advantage in knowing the attitudes, mind-set, and opinions of their opponents during the Civil War.

The U.S. victory was not without its negative consequences, however, as the newly gained territories had to grapple with the thorny issue of whether or not to allow slavery to exist within their respective borders. In the years after the Mexican-American War, repeated, short-term compromises on slavery issues provided only temporary relief. Ultimately, the American Civil War ensued from 1861 to 1865. Indirectly, one root cause of the American Civil War was surely the outcome of the Mexican-American War. In the words of philosopher Ralph Waldo Emerson, absorbing so much Mexican territory was analogous to a man who swallows arsenic, "which brings him down in turn. Mexico will poison us."

From the Mexican perspective, the war had equally profound consequences. Not surprisingly, Mexican politics were greatly disrupted as a result of the war. As Mexican political groups tried to digest the lessons of the conflict, they recalibrated their platforms and policies. Conservatives came to believe that the only way to cure Mexico of its ills and stave off American expansionism was to embrace Mexico's Spanish roots and adopt a monarchical form of government. Liberals, on the other hand, held that Mexico's main problem was the failure of independence to abolish the Spanish colonial legacy. Both sides became more insistent on implementing their own ideology, and consequently another round of political strife ensued—the Three Years' War (1858–1860) and the French intervention (1862–1867). Liberals led by Benito Juárez ultimately won the struggle, and their victory allowed them to turn their ideology into what Charles A. Hale called "a unifying political myth" that helped consolidate Mexico as a nation-state.

The loss of over half of the national territory to the United States in 1848 also exacerbated the economic and population gulf that existed between the United States and Mexico, which to this day remains a sticking point in U.S.-Mexican relations. The conflict left many Mexicans wary of U.S. motives, and contemporary observers believed that the Americans might attempt further seizures of their territory. Although the regime of Porfirio Díaz (1876–1911) largely succeeded in mending Mexico's relationship with the United States, relations between both countries reached a nadir during the 1910 Revolution when U.S. forces occupied Veracruz in 1914 and two years later launched a punitive expedition into northern Mexico.

As relations between the two nations improved beginning in the 1930s, Mexico still found itself as the decidedly junior partner in the relationship. Indeed, its cautious foreign policy, predicated on the rule of law, nonintervention, and the peaceful resolution of conflicts, is a direct consequence of its involvement in the Mexican-American War. Although the 1990s saw an attempt by the Mexican government to find common ground with the Americans and to deemphasize the painful memories of the Mexican-American War, the signing of the North American Free Trade Agreement (NAFTA) in 1993 proved to be controversial among many Mexicans, who continued to fear American perfidy, nearly 150 years after the end of the Mexican-American War. Similar suspicions remain today and leave their mark on issues that affect bilateral relations such as immigration, water resources, and the war on drugs.

PATRICK M. ALBANO AND PAUL G. PIERPAOLI JR.

See also

Expansionism and Imperialism; Guadalupe Hidalgo, Treaty of; Manifest Destiny; Mexican Cession; Mexico; *Patria Chica*; Politics, Mexican; Politics, U.S.; Polk, James Knox; Santa Anna, Antonio López de; Scott, Winfield; Slavery; Taylor, Zachary; United States, 1821–1854.

References

Clary, David A. *Eagles and Empire: The United States, Mexico, and the Struggle for a Continent.* New York: Bantam Books, 2009.

DeLay, Brian. *War of a Thousand Deserts: Indian Raids and the U.S.-Mexican War.* New Haven: Yale University Press, 2008.

Griswold Del Castillo, Richard. *The Treaty of Guadalupe Hidalgo: A Legacy of Conflict.* Norman: University of Oklahoma Press, 1990.

Hale, Charles A. *Mexican Liberalism in the Age of Mora, 1821–1853.* New Haven: Yale University Press, 1968.

Rodríguez O., Jaime E., and Kathryn Vincent, eds. *Myths, Misdeeds, and Misunderstandings: The Roots of Conflict in U.S.-Mexican Relations.* Wilmington: Scholarly Resources, 1997.

Streeby, Shelley. *American Sensations: Class, Empire, and the Production of Popular Culture.* Berkeley: University of California Press, 2002.

Lenni Lenapes

See Delawares (Lenni Lenapes)

León, Antonio

Birth Date: June 4, 1794
Death Date: September 8, 1847

Mexican army general and federalist politician. Antonio León was born on June 4, 1794, at Huajuapam, Oaxaca, Mexico, and joined a provincial militia company in May 1811 as an ensign. Before March 1821, when he joined the independence movement, he fought numerous engagements as a royalist. After Mexico became independent in 1821, he became commanding general at Oaxaca. In 1824 he was elected to the constituent congress and eight years

Mexican general Antonio León served in the Army of the East. He fought at the Battle of Cerro Gordo during April 17–18, 1847, and was killed in the Battle of El Molino del Rey on September 8, 1847. (Library of Congress)

later was elected as a deputy to the national congress (which, however, never assembled).

During the mid-1830s, León helped lead suppressions of several rebellions, including one in Chiapas. In 1838, he became commanding general of Chiapas, concurrent with his role as commanding general of Oaxaca, and in the summer of 1841 he supported General Mariano Paredes y Arrillaga's successful coup against the centralist government of Anastasio Bustamante. The following year, León played a prominent role in the annexation of the Soconusco region (in modern-day Chiapas), for which the government rewarded him with a promotion to general of brigade in January 1843.

When the Mexican-American War began in 1846, León was in command of a brigade from Oaxaca tasked with reinforcing Mexican reserve forces at Cerro Gordo. That force saw action at the Battle of Cerro Gordo on April 17–18, 1847, which ended in an embarrassing defeat for the Mexicans. Thereafter, León's brigade became the nucleus of the reorganized Army of the East, which battled the Americans during the Mexico City Campaign. At the September 8, 1847, Battle of El Molino del Rey, León was badly wounded by an American bullet and died several hours after the engagement. He was posthumously promoted to general of division and is considered one of Mexico's leading war heroes.

PAUL G. PIERPAOLI JR.

See also

Bustamante y Oseguera, Anastasio; Cerro Gordo, Battle of; El Molino del Rey, Battle of; Mexico City Campaign; Paredes y Arrillaga, Mariano; Politics, Mexican.

References

DePalo, William A., Jr. *The Mexican National Army, 1822–1852.* Albuquerque: University of New Mexico Press, 1997.
Roa Bárcena, José María. *Recuerdos de la invasión norteamericana (1846–1848).* 3 vols. 2nd ed. Mexico City: Editorial Porrúa, 1971.

Léperos

The lowest class of the Mexican urban poor that often included vagabonds, criminals, and beggars who usually lived on the streets and were at most sporadically employed. *Léperos* played a part in the Mexican-American War as participants in the street fighting and other informal resistance that occurred at times against U.S. forces in Mexico, most notably during Major General Winfield Scott's Mexico City Campaign and the U.S. occupation of Mexico City, which began in September 1847.

The greatest military challenge from the *léperos* came shortly after Scott's army entered Mexico City on September 14, 1847. While U.S. Army forces entered the city itself unchallenged, before his exit General Antonio López de Santa Anna had ordered prisoners released from the city's jails. They joined with straggling Mexican soldiers, *léperos,* and others of the lower classes in ransacking the National Palace and other buildings and engaging in street fighting. Brigadier General David E. Twiggs and Brevet

Major General William J. Worth each lost men in the melee as their troops engaged in house-to-house and street combat. Order was restored only after the avenues had been swept clear by light artillery. For some time thereafter, U.S. soldiers continued to encounter sniper fire from the city's rooftops and had to take particular care when traveling outside the central city. U.S. troops had also been the occasional targets of attacks from *léperos* before they reached the city, including the stoning and turning back of a supply wagon near El Molino del Rey, which, in part, led to the abrogation of the armistice of August 23–September 6, 1847.

Several times during the 19th century the Mexican government had forced those of the *léperos* class to become unwilling conscripts in the Mexican army, which had chronic difficulties attracting other classes of Mexicans into its ranks. Most elite Mexicans feared putting weapons into the hands of the lower classes under any circumstances, however, because of the possibility of instigating class violence in the politically unstable nation. To the extent that the *léperos* served, they were usually poorly equipped and trained and had little loyalty to their upper-class officers or the government. As a result, many deserted from the army's ranks. Many historians, in fact, point to the strong class divisions of Mexican society as a major reason for Mexico's poor military performance in the war.

Accounts by contemporary U.S. writers on the war and letters home from U.S. soldiers often included descriptions of the *léperos* in colorful but disparaging terms. Emphasizing their difference from any class found in the United States, these descriptions introduced American readers to an exotic and unsavory Mexican type that became part of the popular conception of the country.

SUE E. BARKER

See also

Castes; Guerrilla Warfare; Mexico, Occupation of; Mexico City; Mexico City Campaign; *Patria Chica*; Scott, Winfield; Twiggs, David Emanuel; Worth, William Jenkins.

References

Foos, Paul. *A Short, Offhand, Killing Affair: Soldiers and Social Conflict during the Mexican-American War.* Chapel Hill: University of North Carolina Press, 2002.
Granados, Luis Fernando. *Sueñan las piedras: Alzamiento ocurrido en la ciudad de México, 14, 15, y 16 de septiembre de 1847.* Mexico City: Ediciones Era, 2003.
Henderson, Timothy J. *A Glorious Defeat: Mexico and Its War with the United States.* New York: Hill and Wang, 2007.

Lerdo de Tejada, Miguel
Birth Date: 1812
Death Date: March 22, 1861

Brother of Mexican president Sebastián Lerdo de Tejada (1872–1876), political spokesman for Mexico's Liberal Party, supporter of the Ayutla Rebellion, and key figure during the *Reforma* era that followed President Antonio López de Santa Anna's final ouster in 1855. Miguel Lerdo de Tejada was born in the port city of Veracruz in 1812. He was schooled to enter local and national politics at an early age, as his family was prominent in regional political life in Veracruz. By 1841, after having engaged in various business endeavors, Lerdo had relocated to Mexico City and became involved in public affairs as a member of the more radical faction of the federalist party known as the *puros.*

During the Mexican-American War, however, Lerdo went from being a relatively obscure political figure to one with significant influence. Following the U.S. occupation of Mexico City in September 1847, he and 20 other *puros,* with the help of U.S. authorities, secured election to the *ayuntamiento* (town council) and instituted a program of radical socioeconomic reforms. Those changes, however, encouraged recrimination, and Lerdo's political rivals consequently argued that he had worked to secure Mexico's annexation to the United States.

In 1853 Lerdo joined Santa Anna's administration as minister of development. His family, and that of President Santa Anna, had been neighbors in Jalapa, Veracruz, during Lerdo's early life, and it is possible that those familial connections led to Lerdo's appointment. One year later, Lerdo supported the Ayutla Rebellion that overthrew Santa Anna in 1855. The rebellion's triumph launched the era known as *La Reforma,* which sought to alter Mexico's political and economic structures to create a modern nation-state. Lerdo authored one of the most important pieces of legislation to emerge from that era, the so-called Lerdo Law of 1856. The decree, which banned the Catholic Church from owning real estate not essential to daily operations, aimed to promote agrarian reform by stripping the church of its large landholdings as well as reducing its political and social influence.

Lerdo was elected to Mexico's Supreme Court in 1861 but died on March 22, 1861, in Mexico City.

MARK A. OCEGUEDA AND PEDRO SANTONI

See also

Catholic Church, Mexico; Gadsden Purchase; Juárez, Benito; *Moderados*; Politics, Mexican; *Puros*; Santa Anna, Antonio López de.

References

Blázquez, Carmen. *Miguel Lerdo de Tejada: Un liberal veracruzano en la política nacional.* Mexico City: El Colegio de México, 1978.

Olliff, Donathon. *Reforma Mexico and the United States: A Search for Alternatives to Annexation, 1854–1861.* Tuscaloosa: University of Alabama Press, 1981.

Liberty Party

U.S. political party officially founded in 1839 and based primarily on an abolitionist platform. As the antislavery and abolitionist movements gained momentum in the 1830s, many abolitionists looked to support political candidates who would embrace, at least in part, their agenda. This was especially true during and after the Texas Revolution, which alarmed many abolitionists by the prospect of the U.S. annexation of Texas and the spread of slavery into that state. By the end of the 1830s, many abolitionists were unwilling to support candidates from either the Whig Party or the Democratic Party. Therefore, a number of them decided to establish their own political party.

The Liberty Party was born in 1839 in Warsaw, New York; its first official convention was held in Albany, New York, in April 1840. The Liberty Party was particularly well supported in western New York State, its birthplace. Attorney Alvan Stewart and Myron Holley, a onetime activist with the Anti-Masonic Party, both western New York natives, were early and avid supporters of the party. The Liberty Party nominated James G. Birney, an attorney and abolitionist from Cincinnati, Ohio, as its presidential candidate for the election of 1840. Thomas Earle, from Pennsylvania, was his vice-presidential running mate.

In the November election, the ticket garnered only 7,000 votes. This poor showing did not deter party stalwarts, however. They saw the role of the party as being one of abolitionist promotion rather than political influence. The Liberty Party did not support William Lloyd Garrison's brand of abolitionism.

Birney was again nominated for the presidential slot during the 1844 election, this time running with Thomas Morris, a former U.S. senator from Ohio, as his vice-presidential pick. The ticket attracted a far more respectable 62,000 votes in the election. Ironically, the Liberty Party's fairly strong showing in New York swung that state's electoral vote to proslavery and proexpansionist candidate James K. Polk, a Democrat. Polk won the election.

By 1848, the Liberty Party had all but run its course. Many of its adherents decided to back the new Free Soil Party, although a small group led by Gerrit Smith, a wealthy New York philanthropist and ardent abolitionist, decided to field their own Liberty ticket in the 1848 election. Smith served as the presidential candidate in both the 1848 and 1852 elections. He won few votes, however, and after 1852 the Liberty Party was essentially defunct.

PAUL G. PIERPAOLI JR.

See also

Abolitionism; Democratic Party; Expansionism and Imperialism; Free Soil Party; Freemasonry; Garrison, William Lloyd; Polk, James Knox; Whigs.

References

Johnson, Reinhard O. *The Liberty Party, 1840–1848: Antislavery Third-Party Politics in the United States.* Baton Rouge: Louisiana State University Press, 2009.

Kraditor, Aileen K. *Means and Ends in American Abolitionism: Garrison and His Critics on Strategy and Tactics, 1834–1850.* Chicago: Ivan R. Dee, 1989.

Sewell, Richard H. *Ballots for Freedom: Antislavery Politics in the United States, 1837–1860.* New York: Oxford University Press, 1976.

Lincoln, Abraham

Birth Date: February 12, 1809
Death Date: April 15, 1865

U.S. congressman (1847–1849) and president of the United States (1861–1865). Abraham Lincoln was born near Hodgenville, Kentucky, on February 12, 1809. He grew up in relative obscurity, moving with his family to Indiana when he was seven years old. Lincoln had to work hard throughout his childhood and teen years at manual labor jobs, and so schooling was not a priority. Indeed, he attended a formal school for only 18 months. He was, however, an inquisitive youngster and made up for his educational shortfall by voracious reading.

By the time he was 21, Lincoln had settled in New Salem, Illinois, where he found work as a postmaster and shopkeeper. He also joined a local militia company. For a brief period during the Black Hawk War he served as its captain, although Lincoln saw no action during that conflict.

Lincoln first entered politics when he ran unsuccessfully for the Illinois General Assembly on the Whig Party ticket. Two years later, he ran again—this time successfully—for the state legislature, ultimately serving four consecutive terms in office. About that time, he also began to read for the law. In 1837, he moved to Springfield, Illinois, and opened a successful law practice in partnership with William H. Herndon.

In 1846, Lincoln ran successfully for the U.S. House of Representatives, taking office in 1847. Although Lincoln served only one two-year term in the House, he made a name for himself in Washington. He became known for his outspoken opposition to slavery and the Mexican-American War. As with many other northerners, Lincoln saw the Mexican War as being inextricably linked to the institution of slavery. He distrusted the James K. Polk administration, believing that it had precipitated the Mexican-American War based on false pretenses and sought to extend slavery into formerly Mexican lands.

Lincoln spoke out repeatedly against Polk, accusing him of chasing "military glory." In December 1847, Lincoln, joined by several of his fellow Whigs, introduced the so-called spot resolutions, which challenged the Polk administration to provide the precise location, or spot, where American blood was first spilled in April 1846. Polk had used the Thornton Affair of April 1846 in which U.S. and Mexican forces clashed in southern Texas as a partial pretext for the war declaration that year. Lincoln refused to let the resolutions die, despite the fact that most Democrats and a growing number of Whigs believed them to be counterproductive at best and unpatriotic at worst. Lincoln, however, replied that he was not attacking the war so much as he was attacking the president's execution of it. Nevertheless, Lincoln's actions, and the controversial speeches he gave on the subject, put an effective end to his legislative career. Several colleagues and confidants counseled Lincoln not to stand for reelection in 1848, and he left Congress in 1849.

Abraham Lincoln of Illinois served only one term in Congress (1847–1849) because of his opposition to both slavery and the Mexican-American War. (Library of Congress)

Lincoln, now a member of the new Republican Party, stayed out of elective politics until 1858, when he decided to challenge Democrat Stephen Douglas in a race for the U.S. Senate. Lincoln and Douglas engaged in a lively campaign of debates, during which the two men discussed the future of slavery in the territories. Although Lincoln lost the race, the 1858 election campaign catapulted Lincoln into the forefront of the Republican Party, and in 1860 he won its nomination for president.

The Democratic Party, now hopelessly split, ran two candidates for president, and the upstart Constitutional Union ran a compromise candidate. This four-way race resulted in Lincoln's victory, albeit with only 40 percent of the popular vote. Most southern Democrats refused to acknowledge Lincoln's victory, and the sectional crisis deepened when the states of the Deep South began to secede from the Union.

When Lincoln became president in March 1861, the Civil War was less than a month away. The first shots were fired at Fort Sumter on April 12, and Lincoln, with virtually no prior military experience, became a wartime president. Lincoln, who believed in the inviolability of the Union, chose to fight the war vigorously and in so doing earned the enmity and criticism of many, including some in his own administration. Lincoln's initial choices for commanders proved problematic, but as the war progressed, his choices became far wiser. He also became an excellent military strategist.

An orator of unequaled skill, Lincoln used his speaking ability to rally the nation and prepare it for a postwar world.

Challenged by a disgruntled Major General George B. McClellan, a Democrat, in 1864, Lincoln won reelection in spite of the pundits who had written his political epitaph. By then, Lincoln had already begun to lay out his plans for Reconstruction, the spirit of which was enunciated in his Second Inaugural Address, which promised "malice toward none" and "charity for all." His plans were derailed when he died from an assassin's bullet on April 15, 1865, in Washington, D.C., virtually ensuring that the Radical Republicans' Reconstruction policies would prevail.

PAUL G. PIERPAOLI JR.

See also
Congress, U.S.; Democratic Party; Opposition to the Mexican-American War, U.S.; Polk, James Knox; Republican Party; Slavery; Thornton Affair; Whigs.

References
Donald, David Herbert. *Lincoln.* New York: Simon & Schuster, 1996.
Goodwin, Doris Kearns. *Team of Rivals: The Political Genius of Abraham Lincoln.* New York: Simon & Schuster, 2006.

Lipantitlán, Battle of
See Fort Lipantitlán, Battle of

Literature

Although there is debate over the exact impact of the Mexican-American War on significant creative literature on the part of North American authors, the conflict certainly energized writers, novelists, and intellectuals—including such significant American intellectuals as Ralph Waldo Emerson and Henry David Thoreau—to cast a critical eye not only on the concept of Manifest Destiny but also on the validity and morality of the war effort and of the institution of slavery. While the Mexican War did not give birth to the transcendentalist movement, which began in Massachusetts in the mid-1830s, it did spur progressive thinking and reform, which in turn fueled the antiwar messages of numerous writers of the era.

Although war correspondents introduced the American public to sensationalist war coverage and largely propagated the concept of Manifest Destiny, or a belief in U.S. territorial expansion, the scene on the nonjournalistic front was more divided. On one side, a "poetical mania" overtook the nation, reflected in jingoistic poetry and a proliferation of now-forgotten narratives, letters, and diaries. Publishers raced to feed a reading public hungry for war chronicles. Nevertheless, in spite of the expansionist spirit that moved the nation before and during the war, the mood waxed increasingly critical, particularly among prominent American intellectuals and writers. Ralph Waldo Emerson claimed in his *Journals* that by

swallowing Mexico, the United States was swallowing a fatal dose of arsenic. Philanthropist and *New York Tribune* editor Horace Greeley raged against the "ruffianly and piratical" treatment of Mexico. James Russell Lowell denounced the war in his satirical *Biglow Papers* as a pretext for the extension of slavery.

Antislavery protests climaxed with the 1848 Treaty of Guadalupe Hidalgo. Walt Whitman, initially a supporter of the war, then joined the ranks of abolitionists such as John Greenleaf Whittier, William Ellery Channing, James Russell Lowell, and William Lloyd Garrison. The most prominent protester was Henry David Thoreau, jailed for his refusal to pay taxes to a government "that condoned slavery and war," later claiming in his treatise "Civil Disobedience" (1849) that governments are tyrannical when they deny the individual's right to integrity.

In the newly conquered borderlands, the literature of the Mexican-American War is important primarily for having fed into a nascent Mexican-American literary tradition, inspiring *corridos,* or popular ballads, that voiced Mexican Americans' political anxieties and resentment about the conflict. *Corridos* were ballads in which border heroes like Ignacio and Jacinto Treviño and Aniceto Pizaña valiantly fought for their rights against Americans. This was a signal that border conflicts would not end with the Treaty of Guadalupe Hidalgo, just as the abolitionist controversies in American literature were to culminate in the years leading to the Civil War.

ANNA M. WITTMANN

See also
Abolitionism; Emerson, Ralph Waldo; Greeley, Horace; Garrison, William Lloyd; Guadalupe Hidalgo, Treaty of; Lowell, James Russell; Manifest Destiny; Opposition to the Mexican-American War, U.S.; Slavery; Thoreau, Henry David; Transcendental Club; War Correspondents; Whitman, Walter (Walt); Whittier, John Greenleaf.

References
Frangaviglia, Richard V., and Douglas W. Richmond, eds. *Dueling Eagles: Reinterpreting the U.S-Mexican War, 1846–1848.* Fort Worth: Texas Christian University Press, 2000.
Johannsen, Robert W. *To the Halls of the Montezumas: The Mexican War in the American Imagination.* New York: Oxford University Press, 1985.
Morison, Samuel Eliot, Frederick Merk, and Frank Freidel. *Dissent in Three American Wars.* Cambridge, MA: Harvard University Press, 1970.
Rodríguez, Jaime Javier. *The Literatures of the U.S.-Mexican War: Narrative, Time, and Identity.* Austin: University of Texas Press, 2010.
Weems, John Edward. *To Conquer a Peace: The War between the United States and Mexico.* New York: Doubleday, 1974.

Lithographs

The Mexican-American War occurred at the same time that lithography was becoming the established art form in America for the production of souvenir prints. In an era just prior to the onset of pictorial journalism and at the dawn of photography, such prints

Lithograph depicting the death of Colonel Pierce M. Butler at the Battle of Churubusco on August 20, 1847. Butler commanded the volunteer South Carolina Palmetto Regiment during the 1847 campaign from Veracruz to Mexico City. (Library of Congress)

were the main source for visual communication of contemporary and historical events. One of the leading practitioners of this reproductive art, Nathaniel Currier (1813–1888), is credited with developing new lithographic techniques in the creation of prints, standardizing the process of production, developing new lithographic crayons for colorization, and above all greatly improving the marketing and distribution of prints.

The beginning of the war with Mexico in 1846 provided a suitable outlet for lithographic prints. Lithographic publishers were eager to produce pictures of the battles and portraits of the leading commanders that would find a ready market among the art-buying public, and the companies of Nathaniel Currier, Napoleon Sarony and Henry B. Major, James S. Baillie, and David W. Kellogg emerged as the leading purveyors of lithographic prints during this period. While the majority of these popular prints were inaccurate from a factual perspective, they were frequently based on newspaper accounts and tried to present a realistic impression of the events, but often veiled in heroic and nationalistic symbolism.

Currier, more than his competitors, single-handedly created a market for prints of the Mexican-American War. He published a total of 70 lithographs depicting scenes of the war, and many of these appeared shortly after the actual events, so they were remarkable for their currency. The fact that so many were published suggests that there was a ready market for such iconography. He employed a large pool of talented artists, but their names were not included on the finished prints with one exception, that of John Cameron, who in fact was not the artist but the lithographer.

Prints showing individual deeds of valor were a popular subject, such as the "Capture of Mexican General Vega by Captain May" at Resaca de la Palma, "Colonel Harney at the Dragoon Fight at Medelin near Vera Cruz," and the deaths of Colonel Pierce M. Butler, Lieutenant Colonel Henry Clay, and Major Samuel Ringgold. Currier also published two naval scenes, one showing the bombardment of Veracruz, the other an attack by U.S. gunboats on the city of San Juan de Ulúa.

In contrast to these pictures of the war is the series of large, high-quality lithographic plates published in portfolio form by George Wilkins Kendall after paintings by Carl Nebel. Both had been in Mexico prior to the fighting, and once the war began, Kendall, who rode as a volunteer with Captain Ben McCulloch's company of Texas mounted rifles, sent back accounts of the fighting that were published in various newspapers. The finished lithographs, accompanied by a text written by Kendall, portrayed major battles such as Monterrey, Buena Vista, Cerro Gordo, Chapultepec, and Palo Alto.

While many of the popular lithographs of the day are inaccurate, they provide a glimpse into contemporary attitudes toward war and soldiering of mid-19th-century America. These include ideas of gallantry, glory, heroes, leadership, and the representation of death, as well as of the enemy. As such, they provided a misleading idea of war to a populace at home.

Peter Harrington

See also
Art; Currier, Nathaniel.

References

Sandweiss, Martha A., Rick Stewart, and Ben W. Huseman. *Eyewitness to War: Prints and Daguerreotypes of the Mexican War, 1846–1848*. Fort Worth, TX: Amon Carter Museum, 1989.
Tyler, Ronnie C. *The Mexican War: A Lithographic Record*. Austin: Texas State Historical Association, 1973.

Logistics, Mexican

Logistics refers to activities that support the strategy and tactics of an armed force, including the mobilization of troops and subsequently supplying them with weapons, ammunition, uniforms, equipment, and such necessities as food, medical services, and pay, both in camp and during military campaigns. In all these matters, the Mexican army of the mid-19th century was woefully inadequate.

Part of the problem was the lack of funds or their diversion away from intended purposes. Mexico was still underdeveloped, and its total government income at the outbreak of the war in 1846 was only one-thirteenth that of the United States. The government was chronically starved for money and laden with debt, and the American naval blockade during the war all but eliminated the flow of income from customs duties. A great deal of the money scraped together for military purposes was spent buying outdated weapons abroad because none were produced in Mexico. Too much of the available money was wasted on the elaborate uniforms and living costs of an officer corps that was too large, complacent, and incompetent, comprising as many as 18 officers for every 5 soldiers. Money for the pay and allowances of enlisted men was frequently skimmed by corrupt generals who pocketed the pay and allowances of "ghost soldiers," men who had died or deserted but were still reported as part of the army. When the soldiers were paid less than they had been promised or only at long intervals, morale declined precipitously and desertions increased.

Another logistical problem was the complete lack of a quartermaster corps to procure and distribute supplies for the army, coupled with an absence of a system of depots for the storage and distribution of supplies and equipment in the field. There was also no ordnance department, which could have standardized arms and ammunition and their distribution. Because Mexico largely lacks navigable rivers that would have made travel and transportation easier, Mexican fighting forces had to struggle to move long distances on crude and difficult roads through harsh and thinly settled terrain and adverse weather conditions. With no quartermasters or depots, armies could not take with them everything they needed, nor could they be supplied from the rear. Troops carried their arms, ammunition, and tools; some baggage wagons were available, but the men lacked even essentials such as hats and blankets and usually took with them only a bit of raw meat and perhaps some corn and tortillas. They were forced to find food and replacement clothing as they moved and were largely responsible for feeding themselves.

Army leaders took with them drafts on the Mexican Treasury to pay merchants and farmers for what they needed, but few suppliers trusted the government enough to accept them. Some merchants and sutlers moved with the army but disappeared when they realized that the soldiers had little or no money and the generals were paying them with potentially worthless treasury drafts. This meant that soldiers had to be sent out daily to procure food and clothing from mistrustful locals who were experienced at hiding what they owned from tax collectors and other officials. A great deal of time and effort was wasted in this way, and armies often arrived at their destination half-starved, exhausted, and in tatters. Some transport of necessary supplies was achieved by hiring *cargadores,* men who could carry huge loads on their backs for great distances. In the case of artillery, civilian contractors were engaged not only to transport the guns on the line of march but even to haul them onto the field and reposition them during battles.

Medical facilities and services were largely lacking in the Mexican army, leading to unacceptable rates of attrition due to disease and accident during normal service, an excessive rate of deaths among those wounded in battle, and a higher than normal death rate and incidence of health problems among veterans years after the hostilities ceased.

Some experts believe that the armies Mexico put into the field during the war could not have carried out their duties at all without the services supplied by *soldaderas,* the mob of camp followers consisting largely of the women and children of soldiers that moved with the army, foraging for food, cooking, mending uniforms, and tending the sick and wounded. Although they slowed the armies and presented problems to the generals trying to organize the army for battle, they provided almost all the logistical support for some military units and many became casualties themselves.

Joseph M. McCarthy

See also
Army Life, Mexican and U.S.; Camp Followers, Mexican and U.S.; Foraging; Logistics, U.S.; Mexico; Mexico, Army; Mexico, 1821–1854; Military Tactics, Mexican; United States Army; Weapons, Mexican.

References

Chartrand, René. *Santa Anna's Mexican Army, 1821–48*. Oxford, UK: Osprey, 2004.
Clary, David A. *Eagles and Empire: The United States, Mexico, and the Struggle for a Continent*. New York: Bantam Books, 2009.
DePalo, William A., Jr. *The Mexican National Army, 1822–1852*. College Station: Texas A&M University Press, 1997.
Paulus, Robert D. "Pack Mules and Surf Boats: Logistics in the Mexican War." *Army Logistician* 29, no. 6 (1997): 34–40.

Logistics, U.S.

Logistics refers to the development, procurement, receipt, storage, and issuance of military matériel and supplies and the provision of support services. In the U.S. Army during the Mexican-American War, logistics requirements included food, water, uniforms, shoes, leather goods, weapons, ammunition, wagons, horses, and boats, as well as medicine, maintenance, and transportation.

At the national level, logistics were managed by the Commissary, Ordnance, and Quartermaster Departments. The Commissary General procured, stored, and delivered foodstuffs. The Ordnance Department bought, manufactured, stored, maintained, and delivered personal weapons, artillery, and ammunition. The Quartermaster Department procured, stored, issued, and repaired all uniforms and personal items, general supplies, tenting, wagons, and horses and mules. It also provided all transportation services. The Surgeon General provided medical services and medical supplies to include the establishment of hospitals and medical evacuation. The departments were administrative offices that reported directly to the secretary of war. At the beginning of the conflict, each was a small organization staffed and financially resourced for peacetime operations.

Because the logistics departments supported the U.S. Army on the frontier and had just wound down from support of the Second Seminole War (1835–1842), each was accustomed to providing logistics to an army distant from populated areas. The logistics departments were thus highly experienced and blessed with long-term leadership. Brigadier General Thomas S. Jesup had been quartermaster general since 1818, and Colonel George Bomford had been chief of ordnance since 1832.

Each department had officers and enlisted men assigned to it. Officer authorizations were low, however, and the chiefs of the departments often requested additional manpower. In wartime, manpower was insufficient because the department chief would dispatch officers to act as the commissary officer, ordnance officer, or quartermaster officer for armies in the field. These technical officers would establish and run depots and would purchase supplies in the local areas. The departments would, at times, assign officers down to the division level to act as the senior logistics experts in their commodity. At the regimental level and lower, line officers were detailed to perform logistics duties. The more technical the work, such as weapons repair, the more likely that services were consolidated at division and army level in a forward depot.

Prior to the Mexican-American War, the logistics services suffered from two major obstacles that hindered transition to war. First, the War Department did not have a strong logistics requirements planning function. When the Army of Observation was dispatched to Corpus Christi in 1845, no specific logistics requirements had been developed, even though the U.S. Army had been planning for the possibility of war for several years. Second, Congress did not authorize funding for increased purchasing to support a war until May 1846. These shortcomings meant that logistics services were forced to award last-minute contracts and rapidly expand operations to support the field armies. This tended to result in higher costs, shoddy quality of goods, strained transportation, and increased reliance on local purchase and foraging.

The Ordnance Department rapidly met initial requirements because it had ample stored supplies of arms and ammunition. In an interesting development, the Ordnance Department created a rocket and howitzer battery with 12-pounder mountain howitzers and Hale rockets. The battery landed at Veracruz in March 1847 in the first assault wave and fought in every battle in Scott's Mexico City Campaign. The other logistics departments faced greater challenges. The Medical Department had to contract for doctors and purchase supplies. Most medical supplies were procured in New Orleans and were easily delivered to the armies. Although the commissary general struggled with the lack of provisions along the frontier, most foodstuffs were available along the Gulf Coast and could be purchased there or in major U.S. cities and shipped to the war zones. In addition, forces locally procured foodstuffs in Mexico to provide variety and fresh goods.

The Quartermaster Department faced the greatest difficulties as it had to provide uniforms, tents, and transportation. Volunteer units were required by law to arrive with their own uniforms, but most did not. The quartermaster thus had to rapidly expand uniform manufacture and increased by 10 times the number of government-hired tailors and seamstresses. The sizeable expansion of the army resulted in a significant shortage of tents. Heavy canvas was not readily available, so General Jesup awarded contracts using lighter-grade fabric. These tents rapidly disintegrated in harsh winter conditions and led to many complaints.

Transportation became the major logistics issue. Wagon making was a local manufacturing industry; thus, the Quartermaster Department was unable to award contracts for all the wagon requirements to a few major producers and had to decentralize to small companies. Despite using standardized wagon specifications, the delivered wagons came in a large number of sizes; many of the spare parts were not interchangeable. This created problems in repairing wagons in the field. The Quartermaster Department responded by hiring wagonwrights and deployed them to Texas and Mexico. The Quartermaster Department also had to purchase horses and mules either in the United States or locally. Finally, it had to purchase and operate shipping to deliver supplies to the armies up the Rio Grande and in Mexico. In the end, the Quartermaster Department purchased 38 sailing ships and 35 steamers.

All of the logistics departments relied on deploying the best personnel forward and hiring private contractors to meet personnel shortfalls. Despite a slow start, logistics was not a major concern for the U.S. Army during most of the war with Mexico.

GEORGE EATON

See also

Foraging; Logistics, Mexican; Military Contractors, U.S.; Point Isabel; Quartermaster Services, U.S. and Mexican; Scott, Winfield; Surfboats; Taylor, Zachary; United States Army; Veracruz, Landing at and Siege of; Weapons, U.S.

References

Huston, James A. *Sinews of War: Army Logistics 1775–1953*. Washington, DC: Office of the Chief of Military History, 1966.

Kindsvatter, Peter S. "Howitzers, Rockets, and Siege Guns: The Ordnance Department in the Vera Cruz Campaign of 1847." *Ordnance Magazine* (Winter 2000): 8–12 and (Spring 2000): 6–13.

Paulus, Robert D. "Pack Mules and Surf Boats, Logistics in the Mexican War." *Army Logistician* 29, no. 6 (1997): 34–40.

Risch, Erna. *Quartermaster Support of the Army: A History of the Corps, 1775–1939*. Washington, DC: U.S. Army Center of Military History, 1989.

Lombardini, Manuel María
Birth Date: July 23, 1802
Death Date: December 2, 1853

Mexican army general and ally of General Antonio López de Santa Anna. Born on July 23, 1802, in Mexico City, Manuel María Lombardini joined the Spanish army at age 12 during the war for independence, fighting with the Patriots of Tacubaya. He later left the service for a brief time but rejoined the Mexican army in 1832 and became a devotee of General Antonio López de Santa Anna, who came to regard Lombardini with considerable affection. Lombardini successfully commanded a brigade during an uprising at Puebla in 1834, and two years later he marched north to join Santa Anna's army after the debacle at the Battle of San Jacinto during the Texas Revolution. Then, in 1838 Lombardini led a force that repelled the French at Veracruz during the 1838–1839 Pastry War.

When the Mexican-American War began in 1846 Lombardini commanded a division in the Mexican Army of the East, headquartered at Veracruz. After the Mexicans' stunning reversals at the Battles of Palo Alto and Resaca de la Palma in the spring of 1846, he commanded the 1st Division of the newly formed Army of the North, headquartered at San Luis Potosí. His most notable service during the war occurred during the February 22–23, 1847, Battle of Buena Vista, where on the second day he fearlessly spearheaded a frontal assault against the Americans' left flank that brought about its collapse during the early hours of the engagement. In the process, he was seriously wounded and compelled to turn over his command to General Francisco Pérez. Witnesses on the scene, including an American dragoon, marveled at the valor of Lombardini and his men.

Forced to sit out several months of the war while he recuperated from his wound, Lombardini took up command of Mexican defenses at Mexico City in August 1847, just as Major General Winfield Scott's army moved inexorably toward the capital city. Lombardini's men put up a determined resistance, especially after the fall of Chapultepec and the Belén Gate, but ultimately were no match for the Americans. When the collapse of Mexico City's defenses seemed inevitable, Santa Anna gave Lombardini temporary command of the Mexican army with orders to evacuate the capital. In July 1848, shortly after José Joaquín de Herrera had been reinstalled as president, Lombardini took part in the campaign that crushed General Mariano Paredes y Arrillaga's antigovernment coup.

By 1853 Lombardini was in command of the entire Mexican army and that same year served as interim president between February 8 and April 20 after a coup (in which he also participated) toppled the government of General Mariano Arista. He then yielded power to his old friend and benefactor Santa Anna, who had returned from exile in Colombia. Santa Anna then appointed Lombardini commandant general of the Federal District (Mexico City and environs), but Lombardini died unexpectedly in Mexico City on December 2, 1853.

PAUL G. PIERPAOLI JR.

See also

Arista, Mariano; Buena Vista, Battle of; Chapultepec, Battle of; Herrera, José Joaquín de; Mexico City, Battle for; Palo Alto, Battle of; Pastry War; Pérez, Franciso; Resaca de la Palma, Battle of; San Jacinto, Battle of; Santa Anna, Antonio López de; Texas Revolution.

References

DePalo, William A., Jr. *The Mexican National Army, 1822–1852*. Albuquerque: University of New Mexico Press, 1997.

Clary, David A. *Eagles and Empire: The United States, Mexico, and the Struggle of a Continent*. New York: Bantam Books, 2009.

Orozco Linares, Fernando. *Gobernantes de México*. Mexico City: Panorama Editorial, 1985.

Longstreet, James
Birth Date: January 8, 1821
Death Date: January 2, 1904

U.S. and Confederate Army officer. Born in Edgefield District, South Carolina, on January 8, 1821, James Longstreet spent his early years in Augusta, Georgia, but, on the death of his father, moved with his mother to Somerville, Alabama. Longstreet graduated from the U.S. Military Academy, West Point, in 1842. As a second lieutenant in the 4th U.S. Infantry, Longstreet served in Louisiana and in Missouri. He then served with the 8th Infantry in Florida.

During the Mexican-American War, Longstreet first served under Major General Zachary Taylor in northern Mexico, where he took part in the Battles of Palo Alto, Resaca de la Palma, and Monterrey. He ably commanded troops during heavy street fighting in Monterrey. Longstreet then served under Major General Winfield Scott during the Mexico City Campaign. He was brevetted to captain following the Battle of Churubusco on August 20, 1847, and to major after the Battle of El Molino del Rey that September 8. Longstreet was badly wounded in the Battle of Chapultepec four days later, on September 12.

After the war, Longstreet remained in the army. He served on the frontier in Texas, primarily at Fort Martin Scott and at Fort Bliss with the 8th Infantry Regiment. In 1858 he was appointed paymaster and received promotion to major.

Future Confederate lieutenant general James Longstreet was a lieutenant at the start of the Mexican-American War. He was breveted to captain and to major for his roles in the battles of Churubusco and El Molino del Rey. Longstreet was badly wounded at Chapultepec. (Getty Images)

With the beginning of the Civil War, Major Longstreet resigned from the U.S. Army on June 1, 1861, and accepted a commission as a brigadier general in the Confederate Army on June 17. He earned recognition in the First Battle of Bull Run/Manassas, and was promoted to major general on October 7, 1861. Longstreet commanded a division in the Peninsula Campaign and saw action at the Battles of Williamsburg and Seven Pines/Fair Oaks, and at the Seven Days' Battles.

General Robert E. Lee then dispatched Longstreet, in command of five divisions representing over half of Lee's infantry, to join with forces under Major General Thomas J. Jackson and defeat Union Major General John Pope's Army of Virginia in the Second Battle of Bull Run/Manassas. Although he opposed Lee's invasion of Maryland, Longstreet fought well at South Mountain and in the Battle of Antietam/Sharpsburg. Promoted to lieutenant general in October 1862, in the Battle of Fredericksburg (December 13, 1862), Longstreet's I Corps held Marye's Heights, defending it against numerous costly Federal assaults.

In early 1863 Lee sent Longstreet on foraging operations (the Suffolk Campaign), and he thus missed the Battle of Chancellorsville. Following the death of Jackson from wounds sustained in that battle, Longstreet became Lee's chief subordinate, known as Lee's "Old War Horse." Longstreet opposed Lee's decision to fight at Gettysburg and especially Lee's failed frontal assault (Pickett's Charge) on July 3, 1863.

Sent west with his men to reinforce General Braxton Bragg, Longstreet arrived there in time to fight in the Battle of Chickamauga, where he was able to take advantage of Major General William Rosecrans's critical error that shifted a Union division out of the line. Then while Bragg besieged Chattanooga, Longstreet moved against Major General Ambrose E. Burnside at Knoxville, but Longstreet failed to dislodge him and had to begin a siege, which denied Bragg support at Chattanooga.

In April 1864, Longstreet rejoined Lee in Virginia, and he and his men fought effectively against the Union forces in Grant's Overland Campaign of 1864. Wounded in the Battle of the Wilderness, he relinquished command to recuperate. Returning to duty that November, Longstreet fought in the remaining actions of the war near Petersburg and Richmond, serving with Lee's Army of Northern Virginia to the final surrender at Appomattox Court House on April 9, 1865.

After the war, Longstreet alienated southerners when he became a Republican, renewed his old friendship with Ulysses S. Grant, and served in a variety of U.S. government posts, including minister to Turkey (1880). He published his memoirs in 1896. Longstreet initially settled in New Orleans, Louisiana, but he later moved to Gainesville, Georgia, where he died on January 2, 1904.

SPENCER C. TUCKER

See also

Chapultepec, Battle of; Churubusco, Battle of; El Molino del Rey, Battle of; Mexico City Campaign; Monterrey, Battle of; Palo Alto, Battle of; Resaca de la Palma, Battle of.

References

Eckenrode, H. J., and Bryan Conrad. *James Longstreet: Lee's War Horse.* Chapel Hill: University of North Carolina, 1936.

Longstreet, James. *From Manassas to Appomattox.* Philadelphia: J. B. Lippincott, 1896. Reprint edited and with an introduction by James I. Robertson Jr. Bloomington: Indiana University Press, 1960.

Piston, William Garrett. *Lee's Tarnished General: James Longstreet and His Place in Southern History.* Athens: University of Georgia Press, 1987.

Wert, Jeffery D. *General James Longstreet.* New York: Simon and Schuster, 1993.

Loreto

Small port city in Baja California along the Gulf of California (Sea of Cortez). Situated about two-thirds of the way down the Baja Peninsula on the east coast, Loreto is on relatively flat terrain (averaging about 32 feet above sea level); to the west is a large mountain range known as the Sierra de la Giganta. The climate of Loreto is hot and dry, although summers witness a monsoon season that brings elevated humidity and frequent brief but intense thunderstorms. During the Mexican-American War, Loreto was little more than a small fishing village and minor port, probably with fewer than 1,000 people.

On October 4, 1847, U.S. Navy commander Thomas O. Selfridge arrived off the coast of Loreto in the sloop of war *Dale*. The following day, he led ashore a landing party of some 100 marines and sailors to search for weapons. After a thorough search of the town and its environs, Selfridge's force confiscated three cannons, a musket, and numerous lances. The Americans departed the next day, and the town saw no other action during the conflict, although it was subjected to the U.S. naval blockade.

Today, Loreto remains a small town with only 10,250 permanent residents. It has become a minor tourist destination, especially for Americans visiting Baja California, many of whom fly into Loreto's international airport. Loreto is also known for its excellent sports fishing, which attracts many anglers.

PAUL G. PIERPAOLI JR.

See also

Baja California; Blockade, Naval; Gulf of California (Mar de Cortés); United States Navy.

References

Bauer, K. Jack. *Surfboats and Horse Marines: U.S. Naval Operations in the Mexican War.* Annapolis, MD: U.S. Naval Institute, 1969.

Cleary, David A. *Eagles and Empire: The United States, Mexico, and the Struggle for a Continent.* New York: Bantam Books, 2009.

Loring, William Wing
Birth Date: December 4, 1818
Death Date: December 30, 1886

U.S. and Confederate Army officer. William Wing Loring was born on December 4, 1818, in Wilmington, North Carolina. When he was quite young, he moved with his family to Saint Augustine, Florida. At age 14, he joined the Florida militia and saw action against the Seminoles at the beginning of the Second Seminole War (1835–1842). The following year, against his father's admonitions, he went to Texas to fight in the Texas Revolution. His father insisted on his return, and the young Loring came back to Florida, where he saw more action during the Second Seminole War, ultimately rising to the rank of second lieutenant.

Loring then attended boarding school in Virginia and studied at Georgetown University from 1830 to 1840. He then read for the law and was admitted to the bar in 1842. From 1843 to 1845, he served in the Florida House of Representatives while at the same time practicing law.

In 1846, Loring, now a major, commanded the U.S. Mounted Rifles and was dispatched to the Mexican-American War. In 1847, his regiment participated in Major General Winfield Scott's Mexico City Campaign, which began in Veracruz in March 1847. Loring performed poorly at the Battle of Cerro Gordo but redeemed himself at the Battle of Contreras. On September 13, 1847, Loring was severely wounded in the Battle of Chapultepec on the outskirts of Mexico City. The third wound he had sustained since the start of the conflict, it resulted in the amputation of his left arm. In October 1847, Loring was ordered back to the United States for recuperation. For his service during the Mexican-American War, Loring was brevetted first to lieutenant colonel and then to colonel.

Loring remained in the army after his Mexican-American War service, serving as commander of the Oregon Territory for several years and engaging in sporadic skirmishes there with Native Americans. In 1856 he was promoted to colonel, and in 1859 he traveled to Europe where he studied European military tactics. He visited numerous countries, including Egypt and Turkey.

When the Civil War began in 1861, Loring declared for the Confederacy, and he was appointed a brigadier general in the Confederate Army on May 20, 1861. He was given command of troops in western Virginia (now West Virginia). Loring saw action at the Battle of Cheat Mountain in September. In December, Loring's brigade was assigned to Major General Thomas J. "Stonewall" Jackson's division. In January 1862, the two clashed over Jackson's decision to position Loring and three brigades at Romney in western Virginia, which Loring believed to be an exposed and dangerous position. Loring complained to the War Department, which ordered Jackson to recall Loring and his men. Jackson regarded this as an intrusion regarding his command authority and almost resigned over it.

Loring received promotion to major general in February 1862 and was given command of the Army of Southwestern Virginia; that December he was transferred to command the Army of Mississippi. During Ulysses S. Grant's attempt to assault Vicksburg from the north during the winter and early spring of 1863, Loring famously stood on a cotton bale, exhorting his men to "Give them blizzards!," a reference to the heavy fire his troops were concentrating on Union forces at Fort Pemberton. From then on, he was given the nickname "Old Blizzards." Loring stayed on during the ensuing Second Vicksburg Campaign of April 1–July 4, 1863, which ended in a Union victory, but escaped capture.

Loring subsequently served under Lieutenant General Leonidas Polk, and when Polk was killed in action at Pine Mountain, Georgia, in July 1864, Loring took command of his corps in the Army of Tennessee. Loring saw action during the Atlanta Campaign and the Carolinas Campaign. When the Civil War ended in 1865, Loring left the United States, eventually making his way to Egypt, where he served as a senior army officer until 1879. He finally returned home, published *A Confederate Soldier in Egypt* in 1884, and died in New York City on December 30, 1886.

PAUL G. PIERPAOLI JR.

See also

Cerro Gordo, Battle of; Chapultepec, Battle of; Contreras, Battle of; Mexico City Campaign; Scott, Winfield; Texas Revolution.

References

Rankin, Thomas M. *Stonewall Jackson's Romney Campaign, January 1–February 20, 1862.* Lynchburg, VA: H. E. Howard, 1994.

Sauers, Richard A. *The Devastating Hand of War: Romney, West Virginia, During the Civil War.* Glen Ferris, WV: Gauley Mountain Press, 2000.

Wessels, William L. *Born to Be a Soldier: The Military Career of William Wing Loring of St. Augustine, Florida.* Fort Worth: Texas Christian University Press, 1971.

Los Angeles

Founded in 1792 as a pueblo (as opposed to a presidio or a mission settlement) by settlers of mixed nationalities hailing primarily from northwestern Mexico, Nuestra Señora de la Reina de los Angeles de Porciuncula, or simply Los Angeles, was a major town in the Mexican territory of Alta California (modern-day Southern California). It had approximately 1,250 full-time residents at the end of the Mexican era in 1848.

Los Angeles is located several miles east of the Pacific coast in the Los Angeles Basin and is ringed by mountains. It is also partly located in the San Fernando Valley. The Los Angeles River, which is largely dry during the summer and autumn months, bisects the city. Ruled by a town council that shared authority with military officers, mid-19th-century Los Angeles was primarily an agricultural community, although trade and light manufacturing would develop over time.

Residents of Mexican Los Angeles practiced subsistence farming, although by the 1830s brandy and wine produced in the region were exported along with hides and tallow. Although more women than men lived in Los Angeles in the 1820s, by 1844 there were more males than females. Established by settlers with an anticlerical bent, Los Angeles did not claim its first church until 1822. By the middle of the 1830s, nearly a third of the citizens were from areas outside Mexico, and most of them were Americans. By then, the local economy was driven by agriculture and cattle raising, crafts, and a thriving prostitution trade.

Population of Los Angeles, 1800–1870	
Year	Population
1800	315
1810	365
1820	650
1830	1,300
1840	2,240
1850	1,610
1860	4,385
1870	5,730

Los Angeles was initially governed by military commissioners (*comisionados*) until 1822, when the city came under full civilian control. Locals raised cattle on large ranchos, which contributed to the hide and tallow trade, and supplemented their diets and income by hunting and growing crops like wheat and beans. At least a third of the artisans of Los Angeles were non-Mexicans by the mid-1830s, as foreigners came in increasing numbers to the area by sea and via the Overland Route from the United States. Some 30 additional families arrived there from New Mexico in the 1840s. Frequently, the growing town was caught up in the North-South rivalries of Mexican-era California, and for a brief period in 1836 Los Angeles became the provincial capital.

By the 1840s there was a growing American presence in the region, and during the Mexican-American War the Californios

Depiction of Los Angeles, California, in 1853. Founded in 1792, Los Angeles was the site of several battles during the Mexican-American War. (National Oceanic and Atmospheric Administration)

of Los Angeles put up a relatively fierce resistance. After initially surrendering early in the conflict in 1846, the harsh restrictions imposed on the citizenry by the American military occupation led to a revolt organized by José María Flores. On September 24, 1846, U.S. forces were forced to withdraw from the city, and the Californios won fleeting victories at the Battle of the Old Woman's Gun (October 8, 1846) and the Battle of San Pascual (December 6, 1846).

Eventually, U.S. forces combined to suppress the Californios, and the position of the latter in Los Angeles society dissipated during subsequent years. While some of the prominent citizens of the Mexican era, such as Manuel Sepúlveda, managed to hold on to their land and power, others, such as Pío de Jesús Pico, met with economic and social decline.

During the California Gold Rush period Los Angeles turned into a prototypically violent cattle town, with cattle far outnumbering people and the citizens enduring the nation's highest murder rate. The city grew quickly after the Civil War, especially after the Southern Pacific Railway linked it to the rest of the United States in 1876. By 1900, its population had reached 100,000 people, and it was growing rapidly. In the 1920s, the Los Angeles area became prominent for its oil reserves, and by 1923 it was producing one-third of the world's oil. That same decade, the motion picture industry established itself in the city, which proved a major economic boon. Thereafter, millions of Americans were drawn to the city because of its climate and economic opportunities, and by midcentury the region had become well populated with industry and defense-related manufacturers. After World War II, Los Angeles's population exploded, and it is now the second-largest city in the United States with some 3.85 million people.

RANDAL BEEMAN

See also

California; California Theater of War, Overview; Californios; Flores, José María; Gold Rush, California; Pico, Pío de Jesús; San Pascual, Battle of.

References

Caughey, John W. *California: History of a Remarkable State.* Englewood Cliffs, NJ: Prentice Hall, 1982.
Dewitt, Howard A. *The California Dream.* Dubuque, IA: Kendall Hunt, 1999.
Griswold del Castillo, Richard. *The Los Angeles Barrio: A Social History.* Berkeley: University of California Press, 1982.
Pitt, Leonard. *The Decline of the Californios: A Social History of the Spanish Speaking Californians, 1846–1890.* Berkeley: University of California Press, 1966.

Los Niños Héroes

Six young cadets who died defending Mexico City's Chapultepec Castle, which at the time served as the Mexican Military Academy. Los Niños Héroes (the Boy Heroes) were attempting to defend the fortress from attacking U.S. forces during the Battle of Chapultepec on September 12–13, 1847. Six of the cadets died in the struggle—Juan de la Barrera, Juan Escutia, Francisco Márquez, Agustín Melgar, Fernando Montes de Oca, and Vicente Suárez. Although their commanders, Generals Nicolás Bravo Rueda and José Mariano Monterde, had ordered them to fall back from Chapultepec as U.S. forces approached, the six cadets instead supposedly resisted the invaders until all were killed. Popular legend maintains that the last survivor leapt from the Chapultepec Castle wrapped in the Mexican flag to prevent the enemy from taking it.

Although the young men lapsed from the national historic memory for approximately 25 years, the patriotic euphoria that accompanied Mexico's victory over the French invaders in 1867 set the groundwork for the cadets' subsequent commemoration as national heroes. Beginning in 1871 and continuing throughout the 20th century, a host of Mexican military organizations and government officials reworked the legend to fulfill their own particular agendas.

Juan de la Barrera was born in Mexico City in 1828. During the attack on Chapultepec, he was a lieutenant in the military engineers and died defending a gun battery located near the entrance to the academy. Juan Escutia was born in Tepic, Nayarit, in 1827 and was a second lieutenant in an artillery company. Born in Guadalajara, Jalisco, in 1834, Francisco Márquez belonged to the first company of cadets at the time of the battle. Márquez's personnel record states that his bullet-riddled body was found alongside that of Escutia. Only 13, he was the youngest of the six Héroes. Agustín Melgar, who was born in Chihuahua in 1829, tried to stop the Americans on the north side of the castle. He shot and killed one American soldier before taking refuge behind some mattresses. When he was wounded, his comrades placed him on a table, where his body was found on September 15. Fernando Montes de Oca was born in Azcapotzalco in 1829; his role in the battle is unclear. Vicente Suárez, born in Puebla in 1833, was killed defending his sentry post during the battle. Suárez reportedly shot one American attacker and stabbed another in the stomach with his bayonet before being killed at his post in hand-to-hand combat.

The bodies of the six cadets were buried on the grounds at the Chapultepec Castle, in a location that remained uncertain. In 1947, however, their remains were finally located and identified. On September 27, 1952, the cadets were reinterred at the Monument to Heroic Cadets in Chapultepec. In addition to the large monument and park, many buildings and streets in Mexico City are named Los Niños Héroes to memorialize the courage of the cadets.

CHARLENE T. OVERTURF

See also

Bravo Rueda, Nicolás; Chapultepec, Battle of.

References

García Muñoz, María Elena, and Ernesto Fritsche Aceves. "Los niños héroes, de la realidad al mito." Unpublished BA thesis, Universidad Nacional Autónoma de México, 1989.

Marble monument at the entrance of Chapultepec Park in Mexico City dedicated to Los Niños Héroes, the teenage cadets of the Mexican Military Academy who died fighting U.S. forces in the Battle of Chapultepec. (Louise Rivard/Dreamstime.com)

Johnson, Lyman L. "Digging Up Cuauhtémoc." In *Death, Dismemberment, and Memory: Body Politics in Latin America*, edited by Lyman L. Johnson, 207–244. Albuquerque: University of New Mexico Press, 2004.

Louisiana Purchase
Event Date: 1803

Land acquisition by the Thomas Jefferson administration on May 2, 1803, that added approximately 828,800 square miles of territory to the United States. The United States purchased the territory from Napoleonic France for a total cost of $15 million. The Louisiana Purchase encompassed portions of 14 states and 2 Canadian provinces west of the Mississippi River and included the strategic port city of New Orleans. It augmented the U.S. landmass by some 140 percent and included a population of about 200,000 people—most of whom were Native Americans.

At the time, some Americans questioned Jefferson's ability to engage in such a deal, but the president sought to take advantage of the French Revolution and Napoleonic Wars, which had left France strapped for cash. He also asserted that the purchase was

a strategic necessity for the United States, arguing that control of New Orleans and the lower Mississippi River was crucial to American security. Almost immediately after the purchase, Jefferson authorized the Lewis and Clark Expedition to survey the territory. A Lemhi Shoshone woman named Sacajawea provided invaluable guidance to the expedition over the treacherous Rocky Mountains west to Oregon. She also helped secure cordial relations with Native Americans along the way.

Indeed, the Louisiana Purchase offered the United States a golden opportunity to limit the influence of foreign powers in the west, to gain control over the Native American populations of North America, and to secure western lands for future settlement. It also posed some serious challenges. The territory was inhabited by numerous Native American tribes, most of whom were unwilling to simply move out of the way for the growth of the United States. This led to innumerable conflicts over the years that did not come to an effective end until 1891.

Between 1783 and 1803, the possession of Louisiana and Florida by the Spanish had been a persistent problem for the United States. The Spanish could use their territory along the U.S. borders to encourage Native Americans in what was then the western United States (the area between the Appalachians and the

Mississippi River) to raid American settlements. The transfer of Spanish Louisiana back to France in 1800 did not lessen the problems but simply placed a more dangerous foreign power on the U.S. border.

In the years between 1803 and 1819, the United States claimed that Texas was part of the Louisiana Purchase, which Spain refused to concede. The issue was not definitively settled until the signing of the 1819 Adams-Onís Treaty, which placed the western U.S. border at the Sabine River and did not include Texas. Nevertheless, many expansionist-minded Americans believed that Texas was indeed U.S. territory, and numerous attempts were made to annex or buy it from the Mexican government after 1821. This certainly helped fuel the Texas Revolution of 1835–1836 and paved the way for the annexation of the Republic of Texas in 1845.

DONALD E. HEIDENREICH JR. AND PAUL G. PIERPAOLI JR.

See also

Adams-Onís Treaty; France; New Orleans; Spain; Texas; Texas Revolution.

References

Kennedy, Robert G. *Jefferson's Lost Cause: Land, Farmers, and the Louisiana Purchase.* New York: Oxford University Press, 2003.

Kukla, Jon. *A Wilderness So Immense: The Louisiana Purchase and the Destiny of America.* New York: Anchor Books, 2004.

Stewart, Richard W., ed. *American Military History.* Vol. 1, *The United States Army and the Forging of a Nation, 1775–1917.* Washington, DC: Center of Military History, 2005.

Tucker, Robert W., and David C. Henderson. *Empire of Liberty: The Statecraft of Thomas Jefferson.* New York: Oxford University Press, 1992.

Lowell, James Russell

Birth Date: February 22, 1819
Death Date: August 12, 1891

American poet, writer, satirist, professor, diplomat, reform advocate, and opponent of the Mexican-American War. James Russell Lowell was born in Cambridge, Massachusetts, on February 22, 1819, to a socially and politically prominent family. His ancestors were among the Lowells who helped settle Massachusetts beginning in the late 1630s. Despite a reputation as a troublemaker, Lowell graduated from Harvard College in 1838 and from Harvard Law School in 1842. While still in school, Lowell began writing poetry and other works and had already decided to pursue a literary career.

Lowell's first poems were published in 1840 in the *Southern Literary Messenger,* and he soon helped found a periodical titled the *Pioneer,* which failed to find a dedicated audience. He then began to publish extensively in magazines and newspapers and became dedicated to the antislavery cause. Lowell made no secret of his disdain for the Mexican-American War and the reason for which he believed it was waged. Indeed, he saw the conflict as a poorly

disguised excuse to extend slavery into California and the Southwest. His most notable and specific denunciation of the war came in the *Biglow Papers,* published in 1848, in which he made use of fictional individuals, including a fictional volunteer soldier, to tell the "story" of the war and what it meant for the United States and slavery proponents. The *Biglow Papers,* written largely in verse, were popular when they were released and were replete with black humor and biting satire. In the meantime, Lowell had become well acquainted with other New England literary luminaries including Henry Wadsworth Longfellow and Ralph Waldo Emerson.

Lowell subsequently traveled extensively throughout Britain and Europe before taking a position as an endowed professor of literature at his alma mater in 1855. Meanwhile, he continued publishing, and in 1857 he became the first editor of the newly created *Atlantic Monthly* magazine. As editor, he helped advocate for the abolition of slavery, and when the Civil War began in 1861, he became a fervent supporter of President Abraham Lincoln and his efforts to preserve the Union. In 1877, Lowell briefly engaged in politics, serving as a delegate to the 1876 Republican National Convention. From 1877 to 1880, he was U.S. minister to Spain, a post he secured in return for his support of President Rutherford B. Hayes. He was so well received in Spain that in 1880 he also became minister to Great Britain, which post he held until 1885.

Lowell came to embrace numerous reform agendas of his day, including temperance, opposition to capital punishment, and the amelioration of factory working conditions. Some of his critics argued that Lowell had seemed to waver on his antislavery views, however. Although some late critics charged that Lowell's poetry could be uninspiring, his use of satire and employment of dialects could be masterful, and he is credited with having inspired other writers such as Samuel Langhorne Clemens (Mark Twain), William Dean Howells, and H. L. Mencken, among others. Plagued by a variety of health ailments, Lowell died in Cambridge, Massachusetts, on August 12, 1891.

PAUL G. PIERPAOLI JR.

See also

Abolitionism; Emerson, Ralph Waldo; Literature; Opposition to the Mexican-American War, U.S.; Slavery.

References

Heymann, C. David. *American Aristocracy: The Lives and Times of James Russell, Amy, and Robert Lowell.* New York: Dodd, Mead, 1980.

Wagenknecht, Edward. *James Russell Lowell: Portrait of a Many-Sided Man.* New York: Oxford University Press, 1971.

Lower (Baja) California and West Coast of Mexico Campaign

During the Mexican-American War, the campaign for Lower (Baja) California and the west coast of Mexico was part of the larger theater of operations principally centered on present-day California (then known as Upper, or Alta, California). The narrow and sparsely populated Baja Peninsula, the economy of which was based chiefly on cattle ranching and silver mining, extends north–south for some 1,000 miles. Its west coast borders the Pacific Ocean, while its east coast is situated on the Gulf of California (Sea of Cortez). The peninsula's geographic isolation from the remainder of Mexico gave it some autonomy from the remainder of the country.

Because of the distances involved and paucity of troops, the U.S. Navy bore the brunt of the effort against the western coast of Mexico and Baja California. The navy seized many Mexican ships, most of which were merchant vessels, and fought a number of small skirmishes and minor actions on land. During the campaign, many *Bajacalifornios,* as the Baja California natives were known, collaborated with the U.S. forces. Those who believed that Baja California would become part of the United States and cooperated with the U.S. occupation found themselves in some difficulty when Mexico retained Lower California in the 1848 Treaty of Guadalupe Hidalgo.

At the outset of hostilities, on August 19, 1846, U.S. Pacific Squadron commander Commodore Robert F. Stockton proclaimed a blockade of the entire Mexican west coast. But because he lacked the ships to enforce such an extensive operation, it was only a paper blockade and thus contrary to both the laws of war and U.S. policy. Unconcerned about this, Stockton dispatched two sloops to the west coast of Mexico: the 20-gun *Cyane,* under Commander Samuel F. Du Pont, was charged with blockading San Blas; the 24-gun *Warren,* under Commander Joseph B. Hull, was to do the same at Mazatlán, the largest Mexican Pacific port. The ships departed Monterey (Alta California) on August 23 and 28, respectively.

On September 2, Du Pont proclaimed the blockade off San Blas and seized a Mexican sloop, the *Solita.* A landing party then went ashore to spike 24 Mexican cannon. On September 7, boats from the *Warren* cut out the Mexican brig *Malek Adhel* at Mazatlán. The next day the *Warren* took the Mexican brig *Carmelita* off the same port, and on September 9, Hull proclaimed the blockade off Mazlatán. In mid-September, the *Cyane* captured 9 Mexican ships at La Paz and 5 others off Loreto and Mulejé, all three towns being located on the east coast of Baja California. In early October the *Cyane* took 3 Mexican ships at Loreto and 2 others at Mulejé. On October 7, Lieutenant George W. Harrison from the *Cyane* led a boat expedition ashore at Guaymas on the northwestern Mexican coast and there burned the Mexican brig *Condor* and gunboats *Anahuac* and *Sonorense.*

On September 14, 1846, seamen from the *Cyane* went ashore and secured the capitulation of La Paz, capital of Baja California. The Mexican governor, Colonel Francisco Palacios Miranda, chose to collaborate with the United States (for which he was subsequently removed and declared a traitor) and agreed to neutralize the peninsula. Du Pont also seized nine merchant ships found in the harbor—an action that Miranda protested to no avail. Learning that a Mexican gunboat had recently departed from Mulejé, Du Pont sailed on September 28 in an effort to intercept it. The *Cyane*

and another U.S. Navy sloop, the 16-gun *Dale* under Commander William W. McKean, were received without incident at another Baja port, San José de Cabo, in mid-November. The peninsula was then left to fend for itself for some time, Stockton asserting that the United States had command of the sea in both Upper and Lower California.

After the American naval forces had departed and in spite of Miranda's proclamation, an insurgency developed in the northern areas of Baja, buoyed by news that help might soon arrive from mainland Mexico. Local patriots rejected the collaborationist Miranda and began organizing resistance.

With operations in Alta California having ended with satisfactory results for the American cause by January 1847, Stockton turned his attention back to Baja California and the western coast of Mexico. Stockton planned to occupy the west coast port of Acapulco, fearful that the Mexicans might seek to utilize it as a privateer base from which to attack U.S. Pacific merchant shipping. He also hoped that it might be made into a base to be used by U.S. troops to march from the west against Mexico City. Stockton also hoped to take both Mazatlán and San Blas.

Stockton was, however, distracted by his struggle with U.S. Army brigadier general Stephen W. Kearny over who was governor of California. On January 22, Commodore W. Branford Shubrick arrived at Monterey in the 54-gun frigate *Independence* to relieve Stockton as commander of the U.S. Pacific Squadron. Shubrick held his command only six weeks, however; on March 1, the more senior Commodore James Biddle arrived at Monterey in the 74-gun ship of the line *Columbus.* Biddle gave direction of the Baja California/west coast of Mexico campaign to Shubrick, however. The navy was then blockading only Guaymas and Mazatlán.

On February 2, 1847, Stockton ordered Commander John B. Montgomery of the 22-gun sloop *Portsmouth* to reestablish the blockade off Mazatlán. Once this had been accomplished, he was to sail to Baja California and raise the American flag over San José de Cabo, La Paz, Picilinque, and Loreto. *Portsmouth* arrived off Mazatlán on February 17 and subsequently took several prizes. On March 30, Montgomery sent a landing party under Lieutenant Benjamin F. B. Hunter ashore to seize San José de Cabo. On April 1, another landing party from the *Portsmouth,* this time under Lieutenant John S. Missroon, went ashore at La Paz.

In May 1847 orders arrived at Monterey from Secretary of the Navy John Y. Mason. He called on the U.S. Pacific Squadron to take and hold at least one Baja California port. Secretary of War William L. Marcy ordered Kearny to do the same. Such a step was designed to give the United States claim to Baja California in peace negotiations. With the Americans short of supplies, however, any such operation had to await the arrival that summer of the eight-gun storeship *Southampton.* On July 19, meanwhile, Biddle transferred command of the Pacific Squadron back to Shubrick.

There was also no Mexican resistance when, in fulfillment of orders from Washington, Lieutenant Colonel Henry S. Burton came ashore at La Paz in Baja with two companies of New York volunteers on July 21. Burton restored civilian government after securing a promise from the locals to transfer their loyalty to the United States.

The relative peace in Baja was shattered when Mexican army captain Manuel Pineda succeeded in crossing the Gulf of California to the port of Mulejé with a small number of officers and men to take charge of Mexican resistance in the peninsula. Pineda rallied local ranchers who had already begun to resist the American occupation. The Mexicans subsequently repelled a landing force under Lieutenant Tunis A. M. Craven from the *Dale* (commanded by Thomas O. Selfridge) near Mulejé on October 2. This inconclusive skirmish nonetheless helped galvanize local resistance against the Americans. On October 5, Craven and a landing party seized Mexican arms at Loreto in Baja.

On October 19, Captain Elie Augustus Frederick Lavallette arrived in the frigate *Congress* off Guaymas, supported by the sloop *Portsmouth.* The Americans demanded the surrender of the port and the next day opened a bombardment. The Mexican garrison had departed during the night, and the town authorities quickly surrendered. On October 27, the *Portsmouth* captured a Mexican schooner off Guaymas. On November 8, the sloop *Dale* arrived at Guaymas, relieving the *Portsmouth.*

Meanwhile, on November 1, Lieutenant Montgomery Lewis and 28 men departed San José for Todos Santos in Baja. They returned on November 7. Three days later, Commodore Shubrick proclaimed that it was the intention of the United States to retain Baja California after the war.

On November 11, a landing party under Captain Lavallette, formed of men from the *Independence, Congress,* and *Cyane,* seized Mazatlán. On November 16, Mexican captain Pineda mounted a surprise attack on Burton's forces at La Paz. The Mexicans tried to take the town over a 10-day span but were finally forced to break off the effort when they ran short of ammunition. Pineda also sent men to attack U.S. marines under Lieutenant Charles Heywood at San José de Cabo on November 20. Pineda may have harmed his own efforts, however, by taking punitive action against those Mexicans who had cooperated with the Americans.

Through the campaign the Americans were plagued by inadequate numbers of men. Although the Americans lacked the strength to occupy Guaymas, the presence in the harbor of the *Congress,* joined on October 17 by the *Portsmouth,* was sufficient to keep the Mexicans from using the town. Captain Lavallette departed in the *Congress* on October 23. The *Portsmouth* remained until the *Dale* arrived on November 8.

On November 17, learning that Mexican forces had infiltrated Guaymas, Commander Selfridge landed with 50 seamen, 17 marines, and a 6-pounder boat gun in a show of force. They got as far as the fort on Casa Blanca Hill near the shore, when they came under fire from a Mexican force estimated to number about 250 men. Selfridge was seriously wounded in the first exchange of fire, and the Americans were pinned down at the fort until they were able to get a message back to the *Dale,* which opened up with its

guns and forced the Mexicans to withdraw. The *Dale* remained off Guaymas until December 23, when the *Southampton* replaced it.

Meanwhile, late on November 10, Commodore Shubrick arrived off Mazatlán with a powerful squadron consisting of the *Independence, Congress,* and *Cyane,* accompanied by the four-gun storeship *Erie.* The next day he demanded the town's surrender and sent ashore a force of 730 seamen and marines, which met no Mexican opposition. Mexican forces withdrew 10 miles distant to Urias, where they were subsequently defeated by a combined U.S. land and naval attack. U.S. losses were 1 killed and 20 wounded; the Mexican sustained 4 killed and an unknown number of wounded. On January 12, 1848, a landing party from the six-gun U.S. storeship *Lexington,* under Lieutenant Theodorus Bailey, captured San Blas without opposition.

Casualties in these engagements were for the most part light, and superior American artillery, aided by complete U.S. command of the sea that included naval gunfire when required, made U.S. victory a virtual certainty. Captain Pineda, meanwhile, proved an able organizer and, armed by a supply of muskets that had arrived from Sonora, was ready by November 1 to take the offensive against the Americans. With more than 100 men, Pineda led unsuccessful assaults on the U.S. garrison at La Paz on November 11 and again on November 17.

On November 19, Pineda and about 150 men advanced on the small American garrison under Lieutenant Heywood at San José del Cabo. The Mexicans demanded that Heywood surrender. He refused, and fighting began. The Americans occupied a strong position in an old mission building and held out with some two dozen friendly *Bajacalifornios* who had joined them for protection. On the morning of November 21, two ships were sighted on the horizon. Assuming them to be American warships, the Mexicans withdrew. The two vessels in question soon arrived in port but turned out to be whalers.

On November 27, having increased his strength to some 350 men against Burton's La Paz garrison of only 112 men, Pineda tried for a third time to take the Baja California capital. Burton's men beat back this third assault at heavy cost to the Mexicans, in part thanks to U.S. artillery.

On December 12, Lieutenant Montgomery Lewis routed a Mexican force near Mazatlán, and on January 12, 1848, a landing party under Lieutenant Frederick Chatard from the *Lexington* and *Warren* spiked Mexican guns at San Blas and cut out two schooners. On January 17, Chatard led another American party ashore to spike guns at Manzanillo, and the next day the *Lexington* took two Mexican schooners at San Blas. By this time the Americans had disabled most of the guns defending the west coast of Mexico, save for those in the old fort at Acapulco.

Commodore Shubrick's requests from Mazatlán to Major General Winfield Scott for reinforcements were met with the response that no men could be spared. As a consequence, Shubrick lacked the manpower to effectively occupy the Baja Peninsula, which is the principal reason why its cession was not part of the Treaty of

Guadalupe Hidalgo. Fighting continued both along the western Mexican coast and Baja California, however, well after the Treaty of Guadalupe Hidalgo was signed on February 2, 1848.

On January 22, a second Mexican siege of San José de Cabo began; it was not lifted until the arrival of the *Cyane* on February 15. Meanwhile, an American landing party from the *Dale* attacked a Mexican camp at Cochori, Mexico, on January 30. On February 13, a landing party under Lieutenant Fabius Stanly from the *Dale* attacked a Mexican camp at Bocachicacampo, four miles north of Guaymas. On February 20, Stanly led another landing party that destroyed that same camp.

Even while San José de Cabo was under siege, Colonel Burton was preparing a campaign to end all resistance to the Americans in Baja. He seized horses and saddles so that his men might be mounted, but his campaign did not really begin until the arrival of an additional company of 115 New York volunteers at La Paz on March 22. On March 25, Captain Seymour G. Steele and 33 of the volunteers attacked Pineda's principal camp at San Antonio, taking three prisoners and capturing Pineda's correspondence and freeing two American midshipmen and three seamen who had been held prisoner. Pineda was seriously wounded in the fighting and forced to hand over command of Mexican forces in Baja California to the governor, Mauricio Castro.

Determined to put an end to the Mexican resistance, Colonel Burton personally led 217 New York volunteers from La Paz in an attack on the Mexican camp at Todos Santos. On March 31, in a 30-minute engagement, the Mexicans lost 10 men killed; the remainder of the force, including Castro, fled. On April 2, at Santiago, some 25 miles to the east, two detachments of Americans—one landed from the *Cyane* and another under Lieutenant George L. Selden—captured Castro and the remainder of his men. On April 8, Commodore Shubrick reported to Secretary of the Navy Mason that, after a year and a half of sporadic and limited fighting, Baja California was at last secure.

Under terms of the Treaty of Guadalupe Hidalgo, Mexico retained possession of Baja California, however. Those residents of Lower California who had actively supported the American takeover were chagrined at this turn. Several U.S. Army officers, including Lieutenant Henry W. Halleck, pleaded with the authorities in Washington in order to fulfill pledges that had promised Baja residents U.S. citizenship. Nearly 500 people were eventually evacuated to American-held California; most of them relocated to San Francisco. Those Mexican collaborators who remained behind faced persecution for having allied with the United States.

The last fighting near Guaymas occurred on April 9, when Lieutenant Fabius Stanly and a small American detachment skirmished with a Mexican force near the estuary of the Soldado River. U.S. forces evacuated Mazatlán on June 17, Guaymas on June 24, and La Paz on August 31, 1848, the last nearly seven months after the Treaty of Guadalupe Hidalgo had been signed.

RANDAL BEEMAN AND SPENCER C. TUCKER

See also

Baja California; Biddle, James; Blockade, Naval; California; Guadalupe Hidalgo, Treaty of; Gulf of California (Mar de Cortés); Halleck, Henry Wager; Kearny, Stephen Watts; La Paz; Marcy, William Learned; Mazatlán; San José del Cabo; Shubrick, William Branford; Stockton, Robert Field; Todos Santos, Skirmish at.

References

Bauer, K. Jack. *Surfboats and Horse Marines: U.S. Naval Operations in the Mexican War, 1846–1848.* Annapolis, MD: U.S. Naval Institute, 1969.

Gerhard, Peter. *Baja California in the Mexican War.* Berkeley: University of California Press, 1945.

Nardo, Don. *The Mexican-American War.* Farmington Hills, MI: Lucent Books, 1991.

Nunis, Doyce B., Jr., ed. *The Mexican War in Baja California: The Memorandum of Captain Henry W. Halleck Concerning His Expeditions in Lower California, 1846–1848.* Los Angeles, CA: Dawson's Bookshop, 1977.